LAND USE REGULATION

LAND USE REGULATION

Cases and Materials

Second Edition

Daniel P. Selmi
Professor of Law
Loyola Law School

James A. Kushner
Professor of Law
Southwestern University

ASPEN PUBLISHERS

1185 Avenue of the Americas, New York, NY 10036
www.aspenpublishers.com

A Wolters Kluwer Company
www.aspenpublishers.com

Printed in the United States of America

1 2 3 4 5 6 7 8 9 0

Library of Congress Cataloguing-in-Publication Data

Selmi, Daniel P.
Land use regulation : cases and materials / Daniel P. Selmi, James A. Kushner.—2nd ed.
p. cm.
Includes index.
ISBN 0-7355-2716-4
1. Land use—Law and legislation—United States—Cases. I. Kushner, James A. II. Title.

KF5698.A4S45 2004
346.7304'5—dc22 2004000857

About Aspen Publishers

Aspen Publishers, headquartered in New York City, is a leading information provider for attorneys, business professionals, and law students. Written by preeminent authorities, our products consist of analytical and practical information covering both U.S. and international topics. We publish in the full range of formats, including updated manuals, books, periodicals, CDs, and online products.

Our proprietary content is complemented by 2,500 legal databases, containing over 11 million documents, available through our Loislaw division. Aspen Publishers also offers a wide range of topical legal and business databases linked to Loislaw's primary material. Our mission is to provide accurate, timely, and authoritative content in easily accessible formats, supported by unmatched customer care.

To order any Aspen Publishers title, go to *www.aspenpublishers.com* or call 1-800-638-8437.

To reinstate your manual update service, call 1-800-638-8437.

For more information on Loislaw products, go to *www.loislaw.com* or call 1-800-364-2512.

For Customer Care issues, e-mail *CustomerCare@aspenpublishers.com*; call 1-800-234-1660; or fax 1-800-901-9075.

Aspen Publishers
A Wolters Kluwer Company

To the Hon. Manuel L. Real

—DPS

In memory of Solomon Kushner

—JAK

Summary of Contents

Contents

PART THREE

THE LIMITS OF CURRENT LAND USE REGULATION 219

Preface to the Second Edition

The field of land use regulation is hurtling through the early 21st century. New developments continue to appear at a rapid rate, and land use issues seem to engender ever increasing controversy among the public.

Since the first edition was published, for example, the concept of "smart growth" (with all its attendant permutations and imprecision) has become part of the everyday lexicon of land use practitioners. The Supreme Court has continued to issue takings cases on a regular basis, and further action in this area by the Court is very likely in the near future. The past few years also have brought rapid developments at the intersection of land use regulation and First Amendment law, particularly with respect to regulation of churches. And courts are increasingly questioning local government's use of its land use authority to spur economic growth, both through expansive redevelopment projects in economically viable areas as well as through favoring particular industries.

We believe that the overall structure of the book is well suited to address these developments, so we have retained the structure of the first edition in this revision. Where a choice of cases is available, we have continued to use very current cases for inclusion in the book, a practice that allows students to see the cutting edge of land use regulation and thus transition easily into the actual practice of land use law. In addition, the book's structure allows teachers, after they have covered the fundamentals of the subject, to choose among specific topics of particular interest to them, such as economic development, environmental regulation, housing discrimination, and aesthetic regulation.

So the second edition is in the nature of fine-tuning rather than fundamental revision. Among other subjects, we have added new material dealing with annexations, law and economics, First Amendment law, private land use controls, and environmental regulation of land use. We have also included a detailed summary of the so-called "Playa Vista" development in Chapter One, which can be used to give students an early view of the "big picture" of land use regulation.

We express our thanks to Dean David Burcham at Loyola Law School and Dean Leigh Taylor at Southwestern Law School for their continued support of our efforts. We also want to thank Nicole Mieuli for her excellent research assistance, and Paul Howard at the Loyola Law School Library for his extensive efforts to track down non-legal materials for us. Finally, we wish to thank Barbara Roth, Mei Wang, and Jessica Barmack at Aspen Publishers for their help and perseverance.

Daniel P. Selmi
James A. Kushner

April 2004

Preface to the First Edition

The field of land use regulation is a dynamic and intellectually challenging area of law. If the reader wants proof of the vitality of land use law, he or she need only consult the accounts of land use disputes that appear daily in the popular press. The odds are that, in whatever part of the country you reside, today's local paper will include headlines about some land use dispute of vital importance to the citizenry. It might be a major choice affecting the future of the downtown business area of a small city (should a new Wal-Mart be put in?), a dispute over aesthetics (how high should the sign on the McDonald's restaurant be?), or a controversy over the use of an important natural resource (can the new development fill a wetland on the property?). Whatever the decision might be, chances are that local citizens are vigorously debating it.

The dynamic aspect of land use regulation is also reflected in the changing nature of law in the field. The state courts, of course, issue a steady stream of opinions about zoning regulations, subdivision controls, growth management systems, and the like. The United States Supreme Court regularly grants certiorari in takings cases, and some argue that the Court is in the midst of redefining the contours of the Fifth Amendment in a way that will fundamentally change how local governments regulate land use. Furthermore, state legislatures increasingly consider legislation designed to empower increased land use regulation or to constrain it, perhaps by lowering the constitutional minimum under which a court may conclude that property has been "taken" without compensation. During the time this book was written, Congress even considered major intervention in the field; the House of Representatives has passed HR 1534, the "Private Property Rights Implementation Act of 1997," which would greatly expand the ability of landowners to bring takings claims in federal court.

In short, a course in land use regulation should present students with exciting possibilities for exploring legal issues of vital importance to contemporary society. A principal goal of this casebook is to reflect the excitement that we feel about land use and convey that excitement to students. One way we seek to accomplish this goal is by emphasizing, where pedagogically appropriate, the use of very recent case law. Given the fast pace of this field, the factual patterns of cases that are only 25 years old often cannot convey the intensity of the field today.

Another major goal of the casebook is to give the students an overall structure that they can employ in approaching land use issues and placing them in context. After introducing the field in Part One, we have attempted to achieve this goal by crafting a five-part structure for the book. First, all students must gain an understanding of the methods used to control land use, from the traditional zoning ordinance to the most modern regulatory tools, such as the site plan or the expanded use of exactions to finance the infrastructure needed for development. This base of knowledge is found in Part Two of the book.

Part Three then introduces the students to the boundaries or "limits" of the present system. These include the obvious constitutional constraints found in the Fifth and First Amendments to the United States Constitution, as well as the discipline imposed by the courts on local governments through the conduct of judicial review. Another such constraint is the oversight that, in various forms, higher levels of government exercise over local land use decisions. This category of restraints can range from direct control, through a statewide or "critical area" regulatory system established by the state, to much less formal oversight through various state agencies. Finally, the students must consider the constraints that inhere in the model of regulation used. Viewing land use decisions as legislative in nature is very different from seeing them as adjudicative, or as consensual, and the students must determine which of these models is best suited to addressing the land use issues of today.

Part Four of the book asks the student to confront what is probably the central conflict dominating modern land use: the question of how to strike a proper balance between the need for housing, including the imperative that the less well-off in the society receive adequate shelter, and the need to manage growth and shape it to avoid the undesirable consequences of urban sprawl. The student learns the techniques for managing growth and examines the legislative strategies for spurring developers to provide additional housing. The student also examines whether, and how, these two conflicting needs can be reconciled.

Finally, Part Five reflects the fact that, in the last 25 years, land use law has increasingly been shaped through legislative attempts at achieving specific policy goals. The goal might be environmental protection (saving wetlands or endangered species, for instance), preventing discrimination in the housing supply, or siting a land use that is unpopular. To achieve these goals, state legislatures (and Congress to some extent) have placed specific, single-focused provisions in law. The last part of the book examines these various "land use controls to effectuate governmental policy objectives" and asks the student to reach conclusions about whether these laws are both effective and wise.

The five-part structure of the book prepares the student to understand the land use system as presently constituted. At the same time, it will also give a frame of reference from which to confront issues that will arise in the future.

We also intend this casebook to explore a core group of themes that cut across the entire structure of the book and that account for both the dynamism and the doctrinal tension found in the current land use regulatory system. One of these themes is the scope and ramifications of the vast discretion exercised by local government regulators. The system of land use controls is premised on the concept of rationality in administrative regulation and reliance on planning expertise. The problem, however, is that land use decisions themselves are intensely political, and the unbridled exercise of political discretion can result in the most serious economic repercussions upon landowners. How the current land use system evolved into its current state, and the means by which increased legitimacy and rigor might be reintroduced into land use regulation as a means of controlling discretion, are important themes in the casebook.

A second theme in the casebook concerns one of the most significant developments in the field over the last 25 years: the increased recognition of "third party" rights in mechanisms for making land use decisions. The traditional model of land use control saw land use decisions as matters largely between the property owner and the local government where the property was located. Now, however, almost all important land use decisions at the local levelmoland even many unimportant onesmolinvolve three parties: the landowner, the local government, and the neighbors or other groups with a stake in the outcome. Defining the appropriate role for third parties in the land use system is an issue that the students have ample opportunity to explore in the materials.

A third theme is more subtle and has received less attention in the literature: the question of the ethical decisions that those practicing in the field, as well as those individuals who hold regulatory positions, must face. These include problems of corruption at the local level, the effect of campaign contributions on local land use decisions, the ethical constraints under which planning professionals operate, the role of regulatory bias and conflicts of interest, and the function of "open government" in the land use process. On a broader level, the very choices that we make about using land also can be seen as raising questions about the land use "ethic" that society has chosen to follow. That ethic can range from utilitarian to conservationist, with various other possibilities also appearing.

A fourth theme recurring throughout the book is that the present features of the regulatory system are subject to substantial (and even radical) revision, and that students should not assume that the system's central features will remain static in the future. Other heavily regulated sectors of the economy have been substantially deregulated (airlines, natural gas, and electricity come immediately to mind), and there are calls for deregulation of the land use area. The casebook includes a chapter addressing alternative models for land use decisionmaking, including deregulation, but throughout the book we ask students to evaluate the efficacy of the current system. Particularly important is the question of whether placing power over land use in the hands of local government officials is the appropriate choice, and whether certain goals of the system (an increased supply of housing, for instance) would be better met through a relaxing of regulatory standards.

Finally, we hope to instill in students an appreciation for the lawyering skills needed to practice in this field. Traditionally, the land use lawyer must act as the bridge between land use professionals (planners, engineers, etc.) and local decisionmakers. As such, he or she is required to understand the political context in which such decisions are made and advise clients accordingly. The skills currently required of land use practitioners, however, are even greater. For example, local governments often make land use decisions on the basis of negotiated solutions reached with developers, and in increasing instances mediation is used to resolve particularly intractable land use disputes. The lawyering skills needed to represent clients in such proceedings are quite different from the traditional skills required of the land use practitioner. The materials in the book ask the students to consider the types of skills that are needed to successfully practice in today's land use environment.

Writing the book has been enjoyable, not the least because of the support we have received. At Southwestern Law School we thank Dean Leigh H. Taylor for his support and Southwestern University School of Law for the financial support it provided. Christiana E. Dietzel provided valuable research assistance and administration, while Jeanne Nicholson, Director of Faculty Support, constantly provided support and encouragement that enabled the project to progress. In addition, Martha Fink was simply incredible in performing the technical editing and paste-ups of cases and materials during the teaching of tentative drafts of the manuscript. Professor Linda A. Whisman, Director of the Law Library, and her superb staff, including Carole Weiner and David McFadden, provided critical and extraordinary assistance in supporting research for the book. At Loyola Law School we thank Dean Gerald T. McLaughlin for the financial and other support provided, and Usi Meshreky, Mark Polland, Denise Lohmann, and Judy Friedman for providing outstanding research assistance. Mell Banex, aided by Ruth Busch, provided much needed and very able secretarial assistance at Loyola, and Pam Buckles, as always, helped whenever necessary in her role as Director of Faculty Support. We also express our gratitude to the students who studied from tentative editions of the manuscript and provided valuable feedback.

We extend our heartfelt thanks to those individuals at Aspen Law & Business who made this book possible: Carol McGeehan, who initiated the project for Little, Brown; Melody Davies, who brought the book to completion; Lisa Yi, who, with the able help of Jay Boggis, edited the book and gently (but firmly) encouraged us to meet deadlines; and Taylor Huttner, who oversaw the acknowledgments and teacher's manual. We are indebted to all of you.

Daniel P. Selmi
James A. Kushner

April 1999

Acknowledgments

The authors acknowledge the permission kindly granted to reproduce the materials indicated below.

American Planning Ass'n, Smart Growth Project, Model Legislation, Section 8-104 Consistency of Land Development Regulations with Local Comprehensive Plan. Reprinted with permission from American Planning Institute.

Baer, General Plan Evaluation Criteria: Approach to Making Better Plans, 63 J. Am. Planning Ass'n 329 (1997). Reprinted with permission from Journal of the American Planning Association.

Baron, The Great Gate Debate, 21 Builder 92 (Mar. 1, 1998). Reprinted with permission of Builder magazine.

Beatley, Ethical Land Use: Principles of Policy and Planning 23-39, The Johns Hopkins University Press (1994).

Beatley, from Habitat Conservation Planning: Endangered Species and Urban Growth by Timothy Beatley. Copyright © 1994. Courtesy of the University of Texas Press.

Bishop and Tilley, Smart Growth or Dumb Bureaucracy? 32 Envtl. L. Rpt. 10822. Reprinted with permission from Publications of The Environmental Law Institute®.

Blakely and Snyder, Fortress America: Gated Communities in the United States 1-10, 18-23, 28 (1999). Copyright © 1999 The Brookings Institution. Reprinted with permission of the Brookings Institution.

Boerner, Environmental Justice? 4-6 (1994). Copyright © 1994 Center for the Study of American Business. Reprinted with permission of the Center for the Study of American Business.

Bolick, Subverting the American Dream: Government Dictated "Smart Growth" Is Unwise and Unconstitutional, 148 U. Pa. L. Rev. 859 (2000). Reprinted with permission of University of Pennsylvania Law School and William S. Hein & Company, Inc.

Bosselman, Four Land Ethics: Order, Reform, Responsibility, Opportunity, 24 Envtl. L. 1439, 1440-1441 (1994). Copyright © 1994. Reprinted with permission.

Bowman and Pagano, Imagining Cityscapes: The Politics of Urban Development, 8 Land Lines 1, 4-5 (Mar. 1996). Copyright © 1996 Lincoln Institute. Reprinted with permission of the Lincoln Institute.

Commission for Racial Justice, Toxic Wastes and Race in the United States: A National Report on the Racial and Socio-Economic Characteristics of Communities with Hazardous Waste Sites xi-xv, 13 (1987). Copyright © 1987 United Church of Christ.

Costonis, Icons and Aliens: Law, Aesthetics, and Environmental Change 15-19, 76-79 (1989). Copyright © 1989 by the Board of Trustees of the University of Illinois. Used with the permission of the University of Illinois Press.

Dear, Understanding and Overcoming the NIMBY Syndrome, 58 J. Am. Plan. Ass'n 288 (Summer 1992). Reprinted by permission of the Journal of the American Planning Association.

Ferrell, Spielberg Notes Hollywood Twist for Dream Works, Los Angeles Times, Dec. 4, 1995. Copyright © 1995 by The Los Angeles Times. Reprinted with permission of the Los Angeles Times.

Fischel, The Economics of Zoning Laws: A Property Rights Approach to American Land Use Controls (1985).

Fischel, Why are there NIMBYs?, Land Economics Feb. 2001, vol. 77. Copyright © 2001. Reprinted with permission of the University of Wisconsin Press.

Freyfogle, Owning the Land: Four Contemporary Narratives, 13 J. Land Use & Envtl. L. 279 (1988). Reprinted with permission from the Journal of Land Use and Environmental Law.

Frug, Euphemism as a Political Strategy, 30 Envtl. L. Rptr. 11189 (2000). Reprinted with permission.

Gerrard, Whose Backyard, Whose Risk: Fear and Fairness in Toxic and Nuclear Waste Siting 99-107 (1994). Copyright © 1994 by MIT Press. Reprinted with permission of the MIT Press.

Gordon and Richardson, Are Compact Cities a Desirable Planning Goal? 63 J. Am. Plan. Ass'n 232 (1997). Reprinted by permission of the Journal of the American Planning Association.

Hirsh, Law and Economics: An Introductory Analysis (3rd ed. 1999). Reprinted with Permission of Elsevier Ltd.

Houston Trademark Intact: City Remains Largest in the U.S. Without Zoning Ordinance, Nov. 4, 1993. Reprinted with permission of The Associated Press.

Huffman, The Public Interest in Private Property Rights, 50 Okla. Rev. 337 (1997). Reprinted with permission from the University of Okalahoma Law Review.

Hyatt, Declaration of Covenants, Conditions, and Restrictions for Mystic Isle. Copyright © 2002.

Hyman, Empowerment Zones, Enterprise Community, Black Business, and Unemployment 53 Wash. L.J. Urb. & Contemp. L. 143 (1998). Reprinted with permission.

Kelly, Managing Community Growth: Policies, Techniques, and Impacts 8-10. Copyright © 1993 by Praeger Publishers. Reproducd with permission of Greenwood Publishing Group, Inc., Westport, Ct.

Kushner, A Comparative Vision of the Convergence of Ecology Empowerment, and the Quest for a Just Society, 54 U. Miami L. Rev. 301 (1998). Reprinted with permission of the University of Miami Law Review.

Lake, Rethinking NIMBY, 59 J. Am. Plan. Ass'n 87 (Winter 1993). Reprinted by permission of the Journal of the American Planning Association.

Lefcoe, When Government Becomes Land Developers: Notes on the Public Sector Experience in the Netherlands and California, 51 S. Cal. L. Rev. 165. Reprinted with permission.

Marshall, ISTEA Five Years Later: Where Do We Go From Here? 49 Land Use Law and Zoning Digest 3. Copyright © 1997 Land Use Law and Zoning Digest. Reprinted with permission of the Land Use Law and Zoning Digest.

Martin, Hue and Cry Over Colors of Homes in South Gate, L.A. Times, Sept. 22, 1998, at B1. Reprinted with permission of the Los Angeles Times.

Miles, Bernes, and Weiss, Real Estate Development: Principles and Process (2000). Reprinted with permission from the Urban Land Institute.

Morris and Miners, The Destructive Role of Land Use Planning, 14 Tulane Envtl. L.J. 95 (2000). Reprinted with permission from Tulane University Environmental Law Journal.

Moyano, A Tale of Two Wetlands, 52 Or. St. Bar Bull. 39 (Feb./Mar. 1992). Copyright © 1992 Linda D. Moyano. Reprinted with permission of Linda D. Moyano.

National Public Radio, Interview: Jacksonville, Florida, Mayor John Delaney Talks About Problems With Urban Sprawl, B. Edwards host, May 9, 2001. © Copyright NPR® 2001. The interview by NPR was originally broadcast on National Public Radio's Morning Edition on May 9, 2001, and is used with the permission of National Public Radio, Inc. Any unauthorized duplication is strictly prohibited.

Nelson, Privatizing the Neighborhood: A Proposal to Replace Zoning with Private Collective Property Rights to Existing Neighborhoods, 7 George Mason L. Rev. 827 (Summer 1999). Reprinted with permission of Robert H. Nelson and the George Mason Law Review.

Nelson, Pro-Choice Living Arrangements Reality Check, Forbes 6-14 (1999). Reprinted by permission of Forbes Magazine © 2004 Forbes Inc.

Netter, Using Mediation to Resolve Land Use Disputes, 15 Zoning and Plan. L. Rep. 25, 27-28 (1992). Copyright © 1992. Reprinted with permission of West Group.

Nivala, Constitutional Architecture: The First Amendment and the Single Family House, vol. 33 U.S.D. L. Rev. Copyright 1996 San Diego Law Review. Reprinted with permission of the San Diego Law Review.

Ohm, Reforming Land Planning Legislation as the Dawn of the 21st Century: The Emerging Influence of Smart Growth and Livable Communities, 32 Urban Law 181, No. 2, Spring 2000. Reprinted by permission.

Platt, Land Use and Society: Geography, Law and Public Policy 6-22. Copyright © 1996 Island Press. Reprinted with permission of Island Press.

Rose, New Models for Local Land Use Decisions, 79 Nw. U.L. Rev. 1155 (1984-1985). Reprinted by special permission of Northwestern University School of Law, Northwestern University Law Review.

Salvesen, Banking on Wetlands. Urban Land Institute, June 1993, at 36-38. Reprinted with permission from Banking on Wetlands, 1993, published by ULI-the Urban Land Institute, 1025 Thomas Jefferson St. NW, Ste. 500W, Washington, DC 20007-5201.

Sax, Historic Preservation as Public Duty: The Abbe Gregoire and the Origins of the New Idea. 88 Mich. L. Rev. 1142. Reprinted with permission.

Siegel, Is Regional Government the Answer? The Public Interest Fall, 1999. Reprinted with permission.

So and Getzels, The Practice of Local Government Planning 402-403, 422-423. Copyright © 1979 American Planning Association. Reprinted with permission of the International/City County Management Association, 777 North Capitol Street NE, Suite 500, Washington, DC 20002. All rights reserved.

Stark, America, the Gated?, 22 Wilson Quarterly 58 (1998). Copyright © 1998. Reprinted with permission of the author.

Strachan, Concurrency Laws: Water as a Land Use Regulation, 21 J. Land Resources and Envtl. 435. Reprinted with permission.

Williams and Matheny, Democracy, Dialogue, and Environmental Disputes 166-168 (1995). Copyright © 1995 Yale University Press. Reprinted with permission of the Yale University Press.

PART ONE

INTRODUCTION TO LAND USE CONTROLS

1

The Regulatory Setting: Land, Ethics, Economics, and Players

A. THE VITALITY OF CONTEMPORARY LAND USE REGULATION

Land use regulation is probably the area of law that most affects the quality of life in the United States. The design of communities and their development are complex subjects that are fraught with the vicissitudes of politics and factionalism. At various times, developers are pitted against residents, environmentalists against advocates of growth, rich against poor, homeowners against renters, and automobile users against transit users and bicyclists.

Land use law reflects the dynamic process of deciding how land is used. The field is rapidly evolving. In recent years, for example, the United States Supreme Court has issued several opinions that have markedly changed how local governments may condition the approval of new development and limit the uses of land. The courts are also grappling with the intersection between First Amendment rights, such as freedom of religion, and the rights of local governments to regulate the use of churches. And to a large extent, the fields of environmental law and land use law are converging.

From the student's perspective, modern land use cases are exciting. They often tell stories that are reminiscent of soap operas (or old-time melodramas), and the cast of characters is large. There are landowners and developers, neighbors who become involved in every aspect of their community's development, environmentalists concerned about growth, civil rights activists seeking more housing, inspectors and bureaucrats who are part of the local land use governmental machinery, regulatory bodies that are often controlled by elected or appointed officials with declared ideological agendas, and judges who must review local decisions.

A former speaker of the United States House of Representatives once uttered the oft-quoted phrase, "All politics is local." The land use stories from around the country certainly confirm this statement, for land use disputes are intensely political and take the center stage of local politics. The participants care deeply about the issues, and they demand a right to be heard.

The variety of land use issues is extremely broad. A few are extremely important to the future of a region, while others are much smaller in scope. To get a taste of modern land use, consider the following summaries:

- Residents of a development in Scottsdale, Arizona, battled over whether an aquatic center and skate park should be built on a forty-acre park in their area. Plans for the park were originally drawn in 1994 when the area was still sparsely populated. Later, some residents became concerned about the impacts of the project, including traffic and use of the park by juvenile delinquents. According to the local paper, by the time the city council decided the issue, "at least one resident worried about terrorism at the complex." Lesley Wright, "Unified Front" Helped Save Aquatic Center, Scottsdale Republic, March 19, 2003.
- A Virginia dispute over a golf driving range ended with the owner being sent to jail after refusing to obey a court order that he close. The dispute over zoning violations had gone on for years. At the conclusion, the county contended that a screening berm for the facility was too high and that the site did not have the 300 trees that the owner had agreed to plant. Peter Whoriskey, "Defiant Va. Man Returned to Jail," Washington Post, Feb. 21, 2001, at B01.
- Residents of Aberdeen, South Dakota, opposed an application to amend the local zoning ordinance to include a crematorium as a use that could be allowed in a highway commercial district. The applicants planned to open a funeral home in a building that once housed two restaurants and eventually planned to put in a crematorium. The residents cited concerns over smell. As one person put it to the local newspaper, "This is South Dakota." There will be a lot of wind and "[t]his stuff will carry." Elissa Grossell, Crematorium Plan Raises Stink. Residents of Nearby Neighborhood Worried about Smell from Proposed Facility, Aberdeen Am. News, Feb. 4, 2003, at 1.
- The Cottonwood Christian Center and the City of Cypress became locked in a nationally publicized duel over the church's efforts to build a new worship center on a parcel of land. The city resisted the church's efforts because it wanted to use the land to attract a new Costco store. After litigation in federal court, the parties finally reached a land-swap arrangement, which ended the three-year fight. Iris Yokoi, "Cypress Reaches Agreement with Cottonwood," Orange County Register, March 2, 2003, at 2.
- A family that owned 292 acres in a city near Dallas, Texas, requested permission to build apartments on the land. The property, however, was zoned for an industrial park. After a number of years in which they were unsuccessful in obtaining permission to build, the landowners filed a civil rights suit alleging that the city's restrictions on apartments violated federal civil rights laws. Ultimately, each side consented to submitting the case to mediation. Mike Lee, "Dispute over Anti-Apartment Rules Headed for Mediation," Forth Worth Star-Telegram, March 11, 2003, at 3.

B. THE LAND RESOURCE IN AMERICA: DISTRIBUTION AND TRENDS

To understand the context in which the law of land use controls operates, the student must have some sense of the land resources of the United States and how that land is now used.

RUTHERFORD PLATT, LAND USE AND SOCIETY: GEOGRAPHY, LAW AND PUBLIC POLICY

6-22 (1996)

CLASSES OF LAND USE

About three-quarters of the total U.S. land area is devoted to three primary categories of rural land usage: (1) cropland, (2) grazing land (including pasture and range), and (3) forest land. Each of these represents a productive and economically beneficial class of land resource, although the more remote forests and more arid grazing lands may seldom be exploited. . . . Other portions of our undeveloped land resources are managed for specialized purposes, including wetlands, recreation areas, and wildlife sanctuaries.

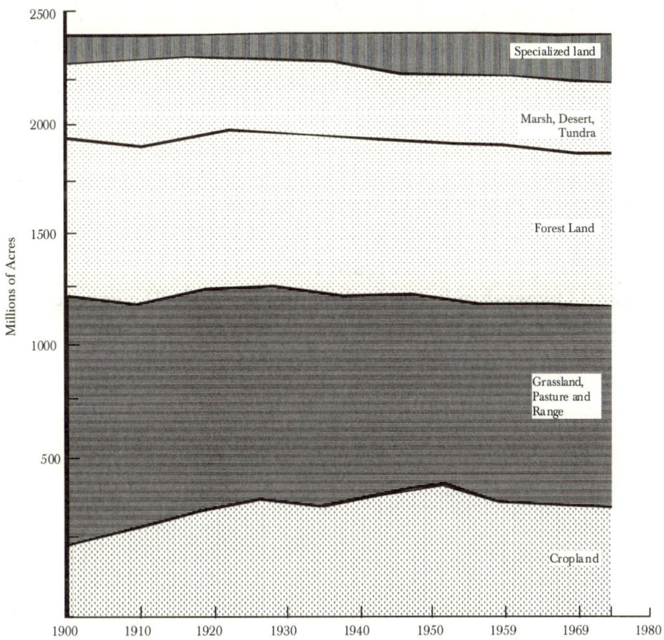

Source: U.S. Council on Environmental Quality, 1979.
Note: *Forest Land* excludes reserved forest land in parks, wildlife refuges, and other special-use areas. *Specialized Land* is urban and built-up areas . . . and nonurban special-use areas (e.g., federal and state wildlife refuges and parks . . .).

Figure 1-1
Major Uses of Land in the United States: 1900-1974

At the other extreme, a small but critical proportion of our nation's land resources is devoted to urban uses, including housing, commercial, industrial, and transportation facilities. Most Americans live out their lives in these metropolitan and urbanized areas.

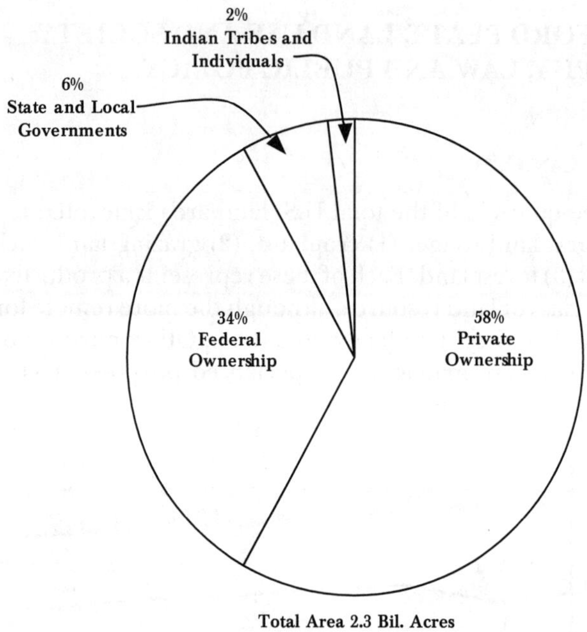

Source: U.S. Department of Agriculture, 1974.

Figure 1-2
Land Ownership in the United States, 1969; 94 percent of federal ownership is in the 11 westernmost states and Alaska (about 50 percent is in Alaska)

The United States census provides voluminous information about current land use trends. Consider the following trends, revealed by the 2000 Census.

Population increases provide a crude but meaningful indicator of land use changes. Here are the states that had the largest increases in population between 1990 and 2000. [See Table 1-1 on p. 7.]

Table 1-1
Census 2000: States Ranked by Numeric Population Change: 1990 to 2000

		Census Population		*Change, 1990 to 2000*	
Rank	*Area*	*April 1, 2000*	*April 1, 1990*	*Number*	*Percent*
1	California	33,871,648	29,760,021	4,111,627	13.8
2	Texas	20,851,820	16,986,510	3,865,310	22.8
3	Florida	15,982,378	12,937,926	3,044,452	23.5
4	Georgia	8,186,453	6,478,216	1,708,237	26.4
5	Arizona	5,130,632	3,665,228	1,465,404	40.0
6	North Carolina	8,049,313	6,628,637	1,420,676	21.4
7	Washington	5,894,121	4,866,692	1,027,429	21.1
8	Colorado	4,301,261	3,294,394	1,006,867	30.6
9	Illinois	12,419,293	11,430,602	988,691	8.6
10	New York	18,976,457	17,990,455	986,002	5.5

Source: U.S. Census Bureau, Census 2000 Redistricting Data (P.L. 94-171) Summary File and 1990 Census.

Other states with "double-digit" increases in the percent of population over that decade were Virginia (14.4 percent), Tennessee (16.7 percent), Nevada (66.3 percent), Oregon (20.4 percent), Minnesota (12.4 percent), South Carolina (15.1 percent), Maryland (10.8 percent), Utah (29.6 percent), Alabama (10.1 percent), Arkansas (13.7 percent), New Mexico (20.1 percent), Idaho (28.5 percent), Mississippi (10.5 percent), New Hampshire (11.4 percent), Delaware (17.6 percent), Montana (12.9 percent), and Alaska (14.0 percent).

Here are the metropolitan areas that experienced the largest percent population change from 1990 to 2000.

Table 1-2
Metropolitan Areas Ranked by Percent Population Change: 1990 to 2000

		Census Population		*Change, 1990 to 2000*	
Rank	*Metropolitan Area Name*	*April 1, 2000*	*April 1, 1990*	*Number*	*Percent*
1	Las Vegas, NV–AZ	1,563,282	852,737	710,545	83.3%
2	Naples, FL	251,377	152,099	99,278	65.3%
3	Yuma, AZ	160,026	106,895	53,131	49.7%
4	McAllen–Edinburg–Mission, TX	569,463	383,545	185,918	48.5%
5	Austin–San Marcos, TX	1,249,763	846,227	403,536	47.7%
6	Fayetteville–Springdale–Rogers, AR	311,121	210,908	100,213	47.5%
7	Boise City, ID	432,345	295,851	136,494	46.1%

cont. on next page

Table 1-2 *(cont.)*
Metropolitan Areas Ranked by Percent Population Change: 1990 to 2000

		Census Population		*Change, 1990 to 2000*	
Rank	*Metropolitan Area Name*	*April 1, 2000*	*April 1, 1990*	*Number*	*Percent*
8	Phoenix–Mesa, AZ	3,251,876	2,238,480	1,013,396	45.3%
9	Laredo, TX	193,117	133,239	59,878	44.9%
10	Provo–Orem, UT	368,536	263,590	104,946	39.8%
11	Atlanta, GA	4,112,198	2,959,950	1,152,248	38.9%
12	Raleigh–Durham–Chapel Hill, NC	1,187,941	855,545	332,396	38.9%
13	Myrtle Beach, SC	196,629	144,053	52,576	36.5%
14	Wilmington, NC	233,450	171,269	62,181	36.3%
15	Fort Collins–Loveland, CO	251,494	186,136	65,358	35.1%
16	Orlando, FL	1,644,561	1,224,852	419,709	34.3%
17	Reno, NV	339,486	254,667	84,819	33.3%
18	Ocala, FL	258,916	194,833	64,083	32.9%

Source: U.S. Census Bureau Internet Release date: April 2, 2001

Land use is not static. Rather, it evolves constantly, and the decisions of local government officials, when viewed as a whole, indelibly stamp how the country will appear for many years to come. In recent decades, the most important development has been the continued expansion of suburban metropolitan areas.

This trend has important implications in a variety of areas, ranging from environmental protection to race. For now, however, you simply need to recognize where the intense pressure to develop land is occurring.

While suburban growth was robust from 1990-2000, not every suburban area grew. The declining suburbs were predominately located in the Northeast and Midwest, in places like the Cleveland, St. Louis, and Philadelphia areas. *See* Suburbs and the Census: Patterns of Growth and Decline, Center on Urban & Metropolitan Policy, the Brookings Institution (Dec. 2001), at 1. The report concluded that "[w]hile it is common to talk about 'the suburbs' as a group of homogenous jurisdictions, careful analysis reveals that suburbs are highly diverse." *Id.* at 2.

Another important trend was that almost two out of three householders in the United States (69.8 million, or 66.2 percent) owned their homes by 2000. From 1990 to 2000, the increase in owner-occupied homes (18.3 percent) far outpaced the increase in renter-occupied units (8.3 percent). More Householders Than Ever Own Their Own Homes According to Census 2000, U.S. Census Bureau, U.S. Dept. of Commerce, (Nov. 27, 2001) (available at *http://www.census.gov/Press-Release/www/2001/cb01cn191.html*).

Notes and Comments

1. *The Distribution of Land Ownership*. Most students undoubtedly understand that some land in the United States, such as the national parks, is owned by the

federal government. You may be surprised, however, to learn that up to one-third of the nation's land is federally controlled. Is this government ownership inconsistent with a private market economy that emphasizes individual home ownership and economic entrepreneurship? Some have vigorously argued that the federal lands should be largely sold off. Do you agree?

2. *Transportation and Urban Development.* In his influential book Edge City: Life on the New Frontier (1991), journalist Joel Garreau documented the development of so-called "edge cities," large new cities just outside of the traditional urban centers. Garreau emphasized the relationship between "edge cities" and the transportation infrastructure, suggesting that cities are always created around the "state of the art" transportation device of the time. According to Garreau, "edge cities" result from a combination of the automobile, the jet plane, and the computer. *Id.* at 32.

Who should make the decisions about where the transportation infrastructure for development, such as expansions of the freeway system, is located? As you will see, while local government continues to make the most important decisions about individual developments, the money to build freeways, and the decisions about the location of those freeways, has been left largely in federal hands (although this is now changing somewhat).

3. *Land Use and the Census.* The census data now available from the 2000 census allowed the Census Bureau to analyze historical trends across the entire twentieth century. Some of the conclusions are fascinating: (1) the U.S. population more than tripled from 76 million in 1900 to 281 million in 2000; (2) the population of the West grew faster than the population for each of the other three regions of the country in every decade of the twentieth century; (3) from 1900 to 2000, the number of non-Southern states with populations of at least 10 percent races other than White increased from 2 to 26, reflecting the increasing diversity of the United States; and (4) while the most common household in 1900 contained seven or more people, from 1940 to 2000, it contained two people. U.S. Census Bureau, U.S. Dept. of Commerce, Demographic Trends in the 20th Century (Nov. 2002) 1-2.

The federal government uses the census data for a wide variety of purposes, including the distribution of some federal funding and political redistricting. Not surprisingly, states and cities are extremely concerned about the methodologies used in the counts, and they will litigate over those issues. *See, e.g.*, City of Los Angeles v. United States Dept. of Commerce, 307 F.3d 860 (9th Cir. 2002) (unsuccessfully seeking to compel the Secretary of Commerce to use statistically adjusted population data as the official census for the purposes of political redistricting).

4. *Regulating Land Use.* Do you see any need for local government to regulate land uses? In the introduction to his 1972 book Land Use Without Zoning, Professor Bernard H. Siegan cogently states his case opposing government intervention:

> For most people, home is where the major part of life is spent. It is the place that occupies the time and attention of the wife and children most of each day. It is also the place where the husband spends most of his time when away from work and the major purpose for which he works. Its characteristics greatly influence the quality of one's life.
>
> For those concerned with the quality of life, housing and local environmental conditions merit the highest priority. I believe one means to achieve these objectives

> is to eliminate one of the principal barriers to production, zoning, and thereby allow the real estate market greater opportunity to satisfy the needs and desires of its consumers. My studies show that zoning is neither necessary to maintain or protect property values nor an aid to "planning"—its principal justifications. On the contrary, it has adverse effects on both. When it impedes the production of housing, it also impedes the achievement of better housing and housing conditions.

Based on your knowledge of how land is used in the United States, do you agree with his position?

5. *Common Law Remedies*. If zoning and the other modern land use regulatory techniques were eliminated, not only would this casebook be unnecessary, landowners could still rely on the common law concept of nuisance to adjust disputes with other landowners. Nuisance, of course, allows a landowner (or occupier) to bring a cause of action alleging that a neighbor's use of property has interfered with the plaintiff's use and enjoyment of his or her property. Would this common law remedy be sufficient?

C. LAND USE AS AN ETHICAL DECISION

A central theme of this text focuses on ethical issues in land use regulation. The word "ethics" is used in a couple of different ways. On its narrowest level, there are legal issues concerning ethics, such as when a decisionmaker has a conflict of interest in rendering a land use decision. There also exist questions regarding the ethics of developers. For example, they may bring litigation against opposing groups to intimidate them, suits known as "strategic lawsuits against public participation" (or "SLAPP" suits). Alternatively, developers may threaten to bring suits against public entities for damages, suits that pose the specter of heavy litigation costs. Opponents of growth have similar choices. Is it ethically justifiable for such opponents to institute litigation challenging *every* discretionary decision made by local government on a development project?

On a broader level, ethical issues underlie the choice about how land is used. When we choose the uses to be allowed on property, those choices either serve or can conflict with an underlying land "ethic": a series of principles that govern our view of the proper role that property is to play in society. An important component of this ethic is the extent to which natural resources should be viewed as available for exploitation by the property owner, or whether those resources are subject to a broader public interest in them.

In the first reading, Professor Fred Bosselman reviews the history of the legal attitude toward land.

■ FRED BOSSELMAN, FOUR LAND ETHICS: ORDER, REFORM, RESPONSIBILITY, OPPORTUNITY

24 Envtl. L. 1439, 1440-41 (1994)

I. Introduction

The term "land ethics" has found a prominent place in environmental literature ever since Aldo Leopold rather casually and cryptically coined it in the 1930s.

If one defines the phrase to mean a system of thought that relates land to ideas of right and wrong, one can identify many prior systems which have achieved prominence at some time or place. . . .

I conclude that only a pluralistic process in which multiple land ethics are debated will be a satisfactory basis for the resolution of many of the current bitter conflicts over land in America. . . . The four land ethics discussed [below] play important roles in the United States today. This section briefly describes these roles.

A. ORDER

[The land policies of the semi-legendary King Arthur were] designed to protect the social order [and] continue to play an important role in the United States. Although class distinction in the United States never attained the rigidity of the English model, land policy in the United States has frequently been used to stabilize existing social relationships.

For example, federal tax policy creates a sharp distinction between homeowners, who receive interest deductions, and tenants, who do not. A new nationally supported system of mortgage commodification has increased the extent to which "homeowners" now hold in an almost tenurial relationship to the pension funds and similar institutions that dominate long-term investment. An Arthurian network of deed restrictions and local zoning protects many residential communities from disruptions in the social order. Gated communities increasingly resemble fortified castles.

B. REFORM

[Demands for reform like David Ricardo's in post-[W]aterloo England] are less shrill in the United States than in many other countries because the privileges attached to land ownership have never been as dramatic as those that prompted Ricardo's call for reform. Nevertheless, substantial privileges exist and have prompted demands for greater equity.

Reformers object that agricultural interests destroy the soil resource and pollute the environment while receiving cash subsidies, property tax abatements, and relief from responsibility for damages caused by pesticides. They question whether mining interests should continue to use the federal lands without making reimbursement to taxpayers. One noted law and economics scholar has characterized urban redevelopment cartels as "feudal."

C. RESPONSIBILITY

Modern [followers of John Muir] have substituted wetlands for Muir's Sierran peaks as the resource most in need of preservation. Moreover, the protection of wilderness has become well-accepted policy in Congress, and a growing recognition of the importance of biodiversity has placed emphasis on the need for preservation of a wide range of habitats. Perhaps the most dramatic recent success of the ethic of responsibility is the legislation imposing responsibility on those who have poisoned the land through careless use of toxic chemicals. . . .

Although those who attempt to model their activities on Muir's are but a small fraction of the population, Muir's influence goes far beyond those who follow directly in his footsteps. Many Americans honor his example intermittently or vicariously. For example, the Outward Bound movement has brought thousands of business executives into the wilderness as an educational experience, and groups like the Nature Conservancy allow people to honor their responsibility to nature vicariously through cash or land donations.

D. OPPORTUNITY

If utilitarians had worried that the entrepreneurial opportunity to create wealth out of land would be stifled by rigid controls, by the ability of privileged vested interests to avoid reform, and by the demands of preservationists for greater responsibility, the free-wheeling business climate of the 1980s proved their worries groundless. Legislation converted many savings and loan associations into governmentally insured entrepreneurial vehicles for the development of real estate that were often operated by developers with little regard for market needs. The result was a taxpayer bailout of unprecedented proportions and a record oversupply of commercial buildings, which may dampen new construction well into the twenty-first century.

Meanwhile, in residential real estate, Ricardo's idea that economic rent was the windfall of the gentry was transformed into the government-subsidized homeownership movement—if you can't beat the gentry, join the gentry! Economists might classify land as just another asset, but the American public thought otherwise.

Landowners continue to be successful in amassing government subsidies for their activities (or inactivities), relying on the Jeffersonian mystique to hide the fact that most of the subsidies are being paid to large corporations. Congress has begun paying farmers to not farm in sensitive areas, and some landowners are seeking higher subsidies against losses in land value.

VII. Conclusion

Each of the land ethics discussed in this article represents an important factor in the way Americans currently think about land. . . . Each will be an element of any public decisionmaking process having a major impact on land. The search for a new land ethic will continue, but in a democratic society the existence of multiple ethics must be accepted.

Since the early 1980s, academics in the planning field have opened up a broad discourse on the role of ethics in land use decisionmaking. In the following excerpt, one of the leaders in that field, Professor Timothy Beatley, discusses the role that ethics should play in such decisions.

■ TIMOTHY BEATLEY, ETHICAL LAND USE: PRINCIPLES OF POLICY AND PLANNING

3-4, 13-16 (1994)

[T]he social allocation of land to different uses and activities is fundamentally and inextricably a problem of ethics. This is so because such land-use decisions have, both individually and cumulatively, tremendous social and environmental impacts. Land-use actions can destroy important elements of the natural environment, and today land development and urban growth are major causes of the loss of such areas as wetlands, habitat for endangered species, and forestlands, among others. Development patterns have much to do with the nature and extent of pollution generated by our society — ozone and carbon monoxide in urban areas due to land-use patterns that rely unduly on the automobile, nonpoint sources of water pollution generated by impervious surfaces, loss of natural vegetation, careless construction practices, and a variety of urban and rural uses such as underground storage tanks, landfills, and agricultural operations. . . .

Land-use practices are even at the core of many of our global environmental problems. . . .

Land-use decisions have tremendous social and economic implications as well. Such decisions influence the distribution of basic goods and services in the society, including access to jobs, schools, transportation, and recreation facilities, among others. Land-use decisions also influence the distribution of *bads*, or hazards and threats to health and safety, including the extent to which individuals and families are placed at risk to cancer-causing toxic waste facilities; to floods, hurricanes, earthquakes, or other natural disasters; to hazardous air and water pollutants; or to dangerous traffic and road conditions. Land-use decisions, moreover, have the capability to isolate and segregate different social and economic groups, and to influence how people view themselves and the value of their lives.

In short, land-use decisions affect the condition and quality of the natural and built environment, and the basic quality of people's lives. Land-use decisions are thus not trivial, and should be the focus of careful and deliberative thought on the part of those individuals and institutions responsible for making or influencing them. All decisions about the use of land, then, are inherently ethical judgments, inherently ethical choices. Land-use decisions and policies raise questions of right and wrong, good and bad. . . .

Central Questions in Land-Use Ethics . . .

DEFINING THE RELEVANT MORAL COMMUNITY

To resolve dilemmas about land-use policy it is important to determine what the relevant moral community is. There are at least three dimensions to this question. The first is *geographical*. Are we, on the one hand, obligated to consider the effects of a land-use decision or policy on the immediate neighborhood or community? Or should we consider the interests and well-being of broader publics — say, of the residents of the surrounding region, state, or nation? . . .

A second dimension to this question is *temporal*. Many land-use decisions and policies clearly have impacts that extend into the future. In considering whether to allow the destruction or degradation of some natural landscape, are we obligated to consider only the interests of the present human population? Or do we have an obligation to consider a much longer time frame, to factor into our moral calculations the effects of such an action on future generations? . . .

A third dimension to the question of how to determine the relevant moral community is *biological*. Must we, when making land-use decisions, consider the interest and well-being of other forms of life? Some have argued that, morally, our only obligations extend to *Homo sapiens*, while others suggest that certain ethical obligations extend to all sentient life- forms. Still others argue that the moral community must include all forms of life, sentient and nonsentient alike, and that land-use and other societal decisions must reflect a certain level of ethical respect for this life.

THE ETHICAL OBLIGATIONS

Once conclusions are reached about the extent and parameters of the moral community, the question then becomes, What are the actual ethical obligations owed to the various members of this moral community? There are numerous ethical principles, standards, and concepts that have been considered and argued for in areas such as moral philosophy and environmental ethics. Is our moral obligation to decide land-use policy dilemmas through the use of utilitarian and economic concepts — choosing those policies or actions which maximize social utility? Or do we have moral obligations that extend beyond economical utilitarian efficiency? . . .

MAKING DECISIONS ABOUT THE LAND AND LAND USE

It is at the stage of making decisions about land use that actual discourse about alternative ethical standards and concepts, and their implication for land-use policy, typically occurs. Several questions arise here, many revolving around alternative notions of what constitutes a democratic process for land-use decisionmaking. Questions include these: What is the correct role to be played by citizens in the land-use decisionmaking process (e.g., direct decisionmaking, as through referenda and public participation)? Must all individuals affected by land-use decisions be involved in the decisionmaking process? What theory of representation should elected officials involved in land-use manners adhere to?

What values does the existing land use system embody? Traditionally, property rights advocates have argued that respect for individual autonomy and the accepted need to foster economic development should lead to a property rights regime that disfavors government intervention, such as governmental regulation of land uses. That view is argued by Professor James Huffman in the article immediately below.

■ JAMES L. HUFFMAN, THE PUBLIC INTEREST IN PRIVATE PROPERTY RIGHTS

50 Okla. L. Rev. 377 (1997)

[P]roperty in scarce resources is inevitable. It would seem to be in the nature of things. That property is in the nature of things does not necessarily mean that it is a morally superior social custom or institution. But there is a persuasive moral case to be made for the legal recognition and protection of private property rights. John Locke wrote at length and with great insight on property as the fundamental among all of the natural rights.

Why, then, are property rights advocates usually on the defensive? Because those who are excluded invariably outnumber those with the right to use or enjoy a particular resource. Property owners are thus easily cast as selfish individualists, while those who are excluded assume the comfortable mantle of the public interest in their efforts to influence the use of resources in which others possess property rights. The case for a public interest in the creation and protection of property rights is not easily made to those who anticipate that they will benefit from governments' interventions. The prospect of getting something for nothing is too much to resist for most self-interested advocates of the public interest.

So the claims of private property owners are often seen as obstacles to the pursuit of the public interest. The debate tends to pit self-interest against the public interest. Never mind that those who advocate for a particular version of the public interest will usually benefit personally from its realization. This is not to say that public interest advocates do not sincerely believe that the objectives they champion are good for the public. But it is the rare individual who does not value personally the ends he or she urges as in the public interest. . . .

The framers of the American Constitution understood both the natural rights and the positivist arguments for private property. They were well instructed in the natural rights philosophy of John Locke. They believed, as articulated in the Declaration of Independence, that individuals are endowed with inalienable rights. Their experience under the Articles of Confederation led them to insist upon the inclusion of a bill of rights in a new constitution, but a bill of rights which derived its content from the nature of things, not from the constitution, the democratic will or the government. Property was understood to be an inevitable consequence of human enterprise and a necessity for the fulfillment of human potential.

The framers of the Constitution also understood that without private property, the abundant resources of their continent would suffer the fate which Garret Hardin would, many years later, describe as the tragedy of the commons. Without secure and transferable property rights, resources would be allocated according to the whim of the self-interested thief or the well-intentioned representative of the democratic majority. In neither case would there exist the incentives requisite to wise use of scarce resources. The framers understood in their own way that a tragedy of the commons results from the individual's recognition that resources not consumed today will almost surely be consumed by someone else in the future.

Contrast the view of property rights just set forth with the following excerpt from an article by Professor Eric Freyfogle in which he attempts to generally categorize the trends in contemporary property rights.

ERIC T. FREYFOGLE, PROPERTY RIGHTS, THE MARKET, AND ENVIRONMENTAL CHANGE IN 20TH CENTURY AMERICA

32 Envtl. L. Rptr. 10254 (2002)

[O]bservers [sometimes] conclude that property rights best promote growth when they are (i) legally secure against interference, particularly governmental interference, (ii) clearly defined so that people know who owns what, and (iii) readily transferable. As some see it, the more that a property-rights regime reflects these principles, the more growth it stimulates. Best of all is a system in which everything is privately owned and transferable. Then, the market's reach is complete and all resources can flow to their highest valued uses.

In this era of transition for so many countries it is pertinent to ask: Do these characteristics describe property rights in the United States, particularly landed property rights? Would a property rights regime based on these principles help foster elsewhere the kind of economic success the United States has enjoyed? And what effects on the environment would such a regime likely produce? . . .

Over the past century, U.S. laws and regulations have increasingly re-embedded property rights in a communal order, aimed in important part at protecting the natural environment. Property law continues to recognize and protect individual rights, as it has for generations, but it recognizes other aims as well, and constraints on the market are pervasive. Aggregate calculations are hard to undertake, yet plentiful evidence suggests that these constraints have served not to contain economic growth, but to help fuel it, both by correcting the market's flaws in pricing and allocation and by fostering the kind of trust, social cohesiveness, and civic stability that any market needs to work well. In the ongoing drama of private property in America, the market is only one of the lead characters. . . .

Though the contemporary scene is distinctly messy, it is possible to identify six major themes or trends in contemporary landed property rights. Briefly stated, they are as follows:

- Landowner rights to use land are increasingly tailored to the land and to the surrounding social context; that is, rights to use land are becoming more context-dependent. In a related shift, rights to use land intensively are being reduced, with corresponding increases in the protections landowners enjoy against disruptive land uses by neighbors.
- Old categories of private ownership versus public ownership are being blurred, with more instances of intermediate ownership forms that mix the categories. Increasingly, rights in a single piece of land are fragmented among various "owners," with some rights held by the prime user of the land while other rights are held by neighbors, private entities, and government bodies.
- Land use planning is taking place on larger spatial scales and covering rural lands, aimed chiefly (although not solely) at urban sprawl, quality-of-life issues, and various land use-related environmental problems.
- American law has made substantial progress toward a complex reconciliation of the unending conflict between the private owner's desire for clearly defined, stable property norms and the community's contrasting need to retain power to redefine ownership rights in light of shifting conditions and values. The reconciliation offers substantial protection for existing land uses but far less protection for landowner desires to devote land to new uses.
- Governments at all levels, from the most local to the national and even global, are becoming involved in the processes of defining and controlling land use rights, albeit with little consensus and much experimentation on

how best to allocate power and responsibility among the various governing levels.

- In the vitally important rhetorical battleground over the meaning of private property, individualistic, commodity-focused images of ownership have gained prominence, and they have significantly impeded efforts to address rural land use problems, particularly land degradation caused by agriculture and other commodity-production activities. Though conservation advocates have been slow to develop alternative images of ownership—ones that draw upon organic, communal understandings of ownership—alternative images are emerging, thus joining the contest over private property as cultural emblem.

Notes and Comments

1. *The Four Land Ethics.* Professor Bosselman argues that understanding the four land ethics is necessary if we are to understand why the current debates over land use are intemperate and ideological. Which of these four ethics best reflects your own personal understanding of the role that land is to play in American society? How did you form that view?

As you read the material in the book, you should consider whether land use laws serve one of the "ethics" identified by Professor Bosselman more than others. For example, many commentators have argued that the laws governing use of the public lands owned by the United States government have traditionally been skewed in favor of development. *See, e.g.*, Arthur McEvoy, *Markets and Ethics in U.S. Property Law* in Harvey M. Jacobs (ed.), Who Owns America? Social Conflict Over Property Rights (1998) 6 (arguing that "[t]he law of property in the United States contains a profound bias toward developmental uses and against such nonmarket values as the health and welfare of the communities that live on the land"). *See also* Lynda L. Butler, The Pathology of Property Norms: Living Within Nature's Boundaries, 73 So. Cal. L. Rev. 927, 928 (2000) ("Th[e] failure to give serious consideration to the connections between land development, water use, and ecosystem health reflects a fundamental problem with American property law").

Professor Bosselman also states that we need "ongoing conflict management systems to cope with regular conflicts between existing ethical systems." What kind of systems might be designed for this purpose? Would they be legislative or adjudicatory? Or would they follow some other model, such as negotiation?

2. *Anthropocentric versus Ecocentric Land Ethics.* Another book on land use ethics has likewise focussed on different land ethics. Professor Kristin Shrader-Frechette argues that viewing land use ethics through the prism of anthropomorphism suggests which types of land ethics are likely to prevail:

> Although both land-use ethics and the earlier land-reform ethics call for a new land philosophy and a new land practice, they are primarily *anthropocentric*. They demand a change in our behavior so as to prevent harm to humans. . . .
>
> The two remaining land ethics, land-community ethics and land-rights ethics, however, are primarily nonanthropocentric or ecocentric. They issue moral imperatives, not for the sake of human well-being alone, but also for the good of the land

> (the entire biosphere) as a whole, apart from human interests. Although humans are included in the biosphere, presumably somewhat different actions might be mandated by an ecocentric or biocentric ethics that attempts to maximize the good of the whole biosphere, as opposed to an anthropocentric ethics that attempts to maximize the good of one subset of inhabitants (humans) of the biosphere.

Kristin Shrader-Frechette, Four Land Ethics: An Overview, in Lynton Keith Caldwell & Kristin Shrader-Frechette, Policy for Land: Law and Ethics, 57-58 (1993).

3. *Land Use and Religious Belief.* For some, religious beliefs are important factors in making land use decisions. For example, some authors have traced the development of a "Judeo-Christian principle of stewardship," with its consequences for such issues as land ownership. See Peter W. Salsich, Jr., *Toward A Property Ethic of Stewardship* in Charles Geisler & Gail Daneker (eds.), Property and Values: Alternatives to Public and Private Ownership (2000). Professor Salsich concludes that, while the principle of stewardship has "waxed and waned over the years," the ideal has survived and "is a consistent part of historical and current Judeo-Christian teachings." *Id.* at 36. He emphasizes that this principle would, for example, encourage the adoption of policies that could help a wide range of families obtain decent housing rather than maximizing advantages for families that do not need governmental assistance. *Id.*

4. *The Significance of the Opportunity Ethic.* How important is the "opportunity" land ethic to the American economy? Is it sufficiently central that greater restrictions on the ability to use land should be resisted on economic grounds? Or are there sufficient other outlets for entrepreneurial activities that the opportunity land ethic should play a less important role in land use law?

Do you agree with Professor Huffman's argument that increased recognition of private property rights will result in better use of natural resources, not increasing degradation? See also James L. Huffman, Land Ownership and Environmental Regulation, 25 Ecol. L. Q. 591, 600 (1999) (arguing that "a well designed system of private property will serve the public interest in many ways").

5. *The Significance of the Muirian Ethic.* Our developing understanding of ecology plainly calls into question the self-contained notion of traditional property law. For example, we now know that species require sufficient habitat for their survival, but this habitat may bear little relationship to the pattern of land ownership now extant. Should the right to use land in private ownership be changed to reflect this ecological knowledge? Professor Joseph Sax has pointed out the significant implications that this "economy of nature" poses for traditional property law:

> Assuming no compensation and a willingness to look anew at the nature of rights in land, what might property rights designed to accommodate both transformational needs and the needs of nature's economy look like? They would, at the least, be characterized by the following features:
>
> 1. Less focus on individual dominion, and the abandonment of the traditional "island" and "castle-and-moat" images of ownership.
> 2. More public decisions, because use would be determined ecosystematically, rather than tract by tract; or more decisions made on a broad, systemwide private scale.
> 3. Increased ecological planning, because different kinds of lands have different roles.

4. Affirmative obligations by owners to protect natural services, with owners functioning as custodians as well as self-benefitting entrepreneurs.

Joseph Sax, Property Rights and the Economy of Nature: Understanding Lucas v. South Carolina Coastal Council, 45 Stan. L. Rev. 1433, 1451 (1993). If this type of model were to become ascendant, can you envision what these "affirmative obligations" to protect natural services would look like? How would government make these types of decisions? Would the landowner be compensated for any loss of uses resulting from the affirmative obligations?

Consider Professor Freyfogle's attempt to summarize the current state of property rights, particularly his claim that American law has made "substantial progress" in reconciling the private owner's desire for stable property norms and the community's need to retain power. This conflict recurs throughout the book, particularly in the dispute over when a developer's right to build has "vested" and thus no regulation can obviate it. See Chapter 3 infra. Your view on when such rights should vest may well reflect your underlying land "ethic," as Professor Bosselman would term it.

In another article, Professor Freyfogle suggests that, for environmental policy to succeed, "ordinary landowners and other citizens must be drawn into the processes by which land-use decisions are made." Eric T. Freyfogle, Owning the Land: Four Contemporary Narratives, 13 J. Land Use & Envtl. L. 279, 307 (1998). He concludes that such participation "can help landowners become more knowledgeable about environmental problems," and the more such knowledge grows, the more likely the landowners are "to see land-use restrictions as legitimate responses to real problems, rather than as the corruption or dismantling of private rights." *Id.* In this casebook, you will see numerous examples of public involvement in land use decisions, and you can test this assertion for yourself.

6. *Defining the "Relevant Moral Community."* Professor Beatley raises the difficulty of determining "what the relevant moral community is." Looking at this issue in the first sense that he discusses, the geographical sense, he asks whether one is obligated to consider the effects of a land use decision only on the immediate neighborhood or whether the residents of the region or perhaps the state also must be considered. Think about this issue in terms of standing to litigate a decision. Who should be allowed to challenge a local government decision? Only those living in the community? Or should other, non-community members be given such rights? As you will see in this book, the land use system now recognizes the rights of "third parties" in land use disputes to an extent unheard of 25 years ago.

7. *The Exclusion of "Undesirables."* Another critical aspect of the ethical questions raised by land use regulation is the relationship between regulation and discrimination. Professor Jerry Frug has charged that local control over land use has resulted in the exclusion of what he terms "the wrong kind of people"—those excluded to make a residential neighborhood seem desirable. Jerry Krug, The Geography of Community, 48 Stan. L. Rev. 1047 (1996). In a more recent article addressing the information produced by the 2000 census, he and a co-author argue that current land use rules "allow the rich to exclude the poor from their jurisdiction and then to spend the money raised from local taxes on schools that admit only local residents and on crime control techniques that protect these residents from outsiders." David J. Barron and Gerald E. Frug, The Census as a Call to

Action, 29 Fordham Urb. L. J. 1387, 1388 (2002). He continues: "In other words, they allow some people to gain privileges by isolating themselves from those across the city line who want the same privileges." *Id.* Do you agree? Or do current land use patterns merely reflect existing consumer preferences, as we might expect in a market economy?

D. LAND USE AND ECONOMIC THEORY

Over the past three decades a considerable body of literature has grown in the field known as "Law and Economics." *See, e.g.*, Richard Posner, Economic Analysis of Law (1998). These writings have attempted to examine the consistency between recognized legal principles and the overriding criterion of microeconomic analysis: the assurance of economically efficient outcomes. Much of this literature is directly relevant to land use, examining whether current land use rules either promote or hinder economic efficiency. Indeed, one of the seminal articles in the field addressed legal entitlements from the perspective of what was, in essence, a land use dispute. See Ronald Coase, The Problem of Social Cost, 3 J. L. & Econ. 1 (1960).

Examining land use from an economic perspective provides a useful counterpart to the viewpoint, discussed above, that land use is an "ethical" issue. In the two excerpts discussed below, you will see how the economist views land use regulation. In particular, economic theory demonstrates how, at least from the standpoint of efficiency, the initial "entitlement" to land use rights is irrelevant. No matter what the entitlement, the parties will reach an economically efficient outcome—an outcome that achieves the result at the lowest possible cost. First, though, a brief word about terminology.

The economic theory we are concerned with addresses how markets take negative externalities into account. These occur when the activity of one individual on land imposes a cost on another individual. For example, if a landowner runs a large pig farm on his or her property (in modern terminology, a "confined animal feeding operation, or "CAFO"), that operation could impose negative externalities on neighbors, such as noise or, most likely, bad smells. More prosaically, a church in a residential neighborhood can impose externalities if large numbers of cars use all the parking on a street.

A related problem here is the question of the so-called tragedy of the commons. This occurs when lands are available for use by the public. In a leading article by that title, the author reasoned that individuals using a common area for grazing would have an economic incentive to keep adding additional animals to their flocks. The reason would be that, while the owner could keep all the benefit from that additional animal, the costs imposed by its grazing on the commons would be spread throughout the other users of the commons. The result would be the destruction of the commons caused by each individual user acting in his or her own self-interest. See Garrett Hardin, The Tragedy of the Commons, 162 Science 1243 (1968).

The concepts of externalities and the tragedy of the commons plainly illustrate the function of much of land use regulation. It is a body of law intended in large part to avoid externalities and damage to common goods. It does so by granting entitlements to individuals who are allowed to undertake land uses. But the question remains whether, in dealing with externalities, the current land use system serves the overriding purpose of economic efficiency.

With these thoughts in mind, consider the following two articles.

WERNER Z. HIRSCH, LAW AND ECONOMICS: AN INTRODUCTORY ANALYSIS

6-7, 14-15, 22, 80-82 (3d Ed. 1999)

LEGAL RULE FORMULATION

Rule formulation seeks to maximize or minimize some specified goal, often allocative efficiency. Normative or welfare economics is ideally suited for this task. This approach usually is applied after a failure to achieve a desired goal. Efforts are then undertaken to prescribe corrective solutions.

Efforts of rule formulation are in the rational intellectual tradition of William Blackstone[15] on the legal side and Adam Smith[16] on the economic side. They can also be traced to Jeremy Bentham's utilitarianism, "in its aspect as a positive theory of human behavior, . . . another name for economic theory."[17]

A modern-day proponent is Posner. His view of the world of economics and to no small extent of law includes the assumption "that man is a rational maximizer of his ends in life, "[18] an assumption he correctly reminds us is "no stronger than that most people in most affairs of life are guided by what they conceive to be their self-interest and that they choose means reasonably (not perfectly) designed to promote it."[19] On the basis of this assumption, three major fundamental economic concepts emerge.[20] The first is the inverse relation between price and quantity; the second is the economist's view of cost as opportunity cost, that is, the price that the resources consumed in making (and selling) the seller's product would command in their next best use — the alternative price; and the third is the tendency of resources to gravitate toward their highest value uses if exchange is permitted. If voluntarily exchanged, resources are shifted to those uses in which the value to the consumer, as measured by the consumer's willingness to pay, is highest. When resources are being used where their value is greatest, they are being employed efficiently; they produce the largest possible output. On the basis of microeconomic arguments — those that allegedly reflect the behavior of firms and households — Posner, for example, is convinced that "it may be possible to deduce the basic formal characteristics of law itself from economic theory";[21] consequently he argues that "the ultimate question for decision in many lawsuits is, what allocation of resources would maximize efficiency?"[22]. . . .

15. William Blackstone, *Commentaries on the Law of England*, 4 vols. (n.p., 1765–1769).
16. Smith, *Wealth of Nations*.
17. Jeremy Bentham, *Theory of Legislation*, R. Hildreth, Ed. (n.p. 1864): 325-326, 357.
18. Posner, *Economic Analysis of Law*, 3d ed.: 1.
19. *Ibid.*: 5.
20. *Ibid.*: 6.
21. *Ibid.*: 393.
22. *Ibid.*: 320.

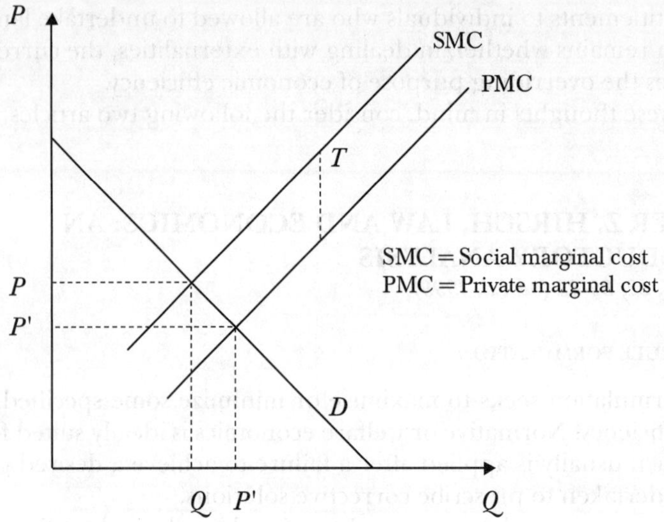

Figure 1-3

Now let us turn to externalities. An externality exists whenever the decision of such economic actors as a household or firm directly affects, through non-market transactions, the utility or production functions of other economic actors. An externality thus results as resources are exchanged in nonmarked situations commonly involving involuntary exchange.

A simple example of externality is shown in Figure [1-3], which depicts the demand and marginal cost curves for the product of a firm that emits smoke into the air in the course of production (the latter also is the firm's supply curve). The market equilibrium output and price levels occur at points *Q'* and *P'*. Yet this equilibrium is not efficient, for it does not consider the social cost imposed on residents who live near the factory and who must bear the discomfort caused by the smoke. If we assume that the discomfort to all the individuals equals *T* dollars per unit of production, then the full social marginal cost of production would be located *T* dollars above the firm's private marginal cost curve. The efficient equilibrium would be at output level *Q* and price *P*. In this case, the firm must pay for its true costs of production (we can assume that the firm directly compensates the individuals in the community). . . .

PROPERTY RIGHTS

The concept of property rights relates to the set of privileges and responsibilities accorded to a person in relation to the owning of property in general and real property in particular. These rights are determined by a long history of property laws, whether common laws or statutory laws. The right to property is the power to exclude others from or give them access to a benefit or use of the particular object. An elaborate system of property, liability, and inalienability rules exists to bolster an owner's claim to the property or good. Property rights to an unexplored area, such as the moon or the sea, are determined by international agreements entered into by bodies that have the power to enforce them. A mere individual without the coercive power of government could not hope to enforce a claim to, for example, the Atlantic Ocean.

The presence of property rights furnishes incentives to use resources efficiently. Given a legal system that enforces property rights, holders can have confidence that they will obtain returns from the use of property.

Under what conditions is a system of property rights efficient? The conditions include universality, exclusivity, and transferability. *Universality* implies that all resources should be owned by someone. *Exclusivity* is defined as the right to exclude people who might want to take part of the property. *Transferability* provides for voluntary exchanges that in general are value enhancing. . . .

Zoning is an area that lends itself more than some others to economic analysis. . . . [Z]oning involves the division of land into districts or zones having different regulations. These regulations impose legal constraints under which the land market must operate and rights and entitlements can be exchanged. The constraints are made in accordance with a comprehensive plan, ostensibly designed to promote the health, safety, and general welfare of the population. . . .

Efficiency of resource allocation and equity in income distribution are major considerations. The efficiency issue arises because, in the presence of externalities, land use controls in general and zoning in particular are designed to improve resource allocation. A major task is to assess the extent to which zoning does or does not accomplish this objective.

The equity issue arises because of direct and indirect influences of zoning. Direct influences relate to zoning's reallocation of rights and entitlements, with the result that some parties gain and others lose. At the same time, there are indirect effects because zoning influences patterns of local government finance, which in turn affect the distribution of income or at least the ability of local governments to redistribute income. . . .

Microeconomic theory can offer some further helpful insights — for example, into the relation between zoning and negative externalities. According to economic theory, the separation of land uses increases the efficiency of property markets to the extent that it causes the price of the parcel of land to equal its true marginal product without causing the prices of equal parcels of land to differ. Thus, for a zoning ordinance to increase the efficiency of the local property market, it should remove any externalities that exist and yet do so without artificially constraining the supply of land in any given use. However . . . increasing efficiency of land use in this manner is not easy.

WILLIAM A. FISCHEL, THE ECONOMICS OF ZONING LAWS: A PROPERTY RIGHTS APPROACH TO AMERICAN LAND USE CONTROLS

82-90 (1985)

The Pulp Mill Example and Efficiency

THE CONTROVERSY

. . . A wood pulp manufacturing company sought to locate a mill along the Connecticut River in New Hampshire. After briefly testing the political sentiments of several towns, it purchased an option to buy a large farm in a town of about three thousand people. . . . The company needed the town government to rezone the property from agricultural to industrial. . . .

Even though the mill might not have contributed to regional air or water pollution, it would still have created a number of *localized* nuisances that caused many townspeople to object to the rezoning proposal. These nuisances included the odors from the mill, the heavy truck traffic, and the disruptions to small-town life occasioned by the influx of newcomers who would work in the mill. . . .

THE MILL'S VALUATIONS

The mill's production process generates some fumes that must be disposed of somehow. An inexpensive way for the mill owner is to deposit them in the atmosphere. In this sense, the atmosphere is an input to producing pulp, just as trees, labor, trucks, and chemicals are inputs to producing the product. Like the use of other resources, the use of the atmosphere *can* be conserved if the mill's owner has some incentive to do so. . . .

Figure [1-4]'s horizontal axis is labeled "Use of Atmosphere Index." On the left side, it is as polluted (in the sense of foul odors) as is profitable for the mill; on the right it is perfectly pure. If we assume that degrees of pollution, the complement of air purity, can be measured accurately and easily, then there are, for the sake of argument, five degrees of air pollution or purity. To move from point 1 to point 2 (i.e., to reduce odors around the village) the mill owner takes some relatively inexpensive steps: he attaches some filters to major smokestacks and reduces some of the chemical spillage around the factory. Let us say that these steps cost $25. Now consider a further reduction in pollution, from point 2 to point 3. This requires a more costly adjustment. (It cannot be less costly; if it were, the firm would have done it first.) The factory may try a more expensive process using less sulfuric acid, it may pay a premium for types of wood that do not need so much processing, and it may cut back operations during temperature inversions. This costs an *additional* $50. To move from point 2 to point 3 costs the mill $50, but to move from point 1 to point 3 costs the mill $75 (= $25 + $50). . . .

Moving from point 3 to point 4 involves still greater expense (special precipitators, severely reduced operating hours, hiring more labor to monitor containments), of $75 extra. Moving from point 4 to point 5 involves looking for the next-best site—not locating there at all—at a cost of an additional $100.

THE VILLAGE'S VALUATIONS

Now consider the village residents who (alone) are affected by the atmospheric pollution. What is good-smelling air worth to them? Using figure [1-5], whose axes are the same as those in figure [1-4], begin at the left side again, where the air is (hypothetically) heavily polluted by the mill's fumes. What would it be worth to the villagers, all together, to reduce pollution from point 1 to point 2? Let us say $125. This might be inferred from increased housing values as the place became more pleasant (assuming the mill had already located there), but one must confess even at this early stage in the analysis that the collective value is difficult to determine: "I'd give one dollar to have a little less of those fumes," says one of the 125 villagers, and the sentiment is unanimous.

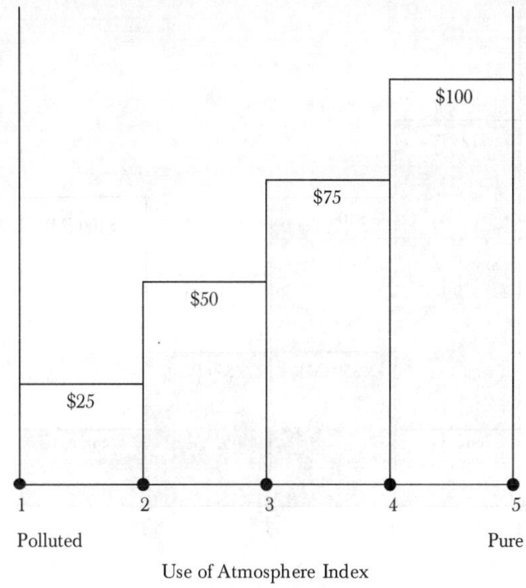

Figure 1-4
The Mill Owner's Valuation of the Atmosphere

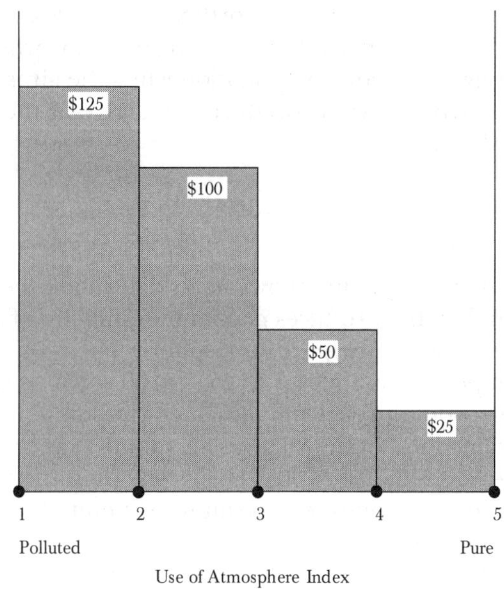

Figure 1-5
Village Residents' Valuation of the Atmosphere

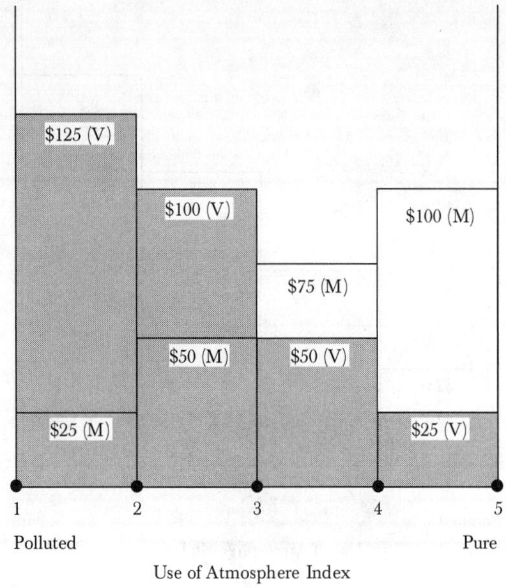

Figure 1-6
Mills' (M) versus Villagers' (V) Valuation of the Atmosphere

Suppose now that the villagers desire to have the factory reduce the pollution still more, from point 2 to point 3. That is worth \$100. Why less than \$125? Because of the law of diminishing marginal utility: reducing pollution when the air is usually pure is less compelling than reducing pollution when the air is palpably foul.

Using the same hypothetical procedure, we arrive at the remaining dollar values in figure [1-5]. . . .

VALUE MAXIMIZATION, COST MINIMIZATION

The next step in the analysis is to superimpose figure [1-4] on figure [1-5], which is done in figure [1-6]. This allows us to determine the point on the use of the atmosphere index that produces maximum valuation of air resources. The villagers would prefer point 5, the pure atmosphere. Their total valuation of point 5, as compared with point 1, is \$300 (= \$125 + \$100 + \$50 + \$25).

The mill owners would prefer an entitlement to point 1. Their valuation of the right to unrestrained use of the village's air (point 1) as compared with point 5, is \$250 (= \$25 + \$50 + \$75 + \$100). This is less than the \$300 valuation the residents would put on the opposite extremum. If points 1 and 5 were the only choices, the mill should not locate there.

If all of the points were realistic choices, then point 3 would produce the maximum valuation of the atmosphere. The mill's preference for point 3 as opposed to point 5, is \$175, and the villagers' valuation of point 3 as opposed to point 1 is \$225. The total valuation is thus \$400 (= \$175 + \$225), greater than that of either point 1 or point 5. It is also greater than the total valuation at point 4 (\$375) or point 2 (\$350), though either of these is preferable to the endpoints. . . .

ENTITLEMENTS AND EXCHANGE: THE COASE THEOREM . . .

Assume that the state government explicitly authorizes the municipality to make any kind of deal that it wants with the mill. It will freely enforce any arrangement settled on voluntarily. Assume also that the valuations of both parties of the use of the atmosphere (figure [1-6]) are known to both sides.

Now we state a seemingly remarkable result, known as the Coase theorem. Point 3 in figure [1-6], the use of the atmosphere that produces the maximum valuation, will be obtained regardless of whether the factory is initially entitled to pollute (point 1) or the villagers are originally entitled to pure air (point 5). Under our assumptions, in other words, the initial distribution of resource entitlements has no effect on the outcome, and the outcome maximizes the social valuation of the resource. . . .

THE COASE THEOREM GENERALIZED . . .

DIVISIBLE ENTITLEMENTS . . .

I noted earlier that economists' training makes them think of several alternative assignments. A lawyer's training suggests much the same thing. A common metaphor in property law is that property is a "bundle of sticks." The implication is that one can split up entitlement bundles in many ways: private agreements to divide property can involve covenants, easements, and other "equitable servitudes" that divide an interest. Nuisance law and zoning law can also be thought of as dividing up entitlements between the public and private landowners.

Notes and Comments

1. *Zoning and Efficiency*. Economic theory allows the evaluation of zoning against the principal norm offered by microeconomics: efficiency. A principal aim of zoning is to avoid land use conflicts that are nuisance-like in nature. Accordingly, an economist would ask whether the gains made in avoiding such conflicts are greater than the costs that the land use system imposes, and whether they are better than the land use situation that would occur as a result of unfettered operation of the private market.

Some economists have concluded that zoning is not superior. In a leading article, Professor Robert Ellickson sums up the "case against" zoning as follows:

> These locational decisions [imposed through zoning] unquestionably reduce the nuisance costs that would occur if land uses were randomly distributed. Nonzoning allocations, however, may also be better than random. Urban land markets automatically reduce nuisance costs far below the level that would be found with random land use distribution. Industrial plants are not attracted to prime residential areas; instead, they naturally congregate along railroad tracks, just where zoning is likely to put them. . . . It is difficult to disagree . . . that a nonzoning system seems to have allocated these uses as efficiently as any zoning scheme could have. Thus, even if a zoning system is more efficient than random land use, it does not necessarily follow that it reduces nuisance costs more than the market mechanism.

Robert C. Ellickson, Alternatives to Zoning: Covenants, Nuisance Rules, and Fines as Land Use Controls, 40 U. Chi. L. Rev. 681, 693-694 (1973).

2. *Overregulation and Efficiency*. One of the key insights of economic theory is its tendency to look at "mid-points" rather than all or nothing alternatives. For example, the most efficient land use solution to a noise problem may not be to completely ban it at a given location. Rather, efficiency might dictate that noise should be slightly reduced, and the neighboring buildings should have double-paned windows. *See* William A. Fischel, A Property Rights Approach to Municipal Zoning, 54 Land Econ. 64 (1978) (noting that "[e]mpirical investigations by several economists suggest that zoning tends to exclude land uses which have rather small effects on neighboring properties"). Given that land use is a political decision at the local level, are politicians more prone to less-efficient "all or nothing" solutions?

3. *Entitlements and the Coase Theorem*. As explained in the articles excerpted above, Coase's great insight was that the parties would reach the same efficient solution through bargaining no matter which party to a land use dispute is given the initial "entitlement" or right to use. See Robert C. Ellickson, Order Without Law: How Neighbors Settle Disputes (1991) (noting "a central proposition of law and economics [the Coase Theorem] that portrays people as bargaining to mutual advantage from whatever starting points the legal system has bestowed on them"). Does this conclusion mean that the law should be indifferent as to who receives such entitlements? What about considerations of equity? Or concerns about discrimination?

Consider, for example, the famous case of *Spur Industries, Inc. v. Del E. Webb Development Co.*, 494 P.2d 700 (Ariz. 1972). A developer built a retirement community next to a large agricultural feedlot. Then, after the noise and smells from the feedlot bothered the residents, the developer sued the feedlot owner on the grounds that the feedlot was a nuisance. The court held that the feedlot did constitute a nuisance. From a Coasian perspective, that should end the matter — the parties could then negotiate to reach an efficient solution. The court, however, ordered the developer to pay damages to the feedlot owners that would cover the expense of relocating. Arguably, the distributional effects of the initial legal entitlement drove the court's holding in this regard. *See generally*, James E. Krier and Stewart J. Schwab, Property Rules and Liability Rules: The Cathedral in Another Light, 70 N.Y.U.L. Rev. 440, 447 (1995) (suggesting that both "efficiency" and "justice" bear on who should be awarded the initial entitlement).

4. *Land Use Regulation and Public Goods*. Another key concept in economic theory is that of the "public good." If the developer of a good cannot legally protect it, others known as "free riders" may use it freely. Because of this problem, society may not produce such goods in the quantities that are needed. Land use planning and regulation can be seen as a means of ensuring that public goods are produced in sufficient amounts. See Christopher J. Weber, Public Choice, Pigouvian and Coasian Planning Theory, 35 Urb. Studies 53, 54 (1998) ("Land-use planning produces several types of public goods . . . in its control of urban development. It reserves land for public utilities and social infrastructure: the market would underallocate. . . . It produces policies for minimizing externalities (local spillover costs): . . . the market would undersupply such agreements largely because of the transaction costs of making and enforcing them . . . ").

5. *Economic Analysis and Information*. To make an efficient decision, a consumer must have accurate information about the choice before her. One of

the assumptions of microeconomic theory is that consumers have "perfect information" in making decisions. To the extent that they do not, government intervention may correct that imbalance.

Consumer choices, of course, have important implications for land use. For example, the materials set forth above in this chapter concerning the census show the great migration to the suburbs that has occurred and continues to occur. Consumers, presumably, are simply exercising their preference for cheaper housing in these areas and the amenities that go with them, and they are willing to put up with longer commutes to do so. What if, however, they are acting on flawed or incomplete information? *See* Mark S. Davies, Understanding Sprawl: Lessons from Architecture for Legal Scholars, 99 Mich. L. Rev. 1520, 1527 (2001) (suggesting "the possibility that consumer errors are contributing to sprawl" and that the field of "behavioral law and economics" may help scholars understand sprawl).

6. *Implications of Economic Analysis*. Economic analysis is a tool that can be used to make judgments about whether various land use regulations produce gains in the public interest. As you read the materials in the book, economic analysis will suggest a preference for certain kinds of processes as well. For example, the economist would favor bargaining between parties that will result in a more optimal or efficient result. Thus, the economist would likely favor the recent trend in land use law, examined in detail in Chapter 10, toward the use of "development agreements" that result from bargaining between developers and local governments. *See* Donald C. Guy & James E. Holloway, The Recapture of Public Value on the Termination of the Use of Commercial Land under Takings Jurisprudence and Economic Analysis, 15 B.Y.U. J. Pub. L. 183, 217-218 (2001) (noting economists' preference for market-based solutions such as development agreements).

E. THE PLAYERS IN THE REGULATORY PROCESS

One fundamental aspect of the current regulatory system is the location of governmental power. Unlike many other areas of modern law in which the federal government has played a key role, land use regulation remains principally a matter for local governments. It is critical for the student to recognize the implications of this institutional arrangement. For example, many important regulatory decisions in American society are entrusted to administrative agencies, often located at the state or federal level. Land use decisions, in contrast, are made by elected officials at the local level.

ANN O'MALLEY BOWMAN & MICHAEL PAGANO, IMAGINING CITYSCAPES: THE POLITICS OF URBAN DEVELOPMENT

8 Land Lines 1, 4-5 (March 1996)

CITY TYPES

A city government's orientation reflects both its leaders' aspirations and its tax-services balance. We have defined four city types based on levels of economic stress and political activism to promote development. In "survivalist cities" development decisions are triggered by a tax-services imbalance. These cities experience economic and fiscal stress and employ a greater-than-average number of development tools. In "market cities" that also suffer economic and fiscal stress, officials do not implement many economic development tools but instead leave the city's economic fortunes to the private marketplace. "Expansionist cities" are in fairly healthy economic shape, but they mobilize more economic development tools than the average city out of the desire to become a higher order city. "Maintenance cities" also enjoy economic and fiscal health, but city officials refrain from mobilizing many economic development tools because they want to control or manage growth.

Politics Matters

. . . A change in city leadership and the governing elite, the closing or downsizing of a large firm, or a substantial change in state aid or in unfunded mandates will, among other factors, influence the vision of the city's leaders and affect the underlying economy. These changes in vision and market adjustments, then, profoundly affect a city's approach to economic development. The mobilization of public capital as a mechanism for achieving the vision may change as well.

When voters replaced the leadership of Boise, Idaho, with more proactive officials in the mid-1980s, for example, a new vision was one of the most obvious results. The new mayoral-led coalition talked about regional prominence, and boldly marshaled public capital in support of development projects. The city used development tools and sponsored projects that were vastly different from those of the previous regime. In effect, Boise was transformed from a "maintenance city" to an "expansionist city."

Thus, politics plays an important role in explaining the path and direction a city chooses. Local officials may perceive a relevant orbit and then try to mobilize public capital in order to keep their city in (or move it to) that orbit. Or, they may choose to allow the workings of the marketplace to determine the city's orbit. In either case, market forces, a city's comparative advantage, the relative factor prices of land, labor, and capital — in short, the underlying local economy — influence these perceptions and the city's approach to development policy.

The next excerpt introduces you to the governmental jurisdictions that regulate land use at the local level.

■ ERIC DAMIAN KELLY, MANAGING COMMUNITY GROWTH: POLICIES, TECHNIQUES AND IMPACTS

8-11 (1994)

Planning and land use control in the United States take place largely at the local government level (a small number of states are also heavily involved in planning . . .). The United States contains more than 3100 counties and 19,000 municipalities. Not all local governments are active in planning. Many municipalities are too small: 70 percent of the total (about 13,000) serve fewer than 2500 people; another 19 percent (about 3700) serve more than 2500 but fewer than 10,000. Few of the very small local governments are likely to be active in planning, although some certainly are. Virtually all municipalities with populations of more than 25,000—numbering about 1000—have some sort of land use controls.

Counties participate in the land use control system in some states. In other states counties have little or no land use authority. . . . Allowing for all those local governments that do not exercise such power, it is safe to estimate that well over 3000 local governments in the United States are involved in planning decisions, and perhaps as many as 10,000.

Having several thousand local governments involved in planning over the vast land area of the United States may not seem significant. In heavily populated and growing areas, however, virtually all local governments are likely to be involved in their own separate planning and land use decisions. . . .

As if the system of land use controls itself were not complicated enough, the task assigned to that system poses enormous difficulties. Through the planning process, a local government attempts to plan for the use of land within its jurisdiction. Most of that land is privately owned, and many landowners have no idea what they will do with their land in the future. Some are happy farming it now and have no plans to do anything else, although one or more of them may cheerfully sell out to a developer within a year or a decade. Other landowners may be holding the land primarily for investment. . . .

A local government must try to plan for the future of such land, even though its owners, who are more intimately familiar with it, have no plans, impractical plans, impossible plans, or plans that simply may change. Although some local planners would resolve that situation by simply dictating future land uses to private owners, residents of the United States relate closely to land, emotionally as well as financially and legally; and they generally resent perceived intrusions on their ownership rights. . . . Thus, although most responsible owners recognize the need for some system of controls as a part of creating an orderly society, the political burden of proof generally remains on the local government to demonstrate why a particular restriction is necessary and reasonable. The system itself thus remains, in most cases, largely a reactive one.

As for all other types of lawyers, a critical issue for land use lawyers is understanding the background and make-up of the decisionmaking body as well as the motivations and background of others who participate in the process. Within the local government are various "players" that affect the outcome of a land use decision. The following article describes the planning commission, the administrative officer, and the legislative body at the local level. After first summarizing the origin of the planning commission and criticism of its function that emerged in early 1940s, the discussion continues:

■ THE PRACTICE OF LOCAL GOVERNMENT PLANNING (FRANK S. SO & JUDITH GETZELS eds.)

43, 422-424 (2d ed. 1988)

The role of planning commissions include the following: holding public hearings on comprehensive plans or elements of comprehensive plans; holding public hearings on zoning amendments; reviewing new land subdivision plats to ensure conformance with subdivision regulations; and, in some cities, holding public hearings on and discussing the capital improvements program. . . .

Independent planning commissions have probably persisted because government officials find that they serve some useful purposes. A commission can act as a buffer between government officials and the general public; can relieve the local legislative body of time-consuming public hearings and details; can serve as a sounding board for new ideas; and can add a fresh perspective to competing viewpoints of staff, citizens, and developers.

Along with the planning commission, another common local government advisory body is the zoning board of appeals (sometimes called board of adjustment). The board was created in very early zoning laws as a mechanism to hear appeals for variance from the strict interpretation of an ordinance. . . .

THE CHIEF ADMINISTRATOR

The relationship between the planning agency and the chief administrator is extremely important, especially in municipalities with the council-manager or strong mayor form of government. The influence of the chief administrator ranges from immediate operational issues to long-range policy questions. As the single person with the broadest influence on community decisions, the chief administrator can initiate new programs, lead publicly in the reconsideration of priorities, and throw the full weight of the local government administrative machinery behind a planning initiative. . . .

THE LOCAL LEGISLATIVE BODY

The local legislative body interacts with the planning agency in several ways. Because the council adopts the budget and passes local laws (including zoning ordinances), it is the final decisionmaker on the most fundamental policy issues in the community. . . . In effect, the council is the ultimate audience for the recommendations that emerge from planning activities.

Most of the interaction between the planning agency and the legislative body occurs in the context of zoning decisions. This is important for two reasons: First, the cumulative effect of zoning decisions has a profound impact on the physical development of the community. Second, the intensity and frequency of zoning activity make it the primary context for contact between the planning agency and the legislative body; it is here that the legislative body is most likely to observe the planning agency in action. Opinions that council members form about staff competence and integrity in the context of zoning actions may influence their willingness to accept planning agency advice in other contexts. Because zoning actions tend to be controversial and can be time-consuming and distasteful to the council, the conduct of the planning agency is particularly important.

Local Boards and Commissions

While the planning department has direct, formal relationships with the planning commission and the zoning board, it also has to interact with numerous boards and commissions in the governmental fabric of every urban community, many of which have responsibilities that relate to community growth and development. The list would typically include local school district boards, park and recreation commissions, and water or sewer utility district boards.

Finally, a key player in the land use process is, of course, the developer of the property. Completing a development in today's land use regulatory environment can be a difficult undertaking fraught with uncertainty. Consider the "eight-stage" model of real estate development posed in the following excerpt.

MIKE E. MILES, GAYLE BERENS, & MARC A. WEISS, REAL ESTATE DEVELOPMENT: PRINCIPLES AND PROCESS

6 (2000)

The Eight-Stage Model of Real Estate Development

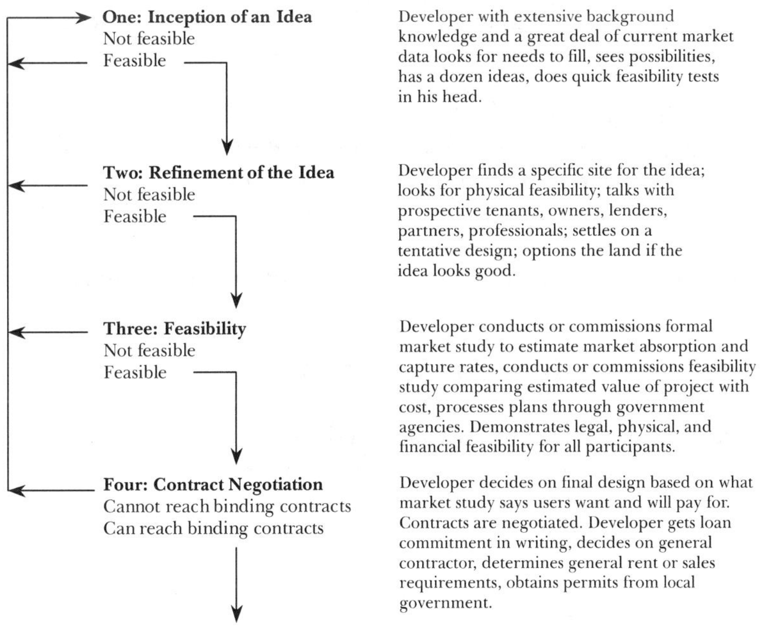

(*chart continues on next page*)

The Eight-Stage Model of Real Estate Development (*cont.*)

Five: Formal Commitment ↓	Contracts, often contingent on each other, are signed. Developer may have all contracts signed at once; joint venture agreement, construction loan agreement and permanent loan commitment, construction contract, exercise of land purchase option, purchase of insurance, and prelease agreements.
Six: Construction ↓	Developer switches to formal accounting system, seeking to keep all costs within budget. Developer approves changes suggested by marketing professionals and development team, resolves construction disputes, signs checks, keeps work on schedule, brings in operating staff as needed.
Seven: Completion and Formal Opening ↓	Developer brings in full-time operating staff, increases advertising. City approves occupancy, utilities are connected, tenants move in. Construction loan is paid off, and permanent loan is closed.
Eight: Property, Asset, and Portfolio Management	Owner (either developer or new owner) oversees property management (including re-leasing), reconfiguring, remodeling, and remarketing space as necessary to extend economic life and enhance performance of asset; corporate management of fixed assets and considerations regarding investor's portfolios come into play.

Notes and Comments

1. *Other Players*. Of course these are not the only "players" in the land use field. Most importantly, in most modern land use disputes a neighborhood association or perhaps an environmental group will play a role. For a famous, if now somewhat dated, look at the players in the land use business, *see* Richard F. Babcock book, The Zoning Game (1966). For a humorous look, consult Tom Paine, Unapproved Minutes of the Carthage, Vermont, Zoning Board of Adjustment, Harper's Magazine, Apr., 1998, at 77.

2. *Administrative Law*. Because most land use decisions are made by governmental bodies, the lawyer practicing in this field must be aware of the general procedures that local government entities follow in making decisions. They must also be cognizant of the principles that courts apply in reviewing such decisions. Much of this body of law is covered in the law school course on administrative law.

F. A CASE STUDY: THE PLAYA VISTA PROJECT

Now that you are generally familiar with the players and the process, it is time to take a look at a real land use project, the so-called Playa Vista Project proposed for a property along the coast in Los Angeles. Our reasons for using the Playa Vista Project as an exemplar are several. First, it is interesting, involving such famous names as Steven Spielberg and Howard Hughes. Second, it allows you to see how the development process actually works in a current situation.

You must realize that Playa Vista is much more complex than the typical, single-jurisdiction development approval process. But the project offers the advantage of showing you the wide array of agencies and individuals that can affect a development project. As you read the various chapters in the book, you will learn about the legal authority under which these agencies operate and the legal options available to the various interests that you meet in the description of Playa Vista.

We start with an article from the *Los Angeles Times* describing an important land use announcement about the Playa Vista property. The facts in the remainder are taken from various newspaper and magazine accounts.

DAVID FERRELL, SPIELBERG NOTES HOLLYWOOD TWIST FOR DREAM WORKS

L.A. Times, Dec. 14, 1995, Metro Part-B

Where Howard Hughes once tread, now comes Steven Spielberg and company.

That bit of symbolism was as vivid as a Hollywood sunset Wednesday in the vast aircraft hangar where, half a century ago, Hughes built his fabled Spruce Goose. With that relic now packed off to a museum in Dayton, Ore., and the aerospace industry still reeling like one of Jurassic Park's ill-fated tyrannosaurs, Spielberg took over the dim, dank and drafty hangar and proclaimed it home to the future of movie-making.

"This was so ideal it was almost meant to be," Spielberg said during a ceremonial unveiling of the proposed new DreamWorks SKG studio complex at Playa Vista, a high-tech entertainment center expected to break ground in June. "There must be some kind of karmic relevance to the fact that we are here in a hangar that Howard Hughes built to bring his dreams to life." . . .

The DreamWorks studios, built around an eight-acre lake, will form the anchor for a $750-million, 100-acre campus of studio facilities. And that complex, in about 10 years, will be part of a small town of more than 1,000 acres that will house 30,000 people and contain, among other things, more than 5 million square feet of office space. The massive project is being developed by Maguire Thomas and the Howard Hughes Corporation on oceanfront land north of Los Angeles International Airport.

A day after the Los Angeles City Council gave its conceptual approval to the plan, the three moguls of DreamWorks took to a makeshift stage on Wednesday, dwarfed by the size of the hangar and, illuminated by portable spotlights, pronounced their faith in the high-tech future of Hollywood. . . .

"It's the biggest business win that any city has ever had," Mayor Richard Riordan gushed, before a luncheon that included smoked salmon and pasta salad. "It sends a message to the rest of the world that Los Angeles is back."

Gov. Pete Wilson was equally effusive, alluding to the DreamWorks triumvirate as the "Three Wise Men" and saying, "To say I'm pleased and proud would be a terrible understatement. I'm excited as hell."

Wilson made it clear that the entertainment industry represents important hope to a state hard hit by cuts in the aerospace and defense industries.

"In my prior incarnation as a mayor [of San Diego], I would have sold my family to get a project like this. . . . Unlike Howard Hughes' Spruce Goose, this one's going to fly and soar for a long time."

Not every observer was so enthusiastic. About a dozen protesters, standing in a light rain outside the Playa Vista gates, held picket signs saying, "DreamWorks Wake Up," and "Spielberg Phone Home 2 Stop This Project." . . .

Those groups are fearful that the development will create substantial additional traffic in an area already badly congested and threaten sensitive wetlands nesting sites, despite a pledge by developers to restore the Ballona Wetlands.

Those concerns seemed far from the minds of those with embossed credentials in the hangar. . . .

George Clooney, star of television's "ER," met briefly with Spielberg, having recently made a deal to appear in one of the director's films. Clooney said it was his day off, and so "I thought I'd come over and see where I'd be coming to work every day."

Director Jim Cameron, noted for his special effects in "Terminator II," was there contemplating a new home for his rapidly expanding production company, Digital Domain. . . .

As we shall see, however, this was not the beginning of the story, and the end of it has not yet occurred.

Note on the Playa Vista Project

1. *The Property.* The Playa Vista property is 957 acres in size and is ideally located. Not only is it near Los Angeles International Airport, it fronts on the San Diego Freeway, a main transportation artery, and ends at the Pacific Ocean at the other end. The Playa Vista property was purchased by Howard Hughes in the 1940s. Hughes built an airplane hanger on the site and constructed his famous airplane, the "Spruce Goose," on the land. Most of the site, however, was left vacant.

On one part of the property is the so-called Ballona (pronounced "buy-owna") Wetlands. The wetlands are thought to have originally covered about 1,750 acres of property around 1850, but over the years urban development and encroachment has greatly reduced the area. By 1980, the wetlands only covered an area of somewhere between 175 to 325 acres. But the area was environmentally significant, for the wetlands area is one of the last remaining tidal marshes in the state and is home to a large amount of bird and animal life.

When the billionaire Hughes died in 1976, he left no will, and the Summa Corporation controlled the property and began planning to develop it. The property was considered the largest and most valuable undeveloped urban land parcel in the country. As of 1984, some speculated that its value was about $1 billion.

2. *The Initial Summa Plans.* Summa planned a gigantic development for the property. It envisioned 3 million square feet of new office construction, a 950,000 square-foot industrial park, 870,000 square feet of retail shops, and a 40-acre boat marina. The development would include a planned community of 20,000 residents living in apartments and condominiums.

To secure approval of the project, Summa faced a formidable regulatory gauntlet. The property itself was not part of the City of Los Angeles and would have to be annexed to the city. Development approval would require that the city's general plan call for such a project. Zoning would have to change to allow the development, and subdivision maps would have to be approved. For the marina to be built, the County of Los Angeles would have to allow Summa to cut through a parcel of county-owned property to connect the Summa land with a channel leading to the ocean. The development also would need approval from the California Coastal Commission, since it was located in the coastal zone, and from some federal agencies, most notably the Army Corps of Engineers, which regulates the filling of wetlands under Section 404 of the federal Clean Water Act.

The wetlands posed a significant problem for Summa. To alleviate environmental concerns about it, Summa soon agreed to pay over $10 million that would be used to restore about 175 acres of the marsh. In return, it would be allowed to fill the remaining acreage outside of the marsh. The State Coastal Commission approved the development. . . .

This approval, however, was followed by litigation. Concerned over the future of the wetlands, a group known as the Friends of the Ballona Wetlands filed a lawsuit seeking to block the Coastal Commission's approval of a wetlands area totalling only 175 acres. The group argued that between 250 and 325 acres should be set aside.

Summa otherwise continued to make headway on the project. In November 1985, the Los Angeles City Council voted unanimously to approve the annexation of the property. The city councilperson for the area, Pat Russell, praised the development as "such a prize to have within our area."

Then the politics began to change.

3. *The Shifting Political Winds.* During the building boom of the mid-1980s, traffic congestion in Los Angeles greatly increased, and a "slow growth" movement began to take form. In November 1986, the city's voters overwhelmingly passed Proposition U, which limited construction of commercial buildings in some areas. Councilperson Russell opposed the proposition, and many expected that she would have a tough campaign for reelection in April 1987.

In the April 1987 election, an antigrowth candidate, Ruth Galanter, forced Russell into a runoff by attacking her pro-growth record. Galanter, who had never run for office before, received large support from neighborhood and environmental groups, although her $32,000 in campaign contributions was but a fraction of the $262,000 raised by Russell. Russell argued that Playa Vista was substantially smaller than it would have been had she not forcefully advocated controlled development, but the voters were not convinced. Galanter won a sweeping victory over Russell.

4. *The Negotiations.* Galanter's election posed a significant problem for Summa, since in Los Angeles the councilperson in whose district a development is slated traditionally wields much informal control over it. Summa still needed to secure various approvals for the property from the city, so Galanter and Summa representatives began a series of negotiations over the proposal. Although Summa had the option of trying to seek city approval over Galanter's objections, that course of action might be difficult.

By May 1988 the negotiations had collapsed. Galanter had been seeking to cut the project by about 40 percent but was unable to persuade Summa to scale down its development. Summa decided to submit some of its so-called "tentative tract maps" — the legal documents required for subdivision approval — to the city. The maps covered 3,500 residential units, 5 million square feet of commercial development, and 600,000 feet of retail office space.

Galanter responded two months later by writing to the city's Planning Department and calling for a new environmental impact report on the project. She claimed that the 1985 report, which formed the basis for the earlier approvals, was "flawed" and based on "inadequate and inaccurate information." She said that changes that had occurred in the interim required a thorough reassessment of the project. If such a plan were prepared, it would mean a considerable delay for Summa, and the project and its impacts would be re-opened to intense public scrutiny.

The delays and difficulties in seeking approval apparently took a toll on Summa. A major change in the circumstances of the project was in the offing.

5. *The Maguire Thomas Partnership.* In February 1989, Summa announced that Maguire Thomas Partners had acquired a large interest in Playa Vista and would become the managing partner for the development. The partnership was well-known, indeed almost legendary in Los Angeles. Maguire Thomas had a deserved reputation as "enlightened developers" who listened to community concerns about development and shaped projects in a way that won widespread approval.

Maguire Thomas immediately set about meeting with all interests concerned with the project, from public officials down to neighborhood groups. It hired a public relations firm, which built a mailing list of about 25,000 names, and it produced a direct-mail newsletter on the project. By the end of June 1989, Nelson Rising, a lawyer who headed the development team for Maguire Thomas, announced that he did not expect any residential complex in the project to be taller than six stories, or any commercial office building to be taller than 10 stories, which was below the ridgeline of the adjacent homes on the bluffs. The amount of commercial space would be cut, and the number of residential units increased.

Maguire Thomas set about systematically solving the regulatory hurdles and opposition that it faced. By the end of 1989, Maguire Thomas believed that it had solved one large piece of the puzzle. It reached a tentative settlement with the Friends of the Ballona Wetlands to end the five-year-old lawsuit over the Ballona Wetlands. Maguire Thomas agreed to save 270 acres of wetlands and to drop the extension of a road through the wetlands. The parties agreed to hire a referee to mediate remaining issues. In exchange for the settlement, Maguire Thomas sought a promise that government agencies would expeditiously process all applications for zoning approvals and building permits. The plaintiffs in the case, the Friends of Ballona Wetlands, agreed to provide written and oral testimony supporting the project at public hearings.

The Maguire Thomas Partners began the preparation of a new environmental impact report for the project, and the partners continued the series of public meetings over the project. While the project received much support, it became clear that opposition continued to exist. Nevertheless, by September 1990, the partners had reached a deal with the State of California, which agreed to sell to Maguire Thomas the 70 acres of land it had received in payment for the tax liability of the Hughes' Estate.

In October 1992, Maguire Thomas released the draft environmental impact report for the project, which included documents totaling more than 2,000 pages and weighing 18 pounds.

6. *The Approval Process.* In January 1993, the developers received a surprise: Councilwoman Galanter announced that she opposed the first phase of the Playa Vista development. In a 19-page letter to the City's planning department, she raised numerous questions about the project's environmental impact report. At the same time, other critics of the project continued to blast away at it, emphasizing its size and the traffic impacts.

Responding to the criticism, in March 1993 Maguire Thomas indicated that it was making more changes in its project. In the final environmental impact report for the project, the partners agreed to construct further road and highway improvements, to alter their plans for handling traffic, and to limit the amount of office space in future stages of the development if the afternoon rush-hour traffic could not be reduced. It also promised to finance an unprecedented series of steps to widen streets and improve more than five dozen intersections.

Maguire Thomas also countered by releasing an economic study of the project, which it had commissioned from an accounting firm. When completed, the Playa Vista project would generate $39 million per year in tax revenue for Los Angeles, and $30 million more for Los Angeles County. The project would create up to 137,000 jobs and pump nearly $13 billion into the local economy in the next ten years.

In July 1993 the City of Los Angeles Planning Commission approved the project by a three to one vote. Later, Councilperson Galanter finally came out in favor of the project, praising it as a "model development" and stating that it "will play a major role in the economic revitalization of Los Angeles." With this last possible roadblock cleared, the full city council voted ten to one to approve the project.

7. *The Coming of DreamWorks.* The city council's action approving the project did not end the opposition. Less than one month later, opponents of the project filed suit in superior court claiming that the environmental review of the project was inadequate. The plaintiff was a group known as Save Ballona Wetlands, which was not to be confused with Friends of the Ballona Wetlands, which had sued earlier and whose case had been settled by the agreement with Maguire Thomas.

About a month later, the City's Ethics Commission released a report on lobbying expenditures before the City. The report noted that Maguire Thomas had paid $93,265 to lobbyists advocating the Playa Vista development.

The lawsuit by Save Ballona Wetlands went to trial in May 1994. Three months later, the trial judge rejected all the claims.

In the meantime, however, Maguire Thomas was encountering difficulties moving the project forward. By January 1995, financing for Playa Vista was still not in place, although the City was making plans to market bonds to be used to finance public improvements on the site. But during the same month, the Los Angeles Times first reported an intriguing development: Robert Maguire III of Maguire Thomas was negotiating with Steven Spielberg, Jeffrey Katzenberg, and David Geffen to have them locate the campus of a proposed studio on the Playa Vista property.

Negotiations with DreamWorks SKG continued throughout 1995. In the meantime, the City of Los Angeles jumped in to help. The economic recession of the early 1990s had hit the city hard, and it wanted to ensure that the DreamWorks SKG studio would locate within the city. To do so, it put together what was described as an "unprecedented series" of tax breaks and other economic concessions designed to lure DreamWorks SKG.

By the fall of 1995, the deal started to come together. However, if part of the property was to become the DreamWorks studio, changes were required in the approvals which Maguire Thomas had previously secured from the City. Accordingly, the partners applied to the City for permission to alter its street and subdivision maps and to expand the first phase of its project from 280 to 336 acres. The City approved the changes, and it also gave preliminary approval to the $70 million package of tax and development incentives.

In December 1995, DreamWorks SKG agreed to become the anchor tenant and to take a $200 million equity stake in the $750 million needed to begin the first phase of construction.

Once again things seemed to be looking up for the Playa Vista project. Then another bombshell hit.

8. *The Break-Up.* On August 13, 1996, Maguire Thomas Partners issued a press statement announcing that its founders were splitting up the partnership. Observers declared that the real estate recession, which greatly depressed office rents in Los Angeles, was at least partly responsible for the breakup. By November 1996, a U.S. News and World Report article was gloomy about the prospects for DreamWorks' Playa Vista project. The problem, said the article, was the money needed for infrastructure.

A month later, another group of environmentalists, called the Wetlands Action Network, filed suit, this time in federal court. The group claimed that the U.S. Army Corps of Engineers had violated the Clean Water Act and other federal laws when it approved the developer's permit to fill, dredge, or pave over about 28 acres of wetlands.

9. *The Project in Limbo.* Throughout 1997, as the real estate recovery in Southern California blossomed, the future of the Playa Vista project remained uncertain. In October 1997, an agreement to transfer ownership of the development to a consortium of new owners, including real estate affiliates of New York investment banks Goldman Sachs & Co., and Morgan Stanley & Co., was announced.

In February 1998, the project was back before the city council, which refused to help secure government-financed bonds to fund the project's housing component. City Councilwoman Galanter withdrew her support of the $70-million state bond application when she could not persuade the developers to include more low and moderate-income housing in their plans.

10. *More Litigation and No DreamWorks.* In January 1998, three environmental groups filed a lawsuit in federal court, claiming that the U.S. Army Corps of Engineers had violated the Endangered Species Act when it issued permits for the construction of the Playa Vista development. The suit claimed that the U.S. Fish and Wildlife Service failed to ensure "non-jeopardy" of the California brown pelican and nine other endangered or threatened species. During the same month, the developers began construction on the freshwater marsh part of the development.

In June of that year, a federal district judge ordered a halt to the filling of the wetlands. He ruled that the Corps had failed to consider the total impact of the project and had relied on environmental reviews that were insufficiently detailed. The company responded that it would continue its building of infrastructure on the part of the site which was unrelated to the wetlands.

Protests around the site became commonplace, including one by a 25-year old man staging a hunger strike. In December, the Los Angeles City Council, by a ten to two vote, approved $87 million in tax-free housing bonds for the development of Playa Vista. The developers had agreed to build 417 apartments for very-low, low, and moderate-income tenants.

In July 1999, DreamWorks canceled plans to build its studio headquarters at Playa Vista.

In August 2000, the U.S. Court of Appeals for the Ninth Circuit reversed the District Court's decision that had barred filling of a portion of the wetlands on the project. The Supreme Court thereafter denied review. But a new issue emerged: the possibility of dangerous levels of methane gas. City of Los Angeles officials, involved because of the bond funding for the project, began studying the issue. They later reported that the project could be built safely.

11. *New Directions and First Tenants.* A new star then arose. In July 2001, Architect Frank O. Gehry, internationally renowned for his work on projects such as the Guggenheim Museum in Bilbao, Spain, and the Experience Music Project in Seattle, agreed to design at least four buildings on the site. In the meantime, construction was underway on the first residential units. Plans for the second phase remained uncertain, with more regulatory approvals required.

The next month, developers of the project signed an agreement with the Trust for Public Land, giving that group an option to buy 193 acres of property. If the deal went through, the overall project would be scaled back so that wildlife habitat in the Ballona Wetlands could be preserved. The parties, however, had not yet agreed on a price, and the Trust had to figure out how to come up with the money.

Meanwhile, some protested Architect Gehry's involvement, including an old friend who chained herself to the doors of his studio. Another lawsuit also complicated matters. A coalition of homeowners had filed suit claiming that the City's general plan was legally inadequate. But the California Coastal Commission approved the street improvements needed to complete the project. It did so after a public hearing in a room filled with over 300 opponents and supporters of the development. Opponents unsuccessfully challenged the approval in court.

Building continued on the site. Now, however, the project was styled as a good example of what was called "the New Urbanism."

In April 2002, the first residents moved into apartments at the Playa Vista development. Ultimately, the first phase would result in 3,246 dwellings. Councilwoman Galanter was quoted as saying that Playa Vista "is a project designed to do smart growth" with "jobs and housing in the same place."

In July 2002, yet more litigation started. Two environmentalists sued the California Department of Transportation over a freeway project designed to serve the development. Soon thereafter, Architect Gehry decided not to move his studio to Playa Vista.

In December 2002, the Los Angeles Planning Department opened hearings on Playa Vista's next and final phase of development. This phase, which the developer described as "smaller, greener," planned for 2,600 homes as well as retail shops and restaurants. It would have 55 percent less housing than the originally proposed 13,000 units.

Notes and Comments

1. *The Project in Perspective.* Why has the Playa Vista Project taken so long to build? Is the project simply too large? Was the approval process too convoluted? If so, what would you change in the process?

2. *Levels of Governmental Authority.* Note that while local government retains by far the most important role in this process, other governmental entities have critical roles in the approval process. For example, the county had to approve the yacht channel connecting to the ocean, the coastal commission had to approve the project, and the federal government had approval power over filling the wetlands. What level of government should have the bulk of the approval power over this project?

3. *Tax Breaks for Hollywood?* The City of Los Angeles approved a package of tax breaks and other incentives designed to lure DreamWorks into locating at Playa Vista. In addition, the State of California is providing over $40 million in free benefits. Is this an appropriate use of government money? What criteria should the government use in deciding to "invest" in this project in comparison to other projects? Shouldn't projects in the inner, decaying part of Los Angeles, devastated by riots in the early 1990s, take priority over this one?

4. *The Environmental Splinter Groups.* Consider the numerous lawsuits brought by environmental groups. Were any of these lawsuits frivolous? If so, how should the legal system deter them? After the original lawsuit brought against the project was settled, that group of plaintiffs supported the project. New groups, however, soon sprung up. Should these "splinter" groups somehow be barred from litigating?

5. *The "Consensus" Approach to Development.* The approach of Maguire Thomas to developing the project was very different from the Summa Corporation. Do you think that a process by which the developer consults with all interested parties and tries to meet their interests is one that is preferable for a developer? Did Maguire Thomas gain anything by proceeding in this fashion?

6. *Analyzing and Mitigating Traffic.* The chief complaint about the Playa Vista project was that it would cause too much traffic. Was this impact sufficiently analyzed? Transportation infrastructure is put in by cities, counties, the state, and the federal government. Can their efforts be coordinated to ensure that the traffic impacts from the Playa Vista project are sufficiently mitigated? Should a developer have to pay to mitigate those impacts?

G. ORGANIZATION AND THEMES OF THIS CASEBOOK

1. Organization

The casebook is designed to provide the student with a comprehensive understanding of the law of land regulation in a practical, contemporary context. The materials emphasize the theoretical foundation for contemporary regulation and touch on the most controversial and significant applications of land use law doctrine. In line with this approach, with the exception of a selected group of "classic" cases of which every student of land use must be aware, the cases selected for use in the book are of very recent vintage. The goal is to put you in the midst of the currents swirling through land use regulation as it is now practiced throughout the country.

At the outset, you should spend a few minutes thinking about the overall structure of the book. Part Two of the materials begins with the basic building blocks of public regulation. Thus, Chapter 2 covers zoning and its various permutations, while Chapter 3 is an overview of the administration of subdivision regulation. Chapter 4 deals with the financing of infrastructure, and Chapter 5 lays out the role that the comprehensive planning process plays in regulation.

With the basic tools of land use regulation in mind, Part Three of the book turns to the limits of land use regulation, which are found in several places. First, Chapter 6 looks at the various doctrines that govern judicial review of local land use decisions, the procedures followed by local governments, the use and misuse of litigation (by opponents and proponents), and the availability of relief in the federal courts. Chapter 7 builds on the discussion of infrastructure financing in Chapter 4 by completing the analysis of the Takings Clause of the Fifth Amendment. This clause sets the outermost constitutional limits of land use regulation. In Chapter 8, we turn to those limits found in the First Amendment's protections of freedom of speech and freedom of religion. Finally, the last two chapters of this part look at limits of a different sort. Chapter 9 focuses on the restrictions that the regional, state, and federal governments place on local governmental control of land use. Chapter 10 then asks the student to step back and consider alternatives to the present model of land use control. Since we may well be in a state of transition from a legislative or adjudicative model of land use controls to one based on bargaining, this chapter is a critical bridge to the future.

Part Four of the book centers on the critical tradeoff between housing and controlling growth. Chapter 11 covers the issues presented by the contemporary growth management policies that are increasingly followed in various jurisdictions. Chapter 12 then addresses the means now found in the law for securing a sufficient supply of housing, particularly housing for those of low or moderate income.

The last part of the book then turns to how the land use system effectuates specific policy objectives. Chapter 13 examines those laws established to prevent discrimination and to ensure equal opportunity in the land development process. Chapter 14 focuses on environmental protection, particularly on how federal and state laws designed to protect the environment have affected the development of land. Chapter 15 addresses planning issues in redevelopment, emphasizing economic development and issues of anticompetitiveness in land planning regulation. Chapter 16 addresses the siting of unpopular land uses, while Chapter 17 concludes the book by looking at how the land use system is used to protect aesthetic values.

2. *Themes*

While the casebook is organized in chapters that cover discrete topics, you will find certain themes in the materials that recur throughout the book. These themes create a lens through which to examine land use regulation.

The Benefits and Dangers of Discretion. Perhaps the most obvious recurring theme is the benefits and dangers of discretion. Because of the need to identify the environmental harms and infrastructure costs generated by individual projects, land use regulation has evolved to establish legislative and administrative review techniques. These techniques allow local governments to exercise a great deal of discretion in approving projects. In addition to authorizing the local government to approve or reject the project, the land use regulatory system also allows the government to impose permit conditions, including conditions to mitigate identified environmental harms or infrastructure needs, to alter the project and its site design, to require other improvements, and to require the developer to finance facilities. The authority to exercise discretion is found in subdivision ordinances, review procedures for site plans, and other types of permit-granting functions.

With the exercise of this type of vast discretion, however, comes the possibility that it will be exercised arbitrarily. Students must carefully consider whether such discretion is advisable and how the legal system can be structured to ensure that it is exercised properly.

The Dynamic Nature of Land Use Regulation. Another important theme is the dynamic nature of land use regulation. Almost every area of the field of land use regulation is undergoing evolutionary changes. These changes reflect not only the rapidly changing discipline of land use planning, but also the fast pace of changing doctrine in the courts and the perennial modification of procedures and standards by state legislatures. Moreover, judicial review of the land use process has been active.

All of this means that practicing in the field requires considerable flexibility. The ability to recognize trends and take advantage of rapidly changing circumstances becomes critical.

Land Use and Unattainable Political Goals. Land use regulation is often designed to undertake goals that may be very difficult for communities to attain. For example, the land use regulatory process must secure sufficient housing for all segments of the community while, at the same time, providing environmental protection and saving open space. If the goals themselves are in conflict, attaining those goals can be impossible.

In addition, the political nature of the regulatory process can impede rational efforts to attain goals. For example, elected politicians may restrict the ability of the local planning commission or board to carry out its responsibilities.

The Tension Between Regulatory Methods and Constitutional Protections. Another broad theme in land use regulation is the tension between regulatory methods and constitutional protections. The recent United States Supreme Court cases on takings underscore the escalating conflict between constitutional commands and government's ability to regulate land use and the development process effectively. The trend is clearly toward more constitutional protection; increasingly, developers are going to court and finding an attentive judiciary. At the same time, First Amendment rights, put at risk by actions such as municipal attempts to preserve church structures and to regulate adult businesses, are increasingly being litigated in the courts.

The Rise of Third-Party Rights. Third parties such as citizen and environmental groups are key players in the development process. The range of interests represented by third parties varies widely. These parties include neighborhood residents, business associations, advocates for affordable housing, civil rights activists, construction trade unions, civic groups promoting democracy, environmental groups, and so-called conservative public interest organizations seeking to preserve property rights.

When you read the materials in the casebook, you will see how the actions of these groups affect the development process, both directly through participation in a particular decision, and indirectly through political activity. What is debatable is the extent to which such participation is useful and should be encouraged, or is counterproductive and contributes only to economic inefficiency and delay. The materials in this casebook will put you in a position to make judgments about issues associated with third-party participation.

The Cost of Growth. As municipalities throughout the United States are now well aware, there is no "free lunch" associated with growth. It is possible for growth to be well planned so that its costs are paid by tax-financed public or private sources, such as exactions imposed on the developer or assessments imposed upon the ultimate homeowner. It is also possible to analyze possible environmental threats to determine if they will actually occur and to design measures to mitigate their effects. Current principles of growth management emphasize the concept of ensuring that development and the infrastructure to support it—roads, schools, water, sewer services, and so forth—are "concurrently available."

Sprawl, however, imposes other opportunity costs, which may not be so obvious. For example, the approval of a particular type of development may constitute a "lost opportunity" to develop convenient public transit. The density of the project may be too low, or the design of the project too spread out, to locate transit conveniently to the development. Sprawl may also mean that new suburban employment centers are inaccessible for those individuals who live in the central city and who are most in need of access to employment.

As you consider the land use regulatory system, you must decide whether it adequately addresses the costs that such development imposes.

Regulation and Social Equity. If there are clear losers in the land use regulatory process, it is the poor and most minority racial groups. Their economic plight often leaves them confined to the declining central city, without access to economic opportunities available in the wider region, to the training and education necessary to compete in the limited employment market, and to higher education. In some instances, the land use regulatory system operates to exclude such groups—so-called exclusionary zoning. In other instances, poor residents find that they are exposed to greater risks from facilities that have externalities associated with them, such as landfills and hazardous waste disposal operations.

The Friction Between Urbanization and Environmentalism. The most fundamental part of the debate over contemporary land use regulation is whether to maintain and extend the pattern of suburban development so prevalent over the last 25 years, or to pursue a more dense development pattern. Such a pattern, for example, might emphasize the planning of villages located near transit stations. It likely would emphasize so-called sustainable development, a concept that includes such features as maximizing recycling of solid wastes, using reclaimed water, and minimizing the use of toxic chemicals such as pesticides.

Whether the movement toward sustainable development will result in extensive changes in how development occurs is a theme that recurs throughout the book, and it is one that the student must carefully consider.

Regionalism and the Appropriate Level of Government for Land Use Regulation. For some time, it has been apparent that the traditional model of land use regulation at the local level may no longer be appropriate. Problems are often insoluble at the neighborhood or municipal level, particularly where a community has sited many uses that demand services that the community's tax base cannot support. Another problem is that cities compete for tax-generating development, such as large shopping malls, while seeking to exclude other uses, such as low and moderate income housing, that generate insufficient taxes to fund needed services and facilities. Moreover, as our concern over environmental protection has grown, environmentalists have increasingly argued that an institutional arrangement for land use control that is premised on local government jurisdictional lines is inadequate to respond to the larger effects of development on ecosystems.

As you read the cases and other materials in this book, you must evaluate the pros and cons of situating land use regulatory authority at the local level.

Regulation, Deregulation, and Economic Efficiency. An understanding of the land use regulatory process cannot be achieved without an appreciation for economics. Regulations can greatly affect the desirability of sites by either increasing or decreasing land uses.

For example, "over-zoning"—the practice of zoning many more acres in a community for a single use, perhaps industrial, than is needed—may tend to reduce the price of such land and increase the community's attractiveness to industrial development. Alternatively, regulations that increase the size of home sites, reduce density by placing fewer homes on larger tracts, or increase the developer's obligation to fund infrastructure and mitigate environmental impacts, may tend to increase the cost of housing. The law of supply and demand is operative.

Law reform of the existing land use system must balance the need for affordable housing and for reasonable land prices that will attract developers with the need to ensure a high quality of life through the provision of adequate infrastructure and sufficient environmental safeguards. The tradeoff is inevitable.

The Future—Evaluation and Reform. Ultimately, the land use regulatory process must be evaluated for its ability to achieve these types of societal objectives. A realistic appraisal of the current law reveals that the democratic majority may not favor many of the objectives that such laws are designed to serve, such as ensuring adequate housing, assuring access to employment for the poor, or siting unwanted facilities. Can the land use system overcome the determined opposition of some individuals to these goals? Can it bring about housing for the poor, protection of natural resources, assurance of adequate infrastructure, and the siting of unpopular land uses such as landfills, incinerators, prisons, and homes for the disabled? If not, how can the system be reformed to achieve these goals?

These are questions that you must ponder as you encounter the materials ahead.

PART TWO

THE LAND USE REGULATORY TOOLS

2

Zoning

A. INTRODUCTION

1. In the Beginning: Euclidian Zoning

The materials that you read in Chapter 1 provide more than just the usual interdisciplinary perspective on the law that is included at the beginning of many law school casebooks. They also illuminate the environment in which land use regulation takes place, an environment that the land use lawyer must be cognizant of at all times in order to serve clients properly. Thus, as the person who often heads a team of individuals working on a land use problem, the lawyer must fully understand the politics of the local government officials who must approve or disapprove a development. Economics also plays an important role in the process. If, as is often the case, the lawyer ends up negotiating with the local jurisdiction over the various conditions that will be imposed on the project, or represents the local government in such negotiations, a firm understanding of the economic tradeoffs involved in those conditions is essential. It goes without saying that the lawyer must understand the planning profession and the discipline its members practice.

Most importantly, however, the lawyer must understand the legal tools of land use regulation, the fundamental building blocks found in the ordinances of every local jurisdiction, and the statutes of every state. Fortunately, although they vary slightly from jurisdiction to jurisdiction, the basic forms and functions of land use controls are relatively consistent. The student must do more than recognize them, however; he or she must understand how they have evolved to the present and, based on that evolution, how they are likely to develop in the future. The historical context of land use regulation is important, for it offers fundamental lessons about today's land use regulatory system.

Accordingly, although common law methods of controlling land uses through such mechanisms as covenants and nuisance law have existed for centuries, the chapter starts with the most famous zoning case, *Village of Euclid v. Ambler Realty*, 272 U.S. 365 (1926). In this decision the United States Supreme Court upheld the constitutionality of a local government zoning ordinance, even though it caused a large diminution in the property value of the plaintiff's property. Two years later in *Nectow v. City of Cambridge*, 277 U.S. 183 (1928), the Court handed down a decision demonstrating how a zoning regulation can go too far and be found unconstitutional. The Supreme Court then largely disappeared from the land use field for decades, surfacing in significant fashion only in the late 1980s when it issued a series of rulings on the Takings Clause, discussed in Chapters 4 and 7. After *Village of Euclid* and *Nectow*, the state courts were left to sort out the huge volume of land use cases that arose throughout the ensuing decades as the tentacles of local land use regulation spread.

The *Village of Euclid* case is important for another reason: it introduces the student to the features of the classic zoning ordinance, often referred to as "Euclidian zoning." The theory behind this type of ordinance seems almost quaint in retrospect; the local government rationally decides which types of uses and densities should be allowed throughout the city, and it then passes a zoning ordinance implementing its conclusions. The local government thereafter is to act largely as an observer as the operation of the ordinance shapes a rational development pattern throughout the jurisdiction.

2. *The Need for Flexibility*

This ideal, of course, was not fulfilled. For one thing, the economic interests at stake in land use regulation are extraordinarily large, a fact clearly illustrated by the effect of the ordinance on the plaintiff in *Village of Euclid*. The existence of such large economic stakes make it inevitable that landowners will push for changes to a zoning ordinance if it does not allow for the intensity or type of development they wish to pursue. Moreover, the concept of zoning plainly clashes with the celebrated American ideal of the individual entrepreneur, a person who recognizes a market for a development, buys the land, and wants to build — only to find that the property's zoning will not allow the development. The power of these economic and entrepreneurial forces pushing for change in existing land use regulations means that some flexibility in the system is necessary to accommodate change.

Other reasons besides the political need to accommodate the economic and entrepreneurial forces of land development support the need for flexibility. In particular, classic Euclidian zoning assumes that the zoning authorities can foresee how development will unfold in the jurisdiction and, based on that knowledge, will zone accordingly. That degree of foresight, however, rarely exists in a dynamic, constantly changing economy. Thus, the zoning map becomes less a plan for future development than a hopeful but slightly tentative model of future direction.

One example from the 1990s, the "home business," illustrates how unforeseen economic developments can require change in local land use regulation.

Citizens in a given locality might theoretically agree that business and residential uses should be separated; homes should not be subjected to the kinds of externalities often associated with businesses, such as noise from traffic, parking problems, employees coming and going during evening hours, and so forth. In the 1990s, however, computer technology has, in rapid-fire fashion, brought us faxes, the Internet, electronic mail, and computerized research, all of which allow individuals to work more easily from their homes. Indeed, air quality regulators vigorously promote the idea of "telecommuting" from home as a means of controlling air pollution. However, many who answer the call to work at home are surprised to find themselves in violation of local zoning laws that do not allow their business as a permitted use where they live. Change in the existing ordinances is then sought to accommodate the right to work out of the home.

In the decades after *Village of Euclid*, then, local jurisdictions attempted to introduce a measure of flexibility into their land use systems through a variety of regulatory devices. Another function of this chapter is to introduce such devices to the student. The earliest flexibility devices were zoning amendments, variances from the zoning ordinance, and use permits. Later, the local governments sought and received permission from the courts to use floating zones and planned unit developments. All of the flexibility devices have the common characteristic of focusing on the individual impacts from a particular development or use, rather than on the needs of the jurisdiction as a whole.

3. *Flexibility and Discretion*

A fundamental purpose of this chapter is simply to familiarize the student with these devices. You must learn to recognize them, to understand their features, and to see their limitations. They are the basic tools of the land use lawyer's trade.

In learning about how these devices work, however, the student soon encounters perhaps the most important underlying conundrum in the land use system: the question of how to give local governments sufficient discretion while, at the same time, constraining the exercise of that discretion to avoid administrative arbitrariness and inconsistent decisionmaking. Flexibility is a slippery slope; one person's valid zoning amendment or use permit is another's arbitrary change that conflicts with the overall land use regulatory pattern.

One means of controlling discretion is through judicial review, and Chapter 6 examines the techniques that courts use to control judicial discretion. In the meantime, you must be aware that the concern over excessive local government discretion early on led to prohibitions against "spot zoning" and "contract zoning." In the case of spot zoning, certain zoning amendments were deemed illegal because they lacked a comprehensive viewpoint, while contract zoning was seen as an impermissible bargaining away of the local government's police power. The judicial conclusion was that both spot zoning and contract zoning necessarily were enactments made for the benefit of the individual landowner rather than in the public interest.

Spot zoning cases continue to appear regularly in the courts, but defining spot zoning in the abstract and "spotting" it (pardon the pun) in the real world are two very difficult undertakings. The case law sometimes seems a morass of cases applying vague standards to reach inconsistent results, a state of affairs that puts a premium on the advocacy skills utilized by land use lawyers.

4. *Flexibility and the "Slippery Slope"*

The slippery slope of "flexibility" grew even steeper in the 1980s and 1990s as development proposals became increasingly complex, and municipalities began to mitigate their impacts through negotiating various conditions on the project. It is not a big step from negotiating marginal aspects of a proposal to negotiating a complete land use "deal" between a developer and a municipality. Furthermore, even though something about a negotiated "deal" between a developer and a local jurisdiction can give cause for alarm, negotiated agreements are not necessarily a bad idea. In a later chapter of this casebook, the student will examine in more detail the "negotiation" model for land use decisions and have the opportunity to reach conclusions about its efficacy. In the meantime, you must keep in mind that the greater the range of the negotiations, and the larger the number of conditions placed on individual projects as a result of the negotiations, the farther the land use system moves from its original moorings in the Euclidian model.

B. THE TRADITIONAL ZONING ORDINANCE

The most long-lasting (if not most important) legislative device for regulating land uses is the zoning ordinance. If you ask laypersons to explain what they understand the term "land use controls" to mean, they will likely mention zoning first. We start our exploration of zoning with what is probably the most famous American land use decision of the twentieth century, a decision that continues to have important implications today.

■ VILLAGE OF EUCLID v. AMBLER REALTY
272 U.S. 365 (1926)

MR. JUSTICE SUTHERLAND delivered the opinion of the Court.

The Village of Euclid is an Ohio municipal corporation. It adjoins and practically is a suburb of the City of Cleveland. Its estimated population is between 5000 and 10,000, and its area from twelve to fourteen square miles, the greater part of which is farm lands or unimproved acreage. It lies, roughly, in the form of a parallelogram measuring approximately three and one-half miles each way. East and west it is traversed by three principal highways: Euclid Avenue, through the southerly border, St. Clair Avenue, through the central portion, and Lake Shore Boulevard, through the northerly border in close proximity to the shore of Lake Erie. The Nickel Plate railroad lies from 1500 to 1800 feet north of Euclid Avenue, and the Lake Shore railroad 1600 feet farther to the north. The three highways and the two railroads are substantially parallel.

Appellee is the owner of a tract of land containing 68 acres, situated in the westerly end of the village, abutting on Euclid Avenue to the south and the Nickel

Plate railroad to the north. Adjoining this tract, both on the east and on the west, there have been laid out restricted residential plats upon which residences have been erected.

On November 13, 1922, an ordinance was adopted by the Village Council, establishing a comprehensive zoning plan for regulating and restricting the location of trades, industries, apartment houses, two-family houses, single family houses, etc., the lot area to be built upon, the size and height of buildings, etc.

The entire area of the village is divided by the ordinance into six classes of use districts, denominated U-1 to U-6, inclusive; three classes of height districts, denominated H-1 to H-3, inclusive; and four classes of area districts, denominated A-1 to A-4, inclusive. The use districts are classified in respect of the buildings which may be erected within their respective limits, as follows: U-1 is restricted to single family dwellings, public parks, water towers and reservoirs, suburban and interurban electric railway passenger stations and rights of way, and farming, non-commercial greenhouse nurseries and truck gardening; U-2 is extended to include two-family dwellings . . . [The court then described zones U-3 through U-6, which gradually increase in intensity of use. For example, U-6 includes sewage disposal plants, scrap iron storage, and manufacturing and industrial uses not included in zones U-1 through U-5. A seventh class of uses is totally prohibited.]

Class U-1 is the only district in which buildings are restricted to those enumerated. In the other classes the uses are cumulative; that is to say, uses in class U-2 include those enumerated in the preceding class, U-1; class U-3 includes uses enumerated in the preceding classes, U-2 and U-1; and so on. In addition to the enumerated uses, the ordinance provides for accessory uses, that is, for uses customarily incident to the principal use, such as private garages. Many regulations are provided in respect of such accessory uses.

The height districts are classified as follows: In class H-1, buildings are limited to a height of two and one-half stories or thirty-five feet; in class H- 2, to four stories or fifty feet; in class H-3, to eighty feet. To all of these, certain exceptions are made, as in the case of church spires, water tanks, etc.

The classification of area districts is: In A-1 districts, dwellings or apartment houses to accommodate more than one family must have at least 5000 square feet for interior lots and at least 4000 square feet for corner lots; in A-2 districts, the area must be at least 2500 square feet for interior lots, and 2000 square feet for corner lots; in A-3 districts, the limits are 1250 and 1000 square feet, respectively; in A-4 districts, the limits are 900 and 700 square feet, respectively. . . .

Appellee's tract of land comes under U-2, U-3 and U-6. The first strip of 620 feet immediately north of Euclid Avenue falls in class U-2, the next 130 feet to the north, in U-3, and the remainder in U-6. The uses of the first 620 feet, therefore, do not include apartment houses, hotels, churches, schools, or other public and semi-public buildings, or other uses enumerated in respect of U-3 to U-6, inclusive. The uses of the next 130 feet include all of these, but exclude industries, theatres, banks, shops, and the various other uses set forth in respect of U-4 to U-6, inclusive. . . . Annexed to the ordinance, and made a part of it, is a zone map, showing the location and limits of the various use, height and area districts, from which it appears that the three classes overlap one another; that is to say, for example, both U-5 and U-6 use districts are in A-4 area districts, but the former is in H-2 and the latter in H-3 height districts. . . .

The lands lying between the two railroads for the entire length of the village area and extending some distance on either side to the north and south, having an average width of about 1600 feet, are left open, with slight exceptions, for industrial and all other uses. This includes the larger part of appellee's tract. Approximately one-sixth of the area of the entire village is included in U-5 and U-6 use districts. That part of the village lying south of Euclid Avenue is principally in U-1 districts. The lands lying north of Euclid Avenue and bordering on the long strip just described are included in U-1, U-2, U-3 and U-4 districts, principally in U-2. . . .

Before proceeding to a consideration of the case, it is necessary to determine the scope of the inquiry. The bill alleges that the tract of land in question is vacant and has been held for years for the purpose of selling and developing it for industrial uses, for which it is especially adapted, being immediately in the path of progressive industrial development; that for such uses it has a market value of about $10,000 per acre, but if the use be limited to residential purposes the market value is not in excess of $2500 per acre; that the first 200 feet of the parcel back from Euclid Avenue, if unrestricted in respect of use, has a value of $150 per front foot, but if limited to residential uses, and ordinary mercantile business be excluded therefrom, its value is not in excess of $50 per front foot.

It is specifically averred that the ordinance attempts to restrict and control the lawful uses of appellee's land so as to confiscate and destroy a great part of its value. . . .

It is not necessary to set forth the provisions of the Ohio Constitution which are thought to be infringed. The question is the same under both Constitutions, namely, as stated by appellee: Is the ordinance invalid in that it violates the constitutional protection "to the right of property in the appellee by attempted regulations under the guise of the police power, which are unreasonable and confiscatory?" . . .

The ordinance now under review, and all similar laws and regulations, must find their justification in some aspect of the police power, asserted for the public welfare. The line which in this field separates the legitimate from the illegitimate assumption of power is not capable of precise delimitation. It varies with circumstances and conditions. A regulatory zoning ordinance, which would be clearly valid as applied to the great cities, might be clearly invalid as applied to rural communities. In solving doubts, the maxim *sic utere tuo ut alienum non laedas*, which lies at the foundation of so much of the common law of nuisances, ordinarily will furnish a fairly helpful clew. And the law of nuisances, likewise, may be consulted, not for the purpose of controlling, but for the helpful aid of its analogies in the process of ascertaining the scope of, the power. Thus the question whether the power exists to forbid the erection of a building of a particular kind or for a particular use, like the question whether a particular thing is a nuisance, is to be determined, not by an abstract consideration of the building or of the thing considered apart, but by considering it in connection with the circumstances and the locality. *Sturgis v. Bridgeman*, L. R. 11 Ch. 852, 865. A nuisance may be merely a right thing in the wrong place,—like a pig in the parlor instead of the barnyard. If the validity of the legislative classification for zoning purposes be fairly debatable, the legislative judgment must be allowed to control. *Radice v. New York*, 264 U.S. 292, 294.

There is no serious difference of opinion in respect of the validity of laws and regulations fixing the height of buildings within reasonable limits, the character of materials and methods of construction, and the adjoining area which must be left open, in order to minimize the danger of fire or collapse, the evils of over-crowding, and the like, and excluding from residential sections offensive trades, industries and structures likely to create nuisances. See *Welch v. Swasey*, 214 U.S. 91; *Hadacheck v. Los Angeles*, 239 U.S. 394; *Reinman v. Little Rock*, 237 U.S. 171; *Cusack Co. v. City of Chicago*, 242 U.S. 526, 529-530.

Here, however, the exclusion is in general terms of all industrial establishments, and it may thereby happen that not only offensive or dangerous industries will be excluded, but those which are neither offensive nor dangerous will share the same fate. But this is not more than happens in respect of many practice-forbidding laws which this Court has upheld although drawn in general terms so as to include individual cases that may turn out to be innocuous in themselves. *Hebe Co. v. Shaw*, 248 U.S. 297, 303; *Pierce Oil Corp. v. City of Hope*, 248 U.S. 498, 500. This inclusion of a reasonable margin to insure effective enforcement, will not put upon a law, otherwise valid, the stamp of invalidity. . . .

It is said that the Village of Euclid is a mere suburb of the City of Cleveland; that the industrial development of that city has not reached and in some degree extended into the village and, in the obvious course of things, will soon absorb the entire area for industrial enterprises; that the effect of the ordinance is to divert this natural development elsewhere with the consequent loss of increased values to the owners of the lands within the village borders. But the village, though physically a suburb of Cleveland, is politically a separate municipality, with powers of its own and authority to govern itself as it sees fit within the limits of the organic law of its creation and the State and Federal Constitutions. Its governing authorities, presumably representing a majority of its inhabitants and voicing their will, have determined, not that industrial development shall cease at its boundaries, but that the course of such development shall proceed within definitely fixed lines. If it be a proper exercise of the police power to relegate industrial establishments to localities separated from residential sections, it is not easy to find a sufficient reason for denying the power because the effect of its exercise is to divert an industrial flow from the course which it would follow, to the injury of the residential public if left alone, to another course where such injury will be obviated. It is not meant by this, however, to exclude the possibility of cases where the general public interest would so far outweigh the interest of the municipality that the municipality would not be allowed to stand in the way.

We find no difficulty in sustaining restrictions of the kind thus far reviewed. The serious question in the case arises over the provisions of the ordinance excluding from residential districts, apartment houses, business houses, retail stores and shops, and other like establishments. . . . Upon that question this Court has not thus far spoken. The decisions of the state courts are numerous and conflicting; but those which broadly sustain the power greatly outnumber those which deny altogether or narrowly limit it. . . .

The decisions enumerated in the first group cited above agree that the exclusion of buildings devoted to business, trade, etc., from residential districts, bears a rational relation to the health and safety of the community. Some of the grounds for this conclusion are — promotion of the health and security from injury of children and others by separating dwelling houses from territory devoted to trade and industry; suppression and prevention of disorder; facilitating the extinguishment of fires, and the enforcement of street traffic regulations and other general welfare ordinances; aiding the health and safety of the community by excluding from residential areas the confusion and danger of fire, contagion and disorder which in greater or less degree attach to the location of stores, shops and factories. Another ground is that the construction and repair of streets may be rendered easier and less expensive by confining the greater part of the heavy traffic to the streets where business is carried on.

The matter of zoning has received much attention at the hands of commissions and experts, and the results of their investigations have been set forth in comprehensive reports. These reports, which bear every evidence of painstaking consideration, concur in the view that the segregation of residential, business, and industrial buildings will make it easier to provide fire apparatus suitable for the character and intensity of the development in each section; that it will increase the safety and security of home life; greatly tend to prevent street accidents, especially to children, by reducing the traffic and resulting confusion in residential sections; decrease noise and other conditions which produce or intensify nervous disorders; preserve a more favorable environment in which to rear children, etc. With particular reference to apartment houses, it is pointed out that the development of detached house sections is greatly retarded by the coming of apartment houses, which has sometimes resulted in destroying the entire section for private house purposes; that in such sections very often the apartment house is a mere parasite, constructed in order to take advantage of the open spaces and attractive surroundings created by the residential character of the district. Moreover, the coming of one apartment house is followed by others, interfering by their height and bulk with the free circulation of air and monopolizing the rays of the sun which otherwise would fall upon the smaller homes, and bringing, as their necessary accompaniments, the disturbing noises incident to increased traffic and business, and the occupation, by means of moving and parked automobiles, of larger portions of the streets, thus detracting from their safety and depriving children of the privilege of quiet and open spaces for play, enjoyed by those in more favored localities,—until, finally, the residential character of the neighborhood and its desirability as a place of detached residences are utterly destroyed. Under these circumstance, apartment houses, which in a different environment would be not only entirely unobjectionable but highly desirable, come very near to being nuisances.

If these reasons, thus summarized, do not demonstrate the wisdom or sound policy in all respects of those restrictions which we have indicated as pertinent to the inquiry, at least, the reasons are sufficiently cogent to preclude us from saying, as it must be said before the ordinance can be declared unconstitutional, that such provisions are clearly arbitrary and unreasonable, having no substantial relation to the public health, safety, morals, or general welfare. *Cusack Co. v. City of Chicago, supra*, pp. 530-531; *Jacobson v. Massachusetts*, 197 U.S. 11, 30-31.

It is true that when, if ever, the provisions set forth in the ordinance in tedious and minute detail, come to be concretely applied to particular premises, including those of the appellee, or to particular conditions, or to be considered in connection with specific complaints, some of them, or even many of them, may be found to be clearly arbitrary and unreasonable. But where the equitable remedy of injunction is sought, as it is here, not upon the ground of a present infringement or denial of a specific right, or of a particular injury in process of actual execution, but upon the broad ground that the mere existence and threatened enforcement of the ordinance, by materially and adversely affecting values and curtailing the opportunities of the market, constitute a present and irreparable injury, the court will not scrutinize its provisions, sentence by sentence, to ascertain by a process of piecemeal dissection whether there may be, here and there, provisions of a minor character, or relating to matters of administration, or not shown to contribute to the injury complained of, which, if attacked separately, might not withstand the test of constitutionality. . . .

Under these circumstances, therefore, it is enough for us to determine, as we do, that the ordinance in its general scope and dominant features, so far as its provisions are here involved, is a valid exercise of authority, leaving other provisions to be dealt with as cases arise directly involving them. . . .

Decree reversed.

MR. JUSTICE VAN DEVANTER, MR. JUSTICE MCREYNOLDS and MR. JUSTICE BUTLER, dissent.

Notes and Comments

1. *Euclidian Zoning.* The zoning ordinances at issue in *Village of Euclid* were typical of those adopted throughout the country at that time. They divided property into use, height, and area districts. This type of model became known as "Euclidian Zoning," a reference to the seminal Supreme Court opinion in the *Village of Euclid* case. *See KCI Management, Inc. v. Board of Appeal of Boston,* 764 N.E.2d 377, 381 (Mass. App. 2002) (referring to "this Traditional Euclidian classification scheme that divides the city of Boston into residential, business, industrial, and other uniform zoning districts . . . "). The traditional zoning ordinance has text accompanied by maps showing the classification scheme. *See Hatch v. Boulder City Council,* 21 P.3d 245 (Utah App. 2001) (finding zoning ordinance invalid because it failed to contain a map to accompany the text).

The *Village of Euclid* opinion culminated a remarkable ten-year period in which the use of zoning spread rapidly among local jurisdictions and was immediately challenged by landowners as violating their due process rights. The cycle effectively began in 1916 when New York adopted the first comprehensive zoning ordinance. See generally Seymour Toll, Zoned American (1969).

2. *Common Law Doctrines.* Zoning was certainly not the first legal control over land use. Two important common law doctrines, nuisance and restrictive covenants, were available to regulate land uses. Nuisance law involves a judicial determination as to whether one person's use of property has substantially impaired another's use and enjoyment of property. *See 44 Plaza Inc. v. Gray-Pac Land Co.,* 845 S.W.2d 576, 578 (Mo. App. 1992) ("a private nuisance is the unreasonable, unusual, or unnatural use of one's property which substantially impairs the right of another to enjoy his property").

Furthermore, as you will recall from your property law course, restrictive covenants are devices that can prohibit certain types of land uses through deed restrictions. *See, e.g., Pelosi v. Wailea Ranch Estates,* 876 P.2d 1320 (Haw. Ct. App. 1994) (defendants violated covenants restricting use to "residential purposes" by constructing a roadway to an adjoining subdivision and a tennis court for use of residents of the adjoining subdivision); *Corner v. Mills,* 650 N.E.2d 712 (Ind. Ct. App. 1995) (enforcing restrictive covenants that establish set-back requirements and prohibit certain commercial and trade behavior, and that impose restrictions against certain structures such as trailers, barns, and garages from being used as residences even on a temporary basis). For a general discussion of the potential employment of nuisance and covenants as land use control mechanisms, see Robert C. Ellickson, Alternatives to Zoning: Covenants, Nuisance Rules, and Fines as Local Land Use Controls, 40 U. Chi. L. Rev. 681 (1973).

3. *Zoning and Nuisances.* What is the relationship between zoning and nuisance law? Is zoning merely another means of preventing nuisances on a prospective basis, or does it offer a useful analogy to justify a far more extensive regulatory system? Nuisance law continues to be used as a means of addressing land use disputes. *See, e.g., Brenton v. Young*, 596 So. 2d 577, 578 (Ala. 1991) (nuisance existed where the neighbors testified that the use and enjoyment of their homes "was significantly impaired by the presence of at least 50 dogs on [defendant's] property and that the barking was constant and the smell unbearable on warm days"); *Village of Wilsonville v. SCA Services, Inc.*, 426 N.E.2d 824 (Ill. 1981) (defendant's waste disposal facility could be enjoined as a nuisance although it had received approvals from all required governmental agencies); *Boomer v. Atlantic Cement Co.*, 257 N.E.2d 870 (N.Y. 1970) (court finds that cement facility constitutes a nuisance but refuses to issue an injunction). In *Perkins v. Madison County Livestock & Fair Association*, 613 N.W.2d 264 (Iowa 2000), the Iowa Supreme Court found that a racetrack at a fairgrounds constituted both a violation of the local zoning ordinances and a nuisance as to the property owner nearest the racetrack. Owners located further away, however, could not establish sufficient interference with the use and enjoyment of their property to prove a nuisance.

4. *Zoning as a Legislative Act.* If zoning is a legislative act, a court would traditionally accord it a presumption of constitutionality. The court would defer to the legislative judgment, and the burden of proof would be on the party challenging a zoning ordinance. The *Village of Euclid* opinion continues to be regularly cited by courts for this proposition. *See, e.g., Schrank v. Pennington County Bd. of Commissioners*, 610 N.W.2d 90, 92 (S.D. 2000) ("Once a zoning ordinance has been properly enacted it is given a strong presumption of legitimacy."); *Sanders Orchard v. Gem County*, 52 P.3d 840, 843 (Idaho 2002) ("There is a strong presumption of favoring the validity of the actions of zoning boards, which includes the application and interpretation of their own zoning ordinances."); *Goldberg Cos., Inc. v. Richmond Heights City Council*, 690 N.E.2d 510, 514 (Ohio 1998) ("reestablishing" the *Village of Euclid* test as "the appropriate standard applicable to constitutional challenges of zoning" and holding that the test is whether the ordinance is "clearly arbitrary and unreasonable, having no substantial relation to the public health, safety, morals, or general welfare" (citing *Euclid*)). As a practical matter, how important is this presumption in legal challenges to zoning ordinances?

Furthermore, if a regulation substantially advances a legitimate state interest, it will survive a challenge alleging that it violates substantive due process and thus is unconstitutional. *See, e.g., Pro-Eco, Inc. v. Board of Commissioners of Jay County*, 57 F.3d 505, 514 (7th Cir. 1995) (in order to claim a substantive due process violation, "Pro-Eco must be able to demonstrate either that the [zoning] ordinance infringes a fundamental liberty interest . . . or that the ordinance is 'arbitrary and unreasonable,' having no substantial relation to the public health, safety, morals or general welfare").

You should note that Justice Sutherland's opinion refers in a positive manner to studies of zoning by "commissions and experts" whose investigations have been set forth in "comprehensive reports." Is the Court intimating that studies and plans are needed before a zoning ordinance can be constitutional?

5. *Zoning, Wipeouts, and Takings*. The diminution in property values alleged by the plaintiff in *Village of Euclid* was substantial: on the order of a 75 percent loss in value. Zoning law today can still cause large losses in value before crossing the line into unconstitutionality. *See, e.g., Gwinnett County v. Davis*, 492 S.E.2d 523, 525 (Ga. 1997) (evidence that property under existing classification was worth substantially less than if rezoned to "residential lakeside" was insufficient to overturn the zoning). Why not require compensation for such a large "wipeout"?

Interestingly, a 1915 Minnesota statute authorized payment for injuries caused by zoning use restrictions. However, the effort was not a success and was not followed. See Edward M. Bassett, Zoning 27 (1940). In the mid-1990s, however, states have again begun enacting legislation that requires compensation where government regulations diminish property past a certain threshold. You will study the takings issue in Chapter 4, as part of the examination of infrastructure finance and permit conditions, and in Chapter 7, as part of the examination of the limits of land use regulation.

6. *Justice Sutherland's Turnaround*. Although the constitutionality of zoning was settled in *Village of Euclid*, it was a close issue. The Court had previously considered two local land use regulations that prohibited certain land uses and upheld them from charges that they effected a taking of property without compensation. *See Hadacheck v. Sebastian*, 239 U.S. 394 (1915); and *Reinman v. Little Rock*, 237 U.S. 171 (1915). The *Village of Euclid* case, however, was the first to squarely consider a due process and equal protection challenge to a zoning ordinance.

The case was decided on rehearing after Justice Sutherland, who was considered a staunch defender of property rights, had earlier prepared a draft opinion that would have overturned the Euclid ordinance. A former supreme court law clerk has suggested that "talks with his dissenting brethren (principally [Justice] Stone, I believe) shook his [Sutherland's] convictions and led him to request a reargument, after which he changed his mind." Alfred McCormack, A Law Clerk's Recollections, 46 Colum. L. Rev. 710, 712 (1946). If you had dissented in *Village of Euclid*, what points would you have emphasized in your opinion?

The history of the case is fascinating and has been thoroughly analyzed in a number of books and articles. One of the most interesting is Zoning and the American Dream (Charles M. Haar & Jerold S. Kayden eds. 1989), written to commemorate the sixtieth anniversary of the *Village of Euclid* decision. *See also* Symposium on *Village of Euclid v. Ambler Realty*, 51 Case Wes. Res. L. Rev (2001).

7. *The Extent of the Police Power*. Zoning is grounded in the local government's exercise of the police power. What types of land use regulation will the police power support? Consider the Supreme Court's statement in its 1974 decision *Village of Belle Terre v. Boraas*, 416 U.S. 1, 9 (reprinted in Chapter 13): "The police power is not confined to elimination of filth, stench, and unhealthy places. It is ample to lay out zones where family values, youth values, and the blessings of quiet, seclusion and clean air make the area a sanctuary for people." What does this statement suggest about the extent of a city's authority to regulate land uses? For example, would it include the right to enact a "view ordinance" preventing new development from blocking the views of the ocean, from existing houses? *See*

Kucera v. Lizza, 69 Cal. Rptr. 2d 582 (Ct. App. 1997) (preservation of views and sunlight is a legitimate purpose of the exercise of the police power).

8. *Zoning and Housing*. Justice Sutherland's opinion states that the "serious question in the case" arises over the provisions of the ordinance that exclude apartment houses and the like from residential uses. Why did this provision pose the most serious question in the case? Were you surprised by Justice Sutherland's attitude toward apartments ("very often the apartment house is a mere parasite")? What does this statement suggest about whether local governments have an obligation to use their zoning power to ensure that all economic segments of the community can find housing? See generally the cases and discussion in Chapter 12 concerning securing a sufficient supply of housing.

9. *The* Nectow *Decision*. The *Village of Euclid* decision was an important victory for local governments that were adopting zoning ordinances. What is particularly striking about the case is the extent of the diminution in value that the zoning ordinance caused to the plaintiff's property. After the case was handed down, the obvious question was whether the Court would attempt to set further limits on the zoning power whose constitutionality was now generally confirmed. The Supreme Court soon decided another case that set at least some limits on the broad affirmance of zoning in *Village of Euclid*.

In *Nectow v. City of Cambridge*, 277 U.S. 183 (1928), part of plaintiff's land was put in an R-3 zone, which was restricted to dwellings, hotels, clubs, churches, and the like. It fronted on Brookline Street to the west, and on Henry Street, to the north. The land to the south was owned by Ford Motor Company, which operated an auto assembly factory there. There was also a soap factory and railroad tracks nearby. The lands beyond Henry Street to the north and beyond Brookline Street to the west were in a residential district and had some residences on them, while the land to the south and east was unrestricted. The result was that business and industry was excluded from this part of plaintiff's land, while the remainder of the tract was unrestricted.

A master assigned to the case found that the zoning did not promote the health, safety, convenience and general welfare, concluding that because of the adjacent industrial and railroad uses, the land was of little value for the limited uses permitted by the ordinance. The Supreme Court agreed. Although noting that the zoning determination should not be set aside unless it "has no foundation in reason and is a mere arbitrary and irrational exercise of government power," the Court nonetheless found that the master's finding was dispositive of the case. The Court particularly noted that the boundary line of the residential district, before reaching the plaintiff's property, ran along the streets. Thus, "to exclude the locus from the residential district requires only that such line shall be continued 100 feet further along Henry street and thence south along Brookline street." 277 U.S. at 188.

10. *Judicial Scrutiny of Land Use Enactments*. After *Village of Euclid* and *Nectow*, how easy will landowners find it to challenge the constitutionality of zoning on their property? The *Nectow* decision illustrates how a zoning ordinance can be attacked on substantive due process grounds, but most challenges to such ordinances will fail.

After these first two zoning decisions, the Supreme Court largely abandoned the field of land use regulation. As a result, land use law has largely been left to the state courts, which often undertake more rigorous scrutiny. A higher level of scrutiny is particularly evident when plaintiffs allege that land use ordinances exclude minorities or low and moderate income households, an issue taken up in Chapter 11 (dealing with growth management), Chapter 12 (dealing with securing a sufficient housing supply), and Chapter 13 (dealing with housing and discrimination).

While zoning is generally thought of as restricting uses on property, it does so by listing certain uses that are "permitted" on a property, thus excluding all others. What does it mean when zoning authorizes a "permitted use" on a particular piece of property?

BOARD OF SUPERVISORS OF MADISON COUNTY v. GAFFNEY

422 S.E.2d 760 (Va. 1992)

HASSELL, Justice.

In this appeal, we consider whether the Madison County zoning ordinance permits landowners to operate a nudist club on their property, which has a conservation zoning classification.

L. Patrick Gaffney, Jr., Phyllis J. Gaffney, and Leighton B. Brown (landowners) own approximately 200 acres of land in the Criglersville area of Madison County. The property is adjacent to the Blue Ridge Mountains and is accessed by State Route 642.

On a portion of their property, the landowners operate a nudist club, consisting of 170 paying members. In 1990, the nudist club collected fees of approximately $20,000 to $25,000 and realized a profit. Members of the club and their guests participate, while nude, in such activities as volleyball, frisbee, croquet, horseshoes, picnics, barbecues, swimming, hiking, and "sing-alongs." Facilities at the nudist club site include a solar shower, a swimming pond with a cement bottom, hiking trails, barbecue and horseshoe pits, a sandbox, play swings, three campsites, and an outhouse.

Persons who live adjacent to the landowners' property complained to the Board of Supervisors of Madison County about the operation of the nudist club. From his property, Lee R. Knighting is able to see nude persons sunbathing and playing volleyball and frisbee. Thomas Lee Utz, another landowner, observed nude members of the club playing volleyball. According to Utz, nude persons can be seen from State Route 642, a public highway. Additionally, Steven Smith Hoffman, a member of the Board of Supervisors of Madison County, received complaints from citizens who informed him that they observed nude persons on the landowners' property. Hoffman, while visiting Knighting's property, saw approximately 25 nude persons at the nudist club.

The landowners deny that nude persons can be seen from State Route 642. They claim that "little can be seen from any occupied, neighboring property with the unaided eye."

In January 1987, the landowners requested, and were granted by the planning commission, a special use permit to develop a campground and lodge on their property. However, the planning commission did not know that the landowners planned to operate a nudist club on their property. The Board of Supervisors revoked the special use permit in January 1989, on the ground that the landowners had not disclosed, in their original application, that they would operate a nudist club.

Subsequently, the landowners filed suit challenging the County's actions. The trial court held that the planning commission's actions were invalid because the Board of Supervisors could not legally delegate to the planning commission the power to grant special use permits. Later, the Board of Supervisors amended the County's zoning ordinance to vest in itself the power to issue special use permits. The landowners have sought no further special use permit, nor have they requested a change in the zoning classification of their property.

The Board of Supervisors initiated this zoning enforcement proceeding by filing a petition to enjoin the landowners from operating a nudist club on their property, which enjoys a Conservation, C-1 zoning classification. Following a bench trial, the court refused to grant the injunction and held that the use of the property as a nudist club is consistent with the zoning status of the property. We awarded the County an appeal.

The Board of Supervisors argues that the trial court erred because a nudist club is not an articulated permissive use in the Conservation, C-1 zoning district. The landowners argue, and the trial court held, that the landowners' use of their property qualifies as "preserve and conservation area" which is permitted by right in the Conservation, C-1 zoning district. . . .

Article 2 of the Madison County zoning ordinance divides the County into numerous zoning districts, including Conservation, C-1. Article 3 of the County's ordinance describes the purpose of the Conservation, C-1 zoning classification:

> This district is established for the specific purpose of facilitating the conservation of water, timber, and other natural resources, reducing soil erosion, protecting upland watersheds, lessening the hazards of flood and fire, and enhancing existing and future farming operations. The district covers steep slopes, hardwood forests, areas of erosive soils, and those portions of the county which are occupied by various open spaces such as parklands, farms, lakes or mountains. Because of the fragile nature of the district, intensive residential or urban development and uses not consistent with the existing character of the district are inappropriate.

Article 3 of the ordinance also identifies the land uses permitted by right:

Single-family detached dwelling (excluding mobile home)

General farming, agriculture, horticulture, dairying and forestry

Public school, public park and public playground

Preserve and conservation area

Hunting or fishing club

Sawmill

Small boat dock (with repair)

Cemetery and graveyard

> Church, parish hall and rectory
>
> Accessory use and building
>
> Public service corporation transmission lines, poles, pipes, meters, transformers and other facilities necessary for the transmission and maintenance of public service utilities. . . .
>
> Farm winery with wholesale sales

This article also enumerates certain special permit uses, none of which are implicated here.

Article 2-4 of the ordinance states:

> Any use not specifically permitted as a matter or [*sic*] right or by special use permit is prohibited. Requests for such prohibited uses shall be governed by the terms of the ordinance specified in Section 15-7 (Uses Not Provided For) and Article 19 (Amendments).

Furthermore, Article 15-7-1 of the ordinance, entitled "Uses Not Provided For," states, in relevant part:

> If in any zone established under this ordinance a use is not specifically permitted, it is prohibited. If an application is made by a property owner to the administrator fur [*sic*] such use, the administrator shall refer the application to the Planning Commission. After a public hearing in accordance with Section 15.1-431 of the Code of Virginia (1950, as amended), the Planning Commission shall make its recommendations to the Board of Supervisors to (a) amend the ordinance to allow the use within the zone by right, (b) amend the ordinance to allow the use within the zone with a special use permit, (c) rezone the area and thereby allow the use, or (d) deny the use in that zone.

The County's zoning ordinance makes it abundantly clear that only uses specifically enumerated within a zoning district are permitted without a special use permit. We have approved the use of inclusive zoning ordinances.

> In the drafting of comprehensive zoning ordinances two classifications are generally employed: the *inclusive* type which permits only those uses specifically named, and the *exclusive* type which prohibits specified uses and permits all others. Such ordinances utilize both forms and all three are recognized as valid classifications. . . .

We hold that under the facts and circumstances of this case, the landowners failed to prove that use of their property to operate a nudist club constitutes a use, permitted by right, in accordance with Article 3 of the County's zoning ordinance. The zoning ordinance is inclusive in that it specifies the uses that are permitted in each zone. The zoning ordinance, in at least two provisions, Articles 2-4 and 15-7-1, states that a use not specifically permitted in a zone is prohibited. The operation of a nudist club is not a use specifically permitted by right in the Conservation, C-1 district.

Next, the landowners argue that the nudist club is operated "as an open space recreational area," that the Madison County Comprehensive Plan "places a heavy emphasis upon conservation and recreation," and that the operation of their particular nudist club is consistent with conservation and recreation which, they say, the County encourages in the conservation zone. The fallacy in this argument is that the operation of a nudist club constitutes a land use and, thus, we must look to the specific language contained in the County's ordinance and ascertain if the use is an articulated use permitted by right. Because the operation of a nudist club is not such a use, the landowners may not conduct such activity on their property.

Accordingly, we will reverse the judgment of the trial court and remand this case for the entry of a decree consistent with this opinion.

Reversed and remanded.

KEENAN, J., with whom LACY, J. joins, concurring.

WHITING, Justice, concurring in the result.

I note that in holding the operation of a nudist club is not a use specifically permitted by right in the ordinance, the majority recites specific testimony of witnesses Knighting, Utz, and Huffman indicating that nude persons could be observed without binoculars from various vantage points off the property. If my understanding of the holding is correct, it is that the operation of a nudist club is not a use permitted by right, nor would it qualify for a special use permit under the terms of the ordinance as written. Should this be the holding, it seems to me that it would make no difference whether persons off the property could ascertain that club members were unclothed.

KEENAN, Justice, with whom LACY, Justice, joins, concurring. . . .

"Use," as defined in the Ordinance, is "[t]he principal purpose for which a lot . . . is or may be used, occupied or maintained." Madison County Zoning Ordinance §21-202. Thus, by definition, a "use" describes the purpose for which a parcel of land is or may be utilized. The term "use" has also been defined as including "occupations and activities of persons occurring on the land." 8 Eugene McQuillin, *The Law of Municipal Corporations* §25.01, at 9 (3d ed. rev. vol. 1991).

In the case before us, the purpose for which the land is being used is that of a private, recreational facility. The fact that the users of this recreational facility are unclothed does not alter the character of the land use. . . .

The majority's characterization of the above land use as a "nudist club" improperly focuses on whether the people participating in these activities are attired, rather than on the activities and facilities which themselves impact the land. This distinction is critical in the analysis of an "inclusive" ordinance, such as the one before us because, under the majority's view, a governmental entity can secure the exclusion of any land use simply by assigning it a label not found in the ordinance. Here, the majority's characterization of the land use as a "nudist club" bears no relationship to how the land itself is being used. Lacking such a nexus, this use classification is invalid.

Notes and Comments

1. *A "Nudist Club" or a "Recreational Facility"?* To determine whether the landowner's use was a "permitted use" under the county zoning ordinance, the

court had to characterize the activities that the club members were undertaking. Which contains the better characterization: the majority opinion, which concluded that the land use was "operating" a nudist club, or Justice Keenan's concurring opinion, which finds that the land use is a "private, recreational facility"? If Justice Keenan is correct, will the fact that the club members conduct activities in the nude *ever* be relevant under a zoning ordinance? Does this power of the court to characterize land uses mean that judicial conceptions of morality can overtly dictate case outcomes? Judicial line drawing of a similar type is found in the adult zoning cases discused in Chapter 8, which involve distinctions between "adult" and other movies, and taverns versus "topless" bars.

2. *Territories and Uses*. The relationship between the zoning ordinance in *Village of Euclid* and the modern ordinance in *Gaffney* should be evident. As one court summarized, "The traditional zoning law divides the community into specific, territorial districts and prescribes the uses that are permitted (or not permitted) in each district. The boundaries of these districts are fixed by law, usually by reference to a map. Thus, in comprehensive zoning, every square foot of the community is within some fixed zone and is subject to the predetermined set of land use restrictions applicable to that zone." *Wheaton Moose Lodge No. 1775 v. Montgomery County*, 397 A.2d 250, 252 (Md. Ct. Spec. App. 1979).

3. *The Standard Zoning Enabling Act*. Zoning ordinances throughout the United States tend to be remarkably similar in their features despite the fact that no overarching federal law dictates uniformity. This similarity is largely due to an unlikely source: the United States Department of Commerce. In the early 1920s, Herbert Hoover, who later became president of the United States, headed the department. Although today he is remembered largely for presiding as president over the onset of the great Depression that began in 1929, Hoover in fact held progressive views and was particularly concerned with promoting home ownership and protecting residences from adverse urban impacts. To further these goals, he appointed the Advisory Committee on City Planning and Zoning.

The Advisory Committee drafted a Model Act, the "Standard Zoning Enabling Act," whose final version was published in 1924. This draft was intended to serve as a model for state legislation that would authorize the adoption of local zoning ordinances, and it set forth various concepts, which today are well known. For example, the Act defined the concept of a variance, which is discussed below in this chapter.

The Standard Zoning Enabling Act struck a chord throughout the country and served as a unifying force for the development of modern land use regulation. By 1930, 35 states had adopted legislation based upon it, and a leading treatise declares that at one point it was adopted in all 50 states. Norman Williams, Jr., American Land Planning Law, §18.01 (1988). *See Symmes Township Bd. of Trustees v. Smyth*, 721 N.E.2d 1057, 1062-1063 (Ohio 2000) ("Since the Standard State Zoning Enabling Act of 1922 . . . the law of zoning has developed a unique vocabulary of 'uses,' 'districts,' 'parcels,' 'variances,' 'cumulative zoning,' 'comprehensive plans,' 'PUDs,' and other specialized terms."). For a discussion of the Act and its origins, see Ruth Knack, et al., The Real Story Behind the Standard Planning and Zoning Acts of the 1920s, 48 Land Use L. & Zoning Dig. 3 (Feb. 1996).

4. *Sources of and Limits on Local Government Authority*. Traditionally, under American law local governments receive their authority from the state, through enabling legislation (such as, if enacted, the Standard Zoning Enabling Act). Absent

such authority, local governments have no power to act. This limitation is reflected in a doctrine known as "Dillon's Rule," which requires courts to construe state grants of authority narrowly. *See, e.g., City of Virginia Beach v. Hay,* 518 S.E.2d 314, 316 (Va. 1999) ("Under Dillon's Rule, municipal governments have only those powers which are expressly granted by the state legislature, those powers fairly or necessarily implied from expressly granted powers, and those powers which are essential and indispensable."); *Southern Constructors, Inc. v. Loudon County Bd. of Education,* 58 S.W.2d 706, 709 (Tenn. 2001) ("Dillon's Rule is a canon of statutory construction that calls for the strict and narrow construction of local government authority").

Although not followed in some states, Dillon's Rule can still be important in the land use area, because it allows parties to argue that local governments have exceeded their authority. *See, e.g., Board of Supervisors of Augusta County v. Countryside Investment Co.,* 522 S.E.2d 610 (Va. 1999) (citing Dillon's Rule in holding that the state Land Subdivision and Development Act did not authorize a county subdivision ordinance which prohibited a subdivision if the proposed subdivision was not conducive to the preservation of the rural environment); *T & S Signs, Inc. v. Village of Wadsworth,* 634 N.E.2d 305, 310 (111. App. 1994) (in which plaintiff unsuccessfully argued that "[s]ince Dillon's rule limits the powers of a non-home-rule municipality to those expressly granted by the Constitution or by statute, the plaintiff asserts that when there is a State law regulating a certain field, such as outdoor advertising, a non-home-rule municipality may not adopt ordinances which conflict or infringe upon the spirit of the State law.").

Some cities and counties are so-called charter or home rule jurisdictions, set apart by the fact that they have their own charters pursuant to the particular state constitution. These jurisdictions have somewhat more power to act than other cities and counties that lack a charter. However, state law can still preempt local action in a field of "statewide concern." *See, e.g., Munrow v. Town of East Greenwich,* 733 A.2d 703, 710 (R.I. 1999) ("Zoning, land development and subdivision regulations constitute a valid exercise of police power, and are matters of statewide concern").

The upshot of these doctrines is that, in general, local governments must depend upon state law to act in the land use field. Correspondingly, state law operates as a limit on that authority. It can either prohibit local action in conflict with the state authorization or, as is discussed in Chapter 9, preempt local action. For a discussion of local lawmaking power, *see* Daniel B. Rodriguez, Localism and Lawmaking, 32 Rutgers L.J. 627 (2001).

5. *Zoning and Controversy*. How likely is it that zoning ordinances, which set out rigid requirements for uses and restrictions on particular pieces of property, will ever be free from controversy? The common law of property has long emphasized the maxim that "all property is unique." Does this maxim suggest that municipalities will always encounter difficulties in regulating the use of land prospectively through zoning?

Consider also the emphasis in the United States upon the "entrepreneur," the individual who recognizes an economic opportunity and seizes it to create a successful enterprise. How likely is it that, if the project is impeded by the local zoning, the entrepreneur will simply give up and turn attention to another property?

6. *The Meaning of "Permitted Uses."* What does it mean when we say that a particular use of property is "permitted as of right" under the zoning ordinance? Courts often grapple with the plain meaning of a permitted use within the text of a zoning ordinance. *See, e.g., Marzulo v. Kahl,* 783 A.2d 169 (Md. Ct. App. 2001) (business of breeding and selling snakes was not "commercial agriculture"); *Lovers Lane & Co. v. Village of Libertyville,* 128 F. Supp. 2d 1126 (N.D. Ill. 2000) (lingerie and gift shop was both an "Apparel and Accessory Store" and a "Miscellaneous Retail Store"); *Harry v. Mecklenburg County,* 523 S.E.2d 135 (N.C. App. 1999) (a pier was not a permitted "principal structure" in a single-family residential area). Prohibitions of uses are also fodder for litigation. *See Kissell v. Ferguson Township Zoning Hg. Bd.,* 729 A.2d 194 (Pa. Commw. Ct. 1999) (display of riding and self-propelled lawn mowers and tractors did not violate prohibition against the display of "motor vehicles" in a setback area).

7. *Meaning II: "Adult Uses." In Voyeur Dorm, L. C. v. City of Tampa,* 265 F.3d 1232 (11th Cir. 2001), the court considered how the purposes of land use regulation affected the meaning of a use permitted under the Tampa, Florida zoning ordinance. The operator of an internet site transmitted pictures from webcams situated in what the operator termed the "Voyeur Dorm," a residence in the City of Tampa. Patrons would pay for access to the web site. After the City sought to enforce its ordinance, claiming that the property was not zoned as an "adult entertainment establishment," the plaintiff brought an action for declaratory relief that it was not subject to the zoning ordinance.

The Eleventh Circuit Court of Appeals found for the plaintiff. It reasoned that "[t]he City Code cannot be applied to a location that does not, itself, offer adult entertainment to the public." *Id.* at 1236. Rather, the offering occurred only when the videotaped images were dispersed over the internet and into the public eye. The Court also noted that the consumers of the pictures "do not go to 2312 West Farwell Drive or congregate anywhere else in Tampa to enjoy the entertainment." Rather, the public offering "occurs over the Internet in 'virtual space.'" *Id.* at 1237. Was the Court's interpretation correct? *See, generally,* Francesca Ortiz, Zoning the Voyeur Dorm: Regulating Home-Based Voyeur Web Sites Through Land Use Laws, 34 U.C. Davis L. Rev. 929 (2001).

8. *The Baby-Bouncing Outlaw at the Home Computer.* With the advent of faxes, electronic mail, and the internet, it is now possible for many individuals to work out of the home. This development, of course, has both environmental benefits and benefits for families. Such businesses, however, may run afoul of zoning laws that zone the property for residential use only. Local jurisdictions may respond by crafting "home business" zoning regulations, but these too are open to interpretation.

In *Sundberg v. Greenville Bd. of Adjustment,* 740 A.2d 1068 (N.H. 1999), a family member who did the paperwork (without salary) for the family welding supply business, which was operated from the family's mobile home, was "employed" within the meaning of the city's "customary home occupation" ordinance. Under that ordinance, such a "customary home occupation" could employ no more than two people. *See* Nicole Stelle Garnett, On Castles and Commerce: Zoning Law and the Home-Business Dilemma, 42 Wm. and Mary L. Rev. 1191 (2001) ("As I write this sentence, I am bouncing my six-month-old daughter on my knee . . . and pondering the best way to explain the difference between springing and shifting executory interests to my first-year property class. I might also be breaking the law.").

9. *The Attack on Euclidian Zoning*. As you have seen, the primary thrust of traditional Euclidian zoning was to separate uses. Some critics have found that this idea behind zoning is responsible for much of the poor land use and urban sprawl so common in the late twentieth century. See, e.g., James Howard Kunstler, Home From Nowhere, Atlantic Monthly, Sept. 1996, at 43 (finding that after World War II, the effects of zoning began to overshadow the historic elements of civic life); and Nicolas M. Kublicki, Innovative Solutions to Euclidian Sprawl, 31 Envtl. L. Rptr. 11001 (Aug. 2001) (cataloguing the effects of "Euclidian sprawl," including increased commuting costs, inefficient use of land, intensified sociological detachment of suburbanites, and exacerbation of the housing shortage).

Criticism of Euclidian zoning has resulted in support for what has become known as the "New Urbanism" school of planning, which attempts to center development around the creation of new neighborhoods with mixed-uses. *See* Peter Katz (ed.), The New Urbanism: Toward an Architecture of Community (2003); Special Series: The New Urbanism and Smart Growth, 29 Fordham Urb. L.J. 1445 (2002). In S. Mark White & Dawn Jourdan, Neotraditional Development: A Legal Analysis, Land Use L. & Zoning Dig., Aug. 1997, at 3 the authors state: "Responding to a perceived loss of community and the decline in quality of life occasioned by the automobile and urban sprawl, 'New Urbanism' and neotraditional development have challenged the assumptions of Euclidian zoning and conventional suburban development that residential and nonresidential uses must be separated, that streets should be wide and curvilinear, and that densities must be low."

Do you agree?

A Note on Nonconforming Uses

When local governments pass zoning ordinances or zoning amendments, they do not write on a clean "development slate." Existing land uses on the properties that the zoning affects may not be authorized under the new zoning. In that situation, they are deemed "nonconforming" uses (that is, uses that do not conform to those allowed by the zoning ordinance).

The Theoretical Conundrum. Nonconforming uses obviously pose the danger of disrupting the zoning plan that the ordinance seeks to implement. At the same time, however, landowners have legitimate expectations that their investments in a given use will not be disrupted by changes in the allowed zoning.

The concept of nonconforming uses posed a considerable theoretical problem for the early proponents of Euclidian zoning. As we have seen above in this chapter, Euclidian zoning envisioned an orderly pattern of development in which various conflicting uses would be separated. The zoning theorists believed that nonconforming uses would naturally vanish over time. They erred in failing to recognize that the economics of the nonconforming use gives rise to an incentive to maintain both the structure and the monopolistic status enjoyed by the owner.

Continuation of a nonconforming use after the adoption of a new zoning ordinance would jeopardize the benefits that the proponents of Euclidian zoning foresaw. They feared, however, that if zoning attempted to outlaw all pre-existing nonconforming uses, this prohibition would raise such significant constitutional questions that it might jeopardize the constitutionality of all zoning.

The compromise was to allow nonconforming uses to continue after the new zoning was passed but to restrict expansions of them and eventually to require their removal. *See* Edward M. Basset, Zoning, 115-116 (1936).

Nonconforming Uses: The Issues. The result of this compromise has been a steady stream of litigation over the validity of nonconforming uses. One author has usefully divided the issues raised by nonconforming uses into four categories: (1) disputes over the essential factors required to establish that a use existed prior to the time a zoning enactment became effective; (2) disputes over the ways in which the right to continue a nonconforming use can be lost; (3) disputes over the scope of the nonconforming use; and (4) disputes over devices by which a jurisdiction may eliminate such uses. 6 Patrick J. Rohan, Zoning and Land Use Controls §41.01[5], 41-14 (1996).

The following is a thumbnail sketch of a large and relatively intricate area of land use law.

(1) *Establishing Nonconforming Uses.* To obtain recognition of a valid nonconforming use, the landowner must establish that the use actually existed when the zoning restriction became effective. *See, e.g., Conforti v. City of Manchester*, 677 A.2d 147 (N.H. 1996) (prior use of premises as a movie theater did not mean that the property could be used for live entertainment under the status of a nonconforming use).

Nonconforming uses essentially become vested rights. Many states accord these uses constitutional protection, while in others statutes or local ordinances authorize the continuation of the nonconforming use. *See, e.g., Cicerella, Inc. v. Jerusalem Township Bd. of Zoning Appeals*, 392 N.E.2d 574, 577 (Ohio Ct. App. 1978) ("Any attempt by zoning legislation to deprive the owner of a pre-existing lawful use is generally regarded as an unconstitutional taking of property without compensation and without due process of law").

(2) *Losing Nonconforming Uses.* To maintain the nonconforming use, the landowner cannot alter the use on the property, a rule that has generated legions of cases analyzing whether the use on the property has stopped or changed. *See, e.g., Toys "R" Us v. Silva*, 676 N.E.2d 862 (N.Y. 1996) (nonconforming use status lapsed where, under a statute declaring that a nonconforming use lapses if discontinued during a two-year period, the warehouse was completely unused for 20 months and then used only slightly for the remainder of that period); *Board of Zoning Appeals of Spotsylvania County v. McCalley*, 300 S.E.2d 790 (Va. 1983) (metal forge and machine shop that fabricated metal railings was not the same use as an auto body shop that existed when the zoning ordinance became effective).

One difficult situation that recurs involves the accidental destruction of the property through a fire or natural disaster. Some ordinances allow the property owner to replace the structure and continue the nonconforming use. *Krul v. Board of Adjustment of the City of Bayonne*, 298 A.2d 308 (N.J. Sup. Ct. Law Div. 1972), *aff'd*, 313 A.2d 220 (N.J. Super. Ct. App. Div. 1973) (statute authorized repair of a building destroyed by fire without loss of nonconforming use status). Many other ordinances, however, terminate the nonconforming use where the fire or natural disaster has resulted in complete or substantial (as opposed to partial) destruction.

(3) *Scope of Nonconforming Uses*. As a general rule, the nonconforming use cannot be expanded or enlarged, nor can the structure in which it is being carried on be expanded. *See, e.g., City of Marion v. Rapp*, 655 N.W.2d 88 (S.D. 2002) (replacing old 14 by 70 foot trailer with a 16 by 76 foot trailer is a prohibited enlargement of a nonconforming use); *State ex rel. Dierberg v. St. Charles County Board of Zoning Adjustment*, 869 S.W.2d 865 (Mo. Ct. App. 1994) (landowners unlawfully expanded a private hunting club, which was a nonconforming use, when they opened it to the public for, among other activities, clay pigeon shooting). However, some states allow the "natural expansion" of an existing use, while others will allow a change to a "less offensive" nonconforming use. *See, e.g., Pappas v. Zoning Bd. of Adjustment of Philadelphia*, 589 A.2d 675 (Pa. 1991) (full-service pizza restaurant was a natural expansion from a take-out sandwich shop and restaurant). Moreover, merely increasing the volume of business does not, by itself, violate the nonconforming use status.

A land user with a valid nonconforming use is entitled to make normal repairs on the property. *See, e.g., Social Spirits, Inc. v. Town of Colonie*, 426 N.Y.S.2d 148 (Sup. Ct. App. Div. 1980) (restaurant retained nonconforming use status even though it remodeled its exterior and installed new electrical wiring, plumbing, and insulation). Moreover, the general rule is that a change of ownership, occupancy or name of an operating business facility does not eliminate its status as a legal nonconforming use. *Budget Inn of Daphne, Inc. v. City of Daphne*, 789 So. 2d 154, 160 (Ala. 2000).

(4) *Eliminating Nonconforming Uses*. Courts often express the view that while nonconforming uses must be tolerated, the purposes of zoning require them to be eliminated as soon as possible. *See, e.g., P.M.S. Assets, Ltd. v. Zoning Bd. of Appeals of Village of Pleasantville*, 774 N.E.2d 204, 205 (N.Y. 2002) ("While nonconforming uses of property are tolerated, the overriding policy of zoning is aimed at their eventual elimination").

While nonconforming uses are protected against immediate prohibition by the local jurisdiction, they can be terminated after a sufficient period during which the investment in the property can be amortized. Many states follow the rule that the reasonableness of the amortization period is based on a balancing of public good against private loss. *See, e.g., City of Los Angeles v. Gage*, 274 P.2d 34, 44 (Cal. Ct. App. 1954) ("Use of a reasonable amortization scheme provides an equitable means of reconciliation of the conflicting interests in satisfaction of due process requirements"). A minority of courts find such amortization provisions unconstitutional on their face. *See Ailes v. Decatur County Area Planning Comm'n*, 448 N.E.2d 1057 (Ind. Ct. App. 1983), *cert. denied*, 465 U.S. 1100 (1984) (ordinance providing for three and five-year periods for amortization of nonconforming junkyards is unconstitutional). *See also McDowell v. Board of Adjustment of Township of Wall*, 757 A.2d 822, 829 (N.J. App. Div. 2000) ("a municipality may not take active steps to extinguish nonconforming uses . . . but instead must wait with 'fervent hope that they in time wither and die . . . '") Much of the litigation in this area centers on the legality of the amortization period provided, with the outcome depending on the facts of the individual use to which the time period is applied. *See, e.g., Collins v. City of Spartanburg*, 314 S.E.2d 332 (S.C. 1984) (five-year amortization period for junkyard is reasonable); *Rives v. City of Clarkesville*, 618 S.W.2d 502 (Tenn. Ct. App. 1981) (two-year period for amortization of junkyard allowed).

C. AMENDMENTS, VARIANCES, AND SPOT ZONING

The Euclidian zoning ordinance is legislative in nature, and a landowner who is not satisfied with the permitted uses on his or her property retains the right to seek a change in those uses through subsequent local legislation. However, because zoning is to be "in accordance with a comprehensive plan," an amendment to the zoning ordinance that affects only a single parcel of property poses the distinct possibility of damaging or destroying the overall plan. The courts thus had to decide whether amendments to zoning ordinances would be treated with the deference generally accorded other legislation or examined more closely.

COVINGTON v. TOWN OF APEX
423 S.E.2d 537 (N.C. App. 1992)

JOHNSON, Judge.

On 26 March 1990, C & D Investment Company, Inc. (hereinafter C & D) petitioned the Town of Apex to rezone the property located at 212 S. Salem Street, Apex, N.C. from Office & Institutional-1 to Conditional Use Business-2. The rezoning was sought to permit electronic assembly by a prospective tenant, A & E Electronic, Inc. (hereinafter A & E), within the former post office building located on the subject property.

The subject property is bordered by property zoned as follows: to its immediate north by property zoned Office & Institutional-1; to its immediate east by property zoned Business-1; to its immediate south-east by property zoned Business-2; to its immediate south by property zoned Office & Institutional-1; and to its immediate west by property zoned Residential-6.

On 7 May 1990, the Apex Planning Board held a public hearing on the rezoning application. The Apex Planning Director, David Rowland, recommended approval of the rezoning petition in his memorandum given to the Planning Board and Board of Commissioners. On 4 June 1990, the Planning Board voted 5-2 to recommend approval of the rezoning.

On 10 May 1990, several persons, including Donald W. Grimes who resides next to the subject property, submitted a valid protest petition to the Town of Apex. The Apex Board of Commissioners held public hearings on 15 May 1990 and 5 June 1990. After hearing the testimony, the board voted 4-1 to amend the zoning ordinance to rezone the subject property to a Conditional Use Business-2 district with the condition that use of the tract be restricted to the uses permitted in Office and Institutional-1 plus the use of electronic assembly. The mayor executed the ordinance effecting the rezoning on 19 June 1990. Plaintiffs instituted this action. . . .

Defendants supported their motion for summary judgment by providing affidavits which identified the public purposes of the rezoning ordinance. Mr. David Rowland's affidavit stated that the rezoning ordinance serves legitimate public purposes in that it contributes to the revitalization of downtown, it promotes economic stability, and it serves to promote the express statutory goal of conserving the value of buildings.

Plaintiffs' pleadings and supporting affidavits showed that C & D, the owners of the subject property, voluntarily terminated their lease with their former tenant, the postal service, in order to execute a lease with A & E. Because A & E's line of business involved electronic assembly, the property had to be rezoned in order to permit use of the property by A & E. C & D, with the execution of the lease, would realize a $10,000.00 increase in rental profits, and A & E would pay less money in rent for more space. When they executed the lease agreement, A & E was under a present lease until the year 1993 in an area zoned for light industry. C & D, in order to effectuate the lease agreement, petitioned the Town of Apex for a zoning change.

The only public interest cited in the petition and in the Town of Apex's Planning Administrator's recommendation was "occupancy of a vacant building." No other explanation was provided for a zoning change that would implement an industrial use into a neighborhood heavily populated by residential dwellings.

Plaintiff also showed that the enactment of the zoning ordinance would produce minimal benefit to the community. The only benefit to the community provided by the rezoning ordinance was aesthetic in nature in that the prospective tenant would have to provide streetscaping for the general area around the property.

No jobs were to be created by the zoning change. In fact, Ann Sears, president of A & E, stated in her deposition that she did not intend to increase her staff. No services or other benefits were to be provided for the community by the implementation of the zoning change. There is no indication that the enactment of the zoning ordinance without the creation of jobs, services or other benefits would revitalize downtown or provide economic stability to the community.

A fact more suggestive of the unreasonableness and arbitrariness of the rezoning ordinance was the lack of effort by the owners to find other tenants that could have leased the building and helped to conserve its value without rezoning the subject tract. Plaintiffs provided supporting materials illustrating that fact.

Mr. Billy Johnson, owner of Apex Realty, indicated in his affidavit that he advertised the property for two weeks and had six to seven inquiries concerning the subject tract. Mr. Johnson's activities were on behalf of the tenant, the postal service. After Mr. Johnson informed the postal services that he had a potential tenant (other than A & E) ready, willing, and able to sub-lease the premises, he determined that the postal service would or could not pay a real estate commission. He then contacted one of the owners, an attorney, who advised Mr. Johnson that he wanted to terminate the lease with the postal service since the property was capable of producing higher rents. The affidavit of Mr. Dixon, president of C & D, does indicate that a law firm contacted him about purchasing the building, but the deal never materialized. The affidavits of Mr. Johnson and Mr. Dixon indicate that potential tenants were interested in the subject tract. The express statutory goal of conservation of buildings could have been accomplished without the rezoning necessary to accommodate the prospective tenant, A & E. We, therefore, conclude that plaintiffs provided sufficient evidence that the zoning change from Office & Institutional to Conditional Use Business-2 was unreasonable, arbitrary, and not in the public interest.

Defendants also argue that plaintiffs failed to present sufficient evidence that the conditional use zoning enacted constituted spot zoning. We disagree. . . .

The North Carolina Supreme Court has defined spot zoning as

> A zoning ordinance, or amendment which singles out and reclassifies a relatively small tract owned by a single person and surrounded by a much larger area uniformly zoned . . . so as to relieve the small tract from restrictions to which the rest of the area is subjected is called spot zoning.

Dale v. Town of Columbus, 101 N.C. App. 335, 338, 399 S.E.2d 350, 352 (1991). . . .

An essential element of spot zoning is a small tract of land owned by a single person and surrounded by a much larger area uniformly zoned. Plaintiffs' supporting materials showed that the parcel of land was a small rectangular lot, 100′ × 275′ in size, and owned by a single owner, C & D. They also presented materials which showed that the vast majority of the land surrounding the subject tract is uniformly zoned. . . .

In the case *sub judice*, plaintiffs used zoning maps to show that the subject tract is surrounded by a vast majority of property zoned either Residential-6 or Office & Institutional. Property adjacent to the subject tract is zoned Business-1 and Business-2. The two isolated pockets of property zoned Business-1 and Business-2, at the time they were implemented, were both surrounded by Residential-6 and Office & Institutional zoning. The properties zoned Business-1 and Business-2 are themselves examples of spot zoning. On the basis that the property is surrounded by property uniformly zoned Residential-6 and Office & Institutional, the zoning ordinance enacted by the Town of Apex is spot zoning as defined by the North Carolina Courts.

The North Carolina Supreme Court, however, has established that spot zoning is not invalid per se. *Chrismon*, 322 N.C. at 627, 370 S.E.2d at 589. . . .

[S]everal factors . . . are relevant to a showing of the existence of a sufficient reasonable basis for spot zoning.

1. The size of the tract in question.
2. The compatibility of the disputed action with an existing comprehensive zoning plan.
3. The benefits and detriments for the owner, his neighbors and the surrounding community.
4. The relationship of the uses envisioned under the new zoning and the uses currently present in adjacent tracts.

Chrismon, 322 N.C. at 628, 370 S.E.2d at 589.

The first factor is the size of the tract in question. Plaintiffs provided evidence that the tract is a single rectangular lot, 100′ × 275′ in size, with a one-story masonry building containing 3,780 square feet of net interior floor space. The lot is surrounded by residences on three sides and is uniformly zoned Residential-6 and Office & Institutional.

The second factor is the compatibility of the disputed action with an existing comprehensive zoning plan. . . .

In the present case, a comprehensive zoning plan entitled 2010 Land Use Plan was adopted on 5 December 1989. The plan list [*sic*] several guidelines for future development in the Town of Apex. The two that are relevant to this appeal are the following: (1) Use buffer areas and transitional zoning to protect adjacent existing residential development and (2) Industrial uses should be located adjacent to or near the major railroad corridors and away from residential areas. The 2010 Land Use Map also provides that South Salem Street should continue to be zoned and developed for Office & Institutional uses to provide a transition between residential and more intensive uses. Although the property is zoned Conditional Use Business-2 with the same features as Office & Institutional, the uses to be employed are industrial in nature. The Town of Apex enacted a zoning ordinance in direct contravention of its comprehensive zoning plan.

The third relevant factor is the benefits and detriments to the owner, his neighbors and the surrounding community. . . .

. . . The benefits to the owner are monetary in nature. When C & D leased the premises to the postal service in December 1989, the rent was $8000.00 per year. The lease between C & D and A & E, dated 1 June 1990, fixed the rent at $18,000.00 per year. By leasing the premises to A & E, C & D will receive a $10,000.00 increase in rental profits. C & D will also benefit from the special conditions of the permit which required additional streetscaping to be performed by the tenant around the subject property. The zoning change presents no detriment to C & D.

The only benefit to the community provided by the zoning change is one of an aesthetic nature. Again, the prospective tenant, in accordance with the conditions listed in the zoning ordinance, is obligated to perform streetscaping around the premises. No jobs will be created by the zoning change nor services provided which would specifically benefit the community. The main detriment to the community would be the placement of an industrial use in an area where the property is used for residential and professional purposes.

In *Chrismon*, the Court considered the community's support of the rezoning ordinance in order to assess the benefit of the zoning change to the community. In the case *sub judice*, there was no support for the purported zoning change. In fact, sixty Apex residents signed a protest petition in opposition to the proposed zoning change.

The final factor listed by the *Chrismon* Court in determining whether or not a reasonable basis exists for spot zoning focuses on the compatibility of the uses envisioned in the rezoned tract with the uses already present in adjacent tracts. The use envisioned under the new zoning change is electronic assembly. Present uses of property surrounding the subject tract include: residential dwellings on three sides, medical offices, a bank, a pharmacy and a jewelry store.

Plaintiffs correctly contend that the use envisioned by A & E is a drastic change from the uses already present in the surrounding area. Electronic assembly is manufacturing which is totally different from the various uses that are already present in the surrounding areas. Ann Sears, president of A & E, stated in her deposition that at various times automobiles, vans and tractor trailer trucks would create a flow of traffic in and out of the premises. This type of activity would totally destroy the tenor of the basically residential and professional area. . . .

For the foregoing reasons, the trial court correctly granted the plaintiffs' motion for summary judgment and denied defendants' motion for summary judgment. Accordingly, we

Affirm.

EAGLES and PARKER, JJ., concur.

Notes and Comments

1. *Two Types of Zoning Amendments*. Note that an "amendment" to a zoning ordinance can take one of two forms. The jurisdiction can amend the text of the zoning ordinance to create a new district, expand the uses allowed in a district, and so forth. Alternatively (or concurrently), it can amend the zoning map to change the zoning designations that apply to a specific piece of property.

2. *Spotting "Spot Zoning."* How does the court determine whether the rezoning "furthers" the comprehensive zoning plan, and thus is legitimate, or constitutes spot zoning and is invalid? In an early leading case, *Bartram v. Zoning Commission of the City of Bridgeport*, 68 A.2d 308 (Conn. 1949), the Connecticut Supreme Court stated:

> Action by a zoning authority which gives to a single lot or a small area privileges which are not extended to other land in the vicinity is in general against sound public policy and obnoxious to the law. It can be justified only when it is done in furtherance of a general plan properly adopted for and designed to serve the best interests of the community as a whole.
>
> The vice of spot zoning is in the fact that it singles out for special treatment a lot or a small area in a way that does not further such a plan.

Id. at 310-311.

3. *Defining Spot Zoning*. The appellation "spot zoning" is one of those terms that is more easily defined than applied. Consider the following explanations of the term:

> Spot zoning results when a zoning ordinance creates a small island of property with restrictions on its use different from those imposed on the surrounding property. *Kane v. City Council of Cedar Rapids*, 537 N.W.2d 718, 723 (Iowa 1995).
>
> Spot zoning consists of zoning that "single[s] out a small parcel or perhaps even a single lot for a use classification different from the surrounding area and inconsistent with any comprehensive plan, for the benefit of the owner of such property." *Granger v. Town of Woodford*, 708 A.2d 1345, 1346 (Vt. 1998).
>
> Spot zoning is "a change in zoning applied only to a small area, which is out of harmony with comprehensive planning for the good of the community." *Hanna v. City of Chicago*, 771 N.E.2d 13, 23 (Ill. App. 2002) (*quoting Bossman v. Village of Riverton*, 684 N.E.2d 427 (Ill. App. 1997)).

Spot zoning usually consists of a rezoning to a new use that is markedly different from surrounding uses. But "reverse" spot zoning is also a possibility. *See Debes v. City of Key West*, 690 So. 2d 700 (Fla. Dist. Ct. App. 1997) ("reverse spot zoning" occurred when the city refused to rezone to commercial a residentially zoned parcel that was surrounded by commercial uses).

4. *Zoning Intent and Psychoanalysis*. At its core, the spot zoning doctrine requires the court to resolve whether a zone change is in the public interest or merely benefits a private landowner. *See, e.g., Gallo v. Mayor and Township Council of Lawrence Township,* 744 A.2d 1219, 1225 (N.J. Super. Ct. App. Div. 2000) ("'Spot zoning'

is the use of the zoning power to benefit particular private interests rather than the collective interests of the community."). All zone changes initiated by a private landowner, however, provide benefit to that individual, so deciding which are in the public interest as well, and whether the public interest outweighs the private benefit, is a problematic exercise. Further, deciding the "intent" behind a rezoning is nearly impossible; as the late Professor Williams noted, the test of motivation is "purely subjective" and "would tax the psychoanalytic capabilities of the most sophisticated court." 1 Norman Williams, Jr., American Planning Law §27.05, 743 (1988).

Perhaps in response to this difficulty, many courts have looked to whether comprehensive planning preceded the zone change and to the procedures used in changing the zoning. *See Jones v. Zoning Board of Adjustment of the Township of Long Beach*, 108 A.2d 498, 502 (N.J. Super. Ct. App. Div. 1954) (" 'spot zoning' is the very antithesis of planned zoning"); *Kravetz v. Plenge*, 446 N.Y.S.2d 807, 811 (Sup. Ct. App. Div. 1982) ("A determining factor in deciding whether zoning is part of a comprehensive plan is whether forethought has been given to the community's land use problems").

5. *Factors in the Analysis.* Courts determining whether a zoning amendment constitutes spot zoning examine a variety of factors. The size of the area reclassified is perhaps the most important factor, as many courts refer to spot zoning as the reclassifying of a small parcel of land. As the size of the rezoned parcel increases, it becomes less likely that the court will find spot zoning. Another important factor is the uses of the lands surrounding the reclassified parcel, while the court also may evaluate the history of zoning and zoning patterns in the area.

6. *Changes, Mistakes, and Presumptions.* State rules vary on the showing necessary to support an amendment to a zoning ordinance. The most stringent showing required for an amendment is in Maryland, which follows the rule that only a mistake in the original zoning or a change in conditions subsequent to the enactment of the original ordinance can justify an amendment. *See, e.g., Howard County v. Dorsey*, 438 A.2d 1339, 1345 (Md. 1982). *See also Fondren North Renaissance v. Mayor and City Council of Jackson*, 749 So. 2d 974, 977 (Miss. 1999) (requiring either a mistake in the original zoning or "that the character of the neighborhood has changed to such an extent as to justify reclassification, and there was a public need for rezoning").

Another approach is presented in *Fasano v. Board of County Commissioners*, 507 P.2d 23 (Or. 1973), which is reprinted and discussed in Chapter 6. The court in *Fasano* treats small-tract rezonings as quasi- judicial rather than quasi-legislative in nature. The municipality must reflect this characterization in the procedures by which it adopts zone changes (for instance, findings of facts will be required), and the court's review of the decision will be less deferential than if the court were to treat the rezoning as quasi-legislative in nature. Most courts follow the traditional approach to judicial review of legislative actions by a municipality. They presume that the rezoning is valid, place a heavy burden on the challenging party, and overturn the rezoning only if it is arbitrary and capricious.

Other courts, a minority, refuse to apply the normal presumptions to rezonings. *See, e.g. Citizens for Mount Vernon v. City of Mount Vernon*, 947 P.2d 1208, 1215 (Wash. 1997). Is this a better approach to judicial review of rezonings?

7. *The Feed Store*. Consider the following excerpt from the very short opinion in *Bird-Kendall Homeowners Ass'n v. Metropolitan Dade County Commissioners*, 695 So. 2d 908, 909 (Fla. Dist. Ct. App. 1997):

> The Dade County Commission rezoned a tiny, 0.23 acre tract in the middle of a West Dade area known as "Horse Country" from AU (Agricultural Use) to BU-3 (Business Use-3) solely and admittedly so the owner could operate a feed store—which is forbidden in an AU zone, but permitted (along with many other uses) in BU-3. No other BU zoning is anywhere close. On the face of it, the rezoning resolution embodies, to the nth degree, all the evils of spot zoning . . . which have been universally proscribed.

Do you agree with the court that this must be spot zoning? Or are there other facts you would need to know first?

8. *Spot Zoning and Invalidation*. Most courts treat "spot zoning" as a conclusion that requires invalidation of the ordinance. However, a minority, including the *Covington* Court, hold that spot zoning is not illegal per se. *See Save Our Rural Environment v. Snohomish County*, 662 P.2d 816, 819 (Wash. 1983) ("When faced with a challenge to a . . . rezone action on the grounds the rezone constitutes an illegal spot zone, the main inquiry of the court is whether the zoning action bears a substantial relationship to the general welfare of the affected community. . . Only where the spot zone grants a discriminatory benefit to one or a group of owners to the detriment of their neighbors or the community at large without adequate public advantage or justification will the county's rezone be overturned").

9. *Looking to the East*. The *Covington* Court declares that the town's zoning amendment is presumed valid and that, to prevail, the plaintiff must show that the town acted arbitrarily or capriciously. *See also Gregory v. Board of Supervisors*, 514 S.E.2d 350, 354 (Va. 1999) ("A property owner seeking rezoning bears the burden of clearly demonstrating that the existing zoning classification is no longer reasonable"). How could the court conclude that the rezoning to Conditional Use Business-2 was arbitrary and capricious when the property to the east was zoned Business-1 and the property to the southeast was zoned Business-2?

10. *"Minimal Benefit"*? The court in *Covington* emphasizes that the rezoning would produce "minimal benefit" to the community and would create no jobs. Is that conclusion realistic today? If A & E Electronics needed larger quarters and could not move into this building, would it remain within the town or move elsewhere? Should the court have considered this latter possibility?

Why did the court in *Covington* expressly note that "there was no support for the zone change" in the community and that 60 residents had signed a protest petition opposing it? Is that petition relevant to the court's determination?

11. *Relevant Facts*. Setting forth a general rule about the type of proof that will support a rezoning is not possible; the cases are very fact- oriented. The following list of factors from the Illinois case of *Rodriguez v. Henderson*, 578 N.E.2d 57, 60 (Ill. App. Ct. 1991) can serve as a good general summary:

(1) the existing uses and zoning of nearby property;
(2) the extent to which property values are diminished by the particular zoning restrictions;
(3) the extent to which the destruction of a plaintiff's property values promotes the health, safety, morals, or general welfare of the public;

(4) the relative gain to the public as compared to the hardship imposed upon the individual property owner;
(5) the suitability of the subject property for the zoned purposes;
(6) the length of time the property has been vacant as zoned, considered in the context of land development in its vicinity;
(7) the evidence or lack of evidence of community need for a proposed use.

The court also observed that whether the government has a comprehensive zoning plan for land use and development, and whether the ordinance is in harmony with it, are also relevant.

The drafters of the Standard Zoning Enabling Act recognized that situations regarding particular properties would arise in which certain uses would cause externalities in particular situations. Accordingly, they built into the Act certain devices designed to accommodate those situations. The devices are known as variances or "special exceptions," and virtually every local zoning ordinance includes them.

■ JANSSEN v. HOLLAND CHARTER TOWNSHIP ZONING BOARD OF APPEALS

651 N.W.2d 464 (Mich. App. 2002)

Before: RICHARD ALLEN GRIFFIN, P.J., and HOLBROOK and HOEKSTRA, JJ.

PER CURIAM.

John W. Janssen and others appeal by leave granted from the March 22, 2000, order of the circuit court affirming the decision of defendant Holland Charter Township Zoning Board of Appeals (ZBA) granting a use variance permitting the construction of a 250-unit residential development in an area zoned agricultural. We affirm.

In September 1996, appellees Henry A. and Doris J. Pyle and Baker Brokerage & Development, Inc., filed an application with the Holland Charter Township Board requesting that certain parcels of property consisting of approximately 115 acres be rezoned from the A-Agricultural Zoning District to the R-1 Single Family Residential Zoning District. The township's planning commission voted to recommend that the board deny the rezoning application. Subsequently, these appellees amended their application by removing one fifteen-acre parcel, which left two contiguous parcels consisting of approximately one hundred acres. Again, the planning commission voted to deny the amended petition. Thereafter, the Pyles and Baker filed a use variance request with the ZBA. They sought to have the density requirements changed so as to allow them to build a 400-unit residential development on the property. After appellee Vistiana Properties, LLC, purchased the property, it and the Pyles filed an amended use variance petition, in which they reduced the number of residential units from 400 to 250. Eventually, after holding public hearings, the ZBA granted the use variance petition. Appellants then contested the ZBA's decision in the circuit court, and the court upheld the ZBA's decision.

Appellants first argue that the circuit court erred in concluding that defendant ZBA's decision to grant the use variance did not constitute impermissible rezoning because a one hundred-acre parcel is too large a parcel of land to be the subject of a use variance. Upon review de novo, we disagree. . . .

M.C.L. §125.293 provides, in pertinent part, as follows:

> Where there are practical difficulties or unnecessary hardship in the way of carrying out the strict letter of the zoning ordinance, the board of appeals in passing upon appeals may vary or modify any of its rules or provisions so that the spirit of the ordinance is observed, public safety secured, and substantial justice done.

Likewise, Holland Charter Township's zoning ordinance provides as follows:

> Sec. 20.2. Jurisdiction and powers.
>
> The board of appeals shall have all powers and jurisdiction granted by the zoning act, all powers and jurisdiction prescribed in other articles of the ordinance and the following specific powers and jurisdiction. . . .
>
> C. The jurisdiction and power to authorize, upon appeal, a variance or modification of this ordinance where there are practical difficulties or unnecessary hardship in the way of carrying out the strict letter of this ordinance so that the spirit of this ordinance shall be observed, public safety secured and substantial justice done.

The plain and ordinary language of both the statute and the ordinance do not set forth any limitations based on the size of the property owner's parcel of land. To conclude, as appellants urge, that the granting of a use variance to a large parcel of land constitutes de facto rezoning, we would have to, in effect, add an exclusion for such parcels to the above statute and ordinance. . . .

Appellants next contend that the ZBA's decision to grant the use variance was not supported by competent, material, and substantial evidence on the record. . . . To conclude that a property owner has established unnecessary hardship, a zoning board of appeals must find on the basis of substantial evidence that (1) the property cannot reasonably be used in a manner consistent with existing zoning, (2) the landowner's plight is due to unique circumstances and not to general conditions in the neighborhood that may reflect the unreasonableness of the zoning, (3) a use authorized by the variance will not alter the essential character of a locality, and (4) the hardship is not the result of the applicant's own actions. *Johnson v. Robinson Twp.*, 420 Mich. 115, 125-126, 359 N.W.2d 526 (1984); *Puritan-Greenfield Improvement Ass'n v. Leo*, 7 Mich. App. 659, 672-673, 677, 153 N.W.2d 162 (1967). We conclude that the Pyle appellees presented sufficient evidence to establish each of these criteria.

"Whether property used in trade or business or held for the production of income can reasonably be used for a purpose consistent with existing zoning will, no doubt, ordinarily turn on whether a reasonable return can be derived from the property as then zoned." *Puritan-Greenfield* at 673-674, 153 N.W.2d 162. Contrary to appellants' argument on appeal, the ZBA's conclusion that appellee Vistiana could not receive a reasonable economic return was not based on some "hypothetical value." Rather, the ZBA's finding was based on an analysis of the rental income received and the taxes assessed on the property as zoned. In concluding that the applicants established by substantial evidence that they could receive no reasonable economic return for the property as zoned, the ZBA noted that the annual rental income for the farm was $6,000, and the annual rental income for the two residences on the property yielded $12,900. The ZBA further pointed out that the 1998 taxes on the property amounted to $7,867.42. Thus, the ZBA concluded that the applicants could not realize a reasonable economic return, given the rental income from leasing the farm and the two houses. We hold that the ZBA's conclusion that the property cannot reasonably be used in a manner consistent with existing zoning was supported by competent, material, and substantial evidence on the record.

We also believe this evidence supports the finding that the hardship is not the result of the applicants' own actions. The increasing taxable value of the property and the comparatively low rental income derived are not "self-created" burdens.

In addition, we hold that there was competent, material, and substantial evidence to support that ZBA's conclusion that the use authorized by the variance would not alter the essential character of the locality. In considering the essential character of this locality, one cannot, and should not, just look at the immediate neighboring properties. The character of the locality is defined in broader strokes than such a myopic viewpoint would provide.

The underlying situation presented in the case at bar involves the changing circumstances and character of this community. With the growing consolidation of farming operations throughout that country and the fewer children willing to follow their parents into farming, the family farm, once a mainstay of both the economic and cultural landscape in rural America, has begun to disappear. . . . Appellants and appellees have found themselves caught in the tide of this rural transformation. In other words, the essential character of this community is not immutable, and is, indeed, in a state of transition.

The use to be made of the subject property not only recognizes this unfolding change in circumstances, but it also takes measured steps to balance the pressures inherent in this course of development. In granting the variance, the ZBA explained that the proposed cluster housing development will provide "a large area of open space around the perimeter of the property, thereby maintaining a buffer area between the proposed residential uses and the surrounding agricultural property," and further concluded that this factor, as well as the other conditions imposed, will ensure that the variance will not alter the locality's essential character. . . .

This leaves the question whether Vistiana's plight was unique to the property. The requirement that the landowner's plight be due to unique circumstances does not mean that the circumstances must exclusively affect only the single landowner. Rather, "[t]he courts have repeatedly emphasized that the hardship to be unique is 'not shared by *all* others.' "

While the subject property has no defining physical characteristics such as size or topographical peculiarities that make it unique, we do not believe this necessarily ends the inquiry . . . The uniqueness inquiry should not in all cases be limited to an examination of whether there is a uniqueness that inheres in the land itself.

Appellees' claim of "uniqueness" invites consideration of their plight in light of the situation of other landowners in the surrounding area. In making such a comparison, it quickly becomes evident that it is not the unreasonableness of the zoning ordinance that has led to appellees' plight. As the circuit court recognized, when the use variance was granted, the township's then current master plan envisioned that, although zoned agricultural, the subject land should eventually be used for residential purposes. Indeed, before appellees' request, the township had approved approximately fifty other instances of residential use of land in areas zoned agricultural. Thus, change in the character of the locality has not only been countenanced by the master plan, but the zoning history of the case reveals a steady, incremental movement in that direction. We believe that this shows that at the time the variance was sought, the hardship alleged was not due to the general conditions then existing in the area. In other words, the remedy does not necessarily lie in amendment of the zoning ordinance itself. Given the master plan's recognition of potential future growth specifically on lands zoned agricultural, we believe that restrained and managed development, in part through the issuance of use variances as the changing conditions create unique hardships for those remaining agricultural lands, is a reasoned approach. It satisfies the goals of upholding the spirit of the ordinance, protects public safety, and assures that substantial justice is done. . . . Further, when a "landowner has made the requisite showing of financial hardship and compatibility of the proposed use with the character of the neighborhood, the variance should be granted since to deny it [solely] on the ground that 'unique circumstances' have not been shown invites a potentially successful assault on the zoning ordinance as being confiscatory." *In re Family of Woodstock, Inc.*, 225 A.D.2d 854, 856, 638 N.Y.S.2d 825 (1996).

Affirmed.

Notes and Comments

1. *Safety Valves.* Variances are a staple of modern land use practice. They are intended to serve as "safety valves" where the strict application of Euclidian zoning causes unfairness to particular property owners. *Tall Trees Construction Corp. v. Zoning Bd. of Appeals,* 735 N.Y.S.2d 873 (2001) (referring to Zoning Boards of Appeals, which grant variances, as a "safety valve"). The origin of variances is traceable to Section 7 of the Standard Zoning Enabling Act, which empowers local "boards of adjustment":

> [t]o authorize upon appeal in specific cases such variance from the terms of the ordinance as will not be contrary to the public interest, where, owing to special conditions, a literal enforcement of the provisions of the ordinance will result in unnecessary hardship, so that the spirit of the ordinance shall be observed and substantial justice done.

Substantial parts of this section have been enacted in a majority of states.

A variance "runs with the land," and its benefit is available to the applicant's successors in title. *Stop & Shop Supermarket Co. v. Board. of Adjustment of Township of Springfield,* 744 A.2d 1169, 1177 (N.J. 2000) (citing numerous state cases).

2. *Use and Area Variances I.* Variances are broken into two general categories: use variances and area (sometimes called "bulk") variances. As indicated by its name, a use variance permits the property owner to use the land in a manner that is different from the uses prescribed in the zoning ordinance. By contrast, an area variance is a catch-all category for all non-use variances and includes such matters as lot size, height, setback, and yard requirements. Distinguishing between the two

categories, however, can be difficult. For example, would you consider a variance authorizing an increase in density to be a use variance or an area variance?

3. *Use and Area Variances II.* The distinction between use and area variances is significant, for the test for an area variance "generally is less onerous than the evidentiary showing required for a use variance." *Metropolitan Bd. of Zoning Appeals v. McDonald's Corp.*, 481 N.E.2d 141, 146 (Ind. App. 1985). Indeed, some states go so far as to prohibit the issuance of use variances. *See* Cal. Govt. Code §65906 (West 1997); Minn. Stat. Ann. §394.27, subd. 7 (West 1997); Va. Code Ann. §15.2-2201 (LexisNexis 2003). What is the reason for this difference?

4. *"Unnecessary Hardships."* In many states, an applicant for a use variance must demonstrate "unnecessary hardship," while an area variance requires a showing of "practical difficulties." *Trent v. German Township Bd. of Zoning Appeals*, 759 N.E.2d 421 (Ohio App. 2001). These tests are taken from Section 7 of the Standard Zoning Enabling Act, quoted above.

An early, leading decision concluded that to meet the "unnecessary hardship" test, an applicant must show:

> (1) [that] the land in question cannot yield a reasonable return if used only for a purpose allowed in that zone; (2) that the plight of the owner is due to unique circumstances and not to the general conditions in the neighborhood which may reflect the unreasonableness of the zoning ordinance itself; and (3) that the use to be authorized by the variance will not alter the essential character of the locality.

Otto v. Steinhilber, 24 N.E.2d 851, 853 (N.Y. 1939). Additionally, courts often declare that a variance must be in the "public interest." *See, e.g., Grey Rocks Land Trust v. Town of Hebron*, 614 A.2d 1048 (N.H. 1992) (variance denied where it would have impaired the natural scenic, recreational, and environmental values of the property surrounding it).

The unnecessary hardship test is most easily satisfied by a showing that the applicant's property has significant physical differences from other similarly situated properties. As the Pennsylvania Supreme Court put it, "Unnecessary hardship is established by evidence that the physical features of the property are such that it cannot be used for a permitted purpose or that the property can be conformed for a permitted use only at a prohibitive expense." *Allegheny West Civic Council, Inc. v. Zoning Board of Adjustment of the City of Pittsburgh*, 689 A.2d 225, 227 (Pa. 1997). Thus, in *Minnick v. Zoning Hearing Board*, 455 A.2d 243, 249 (Pa. Commw. Ct. 1983) the court found "unique hardship" where, due to its peculiar characteristics, a lot could not be developed consistently with the "rear yard" requirements of a zoning ordinance.

In contrast, the prospect of increased economic profit will not support the grant of a variance, as long as the owner can make a reasonable return from the permitted uses allowed by the ordinance. Furthermore, if the hardship is self-created, a variance cannot be granted, although courts generally now conclude that merely purchasing the property with knowledge that a variance would be needed is not self-created hardship that bars the grant of a variance. *Spence v. Board of Zoning Appeals for the City of Virginia Beach*, 496 S.E.2d 61 (Va. 1998).

5. *"Practical Difficulties."* The other test often employed in variance decisions is whether the applicant has demonstrated "practical difficulties." In some states, the practical difficulties test is essentially treated as a restatement of the unnecessary

hardship standard. *See, e.g., State v. Kenosha County Board of Adjustment*, 577 N.W.2d 813, 820 (Wis. 1998) ("this court has already decided that there is no significant distinction between the meaning of the two terms"). Most others, led by New York, have assigned a separate meaning to the term. *See Bronxville v. Francis*, 135 N.E.2d 724 (N.Y. 1956). Most courts now hold that a person who purchases the land with notice of the zoning restrictions may still apply for a variance. *See, e.g., Richard Roeser Professional Builder, Inc. v. Anne Arundel County,* 793 A.2d 545 (Md. 2002). A few courts, however, continue to apply the earlier rule that such a purchase creates the hardship, and thus the owner is not entitled to a variance. *See, e.g., Hill v. Town of Chester,* 771 A.2d 559 (2001).

6. *Lawyering Skills*. In contrast to zoning, which is generally (although not universally) viewed as a legislative act, variances have the characteristics of an adjudicative act. As such, the granting of a variance is often entrusted to a zoning "board of adjustment." Because of its judicial nature, whether a variance is granted often depends upon the specific factual evidence presented by the applicant. The decision on applications for variances thus places a premium on good lawyering on the part of the applicant.

7. *Has the "Safety Valve" Ruptured?* Because variances authorize either uses or other deviations from the zoning ordinance not allowed on other properties, the variance power plainly raises the prospect of abuse and favoritism in the zoning process. *See, e.g., People ex rel. Fordham Manor Reformed Church v. Walsh*, 155 N.E. 575, 578 (N.Y. 1927) (warning by Chief Judge Cardozo that the variance power is "one easily abused"); 5 Norman Williams, Jr., American Land Planning Law, 1 (1985) ("[I]t is common knowledge that zoning boards often ignore the restrictive tone, and sometimes tend to hand out variances just for the asking.") *See* Osborne M. Reynolds, Jr., The "Unique Circumstances Rule" in Zoning Variances—An Aid in Achieving Greater Prudence and Less Leniency, 31 Urb. Law. 127 (1999) (summarizing the criticism of variance law and practice, and concluding "[t]here thus seems widespread agreement that variance procedures in the United States today may often lead to denial of equal protection and that variance practices may have undesirable effects on community planning."). Some have suggested that an ethical problem lies at the heart of abuse of the variance power: ties between those individuals appointed to boards that hear variances and the applicants may lead to insufficient rigor in applying variance standards. *See Topanga Ass'n for a Scenic Community v. County of Los Angeles,* 522 P.2d 12, 19 (Cal. 1974) ("Although we emphasize that we have no reason to believe that such a circumstance exists in the case at bar, the membership of some zoning boards may be inadequately insulated from the interests whose advocates most frequently seek variances").

This concern over municipal abuse of the discretion involved in granting variances has influenced judicial review of variance decisions. Courts have repeatedly warned that the burden on an applicant for a variance is a significant one. *See, e.g., Board of Zoning Adjustment v. Summers,* 814 So. 2d 851, 855 (Ala. 2001) ("We have repeatedly recognized that variances should be granted sparingly, and only under unusual and exceptional circumstances . . . "); *Valley View Civic Ass'n v. Zoning Board of Adjustment*, 462 A.2d 637, 640 (Pa. 1983) ("The reasons for granting a variance must be substantial, serious and compelling."). Despite these judicial warnings, however, it seems clear that variance boards continue to grant variances that do not meet the statutory and judicial standards established for them. Why does this situation persist?

8. *Variations on Variance Tests*. The New Hampshire Supreme Court has found that the definition of "unnecessary hardship" had become "too restrictive" in light of the constitutional rights of property owners. Accordingly, it adopted a new test for this term. Applicants must prove that:

> (1) a zoning restriction as applied to their property interferes with their reasonable use of the property, considering the unique setting of the property in its environment; (2) no fair and substantial relationship exists between the general purposes of the zoning ordinance and the specific restriction on the property; and (3) the variance would not injure the public or private rights of others.

Simplex Technologies, Inc. v. Town of Newington, 766 A.2d 713, 717 (N.H. 2001). Is this formulation an improvement? Is the solution to the variance "problem" the granting of more or fewer variances?

New Jersey's Municipal Land Use Law disallows variances without a showing that the variance can be granted "without substantial detriment to the public good and will not substantially impair the intent and purpose of the zone plan and zoning ordinance." N.J.S.A. §40.55D-70d. In *New Brunswick Cellular Tel. Co. v. Borough of South Plainfield Bd. of Adj.*, 733 A.2d 442, 445 (N.J. 1999), the New Jersey Supreme Court explained these two criteria, which it termed respectively the "positive" and "negative" criteria:

> [T]o satisfy the positive criteria, an applicant must prove that the use promotes the general welfare because the proposed site is particularly suitable to the proposed use. . . . Further, to satisfy the negative criteria, in addition to proving that the variance can be granted without substantial detriment to the public good, an applicant must demonstrate through an enhanced quality of proof . . . that the variance sought is not inconsistent with the intent and purpose of the master plan and zoning ordinance.

Do the "positive" and "negative" criteria better capture the considerations that should go into the grant of a variance?

D. FLEXIBILITY DEVICES

1. Use Permits

As zoning developed, other so-called flexibility devices arose as local governments and developers sought to lessen the rigidity of Euclidian zoning. One such flexibility device is the conditional use permit.

■ JONES v. CITY OF CARBONDALE

576 N.E.2d 909 (Ill. App. Ct. 1991)

Justice CHAPMAN delivered the opinion of the court:

Hill House, Inc., filed an application with the City of Carbondale (City) for a special use permit on May 30, 1989. Thereafter, William Jones filed a petition seeking to invoke the provisions of section 11-13-14 of the Illinois Municipal Code which provides in pertinent part:

> In case of a written protest against any proposed amendment of the regulations or districts, signed and acknowledged by . . . the owners of 20% of the frontage immediately adjoining the frontage proposed to be altered, is [*sic*] filed with the clerk of the municipality, the amendment shall not be passed except by a favorable vote of two-thirds of the aldermen or trustees of the municipality then holding office. [Ill. Rev. Stat. 1989, ch. 24, par. 11-13-14.]

The city council took no formal action on Jones' petition as it determined that section 11-13-14 was inapplicable to the grant of a special use permit. On July 3, 1989, the city council, by a simple majority, adopted a resolution which granted the special use request submitted by Hill House, Inc.

Jones then filed a two-count complaint for declaratory judgment in the circuit court. This appeal concerns the disposition of count I; therefore, we will limit our discussion to that count.

In count I, Jones requested that the court: (1) declare the rights of the plaintiff to invoke the provisions of section 11-13-14 of the Municipal Code; (2) declare the grant of the special use null and void; and (3) enjoin the City of Carbondale from issuing the special use certificate. In its answer to the complaint, the city admitted: (1) that the objection was filed by the requisite percentage of frontage owners; (2) that the city council took no formal action on Jones' petition invoking the two-thirds majority provision of section 11-13-14; and (3) that the city council approved the special use certificate by a vote of three in favor and two opposed. . . .

Zoning ordinances typically provide three mechanisms to accommodate circumstances for which the generalized ordinance regulatory scheme is imperfect: the variance, zoning amendment, and special use permit . . . While these tools are similar in that they all deviate from the principal permitted uses of a zoning ordinance, they differ in their scope and purpose.

A variance is a grant of relief to an owner from the literal requirements of the ordinance where literal enforcement would cause him undue hardship. (*City of Clinton v. Glasson* (1976), 35 Ill. App. 3d 745, 748, 342 N.E.2d 229, 231.) It has been recognized that because the special use may have the same impact upon neighboring property as a variance, procedural safe-guards similar to those prescribed for variances might be desirable for special uses as well. (*Kotrich v. County of Du Page* (1960), 19 Ill. 2d 181, 187, 166 N.E.2d 601, 605.) However, the supreme court determined that the procedural requirements for variances are not, without legislative directive, imposed upon special uses. See *Kotrich*, 19 Ill. 2d at 188, 166 N.E.2d at 605.

An amendment to a zoning ordinance changes or alters the original ordinance or some of its provisions. (*Athey v. City of Peru* (1974), 22 Ill. App. 3d 363, 367, 317 N.E.2d 294, 297.) In the instant case Jones argues that because the special use authorizes use of the property contrary to the ordinance, it is an amendment and the voting requirements attendant to an amendment apply. We disagree.

The ordinance at issue in this case is set forth in section 15-2-24 of the Carbondale Revised Code:

D. Special Uses:

After a public hearing before the Planning Commission, the City Council may permit as special uses the following uses which are subject to: (a) the "Procedures" as prescribed in 15-2-57; (b) the lot area, lot width, yards, and height limitations of this district unless specified otherwise in the special use; (c) the performance standards as prescribed in this district for each special use (if any):

1. commercial agricultural storage operation
2. commercial fishing, hunting lodge, gun club or related operation
3. drive-in theater
4. licensed home or institution which provides for the care or custody or education or welfare of persons, not including hospitals. . . .

(Carbondale Revised Code (1990), section 15-2-24.)

. . . A special use is a permission by the Board to an owner to use his property in a manner contrary to the ordinance provided that the intended use is one of those specifically listed in the ordinance and provided that the public convenience will be served by the use . . . The very nature of a special use, whose origins come from the ordinance itself, is contrasted sharply with the essence of an amendment's nature. A permitted special use authorizes a use of the land pursuant to the existing zoning ordinance. No change or alteration in the ordinance itself is required in order to effect a special use. When the special use was granted in this case, section 15-2-24 of the Carbondale Revised Code was neither altered nor repealed. Rather, the only action necessary was the invocation of that portion of the ordinance which listed the permissible special uses.

Jones points out that the resolution adopted by the city granting the special use requires the applicant to comply with four conditions, none of which are contained within the ordinance. The resolution requires that: (1) the city be given site plan approval; (2) building construction be done in accordance with Illinois and Carbondale building codes; (3) the applicant must connect to city water and sanitary sewer mains; and (4) the applicant must dedicate land to allow for street improvements. Jones argues that the city has clearly amended the zoning regulations by imposing requirements which are not otherwise imposed on other landowners within the zoning district.

The Illinois Municipal Code provides in part that:

a special use shall be permitted only upon evidence that such use meets standards established for such classification in the ordinances, and the granting of permission therefor may be subject to conditions reasonably necessary to meet such standards. . . . (Ill. Rev. Stat. 1989, ch. 24, par. 11- 13-1.1.)

The ordinance at issue provides that a special use may be permitted subject to:

(a) the "Procedures" as prescribed in 15-2-57; (b) the lot area, lot width, yards, and height limitations of this district unless specified otherwise in the special use; (c) the performance standards as prescribed in this district for each special use. . . . (Carbondale Revised Code (1990), section 15-2-24(D).)

We have reviewed the procedures as prescribed in section 15-2-57 of the Carbondale Revised Code and do not find the four conditions imposed upon the special use applicant contrary to the performance standards which are provided in section 15-2-57. Because the plaintiff has otherwise failed to demonstrate how the four conditions imposed upon the special use applicant are not reasonably necessary to meet the standards as provided in the ordinance (Ill. Rev. Stat. 1989, ch. 24, par. 11-13-1.1), we cannot find that the imposition of the conditions constitute[s] an amendment of the ordinance.

Jones also argues that permitted special uses shown on the official zoning map of the City of Carbondale are amendments because changes to the zoning map may only be made via passage or amendment of an ordinance as provided in the Carbondale Revised Code. The city counters that special uses are noted on the official zoning map as a convenience to the public and do not constitute amendments to the zoning ordinances.

Mr. James Rayfield, a planner with the City of Carbondale, testified at a deposition taken on behalf of the plaintiff that the register of amendments to the official zoning map for the city indicates special uses which are identified on the zoning map. He testified that, although a special use such as the one at bar may appear on the zoning map, the zoning district boundary lines do not change.

Section 15-2-9 of the Carbondale Revised Code states that the official zoning map "is the final authority as to the *current zoning status* of land and water areas, buildings, and other structures. . . ." (Emphasis added.) (Carbondale Revised Code (1990), section 15-2-9.) This description of the official zoning map for the city imposes no greater requirement than is mandated by the Illinois Municipal Code, which provides:

> [T]he corporate authorities shall cause to be published no later than March 31 of each year a map clearly showing the existing zoning uses, divisions, restrictions, regulations and classifications of such municipality. . . . (Ill. Rev. Stat. 1989, ch. 24, par. 11-13-19.)

Both the Illinois Municipal Code and the Carbondale Revised Code mandate that zoning uses are to be indicated on the zoning map. When the special use herein was granted, the area remained zoned agricultural. The special use is merely a designated use within the zoned district which is indicated on the official zoning map. Flagging the permitted special uses on the zoning map simply gives notice that a special use is being made of the parcel. . . .

Affirmed.

LEWIS and GOLDENHERSH, JJ., concur.

Notes and Comments

1. *Amendments v. Use Permits*. The case does not tell you what use plaintiff sought to make of the property. Can you make an "educated guess" just from reading the zoning ordinance in question?

The plaintiff argued that the special use permit actually constituted an amendment to the zoning ordinance. Why did it make this argument? Before answering, look at the statute again and note the differences in procedures used for zoning amendments in contrast to use permits.

2. *Use Permits v. Variances*. A variance differs conceptually from a conditional use or special use permit. The latter involves a use that the zoning ordinance envisions to be proper under certain prescribed conditions. A variance, in contrast, is a departure from the specific terms of the zoning ordinance. In other words, the variance allows the landowner to do something that the zoning ordinance forbids, while the special use permit allows a use that the ordinance authorizes. *See Texaco Refining and Marketing, Inc. v. Valente*, 571 N.Y.S.2d 328, 330 (Sup. Ct. App. Div. 1991) ("Unlike a variance, a special use permit does not involve a use of property forbidden by the zoning ordinance but instead constitutes a recognition of a use which the ordinance permits under stated conditions."). Because special use permits authorize uses that are envisioned in the zoning ordinance, while variances depart from the zoning ordinances, the standard for a variance is much more stringent. *Retail Property Trust v. Bd. of Zoning Appeals,* 774 N.E.2d 727, 730 (2002).

3. *Special Uses, Conditional Uses, and Exceptions*. The zoning device used in the *Jones* case is referred to by various names: a special use permit, a conditional use permit, or a special exception. A special use permit is required for certain uses that are authorized by the zoning ordinance but that present special problems in certain locations because of the nature of the use. *City of Chicago Heights v. Living Word Outreach Full Gospel Church and Ministries,* Inc., 749 N.E.2d 916, 926 (Ill. 2001) (special uses provide for those uses that are either necessary or generally appropriate for a community but may require special regulation because of unique or unusual impacts associated with them). Because the use is potentially incompatible with other nearby uses, the applicant must obtain a permit. Examples of uses for which a special use permit is often required are gasoline stations, theaters, junkyards, churches, day care centers, funeral homes, television transmission towers, and adult book stores. Each of these uses poses externalities that, if not controlled, can affect nearby properties.

Some communities differentiate between special use permits and conditional use permits. They authorize a special use permit for uses specified in the specific zoning district, while a conditional use permit is available for certain uses listed under an ordinance that is separate from the zoning ordinance. Uses such as landfills, liquor stores, or adult businesses fall into the latter category. The student also should note that many ordinances provide for small deviations from allowable uses under the zoning ordinance through the granting of a minimal variance of exception. For example, such an approval might allow less than a 10 percent variation from the zoning ordinance, which the zoning administrator can approve without the cost and delay associated with a variance proceeding.

Special uses must be distinguished from another zoning term, "accessory uses." These are uses that are incidental to the permitted use authorized by the zoning ordinance, and thus allowable as a matter of right. For example, the courts have held that a "basketball backboard" is an accessory use and not a separate "building" under the applicable ordinance. *Dyno v. Village of Johnson City,* 690 N.Y.S.2d 325 (A.D. 1999); *See also Eastern Service Centers, Inc. v. Cloverland Farms Dairy, Inc.,* 744 A.2d 63 (Md. Ct. Sp. App. 2000) (convenience store is an accessory use to a gas station). While accessory uses are thought of as minor, some interpretations of that term can be quite broad. *See, e.g., Henley v. City of Youngtown Bd. of Zoning Appeals,* 735 N.E.2d 433 (Ohio 2000) (transitional apartments for homeless women and children are an accessory use to the principal use of a church; thus a convent could be converted to that use).

4. *Procedures for Use Permits*. The granting of a special use permit is an adjudicative decision, and the permit can be granted only after notice and hearing. Local ordinances typically assign the granting of such permits either to a board of adjustment or to the planning commission, with the possibility of appeal to the city council. In granting a special use permit, the board or commission normally must make findings of fact and can place conditions on the permit to protect neighboring properties from such things as excessive noise or traffic.

5. *Legislatively Prescribed Standards*. To avoid the claim that the grant of a special use permits is an exercise of unbounded discretion and thus constitutes an invalid delegation of power, the board or commission must adhere to a set of legislatively prescribed standards. In most cases, however, the courts have approved the use of standards that are quite general. *See, e.g., Whittaker & Gooding Co. v. Scio Township*, 332 N.W.2d 527, 532 (Mich. Ct. App. 1983) (upholding ordinance allowing the board to impose such conditions as it deems necessary "to protect the public interest . . . and the surrounding property, and to achieve the objectives of th[e] Ordinance"); *Anderson v. Peden*, 587 P.2d 59 (Or. 1978) ("purposes in view" was an adequate standard).

6. *Conditions, Conditions*. Special use permits typically are approved with conditions designed to ameliorate the impacts of the particular land use. These conditions can broadly relate to the operation of the site. There are, however, limits on the power to condition. For example, the condition must relate to the use of the property, rather than merely regulating the owners of the property *See Baughman v. Bd. of Zoning Appeals for Harrison Township*, 2002 WL 1773043 (Ohio App. 2002) (condition that any split or transfer of the property would nullify the permit exceeded the township's authority). If the permittee violates the conditions, the permit can be revoked. *See, e.g. Malibu Mountains Recreation, Inc. v. County of Los Angeles*, 79 Cal. Rptr. 2d 25 (App. 1998) (revoking conditional use permit for tennis ranch).

7. *The Neighbors' Veto Power?* As the *Jones* case indicates, some state statutes authorize written protests from neighboring landowners that, if they reach a minimum percentage, change the requirements for the vote needed to amend the ordinance. These provisions are traceable to Section 5 of the Standard Zoning Enabling Act, which declares:

> In case, however, of a protest against such change, signed by the owners of 20 percent or more either of the area of the lots included in such proposed change, or of those immediately adjacent in the rear thereof extending ___ feet therefrom, or of those directly opposite thereto extending ___ feet from the street frontage of such opposite lots, such amendment shall not become effective except by the favorable vote of three-fourths of all the members of the legislative body of such municipality.

A handful of statutes go even further, requiring the consent of certain neighboring land users before the zoning ordinance can be amended. Some courts have held that these types of provisions are an unlawful delegation of legislative power and therefore unconstitutional. *See Town of Gardiner v. Stanley Orchards, Inc.*, 432

N.Y.S.2d 335, 340 (Sup. Ct. 1980); *Williams v. Whitten*, 451 S.W.2d 535, 537-38 (Tex. Ct. App. 1970).

What is the rationale for these statutes? Do they give too much power to neighboring property owners? As you will see, the rights that nearby landowners may exercise in the land use regulatory process and the effect of neighborhood opposition are important issues. For example, in a 1997 New York Court of Appeals case, *Twin County Recycling Corp. v. Yevoli*, 688 N.E.2d 501 (N.Y. 1997), the court overturned the denial of a special use permit for a recycling plant because, "[a]lthough scientific or expert testimony is surely not in every case required to support a zoning board determination, the board may not base its objection on generalized community objections." 688 N.E.2d at 502.

2. *Floating Zones and Contract Zones*

The system of "Euclidian" zoning was very much a visual process centering on the use of a zoning map. Landowners could look at the map, consult the zoning ordinance, and determine the types of land uses allowed on a specific property. The system thus gave prospective notice to landowners of their rights at the time the system was adopted. At the same time, since the zoning map views the city as a whole, some assurance existed that the "benefits and burdens" of zoning were distributed for the good of the entire community.

The need for flexibility of uses on property, however, inevitably meant that pressures would arise for case-by-case determinations of land uses on specific properties. Consider carefully the extent to which the type of zoning in the next case is inconsistent with the principles implicit in Euclidian zoning.

■ RODGERS v. VILLAGE OF TARRYTOWN

96 N.E.2d 731 (N.Y. 1951)

FULD, Judge.

This appeal, here by our permission, involves the validity of two amendments to the General Zoning Ordinance of the Village of Tarrytown, a suburban area in the County of Westchester, within twenty-five miles of New York City.

Some years ago, Tarrytown enacted a General Zoning Ordinance dividing the village into seven districts or zones — Residence A for single family dwellings, Residence B for two-family dwellings, Residence C for multiple dwellings and apartment houses, three business districts and an industrial zone. In 1947 and 1948, the board of trustees, the village's legislative body, passed the two amendatory ordinances here under attack.

The 1947 ordinance creates "A new district or class of zone . . . [to] be called 'Residence B-B' ", in which, besides one- and two-family dwellings, buildings for multiple occupancy of fifteen or fewer families were permitted. The boundaries of the new type district were not delineated in the ordinance but were to be "fixed by amendment of the official village building zone map, at such times in the future as such district or class of zone is applied, to properties in this village." The village planning board was empowered to approve such amendments and, in case such approval was withheld, the board of trustees was authorized to grant it by appropriate resolution. In addition, the ordinance erected exacting standards of size and physical layouts for Residence B-B zones: a minimum of ten acres of land and a maximum building height of three stories were mandated; set-back and spacing requirements for structures were carefully prescribed; and no more than 15% of the ground area of the plot was to be occupied by buildings.

A year and a half after the 1947 amendment was enacted, defendant Elizabeth Rubin sought to have her property, consisting of almost ten and a half acres in the Residence A district, placed in a Residence B-B classification. After repeated modification of her plans to meet suggestions of the village planning board, that body gave its approval, and several months later, in December of 1948, the board of trustees, also approving, passed the second ordinance here under attack. In essence, it provides that the Residence B-B district "is hereby applied to the [Rubin] property . . . and the district or zone of said property is hereby changed to 'Residence B-B' and the official Building Zone Map of the Village of Tarrytown is hereby amended accordingly [by specification of the various parcels and plots involved]".

Plaintiff, who owns a residence on a six-acre plot about a hundred yards from Rubin's property, brought this action to have the two amendments declared invalid and to enjoin defendant Rubin from constructing multiple dwellings on her property. . . .

While stability and regularity are undoubtedly essential to the operation of zoning plans, zoning is by no means static. Changed or changing conditions call for changed plans, and persons who own property in a particular zone or use district enjoy no eternally vested right to that classification if the public interest demands otherwise. Accordingly, the power of a village to amend its basic zoning ordinance in such a way as reasonably to promote the general welfare cannot be questioned.

The Tarrytown board of trustees was entitled to find that there was a real need for additional housing facilities; that the creation of Residence B-B districts for garden apartment developments would prevent young families, unable to find accommodations in the village, from moving elsewhere; would attract business to the community; would lighten the tax load of the small homeowner, increasingly burdened by the shrinkage of tax revenues resulting from the depreciated value of large estates and the transfer of many such estates to tax-exempt institutions; and would develop otherwise unmarketable and decaying property.

The village's zoning aim being clear, the choice of methods to accomplish it lay with the board. Two such methods were at hand. It could amend the General Zoning Ordinance so as to permit garden apartments on any plot of ten acres or more in Residence A and B zones (the zones more restricted) or it could amend that Ordinance so as to invite owners of ten or more acres, who wished to build garden apartments on their properties, to apply for a Residence B-B classification. The board chose to adopt the latter procedure. That it called for separate legislative authorization for each project presents no obstacle or drawback—and so we have already held. . . . Whether we would have made the same choice is not the issue; it is sufficient that the board's decision was neither arbitrary nor unreasonable.

As to the requirement that the applicant own a plot of at least ten acres, we find nothing therein unfair to plaintiff or other owners of smaller parcels. The board undoubtedly found, as it was privileged to find, that garden apartments would blend more attractively and harmoniously with the community setting, would impose less of a burden upon village facilities, if placed upon larger tracts of land rather than scattered about in smaller units. Obviously, some definite acreage had to be chosen, and, so far as the record before us reveals, the choice of ten acres as a minimum plot was well within the range of an unassailable legislative judgment.

The charge of illegal "spot zoning" — levelled at the creation of a Residence B-B district and the reclassification of defendant's property — is without substance. Defined as the process of singling out a small parcel of land for a use classification totally different from that of the surrounding area, for the benefit of the owner of such property and to the detriment of other owners . . . "spot zoning" is the very antithesis of planned zoning. If, therefore, an ordinance is enacted in accordance with a comprehensive zoning plan, it is not "spot zoning," even though it (1) singles out and affects but one small plot *see, e.g.*, Shepard v. Village of Skaneateles, supra, 300 N.Y. 115, 89 N.E.2d 619, or (2) creates in the center of a large zone small areas or districts devoted to a different use. . . . Thus, the relevant inquiry is not whether the particular zoning under attack consists of areas fixed within larger areas of different use, but whether it was accomplished for the benefit of individual owners rather than pursuant to a comprehensive plan for the general welfare of the community. Having already noted our conclusion that the ordinances were enacted to promote a comprehensive zoning plan, it is perhaps unnecessary to add that the record negates any claim that they were designed solely for the advantage of defendant or any other particular owner. Quite apart from the circumstance that defendant did not seek the benefit of the 1947 amendment until eighteen months after its passage, the all-significant fact is that that amendment applied to the entire territory of the village and accorded each and every owner of ten or more acres identical rights and privileges.

In point of fact, there would have been no question about the validity of what was done had the board simply amended the General Zoning Ordinance so as to permit property in Residence A and Residence B zones — or, for that matter, in the other districts throughout the village — to be used for garden apartments, provided that they were built on ten-acre plots and that the other carefully planned conditions and restrictions were met. It may be conceded that, under the method which the board did adopt, no one will know, from the 1947 ordinance itself, precisely where a Residence B-B district will ultimately be located. But since such a district is simply a garden apartment development, we find nothing unusual or improper in that circumstance. The same uncertainty — as to the location of the various types of structures — would be present if a zoning ordinance were to sanction garden apartments as well as one-family homes in a Residence A district — and yet there would be no doubt as to the propriety of that procedure. Consequently, to condemn the action taken by the board in effectuating a perfectly permissible zoning scheme and to strike down the ordinance designed to carry out that scheme merely because the board had employed two steps to accomplish what may be, and usually is, done in one, would be to exalt form over substance and sacrifice substance to form. . . .

The judgment of the Appellate Division should be affirmed, with costs.

Notes and Comments

1. *Floating Zones and Euclidian Zoning*. In *Bellemeade Co. v. Priddle*, 503 S.W.2d 734, 738 (Ky. 1973), the Kentucky Supreme Court noted that "a floating zone is differentiated from a fixed ('Euclidian') zone in that the latter is a specifically defined area under the zoning ordinance, while the boundaries of the former are undefined and it 'floats' over the entire district until by appropriate action the boundaries are fixed and it becomes anchored." Is the concept of a "floating zone" consistent with the underlying theory behind Euclidian zoning? How would Justice Sutherland, the author of the *Village of Euclid* opinion, have reacted to the legal challenge to floating zones made in the *Rodgers* case?

2. *Judicial Approval of Floating Zones*. *Rodgers* is the leading case upholding the concept of the floating zone. In another early decision, *Eves v. Zoning Board of Adjustment*, 164 A.2d 7, 11 (Pa. 1960), the Pennsylvania Supreme Court rejected the concept, reasoning that because floating zones await solicitation by individual landowners, "the development itself would become the plan, which is manifestly the antithesis of zoning 'in accordance with a comprehensive plan.' " Similarly, the New Jersey Supreme Court initially rejected the technique. *Rockhill v. Chesterfield* Township, 128 A.2d 473 (N.J. 1957). Almost every state, however, has refused to follow *Eves* and *Rockhill*, often commenting on the need for flexibility in the development process. *See, e.g.*, *State ex rel. Zupancic v. Schimenz*, 174 N.W.2d 533, 537 (Wis. 1970) ("The virtue of allowing private agreements to underlie zoning is the flexibility and control of the development given to a municipality to meet the ever-increasing demands for rezoning in a rapidly changing area.").

3. *Form, Substance, and Means to the Same End*. The New York Court of Appeals in *Rodgers* notes that the village could have accomplished its zoning aims through two alternative actions: (1) amending the general zoning ordinance to permit garden apartments on any ten-acre plot of land in Residence A and B zones or (2) amending the ordinance to invite owners of ten or more acres to apply for a Residence B-B classification on their property. The court concluded that invalidating the floating zone "merely because the board had employed two steps to accomplish what may be . . . done in one would be to exalt form over substance." Do you see any difference in the two methods? Could a city council pass an amendment to the zoning ordinance establishing and defining a "floating zone" and then delegate to an administrative body, such as the planning commission, the function of approving specific proposals that "anchor" the floating zone on a specific piece of property?

4. *Where's the Plan?* The court rejects plaintiff's spot zoning claim, concluding that the ordinances were enacted to promote a comprehensive zoning plan. How did the ordinance promote such a plan? Indeed, how can you have a comprehensive plan if you use a floating zone? If the adoption of a floating zone does not constitute spot zoning, what other grounds are available to attack a floating zone?

5. *The Evolution of Non-Euclidian Zoning*. The floating zone was an important step in the evolution of land use controls away from the strict application of the Euclidian model. Most significantly, floating zones depart from the traditional Euclidian concept that all uses must be mapped at the time the zoning district is created. Other types of non-traditional zones soon appeared, including: (1) overlay zones (the superimposition of a new zoning district on the zoning map's designations in order to protect specific resources, such as historical buildings),

(2) performance zoning (replacing Euclidian zoning with a system that would determine density in light of various environmental constraints of the site), and (3) transferable development rights (allowing the sale or transfer of rights from one piece of property for use on another).

Does a local government act quasi-legislatively when it "anchors" a floating zone, or is its action quasi-judicial because it is focused on the specific property? *See Heithaus v. Planning and Zoning Commission of the Town of Greenwich*, 779 A.2d 750, 759 (Conn. 2001) ("Unlike the special permit, a floating zone is the product of legislative action.").

3. Planned Unit Developments

If a floating zone for a single use is allowable, should it make any difference whether the zone allows for multiple, mixed uses?

■ PETERS v. SPEARFISH ETJ PLANNING COMMISSION

567 N.W.2d 880 (S.D. 1990)

MILLER, Chief Justice.

Landmark Realty and Development Company (Landmark) and Spring Creek Ranch appeal the trial court's construction of a zoning ordinance and its decision that the Spearfish ETJ Planning Commission (Commission), the Spearfish City Council (City) and the Lawrence County Board of Commissioners (County) exceeded their authority and jurisdiction by approving a proposed planned unit development near Spearfish, South Dakota. We affirm.

FACTS

Landmark owns a 240-acre tract of land in Lawrence County, South Dakota. The land is located within the extraterritorial jurisdiction zoning area governed by the ETJ Planning Ordinances adopted by City and County and overseen by Commission. Landmark's property is zoned A-1, general agriculture.

As required by the ETJ Planning Ordinances, Landmark requested Commission's approval of a planned unit development (PUD), Spring Creek Ranch, to be constructed on the tract of land at issue in this appeal. The proposed PUD consisted of fifty-five single family residence estates, three clusters of single family attached residences containing twenty units, one bed and breakfast inn with six to eight guest rooms, and three to six duplex cabin units. The remainder of the tract was designated as "green space" for developing walking, biking, and cross-country skiing trails, with at least fifty percent of the green space slated as "open space," consistent with the requirements for PUDs. Commission recommended approval of the proposed PUD and, after reviewing the request, City and County approved the same. . . .

Decision

The trial court concluded ETJ Planning Ordinance—4.10.1 was ambiguous. It interpreted the ordinance to limit residential density for PUDs in an A-1, general agriculture district to one dwelling per forty acres. Based on this interpretation, the trial court concluded Commission, City and County exceeded their authority and jurisdiction in approving the proposed PUD. We agree. . . .

ETJ Planning Ordinance §4.10.1 provides:

> A planned residential development, occupying three (3) acres or more shall be permitted in any A-1, PF or SRD District by special permit.
>
> The regulations established in this section are intended to provide optional methods of land development which encourage more imaginative solutions to environmental design problems, such as cluster planning. Residential areas thus established would be characterized by a unified building and site development program, open space for recreation, and the provision for commercial, religious, educational and cultural facilities which are integrated with the treatment. In order to accomplish these objectives the customary district regulations may be modified, provided that overall population densities do not exceed the densities of specific residential districts. . . .

Landmark and Spring Creek argue the emphasized language is unambiguous and a plain reading of the ordinance allows modification of the population density of A-1, general agriculture property to accommodate a PUD. In their brief on appeal, Petitioners argued that the emphasized language is ambiguous. However, in oral argument before this Court, Petitioners switched positions and suggested that the ordinance was unambiguous and a "plain reading" of the ordinance limits the population density of a PUD constructed on A-1, general agriculture property to one dwelling per forty acres.

Our review of ETJ Planning Ordinance §4.10.1 indicates the ordinance is ambiguous as to the meaning of "residential districts." "Residential districts" is not defined in §4.10.1. The term is not applied to A-1 general agriculture property anywhere in the comprehensive zoning plan other than the disputed final sentence of §4.10.1. The only other reference to "residential districts" in the ETJ Planning Ordinances is in §3.1.5(A) to describe suburban residential, rural residential and park-forest residential property. This reference does not pertain to or reference A-1, general agriculture property.

A plain reading of the term "residential districts" results in more than one reasonable definition and leads to more than one interpretation of ETJ Ordinance §4.10.1. The ordinance's language indicates that the customary district regulations may be waived for a proposed PUD but overall population density requirements may not. The ordinance does not make clear whether the population density for a proposed PUD is to be measured by the density governing the three districts which specifically allow PUDs (A-1, general agriculture, park forest, or suburban residential) or the three zoning districts specifically referred to as residential districts (suburban residential, rural residential, or park- forest residential) in other zoning ordinances. Absent an indication of which population density applies to a proposed PUD, the appropriate population density ranges from one dwelling per 7500 square feet in suburban residential districts to one dwelling per forty acres in A-1, general agriculture districts, depending on the understanding of the disputed ordinance. This wide range of possible population densities allowed by the ordinance's language results in an ambiguity. Any argument that the ordinance is not ambiguous belies the reality that the plain language of the ordinance results in more than one reasonable understanding of the PUD requirements. The trial court's conclusion ETJ Ordinance §4.10.1 was ambiguous as a matter of law was proper. Having determined the ordinance to be ambiguous, we must now determine the proper construction to be given to it. . . .

We agree with the trial court's construction of ETJ Planning Ordinance §4.10.1 that a PUD is subject to the population density limitations applicable to the district in which it is proposed. PUDs are allowed by special permit in three districts: A-1, park forest and suburban residential districts. Though the ordinance authorizing PUDs refers to "residential districts" as the basis for determining population density, PUDs are not allowed in all residential districts. A logical reading of the ordinance suggests that the population density limitations apply to those specific districts in which PUDs are allowed. The population density for a PUD is determined based on whether the PUD is proposed in an A-1, park forest or suburban residential district and limited to the population density for that specific district. Accordingly, Landmark's proposed PUD is limited to a population density of one dwelling per forty acres because of the property's status as A-1, general agriculture. . . .

Our interpretation is further supported by the fact that without population density limitations for PUDs in A-1, general agriculture districts, general agriculture districts would effectively be abolished. By removing the population density requirements for agriculture districts, the very nature and customary uses of the districts become unpractical. The exception allowing for PUDs was not intended to abandon A-1, general agriculture districts, as evidenced by the zoning regulations specific recognition of the necessity of agriculture districts in the overall development and planning for the City and County. Our interpretation of ETJ Planning Ordinance §4.10.1 is consistent with the zoning purposes of both A-1, general agriculture districts and PUDs without sacrificing the purpose of one district at the expense of the other.

Despite the population density limitations currently affecting the proposed PUD in this case, Landmark and Spring Creek are not without a remedy. The disputed property may be rezoned as a residential district compatible with the population density necessary to support the PUD. . . . If City and County intended the PUD ordinances to replace the necessity of rezoning to higher population density districts in cases such as the Spring Creek development, we respectfully suggest the zoning ordinances be amended to so indicate. . . .

Affirmed.

SABERS, AMUNDSON, KONENKAMP, and GILBERTSON, JJ., concur.

Notes and Comments

1. *Flexibility Provided by PUDs*. The use of the planned unit development, or "PUD" in common parlance, marked another step away from the rigidity of Euclidian zoning. The PUD concept draws from such land use tools as special use permits and floating zones discussed earlier in this chapter. *See generally* Gail R.

Gudder, A Primer on Planned Unit Developments, 21 Zon. and Plan. L. Rep. Nos. 3 & 4 (March and April 1998), pp. 17, 25.

As you have seen, the traditional zoning ordinance was directed at development on a lot-by-lot basis within the jurisdiction. In later decades, however, particularly after World War II, large-scale developments of subdivisions became the norm. Developers and local jurisdictions were faced with designing the future use of large plots of undeveloped land. PUDs can be used for small pieces of property, but the flexibility that they provide makes them particularly suitable for large, mixed-use developments. *See, e.g.*, *Wooland Manor Associates v. Keeney*, 713 A.2d 806 (R.I. 1998) (describing a PUD that included "various types of buildings to be combined as an integrated whole, with construction to occur in phases: phase 1, an apartment complex, (Woodland Manor I); phase 2, a housing facility for the elderly (Woodland Manor II); phase 3, a nursing home (Coventry Health Center); and phase 4, a condominium complex (Woodland Manor III))." PUDs also allow for increased environmental protection. *See Association of Rural Residents v. Kitsap County*, 4 P.3d 115, 119 n. 3 (Wash. 2000) ("A PUD is essentially a mechanism which allows property owners the option of clustering or configuring lots in a plat to avoid development in sensitive areas, create open space, or achieve other environmental or aesthetic amenities.").

2. *Benefits of PUDs*. In a leading case upholding the use of PUDs, *Cheney v. Village 2 at New Hope, Inc.*, 241 A.2d 81 (Pa. 1968), the Pennsylvania Supreme Court articulated the benefits of PUDs:

> [W]ith the increasing popularity of large scale residential developments, particularly in suburban areas, it has become apparent to many local municipalities that land can be more efficiently used, and developments more aesthetically pleasing, if zoning regulations focus on density requirements rather than on specific rules for each individual lot. . . . The ultimate goal of this so-called density or cluster concept of zoning is achieved when an entire self-contained little community is permitted to be built within a zoning district, with the rules of density controlling not only the relation of private dwellings to open space, but also the relation of homes to commercial establishments such as theaters, hotels, restaurants, and quasi- commercial uses such as schools and churches.

241 A.2d at 83. Other advantages may include lower costs as infrastructure costs are minimized and roads concentrated, additional open space for individual owners, and the inclusion of affordable housing.

3. *Procedures for Approving a PUD*. How must a PUD be implemented? *See Caruso v. Pastan*, 294 N.E.2d 501 (Mass. Ct. App. 1973) (approving use of a special permit to approve PUD); *Peterson v. City of Clemson*, 439 S.E.2d 317 (S.C. Ct. App. 1993) (approving a two-step PUD process in which the city first adopts an ordinance permitting a PUD district and then later rezones a particular parcel of land pursuant to specific plans meeting the city's development regulations). A few jurisdictions use conditional use permits to implement the PUD.

Some decisions hold that a city cannot (1) pass an ordinance that amends the text of the zoning code to generally authorize a planned unit development district, and then (2) leave it to the planning commission to approve the specific location of the PUD. *Lutz v. City of Longview*, 520 P.2d 1374 (Wash. 1974). Could the city enact PUD zoning for a specific parcel of property but then allow the planning commission to approve the specific development plan for that property? In *Bailey v. Zoning Bd. of Adjustment of the City of Philadelphia,* 742 A.2d 247 (Commw. Ct. Pa. 1999), the court held that the planning commission had no power even to make "minor modifications" in a previously approved PUD. The city council retained this authority.

4. *A Slippery Slope Toward Arbitrariness.* Since PUDs can embrace a variety of uses in a development, they could be challenged on the basis that approval or denial of a PUD is a purely arbitrary decision by the local jurisdiction, since there are no standards to guide it. In *Tri-State Generation & Transmission Co. v. City of Thornton,* 647 P.2d 670, 678 (Colo. 1982), the Colorado Supreme Court noted that the "same flexibility which is the primary virtue of a PUD ordinance also results in a loss of certainty and a concomitant concern with the misuse and abuse of discretionary authority. Consequently, courts have generally required that standards be incorporated into a planned development ordinance in order to protect against arbitrary state action."

Another legal challenge to PUDs argues that the mixing of various uses violates the statutory requirement that zones be "uniform" in nature. *See Orinda Homeowners Committee v. Bd. of Supervisors,* 90 Cal. Rptr. 88 (Ct. App. 1970) (rejecting the claim). PUDs are also open to the charge of spot zoning. *See Citizens for Mount Vernon v. City of Mount Vernon,* 947 P.2d 1208, 1216 (Wash. 1997) ("if a planned unit development can be placed at any location within a city regardless of the underlying or surrounding zoning . . . it might raise issues of spot zoning and it might undermine the overall zoning plan"). But if the PUD involves a larger parcel of land, such a claim has much less force.

Finally, PUD zoning can also be found to be spot zoning. In *Greater Yellowstone Coalition, Inc. v. Bd. of County Commissioners of Gallatin County,* 25 P.3d 168 (Mont. 2001), a county changed the zoning on a property to PUD. The court found that, even though the rezoning covered 323 acres, it constituted spot zoning. The PUD zoning, which allowed for a wide variety of uses, conflicted with the rural and residential character of the surrounding properties.

5. *Bargaining and Contract Zoning.* As consideration of land uses on a case-by-case basis increased, such as when PUDs are used, it was inevitable that local municipalities and developers would engage in discussions about the conditions under which a particular land use would be approved. Gradually, the types of conditions that municipalities required for such approvals became quite detailed, and cities sought to ensure the implementation of those conditions through a binding legal document. However, a longstanding principle of constitutional law stood in their way: many state constitutions had been interpreted to prevent cities from "contracting away" or "bargaining away" the police power.

Contract zoning issues arise when a local government enters into an agreement with a developer whereby the government extracts a performance or promise from the developer in exchange for its agreement to rezone the property. *Brandywine Enterprises, Inc. v. County Council for Prince George's County,* 700 A.2d 1216, 1221 (Md. Ct. Spec. App. 1997). If the parties reach a formal agreement prior to the rezoning, third parties (perhaps neighbors) who challenge the rezoning can argue that the agreement constitutes illegal "contract zoning." In the absence of specific statutory authority allowing such agreements, many courts will find such actions illegal.

What is it about "bargaining" over land use approvals that might suggest that the outcome will not serve the public interest? Is it, as some courts conclude, a concern that reaching a bargain will short-cut otherwise required legislative procedures? *Dacy v. Village of Ruidoso*, 845 P.2d 793 (N.M. 1992). *See also McLean Hospital Corp. v. Town of Belmont*, 778 N.E.2d 1016, 1020 (Mass. App. 2002) (applying two-part test asking (1) was contract zoning action contrary to the best interest of the city and hence offensive to general public policy, and (2) did it involve extraneous consideration?); Or is the concern over the substance of the bargain? *See City of Knoxville v. Ambrister*, 263 S.W.2d 528 (Tenn. 1953) (rezoning agreements present opportunities for fraud and undue influence).

6. *Bargaining and Development Agreements*. If a court outlaws contract zoning, will the ruling mean that parties will not be able to bargain with jurisdictions and reach agreements concerning the circumstances under which land use approvals and developments will occur? Or can creative lawyering overcome this "obstacle"?

In recent years the practice of negotiating "development agreements" for both large- and small-scale developments has grown rapidly. Such agreements are discussed in detail in Chapter 10. These agreements are contracts and thus are open to the charge that they are illegal because they constitute a bargaining away of the police power. Many states, however, have passed legislation authorizing development agreements. There are very few decisions directly addressing whether a development agreement constitutes an illegal bargaining away of the police power. Why not?

The law and economics literature discussed in Chapter 1 would encourage bargaining as a means of assuring efficiency. Assuming that the traditional concern over contract zoning has some merit, should the promotion of efficiency outweigh that concern?

7. *The Validity of Conditional Zoning*. Contract zoning is sometimes distinguished from "conditional zoning," in which the municipality rezones property but, as part of that approval, places specific conditions on its use. Because no agreement between the applicant and the jurisdiction is involved (at least in the technical sense), conditional zoning does not involve any question of contracting away the police power. This type of zoning, however, is open to another charge: that it violates the requirement found in many local zoning ordinances that zoning must be "uniform." The states are split on the validity of conditional zoning, although the trend is clearly in favor of upholding it.

Some states have passed statutes that authorize conditional zoning, and in these jurisdictions the technique is very likely to be upheld. If a local jurisdiction could obtain the same result by passing a floating zone or the use of a special use permit, should it make any difference that it chose to use conditional zoning instead?

4. *Site Plan Review*

As we have seen in the development of floating zones, PUDs, and contract zoning, municipalities have utilized new zoning devices that expand their discretion to tailor the approval of developments with specific conditions that ameliorate adverse impacts. This recognition that individual developments pose idiosyncratic problems that must be examined on a case-by-case basis also extends to permitted uses under zoning ordinances. Site plan review serves this function.

■ COLORADO SPRINGS v. SECURCARE SELF STORAGE

10 P.3d 1244 (Colo. 2000)

I.

SecurCare Self Storage, Inc. (SecurCare) owns approximately 4.4 acres of land (the plot) in Colorado Springs. In 1995, SecurCare sought to develop the entire plot by constructing mini-warehouses for self-storage. That year, SecurCare received administrative approval for its initial development plan, outlining SecurCare's intention to place mini-warehouses on its plot.

Shortly thereafter, SecurCare modified its development plan in light of an agreement it had with Amoco Oil Company (Amoco) to build a service station on approximately one acre of the plot, with the remaining 3.4 acres dedicated to the initial proposed use of mini-warehouses. The service station complex was to include a gas station, a convenience store, and an enclosed car wash.

Unlike the first development plan, this amended plan was submitted to the City of Colorado Springs Planning Commission (the Planning Commission) for its approval. At a public hearing before the Planning Commission on the amended development plan, several members of the surrounding community voiced their concerns about constructing a service station on the plot. After hearing arguments in favor of and against the service station, the Planning Commission refused to approve the amended development plan, ruling that the service station was "incompatible" with the surrounding residential neighborhood.

The Planning Commission reached this conclusion despite the fact that Colorado Springs zoned the plot as a Planned Business Center (PBC) in 1972. The Zoning Code of the City of Colorado Springs (Zoning Code) explicitly designates mini-warehouses, service stations, convenience stores and enclosed car washes as permitted uses in a PBC zone . . . The City Council, however, upheld the Planning Commission's denial of the development plan. . . .

II. . . .

B. . . .

The Zoning Code initially creates specific zone districts throughout Colorado Springs. *See* §1-1-105(A), Zoning Code. The Zoning Code then defines the uses allowed within each zone district, specifying whether the use is conditional or permitted . . . A permitted use is defined as "[a]ny use of land or a structure which is allowed by right in a zone district and *subject to the requirements of that district.*" §1-2-201, Zoning Code (emphasis added). . . .

The zone district at issue here is the PBC zone district, which allows for a variety of permitted and conditional uses. . . . Permitted uses within the PBC zone district include those uses proposed by SecurCare. *See* Table 2.2.1, Zoning Code (listing mini-warehouses, convenience stores, enclosed car washes, and service stations as permitted uses in a PBC zone district).

The Zoning Code also establishes certain requirements for developing land in any designated zone district, including the PBC zone district. For example, the construction of any building or structure requires a building permit. *See*

§4-4-402(A), Zoning Code. Moreover, the issuance of a building permit is explicitly conditioned on receiving the approval of a development plan explaining the proposed development. *See id.* . . .

The Zoning Code created the development plan requirement in recognition of the fact that "[a]ll combinations of permitted uses and development standards in a zoning district may not be appropriate at a particular location." §4-6-602(A), Zoning Code. Hence, one key purpose of the development plan requirement is to "ensure . . . use compatibility between the proposed land use and site design and the surrounding properties." *Id.*

When deciding whether to approve a development plan, a detailed list of review criteria, specifically designed for reviewing development plans, guides the decision. *See* §4-6-602(C), Zoning Code. Some important considerations in the review criteria include whether the proposed project is harmonious with the surrounding land use and whether the proposed project complies with the requirements of the zone district. *See id.* As pertinent to this case, the review criteria require the Planning Commission to ask, "Will the proposed land uses be compatible with the surrounding neighborhood?" *Id.*

C. . . .

[T]he plain language of Zoning Code provisions granted the Planning Commission the authority to deny a development plan for a permitted use by means of the development plan review criteria. Initially, we note that the plain language clearly establishes that a permitted use is not an absolute right under the Zoning Code. The plain language provides that all permitted uses are "subject to the requirements of" the various zone districts. §1-2-201, Zoning Code. This language clearly demonstrates that the Zoning Code does not establish an absolute right to development that constitutes a permitted use, but instead applies some limitations on permitted uses.

As previously noted, any development in any zone district is subject to the requirement of obtaining a building permit, which in turn requires approval of a development plan. *See* §4-4-402(A), Zoning Code. The Zoning Code repeatedly makes clear that this requirement specifically applies to any development in a PBC zone district. Section 4-6-602(B)(1) of the Zoning Code simply states, "A development plan shall be approved before any building permits may be issued for property . . . which is located in the . . . PBC . . . zone district." *See also* §4-4-402, Zoning Code (same). Also referring to development in a PBC zone district, section 2-2-202(C)(2) of the Zoning Code provides, "Before building permits may be issued, a development plan which conforms to [s]ection 4-6-602 of this Zoning Code must be approved. . . . All development in a PBC shall be in conformance with the approved development plan." In establishing these requirements, this language makes no distinction between the types of uses, permitted or conditional, that are subject to the requirement of receiving approval of a development plan. . . .

Significantly, the Zoning Code also provides that "[a] development plan *shall* be reviewed using" the development plan review criteria. §4-6-602(C), Zoning Code (emphasis added). More importantly, "[n]o development plan shall be approved unless the plan . . . is consistent with the intent and purpose of the Zoning Code and is compatible with the land uses surrounding the site." *Id.*

The plain language of this last sentence authorizes the Planning Commission to grant, or to deny, a development plan. The provisions also mandate that the Planning Commission review any development plan by using the development plan review criteria. Hence, the plain language of these provisions establishes the legislative intent to retain some discretion over permitted uses by means of the development plan review criteria. In our opinion, this intent is clearly expressed in the Zoning Code provisions.

The plain language of the Zoning Code provisions also puts to rest the court of appeals' concern that this interpretation is "inconsistent with the [Zoning] Code's intent to distinguish between permitted uses and conditional uses." *SecurCare*, 987 P.2d at 854. As Colorado Springs points out in its reply brief, a closer reading of the Zoning Code provisions discloses several key differences between conditional and permitted uses, which maintain a clear distinction between the two different types of uses.

In addition to satisfying the development plan review criteria, conditional uses are subject to several other requirements that do not apply to permitted uses. For example, while development plans for conditional uses are automatically reviewed by the Planning Commission and the City Council, those for permitted uses may be approved administratively or referred to the Planning Commission. *See* § 4-6-603(A), Zoning Code. Also, an approved development plan for a conditional use expires after one year if no building permit has issued. *See* §4-8-806, Zoning Code. Development plans for all other uses, including permitted uses, expire after four years. *See* § 4-6-604(C)(2), Zoning Code. Importantly, these requirements are not reflected in the development plan review criteria. Hence, while it is true that the two types of uses are subject to the development plan review criteria, this similarity alone does not eliminate the distinction between the two types of uses. . . .

III.

Accordingly, we reverse the judgment of the court of appeals, and remand the case to the court of appeals with instructions to return the case to the district court for further proceedings consistent with this opinion.

Justice KOURLIS dissents, and Justice COATS joins in the dissent.

Justice KOURLIS dissenting: . . .

I. . . .

A court should not allow the denial of a development plan on the basis of extraneous considerations when the applicant, as here, meets the legal requirements of the zoning ordinances. . . .

In my view, compatability with neighborhood conditions is an issue that the land use authority should properly determine before the land use entity adopts zoning requirements for a particular area. Therefore, I would affirm the court of appeals and respectfully dissent from the Majority Opinion.

Notes and Comments

1. *Subdivision Approval.* The fact that a developer wants to build a structure that is a permitted use under the zoning ordinance does not necessarily mean that the development will be allowed. The development may still be subject to site plan approval under an ordinance like the one at issue in *Friedman.* Even more significantly, if the development will subdivide land, it will likely be subject to extensive regulation under state subdivision laws, even though the use sought by the development is permitted under local zoning. Subdivision regulation is the subject of the next chapter in this casebook.

There are, however, significant differences between site plan approval and subdivision approval. A subdivision is likely to require new streets and substantial new infrastructure, and the costs can be passed through to new purchasers. Site review, in contrast, often concerns applications to build a single building by the present owner who will continue to hold the property, and the building will rely largely on the existing infrastructure.

2. *The Purpose of Site Plan Approval.* The purpose of site plan approval is to afford the local jurisdiction an opportunity to undertake a detailed analysis of the precise features of the development project. The review focuses on such factors as building layout, placement of roads, and aesthetic features. *Prudential Insurance Co. of America v. Board of Appeals of Westwood*, 502 N.E.2d 137 (Mass. App. Ct. 1986) (site plans disclose "the specifics of the project, including the proposed location of buildings, parking areas, and other installations on the land"); *Mountain Valley Mall Associates v. Municipality of Conway,* 745 A.2d 481 (N.H. 2000) (site plan adequately dealt with parking, off-street loading of goods, pedestrian and wheelchair access, snow storage, and green space). *Compare Kurlanski v. Portland Yacht Club*, 782 A.2d 783 (Me. 2001) (planning board failed to make findings about a number of site plan elements: the driveway, parking, landscaping, and lighting). The actual scope of the review will turn on the provisions of the local ordinance and any state statute governing this area.

A local body acts in a quasi-judicial capacity in considering a site plan. *Willoughby v. Planning Board of the Township of Deptford*, 703 A.2d 668, 671 (N.J. Super. Ct. App. Div. 1997). As a result, it must accord due process to the applicant by giving him or her a fair hearing. *Geiger v. Levo Route 46 Assoc., Ltd.*, 437 A.2d 336 (N.J. Super. Ct. Law Div. 1981). Indeed, the hearing itself can become quite complex if the issues are contested. The result of the site plan evaluation is likely to be a series of additional conditions that the applicant must meet in order to build.

3. *Tension.* There is an obvious tension between the concept of permitted uses under zoning ordinances, which allow a landowner to build as a matter of right, and the locality's retention of discretion under a site review ordinance, which may result in a denial of a project under the site review criteria. Some courts have held that site review ordinances may not be used to deny a project that is a permitted use, while others disagree. *See, e.g., Wesley Inv. Co. v. County of Alameda,* 198 Cal. Rptr. 872, 876 (Ct. App. 1984) ("The ordinances do not provide for an unbridled right to erect a retail store in a C-1 zone. Rather, the listing of permitted uses . . . is qualified by the provision . . . subjecting certain projects to site development review.").

The Connecticut courts have grappled with this issue in a series of cases. In *Beit Havurah v. Zoning Bd. of Appeals,* 418 A.2d 82 (Conn. 1979), the Connecticut Supreme Court declared that the designation of a permitted use "establishes a conclusive presumption that such use does not adversely affect the district and precludes further inquiry into the effect on traffic, municipal services, property values, or the general harmony of the district." Ten years later, the court decided that a local government *could* consider offsite traffic, but "solely as the basis for requiring a *modification* of the proposed site plan," not as a basis for denial. *TLC Development, Inc. v. Planning & Zoning Commission,* 577 A.2d 288, 290 (Conn. 1990). Then, in *Friedman v. Planning & Zoning Commission*, 698 A.2d 1178 (Conn. 1992), the supreme court upheld the denial of a site plan because the applicant had failed to submit a required off-site traffic study.

Could a local government, based on a properly drafted ordinance, reserve the right to deny a site plan for reasons such as cumulative traffic in the area, even if the use were otherwise permitted under the zoning ordinance? Could the plan be denied on the basis that the project was "shoehorned" into the proposed site and "not in keeping with the surrounding area"? *See Home Depot, USA, Inc. v. Town of Mount Pleasant,* 741 N.Y.S.2d 274 (N.Y. App. Div. 2002).

4. *The Scope of Discretion.* If approval of the development is hotly contested by opponents, it is critical to determine the extent of the discretion that the site review ordinance gives to the local entity. In *Richmond Co. v. City of Concord*, 821 A.2d 1059 (N.H. 2003), the New Hampshire Supreme Court upheld the denial of a site plan for a retail shopping center. The court upheld the denial, in part, on evidence that the shopping center would demolish all existing structures on the property, some of which had historical value. The project was consistent with the zoning on the property. Is this an appropriate use of a site plan ordinance?

3

Subdivision Regulation

A. INTRODUCTION

1. Plats and Planning

The historical antecedents of modern subdivision review were the platting statutes. These allowed land transfer and recordation according to the plat and parcel number rather than by metes and bounds property description, which requires deeds and other land record documents to be filed according to distances between surveyor and natural markers. Metes and bounds property descriptions generated mistakes and disputes. It also resulted in time-consuming and expensive property title searches and surveying in order to permit conveyances.

As land development procedures evolved, communities either failed to undertake comprehensive planning or neglected to establish plan implementation techniques to ensure that developments were well planned or consistent with scientific planning techniques. Although communities typically adopted a vague, conceptual comprehensive plan, usually through zoning, local government often did not consider the appropriateness of sites for specific development nor investigate environmental impacts.

In contrast, contemporary subdivision review often generates a de facto specific community plan. This occurs when the governing body first considers the type of uses and structures, as well as their relationship to the site, and then sets planning criteria.

2. *Subdivisions: Substantive Review*

Modern subdivision development review has several purposes. The five central components of subdivision review are: (1) discretionary review to allow disclosure and mitigation of environmental harm; (2) assurance of the adequacy of infrastructure; (3) opportunity to shift the cost of development and infrastructure to the developer through the imposition of conditions on subdivision and permit approval; (4) review to ensure compliance with planning and subdivision standards; and (5) assurance that the site is well planned, attractive, safe, and compatible with adjacent development.

The first component has become increasingly significant over the last 25 years. The process of subdivision review often uncovers any adverse environmental impacts of a proposed project and provides an opportunity to impose mitigation measures to alleviate those impacts. The subdivision review also is typically a trigger point to comply with state environmental assessment laws, which are discussed in Chapter 14 of this casebook.

A second important function of subdivision review is its focus on whether the infrastructure is adequate to support the development. Infrastructure includes the public facilities and services necessary to support development. The subdivision process should identify any problems in providing transit, reducing or managing traffic congestion, and providing other infrastructure components such as water and sewer services, schools, parks, and libraries. Flood control and emergency services, including police and fire protection, also are typically addressed. The subdivision review process provides for the imposition of conditions addressing site design and the developer's obligations to fund or provide necessary infrastructure.

Subdivision review is also central to modern growth management techniques. Growth management, which is discussed in detail in Chapter 11, seeks to restrict growth to accomplish the goals of the community's planning philosophy, particularly with respect to the density and distribution of development. More importantly, growth management often focuses on the carrying capacity of infrastructure and seeks, as its mission, to ensure that development is kept concurrent with adequate roads, schools, and water and sewer services.

The subdivision review process has been successful in affording public officials the opportunity to undertake discretionary review of individual projects, to review the impacts of the project's design, to impose mitigating conditions, to order design modifications, and to shift infrastructure costs and development impacts to the developer. The desirability of this discretionary process has spawned similar procedures for the review of site plans in cases not involving any subdivision approval, as seen in Chapter 2, and for the discretionary review of building permits in the case of large projects.

In the next chapter, you will study a topic closely related to subdivision review: the issue of how infrastructure for a development should be financed. In particular, the chapter will focus on how municipalities shift the costs of new development through the application of permit conditions as well as through other, innovative financing techniques. In two recent decisions, *Nollan v. California Coastal Commission*, 483 U.S. 825 (1987) and *Dolan v. City of Tigard*, 512 U.S. 374 (1994), the United States Supreme Court has restricted the authority of government to impose conditions on subdivision and other permit processes.

3. *Subdivisions: Procedural Review*

One important problem posed by subdivision regulation concerns the timing of the review process, which may take several years to complete. Developers first seek tentative (or preliminary) subdivision tract approval, respond to the problems and conditions identified, and then seek final subdivision tract approval and, ultimately, building permits. Both state and local standards, however, can change during this period, as new zoning, planning, or subdivision design criteria may be under review or adopted. To avoid unwanted change in the regulatory standards, developers may seek to acquire "vested rights" to complete their project or at least to avoid imposition of new development criteria. Conversely, until it completes the review of a proposed subdivision, a community may not be aware of the seriousness of its environmental impacts or the infrastructure problems it presents. Accordingly, local governments often desire to withhold the vesting of any right to complete a development until late in the regulatory process.

The struggle for early or late vesting is going on in every jurisdiction and will be reviewed in this chapter. As you will see, one legislative response has been the passage of so-called permit streamlining legislation setting strict timetables in which local governments must complete their subdivision review process, often changing the vesting rules.

4. *Efficiency, Politics, and Reform*

Theoretically, the subdivision review process provides an effective mechanism for regulating the development of land. The process, however, was designed to achieve goals that may be difficult for communities to attain. For example, local politics may threaten the credibility of the process if politicians attempt to interfere with the planning commission's or the planning board's exercise of its responsibilities. Alternatively, the political appointment process may result in a one-sided commission or a board that reflects only the development community's agenda or the environmental community's agenda.

Another possibility is that political interference may reflect a development policy that is quite different from the officially adopted plan and subdivision regulations in the particular jurisdiction. The technique of variances from subdivision standards, just like variances from zoning as described in Chapter 2, can be employed to depart from planning requirements. Finally, the system of campaign contributions may cause particular developers to be successful in obtaining changes in or exemptions from development criteria.

These situations raise ethical questions, and a central theme of this text is its focus on the ethical issues posed by land use regulation. Conflicts of interest comprise one type of ethical issue. In addition, there also exist questions regarding the ethical behavior both of developers and opponents of development. For example, a developer may threaten to bring bad faith litigation against opposing groups through the use of so-called SLAPP suits (strategic lawsuits against public participation) or through litigation against the regulating agency threatening damage exposure and heavy litigation costs. At the same time, project opponents may oppose development of any sort on a particular property, in apparent disregard of the Fifth Amendment's limitation on the extent of government regulation.

This chapter, as well as later chapters, will explore whether the subdivision system may be reformed to address such concerns. Such reforms might include increased specificity of the regulatory instruments, enhanced scrutiny in judicial review, or even deregulation of the land use control process.

The recent United States Supreme Court cases on development exactions, which you will read in Chapter 4, also underscore an escalating friction between constitutional commands, particularly under the Takings Clause, and governments' ability to effectively regulate land and the development process. Developers are going to court and are finding an increasingly attentive judiciary. It remains to be determined, however, whether the developing constitutional doctrine will result in greater rationality and fairness in the development process or will merely further contribute to the inefficiency of local development planning and control.

Ultimately, the subdivision process must be evaluated for its ability to achieve specific societal objectives. Many of its objectives, such as protecting the environment or ensuring adequate housing, may be goals that are unpopular with the current democratic majority in the jurisdiction. Is it really possible for a planning commission to bring about housing produced for the poor, along with improved schools? To protect natural resources and, at the same time, to ensure adequate infrastructure? You be the judge.

B. JURISDICTION AND DEFINITIONS

A threshold jurisdictional question in subdivision review is one of statutory interpretation. What is the definition of a "subdivision" that triggers subdivision review?

■ LOFTIN v. LANGSDON

813 S.W.2d 475 (Tenn. Ct. App. 1991)

OPINION

LEWIS, Judge. . . .

Loftin purchased a large tract of land in the Rock Springs Community of Maury County in 1988. A farmhouse sat on the back of the property, and an easement for a driveway or lane ran from the public road to the highway. Although the deed showed the easement for this driveway to be 60 feet wide, only a narrow lane was passable at the time Loftin purchased the property.

In preparation of his plan to divide and resell a portion of the property, Loftin made major improvements to the land. He cleared the brush from much of the easement, and he graded and re-cherted the lane. To facilitate drainage, he dug ditches along both sides of the lane. He also installed a six inch water pipe along the length of the easement and made arrangements with representatives of the Duck River Electric Membership Corporation to have two poles and a power line installed on the property adjacent to the easement. Loftin made all of these improvements at great expense to himself in anticipation of realizing a higher profit when the property was sold.

Loftin divided this improved portion of his property into 18 separate tracts. He named the lane to the farm house Beasley Lane. Thirteen of the tracts ranged in size from 5.16 to 7.63 acres and fronted on Beasley Lane. Loftin planned to sell the tracts at auction on 9 June 1990.

Pursuant to this plan, he advertised the upcoming auction in the local newspaper, *The Daily Herald*. The ad displayed a map of the available tracts complete with roads and described the property as follows:

> These tracts lay level to gentle rolling with plenty of good shade trees and are suitable for any style home. All tracts have good building sites, city water available, good building restrictions. These tracts are adjoining 20 tracts that were sold in December 1989 that have several very nice homes already built or under construction.

Judy Langsdon, Director of Community Development for Maury County, became aware of Loftin's plans by reading the ad in the Sunday paper. Her attention was captured by the designation on the map of a road called Beasley Lane. Since she knew there was no road in that area by that name, she assumed that Loftin had constructed a new road. This action, she believed, brought Loftin's project under the Planning Commission's subdivision regulations.

After confirmation from the Maury County Road Superintendent that Beasley Lane was not a public right-of-way, Langsdon contacted Loftin and advised him that he could not proceed with his auction without prior approval from the Planning Commission. . . .

Loftin commenced this action on 1 June 1990. He asked the court for a declaratory judgment that his division and sale of the property did not constitute a subdivision under Tenn. Code Ann. §13-3-401(4)(B) and thus did not come under regulation by the Planning Commission. . . .

This action was heard on 8 June 1990. Both parties agreed that Planning Commission approval was necessary if the proposed division of the property required new street construction or utility construction. Both parties also agreed that the likely use for the property after the sale was residential. The parties agreed on very little else.

Langsdon's position was that substantial road improvements had been made to the "driveway/road" to make it useable to the thirteen lots which fronted on it. Therefore, road improvements were required for subdivision.

Loftin, on the other hand, contended that Beasley Lane had been in existence for at least 35 years and that, while he had graded and re-cherted it, he had not changed or relocated its route. He insisted that the lane was a private easement to which he would grant right of use to all those who chose to purchase property fronting on it. He compared Beasley Lane to private roads within a farm which are necessary to the farm's operations. When asked on cross-examination why the improved portion of Beasley Lane had ditches on both sides while the unimproved portion had none, Loftin replied that he didn't "think any ditches were required back then (when the lane was initially built)."

Loftin admitted that he put the water line in to make water available if the buyers wanted to hook onto it. He also admitted to negotiating with Duck River for the laying of power lines, but he insisted that future buyers could just as easily tie into existing power lines at the north and south ends of the property. When asked on cross-examination whether more power poles would have to be put along or near Beasley Lane "or the people along those thirteen lots couldn't tap on and get electricity to the property," Loftin answered, "Yes, I would suppose so. Yes."

In closing arguments Loftin maintained that the new utility construction which had already been accomplished on the property was not required. He insisted that the new property owners could drill a well rather than tap onto the new water line if they so chose.

Langsdon argued at trial that in order to use the property to build houses, there would have to be a water main and an electric main available to the new buyers. These improvements to the land did not exist when Loftin purchased the land. Loftin had provided, or was in the process of providing, these improvements in order to make the land useable. Langsdon urged the court to consider the probable use of the land in determining whether utility construction was required.

Finding that the wording of Tenn. Code Ann. §13-3-401(4)(B) was "a little bit too imprecise" to grant Langsdon the relief she was seeking, the court issued a declaratory judgment in favor of Loftin. . . .

The Tennessee law referred to by Langsdon is Tenn. Code Ann. §13-3-401(4)(B). This statute provides:

> "Subdivision" means . . . the division of a tract or parcel of land into two (2) or more lots, sites, or other divisions requiring new street or utility construction, or any division of less than five (5) acres for the purpose, whether immediate or future, of sale or building development, and includes resubdivision and when appropriate to the context, relates to the process of resubdividing or to the land or area subdivided.

In order to determine whether Loftin's division of property was a "subdivision," it is necessary for this Court to construe the meaning of this statute. . . .

Loftin would have us focus almost exclusively on the word "requiring." Even though he installed a water line, he argues that this action was not required since any purchaser could choose to dig a well instead of tapping onto this line. He further argues that his grading, resurfacing, and digging ditches along Beasley Lane was not required construction but was merely the clearing of an existing lane. While he admits that the purchaser will still have to add two power poles in order to supply power to these tracts, he insists that this would be "no greater construction of utilities" than would be required on the undisputed tracts which are also for sale. Furthermore, he testified that the reason no ditches were dug along the unimproved portion of the lane was because he did not "think any ditches were *required* back then (when that portion was built)." (Emphasis added.)

The essence of Loftin's argument appears to be: If the seller makes the improvements necessary for the division and sale of his property voluntarily before anyone tells him that those improvements are required, then the improvements are not required. Furthermore, since the improvements were not required, there is no reason for the seller to go before the Planning Commission to inquire as to whether or not the improvements are required. This argument leads ultimately to a "catch 22" which would render the statute meaningless when applied to any division of property over five acres in size and would defeat the intent of the legislation. Such a result is absurd. . . .

Loftin acknowledges that the purpose of his driveway/lane is to provide access to the subdivided lots from the public roadway. The purpose of Planning Commission regulations dealing with road construction is to insure that the roads are built in a manner such as will protect the health, safety, and welfare of the citizens. According to these regulations, the developer must have the road construction plans designed and sealed by a licensed civil engineer. These plans must show drainage tiles, ditches, grades, elevations, and the base and finish in detail. These plans must be approved before the developer can implement them. There is no evidence in the record that Loftin has taken any of the actions necessary to insure that his driveway/lane is safe, and under Loftin's proposed construction of the statute there is no governmental body with oversight to guarantee to the public that his driveway/lane is safe. Yet it is obvious that the intent of the legislature was that roadways traveled by the general public be safe.

Loftin admits that further utility construction is required if these buyers are to receive electricity on their lots from a public utility (only a minute percentage of our society produces its own alternative source of energy). Again, under his proposed construction of this statute, there is no one the public can look to for assurance that the poles have been set and the wires have been strung in a safe manner. The public would just have to take the large developer's word for it.

If one were to follow Loftin's reasoning, small developers (those offering lots of under five acres for sale) would be subject to planning commission regulations if utility or road construction were required, but large developers, who installed these conveniences of modern living before offering their lots for sale, would not be under such constraints. Such a construction of this statute would be absurd. . . .

The phrase Loftin asks us to construe says: "other division requiring new street or utility construction. . . . " Tenn. Code Ann. §13-3-401(4)(B). The phrase does not say: "new street or utility construction required *by a planning commission.*" To add such a phrase to the statute would effectively amend the statute. . . .

This statute, like all statutes, must be applied in its present form unless doing so would result in "manifest injustice." *Scarboro v. First Amer. Nat'l Bank of Nashville*, 619 F.2d 621, *cert. denied*, 449 U.S. 1014 (1980). There is no "manifest injustice" in applying this statute evenhandedly to large and small developers or in applying the statute in a manner that will further enhance the health, safety and welfare of the community. . . .

Loftin admits he made the road and utility improvements "to get the most money for (the land)." These improvements were "required" by the imperatives of the marketplace. These improvements were "required" within the ambit of Tenn. Code Ann. §13-3-401(4)(B). . . .

TODD, P.J., and CANTRELL, J., concur.

Notes and Comments

1. *Definitions and Interpretation.* What is a subdivision? What is the correct interpretation of the word "required" in the statute defining coverage by the

phrase "requiring new street or utility construction?" Does the court's interpretation of this phrase provide sufficient notice to developers as to whether they will be required to comply with the subdivision regulations?

2. *A Surprised Developer?* Was the developer in *Loftin* attempting to evade subdivision regulations by seeking to structure a project so that it would not come within the statutory definition, or was he genuinely surprised when the litigation was initiated? Look carefully at the proposed subdivision and the statutory definition of "subdivision" in reaching your conclusion. If you decide that this was an attempt to evade, would you see any ethical problems in advising a client to achieve that goal?

3. *Evasion Techniques.* Some states define a subdivision as a division into five or more parcels. Would dividing a tract into four parcels without public approval be legal? What if each of the four parcels were subsequently subdivided into four more parcels, for a total of 16 parcels? *Manning v. Fox*, 198 Cal. Rptr. 558 (Ct. App. 1984) (the practice of "four-by-fouring" — that is, making a series of conveyances that individually do not trigger the statutory subdivision definition based on the number of lots created but which cumulatively exceed the standard — resulted in real estate licensing discipline). *See* Tom Bell, Legal Loophole Lets Developers Bypass Town Planners, Maine Sunday Telegram (Aug. 1, 1991), at 1 (describing process by which developers avoid subdivision laws by assigning lots to members of their family). What if the landowner intends to divide the property but to lease rather than sell the parcels as part of a mobile home park? *See Sizemore v. Madison County Fiscal Court*, 58 S.W.3d 887, 889 (Ky. App. 2001) ("Nothing in these definitions requires that divided lots be offered or developed solely for sale in order to constitute a 'subdivision' of property").

Another technique used to avoid or evade subdivision review is to demonstrate that a property was either subject to an antiquated recorded subdivision plat predating passage of subdivision regulation or was a separate lot in ancient times. A California intermediate appellate court in *Gardner v. County of Sonoma*, 112 Cal. Rptr. 2d 386 (Ct. App. 2001), *rev. granted & superseded*, 38 P.3d 432 (Cal. 2002), rejected the concept of awarding ancient subdivision certificates for fragments of legal parcels. The ancient records failed to establish legal lots, even if the earlier map was accurate and detailed. The court construed the subdivision map act liberally to cover as many transfers as possible to facilitate compliance with modern planning standards.

California later passed legislation prohibiting the technique of subdivision exemption for large parcels that at one time had been separate parcels. The widespread practice was publicized when the Hearst family utilized the technique in an attempt to develop a luxury ocean front resort near the famous Hearst Castle. Kenneth R. Weiss & John Johnson, The Nation Battles for the Coast in Hearst Land Fight, Old Papers Are New Weapons, L.A. Times, July 22, 2001, at A1.

4. *Partitions and Devisees.* Would the judicial partition of a tract held by five or more partners or co-tenants trigger mandatory subdivision review? In *Pratt v. Adams*, 40 Cal. Rptr. 505 (Ct. App. 1964), the court ruled that a partition suit triggered the Subdivision Act, as the law simply requires that the actor "caused [the property] to be subdivided."

What if a will divides a tract, leaving it to more devisees than the minimum number exempted from the statutory subdivision definition? *See In re Sayewich*, 413 A.2d 581 (N.H. 1980) (subdivision regulation applies and requires approval to develop, or the court could order the entire tract sold and distribute the proceeds).

5. *Criminal Penalties*. Violation of subdivision laws can be a crime. Where an owner engages in a series of three single or two-lot transfers designed to evade a statutory definition of a subdivision as a three-lot division, how many criminal counts can be sustained? In *McClellan v. State*, 933 P.2d 461 (Wyo. 1997), the court upheld three counts and rejected a claim of double jeopardy. It concluded that a $750 fine and three days imprisonment were within the permissible maximum of 30 days or $500 for each offense, and that the law allows a separate charge for each day of a violation following an illegal subdivision. *Compare Gallegos v. City of Las Vegas*, 957 P.2d 1159 (Nev. Ct. App. 1998). The Nevada subdivision statute covers the division of a parcel into two or more parts. The court, however, ruled that the sale of a long-existing home to the grantor's son was not a subdivision, that the sale of a trailer park was not a sale for development purposes, and that the gift of vacant land to a relative was not shown to be for development. The court also ruled that the repeated sale of individual parcels in the same year constitutes only one division even though portions of the parcels were transferred over the years in 17 separate transactions.

6. *Deterring Lawlessness*. To whom should the subdivision lot purchaser look for assurance that infrastructure is safely and effectively installed? Would the opportunity for tort recovery protect the public or deter lawlessness? Contrast the benefits and costs of a free market approach with those of subdivision review, which follows traditional public regulatory processes. In one interesting case, a homeowner sued the developer of the "Holiday Harbor" subdivision in tort for failing to disclose that the subdivision was created on a former graveyard. *Hickman v. Carven*, 784 A.2d 31, 34 (Md. Ct. App. 2001) (plaintiff "dug a hole in her yard where a yucca plant had been and, about 12 inches below the surface, discovered some bones and a piece of metal that she believed to be a casket handle").

7. *Subdivision Review Purposes*. Which of the following goals of subdivision review might be the most difficult to achieve, and why: (1) discretionary review to allow disclosure and mitigation of environmental harm; (2) assurance of the adequacy of infrastructure; (3) ability to shift the cost of development and infrastructure to the developer through the imposition of conditions on subdivision and permit approval; (4) review to ensure compliance with planning and subdivision standards; and (5) assurance that the site is well-planned, attractive, safe, and compatible with adjacent development. How might politics influence the ability to achieve these goals?

Subdivision review allows for consideration of fiscal issues and concerns about the adequacy of facilities and services, and it protects adjacent property owners from the impact of poorly planned development. Subdivision review also should ensure that infrastructure capacity is adequate to accommodate the project. Tight municipal budgets, however, can influence substantive decisions on subdivision review, giving cities an incentive to approve a project as a means of generating tax revenues. In addition, while the subdivision process is intended to equitably allocate infrastructure costs among various developments, that burden may be distributed inequitably and imposed on politically powerless developers.

8. *Consumer Protection.* While subdivision review was evolving to provide improved community planning, state legislatures were moving to modify the development process to protect both housing consumers as well as the local governing body from developers who fail to carry out conditions of development approvals. Developers may default on obligations to complete infrastructure, leaving purchasers of home sites to cope with sewer system failure, low water pressure, flooding, and poor roads. Overreaching developers also may engage in false promises of community design and project amenities.

State legislation typically requires simultaneous compliance both with local planning requirements and marketing regulations administered by the state. State marketing regulation often requires developers to disclose plans as well as to file disclosure documents with a state real estate regulatory agency. Causes of action for misrepresentation or the failure to complete plans are often provided for, and remedies are authorized. These include public enforcement seeking injunctive relief against further development or marketing, and criminal sanctions for noncompliance or noncompletion. *People v. Pacific Land Research Co.*, 569 P.2d 125 (Cal. 1977) (injunctive relief and restitution available in lawsuit by state). *See also Winant v. Bostic*, 5 F.3d 767 (4th Cir. 1993) (damages may be trebled but restitution is not available under North Carolina law where the developer made false promises of amenities such as a pool, a club, and exotic landscaping).

Congress has enacted the federal Interstate Land Sales Full Disclosure Act, 15 U.S.C. §§1701-20 (2000), requiring disclosure of terms, benefits, and amenities to purchasers, if the subdivision lot they purchased was marketed on an interstate basis. In addition, the Act gives those purchasers who later have "buyer's remorse" an opportunity to rescind their contract. *See, e.g., HUD v. Cost Control Marketing*, 64 F.3d 920 (4th Cir. 1995), *cert. denied*, 517 U.S. 1187 (1996) (sustaining an order to disgorge $8.65 million, representing profits calculated by multiplying sales times the average sales price in excess of market value, and sustaining a freeze on assets where defendant made no attempt to comply with law); *Engle Homes, Inc. v. Krasna*, 766 So. 2d 311 (Fla. Dist. Ct. App. 2000) (failure to provide notice of rescission right extends rescission window to three years under the Act, and buyers did not waive their rights by moving into a home); *United States v. Judd*, 889 F.2d 1410 (5th Cir. 1989), *cert. denied*, 494 U.S. 1036 (1990) (telemarketing of land with "guaranteed" coal deposits and commission of mail and wire fraud through the use of "bird dogs" —agents of sellers who provide fake personal satisfaction testimonials—violated the Act, where the seller offered a falsified geological and financial report, and the subdivider did not own mineral rights). *See also Happy Investment Group* v. *Kaleworld Properties, Inc.*, 396 F. Supp. 175 (N.D. Cal. 1975) (lots in recreational subdivision are not securities under federal securities law); *Becherer v. Merrill Lynch*, 127 F.3d 478 (6th Cir. 1997), *mod. en banc on other grounds*, 193 F.3d 415 (6th Cir. 1999) (nonresidential units in hotel, although called condominiums, did not constitute a subdivision under the Act, as there was no exclusive use by owners who were permitted use of a unit only if there was a vacancy).

9. *Ensuring Completion of Infrastructure.* In small subdivisions, building permits may issue only upon final inspection of the completed infrastructure, with emphasis on roads and utilities. Conditioning building permit issuance upon completion of all subdivision amenities in the case of large subdivisions, however, may be very

costly for the developer. In that instance the developer cannot obtain a cash flow during an extended period of development, and that situation might discourage the installation of expensive amenities due to the high interim financing costs.

One technique used to ensure the completion of infrastructure is requiring the developer to post security or secure a performance bond. *Legion Manor, Inc. v. Municipal Council of the Township of Wayne*, 231 A.2d 201 (N.J. 1967) (performance bonds may be required, and upon completion of the improvement, a maintenance bond may be required to protect against defects in construction of the improvement). *See also Parker v. Board of County Commissioners of Dona Ana County*, 603 P.2d 1098 (N.M. 1979) (suspension of plat approval upon failure to complete road improvements).

C. THE PROJECT APPROVAL PROCESS

Apart from questions concerning the validity of subdivision conditions and exactions, which are covered in Chapter 4, most subdivision litigation centers on the legality of the decision by the governmental entity assigned the obligation of subdivision review.

The subdivision regulatory process is becoming increasingly sophisticated because of the technical nature of environmental and land planning, and the escalating complexities of legislative policies and procedures. These complexities can be further compounded by judicial interpretation. In some instances, the subdivision process may exceed the institutional capacity of the planning department and public officials to perform the tasks legally required.

When you review the following subdivision cases, ask whether local decisions and processes reflect both the potential rationality of the administrative process and planning expertise. Contemporary subdivision review suggests that the promise of implementing "planning expertise" in a systematic way is often unfulfilled.

Another fundamental problem you must consider is that to some degree the system seeks, through the utilization of a planning commission and a planning process, to override local "politics." In actuality, however, politics more frequently overrides the application of planning requirements, despite attempts by the legislature to provide rationality in the statutory scheme. The result is often a system with a veneer of rigor that places vast discretion in the hands of local government.

The following case, *Garipay v. Town of Hanover*, introduces the application of substantive subdivision standards.

GARIPAY v. TOWN OF HANOVER
351 A.2d 64 (N.H. 1976)

GRIFFITH, Justice.

This is an appeal . . . from a decision of the planning board of the town of Hanover denying plaintiffs' agents' requests for preliminary approval of a subdivision in that town. . . . The planning board's denial of the request for approval of the subdivision was based on a finding that Hemlock Road, the access road connecting the proposed subdivision to the main network of town roads, would be inadequate to handle the increased traffic created by forty-nine new homes. The question presented to us is whether the planning board is authorized under RSA ch. 36 and the town ordinances to reject a subdivision proposal which intrinsically conforms to the requirements of the town zoning ordinance and regulations solely because of the inadequacy of an offsite, town-owned road. . . .

The location of the proposed subdivision is on top of a hill to which Hemlock Road provides the only access. This road is described as "narrow, steep and winding, having a width of fourteen to sixteen feet, shoulders only two feet wide, a grade which at times exceeds 15%, and a course which results in "at least one horseshoe curve." Consequently, the planning board found that the road would pose "a serious danger to both pedestrian and vehicular traffic." The town police chief expressed "serious reservations about [his] department being able to respond to an emergency in this area, in the wintertime." There was evidence that in winter the steepness of the road often forces residents to leave their cars at the foot of the hill, and that while the limited available space can accommodate the present vehicles, congestion created by further abandoned cars from the subdivision could cause serious hazards.

The plaintiffs do not contest the accuracy of these findings. Their argument is that the planning board is precluded from considering offsite factors and must limit its investigation to whether the subdivision internally complies with state and town requirements. In our opinion both the state-enabling legislation and the Hanover subdivision regulations provide authority for the board's decision.

RSA 36:21 (Supp. 1975) provides that town planning boards may promulgate regulations which "provide against such scattered or premature subdivision of land as would involve danger or injury to health, safety, or prosperity by reason of the lack of . . . transportation . . . or other public services, or necessitate an excessive expenditure of public funds for the supply of such services." Pursuant to this statute, Hanover has enacted article III (B) of its subdivision regulations, which uses language identical to that quoted above. These provisions plainly empower the planning board to take offsite factors into its consideration, insofar as they render subdivisions "scattered or premature."

The plaintiffs argue that the proposed subdivision cannot be deemed "scattered or premature" because there are already some eighteen homes in the area. Plaintiffs further maintain that such a finding is precluded by language on a map contained in the Hanover master plan, which designates the site "to be developed after 1970." According to this argument once an area is found not to be premature for a particular degree of development, it must be found ripe for all levels of development. In other words, where there are presently some homes in the area, the planning board may not find that an addition of forty-nine homes would be premature, regardless of the amount of public services available.

We reject this interpretation as too narrow, for prematurity is a relative rather than an absolute concept. The statute, by defining a "scattered and premature" development as one which poses a danger to the public through insufficiency of services, sets up a guide for the planning board's determination. The board must ascertain what amount of development, in relation to what quantum of services available, will present the hazard described in the statute and regulations. At the point where such a hazard is created, further development becomes premature. Thus in the instant case, although the available services suffice to meet the need of the present eighteen homes, when an additional forty-nine homes will endanger the well-being of residents both within and contiguous to the development, the statute and regulations authorize the planning board to find the subdivision premature. Thus the action of the Hanover Planning Board was within its statutory mandate. . . .

"Subdivision controls are imposed on the supportable premise that a new subdivision is not an island, but an integral part of the whole community which must mesh efficiently with the municipal pattern of streets, sewers, water lines and other installations which provide essential services and vehicular access. . . . [O]ffsite circumstances may be considered by the reviewing board, and may provide the basis for denying approval of a plat." 3 R. Anderson, American Law of Zoning §19.36 (1968).

Appeal dismissed.

Notes and Comments

1. *On-Site/Off-Site Criteria.* Some jurisdictions require that, in making a decision on a subdivision application, the local governmental entity must restrict its evaluation to "on-site" criteria, that is, considerations stemming solely from the proposed site itself. For example, a planning commission might be foreclosed from considering local school overcrowding as a basis for denying a residential subdivision. *Cf. Steel v. Cape Corp.*, 677 A.2d 634 (Md. Ct. Spec. App. 1996) (rejection of zoning because of inadequacy of school capacity resulted in a taking). Was the plat denial in *Garipay* based on on-site or off-site considerations?

2. *Premature Subdivisions.* What was the standard that the court used to review the Town's decision in *Garipay*? Would rejection of a subdivision as "scattered or premature" be sustained if it was based upon inadequate schools or public transportation service, the environmental impacts of urban sprawl, or the absence of affordable housing in the community?

In *Ettlingen Homes, Inc. v. Town of Derry*, 681 A.2d 97 (N.H. 1996), the planning board denied a residential subdivision application on grounds of "prematurity." The board applied an ordinance that authorized the rejection of scattered or premature subdivisions that would involve danger or injury to health, safety, or prosperity by reason of a lack of facilities or public services. The primary concern of the town appeared to be school capacity. The court reversed, stating that the denial must be based on the impacts of the proposed project itself and not on those of community-wide further development in general. To reject a subdivision on grounds of prematurity, there must be evidence that the proposed project poses a hazard to health, safety, or prosperity.

Can *Garipay* be distinguished from *Ettlingen* on the basis of the inadequate access road in *Garipay*? Larry Gardner, Esq., who represented the Town of Hanover in *Garipay*, informed the authors that the phrase "scattered or premature subdivision," contained in N.H. Stat. Ann. §36:21, was never in issue in the case and had neither been briefed nor argued. The land in question in *Garipay* was eventually purchased by a local conservation group and donated to the town as open space. E-mail from Larry Gardner to James A. Kushner, Sept. 5, 1997.

3. *Judicial Review of Subdivision Approvals.* Subdivision approval involves a discretionary administrative determination focused on a particular parcel and a

proposed development. In comparison, a legislative matter typically sets policy either for the entire community or even for the parcel, as in the case of zoning. As an administrative determination, subdivision approval must conform to certain standards established by statute, ordinance, or regulation, or adopted by the courts, that are designed to aid judicial review of administrative or "quasi-judicial" decisions, that is, decisions in which the local agency engages in fact finding regarding that specific parcel. *See, e.g., C.F.T. Development, LLC v. Bd. of County Commissioners of Torrance County*, 32 P.3d 784 (N.M. Ct. App. 2001) (upholding local government denial of a subdivision on grounds that septic tanks would pose a threat of contamination to the water supply even though the State Environment Department had approved the development); *Sansom v. Board of Supervisors of Madison County*, 514 S.E.2d 345 (Va. 1999) (upholding denial of a subdivision application under an ordinance prohibiting land disturbances within fifty feet of a "substantial surface drainage course").

Decisions must be based on findings that are supported by substantial evidence in the record and that clearly communicate the reasons for the denial. *See Plan Commission of Harrison County v. Aulbach*, 748 N.E.2d 926, 937 (Ind. Ct. App. 2001) ("it was the Plan Commission's duty . . . to furnish the Developers with all of the specific and concrete reasons for disapproval so that the Developers could amend their plat to comply with the applicable ordinances"); *Advantage Development, Inc. v. Board of Supervisors of Jackson Township*, 743 A.2d 1008 (Pa. Commw. Ct. 2000) (applicants have a right to a denial letter describing the requirements that have not been met so they can effectively appeal the denial to a court). Challenges typically allege that the decision is either arbitrary or capricious or is not supported by substantial evidence, or that the decision reflects an error of law. See *Herr v. Lancaster County Planning Comm'n*, 625 A.2d 164 (Pa. Commw. Ct. 1993).

Other than technical violations, most challenges to subdivision approvals allege adverse environmental impacts, inadequacy of supporting infrastructure, or adverse effects on adjacent properties. Is the decision whether an approval was arbitrary or capricious akin to the application of the test for a violation of substantive due process? Is the court faced with Hobson's choice: either excessively deferring to the administrative agency or unnecessarily substituting its judgment for that of the planning agency? *See, e.g., Whitesell v. Kosciusko County Board of Zoning Appeals*, 558 N.E.2d 889 (Ind. Ct. App. 1990) (no de novo judicial review or substitution of court's decision for that of the planning commission and the board of zoning appeals).

4. *Comparing Site Plan Review*. The central benefits of subdivision review derive from the opportunity for a discretionary review of the project to consider site design, environmental impacts, and effects on infrastructure capacity. The benefits include the ability to impose conditions on the project by requiring modifications of the plat, and the ability to impose exactions, such as requiring developers to finance facilities, pay impact fees, or dedicate land for facilities. Where property can be developed without subdividing, however, it is not subject to the subdivision review process. The possibility that large projects with significant impacts akin to those of subdivisions would avoid this type of review prompted many communities to adopt site plan ordinances, as discussed in Chapter 2.

Is subdivision review necessarily subjective and discretionary, or does the obligation for compliance with all laws and regulations ensure objectivity in the review process? The next case, *Burrell v. Lake County Plan Commission*, places the administrative subdivision review process in the context of overall land use planning controls and generally describes the decisionmaking analysis.

BURRELL v. LAKE COUNTY PLAN COMMISSION
624 N.E.2d 526 (Ind. Ct. App. 1993)

SHARPNACK, Chief Judge.

This case concerns the denial of approval by the Lake County Plan Commission (Commission) to the preliminary subdivision plan submitted by Donald and Alice Burrell. The Burrells petitioned the trial court for a writ of certiorari to reverse the denial of plan approval and the trial court, after remanding for findings of fact by the Commission, denied relief and affirmed the Commission action. The Burrells now ask us to reverse the trial court and the Commission. . . .

In 1990, the Burrells filed an application with the Commission for subdivision approval of Rainbow Estates, a residential subdivision to be developed on their property in Lake County, Indiana. The Commission granted tentative approval for the subdivision [and] a public hearing on the Burrells' application for preliminary plan approval was held during the Commission's regular meeting of February 5, 1991. The Burrells' application was denied, consistent with the requirements of the applicable ordinance, based on the Commission's conclusion that the subdivision would have an adverse effect on the health, safety, and general welfare of the community. The Commission made no findings of fact in support of its conclusion. . . .

[T]he Burrells contend that the Commission's findings are not supported by substantial evidence. . . .

In our review of the Burrells' claim that the Commission's findings are not supported by substantial evidence, we may vacate the decision of the Commission " 'only if the evidence, when viewed as a whole, demonstrates that the conclusions reached by the [Commission] are clearly erroneous.' " . . .

At the public hearing on the Burrells' proposed subdivision, the Commission heard a presentation in support of the Burrell's application and received the Commission staff recommendation that the application be approved, as the staff found that the proposed subdivision was "in compliance with the Comprehensive Plan of Lake County and [met] all the requirements of [the Ordinance]." The Commission also received evidence from remonstrators which included an affidavit from an engineer, Rowland Fabian. The remonstrators presented their position, along with supporting documentation, that the existing surface water drainage problem was unacceptable and that the proposed development would increase the problem. The engineer's affidavit discussed, inter alia, alleged deficiencies in the Burrells' plan, risks of leaching and biological contamination from the septic system for the subdivision, the existing excess surface water and flooding problem in the area, and his opinion that the development would contribute to drainage and soil erosion problems in the area. In March, 1992, pursuant to the trial court's instruction, the Commission entered findings in support of its conclusion that the

Burrell's proposed subdivision would have an adverse effect on the health, safety, and general welfare of the community.[8]

The substantial evidence test is not a test of our agreement with the Commission's findings. Instead, our inquiry focuses on whether the Commission's decision is founded on "a reasonably sound basis of evidentiary support." Additionally, we should sustain the Commission's decision if it is correct on any of the grounds stated for disapproval of the plan.

In their argument on this issue, the Burrells dispute the accuracy of the Fabian affidavit, much of which was adopted in the Commission's findings, and question Fabian's expertise. In his affidavit, Fabian states that he is a registered professional engineer and land surveyor in the State of Indiana with over forty years of experience. He further states that in the preparation of his affidavit be reviewed the plans and plats associated with the proposed development, soils studies, U.S. Coast and Geodetic Survey Quadrangle Maps for the area, a federal manual on wetlands conservation, aerial photography of the area, and that he made a personal walking inspection of the project site and surrounding area. In an administrative proceeding involving technical or scientific evidence such as in this case, it is not our task, nor is it within our area of expertise, to determine the credibility or weight to be given technical evidence such as that found in the Fabian affidavit. Our role, instead, is to determine whether the evidence before the Commission *taken as a whole* provides a reasonable evidentiary basis for the Commission's determination, and we conclude that it does.

The Commission received evidence from the remonstrators in a variety of forms at the hearing on the Burrells' plan. This evidence included oral testimony;

8. The Commission made the following findings: "The Plan Commission now finds that the report submitted to the Lake County Plan Commission on January 31, 1991 by Fabian Engineers, Inc. of Hammond, Indiana, describes in Paragraphs 3, 4, 5, 6, 7, and 8 of [*sic*] the inadequacies of the proposed development, specifically the lack of mathermatical computations to support the conclusions that the project, as currently contemplated, is consistent with good engineering practices and will not cause damage to areas in and around the project within one mile; also

That none of the mathematical computations or procedures found and inferred in the State Board of Health Bulletin SE13 of 1988, specifically pages 41 to 46 and 47 to 50 of that manual, have been provided to the Lake County Plan Commission for review regarding this project; also

That even without engineering computations, the following general observations can be made regarding the pending proposal before the Lake County Plan Commission; to-wit

a. That at proposed construction density, no septic system other than a mound system can operate effectively in the soils and topography in question. However, even a mound system is highly questionable and presents a substantial risk of leaching which would result in the biological contamination of both the subdivision and the surrounding areas;
b. That as the area is currently developed, there is already substantial surface water runoff and flooding during normal rains, and during heaving [sic] rains the area around 129th and Tyler Street is subject to excessive water runoff and flooding.
c. That any further development which reduces the existing capacity of the ground to retain surface water (such as the construction of new roadways, large homes, expansive driveways, tennis courts and the like), or the reduction of existing vegetation and trees in the area can only add to the existing problems, further overload the surface water drainage system and contribute to increased soil erosion and related problems of the area.
d. That there is a substantial probability that leaching from the project could result in the biological contamination of any and all of the retention ponds, detention ponds and wetland areas located in the watershed in and about the project; . . .

(Record pp. 298-299). Although we agree with the Burrells that the Commission's findings consist almost entirely of verbatim portions of the engineer's affidavit submitted by Rowland Fabian, the Burrells cite no authority for the proposition that the adoption of portions of the Fabian affidavit vitiates the findings.

a video-tape of the area accompanied by oral explanation; and a three-ring binder containing, among other things, an aerial photograph of the proposed development area and surrounding area, photographs depicting flooding in the area, a photocopy of §V(B) of the applicable subdivision ordinance (discussed *supra*), the engineer's affidavit by Rowland Fabian and accompanying attachments, photocopies of newspaper articles describing flooding and sewage disposal problems in Lake County, and a copy of a street and drainage plan that included soils report information. Our review of this evidence leads us to the conclusion that the Commission's findings are supported by substantial evidence of probative value. . . .

With reference to the Commission's findings regarding risks of leaching and biological contamination from the septic system for the subdivision (findings "a" and "d"), the Commission had before it the engineer's affidavit from Rowland Fabian. Additionally, attached to the Fabian affidavit was a letter from a Purdue University extension agronomist that discussed septic system design in difficult soils and referenced publications forwarded to Fabian dealing with issues of septic system design and installation. Although, as noted by the Burrells, the extension agronomist wrote:

> Whether or not homes in a development with 'small' lot sizes would have a high percentage of successfully operating systems depends on many factors, including the ability to lower seasonal water tables. It is probably impossible to give more than an impression or an estimate of risk without a thorough evaluation of the site and proposed development.

[I]n the next paragraph, he wrote: "However, if the majority of soils in the area are Morley, Pewamo, Wallkill and Carlisle then the area has a high risk of waste disposal problems." The street and drainage plan submitted to the Commission by remonstrators reveals that a significant percentage of the Burrells' property consists of these four problematic soils. With reference to the Commission's findings regarding both existing and anticipated flooding, bad drainage, and excessive surface water (findings "b" and "c"), the Commission had before it the Fabian affidavit, a street and drainage plan, photographs of flooding in the area, photocopies of newspaper articles regarding flooding in the county, and a videotape of the area accompanied by oral explanation.

We conclude that the Commission was presented with substantial evidence that the proposed subdivision presented significant risks of septic system leaching, as well as increased flooding and drainage problems. . . .

The Commission had a reasonable evidentiary basis on which to conclude that the subdivision would have an adverse effect on the health, safety, and general welfare of the community, a conclusion from which denial of the preliminary plan must follow under the Ordinance. . . .

AFFIRMED.

Notes and Comments

1. *Regulatory Criteria and Subdivision Approvals.* *Burrell* stands for the proposition that a subdivision must meet all requirements established through subdivision

regulation, zoning, or the comprehensive plan. *See In re Taft Corners Associates, Inc.*, 758 A.2d 804 (Vt. 2000) (developer received subdivision approval but was subject to a later change in the zoning ordinance); Cal. Govt. Code §66473 (West 1997) (a plat application should be denied unless it complies with all standards, including any adopted comprehensive plan). The correlative of this rule is that when a subdivision application complies with all regulations, it must be approved. *South E. Property Owners Ass'n v. City Plan Comm'n of the City of New Britain*, 244 A.2d 394 (Conn. 1968); *State ex rel. Menkhus v. City of Pevely*, 865 S.W.2d 871 (Mo. Ct. App. 1993) (application becomes ministerial after officials determine plat conforms to regulations); *Herr v. Lancaster County Planning Comm'n*, 625 A.2d 164 (Pa. Commw. Ct. 1993). *See also Board of County Comm'rs of Routt County v. O'Dell*, 920 P.2d 48 (Colo. 1996) (sustaining denial of plat in the face of environmental threats; finding that the board was not required, on its own initiative, to consider mitigation methods; and declaring that the burden is on the applicant to present alternative development proposals that might carry a lesser impact); *Broward County v. G.B.V. Int'l, Ltd.*, 787 So. 2d 838 (Fla. 2001) (if a developer satisfies its initial burden to show that a site plan or plat application meets statutory criteria, the burden shifts to the planning commission to show by competent, substantial evidence presented at the hearing and made a part of the record that the application does not meet the standards and is adverse to public interest).

Burrell also demonstrates the need for comprehensive, formally adopted subdivision regulations setting forth the basis on which a project can be denied. An alternative to such action is the approval of a project generating unacceptable impacts if that approval is subject to modifications or conditions that would mitigate those impacts. *Miles v. Planning Board of Millbury*, 558 N.E.2d 1150 (Mass. App. Ct. 1990); *Western Land Equities, Inc. v. City of Logan*, 617 P.2d 388 (Utah 1980) (reprinted *infra* this chapter).

2. *Building Permits*. Issuance of a building permit is generally thought to be a ministerial act upon the satisfaction of all requirements such as plan and zoning consistency, subdivision approval, building plan check, and payment of administrative, engineering, and inspection fees. In a number of jurisdictions, however, courts have interpreted building permit ordinances to require a discretionary review process, at least in the case of large-scale residential and commercial developments. This review process allows the application of environmental impact review statutes and the imposition of mitigation conditions. *See, e.g., Friends of Westwood, Inc. v. City of Los Angeles*, 235 Cal. Rptr. 788 (Ct. App. 1987) (issuance of a building permit for a 26-story, multiple-use building was discretionary where a plan check was required for major projects and where the project was unusual in size, dimension, and location).

3. *Subdivisions and PUDs*. As discussed in Chapter 2, the planned unit development concept allows implementation of so-called "New Urbanism," a development concept calling for higher density mixed-use with pedestrian friendly streets and walks, and mixed uses in districts (including different housing tenures). It also allows mixed commercial and employment centers so important for modern transit villages and creatively planned subdivisions. Like subdivision and site plan ordinances, the PUD, which is often implemented through a rezoning (see Chapter 2 *supra*), provides an alternative mechanism for addressing environmental and infrastructure problems. The regulatory scheme under PUD ordinances typically mirrors the site plan and subdivision process.

4. *Architectural Design and Consistency with Renderings*. The decision in *Frankland v. City of Oswego*, 517 P.2d 1042 (Or. 1973), illustrates a problem that can arise during subdivision and other types of project review: the final developed project may depart from the description of the project or the design concept and sketches submitted to support an application. At the preliminary stages of the review process, the developer submitted sketches that presented a melange of "garden apartment" buildings varying in height and building shapes with many architectural details. The sketches presented a "woodsy" appearance in which the project appeared well integrated with the surrounding forest. However, the developer later constructed large, monolithic apartment houses of uniform height.

The Oregon court ruled that the sketches submitted became part of the PUD plan, thus committing the developer to the architectural design and building configuration depicted. One lesson from *Frankland* is that communities may wish to enact aesthetic control ordinances requiring final plans to conform to community standards for beauty and aesthetics. See Chapter 17 for a discussion of aesthetic regulation.

5. *Subdivisions and Master Planning*. In *Board of County Comm'rs of Cecil County v. Gaster*, 401 A.2d 66 (Md. 1979), the developer submitted a preliminary plat application for a residential subdivision calling for 408 single-family detached lots on 174.3 acres, or 2.3 units per acre. The officially adopted master plan, however, called for a density at one dwelling unit per acre, together with planning standards for adequate roads, schools, and other facilities and services. The highest court in Maryland, the court of appeals, ruled that consistency was required between the subdivision, the subdivision regulations, and the master plan. The court emphasized that failing to require consistency would leave to the discretion of the developer whether the community would be designed with adequate schools, fire protection, parks, playgrounds, and other public facilities, and whether the delivery of adequate services would constitute a drain on the municipal purse.

The decision in *Gaster*, just as in *Burrell*, instructs that to assure that subdivisions are well planned and served by adequate facilities and services, it is important that the comprehensive plan contain the community's standards of service and facility capacity as well as policies for imposing the costs of service delivery and facilities installation. The court in *Gaster* emphasized that zoning itself fails to present comprehensive planning, as it typically simply calls for a projected use. Zoning does not assure the adequacy of roads, schools, and other services and facilities.

D. VESTED RIGHTS TO DEVELOP

The subdivision review process involves review at various stages, such as the initial sketch plan review, the formal tentative or preliminary tract review, and the final subdivision review. Accordingly, the process may take many years, particularly where a large project is undertaken in phases. During that time, plans, statutes, and subdivision regulations may undergo substantial modification due to changes in the city's development policies.

This possibility of modification poses a significant problem for developers. They seek predictability in their investments and would like to have standards finalized and "locked in" at an early point so that financing and profitability can be forecast. In contrast, local communities prefer to retain the flexibility of imposing conditions at a later stage in the development process, in case new environmental impacts or infrastructure problems are identified at that point. The following case, *Western Land Equities, Inc. v. City of Logan*, asks the question: at what stage in the development process does the developer become entitled to complete a project?

■ WESTERN LAND EQUITIES, INC. v. CITY OF LOGAN

617 P.2d 388 (Utah 1980)

STEWART, Justice: . . .

In February 1969 plaintiffs purchased 18.53 acres of property within the City of Logan. In April 1976, pursuant to a new land use ordinance, the property was zoned M-1, a manufacturing zone which permitted single-family dwellings. Plaintiffs' intent was to use the property for moderately priced single-family housing.

The procedure for securing approval of single-family residential subdivisions is established by city ordinance. The ordinance requires consultation with the city planning commission, preparation and submittal of a preliminary plan showing compliance with minimum requirements of the subdivision ordinance, and approval of both preliminary and final plans by the city planning commission. The planning commission's practice is to introduce the preliminary plan at one meeting ("first reading") and discuss its merits and take action in a second meeting. Plaintiffs' project was introduced on July 13, 1977; the second reading was scheduled for August 10, at which time the advisability of the residential development was questioned and the matter was tabled and referred to the municipal council. On August 18, the municipal council reviewed the matter and referred it back to the planning commission with a recommendation that protective covenants be drawn up and that more roadways in and out of the proposed subdivision be provided. The second reading of the preliminary plan occurred before the planning commission on September 14, and the matter was tabled for 60 days. On October 12 the planning commission went on record as opposing subdivisions in M-1 zones, and on November 9 the commission rejected the proposed subdivision on the following grounds:

(1) Development of the proposed residential subdivision was contrary to the land use ordinance and to the city's master plan;
(2) The access roads provided by the plan were inadequate;
(3) The location of the railroad on three sides of the proposed subdivision made it an inappropriate site for housing.

In November plaintiffs unsuccessfully appealed the decision of the planning commission to the municipal council, and in December plaintiffs filed a complaint in district court. A restraining order was issued on January 3, 1978, enjoining the city from amending its zoning ordinance. The injunction was lifted on April 18,

1978, at which time a change in the zoning ordinance that had been enacted on January 19, 1978, became effective as it applied to plaintiffs' property.

In connection with plaintiffs' motion for summary judgment, the parties submitted stipulated statements of facts and issues. The issues submitted to the court were:

1. Did the M1 Land Use Description as set forth in the Logan City Land Use Ordinance of 1976, prior to the January 31, 1978 amendment, permit the development of subdivisions consisting of single family dwelling units on property zoned M1?
2. Does the amendment to the M1 Land Use Description of the Logan City Land Use Ordinance of 1976, which was adopted January 31, 1978 and which prohibits the development of single family dwelling units in the M1 zone except by special use permit, give Defendants the authority to deny approval of Plaintiff's Willow Creek subdivision which was submitted prior to the amendment . . . ? . . .

The . . . rule generally accepted in other jurisdictions [is] that an applicant for a building permit or subdivision approval does not acquire any vested right under existing zoning regulations prior to the issuance of the permit or official approval of a proposed subdivision. Generally, denial of an application may be based on subsequently-enacted zoning regulations. *See* 8 McQuillin, *Municipal Corporations* §25.155 (1976); 1 Anderson, *American Law of Zoning* §6.23 2d ed. (1976); and cases cited in Annot., 50 A.L.R.3d 596, 607 (1973).

However, for the reasons discussed below, we are of the view that the majority rule fails to strike a proper balance between public and private interests and opens the area to so many variables as to result in unnecessary litigation. We hold instead that an applicant for subdivision approval or a building permit is entitled to favorable action if the application conforms to the zoning ordinance in effect at the time of the application, unless changes in the zoning ordinances are pending which would prohibit the use applied for, or unless the municipality can show a compelling reason for exercising its police power retroactively to the date of application.

In the present case, the trial court found that plaintiffs had acquired a vested development right by their substantial compliance with procedural requirements and that the city was estopped from withholding approval of the proposed subdivision. The court used the language of zoning estoppel, a principle that is widely followed. That principle estops a government entity from exercising its zoning powers to prohibit a proposed land use when a property owner, relying reasonably and in good faith on some governmental act or omission, has made a substantial change in position or incurred such extensive obligations or expenses that it would be highly inequitable to deprive the owner of his right to complete his proposed development.

The focus of zoning estoppel is primarily upon the conduct and interests of the property owner. The main inquiry is whether there has been substantial reliance by the owner on governmental actions related to the superseded zoning that permitted the proposed use. The concern underlying this approach is the economic hardship that would be imposed on a property owner whose development plans are thwarted. Some courts hold that before a permit is issued no action of the owner is sufficient reliance to bar application of changes in zoning ordinances because there has been no governmental act sufficient to support an estoppel. Accordingly, a landowner is held to have no vested right in existing or anticipated zoning. *Avco Community Developers, Inc. v. South Coast Regional Comm'n*, 17 Cal. 3d 785, 132 Cal. Rptr. 386, 553 P.2d 546 (1976). Other courts consider any substantial change of position in determining the estoppel issue. . . .

Generally, "substantial reliance" is determined by various tests employed by the courts—for example, the set quantum test, the proportionate test, and a balancing test. The set quantum test, used by the majority of courts, determines that an owner is entitled to relief from new, prohibitory zoning if he has changed his position beyond a certain point, measured quantitatively. A related test is the proportionate test, which determines the percentage of money spent or obligations incurred before the zoning change as compared with the total cost. The problem with both of these tests is that there is no predictable point short of adjudication which separates reliance that is less than "substantial" from the reliance sufficient to result in a vested right or to support an estoppel.

The balancing test, although likely to produce a more fair outcome in a particular case, also results in little predictability. The test weighs the owner's interest in developing his property and the reasonableness of his proposed use against the interests of public health, safety, morals, or general welfare. If the gain to the public is small when compared to the hardship that would accrue to the property owner, the actions of the owner in preparation for development according to a formerly permitted use may be seen as sufficiently substantial to justify the issuance of a permit or continuation of development despite an amendment to the zoning ordinances. See *Nott v. Wolff*, 18 Ill. 2d 362, 163 N.E.2d 809 (1960).

An additional requirement generally considered in zoning estoppel cases is that of the existence of some physical construction as an element of substantial reliance. Preconstruction activities such as the execution of architectural drawings or the clearing of land and widening of roads are not sufficient to create a vested right, nor generally are activities that are not exclusively related to the proposed project.

If the substantial reliance requirement of zoning estoppel were applied to the facts of the present case, we could not agree with the trial court that plaintiffs' "substantial compliance" with procedural requirements justified the estoppel of the city's enforcement of a new zoning ordinance. Although plaintiffs allege they proceeded with subdivision plans and incurred significant costs with the encouragement of certain city officials, they had not yet received official approval of their plan, and their expenditures were merely for surveying and preliminary plans. The record indicates that plaintiffs spent $1335 for a boundary survey and $890 for the preparation of a preliminary subdivision plat. The boundary survey has value regardless of the city's approval or disapproval of the plaintiffs' proposal. The expenditure of $890 for the plat is not significant in relation to the size of the parcel and is not substantial enough to justify an estoppel with regard to the enforcement of valid zoning ordinances that the same effective before official approval of plaintiffs' proposed subdivision. . . .

Courts in several states have adopted the view, not unlike that stated in *Contracts Funding & Mortgage Exchange v. Maynes*, 527 P.2d 1073 (Utah 1974), that an application for a building permit creates a vested right as of the time of application. Pennsylvania, one of these states, initially followed the general rule that a vested right accrued when an owner could show substantial reliance, made in good faith, on a validly issued permit.

In 1968 the Pennsylvania court in *Gallagher v. Building Inspector, City of Erie*, 432 Pa. 301, 247 A.2d 572 (1968), eliminated the need to show reliance on a permit to create a vested right when the amendment to the zoning ordinance was not considered by the city council until after a permit had been issued. At the present time Pennsylvania follows what is termed the "pending ordinance rule." This rule provides that an application for a permitted use cannot be refused unless a prohibiting ordinance is pending at the time of application. *Boron Oil Co. Kimple*, 445 Pa. 327, 284 A.2d 744 (1971), stated the applicable test as follows:

> [A]n ordinance is pending when a Borough Council has resolved to consider a particular scheme of rezoning and has advertised to the public its intention to hold public hearings on the rezoning. [284 A.2d at 747.] . . .

The State of Washington has also refused to follow the general rule that building permits are not protected against revocation by subsequent zoning change unless a permittee has gained a vested right through a substantial change in position in reliance on the permit. As stated in *Hull v. Hunt*, 53 Wash. 2d 125, 331 P.2d 856, 859 (1958):

> . . . The more practical rule to administer, we feel, is that the right vests when the party, property owner or not, applies for his building permit, if that permit is thereafter issued. This rule, of course, assumes that the permit applied for and granted be consistent with the zoning ordinances and building codes in force at the time of application for the permit. . . .

A vested right in a particular development scheme may be created by statute. For example, in Pennsylvania, §508(4) of the Municipalities Planning Code confers a vested right on property owners who have previously received approval of a subdivision plan in which the lots are too small to conform to the requirements of a newly-enacted ordinance. This vested right has a three-year duration. . . .

In our view the tests employed by most other jurisdictions tend to subject landowners to undue and even calamitous expense because of changing city councils or zoning boards or their dilatory action and to the unpredictable results of burdensome litigation. The majority rule permits an unlimited right to deny permits when ordinances are amended after application and preliminary work. It allows government in many cases broader power with regard to land regulation than may be justified by the public interests involved. A balancing test, though geared toward promoting fairness, must be applied on a case-by-case basis and offers no predictable guidelines on which landowners can intelligently base their decisions regarding extensive development projects. Tests currently followed by the majority of states are particularly unsatisfactory in dealing with the large multistage projects. The threat of denial of a permit at a late stage of development makes a developer vulnerable to shifting governmental policies and tempts him to manipulate the process by prematurely engaging in activities that would establish the substantial reliance required to vest his right to develop when inappropriate.

The economic waste that occurs when a project is halted after substantial costs have been incurred in its commencement is of no benefit either to the public or to landowners. In a day when housing costs have severely escalated beyond the means of many prospective buyers, governmental actions should not be based on policies that exacerbate a severe economic problem without compelling justification. Governmental powers should be exercised in a manner that is reasonable and, to the extent possible, predictable.

On the other hand, a rule which vests a right unconditionally at the time application for a permit is made affords no protection for important public interests that may legitimately require interference with planned private development. If a proposal met zoning requirements at the time of application but seriously threatens public health, safety, or welfare, the interests of the public should not be thwarted.

The above competing interests are best accommodated in our view by adopting the rule that an applicant is entitled to a building permit or subdivision approval if his proposed development meets the zoning requirements in existence at the time of his application and if he proceeds with reasonable diligence, absent a compelling, countervailing public interest. Furthermore, if a city or county has initiated proceedings to amend its zoning ordinances, a landowner who subsequently makes application for a permit is not entitled to rely on the original zoning classification. . . .

In the present case, the zoning of the property in question was found by the trial court to have permitted the proposed use at the time of the application. The owners had received encouragement from city officials, although no official approval was rendered. After the application, the city council members decided to reexamine the pertinent zoning regulation and thereafter voted to amend or "clarify" the zoning ordinance to disallow subdivisions in an M-1 zone and permit residences only by special permit. Their actions may have had a reasonable basis. It was argued that fire protection would be undermined because of limited access roads, but it does not appear the problem would be any less serious if the unarguably–permitted manufacturing facilities were erected instead of single-family houses. Objections as to inadequate sidewalks and other problems can be handled by requiring modification of specifications that do not meet city subdivision requirements. Indeed, the order of the trial court stated that the developers must comply with all the reasonable requirements of the city's subdivision ordinance.

We do not find the reasons given by the city for withholding approval of plaintiffs' proposed subdivision to be so compelling as to overcome the presumption that an applicant for a building permit or subdivision approval is entitled to affirmative official action if he meets the zoning requirements in force at the time of his application.

Notes and Comments

1. *Balancing the Competing Interests*. Does the Utah early vesting policy, which limits regulatory standards to those in place or pending when a development application is submitted — subject to a compelling interest exception — adequately balance interests? Does the developer have predictability? What is a "compelling interest" ? Overcrowded schools? Inadequate sewer treatment capacity or water supply? Road congestion?

How should the balance be struck between the developer's concerns and those of the community? Once a preliminary subdivision plan is approved, the developer then proceeds to spend significant sums of money on the final plan. *See HJS Development, Inc. v. Pierce County*, 61 P.3d 1141 (Wash. 2003) ("Once receiving preliminary plat approval, an owner or developer may proceed to prepare detailed engineering drawings, conduct improvements, and prepare the final plat in compliance with the terms and conditions of the preliminary plat"). The developer has distinct investment-backed expectations, and last minute regulatory changes can result in a substantial increase in cost that may make the project uneconomic. On the other hand, the infrastructure and environmental concerns over development are significant. Cities will point to the need to preserve their flexibility to address unanticipated problems. Should the decision about when a project vests be made by the state legislature in a statute? Should it be left to the city council or board of supervisors for decision on a case-by-case basis? Should the court decide?

2. *Late Vesting*. In *Avco Community Developers v. South Coast Regional Comm'n*, 553 P.2d 546 (Cal. 1976), a leading decision in the area, the California Supreme Court opted for late vesting. The developer had obtained subdivision approval, spent over $2 million, and incurred another $740,468 in liabilities for developing a 74-acre tract that was part of a 5234-acre tract to contain 18,925 residential units. The improvements made to the property included grading pursuant to a grading permit and the installation of utilities. Before the developer had sought a building permit, however, the state adopted coastal zone legislation requiring developers to obtain a coastal commission permit. The developer claimed a vested right to complete the subdivision and, alternatively, argued estoppel premised on a development agreement.

The court held that a developer which had not even sought a building permit could not be vested merely because it previously received permission to subdivide. Just as zoning does not provide a vested right to complete a project, the court observed that the government makes no representation that a developer will be exempt from laws in effect at the time of application for a building permit. The court concluded that a vested right can only be acquired where a developer has performed substantial work and incurred substantial liabilities in good faith reliance upon a building permit issued by the government. The permit must be based on approval of the plans for the specific buildings to be built.

In *Avco*, the developer had never applied for permits for specific buildings. Indeed, the county was unaware of the exact buildings to be built, their proposed placement, or even how many units were to be built. In addition, if the developer's rights had vested with subdivision approval, the project could sit for years, exempting development from future zoning changes for an indefinite period of years. *See also Sahl v. Town of York*, 760 A.2d 266 (Me. 2000) (vested right requires actual physical commencement of significant and visible construction in good faith pursuant to a validly issued building permit).

Is the vesting rule in *Avco* equitable?

In a New Hampshire case, the planning board denied a site plan for a shopping center, and the developer filed suit. While awaiting the court's decision, the city rezoned the parcel to prohibit shopping centers. After obtaining the court's reversal of the site plan denial and mandamus requiring the city to approve the site plan, did the developer obtain a vested right to complete the original project? In *Gosselin v. City of Nashua*, 321 A.2d 593 (N.H. 1974), the court held that as long as the city acted in good faith, meaning without undue delay, the developer did not acquire a vested right absent the construction of actual improvements on the land which changed the use of the land in a tangible manner.

Is the vesting rule in *Gosselin* equitable?

Compare The Village, L.L.C. v. Delaware Agricultural Lands Foundation, 808 A.2d 753 (Del. 2002). The Supreme Court of Delaware held that the issuance of a building permit is just one fact to be taken into account in determining whether a right has vested. ("[G]ood faith reliance on existing standards is the test. In a given situation, the issuance, or non-issuance, of a building permit may be evidence of reliance, or lack thereof").

3. *"Downplanning" After an Approved Map.* In *Youngblood v. Board of Supervisors of San Diego County*, 586 P.2d 556 (Cal. 1978), the California Supreme Court ruled that the amendment of the general plan reducing development density could not be applied to a project with an approved tentative tract map. Language in the opinion suggests a narrow rule: the critical point for determining map consistency with the general plan is at tentative tract review. Other language, however, suggests a broader rule concerning vesting: tentative tract approval is the vesting point, making final map approval ministerial once there is substantial compliance with the tentative map and conditions.

Is *Youngblood* consistent with *Avco*?

4. *Vesting and Special Assessments.* After nearly $1 million was spent in the construction of a sewer system designed to service residential uses under a special assessment district, the city council rezoned the property for agricultural use. Was there a vested right to develop? *Furey v. City of Sacramento*, 780 F.2d 1448 (9th Cir. 1986) (no vesting because improvements under the special assessment were voluntary, and vesting occurs only when a landowner is forced to make improvements that, while valuable to others, are useless to him).

5. *Developer Expectations and the Ballot Box.* After a developer obtained zoning for a resort development, opponents successfully nullified the ordinance by popular referendum. Prior to the election, however, the city issued building permits. Is the developer entitled to a vested right under an *Avco*-type rule? *County of Kauai v. Pacific Standard Life Insurance Co.*, 653 P.2d 766 (Hawaii 1982) (vested right requires good faith reliance by the developer upon the reasonable assurances of officials and the expenditure of substantial sums of money, but the developer's reliance was not in good faith because of its knowledge of the pending referendum).

6. *Subsequent Annexation of the Property.* If an application is vested and subsequently the property is annexed to a different jurisdiction, must the new regulating community honor vesting by the predecessor regulator? The Washington intermediate appellate court ruled in the affirmative. *Schneider Homes, Inc. v. City of Kent*, 942 P.2d 1096 (Wash. Ct. App. 1997).

7. *Vesting in the World of Multiple Permits.* The general rule is that where multiple applications must be submitted, vesting under one application will not relieve the developer from seeking other necessary approvals. However, in *Schneider Homes, Inc. v. City of Kent*, supra, the court held that the submission of a preliminary subdivision plat application vested the developer's right to have not only the plat application, but also its companion PUD application, considered under county

ordinances then in effect. Similarly, in *Weyerhaeuser v. Pierce County*, 976 P.2d 1279 (Wash. Ct. App. 1999), the court held that the landowner's rights vested on submission of a complete application for a conditional use permit, and the development was immune from a subsequently enacted requirement that applicants obtain a wetlands permit.

Is this rule better?

8. *The Scope of Post-Vesting Regulation I.* Where a developer establishes a vested right, should the developer be allowed to develop any use permitted as of right in the district? Or is the vesting limited to the specific development contained in the project application? *See Noble Manor Co. v. Pierce County*, 943 P.2d 1378 (Wash. 1997) (where the application is silent on the requested use, the government entity may consider the application to see if any legal use can be made of the subdivided property).

9. *The Scope of Post-Vesting Regulation II.* Just as the Utah court in *Western Land Equities* ruled that a compelling interest, such as a serious environmental hazard, could justify new restrictions after the right to complete the project has vested, jurisdictions will retain development controls after vesting where a development would cause a nuisance. Is that power likely to satisfy municipalities?

10. *Taking Vested Development Rights.* If a community modifies regulatory obligations following the vesting point, does the new regulation constitute a taking? Absent a compelling justification, most would agree that the development right has been taken. *But see Villa at Greeley, Inc. v. Hopper*, 917 P.2d 350 (Colo. Ct. App. 1996) (initiative measure requiring a referendum for PUDs applied to a PUD subject to a development agreement, with the court rejecting a takings claim).

E. STREAMLINING AND DEVELOPMENT STANDARDS

The length of the permit process, combined with the late vesting rules adopted by judicial decisions, has led numerous states to adopt so-called streamlining legislation. The legislation sets deadlines for public agencies to act, and it can prevent later changes in the rules governing a development. The following case offers a typical illustration of streamlining legislation. Note that, although the effect of streamlining laws often arises in the subdivision review process, these laws apply more broadly to a wide variety of development approvals.

NORCO CONSTRUCTION, INC. v. KING COUNTY
649 P.2d 103 (Wash. 1982)

UTTER, Justice. . . .

In 1975, a citizens' committee was created to formulate a Soos Creek Plateau Communities Plan (Soos Creek Plan) to be adopted as an amendment to the County's comprehensive plan. The committee met during the following 2 years. In May 1977, respondent Norco submitted its Star View Acres plat application with a density of 1 unit per acre. The following month, in June 1977, the citizens' committee submitted a draft Soos Creek Plan to the Council contemplating density of

1 unit per 5 acres in the vicinity of the proposed Star View Acres. The applicant's plat is for 75 acres in the Soos Creek Plateau area, a 73-square-mile area located east of the cities of Renton, Kent and Auburn, and above the Green River Valley in southwest King County.

In August 1977, a county hearing examiner recommended approval of the Star View Acres preliminary plat application while identifying its inconsistency with the prospective Soos Creek Plan. The examiner's recommendation was then forwarded to the King County Council. On October 31, 1977, the plat application was placed on the Council agenda and referred to the planning and community development committee considering the pending Soos Creek Plan. On November 11, 1977, the hearing examiner notified respondent Norco that health department approval of sewage and water systems was required prior to preliminary plat approval. . . .

On January 30, 1978, the Council passed ordinance No. 8579 (King County Code 19.08.250) providing for approval of preliminary plats if the water system is "adequate" but providing for deferral of approval when a hearing examiner has identified the plan as inconsistent with the community plan adopted by "the applicable citizens community plan committee and referred to the County for adoption". On December 11, 1978, respondent received health department approval of its water and sewage facilities.

The County did not act further, and after completing its application on January 8, 1979, Norco filed a petition for writ of mandamus in Superior Court in February 1979. In April 1979, the trial court issued its writ of mandamus. In November 1979, the citizens' committee Soos Creek Plan was adopted by the Council with maximum density for Star View Acres of 1 unit per 5 acres.

The principal complaint of the County is directed to that portion of the Court of Appeals opinion which states: "When the statutory time within which the legislative body of a political subdivision of the State must act on a preliminary plat has expired without the required action being taken, the applicant then acquires certain vested rights in connection with the plat application." . . .

Washington does adhere to the minority rule that a landowner obtains a vested right to develop land when he or she makes a timely and complete building permit application that complies with the applicable zoning and building ordinances in effect on the date of the application. . . . Our vested rights rule also has been applied to building permits, conditional use permits, a grading permit, and a substantial development permit.

The County argues a vesting rule is inappropriate in this context. We agree with the County that the terminology "vested right" is inappropriate, but hold Norco did have a right to a decision on its preliminary plat application based on the factors relevant 90 days after filing its application.

I

The County urges this vesting rule should not be applied to plat applications inasmuch as Council decisions are discretionary. The distinction between ministerial and discretionary acts is not relevant to the validity of procedural limits placed on the decision-making entity. The need for a "date certain" upon which a right vests is to avoid tactical maneuvering between parties and that need would appear equally strong whether the act is discretionary or ministerial. . . .

The basic rule in land use law is still that, absent more, an individual should be able to utilize his own land as he sees fit. U.S. Const. amends. 5, 14. Although zoning is, in general, a proper exercise of police power which can permissibly limit an individual's property rights, it goes without saying that the use of police power cannot be unreasonable . . . While local governments exist to provide necessary public services to those living within their borders and to avoid harms in their protection of the public's health, safety, and general welfare, exercise of this authority must be reasonable and rationally related to a legitimate purpose of government such as avoiding harm or protecting health, safety and general, not local or parochially conceived, welfare. . . .

Not only are local governments limited by due process protections in how they zone communities, they are similarly limited in the decisions they make under the adopted zoning plan. Unreasonable delay in approving plat applications may be just as much an exclusionary device as an unconstitutional exclusionary zoning plan itself. . . .

. . . Consistent with the type of abuse noted . . . above . . . , the unreasonable lapse of time alone, without an express showing of coercion, can prove unconstitutionally detrimental to a developer harmed by this action.

The time limit within which the County was required to act, absent other lawful reasons, is established by RCW 58.17.140.[1] The statute does permit the Council to refer the application to the applicant for modification or correction but this must occur within the 90-day period from filing. Notification by the hearing examiner to Norco of the need for health department approval occurred on November 11, 1977, more than 90 days after the application was filed. The County did not act within that time period and it may not at a later date properly refer the application.

The enactment of a 90-day limitation by the legislature was intended to forestall unwarranted delay. The statute demonstrates a clear determination to hold units of local government within responsible bounds of timeliness in dealing with land use issues.[2] Courts will not be used to circumvent such a legislative policy and we will not do so in this case.

While the trial court and Court of Appeals acted properly in supporting the trial court's restriction upon the County action, the use of the term "vested right"

1. "Preliminary plats of any proposed subdivision and dedication shall be approved, disapproved, or returned to the applicant for modification or correction within ninety days from date of filing thereof unless the applicant consents to an extension of such time period: *Provided*, That if an environmental impact statement is required as provided in RCW 43.21C.030, the ninety day period shall not include the time spent preparing and circulating the environmental impact statement by the local government agency. Final plats and short plats shall be approved, disapproved, or returned to the applicant within thirty days from the date of filing thereof, unless the applicant consents to an extension of such time period. A final plat meeting all requirements of this chapter shall be submitted to the legislative body of the city, town, or county for approval within three years of the date of preliminary plat approval. An applicant who files a written request with the legislative body of the city, town, or county at least thirty days before the expiration of this three-year period shall be granted one one-year extension upon a showing that the applicant has attempted in good faith to submit the final plat within the three-year period." RCW 58.17.140.

2. *Cf. Niichel v. Lancaster*, 97 Wash.2d 620, 647 P.2d 1021 (1982) (holding "shall" is directive and not mandatory in the context of RCW 84.40.040). Appellant has not seriously contended that the time limit within RCW 58.17.140 is not mandatory. The statute indicates its mandatory nature not only by

in the opinion of the Court of Appeals overstates the nature of Norco's right. The only right is that granted by RCW 58.17.140 and that is simply the right to have a decision based upon relevant factors made within 90 days after filing. If the County were to grant the plat application based upon factors relevant during the statutory time period, the provisions of RCW 58.17.170 would become operative. That statute provides, "Any lots in a final plat filed for record shall be a valid land use notwithstanding any change in zoning laws for a period of five years from the date of filing." Due to the unusual posture of this case, the 5-year period should run from the date of final decision of the County, not from date of filing, but in the ordinary process only the rights provided by RCW 58.17.140 are granted and no other rights accrue.

II

Not only is the County's discretion limited by the procedural requirements of the statute, it is also limited by the land use restrictions that existed at the time the statutory time period had run. The County argues that even if it were limited to approving or disapproving Norco's plat application within the statutory time limit, it could have considered the pending Soos Creek Plan as a basis for disapproving Norco's application under RCW 58.17.110. That statute permits the county council to consider such factors as the "public use and interest" and the "public health, safety, and general welfare . . . " But to interpret these terms as conferring unlimited discretion upon the Council would make the other sections of the platting statute meaningless and place plat applicants in the untenable position of having no basis for determining how they could comply with the law. RCW 58.17.010 specifically requires plats to "conform to zoning standards and local plans and policies" while RCW 58.17.100, in turn, requires a plat to conform with "the comprehensive plan and to planning standards and specifications as adopted by the . . . county." If the Council may dictate its own agenda of relevant criteria for plat approval, how are developers to intelligently go about conforming plat applications to the County's requirements? Why bother adopting the Soos Creek Plan if it may be given the full force of law via the Council's exercise of discretion? . . .

. . . In light of the County's failure to use the powers it had at its disposal under law, the trial court's writ of mandamus was an entirely appropriate response to the County's lengthy deferral of a decision on Norco's plat application in violation of RCW 58.17.140.

Notes and Comments

1. *Permit Streamlining and Automatic Approvals*. Most states have passed permit streamlining legislation designed to speed up the delay caused by development review. The legislation typically sets a maximum time for taking action on applications, holding hearings, rendering decisions, and notifying applicants,

---

the use of the word "shall" but by requiring that extensions be consented to by the applicant. Moreover, no governmental purpose is undermined by the mandatory time limitation of the statute. The county need only "approve, disapprove or return to the applicant for modification" the plat application. The statute provides for extensions and accommodates the process of filing an environmental impact statement. Appellant has not contended its functions would be undermined by the 90-day time limit of RCW 58.17.140.

often providing that projects may be "deemed approved" if action is not timely taken.

Such "deemed approved" legislation appears fair when considered against unconscionable local delay. It could, however, result in the automatic approval of projects that carry significant, adverse environmental impacts or present a demand for infrastructure beyond local supply capacity.

2. *"Deemed-Approved" Avoided*. The harshness of deemed-approved permit streamlining has caused some courts to evade its impact. *See Nyack Hosp. v. Village of Nyack Planning Bd.*, 647 N.Y.S.2d 799 (Sup. Ct. App. Div. 1996) (although village failed to act on final site plan application after 62 days in violation of statute, the application is not approved by default as the state Village Law did not explicitly provide for default approval of site plans). If a statutory scheme other than the basic permitting statutes is involved, a court may hold that unless the separate scheme has its own "deemed approved" requirement, a violation of that scheme will not result in automatic approval. *See Eller Media Co. v. City of Los Angeles*, 105 Cal. Rptr. 2d 262 (App. 2001) (permits not deemed approved under Permit Streamlining Act where agency had allegedly violated deadlines under separate law requiring preparation of an environmental analysis). Florida Stat. Ann. §163.3184(8)(a) (West 2000) provides that "the state land planning agency, upon receipt of a local government's adopted comprehensive plan or plan amendment, shall have 45 days for review and to determine if the plan or plan amendment is in compliance with this act." In *Caliente Partnership v. Johnston*, 604 So. 2d 886 (Fla. Dist. Ct. App. 1992) (per curiam), the local government failed to comply with the 45-day notice requirement on a proposed plan amendment. That amendment, however, was not approved by default as the legislation contained no specific "deemed approved" language, and the court found that default approval is too harsh a remedy for noncompliance. *See also Board of Aldermen of Newton v. Maniace*, 711 N.E.2d 565 (Mass. 1999) (finding that the filing of the result of a city board's vote was sufficient to prevent the project from being automatically approved even though the plaintiff alleged irregularities in that filing); Frank C. Huntington and Wiliam J. Connolly, Equitable Considerations in Statutory Construction: Board of Aldermen of Newton v. Maniace, Boston Bar J. (March/April 2000) ("it seems likely that the majority [in *Maniace*] was motivated, at least in part, by a sense that constructive approval was too severe a penalty to impose on a local board for what was, at worst, a mere technical violation of the statute").

Should the court in *Caliente Partnership* have followed the mandatory language of "shall"? Does your opinion change when you compare the statute in question with another Florida statute regulating license administration, which specified that an application not approved or denied within the specified period "shall be deemed approved . . . "?

In *Advantage Dev., Inc. v. Board of Supervisors of Jackson Township*, 688 A.2d 759 (Pa. Commw. Ct. 1997), Pennsylvania's intermediate appellate court ruled that in complex subdivision proceedings where multiple revised plans are submitted, each new submission does not create a clear legal right to another decision within the 90-day statutory period. Where the board of supervisors ultimately rejected the first final plan, the subdivision was not to be deemed approved because the board did not specifically reject a revised final plan. In addition, the statute failed to provide that an application remanded to the board of supervisors was subject to the mandatory 90-day response period.

But in *Board of Appeals of Westwood v. Lambergs*, 677 N.E.2d 270 (Mass. App. Ct. 1997), the court held that the failure to deny application for a zoning variance from a frontage requirement within the 100-day statutory period gave rise to constructive variance even though the board, in the same case, had denied the request for a width variance. The court refused the board's attempted rejection, denominated an "amended decision," as untimely.

Where the applicant applies under the zoning law to expand a prior nonconforming use but is unable to garner a majority for approval, should the applicant enjoy a right to expand the use because the board failed to render or convey its official ruling within the deadlines established by a permit streamlining law? See *In re Newton Enters.*, 708 A.2d 914 (Vt. 1998) (too harsh a result and not the reason for the legislation, but the automatic approval may occur if the board neither held a hearing nor reached a vote).

On the subject of automatic approvals, see generally Gregory G. Brooker & Karen R. Cole, Automatic Approval Statutes: Escape Hatches and Pitfalls, 29 Urb. Law. 439 (1997).

3. *Moratorium and Vesting*. Despite a "deemed approved" project approval, could the community impose a moratorium or other "timing" ordinance regulating the pace of development? *Kelly v. Tahoe Regional Planning Agency*, 855 P.2d 1027 (Nev. 1993) (per curiam) ("deemed approved" statute did not exempt a project from subsequent land use regulations), *cert. denied*, 510 U.S. 1041 (1994).

4. *Post-Vesting Regulation*. If a subdivision application anticipates obtaining zoning variances and is "deemed approved," will the variances also be deemed approved? In *Annand v. Board of Supervisors of Franklin Township*, 634 A.2d 1159 (Pa. Commw. Ct. 1993), the court found that the project was deemed approved when the township failed to notify the landowner of its decision within 90 days after the review meeting. The landowner was entitled to a permit where it submitted required engineering details, but the approval does not include any needed zoning variances. The court reasoned that the recipient of a "deemed approved" permit should be no better off than an applicant receiving an approval.

5. *Remedies for Violations of Streamlining Laws*. What are the remedies available to a developer who believes that a public agency has missed a mandatory deadline, and thus rendered the project automatically approved, but has refused to acknowledge its error? The obvious remedy is a mandamus action ordering the project approved. *See State ex rel. Aspen Group, Inc. v. Washington County Bd. of Comm'rs*, 946 P.2d 347 (Or. Ct. App. 1997) (allowing plaintiff to recover statutory attorney's fees as well). But the delay may also cost the developer money. Is a damage remedy also appropriate? Some courts have said yes. *Schillerstrom Homes, Inc. v. City of Naperville*, 762 N.E.2d 494 (Ill. 2001). The Washington Supreme Court has apparently gone much further by recognizing general delay damages for wrongful refusal to process a permit. *Missions Springs Inc. v. City of Spokane*, 954 P.2d 250 (Wash. 1998). Is this overkill, or is a mandamus remedy insufficient to fully remediate the error?

6. *Waiving the Streamlining Protections*. To what extent can rights under the streamlining laws be avoided by voluntary waiver? Courts may apply the common law waiver doctrine in which an applicant waives its right to a decision within a specific period and agrees to an extension of that period. *Bickel v. City of Piedmont*, 946 P.2d 427 (Cal. 1997). In response to *Bickel*, the state legislature amended the statute to eliminate common law waiver. Cal. Govt. Code §§65940.5, 65950

(West Supp. 1999). Section 65957 provides for a one-time extension by mutual agreement of the applicant and the public agency for up to 90 days. Of course, if the extension period granted by the applicant expires, the "deemed approved" requirement again comes into force. In *Northern States Power Co. v. City of Mendota Heights*, 646 N.W.2d 919 (Minn. Ct. App. 2002), the court of appeal rejected the city's argument that applicant was bound by its actions to a further extension where its written agreement to the extension had expired. Instead, said the court, "the burden was on the city to act within the statutory deadline or to request an additional extension" from the applicant. *Id.* at 926.

Another variation on the time limits established under streamlining are statutes designed to allow the developer to advance the vesting point within the development process.

KAUFMAN & BROAD CENTRAL VALLEY, INC. v. CITY OF MODESTO

30 Cal. Rptr. 2d 904 (Ct. App. 1994)

BUCKLEY, Associate Justice. . . .

In 1987, the City appointed an "Infrastructure Study Committee" to examine various mechanisms for funding certain future public improvements identified in the City's "Capital Improvement Program." In its final report issued in June of that ye1ar, the committee recommended the City establish development impact fees to finance that portion of the improvements made necessary by new development. The committee offered additional recommendations for what it termed "broad based funding" of the remaining unfunded portion attributable to the already existing population. The study identified the following improvements to be supported in whole or in part by impact fees: police buildings and equipment; fire facilities; an expressway loop; street lights; parks and recreation (including a new senior citizens' center); traffic signals; and expansion of city hall. The total estimated cost of these improvements charged to new development was $49,440,000. This cost, in turn, was allocated among different types of development to arrive at an appropriate fee for each. The proposed fee for low-density residential development was $1413 per unit.

On June 23, 1987, the City enacted Ordinance No. 2520-C.S. implementing most of the Infrastructure Study Committee's recommendations with respect to impact fees. . . .

The Infrastructure Study Committee also recommended capital facilities fees be adjusted annually to reflect the increased cost of construction. Although it did not incorporate this recommendation into its original fee ordinance, the City adopted Resolution No. 87-1128 in October 1987 in which it found "it is in the best interests of the City of Modesto for capital facilities fees to be adjusted annually in accordance with changes in the Building Cost Index (BCI) published by the Engineering News Record." On this basis, the City increased the fees by 1.23 percent, making the fee $1434 per unit effective January 1, 1988.

In April 1988, City staff prepared an internal memo entitled "Another Look at the Capital Facilities Fees." The memo concluded the City's capital improvement projects were "woefully underfunded" and recommended the City hire a consultant to consider several options for expanding the scope of the fees.

It was at about this same time that Kaufman & Broad's predecessor, Nineveh, Inc., submitted an application to the City for a vesting tentative subdivision map for a 31-acre residential development known as River Terrace. A contiguous 2.13-acre parcel was designated for future development in what was to become known as River Terrace II. The application was deemed complete on June 22, 1988. . . .

In August 1988, the City issued a request for proposals to develop a new fee schedule. Among the identified objectives of the review were an "[a]djustment of the Capital Facilities Fee to accommodate revised costs for the police building, expressway loop, fire/drill training center, and new assumptions in the role of broad-based funding" as well as "[r]econfiguring the Capital Facilities Fee based on a major shift in assumptions."

In anticipation of a substantial increase in fees, City staff perceived a need "to have the adjusted CFF [capital facilities fee] applicable to any new vesting tentative maps that are accepted for filing from this time forward and to prevent a rush on filing vesting tentative maps which attempt to avoid the adjusted CFF." It therefore recommended the City adopt a policy of attaching the following fee escalator condition to approval of all future vesting tentative maps: " 'The Capital Facilities Fee payable at the time of the issuance of a building permit for any construction in this subdivision map (parcel map) shall be based on the rates in effect at time of issuance of the building permit.' " On August 16, 1988, the City adopted Resolution No. 88-609 implementing this recommendation. The following month, the City by resolution increased its capital facilities fees to reflect changes in the building cost index, raising them effective January 1, 1989, to $1,445.70 per unit.

On October 3, 1988, the City planning commission approved Nineveh's vesting tentative map for 134 lots in River Terrace, subject to several conditions including condition 13, the fee escalator condition quoted above.

The City hired Recht Hausrath & Associates to revise its capital facilities fees. . . .

In February 1989, Recht Hausrath [a consultant] issued its initial report (the Phase I Study). It recommended substantial increases in the City's capital facilities fees based upon a much broader approach to future development than had been taken earlier by the Infrastructure Study Committee. In particular, it expanded the area under consideration from certain portions of the City's urban fringe to the entire area expected to be included within the City's future urban boundaries. It also extended the applicable time period from one ending in the year 2000 to one ending at the point of full "buildout" of the urban area in 2011. The need for future improvements increased correspondingly, as did the ratio of new to existing residents and thus the proportionate cost of those improvements chargeable to new development.

The Phase I Study also added two entirely new components to the list of improvements to be funded by impact fees: wastewater treatment and fee administration. Finally, it revised cost estimates for those improvements already on the list. As a result of these various changes, the total estimated cost of improvements attributable to new development grew from $49,440,000 to $165,012,000. This recomputation, in turn, was reflected in a fee increase from $1445.70 to $2653.72 per unit adopted by the City in February 1989. The City's resolution approving the increase also provided for periodic review of the fees and reserved the right to revise them further to incorporate additional studies.

In May 1989, Nineveh applied to the City for a vesting tentative subdivision map for River Terrace II. The application was deemed complete on June 8 and approved by the planning commission on July 10, subject to the same fee escalator condition imposed on the earlier map at the time it was approved. . . .

In March 1991, Kaufman & Broad acquired River Terrace from Nineveh and thereby succeeded to all rights of the former owners including those conferred by the vesting tentative subdivision maps. In October, Kaufman & Broad began applying for building permits to construct individual units at River Terrace, and was charged capital facilities fees of $4890 per unit by the City. Kaufman & Broad paid the fees under protest and subsequently brought the present action: a complaint and petition for writ of mandate seeking reimbursement of all fees paid in excess of $1434, the rate in effect when the vesting tentative subdivision map for River Terrace was deemed complete. . . .

1. The Vested Rights Doctrine

"It has long been the rule in this state and in other jurisdictions that if a property owner has performed substantial work and incurred substantial liabilities in good faith reliance upon a permit issued by the government, he acquires a vested right to complete construction in accordance with the terms of the permit. [Citations.]" (*Avco Community Developers, Inc. v. South Coast Regional Com.* (1976) 553 P.2d 546.) However, this judicially developed doctrine has generally been held to confer a vested right only at the point the property owner has obtained a building permit or other final discretionary approval, notwithstanding their earlier commitment of substantial resources to the project. . . . Consequently, the Legislature has adopted various measures which confer, at some point earlier in the development process, at least a limited right to proceed with development free from new requirements. The precise scope of this right has yet to be clearly established.

In 1982, the Legislature enacted sections 66474.2 and 65961. Section 66474.2, added to the Subdivision Map Act (§66410 et seq.), permits a local agency considering a developer's application for a tentative map to apply only those "ordinances, policies, and standards" in effect on the date the map application was deemed complete. Moreover, this protection effectively extends to the agency's consideration of the final map, which must be approved if it is in substantial compliance with the previously approved tentative map (§66474.1, *Youngblood v. Board of Supervisors* (1978) 586 P.2d 556). Section 65961 precludes a local agency, subject to certain limitations, from imposing any condition on a building permit which it could have lawfully imposed on a previously approved tentative map.

The Legislature amended the Subdivision Map Act again in 1984 to add sections 66498.1 through 66498.7, the vesting tentative map statutes. Section 66498.1 permits a developer to file a "vesting tentative map" whenever a tentative map would otherwise be required. Approval of the vesting tentative map entitles the developer, subject to certain limitations, to proceed with the project "in substantial compliance with the ordinances, policies, and standards described in

Section 66474.2," that is, those in effect when the map application was deemed complete. . . .

3. The Purpose Behind the Vesting Tentative Map Statutes

The City maintains its attachment of a fee escalator condition to the vesting tentative map for River Terrace entitled it to charge capital facilities fees increased thereafter to reflect *new* assumptions, projects, and cost estimates for future development. We disagree, concluding the City's open-ended fee policy conflicts with the intent of the vesting tentative map statutes. . . .

4. Due Process

The vesting tentative map statutes . . . incorporate a notice requirement consistent with due process. "The private sector should be able to rely upon an approved vesting tentative map prior to expending resources and incurring liabilities without the risk of having the project frustrated by subsequent action by the approving local agency. . . ." (§66498.9, subd. (b).) It follows that a developer is entitled to actual or constructive notice of the ordinances, policies, and standards with which it will be expected to comply. "Quite obviously one cannot rely on what one does not know or cannot reasonably discover. . . ."

We interpret section 66498.1 to apply this general notice requirement to a local agency seeking to pass along a fee increase imposed after a developer's rights have vested. That is, the ordinances, policies, and standards in effect when the developer's vesting tentative map is deemed complete, must include not only a general fee escalation provision but must also provide reasonable notice of the nature of the fee and the manner of its calculation. A developer about to commit substantial time and resources to a project should be able to predict with at least some degree of assurance what the fee will be when the time comes to pay it.

. . . Thus, although the City's fee policy contemplated future increases in the amount of the fees, it did not foretell the comprehensive reevaluation of the fee structure which the City was later to conduct. In fact, the policy suggested the increases would be limited to relatively modest and predictable cost of building adjustments.

The City argues at some length that Kaufman & Broad had actual or constructive notice of the fee increases later in the development process, both when the increases were approved and again when it acquired River Terrace. Be that as it may, the critical point in the process for the purposes of the vesting tentative map statutes is the date on which the map application is complete. Consequently, any notice Kaufman & Broad might have received afterward is of no particular significance to the present discussion. . . .

[I]n this case the City had no policy of charging capital facilities fees for anything other than the specific improvements identified by the Infrastructure Study Committee. Further, it had no policy of increasing the fees for any reason other than to adjust for increases in the cost of construction. Therefore, we conclude section 66498.1 conferred on Kaufman & Broad the vested right to develop its River Terrace subdivision subject only to the capital facilities fees in effect when its vesting tentative map application was deemed complete ($1434), adjusted annually according to the building cost index to reflect increases in the costs of construction.

Notes and Comments

1. *Vesting at the Tentative Map Stage.* In large mixed-use projects, there can be scores of different permit approvals from various state, local, and federal agencies. The approvals are required at various stages of development, all preceding the ultimate final building permit. The California legislature responded to the severe results that can follow under a late-vesting rule by enacting the "Vesting Tentative Subdivision" legislation applied in *Kaufman & Broad*. The Washington Supreme Court adopted a similar rule for that state by judicial decision. *Weyerhaeuser v. Pierce County*, 976 P.2d 1279, 1283 (Wash. 1999) ("developers filing a timely and complete land use application obtain a vested right to develop land in accordance with the land use laws and regulations in effect at the time of application").

The vesting tentative map legislation requires that the subdivider submit specific building plans at the time of application for a vesting tentative tract. Developers, however, frequently do not want to undertake architectural costs for the entire subdivision at the time of subdivision approval. They prefer to follow the market and apply for building permits on a tract when the projected market demand warrants such action. As a result, in those jurisdictions that might require early architectural submissions, some subdividers will continue to operate under the uncertainty of the common law late-vesting rule followed in that state, foregoing the legislative early vesting opportunity.

2. *Development Agreements.* Another response to the vesting problem is to enter into a contract that "locks in" the fee requirements applicable to a development. Specifically authorized by some state legislatures, the development agreement provides an enforceable arrangement between a regulating authority and the developer. It establishes regulatory standards and sets forth the improvements required, and it sets specific conditions and exactions required of the developer. In such an agreement, the municipality gives the developer the right to build its project; in return, the developer agrees to obligations and other conditions. *City of Casa Grande v. Tucker*, 817 P.2d 947 (Ariz. Ct. App. 1991) (development not subject to sewer capacity fees as not set out in development agreement); *Giger v. City of Omaha*, 442 N.W.2d 182 (Neb. 1989) (rejecting illegal contract zoning challenge to development agreement). The courts have generally approved of development agreements, and they are discussed in Chapter 10.

3. *The Vesting Problem in Perspective.* You have now been exposed to the vesting "problem," the policy issues involved, and a variety of proposed solutions. What solution would you recommend? When should vesting occur? If early in the process, should the right encompass an actual right to construct, or just to prevent any later regulatory changes? If a timetable is violated, what should the remedy be: mandamus only, or damages as well? Finally, should the courts recognize a right in the applicant to waive the timetable? If they do not, will local governments faced with the expiration of a mandatory deadline, and facing an automatic approval, simply deny projects? Would such actions be ethical?

4

Financing and Development of Infrastructure

A. INTRODUCTION

1. The End of the "Free Ride"

"Infrastructure" refers to the public facilities necessary to support development. Historically, these facilities have included roads, bridges, sidewalks, water and sewer lines, sewage treatment and pumping works, flood control improvements, parks, and schools. Increasingly, however, a broader range of facilities and services supporting new development have been identified. For example, communities must have police and fire services, libraries, transit, bikeways, hospitals and other health care facilities. They also must have welfare, child day care, and social service programs for the dependent. To some extent, any new development generates a demand for a number of these types of infrastructure, and to an increasing degree, municipalities are requiring developments to pay for them.

It wasn't always this way. Initially, suburban local governments lured developers with a "free ride." Through the 1950s and into the 1960s, local communities often provided developments with free or highly subsidized infrastructure. At the very least, it was assumed that tax revenues generated by the new development would cover the costs of the infrastructure to service that development. For those more expensive facilities that were beyond the locally available fiscal resources, the special assessment district was created. Under this district, the owners of all property in the district that the facility will benefit are assessed an annual charge, and that charge is used to pay off bonds issued to finance the facility's construction.

As the development process evolved, however, communities began to realize that low-density, single-family housing failed to generate sufficient tax revenues to fund the development of adequate facilities and the maintenance of quality municipal services. Communities frequently faced overcrowded schools and declining service delivery. Local property taxes were then raised during a period of rapid inflation to the point that, in some states, homeowners engaged in a "tax revolt."

The effect was to exacerbate infrastructure financing problems and force communities to cut back on services. Maintenance of parks was reduced, and libraries were placed on limited budgets, reducing hours, programs, and operating capacity. Other forces were also at work. In the post-World War II era, the federal government had provided large subsidies for highway construction, and this federally promoted road building had encouraged states and local governments to site new development near roads rather than in areas that would encourage transit. The federal government, however, began to reduce its generous funding of new roads, and with that change came an increase in local responsibility over transportation during a period of pressure on state and local budgets.

2. *Developer-Financed Infrastructure*

As a result of these forces, communities striving to provide stable, attractive environments increasingly have turned to developers and new community residents as sources of funding for infrastructure. Developers are mandated to provide or finance infrastructure such as streets, utilities, parks, and other facilities needed to service subdivisions. Developers also must make improvements in the area adjacent to the new subdivision and mitigate impacts that the project will cause, such as increases in traffic. Finally, communities have looked to developers to support the expansion of off-site area facilities, such as schools, sewer treatment plants or transit works.

Courts typically have sustained the imposition of on-site costs such as utilities, streets, and sidewalks as conditions of permit approval. In addition, they have routinely approved the mandatory dedication of portions of the subdivision for parks, schools, and other public facilities to support the development. More difficult problems have arisen as communities ask developers to pay exactions for off-site improvements, frequently in the form of so-called impact fees. These fees are charges set according to the number of residential dwelling units or the square footage of commercial and industrial projects. They are imposed on developers at a rate that is designed to fund the expansion of infrastructure needed to accommodate a proposed project. See generally 2 James A. Kushner, Subdivision Law and Growth Management, ch. 6 (2d ed. 2001 and Supp. 2002).

3. *State Law Tests for Infrastructure Exactions*

Until the mid-1980s, the United States Supreme Court showed no interest in infrastructure finance issues; instead, the state courts labored with the issues of fairness and with the measurement of project impacts raised by such cases. The states generally adopted one of three models for reviewing development conditions and exactions. The most rigorous standard was developed by the Illinois courts, which required public authorities to demonstrate that the need for conditions imposed and for infrastructure to be financed was "uniquely attributable" to the proposed project. *Pioneer Trust & Savings Bank v. Mount Prospect*, 176 N.E.2d 799, 802 (Ill. 1961). The *Pioneer Trust* "uniquely attributable" test prohibited charging developers where other developments generated the demand for the infrastructure improvement or non-project residents would enjoy the benefits from the conditions imposed.

At the opposite extreme were states, such as California, that merely required a "reasonable" connection between the proposed project and the condition such that project residents would benefit from the improvement and the project would contribute to the demand for it. *See Associated Home Builders v. City of Walnut Creek*, 484 P.2d 606 (Cal. 1971). Under this test courts would uphold conditions that were more tenuously connected to the project and its actual impacts.

Despite the distinct differences in the standards followed in the states, most decisions from courts across the country employed the general principle that development conditions should bear a "rational nexus" to demands generated by the project. In addition, a majority of state legislatures passed laws either restricting developer conditions, authorizing the imposition of certain types of conditions (as in the case of impact fees), or establishing substantive standards for the adequacy of infrastructure (as in the case of Florida). *See* Fla. Stat. Ann. §163.3202(2)(g) (West 2000).

4. *The Constitutionalization of Infrastructure Finance*

Perhaps in response to these trends toward imposing infrastructure costs on developers, the United States Supreme Court suddenly re-entered the picture. In a 1987 decision, *Nollan v. California Coastal Commission*, 483 U.S. 825, the Court restricted the authority of government to impose conditions on discretionary permits, such as approvals of subdivisions, site plans, variances, conditional rezonings, and use permit approvals. Seven years later the Court sought to further refine the constitutional standard in *Dolan v. City of Tigard*, 512 U.S. 374 (1994). As a result of these decisions and of the cities' continual push to extend exactions, the policy, legal, and constitutional issues surrounding exactions form one of the most dynamic challenges facing urban America today.

In *Nollan* the Court established that the Takings Clause of the Fifth Amendment of the United States Constitution requires an "essential nexus" between the condition imposed and impact of the project that it is intended to alleviate. The essential nexus test simply requires that the condition must actually serve a legitimate state police power interest.

In *Dolan*, the Court focused on the constitutionally required "fit" between the condition imposed on the project and the needs generated by the proposed project. Finding the Illinois "uniquely attributable" test from *Pioneer Trust* too demanding and the California "reasonableness" standard overly generous, the Court established a new test of "rough proportionality." However, although the test is phrased in new language, it seems to follow what appears to have been the nearly universal "rational nexus" test developed by the prior state court jurisprudence. Finally, the Court also required local governments to undertake an "individualized determination" of the need for infrastructure generated by the proposed project.

While *Nollan* and *Dolan* brought some measure of certainty to the question of a local government's power to impose conditions, they left some important questions unsettled. Both cases involved government requirements that a landowner dedicate property. In many instances, however, local governments impose fees upon developers rather than (or in addition to) requiring dedications. Does the *Nollan* and *Dolan* framework apply to fees as well as dedications? Furthermore, both cases involved situations in which the regulatory agencies acted in an adjudicative fashion. Often fees or exactions are imposed legislatively by local governments. The question here is whether the underlying basis for the heightened scrutiny found in *Dolan* is present when the fee or exaction is set legislatively and applies across the board. The importance of these questions leads to the conclusion that the Supreme Court will have to decide them in the relatively near future.

5. Imposition of Costs and the Marketplace

There is little evidence to suggest that the Supreme Court's new standards have markedly halted or reduced the trend of imposing the costs of new development upon developers and new residents. Whether developers, in turn, can pass those costs on to the ultimate homebuyers depends upon economics and the state of competition in the local market. Where housing demand is high, costs can be shifted from the developers onto home buyers through higher home prices. However, where demand is weak and home developers must compete strenuously for buyers, the market may preclude a developer from raising home prices to reflect exactions for fear of placing its development at a competitive disadvantage with lower priced, comparable developments.

In the near future, further changes in the financing of infrastructure can be expected. As a result of budgetary forces, state and local government will be under increasing pressure to find the resources needed to develop and maintain quality supporting infrastructure. Privatization of some services will occur, and governments increasingly will charge "user fees" to individuals who actually utilize specific services. Also foreseeable is the enhanced dependence on "pay as you go" financing that will attempt to shift the cost of growth to developers and new residents. Although *Nollan* and *Dolan* were victories by development interests seeking to resist the imposition of exactions, the principles established by the cases nonetheless validate developer-financed infrastructure.

6. Conflicts and Confrontation

It remains to be determined whether the constitutional doctrine of these cases will result in greater rationality and fairness in the development process or will further contribute to the inefficiency of local development planning and control. One thing that is certain, however, is that infrastructure finance will remain controversial. Infrastructure financing, like the subdivision review process, is another situation in which the land use planning process is charged with responsibilities that conflict with both political reality and the pressures of democratic government. Very few communities adopt, through their legislative bodies, a binding capital facilities plan and an accompanying budget that reflects the plan and ensures that the extension of infrastructure is consistent with growth projections. The reason is simple: citizens and, derivatively, their political representatives generally oppose increases in taxes despite rapidly escalating costs associated with facilities construction and service maintenance.

Conflicts in infrastructure financing are generating new confrontations and potential litigation. For example, debates about growth are likely to engage not only the usual combatants — homeowners, environmentalists, low income housing advocates, and public agencies — but also a new list of adversaries. The situation today reflects escalating competition between neighborhoods and regions, as often poor ethnic neighborhoods compete for public services, transit resources, and other infrastructure that supports job development. In addition, infrastructure service providers, such as school boards, sewer districts, and water agencies, are likely to be involved and to initiate litigation as a means of protecting their interests. You will see these conflicts reflected in the cases and notes in this chapter.

B. *NOLLAN* AND *DOLAN*: THE SUPREME COURT FRAMEWORK

Prior to the Supreme Court's decisions in *Nollan v. California Coastal Commission* and *Dolan v. City of Tigard*, the law of exactions was largely state-made. The *Nollan* and *Dolan* decisions, then, marked a sea-change in this area of jurisprudence.

■ NOLLAN v. CALIFORNIA COASTAL COMMISSION

483 U.S. 825 (1987)

JUSTICE SCALIA delivered the opinion of the Court. . . .

I

The Nollans own a beachfront lot in Ventura County, California. A quarter-mile north of their property is Faria County Park, an oceanside public park with a public beach and recreation area. Another public beach area, known locally as "the Cove," lies 1800 feet south of their lot. A concrete seawall approximately eight feet high separates the beach portion of the Nollans' property from the rest of the lot. The historic mean high tide line determines the lot's oceanside boundary.

The Nollans originally leased their property with an option to buy. The building on the lot was a small bungalow, totaling 504 square feet, which for a time they rented to summer vacationers. After years of rental use, however, the building had fallen into disrepair, and could no longer be rented out.

The Nollans' option to purchase was conditioned on their promise to demolish the bungalow and replace it. In order to do so . . . they were required to obtain a coastal development permit from the California Coastal Commission. On February 25, 1982, they submitted a permit application to the Commission in which they proposed to demolish the existing structure and replace it with a three-bedroom house in keeping with the rest of the neighborhood.

The Nollans were informed that their application had been placed on the administrative calendar, and that the Commission staff had recommended that the permit be granted subject to the condition that they allow the public an easement to pass across a portion of their property bounded by the mean high tide line on one side, and their seawall on the other side. This would make it easier for the public to get to Faria County Park and the Cove. The Nollans protested imposition of the condition, but the Commission overruled their objections and granted the permit subject to their recordation of a deed restriction granting the easement.

On June 3, 1982, the Nollans filed a petition for writ of administrative mandamus asking the Ventura County Superior Court to invalidate the access condition. . . . The court . . . remanded the case to the Commission for a full evidentiary hearing on that issue.

On remand, the Commission held a public hearing, after which it made further factual findings and reaffirmed its imposition of the condition. It found that the new house would increase blockage of the view of the ocean, thus contributing to the development of "a 'wall' of residential structures" that would prevent the public "psychologically . . . from realizing a stretch of coastline exists nearby that they have every right to visit." The new house would also increase private use of the shorefront. These effects of construction of the house, along with other area development, would cumulatively "burden the public's ability to traverse to and along the shorefront." Therefore the Commission could properly require the Nollans to offset that burden by providing additional lateral access to the public beaches in the form of an easement across their property. The Commission also noted that it had similarly conditioned 43 out of 60 coastal development permits along the same tract of land, and that of the 17 not so conditioned, 14 had been approved when the Commission did not have administrative regulations in place allowing imposition of the condition, and the remaining 3 had not involved shorefront property.

The Nollans filed a supplemental petition for a writ of administrative mandamus with the Superior Court, in which they argued that imposition of the access condition violated the Takings Clause of the Fifth Amendment, as incorporated against the States by the Fourteenth Amendment. . . .

II

Had California simply required the Nollans to make an easement across their beachfront available to the public on a permanent basis in order to increase public access to the beach, rather than conditioning their permit to rebuild their house on their agreeing to do so, we have no doubt there would have been a taking. To say that the appropriation of a public easement across a landowner's premises does not constitute the taking of a property interest but rather (as JUSTICE BRENNAN contends) "a mere restriction on its use," is to use words in a manner that deprives them of all their ordinary meaning. Indeed, one of the principal uses of the eminent domain power is to assure that the government be able to require conveyance of just such interests, so long as it pays for them. J. Sackman, 1 Nichols on Eminent Domain §2.1[1] (Rev. 3d ed. 1985), 2 *id.*, §5.01[5]; see 1 *id.*, §1.42[9], 2 *id.*, §6.14. Perhaps because the point is so obvious, we have never been confronted with a controversy that required us to rule upon it, but our cases' analysis of the effect of other governmental action leads to the same conclusion. We have repeatedly held that, as to property reserved by its owner for private use, "the right to exclude [others is] 'one of the most essential sticks in the bundle of rights that are commonly characterized as property.'" *Loretto v. Teleprompter Manhattan CATV Corp.*,

458 U.S. 419, 433 (1982), quoting *Kaiser Aetna v. United States*, 444 U.S. 164, 176 (1979). . . .

Given, then, that requiring uncompensated conveyance of the easement outright would violate the Fourteenth Amendment, the question becomes whether requiring it to be conveyed as a condition for issuing a land-use permit alters the outcome. We have long recognized that land-use regulation does not effect a taking if it "substantially advance[s] legitimate state interests" and does not "den[y] an owner economically viable use of his land." . . . Our cases have not elaborated on the standards for determining what constitutes a "legitimate state interest" or what type of connection between the regulation and the state interest satisfies the requirement that the former "substantially advance" the latter.[3] They have made clear, however, that a broad range of governmental purposes and regulations satisfies these requirements. The Commission argues that among these permissible purposes are protecting the public's ability to see the beach, assisting the public in overcoming the "psychological barrier" to using the beach created by a developed shorefront, and preventing congestion on the public beaches. We assume, without deciding, that this is so—in which case the Commission unquestionably would be able to deny the Nollans their permit outright if their new house (alone, or by reason of the cumulative impact produced in conjunction with other construction) would substantially impede these purposes, unless the denial would interfere so drastically with the Nollans' use of their property as to constitute a taking.

The Commission argues that a permit condition that serves the same legitimate police-power purpose as a refusal to issue the permit should not be found to be a taking if the refusal to issue the permit would not constitute a taking. We agree. Thus, if the Commission attached to the permit some condition that would have protected the public's ability to see the beach notwithstanding construction of the new house—for example, a height limitation, a width restriction, or a ban on fences—so long as the Commission could have exercised its police power (as we have assumed it could) to forbid construction of the house altogether, imposition of the condition would also be constitutional. Moreover (and here we come closer to the facts of the present case), the condition would be constitutional even if it consisted of the requirement that the Nollans provide a viewing spot on their property for passersby with whose sighting of the ocean their new house would interfere. Although such a requirement, constituting a permanent grant of continuous access to the property, would have to be considered a taking if it were not attached to a development permit, the Commission's assumed power to forbid construction of

3. Contrary to Justice Brennan's claim, our opinions do not establish that these standards are the same as those applied to due process or equal protection claims. To the contrary, our verbal formulations in the takings field have generally been quite different. We have required that the regulation "substantially advance" the "legitimate state interest" sought to be achieved, *Agins v. Tiburon*, 447 U.S. 255, 260 (1980), not that "the State '*could rationally have decided*' that the measure adopted might achieve the State's objective." Justice Brennan relies principally on an equal protection case, *Minnesota v. Clover Leaf Creamery Co., supra*, and two substantive due process cases, *Williamson v. Lee Optical of Oklahoma, Inc.*, 348 U.S. 483, 487-488 (1955), and *Day-Brite Lighting, Inc. v. Missouri*, 342 U.S. 421, 423 (1952), in support of the standards he would adopt. But there is no reason to believe (and the language of our cases gives some reason to disbelieve) that so long as the regulation of property is at issue the standards for takings challenges, due process challenges, and equal protection challenges are identical; any more than there is any reason to believe that so long as the regulation of speech is at issue the standards for due process challenges, equal protection challenges, and First Amendment challenges are identical. *Goldblatt v. Hempstead*, 369 U.S. 590 (1962), does appear to assume that the inquiries are the same, but that assumption is inconsistent with the formulations of our later cases.

the house in order to protect the public's view of the beach must surely include the power to condition construction upon some concession by the owner, even a concession of property rights, that serves the same end. If a prohibition designed to accomplish that purpose would be a legitimate exercise of the police power rather than a taking, it would be strange to conclude that providing the owner an alternative to that prohibition which accomplishes the same purpose is not.

The evident constitutional propriety disappears, however, if the condition substituted for the prohibition utterly fails to further the end advanced as the justification for the prohibition. When that essential nexus is eliminated, the situation becomes the same as if California law forbade shouting fire in a crowded theater, but granted dispensations to those willing to contribute $100 to the state treasury. While a ban on shouting fire can be a core exercise of the State's police power to protect the public safety, and can thus meet even our stringent standards for regulation of speech, adding the unrelated condition alters the purpose to one which, while it may be legitimate, is inadequate to sustain the ban. Therefore, even though, in a sense, requiring a $100 tax contribution in order to shout fire is a lesser restriction on speech than an outright ban, it would not pass constitutional muster. Similarly here, the lack of nexus between the condition and the original purpose of the building restriction converts that purpose to something other than what it was. The purpose then becomes, quite simply, the obtaining of an easement to serve some valid governmental purpose, but without payment of compensation. Whatever may be the outer limits of "legitimate state interests" in the takings and land-use context, this is not one of them. In short, unless the permit condition serves the same governmental purpose as the development ban, the building restriction is not a valid regulation of land use but "an out-and-out plan of extortion."

III

The Commission claims that it concedes as much, and that we may sustain the condition at issue here by finding that it is reasonably related to the public need or burden that the Nollans' new house creates or to which it contributes. We can accept, for purposes of discussion, the Commission's proposed test as to how close a "fit" between the condition and the burden is required, because we find that this case does not meet even the most untailored standards. The Commission's principal contention to the contrary essentially turns on a play on the word "access." The Nollans' new house, the Commission found, will interfere with "visual access" to the beach. That in turn (along with other shorefront development) will interfere with the desire of people who drive past the Nollans' house to use the beach, thus creating a "psychological barrier" to "access." The Nollans' new house will also, by a process not altogether clear from the Commission's opinion but presumably potent enough to more than offset the effects of the psychological barrier, increase the use of the public beaches, thus creating the need for more "access." These burdens on "access" would be alleviated by a requirement that the Nollans provide "lateral access" to the beach.

Rewriting the argument to eliminate the play on words makes clear that there is nothing to it. It is quite impossible to understand how a requirement that people already on the public beaches be able to walk across the Nollans' property reduces any obstacles to viewing the beach created by the new house. It is also impossible to understand how it lowers any "psychological barrier" to using the public beaches, or how it helps to remedy any additional congestion on them caused by construction of the Nollans' new house. We therefore find that the Commission's imposition of the permit condition cannot be treated as an exercise of its land-use power for any of these purposes.[6] Our conclusion on this point is consistent with the approach taken by every other court that has considered the question, with the exception of the California state courts. . . .

We do not share [dissenting] JUSTICE BRENNAN's confidence that the Commission "should have little difficulty in the future in utilizing its expertise to demonstrate a specific connection between provisions for access and burdens on access," that will avoid the effect of today's decision. We view the Fifth Amendment's Property Clause to be more than a pleading requirement, and compliance with it to be more than an exercise in cleverness and imagination. As indicated earlier, our cases describe the condition for abridgment of property rights through the police power as a "*substantial* advanc[ing]" of a legitimate state interest. We are inclined to be particularly careful about the adjective where the actual conveyance of property is made a condition to the lifting of a land-use restriction, since in that context there is heightened risk that the purpose is avoidance of the compensation requirement, rather than the stated police-power objective.

We are left, then, with the Commission's justification for the access requirement unrelated to land-use regulation:

> Finally, the Commission notes that there are several existing provisions of pass and repass lateral access benefits already given by past Faria Beach Tract applicants as a result of prior coastal permit decisions. The access required as a condition of this permit is part of a comprehensive program to provide continuous public access along Faria Beach as the lots undergo development or redevelopment.

That is simply an expression of the Commission's belief that the public interest will be served by a continuous strip of publicly accessible beach along the coast. The Commission may well be right that it is a good idea, but that does not establish that the Nollans (and other coastal residents) alone can be compelled to contribute to its realization. Rather, California is free to advance its "comprehensive program," if it wishes, by using its power of eminent domain for this "public purpose," see U.S. Const., Amdt. 5; but if it wants an easement across the Nollans' property, it must pay for it.

Reversed.

6. As JUSTICE BRENNAN notes, the Commission also argued that the construction of the new house would "'increase private use immediately adjacent to public tidelands,'" which in turn might result in more disputes between the Nollans and the public as to the location of the boundary. That risk of boundary disputes, however, is inherent in the right to exclude others from one's property, and the construction here can no more justify mandatory dedication of a sort of "buffer zone" in order to avoid boundary disputes than can the construction of an addition to a single-family house near a public street. Moreover, a buffer zone has a boundary as well, and unless that zone is a "no-man's land" that is off limits for both neighbors (which is of course not the case here) its creation achieves nothing except to shift the location of the boundary dispute further on to the private owner's land. It is true that in the distinctive situation of the Nollans' property the seawall could be established as a clear demarcation of the public easement. But since not all of the lands to which this land-use condition applies have such a convenient reference point, the avoidance of boundary disputes is, even more obviously than the others, a made-up purpose of the regulation.

Notes and Comments

1. *Holding Versus Dicta.* Because the Supreme Court's takings jurisprudence can vary over time in its inclinations, it is important for the student to clearly identify the actual holding in a case like *Nollan*. Which statements in Justice Scalia's opinion constitute the holding, and which statements can be characterized as dicta? Consider, for example, the discussions of (1) essential nexus, (2) remaining economic value, (3) whether the condition seeks to mitigate a problem that constitutes a basis to deny the permit, (4) the suggestion of some required nexus between the condition and the need for that condition generated by the proposed project, and (5) the use of language calling for "higher scrutiny" by the courts in takings cases.

2. *Justifications for the Condition.* Did the coastal commission's action attempt to serve any interests other than the psychological concerns cited by Justice Scalia? Would articulation of a broader interest have changed the outcome of the case? Consider interests such as the desire to provide year-round public access, to halt conflicts between beach users and homeowners, to enhance beach access, to provide use and recreation opportunities, and any others you might conjure up.

3. *Easement Plus Viewing Platform?* Justice Scalia suggests that if the *Nollan* home were to block the view of the ocean from the coast highway, the coastal commission could condition the permit on a requirement that the Nollans construct an expensive viewing platform and invite the public on their property to enjoy the scenery. Would the commission be justified in requiring the Nollans to provide a perpendicular easement from the coast highway to the beach to allow public access? In California, the public enjoys rights of access to the ocean and beach areas under the public trust doctrine. *State v. Superior Court of Lake County*, 625 P.2d 239 (Cal. 1981) (nontidal lands between low and high water are held in public trust for navigation and recreation); *Gion v. City of Santa Cruz*, 465 P.2d 50 (Cal. 1970) (tidal waters).

In *La Costa Beach Homeowners Assn. v. California Coastal Comm'n*, 124 Cal. Rptr. 2d 618 (Ct. App. 2002), the commission conditioned permits on a requirement that "[n]o less than 20% of the lineal frontage of the project site shall be maintained as a public view corridor from Pacific Coast Highway to the Pacific Ocean." *Id.* at 622. However, it also provided that the applicant could seek to amend the permit to provide off-site mitigation of the public view corridor. When the applicants sought and received amendments substituting a view corridor on an undeveloped parcel less than a mile away, residents living near that "mitigation" parcel challenged the commission's action. The court of appeal rejected the argument that the acceptance of such offsite mitigation was not within the commission's power. Do you see why the application of *Nollan* was not at issue?

4. *The Rationale for Permit Denial.* In dicta, Justice Scalia agreed with an argument by the coastal commission that a permit condition would be valid if it served the same legitimate police power purpose as the refusal to issue the permit. For example, in *Garipay*, reprinted in Chapter 3, the court upheld the denial of subdivision approval because the road to the subdivision was too narrow and on an incline that would make access in wintertime difficult. Would the Scalia rationale suggest that the town might have conditioned approval on the developer's improving the road to county standards? In *Goss v. City of Little Rock*, 151 F.3d 861 (8th Cir. 1998), *cert. denied*, 526 U.S. 1050 (1999), the Eighth Circuit rejected a condition to

mitigate a problem that would ostensibly have justified denial of the zone change application. In essence, the court's holding indicated that the city should have denied an application for rezoning rather than impose a mitigating condition.

5. *Exaction-Induced Appreciation in Property Value*. Was the Nollan property enhanced in value by the condition? If all beachfront property owners provide lateral easements along the beach, each owner would enjoy an easement to walk or jog to the north and south of their property. Under *Nollan*, however, they do not have this opportunity; they can cross their neighbors' property during periods of high tide only if they obtain individual permission.

On remand, if the coastal commission insists on the taking of a lateral easement, how much would it have to pay? Could you find a comparable lateral easement transaction? What if expert appraisers testify that the property value is actually enhanced due to the "reciprocity of advantage" now enjoyed by the Nollans because of the availability of beach walk easements?

The following case, *Dolan v. City of Tigard*, addresses the quantitative relationship between the demand for infrastructure generated by the project and the cost of any condition or exaction imposed.

DOLAN v. CITY OF TIGARD
512 U.S. 374 (1994)

Chief Justice REHNQUIST delivered the opinion of the Court. . . .

Petitioner Florence Dolan owns a plumbing and electric supply store located on Main Street in the Central Business District of the city. The store covers approximately 9700 square feet on the eastern side of a 1.67-acre parcel, which includes a gravel parking lot. Fanno Creek flows through the southwestern corner of the lot and along its western boundary. The year-round flow of the creek renders the area within the creek's 100-year floodplain virtually unusable for commercial development. The city's comprehensive plan includes the Fanno Creek floodplain as part of the city's greenway system.

Petitioner applied to the city for a permit to redevelop the site. Her proposed plans called for nearly doubling the size of the store to 17,600 square feet, and paving a 39-space parking lot. The existing store, located on the opposite side of the parcel, would be razed in sections as construction progressed on the new building. In the second phase of the project, petitioner proposed to build an additional structure on the northeast side of the site for complementary businesses, and to provide more parking. The proposed expansion and intensified use are consistent with the city's zoning scheme in the Central Business District.

The City Planning Commission granted petitioner's permit application subject to conditions imposed by the city's Community Development Code (CDC). The CDC establishes the following standard for site development review approval:

> Where landfill and/or development is allowed within and adjacent to the 100-year floodplain, the city shall require the dedication of sufficient open land area for greenway adjoining and within the floodplain. This area shall include portions at a suitable elevation for the construction of a pedestrian/bicycle pathway within the floodplain in accordance with the adopted pedestrian/bicycle plan.

Thus, the Commission required that petitioner dedicate the portion of her property lying within the 100-year floodplain for improvement of a storm drainage system along Fanno Creek and that she dedicate an additional 15-foot strip of land adjacent to the floodplain as a pedestrian/bicycle pathway. The dedication required by that condition encompasses approximately 7000 square feet, or roughly 10% of the property. In accordance with city practice, petitioner could rely on the dedicated property to meet the 15% open space and landscaping requirement mandated by the city's zoning scheme. The city would bear the cost of maintaining a landscaped buffer between the dedicated area and the new store. . . .

Petitioner contends that the city has forced her to choose between the building permit and her right under the Fifth Amendment to just compensation for the public easements. Petitioner does not quarrel with the city's authority to exact some forms of dedication as a condition for the grant of a building permit, but challenges the showing made by the city to justify these exactions. She argues that the city has identified "no special benefits" conferred on her, and has not identified any "special quantifiable burdens" created by her new store that would justify the particular dedications required from her which are not required from the public at large.

III

In evaluating petitioner's claim, we must first determine whether the "essential nexus" exists between the "legitimate state interest" and the permit condition exacted by the city. *Nollan* . . . If we find that a nexus exists, we must then decide the required degree of connection between the exactions and the projected impact of the proposed development. We were not required to reach this question in *Nollan*, because we concluded that the connection did not meet even the loosest standard . . . Here, however, we must decide this question.

A

We addressed the essential nexus question in *Nollan*. . . .

. . . Undoubtedly, the prevention of flooding along Fanno Creek and the reduction of traffic congestion in the Central Business District qualify as the type of legitimate public purposes we have upheld . . . It seems equally obvious that a nexus exists between preventing flooding along Fanno Creek and limiting development within the creek's 100-year floodplain. Petitioner proposes to double the size of her retail store and to pave her now-gravel parking lot, thereby expanding the impervious surface on the property and increasing the amount of stormwater run-off into Fanno Creek.

The same may be said for the city's attempt to reduce traffic congestion by providing for alternative means of transportation. In theory, a pedestrian/bicycle pathway provides a useful alternative means of transportation for workers and shoppers: "Pedestrians and bicyclists occupying dedicated spaces for walking and/or bicycling . . . remove potential vehicles from streets, resulting in an overall improvement in total transportation system flow." . . .

B

The second part of our analysis requires us to determine whether the degree of the exactions demanded by the city's permit conditions bear the required relationship to the projected impact of petitioner's proposed development. *Nollan*, quoting *Penn Central Transp. Co. v. New York City*, 438 U.S. 104, 127 (1978) ("'[A] use restriction may constitute a taking if not reasonably necessary to the effectuation of a substantial government purpose'"). . . .

The city required that petitioner dedicate "to the city as Greenway all portions of the site that fall within the existing 100-year floodplain [of Fanno Creek] . . . and all property 15 feet above [the floodplain] boundary." In addition, the city demanded that the retail store be designed so as not to intrude into the greenway area. The city relies on the Commission's rather tentative findings that increased stormwater flow from petitioner's property "can only add to the public need to manage the [floodplain] for drainage purposes" to support its conclusion that the "requirement of dedication of the floodplain area on the site is related to the applicant's plan to intensify development on the site."

The city made the following specific findings relevant to the pedestrian/bicycle pathway:

> In addition, the proposed expanded use of this site is anticipated to generate additional vehicular traffic thereby increasing congestion on nearby collector and arterial streets. Creation of a convenient, safe pedestrian/bicycle pathway system as an alternative means of transportation could offset some of the traffic demand on these nearby streets and lessen the increase in traffic congestion.

The question for us is whether these findings are constitutionally sufficient to justify the conditions imposed by the city on petitioner's building permit. Since state courts have been dealing with this question a good deal longer than we have, we turn to representative decisions made by them.

In some States, very generalized statements as to the necessary connection between the required dedication and the proposed development seem to suffice. We think this standard is too lax to adequately protect petitioner's right to just compensation if her property is taken for a public purpose.

Other state courts require a very exacting correspondence, described as the "specifi[c] and uniquely attributable" test. The Supreme Court of Illinois first developed this test in *Pioneer Trust & Savings Bank v. Mount Prospect*, 22 Ill. 2d 375, 380, 176 N.E.2d 799, 802 (1961). Under this standard, if the local government cannot demonstrate that its exaction is directly proportional to the specifically created need, the exaction becomes "a veiled exercise of the power of eminent domain and a confiscation of private property behind the defense of police regulations." *Id.*, at 381, 176 N.E.2d, at 802. We do not think the Federal Constitution requires such exacting scrutiny, given the nature of the interests involved.

A number of state courts have taken an intermediate position, requiring the municipality to show a "reasonable relationship" between the required dedication and the impact of the proposed development. Typical is the Supreme Court of Nebraska's opinion in *Simpson v. North Platte*, 206 Neb. 240, 245, 292 N.W.2d 297, 301 (1980), where that court stated:

> The distinction, therefore, which must be made between an appropriate exercise of the police power and an improper exercise of eminent domain is whether the requirement has some reasonable relationship or nexus to the use to which the property is being made or is merely being used as an excuse for taking property simply because at that particular moment the landowner is asking the city for some license or permit.

Thus, the court held that a city may not require a property owner to dedicate private property for some future public use as a condition of obtaining a building permit when such future use is not "occasioned by the construction sought to be permitted." . . .

Some form of the reasonable relationship test has been adopted in many other jurisdictions. . . .

We think the "reasonable relationship" test adopted by a majority of the state courts is closer to the federal constitutional norm than either of those previously discussed. But we do not adopt it as such, partly because the term "reasonable relationship" seems confusingly similar to the term "rational basis" which describes the minimal level of scrutiny under the Equal Protection Clause of the Fourteenth Amendment. We think a term such as "rough proportionality" best encapsulates what we hold to be the requirement of the Fifth Amendment. No precise mathematical calculation is required, but the city must make some sort of individualized determination that the required dedication is related both in nature and extent to the impact of the proposed development.[8]

Justice STEVENS' dissent relies upon a law review article for the proposition that the city's conditional demands for part of petitioner's property are "a species of business regulation that heretofore warranted a strong presumption of constitutional validity." But simply denominating a governmental measure as a "business regulation" does not immunize it from constitutional challenge on the grounds that it violates a provision of the Bill of Rights. In *Marshall v. Barlow's, Inc.*, 436 U.S. 307 (1978), we held that a statute authorizing a warrantless search of business premises in order to detect OSHA violations violated the Fourth Amendment. . . . And in *Central Hudson Gas & Electric Corp. v. Public Service Comm'n of N.Y.*, 447 U.S. 557 (1980), we held that an order of the New York Public Service Commission, designed to cut down the use of electricity because of a fuel shortage, violated the First Amendment insofar as it prohibited advertising by a utility company to promote the use of electricity. We see no reason why the Takings Clause of the Fifth Amendment, as much a part of the Bill of Rights as the First Amendment or Fourth Amendment, should be relegated to the status of a poor relation in these comparable circumstances. We turn now to analysis of whether the findings relied upon by the city here, first with respect to the floodplain easement, and second with respect to the pedestrian/bicycle path, satisfied these requirements.

It is axiomatic that increasing the amount of impervious surface will increase the quantity and rate of storm-water flow from petitioner's property. Therefore, keeping the floodplain open and free from development would likely confine the pressures on Fanno Creek created by petitioner's development. In fact, because petitioner's property lies within the Central Business District, the Community

8. Justice STEVENS' dissent takes us to task for placing the burden on the city to justify the required dedication. He is correct in arguing that in evaluating most generally applicable zoning regulations, the burden properly rests on the party challenging the regulation to prove that it constitutes an arbitrary regulation of property rights. *See, e.g., Euclid v. Ambler Realty Co.*, 272 U.S. 365 (1926). Here, by contrast, the city made an adjudicative decision to condition petitioner's application for a building permit on an individual parcel. In this situation, the burden properly rests on the city . . . This conclusion is not, as he suggests, undermined by our decision in *Moore v. East Cleveland*, 431 U.S. 494, 97 S. Ct. 1932 (1977), in which we struck down a housing ordinance that limited occupancy of a dwelling unit to members of a single family as violating the Due Process Clause of the Fourteenth Amendment. The ordinance at issue in *Moore* intruded on choices concerning family living arrangements, an area in which the usual deference to the legislature was found to be inappropriate. . . .

Development Code already required that petitioner leave 15% of it as open space and the undeveloped floodplain would have nearly satisfied that requirement. But the city demanded more—it not only wanted petitioner not to build in the floodplain, but it also wanted petitioner's property along Fanno Creek for its Greenway system. The city has never said why a public greenway, as opposed to a private one, was required in the interest of flood control.

The difference to petitioner, of course, is the loss of her ability to exclude others. As we have noted, this right to exclude others is "one of the most essential sticks in the bundle of rights that are commonly characterized as property." *Kaiser Aetna*, 444 U.S., at 176. It is difficult to see why recreational visitors trampling along petitioner's floodplain easement are sufficiently related to the city's legitimate interest in reducing flooding problems along Fanno Creek, and the city has not attempted to make any individualized determination to support this part of its request.

The city contends that recreational easement along the Greenway is only ancillary to the city's chief purpose in controlling flood hazards. It further asserts that unlike the residential property at issue in *Nollan*, petitioner's property is commercial in character and therefore, her right to exclude others is compromised. . . . The city maintains that "[t]here is nothing to suggest that preventing [petitioner] from prohibiting [the easements] will unreasonably impair the value of [her] property as a [retail store]."

Admittedly, petitioner wants to build a bigger store to attract members of the public to her property. She also wants, however, to be able to control the time and manner in which they enter . . . Petitioner would lose all rights to regulate the time in which the public entered onto the Greenway, regardless of any interference it might pose with her retail store. Her right to exclude would not be regulated, it would be eviscerated.

If petitioner's proposed development had somehow encroached on existing greenway space in the city, it would have been reasonable to require petitioner to provide some alternative greenway space for the public either on her property or elsewhere. See *Nollan*, 483 U.S., at 836. . . . But that is not the case here. We conclude that the findings upon which the city relies do not show the required reasonable relationship between the floodplain easement and the petitioner's proposed new building.

With respect to the pedestrian/bicycle pathway, we have no doubt that the city was correct in finding that the larger retail sales facility proposed by petitioner will increase traffic on the streets of the Central Business District. The city estimates that the proposed development would generate roughly 435 additional trips per day.[9] Dedications for streets, sidewalks, and other public ways are generally reasonable exactions to avoid excessive congestion from a proposed property use. But on the record before us, the city has not met its burden of demonstrating that the additional number of vehicle and bicycle trips generated by the petitioner's development reasonably relate to the city's requirement for a dedication of the pedestrian/bicycle pathway easement. The city simply found that the creation of the pathway "could offset some of the traffic demand . . . and lessen the increase in traffic congestion."

9. The city uses a weekday average trip rate of 53.21 trips per 1000 square feet. Additional Trips Generated = 53.21 × (17,600-9720).

As Justice Peterson of the Supreme Court of Oregon explained in his dissenting opinion, however, "[t]he findings of fact that the bicycle pathway system '*could* offset some of the traffic demand' is a far cry from a finding that the bicycle pathway system *will*, or is *likely to*, offset some of the traffic demand." No precise mathematical calculation is required, but the city must make some effort to quantify its findings in support of the dedication for the pedestrian/bicycle pathway beyond the conclusory statement that it could offset some of the traffic demand generated.

IV

Cities have long engaged in the commendable task of land use planning, made necessary by increasing urbanization particularly in metropolitan areas such as Portland. The city's goals of reducing flooding hazards and traffic congestion, and providing for public greenways, are laudable, but there are outer limits to how this may be done. "A strong public desire to improve the public condition [will not] warrant achieving the desire by a shorter cut than the constitutional way of paying for the change." *Pennsylvania Coal*, 206 U.S. at 416. . . .

Justice STEVENS with whom Justice BLACKMUN and Justice GINSBURG join, dissenting. . . .

III

Applying its new standard, the Court finds two defects in the city's case. . . . Even under the Court's new rule, both defects are, at most, nothing more than harmless error.

In her objections to the floodplain condition, Dolan made no effort to demonstrate that the dedication of that portion of her property would be any more onerous than a simple prohibition against any development on that portion of her property. Given the commercial character of both the existing and the proposed use of the property as a retail store, it seems likely that potential customers "trampling along petitioner's floodplain" . . . are more valuable than a useless parcel of vacant land. Moreover, the duty to pay taxes and the responsibility for potential tort liability may well make ownership of the fee interest in useless land a liability rather than an asset. That may explain why Dolan never conceded that she could be prevented from building on the floodplain. The City Attorney also pointed out that absent a dedication, property owners would be required to "build on their own land" and "with their own money" a storage facility for the water runoff. Dolan apparently "did have that option," but chose not to seek it. . . .

The Court's rejection of the bike path condition amounts to nothing more than a play on words. Everyone agrees that the bike path "could" offset some of the increased traffic flow that the larger store will generate, but the findings do not unequivocally state that it *will* do so, or tell us just how many cyclists will replace motorists. Predictions on such matters are inherently nothing more than estimates. Certainly the assumption that there will be an offsetting benefit here is entirely reasonable and should suffice whether it amounts to 100 percent, 35 percent, or only 5 percent of the increase in automobile traffic that would otherwise occur. If the Court proposes to have the federal judiciary micro-manage state decisions of this kind, it is indeed extending its welcome mat to a significant new class of litigants. Although there is no reason to believe that state courts have failed to rise to the task, property owners have surely found a new friend today.

IV

The Court has made a serious error by abandoning the traditional presumption of constitutionality and imposing a novel burden of proof on a city implementing an admittedly valid comprehensive land use plan. Even more consequential than its incorrect disposition of this case, however, is the Court's resurrection of a species of substantive due process analysis that it firmly rejected decades ago . . .

It applied the same kind of substantive due process analysis more frequently identified with a better known case that accorded similar substantive protection to a baker's liberty interest in working 60 hours a week and 10 hours a day. *See Lochner v. New York*, 198 U.S. 45 (1905).[9] . . .

Even if Dolan should accept the city's conditions in exchange for the benefit that she seeks, it would not necessarily follow that she had been denied "just compensation" since it would be appropriate to consider the receipt of that benefit in any calculation of "just compensation." *See Pennsylvania Coal Co. v. Mahon*, 260 U.S. 393, 415 (1922) (noting that an "average reciprocity of advantage" was deemed to justify many laws); *Hodel v. Irving*, 481 U.S. 704, 715 (1987) (such " 'reciprocity of advantage' " weighed in favor of a statute's constitutionality). Particularly in the absence of any evidence on the point, we should not presume that the discretionary benefit the city has offered is less valuable than the property interests that Dolan can retain or surrender at her option. But even if that discretionary benefit were so trifling that it could not be considered just compensation when it has "little or no relationship" to the property, the Court fails to explain why the same value would suffice when the required nexus is present. In this respect, the Court's reliance on the "unconstitutional conditions" doctrine is assuredly novel, and arguably incoherent. . . .

Notes and Comments

1. *Winners and Losers*. Chief Justice Rehnquist appears to be concerned that the city was demanding that property actually be dedicated to the city for flood control and a public access walk-bikeway. Is *Dolan* like *Nollan* in that the Court's decision is driven by notions of "physical occupation?" Would the Court have less objection if the landowner retained ownership with the city conditioning the permit with a requirement that the developer landscape and improve an access way?

If so, the City of Tigard may have actually been the winner in the litigation. Under the invalidated scheme, the city was to obtain title to the parcel and would landscape and maintain the dedicated parcel. Under the Supreme Court's approach, if the proposed improvements would generate the need for traffic,

9. The *Lochner* Court refused to presume that there was a reasonable connection between the regulation and the state interest in protecting the public health . . . A similar refusal to identify a sufficient nexus between an enlarged building with a newly paved parking lot and the state interests in minimizing the risks of flooding and traffic congestion proves fatal to the city's permit conditions in this case under the Court's novel approach.

access, and flood control, the landowner may retain the property and be required to landscape, maintain, insure, and pay taxes on it.

2. *More Winners and Losers.* Might an even bigger winner in *Dolan* be the planning consulting industry? Won't legions of consultants be mobilized by local governments to make the individualized determinations of the need for infrastructure generated by proposed projects? The government carries the burden to prove rough proportionality, and the individualized evaluation to support that determination may be based on hypothetical conditions with a site-specific focus. Opinion evidence of such conditions is admissible where the degree of proportionality and the potential and hypothetical impacts of the project are necessarily speculative. *State Department of Transportation v. Altimus*, 905 P.2d 258 (Or. 1995).

A survey of local California governments concluded that developers have been grossly undercharged for the supporting infrastructure necessary to mitigate or accommodate the impacts of projects. Regulators are anticipating significant increases in exactions, and impact fees as infrastructure elements are scrutinized. Ann E. Carlson and Daniel Pollack, Takings on the Ground: How the Supreme Court's Takings Jurisprudence Affects Local Land Use Decisions, 35 U.C. Davis L. Rev. 103 (2001). An ironic impact of *Dolan* has been to require an "infrastructure impact" statement, increasing the cost of development but generating improved planning.

3. *What About the Benefit?* The majority opinion in *Dolan* ignores the value of the benefit to the property owner resulting from the conditions imposed, and it does not acknowledge any "reciprocity of advantage." For example, the property will now be adjacent to a publicly maintained and landscaped bikeway and pedestrian walkway. Should this benefit be factored into the taking equation?

4. *Helping Cities Meet the Burden of Proof.* One of *Dolan*'s larger changes was its shift in the burden of proof. Local governments must now justify the conditions they impose. Would this shift prevent a local government from requiring an applicant to submit a "rough proportionality" report by a qualified engineer to aid the government in its determinations? *See Lincoln City Chamber of Commerce v. City of Lincoln City*, 991 P.2d 1080 (Or. App. 1999) (concluding that the "rough proportionality report" is simply an application requirement and thus does not violate *Dolan*).

5. *Measuring the Impact in Calculating Rough Proportionality.* In *Rohn v. City of Visalia*, 263 Cal. Rptr. 319 (Ct. App. 1989), an applicant sought to convert an existing single-family residence to professional offices. The city approved but, consistent with the comprehensive plan, conditioned the site plan on the dedication of 14 percent of the parcel to permit the correction of a street misalignment. The court invalidated the condition on the ground that the need for the realignment was not generated by the proposed project but by prior poor planning.

The conclusion that the project did not contribute to the safety need for correcting the misalignment, however, assumed that the "baseline" condition was the use of the parcel for multi-family housing, as the existing zoning permitted. The court opined that the landowner could have built apartments as of right, and that this use would generate a large amount of traffic. Since the proposed use would generate less traffic than that allowed of right, the court concluded that the proposed project would generate no traffic.

Was the court correct in utilizing the existing zoning rather than the existing use as a baseline? Following such reasoning, a subdivision of 1000 homes on land previously zoned for housing would generate no traffic impacts. Obviously the change in *Rohn* from the existing use as a single-family home to use as professional offices will generate substantial traffic from employees, customers, suppliers, and other business contacts.

The rationale of *Rohn* would encourage communities to zone at very low densities. Then, when a rezoning was required for a development, the city could easily show an obviously increased demand for infrastructure.

6. *Adjacent Street Widening*. *Dolan* may have a significant impact on conditions, often routinely imposed before this case, that require the dedication of land for adjacent street widening. The ruling in *Curtis v. Town of South Thomaston*, 708 A.2d 657 (Me. 1998), may support that conclusion. In *Curtis*, an ordinance required subdivisions to construct a 250,000-gallon fire pond within 2,000 feet of any proposed development in the absence of an adequate water supply. In addition, the ordinance required the dedication of an easement so that the town could maintain and use the pond for hydrant pumping. The ordinance was sustained in light of the fact that the town could have rejected the subdivision. However, in *Goss v. City of Little Rock*, 151 F.3d 861 (8th Cir. 1998), *cert. denied*, 526 U.S. 1050 (1999), the Eighth Circuit invalidated a rezoning condition calling for dedicating 22 percent of the parcel for adjacent street widening. The court called for an individualized determination that the condition was designed to mitigate no more than the project's impacts. *See also Town of Flower Mound v. Stafford Estates Limited Partnership*, 71 S.W.3d 18, 43 (Tex. Ct. App. 2002) ("the Town has not met its burden of demonstrating that the additional traffic generated by the Subdivision bears a sufficient relationship to the requirement that Stafford demolish a nearly new, two-lane asphalt road that was not in disrepair and replace it with a two-lane concrete road.").

In *Sparks v. Douglas County*, 863 P.2d 142 (Wash. Ct. App. 1993), the court rejected a condition requiring dedication of a strip of land for street widening. Adequate capacity already existed, and no evidence was presented suggesting that the projected 25 cars per hour generated by the project would render the existing road less safe from overcrowding. On appeal, the Washington Supreme Court reversed the lower court. The county planning agency had prepared a report that documented deficiencies in the right-of-way width and in the surfacing of adjoining streets, and it calculated the increase in traffic. The report also calculated the specific need for the conditions and the cumulative impact of a series of separate subdivisions. The supreme court found that the report constituted substantial evidence satisfying the *Dolan* rough proportionality standard. *Sparks v. Douglas County*, 904 P.2d 738 (Wash. 1995). *See also Honesty in Envtl. Analysis & Legislation (HEAL) v. Central Puget Sound Growth Management Hearings Bd.*, 979 P.2d 864 (Wash. Ct. App. 1999) (*Dolan* nexus rule restricts development permit conditions designed to mitigate a specific adverse impact of a proposal); *Group v. Clackamas County*, 922 P.2d 1227 (Or. Ct. App. 1996) (reviewing a demand for a 10-foot dedication and street improvement condition, and rejecting the argument that a mathematical analysis showing that project would produce 2.6 percent of the traffic on the road to be widened limited the developer's obligation to 2.6 percent of road improvement costs).

7. *The Alternative of Denying the Permit*. If an individualized determination demonstrates that a doubling of the size of the hardware store, the expansion and surfacing of the parking lot, and the addition of several new businesses generate

impacts that threaten flooding and exacerbate street congestion and parking shortages, do *Nollan* and *Dolan* authorize the denial of the expansion permit? Given the difficulties that communities face in funding infrastructure to accommodate growth, is it possible that *Dolan* will result in refusals by municipalities to approve growth rather than in a shift of the costs of growth from developers and new residents to the general community?

What about Justice Scalia's suggestion in *Nollan* that judicial review in takings cases should be more rigorous, perhaps along the lines of the mid-tier equal protection standard? In *Dolan*, does Chief Justice Rehnquist suggest an enhanced scrutiny of permit conditions or takings in general?

8. *Impact Fees*. Impact fees are requirements that a developer pay a set fee to offset a given impact of the project. *See, e.g., City of Zephyrhills v. Wood*, 831 So. 2d 223, 224 (Fla. Ct. App. 2002) (impact fees "are the method by which a new user . . . pays his or her fair share of the costs that the new use of the system involves"). Such fees are usually based upon the number of housing units or the square footage of commercial or industrial space, a method that arguably meets the "individualized determination" and "rough proportionality" requirements of *Dolan*. Does *Dolan* accordingly encourage the expansion of impact fee ordinances to fund infrastructure?

9. *Effect on State Law*. While some states following different standards for reviewing exactions may have to adjust to *Dolan*'s "reasonable relationship" standard, for most states *Dolan* presents no change in the law. See Robert H. Freilich & David W. Bushek, Thou Shalt Not Take Title Without Adequate Planning: The Takings Equation After *Dolan v. City of Tigard*, 27 Urb. Law. 187 (1995) (arguing that *Dolan* will have little impact on communities that plan). For example, where impact fees were previously established and otherwise comply with the rational nexus standard, no *Dolan* problem is presented. Similarly, where a planning authority denies a project because of inadequate infrastructure, no problem would be encountered. The authors of the article suggest that *Dolan* is appropriately limited to physical occupation situations, such as where a project is conditioned on the dedication of an easement or land itself. *See, e.g., Steel v. Cape Corp.*, 677 A.2d 634, 641 (Md. Ct. Spec. App. 1996) (*Dolan* test adopted ten years earlier in Maryland's reasonable nexus or reasonable relationship test).

10. *Using a Set Percentage Fee In Lieu of Dedication*. In *Call v. City of West Jordan*, 606 P.2d 217 (Utah 1979), the Utah Supreme Court sustained a 7 percent dedication or an in-lieu cash payment for recreation. Other jurisdictions have rejected such a standard. *J.E.D. Assocs. v. Atkinson*, 432 A.2d 12 (N.H. 1981); *Frank Ansuini, Inc. v. City of Cranston*, 264 A.2d 910 (R.I. 1970). *Dolan* would appear to preclude ordinances requiring an automatic dedication of a percentage of the parcel regardless of the proposed use and likely demand for infrastructure. *Dolan* also seems to sound the death knell for extraordinary conditions, such as the construction and dedication of a museum or other "out of the ordinary" public facility.

11. *Rough Proportionality, Actual Mitigation, or Earmarking*? What should be the result where a permit condition is measured to be within the rough proportionality measure of a project's impacts, but the condition fails to actually mitigate the impact? In *Burton v. Clark County*, 958 P.2d 343 (Wash. Ct. App. 1998), the Washington state intermediate appellate court ruled that while the dedication of a right of way for a road that might in the future be opened and connected to a highway would eventually offset only a portion of the impact of traffic to be generated by

the project, it nevertheless was invalid as the condition failed to mitigate current traffic impact. The court ruled that *Dolan* not only requires rough proportionality, it also requires that the condition must actually mitigate those impacts. The court was unimpressed with the fact that the condition would impose an obligation on the developer that was similar to the costs generally associated with street extensions experienced by other similar projects. Instead, the condition must actually mitigate the problem generated by the project.

12. *Exactions and Development Agreements*. As with other unpredictable land use questions, developers and regulating communities are increasingly turning to development agreements to establish predictability in the land use process. *Dolan* will simply encourage the trend, allowing, at least in the absence of unhappy third parties, the avoidance of litigation and constitutional analysis. See David L. Callies & Julie A. Tappendorf, Unconstitutional Land Development Conditions and the Development Agreement Solution: Bargaining for Public Facilities after *Nollan and Dolan*, 51 Case W. Res. L. Rev. 663 (2001). Development agreements are examined in Chapter 10 of this casebook.

13. *The Aftermath of* Dolan. After the Supreme Court's decision in *Dolan*, the City of Tigard proceeded to reevaluate the conditions under the *Dolan* standard. The City then required dedication of an easement within the flood plain for flood and erosion control, and drainage control, and an easement above the flood plain for a bike-pedestrian path. The record was in excess of 1,553 pages, and the findings made by the City in excess of 110 pages. In the meantime, however, the Dolan family filed a civil action against the City seeking monetary damages of slightly less than $2.5 million on various theories.

Ultimately, the City and Dolans settled the matter. The City paid $1.5 million and issued the land use permits to the Dolans. In turn, the City received dedication of the flood plain and bike path area. The City also placed a permanent plaque commemorating the legal action along the bike/pedestrian path site. *See* Richard Duane Faus, Exactions, Impact Fees, and Dedications—Local Government Responses to *Nollan/Dolan* Takings Law Issues, 29 Stetson L. Rev. 675, 676 (2000) (setting forth these facts).

Other literature includes James E. Holloway & Donald C. Guy, The Impact of a Federal Takings Norm on Fashioning a Means-End Fit Under Takings Provisions of State Constitutions, 8 Dick. J. Envtl. L. & Pol'y 143 (1999); James E. Holloway & Donald C. Guy, A Limitation on Development Impact Exactions to Limit Social Policy-Making: Interpreting the Takings Clause to Limit Land Use Policy—Making for Social Welfare Goals of Urban Communities, 9 Dick. J. L. & Pol'y 1 (2000).

C. IMPACT FEES

Dolan is likely to encourage use of the increasingly popular impact fee to finance infrastructure. The two most frequently encountered legal questions concerning such fees focus on the local government's authority under state law to adopt the fee measure and the validity of the calculation of the demand for infrastructure generated by the project.

Impact fees can either be legislatively determined or imposed on an ad hoc, adjudicative basis as part of a particular project review. Do impact fees in either case meet the *Dolan* principles? *Ehrlich v. City of Culver City* addresses both forms of fees.

■ EHRLICH v. CITY OF CULVER CITY

911 P.2d 429 (Cal.), cert. denied, 519 U.S. 929 (1996)

ARABIAN, Justice. . . .

I. FACTUAL AND PROCEDURAL BACKGROUND

A

Between 1973 and 1975, plaintiff acquired a vacant 2.4-acre lot on Overland Avenue in Culver City and obtained city approval to develop the site as a private tennis club and recreational facility. At plaintiff's request, the city amended its zoning and general plan ordinances governing uses on the property from a split zone R-1 (single family residential) and C-2 (retail commercial) to C-3 (commercial). . . .

In 1981, in response to financial losses, plaintiff applied to the city for a change in land use in order to construct an office building on the site; that application was abandoned after the city planning commission recommended against approval on the ground that the existing sports and tennis club provided a needed commercial recreational facility within the city. The club continued in operation under a series of managers until August 1988, when plaintiff closed it as a result of continuing financial losses. The following month, he again applied to the city for an amendment to the general plan, a zoning change and amendment of the specific plan to allow construction of a 30-unit condominium complex valued at $10 million. . . .

Following a closed-door meeting ostensibly to discuss the pending litigation, the city council voted to approve plaintiff's application conditioned upon the payment of certain monetary exactions. In lieu of the construction of four tennis courts as a condition of approval, the city required the payment of $280,000 "to be used" as stated in the ratifying ordinance, "for additional [public] recreational facilities as directed by the City Council." The minutes of the city council meeting state that the $280,000 fee was to be used "for partial replacement of the lost recreational facilities . . . "

In addition to the $280,000 recreation fee, the city also required plaintiff to pay an exaction under the city's "art in public places" program. By municipal ordinance, new residential development projects of more than four units, as well as all commercial, industrial, and public building projects with a building valuation exceeding $500,000, are required to provide "art work" (as defined by the ordinance) for the project in an amount equal to 1 percent of the total building valuation, or to pay an equal amount in cash to the city art fund. The city valued plaintiff's project at $3,200,000. He elected initially to pay the fee, which totaled $33,200, but his successor in interest apparently subsequently placed art of his own choosing on the site rather than pay the in-lieu fee. . . .

. . . The site was subsequently developed and residential units were sold to the public. . . .

IV. Do Nollan and Dolan Apply to Nonpossessory Exactions?

Both *Nollan* and *Dolan* involved regulatory schemes under which the local government had required the *possessory dedication* of real property by the owner as a condition for issuing the necessary development permit. Moreover, language employed by Justice Scalia in his opinion for the majority in *Nollan* has been read by some students of the high court's contemporary takings jurisprudence as *limiting* the operation of the "essential nexus" requirement to cases of possessory exactions. . . .

One of the central promises of the takings clause is that truly public burdens will be publicly borne. When the regulatory land use power of local government is deployed against individual property owners through the use of conditional permit exactions, the *Nollan* test helps to secure that promise by assuring that the monopoly power over development permits is not illegitimately exploited by imposing conditions that lack any logical affinity to the public impact of a particular land use. The essential nexus test is, in short, a "means-ends" equation, intended to limit the government's bargaining mobility in imposing permit conditions on individual property owners — whether they consist of possessory dedications or the exaction of cash payments — that, because they appear to lack any evident connection to the public impact of the proposed land use, *may* conceal an illegitimate demand; may, in other words, amount to " 'out-and-out . . . extortion.' " (*Nollan supra*, 483 U.S. at p. 837.)

Under this view of the constitutional role of the consolidated "essential nexus" and "rough proportionality" tests, it matters little whether the local land use permit authority demands the actual *conveyance* of property or the *payment* of a monetary exaction. In a context in which the constraints imposed by legislative and political processes are absent or substantially reduced, the risk of too elastic or diluted a takings standard — the vice of distributive injustice in the allocation of civic costs — is heightened in either case. . . .

[The court then held that the record did not support the $280,000 recreational fee.]

VI. The Art in Public Places Fee

Under the city's art in public places ordinance, plaintiff could not receive a certificate of occupancy for any of the 30 townhouses in the project until he either paid $32,200 to the city art fund (1 percent of the total building valuation) or contributed an approved work of art of an equivalent value. Under the latter option, the art may either be placed on site, in which case it remains the property of the applicant, or it may be donated to the city for placement elsewhere. Although petitioner initially opted to pay the fee, his successor in interest subsequently placed art of his own choosing on the site and received the 30 certificates of occupancy during the pendency of this action.

Plaintiff contends that the required dedication of art or the cash equivalent thereof constitutes a taking under the *Nollan-Dolan* standards. This follows, he asserts, from the fact that the city made no individualized determination that the art mitigates a need generated by the project. . . .

[W]e agree with the city that the art in public places fee is not a development exaction of the kind subject to the *Nollan-Dolan* takings analysis. As both the trial court and the Court of Appeal concluded, the requirement to provide either art or a cash equivalent thereof is more akin to traditional land use regulations imposing minimal building setbacks, parking and lighting conditions, landscaping requirements, and other *design* conditions such as color schemes, building materials and architectural amenities. Such aesthetic conditions have long been held to be valid exercises of the city's traditional police power, and do not amount to a taking merely because they might incidentally restrict a use, diminish the value, or impose a cost in connection with the property. . . . The requirement of providing art in an area of the project reasonably accessible to the public is, like other design and landscaping requirements, a kind of aesthetic control well within the authority of the city to impose. . . .

Notes and Comments

1. *Open Questions I: Monetary Fees.* The reasoning in *Nollan* initially revolved around a condition that required the dedication of real property. Do *Nollan* and *Dolan* even apply to fees at all? Can you make an argument that the rationale of the two cases applies only to conditions that require dedication of real property, not to the payment of fees? If *Nollan* and *Dolan* do apply to fees, is their constitutional doctrine limited to exactions as a condition for development approval, or does it apply to other fees as well?

2. *Open Questions II: Legislatively Set Fees or Exactions.* The second large question left unanswered by *Nollan* and *Dolan* is whether their doctrines apply to fees or exactions set legislatively rather than adjudicatively. *See Rogers Machinery, Inc. v. Washington County*, 45 P.3d 966, 976 (Or. Ct. App. 2002) ("The two questions that consequently have generated considerable litigation for lower courts are: (1) Does heightened scrutiny apply to nonpossessory exactions, such as development or impact fees . . . ? (2) Does that scrutiny extend to exactions imposed through generally applicable legislation rather than individual adjudicative decisions?") The *Rogers* court also noted that "[w]ith near uniformity, lower courts applying *Dolan* to monetary exactions have done so *only* when the exaction has been imposed through an adjudicatory process. . . . " *Id.*

In *San Remo Hotel L.P. v. City and County of San Francisco*, 41 P.3d 87 (Cal. 2002), the state supreme court found that an ordinance requiring that conversion of a residential hotel to one for tourists needed a conditional use permit and the payment of a conversion fee was not subject to *Dolan*. The court reasoned that the fee was legislatively set rather than in a discretionary fashion, and thus mandated more deference from the courts. Are you convinced? Has the developer generated the need for a residential unit by converting to a tourist hotel? Although the fee is set legislatively, can it nevertheless be disproportionate and extortionate?

The Georgia Supreme Court ruled that the imposition of on-site improvements such as landscaping, including an obligation to plant one tree for every eight parking spaces, is exempt from *Dolan* analysis. *Parking Ass'n v. City of Atlanta*, 450 S.E.2d 200 (Ga. 1994), *cert. denied*, 515 U.S. 1116 (1995). Justice Thomas, joined by Justice O'Connor, dissented from the denial of certiorari, arguing that exactions of general communitywide applicability should not be exempt from *Dolan*. *See* Edward J. Sullivan, *Dolan* and Municipal Risk Assessment, 12 J. Envtl. L. & Litig. 1 (1997). The article concludes that improved planning and process as well as better assessment, along with development agreements, can reduce exposure to risk of noncompliance. The article also recommends that it is prudent to consider that impact fees are subject to *Dolan*.

3. *Community Art.* Can you make an argument that mandatory original art or the payment of an in-lieu fee for an "art in public places" program serves a legitimate state police power interest? Can you make an argument against the claim that housing development generates a need for art? Is the need for art, and the calculation of how much is needed, like the value of aesthetic controls or the amount of essential open space, a policy matter to be determined democratically through the comprehensive planning and legislative processes? For criticism of *Ehrlich, see* Gideon Kanner, Tennis Anyone? How California Judges Made Land Ransom and Art Censorship Legal, 25 Real Estate L.J. 214 (1997), and Douglas W. Kmiec, Inserting the Last Remaining Pieces into the Takings Puzzle, 38 Wm. & Mary L. Rev. 995 (1997).

4. *Rough Proportionality and State Law.* Is "rough proportionality" a new name for "rational nexus"? Is there any remaining vitality to the previously developed state standards ("reasonableness," "rational nexus," "uniquely attributable")? In *Goss v. City of Little Rock*, 90 F.3d 306 (8th Cir. 1996), the Eighth Circuit Court of Appeals reviewed a rezoning conditioned on the dedication, for future street widening, of a 55-foot strip running along the entire 633-foot frontage. The dedication amounted to 0.8 acres, or 22 percent of the parcel. For 20 years, the owner had been using the property as a prior nonconforming use, operating a convenience store, gas station, laundromat, and car wash on a parcel subsequently zoned as residential. The owner wished to obtain conforming commercial zoning to allow a possible sale.

The court reversed the dismissal of the complaint and ordered a trial on whether the dedication was roughly proportional to generated need under *Dolan*. Interestingly, the court appeared to suggest that the dedication might be reasonable if the zone change would permit a different business producing heavy traffic. The court never mentioned any standard that might additionally apply under Arkansas law.

5. *"On the Face" or "As Applied."* Should *Nollan* and *Dolan* be applied to exaction challenges directed to allegedly excessive standards for exactions in ordinances as well as to specific conditions imposed on permit applications? In *Garneau v. City of Seattle*, 147 F.3d 802, 811 (9th Cir. 1998), the Ninth Circuit validated an ordinance requiring landlords to pay one-half of the cost of relocating displaced low-income tenants, finding *Dolan* inapplicable to facial takings challenges.

VOLUSIA COUNTY v. ABERDEEN AT ORMOND BEACH, L.P.

760 So. 2d 126 (Fla. 2000)

QUINCE, J. . . .

Aberdeen at Ormond Beach, L.P., owns Aberdeen at Ormond Beach Manufactured Housing Community (Aberdeen), a mobile home park in Ormond Beach that provides housing for persons at least 55 years of age or older. Aberdeen brought suit against Volusia County and the Volusia County School Board (Volusia County) to challenge the constitutionality of public school impact fees assessed on new homes constructed at Aberdeen.

As a mobile home park, Aberdeen is regulated by Chapter 723, Florida Statutes. Its minimum age requirements comply with the "housing for older persons" exemption of the Federal Fair Housing Act. *See* 42 U.S.C. §3607 (1994 & Supp. 1 1996). Aberdeen's Supplemental Declaration of Covenants, Conditions and Restrictions (Supplemental Declaration) contains the following provisions: exceptions to the minimum age requirement are permitted under limited circumstances; persons under eighteen are prohibited from permanently residing in any dwelling unit; the developer reserves the absolute right to modify or revoke all other covenants; and restrictions are binding upon owners for thirty years from the date of recordation. . . .

Effective October 1, 1992, Volusia County enacted Ordinance No. 92-9, imposing countywide public school impact fees on new dwelling units constructed in Volusia County. The ordinance's definition of "dwelling unit" ("living quarters for one family only") included single and multi-family housing, but excluded nursing homes, adult congregate living facilities and group homes. Volusia County, Fla., Ordinance 92-9, art. 1, §4, (July 2, 1992). In addition, the ordinance furthered the County's policy of ensuring that new development should bear a proportionate share of the cost of facility expansion necessitated by such new development." *Id.* art. 1, §2(*l*). . . .

. . . In calculating the fee, the County utilized the student generation rate, which is the average number of public school students per dwelling unit. Pursuant to the Volusia County impact fee ordinances, Aberdeen has paid $86,984.07 under protest for 84 homes as of July 31, 1998.

Aberdeen filed suit against Volusia County, claiming, inter alia, that public school impact fees were unconstitutional as applied to Aberdeen because of the deed restrictions prohibiting minors from living on the property. In response, the County argued that exempting Aberdeen would convert the impact fee into a "user fee," thereby violating the state constitutional guarantee of a free public school system. Although both parties filed motions for summary judgment, the trial court denied Volusia County's motion and granted Aberdeen's motion. . . .

[T]he trial court reasoned that the rationale underlying *St. John's County* [*v. Northeast Florida Builders Ass'n Inc.*, 583 So. 2d 635 (Fla. 1991)] was inapplicable to housing with land use restrictions prohibiting children. . . . [T]he trial court, applying the dual rational nexus test, held that no substantial relationship existed between the need for new schools and the new development because no children resided in Aberdeen. [T]he trial court held that Aberdeen did not benefit from the construction of new schools for the same reason. . . .

The parties . . . dispute the proper application of the dual rational nexus test. In *St. Johns County*, the Court expressly adopted the dual rational nexus test for determining the constitutionality of impact fees: the local government must demonstrate reasonable connections between (1) "the need for additional capital facilities and the growth in population generated by the subdivision" and (2) "the expenditures of the funds collected and the benefits accruing to the subdivision." Volusia County argues that the test requires needs and benefits to be assessed based on countywide growth, and that the specific-need/special-benefit analysis is limited to the water and sewer line context. This argument, however, is without merit.

The language of the test itself belies the assertion that a countywide standard should be employed. The first prong of the test explicitly requires a nexus between the County's need and the "growth in population generated by the subdivision." Similarly, the test's second prong ensures that "benefits accru[e] to the subdivision." Thus, the explicit references to subdivisions indicate that the standard is not tailored to countywide growth, but to growth of a particular subdivision.

Furthermore, this Court in *St. Johns County* adopted the dual rational nexus test exactly as it was enunciated in *Hollywood, Inc. v. Broward County*, 431 So.2d 606 (Fla. 4th DCA 1983), which applied the test to parks. The test ensures that the *Broward County* requirements—the fee must "offset needs sufficiently attributable to the subdivision" and the fee revenue must be "sufficiently earmarked for the substantial benefit of the subdivision residents"—are satisfied. Moreover, this Court in *St. Johns County* reaffirmed the . . . requirement that the fees must "be spent to benefit those who have paid the fees." [T]he dual rational nexus test has not been limited to the water and sewer line context.

Additionally, in *Collier County v. State*, 733 So.2d 1012 (Fla. 1999), we reaffirmed the specific-need/special-benefit standard. Construing *St. Johns County*, we said, "[T]he fee in *St. Johns County* was invalid because it did not provide a unique benefit to those paying the fee." We further explained that the fee at issue in *Collier County* was an invalid tax because "the services to be funded by the fee are the same general police-power services provided to all County residents." Thus, we expressly repudiated a countywide standard for determining the constitutionality of impact fees.

Nevertheless, Volusia County highlights the dicta in *St. Johns County* as credible support for its position: "Thus, if this were a countywide impact fee designed to fund construction of new schools as needed throughout the county, we could easily conclude that the second prong of the test had been met." Certainly, this statement bolsters Volusia County's contention that a countywide standard should be employed. At the very least, the dicta created ambiguity in determining the application of the test.

Nonetheless, our repeated citations to the special-benefit standard and our interpretation of *St. Johns County* demonstrate that we did not abandon the subdivision-based standard. Indeed, imposing a countywide standard would eviscerate the substantial nexus requirement. This nexus is significant because of the distinction between taxes and fees. As this Court noted in *Collier County*, "[T]here is no requirement that taxes provide any specific benefit to the property; instead, they may be levied throughout the particular taxing unit for the general benefit of residents and property." . . . Fees, by contrast, must confer a special benefit on feepayers "in a manner not shared by those not paying the fee." . . . We likewise noted in *State v. City of Port Orange*, 650 So.2d 1, 3 (Fla. 1994), that "the power of a municipality to tax should not be broadened by semantics which would be the effect of labeling what the City is here collecting a fee rather than a tax." Thus, a liberal reading of the dual rational nexus test would obliterate the distinction between an unconstitutional tax and a valid fee.

Volusia County also contends that *St. Johns County's* refusal to exempt households with no minor children from paying public school impact fees demonstrates that a countywide standard is required. This contention, however, is less persuasive when considered in context. The rationale underlying this Court's statement was that "[d]uring the useful life of the new dwelling units, school-age children will come and go." We were concerned with exempting some units because of the potential in the future that students would be residing in the developments. We did, however, distinguish restricted housing, noting that "[w]e would not find objectionable a provision that exempted from the payment of an impact fee permits to build adult facilities in which, because of land use restrictions, minors could not reside." . . . This statement negates the contention that a countywide standard must be utilized. Thus, the logical conclusion is that where there is no potential for student-generating housing to exist within the subdivision, the subdivision may be exempt from paying public school impact fees. In short, the foregoing analysis demonstrates that the specific-need/special-benefit standard is a more favorable construction of the dual rational nexus test.

Despite this narrow construction, Volusia County contends that the "need" prong of the test is satisfied because Aberdeen's growth directly affects the student generation rate used in calculating the fee, that is, the average number of public school students per dwelling unit. Volusia county notes that all residential dwellings, including adult communities, are considered when determining the student generation rate. Consequently, the County contends Aberdeen affects the student generation rate and amount of the fee because if the number of households without children increases, the rate decreases, and therefore the fee decreases.

The issue, however, is not whether Aberdeen influences the student generation rate or the amount of the impact fee, but whether Aberdeen increases the need for new schools. Indeed, Ordinance 97-7 defines "land development activity" as "any change in land use or any construction or installation of a dwelling unit, or any change in the use of any structure that will result in *additional* students in the public schools of the District." . . . In addition, the test itself clearly frames the issue: whether there is a "need for *additional* capital facilities." Moreover, the student generation rate has remained unchanged since the impact fee was initially assessed in 1992. The ordinance provides that it will be adjusted only to "reflect any inflation or deflation in school construction costs." . . . It does not contemplate adjustments based on variations in countywide demographics. As Aberdeen correctly points out, even if adjustments to the student generation rate were correlative to developmental growth, it would not change the fact that Aberdeen does not generate any students. That all residential units were included in the initial student generation rate is insufficient to establish a substantial nexus between Aberdeen's growth and the need for new schools. Thus, Aberdeen's purported effect on the student generation rate does not satisfy the dual rational nexus test.

Volusia County also contends that Aberdeen contributes to the need for schools because the Volusia County School District is required to provide free schooling to all students with disabilities up to the age of twenty-one. Because Aberdeen's age restrictions only prohibit minors from living on the property, the County asserts that the potential to generate students still exists. Volusia County, however, fails to recognize that both the need for new schools and the site selection process is determined according to enrollment projections for elementary, middle, and high school students. Adult enrollment is not factored into these decisions. Although the remote possibility exists that an adult Aberdeen resident could attend school in some capacity, this is also the case with residents of nursing homes and group homes for disabled persons who are exempt from the fee. As the trial court correctly concluded, "[T]he rational nexus test requires Aberdeen to have more than a possible or an incidental impact on the need for schools. In the final analysis, housing that allows children is the land use that creates the need for new school facilities."

Volusia County is also unable to satisfy the "benefits" prong of the dual rational nexus test. Because no children can live at Aberdeen, impact fees collected at Aberdeen will not be spent for Aberdeen's benefit, but for the benefit of children living in other developments. Volusia County contends that Aberdeen benefits from the construction of new schools because they also serve as emergency shelters and sites for adult education classes. However, the connection between the expenditure of impact fee funds for the construction of new schools and the tangential benefit of having places of refuge in natural disasters is too attenuated to demonstrate a substantial nexus. Put another way, the schools are built primarily for the educational benefit of school-age children and, to the extent that Aberdeen derives any incidental benefit from their construction, it is insufficient to satisfy the dual rational nexus test. . . .

Volusia County contends that the lower court's use of the specific-need/special-benefit standard converted this permissive language into a mandatory exemption, thereby transforming it into a user fee. For purposes of the present inquiry, Volusia County's purported distinction between permissive and mandatory exemptions is inconsequential. That the exemption is mandatory rather than permissive does not resolve the issue of its constitutionality. Further, exempting deed-restricted adult communities cannot be equated to exempting households that do not have children. As previously mentioned, the reason underlying *St. Johns County*'s holding was that some units had the potential to generate students. *See St. Johns County*, 583 So. 2d at 638 ("During the useful life of the new dwelling units, school-age children will come and go."). Thus, where there is no potential to generate students, there is no impact warranting the imposition of fees. Furthermore, this interpretation is wholly consistent with our Court's statement that deed-restricted housing could be exempt. Therefore, the lower court's construction of *St. Johns County* does not convert the impact fee into an unconstitutional user fee. . . .

Notes and Comments

1. *Testing the Logic of Exaction Theory.* Is *Volusia County* consistent with *Ehrlich?* Would a group home for the blind with a restrictive covenant so limiting occupancy be exempt from a visual art fee? Can developers of expensive homes any more than builders of factories, offices, or shopping malls have residents that will require art, parks, schools, or libraries? How will the residents of an office building need affordable housing? *See Home Builders Assn. v. City of Napa*, 108 Cal. Rptr. 2d 60 (Ct. App. 2001), *cert. denied*, 122 S. Ct. 1356 (2002) (sustaining requirement that 10 percent of a development must be affordable).

Is affordable housing distinguishable because commercial development will cause a need for new community residents to perform low-wage jobs that will be generated by the development? That population will also require visual attractiveness to advance a sense of community and urban success. Will not the mobile homes in *Volusia County* or attached condominiums and apartments generate demand for facilities: gardeners, construction trades, domestic servants, the computer repair industry, pizza delivery, urban service delivery, and the myriad of other service work that is generated by urban development? In addition, every detached suburban home, mobile home, or commercial development exhausts a finite supply of developable land, typically inflating the price of remaining available land in the environment of a robust economy. Is it significant that the residents or owners of the senior citizen project will directly benefit from the enhancement of the county's schools? Are property values likely to fall if school quality declines? Finally, what happens in thirty years if retirees are no longer flooding Florida and the owners' association elects to allow families? How will the solution to the lack of school capacity be remedied? *See* Gregory L. Torres, Note, Volusia County v. Aberdeen at Ormond Beach, Ignoring Reality?, 31 Sw. U. L. Rev. 305 (2002). Can group homes or facilities limited to the aged or infirm be exempt from parks, recreation, schools, or museums? Is it significant that if Volusia County's schools are of high quality, that quality would be reflected in the value of the mobile home park?

2. *The Dual Nexus*. In *Home Builders Ass'n v. City of Beavercreek*, 729 N.E.2d 349 (Ohio 2000), the Ohio Supreme Court sustained a roadway impact fee ordinance, adopting the Florida dual rational nexus test in reviewing impact fees under the federal and state constitutional takings clauses. Of course, Ohio does not accept the conclusion in *Ehrlich* that legislatively set impact fees are not subject to *Dolan*. Should specific developments be exempt from a community-wide facilities impact fee because residents will not use the facilities?

3. *State Preemption*. Despite federal constitutional approval and satisfaction of any state nexus variations, some jurisdictions demand express statutory enabling authority to impose impact fees. *See, e.g., Home Builders Ass'n v. City of Apache Junction*, 11 P.3d 1032 (Ariz. Ct. App. 2000) (invalidating school impact fee as city lacks authority over schools and enjoys enabling authority only for necessary public services); and *Idaho Bldg. Contractors Ass'n v. City of Coeur D'Alene*, 890 P.2d 326 (1995). Other jurisdictions find authority within a community's home rule authority. *Home Builders Assn. v. City of Beavercreek*, 729 N.E.2d 349 (Ohio 2000).

4. *Using Averages to Calculate Fees*. The Illinois Supreme Court applied both the *Pioneer Trust* "uniquely attributable" test and *Dolan* in sustaining transportation impact fees. *Northern Ill. Home Builders Ass'n v. County of Du Page*, 649 N.E.2d 384 (Ill. 1995). Does *Dolan* require that impact fees be calculated with regard to each proposed development? *Du Page* rejected that argument, finding that fees may be calculated according to generally accepted traffic engineering practices, which may reflect nationwide use averages.

The Du Page County scheme allowed the developer the option of preparing an independent traffic analysis. However, if the analysis was used, the developer would forfeit a 15 percent discount afforded to developers who accept the fee calculation made pursuant to the ordinance. The Illinois Supreme Court invalidated the discount forfeiture as a violation of equal protection. Does the provision allowing the developer to undertake an independent infrastructure analysis to determine the actual costs generated by the project, as an alternative to the fee as otherwise calculated under the ordinance, offer increased fairness?

A decision of the Utah Supreme Court also took a deferential look at impact fee methodology in *Home Builders Ass'n v. City of American Fork*, 973 P.2d 425 (Utah 1999). In upholding sewer and water hookup fees, the court found first that city council members were not required to personally attend to the basic fact-gathering and analysis conducted by the council's staff in setting impact fees. The court ruled that the fee should reflect reasonable estimates of the cost of existing facilities and projections of future capital costs, as well as the disclosure of other relevant factors, but it need not be based on mathematical formulae. The court established the principle that the regulating body must disclose the calculation basis, and it shifted the burden to the challenger to demonstrate a violation of a constitutional standard of "reasonableness." The Utah court did not cite or refer to *Dolan* or federal law. For a less deferential ruling, see *Vintage Constr. Co. v. City of Bothell*, 959 P.2d 1090 (Wash. 1998), where the Washington Supreme Court invalidated a condition imposing a fee in lieu of dedication on a subdivision because the amount was based on citywide property values and characteristics rather than on the specific property at issue, as required by the state's fee statute.

5. *Excessive Open Space?* How does a court determine how much open space is excessive? In Europe, cities frequently are composed of at least 50 percent open space, with lakes, rivers, parks, and forests. By extreme comparison, Los Angeles allots less than 5 percent of its land to open space, with 60 percent of the downtown and 25 percent of the entire city devoted to just streets. See James A. Kushner, A Tale of Three Cities: Land Development and Planning for Growth in Stockholm, Berlin, and Los Angeles, 25 Urb. Law. 197, 212-213 (1993).

Is the choice of how much recreation and open space is required, or alternatively, how much demand is generated by a proposed project, a function of the community's comprehensive plan? California's "Quimby" law authorizes the dedication of 3 acres of land for recreation for each 1000 residents. Cal. Govt. Code §66477 (West. 1997 & Supp. 2002). Could a state or local community validly set that obligation at 3 acres per 100 residents? Should standards such as the size of classrooms and the student-teacher ratio be left to the discretion of the school board? Might exactions premised on extremely low student-teacher ratios in schools pose problems under *Dolan*?

6. *Earmarking*. One problem that arises with the collection of fees is that they must be earmarked for expenditure so as to benefit the project. Communities that collect fees and place the money in the community's general revenue accounts may find that the impact fee is invalidated as to that project. In addition to earmarking, the improvements should be made within a reasonable period of time. *See* Cal. Govt. Code § 66006 (West 1997) (requiring identification of the facility to be financed by a fee, earmarking use of funds, limiting use to that improvement, and imposing an obligation to identify the approximate commencement date when financing collected or refund fees); *Northern Illinois Home Builders Ass'n v. County of Du Page*, 649 N.E.2d 384 (Ill. 1995) (traffic impact fees must be spent in the district where the fees were raised); *Douglas County Contractors Ass'n v. Douglas County*, 929 P.2d 253 (Nev. 1996) (per curiam) (school impact fee preempted by state impact fee legislation, as the local ordinance failed to earmark proceeds to subdivision where exacted, instead allowing use of funds anywhere in the county).

7. *Permit Denial*. If the county were to determine that impact fees generated from a proposed project were insufficient to fund the school expansion necessitated by the project, could the county deny subdivision approval? *Garipay*, reprinted in Chapter 3, would suggest that as long as school capacity standards are established by regulation, project denial would be appropriate and arguably mandatory under the subdivision review laws. In *Ettlingen Homes, Inc. v. Town of*

Derry, 681 A.2d 97 (N.H. 1996), however, the court failed to extend *Garipay* to allow plat rejection in the face of inadequate off-site school capacity. The court required a health or safety danger to support a denial on the ground that the subdivision was premature.

8. *Fee or Tax?* In some jurisdictions, particularly those with a narrow definition of home rule, impact fees may be characterized as taxes and invalidated. *State v. City of Port Orange*, 650 So. 2d 1 (Fla. 1994) (a transportation utility fee used to finance bonds, but imposed on all owners and occupants of developed properties, is an invalid tax). *See also Home Builders Ass'n of Greater Des Moines v. City of West Des Moines*, 644 N.W.2d 339 (Iowa 2002) (mandatory park dedication fees were taxes); *Greater Franklin Developers Ass'n v. Town of Franklin*, 730 N.E.2d 900 (Mass. Ct. App. 2000) (school impact fees invalidated as an impermissible tax despite the fact that the developer could avoid imposition by not building, as the town failed to provide a unique benefit to the fee payer in a manner not shared by others).

If a proposed project would exceed the capacity of existing schools and thus require construction of a new elementary school, could the developer be required to fund the construction of that school? What if state and local school board standards established a minimum school size that would provide capacity for 50 percent more students than the project would generate?

In *McCarthy v. City of Leawood*, 894 P.2d 836 (Kan. 1995), the Kansas Supreme Court ruled that a traffic impact fee was authorized under the state constitution's home rule provision and not preempted. Furthermore, the fee was not a tax, since it was based on specified land uses and was designed to defray increased costs caused by such uses. Kansas joined the group of jurisdictions excluding impact fees from *Dolan* analysis, with the court finding little evidence to support what it termed the plaintiff landowner's "critical leap from a fee to a taking."

9. *Contest or Protest.* The developer in *Ehrlich* was able to pay the contested art fee and subsequently challenge the exaction on appeal, but in some jurisdictions complying with a permit condition may waive any challenge to the exaction. *Fulling v. Palumbo*, 233 N.E.2d 272 (N.Y. 1967) (dedication challenge waived by dedication). Similarly, where a condition is imposed at the preliminary stage, awaiting final approval may waive any claims to the condition or matters relating to tentative approval. *In re Busik*, 759 A.2d 417 (Pa. Commw. Ct. 2000).

10. *Statutory Requirements.* Students should be aware that many states have enacted statutes dealing with the authority of local governments to impose fees. These statutes impose important limitations on the rights of local governments to set fees and of developers to challenge them. *See, e.g.*, Cal. Govt. Code §66020(d) (West 1997) (requiring impact fee challengers to file a protest within 90 days of approval or imposition, pay the fee or make a satisfactory arrangement to pay the fee when due, and file any judicial action within 180 days following the protest filing); *Cherokee County v. Greater Atlanta Homebuilders Ass'n*, 566 S.E.2d 470, 475-476 (Ga. Ct. App. 2002) ("The Association contends that the county ordinance and CIE do not comply with the enabling statute, which requires that the impact fees not exceed a proportionate share of the cost of system improvements."); *Wellington River Hollow v. King County*, 54 P.3d 213 (Wash. Ct. App. 2002) (plaintiff claimed that the school impact fees were incorrectly calculated because the calculation method did not comply with the applicable statute).

Even more basically, a local government likely needs statutory authority before enacting a fee and often must adopt a local ordinance before it can impose the fee. *See, e.g.*, *Thompson v. Village of Newark*, 768 N.E.2d 856 (Ill. App. 2002) (village lacked statutory authorization to impose school construction fees); *Simonsen v. Town of Derby*, 765 A.2d 1033 (N.H. 2000) (municipality had to adopt an impact fee ordinance before it could charge fees); *Home Builders Ass'n of Central Arizona v. City of Apache Junction*, 11 P.3d 1032 (Ariz. Ct. App. 2000) (city lacked statutory authority to impose fees to finance schools as such fees were not "costs to the municipality" within the meaning of the statute).

11. *Judicial Resistance?* The Supreme Court almost certainly is not through with its work dealing with the constitutionality of exactions. Indeed, at least some members of the Court have expressed frustration over whether the state courts are following the essential nexus standard. In *Lambert v. City and County of San Francisco*, 120 S. Ct. 1549 (2000), the Court denied a petition for a writ of certionari. Dissenting from the denial, Justice Scalia, joined by Justices Kennedy and Thomas, found "reason to believe" that the state courts were not holding state administrators "to the Fifth Amendment standards set forth by this tribunal." *Id.* at 1551.

D. ASSESSMENT DISTRICTS

Special assessment districts were historically popular, as a community could "come together" around a needed facility, such as a park or fire station. Bonds can be sold below market lending rates because interest to the bond purchaser is tax exempt. Each landowner then pays an annual assessment to service the bonds.

The scheme was particularly attractive when facility costs and interest rates were very low. Assessments, however, can be a hardship for those on low or fixed incomes, and they can aggravate the impact of rising real property taxes on modest homebuyers. Not surprisingly, developers may prefer assessment district financing over impact fees, because assessment districts allow them to pass on the cost to new residents. In contrast, if impact fees are used, the developer may not be able to pass them on to buyers as part of the sales price if the real estate market is "soft" and price competition between builders is keen.

STRAUSS v. TOWNSHIP OF HOLMDEL
711 A.2d 1385 (N.J. Super. L. 1997)

LOCASCIO, J.S.C. . . .

Plaintiffs represent approximately 137 property owners who reside in two separate subdivisions, the Estates of Holmdel and the Hills of Holmdel, which were approved for construction in sections in 1963, 1965, 1970 and 1972. Because there were no sewer trunk lines available, nor any plans to install trunk lines in the vicinity, the developers were not required to install sewer lines as a condition of approval, and therefore the houses were built with septic tanks.

Late in 1989, the septic systems began experiencing such serious failures that neither the repair, nor the reconstruction, of the systems was practicable. Because a nearby trunkline was, by then, under construction, making the installation of sewer lines into the Estates of Holmdel and the Hills of Holmdel feasible, defendant Holmdel Township decided, in June 1990, to extend the sewer lines into these developments.

On October 22, 1990, a sewer assessment ordinance, providing for the construction of sewer lines into the subdivisions, was introduced by defendant's township committee; a public hearing on the ordinance was held on November 26, 1990. After the ordinance's unchallenged adoption, bonds were sold to finance the project. A bonding ordinance was passed on December 17, 1990, and published on December 20, 1990, which provided for the issuance of $4,100,000 in bonds and, in order to offset a portion of the sewer installations costs, directed the levy of a special assessment on plaintiffs' properties, in accordance with the sewers' resultant increase in the value of each lot. Any amounts not paid, by those lot owners who received the benefit, would be paid by the township.

The installation of the sewer lines was completed in July, 1993 at a total cost of $2,755,986.00. Pursuant to N.J.S.A. §§40:56-1-89, a Sewer Assessment Commission was established which, after an investigation, which included a real estate appraisal, site visits, and consideration of comments made at a May 17, 1995 public hearing, concluded that this improvement resulted in a benefit of $14,700 per lot. The Commission's report was confirmed by a resolution of the township committee on September 11, 1995.[1] Plaintiffs filed their amended complaint, challenging this assessment, on October 11, 1995. Defendants now move for summary judgment as to count I, alleging equal protection violations, and court II, alleging negligence.

I . . .

The Equal Protection Clause of the United States Constitution, made applicable to the states by the Fourteenth Amendment to the United States Constitution, requires "all persons similarly situated be treated alike and that no State . . . shall deny to any person within its jurisdiction the equal protection of the laws." . . .

[P]laintiffs contend that defendant's conduct fails to meet the "rational basis" standard which, in order to withstand constitutional attack, requires the regulation to be rationally related to a legitimate governmental objective. The rational basis test requires that the regulation (1) not be arbitrary or capricious and (2) have a rational basis in relation to the specific objective to be obtained. . . .

Furthermore, a municipal ordinance, like all legislation, is entitled to a strong presumption of constitutionality. . . . "The burden of demonstrating that a statute contravenes the equal protection clause is extremely formidable, as is attested by the long trial of failure." . . .

When conducting an equal protection analysis under Article 1, Paragraph 1 of the New Jersey Constitution, the Court has employed a balancing test, which requires the Court to consider (1) the nature of the affected right, (2) the extent to which the governmental restrictions intrude upon it, and (3) the public need for the restriction. . . .

In the instant action, an analysis of the Equal Protection Clause of the United States Constitution and of the New Jersey Constitution yields the same result. A

1. Ultimately, the residents of the Estates of Holmdel and the Hills of Holmdel contributed $2,013,900 of the total cost of the sewer installation project, and the township absorbed the balance of $742,086. Had the township not absorbed this balance, the cost to the homeowners would have amounted to approximately $20,116 per lot.

governmental entity may levy special assessments against properties which will benefit from a local improvement, including "the construction . . . of a sewer or drain in, under or along a street, alley or public highway, or portion thereof, or in, under or along any public or private lands." N.J.S.A. 40:56-1. Here, plaintiffs concede that, because the sewer lines increased the value of each home in question, their installation constitutes an improvement and not a service.

It is well-settled that the decision of whether particular improvements should be undertaken as a general improvement, for which the whole township would pay, or a local improvement, for which the specifically benefited property owners will pay to the extent they will be benefited, rests within the sound discretion of the municipality. . . .

Plaintiffs contend that the township's decision to levy a special assessment was arbitrary and capricious because the facts of this case are indistinguishable from previous situations where the township paid for sewers out of general funds. However, important distinctions exist between the Estates of Holmdel and Hills of Holmdel and the three other projects which the township financed.

The first of these three projects, Old Mannor and Newstead, were sewered in the 1960's at a time when the township was not facing the growing population and anticipated sewer costs it is facing today. The second of these three projects, located on Alloco Drive, was a relatively simple, single street project, costing approximately $120,000, which did not require the construction of a pump station because the nearest trunk line was located downhill from the development. In addition, at the time that the Alloco Drive project was approved, the township was in a period of intense development, so developers' connection fees and additional user fees, were generally sufficient to cover the costs of the sewers. The North Beers Street project, the third financed by the township, which cost only $100,000, was, like the two other projects, much less complex than the Estates of Holmdel and Hills of Holmdel. Conversely, the Estates of Holmdel and the Hills of Holmdel are characterized by numerous very hilly streets, rolling terrain, streams, flood plains, steep slopes, and wetlands. While other areas in the township may have some of these characteristics, they generally do not have the severe changes in topography which typify the Estates of Holmdel and the Hills of Holmdel. These distinctions in size and topography are what make a sewer system in the Hills of Holmdel and the Estate of Holmdel more complex and more expensive than the other projects financed by the township.

Plaintiffs also argue that they are being treated differently than those residents who live in developments where the developers were required to install sewers as a condition for approval. However, in all likelihood, the cost of installing those sewers was passed on to the residents of those developments in the purchase price of their homes. Therefore, the residents of those other developments have paid for their sewers in much the same way that the residents of the Estates of Holmdel and the Hills of Holmdel, by virtue of defendant's sewer assessment, have paid for theirs.

The township contends that it was looking toward the future when it decided to levy a special assessment upon plaintiffs. Because a large portion of the township is still unsewered, if the township now sets a precedent by absorbing a large portion of the sewer costs, it will be using township tax monies to install sewer systems in various different neighborhoods. The township's only option, in paying for future sewers, is to increase taxes and sewer rates, or levy special assessments.

To increase taxes and sewer rates for the entire town, in order to benefit only one certain group of citizens, would not be fiscally responsible to the remaining portions of the township. Plaintiffs are seeking to have all the residents of the township pay for a sewer system which benefits only them. This is unfair to the other taxpayers of the township. The township has a duty to be fiscally responsible to all its citizens. . . .

For the aforesaid reasons this court concludes that (1) because sewer lines were not readily available to this section of the township when the subdivisions were originally constructed, the township had a rational basis for not requiring the developer to install sewer lines, and (2) because of the complexity and the higher costs associated with now constructing sewers in the subdivisions, a rational basis exists for the township's decision to levy a special assessment against those directly benefited by the sewers. Because plaintiffs have not demonstrated facts sufficient to overcome the presumption of constitutionality, these decisions of defendant Holmdel are neither arbitrary nor capricious.

Therefore, this court finds that the township has not violated plaintiff's equal protection rights provided by the United States and New Jersey constitutions. Accordingly, defendant township's motion for summary judgment on count I is granted.

Notes and Comments

1. *The Mechanics of Special Assessments*. Under financing by the traditional special assessment district, an area petitions the city to establish the district. The city then sells bonds to undertake capital improvements funded by annual assessments imposed on all those benefited in the district. For example, the city may charge over a ten-year period based on the front footage of each property or the assessed value of each parcel. *See City of Boca Raton v. State*, 595 So. 2d 25 (Fla. 1992) (property assessed must receive a special benefit from the service provided, and the assessment must be reasonably apportioned among the specially benefited properties).

The *Strauss* decision presents the less common involuntary special assessment. In most cases the community or landowner to be benefited petitions the government to establish the district, rendering the process voluntary. As the special assessment in *Straus* does not involve a permit application, *Nollan* and *Dolan* would appear inapplicable, leaving only a claim of excessive regulatory taking, which is discussed in Chapter 7.

2. *Facilities Benefit Assessment Districts*. In *J.W. Jones Companies v. City of San Diego*, 203 Cal. Rptr. 580 (Ct. App. 1984), the county sought to plan for adequate infrastructure in a generally undeveloped area and to shift the primary burden of financing facilities to developers and new residents. The financing device created to implement the county's comprehensive plan was the Facilities Benefit Assessment (FBA). The area in question envisioned 23,130 residential units and 698 acres of commercial and industrial uses. Based on an estimated $55 million for streets and parks, nearly $27 million would be charged to the developer and approximately the same amount would be raised through the FBA. The remaining amount, just under $2 million, would be paid by the city and other sources.

The developer made several legal challenges to the FBA. As the charge was imposed to recoup the cost of public improvements made to specially benefit the property, the court found that the FBA was not a tax or assessment subject to Proposition 13, which would have required supermajority referendum approval by voters. The court also rejected an equal protection claim based on the exemption of already developed properties, concluding that such properties were not similarly situated for they did not generate the need for the new proposed facilities. All undeveloped properties were treated similarly with an FBA assessment.

The FBA differs from the traditional special assessment in several respects. First, the traditional assessment is charged to properties specially benefited on the basis either of (1) an allocation to owners based on the front footage of the parcel in relation to the total frontage in the benefited district, or (2) the percentage of assessed valuation of each parcel. Under the FBA, the assessment is equally divided between each dwelling unit. Second, under the traditional special assessment, payments are made annually over a period, such as ten years, to service bonds sold to finance the facility. Under the FBA, the assessment is paid at the time of building permit application. By comparison, if the financing technique was an impact fee, the fee might be due upon subdivision approval. Thus, under the FBA, the developer can await market demand for units and avoid the higher carrying costs associated with impact fees.

Third, unlike the traditional special assessment, the scheme does not consider the location of an assessed parcel; thus, proximity and contiguity to the facility are not essential. Finally, under the traditional special assessment, all benefited properties are equitably assessed for the benefit enjoyed. Under the FBA, developed properties are exempt.

The FBA is similar to the traditional special assessment in one respect: funds collected are earmarked and spent solely for the purpose for which the assessment was imposed. Both are enforced through lien foreclosure.

3. *FBAs or Special Assessments?* Would the developer and future residents prefer infrastructure financing by FBA or special assessment? Knowledge that they have to pay an annual assessment in addition to property taxes and mortgage payments may upset future homeowners, who may not realize that the price of their home, and thus their monthly mortgage payment, are lower because of the assessment. In addition, the income tax consequences of an assessment may be different from those of a mortgage. From the developer's standpoint, the FBA is superior. It is paid on a per dwelling basis as building permits are sought, while under the traditional special assessment, the assessments for each parcel come due annually regardless of the pace at which the project is actually constructed.

4. *Business Improvement Districts.* A variation on the special assessment district is the Business Improvement District, or "BID." BIDs are typically undertaken as a mini-redevelopment strategy to enhance the attractiveness of commercial districts. Rather than placing the administration within an existing or newly created governmental service district, BIDs are administered by private, nonprofit boards made up of district business owners. BIDs allow businesses in a specific neighborhood to increase the level of services provided by government.

For example, the BID might be used to provide additional security, valet parking, maintenance, expansion of public pedestrian spaces, installation of attractive lighting, or widening of sidewalks for landscaping and outdoor cafes and dining. The BID also might be used for the "calming" of streets, that is, strategies to reduce automobile traffic. In Europe, traffic calming is often initiated to make streets available for pedestrians. Suzanne H. Crowhurst Lennard & Henry L. Lennard, Liveable Cities 98 (1987) (Dutch transportation policy called a "Woonerf" is not so much an auto-free policy as a traffic reduction or calming scheme often calling for the mixed use of streets by pedestrians, children, and residents' automobiles); Eran Ben-Joseph, Changing the Residential Street Scene: Adapting the Shared Street (Woonerf) Concept to the Suburban Environment, 61 J. Am. Plan. Ass'n 504 (1995). See also Donald Appleyard, Liveable Streets (1981).

BIDs are often authorized by statute. *See, e.g.*, Cal. Sts. & High. Code §§36601-36670 (West Supp. 2002). In *Foote Clinic, Inc. v. City of Hastings*, 580 N.W.2d 81 (Neb. 1998), the court found that BIDs were authorized. It concluded, however, that the BID violated state law by failing to specifically set forth the improvements to be made in the district and the estimated costs of those improvements. The Nebraska court ruled that assessment ordinances are to be strictly construed with doubts resolved in favor of the taxpayer. *See also* Kessler v. Grand Cent. Dist. Management Ass'n, 158 F.3d 92 (2d Cir. 1998) (BID district not subject to one-person, one-vote equal protection requirement, sustaining a weighted voting system that guaranteed majority representation by property owners). See generally Richard Briffault, A Government for Our Time? Business Improvement Districts and Urban Governance, 99 Colum. L. Rev. 365 (1999); David J. Kennedy, Restraining the Power of Business Improvement Districts: The Case of the Grand Central Partnership, 15 Yale L. & Pol'y Rev. 283 (1996) (BIDs can be used to generate profits for business and cause gentrification, which may result in displacing or excluding the less wealthy and which may adversely affect adjacent areas or the larger community without participation from citizens or area residents); Daniel R. Garodnick, Comment, "What's the BID Deal? Can the Grand Central Business Improvement District Serve a Special Limited Purpose?," 148 U. Pa. L. Rev. 1733 (2000). Can a BID directed to commercial uses in such a district exempt residential dwellings from assessments? *2nd Roc-Jersey Assocs. v. Town of Morristown*, 731 A.2d 1 (N.J. 1999) (sustaining special improvement district statute exempting residential properties).

5. *Municipal Subdivision Liability for Infrastructure Deficiencies.* In an omitted part of the opinion, the New Jersey Court in *Strauss* held that the Township was immune from liability for negligently permitting construction of the development without sewers. However, other jurisdictions may permit liability exposure. *See Charlie Brown Constr. Co. v. Boulder City*, 797 P.2d 946 (Nev. 1990) (city liable in negligence for failure to obtain payment on performance bond for incomplete developer improvements); *Pickle v. Board of County Comm'rs of County of Platt*, 764 P.2d 262 (Wyo. 1988) (rejecting immunity for approval with inadequate septic system).

5

Planning

A. INTRODUCTION

1. The Allure of Planning

Since the advent of modern zoning in this century, the notion has existed that a planning process resulting in a plan (variously denominated a "master," "general," or "comprehensive" plan) will take place prior to the adoption of zoning. As discussed in Chapter 2, the Standard Zoning Enabling Act served as the model for the first zoning ordinances in many municipalities, and the link between planning and zoning was expressly recognized in the Act. It declared that zoning must be "in accordance with a comprehensive plan."

Furthermore, the concept that zoning must be comprehensive in nature and based upon rational planning is reflected in the seminal *Village of Euclid v. Ambler Realty* opinion upholding the constitutionality of zoning. As we have seen, in that decision the Supreme Court first quoted from an Illinois decision which observed that the exclusion of businesses from a residential district "is part of the general plan by which the city's territory is allotted to different uses." 272 U.S. 365, 392 (1926) (quoting *City of Aurora v. Burns*, 149 N.E. 784, 788 (Ill. 1925)). The Court also referred to "investigations" and "comprehensive reports" of various "commissions and experts," reports that the Court found "bear every evidence of painstaking consideration." 272 U.S. at 394. In effect, the Court described a planning process.

The idea that planning can provide solutions to particular societal problems has always strongly attracted legislative bodies, in part because it allows legislators to claim that, by establishing a planning process, they have "done something" in response to the problem. As one recent study of the planning profession summarized, "[c]onfidence in the efficacy of rational intervention had long been part of the reform tradition that developed earlier in the century and was institutionalized by the federal administration as part of Roosevelt's New Deal." Charles Hoch, What Planners Do: Power, Politics, and Persuasion 36 (1994); see also Robert Fishman (ed.), The American Planning Tradition (2000). Thus, it is not surprising that, during the same time period that the U.S. Department of Commerce produced the Standard Zoning Enabling Act, the department also issued the Standard Planning Enabling Act.

The attraction to planning has only increased in recent decades. When widespread concern over environmental degradation, such as diminishing open space and poor air and water quality, arose around 1970, planning was seen as the long-term solution to those ills. Thus, the federal Clean Air and Clean Water Acts include numerous provisions calling for the adoption of plans, and many states require the preparation of plans for critical land use areas, such as the coastal zone. And recent federal legislation requires planning for the national forests and other federally managed lands.

2. *The Rise of the Consistency Doctrine*

Because planning and zoning both concern how land should be used, it seems logical that some connection would be required between the two. However, as illustrated in *Wolf v. City of Ely*, a recent Iowa decision included in this chapter, most courts have rejected the argument that the language in the Standard Zoning Enabling Act requires that adoption of a separate planning document precede zoning. Planning and later regulatory implementation through tools such as zoning were not linked, with the result that plans rarely had any actual effect on land use decisions.

In the last 20 years, however, a growing number of jurisdictions have reemphasized the concept of planning and, at the same time, altered this traditional relationship between planning and zoning. Many states have adopted statutory provisions requiring local jurisdictions to adopt comprehensive master or general plans. These statutes can be quite precise about the required content of the plan, a development illustrated in this chapter by *Twain Harte Homeowners Ass'n v. County of Tuolumne*.

In addition, significant numbers of states have adopted statutes requiring zoning, subdivision, and other regulatory controls to be "consistent" with the comprehensive general plan adopted by the local jurisdiction. These consistency statutes often have been accompanied by statutory provisions expanding the breadth of the local plan's contents, with the result that planning now encompasses a wide variety of subjects, ranging from economic development to use of natural resources. The push for consistency statutes did not result from uniformity of academic opinion on the subject; there was vigorous debate over whether this linkage is a good idea. But the *results* of using traditional land use controls without any link to a separate planning process were almost universally criticized, and this criticism bolstered arguments that planning and regulatory decisions such as zoning should be linked through consistency requirements.

These statutory requirements requiring linkage have led in turn to litigation over the meaning of "consistency." The principal question is how closely the regulatory mechanism, whether it is zoning or regulation of a subdivision, must follow the general plan. Is "strict" consistency required, or does the local governmental body have discretion to determine what type of development will be consistent?

The Arizona Supreme Court's decision in *Haines v. City of Phoenix*, which you will read in this chapter, squarely addresses the meaning of consistency. You must determine whether the court interpreted the statutes in this jurisdiction correctly, but you must also ask whether "strict" or "loose" consistency will best promote the goals of comprehensive planning.

3. *The Efficacy of Consistency Requirements*

The consistency statutes, which state legislatures began to enact in the early 1970s, have now been in place for a sufficient time to allow the drawing of some conclusions about their usefulness. The consistency requirement ideally allows planning to take place in an environment separated from the day-to-day political concerns that often permeate local regulatory decisions about land use. The theory is that once local governments have undertaken a planning process, made choices about the future course of land use in their jurisdiction, and adopted a plan to reflect those choices, they can then begin the process of implementing the plan. The integrity of the completed planning process will serve to ensure the rationality of zoning, subdivision, and other development decisions that the jurisdiction will make.

As might be expected, however, the reality of the planning process usually has not lived up to this ideal. If the general plan is the vehicle that drives regulatory decisions "on the ground," then it is quite difficult to divorce the planning process from the politics that is part of day-to-day development decisions. Thus, in some instances the process of adopting the general plan has itself given rise to intense political controversy over growth policies in the local jurisdiction. In response, one tendency of the planners has been to deflect the political firestorm by adopting a plan that is either vague on key policy decisions or that includes policies designed to please all concerned factions.

Another outcome of the consistency requirements has been to transform the problem of "spot zoning" into one of "spot planning." If the plan rather than the zoning ordinance is the critical force in the regulatory decision about the land use allowed on a specific property, and the plan's map calls for one type of use while the landowner wants another, the "answer" from the landowner's point seems simple: request the local jurisdiction to amend the plan map. Over the long term, however, such a solution pleases almost no one. Promoters of the plan see parcel-specific amendments as undermining the achievement of the plan's overall policies, while development interests decry the bureaucracy involved. In their view, it now takes two steps to get a development approved—a plan change and then a later zone change, subdivision approval, or other type of permit approval—rather than the one step that was needed before the consistency requirement became effective.

Despite these criticisms, planning and consistency requirements continue to have strong support, and planning has achieved some notable successes, particular in the case of plans addressing specific regional problems or areas of critical concern, such as coastal zones. For example, the plan prepared and implemented by the San Francisco Bay Conservation and Development Commission has achieved significant success in attaining its prime objective of preventing the continued filling of San Francisco Bay. In 1965, when the planning process started, almost one-third of the original bay had been filled, but since the plan was completed and implemented, almost no further filling has occurred. These types of outcomes breed hope that, given the right circumstances, planning can be a success.

4. *Planning in the Future*

As plans become increasingly important, new legal issues involving plans will arise, and old ones will be revisited. One important issue is whether a plan can effect a taking of private property, requiring compensation under the Fifth Amendment. In general, courts have traditionally held that planning, in and of itself, does not effect a taking. Their logic is simple: if the plan is not linked to an actual decision on development, the plan has no actual regulatory effect and thus cannot "take" property in the constitutional sense. But if a consistency requirement is in place and the plan becomes the key document in local development decisions, the argument that the plan actually and directly affects property becomes much stronger.

To date, most courts have continued to find that "planning," even in a strong consistency jurisdiction, does not effect a taking, a line of decisions that gives some breathing room to the planning process. Future litigation on the issue, however, seems certain.

In the end, any determination about the efficacy of planning necessarily must return to many of the concerns raised in Chapter 1 about the political environment in which land use decisionmaking takes place and the role of governmental discretion in making land use decisions. In a recent book on planning, the authors noted the debt that current laws have to the Standard Zoning Enabling Act and the Standard City Planning Enabling Act. They then commented that "[o]ne of the fundamental concepts included in the system was that of removing planning from politics." Eric Damian Kelly and Barbara Becker, Community Planning 21 (2000). The student must decide whether it is possible — or even desirable — to separate a "rational" planning process for land use from the more overtly political side of specific land use regulatory decisions.

If you decide that this separation is both possible and a worthy goal, you must also ponder the possibility that planning may become so specific and rigid that it will result in unfairness to individual landowners, and thus give rise to the same demands for "flexibility" that we examined in Chapter 2 with respect to zoning. But if the plan is too flexible, has the consistency requirement really brought any improvement in land use decisionmaking, or has it just added another layer of bureaucracy?

These are hard questions, but they lie at the core of the modern emphasis on planning as a predicate for regulatory approvals.

B. LAND USE PLANNING IN PERSPECTIVE

Behind the relatively simple idea of separating land uses through the adoption of a zoning ordinance was a set of assumptions regarding the role of government and the rationality of decisionmaking processes. Some of these assumptions were surely utopian, but their influence continues to be felt in land use law today.

The first of the following two excerpts demonstrates how planning was viewed at the outset of modern land use regulation, while the second addresses the same question at a later date.

UNITED STATES DEPARTMENT OF COMMERCE, A STANDARD CITY PLANNING ENABLING ACT

(1928)

Sec. 6. General Powers and Duties
It shall be the function and duty of the commission to make and adopt a master plan for the physical development of the municipality, including any areas outside of its boundaries which, in the commission's judgment, bear relation to the planning of such municipality. Such plan, with the accompanying maps, plats, charts, and descriptive matter, shall show the commission's recommendations for the development of said territory, including, among other things, the general location, character, and extent of streets, viaducts, subways, bridges, waterways, water fronts, boulevards, parkways, playgrounds, squares, parks, aviation fields, and other public ways, grounds and open spaces, the general location of public buildings and other public property, and the general location and extent of public utilities and terminals, whether publicly or privately owned or operated, for water, light, sanitation, transportation, communication, power, and other purposes; also the removal, relocation, widening, narrowing, vacating, abandonment, change of use or extension of any of the foregoing ways, grounds, open spaces, buildings, property, utilities, or terminals; as well as a zoning plan for the control of the height, area, bulk, location, and use of buildings and premises. . . . The commission may from time to time amend, extend, or add to the plan.

Sec. 7. Purposes in View
In the preparation of such plan the commission shall make careful and comprehensive surveys and studies of present conditions and future growth of the municipality and with due regard to its relation to neighboring territory. The plan shall be made with the general purpose of guiding and accomplishing a coordinated, adjusted, and harmonious development of the municipality and its environs which will, in accordance with present and future needs, best promote health, safety, morals, order, convenience, prosperity, and general welfare, as well as efficiency and economy in the process of development; including, among other things, adequate provision for traffic, the promotion of safety from fire and other dangers, adequate provision for light and air, the promotion of the healthful and convenient distribution of population, the promotion of good civic design and arrangement, wise and efficient expenditure of public funds, and the adequate provision of public utilities and other public requirements.

In the following recent article, the author describes the variety of different types of plans that local planners have produced.

■ WILLIAM C. BAER, GENERAL PLAN EVALUATION CRITERIA: AN APPROACH TO MAKING BETTER PLANS

63 J. Am. Plan. Ass'n 329 (1997)

The Plan as Vision. The plan as vision has once again garnered popularity in the profession. Simply put, the vision plan is an elegant attempt to publicly propose a "What if?" — to stimulate thought and elicit comment. Appropriate criteria pertain to communicating the vision in an empathetic, visceral and stimulating way that touches not just the mind, but the soul. . . .

The Plan as Blueprint. There was a tendency in the early days of planning to believe that a vision plan could readily be converted to a blueprint plan. The early term "Master Plan" nicely captures the underlying blueprint sentiment. The physical orientation of a Master Plan as blueprint was reflected in Bassett's (1938) early call to limit the scope of the plan to what can be shown on a municipal map: elements like streets, sidewalks, street trees, parks, lakes, public building sites, and the general districts for which private land should be zoned. . . .

Unfortunately, this approach produced few plan successes in the "real world." Often it was the zoning ordinance that was really the blueprint, while the general plan, if there was one, was strictly advisory. . . .

The Plan as Land Use Guide. The general plan as land use guide appeared in the 1950s. Although there were variants, it took a middle of the road approach to what a plan might be. . . .

The plan was a vision of the future, but not a blueprint; a policy statement, but not a program of action; a formulation of goals, but not schedules, priorities, or cost estimates. It was to be uninhibited by short-term practical considerations. . . .

The Plan as Remedy. The alternative to the plan as vision is the plan as remedy: the cure for an existing problem. Urban slums and the promise of federal moneys for their renewal in the 1950s provided such an alternate route to plan reconceptualization. Redevelopment plans were one result. Unlike general plans, redevelopment plans were short-range and specific, aimed at remedying the problems of slum housing, not at building new housing in the suburbs. The appropriate criteria here were largely federally determined, and were in the form of hurdles to surmount, or tests to pass, in order to receive a grant of funds: Local governments had to demonstrate their need for renewal by producing a comprehensive description of slum problems, and demonstrate their administrative and financial capacity to respond effectively by citing a Workable Program that called for a general plan, building codes, financial capacity — and, for the first time — citizen participation in governance. . . .

Process, not Plans. Beginning in the 1960s, planning as an ongoing process, rather than merely making particular plans, was widely embraced as the profession's true purpose. As Altshuler noted, a common planning principle held that "planning is more important than any plan." Moreover, the technical and factual underpinnings of physical plans were deemed insufficient. The city was no longer thought of as simply an artifact to be shaped by criteria for physical design; it was viewed as a mechanism of inter-related parts to be selectively transformed by applying criteria derived from systems theory. The social sciences were introduced to equip planners with more understanding of urban cause-effect relationships.

Modeling urban processes, not drawing up a blueprint, was the key component shaping the criteria for this system.

Two other facets of a process orientation were citizen participation and planner advocacy for the poor. These concerns, too, introduced their own criteria. And in broadening the planner's perspective, social science also cast doubt on the validity of traditional planning criteria. There was no unitary "public interest," the social sciences reported, nor any possibility of rationalism and comprehensiveness. . . . Planning's legitimacy could be bestowed only by a participatory or advocacy process. . . .

Plans as Pragmatic Action. Discussion about plans during the 1970s tended toward the pragmatic. The American Law Institute's (1976) extensive Model Land Development Code, directed toward revising the enabling laws for planning, provided a streamlined framework for subdivision, zoning, and redevelopment. Its implicit criteria were procedural, focusing on how to mesh these assorted devices, but paying less heed to concern for the plan as overall direction-setter for development. . . .

Plans as Responses to State and Federal Planning Mandates. During the 1970s, state-wide plans came into being, often triggered by environmental concerns. . . . Most recently, in this vein, habitat conservation plans (HCPs) have introduced substantive criteria based on biodiversity and ecology.

Is the emphasis on planning worthwhile? The excerpt from the following article suggests that planning does more harm than good.

ANDREW P. MORRIS & ROGER E. MINERS, THE DESTRUCTIVE ROLE OF LAND USE PLANNING

14 Tul. Envtl. L.J. 95, 96-97 (2000)

Over the past century, land use planning by regulatory agencies has increasingly displaced the decentralized process of private landowners making their own decisions about land use. Local governments, county governments, state governments, and, to an increasing extent, the federal government are all requiring private landowners to modify their plans in order for their land to conform to government plans. Increasingly, such plans are justified as necessary to protect the environment, which extends their reach beyond traditional land use concerns like protecting residential neighborhoods from commercial intrusions.

These steps are justified by the need to account for the public interest in preserving endangered species, protecting the environment, coordinating land use in crowded urban centers, preventing urban sprawl, and curbing countless other alleged environmentally destructive ills. Only by imposing planning, so the argument goes, can the land use be rationalized to prevent destructive, self-interested behavior from creating a sterile series of concrete suburbs populated only by strip malls and sidewalk-less neighborhoods. Unfortunately, the increased scope and complexity of planning has reduced the clarity and certainty of property rights in land without necessarily accomplishing its goals. As the traditional rights of landowners become more dependent upon planners' approval, property rights increasingly resemble feudal tenures rather than the traditional common law notions of property rights.

At the same time as planning increases its reach over private land use decisions, the planning model has fallen into disrepute in the economy generally. The experience of the twentieth century suggests that the use of decentralized markets, not central planners, is the superior means of social coordination. Planned economies on the right (Nazi Germany, Fascist Italy) and the left (the former Soviet and eastern bloc countries, Communist China, North Korea, Cuba) either collapsed or are collapsing.

The obvious question thus presents itself: is land use planning fundamentally different from other forms of central planning? If so, does that difference suggest that land use planning will succeed where other forms of central planning failed? We conclude that land use planning is not fundamentally different from other forms of economic central planning. Further, the working of the market economy, and the long-term success of America's economy, is intertwined in the clear and certain rights and responsibilities generated by the common law of property. The complexity of the modern world does not diminish the need for private property; indeed, it strengthens its imperative. Returning to a feudal conception of property is bad for personal freedom, bad for civil society, and bad for the environment.

Notes and Comments

1. *The Role of the Planning Commission.* Like the Standard Zoning Enabling Act discussed in Chapter 2, the Standard City Planning Enabling Act was drafted under the auspices of the federal Department of Commerce. Although not nearly as influential as the model act for zoning, the planning act included provisions that have influenced the adoption of state planning legislation. Why does the Act call for the planning commission, rather than the local city council or body of elected officials, to adopt the plan? What does this choice say about whether the drafters of the Act envisioned the planning process as political in nature or as involving the application of expertise?

2. *Blueprint and Vision Plans.* Is it possible for a local government to create a blueprint plan, that is, one that is quite precise in terms of what land uses are envisioned for particular properties, and then actually to follow the plan when specific land use decisions, such as rezoning and subdivision approvals, are made? Does the inherently political nature of local governmental control of land use make the implementation of a plan impossible?

Is a blueprint plan even advisable? If the plan is that specific, does it usurp the function of zoning and subdivision regulation, so that the end result is simply more bureaucracy?

What are the benefits of creating a vision plan? Can we expect that, if all the various segments of a community are involved in creating a vision plan, the local elected officials will implement the plan's vision when they later make decisions about specific developments?

3. *"Process, not Plans."* The concept of process as the most important feature of planning has led some commentators, as the Baer article notes, to conclude that there is no single "public interest" with which the plan could be identified. Thus, the plan becomes, as the article indicates, a "side-show." Do you agree? Or

can planning processes based on rationalism reach generally accepted conclusions about land uses?

4. *The Possible Functions of a Plan.* In a classic article on the subject of planning, Professor Charles Haar suggests several functions that the general plan may perform: (1) as a device for serving "notice" on public and private parties as to the probable outcome of their development proposals; (2) as a basis for internal coordination of various governmental actions and programs; (3) as a "framework" for coordinating various land use regulatory devices; (4) as an actual control on private activities upon land; and (5) as a safeguard against arbitrary regulatory action. Charles Haar, The Master Plan: An Impermanent Constitution, 20 Law & Contemp. Probs. 353 (1955). In *Bell v. City of Elkhorn*, 364 N.W.2d 144, 147 (Wis. 1985), the Wisconsin Supreme Court stated that the objectives sought through the development of a comprehensive plan include the following:

> (1) improving the physical environment of the community; (2) promoting the public interest; (3) facilitating the implementation of community policies on physical development; (4) effecting political and technical coordination in community development; (5) injecting long-range considerations into the determination of short-range actions; and (6) bringing professional and technical knowledge to bear on the making of political decisions concerning the physical development of the community.

Which of these rationales for the plan do you find realistic and sufficient to justify the often considerable expenditure of resources needed to prepare a plan?

5. *Planning as a Meaningful (or Meaningless) Exercise.* Consider the reasoning of the Oregon Supreme Court in *Baker v. City of Milwaukie*, 533 P.2d 772, 776 (Or. 1975):

> If that plan is to have any efficacy as the basic planning tool for the City of Milwaukie, it must be given preference over conflicting prior zoning ordinances. To hold otherwise would allow a city to go through the motions and expense of formulating a comprehensive plan and then relegating that document to oblivion through continued reliance on the older zoning ordinances.

Is planning a meaningless exercise if the law does not require that zoning ordinances, subdivision maps, and other regulatory approvals must conform to the plan?

6. *Citizen Participation.* How important is citizen participation to the preparation of the plan? Can we expect citizens to devote the time needed to participate in the plan preparation, or will they only be galvanized into action when a specific development proposal becomes a subject for debate?

Must plans be "democratic," and thus involve extensive citizen participation? Or are they better viewed as technical documents, in which planning experts put their knowledge to work to solve planning problems?

7. *Planning and Bargaining.* As you will see in Chapter 10, one of the key developments in land use law over the past two decades has been the increased use of bargaining between cities and developers as a means of making land use decisions. In Planning and the Law, 20 Vt. L. Rev. 657 (1996), Professor Mandelker posited

that a key issue in land use planning is the tension between the need for flexibility to make decisions and the need to limit discretion. He continued:

> These two needs are often difficult to reconcile. A city council must deal with a dynamic political environment and must engage in political bargaining in which outcomes are unpredictable. Notice that a "political bargaining in which outcomes are unpredictable" requires flexibility and the discretion to shape decisions to problems and opportunities as they arise. A binding comprehensive plan can impede this kind of bargaining by limiting the discretion of decision-makers.

Id. at 657-658. Do you agree? Are comprehensive planning and bargaining inherently irreconcilable?

8. *Is Planning Counterproductive?* The Morris and Miners and article raises an interesting comparison. The Communist Bloc of countries centered their economies on a model of economic planning, and that effort failed miserably. Are land use plans doomed to the same fate? Or, to make just one counterargument, will extensive public participation in plan development give them a legitimacy that was not present in the economic planning efforts of the Communist countries?

9. *Is Planning Irrelevant?* Another question is whether the plans are not so much counterproductive as simply irrelevant. Over twenty years ago, a planning professor argued that most master city plans are seriously defective. In his view, the plans "depict land uses as urban planners wish they could be 20 years hence," not what the body politic wants or will accept. He also charged that plans avoid most critical urban problems, while another set of plans is too short-range. Melville C. Branch, Sins of City Planners, Pub. Admin. Rev. (Jan./Feb. 1982). If Professor Branch is correct, are these simply failures of the planning profession, and thus preventable, or are they inevitable outcomes, given what planning is trying to accomplish?

10. *Plans in the Twenty-First Century*. Can you think of how general societal developments today will affect planning over the next 20 years? One planner sees the following development:

> Twenty-first century plans will also reflect the information age. In recent years, many communities have made use of local access television to introduce community planning issues to the broader public. Similarly, a number of communities are starting to use the Internet to post draft sections of their plans, as well as the final product. In the future, virtual reality images will become commonplace, allowing people to actually "see" how the physical nature of their town or city might change in response to differing policies.

Michael Chandler, The 21st Century Comprehensive Plan, Planning Commissioner's Journal 41 (Summer 1998).

Planners are making imaginative uses of new media, such as the Internet and computer-generated drawings, to visualize planning efforts and to make a wide variety of data available to the public. *See* Karen Finucan, The World of E-Planning, *Planning* 4 (July 2001) (listing some of the most interesting municipal websites).

11. *Commentary*. In addition to the Haar article, cited above in these notes, *see also* Daniel R. Mandelker, The Role of the Local Comprehensive Plan in Land Use Regulation, 74 Mich. L. Rev. 899 (1976). The classic book in the planning literature on general plans is T. J. Kent, The Urban General Plan (1964).

C. THE FORM AND CONTENT OF THE GENERAL PLAN

All regulatory efforts embody planning to some greater or lesser degree. After all, even a poorly executed zoning ordinance does "plan" for land uses on that property. A critical question, however, is whether a municipality must prepare a master or general plan that is separate from the zoning ordinances that it adopts, or whether the plan can be found within those ordinances. As you can see from the case below, although the Standard Zoning Enabling Act raised this question in the 1920s, courts today continue to consider it.

■ WOLF v. CITY OF ELY

493 N.W.2d 846 (Iowa 1992)

ANDREASEN, Justice.

The City of Ely adopted a zoning ordinance in 1978. The district court declared the ordinance invalid because it was not adopted in accordance with a comprehensive plan. Upon review we affirm the district court's declaratory judgment.

I. BACKGROUND.

John and Pat Wolf own three connecting parcels of land in or adjacent to the City of Ely that have been identified as parcels A, B and C. The Wolfs operate a salvage or junkyard on their property. Parcel A is located in an area that was zoned manufacturing; parcel B is located in an area zoned commercial; and parcel C is located in an area zoned residential or agricultural. . . .

The Wolfs filed the present action on April 9, 1990, seeking a court judgment declaring the entire zoning ordinance invalid and their use of their property (parcels A, B and C) lawful. The Wolfs allege the entire zoning ordinance is invalid [because] . . . it was not adopted in accordance with a comprehensive plan. . . .

III. COMPREHENSIVE PLAN.

. . . Iowa Code section 414.3 requires that zoning regulations "shall be made in accordance with a comprehensive plan." The requirement of a comprehensive plan is found in the zoning law of those states that have taken the standard state zoning enabling act as their model. The act did not define the term comprehensive plan.

A majority of courts in states where zoning must be "in accordance with a comprehensive plan" hold a plan external to the zoning ordinance is not required. 2 *The American Law of Real Property*, Planning and Zoning §12.02 (1991). However, an increasing number of legislatures specifically require that a plan be adopted. *Id.* The "comprehensive plan" requirement was imposed to prevent piecemeal and haphazard zoning. Standard State Zoning Enabling Act (United States Department of Commerce, §3 n.22 (1922)). The word "plan" connotes an integrated product of a rational process; the word "comprehensive" requires something beyond a piecemeal approach. . . .

Iowa Code section 358A.5, relating to county zoning, contains the identical requirement. In discussing this requirement, we stated: "If the Board gave full consideration to the problem presented, including the needs of the public, changing conditions, and the similarity of other land in the same area, then it has zoned in accordance with a comprehensive plan." *Montgomery v. Bremer County Bd. of Supervisors*, 299 N.W.2d 687, 695 (Iowa 1980). The Iowa Court of Appeals commented, "nothing in Chapter 358A requires a county to reduce a comprehensive plan to written form." *Webb v. Giltner*, 468 N.W.2d 838, 840 (Iowa App.1991). The comprehensive plan requirement is intended to ensure the county board acts rationally rather than arbitrarily in exercising their delegated zoning authority. *Id.* . . .

Prior to the adoption of the 1978 zoning ordinance, Ely had established a planning and zoning commission. Under a 1976 ordinance, the Ely planning and zoning commission had authority to make such surveys, studies, maps, or plans which the commission believed bears a relation to the general comprehensive plan. The ordinance provided . . . that after adoption of a comprehensive plan by the commission an attested copy of the plan shall be certified to the council. The council could then approve the plan, and it would constitute the City's comprehensive plan. . . .

Contrary to the statutory and ordinance requirements, no comprehensive plan was developed by the commission and appropriately presented to the council. At trial, Thomas M. Tjelmeland, the mayor of Ely, admitted he was unaware of any written criteria used in development of the 1978 zoning ordinance. He testified the comprehensive plan consisted of the City's zoning ordinance combined with its zoning map. There were no other documents that he relied upon in interpreting the zoning ordinance.

A councilman of the City testified that no single person had been designated as administrative officer responsible for the administering of the zoning ordinance. The mayor and members of the Ely council would bring zoning matters to the entire council on an ad hoc basis. The councilman further testified that, in making decisions as to whether a specific use is allowed in a specific zone, he just listened, and if he thought it was right, he would go along with it. He had not heard of a comprehensive zoning plan.

The City offered evidence that, in June of 1975, the Linn County Regional Planning Commission (county commission) prepared a housing and community development study and a Linn County regional land use policy plan. The study recommended Ely and other nonmetropolitan cities use the plan as a guide for future growth and development. Although mayor Tjelmeland represented the City of Ely on the county commission, he testified he was unaware of any studies conducted when the 1978 zoning ordinance was drafted. He was unaware of any writing that set forth any proposed or future land use. He testified the 1975 regional housing and land use policy plans were not used in any of Ely's planning or zoning decisions.

The 1978 zoning ordinance was developed by combining different sections and provisions of two or more "model" municipal zoning ordinances. Throughout the ordinance, specific provisions of the model ordinances were deleted, marked "omit" or additional provisions were added in long-hand. . . .

At least two, and possibly four, different zoning maps have been identified as the official city zoning map. The City offered a crayola-colored zoning map as the official zoning map. This map was different than the zoning map identified as Ely's official zoning map in the first trial in 1989. One of the maps indicates the Wolfs' "tract C" was agricultural; the other indicates it was residential. The City acknowledges the 1978 zoning ordinance and zoning map have not been officially amended, changed, modified, or repealed.

Ely's zoning ordinance and zoning map do not suggest an integrated product of rational planning. The ordinance contains glaring omissions and serious structural problems. Although a significant portion of the land within the city limits is identified as agricultural land, the zoning ordinance makes no provisions regulating its use. Some words and terms that are defined in the ordinance are not used later in the ordinance. Extensive provisions relating to mobile homes are included in the definition section. Under the ordinance provisions, mobile homes are permitted only in an approved mobile home park. However, a mobile home park is not a permitted use or special use in any of the seven districts. Junkyards are specifically defined, although they are not a permitted use or special use in any of the districts. In one part of the zoning ordinance, the City prohibits fences of over five feet; in another part it requires a six-foot fence. The ordinance has twenty-eight separate parking classes for off-street parking, although the population of Ely was 275 in 1970 and 425 in 1980.

The structural problems in the zoning ordinance obviously arose from a careless combining of two or more model ordinances. Although such a clip-and-paste ordinance could produce a valid ordinance if carefully and rationally prepared, here the structure and content of the ordinance suggests a careless and irrational process was employed.

Other evidence demonstrates the City's failure to adopt the zoning ordinance in accordance with a comprehensive plan. Studies and plans developed by the county commission in 1975 were not considered by the council. The Ely Planning Commission failed to comply with the City ordinance requirement that a comprehensive plan be certified to the council as an attested copy of the plan. Although city records indicate the commission had presented a proposed zoning ordinance and zoning map in 1977, the records do not identify the proposed ordinance and map. Because the official zoning map was not clearly identified, there was confusion as to the limitation of uses to be applied to certain parcels of land. Amendments or changes to the ordinance and zoning map were reported in the city records, but council approval was made by resolution, contrary to ordinance and statutory requirements. . . .

. . . We, like the district court, find the City failed to comply with the requirement that zoning regulations be made in accordance with a comprehensive plan.

Notes and Comments

1. *"In Accordance with a Comprehensive Plan."* As the *Wolf* case indicates, the Standard Zoning Enabling Act requires that all zoning be "in accordance with a comprehensive plan." The *Wolf* court interprets this phrase as not requiring a plan that is separate from the zoning ordinance. This interpretation, that the comprehensive plan and the zoning ordinance are one and the same, is sometimes referred to as the "unitary" view and is the one that most jurisdictions have

adopted. *See, e.g., Green v. County Council of Sussex County*, 508 A.2d 882, 889 (Del. Ch. 1986) ("The comprehensive plan with which zoning regulations must be in accordance, in order to satisfy the requirement of non-arbitrary action, does not necessarily refer to a written document or series of written documents distinct from the zoning ordinance. Instead, the plan may be discerned from a review of the regulatory language itself"); and *Bogan v. Sandoval County Planning and Zoning Commission*, 890 P.2d 395, 404 (N.M. Ct. App. 1994) ("a comprehensive plan may be found within the [zoning] ordinance itself where a comprehensive plan has not been enacted and . . . the plan need not even be in the form of a document").

2. *A Historical Dispute*. Most courts and commentators addressing the meaning of the "in accordance with a comprehensive plan" language have concluded that the drafters of the Standard Zoning Enabling Act were not referring to a separate plan. *See, e.g, State of Missouri ex rel. Chiavola v. Village of Oakwood*, 886 S.W.2d 74, 80 (Mo. Ct. App. 1994) (citing the notes accompanying the 1926 version of the Standard Zoning Enabling Act). However, a recent article suggests that this conclusion was in error. The author cites unpublished materials from the time the Act was drafted as well as other published materials at the time. He concludes: "This historical backdrop suggests that preparation of an independent plan or study should be a condition precedent to the adoption of a zoning ordinance." Stuart Meck, The Legislative Requirement That Zoning and Land Use Controls Be Consistent with an Independently Adopted Local Comprehensive Plan: A Model Statute, 3 Wash. U. J.L. & Pol'y 295, 304 (2000).

3. *The Role of Rationality*. If the purpose of the "comprehensive plan," "master plan," or "general plan," as it is variously called, is to ensure the rationality of the zoning process, would this goal be better served by requiring that the plan be a separate document from the zoning ordinance? On the other hand, could a court legitimately hold that the language "in accordance with a comprehensive plan" mandates a separate plan if no statute in the jurisdiction specifically sets forth the content of the plan?

4. *The Reasoning in* Wolf. If a separate plan is not required, why did the *Wolf* court pointedly note that the 1976 ordinance gave the planning commission the authority to prepare a separate plan, but that the commission did not do so? Even if a separate general plan is not required for zoning to be "in accordance with a comprehensive plan," the preparation of such a plan can help a municipality convince a court that its zoning meets this statutory requirement. Note also the *Wolf* court's emphasis on the fact that no other studies were conducted when the 1978 zoning ordinance was drafted.

In an influential 1968 decision, the New York Court of Appeals discussed the requirement that zoning be "in accordance with a comprehensive plan." It concluded that the master plan was relevant to determining whether this requirement was met:

> [T]he "comprehensive plan" requires that the rezoning should not conflict with the fundamental land use policies and development plans of the community. These policies may be garnered from any available source, most especially the master plan of the community, if any has been adopted, the zoning law itself and the zoning map.

Udell v. Haas, 235 N.E.2d 897, 902 (N.Y. 1968) (citations omitted). *See also Boyles v. Town Bd. of Bethlehem*, 718 N.Y.S.2d 430, 433 (N.Y. App. Div. 2000) (comprehensive plan "gleaned from" the Town's zoning code, map, and Land Use Management Advisory Committee plan).

5. *Dueling Plans.* If a jurisdiction does not interpret the language "in accordance with a comprehensive plan" to require a separate plan, what effect does the adoption of such a separate plan have? In another Iowa case, *Webb v. Giltner*, 468 N.W.2d 838 (Iowa 1991), the county enacted a comprehensive plan for part of its jurisdiction. It then approved a rezoning for certain property, and opponents challenged the rezoning, arguing that the rezoning was arbitrary because the county did not consider the separate plan in approving it. The county responded that as long as the rezoning was consistent with the comprehensive plan revealed by the zoning ordinance itself, it was valid.

The court disagreed: "Were we to accept the Board's invitation to ignore The Plan, we would nullify Wapello County's concerns, efforts, and expenditures incorporated into that individualized comprehensive plan. We would, in effect, repeal that enactment—an act which we have no power to perform." *Id.* at 840.

Are you convinced? If a separate plan is not required, why must the county follow it? If there are two plans—one from the zoning ordinance and a separate plan—and the municipality follows the zoning plan, how could that conceivably be arbitrary?

In recent years an increasing number of states have adopted statutes which authorize or require the preparation of a separate general plan. Many of these statutes set forth the requirements of the plan in considerable detail. As you read the following statute, which is representative of those adopted in many states, note especially the variety of different issues—including some only tangentially related to land use—that the plan must address.

NEW JERSEY STATUTES ANNOTATED
§40:55D-28

a. The planning board may prepare and, after public hearing, adopt or amend a master plan or component parts thereof, to guide the use of lands within the municipality in a manner which protects public health and safety and promotes the general welfare.

b. The master plan shall generally comprise a report or statement and land use and development proposals, with maps, diagrams and text, presenting, at least the following elements (1) and (2) and, where appropriate, the following elements (3) through (13):

(1) A statement of objectives, principles, assumptions, policies and standards upon which the constituent proposals for the physical, economic and social development of the municipality are based;

(2) A land use plan element (a) taking into account and stating its relationship to the statement provided for in paragraph (1) hereof, and other master plan elements provided for in paragraphs (3) through (13) hereof and natural conditions . . . (b) showing the existing and proposed location, extent

and intensity of development of land to be used in the future . . . and stating the relationship thereof to the existing and any proposed zone plan and zoning ordinance; and (c) showing the existing and proposed location of any airports and the boundaries of any airport safety zones . . . and (d) including a statement of the standards of population density and development intensity recommended for the municipality;

(3) A housing plan element . . . including, but not limited to, residential standards and proposals for the construction and improvement of housing;

(4) A circulation plan element showing the location and types of facilities for all modes of transportation required for the efficient movement of people and goods into, about, and through the municipality, taking into account the functional highway classification system of the Federal Highway Administration and the types, locations, conditions and availability of existing and proposed transportation facilities, including air, water, road and rail;

(5) A utility service plan element analyzing the need for and showing the future general location of water supply and distribution facilities, drainage and flood control facilities, sewerage and waste treatment, solid waste disposal and provision for other related utilities, and including any storm water management plan required. . . .

(6) A community facilities plan element showing the existing and proposed location and type of educational or cultural facilities, historic sites, libraries, hospitals, firehouses, police stations and other related facilities, including their relation to the surrounding areas;

(7) A recreation plan element showing a comprehensive system of areas and public sites for recreation;

(8) A conservation plan element providing for the preservation, conservation, and utilization of natural resources, including, to the extent appropriate, energy, open space, water supply, forests, soil, marshes, wetlands, harbors, rivers and other waters, fisheries, endangered or threatened species wildlife and other resources, and which systemically analyzes the impact of each other component and element of the master plan on the present and future preservation, conservation and utilization of those resources;

(9) An economic plan element considering all aspects of economic development and sustained economic vitality, including (a) a comparison of the types of employment expected to be provided by the economic development to be promoted with the characteristics of the labor pool resident in the municipality and nearby areas and (b) an analysis of the stability and diversity of the economic development to be promoted;

(10) An historic preservation plan element: (a) indicating the location and significance of historic sites and historic districts; (b) identifying the standards used to assess worthiness for historic site or district identification; and (c) analyzing the impact of each component and element of the master plan on the preservation of historic sites and districts; . . .

(12) A recycling plan element which incorporates the State Recycling Plan goals . . . and;

(13) A farmland preservation plan element, which shall include: an inventory of farm properties and a map illustrating significant areas of agricultural land; a statement showing that municipal ordinances support and promote agriculture as a business; and a plan for preserving as much

> farmland as possible in the short term by leveraging monies made available . . . through a variety of mechanisms including, but not limited to, utilizing option agreements, installment purchases, and encouraging donations of permanent development easements.

In the next case, a court considers whether the local jurisdiction has complied with planning requirements that are quite similar to those in the New Jersey statutes.

TWAIN HARTE HOMEOWNERS v. COUNTY OF TUOLUMNE

188 Cal. Rptr. 233 (Ct. App. 1982)

OPINION

MORONY, Associate Justice.

STATEMENT OF THE CASE

This appeal arises out of challenges to the sufficiency of the Tuolumne County General Plan. . . .

"The Planning and Zoning Law (Govt. Code, tit. 7, div. 1, commencing with §65000) require[s] . . . that the board of supervisors of each county adopt a general plan for the 'physical development' of the county, pursuant to section 65300; that the plan be prepared and adopted according to standards established in section 65300.5 and 65301; and that it include each of nine 'elements' enumerated and described in section 65302." (*Camp v. Board of Supervisors* (1981) 123 Cal. App. 3d 334, 340, fn. omitted, 178 Cal. Rptr. 620.)[1] . . .

DISCUSSION . . .

2. THE GENERAL PLAN.

a. Land Use Element.

Appellant contends that the general plan fails to meet statutory requirements in several of its elements. Initially, appellant contends that the land use element of the general plan does not comply with statutory requirements of Government Code section 65302, subdivision (a).

Section 65302, subdivision (a), provided in 1980 that a general plan mandated by section 65300: . . .

1. Except where otherwise indicated, statutory citations are to provisions of the Government Code as they read in 1980.

Section 65302 provided in pertinent part as follows:

> The general plan shall consist of a statement of development policies and shall include a diagram or diagrams and text setting forth objectives, principles, standards, and plan proposals. The plan shall include the following elements: [¶] (a) A land use element. . . . [¶] (b) A circulation element. . . . [¶] (c) A housing element. . . . [¶] (d) A conservation element . . . [¶] (e) An open-space element. . . . [¶] (f) A seismic safety element. . . . [¶] (g) A noise element . . . [¶] (h) A scenic highway element. . . . [¶] (i) A safety element. . . .

> shall include . . . [¶] A land use element which designates the proposed general distribution and general location and extent of the uses of the land for housing, business, industry, open space, including agriculture, natural resources, recreation, and enjoyment of scenic beauty, education, public buildings and grounds, solid and liquid waste disposal facilities, and other categories of public and private uses of land. *The land use element shall include a statement of the standards of population density and building intensity* recommended for the various districts and other territory covered by the plan. . . . (Emphasis added.)

The initial task faced by this court in determining the adequacy of the land use element is to determine the meaning of the terms "population density" and "building intensity." These terms are not defined in the relevant statutes, regulations or guidelines. The parties have cited no authority to assist this court in determining what the statute requires in this regard.

The general plan states "densities" for "urban residential" uses in terms of the maximum number of "dwelling units per gross acre". With respect to non-urban designations of "residential/agricultural", and "resource" lands, densities are stated in terms of minimum lot sizes. No densities are provided for areas designated "commercial," "open space," "industrial," "park and recreation," or "public/institutional/school. " . . .

The County contends in the instant case that the measurement of dwelling units per acre meets the requirement for a statement of standards for population density and that the omission of a statement of population density for "commercial," "industrial" and "open space" land use designations reflects the fact that no residential development is permitted on those lands.

In a planning context, statements of population density might reasonably be related to residency rather than to the extent of intensity of use of all classifications.

For census purposes "population density" has been calculated as "the number of persons per square mile of land area . . . " and "[e]ach person enumerated was counted as an inhabitant of his usual place of abode. . . . " (U.S. Dept. of Commerce, Bureau of the Census, 1970 Census Users' Guide (Oct. 1970) at p. 93.)

Cases in the zoning context have referred to measures of population density in terms of numbers of people per dwelling unit. (*See Village of Belle Terre v. Boraas* (1973) 416 U.S. 1, 19, 94 S. Ct. 1536, 1546, 39 L. Ed. 2d 797 (dis. opn. of Marshall, J.).)

The term "population density" has also been used to refer to maximum numbers of people living in a residential development. (*See, e.g., Trinity Episcopal School Corporation v. Romney* (S.D.N.Y. 1974) 387 F. Supp. 1044, 1080.). . . .

It could be argued that in the planning arena standards of population density might most usefully be stated in terms of dwelling units per acre where some relationship between an average number of people per household has been established and where distinctions based upon factors such as the size and type of dwelling (e.g., single family residences, multiple family residential, mobile home) are supported in the plan.

Nevertheless, we cannot believe that the Legislature intended the terms "population density" and "building intensity" to be synonymous. . . .

It appears that the reasonable interpretation of the term "population density" as used in Government Code section 65302 is one which refers to numbers of *people* in a given area and not to dwelling units per acre, unless the basis for correlation between the measure of dwelling units per acre and numbers of people is set forth explicitly in the plan.

In the instant case, no statement relating dwelling units to numbers of people is presented in the general plan. Thus, we conclude that appellant's land use element is deficient insofar as it lacks an appropriate statement of standards for population density based upon numbers of people.

With respect to the requirement that the land use element must contain a "statement of the standards of . . . building intensity recommended for the various districts and other territory," there is no statement of building intensity for uses designated in the plan as "commercial," "residential/agricultural," "open space," "industrial," "park and recreation" or "public/institutional/school." At most, the "urban residential" designation with its statement of maximum dwelling units per acre is the only land use designation with any building intensity standard. Minimum lot sizes set for "residential/agricultural" and "resource" areas are not sufficient as a statement of a building intensity. Nor are general use captions such as "commercial-neighborhood," "commercial-shopping center," "commercial-visitor serving," "light industrial" and "heavy industrial," which provide only the vaguest picture of the intensity of development to be permitted in those areas and provide no standards at all as to possible restrictions such as height or size limitations, restrictions on types of buildings or uses to be permitted within a designated area. We therefore conclude that the land use element of the Tuolumne County general plan does not comply with the requirements of Government Code section 65302 as it fails to set forth an adequate statement of standards of population density and building intensity recommended for the various districts and other territory covered by the plan.

b. Circulation Element.

Appellant further contends that the general plan is deficient for its failure to comply with the mandates of Government Code section 65302, subdivision (b) which requires in pertinent part that the plan include "[a] circulation element consisting of the general location and extent of existing and proposed major thoroughfares, transportation routes, terminals, and other local public utilities and facilities, *all correlated with the land use element of the plan*." (Emphasis added.) . . .

Insofar as the Tuolumne County General Plan is concerned, the circulation element is contained in chapter VI: 2-3 and VI: 5 and on the display map which outlines existing and proposed roads designated as "arterial," "major collector," or "minor collector."[9] . . .

9. In its entirety, the textual portion of the transportation-circulation element of the general plan provides as follows:

TRANSPORTATION/CIRCULATION [policy]

7 The street and highway network in the county will be classified according to the function they are intended to serve. The following four functional classifications will be used in Tuolumne County:

Arterial—serves statewide and interstate travel. Primarily federal and state highways.
Major Collector—serves intraregional travel. Average travel distances are shorter than on arterial routes.

In the present case it can be seen that the circulation element does not attempt to describe or discuss the changes or increases in demands on the various roadways or transportation facilities of the County as a result of changes in uses of land which will or may result from implementation of the decision system and the general plan. As stated in a letter from several individuals commenting upon the draft general plan, "The [MEIR] and the MDGP do not address the important issues such as the demographic center of the county, the population centers, the movement habits of users or the traffic counts of the main roads and intersections."

Although the Government Code does not explicitly require that a circulation element contain an inventory and data analysis followed by a locally derived program to solve problems identified in the inventory, and we do not so hold, it seems apparent from a review of the general plan [and] the supporting . . . documentation that there is no way to determine whether in fact the circulation element is correlated with the proposed land use element. . . . The requirement of Government Code section 65302, subdivision (b) is that the land use element be correlated with the circulation element. The Tuolumne County general plan does not comply with the statutory requirements in this regard. . . .

FRANSON, Acting P.J., and ANDREEN, J., concur.

Notes and Comments

1. *Advising the County on Remand.* Think carefully about the grounds upon which the court holds that the general plan does not meet the requirements of state law. As a lawyer, what advice would you give to the county concerning the specific steps that it must take to cure the plan's deficiencies?

2. *The Contents of Plans.* A recent book on planning identifies four parts to the "Typical Organization of a Long-Range Urban General Plan": (1) background material, including a summary of present conditions, assumptions concerning the future, projections of growth or change, and current and emerging issues; (2) goals and general policies; (3) an overview of the major plan proposals; and (4) inclusion of the specific elements in the plan. Anderson, Guidelines for Preparing Urban Plans 11 (1995). In *Town of Jonesville v. Powell Valley Village Limited Partnership,*

Minor Collector—collects traffic from local roads and channels it to major collectors or arterials. Serves to link locally important traffic generators.

Local Roads—provide access to immediately abutting land uses or rural areas. Provide service over relatively short distances compared to collectors and arterials.

8 The County of Tuolumne will ensure that both its existing and proposed street configurations serve the ultimate functions they are intended to serve by protecting their alignments from encroachment.
9 The County of Tuolumne will encourage the development of a balanced transportation system, including public transit as well as privately operated vehicles.
Scenic corridors along scenic routes in the county will be preserved. . . .

TRANSPORTATION/CIRCULATION [implementation]

G Adopt the functional street and highway classification indicated on the General Plan maps.
H Ensure that rights-of-way for future streets are protected from encroachment by current development.
I Designate as scenic routes those roads and highways listed in Appendix F. The appendix also indicates the scenic features and implementation recommendations associated with each scenic route.

487 S.E.2d 207 (Va. 1997), the Virginia Supreme Court emphasized that under Virginia law, prior to a plan's adoption "a local governing body must conduct studies covering a wide range of factors including existing land use and development, trends and growth, population, employment and economic factors, public facilities, transportation facilities, and housing needs."

3. *Statutes and Types of Plans*. Recall the Baer article in which he outlined various types of plans (vision plans, blueprint plans, and so forth) that local jurisdictions might produce. Do the statutes set forth above assume that the plan will be one of these types? Do the statutes preclude the adoption of certain types of plans (that is, preclude the adoption of a vision plan, for instance)?

4. *Internal Plan Consistency*. The preparation of a comprehensive general plan requires tradeoffs among the various resources and interests implicated by the plan. The political difficulty of making such tradeoffs may lead to plans with internally conflicting policies. For example, the plan may promise to preserve open space or agriculture while, at the same time, calling for a level of building within the jurisdiction that is inconsistent with preserving substantial amounts of open space or agricultural land. Some states try to avoid this problem by explicitly providing that the jurisdiction's general plan must be internally consistent. For example, Rhode Island requires that the comprehensive plan "shall be internally consistent in its policies, forecasts, and standards." R.I. Gen. Laws §45-22.2-6.

Could a local jurisdiction adopt elements of a plan that are in conflict but then render them internally consistent by including a clause in the plan which states that, in the event of such internal conflict, the land use element of the plan is to take precedence over all other elements? In *Sierra Club v. Kern County Bd. of Supervisors*, 179 Cal. Rptr. 261 (Ct. App. 1981), the court found such a clause invalid. Do you agree? Didn't the county's plan make the basic policy judgment needed by adopting the precedence clause?

Another related issue is whether each individual element of the plan must be internally consistent. *See Concerned Citizens of Calaveras County v. Calaveras County Bd. of Supervisors*, 212 Cal. Rptr. 273, 278 (Ct. App. 1985) ("[t]he first problem with the Calaveras County General Plan is that its circulation element is internally inconsistent on its face and therefore incomprehensible").

5. *The Scope of the Planning Effort*. The New Jersey statute reproduced above allows a city to undertake an extensive planning effort. In one sense, a broad statute like this one allows a city to tailor its planning efforts to its individual circumstances. Small, rural cities will plan much differently from larger, urban cities.

The scope of the plan, however, raises the question of whether local planners can meaningfully address the topics authorized. As you can see, those range from economic development to recycling to farmland preservation. But if this kind of planning can be meaningfully carried out, perhaps there are other, broader topics that plans should address. For example, some recent literature has strongly argued that planners have paid insufficient attention to race. See Charles Hoch, Racism and Planning, 59 J. Am. Plan. Inst. 451 (1993) ("[M]ost planning professionals, like most Americans, do not give racism much thought. Planners rarely study racism or write about it in their professional journals, even though the rare analysis has uncovered evidence of continuing racial discrimination despite civil rights reforms."). See also Charles Smith, Racism and Community

Planning: Building Equity or Waiting for Explosions, 8 Stan. L. & Pol'y Rev. 61 (1997).

To what extent can planning address problems of racism? Does it depend largely on the type of plan (e.g., vision plan, blueprint plan, etc.) that the jurisdiction adopts?

6. *Planning and Federal Lands*. The emphasis on detailed land use planning, evident in the statutes and case you just read, extends beyond the local level. Congress has required federal land management agencies to engage in planning processes to decide the uses of those lands. See George Cameron Coggins, The Developing Law of Land Use Planning on the Federal Lands, 61 U. Colo. L. Rev. 307 (1989); Chapter 9, *infra*.

D. CONSISTENCY REQUIREMENTS

States that require the adoption of separate general plans often make the plan the primary land use document by requiring that zoning, subdivision maps, and other regulatory approvals conform in some manner to the general plan. Such consistency requirements, however, differ markedly from state to state. Consider the following statutes:

■ RHODE ISLAND GENERAL LAWS §45-24-30
Lexis 1999

Zoning regulations shall be developed and maintained in accordance with a comprehensive plan prepared, adopted, and may be amended, in accordance with chapter 22.2 of this title. . . .

■ NEW JERSEY STATUTES ANNOTATED §40:55D-62A
(West Supp. 2003)

(a) The governing body may adopt or amend a zoning ordinance relating to the nature and extent of the uses of land and of buildings and structures thereon. Such ordinance shall be adopted after the planning board has adopted the land use plan element and the housing plan element of a master plan, and all of the provisions of such zoning ordinance or any amendment or revision thereto shall either be substantially consistent with the land use plan element and the housing plan element of the master plan or designed to effectuate such plan elements; provided that the governing body may adopt a zoning ordinance or amendment or revision thereto which in whole or part is inconsistent with or not designed to effectuate the land use plan element and the housing plan element, but only by affirmative vote of a majority of the full authorized membership of the governing body, with the reasons of the governing body for so acting set forth in a resolution and recorded in its minutes when adopting such a zoning ordinance. . . .

ME. REV. STAT. ANN. TIT. 30-A §4352
(West 1996)

2. Relation to comprehensive plan. A zoning ordinance must be pursuant to and consistent with a comprehensive plan adopted by the municipal legislative body.

Consider also the following section from model legislation produced by the American Planning Association's "Smart Growth" project:

8-104 CONSISTENCY OF LAND DEVELOPMENT REGULATIONS WITH LOCAL COMPREHENSIVE PLAN

(1) Land development regulations and any amendments thereto, including amendments to the zoning map, and land-use actions shall be consistent with the local comprehensive plan, provided that in the event the land development regulations become inconsistent with the local comprehensive plan by reason of amendment to the plan or adoption of a new plan, the regulations shall be amended within [6] months of the date of amendment or adoption so that they are consistent with the local comprehensive plan as amended.

(a) Except as provided in paragraph (1) above, any land development regulations or amendments thereto and any land-use actions that are not consistent with the local comprehensive plan shall be voidable to the extent of the inconsistency.

(3) The local planning agency shall find that proposed land development regulations, a proposed amendment to existing land development regulations, or a proposed land-use action is consistent with the local comprehensive plan when the regulations, amendment, or action:

(a) furthers, or at least does not interfere with, the goals and policies contained in the local comprehensive plan;

(b) is compatible with the proposed future land uses and densities and/or intensities contained in the local comprehensive plan; and

(c) carries out, as applicable, any specific proposals for community facilities, including transportation facilities, other specific public actions, or actions proposed by nonprofit and for-profit organizations that are contained in the local comprehensive plan.

Notes and Comments

1. *Voluntary Consistency.* If no state statute requires that zoning or other approvals be consistent with the master or general plan, could a local government adopt such a requirement voluntarily? In *Board of County Commissioners of Larimer County v. Conder*, 927 P.2d 1339 (Colo. 1996), the county first adopted a master plan, which was advisory only in the state. It then, however, included a requirement of compliance with the master plan in its subdivision regulations

and denied a subdivision application on that ground. The Colorado Supreme Court concluded that, under the Colorado Local Government Land Use Control Enabling Act of 1974, the county had the authority to incorporate master plan density provisions into its subdivision regulations. The master plan provisions at issue, however, "must be drafted with sufficient exactitude so that proponents of new development are afforded due process, the county does not retain unfettered discretion, and the basis for the county's decision is clear for purposes of reasoned judicial review." *Id.* at 1351. *See, e.g., West Bluff Neighborhood Ass'n v. City of Albuquerque*, 50 P.3d 182 (N.M. Ct. App. 2002) (finding that city may voluntarily adopt a consistency requirement but did not do so in this case); *Coffey v. Maryland-National Capital Park and Planning Commission*, 441 A.2d 1041 (Md. 1982) (upholding denial of a subdivision on the basis of inconsistency with the master plan where the consistency requirement was adopted by ordinance rather than compelled by statute).

2. *More Consistency Without a Statute?* Are there some circumstances in which a city *must* follow its master or general plan, even though no statute specifically requires that its actions be consistent with the plan? *Compare Friends of "B" Street v. City of Hayward*, 165 Cal. Rptr. 514 (Ct. App. 1980) (city's public works project must be consistent with its general plan even though no specific statute requires consistency), *with Lake City Corp. v. City of Mequon*, 544 N.W.2d 600 (Wis. Ct. App. 1996) (city could not reject a subdivision on the basis of inconsistency with the recently adopted master plan where a statute allowed disapproval if the subdivision plat did not comply with "[a]ny local master plan which is consistent with any . . . official map" but, in this case, the newly adopted master plan conflicted with the city's official map). *See also Garat v. City of Riverside*, 3 Cal. Rptr. 2d 504 (Ct. App. 1991) (zoning ordinance adopted by initiative did not have to be consistent with the general plan of the defendant, a charter city (i.e., a city incorporated pursuant to its own individual charter) where state law exempted charter cities from the requirement that zoning ordinances be consistent with the general plan).

3. *Statutory Approaches to Consistency.* Consider the statutory consistency requirements that you read. Are they sufficiently clear so that city officials can implement them? Is it better to try and define the term "consistent" or to leave it to local governments to interpret? Does the Smart Growth Model Statute capture more of the policy basis for consistency than the shorter statutes?

The New Jersey approach is markedly different. It allows an approval that is not consistent but imposes voting and findings requirements. Is it better to allow inconsistencies, as New Jersey does, as long as the local officials fully face the inconsistency?

Are courts in that state more likely to apply a "tighter" interpretation of consistency because they know that local officials can approve projects even if they are not consistent with the plan? *See, e.g., Willoughby v. Planning Bd. of Township of Deptford*, 740 A.2d 1097, 1100 (N.J. Sup. App. Div. 1999) (reversing trial court, finding that the project was not consistent, and noting that such a finding "merely triggers two procedural requirements: a majority vote of the full authorized membership of the governing body and a statement of reasons"). The court specifically noted that the statute "does not require amendment of the master plan before an inconsistent ordinance is adopted." Will courts require local governments to fully recognize the inconsistency before they will uphold an action taken inconsistent with the plan? *See Willoughby v. Wolfson Group, Inc.*, 753 A.2d 162 (N.J.

Sup. App. Div. 2002) ("before adopting a zoning amendment inconsistent with the master plan, the governing body must expressly recognize the inconsistency. This will give effect to the significance the Legislature attached to the master plan").

4. *What Must Be Consistent?* As you saw in Chapter 2, local governments make a wide variety of land use decisions. They approve rezonings, subdivisions, variances, use permits, planned unit developments, site plans, etc. If a state has a consistency requirement, which of these decisions are subject to it? The answer will turn on the particular statutory language and on judicial interpretation. *See, e.g., Bragdon v. Town of Vassalboro*, 780 A.2d 299, 302 (Me. 2001) ("No comprehensive plan is required before such a site review ordinance is adopted"); *City of Chicago Heights v. Living Word Outreach Full Gospel Church and Ministeries, Inc.*, 749 N.E.2d 916, 930 (Ill. 2001) (comprehensive plan is advisory, and City's zoning ordinance did not include requirement that special use permit must conform to the comprehensive plan).

The same issue can arise with a subordinate plan, such as a specific plan, which is intended to implement the general plan. *See Napa Citizens for Honest Government v. Napa County Bd. of Supervisors*, 110 Cal. Rptr. 2d 579 (Ct. App. 2001). The court of appeal first held that the consistency doctrines requires the specific plan to "recite goals and policies that are consistent with those set forth in the County's General Plan." *Id.* at 606. According to the court, "The proper question is whether development of the Project Area under the Updated Specific Plan is compatible with and will not frustrate the General Plan's goals and policies." *Id.* Is the difference between the two plans a clear one?

5. *The Case Against Consistency*. Is the requirement of consistency with a general plan a good idea? Consider the views of Professor Dan Tarlock, who argues against such a requirement:

> The legitimacy of a planning choice rests on the assertion that collective intervention produces a net gain in society's aggregate welfare. The planner's claim is that his or her proposal will promote the most fair allocation of available resources. A planning choice would be readily perceived as legitimate if, by curing market imperfections, it achieved an allocation equivalent to that produced by a perfectly competitive market. Too often, however, the aggregate gains of a planning choice cannot be estimated. The planning choice is not designed to force internalization of external costs, which are difficult enough to quantify, but is based upon the assumption that the planner's re-distributive values are superior to those of the market and will result in a net gain to the aggregate welfare.

A. Dan Tarlock, Consistency With Adopted Land Use Plans as a Standard of Judicial Review: The Case Against, 9 Urb. L. Ann. 69, 75-76 (1975). Do you agree?

6. *The Influence of the Plan*. Even if a jurisdiction has not adopted a requirement that zoning must be consistent with the general plan, should the plan be taken into account in determining whether a rezoning is arbitrary or capricious? Or does the fact that the legislature has refused to adopt a consistency requirement mean that a separate, comprehensive plan is irrelevant to all zoning decisions? In *Board of County Commissioners of Johnson County v. City of Olathe*, 263 Kan. 667, 952 P.2d 1302 (1998), the Supreme Court of Kansas commented that cities "are not bound by their comprehensive plans in making these rezoning decisions," but it "urged that

the plans not be overlooked when changes in zoning are under consideration." *Id.* at 1313 (citing *Taco Bell v. City of Mission*, 234 Kan. 879, 894, 678 P.2d 133 (1984)). The court, however, then posed the question whether "this seeming disregard for both the City's officially adopted comprehensive plan and the airport compatibility plan tip the scales toward a finding of unreasonableness [of the rezoning]"? The court concluded that the rezoning was not unreasonable, citing the presumption that the zoning authority acted reasonably.

Did the court give too much deference to the city? What's the point of preparing a plan if a rezoning is flatly inconsistent with that plan but is nevertheless approved? In *Urrutia v. Blaine County*, 2 P.3d 738 (Idaho 2000), the court overturned the County Board's denial of a subdivision based solely on noncompliance with the comprehensive plan. The subdivision ordinance required that the land subdivided "shall conform to the Comprehensive Plan," but there was no statutory consistency requirement. The court first observed that the board "may . . . refer to the comprehensive plan as a general guide in instances involving zoning decisions." *Id.* at 743. However, "a more specific analysis, resulting in denial of a subdivision application based solely on non-compliance with the plan elevates the plan to the level of legally controlling zoning law." *Id.* Thus, the Board erred in relying completely on the comprehensive plan. *Id.*

Does the Court's reasoning make sense?

Even if it is clear from the statute that the state has adopted some form of consistency requirement, applying that requirement may be far from simple. Particularly troublesome are situations in which the general plan is incomplete, a fact pattern that arose in the following case. But even if the plan is complete, the court must determine how much deference it should accord to a city's determination that a land use decision is consistent with the city's general plan.

■ HAINES v. CITY OF PHOENIX
727 P.2d 339 (Ariz. App. 1986)

OPINION

HATHAWAY, Chief Judge.

Appellant contests the trial court's granting of summary judgment in affirmance of the City of Phoenix's (city) authority to rezone the parcel in controversy. . . .

On January 1, 1974, Arizona's Urban Environment Management Act (act) became effective. Laws 1973, Chapter 178; A.R.S. §9-461 et seq. The act requires municipalities to adopt long-range, general plans for urban development. A.R.S. §9-461.05(A). The act also authorizes specific plans. A.R.S. §9-461.08. The act requires municipal zoning ordinances be consistent with the general plans. §9-462.01(E). On July 3, 1979, the city adopted two plans—the Phoenix Concept Plan 2000 and the Interim 1985 Plan. It is disputed whether these plans are general or specific plans as defined by the statute.

This action arose from the Phoenix City Council's granting of a "height waiver" for a highrise office project that is proposed to be constructed by appellee

Adams Group on 14.48 acres of land on Central Avenue between Glenrosa and Turney avenues in Phoenix. The property was zoned C-2H-R (intermediate commercial highrise) and subject to a 250-foot highrise limitation. The 1985 plan also limits to 250 feet buildings in the area in which this parcel is located.

On July 29, 1983, the Adams Group submitted an application to amend the city zoning ordinance to permit a building on the parcel in excess of the 250-foot height limitation. The rezoning application was heard by the planning commission on November 16, 1983. That body recommended denial by a 3 to 2 vote. Pursuant to §108-J.1 of the city zoning ordinance the Adams Group requested the city council to hold a public hearing on the application and not to adopt the planning commission's recommendation. Two hearings were held, on December 19, 1983 and February 6, 1984. On February 6, the city council approved a rezoning which allowed the Adams Group to erect a 500-foot building. Appellant then filed this action alleging the city council's action is inconsistent with the general or specific plans and therefore is in violation of A.R.S. §9-462.01(E). Appellees argue that the city had not adopted either a general or specific plan at the time of the city council action and the only issue before the city council was whether there was compliance with §412-B.2-F(1) of the Phoenix Zoning Ordinance, permitting height amendments.[1] . . .

I. HAS THE CITY ADOPTED A GENERAL OR SPECIFIC PLAN?

The act does not establish a timetable for the adoption of a general plan. Therefore, if the city was found not to have a general plan at this time, it would not be in violation of the act absent a showing of bad faith.

A.R.S. §9-461(1) states a general plan means:

> . . . [A] municipal statement of land development policies, which may include maps, charts, graphs and text which set forth objectives, principles and standards for local growth and redevelopment enacted under the provisions of this article or any prior statute.

A.R.S. §9-461(5) states a specific plan means:

> . . . [A] detailed element of the general plan enacted under the provisions of this article or a prior statute.

It is clear that both the Concept Plan 2000 and the Interim Plan 1985 meet the definition for a general plan. Additionally, Interim Plan 1985 could be viewed as a specific plan for the implementation of the general plan pronounced in Concept Plan 2000. Concept Plan 2000 establishes the policy of dividing the city into villages, each containing a core, gradient and periphery. Interim Plan 1985 establishes specific criteria for the implementation of that policy in the Encanto Area in which this dispute occurred. Additionally, there is not any evidence that these two plans were not adopted under the provisions of the article pursuant to A.R.S. §9-461.06. The real debate concerns A.R.S. §9-461.05, which enunciates the scope of a general plan.

1. We note that subsequent to the filing of this action on October 2, 1985, the city adopted a plan it acknowledges is a general plan. General Plans for Phoenix 1985-2000. That plan, however, is irrelevant to the current dispute.

A.R.S. §9-461.05(C) and (D) require the general plan to contain nine district elements. Those elements are:

1. A land use element.
2. Circulation element.
3. Conservation element.
4. Recreation element.
5. Public services and facility element.
6. Public buildings element.
7. Housing element.
8. Conservation rehabilitation and redevelopment element.
9. Safety element.

A review of the two plans establishes that some of the above-required elements have not been addressed by either Concept Plan 2000 or Interim Plan 1985. The question before this court, therefore, is whether the missing elements negate Concept Plan 2000 and Interim Plan 1985 as general or specific plans or are irrelevant to the existence of a plan and establish only that the city's plans are presently incomplete. We find the latter course of reasoning applies.

While these plans are probably not satisfactory in their completeness, they are clearly plans according to the statutory definition. Appellees' reasoning would permit the city to perpetually avoid urban planning by leaving out any element or any subdivision of an element defined in §9-461.05. This would produce the untenable result of the slightest omission causing the city to have no plan. Additionally, appellees argue that Concept Plan 2000 stated it was only the beginning of the development of a general plan and argue it cannot be interpreted to be a general plan. A rose by any other name, however, still smells as sweet, and the city cannot avoid implementation of the statute by creating a plan and then stating it is not one. Concept Plan 2000 and Interim Plan 1985 fit the statutory definitions and are therefore general and specific plans as defined by A.R.S. §9-461(1, 5).

II. WAS THE REZONING IN CONFORMITY WITH THE PLAN?

A. Applicability of A.R.S. §9-462.01(E). A.R.S. §9-462.01(E) states:

> All zoning ordinances or regulations adopted under this article shall be consistent with the adopted general or specific plans of the municipality. . . .

B. Is the amendment consistent with the general and specific plan? Normally the level of judicial review of a zoning ordinance or amendment is the rational basis test. . . . Under the rational basis test if the court can hypothesize any rational reason why the legislative body made the choice it did, the statute or ordinance is constitutionally valid. . . .

. . . Appellant argues instead that, due to the statute, there be no presumption of legislative validity and the city council be required to make written findings and articulate reasons for any deviation from the general plan. There is support for this approach. *See Roseta v. County of Washington*, supra, and *Love v. Board of County Commissioners of Bingham County*, 105 Idaho 558, 671 P.2d 471 (1983).

We, however, reject both of the above approaches. By the enactment of §9-462.01(E), the legislature has provided a standard by which to review zoning decisions in addition to the usual constitutional standard. That standard is consistency with the general plan. In our review, however, we will not substitute our judgment for that of the duly elected legislative body, the city council. Therefore our review will consist of viewing the record that was before the city council and determining if, from that evidence, the council could have decided that despite the deviation from the letter of the plan there was consistency. The burden of proof will still be on the plaintiff to show inconsistency.

Consistency has been defined as "basic harmony." J. DiMento, the Consistency Doctrine and the Limits of Planning (1980). *See also* Op. Ky. Att'y Gen. 68-558 (1968). Therefore in the current situation if from the evidence before it the city council could have determined that the rezoning was in basic harmony with the general plan, the rezoning is valid. Of course in cases where the rezoning does not deviate from the general plan, rational basis review will still be utilized.

This rezoning did deviate from the general plan in that it surpassed by a large margin the 250-foot height restriction. The plan, however, has other goals for that area. The plan does provide that gradient areas where this proposed building lies will have some concentrations of landuse in sub cores. Also there is a provision for commercial development of the Central Avenue corridor. The building height restrictions are only stated in precatory language. Additionally, the plan provided for open space in the gradient, encouragement of landscaping, areas for people to enjoy and commercial development. The city council had before it evidence that this building would be commercially beneficial, would provide open spaces and recreational areas, landscaping, etc. The council also heard testimony that the developer could build two 20-story buildings which would leave less open space and less potential recreational areas. In viewing the above evidence, we cannot say the city council was wrong in finding the rezoning in basic harmony with the general plan. We do not need specific findings by the council to come to this conclusion since we have viewed the same evidence the council viewed. Certainly written findings would be preferable, but they are not mandatory. . . .

Notes and Comments

1. *Three Possible Interpretations*. Consider three possible interpretations of the consistency requirement:

(1) because the city has not yet adopted a plan that fully complies with the statutory requirements, the question of the consistency of zoning with that plan cannot arise;
(2) because the city has not yet adopted a plan that fully complies with the statutory requirements, no zoning ordinances can be legally found consistent with that plan; and
(3) because the city has not yet adopted a plan that fully complies with the statutory requirements, the city's zoning ordinances need only be consistent with the parts of the plan which the city has already adopted.

Which of these three interpretations did the court adopt? Is it the best of the three possible interpretations? *Compare* with *Haines* the decision in *Camp v. Mendocino County Board of Supervisors*, 176 Cal. Rptr. 620 (Ct. App. 1981). In that case, the court invalidated the approval of two subdivisions on the grounds that, because the county's general plan did not have the contents required by statute, the county could not find the subdivisions consistent with the plan. *See also Heine Farms v.*

Yankton County, 649 N.W.2d 597 (S.D. 2002). South Dakota defines a "zoning ordinance" as "any ordinance adopted by the board to implement the comprehensive plan." S.D.C.L. §11-2-1(10). It also separately defines the "comprehensive plan," and the County had none. The South Dakota Supreme Court held:

> Obviously, the Yankton County Commission could not enact a zoning ordinance implementing the goals, policies and objectives of a comprehensive plan for the development of the County if there was no comprehensive plan setting forth those goals, policies, and objectives.

649 N.W.2d at 602.

2. *"Strict" or "Loose" Consistency I.* How strict should the consistency requirement be? Did the holding in *Haines* "gut" the consistency requirement, or is flexibility in its operation needed if plans are to function properly? If a "strict" consistency requirement is adopted, would that interpretation mean that plans would become overly specific and thus functionally indistinguishable from zoning ordinances?

3. *"Strict" or "Loose" Consistency II.* Does a project have to be consistent with each policy in the general plan in order for a finding of consistency to be sustained, or must it just be consistent with the majority of those policies? In *Families Unafraid to Uphold Rural El Dorado County et al. v. El Dorado County Board of Supervisors*, 74 Cal. Rptr. 2d 1 (Ct. App. 1998), a low-density residential project was plainly inconsistent with the land use designation in the proposed general plan. (A statute required consistency with the draft plan.) The county argued, however, that "inconsistency with simply one general plan policy should not be enough to scuttle a project" and attempted to show other ways in which the project was consistent. How would you rule? The court of appeal overturned the approval, concluding that "the nature of the policy [in the plan] and the nature of the inconsistency are critical factors to consider" but that "the land use policy at issue here is fundamental." 74 Cal. Rptr. 2d at 17. For an example of a court closely scrutinizing and interpreting policies in a plan, *see Cathedral Park Condominium Committee v. District of Columbia Zoning Comm'n*, 743 A.2d 1231 (D.C. Ct. App. 2000).

4. *A Right to Rezoning Based on Consistency?* What if a proposed rezoning will be consistent with the comprehensive plan? Does the developer have a right to demand that the local government rezone the property so it is consistent with that plan? This was one of the issues raised in *Hougham v. Lexington-Fayette Urban County Government*, 29 S.W.3d 370 (Ky. Ct. App. 2000). The landowner sought approval of a rezoning that was consistent with the plan, but the County denied the change on the basis of objections by the neighbors. The court upheld the denial, reasoning that "just because the zone change request complies with the comprehensive plan . . . does not mean the zone request *must* be granted. . . ." *Id.* at 372. Are you convinced? If there is a statutory consistency requirement, does the plan play *any* role in a situation like this one?

5. *The "Shall-Should" Distinction.* In some cases general or comprehensive plans contain "goals" as required by statute, but the goals are phrased in precatory language: "could" or "should" rather than "shall." Does this make a difference in determining whether a development is consistent with the plan? It did in *Haines* and certainly did in *Adelman v. Town of Baldwin*, 750 A.2d 577, 584 (Me. 2000), in which the court concluded:

> These sections do not mandate action but merely suggest recommended conduct. Three of the four terms use the permissive term *should*, but none of the sections use the mandatory language such as *must* or *shall*.

Do you see any problem with plans that use permissive language in this fashion?

6. *"Spot Planning."* If general plans are going to be amended on a piecemeal, "lot by lot" basis, amendments of this type might be labeled "spot planning." This technique is the planning equivalent of spot zoning, a topic discussed in Chapter 2 of this casebook. "Spot planning" means "the process of designating a small island of land for a use different from that permitted in the larger area." Joseph F. DiMento, Taking the Planning Offensive: Implementing the Consistency Doctrine, 7 Zoning & Plan. L. Rep. 41, 46 (1984).

In *Dayton v. City and County of Honolulu*, 462 P.2d 199, 209 (Haw. 1969), the Hawaii Supreme Court held that the procedural safeguards applicable to the original adoption of the plan must be followed for amendments to the plan. The court then continued:

> The record in this case shows that the county failed to follow a course of conduct consistent with the safeguards that are required in the initial adoption of the general plan. These safeguards require that alterations in the general plan must be comprehensive and long-range. More specifically, if the city believes the general plan of 1964 is obsolete, then comprehensive updating of the 1964 plan's studies . . . is in order . . .

Id. Does the *Dalton* decision outlaw "spot planning"? *See also Price v. Payette County Board of County Commissioners*, 958 P.2d 583, 587 (Idaho 1998) ("Although these procedures [a plan amendment and a rezoning] can be done in tandem, the Board should deliberate first on the proposed amendment to the Comprehensive Plan, and consider whether or not a general type of growth should be permitted in a particular area; then, once the Board has made that determination, the Board should decide the appropriateness of a rezone within that area.").

7. *Comprehensiveness.* When is a zoning amendment not sufficiently "comprehensive" to meet the statutory requirement that it be in accord with a "comprehensive plan"? *See Trail Mining, Inc. v. Village of Sun*, 619 So. 2d 118, 120 (La. Ct. App. 1993) (a single, prohibitive zoning regulation restricting gravel mining "does not comply with the comprehensive plan requirement. There is no general plan for use or development of property and no forethought to the development of a general plan.").

8. *Planning and Takings.* Traditionally, the adoption of a master plan could not result in a taking of property under the Fifth Amendment, since the plan had no force or effect. *See, e.g., Cochran v. Planning Board of the City of Summit*, 210 A.2d 99 (N.J. Super. Ct. Law Div. 1965) (adoption of a master plan not implemented by further legislative action could not constitute a taking).

Does the plan's ability to effect the development of property through a strong consistency requirement now mean that the adoption of a general plan can effect a "taking" of private property, and thus require compensation? Most courts to date have held that the general plan, in and of itself, cannot effect a taking. *See, e.g., Sproul Homes of Nevada v. Nevada Department of Highways*, 611 P.2d 620, 621 (Nev. 1980) ("It is well-established that the mere planning of a project is insufficient to constitute a taking for which an inverse condemnation action will lie."). Takings issues are addressed in detail in Chapter 7.

9. *The Standard of Judicial Review.* The standard that courts use to review local government determinations of consistency is important to practitioners. A 1987 Florida court of appeal decision took an approach that was deferential to the local government's consistency determination. In *Southwest Ranches Homeowners Ass'n, Inc. v. County of Broward*, 502 So. 2d 931 (Fla. Dist. Ct. App. 1987), plaintiffs challenged the determination by Broward County that a sanitary landfill and resource recovery plant was consistent with the county's general plan. After rejecting a standard of "strict adherence" to the plan, the court found that the facility was consistent with the plan:

> The Association also contends that the proposed waste disposal facility will be incompatible with the low-intensity agricultural character of the surrounding environment. While there may be some truth in this statement, we note that the proposed use by the County, while being more "intensive" than previous zoning allowed, does not involve a higher population density of use. . . . The area in question is already the location of a high-density use, the Broward Correctional Institution. Certainly the prison facility could also be seen as incompatible with the norms set forth in the agricultural designation of the comprehensive plan. While we do not believe that one inconsistent use justifies another, we do believe this factor weakens the Association's contention that the area cannot support isolated high-intensity uses without losing its essentially agricultural character.

Id. at 938-939.

Is the court correct that one or two "isolated" high-intensity uses will not undermine the plan, or did the approval of the landfill and resource recovery facility compromise the plan's integrity? *See also City of New Smyrna Beach v. Barton*, 414 So. 2d 542 (Fla. Dist. Ct. App. 1982) (applying a "fairly debatable" standard to the review of a consistency determination by the local government).

Other courts apply a "substantial compliance" test in their review of consistency determinations. See *Little v. Board of County Commissioners of Flathead County*, 631 P.2d 1282, 1291 (Mont. 1981). *See also Nova Horizon, Inc. v. City Council of the City of Reno*, 769 P.2d 721, 723 (Nev. 1989) (adopting the substantial compliance test and commenting that "[w]e therefore choose to view a master plan as a standard that commands deference and a presumption of applicability, rather than a legislative straightjacket from which no leave may be taken"). Which of these judicial approaches is the best?

E. REMEDIES FOR INCONSISTENCY

If a court does find that a development is inconsistent with the general plan, what should the remedy be? The following case may surprise you.

■ PINECREST LAKES, INC v. SHIDEL

795 So. 2d 191 (Fla. App. 4 Dist. 2001)

FARMER, J.

The ultimate issue raised in this case is unprecedented in Florida. The question is whether a trial court has the authority to order the complete demolition and removal of several multi-story buildings because the buildings are inconsistent with the County's comprehensive land use plan. We conclude that the court is so empowered and affirm the decision under review.

Some twenty years ago, a developer purchased a 500-acre parcel of land in Martin County and set out to develop it in phases. Development there is governed by the Martin County Comprehensive Plan (the Comprehensive Plan). Phase One of the property was designated under the Comprehensive Plan as "Residential Estate," meaning single-family homes on individual lots with a maximum density of 2 units per acre (UPA). The Comprehensive Plan provides that

> [w]here single family structures comprise the dominant structure type within these areas, new development of undeveloped abutting lands *shall be required* to include compatible structure types of land immediately adjacent to existing single family development. . . .

Phases One through Nine were developed as single-family homes on individual lots in very low densities.

The subject of this litigation, Phase Ten, is a 21-acre parcel between Phase One and Jensen Beach Boulevard, a divided highway designated both as "major" and "arterial." Phase Ten was designated by the Comprehensive Plan as "Medium Density Residential" with a maximum of 8 UPA. . . .

[T]he developer sought to develop 136 units in two-story buildings, with a density of 6.5 UPA. The County's growth management staff recommended that the County Commission approve this second revised site plan for Phase Ten. Following a hearing at which a number of people objected to the proposal, including Shidel, the County Commission approved the Revision and issued a Development Order for Phase Ten permitting the construction of 19 two-story buildings.

Claiming statutory authority, Shidel and another Phase One homeowner, one Charles Brooks, along with the Homeowners Associations for Phases One through Nine, then filed a verified complaint with the Martin County Commission challenging the consistency of the Development Order with the Comprehensive Plan, requesting rescission of the Development Order. In response to the verified complaint, after a hearing the County Commission confirmed its previous decision to issue the Development Order.

Shidel and Brooks then filed a civil action in the Circuit Court against Martin County under the same statutory authority.[5] They alleged that the Development Order was inconsistent with the Comprehensive Plan. . . .

In granting [injunctive] relief, the court found that the developer had acted in bad faith. Specifically, the court found that the developer continued construction during the pendency of the prior appeal and continued to build and lease during the trial—even after losing on the consistency issue. The court found that the developer "acted at [its] own peril in doing precisely what this lawsuit sought to prevent and now [is] subject to the power of the court to compel restoration of the status prior to construction." The relief awarded was:

5. *See* §163.3215(1), Fla. Stat. (1995) ("Any aggrieved or adversely affected party may maintain an action for injunctive or other relief against any local government to prevent such local government from taking any action on a development order . . . which materially alters the use or density or intensity of use on a particular piece of property that is not consistent with the comprehensive plan adopted under this part.").

(1) the Court permanently enjoined Martin County from taking any further action on the subject Development order for Phase Ten, other than to rescind it;

(2) the Court permanently enjoined developer and its successors in interest from any further development of Phase Ten under the subject Development Order; and

(3) the Court ordered developer to remove all apartment buildings from Phase Ten either through demolition or physical relocation by a date certain.

When the Final Judgment was entered, five of the eight-unit buildings had been constructed in Phase Ten (Buildings 8-12). Buildings 11 and 12 had already received their CO's, and fifteen of their sixteen units were actually occupied. Building 10 was fully completed and was awaiting final inspection as of the date the remedies stage of trial began. Buildings 8 and 9 were 50% and 66% completed respectively, also as of that date. . . .

[The court first found that the development was not consistent with the Comprehensive Plan.]

II. Remedy of Demolition

Developer challenges what it terms the "enormity and extremity of the injunctive remedy imposed by the trial court." It argues that the trial court's order requiring the demolition of 5 multi-family residential buildings is the most radical remedy ever mandated by a Florida court because of an inconsistency with a Comprehensive Plan. Specifically, the contention is that the trial judge failed to balance the equities between the parties and thus ignored the evidence of a $3.3 million dollar loss the developer will suffer from the demolition of the buildings. The court failed to consider alternative remedies in damages, it argues, that would have adequately remedied any harm resulting from the construction of structures inconsistent with the Comprehensive Plan. Developer maintains that the trial court erroneously failed to give meaningful consideration to the traditional elements for the imposition of injunctive relief. It contends that the trial court proceeded on an erroneous conclusion that where an injunction is sought on the basis of a statutory violation, no proof is required as to the traditional elements for an injunction. . . .

[W]hen the Legislature provides for an injunction in these circumstances, it has deliberately made the new public duty and its corresponding right of enforcement an integrated statutory prescription. By specifying that the public interest requires that a certain duty be vindicated in the courts and not primarily within other branches of government, the Legislature is well within its powers. Surely the Legislature's primary role in defining public policy under the constitution is broad enough to enable it to specify a legal remedy in an enactment, regardless of whether the traditional judicial restrictions on that remedy in other, non-statutory contexts would limits its usage. As the author of the primary duty, the Legislature alone shapes the form of its effectuating mechanism.

In section 163.3215, we think the Legislature has constructed such a statute. The statute leads off with a declaration that:

> "Any aggrieved or adversely affected party may maintain an action for injunctive or other relief against any local government to prevent such local government from

> taking any action on a development order, as defined in s. 163.3164, which materially alters the use or density or intensity of use on a particular piece of property that is not consistent with the comprehensive plan adopted under this part."

From the plain and obvious meaning of this text we discern only two elements to the granting of an injunction against the enforcement of a development order: (a) the party is affected or aggrieved by (b) an approved project that is inconsistent with the Comprehensive Plan. In short, the existence of an affected neighbor is all that is necessary for the issuance of an injunction against a proposed land use that is inconsistent with the Comprehensive Plan.

We note that the statute does not say that the affected/aggrieved party bringing the action "creates a presumption of irreparable injury" by showing an inconsistency with the Plan. . . . When the Legislature wants to make a lesser intrusion on traditional equitable jurisdiction, it obviously knows how to do so. Here the statutory text makes the injunction the first and preferred remedy to alleviate the affects [sic] of [an] inconsistent land use. Hence, we read the statute to make the injunction the presumed remedy where the conditions prescribed are shown.

We disagree with the developer's contention that this statute was meant to create mere discretion in the court to issue an injunction. If injunctive relief is the specified, primary remedy to correct a violation of a public duty and to vindicate the right of a person affected by the violation of that duty, it can properly be deemed a rule that the Legislature has created, not a grant of discretion. Here the Legislature has devised an entire statutory scheme to insure that all counties have a Comprehensive Plan for the development of land within their respective jurisdictions. The scheme creates mandatory duties to have a plan, mandatory duties to have the plan approved by the state, and once approved mandatory duties to limit all developments so that they are consistent with the plan's requirements. At the end of all these mandatory duties — all these *shalls* — comes a new relaxation of the requirements on standing for citizen suits to enforce comprehensive land use plans and providing for the issuance of injunctions when an inconsistency affects another land owner. Judicial construction of that sole remedy as discretionary strikes us as remarkably inconsistent with not only the text of the statute itself but also with the purpose of the entire legislative scheme.

Developer lays great stress on the size of the monetary loss that it claims it will suffer from demolition, as opposed to the much smaller diminution in value that the affected property owner bringing this action may have suffered. It contends that a $3.3 million loss far outweighs the evidence of diminution in the value of Shidel's property, less than $26,000. Its primary contention here is that the trial judge erred in failing to weigh these equities in its favor and deny any remedy of demolition. Instead, as developer sees it, the court should have awarded money damages to eliminate the objector's diminution in value. . . .

Section 163.3215 says nothing about weighing these specific equities before granting an injunction. If the Legislature had intended that injunctive enforcement of comprehensive plans in the courts be limited to cases where such imbalances of equities were not present, we assume that it would have said so. As important, such balancing if applied generally would lead to substantial noncompliance with comprehensive plans. We doubt that there will be many instances where the cost of the newly allowed construction will be less than any diminution resulting from an inconsistency. Entire projects of the kind permitted here will frequently far exceed the monetary harms caused to individual neighbors affected by the inconsistency. In other words, if balancing the equities—that is, weighing the loss suffered by the developer against the diminution in value of the objecting party—were required before demolition could be ordered, then demolition will never be ordered.

Moreover it is an argument that would allow those with financial resources to buy their way out of compliance with comprehensive plans. In all cases where the proposed use is for multiple acres and multiple buildings, the expenditures will be great. The greater will be its costs, and so will be a resulting loss from an after-the-fact demolition order. The more costly and elaborate the project, the greater will be the "imbalance in the equities." The more a developer is able to gild an inconsistency with nature's ornaments—trees, plants, flowers and their symbiotic fauna—the more certain under this argument will be the result that no court will enjoin an inconsistency and require its removal if already built.

In this case the alleged inequity could have been entirely avoided if developer had simply awaited the exhaustion of all legal remedies before undertaking construction. It is therefore difficult to perceive from the record any great inequity in requiring demolition. Shidel let the developer know when it was just beginning construction of the first building that she would seek demolition if the court found the project inconsistent. When developer decided to proceed with construction in spite of the absence of a final decision as to the merits of the challenge under section 163.3215, the developer was quite able to foresee that it might lose the action in court. It could not have had a reasonable expectation that its right to build what it had proposed was finally settled. It may have thought the decision to build before the consistency question was settled in court a reasonable "business decision," but that hardly makes it inequitable to enforce the rule as written. . . .

We therefore affirm the final judgment of the trial court in all respects.

GUNTHER and GROSS, J.J., concur.

Notes and Comments

1. *The Developer's Nightmare*. What was the developer's mistake? It proceeded on the basis of a government approval, and there was no court order enjoining it from building. As a practical matter, does this decision mean that developers should not build whenever someone challenges the approval of their development on grounds of inconsistency with the comprehensive plan? As a practical matter, lenders often are reluctant to fund a project if litigation is pending against it.

Won't this decision mean that challengers will bring marginal consistency cases knowing that merely filing the suit will delay the development? From the plaintiff's perspective, delay may ultimately kill the project if the economics of it change over time.

2. *Bad Faith and Balancing*. The trial court found that the developer acted in "bad faith" by continuing construction during the pendency of the trial, even after losing on the consistency issue. How does this action show "bad faith" when part of it took place before the trial court had ruled against the developer on the consistency claim? On the other hand, if the court refuses the demolition remedy, doesn't the consistency requirement become meaningless in this case?

Why didn't the trial court abuse its discretion in ordering demolition? Normally, courts "balance the equities" when they grant injunctive relief. Why was no balance against demolition presented here?

3. *The Remedy for Lack of Consistency*. What is the appropriate remedy if a court finds that a zoning ordinance or other enactment is not consistent with the general plan? If a zoning ordinance in a jurisdiction with a consistency statute is inconsistent with the plan in existence at the time of the ordinance's adoption, is that ordinance invalid *ab initio*? Or may the jurisdiction "cure" the deficiency by amending the general plan to eliminate the inconsistency? *See Lesher Communications, Inc. v. City of Walnut Creek*, 802 P.2d 317, 324-335 (Cal. 1990) ("A zoning ordinance that conflicts with a general plan is invalid at the time it is passed. The court does not invalidate the ordinance. It does no more than determine the existence of the conflict. It is the preemptive effect of the controlling state [consistency] statute . . . which invalidates the ordinance.").

If the plan is simply incomplete, rather than in actual conflict with the zoning ordinance, should the result be different? *See Lazy Mountain Land Club v. Matanuska-Susitna Borough Bd. of Adjustment and Appeals*, 904 P.2d 373, 379 n.22 (Alaska 1995) ("We do not hold that all zoning decisions made in the past that were prior to the adoption of a comprehensive plan are invalid. For example, where the municipality has subsequently adopted a comprehensive plan, and the preexisting zoning ordinance rationally complies with that plan, the landowner is not prejudiced and any defect is cured.").

PART THREE

THE LIMITS OF CURRENT LAND USE REGULATION

6

Judicial Review of Land Use Decisions

A. INTRODUCTION

1. The Role of the Courts in Land Use

Although the vast majority of disputed land use decisions proceed to amicable (or, at least, final) resolution at the local government level, judicial review of land use decisions plays a vital role in the land use process. The courts' influence is felt at several levels during the decisionmaking process. First, project proponents recognize that even if they prevail before the local government, litigation challenging the approval can delay the actual implementation of the project for several years, a prospect that can be economically devastating. Opponents of projects often see litigation as just another step in a long battle, perhaps not initially recognizing how expensive it will be. Opponents also may not realize that litigation probably will not produce a definitive outcome, for even if the opponents prevail in court, the project proponent usually can institute new proceedings before the local agency. Finally, local politicians and planning officials dislike the stigma of a court finding that they have violated the law. Their fear of a future adverse ruling can greatly influence how local elected officials and their professional planning staff approach the consideration of a development.

The courts are thus a key player in the local land use process. From the perspective of the practicing lawyer representing a client in the approval process before a local jurisdiction, the prospect of judicial review requires a balancing act. The possibility of future litigation cannot be the ultimate focus of the lawyer's presentation at the local agency level; he or she must principally shape the presentation to convince the local elected officials. However, the lawyer cannot afford to forget that, if the decision ultimately is tested in a court, that test generally will be made on the basis of the administrative record developed before the local government. Thus, the possibility of judicial review must always be kept in mind during the approval process.

The present chapter examines how courts conduct judicial review. In most cases, judicial review will center on the fairness of the procedures followed by local governments. Some of these procedural requirements have constitutional origins; for example, a neighbor opposing a land use decision may be able to claim a due process right to personal notice before the city or county can act. Generally, however, the procedural mandates are of statutory origin, and the issues in litigation over them are somewhat mundane: Did the city publish notice of its proposed action in timely fashion? Did the city make all the required documents available before its decision? Was the hearing conducted properly? Was the city required to make findings explaining its decision, and if so, were they adequate? Was there sufficient evidence in the record before the city or county to support the findings? And, ultimately, if the local government did make a procedural error, does it rise to such a level that the court should invalidate the approval? This is the grist of much of the practical lawyering in land use litigation.

2. *Fairness in Local Procedures*

The chapter particularly emphasizes one aspect of the agency's decisionmaking that is crucial to whether the local decisionmaking process is fair: the question of bias and conflict of interest. This underlying question must be determined: when has a decisionmaker's ability to impartially consider issues become so impaired that a court should intervene?

Consider the hypothetical (but certainly realistic) scenario of a local politician who runs for mayor on a slow growth platform in a vigorously contested election. After taking office, the mayor then must preside over public hearings that concern development projects that the mayor has vigorously opposed during the election. Should the mayor be allowed to participate in the matter? She has obviously reached some judgments about the issues, but after all, these judgments were precisely the reasons why the citizens of that city elected her. Or consider a mayoral candidate who runs on a pro-growth platform and whose campaign is largely and generously funded by real estate interests who wish to develop property within the jurisdiction. Do their contributions taint the development approval process to such an extent that the mayor should disqualify herself from participating?

The answers to these questions lie partly in the nature of the decision that the local government is making. Here, the student must consult the field of administrative law, which offers two important models of how agencies may act: either in a "quasi-legislative" or "quasi-judicial" capacity. If the local decisionmaking body is setting prospective rules for a wide variety of individuals, that action has the earmarks of legislating. In such instances, the courts treat the action with a large amount of deference, overturning the action only if no rational basis exists to support it. Thus, as we have seen in Chapter 2, zoning as conceived of in the Euclidian sense is a legislative activity; city politicians look at the future of a city as whole and establish land uses for the jurisdiction according to a "comprehensive plan."

The legislative model, however, bears little relationship to the reality of many land use decisions, which are plainly judicial in nature. For example, the granting of a conditional use permit essentially adjudicates the terms and conditions to be imposed on a specific project. Indeed, many decisions adopting zoning amendments have the characteristics of adjudication. They come before the local decisionmaking body at the instigation of applicants who have a development proposal in mind for a specific, often relatively small parcel of property. The decision involves the presentation of evidence by the project applicant and perhaps the presentation of countering evidence by project opponents seeking to block the development.

Courts traditionally have treated these types of rezonings as legislative. However, in the groundbreaking case of *Fasano v. Board of County Commissioners of Washington County*, the Oregon Supreme Court departed from this line of precedents. Focusing on how localities actually decide such questions, the court held that small-tract rezonings should be treated as quasi-judicial for purposes of judicial review.

The logic of *Fasano* has considerable appeal. It seems to offer the potential of imposing some rationality and increased fairness upon a local land use process that can be chaotic, overtly political, and often unfair in one sense or the other to concerned parties. But the decision has vast practical ramifications and raises a host of difficult issues. For example, local governments (and later courts on judicial review) must decide which types of decisions are judicial, and thus fall under *Fasano*, and which still retain a legislative character. If a decision is judicial, we will expect more formality in the procedures used to reach the decision. The decisionmaker will have to be impartial, the evidentiary procedures followed at the hearing must be more structured, and the decision will have to be in writing and address the issues raised by the parties. The implications of *Fasano* are numerous and significant. For example, does *Fasano* mean that opponents of a project now have a right to cross- examine witnesses in a hearing before the city council?

Consider again our hypothetical mayor who has been elected on an anti-growth (or pro-growth) platform. If the mayor is legislating, then the concern over decisionmaking fairness disappears. Politicians do not have to be "fair" in taking positions; they are elected *because of* those positions. Democracy is largely about vigorous debate over opposing positions during an election and then implementing the winner's positions during the legislative term. If the mayor is adjudicating, however, her prejudgment of the matter is likely fatal. An impartial tribunal is the most fundamental attribute of a fair process during adjudication, and in this hypothetical, the mayor is anything but impartial.

These types of implications have given other courts pause. The majority of states have refused to follow *Fasano* and continue to treat all zoning decisions as legislative in nature, no matter how small and how specific the particular decision. Nonetheless, the debate about the *Fasano* approach continues, and from the student's perspective, the case serves as a very useful vehicle from which to examine the fundamental nature of the local land use decisionmaking power.

3. *Reviewing the Substantive Decision*

In addition to their focus on the decisionmaking process of the local government, the courts will also review the substance of the local land use decision. Whether the decision is viewed as legislative or judicial, the court will scrutinize the logic of that decision as well as the evidence that supports it. The test may be whether the decision is "arbitrary or capricious," or an "abuse of discretion," or perhaps whether it has a "rational basis." The court's focus is on the reasoning that underlies the decision, given the evidence upon which it rests. The purpose of the judicial function is always the same: to determine whether the agency's discretion was exercised reasonably under the circumstances.

There is an important ethical component to land use decisionmaking that also must be considered: the question of the effect of campaign contributions on local decisionmaking. If local governments are exercising legislative powers, then citizens have constitutional rights to make campaign contributions to those running for office. But when local government elected officials also decide on important development approvals, the campaign contribution can give the appearance of an attempt to indirectly purchase influence.

Issues regarding contributions rarely make it to the courts. One reason is that, in most instances, it is hard for a plaintiff to make the case that a contribution directly affected a vote. Another reason is that contributions implicate constitutionally protected First Amendment rights. *See Buckley v. Valeo*, 424 U.S. 1 (1976). Nonetheless, campaign contributions can cast doubt on the fairness of the decisionmaking process. You will consider this matter in the chapter's materials.

4. *The Role of Neighbors and Project Proponents*

The chapter then moves its focus away from judicial review of the procedures used, and of the substantive decision, to the roles that two particular groups play in that decisionmaking process: neighbors and project proponents. One of the most important developments in the last 20 years of land use law has been the rise in influence of citizen groups. Many important land use decisions at the local level now have three players involved: (1) the project proponent; (2) citizens groups, who are usually neighbors concerned about impacts from the proposal; and (3) the local jurisdiction, particularly its planning staff.

The chapter examines the fundamental question of the weight that the decisionmaking process should accord to the views of these neighbors. Logically, if the decision is legislative in nature, it can be made for purely political reasons. For example, if a large neighborhood group opposes a project, a politician should be able to count potential votes and reflect that tally by voting "no." But other parties, most notably the project proponents, have a vital stake in the decision; after all, it is *their* land at issue.

Most courts conclude that neighborhood opposition to a project is relevant only if it is "factually based." The line between purely political statements and statements based on fact, however, is hard to draw, as illustrated in *Sunderland Family Treatment Services v. City of Pasco*, a principal case in the chapter. Here, the proposed land use, a group home for troubled teenagers, could adversely affect the value of the neighbors' homes, and the neighbors have concerns over their personal safety. When are the neighbors' fears over this project legitimate "facts" for the city's consideration, as opposed to "irrational prejudice" that must be ignored?

5. *The Federal Courts and Local Land Use Decisions*

Finally, no examination of the role that the courts play in reviewing local land use decisions would be complete without an assessment of where the federal courts fit in. For the most part, land use decisions involve only questions of state law over which the federal courts have no jurisdiction. But if a municipality's violation of law can be framed constitutionally as the failure to afford due process or the taking of property without compensation, the landowner may seek relief in federal court under Section 1983 of the federal Civil Rights Act.

A developer often views the federal court as a potentially more hospitable forum for claims than the state court, but federal courts are unquestionably leery of land use litigation. Well aware of the volume of local land use decisions, they fear inundation if the door to the federal courthouse swings open too widely for such cases. Thus, the procedural roadblocks to federal land use litigation are formidable; there are stringent tests for determining the ripeness of the plaintiff's claim, and insistence on complete exhaustion of state administrative remedies is the norm. Moreover, even when the federal court is willing to consider the case on the merits, plaintiffs still have a difficult time prevailing. The Third Circuit's 1995 decision in *United Artists v. Township of Warren* is representative of the trend. Still, plaintiffs keep trying to push the federal door open more widely, and they may yet succeed.

B. FAIRNESS IN THE DECISIONMAKING PROCESS

The procedural requirements a local agency must follow in making a land use decision constitute fertile grounds for litigation challenging the agency's decision. Courts are experts in procedure, and they will insist that local agencies follow the procedures prescribed both by state law as well as by their own local ordinances. The following case presents a complex tangle of facts and statutory requirements relating to an applicant's hearing before a local government.

As you read the case, first make sure you fully understand the various actions that the town did take. Then examine the applicable statutes closely to determine whether those actions were proper. You should also note that lawyers representing clients in such a proceeding must make snap judgments about such questions as whether continuances are proper and whether to object to testimony or actions taken by opposing parties.

FRITO-LAY, INC. v. PLANNING AND ZONING COMMISSION OF THE TOWN OF KILLINGLY

206 Conn. 554 (1998)

Before ARTHUR H. HEALEY, CALLAHAN, Glass, COVELLO and SANTANIELLO, JJ.

ARTHUR H. HEALEY, Associate Justice.

The plaintiff, Frito-Lay, Inc. (Frito-Lay), appealed to the Superior Court from the denial of its application for a special permit and site plan approval (application) by the named defendant, planning and zoning commission of the town of Killingly (commission). . . .

. . . Frito-Lay is, and has been at all times relevant, the record owner of real estate in Killingly, upon which is situated a food processing facility and office. These premises are located in an industrial district as defined in the Killingly zoning regulations (regulations). After some discussions with Killingly town officials, Frito-Lay filed an application for a special permit on November 26, 1984, which was later supplemented by a site plan. This application explicitly proposed "new construction" of a wood chip burning electric "co-generation plant" and this proposed facility included, inter alia, a boiler, generator, silo and chimney.

The commission formally accepted Frito-Lay's application at its regular meeting of December 10, 1984. See General Statutes §8-7d(c). Thereafter, a public hearing was set by the commission for January 14, 1985. This public hearing was duly noticed and held on January 14, 1985. At that hearing, the commission heard testimony, received other evidence and heard oral argument for and against the application. The chairman of the commission specifically declared the public hearing closed at the end of the meeting of January 14, 1985. At that time, Frito-Lay's application was tabled to the commission's next regular meeting on February 11, 1985, pending the receipt of certain information required by the commission.

At its regular meeting of February 11, 1985, the commission, during its "Citizens' Participation"[4] item on its agenda, heard comments on the Frito-Lay application. The trial court found that "fourteen citizens voiced opinions during the course of the meeting on the plaintiff's application." A close examination of the transcript of the remarks made during the "Citizens' Participation" portion discloses that most of those speakers did not view the application with favor. Richard Cunneen, who later intervened and ultimately became a party defendant, was one of the citizens who spoke. After this portion of the meeting was over, commission chairman Vincent Baiocchetti addressed William Walker, Frito-Lay's plant engineer who was present, and told Walker that he had some questions to ask him.[6] Walker responded not only to the chairman's question, but also to a

4. At that time, commission chairman Vincent Baiocchetti said: "All right, the next item on our agenda is Citizens' Participation. It is during this portion of the meeting that any taxpayer or resident of the Town of Killingly may speak on any issue regarding Planning and Zoning. It need not be on the agenda for tonight. As the size of the crowd here, I'm sure there are a few people that want to make comments. I'll ask you to hold your comments to a maximum of three minutes. This is not an opportunity for discussion, arguments, back and forth, it's for you to say what you have to say, that's essentially it. Please state your name, your address, raise your hand, I'll recognize you, we'll go from there. Yes, sir?"

6. At that time, commission chairman Baiocchetti said to William Walker: "Mr. Walker, since you're the rep, and you're the man bearing the brunt of all this, there are some questions that I have, and it may answer some other questions, it may generate some others. In my business, I'm in a situation where I run into a lot of technical people, I asked a few questions of one person. Would it technically be feasible to take the plant exhaust, with the potato and hot oil odors, and use this air for boiler combustion air, as you can tell from what you've heard tonight and other nights, people aren't really opposed to this woodchip idea, what they're really opposed to is the smell, that's been coming, the smell and noise that's been coming since the plant began. That's really been generated, I think, most the aggravation that you're hearing from most of the people. Would it be possible to do this thing, I think it's my understanding that if you're able to do that, you would eliminate the odor completely, by burning it."

Later, during this portion, Baiocehetti said to Walker: "Ok. Now, you've heard the comments that were brought out this evening, are there any in particular that you would like to address, or that you've addressed already, I guess you've already addressed them, of course." Walker did respond with

large number of questions from other members of the commission. At the end of this meeting, the commission voted unanimously to table the application until its next meeting on March 11, 1985.

At the outset of the meeting of March 11, 1985, the town planner, Richard Hubbard, announced that Frito-Lay would not be present that night due to a fatality at its plant and that Frito-Lay had requested an extension until the end of March. The commission determined that a special meeting would be held on March 26, 1985, and, therefore, that no action would be taken that night. Thereafter, the "Citizens' Participation" portion of the agenda preceded the other business of the meeting, as it had on January 14, 1985, and on February 11, 1985. At the "Citizens' Participation" portion, nine persons spoke on the Frito-Lay matter.

On March 26, 1985, the commission held a special meeting.[8] At the outset of this meeting, Baiocchetti, before opening "Citizens' Participation," said that the commission was "limiting discussion based on the information that [had] been gathered at the public hearing, so any comments that the citizens want[ed] to make regarding Planning and Zoning *should not, should not* relate to the matter before us this evening."[9] (Emphasis in original.) This immediately met with a demurrer from a prospective speaker. She was told by the chairman that anything she said "relative to the issue before [the commission that night would] carry no weight because [the commission had] already taken testimony." This woman, however, did speak on the Frito-Lay matter. Attorney Gregory Sharp, representing Cunneen, also spoke, as did Cunneen himself. Despite further statements by the chairman that the commission could accept "no more testimony" because the hearing had been closed in January, that that hearing had been "irrevocably closed," that the commission was not taking "any evidence at this point" and that the commission was "following state statutes exactly," fourteen citizens still spoke on Frito-Lay's operations and the great majority was opposed to its operations. During the "Citizens' Participation" portion, counsel for Frito-Lay, citing the opening statement of the chairman, objected to Sharp's proposal to speak, although he also said that he had no objection to members of the public speaking. After all of the members of the public had spoken, the chairman asked if anyone from Frito-Lay wished to make a comment. Walker indicated that, given the chairman's earlier ruling, Frito-Lay had elected not to comment.

Immediately thereafter, the chairman closed "Citizens' Participation" and the commission itself discussed the Frito-Lay application. That same evening, the commission voted to deny the Frito-Lay application by a vote of three to two. The reasons given for its denial were: (1) the application did not meet the requirements

observations. Thereafter, there followed more questions from commission members and responses to them by Walker.

8. This was noticed as a "special meeting" of the commission and the Frito-Lay application was the sole item noticed in the publication for the special meeting.

9. Baiocchetti's entire opening remarks were: "Up to Citizens' Participation. At this time in the meeting, we open the meeting to citizens' participation relative to any matter regarding Planning and Zoning. I'd like to state that, we are limiting discussion based on the information that has been gathered at the public hearing, so any comments that the citizens want to make regarding Planning and Zoning *should not, should not* relate to the matter before us this evening. Ok, anyone have anything they'd like to bring up, Planning and Zoning?" (Emphasis in original).

of §720.4(c) and (e)[11] of the Killingly zoning regulations; and (2) "the surrounding community has lost faith in Frito-Lay, Inc., due to past performance . . . promises have been made to the community prior to the construction of the facility which were not kept, which resulted in a loss of confidence in Frito-Lay's ability to do what it says it will do." Frito-Lay thereafter appealed to the Superior Court.

At the hearing on the appeal before the Superior Court, Frito-Lay claimed that the commission: (1) either failed to act within the statutory time frame or conducted multiple public hearings, which it claimed invalidated any purported commission action, thus resulting in the automatic approval of its application pursuant to General Statutes §§8-3c[13] and 8-7d;[14] (2) acted improperly from the outset in requiring an application for a special permit; and (3) acted illegally, arbitrarily or in abuse of its discretion in that the grounds assigned for its denial were not reasonably supported by the record. The Superior Court rejected all of these claims. . . .

11. Section 720.4(c) and (e) of the Killingly zoning regulations provide:
720.4 Review of Site and Architectural Plans

The Commission shall review all plans in order to determine that the proposed use or the proposed extension or alteration of an existing use is in accord with the public health, safety and welfare after taking into account, where appropriate . . .

c. The nature of the surrounding area and the extent to which the proposed use or feature will be in harmony with the surrounding area or will serve as a transition between unlike areas and will protect property values and preserve and enhance the beauty of the area. . . .
e. The avoidance of potential nuisance.

13. General Statutes §8-3c provides:

Special Permits and Exceptions. Hearings. Filing Requirements. The zoning commission or combined planning and zoning commission of any municipality shall hold a public hearing on an application or request for a special permit or special exception, as provided in section 8-2. . . . At such hearing any party may appear in person and may be represented by agent or by attorney. Such commission shall decide upon such application or request within the period of time permitted under section 8-7d. . . .

14. General Statutes §8-7d provides:

Hearings and Decisions. Time Limits. Day of Receipt. (a) Except as provided in subsection (b) of this section, in all matters wherein a formal petition, application, request or appeal must be submitted to a zoning commission, planning and zoning commission or zoning board of appeals under this chapter and a hearing is required on such petition, application, request or appeal, such hearing shall commence within sixty-five days after receipt of such petition, application, request or appeal and shall be completed within thirty days after such hearing commences. All decisions on such matters shall be rendered within sixty-five days after completion of such hearing. The petitioner or applicant may consent to one or more extensions of any period specified in this subsection, provided the total extension of any such period shall not be for longer than the original period as specified in this subsection, or may withdraw such petition, application, request or appeal.

(b) Whenever the approval of a site plan is the only requirement to be met or remaining to be met under the zoning regulations for a proposed building, use or structure, a decision on an application for approval of such site plan shall be rendered within sixty-five days after receipt of such site plan. The applicant may consent to one or more extensions of such period, provided the total period of any such extension or extensions shall not exceed two further sixty-five day periods, or may withdraw such plan.

(c) For purposes of subsection (a) or (b) of this section, the day of receipt of a petition, application, request or appeal shall be the day of the next regularly scheduled meeting of such commission or board, immediately following the day of submission to such board or commission or its agent of such petition, application, request or appeal. . . .

We turn first to the issues encompassed by Frito-Lay's claim that its application must be granted as a matter of law because of the commission's failure to adhere to the mandatory time limits set out in §8-7d(a). We do not agree. . . .

. . . There is no question that more than sixty-five days had elapsed from January 14, 1985, to March 26, 1985, when the commission rendered its decision. Having requested this continuance beyond what would have been sixty-five days from January 14, 1985, Frito-Lay has no complaint about extending the sixty-five day limit. Although the record does not indicate that Frito-Lay was represented by counsel until March 26, 1985, as a corporate entity, it was, as much as any individual, chargeable with knowledge of the law. *M & L Homes, Inc. v. Zoning & Planning Commission,* 187 Conn. 232, 244-45, 445 A.2d 591 (1982). Frito-Lay's action in obtaining the extension to March 26, 1985, was a valid waiver of its right to require the defendant commission to make its decision under the statute within sixty-five days after the completion of the hearing of January 14, 1985. *See* General Statutes §§8-7d, 8-3c.

Ordinarily, this fact pattern, with the time for decision properly extended beyond the mandatory sixty-five day limit at the request of the applicant, would settle this phase of the matter. Frito-Lay, however, also contends that, the commission's disregard of the mandatory hearing procedures made the commission's March 26 vote, after the illegal proceedings of February 11, 1985, March 11, 1985, and March 26, 1985, a nullity. This alleged illegality of continuing to hold hearings after the close of the public hearing on January 14, 1985, it asserts, so tainted the proceedings that it resulted in the inability of the commission ever to render a valid decision within the sixty- five day limit. Thus, it maintains that its consent on March 11, 1985, to extend the time limit does not end this issue, but rather, under the circumstances, requires the automatic granting of its application.

Frito-Lay's claim requires that we examine, as the trial court did, the hearings of February 11, 1985, March 11, 1985, and March 26, 1985, to determine their legal significance in this context.

There is no dispute that the commission properly noticed and held a public hearing on the Frito-Lay application on January 14, 1985, and that, at the end of that hearing, the chairman declared the public hearing closed. *See* General Statutes §8-3c, 8-7d. . . . That hearing could properly have been continued and "completed within thirty days after [it] commence[d]," but it was not. We, therefore, must consider the legal effect of the "hearings" of February 11, March 11, and March 26. . . . Our cases consistently recognize the generally adversarial nature of a proceeding considered a "hearing," in which witnesses are heard and testimony is taken. . . . Applying proper principles to the record before us, what occurred on February 11, March 11 and March 26 were "hearings" on the Frito-Lay application, albeit without any sanction in the enabling zoning statutory scheme. After the hearing of January 14, 1985, was held and closed on that date, there could be no further "hearings" on Frito-Lay's application that would be permitted under the enabling statutory scheme on zoning. . . .

Even extending fair deference to the trial court's observation, which, like this court, did not hear testimony or take any evidence, we go on to examine its determination of the effect of what occurred at the post-January 14 hearings especially as to the lengthy "Citizens' Participation." . . . First, neither the trial court nor the defendants point to any statutory or other legal basis for allowing the "Citizens' Participation" phase of any of these three meetings on the Frito-Lay application, once the hearing of January 14, 1985, which was the time and place for such participation, was closed. There is no such basis, and such "Citizens' Participation" constituted a "hearing" on each occasion. Such participation prominently articulated concerns about the noise, odor, traffic problems and the lack of Frito-Lay's credibility, all matters that, in practical terms, addressed Frito-Lay's current application on the merits.

On March 26, 1985, an attorney for a resident "intervened," argued against granting the application, and introduced a photo of the Frito-Lay plant as an exhibit. The trial court observed correctly that commission members may legitimately utilize their personal knowledge in reaching a decision. *See, e.g., Burnham v. Planning & Zoning Commission*, 189 Conn. 261, 267, 455 A.2d 339 (1983). That, however, is not an acceptable explanation for the trial court's determination that "much, if not all," that was said about Frito-Lay's "existing operations" was common knowledge within Killingly, "as well as immaterial to the application." It was hardly "immaterial," especially given the second ground for denying the application, i.e., the community had lost faith in Frito-Lay "due to past performances," its "failure" to keep promises it made before its existing facility was constructed and the resulting loss of confidence in its ability "to do what it says it will do." Even assuming that much of this was common knowledge, these comments were made at hearings not authorized by law. . . .

On March 11, 1985, nine citizens spoke to the Frito-Lay matter during the "Citizens' Participation" portion of the meeting. No Frito-Lay representative attended that meeting because of an accident that had occurred at the plant that day. The trial court's memorandum of decision quotes at length from what it characterizes as the "testimony" of the defendant Cunneen himself given at this meeting about his conversations with "several areas of New England and New York State that have wood-burning facilities" and noted problems that they were having with such facilities. The trial court then observed that "[Cunneen's] testimony was echoed by other concerned residents." What occurred constituted a "hearing," again with no legal sanction.

On March 26, 1985, another "hearing," again without statutory sanction, took place on the Frito-Lay application. Not only did fourteen persons speak to it under the "Citizens' Participation" portion of that meeting, but that included, certainly for practical purposes, the intervention into the proceedings of an attorney representing Cunneen, who spoke, over the objection of Frito-Lay's counsel, against the application and introduced an exhibit. . . .

We do not agree with the defendants' argument that, at the March 26, 1985 hearing, Frito-Lay waived its right to object to any of the citizens' comments because its counsel listened without objection while "citizens made their point about the [Frito-Lay] facility," but only objected when Attorney Sharp began to speak. This is so for two reasons. First, Frito-Lay was entitled to rely on the chairman's statements that such remarks would and could not be considered by the commission. In this connection, we should state that, despite the multiple hearings after January 14, 1985, the entire record would support the view that the commission had maintained an open mind without having made any prejudgment on the Frito-Lay matter . . . Second, Frito-Lay fairly viewed this as a "hearing" beyond the thirty day limit and this was consistent with its position that its consent went only to the extension of the sixty-five day limit for decision and not to any new hearing. We also do not agree with the defendants' contention that Frito-Lay waived its opportunity to rebut "any new submissions" at the March 26, 1985 meeting. At that time, after all the speakers had concluded, the commission chairman asked Walker if he wished to respond. Walker, with counsel present, declined to do so. Here again, Frito-Lay was entitled to rely on the chairman's statements that what had occurred would and could not be considered. . . .

Having held that the post-January 14, 1985 hearings were illegal, we turn now to the relief requested by the plaintiff. Despite these statutory violations, the commission did render its decision within the sixty-five day statutory time limitation which started from January 14, 1985, and which had been properly extended. General Statutes §§8-3c, 8-7d. We do not believe that the automatic approval of an application, which we have said was mandated in such a case as *Vartuli*, where the zoning authority did not render its decision within the sixty-five day limitation, is also mandated in this case because of the failure to observe the thirty day limitation. "A statute should be interpreted according to the policy which the legislation seeks to serve." *Aaron v. Conservation Commission*, 183 Conn. 532, 538, 441 A.2d 30 (1981); see 2A J. Sutherland, Statutory Construction (4th Ed.) §§56.01 through 56.02. Section 8-7d requires "*a* hearing" and that "such hearing . . . shall be completed within thirty days after such hearing commences. . . . " (Emphasis added.) Section 8-3c provides that "[s]uch commission shall *decide* upon such application . . . within the period of time permitted under section 8-7d [the sixty-five day limitation]. . . . " (Emphasis added.) Moreover, §8-7d provides: "All *decisions* on such matters shall be rendered within sixty-five days after completion of such hearing." (Emphasis added.) There is no dispute at all that the commission properly advertised and held "a public hearing"; *see* General Statutes §8-3c; on January 14, 1985, and that it was formally closed on that date. At that time, the "hearing" requirement imposed by statute and the commendable policy of holding "a public hearing" for providing a public forum for citizen input had been satisfied. The commission, however, went further and held additional hearings after January 14, 1985. We do not read this statutory departure by the commission as requiring automatic approval as that does not present the need that this applicant, unlike those relying upon the sixty-five day limitation, "know with certainty that a definite course of statutory action has been taken by a commission, setting in motion clear avenues of appeal." *Carpenter v. Planning & Zoning Commission*, 176 Conn. 581, 597, 409 A.2d 1029 (1979), quoted in *Merlo v. Planning & Zoning Commission*, 196 Conn. 676, 684, 495 A.2d 268 (1985). In addition, we do not believe that the legislature intended automatic approval of the scenario presented to us. Given this view, we have determined that because the commission did act illegally, we should go no further than to sustain Frito-Lay's appeal and remand this entire matter to the commission for a new hearing in accordance with law.

Notes and Comments

1. *Sorting Out the Frito-Lay Events*. This case raises a number of procedural questions that involve the interplay between the statutory requirements set out in General Statutes Section 8-7d and the Planning and Zoning Commission's consideration of the application. In reviewing the case, you should carefully evaluate the following questions, bearing in mind that the attorneys involved (and, where

attorneys were not present, the other representatives of interested parties) were required to make quick decisions about what to do that ultimately affected the outcome of the litigation:

a. Did the Planning and Zoning Commission meet the statutory requirement that it issue a decision within 65 days of the receipt of the plan?
b. When did the "public hearing" end? How can the February 11, March 11, and March 26 proceedings be part of a "public hearing" when the Planning and Zoning Commission expressly closed the public hearing at the end of the January 14 meeting?
c. Why couldn't the Planning and Zoning Commission validly argue that it simply disregarded the information presented at the hearings after January 14 because the "public hearing" had already closed?

2. *Citizens Participation*. The "citizens participation" part of the Planning Commission's proceedings gave rise to much of the defendant's legal difficulties in the case. Many of the comments received at that hearing concerned noise, odor, traffic and Frito-Lay's alleged "lack of credibility." These issues bear directly on the permit application and upon the commission's second ground for denying the application: Frito-Lay's "failure to keep past promises." Thus, Frito-Lay would seem to have a strong argument that the hearing was not really closed on January 14.

Consider how, if you were the commission's lawyer, you would avoid receiving information about the Frito-Lay application during this "citizens participation" proceeding that took place after the hearing was closed. For example, you could attempt to instruct the Commissioners that they must disregard any statements concerning the application if they are made during the "public participation" proceeding. Alternatively, perhaps the safest course legally is not to hold such a "citizens participation" proceeding while the application is pending. But both courses of action, of course, will not please the citizens of that city who oppose the project.

On the other hand, Frito-Lay's representative responded to some of the public comments, and even at the March 26 public hearing, its counsel objected *only* to comments by an attorney, not to comments from the citizens. Why doesn't this partial objection to those comments constitute a waiver of any objection to a continuation of the hearing?

3. *Permit Streamlining*. As discussed in Chapter 3 in the context of subdivision regulation, legislatures in recent years have increasingly adopted stringent time limits requiring governmental agencies to act on applications within a set period of time. If they fail to meet those time limits, those applications will be "deemed approved" as a matter of law. This new type of statute is surveyed in Carolyn W. Poulin, Land Use Applications Not Acted Upon Shall Be Deemed Approved: A Weighing of the Interests, 57 UMKC L. Rev. 607 (1989).

In *Frito-Lay* the court rejects the "automatic approval" remedy sought by Frito-Lay. Was the remedy that the court chose (a new hearing rather than automatic approval) consistent with the statute? The court concludes that, in this type of situation, the applicant does not need to "know with certainty" that a definite course of action was taken within the statutory period. But if that type of certainty isn't the purpose of the time limits in the statute, what is the purpose of those limits?

Should permit applicants be allowed to waive their rights under permit streamlining legislation? The California Supreme Court had quite a workout with this issue in *Bickel v. City of Piedmont*, 946 P.2d 427 (Cal. 1997). In a 4 to 3 decision, the court held that an applicant could waive the statutory deadline in the Act. It concluded that the Act primarily benefits applicants seeking agency approval of a proposed development, rather than evidences a broader public purpose. The dissent was concerned with "coerced" waivers in which public agencies, holding the power to disapprove a project, "free themselves from these strict and mandatory time limits by extracting waivers from applicants." *Id.* at 437 (Baxter, J., dissenting). Do you believe that permit streamlining acts are primarily intended to benefit private applicants, or is a broader public purpose involved?

4. *Process and Substance.* The issues most commonly litigated in cases where judicial review of a land use decision is sought involve allegations of procedural error, such as those brought in the *Frito-Lay* case, or of lack of evidence to support the decision. Plaintiffs, however, also may argue that the substance of the land use decision was illegal (rather than just challenging the procedures followed or the evidentiary support for the decision). The court reviews such claims under various standards of review; the most common test is whether the decision is arbitrary, capricious, or an abuse of discretion. *See, e.g., Whitehead Oil Co. v. City of Lincoln*, 515 N.W.2d 390, 400 (Neb. 1994); *Mahony v. Township of Hampton*, 651 A.2d 525 (Pa. 1994).

5. *Substantive Due Process.* This type of substantive review is closely related to constitutional challenges based on substantive due process. That doctrine remains alive in the state courts despite its demise in the federal courts after the historic decision in *Nebbia v. New York*, 291 U.S. 502 (1934). *See, e.g., Gradous v. Board of County Commissioners of Richmond County*, 349 S.E.2d 707, 709 (Ga. 1986) ("When the governing authority exceeds the police power in regulating land use for zoning, health regulation, abating of nuisance, building standards or for any other purpose, the governing authority runs afoul of not only the constitutional prohibition against condemnation of land for a public purpose without just compensation but also the due process clause of the Georgia Constitution and the United States Constitution.").

The burden on a plaintiff to demonstrate a substantive due process violation is quite heavy. The Washington Supreme Court articulated the test as follows: (1) whether the regulation is aimed at achieving a legitimate public purpose; (2) whether it uses means reasonably necessary to achieve that purpose; and (3) whether it is unduly oppressive on the landowner. *Presbytery of Seattle v. King County*, 787 P.2d 907, 912 (Wash. 1990). As a result, most of the decisions reject such claims. *See, e.g., Smith Investment Co. v. Sandy City*, 958 P.2d 245 (Utah Ct. App. 1998) (downzoning debatably promoted permissible city goals, including reducing oversupply of space zoned for retail and solving traffic problems, and thus did not violate substantive due process); *Brunelle v. Town of South Kingstown*, 700 A.2d 1075 (R.I. 1997) (denial of zone change was not arbitrary where it was based on concerns such as increased traffic, flooding of the road, lack of adequate lot street frontage, and increased pollution of the water table).

Another issue that arises, albeit somewhat infrequently, in local government matters is a basic one of open government: must local decisionmakers deliberate over land use decision in public, or can they retreat beyond "closed doors"? This issue is governed by state "open meetings" acts.

■ KEARNS-TRIBUNE CORPORATION v. SALT LAKE COUNTY COMMISSION

28 P.3d 686 (Utah 2001)

WILKINS, Justice.

This appeal presents the question of whether the Utah Open and Public Meetings Act . . . permits the Salt Lake County Commission to close a meeting to the public in order to consider, with legal counsel, possible courses of action with respect to an annexation petition pending before the Salt Lake County Boundary Commission. . . .

BACKGROUND . . .

The Salt Lake County Commission ("County Commission") held a staff meeting on March 30, 1998. The County Commission customarily treated staff meetings as subject to the Utah Open and Public Meetings Act, and therefore the March 30, 1998 meeting was open to the public. At one point, however, the county attorney's office suggested to the County Commission that part of the meeting be closed. The county attorney's office wanted to discuss in private whether to oppose Riverton City's petition to annex unincorporated county land that was pending before the Salt Lake County Boundary Commission ("Boundary Commission"). The county commissioners voted unanimously to close the meeting, and the public, including the press, was asked to leave.

The county commissioners and their attorneys then met privately and discussed matters pertaining to Riverton City's annexation proposal. The minutes of this closed meeting reflect that legal counsel first explained to the Commissioners the factual and procedural circumstances surrounding the annexation proceeding and the possible results of the annexation petition, namely that islands of unincorporated county land would result. Next, counsel indicated that South Jordan City had protested Riverton City's petition. Finally, counsel outlined three possible courses of action: (1) the County Commission could send a letter to Riverton City listing technical problems with the petition, but refrain from appearing before the Boundary Commission; (2) the County Commission could appear, through counsel, before the Boundary Commission and address only technical problems with the petition; or (3) the County Commission could file a formal protest with the Boundary Commission opposing the annexation. Counsel recommended that the county not protest technicalities. The County Commission voted to appear before the Boundary Commission and to send a letter to Riverton City identifying technical problems. The meeting was then reopened to the public, and adjourned.

The complaint filed by plaintiff Kearns-Tribune Corporation ("Kearns-Tribune"), a newspaper publishing company, insists that the Salt Lake County Commission violated the Utah Open and Public Meetings Act (the "Act"), arguing that the exception to the Act permitting closed meetings for "strategy sessions to discuss pending or reasonably imminent litigation," Utah Code

Ann. §52-4-5(1)(a)(iii)(1998), is inapplicable to annexation or boundary protest proceedings. . . .

Analysis

This case requires the interpretation and application of the Utah Open and Public Meetings Act. Section 52-4-3 of the Act specifies, "Every meeting is open to the public unless closed pursuant to Sections 52-4-4 and 52-4-5." Section 52-4-4 provides the procedure through which a meeting may be closed. It reads, in relevant part: "No closed meeting is allowed except as to matters exempted under Section 52-4-5. . . . " The provision under consideration in this case, section 52-4-5, sets forth seven purposes for which a meeting may be closed. Four of those purposes or circumstances permitting closure to the public of a meeting involve "strategy sessions," and all four require that a record of the closed proceedings be kept. Utah Code Ann. §52-4-5(1)(a)(1998). . . .

. . . The general nature and tone of the seven exceptions in section 52-4-5(1), however, suggest a clear legislative intent to ensure that the public's business is done in full view of the public except in those specific instances where either the public, or a specific individual who is the subject of the meeting, may be significantly disadvantaged by premature public disclosure of sensitive information. The ultimate consequence of closed discussions about the price of real property, collective bargaining, and a public body's approach to pending or reasonably imminent litigation eventually becomes public. Nevertheless, in each of these limited circumstances, the public's general interest was thought by our legislature to be best served by allowing confidential discussions to precede the actions that would disclose the strategy.

In the case before us, the Salt Lake County Commission relies upon the exception for strategy sessions to discuss pending or reasonably imminent litigation. *See* §52-4-5(1)(a)(iii). The Commission argues that it properly closed the meeting to the public because it discussed Riverton City's petition before the Boundary Commission, and matters before the Boundary Commission are quasi-judicial and therefore qualify as "litigation" for purposes of the statute. Kearns-Tribune, to the contrary, argues that the Salt Lake County Commission improperly closed the meeting because the topic discussed by the county commissioners, an annexation dispute, is a legislative or policy matter, and not pending or reasonably imminent litigation. The amici, the Society of Professional Journalists and several news organizations, also argue that the County Commission improperly closed the meeting because the county commissioners discussed policy, not litigation strategy. The amici further contend that the litigation exception must be strictly construed. The plain meaning of the term "litigation" implies court proceedings, they argue, and defining "litigation" to include agency proceedings, like an annexation proceeding, would result in the litigation exception eviscerating the general rule of openness intended by the Act. . . .

I. INTERPRETATION OF EXCEPTIONS TO THE UTAH OPEN AND PUBLIC MEETINGS ACT . . .

The legislature expressly declared its purpose in enacting the Utah Open and Public Meetings Act in section 52-4-1, which reads, "It is the intent of the law that [the] actions [of the state, its agencies and political subdivisions,] be taken openly and that their deliberations be conducted openly." Utah Code Ann. §52-4-1 (1998). As a result, we interpret the Utah Open and Public Meetings Act broadly to further the declared statutory purpose of openness. Because we construe the Act broadly, it therefore follows that the exceptions be strictly construed. In this case we construe the litigation exception narrowly so as to give effect to the legislative intent. We further note the intent of the legislature to permit some meetings to be closed under certain circumstances. In carrying out the purpose of openness, the legislature could have chosen to make the open meetings requirement absolute. It chose, however, to exclude some meetings from the openness requirement.

The statutory provision in question permits an otherwise public meeting to be closed by a public body for "strategy sessions to discuss pending or reasonably imminent litigation." Utah Code Ann. §52-4-5(1)(a)(iii). In order for the Salt Lake County Commission not to have violated the Act by closing the March 30, 1998 meeting, the closed portion of the meeting (1) must have been a strategy session, (2) the strategy session must have been with respect to litigation, and (3) the litigation must have been pending or reasonably imminent.

A. Whether the Closed Portion of the Meeting was a Strategy Session

The trial court, after reviewing the minutes of the March 30, 1998 meeting in camera, concluded that the County Commission "did not conduct a strategy session, rather it discussed the underlying policy question of whether to take any action at all." The district court stated that in order to close a meeting under section 52-4-5(1)(a)(iii), the focus of the public body's discussion must be on litigation strategy, which could include a discussion of claims or defenses, strengths and weaknesses of the public body's position, whether to hire outside counsel, settlement posture, etc.

We conclude that the closed portion of the meeting was a strategy session. In generally accepted terms, to strategize means to devise plans or means to achieve an end. The Salt Lake County Commission devised a plan or course of action and put it in motion during the private portion of the March 30, 1998 meeting. . . . This closed session during which the County Commission was informed of the background of the Riverton City annexation petition, was advised on how to respond to the petition, was given a recommended course of action, and decided on a course of action, constitutes a strategy session.

B. Whether Disputes Before the Boundary Commission Constitute Litigation

Having concluded the closed portion of the meeting was a strategy session, the question becomes whether the meeting was a discussion of *litigation* strategy, or whether it was strategy with respect to a non-litigation process. Essentially, we must decide whether an annexation matter before the Boundary Commission is litigation. . . .

The legislative annexation scheme . . . permits the county legislative body to oppose an annexation petition by filing a protest to the petition, Utah Code Ann. §10-2-407(1)(a)(i) (Supp.2000), thereby creating an adversarial process. The protest is filed with either the county boundary commission,

§10-2-407(2)(a)(i)(B)(I), or with the clerk of the county in which the area proposed for annexation is located if the county has not yet created a boundary commission, §10-2-407(2)(a)(i)(B)(II). . . .

[T]he mandate to resolve disputes between adverse parties by applying rules of law to a particular set of facts is judicial in nature, meaning the boundary commission performs a judicial function.

However, in performing its role of deciding protests, the boundary commission generally retains a "feasibility consultant" to conduct a "feasibility study," *see* §10-2-413, and then holds a public hearing, *see* §10-2-415. . . . As such, the boundary commission considers whether a proposed annexation is good policy. In this sense, the boundary commission acts in a legislative capacity. In sum, the boundary commission functions as both a legislative body and an adjudicative body.

Nevertheless, the role of a county boundary commission is, on the whole, essentially one of resolving disputes between competing parties, the petitioner and the protesting party. Thus, even though the boundary commission engages a consultant to gather information and present recommendations on matters of policy, the county boundary commission is mandated by the legislature to apply the law to the facts and information presented to it by the feasibility consultant, petitioner, and protester. *See* §§10-2-402, 403. For these reasons, we conclude that boundary commissions act as quasi-judicial bodies when considering annexation petitions and protests. . . .

We conclude that while county boundary commissions perform both legislative and adjudicative functions, the method of resolving annexation disputes through county boundary commissions is quasi-judicial, and it constitutes litigation for purposes of the Utah Public and Open Meetings Act.

C. Whether the Dispute before the Boundary Commission was Pending or Reasonably Imminent

In the instant case, it is undisputed that the annexation proceeding discussed by the County Commission was already pending before the Boundary Commission. As a result, the County Commission did not violate the Open and Public Meetings Act by closing the March 30, 1998 meeting to discuss whether to protest Riverton City's annexation petition before the Salt Lake County Boundary Commission. As a matter of law, the closed portion of the meeting constituted a strategy session to discuss pending or reasonably imminent litigation. . . .

Accordingly, the trial court's order granting plaintiff's motion for summary judgment is reversed, and the award of attorney fees to plaintiff is vacated.

Chief Justice Howe, Associate Chief Justice Russon, Justice Durham, and Judge Taylor concur in Justice Wilkins opinion.

Having disqualified himself, Justice Durrant does not participate herein; District Judge Taylor sat.

Notes and Comments

1. *State Open Meeting Acts.* Acts like the one at issue in *Kearns-Tribune* generally presume that all proceedings of local decisionmakers are open to the public except

for certain specified proceedings where secrecy is clearly called for (that is, consultation with the lawyer over litigation). Where a dispute does arise, the courts usually interpret the state open meeting laws broadly to require that meetings be open to the public. *See, e.g.*, *Wesley Chapel Bluemount Ass'n v. Baltimore County*, 699 A.2d 434 (Md. 1997) (county board of appeals, in hearing an appeal from a hearing officer's approval of a development plan, was required to deliberate in public).

Did the Court violate this "broad interpretation" approach in *Kearns-Tribune?* Didn't the court broadly interpret "litigation" when, in part, the supervisors were discussing what policy they should take with respect to this particular annexation? If part of what the commission did was legislative, should the court have made the effort to segregate that portion of the commission's deliberations from the adjudicative portion?

2. *Remedies for Open Meeting Act Violations.* One interesting question is what the remedy is if the local government violates an open meeting law. There may be options. In *Manning v. City of East Tawas*, 593 N.W.2d 649 (Ct. App. Mich. 1999), the city council violated the Open Meeting Act by holding a closed session and then withholding the minutes of the meeting. The Act required their disclosure. The court of appeal held that, where a closed session concerned matters that were both exempt and nonexempt from the public meeting requirements, as a remedy the trial court could "redact" portions of the closed session minutes and release those to the public. Under the Act, the city council was also able to "reenact" its decision, and thus avoid the remedy of having its actions declared invalid by reason of the violation of the Act.

The outcome was a bit different for the city in *Clark v. City of Lakewood*, 259 F.3d 996 (9th Cir. 2001), where the Lakewood Planning Advisory Board formed a task force to examine all aspects of adult entertainment in the city. The task force conducted eleven meetings, most of them closed to the public. It then wrote a report and submitted recommendations. Ultimately the city passed legislation regulating adult businesses.

The court of appeal held that the closed meetings violated Washington's Open Meetings Act. The Act declared that any actions taken at meetings failing to comply with the Act "shall be null and void." The court held that, while the ultimate ordinance passed by the city was not null and void, "[A]ny actions taken at the Task Force's Meetings that were closed to the public are null and void." *Id.* at 1015. The effect of the ruling was to make it more difficult for the City to defend its ordinance, since the evidence compiled by the task force to support it was no longer available.

Under the Maryland State Open Meetings Act at issue in *Wesley Chapel*, supra, the court is authorized to void a public body's action for failing to comply with the Act only if the public body "willfully failed" to comply with it and "no other remedy is adequate." Md. Code Ann., State Gov't, §10-510(d)(4) (1993). The court held that the trial court had to determine whether the board willfully failed to comply with the Act.

3. *Supervising the Local Government's Procedures.* Both *Frito-Lay* and *Kearns-Tribune Corp*. are examples of how courts are called upon to "police" the procedures used by local governments in making land use decisions. The following are typical of the claims of procedural error made in land uses cases:

- A statute required that notice of a public hearing be published "once each week for two successive weeks." The township published the notice twice during the same calendar week: Monday June 26 and Saturday July 1. As a result, the township's new zoning ordinance was invalid. *Stassi v. Ransom Township Zoning Hg. Bd.*, 54 Pa. D. & C. 4th 303 (Ct. Common Pleas 2001). See also *Coleman v. City of Key West*, 807 So. 2d 84, 85 (Fla. Ct. App. 2002) ("Although a tropical storm is an excellent reason to cancel a hearing, it is not a valid reason for noncompliance with the notice requirements.")
- The City Council did not err in restricting each side of a zoning dispute to a ten-minute time limit. The imposition of impartial time limits was reasonable. *Bennett v. City Council for the City of Las Cruces*, 973 P.2d 871 (N.M. Ct. App. 1998).
- The Planning Commission had no authority to allow discovery in proceedings to consider the approval of a subdivision plat. The court thought that, even though the proceeding was technically adjudicatory, the commission in effect acted as a ministerial agency, since it was required to approve a subdivision application which complies with all applicable ordinances. *Hickory Hills Development Co., L.L.C. v. Coffman*, 699 N.E.2d 1214 (Ind. Ct. App. 1998).
- The Court did not err in confining its review of the grant of a conditional use permit to the existing administrative record. Plaintiff asked the court to consider information that was referred to in the conditions for the use permit but was never made part of the record. *R.L. Hexum & Associates, Inc. v. Rochester Township Bd. of Supervisors*, 609 N.W.2d 271 (Minn. Ct. App. 2000).

A Note on Standing, Ripeness, and Exhaustion of Administrative Remedies

Standing to Challenge Local Decisions. Individual standing to challenge local land use decisions is a relatively settled issue. Zoning enabling statutes often authorize judicial review on behalf of "persons aggrieved." *See, e.g.*, Iowa Code §335.18 (1996) (authorizing judicial review of certain county zoning decisions by "persons . . . aggrieved . . . or any taxpayer"). Some statutes contain broader language. *See* N.J. Stat. Ann. §40:55D-17 (West 1996) ("[a]ny interested party"). Even in these cases, however, most courts require the plaintiff to show injury before he or she may sue. *See, e.g., Burgess v. City of Gulfport*, 814 So. 2d 149 (Miss. 2002) (residents lacked standing where they did not allege that they own land around in the property in question "or that the land has been affected in an adverse manner"). A few states require a showing of "special injury" or "special damage" of some sort. *See Massiello v. Town Bd. of the Town of Lake George*, 648 N.Y.S. 2d 330 (App. Div. 1999) (property owner adjacent to "wild west" stables had standing where she alleged that she was subject to odors, flies, and insects because she alleged "direct harm different in kind and degree from any injury to the public at large").

Many states adopt standing tests traceable to United States Supreme Court decisions. In *Sierra Club v. Morton*, 405 U.S. 727, 733 (1972), the Court summarized the principles:

> [I]n Association of Data Processing Service Organizations, Inc. v. Camp, 397 U.S. 150 . . . and Barlow v. Collins, 397 U.S. 159, we held . . . that persons had standing to obtain judicial review of federal agency action under [the Administrative Procedure Act] where they had alleged that the challenged action had caused them "injury in fact," and where the alleged injury was to an interest "arguably within the zone of interests to be protected or regulated" by the statutes that the agencies claimed to have violated.

This test, or close variations of it, often appears in the state courts' jurisprudence on standing. Under the test, the injury that a plaintiff claims can be aesthetic or environmental. *See, e.g., Pye v. United States*, 269 F.3d 459 (4th Cir. 2001) (aesthetic concerns over a historic district are sufficient to constitute injury in fact, citing *Sierra Club v. Morton*).

In recent years, the United States Supreme Court has issued a series of decisions on standing that have narrowed plaintiff's abilities to challenge government programs. *See, e.g., Lujan v. Defenders of Wildlife*, 504 U.S. 555 (1992) (plaintiffs challenging a regulation limiting the Secretary of the Interior's obligation to take certain actions under the Endangered Species Act did not allege sufficient injury where they did not allege "concrete plans" of when they would return to an area they had visited before). As yet, however, the Supreme Court's turn toward restricting standing does not seem to have had a marked effect on the state court decisions regarding standing in land use cases.

Residents' Standing. A primary reason why state law on standing in the land use area remains relatively settled is the nature of the litigation. In most cases, the plaintiffs are individuals who live near the property that was the subject of the land use approval in question. Such plaintiffs can usually show the requisite injury without much trouble. *See, e.g., George v. Timberlake Associates*, 739 A.2d 1207, 1208 (Vt. 1999) ("Because they owned property in the 'immediate neighborhood' of the project under site plan review, petitioners were 'interested person[s]' with standing to challenge the planning commission's decision"); *Sproul v. Town of Boothbay Harbor*, 746 A.2d 368, 371-372 (Me. 2000) ("Because of the abutter's proximate location, a minor adverse consequence affecting the party's property, pecuniary or personal rights is all that is required for the abutting landowner to have standing").

Sufficient Injury. In the case of third parties, such as neighbors or citizens groups, standing also will depend on an allegation of sufficient injury. *See, e.g., Butters v. Hauser*, 960 P.2d 181 (Id. 1998) (neighboring landowner had standing to challenge ordinance amendment and conditional use permit authorizing a radio transmission tower because "the tower looms over her land" and, allegedly, "the tower caused problems with her phones and compact disc player"); *Rattner v. Planning Board of West Tisbury*, 695 N.E.2d 669, 671 (Mass. App. Ct. 1998) (finding that an abutting landowner "enjoys the benefit of a rebuttable presumption of aggrievement").

Economic Injury. An applicant, of course, will have standing to challenge a denial of its project because of the economic injury it will suffer from the denial. However, where the third party is an entity whose interests are economic in nature, such as a competitor of a successful project applicant, that party may have difficulty showing the requisite interest to support standing. *See, e.g., Oceanport Industries, Inc. v. Wilmington Stevedores, Inc.*, 636 A.2d 892, 906 (Del. 1994) (plaintiff stevedoring company did not have standing to contest the issuance of permits for a bulk transfer facility that were issued to a competing company because the statutes that plaintiff alleged to be violated were "designed to protect the environment, not economic interests"). *Compare Burrtec Waste Industries v. City of Colton*, 119 Cal. Rptr. 2d 410 (Cal. Ct. App. 2002) (solid waste disposal and recycling company had standing to challenge adequacy of public notice for permit allowing a competing company to operate a solid waste facility). In *Kroenlein v. Eddington*, 35 P.3d 1207 (Wyo. 2001), the Wyoming Supreme Court drew the following distinction: "[A] party does not have standing to contest issuance of a liquor license by virtue of the party's status as a competitor . . . A party does have standing as a resident even though he or she is a competitor. . . . "

Associational Standing. A citizens organization may obtain standing either by showing that the organization itself has suffered injury or that its members have been injured. Courts have found standing where an association alleged that its members breathed the air near a proposed major expansion of a mill (*In re International Paper Co.*, 363 A.2d 235 (Me. 1976)); where members' views would be blocked by the challenged development, which would lower the members' property values (*Edgewater Beach Owners Ass'n, Inc. v, Walton County*, 833 So. 2d 215 (Fla. Ct. App. 2002)); and where the members would be subject to airplane and helicopter traffic from a nearby airbase (*Glengary-Gamlin Protective Ass'n, Inc. v. Bird*, 675 P.2d 344 (Idaho Ct. App. 1983)). A trade organization, such as a building association, also will have standing if its members will be individually harmed. *See, e.g., Building Industry Ass'n of Lancaster County v. Manheim Township*, 710 A.2d 141, 146 (Pa. Commw. Ct. 1998) (plaintiff met direct injury requirement where it "averred that builders and developers that are members of BIA have paid impact fees as a result of assessments made by the Township pursuant to the Ordinance").

Public Agencies. Public agency plaintiffs, such as municipalities seeking to challenge decisions by their neighbors, also must show they are aggrieved. *See City of Hickory Hills v. Village of Bridgeview*, 367 N.E.2d 1305 (Ill. 1977) (city had sufficient interest to sue and thus was a "person aggrieved" where it was required to furnish sewer and water facilities for the development in question).

Housing Litigation. In *Warth v. Seldon*, 422 U.S. 490 (1975), the Supreme Court held that a variety of plaintiffs, including a developer of low cost housing as well as private individuals who sought to live in such housing, had no standing to challenge the exclusionary zoning practices of a municipality. The Court found that they did not allege demonstrable, particularized injury. However, in *Village of Arlington Heights v. Metropolitan Housing Development Corp.*, 429 U.S. 252 (1977), a case that came down two years after *Warth*, the Supreme Court found that both a developer of low cost housing and private individuals alleging that they were eligible for such housing had standing to challenge a zoning ordinance that prevented the construction of the housing on a specific parcel of land. Plaintiffs also may find it easier to state a claim under the Fair Housing Act. *See Gladstone, Realtors v. Village of Bellwood*, 441 U.S. 91 (1979) (individuals deprived of affordable housing as well as residents of the area deprived of the benefits of living in an integrated area have standing under the Act); *Havens Realty Corp. v. Coleman*, 455 U.S. 363 (1982) (individual plaintiff, who acted as "tester" to determine whether landlord would deny rental to him, and interracial association both had standing to sue under the Fair Housing Act).

Similarly, plaintiffs may have standing under the Civil Rights Act of 1968. *See Trafficante v. Metropolitan Life Insurance Co.*, 409 U.S. 205 (1972) (tenants of an apartment complex who alleged that, because the landlord discriminated, they were denied the benefits of living in an integrated community had standing to sue under the Civil Rights Act of 1968). Nonetheless, in the aftermath of *Warth*, plaintiffs obviously face difficult hurdles to challenge exclusionary zoning ordinances in the federal courts.

The courts of several large states have proved more willing than the U.S. Supreme Court to confer standing on plaintiffs in housing litigation. *See, e.g.*, *Southern Burlington County N.A.A.C.P. v. Township of Mount Laurel* (reproduced as a principal case in Chapter 12). In *Stocks v. City of Irvine*, 170 Cal. Rptr. 724 (Ct. App. 1981), the court rejected *Warth* and concluded that nonresidents had standing to sue. It also noted that under the *Warth* test, the more restrictive that a city's zoning becomes, the less likely it will be that a builder will propose a project and thus have standing.

Ripeness in General. Another procedural doctrine, the concept of ripeness, plays an important role in litigation claiming that a land use regulation has "taken" property without compensation. In the 1970s and 1980s, the Supreme Court issued a series of opinions that required landowners to seek development approvals and variances before asking the court for damages caused by an alleged taking. In *Suitum v. Tahoe Regional Planning Agency*, 520 U.S. 725 (1997) and *Palazzolo v. Rhode Island*, 533 U.S. 606 (2001), the Court's most recent forays into the area, the Court slightly eased the ripeness barrier.

In *Suitum*, the plaintiff owned land on the shore of Lake Tahoe. When she applied to the Tahoe Regional Planning Agency for permission to build the agency determined that her property was located within a "stream environment zone" and denied her request. The agency's regulatory scheme, however, also entitled her to receive certain allegedly valuable "transferable development rights"(TDRs), rights that could be sold to other individuals wishing to develop land. Without seeking to exercise those rights, plaintiff brought an action in federal court claiming that the agency's actions had effected a taking of her property.

The agency responded by seeking to have the case dismissed on the grounds that the takings claim was not ripe, due to the plaintiff's failure to exercise her TDRs. In previous cases, the court had emphasized that a plaintiff must demonstrate that she had received a final decision regarding the application of the challenged land use regulations to the property in question. In this case the agency argued that there remained a "final decision" yet to occur: action on a possible application to transfer the TDRs.

The Supreme Court rejected the claim. It noted that there had been a final decision on the application of land use ordinances to the property; the agency had already determined that it could permit no additional land coverage or other permanent disturbance on the parcel. As to the fact that the plaintiff had not applied to transfer the TDRs, the Court found that this was not the type of "final decision" that its precedents called for the agency to make. The agency agreed that she was entitled to TDRs, and there was no discretionary decision for the agency to make with respect to their sale. The only decision left to the agency, approving a particular sale to a particular buyer, did not render the plaintiff's action unripe. As to how much the TDRs were actually worth, thought the Court, this was simply a matter for trial.

In *Palazzolo*, the plaintiff or his corporate predecessor made a series of applications since the 1960s to develop property on a salt marsh. Part of the property was subject to flooding. Most importantly, in 1983 the plaintiff sought permission to build a wooden bulkhead and fill the entire marshland, while in 1985 he sought to fill 11 of the 18 wetland acres. Both applications were denied.

Plaintiff thereafter brought a takings action, and the state countered that the action was not ripe. According to the state, plaintiff should have sought approval for a development that required less fill than 11 acres.

The Court disagreed. It found that the "unequivocal nature of the wetlands regulations at issue and . . . the council's application of the regulations to the subject property" made it clear what development would not be allowed. *Id.* at 618. Here, the Court found, the council's decisions "make plain that the agency interpreted its regulations to bar petitioner from engaging in any filling or development activity on the wetlands." *Id.* at 621. The key, said the Court, was that there was "no genuine ambiguity in the record as to the extent of the permitted development on petitioner's property, either on the wetlands or the uplands." *Id.* at 625. Finally, the plaintiff was not required to apply for permission to build on the upland part of the property that would not require filling. Here, too, the value of the nonwetlands portion of the property was uncontested.

The Long List of Ripeness Cases. The *Palazzolo* and *Suitum* cases are two of a number of recent Supreme Court cases that address the ripeness issue in the context of a takings claim, and the issue continues to generate considerable litigation. The recurring question is the extent to which an applicant must seek approval of a development before its takings claim will ripen. As you might expect, lack of ripeness is a favored procedural defense by cities and other governmental entities that are defendants in takings cases.

In *Agins v. City of Tiburon*, 447 U.S. 255 (1980), the Court held that a challenge to a zoning ordinance is not ripe until a landowner submits an application to develop the property and the public agency denies that application. In *Williamson County Regional Planning Comm'n v. Hamilton Bank of Johnson City*, 473 U.S. 172 (1985), the Court extended this principle, requiring that before a takings claim will ripen, the applicant also must attempt to secure a variance from the local agency.

One year after *Williamson County*, the Court again considered ripeness in *MacDonald, Somer & Frates v. Yolo County*, 477 U.S. 340 (1986). In that case a developer proposed to build 159 single and multi-family units on lands previously used for agriculture, but the county denied the application, listing a series of objections to the proposal as then envisioned. The developer immediately brought a takings claim, but the Court held that it was not ripe. The Court reasoned that the applicant must secure a "final and authoritative determination of the type and intensity of development" before it may bring a takings action. *Id.* at 348. It also rejected the landowner's claim that future applications would be futile.

Many lower courts have found that this line of ripeness decisions requires both an application for the development and, if that is denied, a later application for a variance before a takings claim based on the denial of those applications will be ripe. *See, e.g.*, *Bonge v. County of Madison*, 573 N.W.2d 448, 451 (Neb. 1998) (citing "two applications" requirement). *Compare Mayhew v. Town of Sunnyvale*, 964 S.W.2d 922 (Tex. 1998). The Texas Supreme Court found that where, in response to the original request, the developer spent a year in negotiations with the town and over $500,000 preparing and developing its application, and then later developed a modified application which was rejected, no variance application was required.

The long list of ripeness cases, and the variations in their application of the doctrine, cannot be captured in a short note. For example, there are differences in its application depending on whether the taking challenge to a zoning ordinance is facial or as applied, as well as differences in the application of the doctrine to equal protection, substantive due process, and procedural due process claims. *See, e.g., McKenzie v. City of White Hall*, 112 F.3d 313 (8th Cir. 1997) (although takings claim challenging a condition that developer give the city an easement over a strip of land to act as a "privacy buffer" was not ripe, due process and equal protection claims challenging that decision were ripe). The subject of ripeness, along with the other procedural nuances of federal court jurisdiction in takings cases, is covered comprehensively in Thomas E. Roberts, Procedural Implications of Williamson County/First English In Regulatory Takings Litigation, 31 Envtl. L. Rptr. 10353 (2001).

The Rationale for the Ripeness Requirement. What is the policy rationale underlying the ripeness requirement? Is it to limit the number of cases brought alleging takings? Or is it that, without a definitive determination of what type of land use *is* allowed, a court cannot determine whether a taking has occurred? Consider the following statement from *City of Riviera Beach v. Shillingburg*, 659 So. 2d 1174, 1180 (Fla. Dist. Ct. App. 1995): The ripeness doctrine acts "both as a means to allow [the dispute] to be resolved politically or administratively outside the judicial process and to prevent the trial court from making decisions in the abstract." If this is the rationale for the doctrine, how many times must a landowner apply for permission to develop before the takings claim will ripen?

Exhaustion of Administrative Remedies. Students also should be aware of a related principle that affects the right to judicial review of local land use decisions: the plaintiff must pursue all administrative procedures to their completion before a court will review the agency's actions. This principle, known as the doctrine of exhaustion of administrative remedies, is a fundamental tenet of administrative law and is covered in courses on that subject. For example, if the zoning administrator denies an applicant's request for permission to develop, but under state law or local ordinance the applicant may appeal the denial to a board of zoning appeals, he or she must take that administrative appeal. In the absence of such an appeal, any request for judicial relief will ordinarily fail. *See, e.g., Lilly v. Caroline County*, 526 S.E.2d 743 (Va. 2000) (plaintiffs barred for failing to appeal decision regarding permitted uses under the zoning ordinance to zoning board of appeals); *Borden v. Planning & Zoning Comm'n. of the Town of North Stonington*, 755 A.2d 224 (Conn. Ct. App. 2000) (abutting landowner required to exhaust administrative remedies by appealing planning and zoning commission approval to town zoning board of appeals).

One exception to the requirement that administrative remedies be exhausted is futility. If the plaintiff can show that the agency has declared what its ruling will be in a particular case, and thus that further participation in the proceeding will be futile, it may be excused from exhausting its administrative remedies. The exception, however, is very narrow and rarely applied. *Compare Hunkins v. City of Minneapolis*, 508 N.W.2d 542 (Minn. Ct. App. 1993) (final determination on a variance was not futile simply because the plaintiff feels ignored and the zoning decision is adverse to plaintiff's desires) *with Orion Corp. v. State of Washington*, 693 P.2d 1369, 1380 (Wash. 1985) (although landowner had not applied for permits, the court found under the "unique set of facts . . . in this case" that the plaintiff had demonstrated futility because the "State and County have made a policy choice to prevent development of Padilla Bay"). The futility exception also applies in takings litigation. *See, e.g., Lost Tree Village v. City of Vero Beach*, 838 So. 2d 563, 574 (Fla. Ct. App. 2002) ("It is now beyond the point of mere speculation that both entities would refuse to remove those [comprehensive plan] provisions. Accordingly, it would be futile to require Lost Tree to apply for amendments to the respective Plans to remove those provisions").

State Process for Obtaining Compensation. In *Williamson County*, the Supreme Court also held that a plaintiff could not bring a takings claim in federal court if the state had provided an adequate process for obtaining compensation. The plaintiff, held the Court, should have availed itself of an inverse condemnation action that would lie under Tennessee law. *See, e.g., Daniels v. The Area Plan Comm'n of Allen County*, 306 F.3d 445, 456 (7th Cir. 2002) ("After utilizing a state remedy, such as a suit for inverse condemnation, if the owner does not receive what he believes is just compensation, he may proceed with a Takings Claim in federal court."); *Macri v. King County*, 110 F.3d 1496 (9th Cir. 1997) (takings claim dismissed because state had adequate procedure for compensation).

C. JUDICIAL CONTROL OF LOCAL DISCRETION

The overarching question the courts face is how to control local discretion while, at the same time, appropriately deferring to true legislative decisions made by local elected officials. In the leading case of *Fasano v. Board of County Commissioners of Washington County*, the Oregon Supreme Court took a new approach to the problem.

FASANO v. BOARD OF COUNTY COMMISSIONERS OF WASHINGTON COUNTY

507 P.2d 23 (Or. 1973)

HOWELL, Justice.

The plaintiffs, homeowners in Washington county, unsuccessfully opposed a zone change before the Board of County Commissioners of Washington County. . . .

The defendants are the Board of County Commissioners and A.G.S. Development Company. A.G.S., the owner of 32 acres which had been zoned R-7 (Single Family Residential), applied for a zone change to P-R (Planned Residential), which allows for the construction of a mobile home park. The change failed to receive a majority vote of the Planning Commission. The Board of County Commissioners approved the change and found, among other matters, that the change allows for "increased densities and different types of housing to meet the needs of urbanization over that allowed by the existing zoning." . . .

According to the briefs, the comprehensive plan of development for Washington county was adopted in 1959 and included classifications in the county for residential, neighborhood commercial, retail commercial, general commercial, industrial park and light industry, general and heavy industry, and agricultural areas.

The land in question, which was designated "residential" by the comprehensive plan, was zoned R-7, Single Family Residential.

Subsequent to the time the comprehensive plan was adopted, Washington county established a Planned Residential (P-R) zoning classification in 1963. The P-R classification was adopted by ordinance and provided that a planned residential unit development could be established and should include open space for utilities, access, and recreation; should not be less than 10 acres in size; and should be located in or adjacent to a residential zone. The P-R zone adopted by the 1963 ordinance is of the type known as a "floating zone," so-called because the ordinance creates a zone classification authorized for future use but not placed on the zoning map until its use at a particular location is approved by the governing body. The R-7 classification for the 32 acres continued until April 1970 when the classification was changed to P-R to permit the defendant A.G.S. to construct the mobile home park on the 32 acres involved. . . .

We granted review in this case to consider the questions — by what standards does a county commission exercise its authority in zoning matters; who has the burden of meeting those standards when a request for change of zone is made; and what is the scope of court review of such actions?

Any meaningful decision as to the proper scope of judicial review of a zoning decision must start with a characterization of the nature of that decision. The majority of jurisdictions state that a zoning ordinance is a legislative act and is thereby entitled to presumptive validity. This court made such a characterization of zoning decisions in *Smith v. County of Washington*, 241 Or. 380, 406 P.2d 545 (1965):

> Inasmuch as ORS 215.110 specifically grants to the governing board of the county the power to amend zoning ordinances, a challenged amendment is a legislative act and is clothed with a presumption in its favor. . . .

However, in *Smith* an exception to the presumption was found and the zoning held invalid. Furthermore, the case cited by the *Smith* court, *Jehovah's Witnesses v. Mullen et al.*, at least at one point viewed the contested zoning in that case as an administrative as opposed to legislative act.

At this juncture we feel we would be ignoring reality to rigidly view all zoning decisions by local governing bodies as legislative acts to be accorded a full presumption of validity and shielded from less than constitutional scrutiny by the theory of separation of powers. Local and small decision groups are simply not the equivalent in all respects of state and national legislatures. There is a growing judicial recognition of this fact of life. . . .

The Supreme Court of Washington, in reviewing a rezoning decision, recently stated:

> Whatever descriptive characterization may be otherwise attached to the role or function of the planning commission in zoning procedures, e.g., advisory, recommendatory, investigatory, administrative or legislative, it is manifest . . . that it is a public agency, . . . a principle [sic] and statutory duty of which is to conduct public hearings in specified planning and zoning matters, enter findings of fact — often on the basis of disputed facts — and make recommendations with reasons assigned thereto. Certainly, in its role as a hearing and fact-finding tribunal, the planning commission's function more nearly than not partakes of the nature of an administrative,

quasi-judicial proceeding, . . . " *Chrobuck v. Snohomish County*, 78 Wash. 2d 884, 480 P.2d 489, 495-496 (1971).

Ordinances laying down general policies without regard to a specific piece of property are usually an exercise of legislative authority, are subject to limited review, and may only be attacked upon constitutional grounds for an arbitrary abuse of authority. On the other hand, a determination whether the permissible use of a specific piece of property should be changed is usually an exercise of judicial authority and its propriety is subject to an altogether different test. An illustration of an exercise of legislative authority is the passage of the ordinance by the Washington County Commission in 1963 which provided for the formation of a planned residential classification to be located in or adjacent to any residential zone. An exercise of judicial authority is the county commissioners' determination in this particular matter to change the classification of A.G.S. Development Company's specific piece of property. The distinction is stated, as follows, in Comment, Zoning Amendments — The Product of Judicial or Quasi-Judicial Action, 33 Ohio St. L.J. 130 (1972):

> . . . Basically, this test involves the determination of whether action produces a general rule or policy which is applicable to an open class of individuals, interest, or situations, or whether it entails the application of a general rule or policy to specific individuals, interests, or situations. If the former determination is satisfied, there is legislative action; if the latter determination is satisfied, the action is judicial. 33 Ohio St. L.J. at 137.

We reject the proposition that judicial review of the county commissioners' determination to change the zoning of the particular property in question is limited to a determination whether the change was arbitrary and capricious.

In order to establish a standard of review, it is necessary to delineate certain basic principles relating to land use regulation.

The basic instrument for county or municipal land use planning is the "comprehensive plan." . . . The plan has been described as a general plan to control and direct the use and development of property in a municipality. *Nowicki v. Planning and Zoning Board*, 148 Conn. 492, 172 A.2d 386, 389 (1961).

In Oregon the county planning commission is required by ORS 215.050 to adopt a comprehensive plan for the use of some or all of the land in the county. Under ORS 215.110(1), after the comprehensive plan has been adopted, the planning commission recommends to the governing body of the county the ordinances necessary to "carry out" the comprehensive plan. The purpose of the zoning ordinances, both under our statute and the general law of land use regulation, is to "carry out" or implement the comprehensive plan. 1 Anderson, American Law of Zoning, §1.12 (1968). . . .

We believe that the state legislature has conditioned the county's power to zone upon the prerequisite that the zoning attempt to further the general welfare of the community through consciousness, in a prospective sense, of the factors mentioned above. In other words, except as noted later in this opinion, it must be proved that the change is in conformance with the comprehensive plan.

In proving that the change is in conformance with the comprehensive plan in this case, the proof, at a minimum, should show (1) there is a public need for a change of the kind in question, and (2) that need will be best served by changing the classification of the particular piece of property in question as compared with other available property. . . .

Because the action of the commission in this instance is an exercise of judicial authority, the burden of proof should be placed, as is usual in judicial proceedings, upon the one seeking change. The more drastic the change, the greater will be the burden of showing that it is in conformance with the comprehensive plan as implemented by the ordinance, that there is a public need for the kind of change in question, and that the need is best met by the proposal under consideration. As the degree of change increases, the burden of showing that the potential impact upon the area in question was carefully considered and weighed will also increase. If other areas have previously been designated for the particular type of development, it must be shown why it is necessary to introduce it into an area not previously contemplated and why the property owners there should bear the burden of the departure.

Although we have said in *Roseta* that zoning changes may be justified without a showing of a mistake in the original plan or ordinance, or of changes in the physical characteristics of an affected area, any of these factors which are present in a particular case would, of course, be relevant. Their importance would depend upon the nature of the precise change under consideration. . . .

What we have said above is necessarily general, as the approach we adopt contains no absolute standards or mechanical tests. We believe, however, that it is adequate to provide meaningful guidance for local governments making zoning decisions and for trial courts called upon to review them. With future cases in mind, it is appropriate to add some brief remarks on questions of procedure. Parties at the hearing before the county governing body are entitled to an opportunity to be heard, to an opportunity to present and rebut evidence, to a tribunal which is impartial in the matter—i. e., having had no pre-hearing or ex parte contacts concerning the question at issue—and to a record made and adequate findings executed. Comment, Zoning Amendments—The Product of Judicial or Quasi-Judicial Action, 33 Ohio St. L.J. 130-143 (1972).

When we apply the standards we have adopted to the present case, we find that the burden was not sustained before the commission. The record now before us is insufficient to ascertain whether there was a justifiable basis for the decision. The only evidence in the record, that of the staff report of the Washington County Planning Department, is too conclusory and superficial to support the zoning change. It merely states:

> The staff finds that the requested use does conform to the residential designation of the Plan of Development. It further finds that the proposed use reflects the urbanization of the County and the necessity to provide increased densities and different types of housing to meet the needs of urbanization over that allowed by the existing zoning. . . .

Such generalizations and conclusions, without any statement of the facts on which they are based, are insufficient to justify a change of use. Moreover, no portions of the comprehensive plan of Washington County are before us, and we feel it would be improper for us to take judicial notice of the plan without at least some reference to its specifics by counsel.

As there has not been an adequate showing that the change was in accord with the plan, or that the factors listed in ORS 215.055 were given proper consideration, the judgment is affirmed.

Notes and Comments

1. *Due Process and the Legislative-Adjudicative Distinction.* The distinction between quasi-legislative acts and quasi-adjudicative acts is fundamental to constitutional and administrative law. In *LC&S, Inc. v. Warren County Area Plan Commn.*, 244 F.3d 601, 602-603 (7th Cir. 2001), Judge Posner opened his opinion with a discussion of the differences between the procedural rights associated with legislating as opposed to adjudicating:

> "Legislative due process" seems almost an oxymoron. Legislation is prospective in effect and, more important, general in its application. Its prospective character offers further, and considerable, protection to any individual or organization that might be the legislature's target by imposing costs on all others who are within the statute's scope. The prospect of such costs incites resistance which operates to protect what might otherwise be an isolated, vulnerable, politically impotent target of the legislature's wrath or greed. . . . The right to notice and a hearing, the essence of [due process], are substitutes for the prospectivity and generality that protect citizens from oppression by legislators and thus from the potential tyranny of electoral majorities. . . .

See also Crispin v. Town of Scarborough, 736 A.2d 241, 247 (Me. 1999) (noting that zoning is a legislative act and that "[g]enerally, members of the public are not entitled to protection under the Due Process Clause when their property rights are adversely affected by the legislative acts of government").

What is the test for determining whether an action generally will be deemed quasi-adjudicative or quasi-legislative? What are likely to be the most important facts in determining whether the approval of a specific zoning amendment is deemed quasi-legislative or quasi-judicial?

2. *The Consequences of Adjudicating.* The determination that a zoning decision is quasi-adjudicative has important effects both on local governments and on courts undertaking judicial review. In practical terms, such a decision raises a host of issues regarding the procedures that the local government now must follow (issues that have been and will continue to be the subject of litigation):

a. Opposing parties will now insist that they have a right to call witnesses under oath and to cross-examine witnesses for the applicant.
b. Decisionmakers such as members of a city council will likely be barred from meeting, outside of the hearing process, with proponents or opponents of zoning changes that are quasi-adjudicative.
c. If the parties to a quasi-judicial zone change are entitled to an "impartial decisionmaker," *Fasano* could mean that decisionmakers who have accepted campaign contributions cannot vote on the matter.
d. The local government probably will have to formalize its hearing procedures, such as by keeping a verbatim transcript of all zoning hearings.

e. Finally, the local government decisionmakers will likely have to adopt "findings of fact" for every quasi- adjudicative zone change.

See, e.g., Guilford Financial Services, LLC v. City of Brevard, 563 S.E.2d 27, 41 (N.C. Ct. App. 2002) (setting forth the "essential elements" of a fair trial as (1) the party whose rights are being determined must be given the opportunity to offer evidence, cross-examine adverse witnesses, inspect documents, and offer evidence in explanation and rebuttal; (2) findings must be based on sworn statements; and (3) findings of fact must be supported by competent, material and substantial evidence).

The right to cross-examine, however, is not unlimited. In *People ex rel. Klaren v. Village of Lisle*, 781 N.E.2d 223, 235 (Ill. 2002), the Illinois Supreme Court emphasized that "a municipality may reasonably restrict the right of cross-examination based on subject matter." Considerations include the complexity of the issue, whether the witness possesses special expertise, whether the testimony reflects a matter of taste or personal opinion or concerns a disputed issue of fact, and "the degree to which the witness's testimony relates to the factors to be considered in approving the proposal." *Id.* at 236.

The characterization of a rezoning decision as quasi-judicial has other important ramifications. For example, in some states this characterization will determine the type of proceeding in which judicial review may be sought, and it will mean that a rezoning is not subject to referendum. *See Copple v. City of Lincoln*, 315 N.W.2d 628 (Neb. 1982) (an action for injunctive relief rather than an appeal is the proper way to challenge legislative determinations).

3. *Fasano in the Other States*. The *Fasano* holding has received some support. The most notable recent decision is the Florida Supreme Court's holding in *Bd. of County Commissioners of Brevard County v. Snyder*, 627 So. 2d 469 (Fla. 1993). *See also Louisville and Jefferson County Planning Commn. v. Schmidt*, 83 S.W.3d 449, 455 (Ky. 2002) ("While zoning is an inherently legislative power . . . it may at times be legislative in nature and at other times adjudicatory in nature, depending upon the nature of the zoning change"). Most states, however, have rejected the *Fasano* rule and continue to treat all rezonings as legislative in nature. *See, e.g. Cabana v. Kenai Peninsula Borough*, 21 P.3d 833, 836 (Alaska 2001) ("[W]e have chosen . . . to treat small-scale rezonings as legislative decisions"). The reasoning in these opinions varies. For example, in *Margolis v. District Court*, 638 P.2d 297, 304 (Colo. 1981), the Colorado Supreme Court stated:

> It appears only logical that since the original act of zoning is legislative, the amendatory act of rezoning is likewise legislative even though the procedures may entail notice and hearing which characterize a quasi-judicial proceeding. Essentially, the city council ultimately amends the zoning ordinance or denies the amendment, a legislative function.

See also Hampton v. Richland County, 357 S.E.2d 463, 467 (S.C. Ct. App. 1987) (treating the rezoning of a single tract as anything other than a legislative act would invite countless challenges to the rezoning of single tracts, and the zoning body's authority to take legislative action "would likely be debased").

Do you agree with these reasons for rejecting *Fasano*?

4. *Application I: Small Tract Plan Amendments.* If the jurisdiction follows *Fasano,* how should it treat small tract plan amendments? The Florida Supreme Court addressed this issue in *Coastal Development of North Florida, Inc. v. City of Jacksonville Beach,* 788 So. 2d 204 (Fla. 2001). The court treated the amendment as legislative. It reasoned that, because the comprehensive plan is a fundamental policy decision, "[a]ny proposed change to that established policy likewise is a policy decision." *Id.* at 209. It distinguished small zoning changes on the ground that "a proposed zoning change ... must be consistent" with the future land use map, "thus requiring policy application instead of policy reformulation." *Id.* Are you convinced? If a state has a consistency statute, under this logic wouldn't all zone changes—large or small—be subject to the plan, and thus "policy application"?

5. *Application II: Ex Parte Contacts.* In some cases, the jurisdiction has unquestionably acted in a quasi-judicial manner, such as when it is granting subdivision approvals or conditional use permits. In those cases, are city council members free to receive ex parte telephone calls from constituents?

In a post-*Fasano* Oregon case, *Neuberger v. City of Portland,* 607 P.2d 722 (Or. 1980), the Oregon Supreme Court held that *Fasano* "should not be read as adopting a mechanical rule that any ex parte contracts touching on a matter before a tribunal acting in a quasi-judicial capacity renders the tribunal, or its affected members, unable to act in that matter." *Id.* at 725. The issue, said the court, is not whether there were any ex parte contacts, but whether there was bias.

But in *Idaho Historic Preservation Council v. City Council of the City of Boise,* 8 P.3d 646 (Idaho 2000), the Idaho Supreme Court voided a decision granting a certificate of appropriateness—a clearly quasi-judicial decision—for demolition of a building in a historic district. The problem, said the court, was that ex parte telephone calls to the city council members were "not, recorded or disclosed at the public hearing," and thus there was "no opportunity to rebut any evidence or arguments the City Council may have received from the callers."

6. *Should the Courts Intervene?* The *Fasano* holding is premised on concerns about the legitimacy of small tract rezonings when they are treated as legislative in nature. But even if you assume that these concerns about the appropriateness of treating small tract rezonings in the same fashion as other types of legislative decisionmaking at the local government level are valid ones, you must consider whether a judicially crafted solution—treating such decisions as quasi-adjudicative—is the best response. Are state legislatures better equipped to consider and respond to such problems? What would you suggest?

7. *The Assault on the Presumption.* As noted in the discussion on zoning in Chapter 2, the courts have traditionally accorded land use regulations a strong presumption of validity. *See, e.g., Harris Bank of Hinsdale v. County of Kendall,* 625 N.E.2d 845, 848 (Ill. 1994) ("A zoning ordinance is presumptively valid, the party contesting the zoning ordinance has the burden of proof, and the party may overcome the presumption of validity only by clear and convincing evidence."). Can *Fasano* be seen as a means of lessening or abolishing the presumption in a large segment of land use cases?

Other recent cases seem to support such a movement, particularly recent Supreme Court takings cases. The Court's decision in *Lucas v. South Carolina Coastal Council,* reproduced as a principal case in Chapter 7, is one of those cases in which "traditional judicial respect for legislative judgments seems to have been replaced by no presumption of validity." Robert J. Hopperton, The Presumption of Validity in American Land-Use Law: A Substitute for Analysis, A Source of Significant Confusion, 23 B.C. Envtl. Aff. L. Rev. 301, 319 (1996). Similarly, in *City of Cleburne v. Cleburne Living Center, Inc.*, a principal case reproduced in Chapter 13, the Court concluded that the denial of a special use permit for a group home for the mentally retarded violated equal protection, a decision that effectively negated the presumption of validity. Other commentators have suggested that the presumption should be reconsidered. See Daniel R. Mandelker & A. Dan Tarlock, Shifting the Presumption of Constitutionality in Land-Use Law, 24 Urb. Law. 1 (1992) (arguing that the traditional presumption should be changed).

If the assault on the presumption of validity is successful, will the amount of litigation over land use decisions become excessive? Will there be any real difference in the outcomes of the litigation? In how local governments approach their land use decisionmaking?

8. *Findings.* Another vehicle employed by some courts to police the rationality of land use decisions is the requirement that local governments make findings to explain their quasi-adjudicatory decisions. In *Topanga Ass'n for a Scenic Community v. County of Los Angeles*, 522 P.2d 12 (Cal. 1974), the California Supreme Court ruled that a city or county "must set forth findings to bridge the analytic gap between the raw evidence and ultimate decision or order." *Id.* at 17. The court declared that such findings "direct the reviewing court's attention to the analytic route the administrative agency traveled from evidence to action." According to the court, such findings (1) conduce the administrative body to draw legally relevant subconclusions supportive of its ultimate decision; (2) facilitate orderly analysis and minimize the likelihood that the agency will randomly leap from evidence to conclusions; (3) allow the reviewing court to trace and examine the agency's mode of analysis; (4) enable the parties to determine whether and on what basis they should seek judicial review; and (5) serve a "public relations" function by helping to persude the parties that administrative decisionmaking is careful, reasoned, and equitable. *Id.* at 18-19. Another obvious purpose of findings is to aid the court in judicial review. *Bernuth v. Zoning Bd. of Review of the Town of New Shoreham*, 770 A.2d 396, 402 (R.I. 2001) (zoning board's findings on a variance were inadequate where "[t]here was no discussion in the written decision of what the board considered to be the hardship suffered by the applicants"); *Broward County v. G.B.V. International, Ltd.*, 787 So. 2d 838, 846 (Fla. 2001) ("We note the Commission did little to facilitate judicial review or to bolster its own decision; it made no findings, stated no formal reason for its decision, and issued no written order").

Which of these separate functions that the findings requirement allegedly serves are realistic, and which are more theoretical than practical?

9. *Litigating a Findings Case.* From the plaintiff's perspective, why would it be worth expending resources to bring a case in which the allegation is that the findings were insufficient? Presumably, the city would merely readopt its decision with new findings that meet the legal requirements. Or can you think of other strategic reasons that might justify such litigation?

Could the city on remand simply readopt the findings? Or are the proceedings vitiated such that the entire hearing process must be restarted?

10. *Findings and Discretion.* An enhanced findings requirement can be seen as another judicial vehicle (similar to *Fasano*) for ensuring rationality in the local

land use system. But consider whether the assumptions underlying the framework are realistic. Will busy city councillors actually consider the evidence, and the legal standard against which that evidence must be measured, in making their decision? In fact, most findings are prepared by the city or county attorney's office prior to the actual decision and are adopted pro forma by the local decisionmaking person or body.

D. ETHICS AND FAIRNESS

Given the economic interests at stake in local land use decisions, as well as the fact that those decisions can shape an area for the foreseeable future, it should not surprise you that important ethical questions can arise in the land use process. One set of issues revolves around the question of whether political campaign contributions skew the local decisionmaking process. Another involves the ethical obligations that lawyers and planners involved in the process may have toward their clients and toward the public.

IN RE CONVERY
765 A.2d 724 (N.J. 2001)

PER CURIAM.

This disciplinary proceeding arises from a Motion for Final Discipline Based Upon a Criminal Conviction filed by the Office of Attorney Ethics ("OAE") before the Disciplinary Review Board ("DRB"). The OAE moved for final discipline against respondent Samuel V. Convery, Jr. pursuant to *Rule* 1:20-13(c)(2). The OAE based its motion on respondent's conviction for promising employment or other benefit as consideration for any "political activity" in violation of 18 U.S.C.A §600 (the Hatch Act). The conviction constitutes a violation of RPC 8.4(b), which states that it is professional misconduct for a lawyer to "commit a criminal act that reflects adversely on the lawyer's honesty, trustworthiness or fitness as a lawyer." Five out of seven participating members of the DRB recommended that respondent be reprimanded on the basis of his guilty plea to the federal misdemeanor of promising employment or other benefit for political activity. Two members dissented and voted to withhold decision and to require the OAE and respondent to submit supplemental briefs on the scope of respondent's unethical conduct and the appropriate discipline.

Under the circumstances of this case, we conclude that a six-month suspension is the appropriate sanction.

I

. . . At the time that the ethics complaint was filed, respondent practiced with the law firm of Convery & Convery, P.C., together with his two sons. A Democrat, respondent had previously served as the Mayor of the Township of Edison from 1991 to 1993, and prior to his term as Mayor he had been counsel to the Board of Adjustment. In his capacity as Mayor, respondent was well acquainted with

Robert F. Engel (Robert F.), a Republican member of the Edison Town Council. During respondent's term as Mayor, a Freeholder had requested that respondent support the effort of Robert J. Engel (Robert J.), the son of Robert F., in obtaining employment with Middlesex County. Respondent agreed to do so. The County's public-property division thereafter hired Robert J. as an at-will employee.

In July 1995, Shobna Patel retained respondent's law firm to represent Pooja M., Inc. ("Pooja") in connection with its purchase and development of real estate in Edison Township. Pooja needed to obtain zoning variances to develop what had been church property. Pooja intended to develop the property as a banquet hall, with a restaurant, a bar, offices, an art gallery and a retail store. The proposed uses required Pooja to obtain use and bulk zoning variances and approval of preliminary site plans from the Township of Edison Board of Adjustment. Respondent's firm was to receive a $100,000 legal fee for the representation, regardless of the success or failure of the project. Respondent's Pre-Sentence Investigation Report reveals that, because of Pooja's financial difficulties, Pooja was unable to pay respondent's entire fee until the project was approved and completed.

In February 1996, respondent filed an application with the Edison Board of Adjustment for variances and site plan approval on behalf of Pooja. There was considerable public opposition to Pooja's project at the first public hearing on April 16, 1996. In his guilty plea to the federal misdemeanor charge, respondent admitted that in August 1996 he promised Robert F. and his son, Robert J., that he would assist the son in obtaining permanent employment with Middlesex County in exchange for the Engels' assistance in obtaining favorable votes for the Pooja project from two zoning board members. At that time, Robert J. worked for Middlesex county as an at-will employee. Respondent acknowledged that, for purposes of the federal charges, his actions in obtaining the Engels' assistance and the members' votes on the project constituted a form of political activity. However, respondent explained that he considered his actions to be permissible lobbying.

Respondent also admitted that after the April 1996 zoning board hearing, he became aware that Gerard Kenny, a member of the Edison Board of Adjustment, had been quoted in a local newspaper article commenting critically about the Pooja project and expressing an intention to vote against it. Kenny then worked as an ironworker out of Ironworkers' Local Union 373 in Perth Amboy. At the time, John Wade was the business agent of Ironworkers' Local Union 373, and usually determined which union members to send out on union jobs. Respondent admitted that he sent a facsimile of the newspaper article, quoting Kenny about the Pooja project, to John Wade, and that he spoke with Wade by telephone about the article. Respondent's Pre-Sentence Investigation Report indicates that after speaking with respondent, Wade visited Kenny at a union job site and showed him a photocopy of the newspaper article. He told Kenny that he should reconsider his opposition to the project because he "was biting the hand that feeds him." However, none of the facts relating to Wade's visit to Kenny formed the basis of defendant's federal plea and, in his objections to the pre-sentence report, respondent denied having asked Wade to make any such comments to Kenny.

Moreover, respondent's Pre-Sentence Investigation Report reveals that, during the summer of 1996, Robert F. told Kenny that respondent would assist Kenny in obtaining a job with the County of Middlesex or the State of New Jersey if Kenny agreed to vote for the Pooja project. The Board of Adjustment's final vote on the Pooja project was scheduled for August 20, 1996, while Robert F. was at the

Republican National Convention. As a result, Robert F. asked his son, Robert J., to meet with Kenny to confirm that he would vote for the Pooja project. During late August, while his father was at the Republican convention, Robert J. spoke to respondent and then met with Kenny to confirm that Kenny would vote for the Pooja project. On August 20, 1996 Kenny voted to approve the Pooja project.

In April 1998, respondent pled guilty to the federal misdemeanor of promising employment or other benefit for political activity in violation of 18 U.S.C.A. §600. . . .

Determining the appropriate discipline for criminal misconduct by an attorney requires a consideration of many factors, including "the nature and severity of the crime, whether the crime is related to the practice of law, and any mitigating factors such as respondent's reputation, his [or her] prior trustworthy conduct, and general good conduct." *In re Lunetta*, 118 N.J. 443, 445-46, 572 A.2d 586 (1989). That respondent's crime directly involved the practice of law is undisputed. He improperly attempted to influence a zoning board's decision in favor of his client, Pooja, by promising Robert F. and his son, Robert J., that he would assist the son in obtaining permanent employment with Middlesex County in exchange for the Engels' assistance in obtaining favorable votes from two zoning board members on the Pooja project. Respondent pled guilty to the Hatch Act offense of promising a benefit in exchange for political activity. Specifically, respondent admitted that he offered Robert J. a permanent job with Middlesex County if Robert J. and his father, Robert F., would use their political influence to obtain the favorable votes of two zoning board members for respondent's client's project. The Hatch Act states in part as follows:

> [w]hoever, directly or indirectly, promises any employment, position, compensation, contract, appointment, or other benefit, provided for or made possible in whole or in part by any Act of Congress, or any special consideration in obtaining any such benefit, to any person as consideration, favor, or reward for any political activity or for the support of or opposition to any candidate or any political party in connection with any general or special election to any political office, or in connection with any primary election or political convention or caucus held to select candidates for any political office, shall be fined under this title or imprisoned not more than one year, or both. [18 U.S.C.A. §600.]

Respondent, as an experienced attorney and ex-counsel to the Edison Board of Adjustment, should have known that influencing two members of a zoning board, a quasi-judicial tribunal, through third parties (the Engels) to vote to grant a variance for the benefit of respondent's client was highly improper.

Zoning boards receive their power directly from the Legislature by virtue of statutory grants of authority contained in the Municipal Land Use Law. N.J.S.A. 40:55D-70. New Jersey courts have recognized that Boards of Adjustment are discretionary governmental administrative agencies that exercise quasi-judicial functions. . . .

Before us respondent's counsel contended that lobbying influential political or public officials in local, county or state government to solicit support for meritorious projects is an accepted practice, and that respondent assumed that his conduct in seeking Engel's assistance with the Board of Adjustment fell within the parameters of permissible lobbying efforts. We reject that contention. Putting to one side the promise of a benefit to the Engels for their assistance, respondent attempted to influence members of the Edison Board of Adjustment to cast votes in the Pooja variance matter on the basis of their political relationship with the Engels, rather than on the basis of the evidence adduced at the hearing before the Board of Adjustment and the applicable legal principles that govern a Board of Adjustment's exercise of its authority in variance matters. The attempt by respondent to compromise the standards that govern Board of Adjustment action in variance matters, and to inject political influence into the Board's deliberative process, was manifestly improper.

We conclude that respondent must be subject to significant discipline for his conduct.

III . . .

Respondent's ethical transgressions were serious, and his actions compromised the integrity of the Edison Board of Adjustment's disposition of the variance application of respondent's client. We conclude that respondent's conduct warrants a six-months suspension from the practice of law. Respondent is also ordered to reimburse the Disciplinary Oversight Committee for appropriate administrative costs.

ZAZZALI, J., concurring and dissenting.

The majority fairly sets forth the facts of this case in a comprehensive opinion. I concur with the determination that respondent's conduct violates R.P.C. 8.4(b). I also agree that a penalty must be imposed upon respondent. I respectfully dissent, however, with regard to the quantum of that penalty. A reprimand and a probationary sanction including additional community service would satisfy the need to protect the public interest while serving the administration of justice. . . .

Justice LONG joins in this opinion.

For suspension — Chief Justice PORITZ and Justices STEIN, COLEMAN and VERNIERO — 4.

Concurring in part, dissenting in part — Justices ZAZZALI and LONG — 2.

Notes and Comments

1. *Lobbying or Illegal "Political Activity"?* Where, exactly, did the lawyer go "over the line" in his advocacy? Is what he did any different from the normal "exchange of favors" that is part and parcel of political life? Was the core of the ethical violation that the proceeding was a quasi-judicial one? If so, would the outcome have been different if the client had sought a rezoning?

2. *Contributions and Influence.* Do you think that local councilmembers are actually influenced by campaign contributions? Or is it a case of developers and others contributing to politicians who already hold beliefs and attitudes toward development that are similar to theirs? You should know that, at the local government level, campaign contributions by development interests can constitute a significant percentage of all the contributions given to local candidates. In an exhaustive study of developer campaign contributions, an "alternative" Los Angeles newspaper concluded that its investigation "raises the distinct possibility" that already pro-development members of the board "have been significantly influenced." Ron

Curran and Lewis MacAdams, The Selling of L.A. County, L.A. Weekly, Nov. 22-28, 1985 at 24, 26. Is there any way to really tell what influence the contributions have?

3. *Disclosure vs. Disqualification.* One case to directly raise the issue of the effect of campaign contributions was the California Supreme Court's decision in *Woodland Hills Residents Ass'n v. City Council,* 609 P.2d 1029, 26 Cal. 3d 938 (1980). The plaintiff, a homeowner's association, challenged the city's approval of a subdivision, contending that certain council members should have been disqualified from voting on the subdivision because the developer had made political contributions to campaign committees controlled by the councilmembers. The plaintiffs argued that they were denied a "fair hearing" within the meaning of the applicable statute because the campaign contribution inevitably results in an appearance of bias.

The court rejected the claim, first noting that to disqualify a city council member because the developer made a constitutionally protected campaign contribution "would threaten constitutionally protected political speech and associational freedoms." 609 P.2d at 1033. The court also held that the state had opted for disclosure of campaign contributions, through the passage of the state Political Reform Act, rather than disqualification when a matter involving the donor comes before the local body. The fundamental policy question that you must consider is whether disclosure is an adequate means of ensuring that the subsequent land use decision is fair and in the public interest.

As the court indicates, there are also constitutional implications that arise from issues concerning campaign contributions. In *Buckley v. Valeo,* 424 U.S. 1 (1976), the Supreme Court held that provisions limiting expenditures by candidates on their own behalf, provisions limiting the total expenditures in various campaigns, and provisions limiting expenditures by individuals independently of candidates, violated the First Amendment. It did uphold limits on the size of political campaign contributions. Most recently, in *McConnell v. Federal Election Commission,* — U.S. — (2003), the Court upheld bans on use of "soft money" for federal election activities. *See also California Medical Ass'n v. Federal Elections Comm'n,* 453 U.S. 182 (1981) (upholding contribution limits of $5000 on gifts to political action committees); *Citizens Against Rent Control v. Berkeley,* 454 U.S. 290 (1981) ($250 limit on contributions to committees supporting or opposing ballot measures held invalid). *Compare Austin v. Michigan Chamber of Commerce,* 494 U.S. 652 (1990) (sustaining prohibition on corporate expenditures of general funds for support of or opposition to a candidate for state office). In *Harwin v. Goleta Water District,* 953 F.2d 488 (9th Cir. 1991), the Court of Appeals for the Ninth Circuit held that an ordinance that prevented a member of a water board from considering an application for a new water connection from a person who contributed $250 or more to that member's election campaign violated the First Amendment. The ordinance's defect was that it did not disqualify a member who received a campaign contribution from an individual *opposing* that application.

4. *Prejudgment and Adjudicative Actions.* If the decision by the local government is legislative in nature, no requirement exists that the decisionmakers be impartial. Thus, city council members are free to meet ex parte with one side to a disputed land issue, plot strategy, announce their position publicly, and seek to influence other votes on the council. These types of political activities are considered a routine and even a commendable part of the political process.

In contrast, where the decision of the local government is quasi-judicial in nature, a quite different model of procedure applies. Due process guarantees the parties a right to a fair hearing; thus, ex parte contacts related to the merits of the matter before the local body can be improper. The key here is disclosure. Courts may not invalidate proceedings on the basis of an ex parte contact if the contact is disclosed to the other parties and they are given a chance to respond. *See McPherson Landfill, Inc. v. Bd. of County Commissioners of Shawnee County*, 49 P.3d 522, 533 (Kan. 2002) ("With respect to the ex parte communications [regarding a use permit for a landfill] . . . the parties must be informed of the evidence submitted for consideration and must be provided an opportunity to respond and rebut the evidence.")

Furthermore, conflicts of interest or bias on the part of the decisionmaker may invalidate the decision. Thus, a decisionmaker may be disqualified if he or she has a financial or personal interest that may be directly affected by the decision or has prejudged the issues, as evidenced by statements made before the matter was decided. *See Jock v. Shire Realty, Inc.*, 684 A.2d 921, 924 (Sup. Ct. App. Div. 1996) (board member's testimony as an expert witness in a variance case "seeking to convince his fellow Board members to allow him to develop his property in violation of the zoning ordinance requirements, created at least the potential for conflict" in violation of the Local Government Ethics Law).

5. *Close Calls*. Situations in which allegations of prejudgment or bias can arise are manifold and often require the courts to make close judgment calls. For example, in *Marris v. City of Cedarburg*, 498 N.W.2d 842, 848 (Wis. 1993), the chairperson of a city board of zoning appeals, which was considering a claim of nonconforming use status, declared that the applicant's position was a "legal loophole" in need of "closing" and suggested that the members of the board "get [the applicant] on the Leona Helmsley rule." (The "Leona Helmsley rule" presumably had to do with Ms. Helmsley's well-publicized tax problems. *See United States v. Helmsley*, 760 F. Supp. 338 (S.D.N.Y. 1991), *aff'd*, 963 F.2d 1522 (2d Cir. 1992); Leona Helmsley Is Found Guilty of Evading Taxes, Wall St. J., Aug. 31, 1989.) The court found that "[t]aken together, these statements overcome the presumption of honesty and integrity that would ordinarily be applied" and that the phrase "get her" constituted prejudgment and a desire to prosecute. *Id.* at 849.

Some of these general rules may be changed by local ordinances that apply more stringent prohibitions against conflicts of interest.

In *De Paolo v. Town of Ithaca,* 288 A.D.2d 68 (N.Y. Ct. App. 1999), Cornell University sought and received zoning approvals to implement a new cooling system on the campus. According to the plaintiff, four members of the town board had undisclosed conflicts of interest. One board member and the spouse of another were employees of Cornell. Another board member was a graduate student. The fourth board member was married to a Cornell retiree. The court held that there was no conflict of interest. Among other things, neither of the employees' work involved the cooling project. Are you convinced? Compare *Nazarko v. Conservation Commn. of the Town of East Lyme*, 717 A.2d 850 (Ct. App. Conn. 1998) (town selectman, ex officio member of town conservation commission, was disqualified from granting a permit for a skeet shoot range on a club's property where he was a member of the club and was the owner of the only gun shop in town).

Finally, in *Griswold v. City of Homer*, 34 P.3d 1280 (Alaska 2001), plaintiff alleged that a city council member intended to start an automobile-related business, and that the member's vote in favor of allowing motor vehicle sales and service in an area was a "step" toward the member's goal. The court thought it wasn't enough. Does it make a difference that the council member did not intend to start his business within the area actually affected by the zoning amendment?

6. *Political Retribution*. Can a plaintiff successfully allege, in a civil rights action brought in federal court, that its application for a development approval was denied because of political views? In *Brady v. Town of Colchester*, 863 F.2d 205 (2d Cir. 1988), plaintiff purchased a building, which it leased to the Borough of Colchester, a political entity controlled by Democrats. The Town of Colchester, however, was controlled by Republicans, and the town refused to issue an occupancy permit for a building. The court of appeal held that this action could violate due process and equal protection. Similarly, in *Esmail v. Macrane*, 53 F.3d 176 (7th Cir. 1995), the plaintiff stated a cause of action when he alleged that the mayor had denied his application for a liquor license for purely political reasons. See also Jules B. Gerard, Land Use Decisions Influenced by Partisan Politics Violate the First Amendment, 20 Zoning & Plan. L. Rep. 81 (1997) (suggesting that because of recent Supreme Court holdings in the free speech area, "those whose land use plans have been frustrated by partisan politics now have a mightier weapon than they ever had before to obtain redress").

7. *Justice by the Hour.* Although not often, it is possible for land use decisions to be heard by administrative hearing officers, who make recommendations to full boards. Assuming that the hearing officer has no ties or connections to the parties, one might assume that conflicts of interest would not be a problem. What if, however, the hearing officer is paid by the hour, and perhaps allows the hearing to go on longer than the government agency budgeted for? *See Haas v. County of San Bernardino*, 45 P.3d 280 (Cal. 2002) (concluding that a hearing officer had a pecuniary interest in the matter requiring disqualification where the county selected, retained, and paid a hearing officer according to the duration or amount of work).

8. *Planners and Conflicts*. In *Los Carneros Community Assocs., Inc. v. Penfield & Smith*, 76 Cal. Rptr. 2d 396 (Ct. App. 1998), the plaintiff hired an engineering firm to represent it in its attempt to win approval of development on 50 acres of land. Later, the engineering firm was hired by another company. Both companies sought approval for "big box retail store" complexes on separate parcels in the city. After the second company found out about the other client, it terminated the firm's services. The company then sought to get this client back, and wrote that its employee, the manager of the first project, "has agreed not to participate in any activities that would involve active opposition to your project."

Finally, when the first client found out about this letter, which it concluded was a secret contract in violation of the engineering firm's ethical duty to it, it terminated Penfield and Smith. The first client then sued for interference with prospective business advantage, among other causes of action. The court rejected defendant's argument that the case should be dismissed.

The American Planning Association has also published a set of ethical obligations for planners to consider. See American Planning Ass'n, Statement of Ethical Principles for Planning, (Apr. 26, 1987).

E. THIRD-PARTY OPPOSITION TO DEVELOPMENT: NEIGHBORS' RIGHTS AND DEVELOPERS' RESPONSES

As you have seen in previous cases, much of the litigation in the land use area is brought by neighbors, citizens groups, and other parties who oppose a particular development or otherwise are challenging action (or inaction) taken by a local government. The next case focuses on the rights of such "third parties." Many have charged that the land use system is now so complicated that opposition to development can effectively block almost any large project. As you consider the following materials, you should try to determine how the legal system should structure the rights of third parties to participate in such decisions and to challenge them in court.

■ SUNDERLAND FAMILY TREATMENT SERVICES v. CITY OF PASCO

903 P.2d 986 (Wash. 1995)

JOHNSON, Justice.

This case requires us to decide whether the City of Pasco's denial of a special use permit to Sunderland Family Treatment Services for a group home for troubled teens was proper. . . .

FACTS

On March 29, 1993, Sunderland Family Treatment Services (Sunderland) applied to the City of Pasco (City) for a special use permit to locate a group home crisis residential center (Home) in a Sunderland-owned residence located in an R-1 zoning district.

Under the Pasco Municipal Code (PMC), the Home could have been classified as a "group care facility" (PMC 22.12.385) or a "community service facility" (PMC 22.12.215). Either was an "unclassified use" under PMC 22.80.020 which was permitted in "any district where not otherwise prohibited" but which required a special use permit no matter where it was proposed to be located. PMC 22.80.010.

The proposed Home was an existing 6-bedroom single-family residence, having 2652 square feet and situated on a 5750-square-foot lot. The Home did not require any physical alterations to the exterior and would have been indistinguishable from the single-family residences in the neighborhood.

Sunderland proposed to house up to eight children (ages 12 through 17), who were abused or neglected by their parents or who had no other place to go. The children would be placed by social service agencies pursuant to RCW 74.13.032,[1] establishing crisis residential centers. Sunderland specifically assured the neighbors and the City the Home would not accept children using drugs or alcohol. No loud music, physical or verbal aggression, or smoking would be

1. This section and those following authorize the establishment of crisis residential centers to provide temporary shelter and services to juveniles with the goal of facilitating their reentry to normal family life. *See also* RCW 13.32A, the Family Reconciliation Act.

permitted. At least two full-time staff members would supervise the children and take them to school and offsite counseling. During the nighttime hours, staff would remain awake to receive placements from Child Protective Services and local police who needed to place children in custody for their own protection.

Neighbors of the proposed Home circulated a petition opposing the special use permit. Many testified at the April 22, 1993, meeting of the planning commission and at the May 17 meeting of the city council. The neighbors questioned whether the children would be properly supervised and cited the high number of elderly persons living in the neighborhood. The planning commission voted to recommend denial of the permit and entered findings of fact supporting its decision.

On June 7, 1993, the city council voted to deny Sunderland's proposed special use permit. Their decision rested on five findings of fact. First, the location, size, and intensity of the proposed use would not be harmonious with the orderly and existing development of the otherwise purely residential character of the neighborhood. Second, the proposed use would house troubled children adjacent to single-family homes and apartment units lived in by many elderly and young families with small children. Third, the operations would impair the value of adjacent properties by diminishing their desirability as single family residential units. Fourth, the proposed use would concentrate juveniles at a single residential site with the high probability of bringing more noise, security concerns, and other nuisance activity. Fifth, the proposed use would be better located in a more transitional neighborhood.

Sunderland petitioned the Franklin County Superior Court for a writ of certiorari pursuant to RCW 7.16, which was granted. Sunderland argued the City's decision violated the Washington Housing Policy Act (WHPA) and was premised on factual findings which were not supported by substantial evidence. . . .

Analysis

The grant or denial of a special use permit by local government is adjudicatory in nature. . . .

Issues of fact are reviewed to determine whether they are supported by competent and substantial evidence. RCW 7.16.120(4)-(5); *Freeburg v. City of Seattle*, 71 Wash. App. 367, 371, 859 P.2d 610 (1993). This review is deferential and requires the court to view the evidence and reasonable inferences therefrom in the light most favorable to the party who prevailed in the highest forum that exercised fact-finding authority. *Freeburg*, 71 Wash. App. at 371-72, 859 P.2d 610; *County of Pierce*, 65 Wash. App. at 618, 829 P.2d 217. We apply this standard to the city council's findings of fact. . . .

FACTUAL BASIS FOR THE CITY'S DENIAL

Sunderland argues the findings of fact (Return of Writ, at 176) are not supported by substantial evidence in the record before the city council. This record consists of the permit application, the determination of non-significance under the State Environmental Policy Act of 1971, correspondence from the applicant and interested citizens concerning the proposed operation, planning commission documents and public hearing transcripts, documents and correspondence regarding the appeal to the city council, and city council documents and public hearing transcripts.

We evaluate each finding against this record.

> Finding of fact 1: The location and size of the proposed use are not harmonious with the orderly and existing development of the residential district where the subject property is located. The intensity of the proposed operations is not harmonious with the otherwise purely residential character of the neighborhood.

Sunderland argues the "location and size" are harmonious because the Home would resemble a single-family home in all physical respects. This argument is consistent with the representations of Sunderland to the City that it would not make any exterior changes. There is no evidence to the contrary.

The City's argument is the Home is commercial, not residential in nature. While true, this argument goes to the "intensity" of the use rather than the "location and size." Furthermore, evidence of "intensity" is sparse. Sunderland testified traffic to and from the Home would be minimal and that friends and families would not be allowed to visit. Counseling would be provided offsite and the home would be used solely as a residence. There was no evidence to the contrary presented by opponents to the project. Although the Home is commercial in nature, there is no evidence to support a greater intensity of use. Therefore, the first finding of fact is not supported by the record.

> Finding of fact 2: The proposed use will house troubled youth on a short-term or temporary basis away from their families. All of the adjacent neighboring properties are developed for single-family homes or a residential apartment housing family units. There are many elderly and young families with small children in the immediate area.

Sunderland argues the Home's residents will not be "troubled" in the sense the City implies, *i.e.*, delinquents or drug users. However, there is ample evidence the residents will be abused or neglected children. The court need not try to read the City's mind. There is substantial evidence supporting the finding that the proposed residents are troubled.

Likewise, planning commission documents show the area is composed primarily of single-family homes, with one apartment building immediately adjacent on the west. Local residents testified to the presence of elderly and young families. There is substantial evidence to support the second finding of fact.

> Finding of fact 3: Although the location and height of the existing structure is consistent with the surrounding neighborhood, the operations involved by the proposed use will impair the value of adjacent properties by diminishing their desirability as single-family residential units due to concerns for the safety of elderly homeowners and young families for their children.

Sunderland and the City agree this finding is based upon fears of neighborhood residents rather than more objective evidence, such as real estate expert opinion. In the past, this court has acknowledged that neighbors' fears may reduce property values. *See Park v. Stolzheise*, 24 Wash. 2d 781, 793-94, 167 P.2d 412 (1946) (location of a sanitorium for mental patients). However, there is an important distinction between well founded fears and those based on inaccurate stereotypes and popular prejudices. *See J.W. v. City of Tacoma, Wash.*, 720 F.2d 1126, 1132 n.7 (9th Cir. 1983). Courts have long held the latter cannot justify zoning restrictions. *E.g., Buchanan v. Warley*, 245 U.S. 60, 79-82, 38 S. Ct. 16, 20-21, 62 L. Ed. 149 (1917) (zoning restrictions based on race).

In this case, there is no evidence the Home would have any effect on the safety of the elderly or children in the area. Any reduction in property values would be based on unsubstantiated fears with regard to teenagers from troubled families. This is not competent nor substantial evidence to support the City's finding.

> Finding of fact 4: The proposed use will concentrate at a single residential site juveniles under the age of eighteen who come from troubled families and backgrounds with the high probability of bringing more objectionable noise, concerns for security, and other nuisance activity to the neighborhood than the existing residential family units provide.

Like finding of fact 3, this finding rests on testimony by neighbors as to their fears about the Home. This testimony was countered by testimony from Sunderland, specifically stating the Home's residents would be supervised at all times by at least two trained adults, that drugs and alcohol would not be tolerated, and friends and relatives would not be allowed to visit. Therefore, this finding also rests on *unsubstantiated* fears rather than substantial evidence.

> Finding of fact 5: The proposed use is better located in a neighborhood more transitional in nature from residential to commerce. This neighborhood is a stable, long-standing residential neighborhood.

The first sentence of this finding is a conclusion rather than a finding of fact. There is no evidence in the record with regard to any alternative sites. Therefore, this sentence is not supported by the evidence.

Although Sunderland argues the second sentence is also unsupported because of commercial uses within a few blocks' radius, the city planning commission adequately documented the residential nature of the immediate area around the proposed Home. Therefore, this part of the finding is supported.

Of the City's five findings, therefore, only the second and a portion of the fifth find support in the record. These remaining findings, in their entirety, provide:

> The proposed use will house troubled youth on a short term or temporary basis away from their families. All of the adjacent neighboring properties are developed for single-family homes or a residential apartment housing family units. There are many elderly and young families with small children in the immediate area. This neighborhood is a stable, long-standing residential neighborhood.

[T]he findings were minimal. The proposed use involved teenagers living away from their families while the existing use involved elderly people and young families. Differences in the age of residents does not seem like a reasonable distinction on which to base the permit denial. The children were "troubled". While this word may suggest a public safety factor, it falls far short of constituting an actual threat on which a decision might be validly based.

In fact, the City's denial appears to rest upon neighborhood opposition. At least one planning commissioner and one city council member so stated. While the opposition of the community may be given substantial weight, it cannot alone justify a local land use decision. Therefore, we hold the City's action in denying the permit was not based on competent and substantial evidence as required by RCW 7.16.120.

Notes and Comments

1. *The Evidence in the Administrative Record.* In studying this case, you must carefully evaluate whether the evidence in the record supports the city's findings in denying the special use permit. Consider, for example, the following issues:

a. The court concludes that the proposed use would be a single-family home and that "there is no evidence to support a greater intensity of use" than other such homes. What about possible "night visits" in which unwilling children are placed in the home at off-hours?

b. The court finds no evidence that the home would have any effect on the safety of the elderly or children in the neighborhood. Is there any such evidence? What about the testimony, noted only in the omitted dissent, regarding "problems" with youths that have run away from group homes and burglarized nearby homes? If this evidence is insufficient, is there any evidence that the neighbors could have produced that would have been sufficient?

c. The court says that it has "acknowledged" that neighborhood fears may reduce property values, but there is an "important distinction between well-founded fears and those based on inaccurate stereotypes and popular prejudices." Why weren't the neighbors fears well-founded in this case?

Also, consider the internal consistency of the city's findings. In particular, is its third finding, that the "location and height" of the house is "consistent with the surrounding neighborhood," consistent with the first finding that the city made?

2. *The Neighbors' Motivations.* Do you think the neighbors' professed concerns over the impact of the group home were legitimate, or is this just another example of the NIMBY phenomenon ("Not In My Backyard") at work? Perhaps it's a fair inference that the neighbors' motivations were a mixture of both. The subject of the NIMBY syndrome and the siting of unpopular land uses is taken up in depth in Chapter 16.

Modern land use processes afford neighbors opposing projects a considerable opportunity to make their views known. One question that arises is whether the opposition of neighbors — in and of itself — should be sufficient to uphold the denial of a project. In this regard, consider the views of the court of appeal in *Ross v. City of Yorba Linda*, 2 Cal. Rptr. 2d 638, 643 (Ct. App. 1991):

> The city appears to be saying that neighborhood opposition to construction on nearby private property is itself a "rational basis" for a local government body to forbid construction.
>
> This argument, carried to its logical conclusion, would be fundamentally destructive of the basic rights guaranteed by our state and federal Constitutions.

> If public opinion by itself could justify the denial of constitutional rights, then those rights would be meaningless.

On the other hand, neighbors have intimate knowledge about the characteristics of the area in which they live (not to mention a significant economic investment in their property, if they are owners). Is it possible to separate this knowledge of the area, which can be used to estimate the impacts that a new development will have in that area, from simple political opposition to a new development?

3. *The Substantial Evidence Test.* As you saw earlier in this chapter, in undertaking a review of the evidence in the record, the court determines whether there is "substantial evidence" to support the local government's decision. "Substantial evidence" means " 'such relevant evidence as a reasonable mind might accept as adequate to support a conclusion.' " *Pittsburgh Cellular Telephone Co. v. Board of Supervisors of Marshall Township*, 704 A.2d 192, 193 n.2 (Pa. Commw. Ct. 1997). If the evidence is mixed, with some evidence supporting the government's conclusion and some contrary to it, the court will uphold the decision. Under the substantial evidence test, which is a staple of administrative law, the local factfinder resolves conflicts in the evidence, and the court does not undertake a *de novo* review of that evidence.

The evidence that is reviewed will be found in the administrative record of proceedings. In this case, the record would include items such as the permit application, the determination of "non-significance" under any State Environmental Policy Act (a subject discussed in Chapter 14), planning commission documents, a transcript of the hearing, and all other materials relied upon by the city council in making its decision.

From a practical standpoint, lawyers representing litigants must ensure that the record contains all the evidence that they intend to rely upon. *See Eastern Outdoor Advertising Co. v. Mayor and City Council of Baltimore*, 739 A.2d 854, 873 (Ct. App. Md. 1999) ("[W]e cannot accept appellee's *post hoc* rationalizations to cure deficient agency actions. . . . Here, the Board did not state in its findings that the two signs were spaced more than two feet . . . Moreover, the record is devoid of any explanation as to how the Board's staff arrived at the[] measurements"). Thus, the case must be shaped before the administrative hearing is completed, since the record is closed at that point. In addition, once litigation is initiated, the lawyers must again ensure that the record includes all the evidence considered by the local government.

4. *Sunderland II.* On remand, Sunderland amended its permit application so that the proposed facility would now be used to house youths aged 12–17 with a diagnosed mental impairment. These children would be referred through mental health professionals and would have a diagnosed mental illness requiring a group setting with 24-hour professional staff supervision as part of a prescribed treatment plan. Children who posed a danger to themselves or others would not be eligible for admission to the facility, nor would children actively using drugs or alcohol, or children with pending criminal charges.

After holding a public hearing, the Pasco Planning Commission recommended approval of the SUP with 14 conditions. The city council denied the application. The plaintiff went back to court. This time, the court of appeal held that the city violated the Washington Housing Policy Act by adopting a regulatory scheme that permitted a "family" to obtain immediate occupancy of a residential structure but required "group care facilities" to obtain a special use permit. *Sunderland Family Treatment Services v. City of Pasco*, 26 P.3d 955 (Ct. App. Wash. 2001).

Would anything have satisfied the neighbors? Were their concerns still valid?

A Note on "SLAPP" Suits

"SLAPP" Suits. The last dozen years or so have seen a counter-attack by developers who were the object of litigation brought by plaintiffs seeking to stop projects. Developers have increasingly instituted legal action against these opponents, seeking damages for delays in the project caused by the opponents, for allegedly defamatory statements made by opponents, or for intentional interference with prospective advantage or contractual relations. This litigation, known as a "strategic lawsuit against public participation" or "SLAPP" suit, raises a variety of issues, not the least of which is the potential "chilling effect" on the exercise of First Amendment rights. For citizens contemplating opposing a project, the specter of paying large damage awards to a developer, or at least of having to bear the expense of defending such litigation, is frightening.

Predictably, the SLAPP suit was soon followed by yet a further round of litigation: the so-called SLAPP-back suit brought by citizen activists seeking damages for injury to their reputations and wallets caused by the SLAPP suit. The development of the whole situation was chronicled in a book and series of law review articles. See George W. Pring & Penelope Canan, SLAPPs: Getting Sued for Speaking Out (1996); George W. Pring, SLAPPs: Strategic Lawsuits Against Public Participation, 7 Pace Envtl. L. Rev. 3 (1989); George W. Pring & Penelope Canan, Strategic Lawsuits Against Public Participation ("SLAPPs"): An Introduction for Bench, Bar and Bystanders, 12 Bridgeport L. Rev. 937 (1992); D. Mark Jackson, The Corporate Defamation Plaintiff in the Era of SLAPPs: Revisiting New York Times v. Sullivan, 9 Wm. & Mary Bill of Rights J. 491 (2001); Thomas A. Waldman, SLAPP Suits: Weakness in First Amendment Law and in the Courts' Responses to Frivolous Litigation, 39 U.C.L.A. L. Rev. 979 (1992).

The Anti-SLAPP Statutes. A number of states have responded to the phenomenon with so-called anti-SLAPP statutes. These include California (Cal. Code Civ. Proc. §425.16), Delaware (Del. Stats., tit. 10, §136-38), Florida (Fla. Stat. Ann. §768.295), Georgia (Ga. Stat. §9-11-11.1), Massachusetts (Mass. Gen. L. 231 §591 H), Minnesota (Minn. Stat. §554.01-05), New York (N.Y. Civ. Rights L. §70-a, 76-a), and Rhode Island (R.I. Gen. L. §69-33-2-3).

The New York statute, for example, reads as follows:

> 1. A defendant in an action involving public petition and participation . . . may maintain an action, claim, cross claim or counterclaim to recover damages, including costs and attorney's fees, from any person who commenced or continued such action; provided that:
>
> (a) costs and attorney's fees may be recovered upon a demonstration that the action involving public petition and participation was commenced or continued without a substantial basis in fact and law and could not be supported by a substantial argument for the extension, modification or reversal of existing law.

N.Y. Civ. Rights L. §70-a. See Marnie Stetson, Reforming SLAPP Reform: New York's Anti-SLAPP Statute, 70 N.Y.U. L. Rev. 1324 (1995); Note, The Empire State SLAPPs Back: New York's Legislative Response to SLAPP Suits, 17 Vt. L. Rev. 925 (1993).

The anti-SLAPP legislation also can authorize a successful defendant to recover attorney's fees for the costs incurred in defending the lawsuit. *MacDonald v. Paton*, 728 N.E.2d 1089, 1094 (Mass. Ct. App. 2003) ("Under the anti-SLAPP statute, once a court grants a special motion to dismiss, the moving party is awarded costs and reasonable attorney's fees. . . . A court has no discretion whether to grant costs and reasonable attorney's fees; under the statute the grant of both is mandatory.").

Balancing the Interests at Stake. The critical issues are both substantive and procedural. On a substantive level, the impacts of a SLAPP suit on First Amendment rights are obviously important. At the same time, however, untrue or malicious opposition to a project can cause the project's demise and, with it, significant economic injury. You must consider what is the appropriate balance between the right to comment and oppose a project, on the one hand, and responsibility for those statements, on the other. Which should be weighed more heavily?

In *Equilon Enterprises, L.L.C. v. Consumer Cause, Inc.*, 52 P.3d 685 (Cal. 2002), the California Supreme Court considered the showing that a defendant must make to receive protection from a SLAPP suit. The matter started when a consumer group served a notice of intent to sue for private enforcement of the California Safe Drinking Water and Toxic Enforcement Act, Cal. H. & Safe. Code §25249.7, subd. (d). The notice alleged that defendants had been polluting the groundwater with discharges of various chemicals. The plaintiff responded by filing a lawsuit for declaratory and injunctive relief seeking, among other relief, an injunction preventing plaintiff from filing an action. Defendant then moved to strike the complaint under the state's anti-SLAPP legislation.

Plaintiff claimed that, to prevail, a defendant must demonstrate that the cause of action "was brought with the intent of chilling the defendant's exercise of constitutional speech or petition rights." 52 P.3d at 688. The court, however, rejected that claim. The court held that under the plain meaning of the statute, it applied to all claims "arising from" protected activity, not just those where a plaintiff sought to "chill" the defendant's rights.

In *Dixon v. Superior Court*, 36 Cal. Rptr. 2d 687 (Ct. App. 1994), a consulting firm brought a lawsuit against an archaeologist who had criticized the consultant's work. The California court of appeal held that if a statute expressly invites public participation, all inquiry into the motives behind the statements or comments were barred:

> Here . . . the statutory invitation for public participation [in the review process] bars any inquiry into the motives behind the statements or comments made. To bring himself within the protection of section 425.16, all [defendant] Dixon had to do was show his statements were made in response to a matter of public concern. He did. Therefore, SRS could not, *as a matter of law*, have established a probability of prevailing at trial because even if it proved Dixon acted with malice, his statements are still entitled to absolute immunity.

36 Cal. Rptr. 2d at 696 (emphasis in original). The Rhode Island Supreme Court reached a similar result in *Hometown Properties, Inc. v. Fleming*, 680 A.2d 56 (R.I.

1996) (statements are protected under anti-SLAPP statute unless they amount to a "sham" petition). Is this standard of protection too broad? *Compare Vultaggio v. Yasko*, 572 N.W.2d 450 (Wis. 1998) (neighbor's statements made in a public hearing about a property owner's upkeep of properties were conditionally privileged, rather than absolutely privileged, and in a defamation action the issue of whether the neighbor abused the privilege was a jury question).

Georgia provided slightly more nuanced relief in *Denton v. Browns Mill Development Co.*, 561 S.E.2d 431 (Ga. 2002). An organization dedicated to preserving the state's natural areas prepared a report documenting the alleged failure of several developers to use proper soil erosion and sedimentation controls. Following the release of the report, two of the companies filed suit alleging trespass, defamation, and intentional interference with business operations. *Id.* at 432.

Defendants responded by trying to dismiss the complaint under the anti-SLAPP legislation. The court held that defendants' conduct did fall under the protection of the legislation. But there was one exception: the cause of action for trespass. The court thought that "[e]ven a trespass for the purpose of collecting information . . . is itself not an act in furtherance of the exercise of free speech. . . . " *Id.* at 434.

Devising an Appropriate Procedural Mechanism. On the procedural level, the issue is how to implement meaningful protection of First Amendment rights. Bear in mind that development interests are, on the whole, more likely to be able to afford large-scale, discovery-intensive SLAPP litigation than are citizens or citizens groups who are defendants. The solution of the California statute is to allow the defendants to bring an early "special motion" to dismiss the suit, a motion that requires the plaintiff to substantiate its claims. Cal. Civ. Proc. Code §425.16 (West 1999). SLAPP plaintiffs argue that this procedure is unfair because it allows a plaintiff no discovery rights before the motion is filed. If you think that some discovery is appropriate, how should it be limited to prevent a crushing burden on individual or citizens group defendants — a burden that in many cases would impel them to a quick settlement requiring them to cease all opposition to the project?

The SLAPP suit issue is also discussed in Chapter 16, infra, which addresses the question of sitting facilities opposed by neighbors — the so-called NIMBY phenomenon.

F. FEDERAL JUDICIAL SUPERVISION: LITIGATION UNDER THE CIVIL RIGHTS ACT

Land use decisions are overwhelmingly the province of local governments in the United States. Thus, judicial review of such actions for the most part occurs in the state courts. Aggrieved landowners, however, often feel that the state courts are not sufficiently attuned to the economic ramifications of local government's land use actions, or to the arbitrariness that they perceive in local government decisionmaking. As a result, they may seek to move the locus of the litigation to the federal courts, which they perceive as a more favorable forum. After all, federal courts are used to adjudicating constitutional claims, and they hear many cases under the federal Civil Rights Act.

The federal courts, however, have been very careful in responding to such cases. They fear that if every local government unfairness in the land use field becomes a potential civil rights violation for failure to accord procedural due process, or if every reduction in land value caused by a rezoning is a potential substantive due process violation, the federal courts could be inundated with lawsuits over such matters. Keep these judicial concerns about institutional consequences in mind as you read the following case, which is illustrative of litigation brought in federal court challenging a local government land use action.

UNITED ARTISTS v. TOWNSHIP OF WARRINGTON

316 F.3d 392 (3d Cir. 2003)

Before: ALITO, COWEN, and LOURIE, Circuit Judges.
ALITO, Circuit Judge. . . .

I.

A.

The dispute underlying this case arises out of a development race between United Artists' proposed multiplex and a competing multiplex theater development proposed by Regal Cinema and developer Bruce Goodman. The record shows that the two companies were competing to obtain approval of their plans by the Township because the market could support only one of the theaters. Goodman agreed to pay the Township an annual "impact fee" of $100,000, but United Artists refused the Township's repeated requests for such a payment. United Artists asserts that, because of Goodman's promise to pay this fee, the Township allowed his project to "sail through the land development process," while United Artists' proposal was repeatedly stalled.

The Board of Supervisors' review process consisted of two phases, preliminary approval and final approval. In January 1996, United Artists submitted a preliminary plan for its theater to the Township Planning Commission, an independent body of local officials that makes recommendations regarding land-use plans to the Board of Supervisors. Along with the preliminary plan, United Artists submitted a traffic impact study, which led the Township to require, as a precondition to the issuance of an occupancy permit, the installation of a separate left-turn lane into the theater. United Artists failed to acquire the property necessary to make this improvement and expressed its intention to request a waiver of the condition or to sue for relief. United Artists claims that its failure to construct the road improvement was a mere pretext for the Township's refusal to support its theater proposal and that this refusal was actually motivated by the Township's desire to obtain an impact fee from Goodman and Regency Cinema.

After granting preliminary approval of United Artists' proposal, the Township attempted to change the terms of that approval by requiring United Artists to obtain an easement for the road improvement and to complete the installation of signals before construction could begin, rather than before the time of occupancy, as was originally provided in the preliminary approval. . . .

In the meantime, the Board granted preliminary approval of the Goodman proposal on February 4, 1997—one month after the initial application was submitted—and final approval was granted on May 21, 1997. By contrast, United Artists did not receive preliminary approval until March 18, 1997, 14 months after submitting its initial application. The Board then tabled its vote on United Artists' application for final approval on three occasions, each time asking if United Artists would pay an impact fee. The Board granted final approval of the United Artists proposal on September 16, 1997. The Goodman/Regal Cinema multiplex was completed in 1999; United Artists never built a theater in Warrington.

B.

United Artists' complaint in this case asserted procedural and substantive due process claims under 42 U.S.C. § 1983, as well as supplementary state law claims. As defendants, the complaint named the Township and the members of the Board of Supervisors—Gerald Anderson, Joseph Lavin, Douglas Skinner, Wayne Bullock, and Katherine Watson ("Supervisors")—in both their official and individual capacities. Asserting the defense of qualified immunity, the Supervisors moved for summary judgment, and in December 1999, the District Court denied the Supervisors' motion with respect to the substantive due process, claim, while granting that motion with respect to the procedural due process claim. . . .

[O]ur task is "'to determine first whether the plaintiff has alleged a deprivation of a constitutional right at all,' before reaching the question of whether the right was clearly established at the time." *Johnson v. Newburgh Enlarged School District*, 239 F.3d 246, 251 (2d Cir. 2001) (quoting *Lewis*, 523 U.S. at 841 n. 5, 118 S.Ct. 1708) . . . To answer this question, we must determine the appropriate legal standard to apply to substantive due process claims.

III.

B.

In *County of Sacramento v. Lewis*, 523 U.S. 833, 118 S. Ct. 1708, 140 L. Ed.2d 1043 (1998), the Supreme Court explained the standard that applies when a plaintiff alleges that an action taken by an executive branch official violated substantive due process. The Court observed that "the core of the concept" of due process is "protection against arbitrary action" and that "only the most egregious official conduct can be said to be 'arbitrary in the constitutional sense.'" *Id.* at 845-46, 118 S. Ct. 1708 (citation omitted). After noting its long history of speaking of "the cognizable level of executive abuse of power as that which shocks the conscience," *id.* at 846, 118 S. Ct. 1708 (citing *Rochin v. California*, 342 U.S. 165, 72 S. Ct. 205, 96 L. Ed. 183 (1952)), the Court continued:

> Most recently, in *Collins v. Harker Heights*, [503 U.S. 115, 128, 112 S. Ct. 1061, 117 L.Ed.2d 261 (1992)], we said again that the substantive component of the Due Process Clause is violated by executive action *only when it "can properly be characterized as arbitrary, or conscience shocking, in a constitutional sense."*

Lewis, 523 U.S. at 847, 118 S. Ct. 1708 (emphasis added). . . . At the same time, however, the *Lewis* Court acknowledged that "the measure of what is conscience-shocking is no calibrated yard stick," *Lewis*, 523 U.S. at 847, 118 S. Ct. 1708, and that "[d]eliberate indifference that shocks in one environment may not be so patently egregious in another." *Id.* at 850, 118 S. Ct. 1708. . . .

Despite *Lewis* and the post-*Lewis* Third Circuit cases . . . United Artists maintains that this case is not governed by the "shocks the conscience" standard, but by the less demanding "improper motive" test that originated with *Bello v. Walker*, 840 F.2d 1124 (3d Cir.1988), and was subsequently applied by our court in a line of land-use cases. In these cases, we held that a municipal land use decision violates substantive due process if it was made for any reason "unrelated to the merits," *Herr v. Pequea Township*, 274 F.3d 109, 111 (3d Cir. 2001) (citing cases), or with any "improper motive." *See, e.g., Woodwind Estates, Ltd. v. Gretkowski*, 205 F.3d 118 (3d Cir. 2000). . . .

These cases, however, cannot be reconciled with *Lewis's* explanation of substantive due process analysis. Instead of demanding conscience-shocking conduct, the *Bello* line of cases endorses a much less demanding "improper motive" test for governmental behavior. Although the District Court opined that there are "few differences between the [shocks the conscience] standard and the improper motive standard," we must respectfully disagree. . . . The "shocks the conscience" standard encompasses "only the most egregious official conduct." *Lewis,* 523 U.S. at 846, 118 S. Ct. 1708. In ordinary parlance, the term "improper" sweeps much more broadly, and neither *Bello* nor the cases that it spawned ever suggested that conduct could be "improper" only if it shocked the conscience. We thus agree with the Supervisors that the *Bello* line of cases is in direct conflict with *Lewis*. . . .

. . . Since *Lewis,* our court has applied the "shocks the conscience" standard in a variety of contexts. . . . There is no reason why land use cases should be treated differently. We thus hold that, in light of *Lewis, Bello* and its progeny are no longer good law.

We note that our holding today brings our Court into line with several other Courts of Appeals that have ruled on substantive due process claims in land-use disputes. *See, e.g., Chesterfield Development Corp.* v. *City of Chesterfield*, 963 F.2d 1102, 1104-05 (8th Cir.1992) (holding that allegations that the city arbitrarily applied a zoning ordinance were insufficient to state a substantive due process claim, and stating in dicta that the "decision would be the same even if the City had knowingly enforced the invalid zoning ordinance in bad faith. . . . A bad-faith violation of state law remains only a violation of state law."); *PFZ Properties, Inc. v. Rodriguez,* 928 F.2d 28, 32 (1st Cir.1991) ("Even assuming that ARPE engaged in delaying tactics and refused to issue permits for the Vacia Talega project based on considerations outside the scope of its jurisdiction under Puerto Rico law, such practices, without more, do not rise to the level of violations of the federal constitution under a substantive due process label.").

Application of the "shocks the conscience" standard in this context also prevents us from being cast in the role of a "zoning board of appeals." *Creative Environments, Inc. v. Estabrook,* 680 F.2d 822, 833 (1st Cir. 1982) (quoting *Village of Belle Terre v. Boraas,* 416 U.S. 1, 13, 94 S. Ct. 1536, 39 L.Ed.2d 797 (1974) (Marshall, J., dissenting)) . . . The First Circuit in *Estabrook* observed that every appeal by a disappointed developer from an adverse ruling of the local planning board involves some claim of abuse of legal authority, but "[i]t is not enough simply to give these state law claims constitutional labels such as 'due process' or 'equal protection' in order to raise a substantial federal question under section 1983." *Estabrook,* 680 F.2d at 833. Land-use decisions are matters of local concern, and such disputes should not be transformed into substantive due process claims based only on allegations that government officials acted with "improper" motives. . . .

We vacate the District Court's denial of the Supervisors' summary judgment motion and remand the case for further proceedings to determine whether United Artists can survive the Supervisors' summary judgment motion. . . .

COWEN, Circuit Judge, dissenting. . . .

[T]ossing every substantive Due Process egg into the nebulous and highly subjective "shocks the conscious" basket is unwise. It leaves the door ajar for intentional and flagrant abuses of authority by those who hold the sacred trust of local public office to go unchecked. "Shocks the conscience" is a useful standard in high speed police misconduct cases which tend to stir our emotions and yield immediate reaction. But it is less appropriate, and does not translate well, to the more mundane world of local land use decisions, where lifeless property interests (as opposed to bodily invasions) are involved. In this regard, it appears rather difficult to analogize the intentional and illegal denial of a building permit to the forced pumping of the human stomach, the infamous fact pattern that begat "shocks the conscience" as a term of constitutional significance. *See Rochin v. California*, 842 U.S. 166, 172-73, 72 S. Ct. 205, 96 L.Ed. 183 (1952). It is the jurisprudential equivalent of a square peg in a round hole. . . .

III.

Even if "shocks the conscience" is the language we must employ to the exclusion of any other (which it is not), the alleged behavior in this case resolutely shocks the conscience. Public officials, sworn to uphold the law, deliberately extracted money, knowing that it was improper for them to do so. In contemporary America, under compelling norms of basic human decency, it would be shocking that such officials improperly and illegally obtained money in matters that come before them. There is little if any distinction between the taking of money for the purposes alleged in this case, and money taken to line the officials' individual pockets. For all of the foregoing reasons, I must dissent.

Notes and Comments

1. *Renewed Interest in the Federal Courts*. After the United States Supreme Court decided the *Village of Euclid* and *Nectow* zoning cases, discussed in Chapter 2, for about the next fifty years the Supreme Court almost universally refused to involve itself in issues arising from state land use regulation. As a result, land use law was largely a matter for the state courts. In recent years, however, the Supreme Court has re-entered the field, issuing a large number of decisions involving the Takings Clause (the most important of which you will examine in Chapter 7). With the Court's renewed concern over the constitutional fairness of land use regulation has come increasing pressure for the federal courts to provide remedies under the Civil Rights Act. The *DeBlasio* case is typical of the challenges brought by plaintiffs seeking a federal forum for their complaints.

2. *The Abstention Doctrine*. A common response by municipal defendants is to ask the federal court to abstain if an issue of state law remains to be decided. *See,*

e.g., *Victor Materials Co. v. City of Tehuacana*, 238 F.3d 382, 390 (5th Cir. 2001) (citing four categories of abstention: (1) *Pullman*-type abstention to avoid decision of a federal constitutional question where the case may be disposed of on questions of state law; (2) *Burford*-type abstention, to avoid needless conflict with the administration by a state of its own affairs; (3) abstention to leave to the states the resolution of unsettled questions of state law; and (4) abstention to avoid duplicative litigation). *Compare Chez Sez III Corp. v. Township of Union*, 945 F.2d 628 (3d Cir. 1991) (abstention was appropriate in case challenging constitutionality of township's zoning ordinance as applied to private video booths) *and Front Royal and Warren County Industrial Park Corp. v. Town of Front Royal*, 945 F.2d 760 (4th Cir. 1991) (abstention was proper because annexation scheme was the particular concern of state and local governments) *with Neufeld v. City of Baltimore*, 964 F.2d 347 (4th Cir. 1992) (district court improperly abstained where the case involved local land use issues only peripherally and there were no difficult interpretations of state law involved) *and Dittmer v. County of Suffolk*, 146 F.3d 113 (2d Cir. 1998) (*Burford* abstention improper where plaintiffs principally argue that Long Island Pine Barrens Protection Act is facially unconstitutional, and their claims are not at issue in a concurrent state court proceeding and do not challenge the determinations of an administrative proceeding).

Where the plaintiff has sought monetary damages and the federal court abstains, it will generally retain jurisdiction over the case rather than dismissing it outright. *See Railroad Comm'n of Texas v. Pullman Co.*, 312 U.S. 496 (1941); *Quackenbush v. Allstate Insurance Co.*, 517 U.S. 706, 721 (1996) (federal courts can dismiss based on abstention only where the relief sought by the plaintiff is equitable or otherwise discretionary); *Carroll v. City of Mount Clemens*, 139 F.3d 1072 (6th Cir. 1998) (trial court properly abstained in action alleging that city ordinance which required rooming houses to have separate bathrooms in each unit violated Fair Housing Act, but the case should have been stayed rather than dismissed).

3. *A Cause of Action for Violation of Procedural Due Process*. The cases in which federal relief is sought include those alleging violations of procedural due process. Perhaps the simplest case is where a defendant acts without granting a hearing at all. In this situation, the court will apply settled Supreme Court law on when a hearing is called for before depriving a plaintiff of property. *See, e.g., Weinberg v. Whatcom County*, 241 F.3d 746 (9th Cir. 2001) (question of fact existed as to whether the county had to provide predeprivation hearing before issuing a stop work order, but the county did have to hold a hearing before vacating the defendant's approved plats).

The review will otherwise center on whether the local government provided adequate process. *See, e.g., Foxy Lady, Inc. v. City of Atlanta, Georgia*, 347 F.3d 1232 (11th Cir. 2003) (to establish a procedural due process violation under Section 1983, plaintiff must establish (1) the deprivation of a constitutionally protected liberty or property interest, (2) state action, and (3) constitutionally inadequate process). Most importantly, however, some circuits have held that if a state provides an adequate opportunity for seeking judicial relief in the state courts, no procedural due process violation will lie. *Id.; see also Tri-County Paving, Inc. v. Ashe County*, 281 F.3d 430, 438 (4th Cir. 2002) ("TCP had remedies available to it in the state courts but chose not to utilize them").

The stringency of these tests is just one example of the federal judiciary's continued resistance to becoming heavily involved in land use cases. *See Sylvia*

Development Corp. v. Calvert County, 48 F.3d 810, 828 (4th Cir. 1995) ("Resolving the routine land-use disputes that inevitably and constantly arise among developers, local residents, and municipal officials is simply not the business of the federal courts").

4. *A Cause of Action for Violation of Substantive Due Process.* Another typical cause of action found in *DeBlasio* is the allegation that the local body violated the plaintiff's substantive due process rights. Here, the court framed its test as whether "the decision limiting the intended land use was arbitrary or irrationally reached."

While a showing meeting this standard will not be easy, it can be done. In *DeBlasio,* for example, the court held that the plaintiff's evidence was sufficient to avoid a motion for summary judgment against him. Do you agree with the court's conclusion regarding the evidence? In particular, what about the significance of the difference in time between the date on which Hoff approached Homes (1988) and the date of the hearing before zoning board of appeals (1991)?

Because the United States Supreme Court has given little guidance on the appropriate standard for a substantive due process violation in the land use area, the law is being developed at the federal court of appeals level. Stating a "general rule" on the federal standard for substantive due process is impossible; many of the circuits have adopted slightly different formulations of what is required. *Compare Licari v. Ferruzzi*, 22 F.3d 344, 347 (1st Cir. 1994) (violation must be "egregiously unacceptable, outrageous, or conscience- shocking") with *Dodd v. Hood River County*, 59 F.3d 852, 864 (9th Cir. 1995) (in putting property into a forest use zone, the county did not act arbitrarily or without a rational basis for its decision, and its decision was "at least debatable"). *See also Pearson v. City of Grand Blanc*, 961 F.2d 1211 (6th Cir. 1992) (cataloguing the standards used by the various circuits in determining whether a land use decision has violated substantive due process); *Natale v. Town of Ridgefield*, 170 F.3d 258, 262 (2d Cir. 1999) ("Arbitrary conduct that might violate zoning regulations as a matter of state law is not sufficient to demonstrate conduct that is so outrageously arbitrary as to constitute a gross abuse of governmental authority that will offend the substantive component of the Due Process Clause. . . . ")

5. *A Protectible Property Interest.* Note also that plaintiff must have a protectible property interest before he or she may seek relief. *See, e.g., Hyde Park Co. v. Santa Fe City Council*, 226 F.3d 1207 (10th Cir. 2000) (plaintiff had no protectable property interest in having the city council approve a subdivision plat for its property); *Tri County Landfill Assn . . . Inc. v. Brule County*, 641 N.W.2d 147 (N.D. 2002) (plaintiff "had no clear entitlement to, or protected property interest in the [landfill] permit"); *Jacobs, Visconsi & Jacobs, Co. v. City of Lawrence*, 927 F.2d 1111 (10th Cir. 1991) (plaintiff lacked a protectable property interest when it was denied a rezoning).

6. *The Relationship Between Takings And Due Process.* As we have seen above in this chapter, the ripeness requirement for a takings claim requires both that the plaintiff receive a final determination from the local government (including, in most instances, a decision on a request for a variance) and exhaust any state court compensation remedy. Some plaintiffs have brought suit in federal court alleging that they could fashion a claim for a due process violation that includes a regulatory taking. For example, in *Villas of Lake Jackson, Ltd. v. Leon County*, 121 F.3d 610, 612 (11th Cir. 1997), the court summarized: "In essence, landowners argue that under the due process clause they may challenge the taking that occurs when a specifically recognized property right, vested under state law, is taken

away — even though they might still retain enough use of the property to avoid a taking under the Takings Clause if you considered the parcel as a whole."

The Eleventh Circuit, however, rejected the argument. The court ruled that if the plaintiff could state a "regulatory taking" claim, "[I]t is a cause of action under the Takings Clause, subject to the ripeness prerequisite of exhaustion of state-court inverse condemnation remedy." *Id.* at 612. The only substantive due process claim, said the court, is for arbitrary and capricious conduct. The effect of the decision, of course, is to limit the scope of the cause of action for violation of substantive due process cognizable in federal courts. Given the difficulty of distinguishing between substantive due process violations and takings claims, however, other courts will be heard on this subject. *See, e.g., John Corp. v. City of Houston*, 214 F.3d 573, 583 (5th Cir. 2000) (rejecting a "blanket rule" that the Takings Clause "subsumes any substantive due process claim relating to a deprivation of property.").

7. *Section 1983 Actions.* Section 1983 of the federal Civil Rights Act of 1871 is the vehicle that plaintiffs use to bring actions in federal court alleging damages for land use decisions. The Act, however, also can be used in the state court. *See Town of Orangetown v. Magee*, 665 N.E.2d 1061 (N.Y. 1996) (New York Court of Appeals affirmed damage award of $5,137,126 in Section 1983 action brought when town arbitrarily revoked developer's building permit). That section provides:

> Every person who, under color of any statute, ordinance, regulation, custom or usage, of any State . . . subjects, or causes to be subjected, any citizen of the United States or other person within the jurisdiction thereof to the deprivation of any rights, privileges or immunities secured by the Constitution and laws, shall be liable to the party injured in an action at law, suit in equity, or other proper proceeding for redress.

Litigation under Section 1983 in the land use context raises a wide variety of technical issues. For example, certain immunities are available to defendants. *See Lake Country Estates, Inc. v. Tahoe Regional Planning Agency*, 440 U.S. 391 (1979) (absolute immunity of state legislators also applies to members of bi-state regional planning agency); *Orange Lake Assocs. v. Kirkpatrick*, 21 F.3d 1214 (2d Cir. 1994) (local legislative body immune in land use case). In contrast, only a qualified good faith immunity may be available in other instances. *See GJR Investments, Inc. v. County of Escambia, Florida*, 132 F.3d 1359 (11th Cir. 1998) (qualified immunity protected county officials and employees from suit for delay in process, which eventually culminated in granting the landowner's application for a permit to build a recreational vehicle campground); *Sullivan v. Town of Salem*, 805 F.2d 81 (2d Cir. 1986) (only qualified good faith immunity for refusal to issue certificates of occupancy).

The general American rule on attorney's fees is that each party bears its own costs for such fees. Under the Civil Rights Attorney's Fees Award Act, 42 U.S.C. §1988, however, prevailing plaintiffs can recover their attorney's fees.

away—even though they might still retain enough use of the property to avoid a taking under the Takings Clause if you considered the parcel as a whole.

4. The Eleventh Circuit, however, rejected the argument. The court ruled that the plaintiffs could state a "regulatory taking" claim. That is a cause of action under the Takings Clause, subject to the ripeness prerequisite of exhaustion of state court inverse condemnation remedy. *Id.* at 1172. The only substantive due process claim, said the court, is for arbitrary and capricious conduct. The effect of the decision, of course, is to limit the scope of the cause of action for violation of substantive due process cognizable in federal courts. Given the difficulty of distinguishing between substantive due process violations and taking claims, however, other courts will be heard on the subject. *See, e.g., John Corp. v. City of Houston*, 214 F.3d 573, 583 (5th Cir. 2000) (rejecting a "blanket rule that the Takings Clause subsumes any substantive due process claim relating to a deprivation of property").

5. *Section 1983 Actions*. Section 1983 of the federal Civil Rights Act of 1871 is the vehicle that plaintiffs use to bring actions in federal court alleging damages for land use decisions. The act, however, also can be used in the state courts. *See Town of Orangetown v. Magee*, 665 N.E.2d 1061 (N.Y. 1996) (New York Court of Appeals affirmed damage award of $5,137,126 in Section 1983 action brought when town arbitrarily revoked developer's building permit). That section provides:

> Every person who, under color of any statute, ordinance, regulation, custom, or usage, of any State . . . subjects, or causes to be subjected, any citizen of the United States or other person within the jurisdiction thereof, to the deprivation of any rights, privileges, or immunities secured by the Constitution and laws, shall be liable to the party injured in an action at law, suit in equity, or other proper proceeding for redress.

Litigation under Section 1983 in the land use context raises a wide variety of technical issues. For example, certain immunities are available to defendants. *See Lake Country Estates, Inc. v. Tahoe Regional Planning Agency*, 440 U.S. 391 (1979) (absolute immunity of state legislators also applies to members of bi-state regional planning agency); *Orange Lake Assocs. v. Kirkpatrick*, 21 F.3d 1214 (2d Cir. 1994) (local legislative body immune in land use case). In contrast, only a qualified good faith immunity may be available in other instances. *See C/R Investments, Inc. v. County of Escambia, Florida*, 182 F.3d 1365 (11th Cir. 1998) (qualified immunity protected county officials and employees from suit for delay in process, which eventually culminated in granting the landowner's application for a permit to build a recreational vehicle campground); [illegible] *v. Town of Salem*, 863 F.2d 31 (2d Cir. 1989) (only qualified good faith immunity for refusal to issue certificates of occupancy).

6. The general American rule on attorney's fees is that each party bears its own costs for such fees. Under the Civil Rights Attorney's Fees Award Act, 42 U.S.C. §1988, however, prevailing plaintiffs can recover their attorney's fees.

7

The Takings Clause: The Fifth Amendment

A. INTRODUCTION

1. *Antecedents I:* Mahon *and* Lochner

At the heart of every land use controversy is the question of private property and the rights of the property owner to its value and to its most productive use. Along with political constraints, the takings clause of the Fifth Amendment determines the limits of the public's power to interfere with those private choices through regulation. The Fifth Amendment applies to the states, as it is incorporated into the Fourteenth Amendment. *Chicago B. & Q.R.R. v. Chicago*, 166 U.S. 226 (1897).

In *Pennsylvania Coal Co. v. Mahon*, 260 U.S. 393 (1922) (reprinted below), the first of the critical takings cases that you must consider, Justice Holmes held that a land use regulation that goes "too far" constitutes a taking. In doing so, Justice Holmes adopted a model by which takings analysis in the lower federal courts and the state courts is to proceed. That model is very similar to the Court's work in defining the limits of substantive due process; the concept is to create a line between allowable regulation and that which is arbitrary or excessive. In both cases, the substantive question is subjective, for we lack calibrating standards to decide it. As a result, the body of takings cases lacks much of an objective explanation, lacks predictability, and ostensibly lacks rationality, as government has little guidance on the limits of its power.

Given the time in which it was handed down, *Mahon* may be a part of the now-discredited federal doctrine of substantive due process under which the Court frequently and subjectively rejected the judgment of legislatures on the wisdom and rationality of their regulatory decisions. *See Lochner v. New York*, 198 U.S. 45 (1905). Like *Lochner*'s condemnation of governmental regulation of the maximum working hours of bakers, *Mahon* may simply be the Court's rejection of the Pennsylvania law that required protection from mining that causes subsidence to surface dwellings. The argument would be that, just as the Court's refusal to recognize the adhesive relationship between employer and employee in *Lochner* had the effect of subjecting the employee to an unhealthful work environment, in *Mahon* the Court failed to acknowledge the adhesive relationship between the mine owner and its workers. It refused to sustain reform legislation designed to protect workers from the owner's monopoly over land and housing in the mine areas. Under that monopoly, workers were precluded from negotiating; they were merely offered an adhesive contract providing for the sale of dwellings conditioned upon a simple 30-day notice for purchasers to vacate before the property was undermined.

Of course much has changed since that time. The New Deal is constitutionally best remembered for having generated a revolution in the Court's role in judicial review. The Supreme Court ultimately acknowledged that the legislature enjoys hegemony in the establishment of regulatory standards. Since *Nebbia v. New York*, 291 U.S. 502 (1934), the Court has generally deferred to Congress and state legislatures on regulatory matters, at least in the absence of discrimination against a powerless minority or where rights involved have been defined as fundamental.

A fundamental debate in the property rights field is whether land regulation should fall within *Nebbia*'s deferential review standard or whether land use regulation's effects on privately held real property suggest a more important fundamental rights status, thus calling for more rigorous judicial scrutiny. Some scholars have suggested that the Court may be using its recent takings decisions to undertake another revolution, perhaps returning to a *Lochner* model where courts enjoy a much greater ability to review legislative policy choices in the land use field. See, e.g., Patrick Wiseman, When the End Justifies the Means: Understanding Takings Jurisprudence in a Legal System with Integrity, 63 St. John's L. Rev. 433, 447-451 (1988).

2. *Antecedents II: Original Intent*

Much of the judicial debate over the meaning of the United States Constitution's various clauses and amendments has centered on the intent of the framers in adopting the instrument. Interestingly, however, the recent takings decisions by the Supreme Court are notable for the lack of any effort by the justices to interpret the Constitution based on the intent of the framers. There may be a good reason for this omission. A number of scholars have suggested that, based on the historical record, a "taking" meant an actual expropriation of property. The effects of land use regulation thus would not result in takings. *See* Peter J. Byrne, Ten Arguments for the Abolition of the Regulatory Takings Doctrine, 22 Ecology L.Q. 89 (1995); John F. Hart, Land Use Law in the Early Republic and the Original Meaning of the Takings Clause, 94 Nw. U. L. Rev. 1099 (2000).

This historical argument would posit that an excessive land use regulation is simply an invalid regulation. It is not, as the *Mahon* case and its progeny would have it, a means by which ownership is transferred to the United States through an implied eminent domain proceeding that requires the government to pay for its acquisition. But see Kris W. Kobach, The Origins of Regulatory Takings: Setting the Record Straight, 1996 Utah L. Rev. 1211 (arguing articulately that state courts had found regulatory takings based on value diminution in the nineteenth century and that it is error to assume that Fifth Amendment takings are historically limited to physical occupation); Andrew S. Gold, Comment, Regulatory Takings and Original Intent: The Direct, Physical Takings Thesis "Goes Too Far," 49 Am. U. L. Rev. 181 (1999).

3. Antecedents III: The "Public Use" Requirement

The Fifth Amendment provides that property will not be taken except for a public use and without payment of just compensation. The requirement of a "public use" has not posed a limitation on the imposition of land use controls, particularly those designed to effectuate redevelopment goals. Older cases from a few jurisdictions restricted the ability of local government to utilize redevelopment programs that provided land for private development. *E.g.*, *City of Owensboro v. McCormick*, 581 S.W.2d 3 (Ky. 1979). However, in *Berman v. Parker*, 348 U.S. 26 (1954), the Court sustained a land acquisition for urban renewal even though the renewal plan called for the acquisition of a department store located on a non-blighted property within the project area. Writing for the Court, Justice Douglas stated:

> The concept of the public welfare is broad and inclusive. . . . The values it represents are spiritual as well as physical, aesthetic as well as monetary. It is within the power of the legislature to determine that the community should be beautiful as well as healthy, spacious as well as clean, well-balanced as well as carefully patrolled.

Id. at 33.

Thus, the interpretation of "public use" under the Fifth Amendment mirrors the modern, deferential standard used to measure violations of substantive due process. Under that standard, the Court defers to Congress's choices in promulgating program standards and to local legislative determinations about the appropriate regulatory strategies for community stabilization. Indeed, the test for the "public use" requirement also appears to mirror the "essential nexus" requirement of *Nollan v. California Coastal Commission* (reprinted in Chapter 4).

In short, determinations of whether social and economic legislation has violated substantive due process, whether condemnation falls within the "public use" provision, and whether conditions meet the "essential nexus" test revolve around a common question: will the legislative means chosen serve a legitimate legislative interest?

Some state courts interpret their constitutions to require a public rather than a private use. *Manufactured Hous. Communities v. State*, 13 P.3d 183 (Wash. 2000) (invalidating the statutory grant of a right of first refusal for mobile home park tenants to purchase park on the grounds that the park served only a private use); *contra Township of West Orange v. 769 Associates, LLC*, 800 A.2d 86 (N.J. 2002) (invalidating condemnation to establish right of way to serve private housing developments as a private use despite most highway improvements representing public use). You should also be aware that the public use doctrine has been subject to intense criticism in assessing the experience of urban renewal and redevelopment. *See* J.J. Lazzarotti, Public Use or Public Abuse, 68 UMKC L. Rev. 49 (1999); Stephen J. Jones, Note, Trumping Eminent Domain Law: An Argument for Strict Scrutiny Analysis under the Public Use Requirement of the Fifth Amendment, 50 Syracuse L. Rev. 285 (2000). Redevelopment law and policy is discussed in Chapter 15.

4. Modern Reforms: Per Se Rules

Most modern rulings from the state and federal courts on the application of the takings clause have been ad hoc and fact-intensive. In *Penn Central Transportation Co. v. City of New York*, 438 U.S. 104 (1978), the Court established a takings rule that is based explicitly on a model of ad hoc balancing of various aspects of the regulation's character and effect. The unpredictability of *Penn Central* balancing and the subjectivity of its standard have driven the Court to frequently revisit the takings doctrine in recent years.

The direction for this reform movement was set in *Loretto v. Teleprompter Manhattan CATV Corp.*, 458 U.S. 419 (1982). In that case, the Court found that requiring landowners to allow cable providers the use of property constituted a taking. In doing so, the Court moved away from balancing and, in its place, articulated a per se rule for takings claims based on "physical occupation." The Court's decision in *Lucas v. South Carolina Coastal Council*, 505 U.S. 1003 (1992), continued the pattern set by *Loretto*, establishing a per se rule for those takings that destroy the parcel's entire economic value. In holding that the denial of all permission to develop two beach-front lots constituted a taking, Justice Scalia's distaste for the subjectivity of ad hoc balancing as a model for takings analysis was evident.

The Court's reform movement, however, so far has failed to overrule, or even discredit, the *Penn Central* bulwark. As you will see, despite criticism and suspicion, *Penn Central* remains the general principle and model for the review of most excessive regulation takings challenges. Of course, the Court's decision in *Dolan v. City of Tigard*, 512 U.S. 374 (1994) (reprinted in Chapter 4), although not establishing a per se rule, does remove a large number of takings claims from balancing. It substitutes the relative objectivity of the "rough proportionality" test in cases involving permit conditions. But the large number of other types of takings claims remains untouched.

Furthermore, despite the Court's effort to find objectivity through per se rules, even the results of this effort arguably have not lived up to the promise that such rules will provide definitive guidance, and thus avoid litigation.

5. Remedies

In addition to the dynamic question of identifying when a "taking" has occurred, the issue of remedies in takings cases remains controversial. In *First English Evangelical Lutheran Church v. County of Los Angeles*, 482 U.S. 304 (1987), the Court ruled that compensation is available upon a finding of a taking caused by excessive land use regulation. Under this holding, the governmental entity imposing the regulation can be liable for the period of a "temporary taking" before the measure is rescinded.

Although compensation for illegal regulation seems fair, there is a downside. The effect of *First English*, with its threat of a damage award if local government regulation turns out to effect a taking, may be to discourage communities from imposing regulation necessary to protect sensitive ecological systems or prevent environmental hazards. If the Court is to hold communities strictly liable in damages for takings caused by excessive regulation, one may conclude that the Court should define an objective standard to provide notice of potential liability exposure.

Finally, the question of measuring the amount of "just compensation" is raised but unanswered by *First English*. How does one measure the damages caused by the temporary taking? Is the measure to be the hypothetical rental value lost by the regulation? Or is it the theoretical value of the property in an unregulated state less the value of the property as regulated?

Very few issues in any legal subject have been subjected to the continuously evolving experience of takings jurisprudence. Takings doctrine permits the student to inquire into whether constitutional doctrine will fulfill the promise of greater rationality and fairness in the development process or will merely further complicate local development planning and control, thereby contributing to its inefficiency.

B. REGULATION AS TAKING

The first critical issue is the definition of a taking. Certainly if the government physically appropriated land, that action would constitute a taking. But should appropriation for a public use be the predicate for a taking? Does the reduction of property value due to a land use regulation constitute a taking? The Supreme Court's seminal decision in *Pennsylvania Coal v. Mahon* raises the fundamental question of whether regulation imposed under the police power can trigger the finding of a taking.

PENNSYLVANIA COAL COMPANY v. MAHON
260 U.S. 393 (1922)

MR. JUSTICE HOLMES delivered the opinion of the Court.

This is a bill in equity brought by the defendants in error to prevent the Pennsylvania Coal Company from mining under their property in such way as to remove the supports and cause a subsidence of the surface and of their house. The bill sets out a deed executed by the Coal Company in 1878, under which the plaintiffs claim. The deed conveys the surface, but in express terms reserves the right to remove all the coal under the same, and the grantee takes the premises with the risk, and waives all claim for damages that may arise from mining out the coal. But the plaintiffs say that whatever may have been the Coal Company's rights, they were taken away by an Act of Pennsylvania, approved May 27, 1921, P. L. 1198, commonly known there as the Kohler Act. . . .

The statute forbids the mining of anthracite coal in such way as to cause the subsidence of, among other things, any structure used as a human habitation, with certain exceptions, including among them land where the surface is owned by the owner of the underlying coal and is distant more than one hundred and fifty feet from any improved property belonging to any other person. As applied to this case the statute is admitted to destroy previously existing rights of property and contract. The question is whether the police power can be stretched so far.

Government hardly could go on if to some extent values incident to property could not be diminished without paying for every such change in the general law. As long recognized, some values are enjoyed under an implied limitation and must yield to the police power. But obviously the implied limitation must have its limits, or the contract and due process clauses are gone. One fact for consideration in determining such limits is the extent of the diminution. When it reaches a certain magnitude, in most if not in all cases there must be an exercise of eminent domain and compensation to sustain the act. So the question depends upon the particular facts. The greatest weight is given to the judgment of the legislature, but it always is open to interested parties to contend that the legislature has gone beyond its constitutional power.

This is the case of a single private house. No doubt there is a public interest even in this, as there is in every purchase and sale and in all that happens within the commonwealth. Some existing rights may be modified even in such a case. But usually in ordinary private affairs the public interest does not warrant much of this kind of interference. A source of damage to such a house is not a public nuisance even if similar damage is inflicted on others in different places. The damage is not common or public. The extent of the public interest is shown by the statute to be limited, since the statute ordinarily does not apply to land when the surface is owned by the owner of the coal. Furthermore, it is not justified as a protection of personal safety. That could be provided for by notice. Indeed the very foundation of this bill is that the defendant gave timely notice of its intent to mine under the house. On the other hand the extent of the taking is great. It purports to abolish what is recognized in Pennsylvania as an estate in land—a very valuable estate—and what is declared by the Court below to be a contract hitherto binding the plaintiffs. If we were called upon to deal with the plaintiffs' position alone, we should think it clear that the statute does not disclose a public interest sufficient to warrant so extensive a destruction of the defendant's constitutionally protected rights.

But the case has been treated as one in which the general validity of the act should be discussed. . . .

It is our opinion that the act cannot be sustained as an exercise of the police power, so far as it affects the mining of coal under streets or cities in places where the right to mine such coal has been reserved. As said in a Pennsylvania case, "For practical purposes, the right to coal consists in the right to mine it." What makes the right to mine coal valuable is that it can be exercised with profit. To make it commercially impracticable to mine certain coal has very nearly the same effect for constitutional purposes as appropriating or destroying it. This we think that we are warranted in assuming that the statute does.

It is true that in *Plymouth Coal Co. v. Pennsylvania*, 232 U.S. 531, it was held competent for the legislature to require a pillar of coal to be left along the line of adjoining property, that, with the pillar on the other side of the line, would be a barrier sufficient for the safety of the employees of either mine in case the other should be abandoned and allowed to fill with water. But that was a requirement for the safety of employees invited into the mine, and secured an average reciprocity of advantage that has been recognized as a justification of various laws.

The rights of the public in a street purchased or laid out by eminent domain are those that it has paid for. If in any case its representatives have been so short sighted as to acquire only surface rights without the right of support, we see no more authority for supplying the latter without compensation than there was for taking the right of way in the first place and refusing to pay for it because the public wanted it very much. The protection of private property in the Fifth Amendment presupposes that it is wanted for public use, but provides that it shall not be taken for such use without compensation. A similar assumption is made in the decisions upon the Fourteenth Amendment. When this seemingly absolute protection is found to be qualified by the police power, the natural tendency of human nature is to extend the qualification more and more until at last private property disappears. But that cannot be accomplished in this way under the Constitution of the United States.

The general rule at least is, that while property may be regulated to a certain extent, if regulation goes too far it will be recognized as a taking. It may be doubted how far exceptional cases, like the blowing up of a house to stop a conflagration, go—and if they go beyond the general rule, whether they do not stand as much upon tradition as upon principle. In general it is not plain that a man's misfortunes or necessities will justify his shifting the damages to his neighbor's shoulders. We are in danger of forgetting that a strong public desire to improve the public condition is not enough to warrant achieving the desire by a shorter cut than the constitutional way of paying for the change. As we already have said, this is a question of degree—and therefore cannot be disposed of by general propositions. But we regard this as going beyond any of the cases decided by this Court. . . .

We assume, of course, that the statute was passed upon the conviction that an exigency existed that would warrant it, and we assume that an exigency exists that would warrant the exercise of eminent domain. But the question at bottom is upon whom the loss of the changes desired should fall. So far as private persons or communities have seen fit to take the risk of acquiring only surface rights, we cannot see that the fact that their risk has become a danger warrants the giving to them greater rights than they bought.

Decree reversed.

MR. JUSTICE BRANDEIS, dissenting. . . .

Every restriction upon the use of property imposed in the exercise of the police power deprives the owner of some right theretofore enjoyed, and is, in that sense, an abridgment by the State of rights in property without making compensation. But restriction imposed to protect the public health, safety or morals from dangers threatened is not a taking. The restriction here in question is merely the prohibition of a noxious use. The property so restricted remains in the possession of its owner. The State does not appropriate it or make any use of it. The State merely prevents the owner from making a use which interferes with paramount rights of the public. Whenever the use prohibited ceases to be noxious,—as it may because of further change in local or social conditions,—the restriction will have to be removed and the owner will again be free to enjoy his property as heretofore.

. . . Furthermore, a restriction, though imposed for a public purpose, will not be lawful, unless the restriction is an appropriate means to the public end. But to keep coal in place is surely an appropriate means of preventing subsidence of the surface; and ordinarily it is the only available means. Restriction upon use does not become inappropriate as a means, merely because it deprives the owner of the only use to which the property can then be profitably put. The liquor and the oleomargarine cases settled that. Nor is a restriction imposed through exercise of the police power inappropriate as a means, merely because the same end might be effected through exercise of the power of eminent domain, or otherwise at public expense. Every restriction upon the height of buildings might be secured through acquiring by eminent domain the right of each owner to build above the limiting height; but it is settled that the State need not resort to that power. If by mining anthracite coal the owner would necessarily unloose poisonous gasses, I suppose no one would doubt the power of the State to prevent the mining, without buying his coal fields. And why may not the State, likewise, without paying compensation, prohibit one from digging so deep or excavating so near the surface, as to expose the community to like dangers? In the latter case, as in the former, carrying on the business would be a public nuisance.

It is said that one fact for consideration in determining whether the limits of the police power have been exceeded is the extent of the resulting diminution in value; and that here the restriction destroys existing rights of property and contract. But values are relative. If we are to consider the value of the coal kept in place by the restriction, we should compare it with the value of all other parts of the land. That is, with the value not of the coal alone, but with the value of the whole property. The rights of an owner as against the public are not increased by dividing the interests in his property into surface and subsoil. The sum of the rights in the parts can not be greater than the rights in the whole. The estate of an owner in land is grandiloquently described as extending *ab orco usque ad coelum*. But I suppose no one would contend that by selling his interest above one hundred feet from the surface he could prevent the State from limiting, by the police power, the height of structures in a city. And why should a sale of underground rights bar the State's power? For aught that appears the value of the coal kept in place by the restriction may be negligible as compared with the value of the whole property, or even as compared with that part of it which is represented by the coal remaining in place and which may be extracted despite the statute. . . . Where the surface and the coal belong to the same person, self-interest would ordinarily prevent mining to such an extent as to cause a subsidence. It was, doubtless, for this reason that the legislature, estimating the degrees of danger, deemed statutory restriction unnecessary for the public safety under such conditions. . . .

A prohibition of mining which causes subsidence of such structures and facilities is obviously enacted for a public purpose; and it seems, likewise, clear that mere notice of intention to mine would not in this connection secure the public safety. Yet it is said that these provisions of the act cannot be sustained as an exercise of the police power where the right to mine such coal has been reserved. The conclusion seems to rest upon the assumption that in order to justify such exercise of the police power there must be "an average reciprocity of advantage" as between the owner of the property restricted and the rest of the community; and that here such reciprocity is absent. Reciprocity of advantage is an important consideration, and may even be an essential, where the State's power is exercised for the purpose of conferring benefits upon the property of a neighborhood, as in drainage projects, or upon adjoining owners, as by party wall provisions. But where the police power is exercised, not to confer benefits upon property owners, but to protect the public from detriment and danger, there is, in my opinion, no room for considering reciprocity of advantage. There was no reciprocal advantage to the owner prohibited from using his oil tanks in 248 U.S. 498; his brickyard, in 239 U.S. 394; his livery stable, in 237 U.S. 171; his billiard hall, in 225 U.S. 623; his oleomargarine factory, in 127 U.S. 678; his brewery, in 123 U.S. 623; unless it be the advantage of living and doing business in a civilized community. That reciprocal advantage is given by the act to the coal operators.

Notes and Comments

1. Mahon *and* Keystone. The effect of the "revolution" commenced by *Nebbia v. New York*, 291 U.S. 502 (1934), can be measured by the Court's ruling, handed down 65 years after *Mahon*, in *Keystone Bituminous Coal Ass'n v. DeBenedictis*, 480 U.S. 470 (1987). The Court sustained a Pennsylvania statute designed to prevent mining, regardless of mineral rights ownership, that would cause the subsidence of buildings. The Court attempted to distinguish *Mahon* as a case involving a single dwelling in conflict with mineral rights ownership, citing the broader environmental and aesthetic concerns involved in the modern Pennsylvania statute at issue in *Keystone*. However, the conclusion is almost obvious that the extent of the Court's deference to the legislature is the real distinguishing factor in the two cases. For a criticism of the *Mahon* model, see Robert Brauneis, The Foundation of Our "Regulatory Takings" Jurisprudence: The Myth and Meaning of Justice Holmes's Opinion in Pennsylvania Coal Co. v. Mahon, 106 Yale L.J. 613 (1996). *Contra*, Michael M. Berger, Vindicating the Rights of Private Land Development in the Courts, 32 Urb. Law. 941, 942 (2000) (*Mahon* the high point of takings jurisprudence). *Compare* William M. Treanor, Jam for Justice Holmes: Reassessing the Significance of *Mahon*, 86 Geo. L.J. 813 (1998) (arguing Holmes wrote of a modern balancing model), *with* Richard A. Epstein, *Pennsylvania Coal v. Mahon*: The Erratic Takings Jurisprudence of Justice Holmes, 86 Geo. L.J. 875 (1998) (arguing Holmes wrote a physical occupation or appropriation model).

2. *Takings Terminology*. When the government seeks to acquire property directly, it files an eminent domain action. The goal is a court judgment requiring transfer of the property for the property's fair market value. One of the key parts of *Mahon*, however, was that a government regulation can deprive a landowner of his or her property, thus requiring compensation. In such instances, the landowner brings suit against the government in an action for "inverse condemnation." *See, e.g., Cumberland Farms, Inc. v. Town of Groton*, 808 A.2d 1107, 1125 (Conn. 2002) ("Inverse condemnation is 'a cause of action against a government defendant to recover the value of property which has been taken in fact by the government defendant, even though no formal exercise of the power of eminent domain has been attempted by the taking agency.'" (citing *United States v. Clarke*, 445 U.S. 253, 257 (1980)).

3. *Nuisance Abatement I*. Even before its decision in *Village of Euclid v. Ambler Realty* (reprinted in Chapter 2), the Supreme Court upheld zoning ordinances that drastically reduced the value of property. In *Hadacheck v. Sebastian*, 239 U.S. 394 (1915), the Court sustained a downzoning of property long used to extract clay for brick manufacturing. The ordinance was enacted in response to environmental and aesthetic concerns over whether the use of the property as a brick manufacturing facility would adversely affect the residential subdivisions soon to be located nearby as the City of Los Angeles urbanized. The law was sustained despite a

"wipeout" of 85 percent of the property value as a result of downzoning, ostensibly because the Court accepted the elimination of the prior use as nuisance abatement.

Cases preceding *Hadacheck* often equated the legitimacy of regulation with the prevention or elimination of an injurious use. For example, in *Mugler v. Kansas*, 123 U.S. 623 (1887), the Court sustained a law prohibiting the sale of liquor, equating a taking with the expropriation of private property. See Catherine R. Connors, Back to the Future: The "Nuisance Exception" to the Just Compensation Clause, 19 Cap. U.L. Rev. 139 (1990). The rationale was not limited to land use regulation. In *Holden v. Hardy*, 169 U.S. 366 (1898), the Court upheld a limit on the maximum hours miners could work. The Court rejected a due process challenge, finding the law to be within the police power, as the statute was implicitly directed at abatement of nuisance-like conditions. Excessive hours working in a mine could result in injury or disease, or constitute a safety and economic hazard to miners and the mine owner. *See also Goldblatt v. Town of Hempstead*, 369 U.S. 590 (1962) (restrictive regulation of a quarry adjacent to a residential district sustained due to the danger posed); and *Miller v. Schoene*, 276 U.S. 272 (1928) (no taking where the state ordered the destruction of diseased cedar trees, which threatened adjacent apple orchards, ostensibly because the cedar rust posed a nuisance-like, injurious externality).

4. *Nuisance Abatement II.* The nuisance abatement issue has arisen in a series of cases in which governments have sought to close businesses or buildings to abate drug sales or other crimes occurring there. Landowners have responded with inverse condemnation claims. In *Keshbro v. City of Miami*, 801 So. 2d 864 (Fla. 2001), the court held that the temporary closure of a motel was not a taking, but the temporary closure of an apartment house was. *See also City of Seattle v. McCoy*, 4 P.3d 159 (Wash. Ct. App. 2000) (drug nuisance statute effected a taking of premises).

5. *The Economic Justifications for the Takings Clause.* In *District Intown Properties Limited Partnership v. District of Columbia*, 198 F.3d 874 (D.C. Cir. 1999), Justice Williams' concurring opinion explored the economists' view of the takings clause. He noted that the clause "provides a check on government's likely tendency to waste resources by treating private property as a free good." *Id.* at 884. This principle, he went on, "is just an application of the general principle that if a firm can externalize costs (e.g., the health costs of polluting the air), it will use more of the unpriced resource" than if it was required to pay. He thought that the framers of the Constitution, although not articulating the purpose of the Takings Clause in economic terms, viewed it as aiming to correct the incentives of the political branches. *Id.* at 885. In current times, concluded Justice Williams, some proposals for restricting land use are driven by "interest-group purposers," commonly known as rent-seeking. Some of these inflict costs outweighing their aggregate benefits, and the Takings Clause "serves to curb such inefficiencies."

Do you agree with his comments? Would his logic support a stronger application of the Takings Clause to maximize its role as a disincentive to wasteful government activities?

A Note on Taking by Physical Occupation

While *Pennsylvania Coal Co. v. Mahon* established that a regulation could effect a taking, *Mahon* suggests that the regulatory effect of the ordinance must be substantial before a court may conclude that a taking has occurred. Would the Court uphold regulation that permits a minimal physical occupation of the landowner's property? The issue was decided in *Loretto v. Teleprompter Manhattan CATV Corp.*, 458 U.S. 419 (1982).

By New York ordinance, landlords were required to accept cable wiring and roof boxes in exchange for a symbolic rent. In *Loretto*, a plaintiff landlord alleged that this regulatory scheme effected a taking. The Court ruled that the wiring constituted a permanent, albeit minor, physical invasion. Citing the examples of flooding, aircraft overflights, and easements required to provide public access, the Court held that such permanent physical occupations constituted a virtual per se taking.

In an earlier case, *PruneYard Shopping Center v. Robins*, 447 U.S. 74 (1980), the Court upheld a state constitutional requirement that shopping center owners permit individuals to exercise free speech and petition rights on their property, to which they had been invited as members of the general public. In *Loretto*, the Court distinguished *PruneYard* on the basis that the invasion of property there was temporary and limited in nature, and the owner had not exhibited an interest in excluding all persons from his property.

Loretto has a number of implications for land use regulation. For example, consider what would happen if the original developer in *Loretto* was required, as a condition of permit approval, to wire the entire building to make each apartment cable-ready. Would such a condition on the right to build be valid under the takings clause? The analysis requires substituting *Dolan* (Chapter 4) for *Loretto*.

As noted in the introduction to this chapter, the student of regulatory takings law must be concerned with the fashioning of a suitable remedy for a taking. What is the appropriate remedy in *Loretto*? Is not Loretto's property worth *more* with cable wiring than without? Who would want to live in Loretto's building without ESPN, the Food Channel, or the Home Shopping Network?

Another physical occupation case was *Kaiser Aetna v. United States*, 444 U.S. 164 (1979). Kaiser Aetna had acquired Kuapa Pond as private property, intending to subdivide and develop it. Kaiser Aetna dredged the pond and created a navigable gateway that eventually opened to the Pacific Ocean. The Army Corps of Engineers determined that no permits were needed for the dredging. Later, however, the United States brought suit asserting that Kaiser Aetna must allow public access to Kuapa Pond pursuant to a federal statute requiring public access to navigable waterways. The Court ruled that, although the government might have constitutionally conditioned a permit on providing public access, the government's present demand for public access interfered with Kaiser Aetna's right to exclude others from the property. This interference constituted a "physical invasion" taking. *See also Bassett, New Mexico LLC v. United States*, 55 Fed. Cl. 63 (Ct. Cl. 2002) (EPA liable for physical taking where, by mistake, it deposited hazardous waste on the claimant's property, and the damage included not only the three acres on which the waste was deposited, but also plaintiff's entire "stigmatized" property); Thomas W. Merrill, Property and the Right to Exclude, 77 Neb. L. Rev. 730 (1998).

The Supreme Court has generally rejected efforts to expand the "physical occupation" or "physical invasion" form of a taking to include certain other types of regulation as "constructive occupation" takings. For example, in *F.C.C. v. Florida Power Corp.*, 480 U.S. 245 (1987), the Court held that a regulation setting a charge for utility pole communications hookups was not an occupation of land because the utility participated voluntarily.

Does a "nuisance exception" (i.e., a government right to enter property to abate a nuisance) exist for physical occupation cases? *See Hendler v. United States*, 36 Fed. Cl. 574 (1996) (recognizing nuisance exception in sustaining entry on private property by EPA to monitor groundwater), *subsequent proceedings*, 175 F.3d 1374 (Fed. Cir. 1999) (not a taking as benefit outweighed burden); *Rohaly v. State Dept. Envtl. Protection*, 732 A.2d 524 (N.J. Super. App. Div. 1999) (rejecting a nuisance exception). In *Boise Cascade Corp. v. United States*, 296 F.3d 1339 (Fed. Cir. 2002), the court took a slightly different approach, reading *Handler* narrowly and holding that federal Fish and Wildlife personnel did not effect a physical taking when they conducted surveys on private property for five months.

C. BALANCING

The decision in *Pennsylvania Coal v. Mahon* suggests that a permissible level of zoning regulatory authority exists that is not a taking. However, *Mahon* does not define how courts or regulators should calculate when the line is crossed into an impermissible taking. Should the Court identify an objective standard for that calculation, such as where regulation reduces the value of property by a set percentage? Or would an ad hoc, subjective evaluation of the public interests and private impacts involved present a more practical analysis?

■ PENN CENTRAL TRANSPORTATION CO. v. NEW YORK CITY

438 U.S. 104 (1978)

MR. JUSTICE BRENNAN delivered the opinion of the Court.

The question presented is whether a city may, as part of a comprehensive program to preserve historic landmarks and historic districts, place restrictions on the development of individual historic landmarks—in addition to those imposed by applicable zoning ordinances—without effecting a "taking" requiring the payment of "just compensation." Specifically, we must decide whether the application of New York City's Landmarks Preservation Law to the parcel of land occupied by Grand Central Terminal has "taken" its owners' property in violation of the Fifth and Fourteenth Amendments.

I

A . . .

New York City, . . . acting pursuant to a New York State enabling Act, adopted its Landmarks Preservation Law in 1965. See N.Y.C. Admin. Code, ch. 8-A, §205-1.0 *et seq.* (1976). The city acted from the conviction that "the standing of [New York City] as a world-wide tourist center and world capital of business, culture and government" would be threatened if legislation were not enacted to protect historic landmarks and neighborhoods from precipitate decisions to destroy or fundamentally alter their character. §205-1.0(a). The city believed that comprehensive measures to safeguard desirable features of the existing urban fabric would benefit its citizens in a variety of ways: *e.g.*, fostering "civic pride in the beauty and noble accomplishments of the past"; protecting and enhancing "the city's attractions to tourists and visitors"; "support[ing] and stimul[ating] business and industry"; "strengthen[ing] the economy of the city"; and promoting "the use of historic districts, landmarks, interior landmarks and scenic landmarks for the education, pleasure and welfare of the people of the city." §205-1.0(b). . . .

. . . The primary responsibility for administering the law is vested in the Landmarks Preservation Commission (Commission), a broad based, 11- member agency assisted by a technical staff. The Commission first performs the function, critical to any landmark preservation effort, of identifying properties and areas that have "a special character or special historical or aesthetic interest or value as part of the development, heritage or cultural characteristics of the city, state or nation." §207-1.0(n); *see* §207-1.0(h). If the Commission determines, after giving all interested parties an opportunity to be heard, that a building or area satisfies the ordinance's criteria, it will designate a building to be a "landmark," §207-1.0(n), situated on a particular "landmark site," §207-1.0(o), or will designate an area to be a "historic district," §207-1.0(h). After the Commission makes a designation, New York City's Board of Estimate, after considering the relationship of the designated property "to the master plan, the zoning resolution, projected public improvements and any plans for the renewal of the area involved," §207-2.0(g)(1), may modify or disapprove the designation, and the owner may seek judicial review of the final designation decision. Thus far, 31 historic districts and over 400 individual landmarks have been finally designated, and the process is a continuing one.

Final designation as a landmark results in restrictions upon the property owner's options concerning use of the landmark site. First, the law imposes a duty upon the owner to keep the exterior features of the building "in good repair" to assure that the law's objectives not be defeated by the landmark's falling into a state of irremediable disrepair. *See* §207-10.0(a). Second, the Commission must approve in advance any proposal to alter the exterior architectural features of the landmark or to construct any exterior improvement on the landmark site, thus ensuring that decisions concerning construction on the landmark site are made with due consideration of both the public interest in the maintenance of the structure and the landowner's interest in use of the property. *See* §207-4.0 to §207-9.0.

In the event an owner wishes to alter a landmark site, three separate procedures are available through which administrative approval may be obtained. First, the owner may apply to the Commission for a "certificate of no effect on protected architectural features": that is, for an order approving the improvement or alteration on the ground that it will not change or affect any architectural feature of the landmark and will be in harmony therewith. *See* §207-5.0. Denial of the certificate is subject to judicial review.

Second, the owner may apply to the Commission for a certificate of "appropriateness." *See* §207-6.0. Such certificates will be granted if the Commission concludes — focusing upon aesthetic, historical, and architectural values — that the proposed construction on the landmark site would not unduly hinder the protection, enhancement, perpetuation, and use of the landmark. Again, denial of the certificate is subject to judicial review. Moreover, the owner who is denied either a certificate of no exterior effect or a certificate of appropriateness may submit an alternative or modified plan for approval. The final procedure — seeking a certificate of appropriateness on the ground of "insufficient return," *see* §207-8.0—provides special mechanisms, which vary depending on whether or not the landmark enjoys a tax exemption, to ensure that designation does not cause economic hardship.

Although the designation of a landmark and landmark site restricts the owner's control over the parcel, designation also enhances the economic position of the landmark owner in one significant respect. Under New York City's zoning laws, owners of real property who have not developed their property to the full extent permitted by the applicable zoning laws are allowed to transfer development rights to contiguous parcels on the same city block. . . .

B

This case involves the application of New York City's Landmarks Preservation Law to Grand Central Terminal (Terminal). The Terminal, which is owned by the Penn Central Transportation Co. and its affiliates (Penn Central), is one of New York City's most famous buildings. Opened in 1913, it is regarded not only as providing an ingenious engineering solution to the problems presented by urban railroad stations, but also as a magnificent example of the French beaux- arts style.

The Terminal is located in midtown Manhattan. Its south facade faces 42d Street and that street's intersection with Park Avenue. At street level, the Terminal is bounded on the west by Vanderbilt Avenue, on the east by the Commodore Hotel, and on the north by the Pan-American Building. Although a 20-story office tower, to have been located above the Terminal, was part of the original design, the planned tower was never constructed.[15] The Terminal itself is an eight-story structure which Penn Central uses as a railroad station and in which it rents space not needed for railroad purposes to a variety of commercial interests. The Terminal is one of a number of properties owned by appellant Penn Central in this area of midtown Manhattan. The others include the Barclay, Biltmore, Commodore, Roosevelt, and Waldorf-Astoria Hotels, the Pan-American Building and other office buildings along Park Avenue, and the Yale Club. At least eight of these are eligible to be recipients of development rights afforded the Terminal by virtue of landmark designation.

On August 2, 1967, following a public hearing, the Commission designated the Terminal a "landmark" and designated the "city tax block" it occupies a "landmark site." The Board of Estimate confirmed this action on September 21, 1967. . . .

On January 22, 1968, appellant Penn Central, to increase its income, entered into a renewable 50-year lease and sublease agreement with appellant UGP Properties, Inc. (UGP). . . .

Appellants UGP and Penn Central then applied to the Commission for permission to construct an office building atop the Terminal. Two separate plans, both designed by architect Marcel Breuer and both apparently satisfying the terms of the applicable zoning ordinance, were submitted to the Commission for approval. The first, Breuer I, provided for the construction of a 55-story office building, to be cantilevered above the existing facade and to rest on the roof of the Terminal. The second, Breuer II Revised, called for tearing down a portion of the Terminal

15. The Terminal's present foundation includes columns, which were built into it for the express purpose of supporting the proposed 20-story tower.

that included the 42d Street facade, stripping off some of the remaining features of the Terminal's facade, and constructing a 53-story office building. The Commission denied a certificate of no exterior effect on September 20, 1968. Appellants then applied for a certificate of "appropriateness" as to both proposals. After four days of hearings at which over 80 witnesses testified, the Commission denied this application as to both proposals. . . .

A

Before considering appellants' specific contentions, it will be useful to review the factors that have shaped the jurisprudence of the Fifth Amendment injunction "nor shall private property be taken for public use, without just compensation." The question of what constitutes a "taking" for purposes of the Fifth Amendment has proved to be a problem of considerable difficulty. While this Court has recognized that the "Fifth Amendment's guarantee . . . [is] designed to bar Government from forcing some people alone to bear public burdens which, in all fairness and justice, should be borne by the public as a whole," this Court, quite simply, has been unable to develop any "set formula" for determining when "justice and fairness" require that economic injuries caused by public action be compensated by the government, rather than remain disproportionately concentrated on a few persons. See *Goldblatt v. Hempstead*, 369 U.S. 590, 594 (1962). Indeed, we have frequently observed that whether a particular restriction will be rendered invalid by the government's failure to pay for any losses proximately caused by it depends largely "upon the particular circumstances [in that] case."

In engaging in these essentially ad hoc, factual inquiries, the Court's decisions have identified several factors that have particular significance. The economic impact of the regulation on the claimant and, particularly, the extent to which the regulation has interfered with distinct investment-backed expectations are, of course, relevant considerations. So, too, is the character of the governmental action. A "taking" may more readily be found when the interference with property can be characterized as a physical invasion by government, *see, e.g., United States v. Causby*, 328 U.S. 256 (1946), than when interference arises from some public program adjusting the benefits and burdens of economic life to promote the common good.

"Government hardly could go on if to some extent values incident to property could not be diminished without paying for every such change in the general law," *Pennsylvania Coal Co. v. Mahon*, 260 U.S. 393, 413 (1922), and this Court has accordingly recognized, in a wide variety of contexts, that government may execute laws or programs that adversely affect recognized economic values. Exercises of the taxing power are one obvious example. A second are the decisions in which this Court has dismissed "taking" challenges on the ground that, while the challenged government action caused economic harm, it did not interfere with interests that were sufficiently bound up with the reasonable expectations of the claimant to constitute "property" for Fifth Amendment purposes. . . .

More importantly for the present case, in instances in which a state tribunal reasonably concluded that "the health, safety, morals, or general welfare" would be promoted by prohibiting particular contemplated uses of land, this Court has upheld land-use regulations that destroyed or adversely affected recognized real property interests. *See Nectow v. Cambridge*, 277 U.S. 183, 188 (1928). Zoning laws are, of course, the classic example, see *Euclid v. Ambler Realty Co.*, 272 U.S.

365 (1926) (prohibition of industrial use); *Gorieb v. Fox*, 274 U.S. 603, 608 (1927) (requirement that portions of parcels be left unbuilt); *Welch v. Swasey*, 214 U.S. 91 (1909) (height restriction), which have been viewed as permissible governmental action even when prohibiting the most beneficial use of the property.

Zoning laws generally do not affect existing uses of real property, but "taking" challenges have also been held to be without merit in a wide variety of situations when the challenged governmental actions prohibited a beneficial use to which individual parcels had previously been devoted and thus caused substantial individualized harm, *Miller v. Schoene*, 276 U.S. 272 (1928). . . . A unanimous Court held that this latter omission did not render the statute invalid. The [Miller] Court held that the State might properly make "a choice between the preservation of one class of property and that of the other" and since the apple industry was important in the State involved, concluded that the State had not exceeded "its constitutional powers by deciding upon the destruction of one class of property [without compensation] in order to save another which, in the judgment of the legislature, is of greater value to the public." *Id.*, at 279.

Goldblatt v. Hempstead, supra, is a recent example. There, a 1958 city safety ordinance banned any excavations below the water table and effectively prohibited the claimant from continuing a sand and gravel mining business that had been operated on the particular parcel since 1927. The Court upheld the ordinance against a "taking" challenge, although the ordinance prohibited the present and presumably most beneficial use of the property and had, like the regulations in *Miller* and *Hadacheck*, severely affected a particular owner. The Court assumed that the ordinance did not prevent the owner's reasonable use of the property since the owner made no showing of an adverse effect on the value of the land. Because the restriction served a substantial public purpose, the Court thus held no taking had occurred. It is, of course, implicit in *Goldblatt* that a use restriction on real property may constitute a "taking" if not reasonably necessary to the effectuation of a substantial public purpose, or perhaps if it has an unduly harsh impact upon the owner's use of the property.

Pennsylvania Coal Co. v. Mahon, 260 U.S. 393 (1922), is the leading case for the proposition that a state statute that substantially furthers important public policies may so frustrate distinct investment-backed expectations as to amount to a "taking." . . .

Finally, government actions that may be characterized as acquisitions of resources to permit or facilitate uniquely public functions have often been held to constitute "takings." *United States v. Causby*, 328 U.S. 256 (1946), is illustrative. In holding that direct overflights above the claimant's land, that destroyed the present use of the land as a chicken farm, constituted a "taking." . . .

B

[A]ppellants make a series of arguments, which, while tailored to the facts of this case, essentially urge that any substantial restriction imposed pursuant to a landmark law must be accompanied by just compensation if it is to be constitutional. Before considering these, we emphasize what is not in dispute. Because this Court has recognized, in a number of settings, that States and cities may enact land-use restrictions or controls to enhance the quality of life by preserving the character and desirable aesthetic features of a city, appellants do not contest that New York City's objective of preserving structures and areas with special historic, architectural, or cultural significance is an entirely permissible governmental goal. They also do not dispute that the restrictions imposed on its parcel are appropriate means of securing the purposes of the New York City law. Finally, appellants do not challenge any of the specific factual premises of the decision below. They accept for present purposes both that the parcel of land occupied by Grand Central Terminal must, in its present state, be regarded as capable of earning a reasonable return, and that the transferable development rights afforded appellants by virtue of the Terminal's designation as a landmark are valuable, even if not as valuable as the rights to construct above the Terminal. In appellants' view none of these factors derogate from their claim that New York City's law has effected a "taking."

They first observe that the airspace above the Terminal is a valuable property interest, citing *United States v. Causby, supra*. They urge that the Landmarks Law has deprived them of any gainful use of their "air rights" above the Terminal and that, irrespective of the value of the remainder of their parcel, the city has "taken" their right to this superjacent airspace, thus entitling them to "just compensation" measured by the fair market value of these air rights. . . .

[T]he submission that appellants may establish a "taking" simply by showing that they have been denied the ability to exploit a property interest that they heretofore had believed was available for development is quite simply untenable. Were this the rule, this Court would have erred not only in upholding laws restricting the development of air rights, but also in approving those prohibiting both the subjacent . . . and the lateral . . . development of particular parcels. "Taking" jurisprudence does not divide a single parcel into discrete segments and attempt to determine whether rights in a particular segment have been entirely abrogated. In deciding whether a particular governmental action has effected a taking, this Court focuses rather both on the character of the action and on the nature and extent of the interference with rights in the parcel as a whole — here, the city tax block designated as the "landmark site."

Secondly, appellants, focusing on the character and impact of the New York City law, argue that it effects a "taking" because its operation has significantly diminished the value of the Terminal site. Appellants concede that the decisions sustaining other land-use regulations, which, like the New York City law, are reasonably related to the promotion of the general welfare, uniformly reject the proposition that diminution in property value, standing alone, can establish a "taking," *see Euclid v. Ambler Realty Co.*, 272 U.S. 365 (1926) (75% diminution in value caused by zoning law); *Hadacheck v. Sebastian*, 239 U.S. 394 (1915) (87 1/2% diminution in value); cf. *Eastlake v. Forest City Enterprises, Inc.*, 426 U.S., at 674 n. 8, and that the "taking" issue in these contexts is resolved by focusing on the uses the regulations permit. Appellants, moreover, also do not dispute that a showing of diminution in property value would not establish a "taking" if the restriction had been imposed as a result of historic-district legislation, but appellants argue that New York City's regulation of individual landmarks is fundamentally different from zoning or from historic-district legislation because the controls imposed by New York City's law apply only to individuals who own selected properties.

Stated baldly, appellants' position appears to be that the only means of ensuring that selected owners are not singled out to endure financial hardship for no reason is to hold that any restriction imposed on individual landmarks pursuant to the New York City scheme is a "taking" requiring the payment of "just compensation." Agreement with this argument would, of course, invalidate not just

New York City's law, but all comparable landmark legislation in the Nation. We find no merit in it. . . .

Next, appellants observe that New York City's law differs from zoning laws and historic-district ordinances in that the Landmarks Law does not impose identical or similar restrictions on all structures located in particular physical communities. It follows, they argue, that New York City's law is inherently incapable of producing the fair and equitable distribution of benefits and burdens of governmental action which is characteristic of zoning laws and historic-district legislation and which they maintain is a constitutional requirement if "just compensation" is not to be afforded. It is, of course, true that the Landmarks Law has a more severe impact on some landowners than on others, but that in itself does not mean that the law effects a "taking." Legislation designed to promote the general welfare commonly burdens some more than others. The owners of the . . . gravel and sand mine in *Goldblatt v. Hempstead* were uniquely burdened by the legislation sustained in those cases.[30] Similarly, zoning laws often affect some property owners more severely than others but have not been held to be invalid on that account. For example, the property owner in *Euclid* who wished to use its property for industrial purposes was affected far more severely by the ordinance than its neighbors who wished to use their land for residences.

In any event, appellants' repeated suggestions that they are solely burdened and unbenefited is factually inaccurate. This contention overlooks the fact that the New York City law applies to vast numbers of structures in the city in addition to the Terminal—all the structures contained in the 31 historic districts and over 400 individual landmarks, many of which are close to the Terminal.[31] Unless we are to reject the judgment of the New York City Council that the preservation of landmarks benefits all New York citizens and all structures, both economically and by improving the quality of life in the city as a whole—which we are unwilling to do—we cannot conclude that the owners of the Terminal have in no sense been benefited by the Landmarks Law. . . .

Appellants' final broad-based attack would have us treat the law as an instance, like that in *United States v. Causby*, in which government, acting in an enterprise capacity, has appropriated part of their property for some strictly governmental purpose. Apart from the fact that *Causby* was a case of invasion of airspace that destroyed the use of the farm beneath and this New York City law has in nowise impaired the present use of the Terminal, the Landmarks Law neither

30. Appellants attempt to distinguish these cases on the ground that, in each, government was prohibiting a "noxious" use of land and that in the present case, in contrast, appellants' proposed construction above the Terminal would be beneficial. We observe that the uses in issue in *Hadacheck, Miller*, and *Goldblatt* were perfectly lawful in themselves. They involved no "blameworthiness, . . . moral wrongdoing or conscious act of dangerous risk-taking which induce[d society] to shift the cost to a pa[rt]icular individual." These cases are better understood as resting not on any supposed "noxious" quality of the prohibited uses but rather on the ground that the restrictions were reasonably related to the implementation of a policy—not unlike historic preservation—expected to produce a widespread public benefit and applicable to all similarly situated property.

Nor, correlatively, can it be asserted that the destruction or fundamental alteration of a historic landmark is not harmful. The suggestion that the beneficial quality of appellants' proposed construction is established by the fact that the construction would have been consistent with applicable zoning laws ignores the development in sensibilities and ideals reflected in landmark legislation like New York City's.

31. There are some 53 designated landmarks and 5 historic districts or scenic landmarks in Manhattan between 14th and 59th Streets. *See* Landmarks Preservation Commission, Landmarks and Historic Districts (1977).

exploits appellants' parcel for city purposes nor facilitates nor arises from any entrepreneurial operations of the city. The situation is not remotely like that in *Causby* . . .

C

Rejection of appellants' broad arguments is not, however, the end of our inquiry, for all we thus far have established is that the New York City law is not rendered invalid by its failure to provide "just compensation" whenever a landmark owner is restricted in the exploitation of property interests, such as air rights, to a greater extent than provided for under applicable zoning laws. We now must consider whether the interference with appellants' property is of such a magnitude that "there must be an exercise of eminent domain and compensation to sustain [it]." *Pennsylvania Coal Co. v. Mahon*, 260 U.S., at 413. That inquiry may be narrowed to the question of the severity of the impact of the law on appellants' parcel, and its resolution in turn requires a careful assessment of the impact of the regulation on the Terminal site.

[T]he New York City law does not interfere in any way with the present uses of the Terminal. Its designation as a landmark not only permits but contemplates that appellants may continue to use the property precisely as it has been used for the past 65 years: as a railroad terminal containing office space and concessions. So the law does not interfere with what must be regarded as Penn Central's primary expectation concerning the use of the parcel. More importantly, on this record, we must regard the New York City law as permitting Penn Central not only to profit from the Terminal but also to obtain a "reasonable return" on its investment.

Appellants, moreover, exaggerate the effect of the law on their ability to make use of the air rights above the Terminal in two respects. First, it simply cannot be maintained, on this record, that appellants have been prohibited from occupying *any* portion of the airspace above the Terminal. While the Commission's actions in denying applications to construct an office building in excess of 50 stories above the Terminal may indicate that it will refuse to issue a certificate of appropriateness for any comparably sized structure, nothing the Commission has said or done suggests an intention to prohibit *any* construction above the Terminal. The Commission's report emphasized that whether any construction would be allowed depended upon whether the proposed addition "would harmonize in scale, material, and character with [the Terminal]." Since appellants have not sought approval for the construction of a smaller structure, we do not know that appellants will be denied any use of any portion of the airspace above the Terminal.[34] . . .

On this record, we conclude that the application of New York City's Landmarks Law has not effected a "taking" of appellants' property. The restrictions imposed are substantially related to the promotion of the general welfare and not only permit reasonable beneficial use of the landmark site but also afford appellants opportunities further to enhance not only the Terminal site proper but also other properties.

Affirmed.

34. Counsel for appellants admitted at oral argument that the Commission has not suggested that it would not, for example, approve a 20-story office tower along the lines of that which was part of the original plan for the Terminal. See Tr. of Oral Arg. 19.

MR. JUSTICE REHNQUIST, with whom THE CHIEF JUSTICE and MR. JUSTICE STEVENS join, dissenting. . . .

. . . Typical zoning restrictions may . . . so limit the prospective uses of a piece of property as to diminish the value of that property in the abstract because it may not be used for the forbidden purposes. But any such abstract decrease in value will more than likely be at least partially offset by an increase in value which flows from similar restrictions as to use on neighboring properties. All property owners in a designated area are placed under the same restrictions, not only for the benefit of the municipality as a whole but also for the common benefit of one another. In the words of Mr. Justice Holmes, speaking for the Court in *Pennsylvania Coal Co. v. Mahon*, 260 U.S. 393, 415 (1922), there is "an average reciprocity of advantage."

Where a relatively few individual buildings, all separated from one another, are singled out and treated differently from surrounding buildings, no such reciprocity exists. The cost to the property owner which results from the imposition of restrictions applicable only to his property and not that of his neighbors may be substantial—in this case, several million dollars—with no comparable reciprocal benefits. And the cost associated with landmark legislation is likely to be of a completely different order of magnitude than that which results from the imposition of normal zoning restrictions. Unlike the regime affected by the latter, the landowner is not simply prohibited from using his property for certain purposes, while allowed to use it for all other purposes. Under the historic-landmark preservation scheme adopted by New York, the property owner is under an affirmative duty to *preserve* his property *as a landmark* at his own expense. To suggest that because traditional zoning results in some limitation of use of the property zoned, the New York City landmark preservation scheme should likewise be upheld, represents the ultimate in treating as alike things which are different. . . .

Penn Central is prevented from further developing its property basically because *too good* a job was done in designing and building it. . . .

Appellees contend that, even if they have "taken" appellants' property, TDR's constitute "just compensation." Appellants, of course, argue that TDR's are highly imperfect compensation. Because the lower courts held that there was no "taking," they did not have to reach the question of whether or not just compensation has already been awarded. . . .

. . . Because the record on appeal is relatively slim, I would remand to the Court of Appeals for a determination of whether TDR's constitute a "full and perfect equivalent for the property taken."

Notes and Comments

1. *Aesthetics and Historic Preservation*. Beyond establishing a guide for calculating the magical *Mahon* line separating reasonable regulation from unconstitutional taking, the Court in *Penn Central* broadly validates regulation for aesthetic reasons and for historic preservation purposes. See Michael A. Wolf, Euclid at Three Score Years and Ten: Is This the Twilight of Environmental and Land Use Regulation?, 30 U. Rich. L. Rev. 961, 965-968 (1996).

2. *Reciprocity of Advantage*. Does the holding in *Penn Central* equitably allocate the costs for planning and historic preservation? In his dissent, Justice (now Chief

Justice) Rehnquist argues that the state can regulate to abate a nuisance or where there is an "average reciprocity of advantage." Is that an appropriate standard for balancing public need and private harm? Can it be argued that Justice Rehnquist's standard was satisfied in *Penn Central*?

3. *The Multi-Factor Balancing Model.* Has Justice Brennan captured the essence of all the relevant considerations in classifying takings? Or does the ad hoc, multi-factor balancing model he endorses simply demonstrate and perpetuate the chaos of takings jurisprudence? Can such a model result in anything but a subjective result in the hands of the balancer? Is *Penn Central* weighted in favor of the regulator?

D. ECONOMIC USE

Dissatisfied with the subjectivity and lack of predictability of the *Penn Central* balancing test, and perhaps perceiving that courts applying the test have favored regulators, the Burger and Rehnquist Courts began a search for a more objective interpretation of the Takings Clause. Pro-property rights advocates cheered the ruling in *Lucas v. South Carolina Coastal Council.*

LUCAS v. SOUTH CAROLINA COASTAL COUNCIL
505 U.S. 1003 (1992)

Justice SCALIA delivered the opinion of the Court.

In 1986, petitioner David H. Lucas paid $975,000 for two residential lots on the Isle of Palms in Charleston County, South Carolina, on which he intended to build single-family homes. In 1988, however, the South Carolina Legislature enacted the Beachfront Management Act, S.C. Code §48-39-250 *et seq.* (Supp. 1990) (Act), which had the direct effect of barring petitioner from erecting any permanent habitable structures on his two parcels. *See* §48-39-290(A). A state trial court found that this prohibition rendered Lucas's parcels "valueless." This case requires us to decide whether the Act's dramatic effect on the economic value of Lucas's lots accomplished a taking of private property under the Fifth and Fourteenth Amendments requiring the payment of "just compensation." U.S. Const., Amdt. 5.

I

A

South Carolina's expressed interest in intensively managing development activities in the so-called "coastal zone" dates from 1977 when, in the aftermath of Congress's passage of the federal Coastal Zone Management Act of 1972, 86 Stat. 1280, as amended, 16 U.S.C. §1451 *et seq.*, the legislature enacted a Coastal Zone Management Act of its own. *See* S.C. Code §48-39-10 *et seq.* (1987). In its original form, the South Carolina Act required owners of coastal zone land that qualified as a "critical area" (defined in the legislation to include beaches and immediately adjacent sand dunes, §48-39-10(J)) to obtain a permit from the newly created

South Carolina Coastal Council (respondent here) prior to committing the land to a "use other than the use the critical area was devoted to on [September 28, 1977]." §48-39-130(A).

In the late 1970s, Lucas and others began extensive residential development of the Isle of Palms, a barrier island situated eastward of the City of Charleston. Toward the close of the development cycle for one residential subdivision known as "Beachwood East," Lucas in 1986 purchased the two lots at issue in this litigation for his own account. No portion of the lots, which were located approximately 300 feet from the beach, qualified as a "critical area" under the 1977 Act; accordingly, at the time Lucas acquired these parcels, he was not legally obliged to obtain a permit from the Council in advance of any development activity. His intention with respect to the lots was to do what the owners of the immediately adjacent parcels had already done: erect single-family residences. He commissioned architectural drawings for this purpose.

The Beachfront Management Act brought Lucas's plans to an abrupt end. Under that 1988 legislation, the Council was directed to establish a "baseline" connecting the landward-most "point[s] of erosion . . . during the past forty years" in the region of the Isle of Palms that includes Lucas's lots. §48-39-280(A)(2) (Supp. 1988).[1] In action not challenged here, the Council fixed this baseline landward of Lucas's parcels. That was significant, for under the Act construction of occupiable improvements[2] was flatly prohibited seaward of a line drawn 20 feet landward of, and parallel to, the baseline, §48-39- 290(A) (Supp. 1988). The Act provided no exceptions.

B

Lucas promptly filed suit in the South Carolina Court of Common Pleas, contending that the Beachfront Management Act's construction bar effected a taking of his property without just compensation. . . . Following a bench trial, the court agreed. . . .

The Supreme Court of South Carolina reversed. It found dispositive what it described as Lucas's concession "that the Beachfront Management Act [was] properly and validly designed to preserve . . . South Carolina's beaches." 304 S.C. 376, 379, 404 S.E.2d 895, 896 (1991). Failing an attack on the validity of the statute as such, the court believed itself bound to accept the "uncontested . . . findings" of the South Carolina legislature that new construction in the coastal zone—such as petitioner intended—threatened this public resource. *Id.*, at 383, 404 S.E.2d, at 898. The Court ruled that when a regulation respecting the use of property is designed "to prevent serious public harm," *id.*, at 383, 404 S.E.2d, at 899 (citing, *inter alia, Mugler v. Kansas*, 123 U.S. 623 (1887)), no compensation is owing under the Takings Clause regardless of the regulation's effect on the property's value. . . .

1. This specialized historical method of determining the baseline applied because the Beachwood East subdivision is located adjacent to a so-called "inlet erosion zone" (defined in the Act to mean "a segment of shoreline along or adjacent to tidal inlets which is influenced directly by the inlet and its associated shoals," S.C. Code §48-39-270(7) (Supp. 1988)) that is "not stabilized by jetties, terminal groins, or other structures," §48-39-280(A)(2). For areas other than these unstabilized inlet erosion zones, the statute directs that the baseline be established "along the crest of the primary oceanfront sand dune." §48-39-280(A)(1).

2. The Act did allow the construction of certain nonhabitable improvements, *e.g.*, "wooden walkways no larger in width than six feet," and "small wooden decks no larger than one hundred forty-four square feet." §§48- 39-290(A)(1) and (2) (Supp. 1988).

III

A

Prior to Justice Holmes' exposition in *Pennsylvania Coal Co. v. Mahon*, it was generally thought that the Takings Clause reached only a "direct appropriation" of property, or the functional equivalent of a "practical ouster of [the owner's] possession." Justice Holmes recognized in *Mahon*, however, that if the protection against physical appropriations of private property was to be meaningfully enforced, the government's power to redefine the range of interests included in the ownership of property was necessarily constrained by constitutional limits. . . .

. . . We have . . . described at least two discrete categories of regulatory action as compensable without case-specific inquiry into the public interest advanced in support of the restraint. The first encompasses regulations that compel the property owner to suffer a physical "invasion" of his property. In general (at least with regard to permanent invasions), no matter how minute the intrusion, and no matter how weighty the public purpose behind it, we have required compensation. . . .

The second situation in which we have found categorical treatment appropriate is where regulation denies all economically beneficial or productive use of land. As we have said on numerous occasions, the Fifth Amendment is violated when land-use regulation "does not substantially advance legitimate state interests or denies an owner economically viable use of his land."[7] . . .

We think, in short, that there are good reasons for our frequently expressed belief that when the owner of real property has been called upon to sacrifice *all* economically beneficial uses in the name of the common good, that is, to leave his property economically idle, he has suffered a taking.[8]

7. Regrettably, the rhetorical force of our "deprivation of all economically feasible use" rule is greater than its precision, since the rule does not make clear the "property interest" against which the loss of value is to be measured. When, for example, a regulation requires a developer to leave 90% of a rural tract in its natural state, it is unclear whether we would analyze the situation as one in which the owner has been deprived of all economically beneficial use of the burdened portion of the tract, or as one in which the owner has suffered a mere diminution in value of the tract as a whole. (For an extreme—and, we think, unsupportable—view of the relevant calculus, *see Penn Central Transportation Co. v. New York City*, 366 N.E.2d 1271, 1276- 1277 (1977), *aff'd*, 438 U.S. 104 (1978), where the state court examined the diminution in a particular parcel's value produced by a municipal ordinance in light of total value of the takings claimant's other holdings in the vicinity.) Unsurprisingly, this uncertainty regarding the composition of the denominator in our "deprivation" fraction has produced inconsistent pronouncements by the Court. *Compare Pennsylvania Coal Co. v. Mahon* (law restricting subsurface extraction of coal held to effect a taking), *with Keystone Bituminous Coal Assn. v. DeBenedictis*, 480 U.S. 470, 497-502 (1987) (nearly identical law held not to effect a taking). The answer to this difficult question may lie in how the owner's reasonable expectations have been shaped by the State's law of property—i.e., whether and to what degree the State's law has accorded legal recognition and protection to the particular interest in land with respect to which the takings claimant alleges a diminution in (or elimination of) value. In any event, we avoid this difficulty in the present case, since the "interest in land" that Lucas has pleaded (a fee simple interest) is an estate with a rich tradition of protection at common law, and since the South Carolina Court of Common Pleas found that the Beachfront Management Act left each of Lucas's beachfront lots without economic value.

8. Justice STEVENS criticizes the "deprivation of all economically beneficial use" rule as "wholly arbitrary," in that "[the] landowner whose property is diminished in value 95% recovers nothing," while the landowner who suffers a complete elimination of value "recovers the land's full value." *Post*, at 2919. This analysis errs in its assumption that the landowner whose deprivation is one step short of complete is not entitled to compensation. Such an owner might not be able to claim the benefit of our categorical formulation, but, as we have acknowledged time and again, "[t]he economic

B

The trial court found Lucas's two beachfront lots to have been rendered valueless by respondent's enforcement of the coastal-zone construction ban. Under Lucas's theory of the case, which rested upon our "no economically viable use" statements, that finding entitled him to compensation. Lucas believed it unnecessary to take issue with either the purposes behind the Beachfront Management Act, or the means chosen by the South Carolina Legislature to effectuate those purposes. The South Carolina Supreme Court, however, thought otherwise. In its view, the Beachfront Management Act was no ordinary enactment, but involved an exercise of South Carolina's "police powers" to mitigate the harm to the public interest that petitioner's use of his land might occasion. 304 S.C., at 384, 404 S.E.2d, at 899. By neglecting to dispute the findings enumerated in the Act or otherwise to challenge the legislature's purposes, petitioner "concede[d] that the beach/dune area of South Carolina's shores is an extremely valuable public resource; that the erection of new construction, *inter alia*, contributes to the erosion and destruction of this public resource; and that discouraging new construction in close proximity to the beach/dune area is necessary to prevent a great public harm." In the court's view, these concessions brought petitioner's challenge within a long line of this Court's cases sustaining against Due Process and Takings Clause challenges the State's use of its "police powers" to enjoin a property owner from activities akin to public nuisances. *See Mugler v. Kansas*, 123 U.S. 623 (1887) (law prohibiting manufacture of alcoholic beverages); *Hadacheck v. Sebastian*, 239 U.S. 394 (1915) (law barring operation of brick mill in residential area); *Miller v. Schoene*, 276 U.S. 272 (1928) (order to destroy diseased cedar trees to prevent infection of nearby orchards); *Goldblatt v. Hempstead*, 369 U.S. 590 (1962) (law effectively preventing continued operation of quarry in residential area).

It is correct that many of our prior opinions have suggested that "harmful or noxious uses" of property may be proscribed by government regulation without the requirement of compensation. For a number of reasons, however, we think the South Carolina Supreme Court was too quick to conclude that that principle decides the present case. The "harmful or noxious uses" principle was the Court's early attempt to describe in theoretical terms why government may, consistent with the Takings Clause, affect property values by regulation without incurring

---

impact of the regulation on the claimant and . . . the extent to which the regulation has interfered with distinct investment-backed expectations" are keenly relevant to takings analysis generally. *Penn Central Transportation Co. v. New York City*, 438 U.S. 104, 124, 98 S. Ct. 2646, 2659, 57 L.Ed.2d 631 (1978). It is true that in at least *some* cases the landowner with 95% loss will get nothing, while the landowner with total loss will recover in full. But that occasional result is no more strange than the gross disparty between the landowner whose premises are taken for a highway (who recovers in full) and the landowner whose property is reduced to 5% of its former value by the highway (who recovers nothing). Takings law is full of these "all-or-nothing" situations.

Justice STEVENS similarly misinterprets our focus on "developmental" uses of property (the uses proscribed by the Beachfront Management Act) as betraying an "assumption that the only uses of property cognizable under the Constitution are *developmental* uses." *Post*, at 2919, n. 3. We make no such assumption. Though our prior takings cases evince an abiding concern for the productive use of, and economic investment in, land, there are plainly a number of noneconomic interests in land whose impairment will invite exceedingly close scrutiny under the Takings Clause. *See e.g., Loretto v. Teleprompter Manhattan CATV Corp.*, 458 U.S. 419, 436, 102 S. Ct. 3164, 3176, 73 L.Ed.2d 868 (1982) (interest in excluding strangers from one's land).

an obligation to compensate—a reality we nowadays acknowledge explicitly with respect to the full scope of the State's police power. . . . We made this very point in *Penn Central Transportation Co.*, where, in the course of sustaining New York City's landmarks preservation program against a takings challenge, we rejected the petitioner's suggestion that *Mugler* and the cases following it were premised on, and thus limited by, some objective conception of "noxiousness":

> [T]he uses in issue in *Hadacheck, Miller*, and *Goldblatt* were perfectly lawful in themselves. They involved no "blameworthiness, . . . moral wrongdoing or conscious act of dangerous risk-taking which induce[d society] to shift the cost to a pa[rt]icular individual." Sax, Takings and the Police Power, 74 Yale L.J. 36, 50 (1964). These cases are better understood as resting not on any supposed "noxious" quality of the prohibited uses but rather on the ground that the restrictions were reasonably related to the implementation of a policy—not unlike historic preservation—expected to produce a widespread public benefit and applicable to all similarly situated property.

"Harmful or noxious use" analysis was, in other words, simply the progenitor of our more contemporary statements that "land-use regulation does not effect a taking if it 'substantially advance[s] legitimate state interests' . . . "

The transition from our early focus on control of "noxious" uses to our contemporary understanding of the broad realm within which government may regulate without compensation was an easy one, since the distinction between "harm-preventing" and "benefit-conferring" regulation is often in the eye of the beholder. It is quite possible, for example, to describe in *either* fashion the ecological, economic, and aesthetic concerns that inspired the South Carolina legislature in the present case. One could say that imposing a servitude on Lucas's land is necessary in order to prevent his use of it from "harming" South Carolina's ecological resources; or, instead, in order to achieve the "benefits" of an ecological preserve.[11] *Compare, e.g., Claridge v. New Hampshire Wetlands Board*, 125 N.H. 745, 752, 485 A.2d 287, 292 (1984) (owner may, without compensation, be barred from filling wetlands because landfilling would deprive adjacent coastal habitats and marine fisheries of ecological support), *with, e.g., Bartlett v. Zoning Comm'n of Old Lyme*, 161 Conn. 24, 30, 282 A.2d 907, 910 (1971) (owner barred from filling tidal marshland must be compensated, despite municipality's "laudable" goal of

11. In the present case, in fact, some of the "[South Carolina] legislature's 'findings' " to which the South Carolina Supreme Court purported to defer in characterizing the purpose of the Act as "harm-preventing," 304 S.C. 376, 385, 404 S.E.2d 895, 900 (1991), seem to us phrased in "benefit-conferring" language instead. For example, they describe the importance of a construction ban in enhancing "South Carolina's annual tourism industry revenue," S.C. Code §48-39- 250(1)(b) (Supp. 1991), in "provid[ing] habitat for numerous species of plants and animals, several of which are threatened or endangered," §48-39-250(1)(c), and in "provid[ing] a natural healthy environment for the citizens of South Carolina to spend leisure time which serves their physical and mental well-being." §48-39-250(1)(d). It would be pointless to make the outcome of this case hang upon this terminology, since the same interests could readily be described in "harm-preventing" fashion.

Justice Blackmun, however, apparently insists that we *must* make the outcome hinge (exclusively) upon the South Carolina Legislature's other, "harm-preventing" characterizations, focusing on the declaration that "prohibitions on building in front of the setback line are necessary to protect people and property from storms, high tides, and beach erosion." *Post*, at 2906. He says "[n]othing in the record undermines [this] assessment," *ibid.*, apparently seeing no significance in the fact that the statute permits owners of *existing* structures to remain (and even to rebuild if their structures are not "destroyed beyond repair," S.C. Code Ann. §48-39-290(B)), and in the fact that the 1990 amendment authorizes the Council to issue permits for new construction in violation of the uniform prohibition, *see* S.C. Code §48-39-290(D)(1) (Supp. 1991).

"preserv[ing] marshlands from encroachment or destruction"). Whether one or the other of the competing characterizations will come to one's lips in a particular case depends primarily upon one's evaluation of the worth of competing uses of real estate. . . . A given restraint will be seen as mitigating "harm" to the adjacent parcels or securing a "benefit" for them, depending upon the observer's evaluation of the relative importance of the use that the restraint favors. *See* Sax, Takings and the Police Power, 74 Yale L.J. 36, 49 (1964) ("[T]he problem [in this area] is not one of noxiousness or harm-creating activity at all; rather it is a problem of inconsistency between perfectly innocent and independently desirable uses"). Whether Lucas's construction of single-family residences on his parcels should be described as bringing "harm" to South Carolina's adjacent ecological resources thus depends principally upon whether the describer believes that the State's use interest in nurturing those resources is so important that *any* competing adjacent use must yield.[12]

When it is understood that "prevention of harmful use" was merely our early formulation of the police power justification necessary to sustain (without compensation) *any* regulatory diminution in value; and that the distinction between regulation that "prevents harmful use" and that which "confers benefits" is difficult, if not impossible, to discern on an objective, value-free basis; it becomes self-evident that noxious-use logic cannot serve as a touchstone to distinguish regulatory "takings"—which require compensation—from regulatory deprivations that do not require compensation. *A fortiori* the legislature's recitation of a noxious-use justification cannot be the basis for departing from our categorical rule that total regulatory takings must be compensated. If it were, departure would virtually always be allowed. . . .

Where the State seeks to sustain regulation that deprives land of all economically beneficial use, we think it may resist compensation only if the logically antecedent inquiry into the nature of the owner's estate shows that the proscribed use interests were not part of his title to begin with. This accords, we think, with our "takings" jurisprudence, which has traditionally been guided by the understandings of our citizens regarding the content of, and the State's power over, the "bundle of rights" that they acquire when they obtain title to property. It seems to us that the property owner necessarily expects the uses of his property to be restricted, from time to time, by various measures newly enacted by the State in legitimate exercise of its police powers; "[a]s long recognized, some values are enjoyed under an implied limitation and must yield to the police power." *Pennsylvania Coal Co. v. Mahon*. And in the case of personal property, by reason of the State's traditionally high degree of control over commercial dealings, he ought to be aware of the possibility that new regulation might even render his property economically worthless (at least if the property's only economically productive use is sale or manufacture for sale), *see Andrus v. Allard*, 444 U.S. 51, 66-67 (1979) (prohibition on sale of eagle feathers). In the case of land, however, we think the notion pressed by the Council that title is somehow held subject to the "implied

12. In Justice BLACKMUN's view, even with respect to regulations that deprive an owner of all developmental or economically beneficial land uses, the test for required compensation is whether the legislature has recited a harm-preventing justification for its action. *See post*, at 2906, 2910-2912. Since such a justification can be formulated in practically every case, this amounts to a test of whether the legislature has a stupid staff. We think the Takings Clause requires courts to do more than insist upon artful harm-preventing characterizations.

limitation" that the State may subsequently eliminate all economically valuable use is inconsistent with the historical compact recorded in the Takings Clause that has become part of our constitutional culture.[15]

Where "permanent physical occupation" of land is concerned, we have refused to allow the government to decree it anew (without compensation), no matter how weighty the asserted "public interests" involved, *Loretto v. Teleprompter Manhattan CATV Corp.* . . . We believe similar treatment must be accorded confiscatory regulations, *i.e.*, regulations that prohibit all economically beneficial use of land: Any limitation so severe cannot be newly legislated or decreed (without compensation), but must inhere in the title itself, in the restrictions that background principles of the State's law of property and nuisance already place upon land ownership. A law or decree with such an effect must, in other words, do no more than duplicate the result that could have been achieved in the courts—by adjacent landowners (or other uniquely affected persons) under the State's law of private nuisance, or by the State under its complementary power to abate nuisances that affect the public generally, or otherwise.

On this analysis, the owner of a lake bed, for example, would not be entitled to compensation when he is denied the requisite permit to engage in a landfilling operation that would have the effect of flooding others' land. Nor the corporate owner of a nuclear generating plant, when it is directed to remove all improvements from its land upon discovery that the plant sits astride an earthquake fault. Such regulatory action may well have the effect of eliminating the land's only economically productive use, but it does not proscribe a productive use that was previously permissible under relevant property and nuisance principles. The use of these properties for what are now expressly prohibited purposes was *always* unlawful, and (subject to other constitutional limitations) it was open to the State at any point to make the implication of those background principles of nuisance and property law explicit. . . . When, however, a regulation that declares "off-limits" all economically productive or beneficial uses of land goes beyond what the relevant background principles would dictate, compensation must be paid to sustain it.

The "total taking" inquiry we require today will ordinarily entail (as the application of state nuisance law ordinarily entails) analysis of, among other things, the degree of harm to public lands and resources, or adjacent private property, posed by the claimant's proposed activities, *see, e.g.*, Restatement (Second) of Torts 826, 827, the social value of the claimant's activities and their suitability to the locality in question, *see, e.g., id.*, §§828(a) and (b), 831, and the relative ease with which the alleged harm can be avoided through measures taken by the claimant and the government (or adjacent private landowners) alike, *see, e.g., id.*, §§827(e), 828(c), 830. The fact that a particular use has long been engaged in by similarly situated owners ordinarily imports a lack of any common-law prohibition (though changed circumstances or new knowledge may make what was previously permissible no

15. After accusing us of "launch[ing] a missile to kill a mouse," *post*, at 2904, Justice BLACKMUN expends a good deal of throw-weight of his own upon a noncombatant, arguing that our description of the "understanding" of land ownership that informs the Takings Clause is not supported by early American experience. . . . Justice BLACKMUN is correct that early constitutional theorists did not believe the Takings Clause embraced regulations of property at all . . . but even he does not suggest (explicitly, at least) that we renounce the Court's contrary conclusion in *Mahon*. Since the text of the Clause can be read to encompass regulatory as well as physical deprivations . . . we decline to do so as well.

longer so, *see* Restatement (Second) of Torts, *supra*, §827, comment *g*. So also does the fact that other landowners, similarly situated, are permitted to continue the use denied to the claimant.

It seems unlikely that common-law principles would have prevented the erection of any habitable or productive improvements on petitioner's land; they rarely support prohibition of the "essential use" of land. The question, however, is one of state law to be dealt with on remand. We emphasize that to win its case South Carolina must do more than proffer the legislature's declaration that the uses Lucas desires are inconsistent with the public interest, or the conclusory assertion that they violate a common-law maxim such as *sic utere tuo ut alienum non laedas*. As we have said, a "State, by *ipse dixit*, may not transform private property into public property without compensation. . . ." Instead, as it would be required to do if it sought to restrain Lucas in a common-law action for public nuisance, South Carolina must identify background principles of nuisance and property law that prohibit the uses he now intends in the circumstances in which the property is presently found. Only on this showing can the State fairly claim that, in proscribing all such beneficial uses, the Beachfront Management Act is taking nothing.

Notes and Comments

1. *Limitations on the Per Se Rule*. Does *Lucas* depart significantly from *Penn Central*? The opinion in *Lucas* first offers a tentative per se rule that regulations denying all economically beneficial or productive use constitute a taking. The Court then backs off the per se rule by acknowledging that regulations designed to abate nuisances constitute valid regulations. *See Smith v. Town of Wolfeboro*, 615 A.2d 1252, 1257 (N.H. 1992) (no taking under *Lucas* where a development poses an "exceptional danger to health," as the landowner has no right to injure others).

In *Palazzolo v. Rhode Island*, 533 U.S. 606 (2001), the Court allowed purchasers to claim a taking despite pre-acquisition regulation. Thus, the reference in *Lucas* to "preexisting" law refers not to pre-existing ordinances but to whether the claimed denial of use was a part of the owner's title under the existing, internal state law. Presumably, rights arising from sources such as prescriptive easements or the public trust doctrine may justify curtailment of an owner's right to develop land. Paul Saraham, Wetlands Protection Post-Lucas: Implications of the Public Trust Doctrine on Takings Analysis, 13 Va. Envtl. L.J. 537 (1994) (recommending growth of trust doctrine).

2. Lucas *and* Penn Central. If *Lucas* is limited to regulation that removes the total value of the parcel, it is limited to rare cases, probably in settings of impacts on sensitive ecological systems or where hillside development is controversial. If so, has the Court reduced the subjectivity of *Penn Central* or simply replaced the calculus of balancing under *Penn Central* with a quest for the definition of nuisance or the public trust? Will takings litigation expand and the doctrine become even more chaotic under *Lucas*?

Does the holding in *Lucas* suggest that *Penn Central* can no longer be relied upon as good law? In *Palazzolo v. Rhode Island*, 533 U.S. at 616, the Supreme Court stated that in the absence of proof that land use regulation denies an economic use under *Lucas*, regulation is to be reviewed under the balancing model of *Penn Central*. For an argument that *Penn Central* represents a superior, nuanced analysis for takings as compared to *Lucas*, and that endorses *Palazzolo*, *see* F. Patrick Hubbard, *Palazzolo*, *Lucas*, and *Penn Central*: The Need for Pragmatism, Symbolism, and Ad Hoc Balancing, 80 Neb. L. Rev. 465 (2001).

While *Lucas* does not appear to threaten most forms of zoning, subdivision, and other development restrictions, it does place in jeopardy environmental and development regulation of sensitive ecological areas. *See also Steel v. Cape Corp.*, 677 A.2d 634, 651 (Md. Ct. Spec. App. 1996) (denial of a rezoning from open space to residential based on inadequate school capacity is a taking under *Lucas* because it left the owner no viable residential or commercial use).

3. *The Dual-Pronged Takings Test.* In *Agins v. City of Tiburon*, 447 U.S. 255, 260 (1980), the Court stated a two-part test for a taking: "if the ordinance does not substantially advance legitimate state interests or denies an owner economically viable use of his land." A plaintiff can theoretically prevail by meeting either prong of the test. *State ex rel. Shemo v. City of Mayfield Heights*, 765 N.E.2d 345, 351 (Ohio 2002) ("[S]atisfaction of either prong of the *Agins* test establishes a taking"). Some have argued, however, that the first prong of the test — the "substantially advance" part — is traceable to the courts' substantive due process holdings and does not belong in the takings test. *See, e.g.*, John Echeverria, Does A Regulation That Fails to Advance a Legitimate State Interest Result in a Regulatory Taking?, 29 Envtl. L. 853 (1999).

4. *The Reach of* Lucas. Is *Lucas* limited to land use regulations? In *Third & Catalina Assocs. v. City of Phoenix*, 895 P.2d 115 (Ariz. Ct. App. 1994), an Arizona appellate court found no taking by a city requirement that commercial high rise buildings exceeding 75 feet in height must retrofit with sprinklers 16 years after construction. The court sustained the regulation despite the expense of the mandated removal of asbestos material after the city had required the use of asbestos in construction: the cost of retrofit was possibly in excess of the building's value. The court based its ruling on the fact that fire protection is a valid interest, and it found *Lucas* inapplicable because the regulation was not a restriction on land use. Can a landowner be required to restore a structure destroyed by fire? *Bernard v. Scharf*, 675 N.Y.S.2d 64 (Sup. Ct. App. Div. 1998) (not where a comparison of cost and anticipated market value demonstrates a denial of a reasonable rate of return, thus constituting a taking), *rev'd for mootness*, 711 N.E.2d 187 (N.Y. 1999).

5. *Exhaustion and Ripeness.* The decision in *Lucas* also must be understood in light of the doctrines, discussed in more detail in Chapter 6, that a landowner must exhaust all available administrative remedies, and the claim must be ripe for adjudication. In *Suitum v. Tahoe Regional Planning Agency*, 528 U.S. 725 (1997), discussed in Chapter 6, *supra*, the United States Supreme Court vacated a ruling that refused to hear a taking challenge based on a permit denial because the owner had yet to apply for available transferable development rights. The Court ruled that the formal application for transfer was not discretionary, like a variance or subdivision request. Thus, the decision denying the right to build is final, and the case is ripe. The Court suggested that the availability of transferable development rights might mitigate or eliminate any obligation to compensate the landowner for the taking, but those rights were not relevant to the existence of a taking.

6. *Nuisance Again*. Are state courts or legislatures free to expand the definition of a nuisance so as to protect certain sensitive ecological systems from exploitation? Would the protections that *Lucas* provides erode as states expanded the definition of nuisance or the public trust doctrine? Louise A. Halper, Why the Nuisance Knot Can't Undo the Takings Muddle, 28 Ind. L. Rev. 329 (1995) (Court was wrong to cut the legislature out of the process of defining nuisances). *See also Kim v. City of New York*, 681 N.E.2d 312 (N.Y. 1997), *cert. denied*, 522 U.S. 809 (1997) (city charter imposing an obligation on property owners to maintain lateral-support for a public highway was a prevailing rule of the state's property law when the owner acquired the property, and thus the city's subsequent enforcement of the obligation by depositing fill along the highway did not constitute a taking under *Lucas*).

7. *Post-Vesting Regulation*. If a community modifies regulatory obligations following the vesting point, does the regulation constitute a taking? Absent a compelling justification, such as avoidance of a nuisance, most would agree that the development right has been taken. However, in *Villa at Greeley, Inc. v. Hopper*, 917 P.2d 350 (Colo. Ct. App. 1996), the Colorado appellate court rejected a taking claim in sustaining an initiative measure that required a referendum on planned unit developments. The referendum applied to PUDs that had received pre-construction approval. Does *Lucas* mandate the finding of a taking in this situation? Or is the right to develop just one of the bundle of property rights, and since there still remains value to develop an alternative project or comply with the new requirements, has no taking occurred? Can a *Lucas* claim be made by arguing that the development right is not part of the property but constitutes *separate* property such that, when vesting is dishonored, the property is extinguished?

8. *Commentary on Lucas*. Some commentators are frustrated by *Lucas*. For example, *Lucas* has been criticized for its vagueness. William W. Fisher, III, The Trouble with *Lucas*, 45 Stan. L. Rev. 1393 (1993). Professor Norman Williams attacked *Lucas* as inconsistent with traditional zoning jurisprudence. Norman Williams, A Narrow Escape?, 16 Zoning & Plan. L. Rep. 113, 122 (1993) (Parts I & II). Others, however, are hopeful that *Lucas* will allow even greater levels of environmental regulation under an expanding public trust doctrine. Jack H. Archer & Terrance W. Stone, The Interaction of the Public Trust and the Takings Doctrines: Protecting Wetlands and Critical Coastal Areas, 20 Vt. L. Rev. 81 (1995); Hope M. Babcock, Should *Lucas v. South Carolina Coastal Council* Protect Where the Wild Things Are? Of Beavers, Bob-o-links, and Other Things that Go Bump in the Night, 85 Iowa L. Rev. 849 (2000) (*Lucas* incorporates common law communal norms so as to protect species and habitat). Still others believe *Lucas* is of slight impact and significance. Dwight H. Merriam, No Norman, the Sky is Not Falling in, 16 Zoning & Plan. L. Rep. 137 (1993); Glenn P. Sugameli, Takings Issues in Light of Lucas v. South Carolina Coastal Council: A Decision Full of Sound and Fury Signifying Nothing, 12 Va. Envtl. L.J. 439 (1993). A narrow view of the case would see it as, at most, resolving a unique group of cases involving the near total wipeout of a landowner. *Waters Landing Ltd. Partnership v. Montgomery County*, 650 A.2d 712, 724 (Md. 1994) (only physical invasion or complete deprivation of value subject to *Lucas* regulatory taking claim). What do you think?

■ TAHOE-SIERRA PRESERVATION COUNCIL, INC. v. TAHOE REGIONAL PLANNING AGENCY, ET AL.

535 U.S. 302 (2002)

Justice STEVENS delivered the opinion of the Court.

The question presented is whether a moratorium on development imposed during the process of devising a comprehensive land-use plan constitutes a *per se* taking of property requiring compensation under the Takings Clause of the United States Constitution. . . .

I

The relevant facts are undisputed. . . . Lake Tahoe's exceptional clarity is attributed to the absence of algae that obscures the waters of most other lakes. Historically, the lack of nitrogen and phosphorous, which nourish the growth of algae, has ensured the transparency of its waters. Unfortunately, the lake's pristine state has deteriorated rapidly over the past 40 years; increased land development in the Lake Tahoe Basin (Basin) has threatened the " 'noble sheet of blue water' " beloved by [Mark] Twain and countless others. 34 F. Supp. 2d, at 1230. . . .

The upsurge of development in the area has caused "increased nutrient loading of the lake largely because of the increase in impervious coverage of land in the Basin resulting from that development." *Ibid.*

Given this trend, the District Court predicted that "unless the process is stopped, the lake will lose its clarity and its trademark blue color, becoming green and opaque for eternity."

Those areas in the Basin that have steeper slopes produce more runoff; therefore, they are usually considered "high hazard" lands. Moreover, certain areas near streams or wetlands known as "Stream Environment Zones" (SEZs) are especially vulnerable to the impact of development because, in their natural state, they act as filters for much of the debris that runoff carries. Because "[t]he most obvious response to this problem . . . is to restrict development around the lake—especially in SEZ lands, as well as in areas already naturally prone to runoff," *id.*, at 1232, conservation efforts have focused on controlling growth in these high hazard areas. . . .

The 1980 Tahoe Regional Planning Compact (Compact) redefined the structure, functions, and voting procedures of TRPA [the Tahoe Regional Planning Agency], App. 37, 94 Stat. 3235-3238; 34 F. Supp. 2d, at 1233, and directed it to develop regional "environmental threshold carrying capacities"—a term that embraced "standards for air quality, water quality, soil conservation, vegetation preservation and noise." 94 Stat. 3235, 3239. The Compact provided that TRPA "shall adopt" those standards within 18 months, and that "[w]ithin 1 year after" their adoption (*i.e.*, by June 19, 1983), it "shall" adopt an amended regional plan that achieves and maintains those carrying capacities. *Id.*, at 3240. The Compact also contained a finding by the Legislatures of California and Nevada "that in order to make effective the regional plan as revised by [TRPA], it is necessary to halt temporarily works of development in the region which might otherwise absorb the entire capability of the region for further development or direct it out of harmony with the ultimate plan." *Id.*, at 3243. Accordingly, for the period prior to the adoption of the final plan ("or until May 1, 1983, whichever is earlier"), the Compact itself prohibited the development of new subdivisions, condominiums, and apartment buildings, and also prohibited each city and county in the Basin from granting any more permits in 1981, 1982, or 1983 than had been granted in 1978.

During this period TRPA was also working on the development of a regional water quality plan to comply with the Clean Water Act, 33 U.S.C. §1288 (1994 ed.). Despite the fact that TRPA performed these obligations in "good faith and to the best of its ability," 34 F. Supp. 2d, at 1233, after a few months it concluded that it could not meet the deadlines in the Compact. On June 25, 1981, it therefore enacted Ordinance 81-5 imposing the first of the two moratoria on development that petitioners challenge in this proceeding. The ordinance provided that it would become effective on August 24, 1981, and remain in effect pending the adoption of the permanent plan required by the Compact. App. 159, 191. . . .

Given the complexity of the task of defining "environmental threshold carrying capacities" and the division of opinion within TRPA's governing board, the District Court found that it was "unsurprising" that TRPA failed to adopt those thresholds until August 26, 1982, roughly two months after the Compact deadline. *Ibid.* Under a liberal reading of the Compact, TRPA then had until August 26, 1983, to adopt a new regional plan. 94 Stat. 3240. "Unfortunately, but again not surprisingly, no regional plan was in place as of that date." 34 F. Supp. 2d, at 1235. TRPA therefore adopted Resolution 83-21, "which completely suspended all project reviews and approvals, including the acceptance of new proposals," and which remained in effect until a new regional plan was adopted on April 26, 1984. Thus, Resolution 83-21 imposed an 8-month moratorium prohibiting all construction on high hazard lands in either State. In combination, Ordinance 81-5 and Resolution 83-21 effectively prohibited all construction on sensitive lands in California and on all SEZ lands in the entire Basin for 32 months, and on sensitive lands in Nevada (other than SEZ lands) for eight months. It is these two moratoria that are at issue in this case. . . .

III

Petitioners make only a facial attack on Ordinance 81-5 and Resolution 83-21. They contend that the mere enactment of a temporary regulation that, while in effect, denies a property owner all viable economic use of her property gives rise to an unqualified constitutional obligation to compensate her for the value of its use during that period. . . .

IV

The text of the Fifth Amendment itself provides a basis for drawing a distinction between physical takings and regulatory takings. . . .

When the government physically takes possession of an interest in property for some public purpose, it has a categorical duty to compensate the former owner, *United States v. Pewee Coal Co.*, 341 U.S. 114, 115, 71 S. Ct. 670, 95 L. Ed. 809 (1951), regardless of whether the interest that is taken constitutes an entire parcel or merely a part thereof. Thus, compensation is mandated when a leasehold is taken and the government occupies the property for its own purposes, even though that use is temporary. . . . Similarly, when the government appropriates part of a rooftop in order to provide cable TV access for apartment tenants, *Loretto v. Teleprompter Manhattan CATV Corp.*, 458 U.S. 419, (1982) . . . ; or when its planes use private airspace to approach a government airport, *United States v. Causby*, 328 U.S. 256 (1946) . . . it is required to pay for that share no matter how small. But a government regulation that merely prohibits landlords from evicting tenants unwilling to pay a higher rent, *Block v. Hirsh*, 256 U.S. 135, (1921); that bans certain private uses of a portion of an owner's property, *Village of Euclid v. Ambler Realty Co.*, 272 U.S. 365 (1926) . . .; *Keystone Bituminous Coal Assn. v. DeBenedictis*, 480 U.S. 470 (1987) . . .; or that forbids the private use of certain airspace, *Penn Central Transp. Co. v. New York City*, 438 U.S. 104 (1978) . . . does not constitute a categorical taking. "The first category of cases requires courts to apply a clear rule; the second necessarily entails complex factual assessments of the purposes and economic effects of government actions." *Yee v. Escondido*, 503 U.S. 519, 523, 112 12 S. Ct. 1522, 118 L. Ed. 2d 153 (1992).

This longstanding distinction between acquisitions of property for public use, on the one hand, and regulations prohibiting private uses, on the other, makes it inappropriate to treat cases involving physical takings as controlling precedents for the evaluation of a claim that there has been a "regulatory taking," and vice versa. For the same reason that we do not ask whether a physical appropriation advances a substantial government interest or whether it deprives the owner of all economically valuable use, we do not apply our precedent from the physical takings context to regulatory takings claims. Land-use regulations are ubiquitous and most of them impact property values in some tangential way — often in completely unanticipated ways. Treating them all as *per se* takings would transform government regulation into a luxury few governments could afford. By contrast, physical appropriations are relatively rare, easily identified, and usually represent a greater affront to individual property rights. "This case does not present the 'classi[c] taking' in which the government directly appropriates private property for its own use," *Eastern Enterprises v. Apfel*, 524 U.S. 498, 522 (1998) . . .; instead the interference with property rights "arises from some public program adjusting the benefits and burdens of economic life to promote the common good," *Penn Central*, 438 U.S., at 124 . . .

Perhaps recognizing this fundamental distinction, petitioners . . . rely principally on our decision in *Lucas v. South Carolina Coastal Council*, 505 U.S. 1003, 112 S. Ct. 2886, 120 L. Ed. 2d 798 (1992) — a regulatory takings case that, nevertheless, applied a categorical rule — to argue that the *Penn Central* framework is inapplicable here. A brief review of some of the cases that led to our decision in *Lucas*, however, will help to explain why the holding in that case does not answer the question presented here.

As we noted in *Lucas*, it was Justice Holmes' opinion in *Pennsylvania Coal Co. v. Mahon*, 260 U.S. 393, 43 S. Ct. 158, 67 L. Ed. 322 (1922), that gave birth to our regulatory takings jurisprudence. In subsequent opinions we have repeatedly and consistently endorsed Holmes' observation that "if regulation goes too far it will be recognized as a taking." *Id.*, at 415 . . . Justice Holmes did not provide a standard for determining when a regulation goes "too far," but he did reject the view expressed in Justice Brandeis' dissent that there could not be a taking because the property remained in the possession of the owner and had not been appropriated or used by the public. After *Mahon*, neither a physical appropriation nor a public use has ever been a necessary component of a "regulatory taking."

In the decades following that decision, we have "generally eschewed" any set formula for determining how far is too far, choosing instead to engage in "'essentially ad hoc, factual inquiries.'" *Lucas*, 505 U.S., at 1015 . . . (quoting *Penn Central*, 438 U.S., at 124). Indeed, we still resist the temptation to adopt *per se* rules in our cases involving partial regulatory takings, preferring to examine "a number of factors" rather than a simple "mathematically precise" formula.[23] Justice Brennan's opinion for the Court in *Penn Central* did, however, make it clear that even though multiple factors are relevant in the analysis of regulatory takings claims, in such cases we must focus on "the parcel as a whole":

> "'Taking' jurisprudence does not divide a single parcel into discrete segments and attempt to determine whether rights in a particular segment have been entirely abrogated. In deciding whether a particular governmental action has effected a taking, this Court focuses rather both on the character of the action and on the nature and extent of the interference with rights in the parcel as a whole—here, the city tax block designated as the 'landmark site.'" *Id.*, at 130-131. . . .

Similarly, our decision in *Lucas* is not dispositive of the question presented. Although *Lucas* endorsed and applied a categorical rule, it was not the one that petitioners propose. . . .

The categorical rule that we applied in *Lucas* states that compensation is required when a regulation deprives an owner of "*all* economically beneficial uses" of his land. *Id.*, at 1019 . . . Under that rule, a statue that "wholly eliminated the value" of Lucas' fee simple title clearly qualified as a taking. But our holding was limited to "the extraordinary circumstance when *no* productive or economically beneficial use of land is permitted." *Id.*, at 1017. . . .

Certainly, our holding that the permanent "obliteration of the value" of a fee simple estate constitutes a categorical taking does not answer the question whether a regulation prohibiting any economic use of land for a 32-month period has the same legal effect. Petitioners seek to bring this case under the rule announced in *Lucas* by arguing that we can effectively sever a 32-month segment from the remainder of each landowner's fee simple estate, and then ask whether that segment has been taken in its entirety by the moratoria. Of course, defining the property interest taken in terms of the very regulation being challenged is circular. With property so divided, every delay would become a total ban; the moratorium and the normal permit process alike would constitute categorical takings. Petitioners' "conceptual severance" argument is unavailing because it ignores *Penn Central*'s admonition that in regulatory takings cases we must focus on "the parcel as a whole." 438 U.S., at 130-131 . . . We have consistently rejected such an approach to the "denominator" question. See *Keystone*, 480 U.S., at 497, 107 S. Ct. 1232. *See also Concrete Pipe & Products of Cal., Inc. v. Construction Laborers Pension Trust for Southern Cal.*, 508 U.S. 602, 644 . . . (1993) ("To the extent that any

23. In her concurring opinion in *Palazzolo*, 533 U.S., at 633. Justice O'CONNOR reaffirmed this approach: "Our polestar instead remains the principles set forth in *Penn Central* itself and our other cases that govern partial regulatory takings. Under these cases, interference with investment-backed expectations is one of a number of factors that a court must examine." *Ibid.* "*Penn Central* does not supply mathematically precise variables, but instead provides important guideposts that lead to the ultimate determination whether just compensation is required." *Id.*, at 634 . . . "The temptation to adopt what amount to *per se* rules in either direction must be resisted. The Takings Clause requires careful examination and weighing of all the relevant circumstances in this context." *Id.*, at 636.

portion of property is taken, that portion is always taken in its entirety; the relevant question, however, is whether the property taken is all, or only a portion of, the parcel in question"). Thus, the District Court erred when it disaggregated petitioners' property into temporal segments corresponding to the regulations at issue and then analyzed whether petitioners were deprived of all economically viable use during each period. 34 F. Supp. 2d, at 1242-1245. The starting point for the court's analysis should have been to ask whether there was a total taking of the entire parcel; if not, then *Penn Central* was the proper framework.

An interest in real property is defined by the metes and bounds that describe its geographic dimensions and the term of years that describes the temporal aspect of the owner's interest. *See* Restatement of Property §§7-9 (1936). Both dimensions must be considered if the interest is to be viewed in its entirety. Hence, a permanent deprivation of the owner's use of the entire area is a taking of "the parcel as a whole," whereas a temporary restriction that merely causes a diminution in value is not. Logically, a fee simple estate cannot be rendered valueless by a temporary prohibition on economic use, because the property will recover value as soon as the prohibition is lifted. . . .

Neither *Lucas* . . . nor any of our other regulatory takings cases compels us to accept petitioners' categorical submission. In fact, these cases make clear that the categorical rule in *Lucas* was carved out for the "extraordinary case" in which a regulation permanently deprives property of all value; the default rule remains that, in the regulatory taking context, we require a more fact specific inquiry. . . .

V

More importantly, for reasons set out at some length by Justice O'CONNOR in her concurring opinion in *Palazzolo v. Rhode Island*, 533 U.S., at 636 . . . , we are persuaded that the better approach to claims that a regulation has effected a temporary taking "requires careful examination and weighing of all the relevant circumstances." In that opinion, Justice O'CONNOR specifically considered the role that the "temporal relationship between regulatory enactment and title acquisition" should play in the analysis of a takings claim. *Id.*, at 632 . . . We have no occasion to address that particular issue in this case, because it involves a different temporal relationship—the distinction between a temporary restriction and one that is permanent. Her comments on the "fairness and justice" inquiry are, nevertheless, instructive:

> Today's holding does not mean that the timing of the regulation's enactment relative to the acquisition of title is immaterial to the *Penn Central* analysis. Indeed, it would be just as much error to expunge this consideration from the takings inquiry as it would be to accord it exclusive significance. Our polestar instead remains the principles set forth in *Penn Central* itself and our other cases that govern partial regulatory takings. Under these cases, interference with investment-backed expectations is one of a number of factors that a court must examine. . . .
>
> The Fifth Amendment forbids the taking of private property for public use without just compensation. We have recognized that this constitutional guarantee is "designed to bar Government from forcing some people alone to bear public burdens which, in all fairness and justice, should be borne by the public as a whole." *Penn Central*, [438 U.S.], at 123-124 . . . (quoting *Armstrong v. United States*, 364 U.S. 40, 49 . . . (1960)). The concepts of "fairness and justice" that underlie the Takings

Clause, of course, are less than fully determinate. Accordingly, we have eschewed "any 'set formula' for determining when 'justice and fairness' require that economic injuries caused by public action be compensated by the government, rather than remain disproportionately concentrated on a few persons." *Penn Central, supra,* . . .

In rejecting petitioners' *per se* rule, we do not hold that the temporary nature of a land-use restriction precludes finding that it effects a taking; we simply recognize that it should not be given exclusive significance one way or the other.

A narrower rule that excluded the normal delays associated with processing permits, or that covered only delays of more than a year, would certainly have a less severe impact on prevailing practices, but it would still impose serious financial constraints on the planning process.[31] Unlike the "extraordinary circumstances" in which the government deprives a property owner of all economic use, *Lucas,* 505 U.S., at 1017 . . . moratoria like Ordinance 81-5 and Resolution 83-21 are used widely among land-use planners to preserve the status quo while formulating a more permanent development strategy. In fact, the consensus in the planning community appears to be that moratoria, or "interim development controls" as they are often called, are an essential tool of successful development. Yet even the weak version of petitioners' categorical rule would treat these interim measures as takings regardless of the good faith of the planners, the reasonable expectations of the landowners, or the actual impact of the moratorium on property values. . . .

. . . Indeed, the interest in protecting the decisional process is even stronger when an agency is developing a regional plan than when it is considering a permit for a single parcel. In the proceedings involving the Lake Tahoe Basin, for example, the moratoria enabled TRPA to obtain the benefit of comments and criticisms from interested parties, such as the petitioners, during its deliberations. Since a categorical rule tied to the length of deliberations would likely create added pressure on decisionmakers to reach a quick resolution of land-use questions, it would only serve to disadvantage those landowners and interest groups who are not as organized or familiar with the planning process. Moreover, with a temporary ban on development there is a lesser risk that individual landowners will be "singled out" to bear a special burden that should be shared by the public as a whole. *Nollan v. California Coastal Comm'n,* 483 U.S. 825, 835 . . . (1987). At least with a moratorium there is a clear "reciprocity of advantages," *Mahon,* 260 U.S., at 415 . . . because it protects the interests of all affected landowners against immediate construction that might be inconsistent with the provisions of the plan that is ultimately adopted. . . .

31. Petitioners fail to offer a persuasive explanation for why moratoria should be treated differently from ordinary permit delays. They contend that a permit applicant need only comply with certain specific requirements in order to receive one and can expect to develop at the end of the process, whereas there is nothing the landowner subject to a moratorium can do but wait, with no guarantee that a permit will be granted at the end of the process. Brief for Petitioners 28. Setting aside the obvious problem with basing the distinction on a course of events we can only know after the fact — in the context of a facial challenge — petitioners' argument breaks down under closer examination because there is no guarantee that a permit will be granted, or that a decision will be made within a year. See, *e.g., Dufau v. United States,* 22 Cl. Ct. 156 (1990) (holding that 16-month delay in granting a permit did not constitute a temporary taking). Moreover, under petitioners' modified categorical rule, there would be no *per se* taking if TRPA simply delayed action on all permits pending a regional plan. Fairness and justice do not require that TRPA be penalized for achieving the same result, but with full disclosure.

It may well be true that any moratorium that lasts for more than one year should be viewed with special skepticism. But given the fact that the District Court found that the 32 months required by TRPA to formulate the 1984 Regional Plan was not unreasonable, we could not possibly conclude that every delay of over one year is constitutionally unacceptable. Formulating a general rule of this kind is a suitable task for state legislatures. Accordingly, the judgment of the Court of Appeals is affirmed.

Notes and Comments

1. *Takings Theory I: Segmentation.* The decision in *Tahoe* is not just the Court's latest takings case in the land use field. It is particularly useful for considering the state of development of takings theory under the Court's modern analysis. To begin with, what does *Tahoe* add to the Court's jurisprudence on defining the relevant parcel for takings analysis? Does the Court's hesitancy in finding a taking here stem from the plaintiff's theory, which would seem to require compensation every time the government imposed a delay on the development of property?

Does the decision reinvigorate *Penn Central*? In recent cases, the Court seemed to be favoring a *per se* rule as a means of giving substance to the Takings Clause. In *Tahoe*, however, the Court once again emphasizes *Penn Central*. Note that Justice Stevens' opinion carefully cites Justice O'Connor's concurring opinion in *Palazzolo v. Rhode Island*, 533 U.S. at 636, in which she stated that the timing of a regulation's enactment was a factor to be considered in a *Penn Central* analysis.

2. *Takings Theory II: Physical Takings.* Why did the Court refuse to use its physical occupation cases as the applicable precedents? If the government had physically occupied the plaintiffs' property for a period of time, would it be required to pay compensation? If so, why is the outcome different simply because the government enacted a moratorium? Wasn't the effect on the landowner exactly the same?

3. *Tahoe and the Planning Process.* Some have seen the *Tahoe* decision as a "win" for land use planning in general. They cite Justice Stevens' statement that, if the court adopted a rule that excluded "normal" delays associated with processing permits, that holding "would still impose serious financial constraints on the planning process." Do you agree? Or would such a holding simply give governments the incentive to act more quickly?

4. *The Importance of* Tahoe. Now that you have read a good assortment of the Court's modern takings cases, can you assess the ultimate importance of the *Tahoe* decision? Those defending municipalities argue that it's a large win for them, emphasizing the Court's refusal to extend its per se rules to include moratoria. They also cite the importance of being able to use moratoria to solve land use problems, a subject discussed in Chapter 13, *infra*. In contrast, those representing landowners note that the Court did not uphold all moratoria. In fact, the Court even suggested that "[i]t may well be true that any moratorium that lasts for more than one year should be viewed with special skepticism." In their view, *Tahoe* simply preserves the status quo of takings law, and is thus relatively unimportant in the long run. *See Walcek v. United States*, 303 F.3d 1349 (Fed. Cir. 2002) (citing *Tahoe* in concluding that the trial court correctly examined plaintiff's entire 14.5 acre parcel in its takings analysis, even though only one part of the property was a restricted wetlands and the rest of the property was subject to development). *See also* J. David

Breemer, Temporary Insanity: The Long Tale of *Tahoe-Sierra Preservation Council* and Its Quiet Ending in the Supreme Court, 71 Ford. L. Rev. 1 (2002); Gregory M. Stein, Takings in the 21st Century: Reasonable Investment-Backed Expectations After *Palazzolo* and *Tahoe-Sierra*, 69 Tenn. L. Rev. 891 (2002).

What do you think?

5. *Jurisdictional Mistakes*. In *Landgate v. California Coastal Comm'n*, 17 Cal. 4th 1006 (1998), the California Supreme Court held that a delay precipitated by an erroneous regulatory action does not give rise to a taking. In that case the Coastal Commission had asserted jurisdiction over a project, but the Court later held that the Commission's assertion of jurisdiction was erroneous. *See also Loewenstein v. City of Lafayette*, 127 Cal. Rptr. 2d 79 (2002) (two-year delay caused by erroneous denial of property owner's lot line adjustment was not compensable under *Landgate*). Is this situation covered by *Tahoe?* Or is *Tahoe* distinguishable, since it involved a moratorium while, in these cases, the agency simply was mistaken in determining its jurisdiction? *Compare Laguna Gatuna, Inc. v. United States*, 50 Fed. Cl. 336 (Ct. Fed. Cl. 2001) (EPA order declaring that a lake was subject to regulation under the Clean Water Act — an order later deemed erroneous in light of a Supreme Court decision — effected a taking).

The *Tahoe* decision examined the issue of segmenting property over a period of time — so-called temporal segmentation. An even more important segmentation issue, however, concerns the choice of the so-called denominator in a takings action. This choice is critical. As the Pennsylvania Supreme Court observed in *Machipongo Land & Coal Co. v. Commonwealth*, 699 A.2d 751, 766 (Pa. 2002), "Resolving the denominator problem profoundly influences the outcome of a takings analysis. . . . [T]he more narrowly the relevant parcel is defined, the more likely is the finding of a taking. . . ." While the Supreme Court has not yet addressed this issue, the lower federal courts are beginning to develop a body of case law. The following opinion is one of the leading decisions.

■ PALM BEACH ISLES ASSOCIATES v. UNITED STATES

208 F.3d 1374 (Fed. Cir. 2000)

PLAGER, Circuit Judge.

Palm Beach Isles Associates, Martin Slifka, Marjorie Margolis and Roberta Franklin, and the Estate of Joseph Slifka (collectively "PBIA") claim that the United States (the "Government") effected a regulatory taking of their property in Florida when the Army Corps of Engineers (the "Corps") refused to grant a permit to dredge and fill the property. The Court of Federal Claims granted the Government's motion for summary judgment of no liability.

PBIA appeals the ruling of the Court of Federal Claims. . . .

BACKGROUND

In 1956, a group of investors bought 311.7 acres of land in Florida for $380,190. With various transfers through the years, primarily by devise and inheritance, this group eventually became PBIA. The property is located north of Palm Beach on a long spit of land which sits between the Atlantic Ocean on the east and Lake Worth on the west. A road traverses the spit from north to south, and splits the property into two parcels. Of the 311.7 acres, 261 acres are east of the road, and constitute upland oceanfront property. This parcel was sold in 1968 to a developer for some $1 million; it is not as such involved in this law suit.

The remaining 50.7 acres are located west of the road. This 50.7 acre parcel consists of 1.4 acres of shoreline wetlands adjacent to the road, and 49.3 acres of submerged land adjacent to the wetlands. The submerged acreage lies below the mean high water mark, in the bed of Lake Worth. It is this 50.7 acre parcel that is the subject of this action.

Lake Worth is a long, narrow, shallow body of water having a north-south orientation. At one time the lake was a land-locked freshwater lake, but years ago a cut, Lake Worth Inlet, was made across the spit that separates the lake from the ocean, and as a result the lake is now a tidal water with direct access to the ocean. Lake Worth serves as a segment of the Atlantic Intracoastal Waterway ("ICW"). A channel has been dredged along the western shore of the lake to provide a readily-navigable passage for vessels. As a part of the ICW, Lake Worth is considered a navigable water of the United States, and thus the submerged portion of PBIA's property lies in the bed of a navigable water of the United States.

. . . Shortly after purchasing the property, in 1957, PBIA applied for and received from the Corps the necessary permits to dredge and fill the 50.7 acres. The permits were renewed in 1960. However, PBIA never performed the work and the permits expired in 1963.

Some twenty-five years later, in 1988, PBIA applied to the State of Florida Department of Environmental Regulation ("DER") for a permit, as now required by state law, to dredge and fill the submerged lake bottom it owned, along with the adjoining wetlands. After the DER in 1990 denied the permit on environmental grounds, PBIA sued the DER and the Trustees of the Internal Improvement Fund of the State of Florida, the state agency from whom PBIA derived its title to the property. Eventually a settlement of the suit was reached. The State acknowledged that, pursuant to the deed from the Trustees, PBIA had the legal right to erect a bulkhead around the submerged land and fill the 50.7 acres. The settlement stipulated that the State would not interfere with PBIA's efforts to obtain permits from the Corps.

PBIA again applied to the Corps for the dredge and fill permits required by the Rivers & Harbors Act. Meanwhile, however, in 1972, Congress had passed the Clean Water Act (codified at 33 U.S.C. §§1251-1376 (1994 & Supp. III 1997)). Section 404 of the Clean Water Act, 33 U.S.C. §1344 (1994), also requires a permit from the Corps for dredging and filling navigable waters of the United States, and requires that environmental concerns be taken into account in deciding whether to grant such a permit. After consulting with the State of Florida, the Corps denied the permits.

The Corps' denial letter made clear that the denial was primarily predicated on environmental grounds and the requirements of the Clean Water Act, but the Memorandum accompanying the denial letter also stated:

> (11) Navigation: Shallow water depths that already exist in the proposed project area have limited boating activities to shallow draft vessels. Therefore, other than

the elimination of [49.3] acres of navigable waters, the project should not have a significant adverse impact on navigation, in general.

After the denial of the permits, PBIA filed suit in the Court of Federal Claims, claiming that the denial of the permits prevents any economically viable use of the 50.7 acres and therefore constitutes a regulatory taking of the parcel. PBIA requested more than $10 million as compensation for the taking.

The Court of Federal Claims found that the 49.3 acres, which lie below the mean high water mark, are part of the bed of Lake Worth and are subject to the federal navigational servitude . . . [T]he Court of Federal Claims ruled that the navigational servitude was a "pre-existing limitation upon the landowner's title," and therefore "the proscribed use interests were not part of [the owner's] title to begin with." In this circumstances, concluded the court, there was no taking despite the total loss of value for the land.

With regard to the 1.4 adjacent acres of wetlands, the Court of Federal Claims again found no taking on three grounds. First, it determined that the 1.4 acres should be viewed not as a separate parcel in itself, but rather as a part of the whole initial 311.7 acre parcel, for which PBIA had received adequate compensation when it sold the 261 acres for $1 million. Second, the Court of Federal Claims held that PBIA knew when it bought the property that it would need permits to develop the land (as evidenced by its 1957 and 1960 filings), and thus the existing statutory regime precluded any reasonable investment-backed expectation of being able to develop the property. Finally, the court found that the 1.4-acre section by itself is insufficient for building homes, and PBIA had not established that all other uses were foreclosed . . .

DISCUSSION . . .

. . . Whether the asserted imposition causes a total wipeout or something less (see *Florida Rock* for a discussion of the implications of "something less") depends in a case such as this on what is the economically relevant parcel—the "denominator problem."[4] We must decide if the whole 311.7 acre parcel is the relevant denominator, as argued by the Government and found by the Court of Federal Claims, or whether the relevant parcel is the 50.7 acres for which the permit was denied, as argued by PBIA. . . .

The Government argues that since the land was purchased together, it should all be treated as one parcel. PBIA should not be allowed to sever the part that is subject to regulation from the part that is not. The value of the part sold in 1968 should be considered as part of the denominator in assessing the proportionate value of the 50.7 acres.

PBIA counters that the two parcels have never been part of a common development scheme; their only link was that they were purchased at the same time. PBIA points out that the two parts are separated by a road, they are different types of property, subject to different zoning, and PBIA applied for its original permits

4. The problem is referred to as the denominator problem because, in comparing the value that has been taken from the property by the imposition with the value that remains in the property "one of the critical questions is determining how to define the unit of property whose value is to furnish the denominator of the fraction" *Keystone Bituminous Coal Assn. v. DeBenedictis*, 480 U.S. 470, 497, 107 S. Ct. 1232, 94 L.Ed.2d 472 (internal notes and citation omitted).

only for the lakeside property because PBIA never planned to develop the entire property as a unit. PBIA also notes that the oceanfront property was sold in 1968, before the now-existing regulatory fabric came into place.

Loveladies Harbor Inc. v. United States, [28 F.3d 1171 (Fed. Cir. 1994)] helps cast some light on this issue. Loveladies Harbor, Inc. ("Loveladies") had purchased 250 acres in 1958, with the intention of development under a comprehensive scheme. By the 1970s, Loveladies had developed 199 of the acres and wished to develop the remaining 51. Loveladies applied to the state of New Jersey for the requisite dredge and fill permits, but the state denied permission. After Loveladies sued the state, the two sides compromised, allowing Loveladies to develop 12.5 acres in exchange for conserving the remainder. Loveladies then applied to the Corps for the necessary federal dredge and fill permits. New Jersey, contrary to the compromise, opposed the permits, and they were denied. . . .

One of the issues on appeal was whether the denial of the permits caused a total wipeout of the economic value of the 12.5 acres, treated as a separate economic entity, or whether the economic value taken as a result of the denial should be considered as a fraction of the total economic value of the entire development, the 250 acres. In the latter case, there would be no denial of all economically viable use of the property, and the full regulatory takings analysis, including the question of distinct investment-backed expectations, would be applicable.

This court agreed with the trial court's conclusion that the proper parcel was the 12.5 acres. The 199 acres were developed over a substantial period of years starting in 1958, at a time when New Jersey had not yet put in place a comprehensive environmental program for wetlands protection. Furthermore, as a result of prior litigation in the case, the State had essentially conceded that under its law the property owner had the right to develop the 12.5 acres independent of any prior development. We concluded that the earlier-developed property was not a part of the denominator.

In the instant case, the Court of Federal Claims found the relevant parcel to be the 311.7 acres. The court based its conclusion, *inter alia*, on the Government's assertion that the regulatory structure under the Rivers and Harbors Act that led to the permit denials was in place before the 261 acres were sold in 1968, and therefore they should be included in the denominator.

The timing of property acquisition and development, compared with the enactment and implementation of the governmental regimen that led to the regulatory imposition, is a factor, but only one factor, to be considered in determining the proper denominator for analysis. As we said in *Loveladies Harbor*, "[o]ur precedent displays a flexible approach, designed to account for factual nuances." In a given case, other factors may be more compelling.

In this case, PBIA never planned to develop the parcels as a single unit. Furthermore, PBIA bought the land in 1956 and sold the 261 acres in 1968, both events occurring before the environmental considerations contained in the Clean Water Act came into play, beginning in 1972. It is inappropriate to consider those transactions to have occurred in the context of the substance of a regulatory structure that was not in place at the relevant times.

The regulatory imposition that infected the development plans for the 50.7 acres was unrelated to PBIA's plans for and disposition of the 261 acres of beachfront upland on the east side of the road. The development of that property was physically and temporally remote from, and legally unconnected to, the 50.7 acres of wetlands and submerged lake bed on the lake side of the spit. Combining the two tracts for purposes of the regulatory takings analysis involved here, simply because at one time they were under common ownership, or because one of the tracts sold for a substantial price, cannot be justified. The trial court's conclusion to the contrary was error.

Once the proper parcel is defined as the 50.7 acres, it becomes clear that, without the dredge and fill permits, the entire 50.7 acres, including the 1.4 acres of wetlands, have no or minimal value. Thus, the facts are uncontrovertible that the permit denial has the effect of denying the property owner *all* economically viable use of the property, and, since the State has stipulated that the property owner under state law has the right to dredge and fill, the denial by the Corps of the permits constitutes a categorical taking of the 50.7 acres by the Federal Government. The Court of Federal Claims erred in holding otherwise.

Since there is a categorical taking of the 50.7 acres, the issue of PBIA's investment-backed expectations under prong (2) of the *Loveladies Harbor* analysis is not applicable. We move to the Government's asserted defense under prong (3).

II. THE GOVERNMENT'S POWER TO REGULATE AND THE NAVIGATIONAL SERVITUDE

The key issue here (and the factor distinguishing it from *Loveladies Harbor*) is whether the navigational servitude defense is available to the Government in this case.

A.

The question to be addressed first in this context is whether the submerged 49.3 acres are subject to the navigational servitude. The "navigational servitude" derives from the Commerce Clause of the Constitution,[7] and gives the United States Government a "dominant servitude"—a power to regulate and control the waters of the United States in the interest of commerce. . . .

[S]ince the parcel at issue lies below the high water mark, is part of the bed of Lake Worth, and Lake Worth is a navigable water of the United States, the parcel is subject to the navigational servitude. The particular water depth over PBIA's land is not controlling. . . .

B. . . .

In light of our understanding of *Lucas* and the other cases we have considered, we hold that the navigational servitude may constitute part of the "background principles" to which a property owner's rights are subject, and thus may provide the Government with a defense to a takings claim. As noted by the Supreme Court, the navigational servitude is "a pre-existing limitation on the landowner's title." . . . In a case in which the navigational servitude applies, a denial of permits to dredge and fill may "do no more than duplicate the result that could have been obtained by the courts." . . .

2. . . .

With regard to what constitutes "proper exercise" of the navigational servitude, the Government takes the position here that the servitude is absolute, and

7. U.S. Const. art. I, §8. cl. 3.

that essentially there never can be a taking of property that is in a waterbody subject to the navigational servitude. The Government concedes that in the case before us its stated rationale for denying the permits was environmental, but it asserts that it also had a navigational purpose, and therefore even if the navigational servitude is not absolute there was no taking. PBIA counters that the navigational servitude only protects the Government when it regulates the use of private property if the purpose of the regulation is related to navigation. In the present case, PBIA argues, the permit denials were predicated on environmental grounds, not navigational grounds.

The precedents clearly establish that the Government's purpose must be related to navigation if it wishes to avoid paying compensation for the regulation or control of private property. . . .

Thus it is clear that in order to assert a defense under the navigational servitude, the Government must show that the regulatory imposition was for a purpose related to navigation; absent such a showing, it will have failed to "identify background principles . . . that prohibit the uses [the landowner] now intends." *Lucas*, 505 U.S. at 1031 . . .

In the present case, we are unable to determine whether the Government has made a sufficient showing of a navigational purpose behind the permit denial. The denial letter itself refers only to the "elimination of 50.7 acres of important Lake Worth shallow water habitat"; it makes no mention of navigation. The Memorandum accompanying the denial letter does discuss navigation, but its findings are contradictory. The Memorandum states that the project area currently allows "limited boating activities to shallow draft vessels" and granting the permit would result in "the elimination of [49.3] acres of navigable waters," language which appears to support a finding of a navigational purpose. However, the Memorandum goes on to conclude that "the project should not have a significant adverse impact on navigation, in general." . . .

Because there is a disputed issue of material fact, we vacate the judgment of the trial court, and remand the case for further development of this issue. . . . If . . . the Government cannot demonstrate that it denied the permit on navigational grounds, then its defense under the navigational servitude fails.

We have focused this discussion on the 49.3 acres of submerged land, though addressing in general the entire 50.7 acres. The trial court concluded that, without development of the 49.3 acres of submerged land, the 1.4 acres of adjoining wetlands would be of little, if any, value. Upon full examination of the record, we see no error in that conclusion. If there is a taking by the Government of the 49.3 acres, then there also must be a taking of the adjoining wetlands as well, and PBIA will be entitled to compensation therefor; if there is no taking because of the navigational servitude, the developmental value of the adjacent wetlands strip standing alone would be at most nominal—the attorney for PBIA admitted as much in oral argument—and in any event PBIA has failed to establish that no other uses are available to it. . . .

Notes and Comments

1. *The Nuisance Exception to* Lucas. Does *Palm Beach* offer an approach to limitations inherent in title that is broader or narrower than that suggested in *Lucas*?

Does the outcome turn on Florida's definition of nuisance? Would the outcome differ in a jurisdiction that considered the filling of wetlands with its adverse environmental impacts to be a nuisance? On rehearing, the Federal Circuit adhered to its earlier ruling that investment-backed expectations were not relevant to a *Lucas* categorical taking. The court remanded the matter for a determination of whether there was a categorical taking of the 1.4-acre parcel. 231 F.3d 1354 (Fed. Cir. 2000).

2. *Identifying the Denominator*. Courts have repeatedly stated that the entire parcel is to be viewed in determining the impact of a regulation, not just the most heavily regulated segment or a portion of the parcel rendered undevelopable. *Keystone Bituminous Coal Ass'n v. DeBenedictis*, 480 U.S. 470 (1987); *Penn Central Transportation Co. v. New York*, 438 U.S. 104 (1978); *Forest Properties, Inc. v. United States*, 177 F.3d 1360 (Fed. Cir. 1999), *cert. denied*, 528 U.S. 951 (1999) (finding the lake-bottom property at Big Bear Lake, together with the previously owned adjacent lake-front property, to constitute the denominator); *K & K Constr. v. Department of Natural Resources*, 575 N.W.2d 531 (Mich. 1998), *cert. denied*, 525 U.S. 819 (1998). In *K&K*, the court treated three parcels pooled for a wetlands development application as one parcel for the denominator. The court held that it should not divide land into segments and seek to determine whether rights in a particular segment have been entirely abrogated. Instead, the court should consider factors such as whether the parcels were contiguous, whether the same party owned all of them, and whether a comprehensive development plan for all parcels existed.

Did the Federal Circuit identify the correct denominator in *Palm Beach* and *Loveladies*? What was the most appropriate "parcel" for the *Lucas* "total loss" analysis? For a discussion of the various factors that might inform the denominator, *see* Marc R. Lisker, Regulatory Takings and the Denominator Problem, 27 Rutgers L.J. 663 (1996) (advocating a subjective rule starting with the landowner's definition of the relevant parcel but subject to modification by several factors such as state law, the avoidance of severance, and consideration of investment-backed expectations, economic viability, and unity of ownership). *See also* Benjamin Allee, Note, Drawing the Line in Regulatory Takings Law: How a Benefits Fraction Supports the Fee Simple Approach to the Denominator Problem, 70 Fordham L. Rev. 1957 (2002) (surveying alternative denominator calculations).

3. Florida Rock. In *Florida Rock Indus. v. United States*, 18 F.3d 1560 (Fed. Cir. 1994), *cert. denied*, 513 U.S. 1109 (1995), the Federal Circuit reviewed the Corps of Engineers' refusal to issue a permit to mine limestone beneath a tract of wetlands. The court found that the permit denial constituted less than a total loss of the value of the property. Nevertheless, the court appeared to apply *Lucas*, given the plaintiff's substantial loss of investment-backed expectations in exploiting the mineral rights.

The "substantial loss" modification of *Lucas* in *Florida Rock* is in tension with the statement in *Penn Central* that takings analysis should not segment the property but should view it as a whole to determine remaining use and value. The model of *Florida Rock* also seems inconsistent with *Palazzolo*'s holding that if a reasonable economic use is possible, the analysis should be under *Penn Central*. *See Rith Energy, Inc. v. United States*, 270 F.3d 1347 (Fed. Cir. 2001), *cert. denied*, 536 U.S. 958 (2002) (regulations suspending coal mining to prevent harmful runoff resulting in a 91 percent reduction in extractable coal caused a mere diminution of value and not a categorical regulatory taking). Chief Judge Nies dissented in *Florida Rock* on the ground that the gist of the majority opinion was to provide compensation for a mere diminution of value.

4. *Strategic Use of Lucas*. Consider the owner of land containing a stand of forest that serves as a habitat for an endangered spotted owl. If the owner conveyed all of the developable portions of the tract, ultimately just retaining the forest, would the owner have a *Lucas* cause of action if regulatory agencies denied a timber cutting permit? Should *Lucas* be modified to establish a "good faith" exception that prevents a finding of a taking where a parcel is subdivided, leaving a segment of the larger parcel unbuildable?

E. REMEDIES

Upon finding that a regulation has gone too far, what is the appropriate remedy? Regulators and environmentalists argue that the remedy should be to invalidate the law and remand for further administrative review. Landowners argue that, as in the case of other constitutional violations, damages are the appropriate remedy, since excessive regulation can be very costly to the landowner who wishes to develop the property. Is it possible for the Court to provide fairness for the landowner and, at the same time, sanction aggressive protection of the environment?

FIRST ENGLISH EVANGELICAL LUTHERAN CHURCH v. COUNTY OF LOS ANGELES

482 U.S. 304 (1987)

CHIEF JUSTICE REHNQUIST delivered the opinion of the Court.

In this case the California Court of Appeal held that a landowner who claims that his property has been "taken" by a land-use regulation may not recover damages for the time before it is finally determined that the regulation constitutes a "taking" of his property. We disagree. . . .

In 1957, appellant First English Evangelical Lutheran Church purchased a 21-acre parcel of land in a canyon along the banks of the Middle Fork of Mill Creek in the Angeles National Forest. The Middle Fork is the natural drainage channel for a watershed area owned by the National Forest Service. Twelve of the acres owned by the church are flat land, and contained a dining hall, two bunkhouses, a caretaker's lodge, an outdoor chapel, and a footbridge across the creek. The church operated on the site a campground, known as "Lutherglen," as a retreat center and a recreational area for handicapped children.

In July 1977, a forest fire denuded the hills upstream from Lutherglen, destroying approximately 3860 acres of the watershed area and creating a serious flood hazard. Such flooding occurred on February 9 and 10, 1978, when a storm dropped 11 inches of rain in the watershed. The runoff from the storm overflowed the banks of the Mill Creek, flooding Lutherglen and destroying its buildings.

In response to the flooding of the canyon, appellee County of Los Angeles adopted Interim Ordinance No. 11,855 in January 1979. The ordinance provided that "[a] person shall not construct, reconstruct, place or enlarge any building or structure, any portion of which is, or will be, located within the outer boundary lines of the interim flood protection area located in Mill Creek Canyon. . . . " The ordinance was effective immediately because the county determined that it was "required for the immediate preservation of the public health and safety. . . ." The interim flood protection area described by the ordinance included the flat areas on either side of Mill Creek on which Lutherglen had stood.

The church filed a complaint in the Superior Court of California a little more than a month after the ordinance was adopted. As subsequently amended, the complaint alleged two claims against the county and the Los Angeles County Flood Control District. The first alleged that the defendants were liable under Cal. Govt. Code Ann. §835 (West 1980) for dangerous conditions on their upstream properties that contributed to the flooding of Lutherglen. As a part of this claim, appellant also alleged that "Ordinance No. 11,855 denies [appellant] all use of Lutherglen." The second claim sought to recover from the Flood Control District in inverse condemnation and in tort for engaging in cloud seeding during the storm that flooded Lutherglen. Appellant sought damages under each count for loss of use of Lutherglen. The defendants moved to strike the portions of the complaint alleging that the county's ordinance denied all use of Lutherglen, on the view that the California Supreme Court's decision in *Agins v. Tiburon*, 598 P.2d 25 (1979), aff'd on other grounds, 447 U.S. 255 (1980), rendered the allegation "entirely immaterial and irrelevant[, with] no bearing upon any conceivable cause of action herein." . . .

In *Agins v. Tiburon, supra*, the California Supreme Court decided that a landowner may not maintain an inverse condemnation suit in the courts of that State based upon a "regulatory" taking. 24 Cal. 3d, at 275-277, 598 P.2d, at 29-31. . . . Under this decision, then, compensation is not required until the challenged regulation or ordinance has been held excessive in an action for declaratory relief or a writ of mandamus and the government has nevertheless decided to continue the regulation in effect. Based on this decision, the trial court in the present case granted the motion to strike the allegation that the church had been denied all use of Lutherglen. . . . Because the appellant alleged a regulatory taking and sought only damages, the allegation that the ordinance denied all use of Lutherglen was deemed irrelevant. . . .

II

Consideration of the compensation question must begin with direct reference to the language of the Fifth Amendment, which provides in relevant part that "private property [shall not] be taken for public use, without just compensation." As its language indicates, and as the Court has frequently noted, this provision does not prohibit the taking of private property, but instead places a condition on the exercise of that power. . . . This basic understanding of the Amendment makes clear that it is designed not to limit the governmental interference with property rights *per se*, but rather to secure *compensation* in the event of otherwise proper interference amounting to a taking. Thus, government action that works a taking of property rights necessarily implicates the "constitutional obligation to pay just compensation."

We have recognized that a landowner is entitled to bring an action in inverse condemnation as a result of " 'the self-executing character of the constitutional provision with respect to compensation. . . .' " . . .

While the California Supreme Court may not have actually disavowed this general rule in *Agins*, we believe that it has truncated the rule by disallowing damages that occurred prior to the ultimate invalidation of the challenged regulation. The California Supreme Court justified its conclusion at length in the *Agins* opinion, concluding that:

> In combination, the need for preserving a degree of freedom in the land- use planning function, and the inhibiting financial force which inheres in the inverse condemnation remedy, persuade us that on balance mandamus or declaratory relief rather than inverse condemnation is the appropriate relief under the circumstances.

We, of course, are not unmindful of these considerations, but they must be evaluated in the light of the command of the Just Compensation Clause of the Fifth Amendment. The Court has recognized in more than one case that the government may elect to abandon its intrusion or discontinue regulations. Similarly, a governmental body may acquiesce in a judicial declaration that one of its ordinances has effected an unconstitutional taking of property; the landowner has no right under the Just Compensation Clause to insist that a "temporary" taking be deemed a permanent taking. But we have not resolved whether abandonment by the government requires payment of compensation for the period of time during which regulations deny a landowner all use of his land. . . .

. . . In such cases compensation would be measured by the principles normally governing the taking of a right to use property temporarily. . . .

These cases reflect the fact that "temporary" takings which, as here, deny a landowner all use of his property, are not different in kind from permanent takings, for which the Constitution clearly requires compensation. . . . It is axiomatic that the Fifth Amendment's just compensation provision is "designed to bar Government from forcing some people alone to bear public burdens which, in all fairness and justice, should be borne by the public as a whole." In the present case the interim ordinance was adopted by the County of Los Angeles in January 1979, and became effective immediately. Appellant filed suit within a month after the effective date of the ordinance and yet when the California Supreme Court denied a hearing in the case on October 17, 1985, the merits of appellant's claim had yet to be determined. The United States has been required to pay compensation for leasehold interests of shorter duration than this. The value of a leasehold interest in property for a period of years may be substantial, and the burden on the property owner in extinguishing such an interest for a period of years may be great indeed. Where this burden results from governmental action that amounted to a taking, the Just Compensation Clause of the Fifth Amendment requires that the government pay the landowner for the value of the use of the land during this period. . . .

. . . Once a court determines that a taking has occurred, the government retains the whole range of options already available—amendment of the regulation, withdrawal of the invalidated regulation, or exercise of eminent domain. Thus we do not, as the Solicitor General suggests, "permit a court, at the behest of a private person, to require the . . . Government to exercise the power of eminent domain. . . . " We merely hold that where the government's activities have already worked a taking of all use of property, no subsequent action by the government can relieve it of the duty to provide compensation for the period during which the taking was effective. . . .

. . . We realize that even our present holding will undoubtedly lessen to some extent the freedom and flexibility of land-use planners and governing bodies of municipal corporations when enacting land-use regulations. But such consequences necessarily flow from any decision upholding a claim of constitutional right; many of the provisions of the Constitution are designed to limit the flexibility and freedom of governmental authorities, and the Just Compensation Clause of the Fifth Amendment is one of them. As Justice Holmes aptly noted more than 50 years ago, "a strong public desire to improve the public condition is not enough to warrant achieving the desire by a shorter cut than the constitutional way of paying for the change." *Pennsylvania Coal Co. v. Mahon.*

Notes and Comments

1. *Reaching the Remedy Issue*. Did the moratorium in *First English* constitute a taking? Was the decision directed to the determination of the presence of a taking, or simply to the striking of damages as a remedy for a regulatory taking under state law?

On remand the state court failed to find a compensatory taking. *First English Evangelical Lutheran Church v. County of Los Angeles*, 258 Cal. Rptr. 893 (Ct. App. 1989), *cert. denied*, 493 U.S. 1056 (1990). Does that outcome surprise you? Given that outcome, was it appropriate for the Supreme Court in *First English* to decide the remedy issue?

2. *Definitional Uncertainty and Its Consequences*. Is it fair to impose the authority, indeed, the obligation, upon government to regulate for the public welfare and to protect the environment, and then to expose government to damage liability when takings law seems unable to objectively define a compensable taking? An alternative strategy is to insure. Douglas Kendall and Matthew Garvey, Successfully Defending Your Takings Challenges: Municipal Insurance Pools, 53 Land Use L. & Zoning Dig. 3 (Jan. 2001).

3. First English *Strategies*. Consider a situation in which a landowner, having unsuccessfully sought approval for its development during legislative or administrative processes before the local government, brings a takings claim under *First English* as a means of forcing further negotiations. The specter of damages for a temporary taking under *First English* may mean that the agency determines to compromise. Thus, the settlement of the matter, which gives the plaintiff certain rights to develop, may take place out of the normal eye of public scrutiny. What are the ethical dimensions of instituting litigation to force such negotiations? Does your conclusion about the ethical correctness of the behavior depend on the motive of the attorney or the strength of the taking claim?

4. *Measuring Damages I*. The measure of damages for a temporary taking can raise some knotty problems. Initially, of course, the plaintiff has to prove that he or she was deprived of all economically viable use of the property. In *Brown v. Legal Foundation of Washington*, — U.S. —, 123 S. Ct. 1406 (2003), the Supreme Court, in a non-land-use case, noted that the pecuniary compensation under the takings clause must be measured by the landowner's net losses rather than by the value of the public's gain. *See also MC Associates v. Town of Cape Elizabeth*, 773 A.2d 439, 445 (Me. 2001) ("The appraisal does not even purport to establish the value of the lot prior to the alleged taking, nor does it address whether the lot retains

substantial uses other than to support a single family residence"). The plaintiff must also prove, as in any other damages case, that the defendant caused the injury. Thus, in *Lost Tree Village Corp. v. City of Vero Beach*, 838 So. 2d 561 (Fla. Ct. App. 2002), the combined effect of city and town ordinances caused a taking.

Is the appropriate measure of damages the market value of the parcel without the offending regulation less the value of the parcel as regulated? One court thought so but later vacated its opinion. *Resolution Trust Corp. v. Town of Highland Beach*, 18 F.3d 1536, *vacated en banc*, 42 F.3d 626 (11th Cir. 1994). Should the court instead award the lost profits or rental income that would reasonably have been derived between the time that the landowner sought development and the time of judgment? Should the current regulated value be compared with the unregulated value or the value of the parcel subject to the greatest level of constitutionally permissible regulation? Should the regulating unit of government be required to elect to pay permanent damages or temporary damages together with invalidation of the offending regulation? *See SDDS, Inc. v. State of South Dakota*, 650 N.W.2d 1, 14 (S.D. 2002) (noting that "[v]arious methods for calculating compensation for temporary takings have been created," including fair rental value, option value, interest on lost profit, before and after valuation, market rate of return, and the "equity interest" approach).

In *Sintra, Inc. v. City of Seattle*, 935 P.2d 555 (Wash. 1997), the Washington Supreme Court held that a temporary regulatory taking allows recovery of simple interest on value taken, despite the general rule that, under 42 U.S.C. §1983, cities are immune from prejudgment interest, as the interest is part of the compensation. The court held that compound interest may be awarded if the landowner demonstrates that simple interest would not offer just compensation.

Under Massachusetts law, a landowner is entitled to a refund of property taxes for the period in which the property was taken. *Lopes v. City of Peabody*, 717 N.E.2d 846, 852 (Mass. 1999) ("Because one hundred percent of the value of Lopes's land was taken for fourteen years, principles of basic fairness compel the same type of refund of property taxes that he would receive if his land had been permanently taken [through an action in eminent domain]").

5. *Measuring Damages II*. As *First English* makes clear, the agency may decide to rescind its regulation, thus rendering the taking a "temporary" one. What if, instead of an affirmative action (e.g., a zoning ordinance) imposing the taking, the government simply denies a permit. How would it act to render the taking temporary? What if the landowner simply decided not to reapply, thereby hoping that the taking remained permanent?

In *Cooley v. United States*, 324 F.3d 1297 (Fed. Cir. 2003), the Corps of Engineers was found to have effected a taking by denying a wetlands permit. Attempting to cut off its damages, the agency then issued a "Provisional Permit" to the plaintiff. The court held that, "[i]f the Corps actually granted Cooley a valid permit permitting development, the government has firm grounds to assert that any taking was only temporary." *Id.* at 1305. Note that, in this kind of situation, the landowner may actually find himself or herself opposing such a permit, if the landowner would prefer to receive compensation for a permanent taking.

6. *Trial by Jury?* In *City of Monterey v. Del Monte Dunes*, 526 U.S. 687 (1999), the United States Supreme Court ruled that liability and valuation issues in excessive regulatory taking claims may be submitted to a jury, at least on "the predominantly factual issue" of whether a land use decision substantially advances a legitimate

governmental interest. The ruling, however, apparently will have limited impact. *See, e.g., Buckles v. King County*, 191 F.3d 1127, 1141 (9th Cir. 1999) (observing that "[f]rankly, we have some difficulty parsing the distinctions laid out by the Supreme Court concerning when a jury trial is required"). One interpretation is that it is restricted to cases such as *Del Monte Dunes*, where the state, at the time of the regulation, lacked a state procedure for recovering in inverse condemnation. As California now has an inverse condemnation remedy, the ruling would have no impact there or in the majority of jurisdictions that have adopted such remedies. To date, courts have not widely held jury trials in inverse condemnation cases. *See, e.g., Cumberland Farms v. Town of Groton*, 808 A.2d 1107 (Conn. 2002) (no right to jury trial in inverse condemnation case); Robert H. Freilich and Jason M. Divilbiss, The Public Interest is Vindicated: *City of Monterey v. Del Monte Dunes*, 31 Urb. Law. 371 (1999); Robert S. Payne, The Current State of Regulatory Takings in Supreme Court Jurisprudence: A Look at *City of Monterey v. Del Monte Dunes at Monterey, Ltd.*, 11 Vill. Envtl. L.J. 349 (2000).

7. *Takings Legislation*. While judge-made law dominates the takings field, since *First English* the increasing political power supporting landowner rights has generated many federal and state legislative efforts. The initiatives address a wide range of issues. For example, in Washington the state attorney general is to issue regulations assisting local governments in evaluating regulatory actions so as to avoid takings. Wash. Rev. Code §36.70A.370 (Supp. 2002). California has passed legislation providing that successful plaintiffs in inverse condemnation actions may recover costs and attorney's fees for trial and appeals. Cal. Civ. Proc. Code §1036 (West 1980 & Supp. 2002).

8. *Literature*. On the subject of takings legislation, see, e.g., David A. Thomas, The Illusory Restraints and Empty Promises of New Property Protection Laws, 28 Urb. Law. 223 (1996) (takings jurisprudence and practice not yet restrained by legislation). See also John Martinez, Statutes Enacting Takings Law: Flying in the Face of Uncertainty, 26 Urb. Law. 327 (1994); Richard L. Settle, J. Taylor Washburn, & Charles R. Wolfe, Washington State Regulatory Reform: Jekyll and Hyde '95, 47 Land Use L. & Zoning Dig. 3 (Sept. 1995) (economic impact studies now required as well as enhanced opportunities for takings compensation under Proposition 164); Lazos Vargas, Florida's Property Rights Act: A Political Quick Fix Results in a Mixed Bag of Tricks, 23 Fla. St. U.L. Rev. 315 (1995); Christian Brooks, Comment, Political Bluff and Bluster: Six Years Later, A Comment on the Texas Private Real Property Rights Preservation Act, 33 Tex. Tech. L. Rev. 59 (2001). But see Robert H. Freilich & RoxAnne Doyle, Taking Legislation: Misguided and Dangerous, 46 Land Use L. & Zoning Dig. 3 (Oct. 1994).

8

The First Amendment: Free Speech and Freedom of Religion

A. INTRODUCTION

The First Amendment is a powerful weapon in challenging land use regulation. Such regulation can touch on freedom of expression or freedom of religion in a myriad of contexts, ranging from the zoning of adult entertainment to the application of historic preservation laws to houses of worship. Since the law of the First Amendment is complex, a knowledge of basic First Amendment principles is essential to understanding and analyzing those land use cases that touch on them, as well as to advising clients on constitutional obligations. Accordingly, the introduction to this chapter begins with a brief primer on First Amendment law.

1. Some First Amendment Principles

The First Amendment to the United States Constitution declares, "Congress shall make no law respecting an establishment of religion, or prohibiting the free exercise thereof; or abridging the freedom of speech, or of the press; or the right of the people peaceably to assemble, and to petition the Government for a redress of grievances." Few legal concepts are as simple to state yet as complex in interpretation as freedom of speech. The complexity of interpretation in part stems from its evolution over generations. The First Amendment has been applied and interpreted during times of national fear as well as during times of peace, during times of both liberal and conservative political leadership, and during times in which the interpretative philosophies of the judiciary have changed markedly.

The Supreme Court has frequently spoken of the freedom of speech as a matter of both the content of speech and the context in which it is uttered. *Schenck v. United States*, 249 U.S. 47 (1919). Thus, certain speech, based on its content, might receive constitutional protection when uttered in one context but not in another. A book containing passages depicting explicit sex may be protected and beyond regulation. In contrast, screening a toned-down film adaptation of that book may result in a criminal prosecution in some jurisdictions or may be subject to zoning that restricts the location of screenings.

Similarly, speech that is innocuous and inoffensive may nevertheless be prohibited because of the context in which it is being uttered. Demonstrators supporting term limits on legislators' terms cannot march down Main Street at the same time that demonstrators opposing such term limits are marching up Main Street. The first group may be awarded a permit, and the second asked to march elsewhere, or at a different time. A political poster containing sexual innuendo may be protected in a museum or on a billboard, but it can be excluded from a public school. *See Bethel School District No. 403 v. Fraser*, 478 U.S. 675 (1986) (school may suspend high school student for use of sexually suggestive language in political speech).

In general, regulation tends to be suspect and likely to be invalidated where the target of the regulation is the message of the speaker. *Cincinnati v. Discovery Network, Inc.*, 507 U.S. 410 (1993) (newsrack ordinance distinguishing commercial publications held invalid). However, where the motive of regulation is not the message of the speaker but other legitimate governmental interests, the regulation is likely to be sustained. *Turner v. Safley*, 482 U.S. 78 (1987) (security concerns support a bar on most inmate-to-inmate mail correspondence).

2. Categories of Speech and Content-Based Regulation

Speech may also be regulated based upon its content. Freedom of expression litigation has always focused on balancing the interests of the speaker and a free society against significant government interests. Historically, the problem has been that the balancing process can be extremely subjective.

The Supreme Court has taken a middle ground between the subjectivity of balancing and the objectivity of an absolute test, using an approach referred to as "definitional balancing." Melville Nimmer, The Right to Speak from Times to Time, 56 Cal. L. Rev. 935 (1968). Under definitional balancing, for each type of expression the Court has developed a test that is designed to reduce subjectivity and protect the values of free expression, yet permit reasonable regulation to advance important government interests. Of course, critics would charge that freedom of speech has been sacrificed or that its protection has damaged our security and quality of life, and that the developed tests retain a broad subjectivity.

To regulate speech that advocates illegal activities, the Supreme Court has required that the speech must be directed toward producing imminent illegal activity and that the illegal activity is likely to occur. *Brandenburg v. Ohio*, 395 U.S. 444 (1969). Similarly, "fighting words"—speech that is likely to be responded to with violence—are unprotected. *Chaplinsky v. New Hampshire*, 315 U.S. 568

(1942). Defamation (words that inflict injury due to their falsity) is not protected if the speaker has actual knowledge of the falsity or has uttered them with reckless disregard for the truth. *New York Times v. Sullivan*, 376 U.S. 254 (1964). Pornography may be punishable as obscenity depending on whether (1) the average person, applying contemporary community standards, would find that the work, taken as a whole, appeals to the prurient interest; (2) the work depicts or describes, in a patently offensive way, sexual conduct specifically defined by the applicable state law; and (3) the work, taken as a whole, lacks serious literary, artistic, political, or scientific value. *Miller v. California*, 413 U.S. 15 (1973). Commercial speech, i.e., speech that offers goods or services for sale, applies still another set of tests that are discussed below.

3. *Equal Protection: An Alternative Model in the Expression Context*

On occasion, the Court has utilized the Equal Protection Clause to vindicate expression claims, particularly where the government has engaged in content discrimination in suppressing particular messages. For example, this standard would apply where the government prohibits picketing (except for labor picketing). Because speech is a fundamental right, the Court applies strict scrutiny, requiring a compelling state interest and the absence of a less restrictive alternative. *Police Department v. Mosley*, 408 U.S. 92 (1972), *followed*, *Carey v. Brown*, 447 U.S. 455 (1980).

At one time the Supreme Court resolved novel expression claims with the doctrine of "clear and present danger," balancing the interests of free expression with the government's interest. Since *Mosley*, however, the Court has replaced the "clear and present danger" test with an equal-protection-based standard. It now requires a compelling state interest and a lack of less restrictive alternatives to uphold regulation of protected speech. *Denver Area Education Tellecommunications Consortium, Inc. v. FCC*, 518 U.S. 727 (1996); *Texas v. Johnson*, 491 U.S. 397 (1989); *Perry Education Ass'n v. Perry Local Educators' Ass'n*, 460 U.S. 37 (1983).

4. *Land Use Controls and the First Amendment*

Land use controls frequently affect the ability to communicate, and thus pose First Amendment issues. A principal area of conflict with the First Amendment is in the regulation of adult entertainment. Is regulation of adult movie theaters, book stores, or topless bars a type of content-based discrimination? Another area of conflict concerns billboards and newsracks. How might the First Amendment limit a community's efforts to achieve aesthetic excellence in part through the removal and prohibition of signs and billboards? How can a community deal with the perceived ugliness of proliferating newsracks?

These are the questions addressed in this chapter. Chapter 13, discussing discrimination in housing, also raises questions about the First Amendment rights of those who may protest and oppose housing developed for protected minorities. Additionally, Chapter 17 will address the subject of aesthetic and architectural controls that can directly or indirectly affect expressive activity.

B. ADULT USE ZONING

Must cities allow adult movie theaters to proliferate because of the First Amendment? Must cities zone a reasonable number of sites to accommodate adult film exhibition?

A Note on *City of Renton v. Playtime Theaters*

In *City of Renton v. Playtime Theaters, Inc.*, 475 U.S. 41 (1985), the United States Supreme Court endorsed the zoning of adult movie theaters. The Renton City Council adopted a moratorium on the establishment of businesses designed to sell, rent, or exhibit adult materials and referred the subject to its planning and development committee. The committee studied reports from Seattle that looked to that city's experience. Those studies, framed largely in response to the United States Supreme Court's earlier ruling in *Young v. American Mini Theaters, Inc.*, 427 U.S. 50 (1976), discussed what are referred to as "secondary impacts" of such theaters, e.g., effects such as crime or neighborhood deterioration. *Young* had sustained a Detroit ordinance that had dispersed uses of this type, prohibiting one use within 1,000 feet from another such use or within 500 feet of a residential zone. Seattle, based on its studies, had elected to disperse such uses under a Detroit-like ordinance.

Renton then adopted an ordinance that permitted the concentration of such uses rather than their dispersal, requiring that they be located 1,000 feet from any school or residential district. Other municipalities, dealing with areas such as Boston's "Combat Zone" or Baltimore's former "Block," concentrated adult uses within a single district.

The Court's decision in *Renton* has several important doctrinal themes. First, it revisited the issue of whether the zoning of adult theaters was a valid time, place, and manner regulation. Conceptually, the zoning turns on the content of the films exhibited, and a principal element of the time, place, manner doctrine is that the regulation must be content neutral. The Court has developed two exceptions to the traditional time, place, and manner doctrine to allow additional content-based regulation. The first exception is found in *FCC v. Pacifica*, 438 U.S. 726 (1978), in which the Court upheld restrictions on the broadcasting of indecent materials. In that case, which involved the classic George Carlin comedy monologue of the "seven dirty words," the Court indicated that the true evil in content-based discrimination was "viewpoint" bias rather than content sensitivity.

Young adopted the rather unique exception that adult zoning is not to be judged solely by traditional time, place, and manner doctrine because the motive for the regulation was not directed at the content of the films but at the "secondary effects" of the land uses. The Court followed this exception in *Renton*.

A second point in *Renton* is that the city was not required to study its own community and establish a record supporting the rationality of its regulation. Instead, it could base its restrictions on studies in other communities. This part of its holding is at odds with the typical state law requirement that zoning must be based on comprehensive planning that studies local conditions. The Supreme Court also found it irrelevant that the City of Renton, basing its ordinance on Seattle's investigation, nonetheless chose a different strategy to deal with secondary effects.

A third important theme of *Renton* is its focus on the obligation of a community's zoning to afford an adequate opportunity for the use to be developed. In

Renton, the City emphasized that 520 acres, or 5 percent of the City, was zoned to permit adult theaters. The respondent argued that much of the land was already occupied by other businesses and that practically none of the zoned land was currently for sale or lease, with no commercially viable theater sites. The Court, however, found that the First Amendment does not compel the government to ensure that adult theaters or other forms of speech-related businesses will be able to obtain sites at bargain prices.

In the following case, the Court revisits the secondary effects doctrine of *Renton*.

CITY OF LOS ANGELES v. ALAMEDA BOOKS, INC.

535 U.S. 425 (2002)

Justice O'CONNOR announced the judgment of the Court and delivered an opinion, in which The Chief Justice, Justice SCALIA, and Justice THOMAS join. . . .

I

In 1977, the city of Los Angeles conducted a comprehensive study of adult establishments and concluded that concentrations of adult businesses are associated with higher rates of prostitution, robbery, assaults, and thefts in surrounding communities. Accordingly, the city enacted an ordinance prohibiting the establishment, substantial enlargement, or transfer of ownership of an adult arcade, bookstore, cabaret, motel, theater, or massage parlor or a place for sexual encounters within 1,000 feet of another such enterprise or within 500 feet of any religious institution, school, or public park.

There is evidence that the intent of the city council when enacting this prohibition was not only to disperse distinct adult establishments housed in separate buildings, but also to disperse distinct adult businesses operated under common ownership and housed in a single structure. The ordinance the city enacted, however, directed that "[t]he distance between any two adult entertainment businesses shall be measured in a straight line . . . from the closest exterior structural wall of each business." Subsequent to enactment, the city realized that this method of calculating distances created a loophole permitting the concentration of multiple adult enterprises in a single structure.

Concerned that allowing an adult-oriented department store to replace a strip of adult establishments could defeat the goal of the original ordinance, the city council amended §12.70(C) by adding a prohibition on "the establishment or maintenance of more than one adult entertainment business in the same building, structure or portion thereof." . . .

Respondents, Alameda Books, Inc., and Highland Books, Inc., are two adult establishments operating in Los Angeles. Neither is located within 1,000 feet of another adult establishment or 500 feet of any religious institution, public park, or school. Each establishment occupies less than 3,000 square feet. Both respondents rent and sell sexually oriented products, including videocassettes. Additionally, both provide booths where patrons can view videocassettes for a fee. Although respondents are located in different buildings, each operates its retail sales and rental operations in the same commercial space in which its video booths are located. There are no physical distinctions between the different operations within each establishment and each establishment has only one entrance. . . .

II

In *Renton v. Playtime Theatres, Inc.*, [475 U.S. 41 (1986)], this Court considered the validity of a municipal ordinance that prohibited any adult movie theater from locating within 1,000 feet of any residential zone, family dwelling, church, park, or school. Our analysis of the ordinance proceeded in three steps. First, we found that the ordinance did not ban adult theaters altogether, but merely required that they be distanced from certain sensitive locations. The ordinance was properly analyzed, therefore, as a time, place, and manner regulation. We next considered whether the ordinance was content neutral or content based. If the regulation were content based, it would be considered presumptively invalid and subject to strict scrutiny. We held, however, that the Renton ordinance was aimed not at the content of the films shown at adult theaters, but rather at the secondary effects of such theaters on the surrounding community, namely at crime rates, property values, and the quality of the city's neighborhoods. Therefore, the ordinance was deemed content neutral. Finally, given this finding, we stated that the ordinance would be upheld so long as the city of Renton showed that its ordinance was designed to serve a substantial government interest and that reasonable alternative avenues of communication remained available. We concluded that Renton had met this burden, and we upheld its ordinance.

The Court of Appeals applied the same analysis to evaluate the Los Angeles ordinance challenged in this case. First, the Court of Appeals found that the Los Angeles ordinance was not a complete ban on adult entertainment establishments, but rather a sort of adult zoning regulation, which *Renton* considered a time, place, and manner regulation. The Court of Appeals turned to the second step of the *Renton* analysis, but did not draw any conclusions about whether the Los Angeles ordinance was content based. It explained that, even if the Los Angeles ordinance were content neutral, the city had failed to demonstrate, as required by the third step of the *Renton* analysis, that its prohibition on multiple-use adult establishments was designed to serve its substantial interest in reducing crime. The Court of Appeals noted that the primary evidence relied upon by Los Angeles to demonstrate a link between combination adult businesses and harmful secondary effects was the 1977 study conducted by the city's planning department. The Court of Appeals found, however, that the city could not rely on that study because it did not "suppor[t] a reasonable belief that [the] combination [of] businesses . . . produced harmful secondary effects of the type asserted." . . .

The central component of the 1977 study is a report on city crime patterns provided by the Los Angeles Police Department. That report indicated that, during the period from 1965 to 1975, certain crime rates grew much faster in Hollywood, which had the largest concentration of adult establishments in the city, than in the city of Los Angeles as a whole. For example, robberies increased 3 times faster and prostitution 15 times faster in Hollywood than citywide.

The 1977 study also contains reports conducted directly by the staff of the Los Angeles Planning Department that examine the relationship between adult establishments and property values. These staff reports, however, are inconclusive. Not surprisingly, the parties focus their dispute before this Court on the report by the Los Angeles Police Department. Because we find that reducing crime is a substantial government interest and that the police department report's conclusions regarding crime patterns may reasonably be relied upon to overcome summary judgment against the city, we also focus on the portion of the 1977 study drawn from the police department report.

The Court of Appeals found that the 1977 study did not reasonably support the inference that a concentration of adult operations within a single adult establishment produced greater levels of criminal activity because the study focused on the effect that a concentration of establishments — not a concentration of operations within a single establishment — had on crime rates. The Court of Appeals pointed out that the study treated combination adult bookstore/arcades as single establishments and did not study the effect of any separate-standing adult bookstore or arcade.

The Court of Appeals misunderstood the implications of the 1977 study. While the study reveals that areas with high concentrations of adult establishments are associated with high crime rates, areas with high concentrations of adult establishments are also areas with high concentrations of adult operations, albeit each in separate establishments. It was therefore consistent with the findings of the 1977 study, and thus reasonable, for Los Angeles to suppose that a concentration of adult establishments is correlated with high crime rates because a concentration of operations in one locale draws, for example, a greater concentration of adult consumers to the neighborhood, and a high density of such consumers either attracts or generates criminal activity. The assumption behind this theory is that having a number of adult operations in one single adult establishment draws the same dense foot traffic as having a number of distinct adult establishments in close proximity, much as minimalls and department stores similarly attract the crowds of consumers. Under this view, it is rational for the city to infer that reducing the concentration of adult operations in a neighborhood, whether within separate establishments or in one large establishment, will reduce crime rates.

Neither the Court of Appeals, nor respondents, nor the dissent provides any reason to question the city's theory. In particular, they do not offer a competing theory, let alone data, that explains why the elevated crime rates in neighborhoods with a concentration of adult establishments can be attributed entirely to the presence of permanent walls between, and separate entrances to, each individual adult operation. While the city certainly bears the burden of providing evidence that supports a link between concentrations of adult operations and asserted secondary effects, it does not bear the burden of providing evidence that rules out every theory for the link between concentrations of adult establishments that is inconsistent with its own.

The error that the Court of Appeals made is that it required the city to prove that its theory about a concentration of adult operations attracting crowds of customers, much like a minimall or department store does, is a necessary consequence of the 1977 study. For example, the Court of Appeals refused to allow the city to draw the inference that "the expansion of an adult bookstore to include an adult arcade would increase" business activity and "produce the harmful secondary effects identified in the Study." 222 F. 3d, at 726. It reasoned that such an inference would justify limits on the inventory of an adult bookstore, not a ban on the combination of an adult bookstore and an adult arcade. The Court of Appeals simply replaced the city's theory—that having many different operations in close proximity attracts crowds—with its own—that the size of an operation attracts crowds. If the Court of Appeals' theory is correct, then inventory limits make more sense. If the city's theory is correct, then a prohibition on the combination of businesses makes more sense. Both theories are consistent with the data in the 1977 study. The Court of Appeals' analysis, however, implicitly requires the city to prove that its theory is the only one that can plausibly explain the data because only in this manner can the city refute the Court of Appeals' logic.

Respondents make the same logical error as the Court of Appeals when they suggest that the city's prohibition on multiuse establishments will raise crime rates in certain neighborhoods because it will force certain adult businesses to relocate to areas without any other adult businesses. Respondents' claim assumes that the 1977 study proves that all adult businesses, whether or not they are located near other adult businesses, generate crime. This is a plausible reading of the results from the 1977 study, but respondents do not demonstrate that it is a compelled reading. Nor do they provide evidence that refutes the city's interpretation of the study, under which the city's prohibition should on balance reduce crime. If this Court were nevertheless to accept respondents' speculation, it would effectively require that the city provide evidence that not only supports the claim that its ordinance serves an important government interest, but also does not provide support for any other approach to serve that interest.

In *Renton*, we specifically refused to set such a high bar for municipalities that want to address merely the secondary effects of protected speech. We held that a municipality may rely on any evidence that is "reasonably believed to be relevant" for demonstrating a connection between speech and a substantial, independent government interest. . . . This is not to say that a municipality can get away with shoddy data or reasoning. The municipality's evidence must fairly support the municipality's rationale for its ordinance. If plaintiffs fail to cast direct doubt on this rationale, either by demonstrating that the municipality's evidence does not support its rationale or by furnishing evidence that disputes the municipality's factual findings, the municipality meets the standard set forth in *Renton*. If plaintiffs succeed in casting doubt on a municipality's rationale in either manner, the burden shifts back to the municipality to supplement the record with evidence renewing support for a theory that justifies its ordinance. This case is at a very early stage in this process. It arrives on a summary judgment motion by respondents defended only by complaints that the 1977 study fails to prove that the city's justification for its ordinance is necessarily correct. Therefore, we conclude that the city, at this stage of the litigation, has complied with the evidentiary requirement in *Renton*. . . .

Our deference to the evidence presented by the city of Los Angeles is the product of a careful balance between competing interests. On the one hand, we have an "obligation to exercise independent judgment when First Amendment rights are implicated." . . . On the other hand, we must acknowledge that the Los Angeles City Council is in a better position than the Judiciary to gather and evaluate data on local problems. We are also guided by the fact that *Renton* requires that municipal ordinances receive only intermediate scrutiny if they are content neutral. There is less reason to be concerned that municipalities will use these ordinances to discriminate against unpopular speech. . . .

Justice SCALIA, concurring. . . .

First Amendment traditions make "secondary effects" analysis quite unnecessary. The Constitution does not prevent those communities that wish to do so from regulating, or indeed entirely suppressing, the business of pandering sex.

Justice KENNEDY, concurring in the judgment. . . .

I . . .

The ordinance may be a covert attack on speech, but we should not presume it to be so. In the language of our First Amendment doctrine it calls for intermediate and not strict scrutiny, as we held in *Renton*. . . .

The plurality's analysis does not address how speech will fare under the city's ordinance. As discussed, the necessary rationale for applying intermediate scrutiny is the promise that zoning ordinances like this one may reduce the costs of secondary effects without substantially reducing speech. For this reason, it does not suffice to say that inconvenience will reduce demand and fewer patrons will lead to fewer secondary effects. . . .

The analysis requires a few more steps. If two adult business are under the same roof, an ordinance requiring them to separate will have one of two results: One business will either move elsewhere or close. The city's premise cannot be the latter. It is true that cutting adult speech in half would probably reduce secondary effects proportionately. But again, a promised proportional reduction does not suffice. Content-based taxes could achieve that, yet these are impermissible.

The premise, therefore, must be that businesses — even those that have always been under one roof — will for the most part disperse rather than shut down. True, this premise has its own conundrum. As JUSTICE SOUTER writes, "[t]he city . . . claims no interest in the proliferation of adult businesses." The claim, therefore, must be that this ordinance will cause two businesses to split rather than one to close, that the quantity of speech will be substantially undiminished, and that total secondary effects will be significantly reduced. This must be the rationale of a dispersal statute. . . .

In this case the proposition to be shown is supported by a single study and common experience. The city's study shows a correlation between the concentration of adult establishments and crime. Two or more adult businesses in close proximity seem to attract a critical mass of unsavory characters and the crime rate may increase as a result. The city, therefore, sought to disperse these businesses. Los Angeles Municipal Code §12.70(C) (1983), as amended. This original ordinance is not challenged here, and we may assume that it is constitutional.

If we assume that the study supports the original ordinance, then most of the necessary analysis follows. We may posit that two adult stores next door to each other attract 100 patrons per day. The two businesses split apart might attract 49 patrons each. (Two patrons, perhaps, will be discouraged by the inconvenience of the separation — a relatively small cost to speech). On the other hand, the reduction in secondary effects might be dramatic, because secondary effects may require a critical mass. Depending on the economics of vice, 100 potential customers/victims might attract a coterie of thieves, prostitutes, and other ne'er-do-wells; yet 49 might attract none at all. If so, a dispersal ordinance would cause a great reduction in secondary effects at very small cost to speech. Indeed, the very absence of secondary effects might increase the audience for the speech; perhaps for every two people who are discouraged by the inconvenience of two-stop shopping, another two are encouraged by hospitable surroundings. In that case, secondary effects might be eliminated at no cost to speech whatsoever, and both the city and the speaker will have their interests well served.

Only one small step remains to justify the ordinance at issue in this case. The city may next infer — from its study and from its own experience — that two adult businesses under the same roof are no better than two next door. The city could reach the reasonable conclusion that knocking down the wall between two adult businesses does not ameliorate any undesirable secondary effects of their proximity to one another. If the city's first ordinance was justified, therefore, then the second is too. Dispersing two adult businesses under one roof is reasonably likely to cause a substantial reduction in secondary effects while reducing speech very little. . . .

Justice SOUTER, with whom Justice STEVENS and Justice GINSBURG join, and with whom Justice BREYER joins as to Part II, dissenting. . . .

I

This ordinance stands or falls on the results of what our cases speak of as intermediate scrutiny, generally contrasted with the demanding standard applied under the First Amendment to a content-based regulation of expression. . . .

[T]he lesser scrutiny applied to content-correlated zoning restrictions is no excuse for a government's failure to provide a factual demonstration for claims it makes about secondary effects; on the contrary, this is what demands the demonstration. In this case, however, the government has not shown that bookstores containing viewing booths, isolated from other adult establishments, increase crime or produce other negative secondary effects in surrounding neighborhoods, and we are thus left without substantial justification for viewing the city's First Amendment restriction as content correlated but not simply content based. By the same token, the city has failed to show any causal relationship between the breakup policy and elimination or regulation of secondary effects. . . .

II . . .

[T]he city apparently assumes that a bookstore selling videos and providing viewing booths produces secondary effects of crime, and more crime than would result from having a single store without booths in one part of town and a video arcade in another. But the city neither says this in so many words nor proffers any evidence to support even the simple proposition that an otherwise lawfully located adult bookstore combined with video booths will produce any criminal effects. . . .

Notes and Comments

1. *The Basis for the Los Angeles Ordinance*. Was the reliance by the City of Los Angeles on its crime statistics or the reliance by the City of Renton on the Seattle experience with adult theater zoning reasonable? Is it significant that Renton adopted a concentration ordinance while Seattle adopted a dispersal strategy? Why is the Court so deferential to the City's ordinance?

2. *Licensing of Adult Businesses*. Communities frequently impose licensing obligations on adult businesses. *FW/PBS, Inc. v. City of Dallas*, 493 U.S. 215 (1990)

(procedures must avoid undue delay); Alan C. Weinstein, Licensing Ordinances as an Adjunct to Zoning Regulation of Sexually-Oriented Adult Businesses (Parts I & II), 22 Zoning & Plan. L. Rep. 1, 17 (1999). *See also* Scott D. Bergthold, How to Avoid the Top Ten Pitfalls of Adult Business Regulation (Parts I & II), 54 Land Use L. & Zoning Dig. 3 (May & June 2002) (include fixed decisionmaking timetables, scienter, and narrowly tailored inspection, and avoid unbridled discretion).

3. *Planning for Adult Businesses.* As we have seen above in this casebook, states authorize zoning based upon a comprehensive planning process. Did Renton or Los Angeles engage in any scientific planning in adopting their ordinances? In *Chambers v. Peach County*, 467 S.E.2d 519 (Ga. 1996), the Georgia Supreme Court overturned an adult entertainment ordinance that required a permit and county approval of employees and the site. The law also regulated conduct between patrons and exotic dancers, and it prohibited exotic dancing where intoxicating beverages were sold on the premises. The court concluded that the regulated actions were expressive conduct and that the county failed to demonstrate that the law advanced an important interest. In particular, the county produced no evidence of increased crime or neighborhood deterioration that might justify the ordinance.

Most other jurisdictions have become much more sophisticated in compiling the kind of evidence that will support an ordinance regulating adult businesses. *Compare DiRaimo v. City of Providence*, 714 A.2d 554 (R.I. 1998) (adopting trial court opinion noting that the staff "turned to the planning advisory service of the American Planning Association, which seems to be a clearinghouse of research material for members of the profession" and detailing the various reports that the staff reviewed from throughout the country). Must this evidence be compiled in a "legislative record" before the local government prior to the adoption, or is post-enactment evidence filed in court sufficient to support the zoning ordinance? *See Phillips v. Borough of Keyport*, 107 F.3d 164 (3d Cir. 1997) (en banc) (post-enactment evidence is sufficient).

Despite the deference displayed in *Renton* and *Alameda Books*, it is possible to challenge secondary effects studies. For a survey of most or all available secondary effects studies, finding that those using credible methods disprove the existence of any secondary effects from adult entertainment, *see* Bryant Paul, Daniel Linz & Bradley J. Shafer, Government Regulation of "Adult" Businesses Through Zoning and Anti-Nudity Ordinances: Debunking the Legal Myth of Negative Secondary Effects, 6 Comm. L. & Pol'y 355 (2001). The Eleventh Circuit rejected enforcement of an alcohol-free adult entertainment ordinance where the statistics actually demonstrated higher crime problems in non-adult entertainment bars. *Flanigan's Enters., Inc. Fulton County*, 242 F.3d 976 (11th Cir. 2001), *cert. denied*, 122 S. Ct. 2356 (2002). Would the Court permit the state legislature to enact a statewide adult entertainment zoning law based on secondary impact studies in various cities? New Jersey has established a 1,000-foot buffer requirement separating adult entertainment from residential districts, schools, and playgrounds. N.J. Stat. Ann. §2C:34-7 (West Supp. 2000); *see Township of Saddle Brook v. A.B. Family Ctr., Inc.*, 704 A.2d 81 (N.J. Super. Ct. App. Div. 1998) (applying the state law and treating a local ordinance excluding all adult entertainment to be preempted or presumptively unenforceable), *aff'd*, 722 A.2d 530 (N.J. 1999) (exclusion decision was based on relevant market, and alternatives outside of township may be considered).

4. *The Extent of the "Secondary Effects" Rationale.* The Court in *Alameda Books*, as well as in *Renton*, avoided the application of traditional First Amendment doctrine.

The Court adopted a theory that the city was not restricting expressive activities because of their content, but was utilizing zoning to prevent "secondary effects" of the theaters. Under this theory, police powers may be exercised to avoid crime, acts of moral turpitude, or neighborhood deterioration despite the "mere" incidental burden on expression. Because under *Renton* the community can use information from other jurisdictions, is the Court actually applying the deferential level of scrutiny typically applied to social and economic regulation reviewed under equal protection and substantive due process?

5. *Alternative Means of Communication*. To satisfy the *Alameda Books* and *City of Renton* requirements, a city must ensure that there are reasonable alternative avenues of communication. In most cases, this requirement means a showing of the physical and legal availability of alternative sites. In part, this showing requires that the zoning ordinance allow adult uses in other areas. *See, e.g.*, *Isbell v. City of San Diego*, 258 F.3d 1108 (9th Cir. 2001) (assuming the existence of demand, dispersal ordinance that permits only existing businesses is suspect); *Young v. City of Simi Valley*, 216 F.3d 807 (9th Cir. 2000), *cert. denied*, 531 U.S. 1104 (2001) ("sensitive interest" exception allows school, church, or other sensitive interests to effectively block the permit for nude dancing in a community with a paucity of reasonable alternative locations and would not be tailored narrowly); *Z.J. Gifts D-2, L.L.C. v. City of Aurora*, 136 F.3d 683, 688 (10th Cir. 1998), *cert. denied*, 525 U.S. 868 (1998) (requirement met where sexually oriented businesses may locate within the city's industrial zones, which comprise approximately 10.9 percent of the city's area, and approximately 3200 acres of this land—3.6 percent of the city's total area—are located near existing water and sewer services); *A.F.M. Ltd. v. City of Medford*, 704 N.E.2d 184 (Mass. 1999) (750-foot set back from certain properties left but one completely occupied block in the city for adult business with no reasonable alternative avenues of communication).

How much evidence must a plaintiff produce to raise a triable issue of fact to rebut such a showing? In *Stringfellow's of New York, Ltd. v. City of New York*, 694 N.E.2d 407 (N.Y. 1998), plaintiffs sought to prove that this requirement was not met by introducing the affidavit of a "land use-planning and local government consultant who actually visited the sites the City identified as potential receptors" of adult businesses. The consultant alleged that many of the sites were actually unavailable because they housed long-term occupants or lacked the necessary infrastructure.

The New York Court of Appeals found that the affidavit did not raise a triable question of fact. It criticized the affidavit's sufficiency on several grounds: its reliance on assumptions (such as that industrial areas are generally unsuitable for generic commercial uses), and the "absence of any attempt to quantify [the consultant's] observations or to make concrete allegations as to precisely how many of the 500 potential receptor sites identified by defendants were, in his estimate, unavailable." 694 N.E.2d at 419. Thus, under the holding in *Stringfellow's*, once the city has initially shown that its zoning sufficiently accommodates adult uses, the plaintiff must shoulder a substantial evidentiary burden to prevail on this issue.

6. *Regulation of Nude Dancing*. In *Barnes v. Glen Theatre, Inc.*, 501 U.S. 560 (1991), a divided Supreme Court upheld the application of an anti-nudity public indecency statute to prohibit non-obscene nude dancing in commercial establishments. Chief Justice Rehnquist's plurality opinion for three members of the Court ruled that nude bar dancing is not expressive conduct. He determined that the

general anti-nudity statute was conduct-based and thus unrelated to the suppression of expression. He was joined by concurring Justice Scalia, who would go further to eliminate all expression-based defenses to general laws. Four dissenting Justices found the activity to be protected expression.

In *Erie v. Pap's A.M.*, 529 U.S. 277 (2000), the Court returned to the subject of nude dancing, this time extending the *Barnes* principle to sustain a local public indecency ordinance. The ordinance made it an offence to knowingly appear in a public place in a state of nudity. The law defined "public place" to include places of entertainment, taverns, restaurants, and clubs, thereby reaching nude dancing. A four-justice plurality found nude dancing to be expressive behavior, but the city's interest in the restriction was found to be unrelated to the suppression of expression. The plurality also employed the secondary effects doctrine in finding that the law was directed to the effects of such establishments rather than at the erotic message of the dance.

Justice Scalia, joined by Justice Thomas, repeated his *Barnes* argument that general laws not targeted at speech are not subject to First Amendment judicial review. Justice Souter formed a majority.

Justice Stevens dissented, joined by Justice Ginsburg. He argued that a total ban could not be a time, place, or manner regulation, that the plurality was too deferential on the issue of secondary effects, and that the law was related to the message conveyed by the nude dancers. To the dissenters it was obvious that the ordinance was targeted and enforced only against nude dancing establishments. *See* Anne E. Mitchell, Nude Dancing and First Amendment Scrutiny, 34 Urb. Law. 277 (2002).

The Seventh Circuit found that restrictions on dance movements that involve fondling or erotic touching interfere with an erotic message and were not a neutral time, place, or manner regulation. *Schultz v. City of Cumberland*, 228 F.3d 831, 846-847 (7th Cir. 2000). The Nebraska Supreme Court upheld an ordinance targeted at nudity in adult entertainment but limited to below the waist nudity, finding the regulation general in nature and less restrictive than the regulation in *Pap's A.M.*, as it permitted topless dancing. *Village of Winslow v. Sheets*, 622 N.W.2d 595 (Neb. 2001). What is the dividing line between general laws and those targeted at particular erotic messages or media?

7. *Time, Place, and Manner Regulation.* Central to the First Amendment is the doctrine of reasonable time, place, and manner restrictions. Like the problem of colliding parades, communities are authorized to regulate the public forum under this doctrine, but only because of the context. The Supreme Court has used a four-part test to determine the legality of restrictions on the forum. The government must demonstrate that a regulation (1) serves a significant government interest, (2) is content neutral, (3) is the least restrictive means to achieve the objective, and (4) leaves alternative channels of communication. Under reasonable time, place, and manner regulations, parades may be subject to permit (*Cox v. New Hampshire*, 312 U.S. 569 (1941)).

How can the zoning of motion picture theaters based on the types of films shown survive the time, place, and manner doctrine, which insists on content neutrality? Has the Court watered down the doctrine by shifting its requirement from content neutrality to "viewpoint neutrality?"

8. *The Public Forum.* Publicly owned streets are, of course, the archetype of the public forum. What happens if a city sells the street to a church, retaining a

pedestrian easement, but as part of the sale bars certain activities, such as demonstrating? This was the fact situation in a high profile case in Salt Lake City. In *First Unitarian Church of Salt Lake City v. Salt Lake City Corp.*, 308 F.3d 1114 (10th Cir. 2002), *cert. denied*, 123 S. Ct. 2606 (2003) the court of appeals held that the city violated the First Amendment when it gave the church the power to ban certain kinds of speech. The court said the city must either relinquish the easement so the parcel becomes entirely private, or permit speech on the easement.

9. *Back to the Voyeur Dorm*. In *Voyeur Dorm v. City of Tampa*, 265 F.3d 1232 (11th Cir. 2001), *cert. denied*, 534 U.S. 114 (2002) (discussed in Chapter 2), the court held that the city could not regulate a house transmitting images over the Internet through use of a camera as an "adult use" under its zoning law. The scenario, which may be the future of adult uses, raises a number of questions. Was the court's ruling *sub silentio* based on a higher level of scrutiny because of the freedom of expression implications? If the city neutrally enforces its zoning laws, can it limit residential districts to residential uses? Is the Voyeur Dorm more like a family home or more like a movie or television studio? Can businesses use single-family homes for their offices, or to store plumbing supplies, as long as the public is not invited to the location? Was the court's ruling based on a reading of the record that the city singled out the Voyeur Dorm based on moral objection to its business? Would the City of Tampa arrest Matt Drudge for a zoning violation because he captains his Web site from his apartment? *See generally* Francesca Ortiz, Zoning the Voyeur Dorm: Regulating Home-Based Voyeur Web Sites Through Land Use Laws, 34 U.C. Davis L. Rev. 929 (2001) (viewing the question through federal constitutional law theories and concluding that nuisance law is available to combat secondary effects).

How will the Internet affect adult entertainment? Although clubs featuring a big screen "Voyeur Dorm" Internet telecast could be characterized as adult businesses and subject to zoning, would the telecast avoid application of public nudity enforcement under *Pap's A.M.*?

10. *Adult Entertainment and Alcoholic Beverages*. Pursuant to the authority recognized in the Twenty-First Amendment, states may exclude nude dancing in establishments serving liquor. *Newport v. Iacobucci*, 479 U.S. 92 (1986); *New York State Liquor Auth. v. Bellanca*, 452 U.S. 714 (1981); *California v. LaRue*, 409 U.S. 109 (1972). In communities where the states have not elected to exercise liquor control authority, may local communities nevertheless regulate liquor consumption in places of adult entertainment based on secondary effects studies? *Artistic Entertainment, Inc. v. City of Warner Robins*, 223 F.3d 1306 (11th Cir. 2000) (endorsing such ordinances yet finding a prior restraint for failure to have the ordinance contain procedural protections from bureaucratic delay).

C. ADVERTISING AND INFORMATION DISSEMINATION

"Commercial speech" is speech that offers goods or services for sale. Such speech may be protected where it concerns lawful activity and is not misleading. To regulate commercial speech, the government must demonstrate that the regulation seeks to implement a substantial government interest, the regulation directly advances that interest, and the goal is not attainable by less restrictive alternatives. *Central Hudson Gas & Elec. Corp. v. Public Serv. Comm'n*, 447 U.S. 557 (1980).

In recognizing that commercial expression is protected by the First Amendment, the Court has called into question the constitutionality of land use restrictions imposed for aesthetic reasons. For example, could a community strategy of revitalizing an area call for reducing the size, design, or placement of commercial signs without violating the First Amendment? Can a new community develop around a plan that includes an aesthetic element excluding commercial signs?

A split Court addressed these issues in the following case. The opinion is a difficult one, so be forewarned. In his dissent, (then) Justice Rehnquist aptly described it as a "Tower of Babel."

METROMEDIA, INC. v. CITY OF SAN DIEGO

453 U.S. 490 (1981)

JUSTICE WHITE announced the judgment of the Court and delivered an opinion, in which JUSTICE STEWART, JUSTICE MARSHALL, and JUSTICE POWELL joined.

This case involves the validity of an ordinance of the city of San Diego, Cal., imposing substantial prohibitions on the erection of outdoor advertising displays within the city.

I

Stating that its purpose was "to eliminate hazards to pedestrians and motorists brought about by distracting sign displays" and "to preserve and improve the appearance of the City," San Diego enacted an ordinance to prohibit "outdoor advertising display signs."[1] . . .

The ordinance provides two kinds of exceptions to the general prohibition: onsite signs and signs falling within 12 specified categories. Onsite signs are defined as those

> designating the name of the owner or occupant of the premises upon which such signs are placed, or identifying such premises; or signs advertising goods manufactured or produced or services rendered on the premises upon which such signs are placed.

1. San Diego Ordinance No. 10795 (New Series), enacted March 14, 1972. The general prohibition of the ordinance reads as follows:

B. OFF-PREMISE OUTDOOR ADVERTISING DISPLAY SIGNS PROHIBITED

Only those outdoor advertising display signs, hereinafter referred to as signs in this Division, which are either signs designating the name of the owner or occupant of the premises upon which such signs are placed, or identifying such premises; or signs advertising goods manufactured or produced or services rendered on the premises upon which such signs are placed shall be permitted. The following signs shall be prohibited:

1. Any sign identifying a use, facility or service which is not located on the premises.
2. Any sign identifying a product which is not produced, sold or manufactured on the premises.
3. Any sign which advertises or otherwise directs attention to a product, service or activity, event, person, institution or business which may or may not be identified by a brand name and which occurs or is generally conducted, sold, manufactured, produced or offered elsewhere than on the premises where such sign is located.

The specific categories exempted from the prohibition include: government signs; signs located at public bus stops; signs manufactured, transported, or stored within the city, if not used for advertising purposes; commemorative historical plaques; religious symbols; signs within shopping malls; for sale and for lease signs; signs on public and commercial vehicles; signs depicting time, temperature, and news; approved temporary, off-premises, subdivision directional signs; and "[t]emporary political campaign signs."...

Billboards are a well-established medium of communication, used to convey a broad range of different kinds of messages....

But whatever its communicative function, the billboard remains a "large, immobile, and permanent structure which like other structures is subject to . . . regulation." Moreover, because it is designed to stand out and apart from its surroundings, the billboard creates a unique set of problems for land-use planning and development....

As construed by the California Supreme Court, the ordinance restricts the use of certain kinds of outdoor signs. That restriction is defined in two ways: first, by reference to the structural characteristics of the sign; second, by reference to the content, or message, of the sign. Thus, the regulation only applies to a "permanent structure constituting, or used for the display of, a commercial or other advertisement to the public." Within that class, the only permitted signs are those (1) identifying the premises on which the sign is located, or its owner or occupant, or advertising the goods produced or services rendered on such property and (2) those within one of the specified exemptions to the general prohibition, such as temporary political campaign signs. To determine if any billboard is prohibited by the ordinance, one must determine how it is constructed, where it is located, and what message it carries.

Thus, under the ordinance (1) a sign advertising goods or services available on the property where the sign is located is allowed; (2) a sign on a building or other property advertising goods or services produced or offered elsewhere is barred; (3) noncommercial advertising, unless within one of the specific exceptions, is everywhere prohibited. The occupant of property may advertise his own goods or services; he may not advertise the goods or services of others, nor may he display most noncommercial messages....

[I]n *Central Hudson Gas & Electric Corp. v. Public Service Comm'n*, 447 U.S. 557 (1980), we held: "The Constitution . . . accords a lesser protection to commercial speech than to other constitutionally guaranteed expression. The protection available for a particular commercial expression turns on the nature both of the expression and of the governmental interests served by its regulation." (citation omitted). We then adopted a four-part test for determining the validity of government restrictions on commercial speech as distinguished from more fully protected speech. (1) The First Amendment protects commercial speech only if that speech concerns lawful activity and is not misleading. A restriction on otherwise protected commercial speech is valid only if it (2) seeks to implement a substantial governmental interest, (3) directly advances that interest, and (4) reaches no further than necessary to accomplish the given objective.

Appellants agree that the proper approach to be taken in determining the validity of the restrictions on commercial speech is that which was articulated in *Central Hudson*, but assert that the San Diego ordinance fails that test. We do not agree.

There can be little controversy over the application of the first, second, and fourth criteria. There is no suggestion that the commercial advertising at issue here involves unlawful activity or is misleading. Nor can there be substantial doubt that the twin goals that the ordinance seeks to further — traffic safety and the appearance of the city — are substantial governmental goals. . . . Similarly, we reject appellants' claim that the ordinance is broader than necessary and, therefore, fails the fourth part of the *Central Hudson* test. . . . Indeed, it has stopped short of fully accomplishing its ends: It has not prohibited all billboards, but allows onsite advertising and some other specifically exempted signs.

The more serious question, then, concerns the third of the *Central Hudson* criteria: Does the ordinance "directly advance" governmental interests in traffic safety and in the appearance of the city? It is asserted that the record is inadequate to show any connection between billboards and traffic safety. . . . We . . . hesitate to disagree with the accumulated, common-sense judgments of local lawmakers and of the many reviewing courts that billboards are real and substantial hazards to traffic safety. There is nothing here to suggest that these judgments are unreasonable. . . .

We reach a similar result with respect to the second asserted justification for the ordinance — advancement of the city's esthetic interests. It is not speculative to recognize that billboards by their very nature, wherever located and however constructed, can be perceived as an "esthetic harm." San Diego, like many States and other municipalities, has chosen to minimize the presence of such structures. Such esthetic judgments are necessarily subjective, defying objective evaluation, and for that reason must be carefully scrutinized to determine if they are only a public rationalization of an impermissible purpose. But there is no claim in this case that San Diego has as an ulterior motive the suppression of speech, and the judgment involved here is not so unusual as to raise suspicions in itself.

It is nevertheless argued that the city denigrates its interest in traffic safety and beauty and defeats its own case by permitting onsite advertising and other specified signs. Appellants question whether the distinction between onsite and offsite advertising on the same property is justifiable in terms of either esthetics or traffic safety. The ordinance permits the occupant of property to use billboards located on that property to advertise goods and services offered at that location; identical billboards, equally distracting and unattractive, that advertise goods or services available elsewhere are prohibited even if permitting the latter would not multiply the number of billboards. Despite the apparent incongruity, this argument has been rejected, at least implicitly, in all of the cases sustaining the distinction between offsite and onsite commercial advertising. . . .

In the first place, whether onsite advertising is permitted or not, the prohibition of offsite advertising is directly related to the stated objectives of traffic safety and esthetics. This is not altered by the fact that the ordinance is under-inclusive because it permits onsite advertising. Second, the city may believe that offsite advertising, with its periodically changing content, presents a more acute problem than does onsite advertising. Third, San Diego has obviously chosen to value one kind of commercial speech — onsite advertising — more than another kind of commercial speech — offsite advertising. The ordinance reflects a decision by the city that the former interest, but not the latter, is stronger than the city's interests in traffic safety and esthetics. The city has decided that in a limited instance — onsite commercial advertising — its interests should yield. We do not reject that judgment. As we see it, the city could reasonably conclude that a commercial enterprise — as well as the interested public — has a stronger interest in identifying its place of business and advertising the products or services available there than it has in using or leasing its available space for the purpose of advertising commercial enterprises located elsewhere. It does not follow from the fact that the city has concluded that some commercial interests outweigh its municipal interests in this context that it must give similar weight to all other commercial advertising. Thus, offsite commercial billboards may be prohibited while onsite commercial billboards are permitted.

. . . In sum, insofar as it regulates commercial speech the San Diego ordinance meets the constitutional requirements of *Central Hudson, supra*. . . .

It does not follow, however, that San Diego's general ban on signs carrying noncommercial advertising is also valid under the First and Fourteenth Amendments. The fact that the city may value commercial messages relating to onsite goods and services more than it values commercial communications relating to offsite goods and services does not justify prohibiting an occupant from displaying its own ideas or those of others.

As indicated above, our recent commercial speech cases have consistently accorded noncommercial speech a greater degree of protection than commercial speech. San Diego effectively inverts this judgment, by affording a greater degree of protection to commercial than to noncommercial speech. There is a broad exception for onsite commercial advertisements, but there is no similar exception for noncommercial speech. The use of onsite billboards to carry commercial messages related to the commercial use of the premises is freely permitted, but the use of otherwise identical billboards to carry noncommercial messages is generally prohibited. The city does not explain how or why noncommercial billboards located in places where commercial billboards are permitted would be more threatening to safe driving or would detract more from the beauty of the city. Insofar as the city tolerates billboards at all, it cannot choose to limit their content to commercial messages; the city may not conclude that the communication of commercial information concerning goods and services connected with a particular site is of greater value than the communication of noncommercial messages.

Furthermore, the ordinance contains exceptions that permit various kinds of noncommercial signs, whether on property where goods and services are offered or not, that would otherwise be within the general ban. A fixed sign may be used to identify any piece of property and its owner. Any piece of property may carry or display religious symbols, commemorative plaques of recognized historical societies and organizations, signs carrying news items or telling the time or temperature, signs erected in discharge of any governmental function, or temporary political campaign signs. No other noncommercial or ideological signs meeting the structural definition are permitted, regardless of their effect on traffic safety or esthetics.

Although the city may distinguish between the relative value of different categories of commercial speech, the city does not have the same range of choice in the area of noncommercial speech to evaluate the strength of, or distinguish between, various communicative interests. With respect to noncommercial speech, the city may not choose the appropriate subjects for public discourse: . . . Because some noncommercial messages may be conveyed on billboards throughout the commercial and industrial zones, San Diego must similarly allow billboards conveying other noncommercial messages throughout those zones.[20]

Finally, we reject appellees' suggestion that the ordinance may be appropriately characterized as a reasonable "time, place, and manner" restriction. The ordinance does not generally ban billboard advertising as an unacceptable "manner" of communicating information or ideas; rather, it permits various kinds of signs. Signs that are banned are banned everywhere and at all times. We have observed that time, place, and manner restrictions are permissible if "they are justified without reference to the content of the regulated speech, . . . serve a significant governmental interest, and . . . leave open ample alternative channels for communication of the information." Here, it cannot be assumed that "alternative channels" are available, for the parties stipulated to just the opposite: "Many businesses and politicians and other persons rely upon outdoor advertising because other forms of advertising are insufficient, inappropriate and prohibitively expensive." . . . It is apparent as well that the ordinance distinguishes in several ways between permissible and impermissible signs at a particular location by reference to their content. . . .

JUSTICE BRENNAN, with whom JUSTICE BLACKMUN joins, concurring in the judgment.

Believing that "a total prohibition of outdoor advertising is not before us," the plurality does not decide "whether such a ban would be consistent with the First Amendment." Instead, it concludes that San Diego may ban all billboards containing commercial speech messages without violating the First Amendment, thereby sending the signal to municipalities that bifurcated billboard regulations prohibiting commercial messages but allowing noncommercial messages would pass constitutional muster. I write separately because I believe this case in effect presents the total ban question, and because I believe the plurality's bifurcated approach itself raises serious First Amendment problems and relies on a distinction between commercial and noncommercial speech unanticipated by our prior cases. . . . In the case of billboards, I would hold that a city may totally ban them if it can show that a sufficiently substantial governmental interest is directly furthered by the total ban, and that any more narrowly drawn restriction, *i. e.*, anything less than a total ban, would promote less well the achievement of that goal.

Applying that test to the instant case, I would invalidate the San Diego ordinance. The city has failed to provide adequate justification for its substantial restriction on protected activity. . . .

Notes and Comments

1. *Advising After* Metromedia. What advice would you give a community that desires to undertake a "city beautiful" movement and wishes to eliminate the

20. Because a total prohibition of outdoor advertising is not before us, we do not indicate whether such a ban would be consistent with the First Amendment. *But see Schad v. Mount Ephraim*, 452 U.S. 61 (1981), on the constitutional problems created by a total prohibition of a particular expressive forum, live entertainment in that case. Despite Justice Stevens' insistence to the contrary, *post*, at 540, 541, and 548, n.16, we do not imply that the ordinance is unconstitutional *because* it "does not abridge enough speech." . . .

ugliness of billboards, marquees, and signs? Would there be greater authority if the sign ordinance was limited to the town's historic district as part of a preservation plan? What if the community were totally residential with only supporting commercial facilities such as convenience stores and filling stations? Could a community allow on-site signs with noncommercial messages, yet order removal of off-site signs with such messages? *Ackerley Communications v. City of Cambridge*, 88 F.3d 33 (1st Cir 1996) (no). *See also Ackerley Communications v. Krochalis*, 108 F.3d 1095 (9th Cir. 1997) (sustaining a Seattle ordinance limiting billboard development under *Metromedia* despite the absence of detailed proof that the ordinance would advance Seattle's interest in traffic safety and aesthetics). Should a motel be permitted to advertise weekly rates? *Suburban Lodges of America, Inc. v. City of Columbus Graphics Commn.*, 761 N.E.2d 1060 (Ohio Ct. App. 2000) (sustaining variance denial from on-premises, freeway-oriented sign ordinance limiting text that may be included).

2. *Neon, Sex, and Flags*. After *Metromedia* numerous issues also arise as to whether a locality can single out specific types of signs for regulation. Consider the following:

a. Can a community prohibit neon signs? *Wallace v. Brown County Area Plan Comm'n*, 689 N.E.2d 491 (Ind. Ct. App. 1998) (yes as regulation was no more extensive than necessary to further interests in safety and aesthetics); *contra*, *State v. Calabria, Gillette Liquors*, 693 A.2d 949 (N.J. Super. Ct. App. Div. 1997) (ban on neon signs was invalid absent evidence as to how it serves aesthetic concern and avoids commercial highway appearance).

b. Can sex-oriented business signs be singled out for regulation? In *Hamilton Amusement Ctr. v. Verniero*, 716 A.2d 1137 (N.J. 1998), *cert. denied*, 527 U.S. 1021 (1999), the New Jersey Supreme Court upheld the constitutionality of a statute placing a cap of two signs on sexually oriented businesses—an identification sign and a notification that premises were off-limits to minors. The court concluded that the statute was not a content-based restriction of free speech but rather a regulation of commercial speech protecting against undesired secondary effects. It also noted that "[v]iewed collectively, a national consensus emerges regarding the secondary effects of sexually oriented businesses." *Id.* at 1145. *See also Excalibur Group, Inc. v. City of Minneapolis*, 116 F.3d 1216 (8th Cir. 1997), *cert. denied*, 522 U.S. 1077 (1998) (upholding adult sign ordinance requiring, among other things, that all signs shall be flat wall signs, that no merchandise or pictures shall be displayed in window areas, and that window areas shall not be covered or made opaque in any way). *See also Pleasureland Museum, Inc. v. Beutter*, 288 F.3d 988 (7th Cir. 2002) (sustaining ordinance regulating facade, font, and color of signage).

Can adult businesses use canvassers to distribute leaflets advertising erotic dance? *S.O.C., Inc. v. County of Clark*, 152 F.3d 1136 (complete ban in large tourist section not narrowly tailored), *aff'd on reh'g*, 160 F.3d 541 (9th Cir. 1998) (suggesting on rehearing that the ban could target smaller problem areas, license canvassers, or limit the number per business).

c. Can a city limit the display of flags? In *Village of Schaumburg v. Jeep Eagle Sales Corp.*, 676 N.E.2d 200 (Ill. App. Ct. 1996), the court invalidated a sign ordinance allowing corporate and official flags of a nation, state, or city, with up to three flagpoles per zoning lot. The automobile dealership had displayed 13 American flags. The court invalidated the ordinance for distinguishing the permitted flags from all other flags under the theory of overbreadth. Traffic safety and visual aesthetics were not compelling interests that would justify such a content-based regulation. In *American Legion Post 7 v. City of Durham*, 239 F.3d 601 (4th Cir. 2001), the court sustained regulation of size and flagpole height in various zoning districts as a valid time, place, and manner regulation. The challenger wished to raise a 238-square foot flag in a district allowing up to a 60-foot flag on a pole no higher than 40 feet.

See generally Charles F. Floyd & Julie Kendig-Schrader, Reducing Billboard Clutter: What Can a Community Do?, 21 Zoning & Plan. L. Rep. 1 (1998).

But see *Skysign Int'l, Inc. v. City of Honolulu*, 276 F.3d 1109 (9th Cir. 2002) (Federal Aviation Administration regulations did not preempt local ban on aerial advertising). *Compare Blockbuster Videos, Inc. v. City of Tempe*, 141 F.3d 1295 (9th Cir. 1998) (Lanham Act, the federal law regulating trademarks, preempts local zoning that attempted to mandate trademark modification to comply with aesthetic standards); *contra Lisa's Party City, Inc. v. Town of Henrietta*, 185 F.3d 12 (2d Cir. 1999) (Lanham Act not intended to interfere with uniform aesthetic regulation that did not require a trademark alteration). *See* Roberta Rosenthal Kwall, Regulating Trademarks on Exterior Signs: Should Local Law Trump the Lanham Act and the Constitution?, 71 S. Cal. L. Rev. 1105 (1998) (arguing that local regulations should prevail).

3. *Racial Justice*. What if a racially integrated community is faced with either "steering," that is, the practice where real estate brokers tend to show homes to minority families while showing white buyers to other areas, or possible "blockbusting," whereby brokers suggest that the area is undergoing racial change to encourage panic sales listings? Can the community ban the posting of "for sale" signs to stifle the panic listings?

In *Linmark Assocs. v. Township of Willingboro*, 431 U.S. 85 (1977), the Supreme Court ruled that such a ban violates the First Amendment. Stressing commercial speech concerns, the Court foreclosed the suppression of speech as a means of achieving the police power interest of avoiding segregation generated by panic sales. Of primary concern to the Court was the lack of an alternative means of communication available to the landowner that is as effective and inexpensive as a sign.

Is *Linmark* hostile to the movement to integrate and stabilize neighborhoods? *See South-Suburban Hous. Ctr. v. Greater S. Suburban Bd. of Realtors*, 935 F.2d 868 (7th Cir. 1991), *cert. denied*, 502 U.S. 1074 (1992), for some judicially approved integrative strategies.

Could a community limit a "for sale" sign to a three-square foot window sign if the property sits within 75 feet of the street? *Cleveland Area Board of Realtors v. City of Euclid*, 88 F.3d 382 (6th Cir. 1996) (content neutral "time, place, and manner" restriction on size, number, and placement of signs in residential neighborhood was invalid as it failed to leave ample alternative channels of communication of information).

4. *"Say No to War."* The City of Ladue, Missouri, passed an ordinance restricting the display of signs on residential property, except for identification, sale, or safety warnings. The ordinance permitted businesses, churches, and nonprofit organizations to have limited signs. A single-family homeowner placed a 24- by 36-inch sign printed with the words "Say No to War in the Persian Gulf, Call Congress Now." Would the ordinance be sustained under *Metromedia* and *Linmark*?

In *City of Ladue v. Gilleo*, 512 U.S. 43 (1994), the Court invalidated the ordinance. The primary defect was that the ordinance precluded noncommercial speech and thus was invalid despite being viewpoint neutral and designed to protect a valid interest in aesthetics. The ordinance failed to leave open adequate alternatives for communication. See Stephanie L. Bunting, Unsightly Politics: Aesthetics, Sign Ordinances, and Homeowners' Speech in City of Ladue v. Gilleo, 20 Harv. Envtl. L. Rev. 473 (1996); Alan C. Weinstein, Sign Regulation After City of Ladue: Still No Answer to the Problem of Content-Based Regulations, 17 Zoning & Plan. L. Rep. 65 (1994). See also Daniel N. McPherson, Municipal Regulation of Political Signs: Balancing First Amendment Rights Against Aesthetic Concerns, 45 Drake L. Rev. 767 (1997); John Nivala, Constitutional Architecture: The First Amendment and the Single-Family House, 33 San Diego L. Rev. 291 (1996) (arguing exterior design is protected by the First Amendment).

Can commercial signs be prohibited in residential districts? *City of Rochester Hills v. Schultz*, 592 N.W.2d 69 (Mich. 1999) (furthers the goal of preserving the residential character of the community). *See also Long Island Bd. of Realtors, Inc. v. Incorporated Village of Massapequa Park*, 277 F.3d 622 (2d Cir. 2002) (sustaining ordinance limiting size, placement, number, and duration of commercial sign placement on residential property under facial challenge).

5. *Protection of Children.* Could a community exclude cigarette or liquor advertisements from publicly viewable locations? In *Lorillard Tobacco Co. v. Reilly*, 533 U.S. 525 (2001), the United States Supreme Court took a broad view of preemption, finding that the Federal Cigarette Labeling and Advertising Act preempts state regulations prohibiting outdoor cigarette advertising within 1,000 feet of a public playground, park, or school, or below five feet from the floor at points of sale. Theoretically, could all local signage regulation as applied to cigarette advertisements be preempted? Would the exclusion of billboards constitute a state restriction on cigarette advertising preempted under *Lorillard*? Presumably not, for it would appear that the trigger for preemption is the targeting of the subject matter of the advertisement to cigarettes. The *Lorillard* Court also found that the extension of the regulation to cigar and smokeless tobacco advertising, although not preempted, nevertheless violated the First Amendment commercial speech doctrine. Thus, local regulations against alcoholic beverage advertising targeted at or particularly accessible to children would appear to be in jeopardy.

6. *Newsracks.* Newsracks pose a classic First Amendment conflict between freedom of expression and preservation of community aesthetics. Newsracks may also represent a metaphor for the regulation of commercial activities by itinerant merchants on streets and sidewalks. In *City of Cincinnati v. Discovery Network, Inc.*, 507 U.S. 410 (1993), the Court invalidated an effort to curtail newsracks. To control the proliferation of newsracks, the City of Cincinnati enforced an ordinance prohibiting the distribution of commercial handbills or publications limited to commercial speech. Newspapers and other publications containing noncommercial speech could be distributed through newsracks. Cincinnati no doubt studied *Metromedia* and was advised not to restrict the dissemination of noncommercial speech. The city believed that aesthetic considerations justified the restriction targeted solely to commercial speech, anticipating application of the more deferential Central Hudson test. The challengers included publishers of free publications; one advertising adult educational, recreational, and social programs; and a real estate listing magazine.

The Court invalidated the restriction on two alternative grounds. Most significantly, the regulation distinguished between speech based on the content of the publication, distinguishing commercial from noncommercial speech and thus subjecting the regulation to exacting scrutiny. The Court treated the regulation as if the restriction turned on the message of the publisher, a notable departure from the treatment in *Renton*. Alternatively, the Court found that the regulation did not meet the *Central Hudson* commercial speech standard, as the city failed to show that the restriction directly advanced the interest in aesthetics.

What regulations, if any, can a community impose on newsracks after *Discovery Network*? Would the Court rule differently if commercial and noncommercial newspapers were not distinguished? Is the central concern of the Court in speech cases equality rather than the freedom of expression?

Could a town construct a newsrack area with ten or twenty attractively designed, permanent racks with applicants chosen by lottery? *See Honolulu Weekly, Inc. v. Harris*, 79 F. Supp. 2d 1186 (D. Haw. 1999) (invalidating lottery system for access to coin-operated newspaper rack in tourism district because, although the allocation of a set number of racks for "free" and "for sale" publications was content neutral, excluding free newspapers from superior, empty coin-operated racks was not narrowly tailored to any interest in aesthetics or safety). Could you make an exception for local daily newspapers or publications, or for newspapers containing legal notices? Could newsracks be excluded from an historic district? *Globe Newspaper Co. v. Beacon Hill Architectural Comm'n*, 100 F.3d 175 (1st Cir. 1996) (yes, sustaining a ban on "street furniture" and emphasizing alternative avenues of newspaper sales such as live vendors).

7. *Vendors, Artisans, Street Performers, and Panhandlers*. How might a town regulate public performances, street musicians, and artisans selling their jewelry, paintings, or objet d'art, or begging by the poor? If newspapers are protected, are tables placed on public sidewalks for distribution of literature similarly protected? *See Turley v. Police Dept. of the City of New York*, 167 F.3d 757 (2d Cir. 1999) (sustaining street musician regulation, including licensing, limits on noise levels, and a permit requirement); *Fanelli v. City of Trenton*, 641 A.2d 541 (N.J. 1994) (sustaining ban on peddlers in special improvement districts as rationally related to revitalizing downtown shopping districts). *Compare* Robert C. Ellickson, Controlling Chronic Misconduct in City Spaces: Of Panhandlers, Skid Rows, and Public-Space Zoning, 105 Yale L.J. 1165 (1996) *with* Stephen R. Munzer, Ellickson on "Chronic Misconduct" in Urban Spaces: Of Panhandlers, Bench Squatters, and Day Laborers, 32 Harv. C.R.-C.L. L. Rev. 1 (1997).

In *Bery v. New York*, 97 F.3d 689 (2d Cir. 1996), *cert. denied*, 520 U.S. 1251 (1997), the Second Circuit Court of Appeals invalidated a condition on vendor licenses barring visual artists from selling wares in public places. The court found that a ceiling of 853 annual licenses was not a narrowly tailored time, place, manner regulation to serve traffic flow and crowding. The regulation also failed to leave open adequate ample alternative channels of communication as applied to the sale of paintings, photographs, prints, and sculpture, in light of exceptions for vendors of printed material.

In *One World One Family Now v. City of Miami Beach*, 175 F.3d 1282 (11th Cir. 1999), the Eleventh Circuit sustained an ordinance establishing five locations in the popular South Beach Art Deco District of Miami Beach where all commercial street activity is prohibited, and nonprofit vending may be conducted from portable tables, but such sales are allowed only between 8:00 A.M. and sunset. The court found that ample alternative channels of communication allowed vendors to communicate their messages and that the regulation was a valid time, place, and manner regulation. Similarly, the Eleventh Circuit also sustained a ban on sidewalk tables as a reasonable time, place, and manner policy furthering the city's interest in keeping sidewalks open for pedestrians. *International Caucus of Labor Comms. v. City of Montgomery*, 111 F.3d 1548 (11th Cir. 1997).

8. *Political Signs*. Although signs and other communication of political messages are typically protected, communities may seek to place time limits on the posting of election campaign signs. Jules B. Gerard, Election Signs and Time Limits, 3 Wash. U. J.L. & Poly. 379 (2000) (arguing the validity of reasonable pre-election time periods and time limits for removal post-election, and possible invalidity of sign limitation periods just prior to elections). *But see Painesville Bldg. Dept. v. Dworken & Bernstein Co., L.P.A.*, 733 N.E.2d 1152 (Ohio 2000) (invalidating limit on political signs, including signs "advocating any type of political action," to 17 days before and 2 days following an election, yet endorsing time limits based on construction and litter dangers without times tied to election dates).

D. CHURCH AND WORSHIP REGULATION

A Note on Freedom of Religion Under the First Amendment

The Establishment Clause. The First Amendment contains two religion clauses: the Establishment Clause, requiring separation of church and state, and the Free Exercise Clause, prohibiting the state from interfering with religious freedom or mandating the practice of religion.

In its interpretation of the Establishment Clause, the Supreme Court appears to be most concerned with public school funding. In *Lemon v. Kurtzman*, 403 U.S. 602 (1971), the Court considered a challenge to state aid to nonpublic schools. The Court articulated a rigorous level of review requiring that (1) the measure must have a secular legislative purpose; (2) its principal or primary effect be one that neither advances nor inhibits religion; and (3) the statute must not foster an excessive government entanglement with religion.

In recent years, however, the Court's evident dissatisfaction with the *Lemon* test has led it to embark on a search for a new doctrine. Sometimes, it is concerned with whether a measure tends to generate coercion upon students to follow or practice religious tenets, as if free exercise of religion was the central issue in Establishment Clause cases. *See Zelman v. Simmons-Harris*, 536 U.S. 639 (2002) (sustaining school voucher program offering unrestricted tuition aid for parents to use at secular or religious schools, finding it neutral and involving free choice); *Lee v. Weisman*, 505 U.S. 577 (1992) (invalidating graduation prayer). At other times the Court has focused on the issue of neutrality, concerned with whether a measure favors or endorses one religion or religious sect over another. *See Allegheny County v. Greater Pittsburgh ACLU*, 492 U.S. 573 (1989) (no nativity scene in courthouse, but a menorah, Christmas tree, and sign saluting liberty approved). Still other opinions seem to engage in an historical search for the original intent of the Constitution. *Lynch v. Donnelly*, 465 U.S. 668 (1984) (nativity scene in municipal Christmas display approved).

The Free Exercise Clause. Government action interfering with religious practices has been reviewed under the First Amendment's Free Exercise Clause. Historically the Court had applied strict scrutiny to such actions, requiring a compelling state interest and no less restrictive alternative to serve that interest, where the effect of state action constituted coercion to engage in religious observance, or interference with an individual's religious observance. *Thomas v. Review Board*, 450 U.S. 707 (1981) (state may not deny unemployment compensation for refusal to work on military armaments due to religious convictions); *Sherbert v. Verner*, 374 U.S. 398 (1963) (violative for state to deny unemployment compensation to one discharged for conscientious refusal to work on the Sabbath).

However, in its 1990 decision *Employment Division v. Smith*, 494 U.S. 872 (1990), the Supreme Court rewrote free exercise doctrine. Smith was denied unemployment compensation following his discharge from a drug rehabilitation organization for ingesting the hallucinogenic drug peyote. Smith had ingested the narcotic for sacramental purposes at a ceremony of the Native American Church. The Supreme Court, in sustaining the denial of benefits, sweepingly endorsed the application of neutral state law to religious activities or over religious objection, at least where the law is not directed at religious practice and is otherwise constitutional. The creation of an exception from neutral laws, such as in the case of religious use of peyote, is solely a decision for the legislature, according to the Court.

The Court reinterpreted the doctrine established in earlier cases such as *Wisconsin v. Yoder*, 406 U.S. 205 (1972), which held that the Free Exercise Clause prevented authorities from requiring the Amish to fully comply with compulsory education laws. *Yoder*, according to Justice Scalia in the *Smith* case, was not a free exercise decision; rather, it was a "hybrid" case combining free exercise concerns with the fundamental right of parents to direct the religious upbringing of their children. 494 U.S. at 881-882.

After *Smith*, the Court no longer searches for the sincerity or religious centrality of the regulated activity. Gone as well is the search for compelling state interests and less restrictive alternatives, the two fundamental components of strict scrutiny analysis. *Sherbert v. Verner*, *supra*, in which the Court invalidated unemployment compensation denial to a Saturday Sabbatarian refusing to work on the Sabbath, was criticized and distinguished. According to the Court, the state law in *Sherbert* allowed the denial of benefits on the basis of an applicant's religion practices without serving any state interest, such as the narcotic laws in *Smith*.

While the *Smith* decision contains language raising its possible limitation to neutral criminal laws, it would certainly appear subject to application or extension to any neutral civil as well as criminal statute or ordinance. Thus *Smith* would apply to challenges to land use ordinances.

The Court adhered to the *Smith* model in its invalidation of an animal sacrifice prohibition in *Church of the Lukumi Babalu Aye, Inc. v. City of Hialeah*, 508 U.S. 520 (1993). *Smith* indicated a stricter scrutiny where laws were targeted at religious practices rather than enacted as neutral exercises of the police power. The city was unable to prove its interests were compelling, and the history behind the ordinance disclosed an intent to suppress religious practice. Under *Hialeah*, a law targeting religious beliefs is presumptively invalid, subject to strictest scrutiny. The Free Exercise Clause demands that the sole reason for imposing the burden of law and regulation be secular.

The Rise and Fall of RFRA. Congress sought to overturn the Court's efforts at free exercise revisionism in *Smith* by quickly approving the Religious Freedom Restoration Act of 1993 ("RFRA"), Pub. L. No. 103-141, 107 Stat. 1488 (codified at 42 U.S.C. §2000bb-1 (2000)). The law specifically reinstated the full decisions in *Sherbert* and *Yoder*, requiring the government to prove (1) that it is acting in furtherance of a compelling state interest whenever government substantially burdens a person's exercise of religion and (2) that it is pursuing the least restrictive means to further that compelling state interest. This led to a number of challenges to governmental land use regulations that affected the practice of religion, with plaintiffs arguing that the regulations, such as a zoning ordinance, violated RFRA.

However, in *City of Boerne v. Flores*, 521 U.S. 507 (1997) (pronounced "Bernie"), the Court ruled that the 1993 Religious Freedom Restoration Act exceeded the scope of Congress's power under Section 5 of the Fourteenth Amendment to "enforce, by appropriate legislation," the amendment's provisions. In a practical sense, the process of reconsidering opinions of the Court, such as *Smith*, and passing legislation designed to reinterpret such rulings, was deemed to constitute a violation of the doctrine of separation of powers. While the Congress possesses the power to pass corrective or preventive legislation to achieve the goals of the Fourteenth Amendment, it lacks the power to pass definitional legislation that invades the Court's jurisdiction and constitutional role of interpreting the Constitution. The Court found the legislative history barren of instances of generally applicable laws passed because of religious bigotry, and thus the law was not seen as remedial or preventive.

See generally Helen M. Maher, Religious Freedom and Zoning, 5 Buff. Envtl. L.J. 309 (1998); Alan C. Weinstein, Conflicts in Regulating Religious Institutions, 52 Land Use L. & Zoning Dig. 3 (March 2000); Elizabeth C. Williamson, City of Boerne v. Flores and the Religious Freedom Restoration Act: The Delicate Balance Between Religious Freedom and Historic Preservation, 13 J. Land Use & Envtl. L. 107 (1997) (endorsing historic preservation but observing that the principle is limited as it requires government initiative); Symposium, Reflections on City of Boerne v. Flores, 39 Wm. & Mary L. Rev. 597 (1998), including Douglas Laycock, Conceptual Gulfs in City of Boerne v. Flores, *id.* at 743, 780-791 (arguing historic preservation laws should not apply to churches and that the church in *Boerne* should be viewed as targeted for hostile regulation, as the law was not generally applicable under *Smith*); Alan C. Weinstein, Zoning and Landmark Regulation of Religious Institutions After City of Boerne v. Flores, 20 Zoning & Plan. L. Rep. 73 (1997) (successful religious challenges likely under state law).

Thus, the Court's decision in *Smith* remains as the foundation of current constitutional protection at the federal level.

Note how the Washington Supreme Court applies free exercise principles in the context of the application of historic preservation laws to churches in *First Covenant Church v. City of Seattle*.

FIRST COVENANT CHURCH OF SEATTLE v. CITY OF SEATTLE

840 P.2d 174 (Wash. 1992)

DORE, Chief Justice.

We reinstate our holding in *First Covenant Church v. Seattle*,[1] that applying the City's ordinances to the church violates the free exercise guaranties of the First Amendment to the federal constitution and article 1, Section 11 of the state constitution. We have fully considered the Supreme Court's holding in *Employment Div., Dep't of Human Resources v. Smith*,[2] and we conclude that *Smith* is distinguishable from this case and does not compel a different result.

ISSUE

Whether applying Seattle's Landmarks Preservation Ordinance to First Covenant violated the church's right to free exercise under the state and the federal constitutions?

FACTS

First Covenant owns the church located at Pike and Bellevue Streets in Seattle. First Covenant uses its church exclusively for religious purposes.

The City of Seattle adopted the Landmarks Preservation Ordinance to:

> designate, preserve, [and] protect, . . . improvements and objects which reflect significant elements of the City's cultural, aesthetic, social, economic, political, architectural, engineering, historic or other heritage. . . . [.]

Seattle Municipal Code (SMC) 25.12.020(B) (1977). Pursuant to that ordinance, the Landmarks Preservation Board nominated First Covenant's church as a landmark in October 1980. First Covenant objected to the nomination at public hearings, but the Board approved designation of the church as a landmark in January 1981. In April 1981, the Board adopted controls to preserve the exterior of the church. . . .

On September 17, 1985, the city council adopted ordinance 112425, which designated First Covenant's church a landmark. The designation ordinance requires that First Covenant get a certificate of approval before it makes certain alterations to the church's exterior. It also provides that:

> [N]othing herein shall prevent any alteration of the exterior when such alterations are necessitated by changes in liturgy, it being understood that the owner is the exclusive authority on liturgy and is the decisive party in determining what architectural changes are appropriate to the liturgy. When alterations necessitated by changes in liturgy are proposed, the owner shall advise the Landmarks Preservation Board in writing of the nature of the proposed alterations and the Board shall issue a Certificate of Approval. Prior to the issuance of any Certificate, however, the Board and owner

1. 114 Wash. 2d 392, 787 P.2d 1352 (1990), *cert. granted, judgment vacated and remanded*, 499 U.S. 901 (1991).
2. 494 U.S. 872 (1990).

shall jointly explore such possible alternative design solutions as may be appropriate or necessary to preserve the designated features of the landmark.

First Covenant filed a declaratory judgment action in January 1986. It sought a judgment that the "religious freedom provisions" of the state constitution prohibited application of the Landmarks Preservation Ordinance to active churches and that application of the Landmarks Preservation Ordinance to its church was void. . . .

. . . A majority of this court concluded, in *First Covenant*, that First Covenant's claims that the Landmarks Preservation and designation ordinances violated the free exercise of religion were not premature. *First Covenant Church v. Seattle, supra* 114 Wash. 2d at 398-400, 787 P.2d 1352. A majority, for different reasons, also concluded that applying the City's ordinances to First Covenant burdened the Church's right of free exercise of religion under the federal and state constitutions. *First Covenant Church v. Seattle, supra* at 405-06, 412, 787 P.2d 1352. And the majority, again for different reasons, concluded that the liturgy exemption did not mitigate the burden on free exercise. *First Covenant Church v. Seattle, supra* at 407, 412, 787 P.2d 1352.

The majority applied the strict scrutiny analysis of *Sherbert v. Verner*, 374 U.S. 398, 83 S. Ct. 1790, 10 L. Ed. 2d 965 (1963), when assessing the free exercise claim. It concluded that landmark preservation was not a "compelling interest" that justified the burden on First Covenant's right to free exercise and, therefore, that applying the City's ordinances to First Covenant violated First Covenant's free exercise rights under the state and federal constitutions. *First Covenant Church v. Seattle, supra* 114 Wash. 2d at 408, 787 P.2d 1352.

The City appealed. The United States Supreme Court vacated the judgment and remanded it to us for "further consideration in light of *Employment Division, Department of Human Resources of Oregon v. Smith* . . . ".[4]

Analysis

. . . First Covenant and the CLS contend that the City's Landmarks Preservation Ordinances are not neutral or generally applicable because the sites, improvements, and objects they govern are arbitrarily selected, and the selection process requires individual evaluation of each building, site, or improvement.

The Landmarks Preservation Ordinance, SMC 25.12, was passed in 1977. The designation ordinance, 112425, was passed pursuant to the general ordinance and "is simply the means by which the Landmarks Ordinance is implemented." . . .

The designation criteria of SMC 25.12 is neutral. It applies to "[a]n object, site or improvement which is more than twenty-five (25) years old" and meets the designation criteria. SMC 25.12.350. The definitions of "object" and "improvement" are also facially neutral. Designation ordinance 112425, however, is not neutral. It alludes to religious facilities in the two references to "liturgy". Because the Landmarks Preservation Ordinances specifically refer to religious facilities, they are not "neutral".

4. 499 U.S. 901, 111 S. Ct. 1097, 113 L. Ed. 2d 208 (1991).

The landmark ordinances must also be "generally applicable" laws. Justice Scalia contrasted "generally applicable" tax laws with statutes that contain "a system of individualized exceptions", that "create[ ] a mechanism for individualized exemptions" or that lend themselves to "individualized governmental assessment" of the conduct governed. The landmark ordinances at issue here are unlike a general tax law because they invite individualized assessments of the subject property and the owner's use of such property, and contain mechanisms for individualized exceptions. The City's Landmarks Preservation Ordinance is not generally applicable.

The City and the National Trust for Historic Preservation (National Trust) insist that *Rector, Wardens, & Members of Vestry of St. Bartholomew's Church v. New York*, compels a different result. St. Bartholomew's owned a church and a community house. Both buildings were designated landmarks in 1967, pursuant to New York's Landmark Law. The law provides a detailed hearings and appeals process for those who object to designation and exempts from designation "interiors utilized as places of religious worship."

In 1983, St. Bartholomew's asked for a certificate of appropriateness to replace the community house with a 47-story tower, some of which it would use, the rest of which it would rent as commercial property. The New York City Landmarks Preservation Commission (Commission) denied approval. The church alleged that the landmark law violated its right to free exercise and was not neutral or generally applicable because it vested discretion in the Commission. The court concluded that the landmark law did not "demonstrate a lack of neutrality or general applicability" and that, absent proof that the Commission exercised its discretion in a discriminatory way, "there [was] no constitutional relevance" to the church's claim. *St. Bartholomew's Church*, at 354-55.

St. Bartholomew's is distinguishable from this case. St. Bartholomew's accepted designation as a landmark, without objection. First Covenant has objected continuously to designation. St. Bartholomew's sought an exception for an adjunct building, not its church building. First Covenant seeks an exception for its church building. St. Bartholomew's sought an exception to use its property for commercial purposes. First Covenant seeks an exemption so that it may continue to use its church for exclusively religious purposes. St. Bartholomew's did not allege that designation reduced its principal asset, only that it impeded its ability to generate additional revenue to expand its programs. Uncontroverted evidence supports First Covenant's claim that designation reduces the values of its principal asset by almost one-half. Finally, the parties in St. Bartholomew's did not challenge the effect of the religious exemption on the New York law's constitutionality, and the religious exemption in the New York law is not "liturgy" based, as is Seattle's. St. Bartholomew's is factually distinguishable and does not control this case.

The rule in *Smith II* also does not apply because First Covenant's claim presents a "hybrid situation." The cases upon which the Supreme Court relied when it formulated the "hybrid claim" exception, as well as other authority, support the view that a "hybrid" case is one in which a single claim encompasses several protected interests. The Church's claim is "hybrid" because designation not only violates First Covenant's right to freely exercise religion, it infringes on First Covenant's rights to free speech.

"Speech" includes nonverbal conduct if the conduct is "sufficiently imbued with elements of communication." *Spence v. Washington*, 418 U.S. 405, 409 (1974). Whether conduct constitutes speech depends on the nature of the activity, combined with the factual context and environment in which the activity is undertaken. *Spence v. Washington, supra*. There must be "[an] intent to convey a particularized message" and a great "likelihood . . . that the message would be understood by those who view it." *Texas v. Johnson*, 491 U.S. 397, 404 (1989).

First Covenant claims, and no one disputes, that its church building itself "is an expression of Christian belief and message" and that conveying religious beliefs is part of the building's function. First Covenant reasons that when the State controls the architectural "proclamation" of religious belief inherent in its church's exterior it effectively burdens religious speech. We agree with First Covenant's reasoning. The relationship between theological doctrine and architectural design is well recognized. The exterior and the interior of the structure are inextricably related. When, as in this case, both are "freighted with religious meaning" that would be understood by those who view it, then the regulation of the church's exterior impermissibly infringes on the religious organization's right to free exercise and free speech. . . .

Applying the *Sherbert* "compelling interest" test, we address the church's contention that subjecting it to the controls of the Landmarks Preservation Ordinance burdens its right to freely exercise religion. . . .

Government regulation is constitutional either if it does not infringe constitutional rights of free exercise, or if any burden on free exercise, direct or indirect, is justified by a compelling state interest in the regulation of subject matter within the State's power to regulate. *Sherbert, supra* at 402-03. The party who alleges that state action restrains his free exercise of religion must "show the coercive effect of the enactment as it operates against him in the practice of his religion." If a party establishes such an infringement on his right to free exercise, the Court will subject the infringement to strict scrutiny. The State then must establish that some compelling state interest justifies the infringement and that the enactment is the least restrictive means to achieve the State's end.

The City's ordinances, as this court held earlier, impermissibly burden First Covenant's right to free exercise in two ways. The ordinances burden free exercise "administratively" because they require that First Covenant seek the approval of a government body before it alter[s] the exterior of its house of worship, whether or not the alteration is for a religious reason. Cf. *Church of St. Paul & St. Andrew v. Barwick*, 67 N.Y.2d 510, 537-38, 496 N.E.2d 183, 194, 200-01, *cert. denied*, 479 U.S. 985 (1986). Further, they burden First Covenant financially, because they reduce the value of the Church's property by almost half. . . .

The City urges that the "liturgy exemption" alleviates any burden on the exercise of religion. We do not believe that the exemption cures either the "administrative" or the financial infringements of First Covenant's right to free exercise.

First, the plain and ordinary meaning of the term "liturgy," which we employ absent a statutory definition of that term, does not provide a workable standard that protects the constitutional rights of the church. "Liturgy" is a "rite or series of rites, observances, or procedures prescribed for public worship in the Christian church in accordance with authorized or standard form." Webster's Third New International Dictionary 1323 (1971). "Liturgy" essentially refers to prescribed conduct that occurs within the structure. The liturgy-focused exemption in this case is constitutionally infirm because it allows the City to control any nonliturgical elements of religious conduct that require architectural change. Further, as we previously observed:

> Would a wider door to permit access by handicapped parishioners comprise a liturgical change? Although . . . widening the door does not relate directly to the rites or procedures of worship in the church, it does facilitate the ability of disabled persons to participate in religious services and activities. The anomalies created by the liturgy exception are cumbersome and would result in . . . delays in carrying out routine church work.

First Covenant, 114 Wash. 2d at 407, 787 P.2d 1352.

Secondly, adopting the City's interpretation of the phrase "necessitated by changes in liturgy" as meaning "for religious purposes" does not resolve the ambiguity. *First Covenant*, supra at 406, 787 P.2d 1352. The City still has the right to determine what is or what is not for a religious purpose and it acknowledged at argument that it reserved the right to determine if the "religious purpose" claim was bona fide. . . .

City reserves the right to oversee and challenge First Covenant's decisions about what is liturgy and what is a valid religious purpose. Further, the City's suggestion that if it did not believe First Covenant's interpretation of liturgy was bona fide it would bring the Church and the religious question before the courts fosters exactly the kind of religious entanglement the constitution seeks to avoid. The governmental oversight of church action that the City reserves to itself, under the liturgy exception, impermissibly burdens free exercise.

Ordinance 112425 also requires that First Covenant seek the City's approval before it alters its church, even for presumptively valid "liturgical" purposes. The exemption states that if the Church proposes an alteration "necessitated by changes in liturgy," the Board and owner shall jointly explore such possible alternative design solutions as may be appropriate or necessary to preserve the designated features of the landmark." The requirement that the Church negotiate with the City constitutes unjustified governmental interference in religious matters and infringes First Covenant's right to free exercise.

Finally, the liturgy exemption does not mitigate the financial burden that designation imposes on First Covenant. Regardless of how the exemption is construed, the Church suffers the same dramatic depreciation in the value of its property and principal asset. In sum, the liturgy exemption does not cure the infringement of free exercise by the Landmarks Preservation Ordinance.

If government action burdens the exercise of religion, but the State demonstrates that it has a compelling interest in enforcing its enactment, that interest will justify the infringement of First Amendment rights. *Sherbert*, 374 U.S. at 406-07. . . . We hold that the City's interest in preservation of esthetic and historic structures is not compelling and it does not justify the infringement of First Covenant's right to freely exercise religion. The possible loss of significant architectural elements is a price we must accept to guarantee the paramount right of religious freedom.

Upon further consideration, in light of *Smith II*, we conclude that applying the City's preservation ordinances to First Covenant's church violates the church's right to freely exercise religion under the First Amendment.

Although we might distinguish this case from *Smith II*, and base our decision solely on federal grounds, we decline to do so. Like the *State v. Hershberger*, 462 N.W.2d 393 (Minn. 1990) court, we eschew the "uncertainty" of *Smith II* and rest our decision also on independent grounds under the Washington constitution. . . .

DOLLIVER, Justice (dissenting). . . .

The Landmarks Preservation Ordinance and its implementing ordinance, like the criminal prohibition against peyote use in *Smith II*, are neutral, generally applicable laws which do not involve other constitutional protections. The ordinances apply neutrally and generally to protect an object, site or improvement which is more than 25 years old and which "has significant character, interest or value, as part of the development, heritage or cultural characteristics of the City, state, or nation." SMC 25.12.350. While the landmark ordinances will affect many religious buildings because of their social and cultural importance, this does not demonstrate a lack of neutrality or general applicability. *See Rector, Wardens, & Members of the Vestry of St. Bartholomew's Church v. New York*, 914 F.2d 348, 354 (2d. Cir. 1990), *cert. denied*, 499 U.S. 905 (1991). Indeed, the majority admits the designation criteria in the Landmarks Preservation Ordinance are neutral. Majority, at 180.

The majority, however, asserts the implementing ordinance's two references to "liturgy," which provide an exemption for religiously motivated exterior changes, transform the otherwise neutral ordinance into a non-neutral one. Majority, at 180-181. The irony, even the perversity, of this position is apparent. The Court in *Smith II* recognized the role the political process could and has played by providing exemptions in generally applicable laws for religiously motivated practices. *Smith II*, 494 U.S. at 890. Particularly, the Court endorsed legislatures which had made, even though it was not constitutionally required, "nondiscriminatory religious-practice exemption[s]" in their criminal drug laws for "sacramental peyote use." *Smith II*, 494 U.S. at 890. In this case, the Landmarks Preservation Ordinance makes no reference to religious facilities. Only the implementing ordinance, which must necessarily focus on the designated church site, is deemed not neutral because of its exception for liturgically required exterior changes. Yet, the majority uses this exemption as the reason the landmark ordinances fail the neutrality test! Incredible. This is bootstrapping of the most egregious nature. . . .

Notes and Comments

1. *Church and Worship Zoning*. Zoning frequently frustrates the ability to worship communally. A community may wish to restrict the number of churches, particularly where traffic and parking problems are generated. Limits on church or religious zoning may also reflect the recognition that the exemption of churches from taxation results in a shrinking tax base, and other uses can generate tax revenues to support infrastructure and services. In single family residential districts, may churches be excluded or limited? What free exercise problems arise from prohibiting regular, organized group worship in private homes? If synagogues are distant and Orthodox Jewish observance prohibits driving on the Sabbath, can zoning be enforced to prohibit group home worship?

Similarly, modern land use regulation often attempts to preserve historically significant buildings. In many instances, these buildings are churches, and the stage for a conflict with First Amendment rights is set. Indeed, such a conflict was present in the *City of Boerne* case, in which the Court invalidated RFRA. Are churches entitled to exemption from general regulatory laws such as historic preservation ordinances? Does the mandate to preserve historically significant buildings or historic districts interfere with the freedom to worship?

2. First Covenant *and* Smith. The Washington Supreme Court finds that the Supreme Court's decision in *Employment Division v. Smith* is not controlling because (1) the landmarks ordinance is not a neutral law of general applicability, and (2) the building itself was an expression of belief. Do you agree with the court's reasoning? Does the case turn on the fact that the restriction will have a severe financial effect on the church?

In *Rector of St. Bartholomew's Church v. City of New York*, 914 F.2d 348 (2d Cir. 1990), *cert. denied*, 499 U.S. 905 (1991), the church received a designation as a landmark. When it thereafter sought to replace a seven-story building next to the principal church building with a 47-story office building, the application was denied because the Church did not prove "necessary hardship." The court affirmed, concluding that the "Landmarks Law is a valid, neutral regulation of general applicability" and that the Church "has failed to prove that it cannot continue its religious practice in its existing facilities." *Id.* at 355-356. Can the two cases be reconciled?

Interestingly, in a later case, *Open Door Baptist Church v. Clark County*, 995 P.2d 33 (Wash. 2000), the Washington Supreme Court found that an ordinance requiring the church to apply for a conditional use permit to operate the church did not violate the Free Exercise Clause. Is this consistent with *First Covenant*?

3. *Zoning I: An Exemption for Churches?* Can communities exempt churches from historic preservation or other zoning laws? Does such special treatment for churches violate the neutrality requirement of the Establishment Clause? *Ehlers-Renzi v. Connelly School of the Holy Child, Inc.*, 224 F.3d 283 (4th Cir. 2000), *cert. denied*, 531 U.S. 1192 (2001) (exemption from special exception requirement for parochial schools located on land owned or leased by a church does not violate Establishment Clause); *East Bay Asian Local Dev. Corp. v. State*, 13 P.3d 1122 (Cal. 2000), *cert. denied*, 532 U.S. 1008 (2001) (sustaining state statute permitting religious entities to exempt certain church properties from landmark designation). *See, e.g.*, Felipe M. Nuñez & Eric Sidman, California's Statutory Exemption for Religious Properties from Landmark Ordinances: A Constitutional and Policy Analysis, 12 J.L. & Relig. 271 (1995-1996) (exception, albeit constitutional, fails to recognize the public interest in preserving significant structures); Laura S. Nelson, Remove Not the Ancient Landmark: Legal Protection for Historic Religious Properties in an Age of Religious Freedom Legislation, 21 Cardozo L. Rev. 721 (1999) (arguing legislation violates the Establishment Clause); Kenneth J. Brown, Comment, Establishing a Buffer Zone: The Proper Balance Between the First Amendment Religion Clauses in the Context of Neutral Zoning Regulations, 149 U. Pa. L. Rev. 1507 (2001) (arguing that churches should be subject to neutral zoning and that an exemption neither serves policy nor is constitutionally supportable under the Establishment Clause). Would exempting a church struggling financially to operate its existing facility be inconsistent with the refusal to grant a permit to operate an adult movie theater

because the exhibitor is unable to obtain any suitable structure at an affordable price?

A Missouri statute enabling local municipalities to enact zoning ordinances reads as follows:

> For the purposes of promoting health, safety, morals or the general welfare of the community, the legislative body of all cities, towns, and villages is hereby empowered to regulate and restrict the height, number of stories, and size of buildings and other structures, the percentage of lot that may be occupied, the size of yards, courts, and other open spaces, the density of population, the preservation of features of historical significance, and the location and use of buildings, structures and land for trade, industry, residence and other purposes.

Mo. Rev. Stat. §89.020(1) (1998). Does this section give municipalities zoning power over churches? The Missouri Court of Appeals held that, while cities may regulate churches for safety reasons, this section did not authorize zoning regulation. *Village Lutheran Church v. City of Ladue*, 935 S.W.2d 720 (Mo. Ct. App. 1996), citing *Congregation Temple Israel v. City of Creve Coeur*, 320 S.W.2d 451 (Mo. 1959). Do you agree?

4. *Zoning II: Zoning and the Free Exercise Clause*. In *Islamic Center of Mississippi v. City of Starkville*, 840 F.2d 293 (5th Cir. 1988), the Court of Appeals for the Fifth Circuit overturned the city's denial of a zoning exception to the plaintiff, which sought to establish a mosque within the city. The court first summarized the general position of the state courts on whether churches may be excluded from allowed uses:

> Many state courts have therefore held that a zoning ordinance that prohibits the construction of church buildings or the use of all existing buildings for public worship in virtually all residential districts violates the free exercise clause. The majority of these state court decisions have held that municipalities may not completely exclude facilities for religious use from such districts, although in many of these cases there was a justification other than free exercise for the invalidation of the ordinance. . . .

Id. at 300.

The court then found that the city had not treated the Islamic Center equally. In particular, it had never enforced its ordinance against a Christian church, with a membership twice as large as the Islamic Center, even though it was located next door on the same allegedly congested street and had only half as many parking spaces. *See also Congregation Kol Ami v. Abington Township*, 161 F. Supp. 2d 432 (E.D. Pa. 2001) (equal protection violated in denial of special use exception for synagogue in residential district where jurisdiction did not explain the denial in terms of traffic, pollution, or noise, and failed to consider whether disruptions warranted denial, and where the zoning permitted other institutions). *Compare Korean Buddhist Dae Won Sa Temple of Hawaii v. Sullivan*, 953 P.2d 1315 (Haw. 1998) (denial of variance to accommodate Buddhist temple upheld). See generally Shelley R. Saxer, When Religion Becomes a Nuisance: Balancing Land Use and Religious Freedom When Activities of Religious Institutions Bring Outsiders into the Neighborhood, 84 Ky. L.J. 507 (1995-1996).

5. *Home Churches.* Would an Orthodox Sephardic Jewish rabbi be entitled to a variance to hold brief daily prayer sessions, requiring ten participants, and services on holy days? The rabbi and members of the prayer group live within one mile of each other but not within walking distance from a house of worship. Their religion prohibits the use of mechanical devices such as automobiles on the Sabbath. On holy days and on the Sabbath, there are from 15 to 25 congregants at the rabbi's home. *Farhi v. Commissioners of the Borough of Deal,* 499 A.2d 559 (N.J. Super. Ct. Law Div. 1985) (activity did not violate single-family zoning as interpreted by the court, considering the strict scrutiny required for free exercise of religion under the state constitution). *See* Colo. Rev. Stat. §29-1-1201 (2001) (local governments prohibited from imposing limits on home worship or religious meetings, subject only to general traffic, parking, noise, or other health, welfare, and safety restrictions); *Tran v. Gwinn,* 554 S.E.2d 63 (Va. 2001) (sustaining neutrally applied special use permit requirement to hold worship services, on property zoned residential conservation). *Cf. Concerned Citizens of Carderock v. Hubbard,* 84 F. Supp. 2d 668 (D. Md. 2000) (making churches and other places of worship a permitted use in single-family residential zones and exempting them from special permit requirement was not an impermissible endorsement of religion and did not violate the Establishment Clause).

See also LeBlanc-Sternberg v. Fletcher, 67 F.3d 412 (2d Cir. 1995), *cert. denied,* 518 U.S. 1017 (1996) (zoning preventing home synagogues violative of First Amendment and Title VIII, the federal Fair Housing Act that prohibits religion-based actions that deny access to housing, as the zoning was part of a conspiracy to discourage residence by religious Jews).

6. *The Future.* Continued litigation in this area is almost a certainty. *See Keeler v. Mayor of Cumberland,* 940 F. Supp. 879 (D. Md. 1996) (historic preservation commission denial of permit to demolish and replace church monastery and chapel violated Free Exercise Clause and constituted a taking, as the existing church was a financial drain and the church was obligated to make repairs); *Munns v. Martin,* 930 P.2d 318 (Wash. 1997) (city demolition permit ordinance that could cause 14-month delay to bishop's plan to demolish school and construct pastoral center violated state constitution's Free Exercise Clause).

State legislatures have embarked on the passage of legislation modeled on RFRA. Douglas Laycock, State RFRAs and Land Use Regulation, 32 U.C. Davis L. Rev. 755 (1999); Robert M. O'Neil, Religious Freedom and Nondiscrimination: State RFRA Laws Versus Civil Rights, 27 Fordham Urb. L.J. 197 (1999). *See also* Mass. Gen. Laws Ann. ch. 40A §3 (West Supp. 2002) (requiring accommodation between protected uses and matters of critical municipal concern); Martin v. Corporation of the Presiding Bishop of the Church of Jesus Christ of Latter-Day Saints, 747 N.E.2d 131 (Mass. 2001) (rigid application of height restrictions to church steeple would impair character of temple without advancing any municipal concern); Jerold S. Kayden, Statutory Preference for Religious Land Use: Divining What Is Religious and What Is Reasonable, 53 Land Use L. & Zoning Dig. 3 (Sept. 2001) (commenting on *Martin* and criticizing it for excessive deference to religion and insufficient search for government zoning interest). Some states are simply interpreting state constitutional free exercise provisions to demand strict scrutiny. *City Chapel Evangelical Free Inc. v. City of South Bend,* 744 N.E.2d 443 (Ind. 2001) (city condemnation of church building subject to defense based upon burden on religious liberty). Despite enactment of a state RFRA, an Illinois intermediate appellate court found that the establishment of an economic revitalization plan was a compelling interest outweighing the claims of a church that had purchased a former Masonic hall and sought a special use permit to operate. *City of Chicago Heights v. Living World Outreach*, 707 N.E.2d 53 (Ill. Ct. App. 1998), *mod.*, 749 N.E.2d 916 (Ill. 2001).

Congress responded to *City of Boerne*, which found RFRA unconstitutional, with passage of the Religious Land Use and Institutionalized Persons Act of 2000 (RLUIPA), Pub. L. No. 106-274, 114 Stat. 803, *codified at* 42 U.S.C.A. §2000cc (Supp. 2001). The following case applies RLUIPA.

■ CIVIL LIBERTIES FOR URBAN BELIEVERS v. CITY OF CHICAGO

342 F.3d 752 (7th Cir. 2003)

Before BAUER, POSNER, and EVANS, Circuit Judges.

BAUER, Circuit Judge.

Appellants, an association of Chicago-area churches and five individual member churches thereof, appeal from the district court's entry of summary judgment in favor of Appellee, the City of Chicago, on Appellants' claims challenging the Chicago Zoning Ordinance ("CZO"), 17 Municipal Code of Chicago, Ill., §§1-11, under the federal Religious Land Use and Institutionalized Persons Act ("RLUIPA"), 42 United States Code §2000cc *et seq.*, and the United States Constitution. For the reasons set forth below, we affirm the decision of the district court.

BACKGROUND

The CZO broadly divides the city into R, B, C, and M zones for residential, business, commercial, and manufacturing uses, respectively. Each zone, in turn, is subdivided into numbered districts and subdistricts. A majority of Chicago land available for development is zoned R. . . . Churches are permitted uses as of right in all R zones, but are termed Variations in the Nature of Special Uses ("Special Use") in all B zones as well as C1, C2, C3, and C5 districts. All Special Uses, whether of a religious or nonreligious nature, require approval by the Zoning Board of Appeals ("ZBA") following a public hearing. *See id.* §§7.3-1(4), 8.4, 9.4, & 11.10. Special Use approval is expressly conditioned upon the design, location, and operation of the proposed use consistent with the protection of public health, safety, and welfare, and the proposed use must not substantially injure the value of neighboring property. *See id.* §11.10-4. Factoring such expenses as application, title search, and legal fees, as well as appraisal and neighbor notification costs, the aggregate cost of obtaining Special Use approval approaches $5000. Before a church may locate in a C4 district or an M zone, the Chicago City Council must vote in favor of a Map Amendment, effectively rezoning the targeted parcel. *See id.* §§9.4-4, 10, & 11.9. Development for church use of land consisting of two or more acres (necessary for congregations exceeding roughly 500 members) requires approval by City Council vote of a Planned Development. *See id.* §11.11-1(a) & 11.11-3.

Civil Liberties for Urban Believers ("CLUB") is an unincorporated association of 40 to 50 Chicago-area religious or not-for-profit Illinois corporations ranging in size from 15 to 15,000 congregants. Five of these individual member churches joined CLUB as plaintiffs in an action challenging the validity of the CZO. The district court summarized as follows the encounters of the five individual plaintiff churches with Chicago's zoning framework as alleged in Appellants' complaint:

> Christ Center began meeting in a high school auditorium in 1990, but soon experienced difficulties at this location due to various school functions that interrupted weekly worship. As a result, Christ Center began searching for a building to purchase. The church was unsuccessful in locating an appropriate building in any R districts. In the summer of 1992, Christ Center located a suitable building at 1139-43 West Madison in Chicago. The building was located in a C district and Christ Center promptly applied for a special use permit. After completing the application process, Christ Center reached out to gain the support of neighbors and Alderman Theodore Mazola. Most neighbors favored a taxpaying entity in the neighborhood rather than a church and Alderman Mazola stated that he would support the church's special use permit on any street but Madison. The Zoning Board eventually convened a special hearing on September 18, 1992. On October 18, 1992, the special use permit was denied. Christ Center subsequently found a second building in an M district at 123 South Morgan. The owner of the building also agreed to provide financing. However, the Chicago Department of Planning and Development informed Christ Center that it would oppose any rezoning application because the particular area was designated to become an entertainment area and the presence of a church would inhibit such development. Christ Center subsequently choose not to file an application for rezoning. In the fall of 1993, Christ Center obtained property at 4445 South King Drive, successfully obtained a special use permit and now operates a church at this location. Christ Center now claims that it paid substantial sums in attorneys fees, appraisal fees, zoning application charges, title charges and other expenses attempting to find suitable property. [Other summaries are omitted.]

In granting summary judgment in favor of Chicago, the district court determined that the February 2000 amendments to the CZO removed "any potential substantial burden" on religious exercise, such that Chicago

> avoid[ed] the preemptive force of any provision of [RLUIPA] by changing the policy or practice that result[ed] in a substantial burden on religious exercise, by retaining the policy or practice and exempting the substantially burdened religious exercise, by providing exemptions from the policy or practice for applications that substantially burden religious exercise, or by any other means that eliminate[ed] the substantial burden. . . .

ANALYSIS . . .

I. RELIGIOUS LAND USE AND INSTITUTIONALIZED PERSONS ACT

Appellants argue that the CZO violates RLUIPA's substantial burden provision, which requires land-use regulations that substantially burden religious exercise to be the least restrictive means of advancing a compelling government interest, *see* 42 U.S.C. §2000cc(a), as well as its nondiscrimination provision, which prohibits land-use regulations that either disfavor religious uses relative to nonreligious uses or unreasonably exclude religious uses from a particular jurisdiction, *see* 42 U.S.C. §2000cc(b).[5]

In order to prevail on a claim under the substantial burden provision, a plaintiff must first demonstrate that the regulation at issue actually imposes a substantial burden on religious exercise. RLUIPA defines "religious exercise" to encompass "any exercise of religion, whether or not compelled by, or central to, a system of religious belief," including "[t]he use, building, or conversion of real property for the purpose of religious exercise." 42 U.S.C. §2000cc-5(7). This definition reveals Congress's intent to expand the concept of religious exercise contemplated both in decisions discussing the precursory RFRA . . . and in traditional First Amendment jurisprudence . . . .

Although the text of the statute contains no similar express definition of the term "substantial burden," RLUIPA's legislative history indicates that it is to be interpreted by reference to RFRA and First Amendment jurisprudence. *See* 146 Cong. Rec. 7774-01, 7776 ("The term 'substantial burden' as used in this Act is not intended to be given any broader interpretation than the Supreme Court's articulation of the concept of substantial burden on religious exercise"). Chicago cites a

5. In relevant part, those provisions read as follows:

§2000cc. Protection of land use as religious exercise.

(a) Substantial burdens.

(1) General rule. No government shall impose or implement a land use regulation in a manner that imposes a substantial burden on the religious exercise of a person, including a religious assembly or institution, unless the government demonstrates that imposition of the burden on that person, assembly, or institution—

(A) is in furtherance of a compelling governmental interest; and

(B) is the least restrictive means of furthering that compelling governmental interest.

(2) Scope of application. This subsection applies in any case in which . . .

(C) the substantial burden is imposed in the implementation of a land use regulation or system of land use regulations, under which a government makes, or has in place formal or informal procedures or practices that permit the government to make, individualized assessments of the proposed uses for the property involved.

(b) Discrimination and exclusion.

(1) Equal terms. No government shall impose or implement a land use regulation in a manner that treats a religious assembly or institution on less than equal terms with a nonreligious assembly or institution.

(2) Nondiscrimination. No government shall impose or implement a land use regulation that discriminates against any assembly or institution on the basis of religion or religious denomination.

(3) Exclusions and limits. No government shall impose or implement a land use regulation that—

(A) totally excludes religious assemblies from a jurisdiction; or

(B) unreasonably limits religious assemblies, institutions, or structures within a jurisdiction.

42 U.S.C. §2000cc.

decision of this Court which held that, within the meaning of RFRA, a substantial burden on religious exercise "is one that forces adherents of a religion to refrain from religiously motivated conduct, inhibits or constrains conduct or expression that manifests a central tenet of a person's religious beliefs, or compels conduct or expression that is contrary to those beliefs." *Mack v. O'Leary*, 80 F.3d 1175, 1179 (7th Cir. 1996) (vacated on other grounds). Substituting RLUIPA's broader definition of religious exercise, which need not be "compelled by or central to" a particular religion, for that articulated in *Mack*, the meaning of "substantial burden on religious exercise" could be read to include the effect of any regulation that "inhibits or constrains the use, building, or conversion of real property for the purpose of religious exercise." Such a construction might lend support to Appellant's contention that the CZO, insofar as it contributes to other existing constraints upon the use of specific parcels as churches, substantially burdens religious exercise. However, this cannot be the correct construction of "substantial burden on religious exercise" under RLUIPA. Application of the substantial burden provision to a regulation inhibiting or constraining *any* religious exercise, including the use of property for religious purposes, would render meaningless the word "substantial," because the slightest obstacle to religious exercise incidental to the regulation of land use — however minor the burden it were to impose — could then constitute a burden sufficient to trigger RLUIPA's requirement that the regulation advance a compelling governmental interest by the least restrictive means. We therefore hold that, in the context of RLUIPA's broad definition of religious exercise, a land-use regulation that imposes a substantial burden on religious exercise is one that necessarily bears direct, primary, and fundamental responsibility for rendering religious exercise — including the use of real property for the purpose thereof within the regulated jurisdiction generally — effectively impracticable.

Appellants contend that the scarcity of affordable land available for development in R zones, along with the costs, procedural requirements, and inherent political aspects of the Special Use, Map Amendment, and Planned Development approval processes, impose precisely such a substantial burden. However, we find that these conditions — which are incidental to any high-density urban land use — do not amount to a substantial burden on religious exercise. While they may contribute to the ordinary difficulties associated with location (by any person or entity, religious or nonreligious) in a large city, they do not render impracticable the use of real property in Chicago for religious exercise, much less discourage churches from locating or attempting to locate in Chicago. . . . Significantly, each of the five individual plaintiff churches has successfully located within Chicago's city limits. That they expended considerable time and money so to do does not entitle them to relief under RLUIPA's substantial burden provision. . . . Otherwise, compliance with RLUIPA would require municipal governments not merely to treat religious land uses on an equal footing with nonreligious land uses, but rather to favor them in the form of an outright exemption from land-use regulations. Unfortunately for Appellants, no such free pass for religious land uses masquerades among the legitimate protections RLUIPA affords to religious exercise.

Though the substantial burden and nondiscrimination provisions are operatively independent of one another, RLUIPA's governmental discretion provision, 42 U.S.C. §2000cc-3(e), upon which the district court relied in order to find that the February 2000 CZO amendments corrected any violation of the substantial burden provision, appears not to reflect this distinction. That subsection provides, in part, that "a government may avoid the preemptive force of *any provision* of [RLUIPA] by changing the policy or practice *that results in a substantial burden* on religious exercise." 42 U.S.C. §2000cc-3(e) (emphasis added). Rather than remove any substantial burden on religious exercise, however, the February 2000 amendments simply place churches on an equal footing with nonreligious assembly uses, thereby correcting any potential violation of the nondiscrimination provision. Despite subsection 2000cc-3(e)'s reference to removal of a "substantial burden," we read it to afford a government the discretion to take corrective action to eliminate a nondiscrimination provision violation, whether or not it was the result of a substantial burden on religious exercise. Thus do we find that, under RLUIPA's governmental discretion provision, the February 2000 amendments to the CZO render RLUIPA's nondiscrimination provision inapplicable to this case.

Insofar as Appellants cannot demonstrate on these facts that the CZO substantially burdens religious exercise, and because the February 2000 Amendments to the CZO bring it into compliance with RLUIPA's nondiscrimination provision, Appellants fail to make a sufficient showing on essential elements of their RLUIPA claims. Chicago is therefore entitled to summary judgment on those claims.

Having found RLUIPA inapplicable to the facts of this case, we need not address the issue of RLUIPA's constitutionality, raised by the parties as well as the United States of America, as Intervenor, and various Amici Curiae. . . .

Notes and Comments

1. *The Effect of RLUIPA.* What types of disputes are likely to arise under RLUIPA? How would RLUIPA affect review of special exceptions, conditional use permits, or requested zone changes? Will traffic, parking, or noise concerns that arise above the pretextual justify denial? What if a neighborhood is saturated with churches outstripping parking resources? Could a church building be subject to a historic preservation ordinance? Could a church be subject to aesthetic controls or approval by an architectural review ordinance?

How would *First Covenant* be resolved under RLUIPA? *See also Murphy v. Zoning Commn. of the Town of New Milford*, 148 F. Supp. 2d 173 (D. Conn. 2001) (town enjoined from enforcing order limiting the number of people that may attend weekly prayer service in a private home under RLUIPA); *Cottonwood Christian Center v. Cypress Redevelopment Agency*, 218 F. Supp. 2d 1203 (C.D. Cal. 2000) (applying a "strict scrutiny" standard under RLUIPA and enjoining the city from carrying out eminent domain proceedings on a site which the city wanted for redevelopment but on which the church wanted to build a facility).

2. *Is RLUIPA Another RFRA?* The constitutionality of RLUIPA remains an open question. In *Freedom Baptist Church of Delaware County v. Town of Middletown*, 204 F. Supp. 2d 857 (E.D. Pa. 2002), the court upheld RLUIPA in a lengthy opinion. RLUIPA was found constitutional because it codified existing free exercise, Establishment Clause, and equal protection rights. *Id.* at 870. The court found that RLUIPA was distinguishable from RFRA because RLUIPA did not attempt any substantive change in constitutional protections.

3. *Writings.* The subject of RLUIPA and RFRA has caught the attention of many commentators. *See* Roman Storzer & Anthony Picarello, Jr., The Religious Land Use and Institutionalized Persons Act of 2000: A Constitutional Response to Unconstitutional Zoning Practices, 9 Geo. Mason L. Rev. 929 (2001); Caroline R. Adams, Note, The Constitutional Validity of the Religious Land Use and Institutionalized Persons Act of 2000, 70 Ford. L. Rev. 2361 (2002); Evan Shapiro, Comment, The Religious Land Use and Institutionalized Persons Act: An Analysis Under the Commerce Clause, 76 Wash. L. Rev. 1255 (2001); Ada-Marie Walsh, Note, Religious Land Use and Institutionalized Persons Act of 2000: Unconstitutional and Unnecessary, 10 Wm. & Mary Bill of Rts. J. 189 (2001).

9

Regional, State, and Federal Limitations on Local Land Use Decisionmaking

A. INTRODUCTION

1. The Quiet (and Slow) Revolution

In a well-known book published in 1972, the authors posited that a fundamental change in land use controls was occurring in the United States. Their thesis was as follows:

> This country is in the midst of a revolution in the way we regulate the use of our land. It is a peaceful revolution, conducted entirely within the law. It is a quiet revolution, and its supporters include both conservatives and liberals. It is a disorganized revolution, with no central cadre of leaders, but it is a revolution nonetheless.
>
> The *ancien regime* being overthrown is the feudal system under which the entire pattern of land development has been controlled by thousands of individual local governments, each seeking to maximize its tax base and minimize its social problems, and caring less what happens to all the others.
>
> The tools of the revolution are new laws taking a wide variety of forms but each sharing a common theme—the need to provide some degree of state or regional participation in the major decisions that affect the use of our increasingly limited supply of land.

Fred Bosselman & David Callies, The Quiet Revolution in Land Use Control 1 (1971).

Now, a quarter-century later, it seems apparent that fundamental change in the governmental level of regulatory control has proceeded more slowly than anticipated. Unlike many other areas of law, which have been substantially "federalized," the field of land use regulation has resisted federal preemption or interference. Moreover, with some well-recognized exceptions, it has also proved resistant to attempts at moving the locus of land use power to the state or regional level.

The student of land use controls must recognize the roots of this deep-seated resistance to change in the level of government that regulates land use. One powerful reason is the pervasive conviction that, because land use decisions have an important impact on living conditions in local communities, those elected representatives who are closest to the community should decide them. Furthermore, because local government operates much of the infrastructure that services new development, local governments have a legitimate claim to authority over decisions about developments that will contribute to and use that infrastructure.

But other potent political forces — forces at odds with each other on many land use issues — also are in agreement on the question of which government should control land use. Local elected officials resist the loss of power that state control or oversight of land use regulation would bring. Land use authority is the most important power remaining at the local government level, particularly in states where state legislation or voter initiative has circumscribed the power to raise property taxes. City councilors tenaciously defend this last bastion of their authority.

The development community is, in general, also satisfied with the current governmental arrangement. Many developers believe that their ability to influence land use decisions is maximized at the local level and would be diminished if those decisions were removed to the regional or state level. Finally, the "third parties" in many land use disputes, citizens' groups and their members, have substantial electoral clout in local elections. Thus, they also worry about a diminution in their influence if state or regional regulation should replace the current system.

2. *The Critiques of Local Regulation*

These various political forces coalesce into a tremendous resistance to proposals that local government should not have the final word on land use decisions. There are, however, strong arguments that complete local autonomy over land use decisions is both illogical and inefficient. Perhaps most importantly, the impacts of land use decisions by cities and counties are not self-contained; instead, those impacts can ripple throughout the region in which the local jurisdiction is situated. For example, the location of a large shopping center in a city will have economic and environmental spillover effects; neighboring jurisdictions may well bear the traffic impacts of such a center, while the region will feel the air quality effects of increased automobile emissions. At the same time, however, the local jurisdiction in which the shopping center is located will likely garner the revenue from any sales taxes accruing to local cities, and the construction of a large shopping center in one city will likely mean that other developers will be uninterested in locating a competing facility anywhere close to this one.

Furthermore, like it or not, the state and the federal governments are already involved in the decisions about how an area develops. They build and maintain the principal transportation arteries in metropolitan regions, and their agencies regulate many development decisions for environmental protection purposes. Integrating these functions with decisions on major development projects, now made by local governments, seems to make sense. Finally, local land use control has often resulted in the type of urban sprawl that many critics have condemned on a combination of economic, environmental, and aesthetic grounds.

3. Regional and State Oversight

These types of problems have led to significant experimentation with state and regional review of certain types of land use decisionmaking. In a few instances, this experimentation has taken the form of direct state intervention into the land use decisionmaking process. Hawaii began the movement in 1961 when it adopted a top-down system of statewide land use regulation that greatly limits the local role in such decisions. This system is unique to Hawaii, which because of its size and politics, is perhaps best suited to a transfer of land use power to the state level. More typical is the bottom-up land use approach adopted in Oregon. Under this system, local governments bear the responsibility of preparing comprehensive land use plans. Those plans, however, must be consistent with a series of goals set at the state level, goals that emphasize protection of forests and farmlands, as well as the securing of affordable housing through increased residential densities inside urban growth boundaries.

An Oregon state agency has the authority to review all local plans for consistency with the statewide goals, and once the local government receives the state's "acknowledgment" that its plan adequately reflects these goals, its development decisions must then be consistent with the plan. Thereafter, a variety of parties are authorized to appeal the local government's decisions to a state land use appeals board, which has authority to review the local agency's determinations of consistency. All of these procedures occur with considerable emphasis on public participation.

A second statewide system, the Vermont system, is explicated in this chapter. While the Oregon system is based on comprehensive planning, in Vermont regional commissions and a statewide agency assess developments against a series of statutory criteria that relate to infrastructure capacity, environmental degradation, and other such impacts. Furthermore, projects in Vermont are not automatically subject to regional and statewide supervision; individuals must appeal local decisions to initiate that oversight.

The Oregon and Vermont approaches involve a statewide land use planning agency overseeing developments in all areas of the state. Other states, however, have chosen to form regional bodies that review local land use decisions for specific areas or for certain projects with significant impacts on natural resources. This regulatory mechanism was championed by the American Law Institute's Model Land Development Code, completed in 1975, which stressed the need to regulate projects with impacts that were not contained within local jurisdictional boundaries. *See* American Law Institute, Model Land Development Code, Art. VII §7-301(1). Other states have formed regional bodies to protect specific areas of environmental significance, such as the Chesapeake Bay region, the San Francisco Bay region, and the Adirondack Mountains. This regional approach is illustrated in this chapter by *330 Concord Street Neighborhood Ass'n v. Campsen*, 424 S.E.2d 538 (S.C. Ct. App.), a 1992 South Carolina case focusing on regulation of the coastal zone in that state.

4. Intergovernmental Disputes and Their Resolution

The efforts of states to alter the traditional model of local government control over land use are important, for over the long run they may be the precursor of fundamental change in how land use is controlled. As the chapter's title implies, however, there are other forms of intergovernmental limitations on local government's discretion over land use. One important area might be termed "boundary" limitations: the extent to which a neighboring city, a special purpose district, or a state agency must respect city or county zoning in implementing a project in that local jurisdiction. The competing policy concerns are obvious. The jurisdiction in which the development will be located has a strong interest in ensuring even-handed implementation of its planning, zoning, and other land use controls. A specific development not called for in the local plan can wreak havoc with a well-considered land use scheme.

At the same time, the agency seeking to site a facility in a city or county's jurisdiction may well face parochial opposition. Certain types of governmental projects produce benefits that are spread throughout the region but impose specific costs on the locality where the project will be sited. For example, every regional area needs at least one facility to serve as a jail, but local opposition to the siting of that jail may be intense. If local governments can use their land use powers to resist the siting of such facilities, and state or regional agencies cannot override that power, the implementation of important public tasks can be stymied.

Resolution of such issues is most appropriately the subject of legislation, but the statutes in many instances are silent. Thus, the matter is often left to the courts by default, which have used a variety of approaches to resolve it. Most recently, the trend is toward the "balancing of interests" approach utilized in *Brown v. Kansas Forestry, Fish and Game Commission*, a principal case in this chapter. This method, under which the court balances the interests of the governmental entities involved to determine which should receive priority, has the merit of avoiding categorical outcomes and of focusing on the specific dispute involved. In performing this balancing process, however, the courts are essentially making a legislative judgment, and their competence to do so can be questioned.

A variation on this form of intergovernmental conflict can occur when one local jurisdiction seeks to annex land outside of its current boundaries. Such action, of course, has important land use implications, as you will see from a principal case included in this chapter, *City of Albuquerque v. State Municipal Boundary Commission*. Disputes over annexations also center on the provision of necessary municipal services.

Another form of intergovernmental conflict arises out of the deluge of environmental legislation adopted by states over the last 25 years. This legislation typically gives a state agency permitting authority over specific types of industrial and business developments, and that permitting authority often requires the state agency to consider factors related to land use before granting the permit. For example, a state regulatory board may have authority over mining activities and may be mandated to consider, among other factors, whether the location of a mine is likely to endanger groundwater or to discharge pollutants that might impact adjoining land uses.

This type of legislation often does not expressly deprive local governments of their traditional land use authority over such facilities. Nonetheless, the overlap in regulatory authority virtually invites claims by applicants that state law preempts local regulation of such developments. In recent years, courts have increasingly grappled with such claims.

5. *The Federal Role*

Finally, in addition to state and regional limitations on local government's land use powers, there is the question of the federal role in land use decisionmaking. In the 1970s, Congress seriously considered enacting some form of national land use planning, and from time to time commentators again float such proposals. Furthermore, the Telecommunications Act of 1996 does contain provisions limiting local power to regulate the siting of certain telecommunications facilities. You will read a case under the Act and use it as a prism to reflect on how the federal government might play a larger role in specific land use decisions.

In general, Congress has refused to intervene in local land use decisionmaking, leaving it to the states and local governments to devise the institutional arrangements that best suit their needs. This refusal, however, does not mean that the federal government exercises no influence on land use. As owner and custodian of one-third of the nation's land, Congress and the federal land management agencies, such as the Bureau of Land Management and the Forest Service, make land use decisions that significantly affect adjoining jurisdictions. The federal influence is particularly great in the western United States, where federal, state, and private land is often intermingled in the trademark "checkerboard" pattern that has existed since the states first entered the Union.

One of the most important developments of the last 25 years has been the passage of federal legislation requiring the principal federal land management agencies, the Bureau of Land Management, in the Department of the Interior, and the Forest Service, in the Department of Agriculture, to create land use plans for federal lands. These planning efforts, undertaken pursuant to the Forest and Rangeland Renewable Resources Planning Act and the National Forest Management Act, both codified at 16 U.S.C. §1600-14 (2000), and the Federal Land Policy and Management Act, 43 U.S.C. §1701-84 (1986 and 2003 Supp.), for the first time have systematically attempted to inventory federal lands and plan for their future.

Even on nonfederal lands, however, the federal government exercises a powerful influence on local land use through its participation in transportation decisions. Most importantly, the interstate transportation system is largely a federally funded undertaking, and the location of freeway extensions, to take one example, can result in pressures to develop adjacent land.

6. *State and Regional Regulation in the Future*

What will the future hold for state and regional regulation of land use? It appears certain that there will be no wholesale movement away from the longstanding emphasis on local control and that the experiments in state and regional regulation will proceed slowly. The problems that arise when land use regulation is left solely at the local level, however, are likely to increase as urbanization makes the use of municipal boundaries as determinants of land use authority appear increasingly illogical.

Furthermore, protection of natural resources continues to be a dominant political theme, and local governments are not well-suited to ensure such protection. Consequently, state and regional approaches will continue to be attractive in the future. Indeed, a number of authors have recently suggested that regionalism is enjoying a resurgence of interest. Peter Calthorpe and William Fulton, The Regional City (2001); Jonathan Barnett, ed., Planning for a New Century: The Regional Agenda (2001); and Bruce Katz, ed., Reflections on Regionalism (2000). If new controls are adopted, they are likely to take the form of the models addressed in this chapter. The forces of jurisdictional change are still at work.

B. DIRECT STATE OVERSIGHT OF LOCAL REGULATION

State oversight of city or county land use regulation could take several forms. For example, the state could simply transfer authority over some (all?) land use decisions from the local government to the state level. Alternatively, the system could allow for selected appeals to a state (regional?) body from decisions that have significant effects outside of the local jurisdiction or that have important environmental effects.

The first two cases in this chapter illustrate the systems in place in Vermont and Oregon, and the notes following discuss in detail how other states have constructed a system of state oversight of local regulation. As you read the cases and the notes, you should begin to make judgments about which of these systems is preferable from the standpoints of planning, politics, and law.

■ FOLAND v. JACKSON COUNTY
807 P.2d 801 (Or. 1991)

VAN HOOMISSEN, Justice.

STATUTORY FRAMEWORK

The underlying dispute in this case can best be understood within the statutory framework in which it arises. The Legislative Assembly has created a broad program for comprehensive land use planning coordination. *See generally* ORS Ch. 197 (Comprehensive Land Use Planning Coordination). To supervise that program, the Legislative Assembly created the Land Conservation and Development Commission (LCDC) and gave that agency certain duties and powers. ORS 197.030 *et seq.* One of LCDC's duties is to adopt state-wide land use planning "goals" (the goals) that LCDC considers necessary to carry out, *inter alia*, the statutory program of land use planning coordination. ORS 197.225; ORS 197.040(1)(c); ORS 197.015(8).

Cities and counties of Oregon generally are required to conduct all land use planning in accordance with the goals adopted by LCDC. ORS 197.175(1). To serve that purpose, the statutes directed each city and county to prepare and adopt a "comprehensive plan" for land use decisions. ORS 197.175(2)(a). A comprehensive plan must comply with the goals. ORS 197.250.

The statutes also provides for LCDC "acknowledgment" of a comprehensive plan's compliance with the goals. ORS 197.251(1), in part, reads: "Upon the request of a local government, [LCDC] shall by order grant, deny or continue acknowledgment of compliance with the goals." The acknowledgment process allows persons to submit written comments and objections to the plan, requires LCDC to prepare a report concerning acknowledgment, and allows an opportunity for the city or county and persons who submitted comments at the earlier stage to submit written exceptions to the report. ORS 197.251(2). The incentive for a city or county to seek acknowledgment is that once LCDC grants acknowledgment, the city or county no longer is technically required to make land use decisions in compliance with the goals; rather, it is required only to make land use decisions in compliance with the acknowledged plan and other acknowledged ordinances adopted by the city or county. ORS 197.175(2)(d); ORS 197.015(11); *compare* ORS 197.175(2)(c) (if comprehensive plan is not acknowledged then city or county must make land use decisions in compliance with the goals). . . .

One of a city's or county's duties in regard to its comprehensive plan is to review that plan and, if necessary, amend and revise it to comply with the goals. ORS 197.250 (compliance required); ORS 197.255 (review required); ORS 197.175(2)(a) (amend and revise). Various procedures, including notice to LCDC, must be followed before an acknowledged plan may be amended. ORS 197.610 *et seq.* LCDC is also required to review periodically acknowledged plans to ensure their continuing compliance with the goals. ORS 197.640(1). LCDC may require a city or county to amend its acknowledged plan. ORS 197.647(4)(b).

If a plan previously has been acknowledged, then an amendment to that plan is also acknowledged by operation of law if no notice of intent to appeal is filed within 21 days from the date on which the city or county mails notice of the amendment to persons who are entitled to such notice. ORS 197.625(1); ORS 197.830(8); *see also* ORS 197.615(2)(a) (identifying persons entitled to notice of adoption of amendment). During the 21 day period, any person who participated either orally or in writing in the proceeding leading to the adoption of the amendment may challenge that decision through an appeal to LUBA. ORS 197.620; ORS 197.830. Filing of an appeal delays acknowledgment of an amendment unless and until LUBA or the appellate courts affirm the decision. ORS 197.625.

Notes and Comments

1. *The Need for State Intervention.* Consider first whether there is any need for state intervention in local land use decisions. What rationales might support such intervention? Factors that you may wish to evaluate include (1) the need to direct growth into specific areas of a state; (2) the arbitrariness of local government boundaries; (3) the possibility that specific projects may cause environmental degradation; (4) the need for large public investments to support new developments; (5) the possibility that all the benefits of a new project will accrue to one local jurisdiction while another local jurisdiction, which receives no benefits, is

significantly burdened; and (6) the local government's possible lack of the expertise needed to regulate large developments.

2. *The Oregon System.* As illustrated in *Foland,* Oregon's State Land Use Act has several key features. The principal requirement is that all local governments must prepare land use plans that must be consistent with goals established by a state agency, the Land Conservation and Development Commission (LCDC). The LCDC, whose members are appointed by the governor and confirmed by the state senate, to date has promulgated 19 such goals. Until a plan is "acknowledged" by the LCDC, decisions by local governments on development projects must be consistent with the state goals. As of 1993, the LCDC had acknowledged the plans of all 241 cities and 36 counties in the state. Edward J. Sullivan, Oregon Blazes a Trail, in State and Regional Comprehensive Planning 54 (1993).

Once the LCDC reviews and acknowledges that the local plan sufficiently takes the statewide goals into account, the city or county is no longer required to make decisions in compliance with those goals. Instead, only compliance with the acknowledged local plan is now mandated; an acknowledgment essentially operates as an affirmation that the statewide policies are being carried out through the local plan. As *Foland* indicates, later amendments to local plans are deemed acknowledged by operation of law unless a notice of intent to appeal is filed with the LCDC.

The Oregon system attempts to integrate state and other public agency actions into the implementation process by requiring state agencies and special districts to carry out the local plans. Cities and counties also are required to undertake a periodic review process to ensure that their plans continue to comply with the statewide planning goals.

The Oregon system includes an enforcement mechanism. Citizens who believe that a local decision is inconsistent with a city or county plan may file an administrative appeal with a special state administrative appeals board, the Land Use Board of Appeals (LUBA). Also given authority to file an appeal is the state Department of Land Conservation and Development, which acts as staff to the LCDC. Judicial review of LUBA decisions may be sought directly in the state court of appeals, bypassing the trial courts.

On the Oregon land use system generally, *see* Symposium on Oregon Land Use, 77 Or. L. Rev. (1998).

3. *"Amendments," "Refinements," and Public Accountability.* Under the Oregon law, an amendment to a plan previously "acknowledged" will be acknowledged by operation of law if no one appeals. Is this a flaw in the system? Will local governments respond to political pressures by adopting small amendments to plans while citizens, having been active in the original acknowledgment process, now turn their attention elsewhere?

The issue arose in a part of the *Foland* case not reproduced. As part of an amendment to its plan, the City adopted a map that included a "refinement clause." This clause stated in essence that the mapping was a "generalized representation" of soils inventory, and that "[m]ore precise soils resource mapping" would be used to interpret the location of some sites. When the City later used the refinement clause to approve a development, citizens challenged it. They found, however, that because the refinement clause had been "acknowledged" by operation of law, they could not attack the City's action, which was taken *under* that acknowledged "refinement clause."

Is the refinement clause an acceptable method of using more precise information about soils as it becomes available? Or does the clause insulate from judicial review actions that are, in reality, changes in the local jurisdiction's plan? As noted above, the Oregon law does call for periodic review of a county's plan for continuing compliance with the state's goals. Is that periodic review sufficient to prevent de facto, piecemeal amendments to the local plan through the use of the refinement clause?

In *Hummel v. Land Conservation and Development Comm'n*, 954 P.2d 824 (Or. Ct. App. 1998), plaintiffs alleged that in approving the city's actions updating its urban growth boundary, so as to be consistent with Goal 14 (the "urbanization goal"), the Land Conservation and Development Commission had erred in failing to consider other goals. The court disagreed, observing that the review process "is designed to be sequential and interactive." 954 P.2d at 827. Thus, concluded the court, "[I]t may well be appropriate for a particular work task to focus on a limited number of goals," with the local government later examining other goals to determine whether the plan remains consistent with those goals as well. *Id*.

4. *Consistency With Goals*. Because the Oregon system depends on the implementation of statewide goals through local plans, the rigor with which LCDC and the courts insist upon compliance with those goals is extremely important. *See, e.g., Department of Land, Conservation and Development v. Yamhill County*, 53 P. 3d 462 (Or. Ct. App. 2002) (Land Use Board of Appeals erred in allowing county to take an "exception" (essentially, a variance) to Goal 3 and thereby rezone land from exclusive farm use to allow construction of a single-family dwelling); *Port of St. Helens v. Land Conservation and Development Commn.*, 996 P.2d 1014 (Or. Ct. App. 2000) (commission's order requiring the county to delete certain provisions of its plan pertaining to mining did not violate Goal 9, which concerns economic development). The case law indicates that the courts have generally required strict adherence to the goals. See also *1000 Friends of Oregon v. Land Conservation and Development Commission*, 752 P.2d 271 (Or. 1988).

5. *The Florida System I*. As noted in the introduction to this chapter, §7-301 of the American Law Institute's Model Land Development Code called for a "State Land Planning Agency" to review "developments of regional impact." These developments were those "which, because of the nature or magnitude of the development or the nature or magnitude of its effect on the surrounding environment," were likely to present issues "of state or regional significance." *Id*. In general, DRIs are large housing or commercial developments, and large public infrastructure projects such as highways, airports, and landfills.

Florida was the leading state to adopt a system implementing the principal features of the Model Code, although several other states, including Massachusetts, Georgia, Colorado, and Washington, have to some extent also incorporated aspects of the DRI model into their land use system. The Florida Environmental Land and Water Management Act of 1972 provided for state oversight of two types of developments: (1) areas of "critical state concern" and (2) developments with regional impacts. Areas of critical state concern are those designated by the Legislature, such as the Florida Keys. *See, e.g.*, the Florida Keys Area Protection Act, Fla. Stats. Ann. §380.0552(1) (West 1997); *Askew v. Cross Key Waterways*, 372 So. 2d 913, 925 (Fla. 1978) (finding that the statute, which then allowed the governor and cabinet, acting as the "Administration Commission," to designate critical areas, was an unconstitutional delegation of legislative power). Regulation of areas of "critical concern" will be discussed below in this chapter.

A "development of regional impact" is defined as a project with a "substantial effect upon the health, safety, or welfare of citizens of more than one county." Fla. Stat. Ann. §380.06(1) (West 1997). *See, e.g., Battaglia Properties, Ltd. v. Florida Land and Water Adjudicatory Commission*, 629 So. 2d 161, 162 (Fla. Dist. Ct. App. 1993) (the magnitude of development sought on a vacant tract of land about 120 acres in size rendered it a DRI).

Whenever a local government issues a development order for a DRI or for a project in a critical area, the owner, the developer, an "appropriate regional planing agency," or the state land planning agency can appeal the order to the Florida Land and Water Adjudicatory Commission. Citizens, however, lack standing to appeal. *Friends of the Everglades, Inc. v. Board of County Comm'rs*, 456 So. 2d 904, 909 (Fla. Dist. Ct. App. 1984). The Commission is made up of the governor of the state and members of his or her cabinet, and hearings before the Commission are de novo. The state bears the burden of proof that an adverse impact will result if the permit is granted, but the burden then shifts to the applicant to prove that the proposed curative measures are adequate. *Graham v. Estuary Properties, Inc.*, 399 So. 2d 1374, 1379 (Fla.), *cert. denied*, 454 U.S. 1083 (1981).

The Florida regulation of DRIs is discussed in Thomas G. Pelham, Regulating Developments of Regional Impact: Florida and the Model Code, 29 U. Fla. L. Rev. 789 (1977). For a discussion of legislation in other states, such as Georgia and Connecticut, implementing the DRI concept, see Marya Morris, Regulating Regional Impacts: Toward Model Legislation, 47 Land Use L. & Zoning Dig. 3 (Aug. 1995).

6. *The Florida System II.* The Florida DRI approach resulted in a great deal of controversy as it was implemented throughout the 1970s and early 1980s. In mid-1985, Florida adopted new legislation that is much closer to the Oregon model.

Under the new law, known as the Local Government Comprehensive Planning and Land Development Regulation Act, Fla. Stat. Ann. §§163.3161–163.3217 (West 2000 and Supp. 2004), each local government must adopt a comprehensive plan, which must contain specific types of goals, objectives, and policies. Fla. Admin. Code §9J-5.005 (2001) (regulations regarding the content of the plans adopted by the Florida Department of Community Affairs). The plans must also provide that adequate public facilities are available when a development is approved. Fla. Stat. Ann. §163.3180 (West 1990) ("concurrency").

The Act provides for state review of the local plans. The local government must transmit its draft plan or any proposed plan amendment to the Department of Community Affairs, which has 30 days to decide whether to conduct a review (although under certain circumstances a review is mandatory). The Department's review will take the form of an "Objections, Recommendations, and Comments Report." After receiving the report, the local government has 60 days to review it and adopt the actual plan or amendment.

After the local government takes action, the Department reviews the actual plan or amendment, and at conclusion of the review it publishes a "Notice of Intent" finding the plan either in compliance or not in compliance with the Act. Fla. Stat. Ann. §163.3184(8) (West 1990). Administrative hearings then follow. *See Florida Wildlife Federation v. Collier County*, 819 So. 2d 200 (Fla. Ct. App. 2002) (admininstrative hearing on whether local plan properly mapped Natural

Resource Protection Areas designed to protect indigenous fauna and flora, especially the highly endangered Florida panther); *St. Joe Paper Co. v. Department of Community Affairs*, 657 So. 2d 27 (Fla. Dist. Ct. App. 1995) (citizens group should not have been allowed to intervene into administrative hearing process resulting in a final order by the Administration Commission). To be in compliance, the plan or amendment must meet certain criteria, including consistency with the now-codified State Comprehensive Plan, regional plans, and other state-imposed criteria. *See 1000 Friends of Florida, Inc. v. State Dept. of Community Affairs*, 824 So. 2d 989 (Fla. Ct. App. 2002) (upholding Department's determination that city's amendments to the intergovernmental coordination element of its general plan were valid).

If the plan or amendment is not in compliance, the Department does not have the authority to render it ineffective or to adopt a substitute plan. Rather, enforcement depends upon financial sanctions, which the government and cabinet, acting as the "Administration Commission," may levy against the noncomplying local government. Fla. Stat. Ann. §163.3184(11) (West 1990). *See Florida League of Cities, Inc. v. Administration Comm'n*, 586 So. 2d 397 (Fla. Dist Ct. App. 1991) (upholding sanctions policy for late submittal of plans). Once the plan is adopted and is in compliance, all actions taken by government agencies with regard to development orders must be consistent with the plan. Fla. Stat. Ann. §163.3194(1)(1) (West 1990). Furthermore, local governments must adopt development regulations that implement and are consistent with the plan.

For a comprehensive review of the Florida process, see Symposium on Florida's Growth Management Legislation, 12 U. Fla. J.L. & Pub Pol'y (2001); Richard Grosso, Florida's Growth Management Act: How Far We Have Come, and How Far We have Yet To Go, 20 Nova L. Rev. 589 (1996). See also John E. Fennelly, Examining the Current State of Post-Comprehensive Plan Land-Use Decision Making in Florida: A Property Owner's Guide to the Local Government Comprehensive Planning and Land Development Regulation Act, 7 St. Thomas L. Rev. 1 (1994).

7. *Evaluating the Florida Systems.* The 1993 amendments to the Act provided for the gradual phasing out of the DRI review. Most significantly, if a project is located within a municipality whose land use plan and regulations have been found consistent with statewide goals, the project is exempt from DRI review. Fla. Stat. Ann. §380.06(27) (West 1990).

Which process has more to commend it from the standpoint of effective and reasonable land use control: the DRI process (Florida System I) or the comprehensive plan process (Florida System II)? In this regard, you may be interested in knowing that more than 90 percent of the development in Florida prior to 1993 did not even go through the DRI process, leading those whose projects did go through the appeals process to complain of unequal treatment. *See* John M. DeGrove, Planning and Growth Management in the States 9-10 (1992); *Leon County v. State Dept. of Community Affairs*, 666 So. 2d 1003 (Fla. Dist. Ct. App. 1996) (pipeline and petroleum storage facility were not subject to DRI review). With respect to the review of local plans, the Department of Community Affairs initially found about half of the local plans to be "not in compliance." Planning and Growth Management, *supra*, at 15. Once the plans achieve compliance, do you think that the implementation measures are sufficient to ensure that the plans are actually followed?

In contrast to the Oregon planning system and the Florida "critical area" approach, under the Vermont Land Use and Development Act, regional and state agencies employ a set of criteria to review development applications. The following case exemplifies this approach.

■ IN RE KISIEL

772 A.2d 135 (Vt. 2000)

DOOLEY, J.

Landowners Mark and Pauline Kisiel appeal the Environmental Board's decision denying their application for an Act 250 permit to subdivide and develop a 158-acre tract of land into five residential lots in the Town of Waitsfield. . . .

The property in question is located at the end of Bowen Road, an unmaintained class 4 town highway, in the Town of Waitsfield on the western side of the Northfield Range. At the time landowners submitted their application for the five-unit subdivision, the Town's zoning ordinance permitted minimum five-acre residential lots on the subject parcel, which is situated within the Town's Forest Reserve District—defined as land in the Northfield Range with an elevation in excess of 1500 feet.[1] The elevation of the project tract ranges from 1500 to 2000 feet, with the proposed construction occurring between 1500 and 1700 feet. To provide vehicular access to the project tract, landowners proposed improving 2400 feet of Bowen Road.

In February 1996, the Waitsfield Planning Commission granted subdivision approval for the proposed project. The Commission noted that its decision to grant a permit followed public discussions of the proposal on four occasions, a site visit, two public hearings, and deliberations by the Commission on four separate dates in late 1995 and early 1996. The subdivision permit contained more than twenty specific conditions, several of which concerned the proposed improvements to Bowen Road. The permit required landowners to pay for the upgrade and maintenance of the road. . . .

In January 1997, the Waitsfield Selectboard approved landowners' request to improve Bowen Road by granting them a Permit for Work in the Public Right of Way. Once again, the permit contained several conditions that reflected the Town's concern with preserving the historic uses of the roadway. The permit required landowners (1) to provide a public trail easement that would allow access to the municipal forest for various recreational uses, (2) to provide easements for logging and natural resources management, and (3) to construct a public parking lot that would facilitate public access to the forest through their property. The permit also stated that the improvements to the road would not "require the Town to upgrade Bowen Road's town highway classification." See 19 V.S.A. §708(b) ("A class 4 highway need not be reclassified to class 3 merely because there exists within a town one or more class 3 highways with characteristics similar to the class 4 highway.").

In November 1997, the District No. 5 Environmental Commission issued a land-use permit authorizing the subdivision under Act 250, 10 V.S.A. §§6001-6108. Notwithstanding the earlier permits granted by the Town, the Town appealed the

1. There was testimony that, after granting landowners a permit to proceed with their development, the Town enacted interim zoning that prohibited residential development above 1700 feet and restricted such development between 1500 and 1700 feet to a conditional use.

Commission's decision to the Board, which received extensive prefiled testimony, conducted a site visit, and held an evidentiary hearing. In June 1998, the Board issued its decision, ruling that the application complied with several of the criteria contained in 10 V.S.A. §6086(a), but failed to comply with others, including criterion (10), which requires "conformance with any duly adopted local or regional plan." *Id.* §6086(a)(10). The Board found, in this regard, that the proposal to upgrade Bowen Road was not in compliance with the plan's goal of maintaining the "status" of class 4 roads, and further found that the proposal was inconsistent with the goal of precluding development on "steep" slopes. In response to a subsequent motion to alter, the Board amended several of its findings, but otherwise reaffirmed its decision denying the application. This appeal followed.

We have decided a number of cases involving the compliance of a development proposal with criterion 10 of Act 250, which requires that the proposed development be "in conformance with any duly adopted local or regional plan." 10 V.S.A. §6086(a)(10). Before we examine the specifics of the plan provisions before us, we find it instructive to review two of those decisions, which we find central to the resolution of this case.

The first is *In re Green Peak Estates*, 154 Vt. 363, 577 A.2d 676 (1990), in which we upheld a decision of the Environmental Board that the second and third phases of a subdivision development were not in conformance with either the town or regional plan. The facts of *Green Peak Estates* have some similarities to the facts of this case because the developer was attempting to develop residential lots in a higher-elevation undeveloped area. Unlike this case, however, the town had no subdivision regulations, and the planning commission opposed the development as inconsistent with the town plan. Moreover, the regional plan specifically provided that "[o]n slopes greater than 20%, residential development should not be permitted." *Id.* at 368, 577 A.2d at 679. The Board found that this specific provision of the regional plan was consistent with the more general provisions of the town plan that established an objective of keeping the "rugged and poorly accessible mountain and forest areas free from development." *Id.* Because at least half of the proposed subdivision was to be located on a slope exceeding 20 percent, the Board found that the development did not conform with the regional plan. We affirmed, holding that "the Board's commonsense interpretation of the plan's policy on this point is consistent with the overall approach to use of the region's intermediate uplands." *Id.* at 369, 577 A.2d at 679.

The second decision is *In re Molgano*, 163 Vt. 25, 653 A.2d 772 (1994), in which the Board also found a development proposal was not in conformance with a town and regional plan. This time, however, we reversed the Board's decision because of two critical elements not present in *Green Peak Estates*. First, the town had adopted specific zoning ordinances consistent with the town plan and had issued a zoning permit to the developer under these ordinances. Second, the language of the town plan on which the Board relied was "broad," "nonregulatory," and "at best, ambiguous" with respect to the issues before the Board. *Id.* at 29-30, 653 A.2d at 775.

Regarding the first difference, we found error in the Board's holding that the zoning ordinances and decisions were irrelevant to criterion 10 review, noting that implementation of a town plan is done through zoning ordinances so that the ordinances control the plan. We concluded:

> Because the Board's interpretation would effectively give nonregulatory abstractions in the Town Plan the legal force of zoning laws, we agree with Molgano that the Board erred as a matter of law in concluding that the Town's zoning bylaws were not germane to the meaning of the Town Plan.
> *Id.* at 31, 653 A.2d at 775.

As suggested in the above quote, we also found error in the Board's holding with respect to the second difference. In discussing language from the regional plan, which we found to be "broad and vague," we distinguished *Green Peak Estates* as involving "a specific policy against [the] type of development" at issue. *Id.* at 31, 653 A.2d at 776 . . . (language of regional plan should be enforced under criterion 10 when it is "clear and unqualified, and creates no ambiguity").

The case can be resolved based on the distinctions between *Molgano* and *Green Peak Estates.* We first turn to the specific plan provisions, and the claims of the parties with respect to them, starting with the Board's holding that the development was not in conformance with the plan's provisions concerning developments on steep slopes. The Board found that the project was not in compliance with Objective 2.a of Goals 1.1 and 1.2 found in section IV of the town plan. The latter goals relate to the preservation and responsible use of the Town's natural features and resources. The Objective in question provides as follows:

> Objective 2. To protect Waitsfield's fragile resources and sensitive natural areas and reduce environmental hazards and prevent the loss of life and property from flooding. a. Prevent the creation of parcels which will result in development on *steep slopes,* critical wetlands and floodplain; and consider amending the Waitsfield Zoning Bylaws to create standards to prevent such development. (Emphasis added.)

In challenging the Board's conclusion that their project failed to comply with Objective 2.a, landowners rely primarily on subsection 1.2 of section III of the Town plan dealing with "fragile features" of the environment. This section cautions that "steep slopes and hillsides" are generally unsuitable for development because of problems relating to sewage disposal and soil erosion, as well as the potential impact on scenic landscape and wildlife habitat. Although the section does not specifically define "steep" slopes, it characterizes certain gradients as follows:

> Generally, slopes with a gradient of 0.6 percent are considered slights; 6-15 percent, moderate; 15-25 percent, severe; and greater than 25 percent, extreme. Consideration of soils conditions and erosion control are extremely important prior to development, with the steepest slopes being unsuitable for development. Resource Map 2 shows those areas which are characterized by severe and extreme slopes.

Landowners emphasize that, with the exception of a portion of one driveway, their project would be confined to slopes ranging between 5-20 percent, and therefore below what the plan characterized as "extreme." The Board rejected this argument below, indicating that construction on gradients characterized as "severe" (15 to 25 percent) was sufficient to establish noncompliance with the Objective to prevent development on steep slopes.

There is no doubt that the Town could limit or preclude development on steep slopes for sound reasons of soil conservation, sewage disposal, view preservation, and the like. This is, of course, the holding of *Green Peak Estates.* But, unlike the regional plan in *Green Peak Estates*, the Waitsfield town plan does not specifically define a "steep" slope; nor does the Town's zoning ordinance provide any specific standards. The parties are thus left to debate the Town's intent, with landowners claiming that the Town intended to apply the prohibition only to "extreme" slopes with grades over 25 percent, and the Town asserting that the prohibition includes slopes characterized as "severe," i.e., having grades between 15 and 25 percent. The Board's decision did not elaborate on the basis of its ruling, and nothing in the plan — or the zoning ordinance — provides contextual guidance on this point.

As we explained in *Molgano*, 163 Vt. at 30, 653 A.2d at 775, zoning bylaws are designed to implement the town plan, and may provide meaning where the plan is ambiguous. Conversely, in the absence of pertinent zoning bylaws, the Board may not "give nonregulatory abstractions in the Town Plan the legal force of zoning laws." *Id.* at 31, 653 A.2d at 775. This is precisely what the Board did here. The town plan sets forth an abstract policy against development on steep slopes, but provides no specific standards to enforce the policy. Indeed, the plan itself acknowledges this deficiency; it expressly recommends within the steep-slope section that the Town "consider amending the Waitsfield Zoning Bylaws to create standards to prevent such development." Nothing in the record, however, indicates that the Town has enacted such standards.[2] Absent some objective measure to guide enforcement of the steep-slope prohibition, there was no basis for the Board to conclude that the project was not in compliance with this policy. Cf. *Green Peak Estates*, 154 Vt. at 368, 577 A.2d at 679 (enforcing specific standard prohibiting development on slopes in excess of 20 percent). Thus, we agree with landowners that the Board erred in concluding that the project was not in compliance with Objective 2.a of the town plan relating to steep slopes.

The Board's second determination that the development does not conform to the town plan concerns the Town's goal of maintaining the "status" of class 4 roads. One of the goals listed in the town plan, Goal 5.2, is: "The improvement and expansion of alternative, non-automobile transportation modes." Among the objectives designed to achieve this goal is Objective 4: "To provide alternatives to the heavy reliance on individual automobiles." Subpart g of this objective provides as follows: "Maintain the current *status* of all class four Town Highways to promote their use for walking, bicycling and horseback riding." (Emphasis added.)

The inventory and analysis section of the town plan (section III) that precedes the stated goals and objectives includes the following paragraphs on roads and residential development within the Forest Reserve District:

> The forest reserve district includes the least accessible areas of town. Few roads provide access, most of those being unmaintained class 4 roads (such as . . . Bowen Road . . .). However, proposals to *upgrade* these roads to *class 3 status* have been made in recent years, and the subdivision of large parcels for residential development has resulted in the construction of private roads. Should these trends continue the current character of the forest reserve district could be significantly altered. Road improvements would likely result in increased pressure to subdivide large parcels for year-round residences, and could lead to the fragmentation of existing habitat. . . .

2. Apparently, as noted above, the interim zoning enacted subsequent to landowners' permit application prohibited residential development above 1700 feet and restricted such development above 1500 feet. There was no evidence that the ordinance addressed steep-slope standards.

> Because of the geographic conditions throughout this district, road improvements are expensive and difficult to maintain. This is exacerbated by the distance from other Town roads and services. Further, emergency vehicle access is difficult on steep, narrow roads, and the potential for conflict between automobile traffic and logging operations exist in this area. Existing class 4 roads, and certain private logging roads, also provide exceptional recreation opportunities, including hiking, biking, horseback riding and hunting access to remote areas. This experience could be diminished through increased automobile access.
>
> . . . In order to limit the adverse impacts of additional residential development in this district, the *upgrade of roads* and subdivision of large forest parcels *should be discouraged.* If residential development does occur, careful site selection and screening of new homes should occur, and landowners should be encouraged to restrict further subdivision of large parcels.
>
> (Emphasis added.)

Another part of the inventory and analysis section of the plan concerning transportation includes the following language:

> Class 4 roads provide excellent walking opportunities, especially in the Northfield Range where such class 4 roads as the Bowen Road . . . offer access to largely undeveloped mountains. . . .
>
> In addition to class 4 roads, many miles of private logging roads and trails are available to the public through the generosity of landowners. However, many of these private roads are at risk of being posted and access prohibited as landowner-user conflicts arise. . . .
>
> In the future the Town may explore the potential for formalizing many of these informal trails through the dedication of permanent easements. The continuing subdivision of land poses both a risk to this informal network *and an opportunity to encourage path easements as a condition to subdivision approval.*

(Emphasis added.) This language supports Objective 3.j (Goal 6.2) of the plan to "secure permanent access to traditional hiking trails in Town, including trail access to the Scrag Municipal Forest from both the north and the south."

In its decision, the Board focused on the word "status" in Objective 4.g, concluding that it was not synonymous with the word "classification." According to the Board, improving a previously unmaintained class 4 highway to the extent that it could handle vehicular traffic would violate the plan's stated objective of "maintain[ing] the current status of all class four Town Highways to promote their use for walking, bicycling and horseback riding."

Landowners argue that the Board has erroneously defined the word status to mean the condition of the road rather than its legal classification. They note that the word "status," when used in connection with highways, often describes legal or statutory standing. . . . Other language in the plan supports this argument. As indicated above, a related section refers to "proposals to *upgrade* these roads *to class 3 status*," thereby suggesting that the word "status" in Objective 4.g means classification.

We recognize that the Board is required to follow ordinary rules of statutory construction in construing the plan, and that we must accord great deference to the Board's decision. *In re MBL Assocs.*, 166 Vt. at 607, 693 A.2d at 700-01. Nevertheless, we conclude that the landowners' position must prevail over the Board's interpretation of the plan in this instance for a number of reasons.

First, although the Board relied upon the most specific and concrete expression of the plan's policy on class 4 roads, other expressions of the policy contained in the plan are far less specific or definitive. As with the policy on steep slopes, there is little specificity on how the class-4-road policy should be enforced and, indeed, the enforcement language is quite tentative. We conclude that the meaning of the plan is ambiguous.[3] This conclusion is underscored by the candid admission of counsel for the Town that differences in meaning urged by it and landowners are "subtle."

In contrast to the town plan in *Green Peak Estates*, which provided that certain development should not be permitted, here the plan provides that the upgrade of roads "should be discouraged." Thus, we are concerned that in addition to attempting to construe and apply an ambiguous plan, the Board has also given "nonregulatory abstractions in the Town Plan the legal force of zoning laws," action that we criticized in *Molgano*, 163 Vt. at 31, 653 A.2d at 775.

Second, and more important, the central teaching of *Molgano* is that where there is ambiguity in the wording of a plan, the Board must look to the interpretation of the plan by the municipal bodies responsible for its implementation and enforcement. When we look at what the Town of Waitsfield has done, and what is has not done, with respect to the development before us, we conclude that this evidence strongly supports landowners' position.

As described above, both the Waitsfield Planning Commission and the Waitsfield Board of Selectmen reviewed this development proposal. Both approved of landowners' plans to improve Bowen Road without upgrading its classification to class 3. Both resolved the conflict between use of the road by automobiles and by hikers, bikers, snowmobilers or horseback riders by requiring landowners to construct a public trail along the road for nonautomobile uses. Both used the permit decisions before them to secure "trail access to the Scrag Municipal Forest," a specific objective of the town plan. In making the many discretionary decisions involved in its evaluation of landowners' subdivision proposal, and in the formulation of the twenty specific conditions it imposed, the planning commission was required to "refer to the goals, objectives, and policies . . . established by the Town plan in making discretionary decisions." Waitsfield Subdivision Regulations §3.1. The selectboard, acting pursuant to its power to control the maintenance of roads, see 19 V.S.A. §303, faced precisely the same decision as the Board—whether to allow landowners to improve Bowen Road for automobile travel to their development—and issued the permit to allow the development. These municipal actions are directly contrary to the plan interpretation accepted by the Board.

We also find that what the Town chose not to do supports landowners' interpretation of the plan. For all practical purposes, the interpretation adopted by the Board would ban further residential development within the Forest Reserve District by the intentional continuation of bad and impassable roads, even though the provisions of the town plan plainly contemplate limited development, and the zoning ordinance in place at the time of landowners' application allowed residential

3. The dissent finds the plan language "concrete and precise," 171 Vt. at —, 772 A.2d at 145, primarily by rephrasing the terminology to say that the plan restricts upgrading the "condition" of the road rather than its "status." We agree that if the drafters of the plan had used the word "condition," it would be precise. They chose instead to use the ambiguous word "status," causing the disagreement.

developments as a permitted use.[5] See *Molgano*, 163 Vt. at 33, 653 A.2d at 776-77 ("where . . . a developer diligently pursues a proposal through the local and state permitting processes before seeking an Act 250 permit, conformance under §6086(a)(10) is to be measured with regard to zoning laws in effect at the time of a proper zoning permit application"). The Town's implementation scheme to allow residential development in the district, but to regulate it through the subdivision and road improvement permit process, is blocked by the Board's determination that no development can occur, a determination based on the Town's own plan.

The purpose of Act 250 "is not to supersede local regulation" of land development. See *In re Trono Constr. Co.*, 146 Vt. 591, 593, 508 A.2d 695, 696 (1986). Although Act 250 gives to the Board, and this Court on appeal from the Board's decisions, the power to override a town's implementation of its own plan, this power should be exercised only when the local construction of the town plan is plainly erroneous. No other policy will maintain local control of land use planning and promote fairness and consistency in state and local regulatory review. We must give deference to the determination of the Board, but the Board in turn must give deference to the determinations of local bodies in applying the plan.

We recognize that we are endorsing the primacy of local determinations as to the meaning of town plans in a case in which the Town is arguing that its implementation of its plan should be ignored. For whatever reasons, the Town is attempting, through Act 250, to undo its own regulatory decisions, without attempting to reopen them in the Town processes. The only explanation in the record lies in the testimony of the chairman of the planning commission that (1) the Town has now adopted an interim zoning ordinance prohibiting residential development on land at an altitude above 1700 feet and requiring conditional use approval for development of land lying between 1500 and 1700 feet, and (2) the Town has more information as a result of the Act 250 process in the way of "environmental impact and scientific knowledge," specifically on the water issues and the visual impact.

The Town is certainly entitled to insist that the Board thoroughly review all the relevant criteria of Act 250 with respect to the development proposal. It is not entitled, however, to use Act 250 to retroactively apply its new zoning regime to a development to which it is not applicable. . . .

We hold that when the language of the Waitsfield town plan is reviewed in light of its application by the regulatory bodies responsible for its implementation within the Town, it cannot be construed to prohibit the improvement of Bowen Road as part of landowners' development proposal. Thus, we conclude that the Board erred in holding that the proposal violated criterion 10.

Reversed and remanded.

AMESTOY, C.J., dissenting. . . .

I do not agree with the majority's conclusion that the Board erred in determining that the road improvements necessary for vehicular access to a proposed five-lot subdivision in the Town's Forest Reserve District would violate the town plan's stated objective of "[m]aintain[ing] the current status of all class four Town

5. We do not agree that the plan bans subdivisions but not single family homes, as the dissent surmises. Whether landowners constructed one home or more, the Board's interpretation of the plan would prevent them from reaching their property by automobile.

Highways to promote their use for walking, bicycling and horseback riding." As the record makes clear, the Board's decision was consistent with the plan, the zoning ordinance, and traditional usage within the Forest Reserve District, which together evinced a clear policy of allowing *limited* residential development and seasonal homes, but discouraging multi-unit subdevelopments of the kind at issue here. Therefore, I would affirm the decision of the Board denying landowners' application for an Act 250 permit.

I.

This case was tried and appealed as a straightforward issue of textual interpretation. In connection with their proposed subdivision project, landowners planned to upgrade approximately 2400 feet of Bowen Road, an unmaintained class four road, through substantial widening and drainage improvements. The issue before the Board was whether the proposed upgrade was consistent with the town plan, one objective of which was to "[m]aintain the current status of all class four Town Highways to promote their use for walking, bicycling, and horseback riding." Landowners argued that "maintain the current status" does not mean "maintain the current physical condition," but rather maintain the class four "legal classification." In support of their contention, landowners cited several cases and statutes which appear to employ the term "status" as the functional equivalent of legal classification, and two other sections of the town plan which arguably provided contextual support for their position.

The Town argued, and the Board found, that the meaning and purpose of the restriction was to restrict the physical improvement of class four roads. Reading the plan as a whole made plain that the goal of the restriction was not merely to maintain Bowen Road's "legal" status, but to preserve the character of the Forest Reserve District. The plan cautioned that improving the few unmaintained roads in the district could significantly alter its unspoiled character by creating pressure for substantial development, and that existing recreational opportunities such as horseback riding, hiking, bicycling, and hunting "could be diminished through increased automobile access."

The majority argues, however, that regardless of the Board's conclusion, the restriction on upgrades of class four roads constitutes little more than a "nonregulatory abstraction" of the kind criticized in *In re Molgano*, 163 Vt. 25, 31, 653 A.2d 772, 775 (1994). The argument was not advanced by landowners at trial or in their appellate briefs. The reason is clear. The provision restricting upgrades on class four roads is concrete and precise. The Town's objective is to *maintain* the existing condition of class four roads, particularly in the Forest Reserve District, in order to limit vehicular access and development, and to preserve existing recreational opportunities and open space. There is nothing abstract about this policy and objective. . . .

Notes and Comments

1. *The Vermont System.* The Vermont Land Use and Development Act, commonly referred to as Act 250, is a prime example of direct state intervention into land use decisionmaking. Unlike the Florida DRI law, which requires state

review only when an appeal is filed on a specific project, Act 250 requires certain applicants to apply directly to one of nine state-created "district environmental commissions." Vt. Stat. Ann. tit. 10 §6026 (1997). The three-member commissions have power to issue permits for all developments under the Act. Any appeals from the commission's decisions are then heard by a nine-member Vermont Environmental Board.

A large number of development applications are subject to Act 250 approval. They include all housing projects of ten or more units; commercial or industrial projects involving more than one acre in towns without land use regulations, or more than ten acres in towns with land use regulations; and all state or municipal projects involving ten or more acres. The state environmental agency reviews all applications for permits and makes recommendations on them to the district environmental commission.

Ten criteria set forth in Act 250 govern permit applications. The criteria embody a wide variety of concerns, ranging from traffic to effects on schools to fiscal impacts. *See* Vt. Stat. Ann. tit. 10 §6086(a) (1997 and Supp. 2003). As a result, many of the judicial decisions under Act 250 turn on whether substantial evidence supports a finding by the Environmental Board that a project meets these criteria and whether the Board's findings support its overall conclusions. *See, e.g., In re Munson Earth Moving Corp.*, 737 A.2d 906, 911 (Vt. 1999) ("the Board's findings do not lead logically to its conclusion that appellant's subdivision would endanger the public investment in government facilities"). As addressed in *Kisiel*, the Act 250 criteria also authorize the commissions to review local decisions for consistency with local and regional plans. *In re Hawk Mountain Corp.*, 542 A.2d 261, 263 (Vt. 1988) (substantial evidence supported Environmental Board's findings concerning the sewage treatment system's deficiencies). *See In re Green Peak Estates*, 577 A.2d 676 (Vt. 1990) (development proposal was properly denied for failing to conform to regional plan containing a policy that prohibited residential development on slopes greater than 20 percent).

The burden of proof under Act 250 is allocated somewhat strangely. Permit applicants bear the burden of showing that the project will not cause undue air pollution, water pollution, soil erosion, or strain on water supplies. In contrast, project opponents bear the burden of demonstrating that a project would unreasonably burden roads and other public services, or would unduly impact natural, aesthetic, or historic sites. Vt. Stat. Ann. tit. 10 §§6086(a), 6088(b) (1997 and Supp. 2003). Appeals from the district environmental commissions to the Board are heard de novo. *See In re Denio*, 608 A.2d 1166, 1170 (Vt. 1992). In turn, decisions of the Board may be appealed directly to the Vermont Supreme Court.

2. *The Environmental Board and Local Plans*. The *Kisiel* case involves the Environmental Board's consideration of one of the criteria: "conformance with any duly adopted local or regional plan." This criteria requires the court to consider how it will approach the plan and what deference, if any, it will give to the local government's interpretation of its own plan. How did the *Kisiel* Court resolve that issue? What about the fact that the local government seems to have changed its position toward the development in question—should this change affect the board's review? The court's review?

The court apparently adopted an interpretation of the plan's restriction on road upgrades that the landowners' did not advance. Is that an appropriate position for the court to take? Why would it do this?

Finally, the Court finds that the plan is vague about development allowed on steep slopes. Do laws such as Act 250, which utilize local plans in state review, encourage local governments to adopt vague policies in plans in the hope that they will retain more discretion over subsequent development decisions?

3. *Jurisdiction, Open Questions, and Malpractice.* Act 250 does not apply to every development. The word "development" in the Act, which triggers jurisdiction, in part is defined as "the construction of improvements on a tract or tracts of land, owned or controlled by a person, involving more than 10 acres of land within a radius of five miles." 10 V.S.A. §6001(3). In *Committee to Save the Bishop's House, Inc. v. Medical Center Hospital of Vermont*, 400 A.2d 1015 (Vt. 1979), a hospital was going to demolish a historic house on a 1.44 acre lot. It proposed to build a parking lot. The hospital itself had two "units." One consisted of 26.7 acres, and a second (which included the lot with the house in question) of 5.9 acres. The two units were separated by a distance of one-half mile at their nearest point.

Does the demolition come within Act 250? Is there any additional information you would need to answer the question? *See also In re Vermont Verde Antique International, Inc.*, 811 A.2d 181 (Vt. 2002) (invalidating rule that allowed district coordinators to issue jurisdictional orders *sua sponte*).

It is, of course, not always entirely clear when a project is subject to certain regulatory requirements, or whether certain kinds of transactions are prohibited. In such instances, the lawyer representing clients must be particularly careful to research the uncertainty fully. Failure to do so can bring unfortunate consequences. *See Roberts v. Chimileski*, —A.2d—(Vt. 2003). In that case the plaintiff brought a malpractice action after he was prosecuted for making an illegal subdivision. He claimed that his lawyer failed to disclose the "inherent risk" of whether the development scheme conformed to Act 250. The court upheld a decision for the defendant that malpractice had not been proven. A dissent argued that "[i]t requires no extensive discussion to establish that the unsettled scope of the term 'controlled' [in the Act] obligated defendants to advise their clients about the risky nature of their scheme, or m.o., to circumvent the Act. . . . " (Morse, J., dissenting).

4. *The Hawaii System.* Hawaii early on turned to a system of direct state land use regulation with a central planning structure. In 1961, the Legislature passed Act 187, the Hawaii Land Use Law, which resulted in the classification of all lands in the state into four categories: urban, agriculture, low-density rural, and conservation. The Act is implemented through a Land Use Commission whose nine members are appointed by the governor. The commission regulates development on urban, agricultural, and low-density rural land. *See Ka Pa'Akai O Ka'Aina v. Land Use Comm'n*, 7 P.3d 1068 (Haw. 2000) (Commission's findings and conclusions do not indicate that it fulfilled its obligation to preserve and protect customary and traditional rights of native Hawaiians).

The role of local government is quite restricted. Only about 4 percent of the state's land is classified as urban, and the counties control development only in this category. The state controls the rest. For example, the Hawaii Department of Land and Natural Resources grants permits for land uses in conservation districts. David L. Callies, Land-Use Planning in the Fiftieth State, in State and Regional Comprehensive Planning 127 (Peter A. Buchsbaum & Larry J. Smith eds. 1993).

In 1978, the Hawaii legislature adopted a statewide land use plan. There are also 12 state "functional plans," which are to implement and conform to the state plan. *See Lum Yip Kee, Ltd. v. City and County of Honolulu*, 767 P.2d 815 (Haw.

1989). Counties are to adopt plans that must "take into consideration" the policies, guidelines, and objectives of the state plan, and local zoning and subdivisions ordinances generally must conform to these county plans.

On the Hawaii system generally, see G. K. Lowry Jr., Evaluating State Land Use Control: Perspectives and Hawaii Case Study, 18 Urb. L. Ann. 85 (1980); Daniel R. Mandelker and Annette B. Kolis, Whither Hawaii? Land Use Management in an Island State, 1 U. Haw. L. Rev. 48 (1979); Michael McPherson, Vanishing Sands: Comprehensive Planning and Public Interest in Hawaii, 18 Ecology L.Q. 779 (1991).

5. *Pros and Cons*. What are the strengths and weaknesses that you see in the institutional structure of the Oregon system in comparison to the Vermont and Florida systems? In evaluating such systems, you must consider them from several perspectives.

(a) *Politics*. From a political standpoint, does the system strike the appropriate balance between local control and state oversight, such that it is likely to stand the test of time? The politics of such a balance can be delicate. In Vermont, for example, the legislature at one point had enacted legislation requiring local land use decisions to conform to 32 statewide goals. The result was revolt; some 200 local jurisdictions voted on town meeting day not to participate in the planning needed to implement that system.

Is the essentially advisory role for the state found in the Colorado system a good compromise between local control and state oversight? Is it surprising that, as one article noted, "no local government has adopted criteria for reviewing matters of state interest before a development that may meet the criteria has been proposed, or before rapid development forces them to look for additional regulatory control"? Marya Morris, Regulating Regional Impacts: Toward Model Legislation (Part II), 47 Land Use L. & Zoning Dig. 3, 6 (Aug. 1995).

(b) *Implementation*. You must also consider the systems from the standpoint of implementation. Which type of system is likely to be more effective in attaining its goals? For example, under the Vermont system the district environmental commissions do not evaluate whether a project adheres to a plan; instead, they apply a set of criteria, such as whether a project will cause "undue" or "unreasonable" effects. 10 Vt. Stat. Ann. tit. 10 §6086(a) (1997) (board or district commission shall find that the subdivision or development will not result in undue water or air pollution, will not cause an unreasonable burden on an existing water supply, will not place an unreasonable burden on the local government's ability to provide municipal or governmental services, etc.). Is this the best type of system to implement effective state oversight of projects?

(c) *Planning*. From a planning standpoint, which state has arranged its processes in the most fair and effective manner? Consider that Oregon's creation of an administrative appeal board, the Land Use Board of Appeals, whose decisions are subject to review directly in the state court of appeals, results in a planning and legal dynamic that is quite different from the norm. One obvious benefit is that LUBA's decisions are more likely to be based on planning expertise than those issued by the courts, and LUBA has the ability to fashion a consistent body of precedent that will do much to shape interpretations of Oregon planning law. Do you see any problems with this institutional arrangement?

An important practical factor is that the Land Conservation and Development Commission, the state agency that oversees the planning process in Oregon, has a staff that aids the commission. The staff is an important player in the plan acknowledgment process, providing both expertise and critical recommendations to the LCDC.

Another aspect of the "planning" issue involves matching the state's role with the kind of institutional planning efforts it will undertake. For example, in larger states, precise mapping of uses for the entire state could be extraordinarily difficult. The state may be better suited to focus on certain policy goals and seeking to ensure that state agencies support those goals throughout the state. *See* Fred Bosselman, A Role for State Planning: Intergenerational Equity and Adaptive Management, 12 U. Fla. J.L. & Pub. Pol'y 311 (2001) (suggesting that state planning should focus on "intergenerational equity"—broadly, giving adequate attention to the needs of future generations—and "adaptive management"—a process "in which the objectives and strategies of the plan are under continuous review" to take into account changes in technology, ecological knowledge, etc.). Do you see any downsides to this approach?

C. REGIONAL LAND USE MANAGEMENT

In addition to some efforts to implement statewide land use management, a few states have implemented controls at the regional level. These efforts, sometimes known as "critical area legislation," often stem from concerns over environmental protection. They are targeted either at areas thought generically to be of particular environmental concern (such as areas along the coast) or at other specific areas whose resources are deemed to be of statewide if not national significance (such as the New Jersey Pinelands, the Chesapeake Bay, the San Francisco Bay, and the Adirondack Mountains). The following case exemplifies this type of system.

■ 330 CONCORD STREET v. CAMPSEN
424 S.E.2d 538 (S.C. Ct. App. 1992)

CURETON, Judge:

This case involves a permit to build a restaurant partly within the critical zone of the waters of the Cooper River in Charleston Harbor. George Campsen sought a permit to construct a restaurant as part of a joint project with the proposed South Carolina Marine Science Museum and the National Park Service Fort Sumter Tour Boat Facility. The South Carolina Coastal Council approved the permit application. An appeal was taken to the circuit court by 330 Concord Street Neighborhood Association and the League of Women Voters of Charleston County. . . .

George Campsen has been a concessionaire with the National Park Service for the Fort Sumter tour boats since the 1960's. The Park Service has been looking for a new landing facility for the tour boats. A proposal was conceived by the National Park Service, the City of Charleston, and Mr. Campsen to construct an aquatic science museum, tour boat facility, and a restaurant at a site on the Cooper River in Charleston County. The restaurant would be privately owned by Mr. Campsen. The tour boat facility would be owned by the National Park Service and the aquatic science museum would be owned by the City of Charleston. The plans envisioned a common parking area and public promenade. All the buildings as planned encroached upon the critical zone in some degree. Permits were issued by the Coastal Council for the aquarium and tour boat facility. These permits are not in issue.

As originally conceived, the restaurant was 31,000 square feet. This concept was downsized to 19,950 square feet and the building was moved landward. Under the revised plan, approximately 3200 square feet are within the mudflat area. Of this amount 1400 square feet is above mean high water in an area covered by concrete rubble and 1800 square feet is below mean high water. The environmental impact is the effect on primary productivity from shading caused by the restaurant. Shading would affect organisms that use sunlight for photosynthesis.

The parties agree the restaurant is a "nonwater dependent structure" as defined by Coastal Council regulations. *See* 23A S.C. Code Ann. Regs. 30-1(C)(10) (1983). Under council's regulations, a "nonwater dependent structure" is prohibited from being constructed in critical areas "unless there is no significant environmental impact, an overriding public need can be demonstrated and no feasible alternatives exist." *Id.* at 30-12(M).

Coastal Council issued a permit for the restaurant after finding the project satisfied the three criteria under the regulation. . . .

I.

The first criterion is "no significant environmental impact." Both sides presented expert witnesses in the field of biology. These witnesses examined the site and analyzed the effect of shading upon the productivity of the estuarine system. They disagreed about the significance of the environmental impact.

The appellants also assert the Coastal Council failed to follow its precedent. The appellants introduced evidence of a prior administrative decision of Coastal Council which denied a permit for an already built packing plant that shaded less area in the mudflats than would be covered by the Campsen restaurant. Coastal Council denied the permit finding there was a significant environmental impact from the shading and "the possible cumulative effects of this type of development could be devastating to the coast line of South Carolina." Appellants assert Coastal Council ignored this precedent and did not consider the cumulative effects of similar development when considering the restaurant permit.

Under the substantial evidence test, the possibility of drawing two inconsistent conclusions from the evidence does not prevent the agency's decision from being supported by substantial evidence. *Lark v. BiLo Inc.*, 276 S.C. 130, 136, 276 S.E.2d 304, 307 (1981). An administrative agency is generally not bound by the principle of *stare decisis* but it cannot act arbitrarily in failing to follow established precedent. *Courtesy Motors Inc., v. Ford Motor Co.*, 9 Va. App. 102, 384 S.E.2d 118 (1989). Given the conflicting expert opinions, we find the conclusion of the agency on the issue of environmental impact is supported by substantial evidence. As to the precedential effect of the prior administrative decision, we have examined the record in this case and the order from the prior case. While they both deal with mudflat areas, there appear to be distinguishing factors between the cases. Most notably, nothing in the prior case suggests any of the public benefits involved in this case. We do not find Council acted arbitrarily in failing to follow its prior decision.

II.

The second criterion is whether "an overriding public need can be demonstrated." Both the Coastal Council and the circuit court found the record established the public need for the restaurant at the proposed site. The term "overriding public need" is not defined in Coastal Council's statutes and regulations.

In finding "public need," the Coastal Council and the circuit court outlined the testimony of various witnesses at the hearing. Only the respondents presented evidence on this point. The witnesses stated the restaurant was an integral part of the three phase development consisting of the aquatic science museum, tour boat facility, and restaurant. The plans had been coordinated to have a common use parking facility and public promenade between the buildings. Although the museum and tour boat facility would still be built if the permit for the restaurant was denied, the witnesses stated the restaurant would provide a needed food service to the public. No other restaurant was within walking distance and the witnesses testified their expectation was people would spend several hours visiting the museum and taking the boat tour. The presence of the three facilities in one location was considered an advantage to tourism. Several witnesses also testified the restaurant would provide jobs for people living in a nearby economically depressed area. Development of this area in this manner was consistent with the City of Charleston's tourism management plan.

Appellants assert the Council and court improperly evaluated "public need" by equating it with "public want" and "public support." In other words, they contend public need is not established simply because the public may want or generally support a project. . . .

In considering whether there is substantial evidence of an overriding public need, we find persuasive prior case authority which holds evidence of a purely economic benefit is insufficient as a matter of law to establish an overriding public interest. *S.C. Wildlife Fed'n v. S.C. Coastal Council*, 296 S.C. 187, 371 S.E.2d 521 (1988). The council viewed the restaurant in conjunction with the museum and tour boat facility on this issue. There was no challenge by the appellants to the "public need" for the aquatic science museum and the tour boat facility. Considered in this context, we find substantial evidence to support the finding of the agency and the circuit court that "public need" had been established. The museum and tour boat facility will provide educational and recreational benefits to the public as well as an economic benefit to the community. Unlike the *S.C. Wildlife Federation* case, there is evidence of more than a purely economic benefit.

III.

The third criterion is "no feasible alternatives exist." In reviewing the evidence, the Coastal Council and the circuit court found the criterion had been met.

The respondents presented the testimony of the restaurant architect, restaurant consultant, and a real estate appraiser. Their testimony related to alternative floor plans for the restaurant, the need for service access, problems with setback restrictions, the value of offstreet parking in the city and the potential loss of parking spaces by further moving the restaurant, and the economic viability of a smaller restaurant. The appellants cross-examined these witnesses but did not offer evidence on this matter. Based upon the evidence, the agency and circuit court found the criterion was met.

Appellants' main argument is the evidence presented by the respondents was opinion testimony which lacked a proper factual foundation and, thus, had no probative value. They assert the restaurant plan is an effort to put too much private commercial space into too small an area and there is no reason why the restaurant cannot be further downsized and removed entirely from the critical area. We have reviewed the testimony of the witnesses and cannot say as a matter of law the testimony has no probative value. Given our standard of review, we find no error since the conclusion reached by Coastal Council based upon the record before it is one a reasonable mind might have reached.

AFFIRMED.

Notes and Comments

1. *The Impetus for Regional Regulation*. What rationales might support regional regulation? When might a regional system of regulation be more appropriate than a statewide system? See Richard Briffault, The Local Government Boundary Problem in Metropolitan Areas, 48 Stan. L. Rev. 1115 (1996) (discussing the various problems associated with local government boundaries). Note that with the exception of Florida and perhaps Maine, the states that have undertaken efforts at statewide land use regulation tend to be relatively small. In those states, the move toward statewide regulation does not present the same type of drastic change in institutional structure that it would in states like New York or California.

2. *Economics and the Response to Sprawl*. Most recently, the concept of urban "sprawl" has received enormous attention in both the press and the academic literature. Regional government, of course, is one suggested response to curbing sprawl. But is "sprawl" such a bad thing? For an economist, the answer would depend on both costs and benefits:

> [E]conomists emphasize the point that the metropolitan decentralization of people and economic activity in the US has occurred for well over 50 years and has been driven in large part by population increases, real income increases, and decreases in the cost of automobile use. To most economists, decentralization is only an undesirable pattern of urban land use if the total costs it imposes upon a metropolitan region are greater than the total benefits generated from it.

Robert W. Wassmer, Fiscalization of Land Use, Urban Growth Boundaries and Non-Central Retail Sprawl in the Western United States, 39 Urb. Studies 1307, 1308 (2002). The article concludes that when cities attract retailers, a "fiscal surplus" in sales tax revenue is generated that exceeds the city's costs of providing additional local services to those retailers.

A good number of states have passed legislation authorizing the preparation of regional plans by regional planning commissions. *See, e.g.*, N.Y. Gen. Mun. Law §239-d (McKinney 1986) ("comprehensive master plan for the development of the entire area of the county or counties or municipalities participating"). Until the early 1970s, however, those statutes almost never required that the plans be implemented or gave regional planning bodies actual authority over land use decisions. *See, e.g.*, Cal. Govt. Code §65060.8 (West 1997) (a regional plan "shall be advisory only and shall not have any binding effect on the counties and cities located within the boundaries of the regional planning district . . .").

This situation began to change slightly with the rise of the environmental movement in the late 1960s. As concern grew about environmental degradation, efforts to preserve specific resources led to legislation designed to protect and manage those resources. Because the natural resources involved generally overlapped numerous local jurisdictions, regulation on a regional basis was the only realistic solution. Two of the earliest efforts established regulatory systems managing land uses in San Francisco Bay and the Adirondack Mountains, and these efforts formed the models for later legislation that proceeded along the same lines.

3. *The Model Act and "Critical Area" Regulation*. Another important impetus for change was the American Law Institute's Model Land Development Code adopted in 1975. Section 7-201 of the Model Act called for regulation of "areas of critical state concern."

As noted above in this chapter, in addition to regulating developments of regional impact, Florida also followed the Model Act's scheme by implementing state regulation of developments in "areas of critical state concern." *See* Fla. Stat. Ann. §§380.05, 380.07(2) (West 2000); *Askew v. Cross Key Waterways*, 372 So. 2d 913 (Fla. 1978) (describing the process leading to the designation of the Florida Keys as an area of critical state concern). See also Thomas G. Pelham, Regulating Areas of Critical State Concern: Florida and the Model Code, 18 Urb. L. Ann. 3 (1980). Under the Florida scheme, four such areas have been designated. Likewise, the Chesapeake Bay is protected under the Chesapeake Bay Critical Area Protection Program. *See Bucktail v. County Council of Talbot County*, 723 A.2d 440 (Md. Ct. App. 1999) (developer applied for reclassification of property within critical area from a "Resource Conservation Area" to a "Limited Development Area").

Other systems are similarly designed around the resource to be protected. The San Francisco Bay Conservation and Development Commission was instituted because San Francisco Bay was being filled in at an alarming rate. The Commission's regulatory jurisdiction encompasses the bay and areas on the shore that are adjacent to it.

4. *Regional and Coastal Zone Regulation: The Federal Influence*. The federal government must be involved if the resource in question is interstate in nature or if the federal government owns any of the land in question. The federal government also has strongly encouraged states to regulate coastal areas. The Coastal Zone Management Act (CZMA), 16 U.S.C. §§1451-§§1465 (2000 and Supp. 2003), authorizes the National Oceanic and Atmospheric Administration in the Department of Commerce to award grants to states that are used to complete coastal zone management plans. The planning requirements are quite stringent. *See* 15 C.F.R. Part 923 (2003). For example, a state must establish a planning process for energy facilities to be located within the coastal zone that may "significantly affect" that zone. 16 U.S.C. §1455 (d)(2)(2000). After a state's plan is completed, it must be approved by the Secretary of Commerce. *See American Petroleum Institute v. Knecht*, 456 F. Supp. 889 (C.D. Cal. 1978), *aff'd*, 609 F.2d 1306 (9th Cir. 1979) (California plan complied with CZMA requirements relating to energy facility siting). After certification, every applicant for a federal license or permit seeking to conduct an activity affecting the coastal zone must certify that the proposed activity comports with the state's program.

5. *The Contours of Regional and Critical Area Regulation*. Regional and critical area land use regulatory systems raise the following issues:

a. *Designating the Regulated Area*. Critical area regulation must begin by defining the area that is subject to regulation. This identification can occur either in a statute that specifically sets forth the precise boundaries of the agency's jurisdiction or through the agency's subsequent administrative implementation of a broader statutory definition. The agency usually will prepare a map that outlines with particularity its jurisdictional limits.

b. *The Administering Body*. Any regional system requires the establishment of a regulatory body. In some instances, that body is a statewide commission, such as the South Carolina Coastal Council in the principal case just read. The Adirondack Park Agency consists of three state cabinet-level officials and eight members appointed by the governor with the advice and consent of the state Senate, while the San Francisco Bay Conservation and Development Commission has 27 members, almost half of whom are representatives of local governments.

The California Coastal Commission operated for almost thirty years under a structure in which a majority of its members were appointed by legislative officials and all members were removable at will. However, in *Marine Forests Society v. California Coastal Comm'n*, 128 Cal. Rptr. 2d 869 (Ct. App. 2002), pet. for review granted (Apr. 9, 2003), a California court of appeal found that this arrangement violated the separation of powers doctrine because the members could be appointed or removed at will. The opinion is not clear about whether the fact that the legislative branch appointed a majority of members posed a constitutional problem. Do you see any practical problems if members are removable at will? Would it bother you if, during a heated controversy, the governor fired his appointees and replaced them before a vote on the issue?

c. *Planning*. How should the agency go about its task of regulating? The typical pattern of regional regulation requires the agency to prepare a comprehensive land use plan for the area in question. Thus, New York legislation required the Adirondack Park Agency to create a "land use and development plan" for the entire area of the park, including private lands, as well as another plan for state lands only. N.Y. Exec. Law §805 (McKinney 1996). In the New Jersey Pinelands, protection is to occur through implementation of the New Jersey Pinelands Comprehensive Management Plan. N.J. Stat. Ann. §13:18A-8 (West 2003). Depending on the significance of the resource and the politics of the situation, approval of the plan by the state legislature may be required. In the Adirondacks, for example, the New York State Legislature ratified the Park Agency's plan for regulating development on private lands.

d. *Regulatory Controls*. The principal implementation method used is a permitting system. *See, e.g.*, N.Y. Exec. L. §809(subd. 2) (McKinney 1996) (person intending to begin a Class A regional project must obtain a permit from the Park Agency). *Kirkorwicz v. California Coastal Comm'n*, 100 Cal. Rptr. 2d 124 (Cal. Ct. App. 2000) (substantial evidence supported Commission's decision to deny permit to protect wetland). Typically, such agencies place conditions on project approvals to mitigate the environmental consequences of development. *See, e.g.*, N.Y. Exec. Law §809(subd. 13) (McKinney 1996); *Friedman v. Adirondack Park Agency*, 565 N.Y.S. 2d 607 (Sup. Ct. App. Div. 1991) (upholding a condition on the sewage system employed for a subdivision and a reduction in the number of lots from the 33 proposed to 15); *McCormick v. Lawrence*, 372 N.Y.S.2d 156 (Sup. Ct. 1975), *aff'd*, 387 N.Y.S.2d 919 (Sup. Ct. App. Div. 1976) (upholding a condition on the approval of development of lakefront lots, which prohibited the construction of boat houses).

e. *The Local Role*. Any system of regional controls must determine the relationship between the local governments in the jurisdictional area, which traditionally have power over land use, and the state or regional body that now is also given regulatory authority. Under the Lake Tahoe arrangement, any political subdivision within the region may adopt higher standards than the regional agency, but the regional agency's standards act as a regulatory floor. Cal. Govt. Code §66801, art. VI(a) (West Supp. 2004). Another possibility is that the local governments may be required to revise their own plans and ordinances to conform to the regional planning effort. *See* N.J. Admin. Code tit. 7 §7:50-3.11 (1996) (counties must conform master plans and ordinances to Pinelands Comprehensive Master Plan); *City of Des Moines v. Puget Sound Regional Council*, 988 P.2d 993, 998 (Wash. Ct. App. 1999) (Growth Management Act "evinces the Legislature's intent to discard the traditional land use system in which each jurisdiction functioned as an isolated entity in favor of a scheme which stresses coordination, cooperation and integration . . . [I]f the coordinated planning process does not result in consistency between regional and local plans, the regional plans must prevail.").

The regulatory system for the region or the critical area may not make every land use decision subject to regional or statewide control. For example, the North Carolina Coastal Area Management Act authorizes the Division of Coastal Resources to grant permits for "major" developments, while "minor" developments remain exclusively within the province of local government. N.C. Gen. Stat. §113A-118(d)(1) (2003); *see also* N.Y. Exec. Law §810 (McKinney 1996) (local governments may be given authority to regulate "Class B regional projects" in the Adirondack Park if their land use programs are approved by the park agency, but "Class A regional projects" must be approved by the Park Agency). Another method is the straightforward "double-veto" system: a project must obtain approval from both the local government and the regional body.

6. *Critical Areas and Takings*. Where the regional agency is charged with protecting a "critical area" or an environmentally sensitive area, it may find itself denying development proposals outright. In such instances, the question of whether the regulatory action constitutes a taking arises quite often. For example, in *Candlestick Properties, Inc. v. San Francisco Bay Conservation and Development Comm'n*, 89 Cal. Rptr. 897 (Ct. App. 1970), the plaintiff was denied permission to fill in part of San Francisco Bay. The court rejected a contention that the denial constituted a taking, even though the parcel was submerged at high tide and, according to the owners, could not be used unless it was filled. Is this holding still good law after *Lucas v. South Carolina Coastal Council*, a principal case discussed in Chapter 7?

7. *Commentary*. Articles on regional and critical area regulation include Symposium on Regionalism, 48 Buff. L. Rev. 1 (2000); Symposium, State and Regional Land Use Planning: An Idea Whose Time Has Come, 73 St. John's L. Rev. 1007 (1999); Carrie Daniel, Land Use Planning—The Twin Cities Metropolitan Council: Novel Initiative, Futile Effort, 27 Wm. Mitchell L. Rev. 1941 (2001); David L. Callies, Land Use and Critical Areas: Preservation and Development Compromise in England and Australia, 5 Colum. J. Envtl. L. 265 (1979); Daniel R. Mandelker, Critical Area Controls: A New Dimension in American Land Development Regulation, 41 J. Am. Inst. Plan. 21 (1975); Comment, Area of Critical State Concern: Its

Potential for Effective Regulation, 26 U. Fla. L. Rev. 858 (1974). Articles on coastal zone management include; Richard G. Hildreth, Coastal Natural Hazards Management, 59 Or. L. Rev. 201 (1980); Steven R. Schell, Living With the Legacy of the 1970's: Federal State Coordination in the Coastal Zone, 14 Envtl. L. 751 (1984).

D. JURISDICTIONAL CONFLICTS AND ADJUSTMENTS: ANNEXATION, PREEMPTION, AND ACCOMMODATION

■ CITY OF ALBUQUERQUE v. STATE OF NEW MEXICO MUNICIPAL BOUNDARY COMMISSION

41 P.3d 933 (N.M. 2002)

OPINION

PICKARD, Judge.

West Tijeras Canyon Ltd. filed an annexation petition with the Municipal Boundary Commission, seeking to have its property annexed to the City of Albuquerque. The Commission determined that the annexation met the requirements of NMSA 1978, §3-7-15(A) (1965) and ordered the property annexed to the City. . . . We hold that the Commission was required to not only consider, but give substantial deference to, the City's opposition to the annexation petition. We therefore affirm the district court's decision reversing the Commission's order.

FACTS AND PROCEEDINGS

The Municipal Boundary Commission is an independent administrative board vested with the authority to hear petitions for annexation. *See* NMSA 1978, §3-7-11 (1995). The Commission may hear petitions from either municipalities seeking to annex new territory or from landowners hoping to strctch the boundaries of a municipality to include their property. The Commission's decision-making process is governed by Section 3-7-15(A), which provides that:

> At the public hearing held for the purpose of determining if the territory proposed to be annexed to the municipality shall be annexed to the municipality, the municipal boundary commission shall determine if the territory proposed to be annexed:
>
> (1) is contiguous to the municipality; and
> (2) may be provided with municipal services by the municipality to which the territory is proposed to be annexed.

If the Commission finds that the two requirements of Section 3-7-15(A) are met, then under Section 3-7-15(B) it must approve the annexation.

West Tijeras owns a 165 acre parcel of land in Bernalillo Country. The property lies south of Interstate 40, sharing its borders with the Four Hills neighborhood in Albuquerque on the west and the Canon de Carnue Land Grant to the east. In 1998, West Tijeras approached the Albuquerque City Council, asking the City to annex the property and change the property's "Country A-1" zoning designation to allow for denser development. The Council voted to deny annexation. About six months later, West Tijeras presented a petition to the Commission seeking to have 101 acres of the property annexed into the City. West Tijeras's main purpose in seeking annexation is to gain access to City water and sewer services. If the property remains county land, West Tijeras can only develop using water wells and septic tanks.

At the Commission's hearing on the petition, the City maintained its opposition to the annexation. The Commission examined the two statutory requirements set out in Section 3-7-15(A). The first requirement, contiguity, was not at issue. A difference of opinion arose, however, as to whether the second requirement was met. The Commission Chairman indicated that West Tijeras need only show that the City was capable of providing services to the area, stating that "the criteria is not whether the City will or wants to . . . it's whether they can. . . . " The City, however, argued that the second requirement would not be met as long as the City was opposed to providing services to the property. Rejecting this interpretation, the Commission voted unanimously in favor of the annexation. . . .

[The district court overturned the annexation. West Tijeras and the Commission jointly appealed.]

Discussion

Appellants argue that the Commission's initial interpretation of the statute was correct, and therefore the Commission was required to approve the annexation once West Tijeras demonstrated that the City was able to provide services to the area. Appellees, on the other hand, assert that the Commission erred in substituting the word "can" for "may," and argue that the annexation can only be approved with the City's consent. This is a case of first impression. It appears that the Commission has never before been asked to approve the annexation of territory to a municipality over the objection of that municipality. We must now determine the implications of the legislature's use of the world "may" within this statute.

. . . "When appropriate, we will rely on rules of grammar to aid our construction of the plain language of a statute." *Wilson v. Denver*, 1998-NMSC-016, ¶16, 125 N.M. 308, 961 P.2d 153. Appellants cite to numerous dictionaries, including Black's Law Dictionary, to support their argument that the two words are sometimes used interchangeably. On the other hand, NMSA 1978, §12-2A-4(B) (1997) instructs us that " '[m]ay' confers a power, authority, privilege or right." In contrast, "can" connotes ability. *See, e.g., William Strunk Jr. & E.B. White, The Elements of Style 42* (4th ed. 2000) ("*Can*. Means 'am (is, are) able.' Not to be used as a substitute for *may*."). In the context of the annexation statutes and the statutes relating to municipal planning, the word "may" in Section 3-7-15(A) cannot reasonably be interpreted as "can" in the manner Appellants suggest.

We acknowledge that our Supreme Court indicated in *Mutz* that the statutory test could be satisfied "if the municipality demonstrates the ability to provide services to the territory to be annexed." *Mutz*, 101 N.M. at 701, 688 P.2d at 19. In *Mutz*, however, it was the municipality, not landowners, petitioning for annexation. The municipality's willingness to provide services was not at issue. The *Mutz* Court, in explaining the difference in meaning between "may" and "must," recognized that "may," as used in this particular statute, is permissive. *Id*. We are confident that the legislature intended that the Commission find something more than mere physical ability when the legislature directed the Commission to insure that services "may be provided" rather than "can be provided."

Nonetheless, we do not read the statute as requiring landowners to seek a municipality's consent to annexation when presenting an annexation petition to the Commission. The legislature provided two options for landowners who wish to see their property annexed to a municipality. The most commonly exercised option is the "petition method," which is set out in NMSA 1978, §§3-7-17 and 17.1 (1998). Using that method, if landowners holding a majority of the acres in the territory proposed to be annexed are in favor of annexation, they can petition directly to the governing body of the municipality. The municipality may then "express its consent or rejection" by ordinance. *See* §§3-7-17(A)(4);-17.1(B)(2). This was the approach first taken by West Tijeras in seeking to have its property annexed. The alternative option is the "boundary commission method," which is governed by NMSA 1978, §§3-7-11 through 16 (1965, as amended through 1995). Once again, approval is required from landowners holding a majority of the acres in the territory proposed. Unlike the petition method, however, the statutes governing the boundary commission method provide no mechanism through which a municipality can express its consent.

If the legislature had intended to require municipal consent under the boundary commission method, it would have included a consent provision in the governing statutes, just as it did in the petition method statutes. Moreover, if municipal consent was required under the boundary commission method, then there would be no meaningful difference between the two options available to landowners. If a municipality was withholding its consent to annexation, there would be no reason for landowners to approach the Commission. Since we presume that the legislature does not intend to enact useless statutes, . . . we do not think this is a correct interpretation of Section 3-7-15.

The City argues that the legislature could not have intended to give landowners the power to force a municipality to annex property despite the municipality's objection, or to allow the Commission to override the City's planning decisions. The Commission, however, does have that power. The state legislature has the power to create and to destroy municipal corporations, and to enlarge or diminish their boundaries, with or without consent of either the municipalities or the affected residents. . . . The legislature delegated its authority to determine municipal boundaries to the Commission. *See* §3-7-11(A). When it did so, it provided a defined set of guidelines for the Commission to follow under Section 3-7-15. The Commission, therefore, has the authority to annex property over the objections of the municipality involved.

In sum, we cannot adopt either party's position wholesale. In our opinion, the City could not unilaterally defeat West Tijeras's petition by withholding its consent to the annexation, but the Commission could not annex property over the City's objection upon a mere showing that the City is capable of providing services to the area. We are still left, then, with some ambiguity as to the meaning of the statutory language. The ambiguity arises, in part, from the use of passive voice in the statutory language. The statute instructs the Commission to determine "if the territory proposed to be annexed . . . may be provided with municipal services by the municipality to which the territory is proposed to be annexed." *Id.* While may is permissive, it is not clear whose permission is required in this context.

THE COMMISSION SHOULD HAVE DEFERRED TO THE CITY'S OPPOSITION TO THE ANNEXATION

. . . The statutes governing annexation, when read together, demonstrate an overall intent to assure that residents who are annexed into a municipality receive services from that municipality. . . .

In keeping with the legislature's intent to assure that residents within an annexed territory have access to municipal services, we think that when the legislature directed the Commission to determine that services "may be provided," it wanted to assure that residents would have the right to demand such services if the territory was annexed. . . .

When a municipality petitions the Commission, there is again no question that the municipality is willing to annex the territory, so the Commission's task is to insure that the provision of services is physically possible. . . . When landowners present annexation petitions, the Commission must make further inquiries and consider the municipality's position regarding annexation. As part of that inquiry the Commission should have not only considered the City's opposition to the annexation, but should have given the City's position considerable deference.

The City's objection to the annexation relates directly to the statutory requirement that services "may be provided" to the area proposed to be annexed. Much of the City's time and resources are directed toward planning and growth management efforts. In doing so, City officials have evaluated how best to provide service to existing territory and where it would be best able to expand services to meet anticipated population growth. Appellants' arguments that the City is capable of providing services to the area disregards the City's right to determine where and how those services should be provided. As one example, West Tijeras presented testimony that the City could provide social services to residents if the land is developed. The City, however, is already concerned that it is not providing sufficient services to seniors living in the nearby area. Annexation would also impact the City's provision of police, fire, and emergency services; schools; social services; street maintenance; refuse pickup; and many other services. Annexation of the West Tijeras land would put an additional burden on the City and undermine its efforts to provide an adequate level of services to those areas already within its municipal boundaries.

The City presented evidence that annexation of the West Tijeras property conflicted with a number of its established policies. The annexation conflicts with the Albuquerque Bernalillo County Comprehensive Plan, which designated the land as Rural Area. The Comprehensive Plan states that Rural Areas "shall generally retain their rural character with development consisting primarily of ranches, farms and single-family homes on large lots." Annexation of the West Tijeras property conflicts with the City's infill policy, Resolution 70, which expresses a strong preference that development occur within existing infrastructure so that the City's resources are not directed toward extending its infrastructure to new areas. These policies reflect the City's considered evaluation of how best to provide services to current and future residents. Based on these policies, the City expressed its opinion that it did not want to extend its service area to include the West Tijeras property. The Commission should have deferred to the City's opinion as to the wisdom of extending its services to the area.

Appellants contend the City's planning policies are not relevant to the Commission's inquiry, because the City can control the level of development in the area through its zoning power. Annexation alone, however, will obligate the City to provide some services to the area, including police and fire services. Roads may need to be built to provide access for emergency services. School services may have to be provided if families with children move into the area. In addition, municipal zoning authority is not unlimited, so the City may not be able to accomplish by zoning what it wishes to accomplish.

THE COMMISSION'S DECISIONS MUST BE REASONABLE

Appellants also contend it would be unfair to consider the City's opposition to annexation when the Commission is required to disregard the concerns of residents who oppose annexation. . . .

. . . [W]hen the provision of services is at issue, the Commission must apply a reasonableness standard rather than rely solely on a technical determination that it is physically possible to extend municipal services to the proposed area. As one City official explained during the hearing on this annexation, "You can make anything feasible if you spend enough money." Yet the City could reasonably argue that the provision of services would be so expensive or burdensome as to be prohibitive. Thus, even when looking at whether the provision of services is physically possible, the decision must be made within reason. Similarly, when the City argues that annexation would be inconsistent with its planning decisions regarding the provision of services to the area, it is unreasonable for the Commission to find that services may be provided to the area. The Commission should only exercise its authority to annex property over a municipality's objections based on a finding that those objections are unreasonable under the circumstances. Because we think it is clear that the City was raising reasonable concerns based on well-established policies, we hold that it was unreasonable for the Commission to approve the annexation.

We recognize that many residents who have been subject to forced annexation have felt that the statutory scheme unfairly denies them the opportunity to object on reasonable grounds because those grounds fall outside the two statutory requirements. To the extent that the residents' objections relate to the two statutory requirements, the Commission should hear and consider those objections. The statute as written, however, leaves no room for consideration of other matters. For that reason, the district court was incorrect when it held that the Commission was required to make an overall determination that the annexation was reasonable and that the Commission could not order the territory annexed over the objections of "the people." In this case in particular, the residents who spoke in opposition to the annexation lived outside the annexation territory, so their objections were beyond the scope of the Commission's inquiry.

Notes and Comments

1. *Questioning* City of Albuquerque. Municipalities become larger when they annex new territories. Should a city have to affirmatively agree to an annexation before it can be approved? In *City of Albuquerque*, the opinion indicates that the proposed annexation would violate the city's growth policies. Is the city in the best position to make this growth determination, or is a regional body better suited to independently look at the facts?

Did the court read the applicable statutes correctly? Where does it include the condition of "reasonableness" that the court finds? In an omitted part of the opinion, the court noted that an alternative method of annexation required the Commission "to determine if the benefits of the government . . . are or can be available within a reasonable time to the territory proposed to be annexed." Will this support the "reasonableness" requirement? What about the fact that this language was not applicable to the annexation methods at issue in this case?

2. *More Questions.* The Court declares that the Commission "should have deferred to the City's opinion about the wisdom of extending its services to the area." Why? What reasons for deference are present? If the Commission has its own staff, shouldn't the Commission take its own, independent look at the facts? More broadly, can you state exactly what is the Court's holding in this case?

3. *Who's Got the Power?* Annexations are handled in a variety of different ways. In some instances, a commission of local officials makes the decision. Other arrangements are possible. *See, e.g., McNamara v. Office of Strategic and Long Range Planning*, 628 N.W.2d 620 (Minn. Ct. App. 2001) (administrative law judge, employed by a state agency, had the power to hold hearings and issue a decision on annexation petitions). Some jurisdictions provide for annexation agreements. *City of Springfield v. Judith Jones Dietsch Trust*, 746 N.E.2d 1272, 1276 (Ill. Ct. App. 2001) ("Preannexation agreements serve to further important governmental purposes, such as the encouragement of expanding urban areas uniformly, economically, efficiently, and fairly").

The procedure under which an annexation can occur, however, is up to the state legislature. That body, often guided by state constitutional provisions, has the power to establish the conditions under which municipalities can grow. The subject is covered more generally in courses on Local Government Law.

4. *Services and the Land Use Connection.* As the discussion of the City's policies in *City of Albuquerque* indicates, annexation decisions have important land use effects. Depending on which jurisdiction annexes land, the property either can be more intensively developed or allowed less intense uses. Annexation is thus highly political.

At the same time, however, annexation involves questions of efficiency. The most important issue is what services will be provided to the territory being annexed. Statutes often require the body considering the annexation question to examine a variety of services. *See Brahm v. Beavercreek Tp. Bd. of Trustees*, 757 N.E.2d 857 (Ohio Ct. App. 2001) (County Board of Commissioners acted arbitrarily in concluding that one service factor—superior snow and ice removal services—outweighed the other evidence on services); *Sonopress, Inc. v. Town of Weaverville*, 562 S.E.2d 32 (N.C. App. 2002) (town's standards of service report adequately described the services that would be provided to the newly annexed area).

5. *Annexation and Conditions*? Because cities supply services, can they agree to do so only on condition that the landowner seek annexation to the city? The cases are split. *Compare Sloan v. City of Conway*, 555 S.E.2d 684, 688 (N.C. App. 2001) (finding such a condition valid "as a means of broadening City's tax base") *with Verry v. City of Belle Fourche*, 598 N.W.2d 544 (S.D. 1999) (contra).

6. *Surprising "Non-Cities."* You may be surprised to learn that not every large, urbanized area in the United States has been incorporated into a municipality. For example, Reston, Virginia (pop. 56,407) and Silver Springs, Md. (pop. 76,540) are not cities. Nor is a large part of the so-called Las Vegas, Nevada "strip," which is known as Paradise, Nevada, and is the place where the legendary Bugsy Siegel

started the famous Flamingo Hotel. Residents of these areas rely on county governments for services. Haya El Nasser, Some Big Places Find Paradise in *Not* Being Real Cities, U.S.A. Today, June 25, 2003, 1A.

Another set of limitations on local governmental land use powers arises from the relationship of local governments to adjacent governmental entities, to special districts, or to state agencies. Surprisingly often, state legislatures have not clearly delineated the split of authority between the respective governmental authorities. In many instances, a dispute is nonetheless settled amicably; for example, local governments and school districts rarely find themselves at odds for long periods of time. Where it is not, however, the courts must devise a solution.

In the following case, the court rejects the past legal framework for resolving such disputes. But is the new framework any better?

■ BROWN v. KANSAS FORESTRY, FISH AND GAME COMMISSION

576 P.2d 230 (Kan. Ct. App. 1978)

FOTH, Chief Judge:

The issue presented in this appeal is whether, in the absence of any clear legislative direction one way or the other, a state agency must conform its land use to local zoning regulations. . . .

The agency involved here is the state forestry, fish and game commission. In 1975 it purchased two lots in the middle of a twenty-three lot subdivision near Manhattan, Kansas, which had been zoned for single family residences. The commission intended to use the land for a public parking lot, complete with toilet facilities, for the convenience of its patrons using a fishing and recreation facility on the adjacent Big Blue River.

The plaintiffs own and reside on fourteen of the twenty-one other lots in the subdivision. They brought this action to enjoin the commission from its proposed use of its land, alleging that such use would violate both Riley county zoning regulations and certain restrictive covenants governing the subdivision. . . .

In this court, as in the court below, the commission argues that it is exempt from local zoning regulations for two reasons. First it says that as an agency of the state itself, performing a governmental function, it is immune from regulation by a mere political subdivision in the absence of a legislative declaration to the contrary. Second, it relies on its possession of the power of eminent domain as indicating a legislative intent that its use of land not be subject to control by local authorities.

A concise review of the terms in which courts have traditionally analyzed conflicts between governmental agencies over land use regulations is found in *City of Temple Terrace v. Hillsborough Ass'n, Etc.*, 322 So. 2d 571 (Fla. App. 1975), *affirmed on opinion below*, *Hillsborough Ass'n, Etc. v. City of Temple Terrace*, 332 So. 2d 610 (Fla. 1976). The Florida Court of Appeals there noted:

> In deciding this type of case, the courts have used varying tests. One approach utilized by a number of courts is to rule in favor of the superior sovereign. Thus, where immunity from a local zoning ordinance is claimed by an agency occupying a superior

position in the governmental hierarchy, it is presumed that immunity was intended in the absence of express statutory language to the contrary. *E.g., Aviation Services, Inc. v. Board of Adjustment*, 1956, 20 N.J. 275, 119 A.2d 761. A second test frequently employed is to determine whether the institutional use proposed for the land is "governmental" or "proprietary" in nature. If the political unit is found to be performing a governmental function, it is immune from the conflicting zoning ordinance. *E.g., City of Scottsdale v. Municipal Court*, 1962, 90 Ariz. 393, 368 P.2d 637. On the other hand, when the use is considered proprietary, the zoning ordinance prevails. *E.g., Taber v. City of Benton Harbor*, 1937, 280 Mich. 522, 274 N.W. 324. Where the power of eminent domain has been granted to the governmental unit seeking immunity from local zoning, some courts have concluded that this conclusively demonstrates the unit's superiority where its proposed use conflicts with zoning regulations. *E.g., Mayor of Savannah v. Collins*, 1954, 211 Ga. 191, 84 S.E.2d 454. Other cases are controlled by explicit statutory provisions dealing with the question of whether the operation of a particular governmental unit is subject to local zoning. *E.g., Mogilner v. Metropolitan Plan Commission*, 1957, 236 Ind. 298, 140 N.E.2d 220.

When the governmental unit which seeks to circumvent a zoning ordinance is an arm of the state, the application of any of the foregoing tests has generally resulted in a judgment permitting the proposed use. This has accounted for statements of hornbook law to the effect that a state agency authorized to carry out a function of the state is not bound by local zoning regulations. 2 Anderson, American Law of Zoning §9.06 (1968); 8 McQuillin, Municipal Corporations §25.15 (1965)." (p. 574.) . . .

There being no "explicit statutory provision" applicable here, the commission relies on the other three common tests: in its first argument it combines the "superior sovereign" with the "governmental-proprietary" test; in its second it asserts the "eminent domain" test. All have been subject to scholarly criticism as too simplistic, avoiding the kind of analysis needed for rational resolution of the complex issues posed by land use problems in a modern, urban-oriented society. . . .

Recent judicial pronouncements are increasingly in the same vein. . . .

Pennsylvania's way in this area was indicated by the leading case in the new wave of intergovernmental zoning decisions, *Rutgers v. Piluso*, 60 N.J. 142, 286 A.2d 697 (1972). There the question was whether Rutgers, the state university, could build student housing units in excess of the maximum number permitted by a township zoning ordinance. . . .

After recognizing the three common tests (asserted by the commission here) and reviewing its own prior decisions, the court formulated its own test:

> The rationale which runs through our cases and which we are convinced should furnish the true test of immunity in the first instance, albeit a somewhat nebulous one, is the legislative intent in this regard with respect to the particular agency or function involved. That intent, rarely specifically expressed, is to be divined from a consideration of many factors, with a value judgment reached on an overall evaluation. All possible factors cannot be abstractly catalogued. The most obvious and common ones include [1] the nature and scope of the instrumentality seeking immunity, [2] the kind of function or land use involved, [3] the extent of the public interest to be served thereby, [4] the effect local land use regulation would have upon the enterprise concerned and [5] the impact upon legitimate local interests. . . . In some instances one factor will be more influential than another or may be so significant as to completely overshadow all others. No one, such as the granting or withholding of the power of eminent domain, is to be thought of as ritualistically required or controlling. And there will undoubtedly be cases, as there have been in the past, where the

> broader public interest is so important that immunity must be granted even though the local interests may be great. The point is that there is no precise formula or set of criteria which will determine every case mechanically and automatically. (pp. 152-53, 286 A.2d p. 702. Numbers inserted.)

The court went on to find that the state university performed an essential governmental function for the benefit of all the people of the state, and that the legislature would not intend its growth to be subject to restriction or control by local land use regulation. After observing that the same reasoning would generally be true of all state functions and agencies, the court added the following caveat:

> It is, however, most important to stress that such immunity in any situation is not completely unbridled. Even when it is found to exist, it must not, as this court said in *Washington Township v. Village of Ridgewood, supra*, 26 N.J. [578] at 584-586, 141 A.2d 308, be exercised in an unreasonable fashion so as to arbitrarily override all important legitimate local interests. . . .

The test applied in *Rutgers* has come to be known as the "balancing of interests" test. . . .

If we look at the factors suggested as relevant by the *Rutgers* court we find: (1) The instrumentality seeking immunity is a state agency, and its judgment is entitled to considerable deference. (2) The general function being performed — promoting recreation — is one of recognized public utility but hardly on a level of importance with public education. The specific use, providing parking space near but not in a recreation area, is of a more marginal public interest. (3) While there is public interest in the proposed use in that some people will find this parking lot more convenient than other available lots, the segment of the population affected is relatively small. (4) Regulation, if rezoning is refused, would have the effect of requiring the parking lot to be located in some area other than a residential subdivision. Such a move might make the lot less convenient, but would probably not substantially impair the usefulness of the recreation area. (5) The proposed use would, prima facie at least, have a substantial adverse impact on the surrounding householders and on the existing land use plan.

As noted above, these factors were not weighed on the basis of evidence either by a zoning body or by the court below, and our observations are based on a skimpy record and our own general knowledge. The commission simply asserted its immunity, without attempting to justify the reasonableness of its decision, while the court looked no further than the admitted violation of the zoning regulation.

It seems to us that, on balance, the initial decision on reasonableness in this case can be made more expeditiously and with greater discernment by the local zoning authority — here the county. That being so, we infer a legislative intent that the responsibility should be imposed on that body. If rezoning is arbitrarily denied, that decision can be reviewed by the courts at the commission's behest through normal channels. If, on the other hand, we were to hold that the commission's status as superior sovereign immunizes it from the normal zoning processes as it urges, then the burden of going forward with a lawsuit would fall on either the county or the affected landowners. In such a suit they would be required to show arbitrariness on the part of the commission. While it is true the landowners would have much the same burden if dissatisfied by an order *granting* rezoning, that would be because two administrative agencies at different levels have concurred in finding the proposed use appropriate. The zoning route strikes us as cheaper and faster, and it puts the local land use decision in local hands where, in this case, it belongs.

In this case the district court ordered the commission to seek rezoning. It can still do so. In our opinion that is the proper course for it to take, and the trial court properly so ordered.

Affirmed.

Notes and Comments

1. *The Extent of Municipal Jurisdiction.* In general, a city's police power does not extend outside its boundaries, and its land use regulatory authority is likewise limited. The power to zone is coextensive with the boundaries of local jurisdiction. *See, e.g., Manorhaven v. Ventura Yacht Servs.*, 561 N.Y.S.2d 277, 278 (Sup. Ct. App. Div. 1990) ("[a]s a general rule, the jurisdiction of an incorporated village is confined to its territorial limits"); *City of Eugene v. Nalven*, 955 P.2d 263, 265 (Or. Ct. App. 1998) ("A city generally may exercise authority only within its corporate limits"). This limitation, however, can raise problems when a neighboring jurisdiction approves a land use near the boundary that has effects on the adjacent jurisdiction. *See, e.g., City of Walnut Creek v. County of Contra Costa*, 162 Cal. Rptr. 224 (Ct. App. 1980) (city sued to overturn the county's approval of an apartment complex located on county land adjacent to the city); *Town of Bedford v. Village of Mount Kisco*, 306 N.E.2d 155 (N.Y. 1973) (town sued adjoining village for adopting an ordinance rezoning an area from single family dwellings to permit six-story multiple dwellings).

What if the actual homes and most of a subdivision lie outside the municipal jurisdiction, but part of the subdivision plan marked "[r]eserved for a road" is within that jurisdiction? *Town of North Yarmouth v. Moulton*, 710 A.2d 252 (Me. 1998) (town had jurisdiction over entire subdivision).

2. *Extraterritorial Planning and Zoning.* In some situations where the area outside the city has not been annexed to a municipality, states attempt to deal with these "border" problems by enacting statutes authorizing the limited, extraterritorial exercise of land use authority. Many states allow municipalities to "pre-plan" for areas outside of their current regulatory jurisdictions. *See, e.g.*, N.Y. Gen. Mun. Law §237 (McKinney 1999); Marygold Shire Melli & Robert S. Devoy, Extraterritorial Planning and Urban Growth, 1959 Wis. L. Rev. 55. But planning in and of itself has no regulatory effect. Accordingly, numerous states provide for extraterritorial zoning, and about half of these statutes also authorize municipal regulation of subdivisions outside the municipality's jurisdiction. *Wood v. City of Madison*, 2002 WL 535416 (Wis. App. 2002) (suggesting that city's powers over a subdivision in its extraterritorial jurisdiction extend to both zoning and subdivision platting).

How far should such a power extend? Should the geographical limitation be flexibly determined on a case-by-case basis, or should a "flat" mileage limitation be placed on the exercise of extraterritorial zoning? *See* Iowa Code Ann. §414.23 (West Supp. 2003) (two miles); N.C. Gen. Stat. §160A-360 (2003) (one mile); Ky. Rev. Stat. Ann. §100.131 (Michie 1993 and Supp. 2003) (five miles); Tenn. Code Ann. §13-7-302 (1999) (areas adjoining the city where the municipal planning commission has been designated as the regional planning commission). Should the power be limited only to areas that are likely to be annexed to the city in the future?

3. *Extraterritorial Effects and the Presumption of Validity*. The use of extraterritorial planning and zoning usually takes place where the land outside of the municipality has not been annexed and is undeveloped. The disputes among adjacent local governments, however, also occur when two cities that are urbanized disagree over a particular project, or where a particular project—although located entirely within the jurisdictional boundaries of the local governmental entity approving it—has regional impacts.

One way to approach such disputes is to alter the way in which the court undertakes judicial review of such actions. For instance, in *Associated Home Builders v. City of Livermore*, 557 P.2d 473 (Cal. 1976), the California Supreme Court devised a test for determining whether a local zoning enactment served the "regional welfare." *See also Lusardi v. Curtis Point Property Owners Ass'n*, 430 A.2d 881 (N.J. 1981) (single-family zoning for beachfront property was invalid in part because it ignored the statewide policy that favored emphasizing the recreational use of beachfront property); *Save A Valuable Environment v. City of Bothell*, 576 P.2d 401 (Wash. 1978) (where zoning ordinance will have a serious environmental effect outside the enacting city's jurisdictional boundaries, the zoning must serve the welfare of the entire affected community).

4. *The City as Landowner*. Another situation that can lead to an intergovernmental conflict occurs when a city owns property outside of its jurisdiction and wants to construct a municipal project on that property. Will the project be subject to the land use controls of the jurisdiction in which the property is located (providing that those controls exist)? The answer, usually found in a statute, varies.

For example, in *County of Will v. City of Naperville*, 589 N.E.2d 1090 (Ill. App. Ct. 1992), the city wanted to build a fire station outside of its own limits but within the jurisdiction of the county. The city relied on a state statute that apparently gave it authority over city-owned property outside the city limits, but the court held that the county's land use authority controlled. In contrast, in *City of Washington v. Warren County, Missouri*, 899 S.W.2d 863 (Mo. 1995), the Missouri Supreme Court concluded that, under the "power of eminent domain test" mentioned in *Brown*, the city was not subject to the county's zoning ordinance in constructing an addition to airport property that the city owned and operated.

5. *School Districts and Public Utilities*. Another important, recurring question is whether school districts are subject to local zoning ordinances and regulatory controls. Here, statutes are likely to provide the answer, with the court deciding if the statutes are not clear. *See Normandy School Dist. v. City of Pasadena Hills*, 70 S.W.3d 488 (Mo. Ct. App. 2002) (city could not deny a building permit on the basis that school construction did not comply with city's height restrictions); *Sto-Rox School District v. Zoning Hearing Board of Kennedy Township*, 674 A.2d 352 (Pa. Commw. Ct. 1996) (school board's authority superseded local zoning power); *City of Addison v. Dallas Independent School District*, 632 S.W.2d 771 (Tex. Ct. App. 1982) (a school district can place any school facility within an area zoned residential, unless the school district action is unreasonable or constitutes a nuisance). Finally, public utilities may be statutorily exempted from complying with local zoning laws. *See Trustees of Washington Tp. v. Davis*, 767 N.E.2d 261 (Ohio 2002) (while statute exempts a "public utility" or railroad from local zoning or land use regulation, an AM radio station constructing a transmission tower was not a public utility).

6. *Constitutional Questions*. The exercise of extraterritorial zoning or subdivision powers raises some obvious constitutional questions. For example, do residents of an area have a constitutional right to vote when their land is located outside of a local jurisdiction's boundaries but is subject to that jurisdiction's extraterritorial zoning power? In *Holt Civic Club v. City of Tuscaloosa, Alabama*, 439 U.S. 60 (1978), a statute authorized the city to exercise its police jurisdiction (but not its land use power) over areas beyond the city's boundaries. The Supreme Court held that this arrangement did not violate the constitutional voting rights of those citizens who were subject to the police jurisdiction but who, because of their location outside the city limits, were not allowed to vote in the municipal elections.

7. *Cooperative Agreements*. Yet another approach to the problem of extraterritorial impacts is to authorize municipalities to reach agreements to carry out land use regulation jointly. *See* N.Y. Gen. Mun. Law §119-u (McKinney Supp. 1997) ("each city, town or village is hereby authorized to enter into, amend, cancel and terminate agreements with any other municipality or municipalities to undertake all or a portion of such [land use] powers, functions and duties"). Does a city have the power to reach such an agreement without express statutory authority? *See Alameda County Land Use Ass'n v. City of Hayward*, 45 Cal. Rptr. 2d 752 (Ct. App. 1995) (memorandum of understanding between cities and counties, under which each city agreed that individual general plan amendments would be ineffective in their jurisdiction unless like amendments were made in all other cities, was an invalid divestment of local power). *Compare Dateline Builders, Inc. v. City of Santa Rosa*, 194 Cal. Rptr. 258 (Ct. App. 1983) (city could refuse to extend its utility service to an area outside its city limits where it had entered into an agreement with the county to implement a joint general plan for the county area in question).

Should a city be able to reach an agreement with a *landowner* outside the city's jurisdiction in order to resolve a dispute about land use on that property? *See People v. City of Batavia*, 414 N.E.2d 916, 920 (Ill. App. Ct. 1980) ("there is no independent power to enter into restrictive covenants to regulate use of land beyond the city's borders").

An interesting variation of the agreement theme is found in *Bd. of County Commissioners of Adams County v. City and County of Denver*, 40 P.3d 23 (Colo. Ct. App. 2001). In order to solve disputes over annexation when it was attempting to construct Denver International Airport, the City of Denver entered into an "intergovernmental agreement" with a city. Under that agreement, the city and other "third party beneficiary" cities were entitled to payments as liquidated damages if the airport exceeded certain noise levels. When just that situation occurred, Denver resisted the payments. The court upheld the contract and the damages.

8. *Resolving "Vertical" Intergovernmental Conflicts*. In addition to "horizontal" intergovernmental conflicts between neighboring jurisdictions, "vertical" conflicts between a state or its agencies and a local government are also possible. These types of conflicts, exemplified by the *Brown* case, occur when the state government or one of its agencies wants to implement a land use that is inconsistent with the uses authorized by the local government's land use controls. *See, e.g., City of Malibu v. Santa Monica Mountains Conservancy*, 119 Cal. Rptr. 777 (Ct. App. 2002) (city sought to regulate commercial uses on 22 acres of property that was part of the [Barbara] Streisand Center for Conservation Studies owned by a state agency). Obviously, the state can legitimately argue that it cannot allow local, parochial land use controls to stymie its project. What governmental interests may be damaged

if state projects are automatically exempt from local regulation? What about the effective implementation of the local master or general plan?

The *Brown* case sets forth a variety of tests that courts have used to resolve such state-local conflicts, including the "governmental-proprietary" test and the "balancing of interests" test. *See Town of Bourne v. Plante*, 708 N.E.2d 103 (Mass. 1999) (applying "essential government function" test to conclude that a steamship authority did not have to comply with local zoning regulations). Which of these tests do you believe is best suited to resolve this type of conflict? One important factor that must be considered is whether the test provides realistic guidance to state and local decisionmakers in determining that future projects are or are not subject to local controls. Does the "governmental-proprietary" test or the "balancing of interests" test provide more guidance of this type? Under the latter type of test, is a court equipped to determine the weight of the "public interest" behind a particular land use proposed by the state?

In *Hazelton Area School Dist. v. Zoning Hg. Bd.*, 778 A.2d 1205 (Pa. 2001), the Pennsylvania Supreme Court rejected a balancing approach and instead used rules of statutory construction to determine legislative intent. Earlier, in *Commonwealth, Dept. of Gen. Serv. v. Ogontz Area Neighbors Ass'n*, 483 A.2d 448, 454 (1984), that court explicitly observed that balancing "amounts to a judicial determination that since the legislature did not provide for the situation at hand, the court will. . . . " The *Hazelton* court concluded that the school district had to exercise its statutory authority to rent its athletic fields consistently with local zoning regulations. *Compare Schultz v. Northville Public Schools*, 635 N.W.2d 508 (Mich. Ct. App. 2001) (statute giving superintendent sole jurisdiction over school plans exempts school construction from local zoning).

Are these cases simply outcome-driven? Are the courts looking at the particular project at issue and, based on their assessment of its impacts, reaching a conclusion regarding preemption that fits their assessment?

A Note on State Law Preemption of Local Land Use Regulation

As state environmental regulation has greatly expanded in the last 25 years, so have claims that state statutes or regulations preempt certain local government regulations of private facilities. Preemption claims have centered on landfills and solid waste disposal facilities, public utilities, billboards, hazardous waste sites, group homes, and airports. *See, e.g., IT Corp. v. Solano County Bd. of Supervisors*, 820 P.2d 1023 (Cal. 1991) (state hazardous waste law did not preempt county enforcement of a conditional use permit requiring a buffer around a hazardous waste facility); *Bd. of County Commissioners, La Plata County v. Bowen/Edwards Assoc.*, 830 P.2d 1045 (Colo. 1992) (state Oil and Gas Conservation Act did not preempt county's authority to enact land use regulations applicable to oil and gas operations); *Scadron v. City of Des Plaines*, 606 N.E.2d 1154 (Ill. 1992) (Illinois Highway Advertising Act did not preempt home rule municipality's total ban on outdoor advertising signs).

1. *Express Preemption.* Preemption can either be express or implied. A state statute expressly precluding local regulation or authorizing a state agency to preempt local action generally will settle the question. For example, express preemption was found in *Planning Bd. of Braintree v. Department of Public Utilities*, 647

N.E.2d 1186 (Mass. 1995), in which the Supreme Judicial Court of Massachusetts affirmed a decision by the state Department of Public Utilities under a statute allowing the department to except public utilities from local zoning ordinances. *See also City of Miami Beach v. Amoco Oil Co.*, 510 So. 2d 609 (Fla. Dist. Ct. App. 1987) ("We hold that by enacting section 563.02, Florida Statutes (1985), the legislature has expressly preempted the city's authority to enact zoning ordinances prohibiting the sale of beer, by state-licensed, gasoline filling stations, for off-premises consumption.").

2. *Implied Preemption*. In the absence of language expressly preempting local regulation, the outcome of the implied preemption analysis will turn on a careful reading of the state statutory language and a consideration of the legislative intent. *See, e.g., Tumino v. Long Beach Township*, 725 A.2d 1173 (N.J. Super. App. Div. 1999) (court's review of state regulatory scheme concerning docks "demonstrates that these rules are intended to exclusively govern the field"). In *Bauer v. Waste Management, Inc.*, 662 A.2d 1179 (Conn. 1995), a solid waste company argued that the state's solid waste management act preempted a 90-foot height limitation imposed on landfills by a local government. The Connecticut Supreme Court disagreed, concluding that the legislature had not demonstrated an intent to occupy the entire field of regulation and that the local regulation did not irreconcilably conflict with the state law. Similarly, in *St. Charles Gaming Co. v. Riverboat Gaming Comm'n*, 648 So. 2d 1310 (La. 1995), the Louisiana Supreme Court concluded that the Riverboat Economic and Gaming Control Act did not preempt a local government from exercising its home rule powers to adopt and enforce a local zoning ordinance. In contrast, in *City of Shelton v. Commissioner of Department of Environmental Protection*, 479 A.2d 208, 215 (Conn. 1984), the court invalidated a local zoning ordinance on the grounds that it frustrated the legislative intent "to commit the difficult regional problems of solid waste disposal to regional and statewide solution."

3. *Dual Authority*. Finally, some statutory schemes attempt to accommodate both state and local regulation. Thus, in *Sawyer Environmental Recovery Facilities, Inc. v. Town of Hampden*, 760 A.2d 257 (Me. 2000), the Maine Supreme Court first found that any local ordinance banning the location and expansion of a landfill was preempted by state law. However, the local government could still regulate the external impacts of landfills. New York law on local regulation of mining has the opposite allocation: cities may prohibit the use of land within its boundaries for mining operations through its zoning laws, but they cannot regulate the "actual operation and process of mining." *Town of Riverhead v. T.S. Haulers*, 713 N.Y.S.2d 740, 741 (Sup. Ct. App. Div. 2000).

If a local government is opposed to a landfill, will this type of statutory allocation of power work well?

E. THE FEDERAL INFLUENCE OVER LAND USE

As this book has stressed, land use regulation largely remains within the province of local governments. While some regional and state controls over land use have been enacted, the federal government (except with respect to the federal lands, such as national forests) has mostly left the matter to state law. One exception to this is the Telecommunications Act of 1996, which allows federal courts to review certain local government land use decisions regarding telecommunications technology—in particular, the siting of cell phone towers. The Act has generated a significant amount of litigation. The following case is typical.

■ PREFERRED SITES, LLC v. TROUP COUNTY

296 F.3d 1210 (11th Cir. 2002)

BLACK, Circuit Judge:

This case involves an application of the Telecommunications Act of 1996 (TCA) to the land use decisions of a local government. Pub.L. No. 104-104, 110 Stat. 56 (codified in scattered sections of 15 and 47 U.S.C.). Preferred Sites, LLC (Appellee), filed suit against Troup County, Georgia (Appellant), alleging the county's Zoning Appeals and Planning Board (the Board) violated §704(a) of the TCA by denying its application for conditional use approval to construct a multiple user-wireless communication tower. Appellee alleged the Board's decision was not supported by substantial evidence contained in a written record, as required by §704(a). The district court agreed, granting summary judgment in favor of Appellee and ordering Appellant to approve the conditional use permit. We affirm.

I. BACKGROUND

A. FACTUAL AND PROCEDURAL BACKGROUND

Appellee owns, operates, and manages free-standing wireless communication towers, which typically are used to provide cellular telephone service. Appellee also acts as a site selection firm for the wireless communication industry. As part of this business, Appellee sought to construct a 250-foot tower on a 7.6 acre parcel of property owned by Charles and Ruth Bailey in LaGrange, Georgia, which is located in Troup County. To obtain permission to construct the tower, Appellee, through its agent, applied to the Board for conditional use approval. Appellee's application was required by the Troup County Zoning Ordinance, which sets forth the standards for placement, design and removal of telecommunications antennas and towers. Troup County, Ga., Comprehensive Zoning Ordinance, Appendix A, Art. IV, §14 (1999).[1]

On June 8, 2000, the Board held a public hearing at which it considered Appellee's conditional use application. The minutes of the hearing do not contain

1. The ordinance specifies the following requirements for a proposed tower: (1) the tower must be constructed on property in an approved zoning district; (2) the tower must be set back from any off-site structure the more restrictive distance of (a) 500 feet or (b) the full height of the tower from any off-site structure and/or be designed to collapse within a specific clear area; (3) the tower must be enclosed by security fencing not less than 6 feet in height and must be equipped with an appropriate anti-climbing device; and (4) the tower must meet or exceed the standards and regulations of the Federal Aviation Administration and the Federal Communications Commission at the time of erection. *Id.* §§14(e), 14(b)(1)-(3). In addition to these requirements, the ordinance provides the following information must be in the conditional use request: (1) the height of the proposed tower; (2) the proximity of the tower to residential structures and residential district boundaries; (3) the nature and uses on adjacent and nearby properties; (4) the surrounding topography; (5) the surrounding tree coverage and foliage; and (6) the design of the tower, with particular reference to design characteristics which have the effect of reducing or eliminating visual obtrusiveness. *Id.* §§14(e)(1)-(6). Finally, the ordinance provides the Board, in granting a conditional use permit, may impose additional conditions as necessary to minimize any adverse effects of the tower on adjoining properties. *Id.* §14(c).

the contents of any discussion or debate concerning the application. Appellant, however, submitted to the district court the affidavit of Mike Dobbs, the Zoning Administrator of Troup County, who attended the meeting. The affidavit stated several members of the public verbally opposed construction of the tower. These individuals apparently opposed the visual obtrusiveness of the proposed tower. The affidavit, however, contained no further information concerning these citizens' objections.

In addition, five petitions, which collectively contained the signatures of 58 individuals, were submitted to the Board. The petitions objected generally to the construction of the tower. All five standard form petitions had three groupings of blank lines: (1) a set of blank lines to write in the purpose of the petition, the opinion being expressed, the property concerned, and the property's specific location; (2) a set of blank lines to write in an explanation of the proposal for which the petition was being circulated; and (3) a set of lines for individuals' full signatures and complete addresses. Despite the presence of these blank lines, only two of the petitions were complete, indicating both the purpose of the petition was to oppose the tower and the proposal for which the petition was circulated was to object to the construction of the tower. The third petition merely noted the location of the proposed tower and indicated the proposal for which the petition was circulated was to object to the construction of the tower. Finally, the fourth and fifth petitions submitted to the Board contained no information other than the signatures and addresses of people who live in LaGrange, Georgia. Other than the five petitions, no evidence objecting to Appellee's construction of the tower exists in the record.

At the conclusion of the hearing, the Board voted unanimously to deny Appellee's request for conditional use approval. Thereafter, in a letter dated June 12, 2000, the Troup County Zoning Department provided written notification to Appellee that the Board denied its application. . . .

B. BACKGROUND OF THE TELECOMMUNICATIONS ACT OF 1996

The TCA was enacted "to provide for a pro-competitive, de-regulatory national policy framework designed to accelerate rapidly private sector deployment of advanced telecommunications and information technologies and services to all Americans by opening all telecommunications markets to competition." H.R. Conf. Rep. No. 104-458, at 113 (1996), *reprinted in* 1996 U.S.C.C.A.N. 124, 124. In addition, the TCA was intended "to promote competition and reduce regulation in order to secure lower prices and higher quality services for American telecommunications consumers and encourage the rapid deployment of new telecommunications technologies." Telecommunications Act of 1996, Pub.L. No. 104-104, 110 Stat. 56, 56 (1996). Wireless telephone service was one of the many telecommunications technologies Congress considered when enacting the TCA.

With respect to the construction of telecommunications facilities, Congress recognized zoning decisions by state and local governments had created an inconsistent array of requirements, which inhibited both the deployment of personal communications services and the rebuilding of a digital technology-based cellular telecommunications network. H.R. Rep. No. 104-204, at 94 (1995), *reprinted in* 1996 U.S.C.C.A.N. 10, 61. Despite this recognition, Congress also acknowledged "there are legitimate State and local concerns involved in regulating the siting of such facilities . . . , such as aesthetic values and the costs associated with the use and maintenance of public rights-of-way." *Id.* at 94-95, *reprinted in* 1996 U.S.C.C.A.N. 10, 61. As a result, Congress enacted §704(a) to "preserve[ ] the authority of State and local governments over zoning and land use matters except in . . . limited circumstances. . . ." H.R. Conf. Rep. No. 104-458 (1996), at 207-08, *reprinted in* 1996 U.S.C.C.A.N. 124, 222.

In §704(a), codified at 47 U.S.C. §332(c)(7), Congress enunciated a number of substantive and procedural limitations upon the authority of state or local governments to regulate the construction of facilities for wireless communication services. Local zoning authorities may not unreasonably discriminate among providers of functionally equivalent services, may not make zoning decisions which prohibit or effectively prohibit the provision of personal wireless services, and may not make zoning decisions premised on concerns regarding the environmental effects of radio frequency emissions associated with wireless telephone service. 47 U.S.C. §§332(c)(7)(B)(i)(I), 332(c)(7)(B)(i)(II), 332(c)(7)(B)(iv) (1994).

To ensure the enforcement of these limitations, Congress delineated the manner in which zoning decisions are to be made and also provided a mechanism for judicial relief for persons aggrieved by decisions inconsistent with §704(a)'s requirements. §§332(c)(7)(B)(iii), 332(c)(7)(B)(v). For example, decisions to deny approval for the placement, construction, or modification of personal wireless service facilities must be both "in writing and supported by substantial evidence contained in a written record." §332(c)(7)(B)(iii). In addition, if a state or local government acts in a manner inconsistent with §704(a)'s statutory requirements, any person adversely affected by the action may, "within 30 days after such action . . . commence an action in any court of competent jurisdiction." §332(c)(7)(B)(v). By structuring the TCA in this manner, Congress explicitly preserved local zoning authority over the siting of wireless facilities, while permitting judicial oversight as to the manner in which such decisions are made. §§332(c)(7)(A), 332(c)(7)(B)(v).

II. Discussion . . .

B. Substantial Evidence for the Board's Denial

. . . Appellant contends the district court erred in holding its decision to deny Appellee's application for conditional use approval was not supported by substantial evidence contained in a written record.

Although §704(a) requires a local zoning board's decision to be both in writing and supported by substantial evidence, it does not statutorily define the term "substantial evidence."[8] The Conference Committee for the TCA, however, expressly noted "substantial evidence" is meant to be "the traditional standard used for judicial review of agency actions." H.R. Conf. Rep. 104-458, at 208, *reprinted in* 1996 U.S.C.C.A.N. 124, at 223. . . .

. . . We have reviewed the record in its entirety and conclude the Board's decision to deny Appellee's application for conditional use approval was unsupported by substantial evidence. The record reveals Appellee submitted an application

8. The TCA also fails to define what is required for a decision to be "in writing." We recognize the district court held Appellant's decision failed to meet the "in writing" requirement of §332(c)(7)(B)(iii). We express no opinion on the issue, however, because it is not necessary for the resolution of this case, as we conclude the decision was not supported by substantial evidence.

for conditional use approval to construct a 250-foot wireless telecommunications tower on property with an appropriate zoning classification approved for the construction of a tower. Appellee's application included all the information required by the Troup County zoning ordinance. Although a public hearing on Appellee's application was held on June 8, 2000, the minutes of the hearing do not reflect that any opposition to the application was raised.

The only evidence of opposition to Appellee's application contained in the written record are the five petitions signed by a total of 58 citizens of LaGrange, Georgia. Of the five petitions, two contained only individuals' signatures and addresses. Nowhere on these two petitions was there even an indication of the reason the individuals signed the petitions. Of the other three petitions, one was only partially completed. It noted only the location of the proposed tower, but not the purpose of the petition nor the opinion being expressed. The petition did, however, indicate the proposal for which the petition was circulated was to object to the construction of the tower. Only two of the petitions were complete, indicating both that the purpose of the petition was to express an opinion opposing the specific tower Appellee intended to build and that the proposal for which the petition was circulated was to object to the construction of that tower. Even these two petitions, however, provided only generalized objections with no articulated reasons for the opposition. Based on the entire written record, we conclude the scant evidence of opposition to the construction of Appellee's proposed tower did not amount to substantial evidence.

Although the written record does not reflect any opposition to Appellee's conditional use application other than the petitions, we recognize Appellant submitted the affidavit of Michael Dobbs to the district court. Dobbs' affidavit explains that he attended the hearing and recalls several members of the public, who resided in the vicinity of the site for the proposed tower, verbally opposed construction of the tower. Their opposition apparently consisted of general concerns about the negative aesthetic impact of the proposed tower.

Even if Dobbs' affidavit could be construed as part of the written record, we conclude the citizens' generalized concerns about aesthetics are insufficient to constitute substantial evidence upon which the Board could rely. Aesthetic concerns may be a valid basis for denial of a permit *if* substantial evidence of the visual impact of the tower is before the board. . . . Mere generalized concerns regarding aesthetics, however, are insufficient to create substantial evidence justifying the denial of a permit under §704(a) of the TCA. . . . Consequently, even construing the concerns voiced about aesthetics at the hearing as opposition contained in the written record, we conclude such meager evidence is insufficient to support the Board's denial of Appellee's application. There being no other evidence in the written record opposing the approval of Appellee's application, the Board's decision was unsupported by substantial evidence.

C. REMEDY FOR VIOLATION OF REQUIREMENTS OF §704(a)

Section 704(a) does not specify the appropriate remedy if a court of competent jurisdiction determines a state or local authority violated the requirements contained therein. Appellant contends, however, the district court erred by granting mandamus relief requiring Appellant to grant Appellee's application for conditional use approval. . . .

Although the TCA does not statutorily provide a remedy for a violation of §704(a), it does require a "court of competent jurisdiction" to "hear and decide [an action arising from a violation of §704(a)] on an expedited basis." 47 U.S.C. §332(c)(7)(B)(v) (1994). A number of courts have considered this issue and held an injunction (or other equitable relief) in the form of an order to issue the relevant permits is a proper form of relief under §704(a). . . .

In this case, the district court found Appellant violated §704(a), thereby entitling Appellee to relief. As a result, the district court granted Appellee's petition for summary judgment, which included a request for a writ of mandamus ordering Appellant to grant the application for conditional use approval. Although the district court's order did not specify the type of relief granted, the nature of the relief granted was in the form of an injunction. We conclude an injunction ordering issuance of a permit is an appropriate remedy for a violation of §704(a). . . .

AFFIRMED.

Notes and Comments

1. *"Substantial Evidence" and Aesthetic Concerns.* Fifteen days before it issued the *Preferred Sites* decision, the Eleventh Circuit handed down *American Tower LP v. City of Huntsville*, 295 F.3d 1203 (11th Cir. 2002). The plaintiff challenged a local zoning board's denial of a special exception and variance for a proposed communication tower. The court first noted that the Board of Zoning Appeals (BZA) was "authorized to consider . . . the proposed tower's negative aesthetic impact." *Id.* at 1208. The BZA heard testimony from several residents on the negative aesthetics and impact on values of the proposed tower. A realtor testified that in her 16 years of experience, she had learned that a proposal to build a cell tower made it harder to sell homes in the neighborhood. She testified she had lost potential buyers for her own property in the area because of the proposed tower. The Board also heard testimony on "safety questions tied to the proposed tower's proximity to two schools and several soccer fields used by children." *Id.* at 1209. There was contrary evidence presented. The court held that substantial evidence supported the BZA's decision.

Are *Preferred Sites* and *American Tower* reconcilable? Is the problem that in the latter case, opponents did not present testimony about economic impacts? That the Troop Affidavit was insufficiently specific? That the meeting was not recorded and submitted to the Court? If you had represented the neighbors in *Preferred Sites* before the Board, what steps would you have taken to present your clients' position? Do the cases indicate that, if cell towers are proposed for affluent areas, there is more likely to be "substantial evidence" in the record supporting a denial than if the tower is proposed for a poor area?

2. *Other TCA Substantive Issues.* The TCA declares that no siting regulation may have "the effect of prohibiting" service. 47 U.S.C. §332(c)(7)(B)(i)(II). When do local actions have the "effect" prohibited in the statute? *See Town of Amherst, New Hampshire v. Omnipoint Communications Enterprises, Inc.*, 173 F.3d 9 (1st Cir. 1999) (criteria could effectively amount to a ban even though substantial evidence exists for a denial, but here "there is no showing of such fixed hostility by the Board that one can conclude that further applications would be useless"). The TCA also bars discrimination against a provider. *See Aegeter v. City of Delafield,*

Wisconsin, 174 F.3d 886 (7th Cir. 1999) (in a "pager versus cell phone" controversy; no violation of antidiscrimination rule because no evidence that city was giving preferential treatment to anyone who offered a service "functionally equivalent" to the applicant). If a town ordinance restricts location of cell towers to certain districts only, does this create a prohibited "significant gap" in service amounting to a prohibition? *Second Generation Properties, L.P. v. Town of Pelham*, 313 F.3d 620 (1st Cir. 2002) ("dead spots" are permissible, larger gaps can be prohibitions, but here the possibility of a variance existed).

A third issue concerns the TCA's requirement that a local government's decision to deny "shall be in writing." Does this impose a new, particularized requirement on zoning decisions? *New Par v. City of Saginaw*, 301 F.3d 390 (6th Cir. 2002) (describing a variety of different judicial views).

Can an applicant combine a violation of the TCA with a claim for damages under the Civil Rights Act? The Third Circuit said no in *Nextel Partners, Inc. v. Kingston Tp.*, 286 F.3d 687, 694 (3d Cir. 2002) ("the TCA implicitly precludes an action under §1983 by creating a comprehensive remedial scheme that furnishes private judicial remedies"). Could a neighbor bring an action alleging that operation of a cell tower was a nuisance? A Texas court of appeal saw no preemption problem in *GTE Mobilnet of South Texas Limited Partnership v. Pascourt*, 61 S.W.3d 599 (Tex. Ct. App. 2001).

3. *The Injunctive Remedy*. Almost every court to address the question has held that an injunction requiring the issuance of permits is an appropriate remedy under the TCA. Why isn't the appropriate remedy a remand to the local agency? Does the conclusion of a lack of substantial evidence suggest that the agency was not acting in good faith?

4. *The Case for Preemption*. The Telecommunications Act stands out "like a sore thumb" in the area of land use regulation. Was the need for preemption so great that Congress should have made an exception to its general approach in this one case? Is the Act already a relic of the excesses of the telecommunications "boom" of the mid-1990s? Or is the "limited preemption" found in the Act—largely requiring that decisions be supported by substantial evidence, a requirement that duplicates most state laws—so minor that the Act is of no long-term importance? In this respect, will the technology advance so it will no longer be an issue? Are there constitutional issues? *See Petersburg Cellular Partnership v. Bd. of Supervisors of Nottoway County*, 205 F.3d 688 (4th Cir. 2000) (opinion by Judge Niemeyer, not joined by other judges, concluding that the "substantial evidence" part of the TCA violates the Tenth Amendment because of "coercive choice" of complying or ending role as land use regulator). In the meantime, the federal courts have heard a significant number of cases brought by telecommunications providers denied permits at the local level.

A Note on Federal Laws that Affect Land Use

Congress to date has rejected almost all incursions of federal law into the bulk of local government's land use authority. But the sheer size and variety of functions performed by the federal government means that actions by Congress and the President have important effects on land use. Sometimes the federal government acts as a land manager over the one-third of the nation's lands within its ownership.

At other times it performs functions—building highways, funding sewage systems, locating military bases and other federal facilities, and so forth—that markedly affect local land use.

1. *Land Use Planning on Federal Lands.* Lands owned by the federal government constitute one-third of the nation's land, although those lands are largely distributed in the western part of the country. How the United States government uses this property is of significant concern to private property owners who live nearby, as well as to municipalities and other local government entities. In the western part of the United States, the importance of the use of federal lands is further complicated by the pattern of intermixed federal, state, and landownership—the famous "checkerboard" pattern common in that part of the country. *See* Public Land Law Review Comm'n, One-Third of Our Nation's Land (1970).

A variety of federal laws affect land use on federal properties. Students usually examine these laws in a separate course on public land law or natural resources law, or sometimes in the environmental law course.

Since 1970, however, Congress has passed several new laws that emphasize the completion of land use plans for federal lands. The most important of these new laws are the Forest and Rangeland Renewable Resources Planning Act (RPA) and the National Forest Management Act ("NFMA"), both codified at 16 U.S.C. §§1600-1687 (2000 and Supp. 2003), and the Federal Land Policy and Management Act (FLPMA), 43 U.S.C. §§1701-1785 (1986 and Supp. 2003). (Another federal law that has significant effects on federal land uses is the Endangered Species Act, which is discussed below in Chapter 14 of this casebook.)

a. *RPA and NFMA.* Enacted in 1974, the RPA requires the U.S. Forest Service to develop long-range land use plans for the national forest lands. Every ten years, the Forest Service is to prepare an assessment of the renewable resources throughout the national forests, and every five years the Service is to prepare a program proposing long-range planning objectives for the Service's activities. This information provides the backdrop for the NFMA, which requires the Forest Service to prepare forest-by-forest plans. Management decisions must then conform to those plans; permits, contracts, and other vehicles authorizing use of the National Forest lands must "be consistent with" the "land and resource management plans." 16 U.S.C. §1604(i) (2000). *See, e.g. Native Ecosystems Council v. Dombeck*, 304 F.2d 886 (9th Cir. 2002) (Forest Service did not violate NFMA when it amended its management plan to allow more roads to remain open after a timber sale).

b. *FLPMA.* FLPMA's land use planning provisions are not as extensive as those under the RPA and NFMA. Under FLPMA, the Bureau of Land Management (BLM) is required to develop land use plans for the public lands under the agency's jurisdiction. 43 U.S.C. §1712(c) (1986). Section 1712 mandates that BLM utilize "multiple use, sustained yield" management principles and "give priority to the designation and protection of areas of critical environmental concern." *See, e.g., Public Lands Council v. Babbitt*, 529 U.S. 728, 738 (2000) ("FLMPA strengthened the Department's existing authority to remove or add land from grazing use, allowing such modification pursuant to a land use plan"); *Natural Resources Defense Council, Inc. v. Hodel*, 624 F. Supp. 1045, 1059 (D. Nev. 1985) (finding that BLM land use planning was to deal with "broader issues" [such as] long-term resource conflicts, long-term range trends, [and] planning of range improvements"), *aff'd*, 819 F.2d 927 (9th Cir. 1987). Once the plans are prepared, the agency is required to manage the public lands "in accordance with land use plans developed . . . under section 1712." 43 U.S.C. §1732(a) (2003). *See Southern Utah Wilderness Alliance v. Norton*,

301 F.3d 1217 (10th Cir. 2002), *cert. granted,* 124 S. Ct. 462 (2003) (BLM has mandatory duty to implement land use plan). *See* Jan. G. Laitos and Thomas A. Carr, The Transformation of the Public Lands, 26 Ecol. L.Q. 140 (1999) (arguing that recreational rather than commodity development is now the predominant federal land use).

2. *Local Land Use Control and Federal Lands.* The "Property Clause" of the United States Constitution gives Congress plenary power to make rules and regulations respecting the federal lands. In *Kleppe v. New Mexico*, 426 U.S. 529, 543 (1976), the Court stated that "[a]bsent consent or cession, the state undoubtedly retains jurisdiction over federal lands within its territory, but Congress equally surely retains the power to enact legislation respecting those lands pursuant to the Property Clause." Thus, the question becomes whether Congress has preempted local control in the situation in question.

In *Ventura County v. Gulf Oil Co.*, 601 F.2d 1080 (9th Cir. 1979), *summarily aff'd without opinion*, 445 U.S. 947 (1980), the Ninth Circuit Court of Appeals rebuffed a county's attempt to require that a lessee of federal land obtain an "open space use permit" for its oil exploration and extraction activities.

Eight years later, the Supreme Court considered a somewhat similar situation in *California Coastal Comm'n v. Granite Rock Co.*, 480 U.S. 572 (1987). The Granite Rock Company had a "location claim" under the Mining Act to mine limestone in a national forest and had secured all necessary federal approvals to begin mining. The California Coastal Commission, however, contended that Granite Rock was subject to the state's regulatory jurisdiction and was required to secure a permit from it. Like Gulf Oil Company in *Ventura*, Granite Rock claimed that federal law preempted the state and local regulation.

Although you might think the outcome obvious after *Ventura*, a five-member majority of the Court held that federal law did not preempt the state permit requirement on its face, although conditions actually placed on the project by the Coastal Commission might result in preemption. The Court found that state land use planning was preempted, but it distinguished such planning from state "environmental regulation," which was not. Interestingly, the majority did not even cite *Ventura*; the case was mentioned only in passing in Justice Scalia's dissent. Do you think that "land use regulation" and "environmental regulation" are distinct classes of regulation, or do they overlap to a significant degree?

3. *Land Use Regulation and Indian Lands.* An interesting if complicated aspect of the federal influence on land use regulation involves the question of whether local governments have any right to impose land use regulations on Indian reservations. The area of law is a complex one that is further complicated by the fact that parcels of land within Indian reservations may be owned by nonmembers of the tribes.

It appears clear that only the Indian tribe has authority to control the use of land on a reservation when that land is owned by the tribe itself or its members. In recent years, Indian tribes have exercised their prerogatives by authorizing large or environmentally significant land use projects on Indian land. *See, e.g.*, Judy Pasternak and Eric Bailey, A Game of Casino Hardball: Corruption Charges Fly in a Tribal Dispute Over Land Use and Lots of Income, L.A. Times, Nov. 5, 2002, at A1 (describing various casinos proposed on tribal land in California, and noting that tribal casinos brought in $12 billion in revenue during 2001).

The result is less clear if Indian land is owned by a corporation; the outcome may turn on whether the corporation is controlled by tribal members or not. With respect to land owned by nonmembers of the tribe, a majority of the Supreme

Court could not agree on an opinion in *Brendale v. Confederated Tribes and Bands of Yakima Indian Nation*, 492 U.S. 408 (1989). Four judges essentially concluded that tribes lack authority — and thus a municipality would have the authority — to zone reservation land owned in fee by nonmembers, while three others reached the opposite conclusion. Justice Stevens, joined by Justice O'Connor, concurred with the three justices but believed that the tribe's zoning authority depends on the extent to which the nonmember's acquisition of land has deprived the tribe of the ability "to establish the essential character of the region" and to establish "a coherent scheme of land use." *Id.* at 446. *See also Gobin v. Snohomish County*, 304 F.3d 909 (9th Cir. 2002). In this case, the tribe approved a tribal member's residential subdivision on tribal land. The county, however, also claimed jurisdiction because the subdivision, which would be sold to members of the public, was larger than the county would have approved. The court held that the county had no jurisdiction over the subdivision, rejecting the claim that Congress authorized state land use regulation when it made the lands freely encumberable. The court also refused to apply the "exceptional circumstances" exception, which allows state regulation notwithstanding express congressional intent, rejecting the argument that the county's environmental interests met the test for the exception.

4. *The Sagebrush Rebellion.* In the last 25 years, the federal government's paradigm for control of federal lands has changed from one of disposal and consumption to one more oriented toward preservation and environmental protection, with a concomitant increase in regulation and bureaucracy. In reaction to this change, some western local governments began to argue not only that the federal government was mismanaging the federal lands, but also that local government has significant legal rights to control land uses on federal lands. The part of this movement led by governmental entities and public officials has been denominated the "Sagebrush Rebellion" or sometimes the "County Supremacy" movement, while action by private citizens seeking increased economic uses of the public lands has been pushed under the rubric of the "Wise Use" movement.

From a legal standpoint, the courts have rejected the local governments' claims of increased rights to control land uses on federal lands. In *Boundary Backpackers v. Boundary County*, 913 P.2d 1141 (Idaho 1996), the Idaho Supreme Court considered a county land use plan that, among other provisions, purported to require the federal government to give notice to the county before taking actions "that would affect the economic stability, custom, or culture" of the county. The plan also prohibited any further designations of wilderness areas in the county and stated that federally managed lands "that are difficult to manage or which lie in isolated tracts shall be targeted for disposal." *Id.* at 1144. The Idaho Supreme Court found that federal land use statutes preempted these provisions and struck them down.

The Bush Administration, however, has reached agreements with the State of Utah that signal its intent to open more of the public lands to wider use. Michael Janofsky, U.S.-Utah Land Accord Incites Unlikely Critics, N.Y. Times, May 23, 2003 (the efforts "reflect the strong desire of the Bush administration . . . to place more control of public lands in the hands of states and counties, and to make federal lands outside of parks and monuments more accessible for a wider range of uses").

5. *National Land Use Legislation?* Unlike other areas of law which are substantially influenced by federal legislation, land use authority remains principally a

local activity (with some regional and state inroads as detailed in this chapter). Not that long ago, however, it seemed likely that federal legislation would play a much stronger role in the development of land use law. In the early 1970s, several bills mandating increased state and local efforts in the land use field received serious consideration in Congress, and President Nixon even indicated some support for them. The Land Use Policy and Planning Assistance Act (S. 268, 93rd Cong., 1st Sess. (1973)), which passed the Senate, would have offered states certain monetary incentives to plan and mandated increased coordination between federal activities and those plans. The bills, however, were defeated in 1974 and 1975, and efforts at congressional action in this area have not received serious consideration since then. As a result, any efforts to make land use more "national" have been informal. Edward J. Sullivan and Carrie Richter, Out of the Chaos: Towards a National System of Land-Use Procedures, 34 Urb. Law. 449, 450 (2002) (noting there is "no national system of land-use planning or regulation" but there have been "three major efforts to systematize the procedures connected with land-use planning and regulation").

6. *The Federal Government and Transportation Policy: "ISTEA — or SAFETEA — Anyone?"* Federal law has shaped the interstate freeway system, which has been federally funded and designed. The effect of the freeway system on local land use has long been recognized. *See, e.g.*, Bruce Katz, The Federal Role in Curbing Sprawl, Annals of Am. Academy of Pol. and Soc. Science 67 (Nov. 2000) ("Federal and state transportation policies generally support the expansion of road capacity at the fringe of metropolitan areas and beyond, enabling people and businesses to live miles from urban centers but still benefit from metropolitan life"). Critics have charged that federal transportation policy has resulted in urban sprawl and over-reliance on the automobile as a means of transportation.

Federal transportation law is a complex subject that defies short description. Planning has been at the core of the law. Both the Federal Highway Administration and the Federal Transit Administration have required large urban areas to undertake a transportation planning process in order to qualify for federal funds.

In 1991, Congress passed a new law, the Interstate Surface Transportation Efficiency Act, Public L. No. 102-240, 105 Stat. 1914 (1991). This law, known as "ISTEA" (pronounced "ice-tea"), was intended to profoundly change transportation planning, and thus, if implemented as intended, would have important effects on land use. A recent article summarized the changes it brought as follows:

> Since their creation in 1975, MPOs have been required to plan for alternative transportation modes, as well as encourage public participation in the transportation planning process. Under ISTEA, however, this focus broadened to include better integration of modes, increased public involvement, adherence to clean air standards, and development of congestion management strategies. . . . The legislation shifted the focus of planning away from increasing capacity through new highway construction, to solving congestion by expanding travel options. ISTEA required that all modes of transportation — highways, mass transit, bikeways, and pedestrian ways — as well as airports, seaports, and intermodal facilities, be considered as an integrated system.
>
> ISTEA also charged metropolitan and state transportation agencies with improving coordination of their planning efforts. The act stressed roadway connectivity within and outside the boundaries of urbanized areas, as well as analysis of the impacts of transportation policy decisions on land use. Long-range transportation plans and

> programs were to be consistent with land development plans. State and metropolitan planning agencies were also obligated to consider the overall social, economic, energy and environmental effects of their transportation decisions.
>
> Underlying all of these planning considerations was the mandate that long-range transportation plans be financially constrained and balanced against future revenue sources.

Margaret A. Marshall, ISTEA Five Years Later: Where Do We Go From Here? 49 Land Use L. & Zoning Dig. 3 (July 1997).

ISTEA expired at the end of 1997 and was replaced by the Transportation Equity Act (TEA-21), Pub. L. No. 102-240, 105 Stat. 1914 (1998). See Dennis C. Gardner, Transportation Reauthorization: A Summary of the Transportation Equity Act (TEA-21) for the Twenty-First Century, 30 Urb. Law. 1097 (1998). The Fifth Circuit has held that TEA-21 precluded judicial review in an action brought by a bicyclist to review a transportation funding decision under the Act. *Lundeen v. Mineta*, 291 F.3d 300 (5th Cir. 2002). The Bush Administration has proposed the "Safe, Accountable, Flexible and Efficient Transportation Equity Act" (SAFETEA) to reauthorize highway and transit programs for the years 2004 to 2009. Article, Transportation DOT Says Highway, Transit Proposal Will Advance Major Environmental Goals, BNA Daily Envt. Report, May 15, 2003, at A-13.

7. *Other Preemption Questions*. The student should remember that other federal laws may provide a basis for claims that local regulation is preempted. For example, federal regulation of aircraft and airspace limits the ability of local governments to regulate noise levels at airports. *See, e.g., National Helicopter Corp. v. City of New York*, 137 F.3d 81 (2d Cir. 1998) (upholding some locally imposed conditions but concluding that the city could not impose a condition restricting the use of certain sightseeing routes by helicopters). *Compare In re Commercial Airfield*, 752 A.2d 13 (Vt. 2000) (federal aviation law did not preempt land use controls governing improvement to airfields because Environmental Board was not regulating air safety or airport noise); *Village of Ridgefield Park v. New York, Susquehanna & Western Ry.*, 750 A.2d 57 (N.J. 2000) (Interstate Commerce Commission Termination Act (ICCTA) of 1995 preempted local government's power to require railroad to secure site plan approval for certain railroad facilities); *Florida East Coast Ry. Co. v. City of West Palm Beach*, 266 F.3d 1324 (11th Cir. 2001) (city's regulation of activities under a railroad's lease was not preempted because it was not "regulation of rail transportation" under the ICCTA); *Koor Communication, Inc. v. City of Lebanon*, 813 A.2d 418 (N.H. 2002) (federal communication law preempts local law restricting height of antenna for commercial radio station where federal license required a higher antenna).

8. *Treaties and Land Use*. Finally, although land use questions rarely rise to the level of impacting international law, the increasing number of international trade agreements may eventually affect local discretion in the land use field. The North American Free Trade Act (NAFTA), for example, contains a provision requiring governments to compensate property owners if a government either expropriates property or takes measures "tantamount to . . . appropriation." *See* Vicki Been, NAFTA's Investment Protections and the Division of Authority for Land Use and Environmental Controls, 20 Pace Envtl. L. Rev. 19, 20 (2002) ("pending NAFTA regulatory takings claims have the potential to upset many aspects of land use and environmental law").

10

Alternative Methods for Land Use Decisionmaking

A. INTRODUCTION

1. Models of Land Use Regulation

This chapter examines alternative means of making land use decisions: popular decisionmaking by initiative and referendum, employing private land use instruments such as covenants, negotiating agreements between developers and local jurisdictions, using alternative dispute resolution mechanisms such as mediation to reach decisions, and the most radical alternative, deregulating the current system.

From the student's perspective, analysis of these alternatives serves an important practical purpose. Many of the alternative decisionmaking mechanisms examined in this chapter are increasingly being used, and the practitioner must adapt to them. The types of skills needed to represent clients professionally and successfully in such systems can be quite different from those needed to participate in the traditional land use regulatory process. A lawyer preparing a set of covenants, conditions, and restrictions, negotiating a development agreement, or participating in a mediation session performs quite different functions from one representing a client in a public hearing.

In an article entitled New Models for Local Land Use Decisions, 79 Nw. U.L. Rev. 1155 (1984-1985), Professor Carol Rose employed the concept of models as a vehicle for examining the operation of the land use regulatory system. She summarizes this view of land use controls as follows:

> [O]ne quite fruitfully can . . . envision[] the whole field of local land use processes as a series of variations on a theme of dispute resolution. Since the beginning of

> modern land use regulation, courts, legislators, administrative bodies, and academic commentators have struggled to define procedures appropriate for controversies that arise over local governmental control of land use. To a very considerable degree, their efforts can be grouped and classified as alternative patterns or models for resolving disputes.

Id. at 1155.

As used in this context, a model generalizes the features found in decision-making processes, thus facilitating both critical thinking about those processes and comparisons with alternative ways of making decisions. Thinking in terms of models lends perspective to the study of land use regulation by aiding students in reaching conclusions about the strengths and weaknesses of the current system, an important pedagogical goal of the class. That type of perspective is particularly important as land use regulation evolves in the twenty-first century, for the law may be in the midst of long-term shift toward a new model that emphasizes bargaining as a central means of making important land use decisions.

2. *The Legislative and Adjudicative Models*

Students using this casebook are already familiar with the features of two models of dispute resolution employed in the land use field: legislation and adjudication. At its inception in the 1920s, modern land use regulation embraced the idea that local jurisdictions act in a legislative capacity, in the same sense as state legislatures and Congress, when they adopt most land use regulations. But do local bodies truly act legislatively when they make most land use decisions? The Oregon Supreme Court considered this issue in *Fasano v. Board of County Commissioners of Washington County*, a principal case included in Chapter 6. The *Fasano* court concluded that a second model, adjudication, was a better lens through which to view much of local land use regulation. The adjudicative model sees the local body as acting more like a court than as a legislature; it is applying standards—perhaps, most significantly, the policies found in the general plan—to determine how specific parcels of land may be used.

The first alternative means of making land use decisions that is studied in this chapter, use of the initiative and referendum, is a variant on the legislative model of land use regulation. If land use decisions are legislative in nature, then citizens should be able to use both the initiative power to enact legislation and the referendum power to examine legislative decisions previously made by local elected officials. As in other legislative processes, however, use of the initiative and referendum means that the voices of individual landowners will not be heard to the same extent that they will be if, for example, the adjudicative model is used. Do landowners have any due process rights when the initiative or referenda is used? In *City of Eastlake v. Forest City Enterprises, Inc.*, 426 U.S. 668 (1976), the case that begins this chapter, the Supreme Court held that the use of an Ohio referendum did not violate due process.

Perhaps the most troublesome question about initiatives and referenda is their effect on orderly land use planning, a concept that underlies the "consistency doctrine" explored earlier in Chapter 5. What will become of the use of expertise in planning, as envisioned in the Standard Planning Enabling Act and embodied in the requirement that planning commissions must examine planning and zoning decisions, if the electorate zones or plans through initiatives? Will citizens employ their powers of direct democracy to block needed projects? Will the devices be used arbitrarily? These questions lie at the heart of the debate over initiatives and referenda.

3. Private Law: Covenants, Conditions, and Controversy

The assumption of this casebook, as reflected in the development of land use law over most of the last century, is that land use is generally governed by a public law system. The local government decides uses of land and is largely responsible for maintaining those uses. Cities and counties provide trash disposal, water, sewage treatment, road maintenance, and all the other services commonly associated with municipal government.

This model of providing services is not preordained, however, and in some areas of the country another model is supplanting it: private government. The phenomenon can be seen in new "gated" developments whose streets, unlike those of traditional developments, are not open to the public. Services within those gates are provided by contractual arrangement, and homeowners associations rather than popularly elected officials administer the system. In sum, private law has largely supplanted public regulation and administration.

In this chapter you will examine the workings of such systems, starting with a reading of some actual "covenants, conditions, and restrictions." But you will also examine the social consequences of using such systems, for their use has touched off a raging debate. Are private communities the logical successor to the kinds of gated communities that have been with us since the middle ages, and simply an alternative, more economically efficient means of meeting the desires of homeowners? Or do such communities pose a direct threat to both the vitality of local government and the American tradition of (and need for?) community involvement?

4. The Bargaining Model: Development Agreements and Mediation

Another model of land use decisionmaking, related to the private law model, is bargaining. One of the most important developments in the last 25 years of land use regulation has been the ascendancy of this model through the widespread use of development agreements and negotiations between developers and municipalities to determine the conditions under which annexations and developments will take place. Development agreements are the direct descendants of contract zoning, examined in Chapter 2 of this casebook, which the courts have approved so long as the formal structure of the agreement reached is not that of a contract. But if the practical result of the bargaining that takes place in the contract zoning cases is the same as if the parties *had* entered into a contract, why not allow localities to formalize the agreement in such a document?

Two major obstacles stood in the way. One was the influential concept underlying Euclidian zoning that the government establishes the ground rules for development through the adoption of a zoning and land use scheme, and development follows that scheme. Negotiating land uses is at least partially inconsistent with this theory, for the outcome may depend more upon the bargaining skills of the parties and the relative strengths of their bargaining positions than upon the agreement's adherence to a set of specific, preordained standards established by the municipality. Second, there has long existed the feeling, often articulated under the rubric that a city cannot "bargain away its police power," that bargaining in the land use context poses some vague but unacceptable risks to the public interest.

Strong countervailing considerations have pushed the latter concern to the side but have not entirely obliterated it. These considerations include the perceived need for governments to impose precise conditions that tailor the design of a development, the realization that mixed land use developments bring benefits that Euclidian zoning cannot, and—perhaps more importantly—the desire of localities to shift the costs of new public infrastructure to developers. Moreover, if "all property is unique," as the property law maxim has it, then prospective, Euclidian-type regulation cannot foresee all the problems that might arise at the individual development stage, and these can be dealt with by bargaining.

A shift to a new model seldom can be made without the need to resolve a host of anticipated (and often unanticipated) issues that arise. If bargaining will take place, who will be authorized to undertake it? How will the system ensure that deals do not violate the public interest? If conditions underlying a previously reached agreement change at some time later, will the local government have the right to break the contract because a larger public interest is involved? What remedies will be provided for breach of contract? These types of issues are explored in *Sprenger, Grubb & Associates v. City of Hailey*, 903 P.2d 741 (Idaho 1995), set forth later in this chapter.

There are other important questions. The agreement reached in each set of negotiations is idiosyncratic; it depends upon the negotiators' bargaining skills and upon the relative strengths and weaknesses of the positions that the parties bring to the table. Because of these characteristics of bargaining, one landowner may negotiate a much better deal than another landowner, perhaps in the amount or types of exactions required of them, even though their lands are similarly situated. Are we prepared to accept these unequal results because of the value we place on the bargaining process as a whole to achieve important societal goals? Additionally, while a key component of the current regulatory process is the public's right to participate in the decisionmaking, integrating public participation into the bargaining process between a developer and a local jurisdiction is not easy. Finally, if there is concern that local decisionmaking has ethical flaws, perhaps because of the influence of campaign contributions, questions will arise about whether the negotiated bargain was fairly reached.

The use of mediation is a variant on the bargaining model. In mediation, a third party facilitates efforts by the parties to a dispute to reach an agreement. In this sense, mediation is closely related to the bargaining model; both assume that the "give and take" of negotiation will produce a mutually agreeable outcome. In mediation, however, the ultimate choice about whether to enter into an agreement lies with the local government. In contrast, if another form of alternative dispute resolution, arbitration, is used, the actual decision is ceded to a neutral third party. For this reason, arbitration in this context has not proved popular.

Mediation raises the same types of problems as negotiation concerning the consistency of its procedures with the accepted and legally required norms of public decisionmaking. For example, mediation poses a potential conflict with state open-meeting laws, as the desire for frank exchanges of views clashes with the public's right to know. Despite these types of issues, however, the use of mediation is on the rise. Developers increasingly recognize that resolving problems through the normal regulatory process often results in long delays and tremendous costs, and localities are eager to gain greater control over the details of projects.

5. The Market Model: Deregulation

A final model of land use regulation is the market model. In the land use context, this model suggests that the current land use system must be radically changed through deregulation. The goal, here, is both increased efficiency in the provision of land uses and less government interference in the market.

With the exception of Houston, Texas, which continues to be the only major United States city refusing to zone, current land use regulation has largely rejected the use of this model. Students, however, should not quickly dismiss it as impractically academic. Regulation in other sectors of the economy, such as telecommunications and electric utilities, was long thought to be settled, but these areas have been at least partly deregulated in the past decade. Moreover, discomfort with the inefficiencies of the present regulatory system, which the student has already seen in the discussions in this casebook on issues such as permit streamlining and the vested rights rules, continues to grow. Complete deregulation is not likely, but experiments with it in various states are distinct possibilities.

B. POPULAR DECISIONMAKING: INITIATIVES AND REFERENDA

The 1970s and 1980s saw an explosion of the use of popular decisionmaking devices in the land use field. Unhappy with the performance of local government officials, citizens circulated initiative petitions designed generally to control growth in some fashion. In addition, they second-guessed the decisions of local officials by utilizing the referendum process to instigate votes on those decisions. In *City of Eastlake v. Forest City Enterprises*, the United States Supreme Court considered the constitutionality of a use of the referendum that, in effect, ensured that the voters would pass on all important land use decisions in that community. As you read the decision, ask yourself whether the Court grappled sufficiently with the consequences of its holding.

CITY OF EASTLAKE v. FOREST CITY ENTERPRISES, INC.

426 U.S. 668 (1976)

Mr. Chief Justice Burger delivered the opinion of the Court.

The question in this case is whether a city charter provision requiring proposed land use changes to be ratified by 55% of the votes cast violates the due process rights of a landowner who applies for a zoning change.

The city of Eastlake, Ohio, a suburb of Cleveland, has a comprehensive zoning plan codified in a municipal ordinance. Respondent, a real estate developer, acquired an eight-acre parcel of real estate in Eastlake zoned for "light industrial" uses at the time of purchase.

In May 1971, respondent applied to the City Planning Commission for a zoning change to permit construction of a multi-family, high- rise apartment building. The Planning Commission recommended the proposed change to the City Council, which under Eastlake's procedures could either accept or reject the Planning Commission's recommendation. Meanwhile, by popular vote, the voters of Eastlake amended the city charter to require that any changes in land use agreed to by the Council be approved by a 55% vote in a referendum.[1] The City Council approved the Planning Commission's recommendation for reclassification of respondent's property to permit the proposed project. Respondent then applied to the Planning Commission for "parking and yard" approval for the proposed building. The Commission rejected the application, on the ground that the City Council's rezoning action had not yet been submitted to the voters for ratification.

Respondent then filed an action in state court, seeking a judgment declaring the charter provision invalid as an unconstitutional delegation of legislative power to the people. While the case was pending, the City Council's action was submitted to a referendum, but the proposed zoning change was not approved by the requisite 55% margin. Following the election, the Court of Common Pleas and the Ohio Court of Appeals sustained the charter provision. The Ohio Supreme Court reversed. . . .

I

The conclusion that Eastlake's procedure violates federal constitutional guarantees rests upon the proposition that a zoning referendum involves a delegation of legislative power. A referendum cannot, however, be characterized as a delegation of power. Under our constitutional assumptions, all power derives from the people, who can delegate it to representative instruments which they create. *See, e.g.*, The Federalist No. 39. In establishing legislative bodies, the people can reserve to themselves power to deal directly with matters which might otherwise be assigned to the legislature. *Hunter v. Erickson*, 393 U.S. 385, 392 (1969).

The reservation of such power is the basis for the town meeting, a tradition which continues to this day in some States as both a practical and symbolic part of our democratic processes. The referendum, similarly, is a means for direct political

1. As adopted by the voters, Art. VIII, §3, of the Eastlake City Charter provides in pertinent part:

> That any change to the existing land uses or any change whatsoever to any ordinance . . . cannot be approved unless and until it shall have been submitted to the Planning Commission, for approval or disapproval. That in the event the city council should approve any of the preceding changes, or enactments, whether approved or disapproved by the Planning Commission it shall not be approved or passed by the declaration of an emergency, and it shall not be effective, but it shall be mandatory that the same be approved by a 55% favorable vote of all votes cast of the qualified electors of the City of Eastlake at the next regular municipal election. . . .

participation, allowing the people the final decision, amounting to a veto power, over enactments of representative bodies. The practice is designed to "give citizens a voice on questions of public policy." *James v. Valtierra, supra*, 402 U.S., at 141, 91 S. Ct., at 1333.

In framing a state constitution, the people of Ohio specifically reserved the power of referendum to the people of each municipality within the State.

> The initiative and referendum powers are hereby reserved to the people of each municipality on all questions which such municipalities may now or hereafter be authorized by law to control by legislative action. . . .

Ohio Const., Art. II, §1f.

To be subject to Ohio's referendum procedure, the question must be one within the scope of legislative power. The Ohio Supreme Court expressly found that the City Council's action in rezoning respondent's eight acres from light industrial to high-density residential use was legislative in nature. Distinguishing between administrative and legislative acts, the court separated the power to zone or rezone, by passage or amendment of a zoning ordinance, from the power to grant relief from unnecessary hardship. The former function was found to be legislative in nature.

II

The Ohio Supreme Court further concluded that the amendment to the city charter constituted a "delegation" of power violative of federal constitutional guarantees because the voters were given no standards to guide their decision. Under Eastlake's procedure, the Ohio Supreme Court reasoned, no mechanism existed, nor indeed could exist, to assure that the voters would act rationally in passing upon a proposed zoning change. This meant that "appropriate legislative action [would] be made dependent upon the potentially arbitrary and unreasonable whims of the voting public." 324 N.E.2d, at 746. The potential for arbitrariness in the process, the court concluded, violated due process.

Courts have frequently held in other contexts that a congressional delegation of power to a regulatory entity must be accompanied by discernible standards, so that the delegatee's action can be measured for its fidelity to the legislative will. *See, e.g., Yakus v. United States*, 321 U.S. 414 (1944); *Amalgamated Meat Cutters v. Connally*, 337 F.Supp. 737 (DC 1971). Assuming, *arguendo*, their relevance to state governmental functions, these cases involved a delegation of power by the legislature to regulatory bodies, which are not directly responsible to the people; this doctrine is inapplicable where, as here, rather than dealing with a delegation of power, we deal with a power reserved by the people to themselves.

In basing its claim on federal due process requirements, respondent also invokes *Euclid v. Ambler Realty Co.*, 272 U.S. 365 (1926), but it does not rely on the direct teaching of that case. Under *Euclid*, a property owner can challenge a zoning restriction if the measure is "clearly arbitrary and unreasonable, having no substantial relation to the public health, safety, morals, or general welfare." *Id.*, at 395. If the substantive result of the referendum is arbitrary and capricious, bearing no relation to the police power, then the fact that the voters of Eastlake wish it so would not save the restriction. . . .

But no challenge of the sort contemplated in *Euclid v. Ambler Realty* is before us. The Ohio Supreme Court did not hold, and respondent does not argue, that the present zoning classification under Eastlake's comprehensive ordinance violates the principles established in *Euclid v. Ambler Realty*. If respondent considers the referendum result itself to be unreasonable, the zoning restriction is open to challenge in state court, where the scope of the state remedy available to respondent would be determined as a matter of state law, as well as under Fourteenth Amendment standards. That being so, nothing more is required by the Constitution.

Our decision in *James v. Valtierra*, upholding California's mandatory referendum requirement, confirms this view. Mr. Justice Black, speaking for the Court in that case, said:

> This procedure ensures that *all the people* of a community will have a voice in a decision which may lead to large expenditures of local governmental funds for increased public services. . . . 402 U.S. at 143 (emphasis added).

. . . As a basic instrument of democratic government, the referendum process does not, in itself, violate the Due Process Clause of the Fourteenth Amendment when applied to a rezoning ordinance. . . .

The judgment of the Ohio Supreme Court is reversed, and the case is remanded for further proceedings not inconsistent with this opinion.

Reversed and remanded.

Notes and Comments

1. *The Terminology of Direct Democracy.* In considering the use of direct democratic devices to make land use decisions, you must first get the terminology straight. An initiative is legislation drafted by individual citizens that is circulated among voters by petition. When a certain number of signatures of registered voters (mandated by state law) is gathered, the initiative is then placed on the ballot for the voters to consider at the next election. In contrast, a referendum occurs after the local elected body, such as a city council, has adopted legislation. Voters then circulate a petition to repeal the new legislation. Once again, if the required number of signatures among registered voters is secured, the local elected body then faces the choice of either rescinding the legislation voluntarily or submitting it to a vote. See, e.g., Eugene McQuillan, The Law of Municipal Corporations §§16.48-.70 (3d ed. 1988).

The "political wars" fought over local initiatives and referenda are fierce. *See* Peter Grant, The Debate Over Sprawl Has Only Just Begun: Various Ballot Initiatives in the West Illustrate Growing Rift in U.S., Wall St. J., Nov. 8, 2000, at B14 (on the local level, the disputes over ballot measures are like civil wars).

2. *Ferreting Out The* Eastlake *Holding*. What precisely was the holding in *Eastlake*? Some have cited the holding for the general proposition that use of the referendum power and, by inference, use of the initiative power do not violate due process. Others have suggested that the actual holding is much narrower. See Robert H. Freilich & Derek B. Guemmer, Removing Artificial Barriers to Public Participation in Land-Use Policy: Effective Zoning and Planning by Initiative and Referenda, 21 Urb. Law. 511, 513 (1976).

3. *More Ramifications of* Fasano. It is hornbook law that the initiative and referendum are available only to enact or repeal legislation. Julian Conrad Juergensmeyer & Thomas E. Roberts, Land Use Planning and Control Law, §5.5, p. 182 (1988). As a consequence, legal issues concerning the use of the initiative or referendum are closely related to the materials, discussed in this casebook in Chapter 6, on whether a land use decision is deemed legislative or adjudicative in nature. If a state follows the decision in *Fasano v. Board of County Commissioners of Washington County* and finds that small-tract rezonings are quasi-judicial in nature, that holding will also limit the rights of citizens to enact initiatives or pass referenda relating to decisions of this type. *See, e.g., Fritz v. City of Kingman*, 957 P.2d 337, 338 (Ariz. 1998) ("In multiple decisions over a lengthy period, this court has consistently held that zoning decisions are legislative acts subject to referendum."); *The Greens at Fort Missoula, LLC v. City of Missoula*, 897 P.2d 1078, 1082 (Mont. 1995) (because a rezoning ordinance is a legislative enactment, "we do not find it necessary to attempt to distinguish between a zoning and rezoning ordinance for referendum purposes").

Should a state court's rejection of the *Fasano* rule and its determination that rezonings are quasi-legislative in nature necessarily mean that *no* rezoning is treated as quasi-judicial for purposes of whether initiative or referendum rights can be used? In *Eastlake*, the majority deferred to the Supreme Court of Ohio's "binding interpretation" that the rezoning in question was legislative. In his dissent to the holding in *Eastlake*, Justice Stevens declared that, for federal constitutional purposes, he would not grant a high degree of deference to the state's determination that a rezoning is legislative in nature. 426 U.S. at 686.

4. *The* City of Cuyahoga Falls *Decision*. In a 2003 decision—involving yet another Ohio referendum—the Supreme Court tangentially returned to the subject of direct democracy. In *City of Cuyahoga Falls, Ohio v. Buckeye Community Hope Foundation*, 538 U.S. 188, 123 S. Ct. 1389 (2003), the City of Cuyahoga Falls approved the site plan for a low-income housing complex. The citizens overturned the approval in a referendum, and the project developers brought suit. In *Buckeye Community Hope Foundation v. City of Cuyahoga Falls*, 607 N.E.2d 181 (Ohio 1998), the Ohio Supreme Court held that a referendum was unavailable because the approval of the site plan was an administrative rather than a legislative act.

The project developers also brought suit in federal court, claiming violation of the Equal Protection and Due Process Clauses, as well as the Fair Housing Act. They also sought damages. In part, they alleged that the City's submission of an administrative land-use determination to the charter's referendum procedures constituted *per se* arbitrary conduct.

The United States Supreme Court held this claim could not withstand scrutiny. The Court first found that the refusal to issue permits while the referendum was pending "in no sense constituted egregious or arbitrary government conduct." 123 S. Ct. at 1396. Indeed, the law director's order not to issue the permits "represented an eminently rational directive." The Court then went on to state:

> As a matter of federal constitutional law, we have rejected the distinction that respondents ask us to draw, and that the Ohio Supreme Court drew as a matter of state law, between legislative and administrative referendums. In *Eastlake v. Forest City Enterprises, Inc.*, 426 U.S., at 672, 675, we made clear that because all power stems from the people. . . . The people retain the power to govern through referendum " 'with

> respect to any matter, legislative or administrative, within the realm of local affairs.' " *Id.*, at 674, n.9. Cf. *James v. Valtierra*, 402 U.S., at 137. Though the "substantive result" of a referendum may be invalid if it is "arbitrary and capricious," *Eastlake v. Forest City Enterprises, supra*, at 676, respondents do not challenge the referendum itself. The subjection of the site-plan ordinance to the City's referendum process, regardless of whether that ordinance reflected an administrative or legislative decision, did not constitute *per se* arbitrary government conduct in violation of due process.

Id. Is the Court saying that, as a matter of constitutional law, even administrative matters are subject to referendum if state law allows? Or is it simply affirming that the submission of an administrative (or quasi-judicial) matter to voters cannot, as a matter of law, rise to the level of "egregiousness" that would support a due process violation? Justice Scalia's concurring opinion would solve the problem differently. In his view, even if there had been arbitrary government conduct, as plaintiffs claimed, that would not establish a substantive due process violation. 123 S. Ct. at 1396 (Scalia, J., concurring).

5. *Criticism I: Abrogation of Process*. In general, commentators have strongly criticized the use of initiatives and referenda in the land use field. See, e.g., David L. Callies et al., Ballot Box Zoning: Initiative, Referendum, and the Law, 39 Wash. U. J. Urb. & Contemp. L. 53, 54 (1991) ("On balance, it is difficult to make a consistent case for the use of initiative or referendum to rezone land."). See also Jon E. Goetz, Direct Democracy in Land Use Planning: The State Response to Eastlake, 19 Pac. L.J. 793 (1987); Mark A. Nitikman, Instant Planning—Land Use Regulation by Initiative in California, 61 S. Cal. L. Rev. 497 (1988). *Compare* Daniel P. Selmi, Reconsidering the Use of Direct Democracy in Making Land Use Decisions, 18 UCLA J. Envtl. L. & Land Use 293 (2002) (arguing that the objections to the use of direct democracy in the land use field are overstated).

One objection to the use of initiatives is that they are inconsistent with the procedural rights found in state land use law. Such rights include the right to a public hearing before enactments like zoning ordinances may be passed. In some states these procedures may require the preparation of so-called environmental impact statements before land use legislation is passed. Because initiatives are circulated directly to the people, these processes are bypassed. *Compare, e.g., Heitman v. City of Mauston Common Council*, 595 N.W.2d 450 (Wash. Ct. App. 1999) (initiative to preclude city from approving treatment facility for sexually violent persons was either a zoning ordinance or zoning amendment, and it could be passed only by using procedures in the zoning enabling legislation); *I'on L.L.C. v. Town of Mount Pleasant*, 526 S.E.2d 716, 721 (N.C. 2000) (finding an "obvious incompatibility between the initiative and referendum process" and zoning) *with Associated Home Builders of Greater Eastbay, Inc. v. City of Livermore*, 557 P.2d 473 (Cal. 1976) (notice and hearing provisions of state zoning and planning law did not apply to a zoning ordinance that was enacted by initiative).

The standard answer to the objection that direct democracy abrogates important procedures is that the political dialogue taking place during the electoral process more than compensates for other public participation rights that cannot be exercised during the initiative process. Do you agree that public dialogue during an election is a sufficient replacement for the public hearings that would otherwise take place? What about the "expertise" (such as scrutiny by the planning commission and the staff) that is unavailable during an election?

These same objections, of course, cannot be made with respect to referenda (do you see why?). As a result, should courts favor the use of referenda to make land use decisions over the use of the initiative power?

6. *Criticism II: Interference with Planning*. Another objection to the use of initiatives and referenda is that they are inconsistent with the principle that land use regulation must be based upon proper planning. See, e.g., *Nordmarken v. City of Richfield*, 641 N.W.2d 343, 349 (Minn. Ct. App. 2002) ("Unlike the process provided in the MPA [Municipal Planning Act] . . . referendum would necessarily proceed without an overriding concept of current and future development and land use needs of the community and of neighboring communities and without benefit of the expertise of land use professionals"); David L. Callies et al., Ballot Box Zoning: Initiative, Referendum, and the Law, 39 Wash. U. J. Urb. & Contemp. L. 53, 87 (Spring 1991) ("Both the plans and the process of planning become irrelevant when land use mapping decisions are made through popular democracy."). This objection assumes that the "rational planning model," discussed in Chapter 5 of this casebook, actually prevails when most land use decisions are made. Do you agree? Or does the political component of such decisions made at the local government level far outweigh any planning expertise that goes into them?

The objection that use of the initiative power conflicts with proper planning would not seem to have as much force for rezonings by initiative or referenda in jurisdictions that have adopted a "consistency" requirement of the type discussed in Chapter 5. In such states, any rezoning must be consistent with the general plan, and a rezoning by initiative (or a referenda) could be challenged on the basis that it was inconsistent with the general plan. *See deBottari v. Norco City Council*, 217 Cal. Rptr. 790 (Ct. App. 1985) (zoning initiative must be consistent with the general plan).

7. *Planning Flexibility*. If citizens are allowed to enact land use regulations by initiative, what mechanisms should be available to make changes in those regulations? In *DeVita v. County of Napa*, 889 P.2d 1019 (Cal. 1995), the California Supreme Court upheld an initiative that reenacted a county's general plan and mandated that the plan could not be changed for 30 years without a vote of the people. Is flexibility in a plan preferable? Or will the city's planning process be enhanced if the plan actually is implemented without change over a long period of years?

C. THE PRIVATE LAND USE MODEL: COVENANTS, CONDITIONS, AND RESTRICTIONS

Before the advent of zoning, and before *Village of Euclid v. Ambler Realty*, reprinted in Chapter 2, the common law had means for implementing land use restrictions. Covenants and easements, for example, could be used to restrict landowners' abilities to use property. The common law doctrine of nuisance was available to adjust conflicting land uses on adjacent properties.

Covenants provide a means of regulating land that is separate from the public regulatory system. *See, e.g., Mannweiler v. LaFlamme*, 700 A.2d 57 (Conn. Ct. App. 1997) (although city approved applicant's request to subdivide property and construct two houses, the property was still subject to a covenant and restriction allowing only one private residence for the use of one family, although certain defenses might be available). They remain very important in the modern land use practice because of the increasing "privatization" of some developments.

A Note on the Common Law and Land Use

Public legislative mechanisms for regulating land use are a twentieth-century development. The common law, however, had devices for adjusting and restricting the rights to use land. These devices, while largely supplanted by zoning and public regulation, nonetheless continue to play an important role in "filling gaps." Most importantly, the common law mechanism of covenants is increasingly used to restrict land use in private developments.

1. *Nuisance*. The common law cause of action for nuisance resolves competing land uses. Nuisances are divided into two categories: (1) private nuisance, which is a substantial and unreasonable inference with the use and enjoyment of land, and (2) public nuisance, which is the interference with a right common to the general public. The difference between the two is largely one of degree. Traditionally, however, a private individual could not sue for public nuisance unless the plaintiff had suffered harm of a "different kind" from that suffered by the public generally. *See, e.g., Philadelphia Electric Co. v. Hercules Inc.*, 762 F.2d 303 (3d Cir. 1985), *cert. denied*, 474 U.S. 980 (1985) (plaintiff could not bring a public nuisance claim to recover for hazardous waste pollution because it did not suffer particular damage).

Courts have labeled some activities as "nuisances per se," or nuisances under all circumstances. In most cases, however, whether an activity is a nuisance depends upon the circumstances under which it is undertaken. *Town of Carter Lake v. Anderson Excavating & Wrecking Co.*, 241 N.W.2d 896, 901 (Iowa 1976) (a refuse disposal operation is not a nuisance per se). Thus, courts will label an activity as a nuisance only after examining the specific circumstances of the property's use in that case and the effect of the particular use on neighboring properties.

The central function in determining whether an activity on land is a nuisance is deciding whether the activity constitutes "a substantial and unreasonable interference" with the use or enjoyment of land. *Dunlop v. Daigle*, 444 A.2d 519, 520 (N.H. 1982). The interference must offend "normal" persons in a particular locality. This determination requires a balancing, and under nuisance law that balancing weighs the utility of the defendant's conduct against the harm that the plaintiff has suffered. Restatement (Second) of Torts §826 (1989). The Restatement sets forth a variety of factors that are pertinent to determining the "gravity of harm" to the plaintiff: (1) the extent of the harm; (2) the character of the harm; (3) the social value that the law attaches to the type of use or enjoyment invaded; (4) the suitability of the particular use or enjoyment invaded to the character of the locality; and (5) the burden on the person harmed of avoiding the harm. Restatement (Second) of Torts, §827 (1989).

At the same time, the court examines the defendant's actions, and the Restatement sets forth a number of factors that are relevant to this examination: (1) the social value that the law attaches to the primary purpose of the conduct; (2) the suitability of the conduct to the character of the locality; (3) whether it is practical to prevent or avoid the invasion, if the activity is maintained; and (4) whether it is impractical to maintain the activity if it is required to bear the cost of compensating for the invasion. Restatement (Second) §828 (1989). *See Thomsen v. Greve* 550 N.W.2d 49, 53-54 (Neb. Ct. App. 1996) (citing both 827 and 828).

As far as remedies are concerned, courts often have ordered defendants to pay damages. *See, e.g., City of Uvalde v. Crow*, 713 S.W.2d 154, 158 (Tex. Ct. App. 1986) ("The usual measure of damages in a nuisance case is the difference in market value of the property immediately before and immediately after the injury."). In balancing the rights of the parties, some courts have placed significance on whether the defendant's activities pre-date those of the plaintiff, that is, whether the plaintiff has "come to the nuisance." For example, in one famous case, *Spur Industries, Inc. v. Del E. Webb Development Co*, 494 P.2d 700 (Ariz. 1972), the court agreed to enjoin the defendant's agricultural operation, which caused a nuisance to a retirement community located nearby. However, because the plaintiff retirement community had "come to the nuisance," the court ordered that the plaintiff compensate the defendant. *Id.* at 708 ("It does not seem harsh to require a developer, who has taken advantage of the lesser land values in a rural area . . . to indemnify those who are forced to leave as a result.").

Courts also have the power to grant injunctive relief as well. Here, however, the courts will engage in the well-established process of "balancing the equities" in deciding whether such equitable relief is appropriate. *See Boomer v. Atlantic Cement Co.*, 257 N.E.2d 870 (N.Y. 1970).

2. *Easements*. You are undoubtedly familiar with the concept of easements from your real property class. Easements are divided into two categories: affirmative and negative. An affirmative easement is a nonpossessory right to use land that belongs to another, while a negative easement is a restriction that the owner places on her own land to benefit another person or other land. *See Gambrell v. Schriver*, 440 S.E.2d 393, 395 (S.C. Ct. App. 1994) ("Ordinarily, four elements must be established to show a reciprocal negative easement. There must be: (1) a common grantor, (2) a designation of land subject to restrictions, (3) a general plan or scheme of restrictions, and (4) covenants running with the land in accordance with such plan or scheme."). Easements can be express or implied. *See, e.g., Evans v. Pollock*, 796 S.W.2d 465, 466 (Tex. 1990) (discussing "Implied Reciprocal Negative Easement Doctrine"). They can also be prescriptive. *See Dieck v. Landry*, 796 So. 2d 1004, 1007 (Miss. 2001) (use must meet five requirements, including "open, notorious, and visible," hostile, and under a claim of ownership).

Various technical rules of property law govern easements (and, to a greater extent covenants, as is discussed below). *See* Susan F. French, Toward a Modern Law of Servitudes: Reweaving the Ancient Strands, 55 S. Cal. L. Rev. 1261 (1982) ("The law of easements, real covenants and equitable servitudes is the most complex and archaic body of American property law remaining in the twentieth century."). For example, an easement may be "appurtenant" to the land, a term meaning that the easement benefits land that the holder of the easement owns. *Lake Arrowhead Community Club, Inc. v. Looney*, 770 P.2d 1046, 1049 (Wash. 1989) ("Appurtenant easements are those that primarily benefit another piece of land rather than a particular individual."). This benefited land is known as the "dominant estate." In contrast, an easement "in gross" is not attached to land but is for the personal benefit of the person who holds it. *Gowen v. Cote*, 875 S.W.2d 637, 640 n. 4 (Mo. Ct. App. 1994) ("By definition, an easement appurtenant is created for the advantage of the owner of the dominant estate. When an easement is in gross, no dominant estate exists.").

Historically, the courts at common law limited negative easements to four categories: light, air, drainage of an artificial stream, and lateral support. Thus, from a land use perspective, negative easements are less important than affirmative easements.

3. *Covenants and Servitudes*. The third principal type of common law device for affecting land use has its origin in contract law. Parties could contract to restrict other uses of land, and this restriction would be enforceable either through a covenant that would "run with the land" or an equitable "servitude."

The key point to remember is that individuals who are not parties to the original contracts can enforce the terms of that contract through property law. Typically, such restrictions are recorded as part of deeds conveying property. Subsequent owners are thus charged with constructive notice of the restriction. Equitable servitudes, in contrast, may be created by implication.

Like easements, covenants can be affirmative (e.g., requiring an owner to contribute to a share of the neighborhood's maintenance expenses) or negative (e.g., requiring an owner to refrain from using the property for certain kinds of businesses). Historically, courts were inclined to disallow the running of affirmative covenants, but the modern trend is decidedly to the contrary.

For a covenant to "run with the land," certain technical requirements of property law (with which, again, you are undoubtedly familiar) must be met. For example, in *1515-1519 Lakeview Boulevard Condominium Ass'n v. Apartment Sales Corp.*, 43 P.3d 1233 (Wash. 2002), the City of Seattle approved a condominium on condition that the owners record a covenant releasing the city from potential liability for landslide damages. (The City thought this alternative was better than a denial of the project, which would likely bring a takings claim.) When, almost inevitably, the development slid, the court had to consider whether the covenant "ran with the land" and thus bound future property owners.

A restrictive covenant is a real covenant that runs with the land of the dominant and servient estates only if (1) the subject of the covenant touches and concerns the land, (2) there is privity of estate between the party enforcing the contract and the party against whom the covenant is being enforced, and (3) the original covenanting parties intended the benefits and burdens of the covenant to run with the land. *Runyon v. Paley*, 416 S.E.2d 177, 182 (N.C. 1992) (citing 5 Powell on Real Property ¶673[1], at 60-41 (Patrick S. Rohan, ed. 1996)); *Vulcan Materials Co. v. Miller*, 691 So. 2d 908, 912 (Miss. 1997) (same). A covenant will be unenforceable unless it is written. *Estate of Wallis*, 659 N.E.2d 423, 427 (Ill. App. Ct. 1995). If it is not in writing, it may be considered an equitable servitude.

The "touch and concern" requirement is perhaps the most difficult requirement to explain. As one commentator put it, the requirement is one "that can be explored and felt better than it can be defined." William B. Stoebuck, Running Covenants: An Analytical Primer, 52 Wash. L. Rev. 861, 869 (1977). One court, citing this article, noted that a covenant meeting this requirement "can be one that calls for either doing physical things to the land such as building a wall, or refraining from doing physical things to the land such as a promise '. . . , not to build a structure, or not to build multifamily dwellings.' . . . " *Cypress Gardens Ltd. v. Platt*, 952 P.2d 467, 470 (N.M. Ct. App. 1997).

Both covenants and easements are employed in many modern developments, and considerable legal skills are required to craft them. For example, both condominiums and large-scale private developments, which have individual homes and "common areas" all owners can use, are subject to "Covenants, Conditions and

Restrictions" that are recorded and run with the land. *See Westwood Homeowners Ass'n, Inc. v. Lane County*, 864 P.2d 350, 355 (Or. 1993) ("Each lot within Westwood PUD is, therefore, both the dominant and the servient estate or tenement with respect to the CC&Rs involved; the benefits and burdens of mutual promises attach to the ownership of each lot."). In *Daniels v. Area Plan Comm'n of Allen County*, 306 F.3d 445 (7th Cir. 2002), a county plan commission, pursuant to a state statute, attempted to vacate a covenant restricting uses to residential and thereby to allow a commercial development. The court found a taking had occurred.

The following materials will introduce you to some of the issues involved in this type of private land use control. First, read carefully the excerpt from a large set of "CC&Rs." As you do so, note the important restrictions on land ownership as well as the rights and obligations which they impose. Then you will read a case in which restrictions of this type resulted in litigation.

WAYNE S. HYATT, DECLARATION OF COVENANTS, CONDITIONS, AND RESTRICTIONS FOR MYSTIC ISLE

SG074 ALI-ABA 285 (2002)

ARTICLE I CREATION OF THE COMMUNITY

Declarant, as the owner of the real property described in Exhibit "A," intends by Recording this Declaration to establish a general plan of development for the planned community known as Mystic Isle. . . .

1.2. **BINDING EFFECT.**

All property described in Exhibit "A," and any additional property which is made a part of the Properties in the future by Recording one or more Supplemental Declarations, shall be owned, conveyed, and used subjects to all of the provisions of this Declaration which shall run with the title to such property. This Declaration shall be binding upon all Persons having any right, title, or interest in any portion of Mystic Isle, their heirs, successors, successors-in-title, and assigns. . . .

ARTICLE II CONCEPTS AND DEFINITIONS. . . .

"Board of Directors" or "Board": The body responsible for administration of the Association, selected as provided in the By-Laws. . . .

ARTICLE III USE AND CONDUCT

3.1. **FRAMEWORK FOR REGULATION.**

The Governing Documents establish, as part of the general plan of development for Mystic Isle, a framework of affirmative and negative covenants, easements, and restrictions which govern Mystic Isle. Within that framework, the Board and the Members must have the ability to respond to unforeseen problems and changes in circumstances, conditions, needs, desires, trends, and technology. Therefore, this Article establishes procedures for modifying and expanding the initial Restrictions and Rules set forth in Exhibit "C."...

3.4. **PROTECTION OF OWNERS AND OTHERS....**

(b) Displays. The rights of Owners to display religious and holiday signs, symbols and decorations inside structures on their Units of the kinds normally displayed in dwellings located in single-family residential neighborhoods shall not be abridged, except that the Association may adopt time, place, and manner restrictions with respect to displays visible from outside the dwelling.

No rules shall regulate the content of political signs; however, rules may regulate the time, place, and manner of posting such signs (including design criteria).

(c) Household Composition. No rule shall interfere with the freedom of Owners to determine the composition of their households, except that the Association shall have the power to require that all occupants be members of a single housekeeping unit and to limit the total number of occupants permitted in each Unit on the basis of the size and facilities of the Unit and its fair use of the Common Area....

ARTICLE IV ARCHITECTURE AND LANDSCAPING

4.1. **GENERAL.**

No structure or thing shall be placed, erected, or installed upon any Unit and no improvements or other work (including staking, clearing, excavation, grading and other site work, exterior alterations of existing improvements, or planting or removal of landscaping) shall take place within Mystic Isle, except in compliance with this Article and the Architectural Guidelines.

No approval shall be required to repaint the exterior of a structure in accordance with the originally approved color scheme or to rebuild in accordance with originally approved plans and specifications. Any Owner may remodel, paint, or redecorate the interior of his or her Unit without approval. However, modifications to the interior of screened porches, patios, and similar portions of a Unit visible from outside the structure shall be subject to approval....

4.3. **GUIDELINES AND PROCEDURES...**

(b) Procedures. Except as otherwise specifically provided in the Architectural Guidelines, no activities shall commence on any portion of Mystic Isle until an application for approval has been submitted to and approved by the Reviewer. Such application shall include plans and specifications showing site layout, structural design, exterior elevations, exterior materials and colors, landscaping, drainage, exterior lighting, irrigation, and other features of proposed construction, as applicable. The Architectural Guidelines and the Reviewer may require the submission of such additional information as may be reasonably necessary to consider any application.

In reviewing each submission, the [Architectural Guidelines] Reviewer may consider any factors it deems relevant, including, without limitation, harmony of external design with surrounding structures and environment. Decisions may be based on purely aesthetic considerations. Each Owner acknowledges that determinations as to such matters are purely subjective and opinions may vary as to the desirability and/or attractiveness of particular improvements. The Reviewer shall have the sole discretion to make final, conclusive, and binding determinations on matters of aesthetic judgment and such determinations shall not be subject to review so long as made in good faith and in accordance with the procedures set forth herein. . . .

4.4. **NO WAIVER OF FUTURE APPROVALS.**

Each Owner acknowledges that the persons reviewing applications under this Article will change from time to time and that opinions on aesthetic matters, as well as interpretation and application of the Architectural Guidelines, may vary accordingly. In addition, each Owner acknowledges that it may not always be possible to identify objectionable features until work is completed, in which case it may be unreasonable to require changes to the improvements involved, but the Reviewer may refuse to approve similar proposals in the future. Approval of applications or plans, or in connection with any other matter requiring approval, shall not be deemed to constitute a waiver of the right to withhold approval as to any similar applications, plans, or other matters subsequently or additionally submitted for approval.

4.5. **VARIANCES.**

The Reviewer may authorize variances from compliance with any of its guidelines and procedures when circumstances such as topography, natural obstructions, hardship, or aesthetic or environmental considerations require, but only in accordance with duly adopted rules and regulations. No variance shall (a) be effective unless in writing; (b) be contrary to this Declaration; or (c) estop the Reviewer from denying a variance in other circumstances. For purposes of this Section, the inability to obtain approval of any governmental agency, the issuance of any permit, or the terms of any financing shall not be considered a hardship warranting a variance. . . .

ARTICLE XI EASEMENTS

11.1. **EASEMENTS IN COMMON AREA.**

Declarant grants to each Owner a nonexclusive right and easement of use, access, and enjoyment in and to the Common Area, subject to:

(a) The Governing Documents and any other applicable covenants;

(b) Any restrictions or limitations contained in any deed conveying such property to the Association;

(c) The Board's right to:

(i) adopt rules regulating use and enjoyment of the Common Area, including rules limiting the number of guests who may use the Common Area;

(ii) suspend the right of an Owner to use recreational facilities within the Common Area (A) for any period during which any charge against such Owner's Unit remains delinquent, and (B) for a period not to exceed 30 days for a single violation or for a longer period in the case of any continuing violation, of the Governing Documents after notice and a hearing pursuant to the By-Laws. . . .

ARTICLE XV DISPUTE RESOLUTION AND LIMITATION ON LITIGATION

15.1 **AGREEMENT TO ENCOURAGE RESOLUTION OF DISPUTES WITHOUT LITIGATION.**

(a) Declarant, the Association and its officers, directors, and committee members, all Persons subject to this Declaration, and any Person not otherwise subject to this Declaration who agrees to submit to this Article (collectively, "Bound Parties"), agree that it is in the best interest of all concerned to encourage the amicable resolution of disputes involving the Community without the emotional and financial costs of litigation. Accordingly, each Bound Party agrees not to file suit in any court with respect to a Claim described in subsection (b), unless and until it has first submitted such Claim to the alternative dispute resolution procedures set forth in Section 15.2 in a good faith effort to resolve such Claim. . . .

15.2. **DISPUTE RESOLUTION PROCEDURES.**

(a) Notice. The Bound Party asserting a Claim ("Claimant") against another Bound Party ("Respondent") shall give written notice to each Respondent and to the Board stating plainly and concisely:

(i) the nature of the Claim, including the Persons involved and the Respondent's role in the Claim;

(ii) the legal basis of the Claim (i.e., the specific authority out of which the Claim arises);

(iii) the Claimant's proposed resolution or remedy; and

(iv) the Claimant's desire to meet with the Respondent to discuss in good faith ways to resolve the Claim.

(b) Negotiation. The Claimant and Respondent shall make every reasonable effort to meet in person and confer for the purpose of resolving the Claim by good faith negotiation. If requested in writing, accompanied by a copy of the Notice, the Board may appoint a representative to assist the parties in negotiating a resolution of the Claim.

(c) Mediation. If the Parties have not resolved the Claim through negotiation within 30 days of the date of the notice described in Section 15.2(a) (or within such other period as the parties may agree upon), the Claimant shall have 30 additional days to submit the Claim to mediation. . . .

If the Claimant does not submit the Claim to mediation within such time, or does not appear for the mediation when scheduled, the Claimant shall be deemed to have waived the Claim, and the Respondent shall be relieved of any and all liability to the Claimant (but not third parties) on account of such Claim.

If the Parties do not settle the Claim within 30 days after submission of the matter to mediation, or within such time as determined reasonable by the mediator, the mediator shall issue a notice of termination of the mediation proceedings indicating that the parties are at an impasse and the date that mediation was terminated. The Claimant shall thereafter be entitled to file suit or to initiate administrative proceedings on the Claim, as appropriate. . . .

■ TURUDIC v. STEPHENS

31 P.3d 465 (Or. Ct. App. 2001)

HASELTON, P.J. . . .

Plaintiffs Andy and Luisa Turudic are the owners of two American mountain lions, more commonly known as cougars. In 1993, plaintiffs decided to move from Missouri to Oregon, in part because Oregon law, subject to certain statutory restrictions and local ordinances, permits the keeping of exotic animals such as cougars.

Plaintiffs purchased property in Susan Estates, a small subdivision in rural Yamhill County, in an area zoned "very low density, 5 acre minimum." There are no zoning restrictions on the type of animals that can be kept on a particular piece of property.

Before moving to Susan Estates, in researching the property, plaintiffs obtained copies for two sets of CCRs. The first set, entitled "Declaration of Covenants and Restrictions of Susan Estates" (original CCRs), was adopted at the time of the original development in 1981. The second set, entitled "First Amendment to Declaration of Covenants and Restrictions" (amended CCRs), was adopted in 1987 as a comprehensive revision to the original CCRs. The parties agree that the amended CCRs apply to plaintiffs' property and the issues regarding both plaintiffs' cougars and the holding pen. . . .

Plaintiffs began building their home in late spring 1994. Construction of the cougar holding pen, which meets or exceeds state standards for animal care and public safety and has been approved by the Oregon Department of Fish and Wildlife, began in mid-September and was completed on October 13, 1994. Plaintiffs did not obtain the approval of the Susan Estates Homeowners' Association board before undertaking or completing either their home or the cougar pen project.

At 3:00 in the morning on October 19, 1994, plaintiffs, without notice to their neighbors, moved the cougars into the holding pen. Two days later plaintiffs first became aware of their neighbors' concerns about the cougars when a deputy sheriff contacted them in response to a neighbor's complaint.

On November 8, 1994, a majority of the members of the Susan Estates homeowners' association met to discuss the cougar issue. Plaintiffs were not invited. At that meeting, the members agreed that the cougars were a nuisance and should be removed from plaintiffs' property. They also resolved to disapprove any "cougar-cage outbuildings." Consequently, on November 30, 1994, counsel for the Association wrote to plaintiffs, expressing concerns both about the cougars and about plaintiffs' failure to seek Board approval for both their house and the cougar pen.

Plaintiffs responded by offering to build a secondary safety fence around the existing cougar pen, and by submitting house plans to the Board. Plaintiffs did not submit plans for the cougar pen. On February 22, 1995, a representative for the Association wrote to plaintiffs, stating that plaintiffs' house plans had been approved but that the cougar pen was rejected under the "nuisance provisions" of the CCRs. . . .

In March 1995, plaintiffs brought this action. Plaintiffs sought a declaratory judgment that neither the pen nor the cougars could be prohibited under the amended CCRs and that, in all events, the Association was precluded from enforcing the CCRs because of the doctrine of laches. Plaintiffs further argued that the Association breached its obligations when it failed to follow the annual meeting provisions of the amended CCRs, failed to enforce the nuisance provisions as to other lot owners, and acted unreasonably and capriciously in denying approval for the cougar pen. . . .

Defendants counterclaimed, alleging that the cougars were a nuisance under both the CCRs and common law. . . .

The trial court subsequently issued a detailed letter opinion addressing the remaining cougar- and holding pen-related issues. That opinion rested on three determinations that are central to this appeal. *First*, plaintiffs' maintenance of the cougars was not a nuisance under either the common law or the amended CCRs. *Second*, nevertheless, plaintiffs' maintenance of the cougars was not a permitted "residential use" under the CCRs. *Third*, construction of the cougar pen without the Board's prior approval violated the amended CCRs.[8] Consequently, given its determination that the maintenance of the cougars was not a nuisance but that plaintiffs had otherwise violated the amended CCRs, the court entered a judgment rejecting plaintiffs' claims for declaratory relief and breach of contract, and rejecting defendants' nuisance-related counterclaims, but directing that both the cougars and the holding facility be removed from plaintiffs' property. . . .

We begin with the cougars. The amended CCRs, which all parties agree apply to plaintiffs' property, authorize the Board to regulate "the use . . . of the Property in such a manner as to preserve and enhance lot and structure values, farming, and to maintain the natural vegetation and topography." Amended CCRs, Art. IV, sec.2. Limitations on "use" are set forth in Article V, section 1, which provides, in pertinent part:

> "(b) *Use of the property*. Property may be reasonably and normally used for agricultural farming, tree farming or residential use only.
>
> "(c) *Nuisances*. No nuisance shall be permitted to exist or operate upon any Property so as to be detrimental to any other Property in the vicinity thereof or to its occupants. The decision of the Association as to what is a nuisance is presumptively correct. No normal or reasonable use of the Property, as described in subparagraph (b) above, shall be a nuisance."

Here, as noted, the trial court concluded that the cougars were not a nuisance under either the amended CCRs or common law.

Defendants do not challenge those determinations on appeal. Thus, for purpose of this appeal, we necessarily assume that plaintiffs' keeping of the cougars is *not* a nuisance under either the common law or the CCRs.

Given that posture, the issue narrows to whether keeping the cougars is a permissible "residential use" within the meaning of Article V, subsection 1(b). In construing the "residential use" provision of the amended CCRs, we follow the methodology prescribed in *Yogman v. Parrott*, 325 Or. 358, 361-66, 937 P.2d 1019 (1997). Under *Yogman*, "[t]o interpret a contractual provision, including a restrictive covenant, the court follows three steps." 325 Or. at 361, 937 P.2d 1019. First, the court must examine "the text of the disputed provision, in the context of the

8. The court also determined that enforcement of the CCRs was not barred by laches both because the delay was insufficient and because plaintiffs had "unclean hands" by virtue of failing to warn their neighbors about the cougars and then surreptitiously moving the animals onto the property.

document as a whole. . . . If the provision is clear, the analysis ends." *Id.* If, however, the provision, when so viewed, remains ambiguous, the court must look to "extrinsic evidence of the contracting parties' intent" to resolve the ambiguity. *Id.* at 363, 937 P.2d 1019. Finally, if that analysis is not dispositive, the court must look to relevant maxims of construction, including the maxim that restrictive covenants should be "'construed most strictly against the covenant.'" *Id.* at 364-65, 937 P.2d 1019 (quoting *Scott Co. v. Roman Catholic Archbishop*, 83 Or. 97, 105, 163 P. 88 (1917); *see also Swanson v. Warner*, 125 Or. App. 524, 526, 865 P.2d 493 (1993).

We begin, then, with the text and context of the "residential use" provision. Article V, subsection 1(b) of the amended CCRs describes, and limits, permitted uses of property within the subdivision:

> "*Use of the Property*. Property may be *reasonably and normally* used for agricultural farming, tree farming or *residential use only*."

(Emphasis added.)

"Residential," as commonly understood, means "of, relating to, or connected with residence or residences." *Webstar's Third New Int'l Dictionary*, 1931 (unabridged ed 1993). "Residence," in turn, means "the place where one actually lives or has his home. . . . " *Id.* Thus, a "residential use" is one that involves activities generally associated with a personal dwelling.

Plaintiff assert—and we agree—that keeping family pets is a "residential activity." *See Aldridge v. Saxey*, 242 Or. 238, 249, 409 P.2d 184 (1965) (concluding that covenant precluding the use of property for nonresidential purposes did not preclude the landowners from keeping 16 German Shepherds and 5 smaller dogs on their property). Plaintiffs further offered uncontradicted testimony that they keep and care for the cougars as pets and not for any commercial purpose, such as breeding or exhibiting the animals for pay. Andy Turudic described the role that the cougars play in plaintiffs' lives:

> "[They] are an integral part of our family life. We have a very strong bond with our animals. . . . They give me and my wife both immense pleasure."

Thus, although the cougars may be more exotic than goldfish or hamsters, they are, nevertheless, indisputably family pets. Given that the cougars are family pets, and that their presence does not present a nuisance, the maintenance of the cougars constitutes a "residential use" within the meaning of the amended CCRs.

Defendants argue, however, that the amended CCRs permit only "reasonable" and "normal" residential uses—and assert that the keeping of cougars is neither. Defendants' argument fails for several reasons. First, as a textual matter, subsection 1(b) does not refer to "reasonable and normal. . . . residential use." Rather, it states that the property may be "*reasonably and normally* used for [farming] or residential use only." (Emphasis added.) Thus, defendants' argument transforms adverbs into adjectives—a transformation that is particularly significant with respect to "normally" and "normal." It is one thing to say that property shall "normally"—*i.e.*, typically or usually—be used for farming and residential purposes. It is quite another to say that property can only be used for "normal"—*i.e.*, presumably ordinary or decidedly nonexotic—uses. Here, plaintiffs "normally" use their property for residential uses.

Second, to the extent that defendants claim contextual support for their "reasonable and normal" use argument, they point to the language of the nuisance provision, subsection 1(c). That reliance is, however, unavailing. Subsection 1(c) refers to "normal *or* reasonable" use—that is, it is phrased in the disjunctive, not defendants' putative conjunctive. . . . Thus, any use described in subsection 1(b) that is *either* "reasonable" *or* "normal" is not a nuisance under subsection 1(c); a use that is not "normal," but is nevertheless "reasonable," must be permitted. Moreover, as noted, the trial court explicitly determined that the use here was not a "nuisance" under subsection 1(c). Logically, in so holding, the court necessarily determined that the use was either "normal" or "reasonable," or both. As noted, defendants do not contest that determination. . . .

Third, to the extent that the phrase "may be reasonably and normally used. . . . for residential use only" remains ambiguous after resort to context, including subsection 1(c), the covenant is to be "construed most strictly against the covenant." *Yogman*, 325 Or. at 364-65, 937 P.2d 1019. Here, that canon assumes special significance because of the conduct of the Association, which seeks to enforce the covenant. As noted, plaintiffs have undertaken considerable efforts to eliminate potential risks associated with keeping the cougars. Those efforts have been highly successful—so successful that the trial court found that any risk from the cougars did not rise to the level of a common-law nuisance. "[T]he potential for actual injury to a person is so remote that the fear of the neighbors cannot be said to be objectively reasonable." Nevertheless, marginal risks remain—*e.g.*, the risk of a trespassing child thrusting his or her hand into the cage or of a stranger releasing the cougars—and plaintiffs offered to undertake additional measures that would have eliminated even that potential. But the Association refuses to approve those reasonable measures. . . .

In effect, the Association contends that plaintiffs' maintenance of the cougars is not "reasonable" because of the Association's own refusal to approve reasonable safety measures. The self-serving circularity is patent. Such a construction of subsection 1(b) cannot be squared with the "construed most strictly against the covenant" canon.

We thus conclude that the keeping of the cougars in their holding pen is a permitted residential use under Article V, subsection 1(b) of the amended CCRs. That conclusion, however, necessarily depends on the premise that the cougars' holding pen lawfully exists, and will continue to exist, on plaintiffs' property. Consequently, we turn to the trial court's determination that the cougar pen must be removed from the property. . . .

We agree that, at least in the abstract, the amended CCRs give the Board the authority to either approve or disapprove construction of structures such as the cougar pen. In particular, the amended CCRs provide:

> No . . . building, fence or other structure shall be erected, placed or altered on any lot or parcel until the proposed building plans, plot plans showing the proposed location of such building or structures . . . have been approved in writing by the Board, its successors or assigns. Refusal or approval of plans or location may be based by the Board upon any reason, including purely aesthetic conditions, which, in the sole discretion of the Board, shall be deemed sufficient.

Amended CCRs, Art. V, sec. 1(e)(2).

That broad authority to approve or disapprove a structure for "any reason" is balanced, however, by Article IV, section 8 of the amended CCRs, which requires that, "In all matters relating to their duties as the Board of the Association, the Board must act reasonably and not capriciously." It is in light of those contractual rights and obligations that we assess the Board's actions here.

In its February 22, 1995, letter, the Board notified plaintiffs that structural approval for their cougar pen had been denied and that the cougar pen had to be removed. The letter further stated:

> "[N]o further construction of cages for housing cougars or any other felid shall be constructed. *This action is predicated on the basis of the nuisance provisions of the Susan Estates Covenants and Restrictions.*" (Emphasis added.)

No alternative explanation was given, and the evidence at trial did not show any additional bases for the Board's decision to deny approval of the plans. For example, there was no evidence that the Board denied approval because the cougar pen violated any "aesthetic" or design requirements of the CCRs or because the cougars or their holding pen might adversely affect property values. Thus, the sole basis of the Board's denial of approval was its belief that maintenance of the cougars was a nuisance.

The trial court concluded that that denial was sufficient basis for enjoining plaintiffs to remove the cougar pan. We respectfully disagree for two related reasons. First, . . . defendants do not dispute on appeal [that] the cougars here are not a nuisance under the CCRs. Thus, while the Board may deny approval of a structure for any reasonable and not capricious reason, the sole basis for disapproval here was legally erroneous—and, indeed, objectively unreasonable: "[T]he fear of the neighbors cannot be said to be objectively reasonable." Denial on such a basis is unreasonable and capricious.

Second, in a related sense, the Board's disapproval was, in purpose and effect, a collateral preclusion of a lawful permitted use under the CCRs. That is, the Board's disapproval was not, actually, of the structure *qua* structure but of the structure's function. The disapproval of the holding pen here is analogous to a homeowners' association refusing to approve plans for a home that includes a billiard room because the association's members disapprove of billiards. Here, the keeping of pets, including exotic pets, in safe facilities is a permitted "residential use." *See* 176 Or. App. at 185-88, 31 P.3d at 470-71. Consequently, so long as the structure for holding such pets does not violate some other (*e.g.*, design-related) requirement of the CCRs, the preapproval process cannot be employed as a subterfuge to preclude that permitted use. Such a denial is unreasonable and capricious. . . .

Notes and Comments

1. *The Breadth of CC&Rs*. Were you surprised by the stringency of the restrictions that the *Mystic Isle* CC&Rs place on use of the property? Do you think most homeowners, who are certainly on constructive notice of these provisions, are actually aware of them before they purchase the property?

The breadth of CC&Rs is illustrated by the myriad disputes that have arisen between owners in the same development, or between owners and the homeowners association. For example, there was the case of the manufactured home alleged to constitute a "trailer" (*Hutchison v. Hill*, 3 P.3d 242 (Wyo. 2000)); the case of the three-inch fence and "private drive" sign (*Skow v. Goforth*, 618 N.W.2d 275 (Iowa 2000)); the case of the "three cats" ("Boo-Boo, Dockers, and Tulip") (*Nahrstedt v. Lakeside Village Condominium Ass'n*, 878 P.2d 1275 (Cal. 1994)); the case of the "bowed roof" which blocked the neighbors' view (*Castonguay v. Plourde*, 699 A.2d 226 (Conn. Ct. App. 1997)); and the case of the "smoking ban" at the club (*Laganella v. Boca Grove Golf and Tennis Club, Inc.*, 690 So. 2d 705 (Fla. Dist. Ct. App. 1997)). *See* Paula A. Franzese, Does It Take a Village? Privatization, Patterns of Community Restrictiveness and the Demise of Community, 47 Vill. L. Rev. 553, 555-556 (2002) (covenants regulate the permissibility and style of one's screen and storm doors, the ratio of grass, trees, and shrubs allowed on one's property, the mounting of basketball hoops, the retrieval of dog droppings, the posting of for-sale signs, the trimming of bushes, and the color of window curtains (citing cases)).

Other disputes are more poignant, such as when a Tampa Florida community association sought to remove a treehouse. The treehouse was built for a six-year old boy battling leukemia. Many were not sympathetic to the association's case, and the association relented. Amy Herdy, Sick Boy's Retreat Violates Rules, St. Petersburg Times, Jan. 9, 2000, at 1B.

2. *Close Reading*. A dispute involving the interpretation of CC&Rs requires much the same type of legal skills that are needed for working with statutes. It also requires adept use of the facts of the case, particularly the ability to raise facts that support equitable arguments when a covenant on its face appears to apply. Consider the following two situations:

a. A covenant in a residential subdivision stated that "[n]o lot shall be used for anything except residential purposes." Here is a picture of the six lots involved:

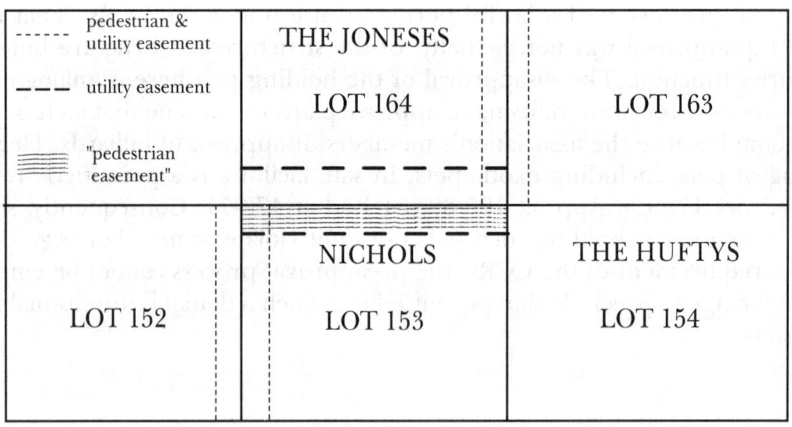

Ten-foot wide pedestrian and utility easement ran vertically between lots 163 and 164, and between lots 152 and 153. Then the developer, Nichols, granted a 15-foot wide pedestrian easement along the inside edge of lot 163 (apparently to fulfill a condition on the subdivision that it provide access to a park). The easement was for "foot traffic only (including the placement of a concrete sidewalk within the easement) by residents of Prairie Stream Estates. . . . " The Joneses and the Huftys sued. Does the easement violate the restrictive covenant? See *Jones v. Nichols*, 765 N.E.2d 153 (Ind. Ct. App. 2002).

b. A set of restrictive covenants that apply to a subdivision contain the following provision:

> **Nuisances**
>
> No business or trade or offensive or noxious activity shall be carried on upon any lot in the Subdivision, nor shall anything be done thereon which may become an annoyance or a nuisance to the neighborhood by unreasonably interfering with the use and enjoyment of other property within the Subdivision, nor shall any residence be utilized for public purposes or services including public worship or church services.

The owners of one home taught swimming lessons at their backyard pool during the summer months from 1988 through 1995. Each summer they conducted 18 lessons over four or five days a week for ten weeks, earning approximately $10,000. The lessons resulted in a substantial increase in traffic and parking in the neighborhood. The owners maintained a portable chemical toilet for the convenience of the swimming students. In addition, at least two other families in the subdivision conduct swimming lessons, and the traffic is well within the capacity of the streets in the subdivision.

The plaintiffs live across the street and sue the owners for injunctive relief. Should the court order that relief? *See Gabriel v. Cazier*, 938 P.2d 1209 (Idaho 1997).

3. *Technical Requirements*. As you know from your property law course and from the Note above, compliance with the law of covenants is quite technical and requires attention to detail by the lawyer and close research of the property law in a particular state. For example, in *Citizens for Covenant Compliance v. Anderson*, 906 P.2d 1314 (Cal. 1995), defendants sought to plant and harvest grapes, operate a winery, and keep llamas on their property. The neighbors brought suit, claiming that the CC&Rs for the subdivision limited the activities on defendants' property. Defendants raised a technical defense: since the CC&Rs were recorded *before* any of the properties they purport to govern were sold, defendants claimed that they were not bound because the restrictions were not mentioned in any deed or other document when the property was sold.

After saluting the properties of wine ("In vino veritas"), Justice Arabian proceeded to wade through the thickets of covenant law to conclude that subsequent purchasers were bound. 906 P.2d at 1316. The court's ruling had a practical bent to it: the rule simplifies the enforcement of CC&Rs by necessitating the recording of only one document containing them.

4. *Enforcement*. When a dispute between owners or between the association and an owner turns nasty, the enforcement provisions of the CC&Rs become important. What restrictions are placed on the ability of the homeowners' association to enforce the Mystic Isle CC&Rs set out above? What restrictions are placed on owners who wish to contest decisions or raise issues? Are those restrictions reasonable?

The association's enforcement "arsenal" normally consists of the power to fine as well as the power to seek injunctive relief. *See, e.g., Liebler v. Point Loma Tennis Club*, 47 Cal. Rptr. 2d 783 (Cal. App. 1995) (association had power to impose fines against an owner who violated a rule that prohibited nonresident owners from using the common area recreational facilities); *Taylor v. McCollom*, 958 P.2d 207, 213 (Or. Ct. App. 1998) (refusing injunctive relief for a violation of a covenant protecting plaintiff's view where the cost to defendants of tearing off and lowering their roof would be "very substantial," and defendants did not willfully violate the covenant).

If a court is reviewing a decision by a community association, the case may well turn on the test that the court applies. *See* Paula A. Franzese, Common Interest Communities: Standards of Review and Review of Standards, 3 Wash. U. J. L. & Pol'y 663 (2000) (arguing for a "multi-factored reasonableness test anchored in whether the restriction or board decision at issue is rationally related to the association's purposes or imposes burdens that are disproportionate to any benefits").

5. *Defenses*. What rights and defenses are available to an owner when he or she believes that a homeowners association has acted arbitrarily? The place to start, as always, is with the provisions of the covenants and restrictions themselves. In the case of the Mystic Isle CC&Rs, what rights does an owner have to contest an arbitrary decision?

The case law does recognize some ability to resist when the association's application of the rules has not been evenhanded. For example, what if the homeowners' association has acquiesced in prior violations of a provision, but now seeks to enforce that provision against an owner not involved in the previous violations? *See Ridgewood Homeowners Assn. v. Mignacca*, 813 A.2d 965 (R.I. 2003) (no waiver where "no evidence was presented that these infractions were brought to the attention of the association or its board as a whole, or that the association considered and declined to enforce the covenant").

If the covenants so provide, the enforcing party may be able to recover its attorney's fees as well. *See Piepkorn v. Adams*, 10 P.3d 428 (Wash. Ct. App. 2000) (awarding fees in a dispute over a fence).

Do these holdings give too much weight to the property rights created by the covenant? If you think so, what rule should the court adopt? Should the court give more deference to the day-to-day interpretation of that use covenant by the affected landowners?

Can lack of enforcement of one covenant bar enforcement of another? In *Mountain Park Homeowners Ass'n Inc. v. Tydings*, 883 P.2d 1383 (Wash.1994), a provision of the CC&Rs stated that invalidating a covenant or restriction "by judgment or court order shall not affect any other provisions. . . . " The court held that this clause mandated separate treatment of covenants in an enforcement action. Did the court read the provision correctly?

What if the allegation is that the homeowners association, perhaps through its architectural review board, has simply acted arbitrarily in denying an application? Can the CC&Rs provide that an architectural control board *may* act arbitrarily? *See Lakeridge Greens Homeowners Assn. Inc. v. Silberman*, 765 So. 2d 95 (Fla. Ct. App. 2000) (homeowner may show arbitrary action by architectural control board in enforcing, but it was not shown here where plaintiffs "terra cotta wall plaque" was larger than those of the neighbors that had been allowed); *Raintree Homeowners Ass'n, Inc. v. Bleimann*, 449 S.E. 2d 13 (N.C. Ct. App. 1994) (upholding a jury determination that an architectural review committee acted unreasonably and in bad faith in denying plaintiffs' application to replace wood clapboard siding with vinyl siding).

Covenants, easements, and the like are conceptually different from the types of public regulation of land use that we have spent our time on in this casebook. Most significantly, they allow parties to decide contractually how they wish to restrict their uses of land. As such, proponents argue that private land use arrangements promote freedom of choice in land use matters and are consistent with the market system. But as more and more developments become "privatized," critics have claimed that so-called private or "gated" communities have significant detriments associated with them.

EDWARD J. BLAKELY & MARY GAIL SNYDER, FORTRESS AMERICA: GATED COMMUNITIES IN THE UNITED STATES

2-3 (1997)

. . . Gated communities are residential areas with restricted access in which normally public spaces are privatized. They are security developments with designated perimeters, usually walls or fences, and controlled entrances that are intended to prevent penetration by nonresidents. They include new developments and older areas retrofitted with gates and fences, and they are found from the inner cities to the exurbs and from the richest neighborhoods to the poorest. Their gates range from elaborate two-story guardhouses staffed twenty-four hours a day to roll-back wrought-iron gates to simple electronic arms. Guardhouses are usually built with one lane for guests and visitors and a second lane for residents, who may open the gates with an electronic card, a code, or a remote control device. Some communities with round- the-clock security require all cars to pass the guard, issuing identification stickers for residents' cars. Others use video cameras to record the license plate numbers and sometimes the faces of all who pass through. Entrances without guards have intercom systems, some with video monitors, that residents may use to screen visitors.

The residences we are discussing are not multi-unit, high-density apartment and condominium buildings with security systems or doormen in which gates or guards prevent public access to lobbies, hallways, and parking lots. Gated communities are different: their walls and fences preclude public access to streets, sidewalks, parks, beaches, rivers, trails, playgrounds—all resources that without gates or walls would be open and shared by all the citizens of a locality.

We estimate that more than 3 million American households have already sought out this new refuge from the problems of urbanization. In 1985 gated communities existed in only a handful of places. Today they can be found in every major metropolitan area. These developments in part reflect the notion of community as an island, a social bulwark against the general degradation of the urban social order; they also reflect the increasing attempt to substitute private controls for public organization, for the joint responsibilities of democratic citizenship all of us share. Gates and walls are not necessary or natural consequences of these social trends, or causes of them; they are, rather, a dramatic manifestation of them.

Gates and fences around our neighborhoods represent more than simply physical barriers. Gated communities manifest a number of tensions: between exclusionary aspirations rooted in fear and protection of privilege and the values of civic responsibility; between the trend toward privatization of public services and the ideals of the public good and general welfare; and between the need for personal and community control of the environment and the dangers of making outsiders of fellow citizens. . . .

■ ROBERT H. NELSON, PRO-CHOICE LIVING ARRANGEMENTS REALITY CHECK

Forbes, June 14, 1999, 222

A recent episode of TV's X-Files featured a neighborhood association that threatens to kill a resident for having a burned-out lightbulb in the yard. The plot was over the top, as usual—but it reflects a growing, real-life fear about the power of residential neighborhood associations. Today 15% of Americans belong to condominium, cooperative or homeowner associations and one-third of new housing is being built under such private governance . . .

As more Americans privatize their communities, I predict, the associations will want to control their social environments as well—ultimately trying to create whole neighborhoods of people of the same age, profession, sexual orientation, religion or even ethnic origin. How far will they be allowed to go?

The very idea of an exclusive community makes some civil libertarians cringe. What's next, they'd ask, racial covenants? These were rightly banned by the Supreme Court in 1948.

But while ruling out the kind of bigotry that once poisoned housing all across the country, we ought to be able to tolerate a lot more experimentation in voluntary homeowner groups than we do now. Freedom from racial discrimination is a basic American right—but so is freedom of association. . . .

Former Labor Secretary Robert Reich not long ago called the spread of private communities a "secession of the successful" from full participation in American life. But in a nation built on the strength and individuality of local communities, when was it decided—and by whom—that it is bad for people of the same background and interests to live together? Reich's thinking exemplifies the sour grapes attitude of the governing elite, worried it will have less control over other people's lives. . . .

Editorialists of all stripes complain that a sense of community is lost from American life. . . .

Private communities can help fill this void. To do so, they will have to be given greater legal powers to control their social environments and to insist that residents conform. . . .

To be clear: I am taking here about private residential communities, not municipalities. Public government should never favor a particular class of resident. People should never be made to leave their homes by any entity, public or private. And there are some forms of exclusion—based on physical handicap, for example—that must remain unacceptable in any context. But it would be a big mistake to reflexively ban all kinds of discrimination.

It is time to give community associations discretion, within reason, to choose members. Given the diversity of culture in this country, I am confident that few Americans would be unable to find a group of like-minded neighbors. In a society where people fear for their children's safety even at school, it is clear that a key institution for forming and defending ethical values — the local community — is in desperate shape. We must allow Americans the freedom to constitute their neighborhoods according to deeply felt personal bonds.

Notes and Comments

1. *Cost Minimization and Social Capital*. One recent article suggested that there are two principal arguments in favor of the "privatization" of land uses like that described in the excerpt above: (1) private production is assumed to be less costly due to the salutary impact of market incentives on efficiency; and (2) privatization will enhance the level of "social capital" — i.e., the "features of social organization such as networks, norms, and social trust that facilitate coordination and cooperation for mutual benefit" — among members of a community. Dell Champlin, The Privatization of Community: Implications for Urban Policy, 32 J. of Econ. Issues 595 (1998). There is a strong argument that privatization should be preferred for economic efficiency reasons. *See* Clayton P. Gillette, Courts, Covenants, and Communities, 61 U. Chi. L. Rev. 1375, 1390 (1994).

Do you agree with these arguments? Are there other benefits of privatization that you see? What about allowing individuals to maximize their feeling of security in an era in which public institutions are seen as unable to prevent crime?

2. *Segregation*. Some have criticized gated communities as symbols of segregation. Consider the following excerpt:

> Meanwhile, critics have seized on gated communities as symbols of social segregation. Evan McKenzie, author of "Privatopia: Homeowner Associations and the Rise of Residential Private Government," thinks gates cause social and economic segregation the same way race-restricted covenants did in an earlier era. People who live in gated communities are saying that they don't support public services that support a community.

Lois M. Baron, The Great Gate Debate, 21 Builder Magazine, Mar. 1, 1998, at 92. Do you agree, and if so, is the remedy to deny approval to gated communities? *See* Henry Stern, County Places Library Levy on November Ballot, The Portland Oregonian, June 26, 2002, at E01 (reporting that the Board of Washington County Commissioners, by a 3-2 vote, decided not to put a commissioner's proposal to prohibit new gated communities on the ballot. The commissioner advocating the measure contended that gated developments were "out of keeping with Oregon's inclusive feel").

What about the freedom of association that Nelson advocates in his article? *See* also Laura T. Rahe, The Right to Exclude: Preserving the Autonomy of the Homeowners' Association, 34 Urb. Law. 521 (2002) (supporting the rights of homeowners' associations to exclude).

3. *The Appropriate Model*. One aspect of the debate is over what exactly is the role that homeowners associations are to play in the governance of gated communities. There are a number of possible models: (1) the Corporate Model, because

the powers, duties, and liabilities of the directors of organizations in the for- profit and nonprofit sectors are much the same; (2) the Trust Model, because the homeowners association performs duties that are analogous to that of a trustee; and (3) the Municipal Model, because the homeowners association performs many of the same duties as a local government. See Wayne S. Hyatt & Jo Anne P. Stubblefield, The Identity Crisis of Community Associations: In Search of the Appropriate Analogy, 27 Real Prop., Prob., & Trust J. 589, 622-641 (1993) (examining these and several other models). Which of these models, if any, seems to fit the homeowners association best?

How the law views the homeowners association (i.e., what "model" is appropriate) has important ramifications. For example, one author has suggested that, for constitutional purposes, courts should view residential associations as "state actors" under the state action doctrine. David J. Kennedy, Residential Associations as State Actors: Regulating the Impact of Gated Communities on Nonmembers, 105 Yale L.J. 761 (1995). Which model does this view advocate? What would be the consequences of treating homeowners associations as state actors? *See also* Susan F. French, The Constitution of a Private Residential Government Should Include a Bill of Rights, 27 Wake Forest L. Rev. 345 (1992) (observing that "one promising line of thought is to pursue the analogy that has been drawn between community associations and governments," and suggesting that in drafting the "constitutions" of private residential governments, developers "should include a bill of rights"). Is such a "bill of rights" necessary? If so, what should it include?

4. *Privatization and Taxes*. Homeowners' associations, through the assessment of dues, provide benefits (street maintenance, street lighting, recreation facilities, and so forth) that municipalities normally provide and pay for through the assessment of property taxes. Residents may deduct such property taxes from their federal income taxes, thus receiving a tax benefit. Dues paid by those in homeowners associations, however, are not deductible. Does fairness require that those dues be made deductible?

5. *Privatization and Governance*. Consider the situation in which the City of Hidden Hills, California, found itself. Hidden Hills, an "entirely-gated" jurisdiction, needed to build a city hall:

> There is only one public space that Hidden Hills cannot privatize, cannot fund and operate through its private government: city hall, the seat of its public government, an eradicably public place where anyone from anywhere can legally demand to go. That is why it had to be moved outside the city's gates. "If people could get into town just by saying "we're going to city hall," explains [the] City Attorney . . . "then the residents of Hidden Hills would have no security."

Andrew Stark, America, the Gated?, 22 Wilson Q., Jan. 1, 1998, at 58. Does this situation, as the article suggests, illustrate "a vast and largely unrecognized transformation: the radical redefinition at the grassroots level of the boundary between the public and private realms."? What, if anything, is the problem with such a development from a governmental standpoint?

6. *The Future*. It is clear that private associations are rapidly growing. As of June 2001, the Community Associations Institute reports that 47 million Americans live in community associations. Http://www.caionline.org/about/facts.cfm. The market

is accepting this model, and its implications are profound. *See, generally*, Michael A. Heller, The Boundaries of Private Property, 108 Yale L.J. 1163 (1999); Patrick J. Rohan, Preparing Community Associations for the Twenty-First Century: Anticipating the Legal Problems and Possible Solutions, 73 St. John's L. Rev. 3 (1999); Symposium, New Forms of Governance: Ceding Power to Private Actors, 49 UCLA L. Rev. 1687 (2002).

D. BARGAINING: DEVELOPMENT AGREEMENTS

Another alternative method for land use decisionmaking is bargaining, and the principal vehicle used in such bargaining is the development agreement. In *Bollech v. Charles County, Maryland*, 166 F. Supp. 2d 443 (D. Md. 2001), the court adopted the following definition of the term:

> Development agreements are defined as agreements between a municipality and a developer under which site conditions may be imposed but the right to develop in compliance therewith is vested at least for a certain period of time.

Id. at 453 (internal quotations omitted). To begin looking at these agreements, whose use is rapidly expanding, we examine excerpts from statutes in several states authorizing local jurisdictions and developers to enter into such agreements.

FLORIDA STATUTES ANNOTATED §§163.3223–163.3235
(West 2000)

163.3223. APPLICABILITY

Any local government may, by ordinance, establish procedures and requirements, as provided in §§163.3220-163.3243, to consider and enter into a development agreement with any person having a legal or equitable interest in real property located within its jurisdiction. . . .

163.3225. PUBLIC HEARINGS

(1) Before entering into, amending, or revoking a development agreement, a local government shall conduct at least two public hearings. At the option of the governing body, one of the public hearings may be held by the local planning agency. . . .

163.3227. REQUIREMENTS OF A DEVELOPMENT AGREEMENT

(1) A development agreement shall include the following:

(a) A legal description of the land subject to the agreement, and the names of its legal and equitable owners;

(b) The duration of the agreement;

(c) The development uses permitted on the land, including population densities, and building intensities and height;

(d) A description of public facilities that will service the development, including who shall provide such facilities; the date any new facilities, if needed, will be constructed; and a schedule to assure public facilities are available concurrent with the impacts of the development;

(e) A description of any reservation or dedication of land for public purposes;

(f) A description of all local development permits approved or needed to be approved for the development of the land;

(g) A finding that the development permitted or proposed is consistent with the local government's comprehensive plan and land development regulations;

(h) A description of any conditions, terms, restrictions, or other requirements determined to be necessary by the local government for the public health, safety, or welfare of its citizens; and

(i) A statement indicating that the failure of the agreement to address a particular permit, condition, term, or restriction shall not relieve the developer of the necessity of complying with the law governing said permitting requirements, conditions, term, or restriction.

(2) A development agreement may provide that the entire development or any phase thereof be commenced or completed within a specific period of time.

163.3229. DURATION OF A DEVELOPMENT AGREEMENT AND RELATIONSHIP TO LOCAL COMPREHENSIVE PLAN

The duration of a development agreement shall not exceed 10 years. It may be extended by mutual consent of the governing body and the developer, subject to a public hearing in accordance with §163.3225. No development agreement shall be effective or be implemented by a local government unless the local government's comprehensive plan and plan amendments implementing or related to the agreement are found in compliance by the state land planning agency.

163.3233. LOCAL LAWS AND POLICIES GOVERNING A DEVELOPMENT AGREEMENT

(1) The local government's laws and policies governing the development of the land at the time of the execution of the development agreement shall govern the development of the land for the duration of the development agreement.

(2) A local government may apply subsequently adopted laws and policies to a development that is subject to a development agreement only if the local government has held a public hearing and determined:

(a) They are not in conflict with the laws and policies governing the development agreement and do not prevent development of the land uses, intensities, or densities in the development agreement;

(b) They are essential to the public health, safety, or welfare, and expressly state that they shall apply to a development that is subject to a development agreement;

(c) They are specifically anticipated and provided for in the development agreement;

(d) The local government demonstrates that substantial changes have occurred in pertinent conditions existing at the time of approval of the development agreement; or

(e) The development agreement is based on substantially inaccurate information supplied by the developer.

163.3235. PERIODIC REVIEW OF A DEVELOPMENT AGREEMENT

A local government shall review land subject to a development agreement at least once every 12 months to determine if there has been demonstrated good faith compliance with the terms of the development agreement. For each annual review conducted during years 6 through 10 of a development agreement, the review shall be incorporated into a written report which shall be submitted to the parties to the agreement and the state land planning agency. The state land planning agency shall adopt rules regarding the contents of the report, provided that the report shall be limited to the information sufficient to determine the extent to which the parties are proceeding in good faith to comply with the terms of the development agreement. If the local government finds, on the basis of substantial competent evidence, that there has been a failure to comply with the terms of the development agreement, the agreement may be revoked or modified by the local government.

HAWAII REVISED STATUTES ANNOTATED §46-125
(Matthew Bender & Co. 2002)

46-125. PERIODIC REVIEW; TERMINATION OF AGREEMENT

(a) If, as a result of a periodic review, the designated agency finds and determines that the principal has committed a material breach of the terms or conditions of the agreement, the designated agency shall serve notice in writing, within a reasonable time period after the periodic review, upon the principal setting forth with reasonable particularity the nature of the breach and the evidence supporting the finding and determination, and providing the principal a reasonable time period in which to cure such material breach.

(b) If the principal fails to cure the material breach within the time period given, then the county unilaterally may terminate or modify the agreement; provided that the designated agency has first given the principal the opportunity, (1) to rebut the finding and determination; or (2) to consent to amend the agreement to meet the concerns of the designated agency with respect to the finding and determination.

Notes and Comments

1. *The Benefits of Bargaining*. Development agreements offer significant benefits both to local jurisdictions and to developers. From the developer's perspective, the agreement provides certainty that the regulatory conditions for a project will not change as the project is implemented. From the local jurisdiction's viewpoint, the development agreement offers an attractive vehicle for funding infrastructure and other improvements in an era in which public funding has been curtailed. See Barry R. Knight & Susan P. Schoettle, Current Issues Related to Vested Rights and Development Agreements, 25 Urb. Law. 779, 788 (1993) ("[T]he developer

obtains vested rights and a degree of certainty regarding the land development regulations applicable to his project while the local government receives assistance in the provision of public facilities and infrastructure and may achieve long-range planning goals such as open space conservation, water and air quality protection, environmental mitigation, and affordable housing.").

2. *Bargaining as a Function of Local Government.* Bargaining of the scope contemplated in development agreements is a significant departure from the previous land use decisionmaking process. In one article on the subject, a local member of the board of supervisors observed in commenting on a completed development agreement: "We wanted something developed there . . . but we wanted something beneficial to the city. It's no different from two large corporations getting together. We're just a municipal corporation." William Fulton, Building and Bargaining in California, Cal. Law., Dec. 1984, at 37, 41. Notice how that view of the local government's function in approaching land use decisions differs from the traditional view of local government regulating in the public interest.

3. *Bargaining and Planning.* In earlier chapters, you have learned about the emphasis in many jurisdictions on the need for comprehensive planning to precede development. Is the notion of "bargaining" to reach an agreement inconsistent with the notion of comprehensive land use planning?

Some states specifically require that development agreements be consistent with the general plan. *See* Ariz. Rev. Stat. Ann. §9-500.05 (B) (West 1996). One expert has suggested that local politicians may be more eager to engage in bargaining for development agreements than in long-range planning because long-range, comprehensive planning, which necessarily involves somewhat abstract policies and objectives, "appears a less than useful exercise to many political leaders who win or lose elections by what they can achieve in two-year terms." Douglas R. Porter, The Relation of Development Agreements to Plans and Planning, in Development Agreements: Practice, Policy, and Prospects 149 (Douglas R. Porter & Lindell L. Marsh eds., 1989).

4. *Bargaining and Third Parties.* Earlier chapters of this casebook have noted the rise of third-party influence in land use decisions and examined the role that neighbors and citizens groups play in the process. The development agreement statutes, however, do not specifically provide for third-party participation in the negotiation of such an agreement. Does the public's right to participate in any later public hearing at which the agreement is ratified provide sufficient participation for third parties? Could third parties claim under state "open meetings" laws that they have a right to be present (if not to participate) during the negotiations?

5. *Bargaining and Democracy.* In *216 Sutter Bay Associates v. County of Sutter*, 68 Cal. Rptr. 2d 492 (Ct. App. 1997), the board of supervisors passed a general plan amendment allowing for large-scale development in the southern part of the county. Opponents then collected enough signatures to place a referendum on the general plan amendment on the ballot. In the meantime, elections had resulted in a new board majority opposing the plan amendment, and the new members would take office on January 4, 1993.

In December 1992, the old board approved 18 development agreements based on the pro-growth general amendment, and "[f]or good measure, the old Board approved another development agreement on the morning of January 4, just hours before leaving office." 68 Cal. Rptr. 2d at 495. After the new board took office, it enacted a moratorium and repealed the development agreements, actions which the court upheld.

The political situation was somewhat similar in *Nicolet Minerals Co. v. Town of Nashville*, 641 N.W.2d 497 (Wis. Ct. App. 2002). Here, a local government reached agreement with a mining company granting it the required approvals. Public sentiment opposed the agreement, and the incumbent members of the board were then defeated. When the new board tried to rescind the agreement, the court upheld it.

Are these idiosyncratic situations or do they illustrate any dangers that development agreements may pose?

6. *Issues*. Negotiating development agreements requires a close reading of the statutes authorizing the local jurisdiction to enter into the agreement. Interestingly, although development agreements have been used extensively in some states, there are relatively few appellate opinions discussing them, and some key legal questions regarding their use remain unanswered. In particular, consider the following issues:

(a) *Authority*. The statutes that you just read authorize local jurisdictions to enter into development agreements, although at least one court has upheld a local jurisdiction's ability to enter into an agreement without such authority. *See Giger v. City of Omaha*, 442 N.W.2d 182 (Neb. 1989). However, given the significant legal concerns that they raise, and their departure from traditional land use processes, entering into such agreements without explicit statutory authority is problematic.

(b) *Vested Rights*. From the developer's standpoint, perhaps the key issue is whether the local jurisdiction can later impose additional conditions on the project. *See Country Meadows West Partnership v. Village of Germantown*, 614 N.W.2d 498 (Wis. Ct. App. 2000) (village exceeded the scope of the parties' subdivision agreements when it imposed fees for parks, libraries, storm and sewage treatment systems, fire and police protection facilities, and emergency medical facilities that were not set forth in the agreements). The development agreement statutes vary somewhat on this point. While all of them provide for a "freeze" on existing regulations, many list certain "exceptions" to this general principle.

(c) *Duration*. The duration of the agreement is another key issue. One thought to keep in mind is the possibility that the longer the term of the contract, the greater the chance that a court will find that the local government has "contracted away" the police power.

(d) *Amendments*. In some instances the land that is the subject of the development agreement will later be annexed to a city (perhaps a newly formed city) that is not a party to the original agreement. Can the agreement itself bind the annexing city to its terms (particularly the promise not to impose conditions on the development not spelled out in the development agreement) if that city is not a signatory to the agreement?

(e) *Secrecy*. Is it possible to keep any part of the agreement or the supporting documents secret? Under state "right to know" or "public records" acts, secrecy is quite unlikely. *See Union Leader Corp. v. New Hampshire Housing Finance Authority*, 705 A.2d 725, 737 (N.H. 1997) (development agreement and construction loan agreement entered into by a finance authority are not exempt from disclosure where the authority was a named party in both agreements and the strong public policy interest in disclosure overrides the intervenors' interests in nondisclosure).

In *Ogden v. Premier Properties, USA, Inc.*, 755 N.E.2d 661 (Ind. Ct. App. 2001), plaintiffs alleged that individual members of the city council met privately to negotiate the terms under which they would approve a proposed rezoning. The court dismissed the complaint, reasoning that "any alleged verbal promises by a council member outside a duly organized meeting cannot contractually bind the council." *Id.* at 669. That conclusion is undoubtedly correct. But does the core problem—the clash between private negotiations and public governance—remain?

(f) *Referenda.* The Florida legislation identifies development agreements as administrative in nature, while California makes them subject to referendum. Thus, in California development agreements may be overturned by referendum, while in Florida they cannot be. *See Midway Orchards v. County of Butte*, 269 Cal. Rptr. 796 (Ct. App. 1990) (filing of a referendum petition prevents a development agreement from becoming effective).

In *Santa Margarita Area Residents Together v. San Luis Obispo County*, 100 Cal. Rptr. 2d 740 (Ct. App. 2000), the county and a developer signed a development agreement, following mediation, which froze zoning in return for the developer's commitment to submit a specific plan. The agreement specifically envisaged a second development agreement pertaining to actual construction. The court rejected plaintiff's contention that the agreement did not approve an "actual development project," reasoning that it "establishes the scope of the Project and precise parameters for future construction as well as procedure to process Project approvals." *Id.* at 745. The agreement had the effect of avoiding any initiative that might affect the property. Is that a valid use of the development agreement power?

(g) *Enforcement.* Who can enforce the agreements? Hawaii allows enforcement by any parties or by successors in interests, Haw. Rev. Stat. §46-127(a) (Michie 1993), while Florida authorizes "any party, any aggrieved or adversely affected person, or the state land planning agency" to seek injunctive relief or challenge compliance with the development agreement statute. Fla. Stat. Ann. §163.3243 (West 2000).

The negotiation and implementation of a development agreement involves a unique combination of private, common law contractual principles and public law governance principles, such as compliance with open meetings laws and adherence to limitations on land use authority found in state law. The following case illustrates some of these problems.

■ SPRENGER, GRUBB & ASSOCIATES, INC. v. CITY OF HAILEY

903 P.2d 741 (Idaho 1995)

SILAK, Justice

I. NATURE OF THE CASE

This appeal concerns a decision by the Hailey City Council to change the zoning classification of certain land owned by appellant Sprenger, Grubb & Associates (SGA) from "Business" to "Limited Business." SGA appealed to the district court, and the district court upheld the City Council's action. SGA again appeals. . . .

III. FACTS & PROCEDURAL BACKGROUND

In 1973, the City of Hailey and McCulloch Properties, Inc. (MPI), the predecessor to SGA, entered into a development agreement which provided for the annexation of 654 acres of MPI's property into the City and the development of a "master planned residential-recreational neighborhood." The property, today known as Woodside Subdivision (Woodside), consisted of certain areas specifically designated as residential areas, and other areas designated for business development. The subject of this appeal is 12.6 acres within Woodside, which had been classified as a Business District from 1973 until 1993, when the Hailey City Council adopted Hailey City Ordinance No. 623, rezoning the 12.6 acres to a Limited Business District. The 12.6 acres is completely surrounded by property zoned and developed as General Residential and is one and a half miles south of Hailey's downtown business area.

The MPI-Hailey development agreement set forth certain fees and obligations for MPI, ranging from cash contributions, to building a recreation center and a sewage treatment facility. Hailey has acknowledged that MPI fulfilled its obligations under the development agreement. Hailey's obligations under the agreement included the annexation and zoning of the Woodside property, along with other action to aid in the development of Woodside. Paragraph 9 of the development agreement provided that the agreement "shall inure to the benefit of and be binding upon HAILEY and upon MPI and upon its successors and assigns."

Since 1973, Hailey has grown and developed, including substantial development in various portions of Woodside. In 1977, MPI sold its interest in Woodside to SGA. SGA supported various favorable rezoning changes throughout Woodside from 1978 to 1989. In June 1991, the Hailey City Council annexed other properties located next to Hailey's downtown business area, and these properties were also classified as "Business District."

In 1990, Hailey's Mayor R. Keith Roark supported "downzoning" the 12.6 acres in Woodside based upon the property's distance from the "downtown business core." In July, 1990, the Hailey City Council amended its comprehensive plan, defining the existing business core as a discrete area demarcated by certain city streets within Hailey. The ordinance further prescribed that expansions of the Business and Limited Business Districts were to occur around the "existing core," as defined. The Hailey Planning and Zoning Commission (Zoning Commission) was requested to "downzone" the property in question from Business District to General Residential District in 1990 and again in 1992, and the Zoning Commission denied both requests. Later in 1992, Mayor Roark directed the City Planning and Zoning Administrator to request the Zoning Commission to rezone the 12.6 acres from Business to Limited Business District. Again, the Zoning Commission denied the request. The Zoning Commission decided that the existing Business District classification conformed to the City's comprehensive plan, and that the proposed zone change to Limited Business did not conform to the comprehensive plan.

The City Planning and Zoning Administrator appealed the Zoning Commission's decision to disallow the rezoning request. This appeal was heard by the Hailey City Council in July 1993, in conjunction with a public hearing. The public comment at the hearing was overwhelmingly in favor of rezoning the 12.6 acres in Woodside. At the hearing, SGA requested Mayor Roark to recuse himself from being the presiding officer on the basis of his alleged lack of impartiality.

Mayor Roark denied that request. However, Mayor Roark did not vote at the July 1993 hearing because three City Council members were present, and it would be unnecessary for him to cast a tie-breaking vote.

At the conclusion of the hearing, the three attending Hailey City Council members unanimously voted to reverse the Zoning Commission's decision, and thus, to rezone (or downzone) the 12.6 acres in Woodside to Limited Business. Subsequently, in August 1993, the City Council issued its written Findings of Fact and Conclusions of Law, relative to its prior verbal decision rendered after the hearing. In its conclusions of law, the City Council concluded among other things that "the existence of a large retail commercial property outside the Hailey Business Core, as defined in the Hailey Comprehensive Plan, is not in accordance with the current Hailey Comprehensive Plan, adopted in 1983." . . . The district court upheld the City Council's action, and SGA again appeals. . . .

V. Analysis

A. Development Agreement

SGA argues that the development agreement between the City and MPI was a binding contract, wherein the City agreed to a regulatory freeze, or to zone consistent with MPI's development plan. SGA contends the rezoning is a breach of the development agreement.

We have reviewed the provisions of the development agreement which SGA cites in support of its argument, and do not believe the development agreement created the claimed regulatory freeze. Paragraph 4(a) of the development agreement says generally that Hailey shall "take all other action as may be required by MPI to develop the annexed real property in accordance with the terms and provisions of the MPI Master Plan and this agreement." Paragraph 8, under the heading "Interpretation of Agreement" provides that "[i]t is understood that the development of the annexed real property in accordance with the terms of this Agreement and exhibits attached hereto shall be in substantial compliance with the MPI Master Plan. . . ." At most, these provisions seem to indicate the City's general agreement that the development will move forward in "substantial compliance" with the MPI Master Plan. At issue, therefore, is whether the City's rezoning action is *not* in substantial compliance with the MPI Master Plan.

We have reviewed the MPI Master Plan, which was attached as Exhibit A to the development agreement. The primary features of the planned 650 acre development included approximately 418 acres for residential lots, 22 acres of neighborhood parks, an 18-acre school site, and a 9-acre tennis club/recreation facility. About 32% of the gross area was to be open space, parks, greenbelts, and recreation areas. (Master Plan p. 5)

However, the MPI Master Plan also speaks of "[a]dequate commercial areas to serve the daily needs of the project's inhabitants." (MPI Master Plan p. 6) It mentions "[n]eighborhood convenience shopping locations designed to serve local residents within 'walking distance' to minimize needless vehicle traffic." (Master Plan p. 6) The "central commercial area" was located so as to "minimize pedestrians crossing a major street when walking from shop to shop." (Master Plan p. 7)

We conclude that the MPI Master Plan did envision a comparatively small commercial area for some "convenience shopping locations" for the "project's inhabitants." However, the MPI Master Plan did not foretell a major retail shopping center, such as a "K-Mart" or "Shopko." We believe that the Woodside development may proceed in "substantial compliance" with the MPI Master Plan despite Hailey's rezoning of the central commercial area to a Limited Business zone. Permitted uses within the Limited Business zone include: motels, boarding houses, professional offices, hospitals, medical clinics, daycare facilities, personal service establishments, churches, schools, and recreation facilities. (Hailey Ordinance No. 532, Section 4.5.2) Moreover, the Limited Business zone allows other "conditional uses" upon receipt of a conditional use permit, which include: convenience stores, service stations, pharmacies and medical supply stores, indoor restaurants, electrical and plumbing contractors, and garden supply nurseries. (Hailey Ordinance No. 532, Section 4.5.3) With such uses allowed in Woodside's central commercial area, we believe the development may proceed in substantial compliance with the MPI Master Plan. We do not find in either the development agreement or the MPI Master Plan any explicit language amounting to a "regulatory freeze" or an agreement for permanent zoning. Hence, we reject SGA's contention that Hailey breached the development agreement.

Having found no breach of a "regulatory freeze" or permanent zoning obligation in the development agreement, we need not decide whether such a provision could even be enforced against a City Council exercising its police powers many years later. *See Idaho Falls v. Grimmett*, 63 Idaho 90, 97, 117 P.2d 461, 464 (1941) (police power of a municipality cannot be bartered away even by express contract).

Notes and Comments

1. *Project Size.* Would you expect large, multi-year and multi-phased developments or small developments to be the subject of the most development agreements? Given the certainty that such agreements provide to developers, one might expect that only the first category of projects would employ development agreements as a vehicle for approval, since these types of long-term developments are more in need of protection against later regulatory changes. The empirical evidence, however, indicates that such agreements are often used for smaller projects as well. See Richard Cowart, Experience, Motivations, and Issues, in Development Agreements: Practice, Policy and Prospects 26 (Douglas R. Porter & Lindell L. Marsh eds. 1989) (survey collecting over 100 development agreements in California and reviewing a sample of 40 projects in detail "showed a wide variety of types of projects, size of projects, and provisions in the agreements").

2. *"Contracting Away the Police Power."* In Chapter 2 of this casebook, you learned that one of the principal concerns with contract zoning was the objection that such zoning "contracted away" the city's police power. The same objection can be raised with respect to development agreements. There are now a few related decisions on this issue. *See Morgran Co., Inc. v. Orange County*, 818 So. 2d 640, 643 (Fla. Dist. Ct. App. 2002) ("The problem in this case lies with Orange County's obligation to 'support' Morgran's request for rezoning, as part of that development agreement. If the Board . . . has already contracted to 'support' Morgran's request for rezoning, it has invalidly contracted away its discretionary power. . . . "); *P.C.B. Partnership v. City of Largo*, 549 So. 2d 738 (Fla. Dist. Ct. App. 1989) (overturning

an agreement entered into prior to the state's development agreement statute on the grounds that the local government had contracted away its police powers).

3. *Breach*. Although development agreements are contracts, they have significant public policy ramifications associated with them. If a party breaches a contract, what should the remedy be?

An interesting situation arises where a developer who has entered into a development agreement later decides that it cannot go through with the project. In such a circumstance, is the developer subject to a lawsuit by the local government for specific performance of the contractual terms obligating the developer to put in certain site improvements? *See River Vale Planning Board v. E. & R. Office Interiors, Inc.*, 575 A.2d 55 (N.J. Super. Ct. App. Div. 1990) (agreement was subject to an implied condition that the improvements were required only if the developer proceeded with its project).

The *Sprenger* court held that the city did not violate the law by promising to cooperate. A similar issue arose in *City of Corpus Christi v. Bayfront Assocs., Ltd.*, 814 S.W.2d 98 (Tex. Ct. App. 1991), in which the court held that a city's refusal to attend meetings with the U.S. Army Corps of Engineers was not a breach of a contractual provision to provide "assistance" to the developer.

The *Sprenger* case continued on. The city thereafter voted to amend the city's zoning to redesignate the property in question from "B" to "GR"—general residential. In *Sprenger, Grubb & Associates*, 936 P.2d 343 (Idaho 1999), the Idaho Supreme Court invalidated the action because the general plan did not meet the statutory requirements. See discussion of planning and consistency in Chapter 5, *supra*.

4. Nollan *and* Dolan *Redux*. Do the Supreme Court's *Nollan* and *Dolan* decisions, which you read in Chapter 4, constrain the types of exactions that a local government can negotiate with a developer? Or does the fact that the agreement is "voluntary" free the parties from the constitutional constraints that would otherwise apply if the exactions were imposed as conditions on a development approval? Most development agreements have proceeded on the assumption that *Nollan* and *Dolan* are not binding, and to date no case law has developed on the point. (Would you expect any? Who would have the incentive to challenge such provisions?) One recent article argues that, in entering a development agreement, the municipality "is not granting the landowner the right to develop nor imposing conditions on such development, but instead is promising to protect the developer's investment by not enforcing any subsequent land use regulation. . . ." Thus, it concludes, the municipality "should therefore be free to negotiate its best terms . . . regardless of nexus." David L. Callies and Julie A. Tappendorf, Unconstitutional Land Development Conditions and the Development Agreement Solution: Bargaining for Public Facilities After Nollan and Dolan, 51 Case W. Res. L. Rev. 663, 695 (2001).

One leading article, however, has suggested that "[a] respectable case can be made for the proposition that development agreements quite simply constitute a novel packaging of regulatory requirements, one that implicates very little contract doctrine." Judith Welch Wegner, Moving Toward the Bargaining Table: Contract Zoning, Development Agreements, and the Theoretical Foundations of Government Land Use Deals, 65 N.C. L. Rev. 957, 1000 (1987). If a development agreement is less like a contract and more like traditional regulation, the constitutional restrictions in *Nollan* and *Dolan* cannot be dismissed so easily. Furthermore, is it really accurate to conclude, as suggested above, that the development agreement does not guarantee the right to develop? The conclusion is based on the technical distinction that the municipality must still go through a separate approval process.

On this subject *see also* David L. Callies, Solutions After Dolan: Land Development Agreements, 10 Land Use L. & Zoning Dig., Oct. 1997, at 3, 9 ("The issue here is whether the local government may go further because the development or annexation agreement is a voluntary agreement that neither government nor landowner is compelled to either negotiate or execute. So long as the agreement is indeed voluntary, the answer is almost certainly yes."); Sam D. Starritt & John H. Mcclannahan, Land-Use Planning and Takings: The Validity of Conditional Exactions to Conserve Open Space in the Rocky Mountain, 30 Land & Water L. Rev. 415 (1995) (the constitutional limitations apply to such situations).

5. *Literature*. The literature on development agreements is growing. In addition to the books and articles cited in the notes above, see David L. Callies, Developers' Agreements and Planning Gain, 17 Urb. Law. 599 (1985); Daniel J. Curtin, Jr. & Scott A. Edelstein, Development Agreement Practice in California and Other States, 22 Stetson L. Rev. 761 (1993); Brad K. Schwartz, Development Agreements: Contracting for Vested Rights, 28 B.C. Envtl. Aff. L. Rev. 719 (2001); R. Alan Haywood and David Hartman, Legal Basics for Development Agreements, 32 Tex. Tech. L. Rev. 955 (2001); David S. Goldwich, Development Agreements: A Critical Introduction, 4 J. Land Use & Envtl. L. 249 (1989); Bruce M. Kramer, Development Agreements: To What Extent Are They Enforceable?, 10 Real Est. L.J. 29 (1981); Ted Taub, Development Agreements, 10 Land Use L. & Zoning Dig., Oct. 1990, at 3.

E. DISPUTE RESOLUTION: MEDIATION

The increasingly controversial nature of land use has led to an explosion of litigation over many highly controversial decisions. This litigation has overwhelmingly addressed the procedural regularity of the approval process, not the underlying concerns of the plaintiff. Moreover, like other forms of litigation, land use litigation has caused delays in project implementation even if it is ultimately unsuccessful.

This model of opposition has caused commentators to suggest that alternative means of resolving the dispute would result in better outcomes for all parties. The following materials discuss the primary method suggested: mediation.

The attractiveness of mediation in this context is obvious. It can lead to a mutually agreeable compromise or settlement, which will save the costs and attendant delay of litigation. Given these benefits, although mediation is growing, why isn't it used more widely in land use disputes? Keep this fundamental question in mind as you review the following materials.

EDITH M. NETTER, USING MEDIATION TO RESOLVE LAND USE DISPUTES

15 Zoning & Plan. L. Rep. 25, 27-28 (April 1992)

WHEN AND WHY SHOULD MEDIATION BE USED? . . .

Any case can be mediated if the parties have something to gain from settling instead of going to trial and if each has something it can offer the other side. The attorneys or their clients also must believe that negotiations will not be successful without the assistance of a third party. Since many attorneys are (or consider themselves to be) skilled negotiators, why use a mediator? Circumstances where mediation is useful include where:

- there is a history of failed negotiations between the attorneys or their clients;
- the attorney is having difficulty convincing his or her client that the case is not as "good" as the client makes it out to be;
- the outcome of the case is uncertain and it makes sense, therefore, to retain control.

Mediation also can be used before a permit is issued or a zoning ordinance or plan is created. It should be considered where negotiation already is being used and is deemed appropriate from legal and policy vantage points. The following example illustrates how mediation can be beneficial where a developer submits an application for a controversial development approval. In this example, the neighbors vehemently oppose the proposed project, which includes twenty-five residential buildings. They say they will agree not to oppose a project with ten or fewer buildings. A mediation process is commenced at the suggestion of the city planner. The mediator, brought in by the planner because he foresees considerable controversy over the proposed project, involves the developer, the neighbors, and the planner in a negotiation process. The developer then agrees to revise the plan so that it now provides for a mixed-use project (mostly residential with some commercial), which includes ten buildings and a new site design. The developer is satisfied with the result because the commercial uses would provide a higher return on his investment than would the residential uses alone. The neighbors have agreed not to oppose the project because it is less dense, there is more green space, and the site design reflects the characteristics of the community. The developer then submits the revised plan for special permit approval. The public hearings are held, the neighbors do not oppose and the project is approved with some modifications.

The period before an application is submitted is one stage in the development review process where mediation can occur. Another could be after the permit application is made. Whereas a mediation that occurs before an application is submitted may lead to a developer revising an application, the parties to a post-application mediation process must understand that the decision-making entity still has the authority to approve, deny, or modify the plans. In both instances, mediation is being used to supplement the public hearing process instead of as an alternative to litigation. Regardless of the point at which mediation occurs (so long as it is before a decision is made), it offers the following advantages:

- Positions have not hardened. At this juncture it is easier to engage in joint problem-solving.
- Improved communications and creative problem-solving. Often public hearings do not offer opportunities for meaningful dialogue. More often than not, the parties are showcasing their positions for the benefit of the media.
- Cost savings. If parties are invested in the process that leads to settlement and they feel the decision is satisfactory, they will not bring a lawsuit.

- Improved community relationships. If parties are satisfied with an outcome, they are more likely to work cooperatively in the future.
- Less political fallout. Where a project or policy is controversial, a mediated outcome will mean board members are still responsible for the decision, but there has been a process, in addition to the public hearing, which has carefully taken into account divergent points of view.

The disadvantages of using mediation include that the decision-makers may not accept the recommendation that arises out of the mediation process or that they may accept the recommendation because they want consensus, not because it promotes the public interest as reflected in the underlying regulatory scheme.

In the pre-permit setting, mediation should be considered for those land use disputes that allow discretion on the part of decision-makers. A good example of a discretionary or flexible permitting process is a planned unit development (PUD). Typically involving some combination of a zone change, special permit and site plan review, PUDs are designed to allow decision-makers a great deal of flexibility when they make decisions. There is room, therefore, to negotiate so long as the negotiations remain within the confines of the permit standards. Other types of permits, such as variances, do not allow for discretion. A decision on a variance concerns whether or not a project meets a statutory standard of hardship. Either the standard is or is not met, so negotiation should not be considered. On the other hand, there are many instances where land use decision-making involves considerable discretion and therefore, provides opportunities for negotiation.

Special permits also may be appropriate for mediation. For example, a special permit standard stating that developments shall be "in harmony with the neighborhood" can be interpreted in different ways. . . . Considerable leeway is left for negotiation, if a commission chooses to do so. Another example is a garden-variety rezoning, such as a change from residential to commercial. Here planning commissions, when rendering advice to local legislative bodies, such as city councils, generally have a great deal of discretion. In this context, the use of a mediator to resolve disputes between various factions in the community may not only be appropriate but beneficial as well.

Florida has passed legislation directly addressing the use of mediation in land use disputes. As you consider the provisions of the Florida Dispute Resolution Act, ask yourself whether mediation using the procedures set out in the Act is likely to be successful.

THE FLORIDA LAND USE AND ENVIRONMENTAL DISPUTE RESOLUTION ACT

Fla. Stat. Ann. §70.51 (West Supp. 2003)

70.51. LAND USE AND ENVIRONMENTAL DISPUTE RESOLUTION

(3) Any owner who believes that a development order, either separately or in conjunction with other development orders, or an enforcement action of a

governmental entity, is unreasonable or unfairly burdens the use of the owner's real property, may apply within 30 days after receipt of the order or notice of the governmental action for relief under this section.

(4) To initiate a proceeding under this section, an owner must file a request for relief with the elected or appointed head of the governmental entity that issued the development order or orders, or that initiated the enforcement action. The head of the governmental entity may not charge the owner for the request for relief and must forward the request for relief to the special master who is mutually agreed upon by the owner and the governmental entity within 10 days after receipt of the request. . . .

(15) (a) The special master shall hold a hearing within 45 days after his or her receipt of the request for relief unless a different date is agreed to by all the parties. . . .

(17) In all respects, the hearing must be informal and open to the public and does not require the use of an attorney. The hearing must operate at the direction and under the supervision of the special master. The object of the hearing is to focus attention on the impact of the governmental action giving rise to the request for relief and to explore alternatives to the development order or enforcement action and other regulatory efforts by the governmental entities in order to recommend relief, when appropriate, to the owner.

(a) The first responsibility of the special master is to facilitate a resolution of the conflict between the owner and governmental entities to the end that some modification of the owner's proposed use of the property or adjustment in the development order or enforcement action or regulatory efforts by one or more of the governmental parties may be reached. Accordingly, the special master shall act as a facilitator or mediator between the parties in an effort to effect a mutually acceptable solution. The parties shall be represented at the mediation by persons with authority to bind their respective parties to a solution, or by persons with authority to recommend a solution directly to the persons with authority to bind their respective parties to a solution.

(b) If an acceptable solution is not reached by the parties after the special master's attempt at mediation, the special master shall consider the facts and circumstances set forth in the request for relief and any responses and any other information produced at the hearing in order to determine whether the action by the governmental entity or entities is unreasonable or unfairly burdens the real property. . . .

(19) Within 14 days after the conclusion of the hearing, the special master shall prepare and file with all parties a written recommendation.

(a) If the special master finds that the development order at issue, or the development order or enforcement action in combination with the actions or regulations of other governmental entities, is not unreasonable or does not unfairly burden the use of the owner's property, the special master must recommend that the development order or enforcement action remain undisturbed and the proceeding shall end, subject to the owner's retention of all other available remedies.

(b) If the special master finds that the development order or enforcement action, or the development order or enforcement action in combination with the actions or regulations of other governmental entities, is unreasonable or unfairly burdens use of the owner's property, the special master, with the owner's consent to proceed, may recommend one or more alternatives that protect the public interest served by the development order or enforcement action and regulations at issue but allow for reduced restraints on the use of the owner's real property. . . .

(21) Within 45 days after receipt of the special master's recommendation, the governmental entity responsible for the development order or enforcement action and other governmental entities participating in the proceeding must consult among themselves and each governmental entity must:

(a) Accept the recommendation of the special master as submitted and proceed to implement it by development agreement, when appropriate, or by other method, in the ordinary course and consistent with the rules and procedures of that governmental entity. . . .

(b) Modify the recommendation as submitted by the special master and proceed to implement it by development agreement, when appropriate, or by other method, in the ordinary course and consistent with the rules and procedures of that governmental entity; or

(c) Reject the recommendation as submitted by the special master. Failure to act within 45 days is a rejection unless the period is extended by agreement of the owner and issuer of the development order or enforcement action.

(22) If a governmental entity accepts the special master's recommendation or modifies it and the owner rejects the acceptance or modification, or if a governmental entity rejects the special master's recommendation, the governmental entity must issue a written decision within 30 days that describes as specifically as possible the use or uses available to the subject real property.

Notes and Comments

1. *Terminology*. Arbitration is a system in which a neutral party hears evidence and makes a decision about which party should prevail. In contrast, mediation attempts to facilitate a negotiated agreement among the parties. Which category does the Florida Dispute Resolution Act fall under?

2. *Role Conflicts*. Does the Florida Act combine roles in a way that may hinder the accomplishment of either role? Would the process be improved by eliminating the requirement that the mediator issue a "nonbinding recommendation"? See Lela P. Love, The Top Ten Reasons Why Mediators Should Not Evaluate, 24 Fla. St. U. L. Rev. 937, 938 (1997) (arguing that an "evaluative" mediator—one who "gives advice, makes assessments, states opinions . . . including opinions on the likely court outcome, proposes a fair or workable resolution to an issue or the dispute, or presses the parties to accept a particular resolution"—plays a role that is inconsistent with the role of a mediator).

On the other hand, shouldn't a mediator be able to suggest a "workable resolution," as long as the parties trust the mediator's impartiality?

3. *Mediation versus Litigation*. Lawyers representing clients in a land use dispute often will not consider the possibility of using mediation to settle the dispute. The use of mediation in such disputes, however, appears to be on the rise. For example, the Oregon Department of Land Conservation and Development has actively promoted the use of mediation, and the State of Massachusetts has retained a mediator to seek settlement of disputes over decisions by local conservation

commissions regarding the filling of wetlands. *See* Lawrence Susskind, Using Assisted Negotiation to Settle Land Use Disputes (1999) (5 case studies of land use mediations).

Consider also the following comparison of a case settled by mediation with another case that is being litigated. Both cases occurred in Oregon:

Bott's Marsh

The Bott's Marsh case is a dispute over the development of a wetland area. . . . A developer proposed filling a wetland area large enough to allow for the development of a marina, motel-boatel, restaurant, shops and parking facilities. There has been much opposition, which so far has resulted in one trip to the Oregon Supreme Court. . . .

Results: Time spent to date on obtaining permits has been seven years and five months. Costs to DSL in attorneys fees alone has been $12,665, and costs to the developer for attorney and consulting fees is estimated to be approximately $250,000.

Hedges Creek Marsh

This case involves the proposed development by Zidell Resources of a 140-acre parcel, including 48 acres of freshwater wetlands, into a residential and light industrial area. Tualitin's Wetlands Protection Ordinance required that before Zidell could get the city's approval of the proposed development, it had to work out all conflicts with the applicable state agencies and interest groups. . . . This process began in early 1988 with unassisted negotiations between the various interested parties and progressed into mediated negotiations. By March 1990 the parties had reached a final agreement on all outstanding issues. . . .

Results: Time spent to date has been two years and six months. The costs of mediation were $3,000, half paid by DSL and half by Zidell. Attorneys fees, consulting fees and staff time costs for Zidell were approximately $14,000.

Lucinda D. Moyano, A Tale of Two Wetlands, 52 Or. St. Bar Bull. 39 (1992).

What are the kinds of factors that might lead you to consider recommending the use of mediation to a client? See, e.g., C. Gregory Buntz & Susan Sherry, A Continuum of Dispute Resolution Approaches in Symposium, Resolving Land Use & Environmental Disputes, Land Use Forum 181, 184 (Summer 1993) ("Traditional dispute resolution approaches, particularly judicial and administrative procedures, simply are not designed to explore the interests of the parties or assess the trade-offs disputants would be willing to make. Furthermore, the named dispute often masks the real issue."). Think carefully about the difference between "rights," which may be enforced through litigation, and "interests" of the parties. The two may or may not coincide.

4. *Advantages and Disadvantages*. The Netter article lists the following benefits of using mediation: (1) ease of problem solving because parties' positions have not hardened; (2) opportunities for meaningful dialogue among parties; (3) cost savings over litigation as an alternative; (4) improved relations among the parties in the future; (5) less political fallout.

Critics list a number of possible disadvantages to mediation: (1) there is no certainty that the process will result in a settlement; (2) the outcome of the dispute does not have to be "principled," i.e., based on law; (3) an imbalance of negotiation skills could be reflected in the solution; (4) no one is accountable for the result of a mediation, and city council members may somehow "abrogate their responsibility" by agreeing to a mediated settlement. Barbara McAdoo & Larry Bakken, Mediation in Public Interest Law, 22 Urb. Law. 179, 189-190 (1990).

Which of these benefits and criticisms, if any, do you find convincing?

5. *Issues Raised by the Florida Dispute Resolution Act*. Consider the following issues raised by the Florida Dispute Resolution Act or (in some instances) by mediation generally:

(a) *Enabling Legislation*. Does a municipality need a state statute enabling it to enter into mediation before it may do so?

(b) *Triggering the Process*. What action on the part of the government triggers the Act's processes? In *Hanna v. Envt'l Protection Comm'n*, 735 So. 2d 544 (Fla. Dist. Ct. App. 1999), a developer pulled a building permit and began clearing his land. The Commission then advised him by letter that this action might be in violation of wetlands regulations. The developer sought to use the dispute resolution mechanism in the Act. The court found that it was not yet available to him, given the stage of proceedings.

(c) *Choosing the Special Master*. What if the parties do not agree on a special master? Does the court have the power to impose one? Would you be willing to accept a special master who was not an attorney?

(d) *Timing*. What if the timetable for the use of a mediator is inconsistent with the timetable for either completing a judicial proceeding or initiating judicial review? The Florida Act tolls the time for seeking judicial review of a local government action until the local government acts upon the special master's recommendation. If an administrative appeal is available that will take less than four months to complete, that appeal must be pursued. Within thirty days of the conclusion of that appeal, or within thirty days after the four-month period expires, a request for relief can be filed.

(e) *Delay*. If you represent a project proponent, how will you ensure that the negotiation does not drag out for a lengthy period of time? Under this scenario your client is hurt financially, because it must pay the carrying costs on its investment in land while the return on that investment is delayed. *See* Pa. Stat. Ann. tit. 53, §10908.1 (West 1997) (if a municipality offers mediation, it shall specify "development terms and conditions" for completing mediation, "including time limits for such completion").

(f) *The Role of Third Parties*. Should third parties, such as neighbors who object to a proposal, be given a formal role in a mediation? Consider that any party who is not a signatory to any mediated settlement retains the right to initiate litigation against a project. *See Thomas v. Lima Township Board of Trustees*, Nos. 95CA83, 95CA84 1996 WL 243804 (Ohio Ct. App. 1996) (unpublished court of appeal decision in which opponents sought to intervene in litigation after board reached a settlement with project applicants through mediation).

(g) *Admissions*. Can facts that come out in an unsuccessful mediation be used later in litigation? *See Medeiros v. Hawaii County Planning Commission*, 797 P.2d 59, 64 (Haw. Ct. App. 1990) (president of community association wrote a letter to the Planning Commission "pointing out that, during mediation, Applicants revealed there will be hydrogen sulfide emission from the wells, contrary to their statement in the application").

In *Wilmington Hospitality v. New Castle County*, 788 A.2d 536 (Del. Ch. Ct. 2001), *appeal refused, Wilmington Hospitality v. Republic Bank*, 781 A.2d 697 (Del. 2001), a developer sought court enforcement of a purported agreement arrived at in a dispute resolution process. The court held that the mediation was confidential, and the plaintiff could not rely on discussions in that process to prove an agreement.

(h) *Unfair and Unreasonable Burdens*. Under the Florida Act, if the parties fail to reach agreement, must the Special Master determine whether the government's action burdens the property "unfairly" or is "unreasonable"? Fla. Stat. Ann. §70.51(17)(b) (West Supp. 2003). What is an unfair or unreasonable burden?

In *Scott v. Polk County*, 793 So. 2d 85 (Fla. Dist. Ct. App. 2001), mediation failed. There was an ongoing lawsuit at the time. The special master then issued a report stating that whether the master proceeded to the non-binding recommendation stage would depend on either the parties or the court providing direction. Is that action consistent with the statute?

If the parties do not accept a mediated settlement, the outcome of the Florida process is that the government entities must issue a written decision "describing the available uses of the property." The parties are then free to litigate the matter. Do you think that in most cases litigation will still occur after the mediation process is exhausted, or is settlement the most likely outcome of mediations under the law?

The Florida legislation is discussed in Martin R. Dix et al., Land Use and Environmental Dispute Resolution: The Special Master, 69 Fla. Bar J. 63 (Nov. 1995); David L. Powell et al., A Measured Step to Protect Private Property Rights, 23 Fla. St. U.L. Rev. 255 (1995).

6. *Open Meeting Laws and Mediation*. The techniques used by mediators can include caucusing with individual parties and shuttling from "room to room" to seek an acceptable resolution. The parties must decide which tradeoffs to accept, and which to reject, at that moment. The model of land use regulation reflected in most state laws, however, is one of open decisionmaking in a public forum. Can the two be reconciled? Should so-called public meetings laws, which generally require that meetings of a quorum of public officials must be held publicly, apply to mediations?

The issue arose in *Sovereign v. Dunn*, 498 N.W.2d 62 (Minn. Ct. App. 1993), in which two of the five members of the city council of the City of Lake Elmo attended a series of nonpublic mediation sessions in an attempt to resolve a border dispute with a neighboring city. The court held that the meetings did not constitute a "committee, subcommittee, board, department or commission" under the act because the group was not capable of exercising the decisionmaking powers of a governmental body (a capacity presumed where a quorum exists), and there was no delegation of power from the governing body. *Id.* at 67.

What would be necessary for a plaintiff to prove that there was a "delegation of power" from the governing body? Does the court's decision virtually invite situations in which the council delegates the negotiating to less than a majority with the "tacit understanding" that the non-quorum is speaking for the entire council? Or, since any result of the mediation must be formally ratified in open hearing, is the public interest fully protected?

What would be wrong with requiring all mediation discussions to be open to the public?

7. *Settlement Parameters*. Any settlement among the parties cannot violate the substantive law of either the state or the local jurisdiction. For example, in *Ad-Ex, Inc. v. City of Chicago*, 617 N.E.2d 333 (Ill. App. Ct. 1993) the court refused to accept a settlement in which the city agreed to waive a set-back requirement for signs. *Compare Summit Township Taxpayers Assoc. v. Summit Township Board of Supervisors*, 411 A.2d 1263 (Pa. Commw. Ct. 1980) (settlement upheld even though it required the grant of a variance).

8. *Literature*. Other articles on mediation include Jonathan M. Davidson & Susan L. Trevarthen, Land Use Mediation: Another Smart Growth Alternative, 33 Urb. Law. 705 (2001); Rosemary O'Leary, Tracy Yandle, & Tamilyn Moore, The State of the States in Environmental Dispute Resolution, 14 Ohio St. J. on Disp. Resol. 515 (1999) (surveying environmental dispute resolution mechanisms in all fifty states); Lawrence Susskind, Mieke Vander Wansen, & Armand Ciccarelli, Mediating Land Use Disputes: Pros & Cons, Lincoln Institute of Land Policy (2000); William B. Fulton, Reaching Consensus in Land Use Negotiations (Washington DC: American Planning Ass'n, 1989); Jeffrey B. Groy & Donald L. Elliott, Using Arbitration and Mediation to Resolve Land Use Disputes, 1988-1989 Current Mun. Probs. 190; Edith M. Netter, Using Mediation To Supplement Zoning Hearings, Land Use L. 3 (Oct. 1992); Joseph P. Tomain, Land Use Mediation for Planners, 7 Mediation Q. 163 (1989). On the Florida Act, *see, e.g.*, Vivian J. Monaco, The Harris Act: What Relief from Government Regulation Does It Provide for Private Property Owners?, 26 Stetson L. Rev. 861 (1967); Nancy E. Stroud & Thomas G. Wright, Florida's Private Property Rights Act — What Will It Mean for Florida's Future, 20 Nova L. Rev. 683 (1996).

F. MARKET-BASED SYSTEMS: DEREGULATION

As your study of land use controls has revealed, the ability to make use of privately held land is heavily regulated in the United States. By this point you should have a good understanding of the tools by which such regulation is undertaken and the goals of the regulatory system. You should also have some sense, especially from the takings cases, of the costs that regulation imposes, both on landowners and, ultimately, on homebuyers.

Are these costs worthwhile? Or could a system with much less government intervention accomplish the goals sought while, at the same time, reducing the costs of land development?

HOUSTON TRADEMARK INTACT: CITY REMAINS LARGEST IN U.S. WITHOUT ZONING ORDINANCE

Associated Press, Nov. 4, 1993

HOUSTON — Things hadn't changed much when Houstonians woke up Wednesday, the day after the election.

Mayor Bob Lanier overwhelmingly was re-elected to a second two-year term and Houston remained the largest U.S. city without a zoning ordinance.

For the third time in 45 years, voters rejected an effort to zone Houston's erratic development.

With all precincts counted, 86,060, or 52 percent, voted against zoning, while 79,063, or 48 percent, were for it.

It was a narrow victory, but a win all the same for zoning foes who waged a fierce campaign and outspent their opponents.

"The election shows how reluctant Houstonians are to give up their free enterprise instincts. They're extreme believers in the free-market forces," said Stephen Klineberg, a sociology professor at Rice University.

Although many neighborhoods are protected by deed restrictions, Houston has had no overall zoning ordinance since it was founded more than 150 years ago.

Over the past several years, zoning proponents had been crafting an ordinance to zone every inch of the city's 586 square miles.

The city council approved the ordinance, but anti-zoning forces gathered enough signatures to get the issue put on the Tuesday ballot so the voters could have the final say.

They spoke as they have in the past, saying no to zoning.

Zoning proponents—including Mr. Lanier—claimed the ordinance was needed to protect neighborhoods.

A lack of zoning has been Houston's trademark of sorts. In some areas, bars, liquor stores, tattoo parlors, auto shops and other businesses exist in residential neighborhoods. High-rise office buildings also tower over other neighborhoods.

But opponents claimed zoning would raise taxes, cost jobs and restrict growth in the nation's fourth-largest city. They also criticized their opponents for coming up with a zoning ordinance without a comprehensive planning proposal. . . .

■ ROBERT H. NELSON, PRIVATIZING THE NEIGHBORHOOD: A PROPOSAL TO REPLACE ZONING WITH PRIVATE COLLECTIVE PROPERTY RIGHTS TO EXISTING NEIGHBORHOODS

7 Geo. Mason L. Rev. 827 (1999)

In the second half of the twentieth century, new economic forces wrought yet another transformation in private property ownership. These forces included: (1) higher densities of development, (2) the desire for precise control over neighborhood character, (3) more economical private provision of common neighborhood services, and (4) greater interest in common recreational and other facilities. They made private neighborhood associations the choice for millions of people for their residential property. . . .

To date, almost all neighborhood associations have arisen as part of the development of a new neighborhood. . . . However, in neighborhoods previously developed with individual ownership of the land and structures, there is little prospect for the formation of a neighborhood association. Doing so would require the individual members of the neighborhood to surrender voluntarily part of their individual rights and accept collective control over the use of the exterior parts of their property by their neighbors. Obtaining such voluntary consent from several hundred or more property owners is extremely time consuming and almost certainly would involve major problems with holdouts and other high transactions costs. Few existing neighborhoods have even considered making such an effort.

. . . I propose enactment of legislation to facilitate the establishment of neighborhood associations in existing neighborhoods. The establishment of a new legal mechanism for this purpose would allow existing neighborhoods to take advantage of collective control over the neighborhood common environment and the private provision of common services, just as new neighborhoods are doing in such large numbers. Moreover, such an approach would facilitate the "deregulation" or "privatization" of zoning. Private neighborhood associations could administer the collective controls over neighborhood quality now exercised through land use regulations at the municipal level. Compared with a private property right regime, and as described below, the government exercise of zoning powers has several major disadvantages. . . .

To offer the advantages of neighborhood associations to existing neighborhoods, state governments should enact a new law to allow self-governance in these neighborhoods, through new collective private ownerships. For purposes of discussion, I propose the following five-step process, recognizing that many variations are possible.

1. A group of individual property owners in an existing neighborhood could petition the state government to form a neighborhood association. . . .

2. The state government would then certify that the proposed neighborhood met certain standards of reasonableness. . . .

3. If the application met state requirements, the state would authorize a neighborhood committee to negotiate a service transfer agreement with the appropriate municipal government. . . .

4. Once the state certified the neighborhood's proposed municipal transfer agreement, the state would schedule a neighborhood election. . . .

5. The state would supervise the neighborhood election. Approval of the neighborhood association would require both of the following: (1) an affirmative vote of property owners cumulatively representing 90% or more of the total value of the proposed neighborhood; and (2) an affirmative vote by 75% or more of the individual unit owners in the neighborhood. If the election met these conditions, all property owners in the neighborhood would be required to join the neighborhood association and would be subject to the full terms and conditions . . . in the neighborhood association charter. The neighborhood association would have the right to collect assessments to fund its operation from each association member.

III. Advantages over Zoning . . .

While zoning and neighborhood association control over neighborhood environmental quality do overlap in a number of key respects, the private neighborhood has several major advantages. For example, except where an historic or other special district can be justified, zoning does not cover the fine details of neighborhood architecture, trees and shrubbery, yard maintenance, and other aesthetic matters that may have a major impact on the character of the neighborhood. Thus, neighborhood associations have a considerably greater degree of authority over actions potentially influencing the character of the neighborhood than zoning typically affords.

In addition, the administration of zoning takes place at the municipal level, where political considerations often include many people who are not residents of the neighborhood. But, in matters such as the control of fine details of neighborhood architecture, there is no need or justification for broader municipal involvement. Indeed, under zoning the substantial influence on such matters by outsiders leaves the neighborhood exposed to regulatory actions that it does not want. This lack of secure control over the details of the administration of neighborhood zoning leads to neighborhoods' reluctance to accept more precise and comprehensive zoning controls over aesthetic matters.

Moreover, because zoning is a form of public regulation, the direct sale of zoning is not considered permissible (it would be "bribery"). However, if the exclusion of a use was an ordinary exercise of a private property right, neighborhoods could sell rights of entry (say for a new neighborhood convenience store) into the neighborhood, sell rights to make certain broader changes in land use within the neighborhood, or even sell all the neighborhood property in one package for comprehensive redevelopment. The private neighborhood's ability to put rights of entry into the neighborhood in the market would introduce greater flexibility in metropolitan land markets, significantly improving the efficiency of their operation.

Furthermore, the ability to sell zoning allows the neighborhood to manage a transition to a different use of the neighborhood. Currently, because an entity outside the neighborhood controls changes in land uses under zoning, and because these changes often do not bring financial gains to the neighborhood collectively (and may involve losses for some individuals), the residents of existing neighborhoods typically resist almost all land use change. Zoning serves many neighborhoods well as a protective instrument for maintaining the existing character of the neighborhood, but fails wherever the objective is the transition from one type of use to another. Similarly, the legal mechanism of private neighborhood ownership could usefully be extended to "neighborhoods" of farmers owning large tracts of vacant land in transitional developing areas on the fringes of metropolitan regions.

Lastly, the advantages of neighborhood associations extend beyond improvements on zoning. Neighborhood associations can serve as a vehicle to provide more efficient and effective garbage collection, recreation facility maintenance, and many other common services. Creating a neighborhood association can establish and sustain a strong spirit of community in the neighborhood, not usually found in neighborhoods without a formal institutional status. Private neighborhoods might also encourage residents' involvement in political affairs, both locally and at higher levels of government. . . .

Notes and Comments

1. *The Houston Zoning Campaign.* Analysis of the November 1993 Houston vote revealed some interesting facts about the election. One important fact was that voters rejecting zoning came from quite different backgrounds; both affluent and low income neighborhoods of Houston voted decisively against the measure. Another (perhaps ironic) fact was that, according to one of the leading opponents of zoning, "television ads critical of comprehensive planning in conjunction with the proposed ordinance were perhaps his group's most effective campaign messages."

The opponent stated that his polls showed pro-zoning sentiment dropped 26 points after the ads began their initial run. Julie Mason, Haves, Have-Nots Joined Same Side to Defeat Zoning, Houston Chronicle Nov. 4, 1993, at 25.

2. *Criticism of Land Use Regulation*. A substantial body of academic articles and books strongly suggests that the time has come to do away with zoning and other similar land use regulations. See, e.g., Bernard H. Siegan, Land Use Without Zoning (1972); Douglas Kmiec, Deregulating Land Use: An Alternative Free Enterprise Development System, 130 U. Pa. L. Rev. 28 (1981); Jan Z. Krasnowiecki, Abolish Zoning, 31 Syracuse L. Rev. 719 (1980). A particularly important article is Robert C. Ellickson, Alternatives to Zoning: Covenants, Nuisance Rules, and Fines As Land Use Controls, 40 U. Chi. L. Rev. 681 (1973). Professor Ellickson believes that a mechanism for internalizing land use externalities is needed but advocates use of private deed restrictions and enforcement of nuisance laws.

This body of criticism is joined with another stream of criticism coming from a different perspective: the argument that land use controls are tools to promote the exclusion of the poor and minorities. See, e.g., J. Peter Byrne, Are Suburbs Unconstitutional?, 85 Geo. L.J. 2265 (1997). Others, advocating the need for increasing housing opportunities, also strongly criticize land use controls. See, e.g., United States President's Commission on Housing, The Report of the President's Commission on Housing 202 (1982) (recommending reconsideration of the decision in *Village of Euclid v. Ambler Realty*, read in Chapter 2 of this casebook, which sustained the constitutionality of zoning).

3. *Houston As a Free Market Exemplar*. Many of these articles cite the Houston experience as evidence that zoning is unnecessary. *See* Bernard H. Siegan, Non-Zoning Is the Best Zoning, 31 Cal. W.L. Rev. 127, 130 (1994). The criticism aligns itself with the economist's stress on markets bringing increased economic efficiency.

But at what price? One article has suggested that Houston is not a good example of a free market in land use. Jane E. Larson, Free Markets Deep in the Heart of Texas, 84 Geo. L. J. 179 (1995). Professor Larson notes that, although Houston has no planning agency or zoning ordinance, it has adopted other land use regulations such as controls on lot sizes, business placement, and setback requirements. Her article asserts that a "better example" of an unregulated market exists in the unincorporated Texas counties ("colonias") that border Mexico, where there are no zoning laws and, until recently, no subdivision or infrastructure requirements. She found that "average housing conditions fall below minimum standards of human habitability that apply in other communities," endangering the health and safety of residents and those of surrounding communities. *Id.* at 185. Professor Larson also wonders "why the kind of empirical evidence presented in this article has been so rare in the land use debate." *Id.* at 228.

4. *Privatizing Zoning*. Professor Nelson's article presents a different alternative: encouraging the formation of private associations. In essence, he argues that private associations can perform many of the same functions as zoning, but more efficiently. Do you agree with that premise? What would be lost, if anything, if such a proposal were implemented?

Nelson also argues that the creation of private neighborhoods would go far towards solving two social problems. It would improve inner-city areas by reducing the rate of crime, and in rural areas that will soon face development, groups of farmers would open large areas for lower and moderate income housing. 7 Geo Mason L. Rev. at 827. Would inner city areas have the resources needed to accomplish the goal of reducing crime? Would efficiencies and collective neighborhood effort make up for this lack of resources? As far as the housing is concerned, should concerns over sprawl and its environmental effects (addressed in Chapter 11) cause second thoughts? *See* Steven J. Eagle, Privatizing Urban Land Use Regulation: The Problem of Consent, 7 Geo. Mason L. Rev. 905 (1999) (questioning whether non-unanimous privatization can be efficient and whether the proposal will really further individual liberty).

Is the Nelson proposal in some way logically inexorable, given the rapid growth of homeowners' associations?

5. *Privatizing Water Quality Protection.* The Texas legislature passed a law that has overtones of privatization of land use decisions. Under its provisions, landowners in the "extraterritorial" jurisdiction of certain cities could create "water quality protection zones." They would designate a zone by filing with the state a general description of water quality protection facilities and proposed land uses for the zone. The Texas Natural Resource Conservation Commission would have to approve. If it did, the adjoining municipality could not enforce a large variety of ordinances, including subdivision requirements or environmental regulations, that are inconsistent with or impair the ability to implement and operate the land use plan and water quality plan as filed. Tex. Water Code §26.179(i).

The Texas Supreme Court concluded that the legislation was an unconstitutional delegation of legislative powers to a private landowner. *FM Properties Operating Co. v. City of Austin*, 22 S.W.3d 368 (Tex. 2000). A livid dissent argued that the legislature was merely restoring private property rights to landowners. Are the efficiencies involved in authorizing private plans outweighed by risks to the public health or environment?

6. *The Persistence of Zoning*. In other areas of the economy, such as the airline, telecommunications, and electric industries, academic criticism of a regulatory regime has brought about extensive deregulation. Despite the academic criticism of zoning, however, there have been very few political attempts to repeal all zoning. See Eric H. Steele, Participation and Rules—The Functions of Zoning, 1986 Am. B. Found. Res. J. 709, 713 (1987) (noting that resistance to changing the basic nature of zoning "springs from a widespread, if unarticulated, perception that the institution is serving some vital social function"). Indeed, land use regulation appears to be growing more complex.

Does the resistance to changing the present system confirm the contention of some critics that zoning simply reflects the majority's economic self-interests, or does it demonstrate that zoning (and other related types of land use regulation) serve valid public purposes? Does it validate the underlying theory of the Nelson article? *See* Bradley C. Karkkainen, Zoning: A Reply to the Critics, 10 J. Land Use & Envtl. L. 45, 47 (1994) (arguing that "many of the critiques, despite the broad claims of their authors, should not be taken as general indictments of zoning, but rather as indicators of particular dysfunctions that must be addressed if zoning is to work effectively").

PART FOUR

BALANCING GROWTH MANAGEMENT AND THE NEED FOR HOUSING

11

Growth Management

A. INTRODUCTION

1. The New Experiments in "Growth Control"

Growth controls are of relatively recent vintage. Until the early 1970s, only a handful of jurisdictions had adopted growth control measures. Certain forces then coalesced to cause cities to reexamine how their land use authority might be used. One impetus was a "first wave" of criticism of "urban sprawl," a by-product of the strong economic development that took place in the 1950s and 1960s. During the now-famous baby boom that followed World War Two, families with children fled the cities for new houses in the suburbs. In time, the by-products of such development became evident: increased air pollution, decay of inner cities, decreased open space, and loss of the amenities of "small town" life. With recognition of these new environmental and aesthetic concerns came an equally powerful economic worry: the realization that new developments were not paying their own way with respect to the public facilities that they required. Cities increasingly found it difficult to fund the municipal services needed by new developments.

For all these reasons, the attraction of "managing" or "limiting" growth in some way gradually grew, and various experiments by local governments in growth control began in earnest. This chapter introduces the student to the legal issues raised by the principal modern mechanisms used for controlling growth — mechanisms whose use has become widespread over the past 25 years.

2. *The Growth Control Techniques*

In the beginning, there were the temporary moratoria: short-term "freezes" on development while a planning process determined what permanent steps should be taken. This type of moratorium is the subject of the decision in *Naylor v. Township of Hellam*, a principal case in this chapter. Short-term moratoria can provoke bitter opposition, because they are often passed in response to particular development proposals that would be allowable under the existing zoning and regulatory standards. Developers feel that the rules are being changed unfairly; the local government, in contrast, sees the need to re-examine its policies before long-term development commitments are made. Statutes increasingly regulate the ability of local jurisdictions to adopt short-term moratoria, and the cases often turn on the wording of the statute in the particular jurisdiction.

In the 1980s, a sort of low-volume debate began about whether a total moratorium on development could constitute a taking. Some argued that the Supreme Court's recognition of a "temporary taking" in *First English Evangelical Lutheran Church*, 482 U.S. 304 (1987) (reprinted in Chapter 7), meant that a moratorium was a taking of property, because it deprived the landowner of all reasonable use. In 2002, the Supreme Court settled the dispute by holding that a reasonable moratorium was not a taking. *Tahoe-Sierra Property Owners Ass'n v. Tahoe Regional Planning Agency*, 535 U.S. 302 (2002) (reprinted in Chapter 7).

On a long-term basis, some jurisdictions adopted so-called tempo controls, absolute caps on the number of building permits to be issued in a particular year. Among other questions, these types of controls raise interesting issues about how a limited number of building authorizations should be allocated. By lottery? By a point system of some sort? Other systems tie further development to improvements in infrastructure, such as roads, sewage systems, schools, and so forth.

Yet another set of jurisdictions established urban growth boundaries, attempts to separate areas in which growth would be encouraged from those areas, outside the boundary limits, where agriculture, natural resource production, and open space would take precedence. In *1000 Friends of Oregon v. Wasco County Court*, reprinted in this chapter, you will see how such limits operate in Oregon, whose land use system emphasizes them. The Oregon experience has provoked a national debate about whether the results in Oregon are good indicators of the efficacy of urban growth limits in general, or whether the situation in Oregon, particularly in the Portland area, is idiosyncratic.

3. *Classic Cases*

These legal instruments predictably raised new issues about the statutory authority of local governments to adopt them and the constitutional limits of land use authority under the police power. The legal challenges brought against the new growth control ordinances led to "classic" landmark decisions on their legality, several of which are included in this chapter. One is *Golden v. Planning Board of the Town of Ramapo*, in which the New York Court of Appeals upheld the famous

Ramapo ordinance, a regulatory scheme that tied residential building to the completion of infrastructure and capital improvement benchmarks over an 18-year cycle. Another is *Construction Industry Ass'n v. City of Petaluma*, also a principal case in this chapter. This decision by the United States Court of Appeals for the Ninth Circuit rejected various constitutional challenges to Petaluma's yearly cap on the number of building permits that it would issue.

These cases set the pattern for judicial decisions upholding a variety of growth control mechanisms over the next two decades. Because the courts in each case upheld the growth control devices at issue, many local jurisdictions patterned their own ordinances after them. Thus, these cases have had nationwide effects on land use practices.

These types of growth control measures, so different in purpose from most traditional land use controls, inevitably caused much criticism, and a backlash against them began to develop. The criticism centered around the charge that such ordinances unduly hamper the supply of housing and have a particularly deleterious effect on the underprivileged. Critics also weighed in with economic arguments that growth controls were a prime contributor to the skyrocketing housing prices found in many parts of the country during the late 1980s and that they unduly inhibit job creation and economic development.

4. *The Debate Resumes: Sprawl and "Smart Growth"*

In the late 1990s, the tide in the debate turned again. Fueled by the economic boom of the mid-1990s, growth boomed throughout the United States, particularly in the western United States and in the suburbs of large cities. "New towns" sprung up outside of older ones, and commuting distances to work lengthened. Soon, the criticism of "urban sprawl" gathered steam, and articles appeared in newspapers and magazines. A so-called smart growth reform movement led by the American Planning Association emerged, advocating certain principles and reforms. Some legislators and elected officials led political movements based on "smart growth." And, in predictable response, critics of the "smart growth" movement emerged.

The last part of this chapter contains a variety of current views on the growth debate. The excerpts will give you a snapshot of the debate and help clarify your own views on this contentious subject.

B. MORATORIA AND INTERIM FREEZES

The moratorium is the simplest kind of growth control device. It is traditionally used as a stop-gap measure, designed to "buy time" while the jurisdiction completes a planning process. In the meantime, the local jurisdiction avoids making land use decisions that may be inconsistent with the final plan then under preparation.

The following case illustrates the application of a "short-term" moratorium and some of the issues that this type of moratorium presents.

■ NAYLOR v. TOWNSHIP OF HELLAM

565 Pa. 397, 773 A.2d 770 (2001)

ZAPPALA, Justice.

This appeal presents the issue of whether a municipality may enact a temporary moratorium on certain types of subdivision and land development while the municipality revises its zoning and subdivision land development ordinances. We hold that the Municipalities Planning Code (MPC), Act of July 31, 1968, P.L. 805, *as reenacted and amended*, 53 P.S. §§10101-11202, does not grant a municipality such power. . . .

. . . Appellants, Irvin S. Naylor, Harry H. Fox., Jr., and Valley Acres, Inc., each own or have an interest in tracts of undeveloped land in Hellam Township, York County. On July 20, 1995, the Hellam Township Board of Supervisors (Board) enacted Ordinance No. 1995-10, which imposed a moratorium on new residential subdivision and land development for a period of one year. . . . The express purpose of the ordinance was to suspend certain subdivision and land development approvals while the Township completed the process of revising its comprehensive plan, so as to prevent development that is inconsistent with proposed revisions. *Id.* at §1. The moratorium expired by its own terms on July 25, 1996, but was extended by ordinance for an additional two month period on August 1, 1996. Hellam Township Ordinance No. 1996-5. . . .

Appellants subsequently filed the instant action, seeking a declaratory judgment that the moratorium was invalid . . .

Initially, we note that it is fundamental that municipalities are creatures of the state and that the authority of the Legislature over their powers is supreme. *Denbow v. Borough of Leetsdale*, 556 Pa. 567, 729 A.2d 1113, 1118 (1999). Municipal corporations have no inherent powers and may do only those things that the Legislature has expressly or by necessary implication placed within their power to do. *Id.*; *In re Gagliardi*, 401 Pa. 141, 163 A.2d 418 (1960). . . .

The parties agree that neither the MPC nor the SCTC [Second Class Township Code] expressly grants a municipality the power to impose a moratorium on subdivision approvals. Our inquiry therefore becomes whether such power is implicitly granted or is incidental to those powers expressly conferred.

We begin our analysis by examining the relevant provisions of the MPC. In doing so, we recognize that zoning enabling legislation, as opposed to zoning ordinances themselves, must be liberally construed in order to effect its purposes. . . .

Section 105 of the MPC sets forth the broad purpose of the Act, which is to protect and promote citizen safety, health and morals, accomplish coordinated development, promote energy conservation, provide for the general welfare by guiding and protecting development and growth and permit municipalities to minimize such problems as may presently exist or which may be foreseen. 53 P.S. §10105. To carry out some of these objectives, the statute expressly grants municipalities the authority to create and adopt a comprehensive development plan, *id.* at §§10301 and 10302, and to regulate development by enacting subdivision and land development ordinances. *Id.* at §§10501 and 10601. The MPC provides that such ordinances may include, among other things, provisions for insuring that the layout of the subdivision and land development conforms to the comprehensive plan, *id.* at §10503(2)(i), and provisions for encouraging and promoting flexibility, economy and ingenuity in the layout and design of subdivisions. *Id.* at §10503(5). The MPC further states that zoning ordinances may permit, prohibit and regulate uses of land, areas and dimensions of land as well as the density of population and intensity of use. *Id.* at §§10603(b)(1), (3) and (4). A catch-all provision states that zoning ordinances may contain "such other provisions as may be necessary to implement the purposes of [the MPC]." *Id.* at §10603(c)(4).

[T]he Commonwealth Court found that the power to enact a temporary moratorium while the Township revises its comprehensive plan is incidental to these expressly granted powers. We disagree. The practical effect of the enactment of the moratorium was to suspend the existing zoning ordinances applicable to subdivision approval until the revised ordinances became effective. Even construing the provisions of the MPC liberally, we find that the power to *enact* a zoning ordinance, for whatever purpose, does not necessarily include the power to *suspend* a valid zoning ordinance to the prejudice of a land owner. *Compare* 53 P.S. §10609.2 (express grant of authority for municipality to invalidate zoning ordinance for period not to exceed 180 days while it enacts curative amendment). More significantly, the power to *suspend* land development has historically been viewed in this Commonwealth as a power distinct from and not incidental to any power to *regulate* land development. Accordingly, as the MPC is silent regarding land planning through the temporary suspension of development, we decline to condone a municipality's exercise of such power.

We find support for our decision in prior case law. In *Kline v. Harrisburg*, 362 Pa. 438, 68 A.2d 182 (1949), property owners applied for a building permit authorizing the construction of an apartment building. While the application was pending, the City of Harrisburg enacted an ordinance prohibiting all construction other than single family dwellings in an attempt to preserve the status quo of residential districts while the city completed its new zoning plan. The property owners sought to restrain the city from enforcing the provisions of what they referred to as an "interim" zoning ordinance, and to direct the city to issue the requested building permit.

Our Court . . . rejected the city's argument that the Third Class City Law included an implied or inherent power to pass an interim ordinance suspending development. The city contended, as does the Township in the instant case, that if it did not possess such power, property owners could always defeat the local governing body's efforts in establishing a new comprehensive zoning plan by racing to get their projects approved before the enactment of a new zoning ordinance.

Our Court's response to this argument was two-fold. We stated:

> In the first place, although the argument is not entirely without merit, it is one which must be directed to the legislature and not to the courts. If the legislature wishes to authorize the enactment of a "temporary" or "interim" ordinance to maintain the status quo it can so provide by legislation with proper safeguards. In the second place, apparently experience has not indicated that the failure to pass a "temporary" or "interim" ordinance has been any substantial menace to zoning. . . . Although there are scores and possibly hundreds of municipalities in Pennsylvania which have enacted zoning ordinances in accordance with the expressed provisions of the relevant statutes, all of which are similar in nature, there is no indication that we could find either by proposed legislation or by cases in any of the courts of this State that

> these municipalities have suffered from inability to maintain the status quo during the enactment of zoning ordinances.

68 A.2d at 189.

We recognize that *Kline* is not dispositive of the instant matter since it predated the MPC and instead interpreted the Third Class City Law. What is clear from the decision, however, is that the power to impose a moratorium is not essential and necessary for the effectuation of a municipality's power to regulate land use. . . .

Despite our Court's previous pronouncements rejecting the existence of an implicit power of imposing a moratorium, the legislature has not acted to authorize municipalities to meet their planning objectives through the suspension, temporary or otherwise, of the process for reviewing land use proposals. As we stated in *Kline* over fifty years ago, "[i]f the legislature wishes to authorize the enactment of a "temporary" or "interim" ordinance to maintain the status quo it can so provide by legislation with proper safeguards." 68 A.2d at 189. The General Assembly is better suited to examine the significant policy issues at stake and to determine the appropriate legal standards to govern the application of such a powerful planning tool.

We are fully aware that many other states have approved the enactment of a temporary moratorium on land development absent express language in the municipality's enabling act. We conclude, however, that the cases of each jurisdiction rest upon the constitution, statutes and case law of the particular state. As our own case law views the power to impose a moratorium as distinct from rather than incidental to the power to regulate land development, we find the cases of our sister jurisdictions unpersuasive. . . .

NEWMAN, Justice, dissenting. . . .

I believe that "implicit in or incidental to the broad powers expressly conferred upon municipalities is the authority to impose moratoria on development while land use regulations are in the process of being revisited." *Naylor v. Township of Hellam*, 717 A.2d 629, 633 (Pa.Cmwlth.1998). Section 503(2)(i) authorizes the Hellam Township Board of Supervisors (Board) to adopt provisions for insuring that "the layout or arrangement of the subdivision or land development shall conform" to the Board's comprehensive plan. 53 P.S. §10503(2)(i). The trial court aptly stated, "[a] logical means of ensuring that subdivision and development conform with a municipality's comprehensive plan during such time as an existing comprehensive plan and subdivision and land development ordinance are being revised and enacted would be to maintain the status quo by enacting a moratorium on subdivision and development." Trial Court Op., p, 10.

It is clearly the responsibility of the Board to monitor community growth and to provide adequate public necessities, such as transportation, water, sewage, schools and parks. In 1990, the Board noticed that development patterns in the township were changing and that the public sewage system could no longer service additional residences. In response, the Board began developing a new comprehensive plan. After the Board invested five years to research and develop this new comprehensive plan, the pace of subdivision and development within the township escalated dramatically. The Board knew that once they announced a new proposed comprehensive plan that substantially altered the existing plan, landowners and developers would flood the Board with applications for subdivision and development pursuant to the existing plan. Recognizing that the proposed comprehensive plan would soon be obsolete, the Board invoked the only tool that would allow them to enact such a plan as they are authorized to do under the MPC. The Board imposed a temporary moratorium on subdivision and development that was nondiscriminatory, limited in duration, and enacted in good faith.

. . . The objectives underlying the use of temporary moratoria are consistent with the purposes of the MPC. A moratorium allows the municipality time in which to create a new comprehensive plan. . . .

"Maintaining the status quo serves to protect and promote the health and welfare of the municipality's citizens by ensuring that proposed development conforms to rather than defeats the revised plans and regulations and by preventing further uncoordinated or hazardous development stemming from the regulations in effect prior to the moratorium." *Naylor*, 717 A.2d at 633. Temporary moratoria also ensure that residents and landowners will have the opportunity to voice their opinions regarding the proposed comprehensive plan. . . .

The Majority [states] that the power to enact a zoning ordinance is distinct from the power to suspend an ordinance, and that the latter cannot be implicitly authorized under the MPC. I disagree. The ordinance affected by the moratorium was not suspended. Rather, it is as if the municipality had rezoned the area to exclude residential building in the traditional manner, with the intent of again amending the ordinance in thirteen months to reflect the new comprehensive plan. . . . Under such a procedure, the landowner is in the same position as if the ordinance was subject to a municipality-issued moratorium. . . .

Notes and Comments

1. *Types of Moratoria.* The moratorium is not a new device. *See Miller v. Board of Public Works*, 234 P. 381 (Cal. 1925) (interim zoning ordinance prohibiting multi-family housing). However, it continues to be an important tool used by local governments confronting growth issues. Moratoria generally fall into two categories: (1) freezes on construction for a period of time or (2) interim zoning restrictions that allow low-level development. Because the purpose of a moratorium is to prevent development until a planning process is completed and a recommended land use change made, or until infrastructure improvements take place (a situation that is the subject of a later case in this chapter), the freeze or stop-gap method is more commonly used.

2. Naylor *and the Authority Issue.* Enactments of moratoria raise several legal issues. An initial issue, the subject of *Naylor*, is whether the local jurisdiction needs specific statutory authority authorizing the enactment of a moratorium or whether general authority to zone is enough.

State statutes commonly govern the enactment of moratoria, and without statutory authorization to enact a moratorium, the local jurisdiction may be unable to do so. Most courts, however, find that the general authorization to adopt zoning ordinances includes the power to adopt moratoria. *See Arnold Bernhard & Co. v. Planning and Zoning Commission of the Town of Westport*, 479 A.2d 801, 806 (Conn. 1984) (upholding moratorium under general zoning authority and citing cases from other states).

Who has the better argument in *Naylor*? How significant is it that the legislature did not appear to have acted since the *Kline* case? Is the better view that the Legislature *did* act when it passed the MPC Act in 1968?

A few states have gone so far as to flatly prohibit the adoption of moratoria in certain circumstances. *See, e.g.*, N.J. Stat. Ann. §40:55D-90(a) (West 1991) ("The prohibition of development in order to prepare a master plan and development regulations is prohibited"); N.M. Stat. Ann. §5-8-42 (Michie 2001) ("A moratorium shall not be placed on new development for the sole purpose of awaiting the completion of all or any part of the process necessary to develop, adopt or update impact fees.").

3. *Is Notice Required*? An important issue is the procedure that the local government must follow in enacting the moratorium. If the full notice and hearing procedures common to the enactment of zoning ordinances must be followed, the very type of development sought to be prevented by the moratorium may become vested in the interim period before the local jurisdiction can enact the moratorium. Thus, the local government may attempt to adopt the moratoria as an emergency measures, bypassing the usual procedures.

Again, the legality of such a step may well depend on whether a statute authorizes emergency zoning of this type. *See* Ariz. Rev. Stat. Ann. §9-463.06(A)(1) (West Supp. 2003) (city shall not adopt a moratorium on construction or land development unless it first provides at least 30-days notice before a final public hearing); *City of Roswell v. Outdoor Systems, Inc.*, 549 S.E.2d 90 (Ga. 2001) (because the city's temporary moratorium on billboard construction was not "final legislative action," the action was not of the type for which the statute required notice). *Compare Gary-Wheaton Bank v. Village of Lombard*, 404 N.E.2d 1115, 1118 (Ill. App. Ct. 1980) (municipality must comply with notice and public hearing requirements).

4. *Time and Takings*. Another issue is the length of time that the moratorium may remain in place. The local jurisdiction may in good faith believe that it can complete its plan and adopt new land use controls within a fixed period only to find that unforeseen delays require the extension of the moratorium. Again, a state statute is likely to provide an answer.

A Massachusetts appeals court found that a 23-month moratorium was valid in *W.R. Grace & Co.–Conn. v. Cambridge City Council*, 779 N.E.2d 141 (Mass. Ct. App. 2002). However, in rejecting the argument that a moratorium is a per se taking in *Tahoe-Sierra Property Owners Assn. v. Tahoe Regional Planning Agency*, reprinted in Chapter 7, Justice Stevens inferred that a moratorium of more than a year could constitute a taking. At the least, lengthier moratoria will likely require much more justification by the local government.

Of course, if the court finds that the municipality adopted the moratorium in bad faith, it will be invalidated. *Home Depot U.S.A., Inc. v. Village of Rockville Centre*, 743 N.Y.S.2d 541 (Sup. Ct. App. Div. 2002) (rejecting Home Depot's claim of bad faith and undue delay in processing permits until the moratorium was enacted). See also *City of Glenn Heights v. Sheffield Development Co.*, 61 S.W.3d 634 (Tex. Ct. App. 2001) (a taking occurred where, once the city had all the information to make a decision, "the [political] stalemate on the council was not a legitimate reason to continue the moratorium which prevented development of the property").

5. *Level of Judicial Scrutiny.* Given the significant economic effects of a moratorium, should a court closely scrutinize the local government's decision, or should it defer to any finding of "emergency" or "harm" made to justify the moratorium?

In a 1991 Oregon case, the city found that harm existed because of the "strong likelihood that current efforts to secure federal and state funding" to purchase the plaintiff's property for a park "would be abandoned or unsuccessful" if residential development occurred. Should that finding be sufficient to meet the statutory mandate requiring a city to find that existing regulations are "inadequate to prevent irrevocable public harm" before it may declare a moratorium? *See Davis v. City of Bandon*, 805 P.2d 709 (Or. Ct. App. 1991) (upholding the moratorium). On the other hand, in *Matson v. Clark County Bd. of Commissioners*, 904 P.2d 317 (Wash. Ct. App. 1995), the court stated that it would undertake only a very limited review of a legislative declaration of emergency. The court would not inquire into the facts, it said, but only examine what appears on the face of the local ordinance "and its judicial knowledge."

Which approach — more intensive review or the extremely deferential review found in *Matson* — is most appropriate for reviewing a moratorium?

6. *The "Single Project" Moratorium.* There are various reasons why a jurisdiction might decide that a moratorium is appropriate. For example, the impetus might be concern that the implementation of a general plan may be jeopardized by development that occurs in the interim, or a belief that infrastructure is unavailable to serve pending development applications. Should it make any difference if only a single project (perhaps a controversial one) leads to the moratorium? *See Duncanson v. Board of Supervisors of Danville Township*, 551 N.W.2d 248, 252 (Minn. Ct. App. 1996) ("The Duncansons' proposal [to operate a feedlot] demonstrated the need for Danville to address a topic that had not previously been relevant to a primarily rural community. . . . It is the good faith effort demonstrated here to plan for orderly development that must . . . defeat any objection that this ordinance is directed at a single project.").

7. *Associated Home Builders v. City of Livermore I.* A second type of moratorium serves a function a bit different from the "short-term" measure at issue in *Naylor*. In *Associated Home Builders v. City of Livermore*, 557 P.2d 473 (Cal. 1976), the California Supreme Court considers the legality of a moratorium designed to stop development until certain infrastructure deficiencies are corrected. The court held that the moratorium would be judged under the traditional test for a measure's validity under the police power: whether it was reasonably related to the general welfare. It then declared, however, that because the measure arguably affected the regional housing supply, the welfare to be considered was not limited to individuals currently residing in Livermore.

The *Livermore* ordinance on its face would have extended the moratorium indefinitely and did not explicitly provide for remedying the alleged infrastructure deficiencies. The California Supreme Court presumed good faith efforts on the part of the City to solve these deficiencies: "We must presume that the City of Livermore . . . will attempt in good faith to provide that community with adequate schools, sewage disposal facilities, and a sufficient water supply." 557 P.2d at 489.

In dealing with growth controls, a few courts have similarly dampened the impact of the ordinance by reading implied restrictions into it that required specific efforts by the enacting jurisdiction. For example, in *Steel Hill Development, Inc. v. Town of Sanbornton*, 469 F.2d 956 (1st Cir. 1972), a small town with a year-round population of about 1000 residents adopted an ordinance that enlarged the Forest Conservation areas and imposed a 6-acre minimum lot size. The court first found that the goals of the ordinance were valid but noted that it was "disturbed by the admission here that there was never any professional or scientific study made as to why six, rather than four or eight, acres was reasonable." *Id.* at 962. The court concluded that "this is a very special case which cannot be read as evidencing a general approval of six-acre zoning" and that the ordinance "may well not indefinitely stand without more homework by the concerned parties." *Id.*

What attitude should a court adopt in reviewing a growth control ordinance such as the one in *Livermore*? Should it defer to the legislative decision (particularly if, as in this case, the decision is made through use of the initiative power?) Or should the court closely scrutinize the ordinance, perhaps on the grounds that it may exclude residents or arbitrarily limit economic opportunities?

8. *Livermore II.* The *Livermore* opinion is also notable for the framework it constructs to review whether the ordinance in question was within the city's police power. It is axiomatic that, to pass constitutional muster under the police power, a local ordinance must bear a "reasonable relationship to the public welfare." *See, e.g., Dateline Builders, Inc. v. City of Santa Rosa*, 194 Cal. Rptr. 258, 264 (Ct. App. 1983). The *Livermore* court's innovation was its recognition that, in some instances, the "public welfare" at issue was the region's welfare, not just the municipality's. To determine whether the regional welfare is met, the court adopted a three-fold test under which the court (1) determines the "probable effect and duration of the restriction," (2) identifies the "competing interests" affected by it, and (3) decides whether the ordinance represents a "reasonable accommodation of the competing interests." *Livermore*, 557 P.2d at 488.

Is this a meaningful test for measuring the impact on the regional welfare? Will it ensure that a municipality considers the effect of an ordinance on the region before adopting a moratorium like the one at issue in *Livermore*?

The dissent's approach is quite different. Justice Mosk would find such measures presumptively invalid, at least if they operate in an urban area. Does his approach provide a better approach to testing ordinances like the one in *Livermore*?

C. TEMPO CONTROLS AND CAPS

Probably the most direct way to control growth is simply to limit the number of building permits that a jurisdiction may issue over a given period of time. The following decision was one of the first major decisions to address such a system, and it continues to be influential today.

■ CONSTRUCTION INDUSTRY ASSOCIATION OF SONOMA COUNTY v. THE CITY OF PETALUMA

522 F.2d 897 (9th Cir. 1975)

CHOY, Circuit Judge:

The City of Petaluma (the City) appeals from a district court decision voiding as unconstitutional certain aspects of its five-year housing and zoning plan. We reverse.

STATEMENT OF FACTS

The City is located in southern Sonoma County, about 40 miles north of San Francisco. In the 1950s and 1960s, Petaluma was a relatively self-sufficient town. It experienced a steady population growth from 10,315 in 1950 to 24,870 in 1970. Eventually, the City was drawn into the Bay Area metropolitan housing market as people working in San Francisco and San Rafael became willing to commute longer distances to secure relatively inexpensive housing available there. By November 1972, according to unofficial figures, Petaluma's population was at 30,500, a dramatic increase of almost 25 per cent in little over two years.

The increase in the City's population, not surprisingly, is reflected in the increase in the number of its housing units. From 1964 to 1971, the following number of residential housing units were completed:

1964	270	1968	379
1965	440	1969	358
1966	321	1970	591
1967	234	1971	891

In 1970 and 1971, the years of the most rapid growth, demand for housing in the City was even greater than above indicated. Taking 1970 and 1971 together, builders won approval of a total of 2000 permits although only 1482 were actually completed by the end of 1971.

Alarmed by the accelerated rate of growth in 1970 and 1971, the demand for even more housing, and the sprawl of the City eastward, the City adopted a temporary freeze on development in early 1971. The construction and zoning change moratorium was intended to give the City Council and the City planners an opportunity to study the housing and zoning situation and to develop short and long range plans. The Council made specific findings with respect to housing patterns and availability in Petaluma, including the following: That from 1960-1970 housing had been in almost unvarying 6000 square-foot lots laid out in regular grid patterns; that there was a density of approximately 4.5 housing units per acre in the single-family home areas; that during 1960-1970, 88 per cent of housing permits issued were for single-family detached homes; that in 1970, 83 per cent of Petaluma's housing was single-family dwellings; that the bulk of recent development (largely single-family homes) occurred in the eastern portion of the City, causing a large deficiency in moderately priced multi-family and apartment units on the east side.

To correct the imbalance between single-family and multi-family dwellings, curb the sprawl of the City on the east, and retard the accelerating growth of the City, the Council in 1972 adopted several resolutions, which collectively are called the "Petaluma Plan" (the Plan).

The Plan, on its face limited to a five-year period (1972-1977),[1] fixes a housing development growth rate not to exceed 500 dwelling units per year. Each dwelling

1. The district court found that although the Plan is ostensibly limited to a five-year period, official attempts have been made to perpetuate the Plan beyond 1977. Such attempts include the urban extension line (*see* text *infra*) and the agreement to purchase from the Sonoma County Water Agency only 9.8 million gallons of water per day through the year 1990. This flow is sufficient to support a population of 55,000. If the City were to grow at a rate of about 500 housing units per year (approximately three persons per unit), the City would reach a population of 55,000 about the year

unit represents approximately three people. The 500-unit figure is somewhat misleading, however, because it applies only to housing units (hereinafter referred to as "development-units") that are part of projects involving five units or more. Thus, the 500-unit figure does not reflect any housing and population growth due to construction of single-family homes or even four-unit apartment buildings not part of any larger project.

The Plan also positions a 200 foot wide "greenbelt" around the City, to serve as a boundary for urban expansion for at least five years, and with respect to the east and north sides of the City, for perhaps ten to fifteen years. One of the most innovative features of the Plan is the Residential Development Control System which provides procedures and criteria for the award of the annual 500 development-unit permits. At the heart of the allocation procedure is an intricate point system, whereby a builder accumulates points for conformity by his projects with the City's general plan and environmental design plans, for good architectural design, and for providing low and moderate income dwelling units and various recreational facilities. The Plan further directs that allocations of building permits are to be divided as evenly as feasible between the west and east sections of the City and between single-family dwellings and multiple residential units (including rental units), that the sections of the City closest to the center are to be developed first in order to cause "infilling" of vacant area, and that 8 to 12 per cent of the housing units approved be for low and moderate income persons. . . .

Purpose of the Plan

The purpose of the Plan is much disputed in this case. According to general statements in the Plan itself, the Plan was devised to ensure that "development in the next five years, will take place in a reasonable, orderly, attractive manner, rather than in a completely haphazard and unattractive manner." The controversial 500-unit limitation on residential development-units was adopted by the City "[i]n order to protect its small town character and surrounding open space." The other features of the Plan were designed to encourage an east-west balance in development, to provide for variety in densities and building types and wide ranges in prices and rents, to ensure infilling of close-in vacant areas, and to prevent the sprawl of the City to the east and north. The Construction Industry Association of Sonoma County (the Association) argues and the district court found, however, that the Plan was primarily enacted "to limit Petaluma's demographic and market growth rate in housing and in the immigration of new residents." *Construction Industry Assn. v. City of Petaluma*, 375 F. Supp. 574, 576 (N.D. Cal. 1974).

Market Demand and Effect of the Plan

. . . For purposes of this decision . . . we will assume that the 500 development-unit growth rate is in fact below the reasonably anticipated market demand for such units and that absent the Petaluma Plan, the City would grow at a faster rate.

1990. The 55,000 figure was mentioned by City officials as the projected optimal (and maximum) size of Petaluma. *See, e.g.*, R.T. at 135-43, 145-46.

According to undisputed expert testimony at trial, if the Plan (limiting housing starts to approximately 6 per cent of existing housing stock each year) were to be adopted by municipalities throughout the region, the impact on the housing market would be substantial. For the decade 1970 to 1980, the shortfall in needed housing in the region would be about 105,000 units (or 25 per cent of the units needed). Further, the aggregate effect of a proliferation of the Plan throughout the San Francisco region would be a decline in regional housing stock quality, a loss of the mobility of current and prospective residents and a deterioration in the quality and choice of housing available to income earners with real incomes of $14,000 per year or less. If, however, the Plan were considered by itself and with respect to Petaluma only, there is no evidence to suggest that there would be a deterioration in the quality and choice of housing available there to persons in the lower and middle income brackets. Actually, the Plan increases the availability of multi-family units (owner-occupied and rental units) and low-income units which were rarely constructed in the pre-Plan days.

COURT PROCEEDINGS . . .

Appellees claim that the Plan is arbitrary and unreasonable and, thus, violative of the due process clause of the Fourteenth Amendment. According to appellees, the Plan is nothing more than an exclusionary zoning device, designed solely to insulate Petaluma from the urban complex in which it finds itself. The Association and the Landowners reject, as falling outside the scope of any legitimate governmental interest, the City's avowed purposes in implementing the Plan — the preservation of Petaluma's small town character and the avoidance of the social and environmental problems caused by an uncontrolled growth rate.

In attacking the validity of the Plan, appellees rely heavily on the district court's finding that the express purpose and the actual effect of the Plan is to exclude substantial numbers of people who would otherwise elect to move to the City. 375 F. Supp. at 581. The existence of an exclusionary purpose and effect reflects, however, only *one* side of the zoning regulation. Practically all zoning restrictions have as a purpose and effect the *exclusion* of some activity or type of structure or a certain density of inhabitants. And in reviewing the reasonableness of a zoning ordinance, our inquiry does not terminate with a finding that it is for an exclusionary purpose.[11] We must determine further whether the *exclusion* bears any rational relationship to a *legitimate state interest.* If it does not, then the zoning regulation is invalid. If, on the other hand, a legitimate state interest is furthered by the zoning regulation, we must defer to the legislative act. Being neither a super legislature nor a zoning board of appeal, a federal court is without authority to weigh and reappraise the factors considered or ignored by the legislative body in passing the challenged zoning regulation. . . .

11. Our inquiry here is not unlike that involved in a case alleging denial of equal protection of the laws. The mere showing of some discrimination by the state is not sufficient to prove an invasion of one's constitutional rights. Most legislation to some extent discriminates between various classes of persons, business enterprises, or other entities. However, absent a suspect classification or invasion of fundamental rights, equal protection rights are violated only where the classification does not bear a rational relationship to a legitimate state interest. *See Ybarra v. City of Town of Los Altos Hills*, 503 F.2d 250, 254 (9th Cir. 1974).

In determining whether the City's interest in preserving its small town character and in avoiding uncontrolled and rapid growth falls within the broad concept of "public welfare," we are considerably assisted by two recent cases. *Belle Terre [v. Boraas*, 416 U.S. 1 (1974)] and *Ybarra v. City of Town of Los Altos Hills*, 503 F.2d 250 (9th Cir. 1974), each of which upheld as not unreasonable a zoning regulation much more restrictive than the Petaluma Plan, are dispositive of the due process issue in this case.

In *Belle Terre* the Supreme Court rejected numerous challenges to a village's restricting land use to one-family dwellings excluding lodging houses, boarding houses, fraternity houses, or multiple-dwelling houses. By absolutely prohibiting the construction of or conversion of a building to other than single-family dwelling, the village ensured that it would never grow, if at all, much larger than its population of 700 living in 220 residences. Nonetheless, the Court found that the prohibition of boarding houses and other multi-family dwellings was reasonable and within the public welfare because such dwellings present urban problems, such as the occupation of a given space by more people, the increase in traffic and parked cars and the noise that comes with increased crowds. . . .

Following the *Belle Terre* decision, this court in *Los Altos Hills* had an opportunity to review a zoning ordinance providing that a housing lot shall . . . contain not less than one acre and that no lot shall be occupied by more than one primary dwelling unit. The ordinance as a practical matter prevented poor people from living in Los Altos Hills and restricted the density, and thus the population, of the town. This court, nonetheless, found that the ordinance was rationally related to a legitimate governmental interest—*the preservation of the town's rural environment*—and, thus, did not violate the equal protection clause of the Fourteenth Amendment. 503 F.2d at 254.

Both the Belle Terre ordinance and the Los Altos Hills regulation had the purpose and effect of permanently restricting growth; nonetheless, the court in each case upheld the particular law before it on the ground that the regulation served a legitimate governmental interest falling within the concept of the public welfare: the preservation of quiet family neighborhoods (Belle Terre) and the preservation of a rural environment (Los Altos Hills). Even less restrictive or exclusionary than the above zoning ordinances is the Petaluma Plan which, unlike those ordinances, does not freeze the population at present or near-present levels.[15] Further, unlike the Los Altos Hills ordinance and the various zoning regulations struck down by state courts in recent years, the Petaluma Plan does not have the undesirable effect of walling out any particular income class nor any racial minority group.[16]

15. Under the Petaluma Plan, the population is expected to increase at the rate of about 1500 persons annually. This rate approximates the rate of growth in the 1960s and represents about a 6 per cent increase per year over the present population.

16. Although appellees have attempted to align their business interests in attacking the Plan with legitimate housing needs of the urban poor and racial minorities, the Association has not alleged nor can it allege, based on the record in this case, that the Plan has the purpose and effect of excluding poor persons and racial minorities. *Cf. Board of County Supervisors of Fairfax County v. Carper*, 200 Va. 653, 107 S.E.2d 390 (1959). Contrary to the picture painted by appellees, the Petaluma Plan is "inclusionary" to the extent that it offers new opportunities, previously unavailable, to minorities and low and moderate-income persons. Under the pre-Plan system single family, middle-income housing dominated the Petaluma market, and as a result low and moderate income persons were unable to secure housing in the area. The Plan radically changes the previous building pattern and requires that

Although we assume that some persons desirous of living in Petaluma will be excluded under the housing permit limitation and that, thus, the Plan may frustrate some legitimate regional housing needs, the Plan is not arbitrary or unreasonable. We agree with appellees that unlike the situation in the past most municipalities today are neither isolated nor wholly independent from neighboring municipalities and that, consequently, unilateral land use decisions by one local entity affect the needs and resources of an entire region. It does not necessarily follow, however, that the *due process* rights of builders and landowners are violated merely because a local entity exercises in its own self-interest the police power lawfully delegated to it by the state. *See Belle Terre, supra; Los Altos Hills, supra.* If the present system of delegated zoning power does not effectively serve the state interest in furthering the general welfare of the region or entire state, it is the state legislature's and not the federal courts' role to intervene and adjust the system. . . . [T]he federal court is not a super zoning board and should not be called on to mark the point at which legitimate local interests in promoting the welfare of the community are outweighed by legitimate regional interests.

We conclude therefore that under *Belle Terre* and *Los Altos Hills* the concept of the public welfare is sufficiently broad to uphold Petaluma's desire to preserve its small town character, its open spaces and low density of population, and to grow at an orderly and deliberate pace. . . .

Reversed.

Notes and Comments

1. *Legislative Purpose and the "Stupid Staff."* As the court observes, the parties dispute the purpose of the Petaluma ordinance. Why is that purpose important to the outcome of the litigation? Furthermore, in cases like this one, is it really possible for a court to determine definitively what *the* purpose of such a measure is, given the wide variety of purposes such an ordinance can serve (such as preventing urban sprawl, ensuring that infrastructure is in place to support development, protecting the environment, preserving the "quality of life," etc.)? Consider the comment of Justice Scalia in *Lucas v. South Carolina Coastal Council*, 505 U.S. 1003, 1025-1026 n.12 (1992), when he considered a claim by the dissent that the Court should give determinative weight to the purpose of a statute set forth on its face:

> In [the dissent's] view, . . . the test for required compensation is whether the legislature has recited a harm-preventing justification for its action. Since such a justification can be formulated in practically every case, this amounts to a test of whether the legislature has a stupid staff. We think the Takings Clause requires courts to do more than insist upon artful harm-preventing characterizations.

2. *Legitimate Goals, Illegitimate Application.* In *Pheasant Bridge Corp. v. Tp. of Warren*, 777 A.2d 334 (N.J. 2001), the New Jersey Supreme Court considered an "as applied" challenge to a zoning ordinance establishing an "environmental

---

housing permits be evenly divided between single-family and multi-family units and that approximately eight to twelve per cent of the units be constructed specifically for low and moderate income persons.

protection zone." The zone was for areas of significant environmental constraints and limited the density of development. The court noted that the plaintiff "concedes, as it must, that defendant pursued legitimate goals in zoning to preserve the environment, open space, and agriculture." *Id.* at 339. Plaintiff claimed, however, that none of the "environmental constraints" in the zoning actually existed on its property.

The court agreed. It cited the trial court's findings that "the environmental concerns that justified passage of the EP-250 zone did not pertain to plaintiff's property." To take just one example, the trial court noted that the city's concerns with steep slopes "has no application to the property since it contains no steep slopes." *Id.*

The case contains an important lesson for practitioners. Litigation over the constitutionality of growth management ordinances is not just a question of constitutional law and positing "goals" that a growth management ordinance could meet. The ordinance must be carefully correlated with the actual factual situation in the jurisdiction. Thus, in *Martin County v. Section 28 Partnership, Ltd.*, 772 So. 2d 616 (Fla. Ct. App. 2000), the court summarized the expert testimony about the factual situation in the county supporting the county's refusal to amend its plan as plaintiff had requested. The court then concluded, "The record before us contains abundant evidence supporting the County's decision, which was based upon its legitimate interest in maintaining low densities in an environmentally sensitive area and accomplishing growth management goals." *Id.* at 621. On the importance of facts in growth management litigation, *see also Clark County Nat. Res. Council v. Clark County Citizens United, Inc.*, 972 P.2d 941 (Wash. Ct. App. 1999) (rejecting claim that the Growth Management Act required the regional growth management board to use population projections by the Office of Financial Management as a "cap" on non-urban growth).

3. Livermore *or* Petaluma? The *Petaluma* court quickly rejects plaintiff's suggestion that it evaluate the Petaluma ordinance's adverse effect on the region, emphasizing that considering such effects is the job of the legislature, not that of the courts in deciding due process claims. *Associated Homebuilders v. Livermore*, discussed in the notes after *Naylor*, took a different approach in determining whether the Livermore ordinance was within the police power. Which of the two approaches do you believe has more to commend it?

4. *The Empirical Evidence.* Do you understand fully how the "point system" under the city's "residential development control system" will operate? Does the court know enough about it to determine that it is constitutional? While the rhetoric often flies about the effects of growth control ordinances, the actual empirical evidence about their implementation is far harder to find.

In one article, a planning professor examined how cities in the San Francisco Bay region had actually implemented various growth management systems. Richard T. Legates, The Emergence of Flexible Growth Management Systems in the San Francisco Bay Area, 24 Loy. L.A. L. Rev. 1035 (1991). The results were surprising. In one city where the system "functioned more or less as planned," Morgan Hill, the growth rate was reduced from a rate of over 20 percent in the year before the measure was passed to 4 percent after the growth management system was in place. In other cities, however, the system never actually limited growth. For example, four cities and one county enacted but never used their residential point systems. One city exempted projects which would have brought the tempo control system into play. In two others, sewer moratoria imposed by state agencies prevented any curbs from happening.

In short, the results were not what one would expect from examining just the legal mechanics of the growth management systems. Do these conclusions suggest that the legal battles over these systems have less practical significance than they might appear to have at first blush? Should these findings affect how courts review the ordinance? Would they call for more deference? Less deference?

5. *Absolute Caps on Units*. Would the logic of *Petaluma* support a total "cap" on the number of units allowed in a jurisdiction so that once the jurisdiction was "built out," it would grow no further? In the few cases in which cities have adopted absolute caps, courts have treated them unfavorably. For example, in *City of Boca Raton v. Boca Villas Corp.*, 371 So. 2d 154 (Fla. Dist. Ct. App. 1979), the city voters passed a charter amendment limiting the total number of dwelling units within the existing boundary of the city to 40,000. After an extensive trial the judge held that the cap violated due process because it did not bear a rational relationship to a legitimate public purpose. The court of appeal affirmed, largely on the basis of the trial court's factual findings.

6. *The Influence of the* Petaluma *Decision*. For growth control measures that simply limit the number of units, the decision in *Petaluma* continues to be very influential. For example, in *Schenk v. City of Hudson*, 114 F.3d 590 (6th Cir. 1997), applicants seeking to build had to receive a "residential development allotment," which was allocated through a lottery. Eighty percent of the allotment is reserved for a "priority development pool," which includes affordable housing and lots that received preliminary or final subdivision approval before the ordinance's effective date.

The court of appeal sustained the ordinance. The court cited *Petaluma*, among other familiar cases, and then concluded that, "to survive a substantive due process challenge, Chapter 1207 must merely be rationally related to its purpose." *Id* at 594.

It then found that the ordinances met this test, declaring:

> The City of Hudson wishes to control growth of residential areas until such time as its infrastructure is able to meet current and future needs. A cap on the number of homes built in the City unquestionably bears a rational relationship to this concern.

Id.

7. Tahoe-Sierra *and* Lucas *(Again)*. If a city uses the Petaluma system, do landowners who must wait for issuance of residential building permits have a takings claim under *Tahoe-Sierra*? If they do not qualify for permits under the Petaluma point system, do they have a takings claim under *Lucas*? Would your conclusion depend on the existing use of the property?

D. INFRASTRUCTURE CONTROLS AND CONCURRENCY REQUIREMENTS

Another branch of the growth control movement focuses on the infrastructure needed to support growth rather than directly on the number of units allowed by the local government. Just as in *Petaluma*, the following decision was one of the first to deal with this new type of issue, and it had a significant impact on how courts in other states viewed similar ordinances.

As you read the case, pay special attention to the process followed by the Town of Ramapo in enacting the ordinance and the way in which it was structured. While similar ordinances abound today, at the time that the town was drafting the ordinances at issue, it (and its lawyers) were entering uncharted territory.

■ GOLDEN v. PLANNING BOARD OF THE TOWN OF RAMAPO

285 N.E.2d (N.Y. 1972)

SCILEPPI, Judge.

Experiencing the pressures of an increase in population and the ancillary problem of providing municipal facilities and services, the Town of Ramapo, as early as 1964, made application for grant under section 801 of the Housing Act of 1964 (78 U.S. Stat. 769) to develop a master plan. The plan's preparation included a four-volume study of the existing land uses, public facilities, transportation, industry and commerce, housing needs and projected population trends. The proposals appearing in the studies were subsequently adopted pursuant to section 272-a of the Town Law, Consol. Laws, c. 62, in July, 1966 and implemented by way of a master plan. The master plan was followed by the adoption of a comprehensive zoning ordinance. Additional sewage district and drainage studies were undertaken which culminated in the adoption of a capital budget, providing for the development of the improvements specified in the master plan within the next six years. Pursuant to section 271 of the Town Law, authorizing comprehensive planning, and as a supplement to the capital budget, the Town Board adopted a capital program which provides for the location and sequence of additional capital improvements for the 12 years following the life of the capital budget. The two plans, covering a period of 18 years, detail the capital improvements projected for maximum development and conform to the specifications set forth in the master plan, the official map and drainage plan.

Based upon these criteria, the Town subsequently adopted the subject amendments for the alleged purpose of eliminating premature subdivision and urban sprawl. Residential development is to proceed according to the provision of adequate municipal facilities and services, with the assurance that any concomitant restraint upon property use is to be of a "temporary" nature and that other private uses, including the construction of individual housing, are authorized.

The amendments did not rezone or reclassify any land into different residential or use districts, but, for the purposes of implementing the proposals appearing in the comprehensive plan, consist, in the main, of additions to the definitional sections of the ordinance, section 46-3, and the adoption of a new class of "Special Permit Uses", designated "Residential Development Use." "Residential Development Use" is defined as "The erection or construction of dwellings or any vacant plots, lots or parcels of land" (§46-3, as amd.); and, any person who acts so as to come within that definition, "shall be deemed to be engaged in residential development which shall be a separate use classification under this ordinance and subject to the requirement of obtaining a special permit from the Town Board" (§46-3, as amd.).

The standards for the issuance of special permits are framed in terms of the availability to the proposed subdivision plat of five essential facilities or services: specifically (1) public sanitary sewers or approved substitutes; (2) drainage facilities; (3) improved public parks or recreation facilities, including public schools; (4) State, county or town roads—major, secondary or collector; and, (5) firehouses. No special permit shall issue unless the proposed residential development has accumulated 15 development points, to be computed on a sliding scale of values assigned to the specified improvements under the statute. Subdivision is thus a function of immediate availability to the proposed plat of certain municipal improvements; the avowed purpose of the amendments being to phase residential development to the Town's ability to provide the above facilities or services.

Certain savings and remedial provisions are designed to relieve of potentially unreasonable restrictions. Thus, the board may issue special permits vesting a present right to proceed with residential development in such year as the development meets the required point minimum, but in no event later than the final year of the 18-year capital plan. The approved special use permit is fully assignable, and improvements scheduled for completion within one year from the date of an application are to be credited as though existing on the date of the application. A prospective developer may advance the date of subdivision approval by agreeing to provide those improvements which will bring the proposed plat within the number of development points required by the amendments. And applications are authorized to the "Development Easement Acquisition Commission" for a reduction of the assessed valuation. Finally, upon application to the Town Board, the development point requirements may be varied should the board determine that such a variance or modification is consistent with the on-going development plan.

The undisputed effect of these integrated efforts in land use planning and development is to provide an over-all program of orderly growth and adequate facilities through a sequential development policy commensurate with progressing availability and capacity of public facilities. While its goals are clear and its purposes undisputably laudatory, serious questions are raised as to the manner in which these ends are to be effected, not the least of which relates to their legal viability under present zoning enabling legislation, particularly sections 261 and 263 of the Town Law. The owners of the subject premises argue, and the Appellate Division has sustained the proposition, that the primary purpose of the amending ordinance is to control or regulate population growth within the Town and as such is not within the authorized objectives of the zoning enabling legislation. We disagree.

In enacting the challenged amendments, the Town Board has sought to control subdivision in all residential districts, pending the provision (public or private) at some future date of various services and facilities. A reading of the relevant statutory provisions reveals that there is no specific authorization for the "sequential" and "timing" controls adopted here. That, of course, cannot be said to end the matter, for the additional inquiry remains as to whether the challenged amendments find their basis within the perimeters of the devices authorized and purposes sanctioned under current enabling legislation. Our concern is, as it should be, with the effects of the statutory scheme taken as a whole and its role in the propagation of a viable policy of land use and planning.

Of course, zoning historically has assumed the development of individual plats and has proven characteristically ineffective in treating with the problems attending subdivision and development of larger parcels, involving as it invariably does, the provision of adequate public services and facilities. To this end, subdivision control (Town Law, §§276, 277) purports to guide community development in the directions outlined here, while at the same time encouraging the provision of adequate facilities for the housing, distribution, comfort and convenience of local residents (*Village of Lynbrook v. Cadoo*, 252 N.Y. 308, 314, 169 N.E. 394, 396). It reflects in essence, a legislative judgment that the development of unimproved areas be accompanied by provision of essential facilities. And though it may not, in a definitional or conceptual sense be identified with the power to zone, it is designed to complement other land use restrictions, which, taken together, seek to implement a broader, comprehensive plan for community development.

It is argued, nevertheless, that the timing controls currently in issue are not legislatively authorized since their effect is to prohibit subdivision absent precedent or concurrent action of the Town, and hence constitutes an unauthorized blanket interdiction against subdivision.

It is, indeed, true that the Planning Board is not in an absolute sense statutorily authorized to deny the right to subdivide. That is not, however, what is sought to be accomplished here. The Planning Board has the right to refuse approval of subdivision plats in the absence of those improvements specified in section 277, and the fact that it is the Town and not the subdividing owner or land developer who is required to make those improvements before the plat will be approved cannot be said to transform the scheme into an absolute prohibition any more than it would be so where it was the developer who refused to provide the facilities required for plat approval. Denial of subdivision plat approval, invariably amounts to a prohibition against subdivision, albeit a conditional one . . . and to say that the Planning Board lacks the authority to deny subdivision rights is to mistake the nature of our inquiry which is essentially whether development may be conditioned pending the provision by the municipality of specified services and facilities. Whether it is the municipality or the developer who is to provide the improvements, the objective is the same—to provide adequate facilities, off-site and on-site; and in either case subdivision rights are conditioned, not denied. . . .

[T]hough the issues are framed in terms of the developer's due process rights, those rights cannot, realistically speaking, be viewed separately and apart from the rights of others " 'in search of a [more] comfortable place to live.' " (*Concord Twp. Appeal*, 439 Pa. 466, 474, n.6, 268 A.2d 765, 768). . . .

There is, then, something inherently suspect in a scheme which, apart from its professed purposes, effects a restriction upon the free mobility of a people until sometime in the future when projected facilities are available to meet increased demands. Although zoning must include schemes designed to allow municipalities to more effectively contend with the increased demands of evolving and growing communities, under its guise, townships have been wont to try their hand at an array of exclusionary devices in the hope of avoiding the very burden which growth must inevitably bring . . . Though the conflict engendered by such tactics is certainly real, and its implications vast, accumulated evidence, scientific and social, points circumspectly at the hazards of undirected growth and the naive, somewhat nostalgic imperative that egalitarianism is a function of growth.

Of course, these problems cannot be solved by Ramapo or any single municipality, but depend upon the accommodation of widely disparate interests for their ultimate resolution. To that end, State-wide or regional control of planning would insure that interests broader than that of the municipality underlie various land use policies. Nevertheless, that should not be the only context in which growth devices such as these, aimed at population assimilation, not exclusion, will be sustained. . . .

Hence, unless we are to ignore the plain meaning of the statutory delegation, this much is clear: phased growth is well within the ambit of existing enabling legislation. And, of course, it is no answer to point to emergent problems to buttress the conclusion that such innovative schemes are beyond the perimeters of statutory authorization. These considerations, admittedly real, to the extent which they are relevant, bear solely upon the continued viability of "localism" in land use regulation; obviously, they can neither add nor detract from the initial grant of authority, obsolescent though it may be. The answer which Ramapo has posed can by no means be termed definitive; it is, however, a first practical step toward controlled growth achieved without forsaking broader social purposes.

The subject ordinance is said to advance legitimate zoning purposes as it assures that each new home built in the township will have at least a minimum of public services in the categories regulated by the ordinance. The Town argues that various public facilities are presently being constructed but that for want of time and money it has been unable to provide such services and facilities at a pace commensurate with increased public need. It is urged that although the zoning power includes reasonable restrictions upon the private use of property, exacted in the hope of development according to well-laid plans, calculated to advance the public welfare of the community in the future, the subject regulations go further and seek to avoid the increased responsibilities and economic burdens which time and growth must ultimately bring.

What we will not countenance, then, under any guise, is community efforts at immunization or exclusion. But, far from being exclusionary, the present amendments merely seek, by the implementation of sequential development and timed growth, to provide a balanced cohesive community dedicated to the efficient utilization of land. The restrictions conform to the community's considered land use policies as expressed in its comprehensive plan and represent a bona fide effort to maximize population density consistent with orderly growth. True other alternatives, such as requiring off-site improvements as a prerequisite to subdivision, may be available, but the choice as how best to proceed, in view of the difficulties attending such exactions . . . cannot be faulted.

Perhaps even more importantly, timed growth, unlike the minimum lot requirements recently struck down by the Pennsylvania Supreme Court as exclusionary, does not impose permanent restrictions upon land use (*see National Land & Inv. Co. v. Easttown Twp. Bd. of Adj.*, 419 Pa. 504, 215 A.2d 597, *supra*; *Concord Twp. Appeal*, 439 Pa. 466, 268 A.2d 765, *supra*). Its obvious purpose is to prevent premature subdivision absent essential municipal facilities and to insure continuous development commensurate with the Town's obligation to provide such facilities. They seek, not to freeze population at present levels but to maximize growth by the efficient use of land, and in so doing testify to this community's continuing role in population assimilation. In sum, Ramapo asks not that it be left alone, but only that it be allowed to prevent the kind of deterioration that has transformed well-ordered and thriving residential communities into blighted ghettos with attendant hazards to health, security and social stability—a danger not without substantial basis in fact.

The proposed amendments have the effect of restricting development for onwards to 18 years in certain areas. Whether the subject parcels will be so restricted for the full term is not clear, for it is equally probable that the proposed facilities will be brought into these areas well before that time. Assuming, however, that the restrictions will remain outstanding for the life of the program, they still fall short of a confiscation within the meaning of the Constitution.

An ordinance which seeks to permanently restrict the use of property so that it may not be used for any reasonable purpose must be recognized as a taking . . . An appreciably different situation obtains where the restriction constitutes a *temporary* restriction, promising that the property may be put to a profitable use within a reasonable time. . . .

Without a doubt restrictions upon the property in the present case are substantial in nature and duration. They are not, however, absolute. The amendments contemplate a definite term, as the development points are designed to operate for a maximum period of 18 years and during that period, the Town is committed to the construction and installation of capital improvements. The net result of the ongoing development provision is that individual parcels may be committed to a residential development use prior to the expiration of the maximum period. Similarly, property owners under the terms of the amendments may elect to accelerate the date of development by installing, at their own expense, the necessary public services to bring the parcel within the required number of development points. While even the best of plans may not always be realized, in the absence of proof to the contrary, we must assume the Town will put its best effort forward in implementing the physical and fiscal timetable outlined under the plan. Should subsequent events prove this assumption unwarranted, or should the Town because of some unforeseen event fail in its primary obligation to these landowners, there will be ample opportunity to undo the restrictions upon default. . . .

In sum, where it is clear that the existing physical and financial resources of the community are inadequate to furnish the essential services and facilities which a substantial increase in population requires, there is a rational basis for "phased growth" and hence, the challenged ordinance is not violative of the Federal and State Constitutions. . . .

Notes and Comments

1. *The Significance of Ramapo's Planning*. The New York Court of Appeals emphasizes the comprehensive planning efforts that preceded the adoption of the Ramapo ordinance. What is the legal significance of these efforts? In *Rancourt v. Town of Barnstead*, 523 A.2d 55 (N.H. 1986), the plaintiff attacked the evidentiary basis for the provision in the town's master plan for a 3 percent annual growth rate. The town offered two exhibits as support for the measure: a state projection of growth for the town and a questionnaire distributed to the town's residents asking them what the "ideal" growth rate would be. The court overturned the measure, finding that the evidence did not constitute a "solid, scientific, statistical basis for the recommended three percent growth rate." *Id.* at 59. *See* John R. Nolon, The Contemporary Relevance of *Golden v. Ramapo*, Am. Bar Assn. Section of State and Local Govt. Law, State and Local Law News, vol. 26, No. 1,

Fall 2002, at 1. The article notes that, at the time, the Ramapo plan's "inventions were sophisticated, controversial, and legally dubious." The article cites the city's "investment in comprehensive planning" as supporting the idea that "land-use laws that conform to objectives contained in adopted master plans are highly successful in overcoming legal challenges." *See also Beck v. Town of Raymond*, 394 A.2d 847, 852 (N.H. 1978) (growth controls "should be the product of careful study and should be reexamined constantly with a view toward relaxing or ending them").

2. *Growth Control as a Zoning Objective?* The Ramapo growth control ordinance was enacted as a zoning ordinance, and the court finds that control or regulation of population growth was not an "authorized objective" of the New York zoning enabling legislation. If growth control was not a zoning objective, how could the court uphold the ordinance? You should closely examine the argument made by the town, centering on its authority to control subdivisions, that the court accepted in upholding the growth control ordinance.

3. *The Principle of Concurrency.* Requiring that infrastructure be available to support housing is a concept known as "concurrency." This concept "endeavor[s] to achieve the orderly sequencing of development within a community." James H. Wickersham, The Quiet Revolution Continues: The Emerging New Model For State Growth Management Statutes, 18 Harv. Envtl. L. Rev. 489, 510 (1994). Concurrency "is a legislative-enacted growth management tool for ensuring the availability of adequate public facilities and services to accommodate development." Ronald L. Weaver, Concurrency, Concurrency Alternatives, Infrastructure, Planning and Regional Solution Issues, 12 U. Fla. J.L. & Pub. Poly. 251 (2001). The concept is a simple one:

> [A] developer applying for a building permit must show the local governing body that the demands of the proposed development will not exceed the maximum capacity of public facilities. If the local government determines that the existing public facilities cannot sustain the additional development, then the application for a permit to build will be denied.

Adam Strachan, Note, Concurrency Laws: Water as a Land-Use Regulation, 21 J. Land Resources & Envtl. L. 435 (2001).

Several states have enacted statutes requiring concurrency. The leading state is Florida, whose Local Government Comprehensive Planning and Land Development Regulation Act has such a provision. Fla. Stat. Ann. §163.3202(2)(g) (West 2000). Washington has also adopted a concurrency requirement for transportation. Wash. Rev. Code Ann. §36.70A.070(6)(e) (West 2003).

Are concurrency measures really "growth control" measures? One book on the subject has stated:

> Florida's concurrency program has generated considerable controversy. . . . While the system is not inherently growth limiting, the failure of the state government to adequately fund improvements to the state roadway network has lead [*sic*] to de facto development moratoria in some urban areas. Critics point out that the concurrency requirements, coupled with inadequate state funding for infrastructure, are encouraging development in rural and exurban areas where excess road capacity exists, contrary to state goals discouraging urban sprawl.

Arthur C. Nelson & James B. Duncan, Growth Management Principles and Practices 97 (1995). *See also* Ruth L. Steiner, Florida's Transportation Concurrency: Are the Tools Adequate to Meet the Need for Coordinated Land Use and Transportation Planning?, 12 U. Fla. J.L. & Pub. Poly. 269, 271 (2001) (concluding that transportation concurrency is not working because "the plans are not vertically consistent, between local, regional and State agencies" and "local governments continue to allow development and do not have a financially feasible capital improvements plan").

4. *No "Right to Sewers."* The *Ramapo* court notes that, if a developer does not want to wait until the town provides the infrastructure for its development, the developer has the option of providing that infrastructure. Note that there is no "right to sewers"; a developer does not have the right to insist that a local jurisdiction engage in deficit financing to pay for infrastructure. On the other hand, some courts have held that cities acting as public utilities cannot deliberately refuse to serve customers as a means of controlling growth. *See, e.g., Brennan Woods Limited Partnership v. Town of Williston*, 782 A.2d 1230 (Vt. 2001) (municipality may allocate capacity of the sewer system, but the allocation may be used to control population and density only "where decisions are based on the load to the sewer system. . . ." Decisions cannot "be based on growth limits in the town plan); *Robinson v. City of Boulder*, 547 P.2d 228 (Colo. 1976) (city could only refuse to serve a new development outside its boundaries for utility-related reasons, not for planning reasons).

5. *Timed Growth and Statutory Limits.* In *Toll Brothers, Inc. v. West Windsor Township*, 712 A.2d 266 (N.J. Super. Ct. App. Div. 1998), the court considered a "timed growth" system. The township determined that its road system did not have the capacity to serve the existing population and future development, so it adopted a capital improvement program to increase that capacity. The time frame for completion of that plan was 50 years; in the meantime, however, the city's complicated system restricted the number of units that could be built. Certain "basic rights" could be exercised at any time, but other "additional rights" could be exercised only at set years in the future.

The city cited both *Ramapo* and *Construction Industry*, but the court held that the zoning ordinance violated a state statute governing moratoria. The statute declared that "[n]o moratoria in applications for development or interim zoning ordinances shall be permitted" except where the municipality demonstrates, on the basis of an opinion by a qualified health professional, that a "clear imminent danger to the health of the inhabitants" exists. N.J.S.A. 40:55D-90. The court concluded:

> [T]he township's timed growth controls constitute a prohibited moratorium with regard to a developer's "additional rights." Exercise of those rights is suspended for periods measuring a year in two districts to more than ten years in other districts. Moreover, additional rights may be exercised only over a period of time from ten years to approximately fifteen years depending on the district. This secondary postponement of full enjoyment of the development rights afforded by the zoning ordinance constitutes an additional level of moratoria.

712 A.2d at 271. The *Ramapo* decision was distinguished on the ground that New York did not have a statutory prohibition equivalent to Section 90.

Did the court apply the statute correctly?

6. *Aftermath*. During the later 1970s, as growth slowed significantly, Ramapo began to follow the program less strictly. For example, it sometimes accepted financial contributions from builders who failed to accumulate the required number of points. The town also fell behind in its capital improvement program. The principal parts of the program ultimately were rescinded in 1983. See Ramapo Marks End of Controlled Growth, Journal News (Rockland County, N.Y.), July 11, 1983, at 1.

E. URBAN GROWTH BOUNDARIES

Another approach to the problem of growth, which has much in common with concurrency requirements, focuses on preventing urban "sprawl," the spread of development into outlying areas of the locality. One method of attempting to avoid sprawl is featured in Oregon: the use of urban growth boundaries. The premise is simply that an urban growth limit should be set, and new development should be directed within that growth boundary.

1000 FRIENDS OF OREGON v. WASCO COUNTY COURT
703 P.2d 207 (Or. 1985)

PETERSON, Chief Justice.

Comprehensive statewide land use planning . . . culminated with the passage of Senate Bill 100 in 1973. The impetus behind Senate Bill 100, codified in ORS chapter 197, the framework within which land use planning occurs, was legislative concern that state intervention was needed to stop a process of cumulative public harm resulting from uncoordinated land use. *See 1000 Friends v. LCDC*, 292 Or. 735, 745, 642 P.2d 1158, 1164 (1982). . . . Senate Bill 100 was intended to substitute a systematic decisional process based on consideration of all relevant facts, affected interests and public policies, for the prevailing practice of inconsistent land use decision-making. *See 1000 Friends v. LCDC, supra*, 292 Or. at 746, 642 P.2d at 1164.

This case involves a question of whether the Statewide Land Use Planning Goals, and particularly the Urbanization Goal (Goal 14), apply to a county's decision to approve a petition for the incorporation of a new city (Rajneeshpuram) and to authorize an incorporation election. . . .

[One] question presented [is] . . .

2. Does Goal 14, the "urbanization" goal, prohibit the incorporation of a new city on rural land absent a Goal 2, part II, exception?

We hold that it does not. . . .

I. THE FACTS

In July 1981, Chidvalis Rajneesh Meditation Center, one of the petitioners in this case, purchased a 64,000-acre ranch which lies east of the Cascade Range, in

Wasco and Jefferson Counties. On October 14, 1981, . . . a petition to incorporate 2135 acres within the Wasco County portion of the ranch was filed by registered voters residing in the proposed area of incorporation. On November 4, 1981, the Wasco County Court held a public hearing to consider the petition. At the hearing the county court heard testimony pertaining to whether the proposed incorporation satisfied the requirements of ORS chapter 221 and complied with the statewide planning goals. The county court made extensive findings on the matter of compliance with the statewide planning goals, fixed the boundaries of the proposed city and authorized a special incorporation election. . . .

An "urban growth boundary" (UGB) is a boundary line established under Goal 14 to separate urbanizable land from rural land. *City of Salem v. Families for Responsible Govt,* 298 Or. 574, 577 n.3, 694 P.2d 965, 966 n.3 (1985). The area of the proposed incorporated city of Rajneeshpuram is not within any acknowledged UGB. In that sense, the land is rural as defined by the goal definitions.

Under Goal 14, land is classified into three categories, rural, urbanizable and urban, through the establishment of a UGB. The terms are defined by the Statewide Planning Goal Definitions:

Rural Land:

Rural lands are those which are outside the urban growth boundary and are;

(a) Non-urban agricultural, forest or open space lands or,
(b) Other lands suitable for sparse settlement, small farms or acreage homesites with no or hardly any public services, and which are not suitable, necessary or intended for urban use.

Urbanizable Land:

Urbanizable lands are those lands within the urban growth boundary and which are identified and

(a) Determined to be necessary and suitable for future urban uses
(b) Can be served by urban services and facilities
(c) Are needed for the expansion of an urban area.

Urban Land:

Urban areas are those places which must have an incorporated city. Such areas may include lands adjacent to and outside the incorporated city and may also:

(a) Have concentrations of persons who generally reside and work in the area
(b) Have supporting public facilities and services.

Goal 14 specifies the requirements for conversion of rural land to urban land. The goal provides:

To provide for an orderly and efficient transition from rural to urban land use.

Urban growth boundaries shall be established to identify and separate urbanizable land from rural land.

Establishment and change of the boundaries shall be based upon consideration of the following factors:

(1) Demonstrated need to accommodate long-range urban population growth requirements consistent with LCDC goals;
(2) Need for housing, employment opportunities, and livability;
(3) Orderly and economic provision for public facilities and services;
(4) Maximum efficiency of land uses within and on the fringe of the existing urban area;
(5) Environmental, energy, economic and social consequence;
(6) Retention of agricultural land as defined, with Class I being the highest priority for retention and Class VI the lowest priority; and,
(7) Compatibility of the proposed urban uses with nearby agricultural activities.

The results of the above considerations shall be included in the comprehensive plan. In the case of a change of a boundary, a governing body proposing such change in the boundary separating urbanizable land from rural land, shall follow the procedures and requirements as set forth in the Land Use Planning goal (Goal 2) for goal exceptions.

Any urban growth boundary established prior to January 1, 1975 which includes rural lands that have not been built upon shall be reviewed by the governing body, utilizing the same factors applicable to the establishment or change of urban growth boundaries. . . .

Land within the boundaries separating urbanizable land from rural land shall be considered available over time for urban uses. Conversion of urbanizable land to urban uses shall be based on consideration of:

(1) Orderly, economic provision for public facilities and services;
(2) Availability of sufficient land for the various uses to insure choices in the market place;
(3) LCDC goals; and,
(4) Encouragement of development within urban areas before conversion of urbanizable areas.

The exceptions process is found in part II of Goal 2. A goal exception is necessary where an applicable goal would otherwise prohibit a local government's proposed action. An exception is essentially a variance that allows state land use goal requirements to be waived where, for some compelling reason, it is "not possible to apply the appropriate goal to specific properties or situations." Goal 2 part II.

III. The Applicability of Goal 14

LUBA [the Land Use Board of Appeals] held, in effect, that incorporation of a city on rural land outside an established UGB is *per se* a violation of Goal 14, and is impermissible unless the county can justify a Goal 2, part II, exception. . . .

LCDC's interpretation of Goal 14 in the context of incorporation is claimed to be grounded in the language of the goal and related goal definitions. LCDC makes this simple four-step analysis:

Step 1: The effect of an incorporation is to make land available for urbanization.

Step 2: Goal 14 prohibits urbanization of land outside urban growth boundaries.

Step 3: Therefore, Goal 14 prohibits incorporation of a city on land outside urban growth boundaries.

Step 4: Because Goal 14 prohibits such an incorporation, an exception to the goal must be taken. . . .

On its face, Goal 14 provides a process for the establishment and change of UGBs, and nothing more. On this point, 1000 Friends, LCDC and the *Wasco County II* majority appear to agree. We quote from the majority opinion:

> . . . The goal's seven factors for establishing a UGB are intended to determine *how much* land and *which* land may be included in a UGB. They do not, however, address the threshold question of *whether any land* should be converted to urban uses." 68 Or. App. at 770, 686 P.2d at 378 (footnote omitted; emphasis in original).

Goal 14 concerns urban growth boundaries. The stated purpose of Goal 14 is "to provide for an orderly and efficient transition from rural to urban use." The goal provides a mandatory mechanism for accomplishing that purpose — the establishment of an urban growth boundary to identify and separate urbanizable land from rural land. The goal sets forth seven factors which must be considered before a local governing body can establish a UGB, and the result of the consideration of these seven establishment factors must be included in the comprehensive plan.[18] *See City of Salem v. Families for Responsible Govt, supra*, 298 Or. at 579, 694 P.2d at 967.

"Urbanizable" land within the UGB may be converted over time to urban uses based upon consideration of an additional four conversion factors, which are also set forth in the goal. In order to change an established UGB, the governing body must consider the seven establishment factors of Goal 14 and satisfy the requirements of the Goal 2, part II, exceptions procedure as well.

We find no support in the language of Goal 14 for LCDC's claim that the goal applies to decisions made during the pre-incorporation stage. Nor can we discover any significance in the goal definitions of "urban," "urbanizable," and "rural" land. As noted by the Court of Appeals in *Willamette University v. LCDC*, 45 Or. App. 355, 369, 608 P.2d 1178, 1186 (1980), the most that can be derived from the land use definition of these three terms is that once a city has an acknowledged UGB, land within the boundary is denominated "urban" or "urbanizable," and land without the boundary is denominated "rural."

The definition of "urban land" is central to LCDC's reasoning. Urban land is defined as

> . . . those places which must have an incorporated city. Such areas may include lands adjacent to and outside the incorporated city and may also: (a) Have concentrations of persons who generally reside and work in the area; (b) Have supporting public facilities and services.

Statewide Planning Goal Definitions. Under this definition, the existence of a city is a prerequisite for urban land. LCDC asserts that from this simple statement can be derived the underlying premise in its analysis: that the effect of incorporation

18. LCDC characterizes the first two factors of Goal 14 as the "need" factors, requiring a city to show a need for the amount of land included within the UGB. The last five factors are characterized as "locational," requiring the city to consider which land should be included within the UGB to satisfy the need demonstrated under factors (1) and (2).

by itself is to make available for urbanization land which would otherwise have to be rural, because where a city exists there may be urban land.

LCDC's theory is seductively simple because, realistically, most incorporated cities will eventually draw UGBs and thus have some land available for future urbanization. The problem with LCDC's theory regarding the effect of incorporation is that the analysis fails to distinguish a county's participation in the incorporation process from the subsequent action of a new city exercising its planning responsibilities in accordance with ORS 197.175. The county court's decision authorized the voters in the affected area to determine by election whether to create a municipal corporation. That decision neither authorized nor accomplished any change in the classification or use of the land included within the proposed corporate boundaries. Under Goal 14, it is the establishment of the UGB, and not the city's creation, that makes land available for urbanization.

In sum, before establishment of the UGB, the land within the new city's corporate boundaries retains its previous classifications. Until such time as the new city considers the seven establishment factors and adopts a UGB, pursuant to Goal 14, in cooperation with the affected county or counties, *see* ORS 197.190, and until LCDC acknowledges the comprehensive plan which includes the proposed UGB, ORS 197.251, the designations in the county's comprehensive plan and ordinances will continue to apply to the land within the new city's corporate boundaries. *City of Salem v. Families for Responsible Govt, supra*, 298 Or., at 580, 694 P.2d at 968; ORS 215.130(2). . . .

We recognized in *1000 Friends v. LCDC, supra*, and iterate now, that there is no requirement that a UGB must be coterminous with the city limits. A UGB may be designated larger or smaller than a city's corporate boundary, depending upon the outcome of the city's consideration of the Goal 14 UGB establishment factors. . . . 292 Or. at 740, 642 P.2d at 1161.[22]

This is not to say that a county, in considering an incorporation petition, has no function with respect to Goal 14. The legislature deemed a county's decision in connection with a proposed incorporation a land use decision which must accord with "the goals," without exception. We take this general mandate to mean that to the extent a county can conduct a meaningful inquiry as to all 19 goals, it must do so. A county's responsibility at the time it considers a petition for an incorporation election is no greater with respect to Goal 14 than with respect to the other goals. It is to determine the compatibility of incorporation and its consequences with the criteria stated in the goal.

Incorporation will transfer to the city actual planning authority for some of the land presently within the county's planning authority. Some of the consequences of incorporation may foreseeably affect land that remains the county's responsibility. The county cannot expect the proponents of incorporation to present a concrete or even a tentative comprehensive plan before the election, and we do not believe that the legislature intended this, although proponents may wish to offer their own

22. Cases cited by LCDC do appear to support the agency's contention that Goal 14 has been consistently interpreted to prohibit urbanization outside existing UGBs. *See Ashland v. Jackson County*, 2 Or. LUBA 378 (1981); *Conarow v. Coos County*, 2 Or. LUBA 190 (1981); *Wright v. Marion County Board of Commissioners*, 1 Or. LUBA 164 (1980); *Sandy v. Clackamas County*, 3 LCDC 139 (1979). However, even assuming the validity of the proposition that Goal 14 prohibits urbanization outside UGBs, it does not follow that an action which cannot result in urbanization before a UGB is established is also prohibited.

ideas for a plan in making their record for approval of the proposed incorporation. The county can, however, expect that the proponents present evidence of the purposes sought to be achieved by incorporation insofar as these bear on future land use, such as the kind of municipal services that the city is expected to provide and the projections about future population and tax base that these purposes assume or necessarily imply. The realism of these purposes and projections and the probable consequences for land use are, of course, open to challenge. . . .

The seven establishment factors of Goal 14 are designed to be considered in conjunction with the actual drawing of a proposed UGB. Nonetheless, under the test stated in part II of this opinion, a county can determine whether it is reasonably likely that the newly incorporated city can and will consider and address the Goal 14 factors when the city eventually draws a proposed UGB, and whether it is reasonably likely that the city can and will ensure that future urbanization is appropriate and not incompatible with Goal 14 and the other goals.

Notes and Comments

1. *The Theoretical Basis of Growth Boundaries*. Urban growth areas or boundaries are perhaps the most simple of the basic growth management tools, and for that reason they have been widely used. Oregon, with its emphasis on "Goal 14," has put in place the most detailed urban growth boundary system. The Washington Growth Management Act also requires certain local jurisdictions to adopt urban growth areas. *See* Wash. Rev. Code Ann. §§36.70A.010-.902 (West 2003).

The theory behind urban growth boundaries is fairly obvious. One author summarized the problem that such boundaries address: "Urban sprawl is a land-use pattern characterized by low density and/or uneven physical development occurring at the fringe of the urbanized areas as well as disinvestment and abandonment of older urbanized areas." G. Easley, Staying Inside the Lines — Urban Growth Boundaries 1 (American Planning Ass'n Planning Advisory Serv. Rep. No. 440, 1992). By requiring that developments occur within the boundary, urban growth boundaries attempt to promote efficient development of infrastructure within the boundary and avoid leapfrog development. At the same time, they promote preservation of agriculture and open space outside the urban boundary and allow predictability for development patterns. See George E. H. Gay, State Solutions to Growth Management: Vermont, Oregon and a Synthesis, 10 Nat. Resources & Env't, 73 (Winter 1996) ("Inside the boundary, compact housing, commercial activities, and economic development are encouraged. Outside the boundary, rural industries (logging and forestry), natural resources, and open space are promoted."). See also Greg C. Gustafson et al., The Oregon Land Use Act: Implications for Farmland and Open Space Protection, 48 J. Am. Plan. Ass'n 365 (1982).

2. *Putting Boundaries into Effect*. How should a growth management system ensure that urban growth boundaries are both adopted and effective? As the *1000 Friends of Oregon* case indicates, under the Oregon system the urban growth boundary is not effective until the pertinent state agency reviews it for compliance with statewide Planning Goal 14. *See D.S. Parklane Dev. Co., v. METRO*, 994 P.2d 1205 (Or. Ct. App. 2000) (remanding Portland metropolitan service district's designation of urban reserve areas). By contrast, in Washington the local government

adopts an urban growth boundary that is immediately effective and may be challenged only by appeal to a regional Growth Planning Hearings Board. *See* Wash. Rev. Code Ann. §36.70A.280 (West 2003 & Supp. 2004).

3. *Separating "Urban" from "Rural" Uses.* Quite obviously, a fundamental tenet of the "urban" growth boundary principle is that urban uses should not be allowed outside of the urban growth boundary. But are you sure what an "urban" use is? Given development pressures, the issue is a critical one.

In *Citizens for Responsible and Organized Planning (CROP) v. Chelan County*, 21 P.3d 304 (Wash. Ct. App. 2001), the county approved a subdivision plan for land outside the interim urban growth boundary. The plan included 15 lots averaging 1.08 acres. Concluding it was bound by the decisions of its predecessors, the county board approved the plan.

The court of appeal vacated the approval. First, it found that what the county had done in the past was irrelevant under the new growth boundary regime: "The question is whether the Matthewses' subdivision is urban. Not, have we done this before?" *Id.* at 307. The plaintiffs then jumped in to claim that the subdivision was urban as a matter of law. The court rejected that argument, remanding for the county to make findings of fact and conclusions of law on whether the subdivision was urban. *Id.* at 308.

Could the subdivision be rural at that density? Is this a question of law? Or, in this case, is it a factual question about which reasonable minds could not differ? *See also Diehl v. Mason County*, 972 P.2d 543, 548 (Wash. Ct. App. 1999) (residential lot sizes of .5 acres in "rural activity area," with lots as small as .125 acre, are densities that "would allow for urban-like development, not consistent with primarily agricultural uses").

4. *Land Inside the Growth Boundary.* What is the legal effect of designating land as outside an urban growth boundary? May a city deny a subdivision approval inside such a boundary on the grounds that it wishes to preserve agriculture? In *Philippi v. City of Sublimity, Oregon*, 650 P.2d 1038 (Or. Ct. App. 1982), the court of appeals rejected that contention, holding that "[i]t would be anomalous for a local government to rely on a policy favoring the retention of agricultural land qua agricultural land as a basis for precluding development within the UGB of land designated and zoned for residential use." *Id.* at 1041. The Oregon Supreme Court reversed, concluding that the city retained the power, within its urban growth boundaries, to establish buffer zones that were "urbanizable" but not yet developed. *Philippi v. City of Sublimity, Oregon*, 662 P.2d 325 (Or. 1983).

5. *Land Outside the Growth Boundary.* In *The Cooper Point Ass'n v. Thurston*, 31 P.3d 28 (Wash. Ct. App. 2001), the county proposed to extend a sewer line from an urban treatment line to a rural area. The four-inch line would serve two unincorporated communities comprising a total of 106 homes, each of which was currently served by small treatment plants. Some of the lots, however, were outside the service areas of those plants. Under Washington law, "[i]n general, it is not appropriate that urban governmental services be extended to or expanded in rural areas except in those limited circumstances shown to be necessary to protect basic public health and safety and the environment." *Id.* at 437.

Did the county violate the statute by approving the treatment line? Are there any additional facts you would need to know in order to decide?

6. *The Effectiveness of Growth Boundaries*. Do you think that urban growth boundaries actually will operate to produce concise development? Consider the following assessment of the Oregon program:

> Securing local compliance with these [urban growth boundaries] has been difficult. Market forces and citizen attitudes still favor low-density development, with single-family detached homes and reliance on automobiles remaining prime objectives of many Americans. Translated through the political process to local plans and regulations, these attitudes appear rather intractable. Oregon's experience is telling. Although all municipalities adopted urban growth boundaries as required by the state statute, a considerable amount of development still takes place outside them. A recent evaluation of Oregon's experience found that more development takes place outside some small town boundaries than within them. Widespread development on "exception" lands (deemed not usable for agriculture or forestry) and waivers by local governments have undermined the state's policy.

Douglas R. Porter, State Growth Management: The Intergovernmental Experiment, 13 Pace L. Rev. 481, 497 (1993). See also Keith W. Dearborn & Ann M. Gygi, Planner's Panacea or Pandora's Box: A Realistic Assessment of the Role of Urban Growth Areas in Achieving Growth Management Goals, 16 U. Puget Sound L. Rev. 975, 977-978 (1993).

F. PERSPECTIVES ON GROWTH MANAGEMENT

Now that you have been exposed to the principal techniques that make up "growth management," it is time to put their use into some perspective. The following articles, drawn from the academic literature, the government press, and the popular media, offer distinctly different viewpoints on the efficacy and morality of growth control ordinances, sprawl, and "smart growth."

■ BRIAN W. OHM, REFORMING LAND PLANNING LEGISLATION AT THE DAWN OF THE 21ST CENTURY: THE EMERGING INFLUENCE OF SMART GROWTH AND LIVABLE COMMUNITIES

32 Urb. Law. 181, 190-191 (2000)

Smart growth has no precise definition. An exhibition on smart growth at the National Building Museum in Washington, D.C., describes smart growth as a reaction to the pattern of development in the United States since World War II. According to a commentator for the Urban Land Institute, smart growth is not anti-growth. Rather it focuses on how growth occurs. It is an evolving approach to development that balances economic development with environmental protection and a better quality of life. While smart growth avoids the use of the term "growth management," these descriptions of smart growth sound similar to definitions of growth management and the recognized purposes of growth management. Nonetheless, smart growth is a recognition that the existing growth management programs have not solved the issues of sprawl. The current problems associated with growth and change are similar to the problems communities have faced for decades. While states have passed a variety of laws to address the issues, according to one commentator, success is in the eye of the beholder. Progress has been made on some issues, such as environmental protection. Other issues, such as the concentration of poverty within older cities, have magnified. . . .

The general principles articulated by the Smart Growth Network help define the objectives of smart growth: (1) mix land uses; (2) take advantage of compact building design; (3) create housing opportunities and choices; (4) create walkable communities; (5) foster distinctive, attractive communities with a strong sense of place; (6) preserve open space, farmland, natural beauty, and critical environmental areas; (7) strengthen and direct development toward existing communities; (8) provide a variety of transportation choices; (9) make development decisions predictable, fair, and cost-effective; and (10) encourage community and stakeholder collaboration in development decisions. A common theme behind many of these principles involves increasing the density of development. This poses a major challenge given that the exodus from the cities following the Second World War was a rebellion against density. People want to live in a small community with access to a big city.

TRANSCRIPT, INTERVIEW: JACKSONVILLE, FLORIDA, MAYOR JOHN DELANEY TALKS ABOUT PROBLEMS WITH URBAN SPRAWL

Morning Edition, National Public Radio, May 9, 2001

BOB EDWARDS, host: Urban sprawl continues to cause problems for America's cities. Recent studies have blamed sprawl for increased traffic congestion, environmental pollution and the loss of wildlife areas nationwide. Sprawl can also mean economic growth for cities. And officials from Atlanta to Portland are searching for ways to keep their cities thriving, while keeping sprawl in check. Planners in Jacksonville, Florida, think they've found a way to do that. John Delaney is the mayor of Jacksonville. He says the strategy is to anticipate sprawl problems before they arise.

Mayor JOHN DELANEY (Jacksonville, Florida): One of the things that we've tried to do is to say, "If you know you're going to change, what do you need to do about it?" The downsides of growth are pretty obvious. One, the environment gets impacted, the quality of your water, your land, your air. Secondly, you tend to leave the older neighborhoods behind, the older communities, typically the urban core neighborhoods, etc. And, third, the infrastructure doesn't keep up. You don't deal with the roads, you don't deal with the schools, the playgrounds, the parks, the water lines, the sewer lines, the drainage. So you can come up, thematically, with a healthier approach to dealing with growth.

EDWARDS: So what has your approach been?

Mayor DELANEY: Well, we've had a couple of different modes. One is, if we don't want the growth to go there, let's buy that land and take it out of development. And do it. . . .

EDWARDS: And call them parks?

Mayor DELANEY: Basically, it's a preserve. We're looking to have, frankly, the largest urban preserve system in the country. And there's sort of two types of parks, there's what's [sic] you call active parks or passive parks. The actives, the ballfields and the soccer fields. And we've obviously got those, but those need to be inner, sort of in the inside of the doughnut. The fundamental rule of attacking sprawl is to have density close to your downtown so that a mass transit system can work, so your infrastructure works, and to not allow it to sprawl outside the center of that doughnut. So we're trying to buy, in effect, the doughnut. We're taking all of that out of development.

EDWARDS: Cities like growth, they like more population, they like to increase the tax base, they like to attract jobs. All of that creates sprawl.

Mayor DELANEY: No question. No question. The growth is inevitable. Clearly, what you want to try to do is if you're going to have it, make it the best growth. The buzz phrase now is smart growth, which is to adapt it in a way that costs your community less in the short-term and the long-term. We, in government, so often look to just get through this budget cycle or this election cycle. And it doesn't make much sense to invest in those infrastructure items, to invest in the environment now, when the price can be pushed off into the future. The community said that we want to try to spend for the future, as opposed to right now. And so part of what we did last year is we set aside $100 million to buy a corridor for a rapid transit system, a light rail system. Now you've got to get to about a two, three, four million in population, or metro area, to really make a rapid transit system work.

By the time you get that big, that land's all gone. By definition, it's the most expensive land around because that's where everybody is driving, the shopping is and the residential is. And we said we know we're not going to build this for 20 years, but let's buy the land now when it's the cheapest it's going to be. So if you look ahead at that, then you can make growth work for you as opposed to against you. And you can save those trees, you can save those rivers, you can save the environment.

■ TIMOTHY S. BISHOP & CRISTINA C. TILLEY, SMART GROWTH OR DUMB BUREAUCRACY?

32 Envtl. L. Rptr. 10822 (2002)

In the west Chicago suburb of Sugar Grove—population 4,000, twice what it was 10 years ago—new large-lot developments spread spider-like from the downtown public library, police station, and village hall out into open farmland. The village has no sizeable employers or large shopping centers, and has limited recreational facilities. All those things are available close by in other suburbs and, of course, in the city of Chicago. After elementary school, children travel to neighboring suburbs for high school. When developers come calling with high-density projects and in-fill proposals, they are sent packing. The village administration explains that people who want to live in a town with greater density and with every service right at hand have their choice of numerous other suburbs. Those who choose to live in Sugar Grove do so because they want large lots and plenty of open space and are willing to travel to their jobs and to shopping in order to live in that sort of environment. The village has identified its niche, markets to that niche, and vows to resist the pressure for different types of development that would change its character. . . .

FRED SIEGEL, IS REGIONAL GOVERNMENT THE ANSWER?

The Public Interest (Fall 1999) 85, 86-87

Undoubtedly, the loss of land and the environmental degradation produced by sprawl are serious problems that demand public attention. But sprawl also brings enormous benefits as well as considerable costs. It is, in part, an expression of the new high-tech economy whose campus-like office parks on the periphery of urban areas have driven the economic boom of the 1990s. And it's sprawl that has sustained the record rise in home ownership. Sprawl is not some malignancy to be summarily excised but, rather, part and parcel of prosperity. . . .

Sprawl is part of the price we're paying for something novel in human history—the creation of a mass upper middle class. Net household worth has been increasing at the unparalleled annual rate of 10 percent since 1994, so that while in 1970, only 3.2 percent of households had an annual income of $100,000 (in today's dollars), by 1996, 8.2 percent of American households could boast a six-figure annual income. The new prosperity is reflected in the size of new homes, many of whose owners no doubt decry the arrival of still more "McMansions" and new residents, clogging the roads and schools of the latest subdivisions. In the midst of the 1980's boom, homebuilders didn't have a category for mass-produced houses of more than 3,000 square feet. By 1996, one out of every seven new homes built was larger than 3,000 square feet. . . .

Sprawl also reflects upward mobility for the aspiring lower-middle class. Nearly a half-century ago, Samuel Lubell dedicated *The Future of American Politics* to the memory of his mother, "who pioneered on the urban frontier." Lubell described a process parallel to the settling of the West, in which families on "the Old Tenement Trail" were continually on the move in search of a better life. In the cities, they abandoned crowded tenements on New York's Lower East Side for better housing in the South Bronx, and from there, went to the "West Bronx, crossing that Great Social Divide—the Grand Concourse—beyond which rolled true middle-class country where janitors were called superintendents." . . .

GERALD E. FRUG, EUPHEMISM AS A POLITICAL STRATEGY

30 Envtl. L. Rep. 11189 (2000)

The standard arguments for smart growth rely on "the substitution of an agreeable or inoffensive expression for one that may offend or suggest something unpleasant"—to quote the dictionary's definition of a euphemism. "Smart growth" is, of course, itself a feel-good term. But it is by no means the only one. Almost as pervasive are terms like "sustainability" and "livable communities." Who could be for dumb growth or think that unsustainable, unlivable places were desirable? Moreover, it is not just these general catch-phrases that rely on euphemism for their effect. When the goals of smart growth are defined more precisely, they regularly skirt controversy by omitting any hint of conflict or dissonance. Consider, for example, the Sierra Club's one-sentence definition:

> Smart growth is intelligent, well-planned development that channels growth into existing areas, provides public transportation options, and preserves farm land and open space.

This definition combines an appeal to values as diverse as rationality (intelligent, well-planned), economic vitality (growth), freedom of choice (transportation options), and the love of both cities (existing areas) and nature (open space). But its emphasis, as is true for much of the smart growth literature, is on the environment. . . .

These euphemistic appeals of smart growth are designed to generate support for a revolutionary change in American urban policy. I am very much for this revolutionary change, but smart growth advocates should frankly admit, at least to each other, how revolutionary it would be. No one living in American metropolitan areas would be unaffected if smart growth objectives were actually achieved.

Intelligent, well-planned development would prevent people from moving to where they apparently want to move—farther and farther out of the central city. As a result, it would produce a kind of density that the long-standing dream of a single-family house surrounded by a yard has sought to escape. Moreover, if this increased density is actually to take place in existing areas, it means reviving the central cities—from St. Louis to Detroit, from Camden to Oakland—that are now filled not simply with poor people but with poor African Americans, Latinos, and immigrants from around the world. It thus requires ending the segregation of metropolitan areas by income and ethnicity—a form of segregation that has generated more and more sprawl as the inner suburbs, following the central cities, have begun to diversify. Increasing density, in other words, will mean that the people who are moving to the outer suburbs will need to learn to live with the very kinds of people that they are now running away from. And this reconciliation will have to take place in more than the central cities. If the central cities become more prosperous because that's where growth is channeled—that is, if they gentrify—many poor people will be driven out of them by rising housing prices. They will need places to go. The areas in the metropolitan region now closed to them will therefore have to become places where they can live. . . .

■ CLINT BOLICK, SUBVERTING THE AMERICAN DREAM: GOVERNMENT DICTATED "SMART GROWTH" IS UNWISE AND UNCONSTITUTIONAL

148 U. Pa. L. Rev. 859, 860, 863 (2000)

"Sprawl." It's an ugly word, conjuring images of some unshaven guy with a massive beer-gut in a T-shirt spread out over a ratty sofa in front of a television set droning endless football games.

Given such imagery, "sprawl" is a clever and effective euphemism to denigrate a phenomenon in which tens of millions of Americans have affirmatively taken part: suburbanization. In search of a better life for themselves and their families, many individuals freely choose to endure longer commutes and greater inconveniences in exchange for larger, more affordable homes in safe neighborhoods. The debate among the relative desirability of urban, suburban, and rural lifestyles has raged forever and probably always shall; but in our free society, reconciliation of competing preferences in the realm of habitation always has been entrusted to free individual choice.

Until now. The latest wave of politically correct conventional wisdom holds that government planners, rather than individual choices collectively expressed through the marketplace, should determine where people live. Obviously such a proposition, starkly stated, would make most Americans recoil. After all, homeownership is a cornerstone of the American Dream, and private property rights are its essential foundation.

So, the planning enthusiasts necessarily effect a beneficent facade. They are not against suburbs; they are against urban sprawl. They are not against development; they favor "smart growth." They condemn congestion, which everyone hates, and propose modest-sounding initiatives that promise to solve most of mankind's problems without cost or inconvenience. The dirty, unstated secret, however, is that the core of any effective smart-growth agenda is coercion — substituting free individual choice with government edicts.

Not only is such a program profoundly contrary to core American values, but like many episodes of government planning, it is certain to produce perverse consequences. Moreover, the Constitution places important constraints on coercive government regulation that bestows benefits upon some while imposing burdens on others in the exercise of property rights. One way or the other, free choice will win out. We should direct our energies toward expanding rather than contracting individual autonomy, especially in such an important area as homeownership. . . .

I. Policy Considerations . . .

[U]rban growth boundaries are increasingly popular around the nation. If people vote with their feet by moving to the suburbs, why would they vote politically to prevent further suburbanization? The answer is simple: once people move to the suburbs, they become interested in preventing additional traffic congestion or similar burdens associated with other people who might follow their lead. So they eagerly roll up the welcome mat. Such is the nature of politics.

This approach creates inherent unfairness in that growth restrictions implicitly benefit people who already have what they want, to the detriment of those who aspire to the same. Portland, Oregon . . . provides an example of this phenomenon. Portland's urban growth boundary is "literally a line in the land outside of which growth is heavily discouraged or even prohibited." The policy is implemented by Metro, a regional planning authority. Metro "has not increased the boundary sufficiently to meet new demand," enlarging available space by only 2% in 1997 despite an expected 80% increase in population projected by the year 2040. In trying to defy demographic trends and individual preferences, Portland soon will become a city that is bursting at the seams, with nowhere to expand. Metro has responded to these dire forecasts by planning to "shrink the average lot size for single-family homes by almost a third," thereby squeezing many more people within the same space. It also will restrict retail development to thirty acres, thereby precluding many popular retailers, such as the smart growth advocates' favorite bogeyman, the dreaded Wal-Mart. Predictably, the artificial diminution of suburban housing development has led to sharply escalating prices: Staley reports that Portland's housing prices rose by 63.8% from 1990-1995, much faster than the U.S. median of 18.2% and faster than the price rises experienced by fifty other large metropolitan areas.

The urban growth boundary produces numerous perverse effects. One effect is a system of haves and have-nots: all growth restrictions lead to higher prices, disproportionately impacting lower-income and first-time homebuyers. Another is that while open space outside the boundary is off-limits for development, space inside the city comes increasingly at a premium. . .

Notes and Comments

1. *Defining "Smart Growth."* As you can seen from the excerpts, the recent debate about growth management centers on the implementation of what proponents call "Smart Growth." As the Ohm article notes, "Smart growth has no precise definition." Does that imprecision doom it to failure? Or is the idea itself—*smart* growth—sufficiently intuitive that it can be fleshed out with particulars?

2. *Comes the Revolution?* In another excerpt, Professor Gerald Frug directly confronts the vagueness in the term. He first gives the idea a more precise definition: "Smart growth is intelligent, well-planned development that channels growth into existing areas, provides public transportation options, and preserves farm land and open space." He then suggests that these ideas are truly revolutionary. Do you agree? If so, does their radical nature doom them to failure in a market economy?

3. *Buying Our Way Out of It.* In the National Public Radio transcript, the Mayor of Jacksonville, Florida, says that a large part of channeling growth is through government purchases. *See also* Robert McClure, A Huge Land Deal To Stem Urban Sprawl, Seattle Post-Intelligencer, Jan. 17, 2002 (reporting on an announcement that the nonprofit Evergreen Forest Trust would buy 104,000 acres from the Weyerhaeuser Co., a purchase that appears to be the highest priced land conservation transaction in U.S. history). How useful is this tool for growth management?

4. *The Search for Culprits.* If sprawl is bad, what is causing it? The excerpt from the Bishop and Tilley article discusses a Chicago suburb that is pro-sprawl and proud of it. It believes that it is filling a market niche. If that's true, then can anti-sprawl forces really change this dynamic? In his article "Can Technology Reduce the Energy Cost of Sprawl," 30 Envtl. L. Rptr. 10829 (2000), Professor Fred Bosselman points to various new technologies that can reduce the energy cost of sprawl and, more broadly, how technological changes in transportation can influence land use patterns.

The Siegel excerpt reminds us that sprawl has another side. He finds that sprawl is simply the price to be paid for prosperity—particularly, the creation of a mass upper middle class. Viewed in that light, won't limits on sprawl, if they are made, be even harder to implement?

5. *The Regional Answer.* In Chapter 9, you examined various mechanisms that moved the locus of land use control from the local to the state or regional level. Many have argued that curbing sprawl requires that kind of structural change.

Others suggest that local government's thirst for tax dollars is a major culprit. *See, e.g.*, Eran Razin, Policies to Control Sprawl: Planning Regulations or Changes in the "Rules of the Game"?, 35 Urb. Studies No. 2, 321 (1998) (arguing that changes in the way that local governments are financed are critical). The problem has been recognized before. Why isn't more done about it?

6. *A Cold, Hard Look.* Finally, the excerpt from the Bolick piece gives you the flavor of the Smart Growth critics. *See also* Bernard Siegan, Smart Growth and Other Infirmities of Land Use Controls, 38 S.D. L. Rev. 693 (2001). Is Smart Growth inherently paternalistic? Or is it simply a response to perceived externalities of current growth patterns?

7. *Literature.* The literature in this area is enormous. Here is a sampling of recent pieces: John R. Nolon, Local Land Use Controls That Achieve Smart Growth, 31 Envtl. L. Rep. 11025 (2001); Timothy Beatley and Richard Collins, Smart Growth and Beyond: Transitioning to a Sustainable Society, 19 Va. Envtl. L. J. 287 (2000); Symposium on Urban Sprawl, 17 Ga. St. U. L. Rev. 1019 (2001); William W. Buzbee, Urban Sprawl, Federalism, and the Problem of Institutional Complexity, 67 Urb. L. Rev. 57 (1999); Patricia E. Salkin, Using Smart Growth to Achieve Sustainable Land Use Policies, 32 Envtl. L. Rep. 11385 (2002); Paul J. Boudreaux, Looking the Ogre in the Eye: Ten Tough Questions for the Anti-Sprawl Movement, 14 Tul. Envtl. L.J. 171 (2000); Lee R. Epstein, Choking Slowly: Is Managing (or Smart) Growth Just Planning a Slow(er) Demise (and If It Is, Is There an Alternative?), 33 Envtl. L. Rptr. 10280 (2003); Michel Lewyn, Suburban Sprawl: Not Just An Environmental Issue, 84 Marq. L. Rev. 301 (2000); and Symposium, A Look At Smart Growth and Urban Sprawl, 21 St. Louis U. Pub. L. Rev. 253 (2002).

12

Securing a Sufficient Housing Supply

A. INTRODUCTION

1. Housing and Land Use Regulation

The provision of housing has long been the implicit assumption of land use regulation and a primary purpose for its existence. Initially, concerns about nuisances and similar externalities led to a view of zoning as a means of separating polluting land uses from housing districts. Almost immediately, however, the process was also used to separate different classes of housing occupants. In New York City, the Fifth Avenue gentry invoked zoning policy to exclude the commercial loft and its laborers. Soon, the more affluent of suburbia utilized zoning to distance their community from the noise, smell, and pollution of the factory. In the process, they also distanced themselves from the sight of workers and the poor.

Zoning codes and subdivision regulations speak in neutral tones of environmental concerns, health, safety, and the adequacy of facilities. Implicit in that process, however, is the assumption that the poor will compete in the marketplace for shelter. Indeed, theorists assumed that the poor would always be provided for, as those better off economically moved to bigger and newer housing, leaving existing housing for the less affluent.

This model of "filtration" continues to dominate housing policy today, despite a lack of scientific support for the accuracy of the model. In recent decades, deteriorated housing stock has been diminished by urban renewal, code enforcement of housing conditions, and increasingly expensive mandates to upgrade housing for health, fire, or earthquake safety. Some previously affordable housing has been converted or "gentrified" through rehabilitation to provide housing stock for the affluent. Similarly, affordable multi-family housing in some instances has been converted to condominiums to allow purchasers to take advantage of the tax shelters of homeownership. The increasing presence of the homeless is also a reminder that housing policies have been unsuccessful, and that land use planning for too long has failed to accommodate the rising needs for shelter.

2. *The Suburbs and the Cities*

As suburbs have developed without the provision of housing for the poor, the result has been an increasing concentration of the poor in central cities. At the same time, retail stores, restaurants, and industries have relocated to the suburbs and beyond, leaving the poor in a deteriorating metropolis with limited access to the new job markets. Decisions regarding the deployment of transit also have contributed to the current condition; today, a good part of the transit systems is designed to bring suburban dwellers to downtown financial and service-oriented jobs.

Overall, the result has been destabilized cities with little economic development. Concerns over this situation have been voiced in the legal and planning literature, and occasionally uttered in judicial dissents to the tidal wave of endorsements of zoning as an institution. Zoning has generated a pattern of land use that is frequently compared to a doughnut or a bagel, with the more affluent in the suburbs surrounding a central core of the poor, ethnic minorities, and those dependent on expensive public services including transit, health care, and welfare. This pattern of suburban land use typically contains numerous tracts of single-family, detached homes on lots ranging from one-quarter to three or four acres. The pattern also features the virtual absence of government-subsidized housing and, frequently, little multi-family housing. The imposition of expensive exactions, development conditions, and impact fees contributes to rendering these suburban homes inaccessible to low income individuals.

The lack of decent, safe, and sanitary affordable housing is seemingly intractable and worsening. According to a report of the National Housing Conference based on 1999 American Housing Survey data, more than 13 million households are paying in excess of 50 percent of their income for housing or are living in substandard conditions. One in Seven Households Has Critical Housing Need, Report Says, [Current Developments] Hous. Dev. Rep. (West) 776 (2002). An inadequate supply of affordable rental housing in the suburbs aggravates inflationary rent increases and can discourage potential employers and investors from locating in the region. The lack of adequate, affordable housing also results in other impacts for communities such as heightened racial and economic segregation, long and costly commutes to employment centers often distant from central city housing markets, and exposure to higher incidences of housing discrimination. *See* Justin D. Cummins, Housing Matters: Why Our Communities Must Have Affordable Housing, 28 Wm. Mitchell L. Rev. 197 (2001).

A central focus of state efforts to breach the exclusionary wall of the suburbs, indeed simply to develop affordable housing, has been the availability of financing. In recent decades the federal government has been the primary source of affordable housing subsidies, but the federal government has reduced its role each year since the end of the Nixon Administration. With today's agenda of budget-balancing and deficits, communities must look elsewhere to fund low income housing. *See also* Kristin A. Siegesmund, The Looming Subsidized Housing Crisis, 27 Wm. Mitchell L. Rev. 1123 (2000) (arguing that the ability of subsidized landlords to exit program participation is exacerbating the housing crisis).

3. *The Assault on the Zoning Citadel*

The Supreme Court's decision in *Village of Euclid v. Ambler Realty Co.*, 272 U.S. 365 (1926) (reprinted in Chapter 2), established a model of judicial deference toward zoning that, some have strongly argued, has been responsible for institutionalizing a form of economic segregation. Zoning classifications and cost-inflating development criteria, ranging from large lots to expensive infrastructure conditions, have greatly limited housing choices available to many individuals. At the same time, the zoning decisions of local governmental bodies have enjoyed a presumption of regularity, and considerable deference from the courts. Typically immune from judicial invalidation, zoning constitutes a citadel—an institution largely impervious to plaintiffs' attacks.

In some housing cases, however, that citadel proved vulnerable. In 1965, the Pennsylvania Supreme Court broke with the pattern of general judicial endorsement of local zoning to invalidate large-lot, suburban zoning that precluded the opportunity for apartment development. In *National Land & Investment Co. v. Kohn*, 215 A.2d 597 (Pa. 1965), the court found that such "exclusionary zoning" was incompatible with serving the general welfare and thus was not within the police power authority of the state.

While a few state courts followed the lead of Pennsylvania, New Jersey went beyond the prohibitory nature of the Pennsylvania principle. In the landmark decision *Southern Burlington County NAACP v. Township of Mount Laurel*, 336 A.2d 713 (N.J.), *appeal dismissed*, 423 U.S. 808 (1975), the New Jersey Supreme Court held that states must regulate for the general welfare of all the state's citizens. Communities are obligated to regulate land use in such a way as to make it realistically possible to house all economic segments of the community. Thus, each community had an obligation to affirmatively plan housing for its "fair share" of regional housing needs.

New Jersey's struggle to implement the *Mount Laurel* doctrine has been a long and difficult one. Perhaps the most significant development during this era was that, in response to increasingly militant rulings from the state courts, the New Jersey Legislature passed a law to hasten compliance with the new doctrine. Although the results of this process have not satisfied critics, the efforts to comply have surely generated a significant stock of affordable housing, a performance not replicated in any other jurisdiction.

Litigation involving exclusionary zoning has involved many groups representing a wide array of interests and has resulted in judicial recognition in the state courts of third-party rights in the development process. Standing to litigate has been granted to developers (even to raise the rights of future occupants), taxpayers, civil rights advocates, housing advocates, and homebuilder organizations. *See Southern Burlington County NAACP v. Township of Mount Laurel*, 456 A.2d 390 (N.J. 1983) (*Mount Laurel II*) (any individual or group interested in securing low income housing has standing to challenge exclusionary zoning).

Although a few states have altered housing and zoning policy by judicial decision, numerous reforms have come from the legislatures at the state and local level. California requires local plans to contain housing elements that plan for affordable housing. Cal. Govt. Code §65302(c) (West 1997). A number of other jurisdictions have followed this approach in establishing obligations to plan for affordable housing.

4. Inclusionary Zoning

The term "inclusionary zoning" is simply the opposite of exclusionary zoning. Inclusionary zoning encompasses more than just zoning techniques; it includes such mechanisms as (1) zoning for "least cost" housing by allowing smaller homes to be built on smaller lots with a minimum of amenities consistent with minimum housing code standards; (2) mandatory inclusion requirements, whereby developers must set aside a percentage of project units in a development for affordable housing; (3) the use of density bonuses, whereby developments with a percentage of affordable housing are allotted permission to exceed standard density limits; (4) rent "skewing," whereby rents on unsubsidized units are increased to permit reduction of rents on a percentage of the units; and (5) housing "linkage." *See Mount Laurel II* (reprinted below).

"Housing linkage" is the term used to describe impact fees imposed on a development so as to produce affordable housing. The fees are imposed on the type of development that attracts low income workers, either as employees who build the development or as permanent residents who will work in businesses that occupy the development. The fees also reflect the fact that as available land in the local jurisdiction is used up through development, the cost of acquisition for affordable housing development is likely to be higher. The effect is to discourage the development of affordable housing. *See Commercial Builders v. City of Sacramento*, 941 F.2d 872 (9th Cir. 1991), *cert. denied*, 504 U.S. 931 (1992) (reprinted below).

5. Political Reality and Ethical Obligations

The tension between the need to ensure access to decent housing, the evolving tests for applying the Takings Clause of the Fifth Amendment, and the leaner, deficit-conscious national and state budgets makes the issues in this chapter among the most controversial of our times. The result is an area of law in a dynamic state of flux.

As is described above, one of the most important developments in recent land use planning law has been the emergence of a principle, reflected widely in some statutes, that localities have an obligation to plan for affordable housing. This obligation, however, presents a difficulty that we have seen before in other aspects of land use law: the legal obligation may fundamentally conflict with political reality. In various subtle (or less than subtle) ways, local officials may either refuse to plan or balk at implementing those plans. Is there a fundamental flaw in the theory of mandatory planning for affordable housing, in that the theory seeks to override local "politics"? Compare the experience of compliance with civil rights nondiscrimination laws.

Ultimately, the provision of affordable housing raises fundamental ethical issues that transcend land use. What is the moral obligation of a community toward the poor and the dependent? Should there be an ethical obligation to avoid public policy that adversely affects the poor? Is there a further ethical obligation to study the benefits and adverse impacts or dangers to the community that result from current planning policies and practices towards workers and the poor? The questions are serious and deserve your thought.

B. JUDICIAL INVALIDATION

In the first successful challenge to exclusionary zoning, the Pennsylvania Supreme Court invalidated a scheme of providing for a minimum lot size of four acres in a suburban community located in the path of urban development. *National Land & Investment Co. v. Kohn*, 215 A.2d 597 (Pa. 1965). The basis for the decision was a violation of substantive due process; the community failed to exercise its police powers in a manner beneficial to the general welfare. According to the Pennsylvania court, communities must plan for the future and not simply wall it out.

The court rejected the municipality's offered justification of traffic congestion, because the current street system was adequate. Concerns over sewage also would not support the zoning scheme, since the community had the capacity to develop adequate sewage treatment, and there was no evidence of impending pollution from smaller homesites. Also rejected was the municipality's contention that large lots were useful in retaining the rural character of the community or the setting for the fine old homes in the community, particularly as no market existed for homes on such large lots.

National Land qualified the community's right to regulate and also established an affirmative obligation to not engage in exclusionary zoning. Ten years later, the following case defined the extent of that obligation.

■ SOUTHERN BURLINGTON COUNTY N.A.A.C.P. v. TOWNSHIP OF MOUNT LAUREL

336 A.2d 713 (N.J.), appeal dismissed, 423 U.S. 808 (1975)

HALL, J.

This case attacks the system of land use regulation by defendant Township of Mount Laurel on the ground that low and moderate income families are thereby unlawfully excluded from the municipality. . . .

There is not the slightest doubt that New Jersey has been, and continues to be, faced with a desperate need for housing, especially of decent living accommodations economically suitable for low and moderate income families. . . .

Plaintiffs represent the minority group poor (black and Hispanic) seeking such quarters. But they are not the only category of persons barred from so many municipalities by reason of restrictive land use regulations. We have reference to young and elderly couples, single persons and large, growing families not in the poverty class, but who still cannot afford the only kinds of housing realistically permitted in most places—relatively high-priced, single-family detached dwellings on sizeable lots and, in some municipalities, expensive apartments. We will, therefore, consider the case from the wider viewpoint that the effect of Mount Laurel's land use regulation has been to prevent various categories of persons from living in the township because of the limited extent of their income and resources. In this connection, we accept the representation of the municipality's counsel at oral argument that the regulatory scheme was not adopted with any desire or intent to exclude prospective residents on the obviously illegal bases of race, origin or believed social incompatibility. . . .

I. The Facts

Mount Laurel is a flat, sprawling township, 22 square miles, or about 14,000 acres, in area, on the west central edge of Burlington County. It is roughly triangular in shape, with its base, approximately eight miles long, extending in a northeasterly-southwesterly direction roughly parallel with and a few miles east of the Delaware River. Part of its southerly side abuts Cherry Hill in Camden County. That section of the township is about seven miles from the boundary line of the city of Camden and not more than 10 miles from the Benjamin Franklin Bridge crossing the river to Philadelphia. . . .

The growth of the township has been spurred by the construction or improvement of main highways through or near it. The New Jersey Turnpike, and now route I- 295, a freeway paralleling the turnpike, traverse the municipality near its base, with the main Camden-Philadelphia turnpike interchange at the corner nearest Camden. State route 73 runs at right angles to the turnpike at the interchange and route 38 slices through the northeasterly section. Routes 70 and U.S. 130 are not far away. This highway network gives the township a most strategic location from the standpoint of transport of goods and people by truck and private car. There is no other means of transportation. . . .

Under the present ordinance, 29.2% of all the land in the township, or 4121 acres, is zoned for industry. This amounts to 2800 more acres than were so zoned by the 1954 ordinance. The industrial districts comprise most of the land on both sides of the turnpike and routes I-295, 73 and 38. Only industry meeting specified performance standards is permitted. The effect is to limit the use substantially to light manufacturing, research, distribution of goods, offices and the like. Some non-industrial uses, such as agriculture, farm dwellings, motels, a harness racetrack, and certain retail sales and service establishments, are permitted in this zone. At the time of trial no more than 100 acres, mostly in the southwesterly corner along route 73 adjacent to the turnpike and I-295 interchanges, were actually occupied by industrial uses. They had been constructed in recent years, mostly in several industrial parks, and involved tax ratables of about 16 million dollars. The rest of the land so zoned has remained undeveloped. If it were fully utilized, the testimony was that about 43,500 industrial jobs would be created, but it appeared clear that, as happens in the case of so many municipalities, much more land has been so zoned than the reasonable potential for industrial movement or expansion warrants. At the same time, however, the land cannot be used for residential development under the general ordinance. . . .

The general ordinance requirements, while not as restrictive as those in many similar municipalities, nonetheless realistically allow only homes within the financial reach of persons of at least middle income. The R-1 zone requires a minimum lot area of 9375 square feet, a minimum lot width of 75 feet at the building line, and a minimum dwelling floor area of 1100 square feet if a one- story building and 1300 square feet if one and one-half stories or higher. Originally this zone comprised about 2500 acres. Most of the subdivisions have been constructed within it so that only a few hundred acres remain (the testimony was at variance as to the exact amount). The R-2 zone, comprising a single district of 141 acres in the northeasterly corner, has been completely developed. While it only required a minimum floor area of 900 square feet for a one-story dwelling, the minimum lot size was 11,000 square feet; otherwise the requisites were the same as in the R-1 zone. . . .

The record thoroughly substantiates the findings of the trial court that over the years Mount Laurel "has acted affirmatively to control development and to attract a selective type of growth" and that "through its zoning ordinances has exhibited economic discrimination in that the poor have been deprived of adequate housing and the opportunity to secure the construction of subsidized housing, and has used federal, state, county and local finances and resources solely for the betterment of middle and upper-income persons." . . .

This pattern of land use regulation has been adopted for the same purpose in developing municipality after developing municipality. Almost every one acts solely in its own selfish and parochial interest and in effect builds a wall around itself to keep out those people or entities not adding favorably to the tax base. . . .

II. The Legal Issue . . .

We conclude that every such municipality must, by its land use regulations, presumptively make realistically possible an appropriate variety and choice of housing. More specifically, presumptively it cannot foreclose the opportunity of the classes of people mentioned for low and moderate income housing and in its regulations must affirmatively afford that opportunity, at least to the extent of the municipality's fair share of the present and prospective regional need therefor. These obligations must be met unless the particular municipality can sustain the heavy burden of demonstrating peculiar circumstances which dictate that it should not be required so to do.

We reach this conclusion under state law and so do not find it necessary to consider federal constitutional grounds urged by plaintiffs. . . .

It is elementary theory that all police power enactments, no matter at what level of government, must conform to the basic state constitutional requirements of substantive due process and equal protection of the laws. These are inherent in Art. I, par. 1 of our Constitution, the requirements of which may be more demanding than those of the federal Constitution. . . .

The warning implicates the matter of *whose* general welfare must be served or not violated in the field of land use regulation. Frequently the decisions in this state, including those just cited, have spoken only in terms of the interest of the enacting municipality, so that it has been thought, at least in some quarters, that such was the only welfare requiring consideration. It is, of course, true that many cases have dealt only with regulations having little, if any, outside impact where the local decision is ordinarily entitled to prevail. However, it is fundamental and not to be forgotten that the zoning power is a police power of the state and the local authority is acting only as a delegate of that power and is restricted in the same manner as is the state. So, when regulation does have a substantial external impact, the welfare of the state's citizens beyond the borders of the particular municipality cannot be disregarded and must be recognized and served. . . .

It is plain beyond dispute that proper provision for adequate housing of all categories of people is certainly an absolute essential in promotion of the general welfare required in all local land use regulation. Further the universal and constant need for such housing is so important and of such broad public interest that the general welfare which developing municipalities like Mount Laurel must consider extends beyond their boundaries and cannot be parochially confined to the claimed good of the particular municipality. It has to follow that, broadly speaking, the presumptive obligation arises for each such municipality affirmatively to plan and provide, by its land use regulations, the reasonable opportunity for an appropriate variety and choice of housing, including, of course, low and moderate cost housing, to meet the needs, desires and resources of all categories of people who may desire to live within its boundaries. Negatively, it may not adopt regulations or policies which thwart or preclude that opportunity. . . .

Mount Laurel's zoning ordinance is . . . so restrictive in its minimum lot area, lot frontage and building size requirements, earlier detailed, as to preclude single-family housing for even moderate income families. Required lot area of at least 9375 square feet in one remaining regular residential zone and 20,000 square feet (almost half an acre) in the other, with required frontage of 75 and 100 feet, respectively, cannot be called small lots and amounts to low density zoning, very definitely increasing the cost of purchasing and improving land and so affecting the cost of housing. As to building size, the township's general requirements of a minimum dwelling floor area of 1100 square feet for all one-story houses and 1300 square feet for all of one and one-half stories or higher is without regard to required minimum lot size or frontage or the number of occupants. . . .

Again it is evident these requirements increase the size and so the cost of housing. The conclusion is irresistible that Mount Laurel permits only such middle and upper income housing as it believes will have sufficient taxable value to come close to paying its own governmental way. . . .

Without further elaboration at this point, our opinion is that Mount Laurel's zoning ordinance is presumptively contrary to the general welfare and outside the intended scope of the zoning power in the particulars mentioned. A facial showing of invalidity is thus established, shifting to the municipality the burden of establishing valid superseding reasons for its action and non-action. We now examine the reasons it advances.

The township's principal reason in support of its zoning plan and ordinance housing provisions, advanced especially strongly at oral argument, is the fiscal one previously adverted to, i.e., that by reason of New Jersey's tax structure which substantially finances municipal governmental and educational costs from taxes on local real property, every municipality may, by the exercise of the zoning power, allow only such uses and to such extent as will be beneficial to the local tax rate. In other words, the position is that any municipality may zone extensively to seek and encourage the "good" tax ratables of industry and commerce and limit the permissible types of housing to those having the fewest school children or to those providing sufficient value to attain or approach paying their own taxwise.

. . . We have no hesitancy in now saying, and do so emphatically, that, considering the basic importance of the opportunity for appropriate housing for all classes of our citizenry, no municipality may exclude or limit categories of housing for that reason or purpose. . . .

The propriety of zoning ordinance limitations on housing for ecological or environmental reasons seems also to be suggested by Mount Laurel in support of the one-half acre minimum lot size in that very considerable portion of the township still available for residential development. It is said that the area is without sewer or water utilities and that the soil is such that this plot size is required for safe individual lot sewage disposal and water supply. The short answer is that, this being flat land and readily amendable to such utility installations, the township could require them as improvements by developers or install them under the special assessment or other appropriate statutory procedure. The present environmental situation of the area is, therefore, no sufficient excuse in itself for limiting housing therein to single-family dwelling on large lots. . . .

The composition of the applicable "region" will necessarily vary from situation to situation and probably no hard and fast rule will serve to furnish the answer in every case. Confinement to or within a certain county appears not to be realistic, but restriction within the boundaries of the state seem practical and advisable. (This is not to say that a developing municipality can ignore a demand for housing within its boundaries on the part of people who commute to work in another state.) Here we have already defined the region at present as "those portions of Camden, Burlington and Gloucester Counties within a semicircle having a radius of 20 miles or so from the heart of Camden City." The concept of "fair share" is coming into more general use and, through the expertise of the municipal planning adviser, the county planning boards and the state planning agency, a reasonable figure for Mount Laurel can be determined, which can then be translated to the allocation of sufficient land therefor on the zoning map. . . .

III. The Remedy . . .

We are not at all sure what the trial judge had in mind as ultimate action with reference to the approval of a plan for affirmative public action concerning the satisfaction of indicated housing needs and the entry of a final order requiring implementation thereof. Courts do not build housing nor do municipalities. . . . The municipal function is initially to provide the opportunity through appropriate land use regulations and we have spelled out what Mount Laurel must do in that regard. It is not appropriate at this time, particularly in view of the advanced view of zoning law as applied to housing laid down by this opinion, to deal with the matter of the further extent of judicial power in the field or to exercise any such power. The municipality should first have full opportunity to itself act without judicial supervision. . . . Should Mount Laurel not perform as we expect, further judicial action may be sought by supplemental pleading in this cause. . . .

Notes and Comments

1. *Defining the Doctrine*. How would you define the *Mount Laurel* doctrine? What is the source of power upon which the *Mount Laurel* doctrine is based? What are the specific remedial obligations under which communities must operate? How would you have written the opinion, defined the principle, and structured the

relief? Or would you have dissented, and why? For the history of the *Mount Laurel* litigation, see David Kirp, et al., Our Town: Race, Housing and the Soul of Suburbia (1995) (critical of the practical benefits from the doctrine). For a positive review of the *Mount Laurel* experience, see Charles M. Haar, Suburbs Under Siege: Race, Space, and Audacious Judges (1996).

2. *The "Developing" City*. What is the meaning of "developing" in *Mount Laurel?* Would a redevelopment plan within a developed city that failed to provide for low income housing violate the *Mount Laurel* doctrine? *See Asian Americans for Equality v. Koch*, 527 N.E.2d 265 (N.Y. 1988) (fair share requirements inapplicable to each individual community, neighborhood, redevelopment, or conversion plan).

3. *Exclusionary Per Se*. In addition to the *Mount Laurel* fair share doctrine, New Jersey permits judicial invalidation of certain land use devices deemed exclusionary and invalid per se. In *Home Builders League v. Township of Berlin*, 405 A.2d 381 (N.J. 1979), the New Jersey Supreme Court overturned an ordinance establishing a minimum floor area that applied regardless of the number of occupants living in the home and that was unrelated to any other factor, such as frontage or lot size. The court reasoned that *Mount Laurel* requires regulations to promote the general welfare, and requirements for minimum floor area were seen as merely inflating costs—leading to economic segregation—and unrelated to health. In addition, such regulations do not preclude overcrowding, which could be regulated by a limit on the number of occupants in relation to floor space.

4. *The Traditional and Deferential Zoning Doctrine*. Although a number of jurisdictions adopted the *Mount Laurel* doctrine, or at least the exclusionary zoning principle of *National Land, supra*, many refused to adopt the model of heightened judicial scrutiny of local housing patterns. In *Associated Home Builders v. City of Livermore*, 557 P.2d 473 (Cal. 1976), (discussed in Chapter 6), the California Supreme Court sustained an initiative-created moratorium on development until adequate facilities were available. The challengers urged the court to follow the Pennsylvania and New Jersey exclusionary zoning decisions and invalidate the measure. The court refused to do so:

> . . . Not only do those decisions rest, for the most part, upon principles of state law inapplicable in California, but, unlike the present case, all involve ordinances which impede the ability of low or moderate income persons to immigrate to a community but permit largely unimpeded entry by wealthier persons.

557 P.2d at 486-487. The California Supreme Court expressly refused to adopt the New Jersey jurisprudence. Footnote 23 of the *Livermore* decision, which followed at that point, states:

> The most recent of these decisions, [*Mount Laurel*] invalidated a township zoning ordinance which discriminated against low and moderate cost housing. The court based its decision upon an extensive trial record which convinced the court that deference to local legislative bodies would impede measures it found essential to the regional welfare. In [*National Land*] the Pennsylvania Supreme Court, striking down a four-acre minimum lot requirement, independently determined that the zoning ordinance would not promote the general welfare; as we explain in text, California courts do not claim the authority to invalidate ordinances that they believe undesirable so long as it is fairly debatable that the ordinance is reasonably related to the public welfare. . . .

557 P.2d at 487 n.23.

5. *Non-Housing Exclusionary Zoning*. Is exclusionary zoning limited to affordable housing? In *County of Beaver v. Borough of Beaver Zoning Hearing Bd.*, 656 A.2d 157 (Pa. Commw. Ct. 1995), the borough adopted a zoning ordinance excluding jails and prison uses. The court invalidated the ordinance as exclusionary. It reasoned that the total exclusion of any use shifts the burden to the borough to justify the exclusion by showing that the use excluded would injure the public's health, safety, welfare, or morals. *See also Omnipoint Communications, Enters., L.P. v. Zoning Hearing Bd. of Easttown Township*, 189 F. Supp. 2d 258 (E.D. Pa. 2002) (recognizing that wireless telephone facilities are protected by the exclusionary zoning doctrine under state law if there is a total or de facto exclusion, although the court found no violation in the denial of a permit for a cellular telephone tower).

6. *Surrick*. The Pennsylvania Supreme Court's decision in *Surrick v. Zoning Hearing Board*, 382 A.2d 105 (Pa. 1977), is important to exclusionary zoning law. The court's approach does not depend entirely on fair share allocations or calculations. Instead the court asks three questions:

(1) Is the community in the path of urbanization?
(2) Is the community one that is still developing rather than substantially developed?
(3) Is the impact of the challenged policy partially or totally exclusionary?

Upper Providence Township, a suburb of Philadelphia, is bisected by a major route into the city. With a population over 9200, the township of 3800 acres had but 43 acres, or 1.14 percent, zoned B-Business district, the only classification allowing apartments. The B district, however, was substantially developed, containing the community's commercial uses. Surrick, a developer, sought to develop apartments on a 16.25 acre parcel of which the developer owned four acres and held a contract for sale on the remainder contingent on obtaining zoning for the project. The tract was zoned A-1, allowing single-family dwellings on one acre tracts, but was located just above the intersection where the existing B-Business district was located.

Following a denial by the board of supervisors of the requested zone change for the land subject to the contingent contract, the developer modified the proposal to include the entire tract. After the building inspector denied building permits, the developer unsuccessfully sought a variance.

Applying what it characterized alternatively as a substantive due process theory and a fair share test, the court looked to a multitude of factors, including:

a. Whether the community is a logical area for development and population growth, that is, whether it is in the path of urbanization because of its proximity to a large metropolis and the community's projected population growth;
b. The community's current level of development, such as the percentage of undeveloped land and the percentage available for multi-family dwellings; that is, whether the community is already highly developed;
c. Whether the challenged zoning scheme effects an exclusionary result;
d. Whether the scheme evidences a primary purpose to exclude or to zone out the natural growth of population, although proof of intent is not of critical importance.

The court did not accept the general claim of the township that the project would overburden municipal services.

7. *Per Se Rules Versus Burden Shifts*. Under *Surrick*, the exclusionary character of the land use policy is not per se invalid. Instead, the burden shifts to the government to justify the policy by important concerns. *Fernley v. Board of Supervisors*, 502 A.2d 585, 587 (Pa. 1985). Which is preferable: the New Jersey "fair share" concept or the Pennsylvania test for exclusionary zoning? Under which scheme does the court ensure greater deference to local planning? Does the Pennsylvania rule, which requires the plaintiff to prove the lack of adequate housing in the entire region, impose a greater litigation burden on the plaintiff?

8. *Other State Approaches*. The states take a variety of approaches to the review of zoning ordinances alleged to be exclusionary. As you read about them, ask yourself: what are the favorable features of each approach? The downsides? Which are more likely to result in land use policies that avoid exclusionary practices?

a. *New York*. New York presents a sort of compromise between the approaches of Pennsylvania and New Jersey. It allows a cause of action wherever a community's land use controls fail to accommodate a fair share of regional need. *Berenson v. Town of New Castle*, 341 N.E.2d 236 (N.Y. 1975). The New York approach differs from New Jersey's in that the challenger must offer proof of regional need and the inadequacy of existing land use controls in the challenged community.

b. *Michigan*. For a time, Michigan applied its own version of the Pennsylvania burden-shifting approach to exclusionary zoning. Under this "preferred use" doctrine, exclusion of certain disfavored uses, such as affordable housing, would shift the burden to the locality to justify its planning policy. *Simmons v. City of Royal Oaks*, 196 N.W.2d 811 (Mich. Ct. App. 1972). The Michigan Supreme Court, however, eventually eliminated the burden-shifting rule, and thus traditional scrutiny and the presumption of legislative validity apply. *Kropf v. City of Sterling Heights*, 215 N.W.2d 179 (Mich. 1974).

In *English v. Augusta Township*, 514 N.W.2d 172 (Mich. Ct. App. 1994), a Michigan appellate court found that when a township excluded mobile homes by zoning only one particular parcel that had no chance of development for such use, that zoning constituted illegal exclusionary zoning. The court's theory was that the total exclusion of a legitimate use violates equal protection. The record in *English* also disclosed a pattern of affordable housing exclusion. *But compare Countrywalk Condominiums, Inc. v. City of Orchard Lake Village*, 561 N.W.2d 405 (Mich. Ct. App. 1997) (per curiam) (exclusion of multiple dwellings from the city did not violate equal protection, as the evidence disclosed that the small city was already congested and that multiple dwellings would impact already overburdened roads, thus compromising safety).

c. *New Hampshire*. Without adopting the mathematical fair share analysis of *Mount Laurel* or the same articulated, affirmative obligation that New Jersey imposes on local governments to utilize inclusionary zoning techniques, New Hampshire more closely followed Pennsylvania and New York in invalidating a community's restrictions on apartment development. *Britton v. Town of Chester*, 595 A.2d 492 (N.H. 1991). By limiting apartments to parcels of at least 20 acres and to certain districts, as well as restricting development on steep slope and wetlands areas, the town's regulations left only 1.73 percent of the town's available land for apartments. Although the percentage was not determinative and may have been sufficient to meet the community's affordable housing needs, the challenger prevailed when the de minimis percentage was considered along with the fact that the town planning board was authorized to approve projects without any objective criteria. The decision was based on the statutory enabling requirement that ordinances must promote the general welfare of the "community," which includes the welfare of the entire region.

d. *Literature*. *See* Charles B. Ferguson, Jr., Comment, Hamlets: Expanding the Fair Share Doctrine Under Strict Home Rule Constitutions, 49 Emory L.J. 255 (2000) (suggesting authority for a litigation strategy of establishing an obligation for fair share of affordable housing and other uses in states, such as Colorado, Georgia, and Louisiana, which follow a home rule doctrine).

9. *Site-Specific Relief*. Some courts in various jurisdictions are awarding so-called site-specific relief to successful challengers of exclusionary zoning. *See, e.g.*, *Britton v. Town of Chester, supra*. Site-specific relief typically requires the issuance of a building permit, thus avoiding the uncertainty of remanding the matter to the local legislative and administrative processes, where agencies may have been recalcitrant, engaged in excessive delay, or failed to act in good faith.

C. STATUTORY HOUSING MANDATES

While an assault on exclusionary zoning was being waged in the courts of a few jurisdictions, in others legislative initiatives emerged. The most aggressive approach was taken by New York, which created a powerful agency to develop affordable housing and override local zoning and land use controls. Fiscal difficulties, which were exacerbated by the collapse of federal subsidies and community opposition to subsidized housing in the suburbs, ultimately destroyed the agency, as opponents succeeded in repealing the agency's preemptive powers. Eleanor L. Brilliant, The Urban Development Corporation: Private Interests and Public Authority (1975); Housing for All Under Law: New Directions in Housing, Land Use and Planning Law 505-508 (Richard P. Fishman ed. 1978) (report of the American Bar Association Advisory Commission on Housing and Urban Growth).

New Jersey, with its establishment of the Council on Affordable Housing under the state's Fair Housing Act, has a hybrid approach. It encourages voluntary compliance with agency-calculated affordable housing goals but also authorizes enforcement through litigation.

The two remaining formats for legislative reform have been the establishment of affordable housing goals as a statewide mandatory planning obligation, and the creation of an administrative review process to replace litigation. California's general approach to exclusionary zoning and the need for affordable housing is found in statutory provisions mandating that general plans contain a housing element. This element must plan for the housing needs of all economic segments of the population. Cal. Govt. Code §§65302(c), 65580-65589.8 (West 1997 & Supp. 2002). While most growth management schemes have been endorsed by both state and federal courts under traditional *Euclid* zoning deference, the following case suggests that California's housing laws can change the normal outcome.

■ BUILDING INDUSTRY ASSOCIATION OF SAN DIEGO v. CITY OF OCEANSIDE

33 Cal. Rptr. 2d 137 (Ct. App. 1994)

HUFFMAN, Acting Presiding Justice. . . .

FACTUAL AND PROCEDURAL BACKGROUND

1. ADOPTION OF PROP. A

. . . Prop. A, alternatively referred to as Chapter 32A [and] adopted by the Oceanside electorate in April 1987, adopts a "Residential Development Control System" (RDCS) which, with what may be significant exceptions, adopts a maximum number of dwelling units to be constructed each year, called annual allotments. The allotments are 1000 for 1987 and 800 for each year thereafter until December 31, 1999, with power granted to the City Council to modify the annual allotment by an amount no greater than 10 percent more or less for any given year and a requirement the annual allotment for a next succeeding year be adjusted higher or lower in order to redress any excess or deficit in the preceding year. Excepted from the RDCS are the following:

(a) Projects of not more than four residential dwellings, limited to only one such project per developer per calendar year.

(b) Fourplexes or less numbered multiple dwellings on a single existing lot.

(c) Single family residential units on a single existing lot.

(d) Rehabilitation or remodeling of an existing dwelling, or conversion of apartments to condominiums, so long as no additional dwelling units are created.

(e) Units within the legally designated redevelopment project area.

(f) Those specific Units which are formally dedicated for occupancy by low income persons or senior citizens pursuant to the provisions of applicable federal, state, or local laws or programs provided these types of units are spread equitably throughout the city and not concentrated in one neighborhood. . . . This section does not exempt low-income or senior citizen projects built with density bonuses or other development considerations under any program.

(g) Single family dwelling unit projects with lots an average of which are 10,000 square feet or better, which can achieve a minimum of 70% or better, of the maximum awardable points using the Residential Development Evaluation System are exempt. . . .

Under Prop. A, projects are reviewed by a "Residential Development Evaluation Board" (the Board) made up of members of the City's planning commission, who evaluate proposed projects for their impact upon public facilities and services (the "A" criteria) and site and architectural quality (the "B" criteria). A project which does not receive a score of 51 percent on the "A" criteria and 70 percent on the "B" criteria is eliminated from consideration for an annual allocation. The Board's recommendations are forwarded to the City Council, which makes the annual allocations.

2. OCEANSIDE'S LAND USE REGULATION

. . . Since 1979, the City's general plan had a public facilities and management element (PFME), which stated as its objective "[t]o influence the timing of development and to direct it to those locations within the City that avoid or minimize any adverse fiscal, economic, social or environmental impacts." The PFME divided the City into four areas and gave priority to development in those areas where adequate services were available. The PFME stated a policy of avoiding "direct controls on the number or location of new housing units built. . . ." Neither the [interim growth management element] IGME nor the PFME gave the City the power to regulate the rate, timing or sequencing of development.

The PFME used the method of planning for growth by encouraging assessment districts and impact fees. The PFME was adopted by the City in light of a compound annual growth rate of 6.3 percent since 1970. An environmental impact report (EIR) for the PFME states that development was expected to continue in the range of 900 to 2000 housing units per year through 1995, a range of 2.9 to 7 percent compound annual growth through 1995. The EIR for the PFME points out that that measure rejected the use of a point system, such as would later be used in Prop. A, with the explanation that "[p]oint systems usually are flawed by the potential for a high score for one service to offset a low score for another" and on the theory that "the problem of adding apples and oranges and then considering only the total is difficult to avoid." The EIR also rejected a "periodic comparative evaluation" system, such as Prop. A would later adopt.

In 1986, the year before Prop. A was adopted, the city council adopted a new land use element (LUE) of the general plan, setting forth the city's long-term goals, objectives, and policies for development. The LUE calls for but does not establish a timing mechanism to regulate residential development. At the time the LUE was adopted, the City recognized the PFME had not solved all the City's growth-related problems. However, no official City action had been taken to invalidate the PFME.

3. THE CITY'S GROWTH STATUS AS OF 1987

In the 1970s, the City's growth rate had reached 8.94 percent per year. While the City's population grew by 89.4 percent from 1970 to 1980, the County's population increased by 37.1 percent. The growth rate as of 1987 was 5 percent annual population increase, equivalent to 60 percent growth if sustained for a decade. The City's expert witness, Dr. Myers, a professor of urban and regional planning, testified that a 1 percent growth rate is normal, and 2 percent per year or 25 percent per decade is a healthy growth rate. In his opinion, at 40 percent growth per decade, it is difficult to "keep up" with a city's growing population. "[W]ith rapid growth the needs escalate . . . and you are always playing catch up."

Conflicting evidence was presented about the City's ability to accommodate growth. The trial court heard evidence that there were severe deficiencies in facilities and services, such as the road system, fire, paramedic and police facilities and response times, schools, libraries, parks and recreation facilities. There were drainage and sewer problems. . . .

II. Conflict of Prop. A with the General Plan or State Law

A. INTRODUCTION . . .

. . . Under [Government Code] section 65860, county or city zoning ordinances must be consistent with the entity's general plan, such that "[t]he various land uses authorized by the ordinance are compatible with the objectives, policies, general land uses, and programs specified in such a plan." (§65860, subd. (a)(ii).) "Only the general plan in effect at the time the ordinance is adopted is relevant in determining inconsistency." [*Lesher Communications, Inc. v. City of Walnut Creek*, 802 P.2d 317 (Cal. 1990)] (*Lesher*).

Moreover, "[a] city may not adopt ordinances and regulations which conflict with the state Planning and Zoning Law." . . . (*Lesher*).

C. THE GENERAL PLAN

At the time Prop. A was adopted, the general plan had in effect the PFME, which contained a statement of a number of major policies to be served by the plan. In particular, the PFME stated a policy to "[a]void direct controls on the number or location of new housing units to be built, but provide financial incentives for projects where services can be provided to new and old residents at least cost." . . .

In light of the clear statement in *Lesher*, that a zoning ordinance that conflicts with a general plan is invalid at the time it is passed, and in light of the factual findings that Prop. A adversely affected the availability of low income housing, the only possible finding is that Prop. A does conflict with the City's general plan, specifically the PFME, regarding the imposition of direct controls on the number or location of new housing units to be built. This restriction on land uses is not compatible with the then-existing general plan.

Although the trial court reasoned that the City had the power to adopt a more restrictive type of growth control than that represented by the PFME, it could not do so without validly amending the existing general plan. . . . Finally, the housing element of Oceanside's general plan states as a policy:

Adequate Provision of Housing

> Adequate provision for the housing needs of all economic segments of the community is an issue of the highest priority in Oceanside to meet the low income household assistance goals and to protect, encourage and, where feasible, provide low and moderate income housing opportunities within the intent of State policy to address local needs. . . .

Prop. A does not promote this policy and accordingly must be deemed inconsistent with it. Although we are sympathetic to the goals stated in Prop. A of promoting the quality of life for the citizens of the City, we are bound by *Lesher* to find the ordinance invalid under those standards.

D. CONFLICT WITH STATUTORY PROVISIONS

[Plaintiffs] BIA and Del Oro next assert that Prop. A conflicts with three particular sections in the State Planning and Zoning Law. The text of the sections on which BIA and Del Oro rely is in relevant part, in the version in effect at the adoption of Prop. A in 1987, as follows:

Section 65008, subdivision (c):

> No city, county, or city and county shall, in the enactment or administration of ordinances pursuant to this title, prohibit or discriminate against a residential

development or emergency shelter because the development or shelter is intended for occupancy by persons and families of low and moderate income, as defined in Section 50093 of the Health and Safety Code, or persons and families of middle income.

Section 65913.1:

[A] city . . . shall designate and zone sufficient vacant land for residential use with appropriate standards . . . to meet housing needs as identified in the general plan . . . "appropriate standards" shall mean densities and requirements . . . which contribute significantly to the economic feasibility of producing housing at the lowest possible cost given economic and environmental factors, the public health and safety, and the need to facilitate the development of housing for persons and families of low and moderate income. . . ."

Section 65915:

(a) When a developer of housing agrees to construct at least (1) 25 percent of the total units of a housing development for persons and families of low or moderate income, . . . or (2) 10 percent of the total units . . . for lower income households, . . . a city, . . . shall either (1) grant a density bonus or (2) provide other incentives of equivalent financial value. . . .

(c) . . . "density bonus" means a density increase of at least 25 percent over the otherwise maximum allowable residential density under the applicable zoning ordinance and land use element of the general plan. . . .

The trial court made key findings that since Prop. A took effect in 1988, affordable housing in the City had dramatically declined. Only 415 total low income and senior citizen units had been excepted from the effect of Prop. A in the period between 1987 and 1990, and they were all in the senior category (plus an additional 28 units in the similar fourplex category). Based on those figures, the trial court made an estimate that some 20,000 persons would be denied affordable housing based on the effect of Prop. A. The trial court expressly found that the exception allowing higher priced units on 10,000 square foot lots was not justified by an asserted imbalance in the current housing stock, such that higher end units were needed in the City. . . . [T]he trial court's overall conclusion on the degree of the City's compliance with its obligations to provide low and moderate income regional share units was that its 1986-1991 compliance was not enough, as the court had to go on to the 1991- 1996 period to make a complete analysis, and the City could not show it would meet the regional share for low/moderate income units for that period.

[T]he court further ruled that the evidence showed developers were discouraged from proposing housing that qualified for density bonuses, due to the exclusion of density bonus units from the low income and senior exception. This exclusion, it held, conflicted with the state density bonus law. However, it declined to invalidate the ordinance on that ground, using the theory that section 65915 had not been shown to have been triggered by a developer's specific proposal of a density bonus project.

The three cited Government Code sections, taken together, clearly show an important state policy to promote the construction of low income housing and to remove impediments to the same. Prop. A is such an impediment, and cannot survive such a conflict. Although the City has made efforts to implement a policy to mitigate the harshness of the exemption of density bonus projects from the exception in Prop. A for low income or senior citizen housing, those efforts do not change the text of the initiative measure. . . .

Similarly, when the trial court made its finding that Prop. A did not offend against the provisions of section 65008, subdivision (c), prohibiting discrimination against low income housing, because Prop. A was neutral as to the intended occupants of any development, it disregarded its own factual findings that affordable housing had taken a dramatic decline since the effective date of Prop. A. Prop. A acts to favor the development of larger units on larger lots, with more design and other amenities, through the exemption for 10,000 square foot lots. The City admitted as much, while asserting that such an exemption was needed in order to remedy an imbalance in the current housing supply. The trial court was not persuaded by that argument in Phase I, and we are not persuaded by it at all. . . .

E. CONCLUSION . . .

We find support for our conclusion that Prop. A is in conflict with state housing policy. . . .

FROEHLICH and NARES, JJ., concur.

Notes and Comments

1. *Litigating Housing Issues*. The absence of a housing element renders a general plan invalid and presumably forecloses local land use permit approvals. What happens if a community adopts a housing element that is vague or fails to call for development in accordance with affordable housing goals? Planning objectives may be meaningless unless courts are willing to engage in enforcement or an administrative agency with the authority to sanction local government is established.

One problem with the use of litigation as a means of enforcing housing obligations is that few developers are willing to underwrite test litigation against a community. Successful developers are profit-motivated, and they are not likely to favor shouldering the expense of costly housing litigation. Neighborhood groups or homeowner associations, even if supportive of affordable housing, generally will not have the resources to hire competent, experienced lawyers to pursue what can become intractable litigation. For example, the opinion in *Building Industry Association v. City of Oceanside*, reprinted above, was the second full opinion of the court of appeals in the case, a vivid demonstration that the litigation was prolix.

2. *The Focus of Judicial Review*. In *Hernandez v. City of Encinitas*, 33 Cal. Rptr. 2d 875 (Ct. App. 1994), a different California Court of Appeals panel rejected a housing element challenge based on an allegation that land use devices impeded affordable housing development. The devices included referenda on zone changes, increasing density or converting non-residentially zoned property for residential use, and imposing maximum densities. The plaintiff also claimed that the city would not implement the goals in its plan.

The court in *Hernandez* adopted a deferential standard of review, examining the record for "substantial compliance" with the statutory obligations. Using that standard, it sustained a housing element that facially could satisfy affordable housing need projections by adequate sites zoned for least cost housing. The court also ruled that the use of block grants and federal subsidies adequately addressed the need to conserve the existing affordable housing stock.

In focusing on the facial exclusion of ordinances, rather than on the actual achievement of providing affordable housing, the court appeared to mirror early efforts by New Jersey to implement *Mount Laurel*. *See generally* Brian Augusta, Comment, Building Housing from the Ground Up: Strengthening California Law to Ensure Adequate Locations for Affordable Housing, 39 Santa Clara L. Rev. 503 (1999).

3. *The New Jersey Fair Housing Act*. Following *Mount Laurel I*, *supra*, and *Mount Laurel II*, *infra*, the New Jersey Legislature passed the New Jersey Fair Housing Act (N.J. Stat. Ann. §§52:27D-301 to 52:27D-329 (West 2001 & Supp. 2003)) to implement the judicially mandated principles. The law established a state commission, called the Council on Affordable Housing, to set the "fair share" levels mandated by the New Jersey Supreme Court, to issue guidelines, and to review local implementing plans. Although judicial review was preserved, the initial law temporarily suspended the availability of site-specific relief, or a "builder's remedy," a type of relief which is discussed in the notes after the last principal case in this chapter.

Under the law, communities meeting the obligations of *Mount Laurel* enjoy a ten-year exemption from further review. N.J. Stat. Ann. §52:27D-307 (West Supp. 2003). Controversial provisions authorize limited residency preferences, allowing up to 50 percent of a community's fair share of affordable housing obligation, as allocated by the Council on Affordable Housing, to be set aside for residents and those who work in the community. In addition, the law authorizes Regional Contribution Contracts, which allow communities to transfer up to 50 percent of their obligations to other communities. The law was upheld in *Hills Development Co. v. Township of Bernards*, 510 A.2d 621 (N.J. 1986).

Does the New Jersey Fair Housing Act present an enlightened approach to enforcing the *Mount Laurel* principle?

4. *Growth Management and Housing*. Oregon's legislative growth management scheme, discussed in Chapter 11, calls for each community to establish an urban growth boundary adequate to accommodate projected growth, and to prohibit most forms of urban development outside the boundary. Where a local land use decision is not in conformity with the plan, or where it is alleged that conditions required a plan amendment and the extension of the urban growth boundary, the local decision may be appealed to the Land Use Board of Appeal (LUBA), which is empowered to override local land use control rulings. In *Shelter Resources, Inc. v. City of Cannon Beach*, 879 P.2d 1313 (Or. Ct. App. 1994), the court affirmed a finding by the LUBA that a small city was exempt from obligations to plan for affordable housing. The exemption was based on a statute which required that cities under 2500 in population were only obligated to accommodate "government subsidized housing."

How effective is the legislative scheme? Should the statute be expanded? Should it reach all housing with rents or prices defined as affordable or as a percentage of median income? Should the law specifically apply to housing financed by income tax credits? Would housing financed by a housing trust fund or with revenue from a local redevelopment tax increment qualify as "government subsidized" housing?

Should the law establish an obligation of the community to include a percentage of affordable housing within each project, neighborhood, or district? Does the law suffer from failure to include a fair share requirement?

5. *Other Alternatives*. Massachusetts pioneered an alternative to judicial review or legislative fiat by establishing an administrative mechanism permitting developers to appeal the denials of affordable housing permits to a state agency with power to override local land use controls. *Hanover v. Housing Appeals Comm.*, 294 N.E.2d 393 (Mass. 1973). *See also Mahoney v. Board of Appeals*, 316 N.E.2d 606 (Mass. 1974), *appeal dismissed*, 420 U.S. 903 (1975) (state agency must remand to allow the local jurisdiction to apply subdivision standards rather than the agency issuing site-specific relief in exclusionary zoning cases); Sharon Perlman Krefetz, The Impact and Evolution of the Massachusetts Comprehensive Permit and Zoning Appeals Act: Thirty Years of Experience with a State Legislative Effort to Overcome Exclusionary Zoning, 22 W. New Eng. 381 (2001) (success but insufficient affordable housing, requiring additional subsidies and state regulation).

Connecticut provides a variation on Massachusetts, calling for judicial review of denials of affordable housing proposals. *Wisniowsky v. Planning Comm'n*, 655 A.2d 1146 (Conn. Ct. App. 1995) (granting authority to place multi-family affordable housing in a district zoned for lots of at least an acre, and finding that the proposed project need not be consistent with zoning or the comprehensive plan). *See* Terry J. Tondro, Connecticut's Affordable Housing Appeals Statute: After Ten Years of Hope, Why Only Middling Results?, 23 W. New Eng. L. Rev. 115 (2001); Peter J. Vodola, Connecticut's Affordable Housing Appeals Procedure Law in Practice, 29 Conn. L. Rev. 1235 (1997); Robert D. Carroll, Note, Connecticut Retrenches: A Proposal to Save the Affordable Housing Appeals Procedure, 110 Yale L.J. 1247 (2001) (critical of legislative amendment effective in 2000 limiting appeals).

Finally, Washington's growth management law establishes a statutory mandate for local governments to provide for affordable housing for all segments of the community and calls for a fair share type of obligation. However, the law lacks an implementation mechanism to ensure local performance. Henry W. McGee, Jr., Equity and Efficacy in Washington State's GMA Affordable Housing Goal, 3 Wash. U. J .L. & Poly. 539 (2000), *published in* Evolving Voices in Land Use Law Ch.8 (Washington U. J. L. & Poly. 2000).

6. *Additional Literature. See generally* Michael J. Stewart, Growth and Its Implications: An Evaluation of Tennessee's Growth Management Plan, 67 Tenn. L. Rev. 983, 991-992 (2000) (Tennessee's new growth management legislation mandates a local plan that ensures affordable housing); S. Stonefield, Affordable Housing in Suburbia: The Importance but Limited Power and Effectiveness of the State Override Tool, 22 W. New Eng. L. Rev. 323 (2001) (discussing Connecticut, Massachusetts, Rhode Island, and New Jersey).

D. INCLUSIONARY ZONING

After years of struggle to shape relief that would enforce its housing standards and the failure of judicial orders to generate affordable housing in exclusionary zoning cases, the New Jersey Supreme Court decided the following case. In it, the court returned to the question of whether simply announcing a local obligation principle was adequate or whether modifying the zoning ordinance will generate affordable housing.

SOUTHERN BURLINGTON COUNTY N.A.A.C.P. v. TOWNSHIP OF MOUNT LAUREL

456 A.2d 390 (N.J. 1983)

WILENTZ, C.J.

. . . This Court is more firmly committed to the original *Mount Laurel* doctrine than ever, and we are determined, within appropriate judicial bounds, to make it work. The obligation is to provide a realistic opportunity for housing, not litigation. We have learned from experience, however, that unless a strong judicial hand is used, *Mount Laurel* will not result in housing, but in paper, process, witnesses, trials and appeals. We intend by this decision to strengthen it, clarify it, and make it easier for public officials, including judges, to apply it. . . .

We note that there has been some legislative initiative in this field. We look forward to more. The new Municipal Land Use Law explicitly recognizes the obligation of municipalities to zone with regional consequences in mind, *N.J.S.A.* 40:55D-28(d); it also recognizes the work of the Division of State and Regional Planning in the Department of Community Affairs (DCA), in creating the State Development Guide Plan (1980) (SDGP), which plays an important part in our decisions today. Our deference to these legislative and executive initiatives can be regarded as a clear signal of our readiness to defer further to more substantial actions.

II. Resolution of the Issues

A. DEFINING THE MOUNT LAUREL OBLIGATION

In *Oakwood v. Madison*, this Court held that it was sufficient in *Mount Laurel* litigation for courts to look to the "*substance*" of challenged zoning ordinances and to the existence of "*bona fide* efforts" by municipalities to meet their obligations. . . . Unfortunately, experience has taught us that this formulation is too vague to provide adequate guidance for either trial courts or municipalitites. . . .

Therefore, proof of a municipality's bona fide attempt to provide a realistic opportunity to construct its fair share of lower income housing shall no longer suffice. Satisfaction of the *Mount Laurel* obligation shall be determined solely on an objective basis: if the municipality has *in fact* provided a realistic opportunity for the construction of its fair share of low and moderate income housing, it has met the *Mount Laurel* obligation to satisfy the constitutional requirement; if it has not, then it has failed to satisfy it. Further, whether the opportunity is "realistic" will depend on whether there is in fact a likelihood—to the extent economic conditions allow—that the lower income housing will actually be constructed. Plaintiff's case will ordinarily include proof of the municipality's fair share of the regional need and defendant's proof of its satisfaction. Good or bad faith, at least on this issue, will be irrelevant. The numberless approach encouraged in *Madison*, where neither plaintiffs nor defendants are required to prove a fair share number, is no longer acceptable. . . .

D. MEETING THE MOUNT LAUREL OBLIGATION

1. REMOVING EXCESSIVE RESTRICTIONS AND EXACTIONS

In order to meet their *Mount Laurel* obligations, municipalities, at the very least, must remove all municipally created barriers to the construction of their fair share of lower income housing. Thus, to the extent necessary to meet their prospective fair share and provide for their indigenous poor (and, in some cases, a portion of the region's poor), municipalities must remove zoning and subdivision restrictions and exactions that are not necessary to protect health and safety. . . .

Once a municipality has revised its land use regulations and taken other steps affirmatively to provide a realistic opportunity for the construction of its fair share of lower income housing, the *Mount Laurel* doctrine requires it to do no more. For instance, a municipality having thus complied, the fact that its land use regulations contain restrictive provisions incompatible with lower income housing, such as bedroom restrictions, large lot zoning, prohibition against mobile homes, and the like, does not render those provisions invalid under *Mount Laurel*. . . .

2. USING AFFIRMATIVE MEASURES . . .

Satisfaction of the *Mount Laurel* doctrine cannot depend on the inclination of developers to help the poor. It has to depend on affirmative inducements to make the opportunity real.

It is equally unrealistic, even where the land is owned by a developer eager to build, simply to rezone that land to permit the construction of lower income housing if the construction of other housing is permitted on the same land and the latter is more profitable than lower income housing. . . .

Therefore, unless removal of restrictive barriers will, without more, afford a realistic opportunity for the construction of the municipality's fair share of the region's lower income housing need, affirmative measures will be required.

There are two basic types of affirmative measures that a municipality can use to make the opportunity for lower income housing realistic: (1) encouraging or requiring the use of available state or federal housing subsidies, and (2) providing incentives for or requiring private developers to set aside a portion of their developments for lower income housing. Which, if either, of these devices will be necessary in any particular municipality to assure compliance with the constitutional mandate will be initially up to the municipality itself. Where necessary, the trial court overseeing compliance may require their use. We note again that least-cost housing will not ordinarily satisfy a municipality's fair share obligation to provide low and moderate income housing unless and until it has attempted the inclusionary devices outlined below or otherwise has proven the futility of the attempt. . . .

The implication of the observation that lower income housing cannot be built without subsidies is that if the *Mount Laurel* principle requires municipalities to provide a realistic opportunity for such housing through their land use regulations but leaves them free to prevent subsidies through non-action, that obligation is a charade. *Mount Laurel* was never intended to produce the perfect model of a just zoning ordinance; it was intended to provide a realistic opportunity for the construction of lower income housing. . . .

In evaluating the obligation that the municipality might be required to undertake to make a federal or state subsidy available to a lower income housing developer, the fact that some financial detriment may be incurred is not dispositive. Satisfaction of the *Mount Laurel* obligation imposes many financial obligations on municipalities, some of which are potentially substantial. By contrast, a tax abatement for a low or moderate income housing project will have only a minimal effect on the public fisc. Thus viewed, the asserted fiscal reasons justifying the failure to provide a tax abatement may be nothing more than a red herring. The direct and immediate financial impact of a tax abatement agreement between the municipality and the developer may be unimportant when compared with increases in municipal and school district costs caused by the advent of lower income housing. The trial court in a *Mount Laurel* case, therefore, shall have the power to require a municipality to cooperate in good faith with a developer's attempt to obtain a subsidy and to require that a tax abatement be granted for that purpose pursuant to applicable New Jersey statutes where the abatement does not conflict with other municipal interests of greater importance.

b. Inclusionary Zoning Devices

There are several inclusionary zoning techniques that municipalities must use if they cannot otherwise assure the construction of their fair share of lower income housing. . . . [W]e in no way intend our list to be exhaustive. . . .

(i) Incentive Zoning

Incentive zoning is usually accomplished either through a sliding scale density bonus that increases the permitted density as the amount of lower income housing provided is increased, or through a set bonus for participation in a lower income housing program. *See* Fox & Davis, 3 *Hasting Const. L.Q.* 1015, 1060-62 (1977).

Incentive zoning leaves a developer free to build only upper income housing if it so chooses. Fox and Davis, in their survey of municipalities using inclusionary devices, found that while developers sometimes profited through density bonuses, they were usually reluctant to cooperate with incentive zoning programs; and that therefore those municipalities that relied exclusively on such programs were not very successful in actually providing lower income housing. *Id.* at 1067.

Sole reliance on "incentive" techniques (or, indeed, reliance exclusively on any one affirmative device) may prove in a particular case to be insufficient to achieve compliance with the constitutional mandate.

(ii) Mandatory Set-Asides

A more effective inclusionary device that municipalities must use if they cannot otherwise meet their fair share obligations is the mandatory set-aside. According to the Department of Community Affairs, as of 1976 there were six municipalities in New Jersey with mandatory set-aside programs, which varied from a requirement that 5 percent of developments in a certain zone be composed of low and moderate income units (Cherry Hill, Camden County) to a requirement that between 15 and

25 percent of all PUDs be reserved for low and moderate income housing (East Windsor, Mercer County).

In addition to the mechanisms we have just described, municipalities and trial courts must consider such other affirmative devices as zoning substantial areas for mobile homes and for other types of low cost housing and establishing maximum square footage zones, *i.e.*, zones where developers cannot build units with *more* than a certain footage or build anything other than lower income housing or housing that includes a specified portion of lower income housing. In some cases, a realistic opportunity to provide the municipality's fair share may require over-zoning, *i.e.*, zoning to allow for *more* than the fair share if it is likely, as it usually is, that not all of the property made available for lower income housing will actually result in such housing.

Although several of the defendants concede that simply removing restrictions and exactions is unlikely to result in the construction of lower income housing, they maintain that requiring the municipality to use affirmative measures is beyond the scope of the courts' authority. We disagree . . . If it is plain, and it is, that unless we require the use of affirmative measures the constitutional guarantee that protects poor people from municipal exclusion will exist "only on paper," then the only "appropriate remedy" is the use of affirmative measures. . . .

3. Zoning for Mobile Homes

As the cost of ordinary housing skyrockets for purchasers and renters, mobile homes become increasingly important as a source of low cost housing. The evidence clearly supports a finding that mobile homes are significantly less expensive than site-built housing. . . . Therefore, subject to the qualifications noted hereafter, we rule that municipalities that cannot otherwise meet their fair share obligations must provide zoning for low-cost mobile homes as an affirmative device in their zoning ordinances. . . .

Lest we be misunderstood, we do *not* hold that every municipality must allow the use of mobile homes as an affirmative device to meet its *Mount Laurel* obligation, or that any ordinance that totally excludes mobile homes is *per se* invalid. Insofar as the *Mount Laurel* doctrine is concerned, whether mobile homes must be permitted as an affirmative device will depend upon the overall effectiveness of the municipality's attempts to comply. . . .

4. Providing "Least Cost" Housing

There may be municipalities where special conditions such as extremely high land costs make it impossible for the fair share obligation to be met even after all excessive restrictions and exactions, i.e., those not essential for safety and health, have been removed and all affirmative measures have been attempted. In such cases, *and only in such cases*, the *Mount Laurel* obligation can be met by supplementing whatever lower income housing can be built with enough "least cost" housing to satisfy the fair share. . . . Least cost housing means the least expensive housing that builders can provide after removal by a municipality of *all* excessive restrictions and exactions and after thorough use by a municipality of all affirmative devices that might lower costs. Presumably, such housing, though unaffordable by those in the lower income brackets, will be inexpensive enough to provide shelter for families who could not afford housing in the conventional suburban housing market. At the very minimum, provision of least cost housing will make certain that municipalities in "growth" areas of this state do not "grow" only for the well-to-do. . . .

1. Builder's Remedy

It is within the power of trial courts to adjust the timing of builder's remedies so as to cushion the impact of these developments on municipalities where that impact would otherwise cause a sudden and radical transformation of the municipality. . . .

To facilitate this revision, the trial court may appoint a special master to assist municipal officials in developing constitutional zoning and land use regulations. . . .

These impartial experts use their skills to help the parties formulate a remedy that will comply with the trial court's order and supply information that the parties may not have available to them. . . .

Notes and Comments

1. *Inclusionary Zoning and the Takings Clause*. How might courts evaluate the inclusionary zoning obligations of *Mount Laurel II* under the takings standards of *Dolan*? In *Home Builder's Ass'n of Northern California v. City of Napa*, 108 Cal. Rptr. 2d 60 (Ct. App. 2001), *cert. denied*, 122 S. Ct. 1356 (2001), the California intermediate appellate court rejected a taking claim, as well as a substantive due process claim, brought against the city's inclusionary zoning ordinance that required 10 percent of all newly constructed units to be affordable. The court followed the ruling in *Ehrlich v. City of Culver City* (discussed in Chapter 4) and rejected the facial challenge, finding that the general legislative policy was not an ad hoc condition and was thus exempt from *Dolan*. *Compare San Remo Hotel L.P. v. City of San Francisco*, 41 P.3d 87 (Cal. 2002) (holding that the conversion of a residential hotel to one for tourists required a conditional use permit and that the payment of a conversion fee was not subject to *Dolan* as the fee was legislatively set rather than discretionary).

Was the New Jersey Supreme Court acting within the traditional role of courts, or was the court too activist? Professor Haar believes not. Charles M. Haar, Suburbs Under Siege: Race, Space, and Audacious Judges (1996). He concludes that *Mount Laurel* is a model that other jurisdictions should replicate in seeking better planned communities.

In New Jersey, supreme court justices are appointed for life, while appellate judges and most other judges have to face reconfirmation on an electoral ballot. Does this feature of New Jersey law explain why *Mount Laurel* has rarely been followed? Did the court in *Mount Laurel* simply take on an impossible task for which courts are not suited?

2. *Density Bonuses*. California provides a 25 percent density bonus for developments that include 20 percent of affordable housing. Cal. Govt. Code §65915 (West 1997 & Supp. 2004) (*see* the discussion in *Building Industry Association v. City*

of Oceanside (reprinted *supra*)). California also provides 25 percent density bonuses for development of housing within one-half mile of a mass transit guideway station. Cal. Govt. Code §65913.5 (West 1997). The value of density bonuses, however, may be lost if expensive parking obligations are imposed on the additional units. *See also* Cal. Govt. Code §65589.5 (West Supp. 2002) (limiting the approval of any projects below the maximum allowable density because of the adverse effect on affordable housing); *Sequoyah Hills Homeowners Assn. v. City of Oakland*, 29 Cal. Rptr. 2d 182 (Ct. App. 1993) (Section 65589.5 makes it reasonable for an environmental impact report not to consider an alternative project that reduces density).

In addition, California Health and Safety Code §33334.2 (West Supp. 2004) provides that 20 percent of "tax increment" redevelopment revenue, that is, the higher tax increment produced when a redevelopment project is implemented, must be set aside for increasing, improving, and preserving the community's supply of low and moderate income housing. The percentage can be increased to 25 percent if a court determines that the redevelopment agency has misrepresented the need for affordable housing or other relevant facts. *Id.* §33334.2[c].

3. *Keeping Affordable Housing Affordable*. A problem with affordable housing is that over time it can increase in value and become unaffordable. One technique to maintain housing affordability is through the execution of affordable housing covenants. *See* Me. Rev. Stat. Ann. tit. 33, §§121-126 (West 1999) (jurisdiction may limit the resale price, place a cap on equity accumulation, or limit purchasers or renters to an economic class of consumers based on income). Are these terms easy to implement? *See also ML Plainsboro Ltd. Partnership v. Township of Plainsboro*, 719 A.2d 1285 (N.J. Super. Ct. App. Div. 1998) (holding that the planning board may not dictate in perpetuity who may use, buy, own, or rent property, and applying the principle to development of a corporate campus restricting occupancy to a single-user owner).

E. GOVERNMENT SUBSIDY PROGRAMS AND HOUSING LINKAGE

A Note on Government Housing Subsidy Programs

From the 1960s through the 1980s, the federal government was deeply involved in the provision of low and moderate income housing. Most of these programs are no longer in effect. Despite their general demise, however, the history of federal housing programs provides a rich tapestry of experience with various models for both the building and financing of affordable housing.

1. *Public Housing*. The original and best known program is public housing. Local agencies sold bonds to build rental housing and received grants from the federal Housing and Home Finance Agency, which in 1965 was consolidated within the new cabinet-level Department of Housing and Urban Development (HUD). The low rents charged tenants were used for maintenance and administration.

Unfortunately, the housing was often poorly planned, and projects were often marked by very high density, a total lack of amenities, and poor construction. Public housing attracted the increasingly poorer tenant, generating insufficient rents to pay the escalating costs of maintenance, management, and security.

As progressively poorer tenants inhabited increasingly costly housing, Congress authorized some subsidies to assist the troubled local housing authorities. However, it dealt the final blow to public housing by setting maximum rents at 25 percent, currently 30 percent, of tenant income, as the ever poorer tenants were generating even less rent to cover operating expenses. Indeed, some tenants were so poor that by the rent calculation they actually paid a negative rent. The projects were also stigmatized, for their sites were in the heart of the poorest neighborhoods. High crime, poor schools, and few jobs were available to the residents as the projects marked areas of the city where investment by private developers and entrepreneurs evaporated.

In recent years, both Republican and Democratic administrations have focused federal public housing policy on demolition and privatization of existing projects, selling the units to poor tenants. In addition to being socially disastrous, public housing was very expensive. Its costs included not only construction but also high operating expense. Not only was there a deep annual public subsidy to pay off construction bonds and cover operation costs in the budget, but a further hidden subsidy was the tax-free income received by the investors who originally purchased the local municipal bonds used to finance the construction of public housing. Chester W. Hartman, Housing and Social Policy 113-117, 127-29 (1975); Barry G. Jacobs, *et al.*, Guide to Federal Housing Programs 56-59, 63-65 (1982).

2. *Subsidized Private Housing*. A below market rate loan rental program known as §221(d)(3) allowed the development of housing in the private sector by nonprofits, cooperatives, and limited-dividend, for-profit sponsors. The program became costly as market interest rates rose. While the government was lending at 3 percent under the program, the government was obligated to borrow at dramatically higher interest rates.

In 1968, Congress passed a new housing act creating two major subsidized housing programs, each financed in the same manner. Section 236 was a rental assistance program patterned after §221(d)(3) but altering the financing scheme by having the tenant pay a rent based on the principal and a 1 percent interest rate. HUD provided an annual subsidy to cover the difference in interest from the market rate. Section 235 was an identical program but used for purchasing housing. The new programs, although eliminating federal loans, became very expensive as interest rates were rising. Rising maintenance costs forced Congress to establish an additional operating subsidy for rental projects, similar to the program in public housing.

To make matters much worse, audits of the program demonstrated that privatization was not cost effective. Construction costs, for example, were typically far higher than for similar unsubsidized market rate housing. In addition, scandals racked the §235 homeownership program, with some unscrupulous real estate and mortgage finance operators skimming huge profits. Chester W. Hartman, Housing and Social Policy 136-139 (1975).

3. *The Section Eight Program*. In 1974, Congress enacted a new housing and development act, creating what is known as the §8 program. Although initially designed to construct and rehabilitate existing rental housing, the centerpiece of the program, and the only part still in place, is the program whereby HUD provides what amounts to housing vouchers to eligible tenants. The tenants can locate housing in the private market and use the HUD grant to pay for part of the rent.

At best the §8 program has provided access to private sector housing for low income tenants previously relegated to public or subsidized projects or substandard private sector housing. At worst, the program may provide a subsidy to marginal landlords operating substandard housing. Barry G. Jacobs, *et al.*, Guide to Federal Housing Programs 23-25 (1982). For a general description of federal housing programs, see Charles Daye, *et al.*, Housing and Community Development Law Ch. 3 (2d ed. 1989).

Although state housing and finance agencies have proliferated since the 1970s, except in the case of New York's Mitchell-Lama program, which has produced a significant number of affordable housing units, the other states have failed to appropriate funds to subsidize housing. They have instead simply used bond-issuing power to reduce interest rates and have required the piggy-backing of federal or other subsidies to reduce rents to affordable levels. *See, e.g.*, *Utah Housing Finance Agency v. Smart*, 561 P.2d 1052 (Utah 1977) (sustaining constitutionality of state program).

4. *Low Income Tax Credit Housing*. Currently, the most significant generator of affordable housing is the low income tax credit established under the 1986 Tax Act. Tax Reform Act of 1986, Pub. L. No. 99-514, 100 Stat. 2085, §252, as amended (codified at I.R.C. §42 (2002)). Frequently utilizing the below-market lending of state housing finance agencies or city-issued bonds, investor-developers agree to maintain affordable rents and, in return, enjoy substantial federal income tax credits to shelter project and other ordinary income. See also James E. Wallace, Financing Affordable Housing in the United States, 6 Hous. Pol'y Debate 785, 795, tbl. 3 (1995) (summarizing housing production under the program). The Low Income Tax Credit Housing program has been criticized for its lack of civil rights standards and a pattern of racially segregated site selection. Florence Wagman Roisman, Mandates Unsatisfied: The Low Income Housing Tax Credit Program and the Civil Rights Laws, 52 U. Miami L. Rev. 1011 (1998). See generally David Philip Cohen, Improving the Supply of Affordable Housing: The Role of the Low-Income Housing Tax Credit, 6 J.L. & Pol'y 537 (1998) (arguing for extension of the tax credit program to assist those of very low income); Allison D. Christians, Breaking the Subsidy Cycle: A Proposal for Affordable Housing, 32 Colum. J.L. & Soc. Probs. 131 (1999) (arguing for expansion and extension of the low income tax credit program); Craig A. Emden & Mark I. Siegel, The Low-Income Housing Credit Provides Shelter from the Cold and Taxes, 12 J. Tax'n Investment 99 (1995); Robert C. Jacobs & Ruth Sparrow Ruben, The Reading Room: Tax Credit Program Under Scrutiny—Findings of the GAO Report, 6 J. Affordable Hous. & Commun. Devel. L. 256 (1997) (generally achieving objectives); Janet Stearns, Low-Income Housing Tax Credit: A Poor Solution to the Housing Crisis, 6 Yale L. & Pol'y Rev. 203, 225-26 (1988) (argues program is inefficient as tax revenues foregone greatly exceed benefit).

5. *Some Questions*. Does the nature of the housing market suggest strategies to solve the affordable housing problem? If the accurate economic model for housing is one of "reverse filtration," shouldn't the logical response be to subsidize housing for the affluent so as to encourage moving out? In fact, during a single year there is a larger subsidy to the better-off in the form of tax sheltering, through the deductibility of mortgage interest and property taxes, than the total cost of housing subsidies for the poor from the institution of the New Deal programs under President Roosevelt to recent times. Hearings Before the Task Force on

Human Resources and Block Grants of the House Budget Comm., 97th Cong., 1st Sess. 9 (1981) (testimony of Cushing Dolbeare).

The decline of the federal role in low-income housing subsidy, together with the relatively uninvolved role of state government, underscores the importance of inclusionary programs such as housing linkage. The following case considers the constitutionality of one such program.

COMMERCIAL BUILDERS OF NORTHERN CALIFORNIA v. CITY OF SACRAMENTO

941 F.2d 872 (9th Cir. 1991)

Introduction

Commercial Builders appeals the district court's grant of summary judgment in favor of the City of Sacramento in Commercial Builders' suit challenging a city ordinance to help expand available low-income housing. . . .

The district court . . . . concluded that the ordinance was not infirm under *Nollan v. California Coastal Comm'n*, 483 U.S. 825 (1987). . . .

Discussion

In 1987, the City and County of Sacramento commissioned a consulting firm, Keyser-Marston Associates, to study the need for low-income housing, the effect of nonresidential development on the demand for such housing, and the appropriateness of exacting fees in conjunction with such development to pay for such housing. Keyser-Marston submitted its report, estimating the percentage of new workers in the developments that would qualify as low-income workers and would require housing. As instructed, it also calculated fees for development based on a yearly subsidy of $12,000 per qualified household that would be connected to the development. This figure represented the difference between $42,000, the minimum cost of building a two-bedroom apartment, and $30,000, the maximum rental income expected from a low-income household. Also as instructed, however, in the interest of erring on the side of conservatism in exacting the fees, it reduced its final calculations by about one-half.

Based upon this study, the City of Sacramento enacted the Housing Trust Fund Ordinance on March 7, 1989. The Ordinance lists several city-wide findings, including the finding that nonresidential development is "a major factor in attracting new employees to the region" and that the influx of new employees "create[s] a need for additional housing in the City." Pursuant to these findings, the Ordinance imposes a fee in connection with the issuance of permits for nonresidential development of the type that will generate jobs. The fees, calculated using the Keyser-Marston formula, are to be paid into a fund to assist in the financing of low-income housing. The city projects that the fund will raise about $3.6 million annually, nine percent of the projected annual cost of $42 million for the needed housing. Additional money will come from other sources, such as debt funding and general revenues.

Commercial Builders does not argue that the city lacks a legitimate interest in expanding low-income housing. Rather, it contends that this Ordinance constitutes an impermissible means to advance that interest, because it places a burden of paying for low-income housing on nonresidential development without a sufficient showing that nonresidential development contributes to the need for low-income housing in proportion to that burden. . . .

The appellants content that . . . the Ordinance . . . must be struck down because the Supreme Court has now articulated a more stringent standard under which courts must analyze the imposition of conditions upon development. The appellants point out that in *Nollan v. California Coastal Comm'n*, 483 U.S. 825 (1987), the Court held that such conditions must not only be ones that the government might "rationally have decided" to employ for a given legitimate public purpose; they must also substantially advance such a purpose. They argue that under the standard articulated in *Nollan*, an ordinance that imposes an exaction on developers can be upheld only if it can be shown that the development in question is directly responsible for the social ill that the exaction is designed to alleviate. . . .

. . . We agree with the City that *Nollan* does not stand for the proposition that an exaction ordinance will be upheld only where it can be shown that the development is directly responsible for the social ill in question. Rather, *Nollan* holds that where there is no evidence of a nexus between the development and the problem that the exaction seeks to address, the exaction cannot be upheld. Where, as here, the Ordinance was implemented only after a detailed study revealed a substantial connection between development and the problem to be addressed, the Ordinance does not suffer from the infirmities that the Supreme Court disapproved in *Nollan*. We find that the nexus between the fee provision here at issue, designed to further the city's legitimate interest in housing, and the burdens caused by commercial development is sufficient to pass constitutional muster.

The appellants also place some significance on the fact that this Ordinance is a fee provision. They contend that the fee represents a transfer of property, i.e., the money paid over to the city. *See Webb's Fabulous Pharmacies, Inc. v. Beckwith*, 449 U.S. 155 (1980) (treating a purely financial exaction as a taking). In this respect, they argue, it more closely resembles a physical taking of property, which automatically falls within the purview of the Fifth Amendment, than a land use regulation, which is subject to a reasonableness analysis. Under appellants' theory, however, compensation would be required for every fee; therefore, every fee would be unconstitutional. We see no valid basis for such a rule. . . .

Finally, the appellants contend that, regardless of the standard to be applied in assessing the validity of the Ordinance, they have raised an issue of material fact in their attack on the conclusions of the Keyser-Marston study. This attack came in the form of an affidavit from their planner, David Wade, suggesting that commercial development may be a less decisive factor in worker migration than the Keyser-Marston study indicates. Wade concluded that, in addition to employment opportunity, the availability of low-income housing is itself partly responsible for any influx of low-income employees to Sacramento. Wade also opined that it is at least as true that employers follow the work force as the converse. This affidavit, appellants argue, sufficiently calls into question the city's findings concerning the nexus between its Ordinance and the social ill it sought to cure to preclude summary judgment.

The appellants' argument lacks merit. Even viewing the Wade affidavit in the light most favorable to the developers, it does not rebut the Keyser-Marston conclusion that commercial development is related to an increase in the need for low-income housing. The Ordinance accounts for what the developers characterize as the indirectness of the connection between the creation of new jobs and the need for low-income housing by charging only a small percentage of what the Keyser-Marston study calculated to be the cost of meeting new low-income housing requirements. As we have already noted, nothing in *Nollan* or any other authority cited by the appellants requires the nexus to be more direct than that achieved through the legislative process that the city here employed. . . .

CONCLUSION

The district court correctly found that, as a matter of law, Sacramento's Housing Trust Fund Ordinance does not work an unconstitutional taking. Summary judgment in favor of the city was therefore proper.

AFFIRMED.

BEEZER, Circuit Judge, dissenting:

I respectfully dissent.

As Justice Scalia warned in *Nollan*, a state can leverage its police power to the point where a regulation of land use becomes an "out-and-out plan of extortion." Sacramento's ordinance is a transparent attempt to force commercial developers to underwrite social policy. Apparently, legislators find it politically more palatable to exact payments from developers than to tax their constituents. The Takings Clause prohibits singling out developers to bear this burden. . . .

When the governmental exaction solves a problem actually created by the development (for example, requiring the developer to provide needed infrastructure), it is not coincidence that the exaction results in a benefit to the development as well as the community. . . .

. . . Sacramento would have developers pay not just for public improvements necessitated by development, but for private subsidies with little or no causal connection to development. Not surprisingly, under a scheme requiring no connection, no benefit accrues to the development in return. . . .

Sacramento has commissioned a study that demonstrates at best a tenuous and theoretical connection between commercial development and housing needs. But the Takings Clause requires a cause-and-effect relationship between the two. *Pennell v. San Jose*, 485 U.S. 1, 20 (1988) (Scalia, J., dissenting). In my view, Sacramento has not shown such a relationship. Even the study relied on by the city to support the ordinance states that its "nexus analysis does not make the case that building construction is responsible for growth."

The ordinance is nothing more than a convenient way to fund a system of transfer payments. Although Sacramento attempts to justify the ordinance as an exercise of its police power, the city actually is exercising its taxing power—free of the encumbrances generally thought to limit the exercise of that power. . . .

The new workers attracted by the new jobs associated with the new development surely will increase the demand for all manner of goods and services. If Sacramento has shown a sufficient causal connection in this case, we can be expected next to uphold exactions imposed on developers to subsidize small business retailers, child-care programs, food services and health-care delivery systems.

Notes and Comments

1. *Linkage and* Dolan. The Ninth Circuit Court of Appeals found that the linkage program in *Commercial Builders* complies with *Nollan*. What problems with *Dolan* does linkage pose? Does the court approve of the Sacramento program because the program was conservatively drawn, charging only half of the calculated costs? *See also Barrington Cove Ltd. Partnership v. Rhode Island Hous. & Mortgage Fin. Corp.*, 246 F.3d 1 (1st Cir. 2001) (allegation that state housing agency required developer to make a sizeable charitable contribution to an affordable housing trust fund in order to receive supplemental federal income tax credits for lower-income housing project failed to shock the conscience to establish substantive due process violation, and an equal protection claim was rejected for lack of a showing of treatment different from others similarly situated).

2. *Developers or the Public?* Will programs be suspect unless costs are spread over the public at large, rather than on developers? The New Jersey Supreme Court has approved of linkage and encouraged the Council on Affordable Housing to issue regulations, as such programs carry out the *Mount Laurel* principle. *Holmdel Builders Ass'n v. Township of Holmdel*, 583 A.2d 277 (N.J. 1990). *See generally* John J. Ammann, Affordable Housing: New Opportunities and Challenges for Housing Trust Funds, 8 J. Affordable Housing & Community Dev. L. 198 (1999); Peter W. Salsich, Jr., Affordable Housing: Can NIMBYism be Transformed into OKIMBYism?, 19 St. Louis U. Pub. L. Rev. 453 (2000) (endorsing inclusion through linkage). *See also* Washington State Imposes Document Recordation Surcharge to Provide Funds for Housing, 29 [Current Developments] Hous. Dev. Rep. (West) 788 (2002) (H.B. 2060 to be codified at Wash. Rev. Stat. §36.22) (establishing $10 document recordation surcharge to provide funds for the state and local housing trust funds).

3. *Preemption in Colorado*. In *Town of Telluride v. Lot Thirty- Four Venture, L.L.C.*, 3 P.3d 30 (Colo. 2000), the Colorado Supreme Court invalidated an ordinance that imposed an affordable housing mitigation mandate. The ordinance required property owners to create affordable housing for 40 percent of the employees to be generated from the new development. To assure that units remained affordable, the scheme limited the growth of the rental rate below the market rate.

The court found the scheme to constitute rent control that had been preempted by state legislation. It did so even though the ordinance authorized other alternatives, such as the actual construction of employee housing, recording deed restrictions on existing units, paying an in-lieu fee for up to 15 percent of the obligation, or conveying land to meet the in-lieu partial option. *See also* Nadia I. El Mallakh, Comment, Does the Costa-Hawkins Act Prohibit Local Inclusionary Zone Programs?, 89 Cal. L. Rev. 1847 (2001) (preemption of rent control may preclude some forms of inclusionary zoning).

PART FIVE

THE USE OF LAND USE CONTROLS TO EFFECTUATE GOVERNMENT POLICY OBJECTIVES

13

Housing and Discrimination

A. INTRODUCTION

1. Zoning, Housing, and Discrimination

Zoning is an institution born of discrimination. No one would dispute that discrimination to prohibit homes in an environmentally dangerous area is an appropriate governmental regulation. In the past, however, zoning also has been used to accomplish the separation of people on the basis of both race and economic class. *See Buchanan v. Warley*, 245 U.S. 60 (1917) (invalidating racial zoning that restricted blocks according to permissible race of occupants).

America's suburbs were developed and first marketed with the approval and subsidy of the federal government. Except for very upscale neighborhoods, subdivision sales were financially dependent on government-insured home loans under the Federal Housing Administration and Veterans Administration programs. Those programs, however, originally were available only for subdivisions that were subject to racially restrictive covenants excluding all but single race occupants. FHA Underwriting Manual ¶935 (1938) (¶980 contained a model racial restrictive covenant). *See* Robert C. Weaver, The Negro Ghetto 152-53, 217-222 (1948) (FHA practice of approving segregated subdivisions); James A. Kushner, Apartheid in America 16-22 (1980), *reprinted as* James A. Kushner, Apartheid in America: An Historical and Legal Analysis of Contemporary Racial Residential Segregation in the United States, 22 How. L.J. 547, 563-569 (1979) (hereinafter cited as *Apartheid*). *See also* Deborah Kenn, Institutionalized Legal Racism: Housing Segregation and Beyond, 11 B.U. Pub. Int. L.J. 35 (2001).

Although civil rights laws today prohibit racial and certain other forms of discrimination, housing bias appears to be institutional. In 1979, a national study funded by the federal Department of Housing and Urban Development disclosed that two million acts of housing discrimination were perpetrated annually. Robert E. Wienk, et al., Measuring Racial Discrimination in American Housing Markets (1979). In addition to racial discrimination, land use policy may discriminate against the disabled, religious minorities, families with children, the homeless, and on the basis of sexual orientation.

2. *Equal Protection in the Land Use Context*

The chapter begins with an examination of how the Equal Protection Clause of the Fourteenth Amendment applies in the land use context. In *Washington v. Davis*, 426 U.S. 229 (1976), the Court restricted the use of the Equal Protection Clause by requiring a plaintiff to establish that the defendant's action was intentionally designed to discriminate on the basis of a racial or other improper motive. The first case that you will read, *Village of Arlington Heights v. Metropolitan Housing Development Corp.*, 429 U.S. 252 (1977) (*Arlington I*), established how litigants can prove the intent required by *Washington* in the context of a zoning controversy.

Following the treatment of equal protection and racial bias, the materials take up the problem of nontraditional living arrangements. The first case, *City of Cleburne v. Cleburne Living Center, Inc.*, 473 U.S. 432 (1985), extended the Equal Protection Clause to preclude irrational regulation of housing for the disabled.

While *Cleburne* demonstrates an enhanced legal sensitivity to bias against both the disabled and nontraditional living arrangements, the Court has also endorsed traditional family zoning in *Village of Belle Terre v. Boraas*, 416 U.S. 1 (1974) (reprinted below). Are these rulings inconsistent? The Court's decision in *City of Edmonds v. Washington State Building Code Council*, 514 U.S. 725 (1995), protects group homes for the disabled from the family zoning policies endorsed in *Belle Terre*. The case demonstrates the significance of statutory civil rights protections.

In 2000, the Supreme Court decided a case illustrating that even in the absence of class-based bias, judicial review of land use regulations will not be toothless. In *Village of Willowbrook v. Olech*, 528 U.S. 562 (2000) (reprinted below), the Court ruled that whenever a landowner is treated differently from those similarly situated, an equal protection claim is stated. For a general overview of equal protections and statutory civil rights protections, *see* James A. Kushner, Government Discrimination (West 1988 & Supp. 2003).

3. *Title VIII*

The federal Fair Housing Act, passed in 1968 and popularly referred to as "Title VIII" (*see* 42 U.S.C. §§3601-3631 (2000)), has become the most effective nondiscrimination requirement in land use controversies. Most notably, Title VIII allows a violation to be based on a practice or policy that carries a discriminatory impact. *Huntington Branch NAACP v. Town of Huntington*, 844 F.2d 926 (2d Cir.), *aff'd per curiam*, 488 U.S. 15 (1988) (reprinted below). In 1988, the statute was expanded to extend protection to the disabled and to families with children.

As discussed in the materials on standing in Chapter 6 of this casebook, Title VIII also carries a reduced requirement for standing. Anyone aggrieved by a discriminatory housing practice may bring suit. *Trafficante v. Metropolitan Life Insurance Co.*, 409 U.S. 205 (1972). The reduced standing requirement of Title VIII invites those previously denied party status in public planning disputes to participate fully in administrative proceedings and litigation. It significantly extends the ability of non-owners to challenge development, by creating third-party rights for various community residents, voluntary associations, and activists. *See* Paul A. LeBel, Standing After Havens Realty: A Critique and an Alternative Framework for Analysis, 1982 Duke L.J. 1013.

B. THE FOURTEENTH AMENDMENT

The fundamental source of constitutional equality doctrine is the Fourteenth Amendment, and that amendment is the obvious constitutional provision invoked by minorities who are subjected to unequal treatment through land use decisions. The principal question that the use of this amendment poses is: What does a plaintiff have to prove in order to prevail under equal protection theory?

The Court has applied most constitutional provisions in contexts where the "effect" of action was an interference with constitutional rights, such as under the Takings Clause and the Commerce Clause. Initially, the Court appeared to have adopted a similar approach to the application of the Equal Protection Clause. *See Palmer v. Thompson*, 403 U.S. 217, 224-225 (1971).

However, In *Washington v. Davis*, 426 U.S. 229 (1976), the Court rejected a challenge to police hiring practices that utilized a written test that whites passed with greater frequency than blacks. The Court ruled that the plaintiff must show intent to prove a violation of the equal protection standard. The effect of the decision was to require a search for circumstantial evidence that might establish a finding of intent.

The following case, *Arlington Heights*, builds on the model of intentional discrimination and establishes how a prima facie case of discrimination can be assembled using circumstantial evidence.

■ VILLAGE OF ARLINGTON HEIGHTS v. METROPOLITAN HOUSING DEVELOPMENT CORP.

429 U.S. 252 (1977)

MR. JUSTICE POWELL delivered the opinion of the Court. . . .

I

Arlington Heights is a suburb of Chicago, located about 26 miles northwest of the downtown Loop area. Most of the land in Arlington Heights is zoned for detached single-family homes, and this is in fact the prevailing land use. The Village experienced substantial growth during the 1960s, but, like other communities in northwest Cook County, its population of racial minority groups remained quite low. According to the 1970 census, only 27 of the Village's 64,000 residents were black.

The Clerics of St. Viator, a religious order (Order), own an 80-acre parcel just east of the center of Arlington Heights. Part of the site is occupied by the Viatorian high school, and part by the Order's three-story novitiate building, which houses dormitories and a Montessori school. Much of the site, however, remains vacant. Since 1959, when the Village first adopted a zoning ordinance, all the land surrounding the Viatorian property has been zoned R-3, a single-family specification with relatively small minimum lot-size requirements. On three sides of the Viatorian land there are single-family homes just across a street; to the east the Viatorian property directly adjoins the backyards of other single-family homes.

The Order decided in 1970 to devote some of its land to low- and moderate-income housing. Investigation revealed that the most expeditious way to build such housing was to work through a nonprofit developer experienced in the use of federal housing subsidies under §236 of the National Housing Act, 48 Stat. 1246, as added and amended, 12 U.S.C. §1715z-1.

MHDC is such a developer. . . .

After some negotiation, MHDC and the Order entered into a 99-year lease and an accompanying agreement of sale covering a 15-acre site in the southeast corner of the Viatorian property. MHDC became the lessee immediately, but the sale agreement was contingent upon MHDC's securing zoning clearances from the Village and §236 housing assistance from the Federal Government. If MHDC proved unsuccessful in securing either, both the lease and the contract of sale would lapse. The agreement established a bargain purchase price of $300,000, low enough to comply with federal limitations governing land-acquisition costs for §236 housing.

MHDC engaged an architect and proceeded with the project, to be known as Lincoln Green. The plans called for 20 two-story buildings with a total of 190 units, each unit having its own private entrance from the outside. One hundred of the units would have a single bedroom, thought likely to attract elderly citizens. The remainder would have two, three, or four bedrooms. A large portion of the site would remain open, with shrubs and trees to screen the homes abutting the property to the east.

The planned development did not conform to the Village's zoning ordinance and could not be built unless Arlington Heights rezoned the parcel to R-5, its multiple-family housing classification. Accordingly, MHDC filed with the Village Plan Commission a petition for rezoning, accompanied by supporting materials describing the development and specifying that it would be subsidized under §236. The materials made clear that one requirement under §236 is an affirmative marketing plan designed to assure that a subsidized development is racially integrated. MHDC also submitted studies demonstrating the need for housing of this type and analyzing the probable impact of the development. To prepare for the hearings before the Plan Commission and to assure compliance with the Village building code, fire regulations, and related requirements, MHDC consulted with the Village staff for preliminary review of the development. The parties have stipulated that every change recommended during such consultations was incorporated into the plans.

During the spring of 1971, the Plan Commission considered the proposal at a series of three public meetings, which drew large crowds. Although many of those attending were quite vocal and demonstrative in opposition to Lincoln Green, a number of individuals and representatives of community groups spoke in support of rezoning. Some of the comments, both from opponents and supporters, addressed what was referred to as the "social issue" — the desirability or undesirability of introducing at this location in Arlington Heights low- and moderate-income housing, housing that would probably be racially integrated.

Many of the opponents, however, focused on the zoning aspects of the petition, stressing two arguments. First, the area always had been zoned single-family, and the neighboring citizens had built or purchased there in reliance on that classification. Rezoning threatened to cause a measurable drop in property value for neighboring sites. Second, the Village's apartment policy, adopted by the Village Board in 1962 and amended in 1970, called for R-5 zoning primarily to serve as a buffer between single-family development and land uses thought incompatible, such as commercial or manufacturing districts. Lincoln Green did not meet this requirement, as it adjoined no commercial or manufacturing district.

At the close of the third meeting, the Plan Commission adopted a motion to recommend to the Village's Board of Trustees that it deny the request. The motion stated: "While the need for low and moderate income housing may exist in Arlington Heights or its environs, the Plan Commission would be derelict in recommending it at the proposed location." Two members voted against the motion and submitted a minority report, stressing that in their view the change to accommodate Lincoln Green represented "good zoning." The Village Board met on September 28, 1971, to consider MHDC's request and the recommendation of the Plan Commission. After a public hearing, the Board denied the rezoning by a 6-1 vote. . . .

III

Our decision last Term in *Washington v. Davis*, 426 U.S. 229 (1976), made it clear that official action will not be held unconstitutional solely because it results in a racially disproportionate impact. "Disproportionate impact is not irrelevant, but it is not the sole touchstone of an invidious racial discrimination." Proof of racially discriminatory intent or purpose is required to show a violation of the Equal Protection Clause. Although some contrary indications may be drawn from some of our cases, the holding in *Davis* reaffirmed a principle well established in a variety of contexts.

Davis does not require a plaintiff to prove that the challenged action rested solely on racially discriminatory purposes. Rarely can it be said that a legislature or administrative body operating under a broad mandate made a decision motivated solely by a single concern, or even that a particular purpose was the "dominant" or "primary" one. In fact, it is because legislators and administrators are properly concerned with balancing numerous competing considerations that courts refrain from reviewing the merits of their decisions, absent a showing of arbitrariness or irrationality. But racial discrimination is not just another competing consideration. When there is a proof that a discriminatory purpose has been a motivating factor in the decision, this judicial deference is no longer justified.

Determining whether invidious discriminatory purpose was a motivating factor demands a sensitive inquiry into such circumstantial and direct evidence of intent as may be available. The impact of the official action — whether it "bears more heavily on one race than another," *Washington v. Davis, supra*, at 242 — may provide an important starting point. Sometimes a clear pattern, unexplainable on grounds other than race, emerges from the effect of the state action even when the governing legislation appears neutral on its face. The evidentiary inquiry is then relatively easy. . . .

The historical background of the decision is one evidentiary source, particularly if it reveals a series of official actions taken for invidious purposes. The specific sequence of events leading up to the challenged decision also may shed some light on the decisionmaker's purposes. For example, if the property involved here always had been zoned R-5 but suddenly was changed to R-3 when the town learned of MHDC's plans to erect integrated housing,[16] we would have a far different case. Departures from the normal procedural sequence also might afford evidence that improper purposes are playing a role. Substantive departures too may be relevant, particularly if the factors usually considered important by the decisionmaker strongly favor a decision contrary to the one reached.[17]

The legislative or administrative history may be highly relevant, especially where there are contemporary statements by members of the decisionmaking body, minutes of its meetings, or reports. In some extraordinary instances the members might be called to the stand at trial to testify concerning the purpose of the official action, although even then such testimony frequently will be barred by privilege.

The foregoing summary identifies, without purporting to be exhaustive, subjects of proper inquiry in determining whether racially discriminatory intent existed. With these in mind, we now address the case before us.

IV

This case was tried in the District Court and reviewed in the Court of Appeals before our decision in *Washington v. Davis, supra*. The respondents proceeded on the erroneous theory that the Village's refusal to rezone carried a racially discriminatory effect and was, without more, unconstitutional. But both courts below understood that at least part of their function was to examine the purpose underlying the decision. In making its findings on this issue, the District Court noted that some of the opponents of Lincoln Green who spoke at the various hearings might have been motivated by opposition to minority groups. The court held, however, that the evidence "does not warrant the conclusion that this motivated the defendants."

On appeal the Court of Appeals focused primarily on respondents' claim that the Village's buffer policy had not been consistently applied and was being invoked

16. See, *e.g.*, *Progress Development Corp. v. Mitchell*, 286 F. 2d 222 (CA7 1961) (park board allegedly condemned plaintiffs' land for a park upon learning that the homes plaintiffs were erecting there would be sold under a marketing plan designed to assure integration); *Kennedy Park Homes Assn. v. City of Lackawanna*, 436 F. 2d 108 (CA2 1970), *cert. denied*, 401 U.S. 1010 (1971) (town declared moratorium on new subdivisions and rezoned area for parkland shortly after learning of plaintiffs' plans to build low-income housing). . . .

17. See *Dailey v. City of Lawton*, 425 F. 2d 1037 (CA10 1970). The plaintiffs in *Dailey* planned to build low-income housing on the site of a former school that they had purchased. The city refused to rezone the land from PF, its public facilities classification, to R-4, high-density residential. All the surrounding area was zoned R-4, and both the present and the former planning director for the city testified that there was no reason "from a zoning standpoint" why the land should not be classified R-4. Based on this and other evidence, the Court of Appeals ruled that "the record sustains the [District Court's] holding of racial motivation and of arbitrary and unreasonable action."

with a strictness here that could only demonstrate some other underlying motive. The court concluded that the buffer policy, though not always applied with perfect consistency, had on several occasions formed the basis for the Board's decision to deny other rezoning proposals. "The evidence does not necessitate a finding that Arlington Heights administered this policy in a discriminatory manner." The Court of Appeals therefore approved the District Court's findings concerning the Village's purposes in denying rezoning to MHDC.

We also have reviewed the evidence. The impact of the Village's decision does arguably bear more heavily on racial minorities. Minorities constitute 18% of the Chicago area population, and 40% of the income groups said to be eligible for Lincoln Green. But there is little about the sequence of events leading up to the decision that would spark suspicion. The area around the Viatorian property has been zoned R-3 since 1959, the year when Arlington Heights first adopted a zoning map. Single-family homes surround the 80-acre site, and the Village is undeniably committed to single-family homes as its dominant residential land use. The rezoning request progressed according to the usual procedures. The Plan Commission even scheduled two additional hearings, at least in part to accommodate MHDC and permit it to supplement its presentation with answers to questions generated at the first hearing.

The statements by the Plan Commission and Village Board members, as reflected in the official minutes, focused almost exclusively on the zoning aspects of the MHDC petition, and the zoning factors on which they relied are not novel criteria in the Village's rezoning decisions. There is no reason to doubt that there has been reliance by some neighboring property owners on the maintenance of single-family zoning in the vicinity. The Village originally adopted its buffer policy long before MHDC entered the picture and has applied the policy too consistently for us to infer discriminatory purpose from its application in this case. Finally, MHDC called one member of the Village Board to the stand at trial. Nothing in her testimony supports an inference of invidious purpose.

In sum, the evidence does not warrant overturning the concurrent findings of both courts below. Respondents simply failed to carry their burden of proving that discriminatory purpose was a motivating factor in the Village's decision.[21]

Notes and Comments

1. *Practice and Discriminatory Impact.* What was the practice that was alleged to carry a discriminatory impact? Would the failure to consistently adhere to a land use policy establish a case? What percentage of inconsistency would render application of the policy as pretextual?

21. Proof that the decision by the Village was motivated in part by a racially discriminatory purpose would not necessarily have required invalidation of the challenged decision. Such proof would, however, have shifted to the Village the burden of establishing that the same decision would have resulted even had the impermissible purpose not been considered. If this were established, the complaining party in a case of this kind no longer fairly could attribute the injury complained of to improper consideration of a discriminatory purpose. In such circumstances, there would be no justification for judicial interference with the challenged decision. But in this case respondents failed to make the required threshold showing.

What if the city has a number of objections to a project proposal, including inadequate parking, overcrowded schools, and the likely influx of African-Americans? Would *Arlington Heights* provide a remedy for the disappointed developer? Would race be the motivating factor?

2. *Justifying Discrimination*. Had the prima facie case been established in *Arlington Heights*, the village would have had to defend its policy, practice, or action as necessary to serve a compelling state interest. In addition, under such strict scrutiny the defendant must prove the difficult proposition that the state's interest could not be served by less discriminatory alternatives. *Attorney General v. Soto-Lopez*, 476 U.S. 898 (1986).

3. *The State Action Limitation*. The Fourteenth Amendment is limited to state action. *The Civil Rights Cases*, 109 U.S. 3 (1883). The Court, however, has established what amount to some exceptions to the rule that the Fourteenth Amendment reaches only government discrimination, such as where the private defendant (1) has acted together with a state official or a state agency (*Lugar v. Edmundson Oil Co.*, 457 U.S. 922 (1982) (participation by courts in prejudgment attachment)), (2) has a partnership arrangement with a government entity (*Burton v. Wilmington Parking Authority*, 365 U.S. 715 (1961) (rental to segregated restaurant in public parking garage)), or (3) is carrying out a governmental function, one that traditionally has been carried out exclusively by states or local governments. *Marsh v. Alabama*, 326 U.S. 501 (1946) (company town).

Most land development techniques directly involve the state or a unit of local government. What forms might a privatized land use development scheme take? Could the use of development agreements, contracts, and private covenants immunize development from the Fourteenth Amendment? *Compare Pitt v. Pine Valley Golf Club*, 695 F. Supp. 788 (D.N.J. 1988) (a private golf club membership restriction was state action as it operates as a zoning ordinance under a public function theory) *with Linn Valley Lakes Property Owners Ass'n v. Brockway*, 824 P.2d 948 (Kan. 1992) (enforcement of private restrictive covenant prohibiting placement of signs on property was not improper state action).

4. *The Referendum and Discrimination*. Could a zoning process that included a mandatory referendum for zone changes violate equal protection? In *City of Cuyahoga Falls v. Buckeye Community Found.*, 538 U.S. 188, 123 S. Ct. 1389 (2003), discussed in Chapter 10, the Court rejected a challenge to a vote pursuant to a referendum that repealed a zoning authorization for a low-income housing project. The city charter provided for such a referendum process, and the process was not adopted as part of a discriminatory scheme. The Fourteenth Amendment requires involvement of public officials, and the Court ruled that the discriminatory animus of some voters cannot establish discrimination by the state.

5. *Segregation and Professional Responsibility*. You should consider the role of attorneys in creating housing segregation. It is lawyers' arguments and judges' decisions that have perpetuated segregation and discrimination in housing. Robert Drinan, Untying The White Noose, 94 Yale L.J. 435, 441-443 (1984). Father Drinan would impose a canon that lawyers should not engage in any transaction directly or indirectly involving racial discrimination.

Should attorneys, like city planners, have ethical obligations not to advocate programs or projects that are discriminatory or segregative, or that would have adverse consequences on the poor? Does such an obligation conflict with the principle that everyone is entitled to counsel, not simply when charged with a crime but to support or represent all interests?

6. *Municipal Services Discrimination.* In *Hawkins v. Town of Shaw,* 437 F.2d 1286 (5th Cir. 1971), *aff'd en banc per curiam,* 461 F.2d 1171 (5th Cir. 1972), the Fifth Circuit encountered a stark disparity between the white community of Shaw in the Mississippi Delta and the African-American neighborhoods on the "other side of the tracks." Street paving, sewers, mercury vapor street lighting, and surface water drainage were almost nonexistent in the black community while nearly universal in the white neighborhoods. The city advanced pretextual explanations for the disparity. The Fifth Circuit found a violation of the Equal Protection Clause, but under a theory of disparate effects now rejected by *Arlington Heights.*

How does *Arlington Heights* affect the *Hawkins* form of litigation strategy? Would it be possible to seek municipal services through a Title VIII strategy, thereby applying an effects test for the prima facie case rather than requiring proof of intent?

The Second Circuit has ruled that the disparity of conditions of New York City's urban parks did not prove discrimination because it is not the results but the inputs that must be equal. The court found that lower use levels, higher maintenance costs, and vandalism in minority area parks explained condition disparities. The court accepted the City's argument that greater services and programs were provided in the white affluent areas based on a formula reflecting the past level of use. *Beal v. Lindsay,* 468 F.2d 287 (2d Cir. 1972).

Funding based on levels of use exacerbates discrimination as facilities in poor repair generate lower use statistics and a reduced budget, while heavily used facilities receive increased funding. Consider whether any Title VI (prohibiting discrimination in federally assisted programs) or Title VIII strategies could be used? Would New York's park funding scheme withstand an "impacts" scrutiny?

If the case alleges discrimination that is not racially based, does the prima facie case or defendant's burden to justify the action change? All equal protection claims demand proof of intent. The following case asks what level of scrutiny should be required for classifications based on disability where a court is reviewing the government's justification.

CITY OF CLEBURNE, TEXAS v. CLEBURNE LIVING CENTER, INC.

473 U.S. 432 (1985)

Justice White delivered the opinion of the Court.

A Texas city denied a special use permit for the operation of a group home for the mentally retarded, acting pursuant to a municipal zoning ordinance requiring permits for such homes. The Court of Appeals for the Fifth Circuit held that mental retardation is a "quasi-suspect" classification and that the ordinance violated the Equal Protection Clause because it did not substantially further an important governmental purpose. We hold that a lesser standard of scrutiny is appropriate, but conclude that under that standard the ordinance is invalid as applied in this case.

I

In July 1980, respondent Jan Hannah purchased a building at 201 Featherston Street in the city of Cleburne, Texas, with the intention of leasing it to Cleburne Living Center, Inc. (CLC), for the operation of a group home for the mentally retarded. It was anticipated that the home would house 13 retarded men and women, who would be under the constant supervision of CLC staff members. The house had four bedrooms and two baths, with a half bath to be added. CLC planned to comply with all applicable state and federal regulations.

The city informed CLC that a special use permit would be required for the operation of a group home at the site, and CLC accordingly submitted a permit application. In response to a subsequent inquiry from CLC, the city explained that under the zoning regulations applicable to the site, a special use permit, renewable annually, was required for the construction of "[h]ospitals for the insane or feeble-minded, or alcoholic *[sic]* or drug addicts, or penal or correctional institutions." The city had determined that the proposed group home should be classified as a "hospital for the feeble-minded." After holding a public hearing on CLC's application, the City Council voted 3 to 1 to deny a special use permit. . . .

II

The Equal Protection Clause of the Fourteenth Amendment commands that no State shall "deny to any person within its jurisdiction the equal protection of the laws," which is essentially a direction that all persons similarly situated should be treated alike. *Plyler v. Doe*, 457 U.S. 202, 216 (1982). Section 5 of the Amendment empowers Congress to enforce this mandate, but absent controlling congressional direction, the courts have themselves devised standards for determining the validity of state legislation or other official action that is challenged as denying equal protection. The general rule is that legislation is presumed to be valid and will be sustained if the classification drawn by the statute is rationally related to a legitimate state interest. . . .

The general rule gives way, however, when a statute classifies by race, alienage, or national origin. These factors are so seldom relevant to the achievement of any legitimate state interest that laws grounded in such considerations are deemed to reflect prejudice and antipathy—a view that those in the burdened class are not as worthy or deserving as others. For these reasons and because such discrimination is unlikely to be soon rectified by legislative means, these laws are subjected to strict scrutiny and will be sustained only if they are suitably tailored to serve a compelling state interest. . . .

Legislative classifications based on gender also call for a heightened standard of review. . . .

III

Against this background, we conclude for several reasons that the Court of Appeals erred in holding mental retardation a quasi-suspect classification calling for a more exacting standard of judicial review than is normally accorded economic and social legislation. First, it is undeniable, and it is not argued otherwise here, that those who are mentally retarded have a reduced ability to cope with and function in the everyday world. Nor are they all cut from the same pattern: as the testimony in this record indicates, they range from those whose disability is not immediately evident to those who must be constantly cared for. They are thus different, immutably so, in relevant respects, and the States' interest in dealing with and providing for them is plainly a legitimate one. How this large and diversified group is to be treated under the law is a difficult and often a technical matter, very much a task for legislators guided by qualified professionals and not by the perhaps ill-informed opinions of the judiciary. Heightened scrutiny inevitably involves substantive judgments about legislative decisions, and we doubt that the predicate for such judicial oversight is present where the classification deals with mental retardation.

Second, the distinctive legislative response, both national and state, to the plight of those who are mentally retarded demonstrates not only that they have unique problems, but also that the lawmakers have been addressing their difficulties in a manner that belies a continuing antipathy or prejudice and a corresponding need for more intrusive oversight by the judiciary. . . .

Third, the legislative response, which could hardly have occurred and survived without public support, negates any claim that the mentally retarded are politically powerless in the sense that they have no ability to attract the attention of the lawmakers. . . .

Fourth, if the large and amorphous class of the mentally retarded were deemed quasi-suspect for the reasons given by the Court of Appeals, it would be difficult to find a principled way to distinguish a variety of other groups who have perhaps immutable disabilities setting them off from others, who cannot themselves mandate the desired legislative responses, and who can claim some degree of prejudice from at least part of the public at large. One need mention in this respect only the aging, the disabled, the mentally ill, and the infirm. We are reluctant to set out on that course, and we decline to do so. . . .

Our refusal to recognize the retarded as a quasi-suspect class does not leave them entirely unprotected from invidious discrimination. To withstand equal protection review, legislation that distinguishes between the mentally retarded and others must be rationally related to a legitimate governmental purpose. This standard, we believe, affords government the latitude necessary both to pursue policies designed to assist the retarded in realizing their full potential, and to freely and efficiently engage in activities that burden the retarded in what is essentially an incidental manner. The State may not rely on a classification whose relationship to an asserted goal is so attenuated as to render the distinction arbitrary or irrational. Furthermore, some objectives—such as "a bare . . . desire to harm a politically unpopular group, . . . "—are not legitimate state interests. Beyond that, the mentally retarded, like others, have and retain their substantive constitutional rights in addition to the right to be treated equally by the law.

IV

We turn to the issue of the validity of the zoning ordinance insofar as it requires a special use permit for homes for the mentally retarded. We inquire first whether requiring a special use permit for the Featherston home in the circumstances here deprives respondents of the equal protection of the laws. If it does, there will be no occasion to decide whether the special use permit provision is facially invalid where the mentally retarded are involved, or to put it another way, whether the city may never insist on a special use permit for a home for the mentally retarded in an R-3 zone. . . .

The constitutional issue is clearly posed. The city does not require a special use permit in an R-3 zone for apartment houses, multiple dwellings, boarding and lodging houses, fraternity or sorority houses, dormitories, apartment hotels, hospitals, sanitariums, nursing homes for convalescents or the aged (other than for the insane or feebleminded or alcoholics or drug addicts), private clubs or fraternal orders, and other specified uses. It does, however, insist on a special permit for the Featherston home, and it does so, as the District Court found, because it would be a facility for the mentally retarded. May the city require the permit for this facility when other care and multiple-dwelling facilities are freely permitted?

It is true, as already pointed out, that the mentally retarded as a group are indeed different from others not sharing their misfortune, and in this respect they may be different from those who would occupy other facilities that would be permitted in an R-3 zone without a special permit. But this difference is largely irrelevant unless the Featherston home and those who would occupy it would threaten legitimate interests of the city in a way that other permitted uses such as boarding houses and hospitals would not. Because in our view the record does not reveal any rational basis for believing that the Featherston home would pose any special threat to the city's legitimate interests, we affirm the judgment below insofar as it holds the ordinance invalid as applied in this case.

The District Court found that the City Council's insistence on the permit rested on several factors. First, the Council was concerned with the negative attitude of the majority of property owners located within 200 feet of the Featherston facility, as well as with the fears of elderly residents of the neighborhood. But mere negative attitudes, or fear, unsubstantiated by factors which are properly cognizable in a zoning proceeding, are not permissible bases for treating a home for the mentally retarded differently from apartment houses, multiple dwellings, and the like. . . .

Second, the Council had two objections to the location of the facility. It was concerned that the facility was across the street from a junior high school, and it feared that the students might harass the occupants of the Featherston home. But the school itself is attended by about 30 mentally retarded students, and denying a permit based on such vague, undifferentiated fears is again permitting some portion of the community to validate what would otherwise be an equal protection violation. The other objection to the home's location was that it was located on "a five hundred year flood plain." This concern with the possibility of a flood, however, can hardly be based on a distinction between the Featherston home and, for example, nursing homes, homes for convalescents or the aged, or sanitariums or hospitals, any of which could be located on the Featherston site without obtaining a special use permit. The same may be said of another concern of the Council—doubts about the legal responsibility for actions which the mentally retarded might take. If there is no concern about legal responsibility with respect to other uses that would be permitted in the area, such as boarding and fraternity houses, it is difficult to believe that the groups of mildly or moderately mentally retarded individuals who would live at 201 Featherston would present any different or special hazard.

Fourth, the Council was concerned with the size of the home and the number of people that would occupy it. The District Court found, and the Court of Appeals repeated, that "[i]f the potential residents of the Featherston Street home were not mentally retarded, but the home was the same in all other respects, its use would be permitted under the city's zoning ordinance." Given this finding, there would be no restrictions on the number of people who could occupy this home as a boarding house, nursing home, family dwelling, fraternity house, or dormitory. The question is whether it is rational to treat the mentally retarded differently. It is true that they suffer disability not shared by others; but why this difference warrants a density regulation that others need not observe is not at all apparent. At least this record does not clarify how, in this connection, the characteristics of the intended occupants of the Featherston home rationally justify denying to those occupants what would be permitted to groups occupying the same site for different purposes. . . .

In the courts below the city also urged that the ordinance is aimed at avoiding concentration of population and at lessening congestion of the streets. These concerns obviously fail to explain why apartment houses, fraternity and sorority houses, hospitals and the like, may freely locate in the area without a permit. So, too, the expressed worry about fire hazards, the serenity of the neighborhood, and the avoidance of danger to other residents fail rationally to justify singling out a home such as 201 Featherston for the special use permit, yet imposing no such restrictions on the many other uses freely permitted in the neighborhood.

The short of it is that requiring the permit in this case appears to us to rest on an irrational prejudice against the mentally retarded, including those who would occupy the Featherston facility and who would live under the closely supervised and highly regulated conditions expressly provided for by state and federal law. . . .

Notes and Comments

1. *Interpreting* Cleburne. What is the precise holding of *Cleburne*? Could group homes be restricted to commercial and multi-family districts but excluded from single-family home districts? Could homeowners enforce a restrictive covenant prohibiting group home use? *See Bannum, Inc. v. City of Fort Lauderdale*, 157 F.3d 819 (11th Cir. 1998), *cert. denied*, 528 U.S. 822 (1999) (no denial of equal protection to refuse a special use permit for a custodial facility for a supervised residential program serving former convicts, distinguishing *Cleburne* on the basis of public safety concerns). *See generally* Richard B. Saphire, Equal Protection, Rational Basis Review, and the Impact of Cleburne Living Center, Inc., 88 Ky. L.J. 591 (1999-2000).

2. Cleburne, Euclid, *and Housing Distinctions*. Is *Cleburne* consistent with *Village of Euclid v. Ambler Realty Co.*, 272 U.S. 365 (1926) (reprinted in Chapter 2), the case that established deference to zoning? Does the distinction between single-family and low density, multi-family housing survive the scrutiny of *Cleburne*? Did the city offer a rational explanation for separating group homes from other commercial

or high density housing? Would the case have been decided differently if group homes were treated the same as multi-family housing?

What would be the result if a special use permit was required for group homes in a detached single-family district? Would a requirement that group homes be located 1500 feet from other group homes be valid under *Cleburne*? What if the dispersal policy was designed to avoid segregation of the disabled and to achieve true integration?

3. *Title VIII and Disability Discrimination.* As noted in the introduction to this chapter, the Fair Housing Act was amended in 1988 to extend Title VIII to reach discrimination based on handicap. Fair Housing Amendments Act of 1988, Pub. L. No. 100-430, 102 Stat. 1619, *codified at* 42 U.S.C. §§3601-3619, 3631 (2000). As a result, most challenges to group home regulation and land use practices touching on or affecting disabilities are reviewed under the statutory standard.

Can equal protection claims be maintained in the absence of class-based bias? Does proof that a developer, landowner, or tenant has been treated differently from others when the victim is simply a member of a class of one show a violation of the Fourteenth Amendment? The following case addresses the question.

■ VILLAGE OF WILLOWBROOK v. OLECH

528 U.S. 562 (2000)

PER CURIAM.

Respondent Grace Olech and her late husband Thaddeus asked petitioner Village of Willowbrook (Village) to connect their property to the municipal water supply. The Village at first conditioned the connection on the Olechs granting the Village a 33-foot easement. The Olechs objected, claiming that the Village only required a 15-foot easement from other property owners seeking access to the water supply. After a 3-month delay, the Village relented and agreed to provide water service with only a 15-foot easement.

Olech sued the Village, claiming that the Village's demand of an additional 18-foot easement violated the Equal Protection Clause of the Fourteenth Amendment. Olech asserted that the 33-foot easement demand was "irrational and wholly arbitrary"; that the Village's demand was actually motivated by ill will resulting from the Olechs' previous filing of an unrelated, successful lawsuit against the Village; and that the Village acted either with the intent to deprive Olech of her rights or in reckless disregard of her rights. . . .

Our cases have recognized successful equal protection claims brought by a "class of one," where the plaintiff alleges that she has been intentionally treated differently from others similarly situated and that there is no rational basis for the difference in treatment. In so doing, we have explained that "'[t]he purpose of the equal protection clause of the Fourteenth Amendment is to secure every person within the State's jurisdiction against intentional and arbitrary discrimination, whether occasioned by express terms of a statute or by its improper execution through duly constituted agents.'" . . .

That reasoning is applicable to this case. Olech's complaint can fairly be construed as alleging that the Village intentionally demanded a 33-foot easement as a condition of connecting her property to the municipal water supply where the Village required only a 15-foot easement from other similarly situated property owners. . . . The complaint also alleged that the Village's demand was "irrational and wholly arbitrary" and that the Village ultimately connected her property after receiving a clearly adequate 15-foot easement. These allegations, quite apart from the Village's subjective motivation, are sufficient to state a claim for relief under traditional equal protection analysis. We therefore affirm the judgment of the Court of Appeals, but do not reach the alternative theory of "subjective ill will" relied on by that court.

It is so ordered.

Justice BREYER, concurring in the result.

The Solicitor General and the village of Willowbrook have expressed concern lest we interpret the Equal Protection Clause in this case in a way that would transform many ordinary violations of city or state law into violations of the Constitution. It might be thought that a rule that looks only to an intentional difference in treatment and a lack of a rational basis for that different in treatment would work such a transformation. Zoning decisions, for example, will often, perhaps almost always, treat one landowner differently from another, and one might claim that, when a city's zoning authority takes an action that fails to conform to a city zoning regulation, it lacks a "rational basis" for its action (at least if the regulation in question is reasonably clear).

This case, however, does not directly raise the question whether the simple and common instance of a faulty zoning decision would violate the Equal Protection Clause. That is because the Court of Appeals found that in this case respondent had alleged an extra factor as well—a factor that the Court of Appeals called "vindictive action," "illegitimate animus," or "ill will." . . .

In my view, the presence of that added factor in this case is sufficient to minimize any concern about transforming run-of-the-mill zoning cases into cases of constitutional right. For this reason, along with the others mentioned by the Court, I concur in the result.

Notes and Comments

1. *The Consequences of* Olech. The larger issue raised by *Olech* is, of course, the extent to which an equal protection claim will lie against routine zoning decisions. Does Justice Breyer's concurring opinion put to rest the specter of an avalanche of such actions?

2. *Interpreting* Olech. In *Hilton v. City of Wheeling*, 209 F.3d 1005, 1008 (7th Cir. 2002), the court interpreted *Olech* to require that plaintiff present evidence that the "defendant deliberately sought to deprive him of the equal protection of the laws for reasons of a personal nature unrelated to the duties of the defendant's position." The same circuit applied that principle in *Cruz v. Town of Cicero*, 275 F.3d 579 (7th Cir. 2001), to uphold a jury verdict, concluding that "[h]ostility stemming from a person's failure to contribute to a politician's campaign fund, or otherwise reward her personally for permitting access to government services," falls into the category of a "totally illegitimate animus." *Id.* at 589. *See also McDonald's Corp. v. City of Norton Shores*, 102 F. Supp. 2d 431 (W.D. Mich. 2000) (no equal protection

violation in rejecting rezoning to allow a drive-in restaurant despite approval of such a request for a K-Mart sit-down restaurant on adjacent property, as the uses were not similarly situated, and distinguishing *Olech*).

While *Willowbrook v. Olech* has yet to generate a revolution in land use regulation, it may have spawned *Bush v. Gore*, 531 U.S. 98 (2000). In halting the counting of disputed presidential ballots by the State of Florida, the Court ostensibly found that the challenging candidate constituted a class of one despite identical treatment under the scheme to the opposing candidate.

3. *Literature*. Paul D. Wilson, What Hath *Olech* Wrought? The Equal Protection Clause in Recent Land-Use Damages Litigation, 33 Urb. Law. 729 (2001) (no significant change in judicial deference, finding most challengers are not similarly situated or are unable to demonstrate disparate treatment).

C. NONTRADITIONAL LIVING ARRANGEMENTS

Limiting the occupation of homes to persons sharing a blood or marriage relationship raises the specter of zoning that interferes with fundamental notions of privacy, personal autonomy, and freedom of association. The following case addresses communal living arrangements and defines some of the constitutional limits on the deferential judicial review model first endorsed in *Village of Euclid v. Ambler Realty*.

■ VILLAGE OF BELLE TERRE v. BORAAS
416 U.S. 1 (1974)

MR. JUSTICE DOUGLAS delivered the opinion of the Court.

Belle Terre is a village on Long Island's north shore of about 220 homes inhabited by 700 people. Its total land area is less than one square mile. It has restricted land use to one-family dwellings excluding lodging houses, boarding houses, fraternity houses, or multiple-dwelling houses. The word "family" as used in the ordinance means, "[o]ne or more persons related by blood, adoption, or marriage, living and cooking together as a single housekeeping unit, exclusive of household servants. A number of persons but not exceeding two (2) living and cooking together as a single housekeeping unit though not related by blood, adoption, or marriage shall be deemed to constitute a family."

Appellees the Dickmans are owners of a house in the village and leased it in December 1971 for a term of 18 months to Michael Truman. Later Bruce Boraas became a colessee. Then Anne Parish moved into the house along with three others. These six are students at nearby State University at Stony Brook and none is related to the other by blood, adoption, or marriage. When the village served the Dickmans with an "Order to Remedy Violations" of the ordinance, the owners plus three tenants thereupon brought this action under 42 U.S.C. §1983 for an injunction and a judgment declaring the ordinance unconstitutional. . . .

In *Seattle Trust Co. v. Roberge*, 278 U.S. 116, Seattle had a zoning ordinance that permitted a " 'philanthropic home for children or for old people' " in a particular district " 'when the written consent shall have been obtained of the owners of two-thirds of the property within four hundred (400) feet of the proposed building.' " The Court held that provision of the ordinance unconstitutional, saying that the existing owners could "withhold consent for selfish reasons or arbitrarily and may subject the trustee [owner] to their will or caprice." Unlike the billboard cases, the Court concluded that the Seattle ordinance was invalid since the proposed home for the aged poor was not shown by its maintenance and construction "to work any injury, inconvenience or annoyance to the community, the district or any person."

The present ordinance is challenged on several grounds: that it interferes with a person's right to travel; that it interferes with the right to migrate to and settle within a State; that it bars people who are uncongenial to the present residents; that it expresses the social preferences of the residents for groups that will be congenial to them; that social homogeneity is not a legitimate interest of government; that the restriction of those whom the neighbors do not like trenches on the newcomers' rights of privacy; that it is of no rightful concern to villagers whether the residents are married or unmarried; that the ordinance is antithetical to the Nation's experience, ideology, and self-perception as an open, egalitarian, and integrated society.

We find none of these reasons in the record before us. It is not aimed at transients. Cf. *Shapiro v. Thompson*, 394 U.S. 618. It involves no procedural disparity inflicted on some but not on others. . . . It involves no "fundamental" right guaranteed by the Constitution. . . . We deal with economic and social legislation where legislatures have historically drawn lines which we respect against the charge of violation of the Equal Protection Clause if the law be " 'reasonable, not arbitrary' " and bears "a rational relationship to a [permissible] state objective."

It is said, however, that if two unmarried people can constitute a "family," there is no reason why three or four may not. But every line drawn by a legislature leaves some out that might well have been included. That exercise of discretion, however, is a legislative, not a judicial, function.

It is said that the Belle Terre ordinance reeks with an animosity to unmarried couples who live together. There is no evidence to support it; and the provision of the ordinance bringing within the definition of a "family" two unmarried people belies the charge.

The ordinance places no ban on other forms of association, for a "family" may, so far as the ordinance is concerned, entertain whomever it likes.

The regimes of boarding houses, fraternity houses, and the like present urban problems. More people occupy a given space; more cars rather continuously pass by; more cars are parked; noise travels with crowds.

A quiet place where yards are wide, people few, and motor vehicles restricted are legitimate guidelines in a land-use project addressed to family needs. This goal is a permissible one within *Berman v. Parker*. The police power is not confined to elimination of filth, stench, and unhealthy places. It is ample to lay out zones where family values, youth values, and the blessings of quiet seclusion and clean air make the area a sanctuary for people. . . .

Mr. Justice Marshall, dissenting. . . .

The instant ordinance discriminates on the basis of . . . a personal lifestyle choice as to household companions. It permits any number of persons related by blood or marriage, be it two or twenty, to live in a single household, but it limits to two the number of unrelated persons bound by profession, love, friendship, religious or political affiliation, or mere economics who can occupy a single home. Belle Terre imposes upon those who deviate from the community norm in their choice of living companions significantly greater restrictions than are applied to residential groups who are related by blood or marriage, and compose the established order within the community. The village has, in effect, acted to fence out those individuals whose choice of lifestyle differs from that of its current residents. . . .

. . . The ordinance imposes no restriction whatsoever on the number of persons who may live in a house, as long as they are related by marital or sanguinary bonds — presumably no matter how distant their relationship. Nor does the ordinance restrict the number of income earners who may contribute to rent in such a household, or the number of automobiles that may be maintained by its occupants. In that sense the ordinance is underinclusive. On the other hand, the statute restricts the number of unrelated persons who may live in a home to no more than two. It would therefore prevent three unrelated people from occupying a dwelling even if among them they had but one income and no vehicles. While an extended family of a dozen or more might live in a small bungalow, three elderly and retired persons could not occupy the large manor house next door. Thus the statute is also grossly overinclusive to accomplish its intended purposes. . . .

Notes and Comments

1. Belle Terre *and* Cleburne. Is *Belle Terre* consistent with *Cleburne*? Does the court engage in more rigorous scrutiny in *Cleburne* despite the articulation of a rational basis standard? Can you justify the deference shown in *Belle Terre*? See James A. Kushner, Substantive Equal Protection: The Rehnquist Court and the Fourth Tier of Judicial Review, 53 Mo. L. Rev. 423 (1988) (arguing that *Cleburne* is one of a number of equal protection rulings applying scrutiny greater than rational basis and less than intermediate scrutiny).

2. Moore. In *Moore v. City of East Cleveland*, 431 U.S. 494 (1977), the Court invalidated an ordinance that limited occupancy to members of a single family, a term that was defined according to a narrow definition of related individuals. As applied, the law prohibited a grandmother from living with her two grandsons because, although they were cousins, they were from different children. The law, however, permitted a grandparent to reside with sibling grandchildren.

The Court could not agree on a unifying rationale for the ruling. Four justices invalidated the ordinance on substantive due process grounds, with two of the four also finding an equal protection violation. Justice Stevens believed that the ordinance was simply arbitrary under *Village of Euclid* and *Nectow v. City of Cambridge*, the Court decision that was handed down soon after *Village of Euclid* and that invalidated a city zoning ordinance.

3. *State Constitutional Law*. Some state courts have refused to follow *Belle Terre* and have opted for a broader grant of privacy under state constitutions to protect against the regulation of occupancy based on blood or marriage relationships. *See, e.g.*, *City of Santa Barbara v. Adamson*, 610 P.2d 436 (Cal. 1980); *Charter Township of Delta v. Dinolfo*, 351 N.W.2d 831 (Mich. 1984); *State v. Baker*, 405 A.2d 368 (N.J. 1979); *McMinn v. Town of Oyster Bay*, 488 N.E.2d 1240 (N.Y. 1985). *See also*

Note, Belle Terre and Single-Family Home Ordinances: Judicial Perceptions of Local Government and the Presumption of Validity, 74 N.Y.U. L. Rev. 447 (1999) (endorsing a perceived trend of state courts to reject the traditional deferential model).

D. FEDERAL STATUTORY LIMITATIONS

In addition to the rights available under the Constitution, Congress has passed a wide array of civil rights legislation affecting land use planning and development. Congress enjoys broad authority under §5 of the Fourteenth Amendment to pass civil rights legislation. *Katzenbach v. Morgan*, 384 U.S. 641, 648-660 (1966). Thus, Congress has the ability to modify the challenger's burden, and it has done so.

For example, Congress has (1) reduced standing barriers (*Havens Realty Corp. v. Coleman*, 455 U.S. 363 (1982) (broad reading of "aggrieved")), (2) done away with the need to prove intent (*Griggs v. Duke Power Co.*, 401 U.S. 424 (1971) (effects test used under Title VII employment discrimination statute)), and (3) eliminated the requirement of the presence of state action (*Runyon v. McCrary*, 427 U.S. 160 (1976) (reaching bias in private school admissions under the power of the Thirteenth Amendment)). The following note discusses nondiscrimination statutes frequently encountered in land use and housing discrimination litigation.

A Note on Civil Rights Statutes

1. *Section 1982.* In *Jones v. Alfred H. Mayer Co.*, 392 U.S. 409 (1968), the Supreme Court recognized the reach of the 1866 Civil Rights Act, 42 U.S.C. §1982 (2000), to encompass all acts of racial discrimination in housing as well as acts involving personal and other forms of property. Discrimination involving property is a "badge or incident of slavery"; thus, Congress could reach purely private transactions under its Thirteenth Amendment powers. Section 1982 was the plaintiff's preferred cause of action in fair housing cases based on race until passage of the 1988 Amendments to the Fair Housing Act, which are known as Title VIII. 42 U.S.C. §§3601-20, 3631 (2000). Title VIII, discussed below, is now the preferable strategy for plaintiffs due to relaxed standing requirements, a more liberal statute of limitations period, prima facie proof based on impact, the availability of remedies that include unlimited damages, and a developed jurisprudence supportive of the claims of many challengers.

Section 1982 has been less used to combat discriminatory land use practices because of the Court's insistence that before a cause of action can arise, a practice must result in a tangible reduction of property values or in the actual denial of housing. In *City of Memphis v. Greene*, 451 U.S. 100 (1981), the Court refused to base a violation on the city's closing of a street to prevent traffic access into a large city park, a closure that resulted in shutting off vehicle access into the park from the adjacent black neighborhood. Justice Marshall dissented, emphasizing the city's segregated past.

2. *Section 1983.* Section 1983 of the Civil Rights Act, 42 U.S.C. §1983 (2000), is the primary vehicle for bringing equal protection, due process, takings, and any other constitutional or federal statutory claims against states and local

governments in land use controversies. This provision requires state action (*West v. Atkins*, 487 U.S. 42 (1988)), and certain public officials enjoy absolute immunity. *Bogan v. Scott-Harris*, 523 U.S. 44 (1998) (local legislators, including a mayor exercising legislative powers such as recommending enactment and approving a budget ordinance, are immune); *Tenny v. Brandhove*, 341 U.S. 367 (1951) (state legislators). State and local administrative officers enjoy qualified immunity. *Scheuer v. Rhodes*, 416 U.S. 232 (1974). Qualified immunity requires that the plaintiff must prove bad faith, typically by demonstrating the violation of a clearly established legal right. *Davis v. Scherer*, 468 U.S. 183 (1984).

3. *Section 1985.* Section 1985 of the Civil Rights Act, 42 U.S.C. §1985 (2000), covers private conspiracies involving race discrimination under the Thirteenth Amendment. It also reaches conspiracies based on other classifications where state action is present.

4. *Title VI.* Title VI of the 1964 Civil Rights Act, 42 U.S.C. §2000d (2000), provides a remedy for discrimination on the basis of race, national origin, or religion in programs receiving federal financial assistance, and programs and projects administered or funded by a federal agency. Pursuant to the Civil Rights Restoration Act of 1987, Pub. L. No. 100-259, §6, 102 Stat. 28, 31 (1988), the entire institution receiving federal assistance is subject to Title VI and other civil rights standards. Title VI requires that a plaintiff prove intent in order to recover damages, but the plaintiff must only prove discriminatory impact in order to obtain injunctive relief. *Guardians Ass'n v. Civil Service Comm'n*, 463 U.S. 582 (1983).

5. *Title VIII.* Lending discrimination in housing is prohibited by Title VIII, 42 U.S.C. §3605 (2000), and most forms of lending bias are prohibited by the Equal Credit Opportunity Act. 15 U.S.C. §1691 (2000). The Federal Home Mortgage Disclosure Act, 12 U.S.C. §§2801-2809 (2000), requires large lenders to disclose the race of applicants and borrowers as well as loan performance by census tract or neighborhood. This disclosure allows analysis of minority lender participation. Under the Federal Community Reinvestment Act, federal lending regulators are to consider a lender's record in meeting the entire community's lending needs when reviewing requested approvals for mergers and branch operations' expansion. 12 U.S.C. §§2901-2905 (2000).

In addition to a more liberal statute of limitations and reduced standing requirements under Title VIII, a plaintiff's prima facie case may be based on the impact of a community's land use practices rather than on constitutional intent. Those who can allege how they have been aggrieved by the practice or decision challenged may also institute private litigation. In the event that the Department of Justice institutes litigation, potential parties may intervene or have their lawsuit consolidated. On Title VIII, generally, see James A. Kushner, Fair Housing: Discrimination in Real Estate, Community Development and Revitalization (2d ed. 1995 & Supp. 2000); Robert G. Schwenn, Housing and Discrimination (2000).

The following case demonstrates the efficacy of Title VIII in litigating discriminatory or segregative land use practices and controls.

■ HUNTINGTON BRANCH, NATIONAL ASSOCIATION FOR THE ADVANCEMENT OF COLORED PEOPLE v. TOWN OF HUNTINGTON

844 F.2d 926 (2d Cir.), aff'd per curiam, 488 U.S. 15 (1988)

Before KAUFMAN, OAKES, and NEWMAN, Circuit Judges.

IRVING R. KAUFMAN, Circuit Judge:

. . . Title VIII of the Civil Rights Act of 1968, 42 U.S.C. §§3601-3631 (1982 & Supp. III 1985) ("Fair Housing Act"), was enacted "to provide, within constitutional limitations, for fair housing throughout the United States." 42 U.S.C. §3601. Today, we are called upon to decide whether an overwhelmingly white suburb's zoning regulation, which restricts private multi-family housing projects to a largely minority "urban renewal area," and the Town Board's refusal to amend that ordinance to allow construction of subsidized housing in a white neighborhood violates the Fair Housing Act.

. . . Appellants allege that the Town violated Title VIII by restricting private construction of multi-family housing to a narrow urban renewal area and by refusing to rezone the parcel outside this area where appellants wished to build multi-family housing. Specifically, appellants sought to construct an integrated, multi-family subsidized apartment complex in Greenlawn/East Northport, a virtually all-white neighborhood. The Town's zoning ordinance, however, prohibited private construction of multi-family housing outside a small urban renewal zone in the Huntington Station neighborhood, which is 52% minority. Thus, appellants petitioned the Town to revise its code to accommodate the project. When the Town refused, appellants brought this class-action to compel the change under Title VIII. . . .

Huntington is a town of approximately 200,000 people located in the northwest corner of Suffolk County, New York. In 1980, 95% of its residents were white. Blacks comprised only 3.35% of the Town's population and were concentrated in areas known as Huntington Station and South Greenlawn. Specifically, 43% of the total black population lived in four census tracts in Huntington Station and 27% in two census tracts in the South Greenlawn area. Outside these two neighborhoods, the Town's population was overwhelmingly white. Of the 48 census tracts in the Town in 1980, 30 contained black populations of less than 1%.

The district court found that the Town has a shortage of affordable rental housing for low and moderate-income households. The Town's Housing Assistance Plan (HAP), which is adopted by the Town Board and filed with HUD as part of Huntington's application for federal community development funds, reveals that the impact of this shortage is three times greater on blacks than on the overall population. Under the 1982-1985 HAP, for example, 7% of all Huntington families required subsidized housing, while 24% of black families needed such housing.

In addition, a disproportionately large percentage of families in existing subsidized projects are minority. . . .

Under the Town's zoning ordinance, multi-family housing is permitted only in an "R-3M Apartment District." The relevant portion of section 198-20(A) provides:

> Use regulations. In the R-3M Apartment District, a building or premises shall be used only for the following purposes:
>
> (1) Any use permitted in the R-80, R-15 and R-5 Residence Districts.
>
> (2) Multiple-family dwellings which constitute an approved public housing project to be owned, maintained and operated by the Housing Authority of the Town of Huntington.
>
> (3) Multiple-family dwellings where such dwellings constitute an element in a formally approved land use or a use plan for all or part of an urban renewal area which has been designated as such under the provisions of Article 15 of the General Municipal Law.

On its face, then, this provision limits private construction of multi-family housing to the Town's urban renewal area, where 52% of the residents are minority. It does permit the Huntington Housing Authority (HHA) to build multi-family housing townwide. But HHA's only project, Gateway Gardens, is in the urban renewal zone. The private housing projects are also in or nearby the urban renewal area. . . .

Only one vacant parcel of land in Huntington currently is zoned R-3M and thus would be eligible for the appellants' proposed development: the MIA site, which is at the northeast corner of Broadway and New York Avenue, is partially zoned C-6 and partially zoned R-3M. The Town in 1980 requested pre-approval for 150 units of Section 8 housing on this site.

In response to the great need for subsidized housing in the Town, HHI [Appellant Housing Help, Inc.] decided to sponsor an integrated housing project for low-income families. HHI determined that the project could foster racial integration only if it were located in a white neighborhood outside the Huntington Station and South Greenlawn areas. This decision eliminated consideration of the MIA site, the only vacant R-3M property located in the urban renewal area.

In its effort to create racially integrated, low-cost housing, HHI actively sought the assistance of Town officials. . . . Throughout 1979, [Michael] Miness [Director of Huntington's Community Development agency] assured HHI representatives that existing zoning should not impede their efforts because the Town Board would amend the zoning ordinance if it supported the organization's project.

After a lengthy search, HHI determined that a 14.8 acre parcel located at the corner of Elwood and Pulaski Roads in the Town was well suited for a 162-unit housing project. This flat, largely cleared and well-drained property was near public transportation, shopping and other services, and immediately adjacent to schools.

Ninety-eight percent of the population within a one-mile radius of the site is white. HHI set a goal of 25% minority occupants. The district court found that "a significant percentage of the tenants [at Matinecock Court] would have belonged to minority groups." *Huntington*, 668 F. Supp. at 785. HHI officials determined that the property was economically feasible and offered a lengthy option period. . . .

[W]e start by pointing out that this case requires what has been called "disparate impact" or "disparate effects" analysis, not "disparate treatment" analysis. A disparate impact analysis examines a facially-neutral policy or practice, such as a hiring test or zoning law, for its differential impact or effect on a particular group.

Disparate treatment analysis, on the other hand, involves differential treatment of similarly situated persons or groups. The line is not always a bright one, but does adequately delineate two very different kinds of discrimination claims. . . .

Under disparate impact analysis, as other circuits have recognized, a prima facie case is established by showing that the challenged practice of the defendant "actually or predictably results in racial discrimination; in other words that it has a discriminatory effect." . . . The plaintiff need not show that the decision complained of was made with discriminatory intent. Refusal to require intent in disparate impact cases is entirely consistent with our prior decisions. . . .

The Act's stated purpose to end discrimination requires a discriminatory effect standard; an intent requirement would strip the statute of all impact on de facto segregation. Congress appears not to have resolved this precise question. Nonetheless, the legislative history provides some indication that an intent standard was not contemplated. . . .

Practical concerns also militate against inclusion of intent in any disparate impact analysis. First, as this court noted "clever men may easily conceal their motivations." This is especially persuasive in disparate impact cases where a facially neutral rule is being challenged. Often, such rules bear no relation to discrimination upon passage, but develop into powerful discriminatory mechanisms when applied. Second, inclusion of intent undermines the trial judge's inquiry into the *impact* of an action. . . . Accordingly, we will not require proof of discriminatory intent to establish a prima facie disparate impact case under Title VIII. . . .

Once a prima facie case of adverse impact is presented, as occurred here, the inquiry turns to the standard to be applied in determining whether the defendant can nonetheless avoid liability under Title VIII. . . . [I]n the end there must be a weighing of the adverse impact against the defendant's justification. As phrased by the Third Circuit, the defendant must prove that its actions furthered, in theory and in practice, a legitimate, bona fide governmental interest and that no alternative would serve that interest with less discriminatory effect. We agree with that formulation. . . . The Seventh Circuit adds two other factors that can affect the ultimate determination on the merits. One factor is whether there is any evidence of discriminatory intent on the part of the defendant. Though we have ruled that such intent is not a requirement of the plaintiff's prima facie case, there can be little doubt that if evidence of such intent is presented, that evidence would weigh heavily on the plaintiff's side of the ultimate balance. The other factor is whether the plaintiff is suing to compel a governmental defendant to build housing or only to require a governmental defendant to eliminate some obstacle to housing that the plaintiff itself will build. In the latter circumstance, a defendant would normally have to establish a somewhat more substantial justification for its adverse action than would be required if the defendant were defending its decision not to build. . . .

. . . A town's preference to maintain a particular zoning category for particular sections of the community is normally based on a variety of circumstances. The complexity of the considerations, however, does not relieve a court of the obligation to assess whatever justifications the town advances and weigh them carefully against the degree of adverse effect the plaintiff has shown. Though a town's interests in zoning requirements are substantial, they cannot, consistently with Title VIII, automatically outweigh significant disparate effects. . . .

The discriminatory effect of a rule arises in two contexts: adverse impact on a particular minority group and harm to the community generally by the perpetuation of segregation. In analyzing Huntington's restrictive zoning, however, the lower court concentrated on the harm to blacks as a group, and failed to consider the segregative effect of maintaining a zoning ordinance that restricts private multi-family housing to an area with a high minority concentration. Yet, recognizing this second form of effect advances the principal purpose of Title VIII to promote, "open integrated residential housing patterns."

Seventy percent of Huntington's black population reside in Huntington Station and South Greenlawn. Matinecock Court, with its goal of 25% minorities, would begin desegregating a neighborhood which is currently 98% white. Indeed, the district court found that a "significant percentage of the tenants" at Matinecock Court would belong to minority groups. The court, however, failed to take the logical next step and find that the refusal to permit projects outside the urban renewal area with its high concentration of minorities reinforced racial segregation in housing. This was erroneous. Similarly, the district court found that the Town has a shortage of rental housing affordable for low and moderate-income households, that a "disproportionately" large percentage of the households using subsidized rental units are minority citizens, and that a disproportionately large number of minorities are on the waiting lists for subsidized housing and existing Section 8 certificates. But it failed to recognize that Huntington's zoning ordinance, which restricts private construction of multi-family housing to the largely minority urban renewal area, impedes integration by restricting low-income housing needed by minorities to an area already 52% minority. We thus find that Huntington's refusal to amend the restrictive zoning ordinance to permit privately-built multi-family housing outside the urban renewal area significantly perpetuated segregation in the Town.

On the question of harm to blacks as a group, the district court emphasized that 22,160 whites and 3671 minorities had incomes below 200% of the poverty line, a cutoff close to the Huntington Housing Authority's qualification standards. *Huntington*, 668 F. Supp. at 786. Thus, the district court focussed on the greater absolute number of poor whites compared with indigent minorities in Huntington. The district court, however, did not analyze the disproportionate burden on minorities as required by *Griggs v. Duke Power Co.*, 401 U.S. 424 (1971). By relying on absolute numbers rather than on proportional statistics, the district court significantly underestimated the disproportionate impact of the Town's policy. . . .

The parties have stipulated that 28% of minorities in Huntington and 11% of whites have incomes below 200% of the poverty line. What they dispute is the meaning of these statistics. Judge Glasser found that, as the Town contends, there is no showing of discriminatory effect because a majority of the victims are white. We disagree. . . . [T]he plaintiffs presented even stronger evidence reflecting the disparate impact of preventing the project from proceeding. Under the Huntington HAP for 1982-85, 7% of all Huntington families needed subsidized housing, while 24% of the black families needed such housing. In addition, minorities constitute a far greater percentage of those currently occupying subsidized rental projects compared to their percentage in the Town's population. Similarly, a disproportionately high percentage (60%) of families holding Section 8 certificates from the Housing Authority to supplement their rents are minorities, and an equally disproportionate percentage (61%) of those on the waiting list for such certificates are minorities. Therefore, we conclude that the failure to rezone the Matinecock Court site had a substantial adverse impact on minorities.

In sum, we find that the disproportionate harm to blacks and the segregative impact on the entire community resulting from the refusal to rezone create a strong prima facie showing of discriminatory effect. . .

Once a plaintiff has made a prima facie showing of discriminatory effect, a defendant must present bona fide and legitimate justifications for its action with no less discriminatory alternatives available. . . .

The [test] has two components: (1) whether the reasons are bona fide and legitimate; and (2) whether any less discriminatory alternative can serve those ends. . . .

. . . The Town asserts that limiting multi-family development to the urban renewal area will encourage restoration of the neighborhood because, otherwise, developers will choose to build in the outlying areas and will bypass the zone. The Town's goal, however, can be achieved by less discriminatory means, by encouraging development in the urban renewal area with tax incentives or abatements. The Town may assert that this is less effective, but it may actually be more so. Developers are not wed to building in Huntington; they are filling a perceived economic void. . . . Huntington incorrectly assumes that developers limit their area of interest by political subdivision. In fact, the decision where to build is much more complex. Hence, if the Town wishes to encourage growth in the urban renewal area, it should do so directly through incentives which would have a less discriminatory impact on the Town.

We turn next to the Town's reasons rejecting the Elwood-Pulaski site. The 1980 letter written by Town Supervisor Butterfield detailed seven justifications for the Town's refusal to rezone: (1) inconsistency with the Town's Housing Assistance Plan; (2) inconsistency with zoning; (3) traffic considerations; (4) parking and fire protection problems; (5) proximity to the railroad and Long Island Lighting Company substation; (6) inadequate recreation and play areas; and (7) undersized and unrealistic units. As the judge below noted, the first two beg the question because appellants are challenging the Town's zoning ordinance. More significantly, as we have already indicated, the Town simply relied on the existence of the Housing Assistance Plan and the zoning ordinance and failed to present any substantial evidence indicating why precluding plaintiff from building a multi-family housing project outside the urban renewal area would impair significant interests sought to be advanced by the HAP and the ordinance. The fourth, sixth and seventh problems are "plan-specific" issues which could presumably have been solved with reasonable design modifications at the time appellants applied for rezoning of the parcel. The fifth concern also is largely plan-specific because proper landscaping could shield the project from the railroad and substation.

Thus, only the traffic issue and health hazard from the substation are site-specific. At trial, however, none of Huntington's officials supported these objections. Butterfield, for example, was primarily concerned that the Matinecock Court project would "torpedo" the Town's plan to develop the site at Broadway and New York Avenue in the urban renewal area in Huntington Station. Moreover, Huntington's only expert, planner David Portman, set forth entirely different problems than were contained in Butterfield's letters. Specifically, he noted sewage concerns, lack of conformity with the low density of the surrounding neighborhood, and inaccessibility of the site to public transportation. . . . Accordingly, we find the reasons asserted are entirely insubstantial. . . .

In balancing the showing of discriminatory effect against the import of the Town's justifications, we note our agreement with the Seventh Circuit that the balance should be more readily struck in favor of the plaintiff when it is seeking only to enjoin a municipal defendant from interfering with its own plans rather than attempting to compel the defendant itself to build housing. . . . Bearing in mind that the plaintiffs in this case seek only the freedom to build their own project, we conclude that the strong showing of discriminatory effect resulting from the Town's adherence to its R-3M zoning category and its refusal to rezone the Matinecock Court site far outweigh the Town's weak justifications. . . .

[W]e would ordinarily remand this case to the district court to afford the appellees an opportunity to identify an alternative site, outside the urban renewal area, that would be appropriate for HHI's project and eligible for the same financial arrangements and assistance available at the Matinecock Court site. If the Town identified such a site, it would then have the burden of persuading the district court that there were substantial reasons for using its preferred site and that those reasons did not impose undue hardships on the appellants. If the district court was not persuaded on balance of the benefits of an alternative site, it would then enter an appropriate judgment to enable HHI to proceed with its project at the Matinecock Court site.

This case, however, is not ordinary. First, we recognize the protracted nature of this litigation, which has spanned over seven years. Further delay might well prove fatal to this private developer's plans. Second, . . . the Town has demonstrated little good faith in assisting the development of low-income housing. . . .

Third, the other 63 parcels outside the urban renewal area are not presently zoned for multi-family housing and, indeed, the zoning ordinance presently forbids rezoning of these properties. . . .

Accordingly, we direct the district court to include in its judgment provision ordering the Town to rezone the 14.8 acre Matinecock Court site located at the corner of Elwood and Pulaski Roads in Huntington Township to R-3M status. The judgment should also order the Town to strike from its R-3M zoning ordinance that portion which limits private multi-family housing projects to the urban renewal area.

Notes and Comments

1. *The Appeal*. The Supreme Court affirmed *Huntington* in a per curiam ruling in which the Court refused to reach the question of the appropriate prima facie case under Title VIII. The Court believed that both parties agreed that an impact test was applicable and was satisfied that the record contained sufficient evidence to meet that standard. *Town of Huntington v. Huntington Branch NAACP*, 488 U.S. 15 (1988).

2. *Equal Protection Distinguished*. Would *Arlington Heights* be decided differently under Title VIII? In *Arlington II*, noted in the *Huntington* opinion, the Seventh Circuit found sufficient evidence to prove a violation, and the village was unable to justify its buffer policy prohibiting multi-family housing within a single-family

neighborhood. After remand to the district court, the parties entered into a settlement calling for a modified project to be built on an alternate site, one that was outside of the Village of Arlington Heights but which the village would annex. *Metropolitan Housing Development Corp. v. Village of Arlington Heights*, 469 F. Supp. 836 (N.D. Ill. 1979), *aff'd*, 616 F.2d 1006 (7th Cir. 1980) (consent decree approved).

3. *The Numbers Game*. In *Summerchase Ltd. Partnership I v. City of Gonzales*, 970 F. Supp. 522 (M.D. La. 1997), the trial court granted partial summary judgment to the defendant in a challenge to the denial of a building permit for low-income apartments based upon the imposition of a moratorium on permits. The district court judge found it rational to allow a replanning process and rejected a Title VIII claim. The court did not follow *Huntington*, refusing to use statistical "proportional" numbers to identify discriminatory impact. Instead, the judge used "absolute" numbers: 2,383 or 77.9 percent of eligible families in the Louisiana parish were white, and 613 or 20 percent were black, generating no adverse impact on minorities. The court rejected the plaintiff's claim that was based on the proportional statistical impact. Under those numbers, only 17.7 percent of whites would be eligible for the housing, while 29.7 percent of blacks would be eligible. In addition, of those earning less than the maximum allowed for admission, 22.7 percent were white while 43.6 percent were black. The court explicitly recognized the disparate impact theory but rejected the claim, finding no adverse impact on families with children.

4. *Inclusionary Zoning and Discrimination*. As discussed in Chapter 12, New Jersey imposes an obligation on cities to accept their "fair share" of regional housing need. The state, however, also has adopted legislation that allows communities to avoid this obligation by paying another community to build up to half of the community's obligation under a regional contribution agreement. Do such regional contribution agreements, whereby New Jersey communities may pay another community to build a portion of its fair share obligation, violate Title VIII? What if a predominantly white suburb pays Newark to build additional affordable housing? *See* Patrick Field, et al., Trading the Poor: Intermunicipal Housing Negotiation in New Jersey, 2 Harv. Negot. L. Rev. 1 (1997) (challenging the practice of purchasing compliance from a poorer community through regional cooperation agreements).

New Jersey authorizes communities to set aside a portion of *Mount Laurel* affordable housing for existing town residents. Do residency preferences in a white suburb near a predominantly minority city violate the federal Fair Housing Act? In *In re Township of Warren*, 622 A.2d 1257 (N.J. 1993), the New Jersey Supreme Court overturned a regulation allowing 50 percent of a community's fair share affordable housing allocation to be set aside for households whose members reside or work in the municipality.

The court found that the set-aside conflicts with the allocation formula, which does not count existing lower income residents. The court ruled that a modified allocation model, reflecting such need with set-asides equivalent to the increased allocation, may be valid. But the court expressed concern for the possible conflict with Title VIII due to the effect of discrimination.

Compare United States v. Housing Authority of the City of Chickasaw, 504 F. Supp. 716 (S.D. Ala. 1980) (city residency requirement for admission to public housing violated Title VIII where the City of Chickasaw was 98.8 percent white and was a suburb of Mobile, a city with a substantial minority population).

5. *Religious Exemption*. The Minnesota Supreme Court's decision in *State v. French*, 460 N.W.2d 2 (Minn. 1990), raises a new legal issue: the possibility of exemptions from civil rights laws based on religious beliefs. The case arose when a landlord refused to rent to an unmarried couple. The homeseekers went to the state fair housing agency and filed a complaint on the grounds of bias based on marital status, a bias that is prohibited in Minnesota.

The state supreme court ruled that the landlord cannot be forced to act contrary to religious views, which in this case condemned cohabitation. The court acknowledged an exemption from the fair housing law on behalf of the objecting landlord due to the fact that the state's law makes fornication a criminal act. *See also Thomas v. Anchorage Equal Rights Comm'n*, 165 F.3d 692 (9th Cir. 1999) (violates free exercise clause of First Amendment), *opinion vacated & cause dismissed en banc for ripeness*, 220 F.3d 1134 (9th Cir. 2000) (eschewing pre-enforcement challenges), *cert. denied*, 531 U.S. 1143 (2001). For contrary rulings, *see Swanner v. Anchorage Equal Rights Comm'n*, 874 P.2d 274 (Alaska 1994), *cert. denied*, 513 U.S. 979 (1994); *Smith v. Fair Employment & Housing Comm'n*, 913 P.2d 909 (Cal. 1996), *cert. denied*, 521 U.S. 1129 (1997). Could a community, on the basis of its religiosity, enact a *Belle Terre* ordinance prohibiting cohabitation by other than those related by blood or marriage?

6. *Race and Development Controls*. A Cornell University study of the literature on the correlation of race and development controls found that growth management techniques such as the adequacy of facilities, urban growth boundaries, and moratoria had little effect on racial composition. However, low-density, single-family zoning generated few minority group members and heightened racial segregation. Rolf Pendall, Local Land Use Regulation and the Chain of Exclusion, 66 J. Am. Plan. Ass'n 12 (2000) (building permit caps, however, were associated with lowered proportions of Hispanic residents; and metropolitan areas with residential densities limited to fewer than eight dwelling units per acre experience reduced rental housing, a lack of residential racial integration, and higher levels of racial segregation, suggesting potential exposure to Title VIII liability).

Is suburban exclusionary zoning subject to a Title VIII segregative impact challenge? For a ruling that Title VIII reaches the segregative impacts of exclusionary zoning, *see Dews v. Town of Sunnyvale*, 109 F. Supp. 2d 526 (N.D. Tex. 2000). The court enjoined zoning and subdivision enforcement in a town with one-acre minimum lot sizes and no multi-family housing. The town's refusal to rezone had the effect of excluding affordable housing and maintaining segregation under Title VIII, and the intent needed to prove an equal protection violation was shown by facts allowing a reasonable inference that race was a significant factor in the refusal. *See* Alice M. Burr, The Problem of Sunnyvale, Texas, and Exclusionary Zoning Practices, 11 J. Affordable Hous. & Community Dev. L. 203 (2002) (arguing that Title VIII does not reach segregative impacts of exclusionary zoning).

The federal Fair Housing Act prohibits the panoply of discriminatory practices found in traditional fair housing cases. However, by extending the protections of Title VIII to the disabled, the Act established an affirmative obligation on governments and private housing providers to make reasonable accommodations in rules, policies, and practices necessary to afford the disabled equal opportunity in housing. The following case explores the meaning of reasonable accommodation.

■ ADVOCACY CENTER FOR PERSONS WITH DISABILITIES, INC. v. WOODLANDS ESTATES ASSOCIATION INC.

192 F. Supp. 2d 1344 (M.D. Fla. 2002)

BACKGROUND

Plaintiff, Advocacy Center for Persons with Disabilities, Incorporated (Plaintiff Advocacy Center), is Florida's Protection and Advocacy system, which has standing to sue on its own behalf and on behalf of it[s] constituents. *See* 42 U.S.C. §15043(a)(2)(A)(i) (authorizing an Advocacy and Protection system to pursue legal, administrative, and other appropriate remedies or approaches on behalf of the developmentally disabled). The individual Plaintiffs are developmentally disabled and reside in a group home which is owned by the Upper Pinellas Association for Retarded Citizens (UPARC), located at 110 Arbor Lane, Oldsmar, Pinellas County, Florida. Defendant Woodlands Estates Association, Incorporated (Defendant) is a homeowners' association for East Lake Woodlands Unit One, where the Plaintiffs' group home is located. The property on which the home is located is governed by the Declarations of Covenant and Restrictions for East Lake Woodlands Unit One (the Declarations).

On December 18, 2000, Defendant sent a letter to UPARC, requesting that it take no action in moving Plaintiffs into the home. According to the letter, Defendant claimed that UPARC's proposed use of the home was in violation of Section 2.01, and may potentially violate Section 2.25, of the Declarations. Specifically, Section 2.01 states that:

> The Lots and Buildings shall be used for residential purposes only. . . . No buildings at any time situate[d] on any Lot or Building Plot shall be used for any business, commercial, amusement, hospital, sanitarium, school, clubhouse, religious, charitable, philanthropic, or manufacturing purposes, or as a professional office. . . .

Section 2.25 provides that "no illegal, noxious, or offensive activity, nor shall anything be permitted or done thereon which is or may become a nuisance or a source of embarrassment, discomfort or annoyance to the neighborhood or Development."

On January 18, 2001, Defendant filed a complaint against UPARC in the Sixth Judicial Circuit Court in Pinellas County, Florida to enforce the Declarations. Plaintiffs then filed a complaint with this Court, asking for declaratory and injunctive relief on the grounds that Defendant violated the Fair Housing Act, Title 42, United States Code, Section 3601, *et seq.* . . .

DISCUSSION

The Fair Housing Act, Title 42, United States Code, Section 3601, *et seq.*, enacted as Title VIII of the Civil Rights Act of 1968, was originally enacted to prohibit discrimination in housing practices on the basis of race, color, religion, or national origin. . . . In 1988, Congress extended coverage to disabled persons. . . . In extending the FHAA to disabled persons, Congress intended to prohibit practices that "restrict the choices" of disabled persons to live where they wish or that "discourage or obstruct [those] choices in a community neighborhood or development." . . .

The FHAA defines "handicap" as "a physical or mental impairment which substantially limits one or more of such person's major life activities." Plaintiffs are developmentally-disabled individuals, and this impairment substantially limits some of their major life activities. . . . First, the Plaintiffs receive assistance in daily living from UPARC, an organization that provides services and supports for developmentally-disabled persons. (Buckley Dep., p. 7). Second, Thomas Buckley, UPARC's executive director, stated, in his deposition, that Plaintiffs are "mentally retarded" and have "substantial limitations in functioning." . . .

FHAA'S SECTION 3604

Section 3604(f)(3) of the FHAA provides, in part, that it shall be unlawful:

> (1) To discriminate in the sale or rental, or to otherwise make unavailable or deny, a dwelling to any buyer or renter because of a handicap of . . .
>
> (B) a person residing in or intending to reside in that dwelling after it is sold . . . or made available. . . .
>
> (2) To discriminate against any person in the terms, conditions, or privileges of sale or rental of a dwelling . . . because of a handicap of . . .
>
> (B) a person residing in or intending to reside in that dwelling after it is sold . . . or made available. . . .
>
> (3) For purposes of this subsection, discrimination includes . . .
>
> (B) a refusal to make reasonable accommodations in rules, policies, [or] practices . . . when such accommodations may be necessary to afford such person equal opportunity to use and enjoy a dwelling.

42 U.S.C. §3604(f). Plaintiffs who allege a violation of Section 3604(f) may proceed under any and all of three theories: disparate treatment, disparate impact, and failure to make reasonable accommodations. Plaintiffs have alleged their claim under the theory that Defendant failed to make a reasonable accommodation for Plaintiffs in it[s] attempt to enforce the restrictions under Section 2.01 of the Declarations.

REASONABLE ACCOMMODATION

The FHAA requires accommodations for disabled persons, if the accommodations are reasonable and necessary, to afford disabled persons equal opportunity to use and enjoy housing. . . . An entity must reasonably accommodate a qualified individual with a disability by making changes in rules, policies, practices, or services, when necessary. . . .

The determination of whether an accommodation is reasonable is highly fact-specific and determined on a case-by-case basis. . . . For example, an accommodation is reasonable if it does not impose "undue financial and administrative burdens" or "changes, adjustments, or modifications to existing programs that would be substantial, or that would constitute fundamental alterations in the nature of the program." . . .

In determining whether a requested accommodation is necessary, "[t]he overall focus should be on 'whether waiver of the rule would be so at odds with the purposes behind the rule that it would be a fundamental and unreasonable change.'" . . . Courts generally balance the burdens imposed on the defendant by the contemplated accommodation against the benefits to the plaintiff. . . .

Although the Eleventh Circuit has not addressed what constitutes a "reasonable accommodation" under the FHAA, several federal courts have. In *Trovato v. City of Manchester, New Hampshire,* the United States District Court for the District of New Hampshire found that the defendant city violated the FHAA when it failed to allow a zoning variance for plaintiffs who suffered from muscular dystrophy. 992 F. Supp. 493 (D.N.H. 1997). The plaintiffs requested the city to allow them to build accessible parking in the front of the home because of the difficulty that they had walking. *Id.* at 497. The court held that the reasonable accommodation requirement of the FHAA clearly applied to zoning ordinances; thus, the city's failure to reasonably accommodate plaintiffs violated the FHAA. *Id.; see U.S. v. Village of Marshall, Wisconsin,* 787 F. Supp. 872 (W.D. Wis. 1991) (holding that a Wisconsin statute that established spacing restrictions for proposed community-based residential facilities constituted "rules, policies, practices, or services" under FHAA; thus, the defendant's failure to grant an exception to the statute constituted a failure to make a "reasonable accommodation" under the FHAA).

Conversely, the Fourth Circuit, in *Bryant Woods Inn, Incorporated v. Howard County* Maryland, found that the defendant county did not violate the FHAA's requirement to provide reasonable accommodations when it failed to allow a zoning variance for the expansion of a group home. 124 F.3d 597 (4th Cir.1997). The court reasoned that the expansion would defeat the purpose of the zoning ordinance, resulting in traffic congestion and parking problems; therefore, the accommodation was not reasonable in light of the large burden on the county and the small benefit to the plaintiffs. *Id.* at 604.

Also, in *Groner v. Golden Gate Apartments,* the Sixth Circuit found that the defendant landlord did not violate the FHAA when it failed to renew the lease of a schizophrenic plaintiff. 250 F.3d 1039 (6th Cir. 2001). Because the defendant frequently received complaints from other tenants about the plaintiff's behavior, the court found that renewing his lease was not a reasonable accommodation under the FHAA. *Id.* at 1045. However, the Sixth Circuit did find a violation of the reasonable accommodation requirement when the defendant city failed to amend a zoning ordinance to allow a twelve-person elderly adult foster home to operate in a single-family residence district. *Smith & Lee Associates, Inc. v. City of Taylor, Michigan,* 102 F.3d 781 (6th Cir.1996). . . .

In the instant case, the Court finds that Defendant did not reasonably accommodate Plaintiffs, in violation of the FHAA, when it failed to waive the enforcement of its deed restrictions contained in the Declarations. . . . [T]here is no evidence on the record to show that failing to enforce Section 2.01 of the Declarations would impose an undue financial burden on the Defendant or undermine the basic purpose of the restriction, namely to maintain the residential nature of the neighborhood. . . .

Denied in part and granted in part.

Notes and Comments

1. *Frivolous Enforcement?* Was the Association's filing of a lawsuit in state court, together with pretrial attempts to enforce restrictive covenants or equitable servitudes, a frivolous venture? Can you distinguish the public enforcement of a single-family zoning ordinance from the private enforcement of covenants?

2. *Reasonable Accommodation*. What is a reasonable accommodation? *See Howard v. City of Beavercreek*, 276 F.3d 802 (6th Cir. 2002) (lack of necessity for six-foot-high privacy fence, as denial of a variance would not deny the right to live in housing of choice); *Sanghvi v. City of Claremont*, 328 F.3d 532 (9th Cir. 2003) (refusal to provide sewer connection for an Alzheimer's facility unless the property was annexed to the city did not deny reasonable accommodation). *Compare Regional Econ. Community Action Program, Inc. v. City of Middletown*, 294 F.3d 35 (2d Cir. 2002), *cert. denied*, 123 S. Ct. 74 (2002) (refusal to apply reasonable accommodation obligation to denial of special use permit for two halfway houses for recovering alcoholics); *Lapid-Laurel, L.L.C. v. Zoning Bd. of Adjustment of the Township of Scotch Plains*, 284 F.3d 442 (3d Cir. 2002) (applicant bears the burden to show that a requested accommodation is necessary, with the burden then shifting to defendant to show that the accommodation was unreasonable, where a large assisted-care facility would generate problems of traffic, emergency vehicle access, and interference with wetlands); *Dadian v. Village of Wilmette*, 269 F.3d 831 (7th Cir. 2001) (sustaining rejection of driveway accommodation and concluding it posed a safety threat, as it called for the disabled driver to back out of the requested front garage); *Forest City Daly Hous., Inc. v. Town of N. Hempstead*, 175 F.3d 144 (2d Cir. 1999) (Title VIII does not require the town to issue a permit for 72-unit assisted living facility in a business area of the city in which comparable traditional residences were not permitted); and *Eppler v. City of Cleveland,* 753 N.E.2d 986 (Ohio Ct. App. 2001) (excluding residential uses from an industrial zone and consistently maintaining a buffer was a legitimate nondiscriminatory justification for denying a variance for a group home). *See generally* Robert L. Schonfeld, "Reasonable Accommodation" Under the Federal Fair Housing Act, 25 Fordham Urb. L.J. 413 (1998).

3. *Defining Family.* The City of Edmonds zoning ordinance defined "family" in its single-family districts as a group of persons, without regard to number, related by genetics, adoption, or marriage, or a group of five or fewer unrelated persons. The family definition was a good deal more permissive than that sustained in *Belle Terre*. Oxford House, which operated a group home for ten to twelve recovering alcoholics and drug addicts, was criminally prosecuted for violating the zoning ordinance.

When Oxford House alleged protection under Title VIII, the city filed an action for declaratory relief in federal district court. The parties had stipulated that recovering substance abusers were handicapped within the meaning of Title VIII. The litigation focused on §3607(b)(1), which provides an exemption from Title VIII for reasonable restrictions regarding the maximum number of occupants permitted to occupy a dwelling.

In *City of Edmonds v. Oxford House, Inc.*, 514 U.S. 725 (1995), the United States Supreme Court ruled that a traditional housing code provision linking occupancy or the number of occupants to a per person square footage minimum would qualify for the occupancy exemption. The family definition, which would have authorized the exclusion of group homes for more than five residents from single-family districts, was not an occupancy restriction. Title VIII thus preempts such family occupancy definitions as contained in the Edmonds or Belle Terre ordinances as applied to housing for the disabled.

The Court did not reach a larger claim of the city that this interpretation overturns Euclidean zoning and destroys the effectiveness and purpose of single-family zoning. The dissent argued that despite its limited reach, the family definition did constitute a limit on occupancy.

Is *Edmonds* consistent with *Belle Terre*? May Belle Terre enforce its family definition so as to exclude an *Edmonds*-type of group home (ten to twelve adult recovering alcoholics or addicts)? Will the *Edmonds* ordinance survive substantive Title VIII review?

4. *Group Home Dispersal*. St. Paul, Minnesota, imposed a policy of dispersal of group homes to avoid concentrations on particular streets or neighborhoods. Does the denial of a permit under that policy violate Title VIII? In *Familystyle of St. Paul, Inc v. City of St. Paul*, 923 F.2d 91 (8th Cir. 1991), the Eighth Circuit ruled that the state policy of deinstitutionalization and placement of the mentally ill in the least restrictive environment possible justified a policy of integration.

5. *Preemption*. Can Title VIII preempt local zoning? Is that what happened in *Huntington*? Does Title VIII establish an affirmative duty on communities to amend zoning to reasonably accommodate handicapped persons?

States such as Michigan have passed legislation to permit group homes for six or fewer residents, who can be defined as a single family. What if the economics of group home operation require ten or twelve residents? What if exceptions are made only for not-for-profit operators?

In *Smith & Lee Assocs., Inc. v. City of Taylor*, 13 F.3d 920 (6th Cir. 1993), the court balanced city interests against the need for accommodation and concluded that the city has an obligation even to spot zone where there would be no undue burden. The court remanded the case for consideration of these issues but did state that the district court has the power to order a rezoning. Following remand, the court of appeal found a failure to reasonably accommodate the disability under Title VIII. *See* 102 F.3d 781 (6th Cir. 1996).

In marked contrast to the Eighth Circuit ruling in *Familystyle*, *supra*, the Sixth Circuit in *Larkin v. Michigan Department of Social Services*, 89 F.3d 285 (6th Cir. 1996), ruled that Title VIII preempted a state law seeking to regulate and disperse group homes. The court found an express conflict between state and federal law, as the state law permitted a discriminatory housing practice. *See also Oconomowoc Residential Programs, Inc. v. City of Greenfield*, 23 F. Supp. 2d 941 (E.D. Wis. 1998) (Wisconsin statute providing for 2,500 feet spacing for community living arrangements or adult family homes, while facially valid, was preempted by Title VIII and the Americans with Disabilities Act, with a zoning exception deemed a "reasonable accommodation").

6. *Familial Bias*. The Fair Housing Amendments Act of 1988 extended Title VIII to prohibit discrimination against families with children. However, Section 3607(b)(2) exempts senior citizen housing to be occupied solely by persons over age 62 or intended to be occupied by at least one person over the age of 55. *Massaro v. Mainlands Section 1 & 2 Civic Ass'n*, 3 F.3d 1472 (11th Cir. 1993), *cert. denied*, 513 U.S. 808 (1994). Would a proposed group home for foster children or juvenile delinquents enjoy Title VIII protection? *Keys Youth Servs., Inc. v. City of Olathe*, 248 F.3d 1267 (10th Cir. 2001) (denial of a special use permit for a youth group home not within Title VIII, as a group home is not within "familial status" coverage, and the city did not refuse to make reasonable accommodation). *See also* Michael J. Davis & Karen L. Gaus, Protecting Group Homes for the Non-Handicapped: Zoning in the Post-Edmonds Era, 46 Kan. L. Rev. 777 (1998). Would zoning amendments restricting the opportunity for residential development constitute

familial bias? *Easthampton Ctr. v. Township of Easthampton*, 155 F. Supp. 2d 102 (D.N.J. 2001) (no).

Some states have authorized senior citizen zoning. *See, e.g., Taxpayers Ass'n v. Weymouth Township*, 364 A.2d 1016 (N.J. 1976), *cert. denied*, 430 U.S. 977 (1977) (sustaining zoning requiring the head of household or spouse to be 52 years of age or older). Can New Jersey enforce its statute after the amendments to Title VIII? What if the community has an adequate supply of housing for families with children? What if decent housing is in short supply?

Title VIII was amended by the Housing for Older Persons Act of 1995, Pub. L. No. 104-76, 109 Stat. 787. The law formerly contained a requirement, found in the senior citizen exemption from the provision outlawing familial bias, that housing projects for those age 55 or older must provide "significant facilities and services especially designed to meet the physical or social needs of older persons." The 1995 amendments eliminated that requirement.

To be eligible for the senior citizen exemption now, at least 80 percent of the occupied units must be occupied by at least one person age 55 or older, and the policy must be published and adhered to. In addition, §3 amends §3607(b) so that a housing provider is immune from damages for violation of the familial bias provisions if the provider (1) in good faith has stated in writing that the facility complies with the exemption requirements, and (2) has no actual knowledge that the facility is or will not be eligible.

7. *Section 224 and Occupancy Standards*. Title VIII was also affected by the 1996 appropriations legislation. Pub. L. No. 104-134, 110 Stat. 1321 (1996). Section 224 prohibits the use of funds to enforce Title VIII on the basis of familial status because of an occupancy standard where the standard conforms to a 1991 HUD memorandum on occupancy standards. That memorandum generally endorsed a two-person-per-bedroom standard.

The provision arguably might preempt more permissive local and state occupancy standards, but the provision is merely a restriction on HUD enforcement. Does a two-person-per-bedroom rule have a discriminatory impact on families with children? Could such a rule have a discriminatory impact on minorities that demographically may have larger families? Would a community's zoning or land use approval allowing only single-bedroom apartments and condominiums have a discriminatory impact on families with children?

In *United States v. Tropic Seas, Inc.*, 887 F. Supp. 1347 (D. Haw. 1995), the court reviewed the enforcement of a rule against occupancy of studio or one-bedroom apartments by more than two persons. The court held that the rule violated Title VIII. Evidence demonstrated that the rule would exclude 92 to 95 percent of families with children, but only 19 to 21 percent of families without children in the relevant area. The finding of intent was supported by an attempted management resolution to bar children under age 14, but the court ruled that the exclusion violated the law even if management held a sincere concern for child safety. The court also ruled that the familial bias prohibition was not void for vagueness.

In *Oxford House-C v. City of St. Louis*, 77 F.3d 249 (8th Cir), *cert. denied*, 519 U.S. 816 (1996), the Eighth Circuit upheld an eight-person restriction. The court found that the interests in decreasing congestion, traffic, and noise in residential neighborhoods were valid interests and sustained the restriction under an ostensible rational basis/substantive due process analysis. The court did not apply the developed Title VIII jurisprudence. *Compare Fair Housing Advocates Ass'n v. City of Richmond Heights*, 209 F.3d 626 (6th Cir. 2000) (sustaining, under Title VIII exception, occupancy standards based on minimum square footage per person as found in national building codes), *and Tsombanidis v. City of West Haven,* 180 F. Supp. 2d 262 (D. Conn. 2001) (city regulation limiting the number of unrelated people who could live in a dwelling, rather than limiting total number of permitted occupants, does not come under Title VIII's exemption for maximum occupancy rules, with the court refusing to allow the application of single-family zoning to exclude a group home for recovering alcoholics and drug addicts). *See also* Harry J. Kelly III, Dicrimination and Occupancy Limits: Finding a Middle Ground, 4 J. Affordable Hous. & Community Dev. L. 51 (1994-1995).

A Note on Title VIII, Freedom of Expression, and Political Participation

Could neighborhood opposition to housing for the handicapped violate §3617? What if the form of the opposition was picketing and chanting adjacent to a group home? What if the opposition took the protest to city hall, with members of the protest group speaking in opposition to a use permit? What if they filed a lawsuit challenging the proposed use on environmental grounds? How should the tension with the First Amendment freedoms of expression and petition be resolved? See Michael P. Seng, Hate Speech and Enforcement of the Fair Housing Laws, 29 J. Marshall L. Rev. 409 (1996); Mary C. Lee, Note, The Conflict Between "Fair Housing" and Free Speech, 4 Wm. & Mary Bill Rts. J. 1223 (1996) (valuing expression over interference with civil rights).

The federal Department of Housing and Urban Development (HUD) has issued guidelines for administrative investigation and processing of complaints implicating the First Amendment. The regulations reflect a political compromise by the Clinton Administration to avoid criticism of government action flouting freedom of speech and the right to petition. Generally, the guidelines limit HUD review of complaints concerning §3617 to cases involving force, physical harm, or the clear threat of such harm. The guidelines specifically exempt peaceful demonstrations, distribution of literature, holding meetings, communicating with the government, and participating in public hearings. The guidelines also exempt matters involving litigation, leaving the legal issues surrounding §3617 to the courts.

The guidelines outlaw subpoenas directed to obtaining membership lists, fund-raising information, or financial data of organizations that may be engaged in protected speech activities. The guidelines admittedly err on the side of First Amendment protection, and in doing so, they arguably fail to protect the victims of harassment and interference. See HUD Guidelines, Substantive and Procedural Limitations on Filing and Investigating Fair Housing Act Complaints That May Implicate the First Amendment, Fair Housing-Fair Lending (ALB) ¶5345 (Sept. 2, 1994).

In *White v. Lee*, 227 F.3d 1214 (9th Cir. 2000), a local nonprofit housing developer, Resources for Community Development (RCD), applied for a use permit from Berkeley's Zoning Adjustment Board. RCD sought to convert a motel to a multi-family housing unit for homeless persons. The plaintiffs lived close to the Bel Air Motel and were opposed to its proposed conversion. They expressed their opposition in a variety of ways. They wrote to the Berkeley City Council, spoke out before the Zoning Adjustment Board and at other public meetings, and published a newsletter with articles critical of the project. The plaintiffs discussed their opposition to the project with the local press and also attempted to persuade merchants to oppose the Bel Air project.

A housing rights advocacy group filed an administrative complaint with the federal Department of Housing and Urban Development (HUD). The complaint alleged that three neighbors in Berkeley opposed the conversion of a motel into a multi-family housing unit because they believed that the project would bring people into the neighborhood who were mentally disabled or disabled through substance abuse. The HUD office initiated an eight-month investigation into the neighbors' activities and beliefs. The HUD officials in San Francisco recommended finding that the neighbors had violated the Fair Housing Act, but officials in Washington ultimately concluded that no violation had occurred and that the neighbors had engaged solely in activities protected by the First Amendment.

The three neighbors then filed a civil rights action alleging a violation of their First Amendment rights. In response, the officials argued that the Fair Housing Act required them to investigate whether the neighbors had filed a lawsuit in state court with an unlawful discriminatory motive. At the very least, they argued, they were entitled to qualified immunity. The Ninth Circuit ruled that the investigation into the plaintiffs' activities and beliefs chilled the exercise of their First Amendment rights. The court minimized the interference provision of Title VIII by suggesting, as an analogy, a hypothetical involving the punishment of a newspaper editorial protesting a project. The court also seemed to implicitly interpret the dividing line between constitutional and unconstitutional application of the Title VIII interference provision to be acts involving violence. *Contra Walker v. City of Lakewood*, 272 F.3d 1114 (9th Cir. 2001), *cert. denied*, 122 S. Ct. 1607 (2002) (rejecting any requirement for violence to make out a §3617 interference claim).

The *White v. Lee* decision presents the conflict between free speech and the right to engage in a range of behavior that may be undertaken intentionally or unintentionally as part of an effort to exclude from housing the group or members of a minority group protected under the civil rights laws. How far can protestors go in opposing housing for the disabled or housing that might be occupied by persons of minority ethnic membership? Should speech be absolute or limited as in the case of hostile environmental sexual harassment? Should the same limits apply to housing or land use discrimination? Is the home equivalent to the environment of the workplace, or is it entitled to even more protection? What if the protest comes in the form of a march to say "leave our neighborhood"? What if it is in the form of a civilized protest over parking and traffic subventions before the planning commission? What if the protest takes the form of an environmental lawsuit? *See also Township of West Orange v. Whitman*, 8 F. Supp. 2d 408 (D.N.J. 1998) (rejecting First Amendment claim based on HUD's distribution of a fair housing pamphlet at a meeting of opponents to group homes for the mentally ill); David K. Godschalk, Protected Petitioning or Unlawful Retaliation? The Limits of First Amendment Immunity for Lawsuits Under the Fair Housing Act, 27 Pepp. L. Rev. 477 (2000) (advocating a test of "illegal objective" to determine whether a lawsuit is frivolous, and therefore unprotected).

14

Environmental Protection

A. INTRODUCTION

1. The Environmental Law – Land Use Intersection

This chapter highlights a development that has been responsible for much of the complexity found in modern land use regulation: the integration of environmental protection into land use decisions. If you had taken a course in land use controls 25 years ago, this chapter would not have existed in your casebook. At that time little environmental legislation existed, and the sparse body of environmental law was almost totally separated from the well-established system of land use controls implemented by local governments.

The rise of modern environmental regulation generally dates from 1969, when Congress passed the National Environmental Policy Act, legislation that requires federal agencies to prepare environmental impact statements on projects that may have a significant effect on the environment. This law was followed by a deluge of federal statutes enacted over the next five years, including the Clean Air Act Amendments of 1970, the Federal Water Pollution Control Act Amendments of 1972 (later renamed the Clean Water Act), the Endangered Species Act of 1973, and the Coastal Zone Management Act. Later, during the waning days of the administration of President Jimmy Carter in 1980, Congress enacted the Comprehensive Environmental Response, Compensation, and Liability Act, known as "CERCLA" or more commonly as the "Superfund," which imposes liability for the cleanup of abandoned hazardous waste sites.

2. *The Impact on Applicants for Land Use Approvals*

These laws have important impacts on land use. The predominant regulatory method employed by the legislation is the issuance of permits by either the federal government or by states whose regulatory programs have received federal approval. The changes, however, were much more profound than just adding a new permit or two. States have also established substantive regulatory requirements aimed at protecting the environment.

These requirements take three forms. First, in many instances states attempted to integrate environmental protection into the traditional tools of land use control. For example, local general plans may be required to include provisions that are designed to protect open space and other natural resources, such as agriculture. Second, some states enacted legislation to protect so-called critical areas, regions of a state that are environmentally sensitive, through regional or state agencies with permit power over developments in these areas. Regions such as the Chesapeake and San Francisco Bays were the subject of legislation that removed the final authority for development approvals from its usual situs at the local governmental level and elevated it to regional or state agencies. Third, states passed environmental legislation that duplicated or, in some instances, mandated even greater protection than the federal environmental laws.

This barrage of legislation has fundamentally affected the regulatory requirements that applicants seeking large-scale land use approvals must meet. Major industrial developments, for example, now must secure more than local land use permits; they must also obtain state permits and, in all likelihood, federal permits as well. The lawyer representing a company seeking to site a new industrial facility could well need a general plan amendment, a zone change, and a site approval from a local government; a "prevention of significant deterioration" or "nonattainment" area permit from the state pursuant to the Clean Air Act; a discharge permit issued by a state agency under the Clean Water Act; and a wetlands permit issued by the federal Army Corps of Engineers. A residential developer in a rural area may find that, in addition to contending with local regulatory requirements intended to protect open space, he or she may have difficulty with the federal requirements. Indeed, as the student will see in *Tanglewood East Homeowners v. Charles-Thomas, Inc.*, a case included in this chapter, it is even possible for a residential developer to run afoul of CERCLA, the federal hazardous waste cleanup legislation.

3. *Land Use Tools for Environmental Protection*

In this chapter, you will also see environmental protection requirements implemented through traditional controls. In *State of New Hampshire v. Rattee*, the case on agricultural protection that is included in this chapter, the local jurisdiction utilized an easement for the purpose of agricultural protection. You will examine how regional and state-level critical-area programs implement planning mechanisms to protect sensitive resources.

Students also will see how the federal government's regulatory mechanisms for protecting wetlands and endangered species can profoundly affect the ability to develop land. Two of the cases chosen on these subjects, *Solid Waste Agency of N. Cook County v. U.S. Army Corps of Engineers* and *Babbitt v. Sweet Home Chapter of*

Communities for a Greater Oregon, respectively illustrate the sweep of the so-called Section 404 permitting power of the Corps of Engineers over wetlands and the prohibitions in the Endangered Species Act.

This chapter offers the student a chance to integrate and build upon basic materials covered earlier in the course. For example, planning mechanisms and regulatory tools such as zoning and subdivision controls have been adapted to serve new environmental protection goals. The chapter also relates directly to the material in Chapter 7 on the takings issue, for regulations under environmental protection law can greatly restrict the landowner's ability to use the property.

4. *Currency and Controversy*

The material covered in this chapter is current, interesting, and exciting. If you pick up today's newspaper, the chances are good that you will see some reference to an environmental dispute of the type examined in this chapter. The material is also very controversial. Part of the controversy is philosophical, with development interests and environmentalists simply at odds over the "right" amount of environmental protection. In other respects, however, the controversy stems from complaints about the costs that the system can impose upon particular landowners.

One problem is that there is not necessarily any correlation between the costs imposed by regulation and the ability of the individuals upon whom they fall to bear them. The extent of the costs depends solely on the resource that is found on the landowner's property. If it turns out that one person owns property upon which an endangered species is located, or that vast parts of it are covered by wetlands, the law may restrict development on a large part of the property, with potentially devastating results for that owner. Furthermore, the sheer complexity of trying to clean up hazardous waste sites can delay development for years, and CERCLA imposes liability on whatever "deep pocket" it can find. Thus, the current landowner may be stuck with the entire cost of cleanup even though it largely was not responsible for the contamination.

Partly as a result of these costs, and partly because of disputes over the need for these regulatory requirements in the first instance. Congress continues to debate regulatory reform measures. At the same time, albeit at a much lower level of political attention, it is becoming clear that some of these environmental protection mechanisms are not attaining their goals. In particular, scientists have argued that to be successful, any attempt to protect endangered species must pay more attention to the habitat that the species depend on for survival and must manage the species on an ecosystem basis. The Endangered Species Act, with its focus on preventing individual actions that affect species on particular properties, is not designed to carry out systematic ecosystem protection.

The debate over the future of environmental law suggests the need to look at alternative ways of attaining environmental protection goals. One of the most promising ideas is "transferable development rights," a concept that students encountered earlier in the *Penn Central* takings case. Tradeable rights are a possible means of avoiding the situation where environmental protection benefits, which accrue to the society as a whole, are achieved by imposing large costs on individual landowners. Another interesting possibility is the creation of new wetlands to offset the destruction of wetlands by development.

The information in this chapter allows the student to conceptualize solutions to the dilemmas posed by the current system. What would *you* suggest?

B. WETLANDS

We begin with the controversial subject of wetlands regulation. The importance of this area of environmental regulation to land use is suggested by two factors. First, the range of acreage that fulfills the definition of a "wetland" is probably larger than you think. Second, Section 404 of the federal Clean Water Act vests considerable power in the United States Army Corps of Engineers and the federal Environmental Protection Agency to deny approval to developments that propose to fill wetlands.

■ SOLID WASTE AGENCY OF NORTHERN COOK COUNTY v. UNITED STATES ARMY CORPS OF ENGINEERS

531 U.S. 159 (2001)

Chief Justice REHNQUIST delivered the opinion of the Court.

Section 404(a) of the Clean Water Act (CWA or Act), 86 Stat. 884, as amended, 33 U.S.C. §1344(a), regulates the discharge of dredged or fill material into "navigable waters." The United States Army Corps of Engineers (Corps) has interpreted §404(a) to confer federal authority over an abandoned sand and gravel pit in northern Illinois which provides habitat for migratory birds. We are asked to decide whether the provisions of §404(a) may be fairly extended to these waters, and, if so, whether Congress could exercise such authority consistent with the Commerce Clause, U.S. Const., Art. I, §8, cl. 3. We answer the first question in the negative and therefore do not reach the second.

Petitioner, the Solid Waste Agency of Northern Cook County (SWANCC), is a consortium of 23 suburban Chicago cities and villages that united in an effort to locate and develop a disposal site for baled nonhazardous solid waste. The Chicago Gravel Company informed the municipalities of the availability of a 533-acre parcel, bestriding the Illinois counties Cook and Kane, which had been the site of a sand and gravel pit mining operation for three decades up until about 1960. Long since abandoned, the old mining site eventually gave way to a successional stage forest, with its remnant excavation trenches evolving into a scattering of permanent and seasonal ponds of varying size (from under one-tenth of an acre to several acres) and depth (from several inches to several feet).

The municipalities decided to purchase the site for disposal of their baled nonhazardous solid waste. . . . [B]ecause the operation called for the filling of some of the permanent and seasonal ponds, SWANCC contacted federal respondents (hereinafter respondents), including the Corps, to determine if a federal landfill permit was required under §204(a) of the CWA, 33 U.S.C. §1344(a).

Section 404(a) grants the Corps authority to issue permits "for the discharge of dredged or fill material into the navigable waters at specified disposal sites." *Ibid.*

The term "navigable waters" is defined under the Act as "the waters of the United States, including the territorial seas." §1362(7). The Corps has issued regulations defining the term "waters of the United States" to include

> "waters such as intrastate lakes, rivers, streams (including intermittent streams), mudflats, sandflats, wetlands, sloughs, prairie potholes, wet meadows, playa lakes, or natural ponds, the use, degradation or destruction of which could affect interstate or foreign commerce. . . . " 33 CFR §328.3(a)(3) (1999).

In 1986, in an attempt to "clarify" the reach of its jurisdiction, the Corps stated that §404(a) extends to intrastate waters:

> "a. Which are or would be used as habitat by birds protected by Migratory Bird Treaties; or
> "b. Which are or would be used as habitat by other migratory birds which cross state lines; or
> "c. Which are or would be used as habitat for endangered species; or
> "d. Used to irrigate crops sold in interstate commerce." 51 Fed. Reg. 41217.

This last promulgation has been dubbed the "Migratory Bird Rule."

The Corps initially concluded that it had no jurisdiction over the site because it contained no "wetlands," or areas which support "vegetation typically adapted for life in saturated soil conditions," 33 CFR §328.3(b) (1999). However, after the Illinois Nature Preserves Commission informed the Corps that a number of migratory bird species had been observed at the site, the Corps reconsidered and ultimately asserted jurisdiction over the balefill site pursuant to subpart (b) of the "Migratory Bird Rule." The Corps found that approximately 121 bird species had been observed at the site, including several known to depend upon aquatic environments for a significant portion of their life requirements. Thus, on November 16, 1987, the Corps formally "determined that the seasonally ponded, abandoned gravel mining depressions located on the project site, while not wetlands, did qualify as 'waters of the United States,' . . . based upon the following criteria: (1) the proposed site had been abandoned as a gravel mining operation; (2) the water areas and spoil piles had developed a natural character; and (3) the water areas are used as habitat by migratory bird *[sic]* which cross state lines." . . .

. . . [T]he Corps refused to issue a §404(a) permit. The Corps found that SWANCC had not established that its proposal was the "least environmentally damaging, most practicable alternative" for disposal of nonhazardous solid waste; that SWANCC'S failure to set aside sufficient funds to remediate leaks posed an "unacceptable risk to the public's drinking water supply"; and that the impact of the project upon area-sensitive species was "unmitigatable since a landfill surface cannot be redeveloped into a forested habitat." *Id.*, at 87. . . .

. . . §404(a) authorizes respondents to regulate the discharge of fill material into "navigable waters," 33 U.S.C. §1344(a), which the statute defines as "the waters of the United States, including the territorial seas," §1362(7). Respondents have interpreted these words to cover the abandoned gravel pit at issue here because it is used as habitat for migratory birds. We conclude that the "Migratory Bird Rule" is not fairly supported by the CWA.

This is not the first time we have been called upon to evaluate the meaning of §404(a). In *United States v. Riverside Bayview Homes, Inc.*, 474 U.S.121, 106 S. Ct.

455, 88 L.Ed.2d 419 (1985), we held that the Corps had §404(a) jurisdiction over wetlands that actually abutted on a navigable waterway. In so doing, we noted that the term "navigable" is of "limited import" and that Congress evidenced its intent to "regulate at least some waters that would not be deemed 'navigable' under the classical understanding of that term." *Id.*, at 133, 106 S. Ct. 455. But our holding was based in large measure upon Congress' unequivocal acquiescence to, and approval of, the Corps' regulations interpreting the CWA to cover wetlands adjacent to navigable waters. See *id.*, at 135-139, 106 S. Ct. 455. We found that Congress' concern for the protection of water quality and aquatic ecosystems indicated its intent to regulate wetlands "inseparably bound up with the 'waters' of the United States." *Id.*, at 134, 106 S. Ct. 455.

It was the significant nexus between the wetlands and "navigable waters" that informed our reading of the CWA in *Riverside Bayview Homes*. Indeed, we did not "express any opinion" on the "question of the authority of the Corps to regulate discharges of fill material into wetlands that are not adjacent to bodies of open water. . . ." *Id.*, at 131-132, n. 8, 106 S. Ct. 455. In order to rule for respondents here, we would have to hold that the jurisdiction of the Corps extends to ponds that are *not* adjacent to open water. But we conclude that the text of the statute will not allow this.

Indeed, the Corps' *original* interpretation of the CWA, promulgated two years after its enactment, is inconsistent with that which it espouses here. Its 1974 regulations defined §404(a)'s "navigable waters" to mean "those waters of the United States which are subject to the ebb and flow of the tide, and/or are presently, or have been in the past, or may be in the future susceptible for use for purposes of interstate or foreign commerce." 33 CFR §209.120(d)(1). The Corps emphasized that "[i]t is the water body's capability of use by the public for purposes of transportation or commerce which is the determinative factor." §209.260(e)(1). Respondents put forward no persuasive evidence that the Corps mistook Congress' intent in 1974.

Respondents next contend that whatever its original aim in 1972, Congress charted a new course five years later when it approved the more expansive definition of "navigable waters" found in the Corps' 1977 regulations. In July 1977, the Corps formally adopted 33 CFR §323.2(a)(5) (1978), which defined "waters of the United States" to include "isolated wetlands and lakes, intermittent streams, prairie potholes, and other waters that are not part of a tributary system to interstate waters or to navigable waters of the United States, the degradation or destruction of which could affect interstate commerce." Respondents argue that Congress was aware of this more expansive interpretation during its 1977 amendments to the CWA. . . . The failure to pass legislation that would have overturned the Corps' 1977 regulations and the extension of jurisdiction in §404(g) to waters "other than" traditional "navigable waters," respondents submit, indicate that Congress recognized and accepted a broad definition of "navigable waters" that includes nonnavigable, isolated, intrastate waters.

Although we have recognized congressional acquiescence to administrative interpretations of a statute in some situations, we have done so with extreme care. . . . Because "subsequent history is less illuminating than the contemporaneous evidence," respondents face a difficult task in overcoming the plain text and import of §404(a).

We conclude that respondents have failed to make the necessary showing that the failure of the 1977 House bill demonstrates Congress' acquiescence to the Corps' regulations or the "Migratory Bird Rule," which, of course, did not first appear until 1986. . . . Beyond Congress' desire to regulate wetlands adjacent to "navigable waters," respondents point us to no persuasive evidence that the House bill was proposed in response to the Corps' claim of jurisdiction over nonnavigable, isolated, intrastate waters or that its failure indicated congressional acquiescence to such jurisdiction.

Section 404(g) is equally unenlightening. In *Riverside Bayview Homes* we recognized that Congress intended the phrase "navigable waters" to include "at least some waters that would not be deemed 'navigable' under the classical understanding of that term." *Id.*, at 133, 106 S. Ct. 455. But §404(g) gives no intimation of what those waters might be; it simply refers to them as "other . . . waters." Respondents conjecture that "other . . . waters" must incorporate the Corps' 1977 regulations, but it is also plausible, as petitioner contends, that Congress simply wanted to include all waters adjacent to "navigable waters," such as nonnavigable tributaries and streams. The exact meaning of §404(g) is not before us and we express no opinion on it, but for present purposes it is sufficient to say, as we did in *Riverside Bayview Homes,* that "§404(g)(1) does not conclusively determine the construction to be placed on the use of the term 'waters' elsewhere in the Act (particularly in §502(7), which contains the relevant definition of 'navigable waters'). . . . " *Id.*, at 138, n. 11, 106 S. Ct. 455.

We thus decline respondents' invitation to take what they see as the next ineluctable step after *Riverside Bayview Homes:* holding that isolated ponds, some only seasonal, wholly located within two Illinois counties, fall under §404(a)'s definition of "navigable waters" because they serve as habitat for migratory birds. As counsel for respondents conceded at oral argument, such a ruling would assume that "the use of the word navigable in the statute . . . does not have any independent significance." Tr. of Oral Arg. 28. We cannot agree that Congress' separate definitional use of the phrase "waters of the United States" constitutes a basis for reading the term "navigable waters" out of the statute. We said in *Riverside Bayview Homes* that the word "navigable" in the statute was of "limited import[,]" 474 U.S., at 133, 106 S. Ct. 455, and went on to hold that §404(a) extended to nonnavigable wetlands adjacent to open waters. But it is one thing to give a word limited effect and quite another to give it no effect whatever. The term "navigable" has at least the import of showing us what Congress had in mind as its authority for enacting the CWA: its traditional jurisdiction over waters that were or had been navigable in fact or which could reasonably be so made. . . .

Respondents — relying upon all of the arguments addressed above — contend that, at the very least, it must be said that Congress did not address the precise question of §404(a)'s scope with regard to nonnavigable, isolated, intrastate waters, and that, therefore, we should give deference to the "Migratory Bird Rule." *See, e.g., Chevron U.S.A. Inc. v Natural Resources Defense Council, Inc.*, 467 U.S. 837, 104 S. Ct. 2778, 81 L. Ed. 2d 694 (1984). We find §404(a) to be clear, but even were we to agree with respondents, we would not extend *Chevron* deference here. . . .

Twice in the past six years we have reaffirmed the proposition that the grant of authority to Congress under the Commerce Clause, though broad, is not unlimited. See *United States v. Morrison,* 529 U.S. 598, 120 S. Ct. 1740, 146 L. Ed. 2d 658 (2000); *United States v. Lopez,* 514 U.S. 549, 115 S. Ct. 1624, 131 L. Ed. 2d

626 (1995). Respondents argue that the "Migratory Bird Rule" falls within Congress' power to regulate intrastate activities that "substantially affect" interstate commerce. They note that the protection of migratory birds is a "national interest of very nearly the first magnitude," *Missouri v. Holland,* 252 U.S. 416, 435, 40 S. Ct. 382, 64 L. Ed. 641 (1920), and that, as the Court of Appeals found, millions of people spend over a billion dollars annually on recreational pursuits relating to migratory birds. . . .

These are significant constitutional questions raised by respondents' application of their regulations, and yet we find nothing approaching a clear statement from Congress that it intended §404(a) to reach an abandoned sand and gravel pit such as we have here. Permitting respondents to claim federal jurisdiction over ponds and mudflats falling within the "Migratory Bird Rule" would result in a significant impingement of the States' traditional and primary power over land and water use. *See., e.g., Hess v. Port Authority Trans-Hudson Corporation,* 513 U.S. 30, 44, 115 S. Ct. 394, 130 L. Ed. 2d 245 (1994) ("[R]egulation of land use [is] a function traditionally performed by local governments"). Rather than expressing a desire to readjust the federal-state balance in this manner, Congress chose to "recognize, preserve, and protect the primary responsibilities and rights of States . . . to plan the development and use . . . of land and water resources. . . ." 33 U.S.C. §1251(b). We thus read the statute as written to avoid the significant constitutional and federalism questions raised by respondents' interpretation, and therefore reject the request for administrative deference.

We hold that 33 CFR §328.3(a)(3) (1999), as clarified and applied to petitioner's balefill site pursuant to the "Migratory Bird Rule," 51 Fed. Reg. 41217 (1986), exceeds the authority granted to respondents under §404(a) of the CWA. The judgement of the Court of Appeals for the Seventh Circuit is therefore

Reversed.

Justice STEVENS, with whom Justice SOUTER, Justice GINSBURG, and Justice BREYER join, dissenting.

Notes and Comments

1. *The Biology and Botany of Wetlands.* For years, wetlands were routinely filled with little thought given to the consequences. In the late 1990s, however, the filling of wetlands is subject to extensive regulation by a variety of federal, state, and local agencies. Why this radical change of position?

It has been estimated that there were originally 221 million acres of wetlands in the continental United States. As of 1997, approximately 105.5 million acres remain. According to the most recent statistics available, between 1986 and 1997, approximately 58,500 acres were lost annually. This figure compares to the annual loss of 458,000 acres per year lost between the 1950s and 1970s. U.S. Fish and Wildlife Service, Status and Trends of Wetlands in the Coterminous United States — 1986 to 1997 (2000).

Federal agencies generally look to three factors in determining whether a particular property is a wetlands: hydrophatic vegetation, hydric soil, and hydrology. *See, e.g., Avoyelles Sportsmen's League, Inc. v. Marsh,* 715 F.2d 897, 910-911 (5th Cir. 1983). All three factors must be present under "normal circumstances"; thus, the fact that one of the factors is not actually present does not mean that the area is exempt from regulation.

2. *The Holding of SWANCC.* What exactly did Chief Justice Rehnquist, writing for the majority, hold in *Solid Waste Ass'n* (popularly known as *SWANCC*)? Did the Court simply reject the "Migratory Bird Rule" as a basis for jurisdiction under the Clean Water Act? Did the Court's rationale indicate an even broader holding that rejects jurisdiction over any "isolated waters"? What about wetlands with a significant nexus to navigable waters? After the case, EPA and the General Counsel of the Corps of Engineers issued a memorandum dated January 19, 2001, in which they asserted that *SWANCC* affected only the Corps' ability to regulate isolated, nonnavigable, intrastate waters on the basis of the Migratory Bird Rule. In addition, EPA and the Corps issued an advanced notice of proposed rulemaking on issues associated with the scope of waters subject to jurisdiction after *SWANCC*. 68 Fed. Reg. 1991 (Jan. 15, 2003).

Most courts seem to have read *SWANCC* relatively narrowly. *See, e.g., Headwaters, Inc. v. Talent Irrigation Dist.*, 243 F.3d 526 (9th Cir. 2001) (irrigation canal that receives water from and diverts water to a water of the United States is subject to regulation). *But see Rice v. Harken Exploration Co.*, 250 F.3d 264 (5th Cir. 2001) (only waters actually navigable or adjacent to an open body of navigable water can be regulated, seeming to exempt nonnavigable tributaries and their adjacent wetlands).

The decision in *SWANCC* may seem somewhat dry and technical, but it has enormous practical consequences. It may eliminate between 30 and 60 percent of the nation's wetlands from regulation. *See* Ass'n of State Wetland Managers, The *SWANCC* Decision and State Regulation of Wetlands (2002), posted at www.aswm.org.

3. *Digging Holes.* Another important jurisdictional issue involves the kinds of activities that subject a party to the Act's regulatory provisions. The Clean Water Act prohibits the "discharge of any pollutant" into the nation's waters, which include wetlands (subject to the *SWANCC* case). A discharge is "any addition of any pollutant" from a point source. 33 U.S.C. §1362(12). A pollutant, in turn, is defined to include rock and sand. What if a farmer, in order to put in new crops, engages in "deep ripping"—dragging four- to seven-foot metal prongs through the soil, thereby puncturing the protective clay layer which prevents surface water from penetrating deeply into the soil?

In *Borden Ranch Partnership v. U.S. Army Corps of Engineers* 261 F.3d 810 (9th Cir. 2001), the court held that this activity was subject to the Corps' jurisdiction. The activity also did not fall into the "farming exception," which exempts discharges from "normal farming . . . and ranching activities, such as plowing." 33 U.S.C. §1344(f)(1)(A). That section was subject to yet another exception where the discharge was used to bring the area of the navigable water into a use to which it was not previously subject. *Id.* §1344(f)(2). A divided Supreme Court split 4 to 4, with Justice Kennedy recusing himself, thereby affirming the judgment. *Borden Ranch Partnership v. U.S. Army Corps of Engineers*, 537 U.S. 99, 123 S. Ct. 599 (2002). *Compare National Mining Ass'n v. U.S. Army Corps of Eng'rs*, 145 F.3d 1399 (D.C. Cir. 1998) ("incidental fallback" into water not a regulable deposit).

4. *The Federal Regulatory Agencies.* One of the reasons—but certainly not the sole reason—for the controversy surrounding wetlands regulation lies in the number of federal agencies that have a role in it. The principal federal agency in charge

is the Corps of Engineers, which issues a permit under §404 of the Clean Water Act, 33 U.S.C. §1344 (1986). But the U.S. Environmental Protection Agency also plays a big role. EPA (in conjunction with the Corps) not only develops guidelines that must be satisfied before a permit may be issued (*see* 40 C.F.R. §§230 *et seq.* (1998)), the agency also may "veto" the issuance of a permit by the Corps. Furthermore, the U.S. Fish and Wildlife Service (part of the Department of the Interior) and the National Marine Fisheries Service (part of the Department of Commerce) must be allowed to comment on applications for §404 permits.

5. *Permit Standards: Alternatives.* From the applicant's standpoint the focus of the process is on the standards used to determine whether to grant the §404 permit. The Corps of Engineers uses a "public interest" review to make this determination. Under this standard, the Corps weighs up to 24 different factors, ranging from environmental considerations to economic ones. The evaluation also examines the existence of alternative locations and methods to accomplish the project's objectives. The specific weight given each factor "is determined by its importance and relevance to the particular proposal." 33 C.F.R. §320.4(a) (1998).

Do you think that a plaintiff is likely to prevail in challenging a determination by the Corps under the public interest standard? Consider the court of appeal's conclusion in *Town of Norfolk v. Army Corps of Engineers*, 968 F.2d 1438, 1454 (1st Cir. 1992) ("Under the 'public interest' review, the Corps conducts a general balancing of a number of economic and environmental factors and its ultimate determinations are entitled to substantial deference."). How predictable is this standard for landowners attempting to determine whether they can fill wetlands on their property? *See, e.g., Mall Properties, Inc. v. Marsh*, 672 F. Supp. 561 (D. Mass. 1987), *appeal dismissed*, 841 F.2d 440 (1st Cir. 1988) (rare instance in which the Corps' denial of a permit was overturned).

The Corps also uses the so-called Section 404 Guidelines, developed jointly with EPA, in making its permit determinations. A critical part of the Guidelines places the burden on the applicant to show that there is no practical alternative to the proposed activity that would have a less adverse impact on the aquatic environment. 40 C.F.R. §230.10(a) (1998). Thus, the Guidelines are in part a land use planning mechanism, with a federal agency making the final determination whether alternative potential sites are "available."

What factors should be considered in the determination of the availability of alternatives? How important is the project's purpose, and is that purpose easy for an agency to determine? In *National Wildlife Ass'n v. Whistler*, 27 F.3d 1841 (3d Cir. 1994), plaintiff proposed a housing project on a bluff outside the Corps' jurisdiction, but it needed a Section 404 permit to give boats access to the Missouri River. The Corps limited its alternatives analysis to the boat access area, excluding the housing development and allowing the developer to avoid the presumption against permit issuance for a nonwater-dependent use. The court upheld this decision.

Did the court improperly allow the Corps to truncate the analysis of alternatives? Wasn't the project's "purpose" simply to provide a residential development? The Guidelines emphasize that there is a presumption against permit issuance for nonwater-dependent projects unless no practical alternatives are available that are less environmentally damaging. In this regard, when is an alternative "available"? *See, e.g., Bersani v. Robichaud*, 850 F.2d 36 (2d Cir. 1988) (practical alternative to shopping center was available at the time the developer entered the market, even though it was not available when EPA made its decision to veto the project).

A less demanding showing of alternatives is required for projects that involve only minor impacts. EPA and U.S. Army Corps of Engineers, Memorandum to the Field, "Appropriate Level of Analysis Required for Evaluating Compliance with the Section 404(b)(1) Guidelines Alternatives Requirements" (Aug. 23, 1993).

6. *Permit Standards: "Significant Degradation" and Mitigation.* Another important criteria in the permit determination is whether the proposed discharge will cause or contribute to the "significant degradation" of waters of the United States. 40 C.F.R. §230.10(c) (1998). The Guidelines require specific, quantifiable factors to be evaluated, but they also take into account factors that cannot be quantified, such as aesthetics. *See* 40 C.F.R. §§230.50-.54 (2003).

Finally, an important aspect of the permit process is mitigation of wetlands impacts. *See Cannon v. State*, 807 A.2d 556 (Del. 2002) (finding that the Delaware Department of Transportation had the authority to condemn property to be used as wetlands mitigation in order to secure a permit from the U.S. Army Corps of Engineers).

7. *A Bar Review Hypo.* Given the significance of wetlands regulation, would a seller's failure to disclose certain information about property give the buyer a right to rescind a contract? Consider the following situation. Defendants sell a ten-acre lakeshore lot to plaintiffs knowing that plaintiffs intend to build a residence on the lot. After beginning construction, plaintiffs find that they have violated state and federal wetland regulations, that "as a practical matter" they will not be able to obtain a federal Section 404 permit to place fill on the property, and that state permits are "unavailable." Do plaintiffs have an action to rescind the contract based on a claim of "mutual mistake"? *See Rancourt v. Verba*, 678 A.2d 886, 889 (Vt. 1996) (granting rescission "[b]ecause the clear intent of plaintiffs was to purchase land suitable for lakeshore development, and because it is impossible to do so under state and federal wetlands regulations").

8. Just v. Marinette County *and the Takings Issue.* Because of the nature of federal and state wetlands law, "compromises" allowing some construction on part of a wetland in return for preservation of another part are unlikely. As a result, agencies often refuse permission to build on any part of the property, and landowners increasingly are responding by bringing takings cases.

One of the earliest and most significant takings cases was *Just v. Marinette County*, 201 N.W.2d 761 (Wis. 1972). In *Just*, a conservancy district adopted a zoning ordinance allowing limited conditional uses for certain areas, including shorelands designated as swamps or marshes. A permit was needed for filling, draining, or dredging wetlands. In the litigation that followed, plaintiff raised the claim that the zoning regulation effected a taking. The Wisconsin Supreme Court found that it did not, reasoning in part as follows:

> In the instant case we have a restriction on the use of a citizen's property, not to secure a benefit for the public, but to prevent a harm from the change in the natural character of the citizen's property. . . .
>
> Is the ownership of a parcel of land so absolute that man can change its nature to suit any of his purposes? . . . An owner of land has no absolute and unlimited right to change the essential natural character of his land so as to use it for a purpose for which it was unsuited in its natural state and which injures the rights of others. The exercise of the police power in zoning must be reasonable and we think it is not an unreasonable exercise of that power to prevent harm to public rights by limiting the use of private property to its natural uses.

201 N.W.2d at 767-768. Is *Just* still good law after the Supreme Court's opinion in *Lucas v. South Carolina Coastal Council*, a principal case discussed in Chapter 7?

9. *Mitigation Banking*. Another idea in the initial stages of use is the creation of "mitigation banks" of wetlands. The idea has been summarized as follows:

> [M]itigation banking generally works something like this: a degraded wetland is purchased and restored by one party, such as a government agency or an investor; this site becomes the bank. The values of the restored wetland are somehow quantified and used as "credits" that can later be withdrawn, at a price, to compensate for unavoidable wetland fills elsewhere.

David A. Salvesen, Banking on Wetlands, Urb. Land, June 1993, at 36, 38.

Most recently, EPA and the Corps have issued a guideline on mitigation that is intended to broaden the scope of the agencies' discretion. Traditionally, the Corps has required that acres of wetland lost to development must be replaced by an equal or larger amount of newly created wetlands. Now, the Corps may use a "functional equivalent" measure evaluating the actual value of restoration activities to a watershed. EPA and U.S. Army Corps of Engineers, Regulatory Guidance Letter (Dec. 26, 2002), www.epa.gov/owow/wetlands/guidance/index.html#mitigation.

10. *State and Local Wetlands Protection*. In addition to the federal role in regulating wetlands, large numbers of states also have substantial programs regulating development that might affect wetlands. At least 15 states, primarily located in the northeastern part of the country, have freshwater wetlands protection statutes such as the New Jersey Freshwater Wetland Protection Act, N.J. Stat. Ann. 13:9B-1 to 30 (West 2003). These include Maine, Connecticut, New Hampshire, Rhode Island, Massachusetts, Vermont, New York, New Jersey, Maryland, Virginia, Florida, Minnesota, Michigan, Pennsylvania, and Oregon. Some of these states have passed comprehensive legislation establishing state regulatory bodies whose principal (or even sole) concern is with wetlands. *See, e.g.*, the Connecticut Inland Wetlands and Watercourses Act, Conn. Gen. Stat. 22a-36 to 22a-45 (West 1995 & 2003 Supp.); the Massachusetts Wetlands Act, Mass. Gen. Laws, ch. 131 40A (2002). Other states regulate through their coastal zone regulatory schemes (discussed above in Chapter 9), which limit wetlands covered to specified parts of the state (*see State v. Simpson*, 423 S.E.2d 759 (N.C. 1992) (regulation under North Carolina Coastal Area Management Act)) or through a state agency, which also has other, broader-based responsibilities. *See In the Matter of the Application of Christenson*, 417 N.W.2d 607 (Minn. 1987) (affirming order by the state Department of Natural Resources that rejected an application to drain a wetland).

A large number of local governments (over 2000 by one estimate) have also used their land use authority to adopt zoning ordinances or conservation ordinances intended to protect wetlands. *See, e.g., Rall v. Town of Belmont*, 635 A.2d 1368 (N.H. 1993) (town could deny application for subdivision approval on the basis that the developers failed to comply with the town's wetlands conservation ordinance).

11. *Other CWA Provisions Affecting Land Use*. Other provisions of the Clean Water Act are increasingly affecting the development of land. If a developer engages in a "construction activity" that disturbs more than five acres of land, then it must receive a Storm Water General Permit and have a Storm Water Pollution Prevention Plan. *See* 40 C.F.R. 122.26. EPA also issues permits for wastewater

treatment plants. *See Crutchfield v. County of Hanover*, 325 F.3d 211 (4th Cir. 2003). Finally, for polluted bodies of water, EPA must issue so-called "total maximum daily loads" (TMDLs) of pollutants. These can significantly limit land uses on the body of water. *See Pronsolino v. Nastri*, 291 F.3d 1123 (9th Cir. 2002) (TMDL required for river polluted only by logging runoff and other "nonpoint" sources of pollution).

C. ENDANGERED SPECIES

Anyone who has made an even cursory attempt to follow the news in recent years certainly is aware of the enormous controversy generated by federal efforts to preserve endangered species. The Endangered Species Act (ESA) has almost always been controversial. When first passed in 1973, the Act breezed through Congress, but by 1978 it was the subject of a major Supreme Court case. Now, as you will see, efforts to implement it in a creative fashion that will lessen its economic impacts are leading to cutting-edge "habitat conservation planning" that will have significant effects on the land use practices of local governments that are located within the planning area.

BABBITT v. SWEET HOME CHAPTER OF COMMUNITIES FOR A GREATER OREGON

515 U.S. 687 (1995)

Justice STEVENS delivered the opinion of the Court.

The Endangered Species Act of 1973, 87 Stat. 884, 16 U.S.C. §1531 (1988 ed. and Supp. V) (ESA or Act), contains a variety of protections designed to save from extinction species that the Secretary of the Interior designates as endangered or threatened. Section 9 of the Act makes it unlawful for any person to "take" any endangered or threatened species. The Secretary has promulgated a regulation that defines the statute's prohibition on takings to include "significant habitat modification or degradation where it actually kills or injures wildlife." This case presents the question whether the Secretary exceeded his authority under the Act by promulgating that regulation.

I

Section 9(a)(1) of the Endangered Species Act provides the following protection for endangered species:

> Except as provided in sections 1535(g)(2) and 1539 of this title, with respect to any endangered species of fish or wildlife listed pursuant to section 1533 of this title it is unlawful for any person subject to the jurisdiction of the United States to. . . .
>
> (B) take any such species within the United States or the territorial sea of the United States[.]

16 U.S.C. §1538(a)(1).

Section 3(19) of the Act defines the statutory term "take": "The term 'take' means to harass, harm, pursue, hunt, shoot, wound, kill, trap, capture, or collect, or to attempt to engage in any such conduct." 16 U.S.C. §1532(19). The Act does not further define the terms it uses to define "take." The Interior Department regulations that implement the statute, however, define the statutory term "harm":

> *Harm* in the definition of "take" in the Act means an act which actually kills or injures wildlife. Such act may include significant habitat modification or degradation where it actually kills or injures wildlife by significantly impairing essential behavioral patterns, including breeding, feeding, or sheltering.

50 CFR §17.3 (1994).

This regulation has been in place since 1975.

A limitation on the §9 "take" prohibition appears in §10(a)(1)(B) of the Act, which Congress added by amendment in 1982. That section authorizes the Secretary to grant a permit for any taking otherwise prohibited by §9(a)(1)(B) "if such taking is incidental to, and not the purpose of, the carrying out of an otherwise lawful activity." 16 U.S.C. §1539(a)(1)(B)....

In addition to the prohibition on takings, the Act provides several other protections for endangered species. Section 4, 16 U.S.C. §1533, commands the Secretary to identify species of fish or wildlife that are in danger of extinction and to publish from time to time lists of all species he determines to be endangered or threatened. Section 5, 16 U.S.C. §1534, authorizes the Secretary, in cooperation with the States, *see* 16 U.S.C. §1535, to acquire land to aid in preserving such species. Section 7 requires federal agencies to ensure that none of their activities, including the granting of licenses and permits, will jeopardize the continued existence of endangered species "or result in the destruction or adverse modification of habitat of such species which is determined by the Secretary . . . to be critical." 16 U.S.C. §1536(a)(2).

Respondents in this action are small landowners, logging companies, and families dependent on the forest products industries in the Pacific Northwest and in the Southeast, and organizations that represent their interests. They brought this declaratory judgment action . . . to challenge the statutory validity of the Secretary's regulation defining "harm," particularly the inclusion of habitat modification and degradation in the definition. Respondents challenged the regulation on its face. . . .

II

Because this case was decided on motions for summary judgment, we may appropriately make certain factual assumptions in order to frame the legal issue. First, we assume respondents have no desire to harm either the red-cockaded woodpecker or the spotted owl; they merely wish to continue logging activities that would be entirely proper if not prohibited by the ESA. On the other hand, we must assume *arguendo* that those activities will have the effect, even though unintended, of detrimentally changing the natural habitat of both listed species and that, as a consequence, members of those species will be killed or injured. Under respondents' view of the law, the Secretary's only means of forestalling that grave result—even when the actor knows it is certain to occur—is to use his §5 authority to purchase the lands on which the survival of the species depends. The Secretary, on the other hand, submits that the §9 prohibition on takings, which

Congress defined to include "harm," places on respondents a duty to avoid harm that habitat alteration will cause the birds unless respondents first obtain a permit pursuant to §10.

The text of the Act provides three reasons for concluding that the Secretary's interpretation is reasonable. First, an ordinary understanding of the word "harm" supports it. The dictionary definition of the verb form of "harm" is "to cause hurt or damage to: injure," Webster's Third New International Dictionary 1034 (1966). In the context of the ESA, that definition naturally encompasses habitat modification that results in actual injury or death to members of an endangered or threatened species.

Respondents argue that the Secretary should have limited the purview of "harm" to direct applications of force against protected species, but the dictionary definition does not include the word "directly" or suggest in any way that only direct or willful action that leads to injury constitutes "harm." Moreover, unless the statutory term "harm" encompasses indirect as well as direct injuries, the word has no meaning that does not duplicate the meaning of other words that §3 uses to define "take." . . .

Second, the broad purpose of the ESA supports the Secretary's decision to extend protection against activities that cause the precise harms Congress enacted the statute to avoid.

Third, the fact that Congress in 1982 authorized the Secretary to issue permits for takings that §9(a)(1)(B) would otherwise prohibit, "if such taking is incidental to, and not the purpose of, the carrying out of an otherwise lawful activity," 16 U.S.C. §1539(a)(1)(B), strongly suggests that Congress understood §9(a)(1)(B) to prohibit indirect as well as deliberate takings. The permit process requires the applicant to prepare a "conservation plan" that specifies how he intends to "minimize and mitigate" the "impact" of his activity on endangered and threatened species, 16 U.S.C. §1539(a)(2)(A), making clear that Congress had in mind foreseeable rather than merely accidental effects on listed species. No one could seriously request an "incidental" take permit to avert §9 liability for direct, deliberate action against a member of an endangered or threatened species, but respondents would read "harm" so narrowly that the permit procedure would have little more than that absurd purpose. "When Congress acts to amend a statute, we presume it intends its amendment to have real and substantial effect." *Stone v. INS*, 514 U.S. 386, 387 (1995). Congress' addition of the §10 permit provision supports the Secretary's conclusion that activities not intended to harm an endangered species, such as habitat modification, may constitute unlawful takings under the ESA unless the Secretary permits them.

The Court of Appeals made three errors in asserting that "harm" must refer to a direct application of force because the words around it do. First, the court's premise was flawed. Several of the words that accompany "harm" in the §3 definition of "take," especially "harass," "pursue," "wound," and "kill," refer to actions or effects that do not require direct applications of force. Second, to the extent the court read a requirement of intent or purpose into the words used to define "take," it ignored §9's express provision that a "knowing" action is enough to violate the Act. Third, the court employed *noscitur a sociis* to give "harm" essentially the same function as other words in the definition, thereby denying it independent meaning. The canon, to the contrary, counsels that a word "gathers meaning from the words around it." *Jarecki v. G.D. Searle & Co.*, 367 U.S. 303, 307 (1961).

The statutory context of "harm" suggests that Congress meant that term to serve a particular function in the ESA, consistent with but distinct from the functions of the other verbs used to define "take." The Secretary's interpretation of "harm" to include indirectly injuring endangered animals through habitat modification permissibly interprets "harm" to have "a character of its own not to be submerged by its association." *Russell Motor Car Co. v. United States*, 261 U.S. 514, 519 (1923). . . .

The judgment of the Court of Appeals is reversed.

It is so ordered.

Notes and Comments

1. *Preserving Species*. The first case under the Endangered Species Act to reach the Supreme Court was *Tennessee Valley Authority v. Hill*, 437 U.S. 153 (1978). Then Chief Justice Warren Berger's opinion noted:

> It may seem curious to some that the survival of a relatively small number of three-inch fish among all the countless millions of species extant would require the permanent halting of a virtually completed dam for which Congress has expended more than $100 million. . . . We conclude, however, that the explicit provisions of the Endangered Species Act require precisely that result.

Id. at 172-173. Why put such an emphasis on preserving species? In a recent article Professor Oliver A. Houck suggests that the Endangered Species Act operates as a surrogate for the health of ecosystems, which American laws have not yet attempted to protect in a holistic way. Oliver A. Houck, Why Do We Protect Endangered Species, and What Does that Say About Whether Restrictions on Private Property to Protect Them Constitute "Takings"?, 80 Iowa L. Rev. 297, 301 (1995). Is that a legitimate reason for the stringent protections required by the ESA?

2. *The ESA and Land Use*. In the 30 years since its passage, the Endangered Species Act has produced a series of high-profile confrontations, usually regarding proposed federal projects. These have ranged from the dispute over the construction of the Tellico Dam in Tennessee (pitting the famous "snail darter" against an already completed dam) to the recent headlines over protection of the spotted owl in the old-growth forests of the Northwest and the alleged loss of jobs that protection of the owl caused in the timber industry.

In recent years, however, the ESA's effect on more traditional land use activities, such as subdivision approvals, has become more apparent. *See*, most recently, Douglas Jehl, Rare Arizona Owl (All 7 Inches of It) Is in Habitat Furor, N.Y. Times, Mar. 17, 2003 (developers say proposed designation of critical habitat for the pygmy owl would drive up housing costs by an average of $7,000 per home); *Defenders of Wildlife v. Bernal*, 204 F.3d 920 (9th Cir. 2000) (upholding finding that construction of a school would not "take" any of the endangered pygmy owls). *See also Friends of Endangered Species v. Jantzen*, 760 F.2d 976 (9th Cir. 1985) (effect of Mission Blue butterfly on 2235 unit residential development); *Maine Audubon Society v. Purslow*, 672 F. Supp. 528 (D. Me. 1987), *aff'd*, 907 F.2d 265 (1st Cir. 1990) (effect of bald eagle on residential subdivision). With this knowledge have come loud calls for Congress to amend the Act. *But see* Stephen M. Meyer, The Economic

Impact of the Endangered Species Act on the Housing and Real Estate Markets, 6 N.Y.U. Envtl. L.J. 450, 474 (1998) (concluding that the ESA "has not had a burdensome impact on real estate industry performance or new single family home construction rates").

3. Sweet Home *and the Reach of the ESA*. The reach of the Act, and its potential to affect land use significantly, are apparent from the *Sweet Home* case. A 1994 study by the General Accounting Office found that more than 50 percent of all listed species depend exclusively upon nonfederal land for survival. Additionally, 90 percent of all listed species and candidate species rely to a significant degree on nonfederal habitat. U.S. General Accounting Office, Endangered Species Act: Information on Species Protection, Nonfederal Lands, GAO/RCED 95-16 (Dec. 1994).

Are you convinced that the Court reached the correct conclusion in *Sweet Home*? Could the administration of a new president who opposes the extensive sweep of the ESA repeal the broad definition of "harm" that includes significant habitation modification or degradation?

Developers have also sought, so far unsuccessfully, a ruling that the provisions of the Endangered Species Act exceed Congress's power to regulate under the Commerce Clause. *See Rancho Viejo, LLC v. Norton*, 323 F.3d 1062 (D.C. Cir. 2003); *Gibbs v. Babbitt*, 214 F.3d 483 (4th Cir. 2000).

4. *The ESA Process*. The *Sweet Home* case outlines some parts of the process under the ESA. That process begins with the listing by the Secretary of the Interior of species as endangered or threatened. 16 U.S.C. §1533 (1994 & Supp. 1996).

The key provisions protecting the listed species are found in §§7 and 9 of the Act. Section 7 requires that federal agencies "insure" that their actions are not likely to jeopardize protected species or their habitats. 16 U.S.C. §1536(a)(2) (1994). If protected species are found in the area of the proposed action, the agency must prepare a "biological assessment" analyzing whether the action is likely to affect the species and its "critical habitat." If such an effect is likely, the agency must formally consult with the U.S. Fish and Wildlife Service or the National Marine Fisheries Service.

Additionally, the U.S. Fish and Wildlife Service must specify whether the action will result in an "incidental take" of protected species. 16 U.S.C. §1536(b)(4). If so, it issues an "Incidental Take Statement" specifying the impact of the taking on the species, those measures necessary to minimize the impact, and terms and conditions to implement those measures. This "Incidental Take Statement" is a safe harbor provision that immunizes persons from liability under Section 9 of the Act.

Section 9 prohibits "any person or agency" from "taking" any endangered species of fish or wildlife. 16 U.S.C. §1538(a)(1)(B)-(C) (1994). As you saw in *Sweet Home*, habitat modification is included within the meaning of "harm," and thereby within "take." Any "Incidental Take Statement" issued by the U.S. Fish and Wildlife Service must specify the take that is allowed. *Arizona Cattle Growers' Ass'n v. U.S. Fish and Wildlife*, 273 F.3d 1229 (9th Cir. 2001). A numerical limit is often used. *See, e.g., Fund for Animals v. Rice*, 85 F.3d 535 (11th Cir. 1996) (landfill may take 52 snakes during construction and 2 snakes per year thereafter); *Mt. Graham Red Squirrel v. Madigan*, 954 F.2d 1441 (9th Cir. 1992) (telescope construction may take 6 red squirrels per year).

In considering the effect of the Endangered Species Act on land use, it is important to think about the structure of the Act's regulatory mechanism. Its focus is on preventing actions by private parties and the government that might jeopardize protected species or their habitats. Thus, it proceeds on a project-by-project basis, looking narrowly at the effect that a specific action may have on a specific endangered species.

This reactive approach ensures that confrontation with developers will occur when proposals, some well down the pipeline toward final approval, are delayed or rejected because of impacts on endangered species. At the same time, the approach is insufficient to ensure that the principal goal of the Act, the survival of endangered species, is met. Species survival depends largely on whether the species has sufficient habitat in which to thrive, but the ESA's case-by-case regulatory mechanism does not provide for comprehensive planning for habitat preservation.

The problems with the present approach have led to efforts at comprehensive habitat protection. To qualify for an "incidental take" under §10 of the ESA, the landowner must submit a "conservation plan" whose purpose is to "minimize and mitigate" the impact on the species. These types of plans could preserve species while, at the same time, giving clear signals to developers about areas in which development can occur without running afoul of the ESA.

The following excerpt discusses habitat conservation plans (HCPs) to protect endangered species.

■ TIMOTHY BEATLEY, HABITAT CONSERVATION PLANNING

23-39 (1994)

Process and Methodology

. . . Usually a steering committee, comprised of key stakeholders in the community or region, is formed to guide and oversee the preparation of the plan. HCP committees usually include representatives of the real estate and development communities, the environmental community, the local governments involved, and state and federal resource agencies (e.g., state wildlife agencies, USFWS, and the federal Bureau of Land Management). In addition to the steering committee, which usually acts as the official policymaking body, HCPs often involve a technical or biological committee consisting of experts on the species of concern and other individuals who may have special technical expertise. Much of the background work on the HCP and the nuts and bolts of the conservation measures included in the HCP are undertaken by such technical committees. In addition, a private consultant is typically hired by the steering committee to collect necessary data, and to prepare the plan and the accompanying maps and environmental review documentation (e.g., state environmental impact reports and federal environmental impact statements). . . .

While each of the HCPs has gone through, or is going through, similar processes and methodologies, they differ in a number of respects. The HCPs vary, for instance, according to who is given responsibility for organizing and coordinating the process. In some instances . . . a regional government coordinates the process. . . . [I]n other cases a single jurisdiction, such as a local planning department, coordinates it. And despite the general similarities in the types of groups and interests involved in HCPs (i.e., real estate and development interests, environmental and conservation interests, and local governments) substantial variation exists, depending on the specific local and regional circumstances. Because the individuals and groups having a stake in HCPs will tend to vary from place to place, the composition of HCP steering committees tends to vary as well. . . .

Most HCPs are issued for a period of thirty years. . . .

Number and Type of Species Protected

The number and types of species addressed varies among the regional HCPs, as each plan involves different biological issues and resulting conservation strategies. Species of concern include reptiles, such as the threatened Coachella Valley fringe-toed lizard in the Coachella Valley HCP, the American crocodile in the North Key Largo HCP, the desert tortoise in the Clark County HCP, and the San Joaquin blunt-nosed leopard lizard in the Kern County HCP. . . .

Different species of concern in turn imply different biological factors and characteristics which will need to be considered. Some species like the desert tortoise have wide ranges, while others have very narrow ranges. Some species are migratory, such as the Least Bell's Vireo and Golden-cheeked Warbler, while others are not. These different biological characteristics in turn require different management and conservation measures.

Types of Threats

All habitat conservation plans also vary by the types of threats presented to species of concern. For instance, in Coachella Valley, the primary threats are the direct loss of blowsand habitat (areas of unstable wind-blown sand) due to private urban and resort development . . . and indirect degradation of habitat due to sand shielding. For the desert tortoise, not only is direct loss of habitat from development a problem, but a host of other threats must be addressed, including impacts on the species from a respiratory disease, off-road vehicles, over-grazing, and raven predation. . . .

Size of Planning Areas

Habitat conservation plans also differ by the size of their planning areas, again in large degree a result of biological differences in the species of concern. Planning areas range in size from the relatively small 550 acres for the Marina Dunes HCP to fairly large areas, such as the several hundred-square-mile planning area for the Metro-Bakersfield HCP, and the very large thirty-two hundred-square-mile valley floor HCP being prepared by Kern County. Some HCPs, such as the Kern County HCP, have sought to assume a larger, more regional scale while others have sought a more localized approach. . . .

. . . Many of the more recently initiated HCPs . . . are attempting to take a much more comprehensive biological focus, looking not just at federally listed species but also at state-listed species, federal candidate species, and other species of concern. There is an increasing recognition by those in both the conservation and the development communities that it makes sense, economically and technically, to deal with multiple species in a comprehensive management framework. . . .

IMPLEMENTATION AND MANAGEMENT

. . . All of the HCPs share the basic and central strategy of identifying and protecting certain designated habitat conservation areas, as well as allowing some degree of urban development or non-conservation land uses to occur. The setting aside of habitat conservation areas has been accomplished in different ways. The Coachella Valley HCP, for instance, acquired, with the help of The Nature Conservancy, large privately owned lands. Three preserves were set up for the fringe-toed lizard, encompassing a total of more than sixteen thousand acres. . . .

Other HCPs have taken different approaches to establishing habitat preserves. The original North Ley Largo HCP envisioned setting aside preserves of hardwood hammocks through a somewhat different means, relying heavily on the use of the local jurisdiction's zoning powers, in combination with a plan to allow the transfer of development rights to designated development nodes. While it incorporated a two-year waiting period that provided a window of time for the state to purchase habitat lands, after a certain date (August 1, 1988) the plan was to allow development only in designated development nodes, restricting by way of a conserved habitat zoning category any development outside of these areas (approximately 84% of the habitat). Under the plan a maximum of thirty-five hundred dwelling units would be permitted in the development nodes, with this maximum density achievable only through the transfer of density from the conserved habitat. Additional restrictions were also placed on the extent of hammock clearance permissible even in development nodes. . . .

Notes and Comments

1. *Species by Species Protection*. From an environmental standpoint, HCPs are an improvement over the normal course of regulation under the Endangered Species Act. They approach the problem of preservation from the perspective of what the species needs to survive, rather than from the impact of a specific development or action on that species. Academic commentators have argued that the overall goal must be protection of biodiversity in general. A. Dan Tarlock, Biodiversity Conservation in the United States: A Case Study in Incompleteness and Indirection, 32 Envtl. L. Rep. 10529 (2002) ("The ESA is a backwards approach to biodiversity because it only indirectly addresses the major cause of biodiversity loss, habitat destruction, and does not concern itself with other causes such as the invasion of exotic species and air and water pollution").

2. *Preparing an HCP*. As the Beatley excerpt indicates, the logistics of preparing an HCP are quite complex. For the larger HCPs, not only are a multitude of federal, state, and governmental agencies involved, the process usually must deal with a variety of different landowners. The Balcones Canyonlands Conservation Plan, which encompasses all of Travis County, Texas (including the City of Austin), provides for five preserve areas ranging in aggregate size from 29,159 acres to a

probable maximum of 35,300 acres. The legal skills required for negotiating such agreements and the technical backup required to properly represent a client are quite different from those needed in the typical local land use dispute.

Despite these complexities, however, a surprising number of HCPs have already been completed. *See* Thomas D. Feldman and Andrew E.G. Jonas, Sage Scrub Revolution? Property Rights, Political Fragmentation, and Conservation Planning in Southern California under the Federal Endangered Species Act, Ann. Ass'n of Am. Geo., 90(2), p. 256 (2000) (discussing the habitat conservation planning process undertaken for the Stephens' kangaroo rat in Southern California). What benefits do developers see in supporting HCPs? What about the attitude of local governments towards them? In the State of Washington, two counties, a school district, two cities, and a port district unsuccessfully challenged the state's adoption of a 70-year habitat conservation plan in which the state agreed to manage 1.63 million acres of state-owned timberland as an ecosystem of watersheds. The local governments contended that the plan was fiscally imprudent because it could reduce the amount of money generated by state trust forest lands by millions of dollars. *See* Washington State's High Court Upholds Habitat Conservation Plan, West's Legal News, Dec. 27, 1996, at 13731, 1996 WL 735711.

Consider also the resistance of state legislatures and local governments, covered in Chapter 9 of this casebook, to statewide or regional planning. Has that resistance been circumvented through the back door of habitat conservation planning as a means of complying with the Endangered Species Act?

3. *"No Surprises."* HCPs usually cover areas that are relatively undeveloped. Will landowners enter into an HCP—which may require them to pay large amounts of money to implement the plan—if the possibility exists that, over the life of the plan (perhaps 30 years), circumstances may change and the federal government may seek additional mitigation or dollar contributions from them? This very real concern led the U.S. Fish and Wildlife Service (USFWS) and the National Marine Fisheries Service (NMFS) to promulgate a "No Surprises" policy. The policy recognizes that HCP provisions will have to deal with "unforeseen circumstances" but limits the government's options in future negotiations over those circumstances. Among other limits, "FWS shall not seek any other form of additional mitigation from an HCP permittee except under extraordinary circumstances." Fish and Wildlife Service, Department of the Interior, Preliminary Draft Handbook for Habitat Conservation Planning and Incidental Take Permit Processing App. 4 (1994). The policy has since been adopted in rulemaking form. *See* 50 C.F.R. §§17.22, 17.32.

Is this policy consistent with the provisions against "taking" of species found in Sections 7 and 9 of the ESA?

4. *Applying Economic Incentives.* A repeated criticism of the existing law of endangered species protection—and one often made of environmental regulation in general—is that it overemphasizes regulatory mandates by the government. Critics argue that the system would work much better if it relied less on this type of "command and control" regulation and more on the use of economic incentives. For example, under the current regulatory system for endangered species, it has been suggested that a landowner who wishes to develop his or her property but discovers an endangered species on it sees only economic disaster in that discovery. Any landowner inclined toward lawbreaking might even be tempted to

destroy the species rather than report it. What is needed, say the critics, is a system with economic incentives built in that will reward landowners for preserving the species rather than penalizing them by preventing development of their property. See David Sohn & Madeline Cohen, From Smokestacks to Species: Extending the Tradeable Permit Approach from Air Pollution to Habitat Conservation, 15 Stan. Envtl. L.J. 405 (1996).

Others have suggested that "mitigation banks," like those used under wetlands law, be created for endangered species. *See* Michael J. Bean and Lynn E. Dwyer, Mitigation Banking as an Endangered Species Conservation Tool, 30 Envtl. L. Rep. 10537 (2000).

D. HAZARDOUS WASTE CLEANUP AND LAND USE

Initially, you may find it hard to see how the cleanup of hazardous waste from contaminated property, pursuant to federal and state hazardous waste cleanup laws, is directly related to land use. Three practical aspects of hazardous waste cleanup will help to illuminate the connection. First, you must consider the economics of cleaning up hazardous waste. As parties have implemented the federal Comprehensive Environmental Response, Compensation, and Liability Act (CERCLA), 42 U.S.C. §§9601–9675 (1994 & Supp. 1996), the high cost of cleaning up sites has become all too clear. Moreover, attaining the last percentage of cleanup, so that a site is left in pristine condition rather than with low, background levels of contaminants remaining on it, increases the costs astronomically. This increment of expense has led to the much debated question of exactly "how clean is clean" under CERCLA.

Second, the practical difficulties of carrying out the cleanup are often substantial. For example, the technology for cleanup is not only expensive, in some instances it may not even exist, particularly if the contamination has spread to the groundwater table. Third, CERCLA operates by spreading liability—for the most part, through the imposition of joint and several liability—among all responsible parties, including the owner of the site. The potential for liability under federal and state law merely because of ownership of a site is enough to discourage many prospective purchasers. As a result, rather than re-use existing, contaminated industrial sites that must be cleaned up—areas known as "brownfields"—companies seek to locate on new, undeveloped areas—"greenfields"—that have no potential liability attached to them.

Thus, hazardous waste cleanup laws indirectly drive future land uses on many properties. Initially, though, you need a feel for the breadth of CERCLA liability. The following case will provide that understanding.

■ TANGLEWOOD EAST HOMEOWNERS v. CHARLES-THOMAS, INC.

849 F.2d 1568 (5th Cir. 1988)

Before POLITZ and JOHNSON, Circuit Judges, and BOYLE, District Judge.

POLITZ, Circuit Judge: . . .

Background

. . . Appellant, First Federal Savings & Loan Association of Conroe, is a lending institution. The other defendants against whom appellees have complained are residential developers, construction companies, and real estate agents and agencies. All participated in the development of the Tanglewood East Subdivision in Montgomery County, Texas. The complainants-appellees are owners of property in that subdivision. The subdivision was built on the site upon which the United Creosoting Company operated a wood-treatment facility from 1946 to 1972. During that quarter century substantial amounts of highly-toxic waste accumulated on the property. In 1973 certain of the defendants acquired the property, filled in and graded the creosote pools, and began residential development.

In 1980, Tanglewood homeowners and residents complained to Texas authorities about toxic problems and all development ceased. In 1983 the Environmental Protection Agency placed the site on its National Priorities List for cleaning under the Comprehensive Environmental Response, Compensation and Liability Act (CERCLA), commonly known as the "Superfund Act," 42 U.S.C. §§9601, *et seq.* The cleanup, expected to cost millions of dollars, will require the demolition of six homes and the construction of bunkers to contain the hazardous materials.

The purchasers of the subdivision lots invoked CERCLA . . . and sought damages, response and cleaning costs, and injunctive relief. . . .

Analysis

A. CERCLA . . .

Under 42 U.S.C. §9607(a) (1988), CERCLA provides a private cause of action where a release or threatened release of a hazardous substance causes response costs to be incurred. The persons covered are:

> (1) the owner and operator of . . . a facility,
> (2) any person who at the time of disposal of any hazardous substance owned or operated any facility at which such hazardous substances were disposed of,
> (3) any person who by contract, agreement, or otherwise arranged for disposal or treatment, or arranged with a transporter for transport for disposal or treatment, of hazardous substances owned or possessed by such person . . . , and
> (4) any person who accepts or accepted any hazardous substances for transport to disposal or treatment facilities. . . .

1. Present Owners

Appellant maintains that under §9607(a)(1), the only owner and operator who discharged hazardous materials was the United Creosoting Company, who abandoned the site in 1972. We find nothing in the wording of §9607(a) to exclude present owners of properties previously contaminated . . . . Section 9607(a)(2) expressly applies to past owners and operators who contaminate their surroundings; it is therefore manifest that §9607(a)(1) applies to current owners of adulterated sites. . . .

"Facility" is defined in §9601(9) to include

> (A) any building, structure, installation, equipment, pipe or pipeline (including any pipe into a sewer or publicly owned treatment works), well, pit, pond, lagoon impoundment, ditch, landfill, storage container, motor vehicle, rolling stock, or aircraft, or (B) *any site or area where a hazardous substance has been deposited, stored, disposed of, or placed, or otherwise come to be located*; but does not include any consumer product in consumer use or any vessel. (Emphasis added.)

The statute leaves no room for doubt; the Tanglewood East development is a covered facility. . . .

2. Past Owners

Section 9607(a)(2) applies to persons who owned or operated a facility at the time of the disposal of the toxins. Appellant contends that the only person who qualifies under that section is United Creosoting Company. We do not so read the statute. Referring to 42 U.S.C. §6903(3), we find "disposal" defined to include

> the discharge, deposit, injection, dumping spilling, leaking, or placing of any solid waste or hazardous waste into or on any land or water so that such solid waste or hazardous waste or any constituent thereof may enter the environment or be emitted into the air or discharged into any waters, including ground waters.

We recognize merit in appellees' argument that this definition of disposal does not limit disposal to a one-time occurrence — there may be other disposals when hazardous materials are moved, dispersed, or released during landfill excavations and fillings.

3. Post Arrangers and Transporters

Appellant next argues that defendants neither arranged for nor transported any hazardous material for disposal or treatment under §9607(a)(3) and (4). This argument rests on the narrow interpretation of disposal, which we reject, and a like interpretation of "treatment" which is defined by §6903(34) as

> any method, technique, or process, including neutralization, designed to change the physical, chemical, or biological character or composition of any hazardous waste so as to neutralize such waste or so as to render such waste nonhazardous, safer for transport, amenable for recovery, amenable for storage, or reduced in volume. *Such term includes any activity* or processing *designed to change the physical form* or chemical composition *of hazardous waste* so as to render it nonhazardous. (Emphasis added.)

Appellees argue that the activity of filling and grading the creosote pools constituted treatment to render the waste non-hazardous, and that those involved in that activity are covered persons under §9607(a)(3). Furthermore, since disposal may be merely the "placing of any . . . hazardous waste into or on any land. . . " §6903(3), those who move the waste about the site may fall within the terms of the provision. Under these readings of the terms "disposal" and "treatment," relevant evidence under the complaint may establish that some of the defendants were arrangers for, or transporters of, the toxic materials. . . .

In light of the foregoing, we are satisfied that the complaint may not be dismissed for failure to state a claim upon which relief under CERCLA may be granted. . . .

C. REMEDIES UNDER CERCLA

Section 9607(a)(4) provides that covered persons shall be liable for

> (A) all costs of removal or remedial action incurred by the United States Government or a State or an Indian Tribe not inconsistent with the national contingency plan;
>
> (B) any other necessary costs of response incurred by any other person consistent with the national contingency plan. . . .

. . . Appellees have alleged that their costs are consistent with the national contingency plan. It remains for them to prove such. The issue of consistency cannot be resolved on the pleadings alone, but must await development of relevant evidence. . . .

The judgment of the district court is AFFIRMED.

Notes and Comments

1. *The Range of CERCLA Defendants*. The *Tanglewood* litigation may have introduced you to a whole new legal world that has generated a deluge of litigation: liability under the Comprehensive Environmental Response, Compensation, and Liability Act, otherwise known as "CERCLA." The reach of CERCLA and its state counterparts (almost every state has some version of a mini-CERCLA) is substantial. Consider carefully how this statute, which is intended to impose liability for cleanup costs (and, in some instances, to require parties to clean up sites) applies in the *Tanglewood* factual context.

It is relatively easy to see why the subdivision site in *Tangelwood* is a "facility," although this location is not the type of operation that you might ordinarily associate with the word "facility." Which of the four liability categories would apply to the developer of the property? It certainly did not send waste for disposal on the property; it was simply trying to build homes. What about the operator of the bulldozer: would that person be liable? Note also that, while the homeowners are plaintiffs in this case, they would also be liable for cleanup costs. For a further example of CERCLA liability, *see North Carolina v. W. R. Peele, Sr., Trust*, 876 F. Supp. 733 (E.D.N.C. 1995), in which a party that held ownership of property for only 13 days as a conduit in a sale was subject to "owner" liability under CERCLA.

The *Tanglewood* case is an example of private litigation brought under §107 of CERCLA seeking recovery of cleanup costs. Under CERCLA, the federal Environmental Protection Agency can take action, and the agency has a number of arrows in its enforcement quiver. It can use money from the so-called Superfund to clean up property and then file suit against various responsible parties under §107 of CERCLA seeking reimbursement of its expenditures. It may also issue a §106 administrative order to parties requiring them to clean up, with violation of the order subject to a penalty equal to three times the cleanup costs, or it can seek injunctive relief in federal court.

2. *The Range of CERCLA Liability*. Once you see the range of possible defendants in a CERCLA case, you must consider the scope of liability. Cleaning up hazardous waste sites is a costly business, and the costs skyrocket if the waste has migrated into the groundwater below a site.

What is each defendant liable for? In tort terminology, joint and several liability applies unless the harm is found divisible. *See O'Neil v. Picillo*, 883 F.2d 176 (1st Cir. 1989), *cert. denied*, 493 U.S. 1071 (1990) (small party defendants are jointly and severally liable); *In re Bell Petroleum Services, Inc.*, 3 F.3d 889 (5th Cir. 1993) (joint and several liability improper if defendant meets burden of proving that a reasonable basis for apportioning environmental liability exists). Is the standard strict liability, or must fault be proven? *See Environmental Transp. Systems, Inc. v. Ensco, Inc.*, 763 F. Supp. 384 (C.D. Ill. 1991), *aff'd*, 969 F.2d 503 (7th Cir. 1992) (contractor held strictly liable for release of PCBs resulting from an accident involving the subcontractor's truck).

Finally, you should also know that the number of sites subject to CERCLA liability has turned out to be much larger than was originally thought. Under CERCLA, the federal government may only clean up sites listed on the National Priorities List. Cleanup costs for those sites have averaged $30 million per site. Even if a site is not listed on the NPL, however, the possibility exists that EPA might list the site at some time in the future. Equally important, because CERCLA provides private causes of action, as illustrated by the *Tanglewood* case, even less-contaminated sites are subject to CERCLA. As of 1995, the agency had listed almost 40,000 sites on its Comprehensive Environmental Response, Compensation and Liability Act Information System (CERCLIS), although it later reduced that number.

This is just a short sketch of what is a very complex law. For more information, see Susan Cooke, The Law of Hazardous Waste Management: Cleanup, Liability and Litigation (1995); Donald L. Stever, The Law of Chemical Regulation and Hazardous Waste (1986).

3. *State Property Transfer Laws and Superliens*. CERCLA is a liability statute that does not directly affect property transfers; instead, it principally imposes liability for cleanup costs. Some states take a different approach to solving hazardous waste contamination problems, focusing on property transfers. They have enacted legislation requiring that sellers provide notice of property contamination prior to the transfer. The notice required can vary; some statutes require notice to state authorities or potential purchasers, while others mandate notice in the deed or other transfer instrument. On disclosure statutes generally, see Sarah L. Inderbitzin, Taking the Burden Off the Buyer: A Survey of Hazardous Waste Disclosure Statutes, 1 Envtl. Law. 513 (1995).

The most far-reaching state legislation is New Jersey's Industrial Site Recovery Act ("ISRA," formerly known as the Environmental Cleanup Responsibility Act, or "ECRA"), N.J. Stat. Ann. §13:1K-6 to -14 (2003). ISRA applies when an industrial establishment either closes or transfers ownership or operations, requiring the seller to notify the State of its intentions. Before the sale can occur, the transferor must take steps to ensure that hazardous wastes at the site have been cleaned up or the State has approved a cleanup plan. *See Federal Pacific Electric Co. v. New Jersey Dept. of Envtl. Protection*, 334 N.J. Super. 323 (A.D. 2000) (overturning remedial action workplan designed to comply with ISRA); *Public Interest Research Group of New Jersey v. New Jersey Department of Environmental Protection*, 608 A.2d

288 (N.J. 1992) (department has authority to require cleanup plan under the Act to remediate contamination that is off the property but which has emanated from it). Most significantly, a buyer may void the sale if the seller fails to comply with ISRA's requirements.

When states use money in state "superfunds" to clean up sites, they have a strong interest in obtaining reimbursement for the state fund. A number of states have sought to enhance the chances of recovery by enacting so-called superlien statutes. These are liens that have the highest priority; they take precedence over earlier liens and encumbrances on the property held by mortgagees, title insurers, and the like. *See, e.g.*, N.H. Rev. Stat §147-B:10-b(III)(a)-(b) (Supp. 2003); Conn. Gen. Stat. Ann. §22a-452a(a) (West 1995 & Supp. 2003).

4. *Risk-Based Cleanup*. An important component of the cleanup is defining the cleanup levels required. Many of the state programs require "risk-based" cleanup; in other words, they attempt to define cleanup standards by evaluating the actual risks to human health posed by the site. At the same time, some of these programs emphasize that the intended use of the property must be considered in determining the cleanup level required. If a site will be reused for industry, it does not require cleanup to a level that would be required for, say, a proposed residential use.

These types of cleanup standards would allow for the use of engineering controls, measures designed to contain contamination on the site rather than to remediate it, such as putting a "cap" over contaminated soil. They would also utilize institutional or "managerial" controls on sites such as warning signs and fences, notice requirements in deeds, leases, or property transfer documents, as well as land use controls.

A Note on "Brownfields"

1. *Brownfields and Greenfields*. Hazardous waste laws have particularly important effects on the ability of urban areas to redevelop and re-use industrial sites that are presently abandoned. If a party desires to purchase a piece of property that is contaminated with hazardous wastes, that party risks becoming subject to CERCLA liability. Many of the properties that are contaminated were previously used for industrial purposes and are located in urban areas. The infrastructure for their reuse for business or commercial purposes is already in place, and their locations are often attractive from a transportation standpoint. Nonetheless, if you were contemplating buying or leasing such property, how attractive would it have to be before you would act, given your knowledge of the potential liability under CERCLA?

If you concluded that most business people will shy away from owning or otherwise dealing with land subject to CERCLA liability, your conclusion is the same as that of many business persons who have been properly advised by their counsel about the potential liability under CERCLA. See Resources for the Future, The Impact of Uncertain Environmental Liability on Industrial Real Estate Development: Developing a Framework for Analysis 30 (1994) ("There is a widespread belief that environmental liabilities arising under CERCLA and related law distort the real estate market."). The problem is not just the expensive liability attached to cleaning up hazardous waste (including the possibility that the buyer may underestimate the dollars required); it also includes the delays in getting federal and state agencies to approve the method of cleanup.

Thus, many businesses have avoided what have become known as "brownfields." The term generally refers to abandoned, inactive, or underutilized industrial sites located primarily in urban areas. (Wags have suggested the acronym should be "TOADS" for "temporarily obsolete abandoned derelict sites.") Instead of utilizing brownfields, companies have opened new businesses in "greenfields," areas which are located on the outskirts of a built-up area and which have not been previously used for urban or industrial activities.

The land use implications of these decisions are significant. The existence of brownfields makes redevelopment of urban areas that much more difficult. Cities receive less property tax revenue from brownfields sites, and inner-city neighborhoods fail to benefit from the jobs that location of industry on these sites might provide. As blighted industrial or commercial areas remain vacant, the cycle of deterioration in those areas continues. At the same time, as businesses exhibit a preference for locating in "greenfields," which are suburban areas, they create impacts on the transportation system as well as secondary environmental impacts such as increased air pollution. Finally, the use of greenfields exacerbates urban sprawl.

2. *Solving the Brownfields Dilemma*. As CERCLA's inability to ensure expeditious site cleanup became more and more obvious, individuals began to realize that the key to cleanups was to encourage voluntary actions on the part of site owners. EPA has joined in this effort to encourage voluntary cleanups through its "Brownfields Economic Redevelopment Initiative," as well as other steps it has taken. For example, it removed thousands of sites from its site cleanup list, thus indicating that the federal government has little or no interest in compelling cleanup of those sites.

The principal thrust of this movement, however, has come from states, particularly those located in the northeast and midwest, which have enacted legislation to promote voluntary cleanups and implemented policies designed to promote this goal. *See, e.g.*, the Alabama Land Recycling and Economic Redevelopment Act, Ala. Code 1975 §22-30-E-1; and the Pennsylvania Land Recycling and Environmental Remediation Standards Act, 35 Pa. Stat. §6026.101-908 (Supp. 1998). For a summary of the state efforts, *see* Charles Bartsch et al., Northeast-Midwest Institute, Brownfields "State of the States": An End-of-Session Review of Initiatives and Program Impacts in the 50 States (2001), available at http://www.nemw.org/brown_stateof.pdf.

Seventeen states have entered into a "Memorandum of Agreement" (MOA) with EPA regarding how EPA will treat sites remediated under a state's voluntary treatment program. *See, e.g.*, Delaware Dep't of Nat. Resources & Envtl. Control, Superfund Memorandum of Agreement Between the Delaware Department of Natural Resources & Environmental Control and the United States Environmental Protection Agency Region III Concerning Delaware's Voluntary Cleanup Program, http://www.dnrec.state.de.us/dnrec2000/Divisions/AWM/sirb/docs/fivcpmoa.doc (under the MOA, a site remediated according to the voluntary cleanup program will then be "of no federal interest" under CERCLA, and the EPA will take no further action unless there is an imminent and substantial endangerment to public health, welfare, or the environment that is not being adequately addressed under the State program).

A key component of this effort is changes in the level of cleanup required. Under CERCLA, that level cannot be predicted in advance; CERCLA requires a detailed inquiry to be undertaken for each site. See William H. Rodgers, Jr., Environmental Law §8.5, at 727 (2d ed. 1994). And even when cleanup to pre-contamination levels is required, this decision has brought about a loud debate on the issue "how clean is clean?" The voluntary cleanup programs emphasize the need for more certainty in establishing cleanup standards, so that lenders and investors can determine in advance whether a brownfields development "pencils out." Other important components of the effort include (1) providing certainty that, once a state has "signed off" on a brownfields cleanup, the federal or state governments will not later decide to bring an action against the new landowner; (2) establishing a fast-track process for rapid government approval of cleanups; (3) providing financial incentives to spur interest in brownfields redevelopment; and (4) reducing the possibility that lenders may be held liable for lending on contaminated property.

3. *The Small Business Liability Relief and Brownfields Revitalization Act.* This law was passed by Congress and signed into law in January 2002. Pub. L. No. 107-118, 115 Stat. 2355 (2002) (codified as amended in scattered sections of 42 U.S.C. §§9601-9628). The new law breaks down into two parts. First, it clarifies that bona fide prospective purchasers are exempt from CERCLA liability, even if they have knowledge of contamination, if they meet certain requirements. The Act contains provisions for settlements for low volume or low toxicity waste contributors to CERCLA sites. The law also provides for conditional expedited settlements with persons who can demonstrate an inability or limited ability to pay response costs. The second part of the Act (Title II, called "Brownfields Revitalization and Environmental Restoration") includes various funding mechanisms for brownfields revitalization.

EPA maintains a website devoted to brownfields. *See* http://www.epa.gov/brownfields.

The literature on the brownfields issue is voluminous. Major sources include Michael B. Gerrard, ed., Brownfields Law and Practice: The Cleanup and Redevelopment of Contaminated Land (1999); Brownfields: A Comprehensive Guide to Redeveloping Contaminated Property (Todd S. Davis and Kevin D. Margolis eds. 1997); and Robert H. Abrams, Superfund and the Evolution of Brownfields.

As you can see from the discussion of CERCLA above, a critical question is the extent of the cleanup that will be required for any property in question. The following excerpt sets forth EPA's position on how CERCLA remedies and land use interact.

UNITED STATES ENVIRONMENTAL PROTECTION AGENCY, LAND USE IN THE CERCLA REMEDY SELECTION PROCESS

OSWER Directive No. 9355.7-04, May 25, 1995

Background

Reasonably anticipated future use of the land at NPL sites is an important consideration in determining the appropriate extent of remediation. Future use of the land will affect the types of exposures and the frequency of exposures that may occur to any residual contamination remaining on the site, which in turn affects the nature of the remedy chosen. . . .

Developing Assumptions About Future Land Use

In order to ensure use of realistic assumptions regarding future land uses at a site, EPA should discuss reasonably anticipated future uses of the site with local land use planning authorities, local officials, and the public, as appropriate, as early as possible during the scoping phase of the RI/FS. EPA should gain an understanding of the reasonably anticipated future land uses at a particular Superfund site to perform the risk assessment and select the appropriate remedy.

A visual inspection of the site and its surrounding area is a good starting point in developing assumptions regarding future land use. Discussions with the local land use authorities and appropriate officials should follow. Discussions with the public can be accomplished through a public meeting and/or other means. By developing realistic assumptions based on information gathered from these sources early in the RI/FS process, EPA may develop remedial alternatives that are consistent with the anticipated future use.

The development of assumptions regarding the reasonably anticipated future land use should not become an extensive, independent research project. Site managers should use existing information to the extent possible, much of which will be available from local land use planning authorities. . . .

Land Use Considerations in Remedy Selection

As a result of the comparative analysis of alternatives with respect to EPA's nine evaluation criteria, EPA selects a site-specific remedy. The remedy determines the cleanup levels, the volume of contaminated material to be treated, and the volume of contaminated material to be contained. Consequently, the remedy selection decision determines the size of the area that can be returned to productive use and the particular types of uses that will be possible following remediation.

The volume and concentration of contaminants left on-site, and thus the degree of residual risk at a site, will affect future land use. For example, a remedial alternative may include leaving in place contaminants in soil at concentrations protective for industrial exposures, but not protective for residential exposures. In this case, institutional controls should be used to ensure that industrial use of the land is maintained and to prevent risks from residential exposures. Conversely, a remedial alternative may result in no waste left in place and allow for unrestricted use (e.g., residential use). . . .

Institutional Controls

If any remedial alternative developed during the FS will require a restricted land use in order to be protective, it is essential that the alternative include components that will ensure that it remain protective. In particular, institutional controls will generally have to be included in the alternative to prevent an unanticipated change in land use that could result in unacceptable exposures to residual contamination, or, at a minimum, alert future users to the residual risks and monitor for any changes in use. . . .

Notes and Comments

1. *The CERCLA Presumption and Future Land Use*. The underlying issue in determining the level of cleanup is whether the cost and bureaucratic difficulty of cleaning a site up to background levels is preferable to flexibility in cleanup that may result in a lesser cleanup coupled with land use restrictions. To date, Congress has inclined toward the former. The state voluntary cleanup statutes, in contrast, are much more flexible on cleanup levels. As one author put it, the state statutes "envision voluntary cleanups that trade increased health risks to the affected community for the prospect of new jobs and higher tax revenues." Joel B. Eisen, "Brownfields of Dreams"? Challenges and Limits of Voluntary Cleanup Programs and Incentives, 96 U. Ill. L. Rev. 883, 887 (1996). Another author put the policy issue as follows: "[S]hould institutional controls be used only as a last resort when cleanup is impossible, or should they be used more broadly to maximize reuse of contaminated property?" Susan C. Borinsky, The Use of Institutional Controls in Superfund and Similar Laws, 7 Fordham Envtl. L.J. 1 (1995). What do you think?

2. *Deciding on Future Uses*. A number of the state voluntary cleanup programs provide that the cleanup of a site must be based on the health risk that will be posed by the reasonably anticipated future use of a site. Some of these require land use to be considered explicitly; in others, it is an implicit consideration. *See, e.g.*, Mich. Comp. Laws Ann. §324.20120a(16) (2001) (a cleanup must be for residential use or provide for land use controls).

Do you see how the future land use planned for the contaminated property affects the determination of the residual risk that would remain after various types of cleanups at the site have been completed? How should this future land use be decided? Is it simply a matter for the local government, or do the state and federal governments also play a role? How does the EPA memo on the CERCLA Remedy Selection Process indicate that the agency will determine what the "reasonably anticipated future use" at a particular Superfund site will be?

3. *Implementing the Land Use Restriction*. Assuming you decide that more limited cleanup is appropriate in some instances, what kinds of land use controls should be instituted to ensure that the public health is protected? Relying solely on local land use regulations, such as zoning, is impractical for a number of reasons, including the fact that such restrictions are subject to change. How can the state or federal government ensure that the local government will actually implement the restriction?

The obvious solution is a deed restriction, such as a covenant or easement that runs with the land, or some other similar property instrument. How should the law ensure that these restrictions are implemented?

4. *But Will It Work?* The various states have unquestionably put significant bureaucratic efforts into redeveloping brownfields. A recent article, however, suggests that these efforts miss the broader picture. Heidi Gorovitz Robertson, One Piece of the Puzzle: Why State Brownfields Programs Can't Lure Businesses to the Urban Cores Without Finding the Missing Pieces, 51 Rutgers L. Rev. 1075 (1999).

One problem is that lenders "feel squeamish" about the possibility of becoming liable if they undertake brownfields funding. *Id.* at 1088. Another large problem is that non-environmental factors, such as building size and configuration, construction costs, access to interstate highways, and the ability to attract a suitable workforce, "appear as important to companies making relocation decisions as the environmental status of prospective sites." *Id.* at 1121. In other words, while governments are focused on brownfields issues, businesses may have larger concerns.

E. PROTECTION OF AGRICULTURE AND OPEN SPACE

The next subject addressed in this chapter is the preservation of agriculture and open space. The principal case included below demonstrates how a traditional land use tool is used to protect agriculture and preserve open space.

■ IN RE RATTEE
761 A.2d 1076 (N.H. 2000)

BROCK, C.J.

This is a consolidated appeal from decisions of the New Hampshire Agricultural Lands Preservation Committee (ALPC) and the Superior Court (*Brennan,* J.) denying the request of Steven Rattee to construct a home on land subject to an agricultural preservation restriction (APR). We affirm in part and vacate in part.

. . . In May 1996, Rattee purchased at a foreclosure sale 185 acres of land on the east and west sides of Mountain Road in Concord for $216,000 and approximately $28,000 in back taxes. The deed granted to him stated that the land was subject to the terms of an APR and stated where the APR was recorded in the Merrimack County Registry of Deeds. In 1982, Rattee's predecessor in title, Horace Blood, had granted by deed the APR on approximately 103 acres of the property to the State of New Hampshire (grantee), acting through the ALPC and the commissioner of the department of agriculture (commissioner). The State paid approximately $406,000 to acquire the APR.

The APR states, in pertinent part:

> The Grantor, his heirs, . . . successors and assigns, . . . covenant and agree that they are restrained from constructing on, . . . or otherwise improving the Site for uses that result in rendering the Site no longer suitable for agricultural use. . . . Such restraint . . . shall include prohibition of:
>
> 1. Construction or placement of building or structures except those to be used for agricultural purposes or for dwellings to be used for family living by the landowner, his immediate family or employees. Construction or placement of (a) dwellings to be used for family living . . . shall be subject to the prior approval of the Grantee. Approval for such construction or placement shall be granted only when it will not defeat or derogate from the intent of this restriction. Any building or structure and the land upon which it is situated shall not be sold or otherwise severed from the

Site unless the Grantee releases such dwelling, permanent structure or land from the restriction pursuant to RSA 36-D:7 (Supp.) . . .

The foregoing restriction is intended to conform to and have the benefit of RSA 36-D (Supp.) and RSA 477:45-47 (Supp.).

In 1987, the prior owners constructed on land subject to the APR a small house that remains. Also included in the 185 acres purchased by the petitioner is an adjacent 3.3 acre "farmstead site," which is exempt from the APR and upon which stood a house. According to Rattee, in 1996 he arranged for that house to be burned down as a fire department exercise because it was in very poor condition.

In the fall of 1996, Rattee excavated a field on land subject to the APR to construct a new 5500 square foot home and a 1500 foot driveway that would destroy two acres. He applied for a building permit from the City of Concord, but did not seek building or placement approval from the ALPC. Shortly thereafter, the State advised Rattee that he was in violation of the APR. Rattee asserted that the APR did not apply because the house was going to be his home, and thus was subject to an exception for "dwellings used for family living by the landowner." RSA 36-D:1, II (current version at RSA 432:18, II). . . .

On appeal, Rattee argues that: (1) the State, acting through the ALPC, lacked authority to acquire the right to require prior approval for the construction of owner residences on APR sites; (2) the APR did not effectively convey to the State the right to determine the location of owner residences on the site; (3) the ALPC acted unreasonably in disapproving Rattee's application; and (4) the ALPC and the trial court improperly ruled that sections of the APR site on either side of Mountain Road cannot be sold separately without the ALPC's approval.

With respect to the first argument, we do not agree that the State lacked authority to purchase or acquire more rights than are contained in the statutory definition of an APR, specifically the right to regulate construction of owner residences on APR sites. The provision requiring prior approval for construction or placement of owner residences was part of a voluntary conveyance of property rights to the State. Even if we assume that the prior approval provision exceeds the authority given to the State by RSA chapter 36-D, no rule of law bars the State from purchasing such a right.

We also reject the argument that the APR did not convey to the State the right to determine the location of owner housing on the site. Rattee contends that the statement in the APR that it "is intended to conform to and have the benefit of RSA 36-D" restricts the rights conveyed to those enumerated in RSA chapter 36-D. Therefore, while the APR language requiring prior approval may be clear, Rattee argues that it is rendered ambiguous by the statement that the APR is intended to conform to RSA chapter 36-D, which does not have a prior approval provision. The State counters that the prior approval provision is a "necessary, appropriate and reasonable means for accomplishing the public policy objective of preserving good quality agricultural land for future agricultural production." . . .

The stated purpose of RSA chapter 36-D is to "recognize the importance of preserving the limited land suitable for agricultural production, to safeguard the public health and welfare by encouraging the maximum use of food and fiber producing capabilities of the state's agriculturally suitable land and to ensure the protection of agricultural land facing conversion to non-agricultural uses." Laws

1979, 301:1. Thus, while the APR statute and deed both reserve the right to construct "dwellings to be used for family living," requiring prior approval for such construction is consistent with the statutory purpose. Prior approval ensures that family dwellings will be constructed in a manner that minimizes their impact on agricultural production and prevents potential abuse of the family dwelling exception. Therefore, we conclude that the prior approval provision in the APR conforms to, and indeed strengthens, RSA chapter 36-D. *Cf. Bennett,* 576 N.E.2d at 1368 (APR prior approval provision enforceable, even if the condition of approval did not fall within the statutory definition of APR, because it was consistent with the public policy expressed in the Massachusetts APR statute).

We disagree with Rattee that this conclusion is unreasonable due to the statutory language preserving for the landowner all customary rights of ownership, including the right to carry out all regular agricultural practices not prohibited by the statutory definition of an APR. *See* RSA 36-D:7 (current version at RSA 432:24, 1). We interpret this language in accordance with the statutory purpose of RSA chapter 36-D. While the statute may reserve certain rights for the landowner, it is reasonable for the APR to include a prior approval provision to ensure that the exercise of the family dwelling exception does not defeat the statutory purpose of "preserving the limited land suitable for agricultural production." Laws 1979, 301:1. For the same reason, we disagree that the statement that the APR "is intended to conform to and have the benefit of RSA 36-D" restricts the rights conveyed in the APR to those enumerated in RSA chapter 36-D.

Because we conclude that the prior approval provision conforms to RSA chapter 36-D, we reject the argument that the APR is ambiguous. Accordingly, we interpret the intended meaning of the prior approval provision from the language of the deed and need not consider extrinsic evidence. . . .

Rattee next argues that the ALPC's conclusion that "construction of a house would damage agricultural use of the land was unsupported by any evidence." We disagree. Because both the statute and the deed carve out of their prohibitions on construction an exception for "dwellings used for family living by the landowner," RSA 36-D:1, II, we agree with Rattee that the existence of the small house does not preclude him from constructing another residence. The APR provides, however, that the ALPC shall grant approval for construction "only when it will not defeat or derogate from the intent of [the] restriction." The statutory purpose of an APR is "to recognize the importance of preserving the limited land suitable for agricultural production . . . and to ensure the protection of agricultural land facing conversion to non-agricultural uses." Laws 1979, 301:1. In his application to the ALPC, Rattee proposed constructing a 5500 square foot home. The proposed home and accompanying 1500 foot driveway would remove two acres of productive soil from cultivation. Given the availability of the adjacent 3.3 acre farmstead site that is exempt from the APR, we agree with the ALPC that the proposed construction "is far from the least disruptive alternative available to . . . [Rattee]." Thus, we conclude that sufficient evidence in the record supports the ALPC's decision to deny this particular application, and that the decision is reasonable in light of the standard for approval stated in the APR. *See Petition of Hoyt,* 143 N.H. at 534, 727 A.2d at 1002. We also note that the ALPC's decision was "without prejudice . . . to [Rattee's] submission of a subsequent application containing a construction proposal which is consistent with the purpose of the [APR]."

Rattee next argues that the ALPC's decision was unreasonable because the ALPC improperly and without statutory authority considered several factors not relevant to its decision, including how much time the petitioner would devote to farming. Even if we assume that the ALPC improperly considered these factors, any error was harmless because Rattee did not meet his burden of showing that the alleged error resulted in material prejudice. . . .

We need not decide the fourth issue on appeal. Rattee argues that the ALPC and the trial court improperly ruled that sections of the APR site on either side of Mountain Road cannot be subdivided or sold separately without the ALPC's approval. In his brief, Rattee states that "the question of separate sale or subdivision of [his] land is not directly material to the central question in this case." He also notes that at trial the State argued that the issue was not before the trial court. Rattee argued to the trial court that the separate sale issue was significant because if he could sell the land on the west side of Mountain Road, which includes the existing small house, then the ALPC could not tell him that he could use that house instead of constructing a new one on the east side of Mountain Road. We interpret these statements to mean that the separate sale issue was relevant only if the existing house precludes the construction of an additional house. Because we conclude that it does not, the separate sale issue was not relevant and need not have been reached by the ALPC or the trial court. Accordingly, we vacate the decisions of the ALPC and the trial court to the extent they concluded that the land covered by the APR cannot be sold separately, subdivided, or otherwise severed without obtaining a release.

Affirmed in part; vacated in part.

Notes and Comments

1. *The* Rattee *Holding*. How can the state purchase "more rights" than is contained on the statutory definition of an agricultural preservation restriction? Isn't the state restricted to its statutory authority, even if the conveyance is "voluntary"? Even if this were true, however, would Rattee have standing to raise this issue?

Why wasn't Rattee's proposed house consistent with the purpose of the statute? After all, it would only use two of the 185 acres. Can't a farmer live in style? If the plan was not consistent, what are the parameters of the Commission's ability to reject the landowner's plans?

2. *The Need for Open Space and Agricultural Preservation*. In the early 1970s, a consistent theme in the land use literature was the need to preserve "open space" against rapidly encroaching urbanization. In the years that followed, preservation of open space through traditional means such as low-density zoning became commonplace. In addition, cities and counties used their power to mandate exactions as conditions of development approval as a means of acquiring certain lands for parks and other types of open space.

Somewhat later, others argued that agricultural land was being rapidly converted to urban uses and that government must take action to preserve agricultural land. A 1997 report by the American Farmland Trust, entitled Farming on the Edge, concluded that 79 percent of the nation's fruit crop, 69 percent of its vegetables, and 52 percent of its dairy products are produced on land vulnerable to development.

The need for preserving agricultural land, however, is not universally accepted. The National Association of Home Builders responded to the American Farmland Trust report by asserting that "the conversion of some agricultural land into developable land is simply a fact of life, given the nation's growing population." Economists in particular dispute the notion that any "crisis" exists. They argue that increases in per-acre agricultural productivity are such that no loss of agricultural production has occurred as prime agricultural land has been urbanized. See, e.g., William A. Fischel, The Urbanization of Agricultural Land: A Review of the National Agricultural Lands Study, 58 Land Econ. 236 (1982).

Nonetheless, many states have determined to take action to preserve farmland, using a variety of legal mechanisms described below. Federal legislation, such as the Farmland Protection Policy Act of 1981, 7 U.S.C. §4201 (1994), has promoted this goal by requiring federal agencies to examine the adverse effects of taking actions that would result in the conversion of farmland and to consider alternatives to such actions. This legislative effort was supported by other nonfarm interests, principally environmentalists, who saw any increases in agricultural preservation as gains both in their battles to prevent leapfrog urbanization of land outside the urban core and to preserve additional open space. While the rationales for open space preservation and agricultural protection are not necessarily the same, the efforts to preserve agriculture and open space have much in common, particularly since agriculture can be seen as a type of open space use. See, e.g., Report of the Subcommittee on Innovative Growth Management Measures: Preservation of Agricultural Land and Open Space, 23 Urb. Law. 821 (1991) ("Agricultural land is the open space in some areas of the country."). *Compare* Jim Chen, Get Green Or Get Out: Decoupling Environmental From Economic Objectives in Agricultural Regulation, 48 Okla. L. Rev. 333 (1995) (criticizing the supposed link between environmental protection and agricultural preservation).

Are there any reasons for preserving agriculture other than to ensure the production of food? For example, one recurring theme in the literature of American democracy is the famous Jeffersonian ideal of the family farm. Should land use regulation be mobilized toward the goal of preserving the family farm?

3. *Methods of Preservation.* Consider broadly how legal techniques might be used to promote the goal of preserving agricultural or open space uses. Is the coercion of zoning and other land use controls a necessary means, or even the most effective means, of preserving agricultural land or retaining land in open space? How might private law techniques for restricting uses of property be utilized to attain the desired goals? What about using tax incentives to encourage landowners to retain property in agricultural uses, rather than mandating certain land uses?

In fact, all of the following techniques have been used, sometimes in combination, by both public and private entities:

a. *Open Space Zoning.* Perhaps the most effective method of preservation is to employ the standard zoning ordinance as a means to preserve agricultural land or other types of open space. A city might enact low-density or large-lot zoning techniques. It is also possible to adopt a zoning ordinance that makes agricultural use the exclusive use in an area *See* John C. Becker, Promoting Agricultural Development Through Land Use Planning Limits, 36 Real Prop. & Tr. J. 619 (2002).

Landowners subject to such rezonings may resist them as arbitrary and capricious. *See, e.g., Johnson v. Town of Edgartown*, 680 N.E.2d 37 (Mass. 1997) (upholding three-acre minimum requirement for residential lots in a residential-agricultural zoning district); *Urrutia v. Blaine County*, 2 P.3d 738 (Idaho 2000) (Board erred in relying solely on comprehensive plan to deny a subdivision, even though the plan contained policies to preserve agriculture and zoning permitted subdivisions).

b. *Conservation Easements.* Landowners can use property law to voluntarily restrict other types of uses on their property, thus ensuring that agricultural use of the property will continue. A technique whose use has steadily increased over the last 20 years is the so-called conservation easement. A 1995 study estimated that local organizations own conservation easements covering over 740,000 acres; one national organization alone estimated that it holds conservation easements over 628,000 acres. Land Trust Alliance, 1994 National Land Trust Study Summary 3 (May 1995); The Nature Conservancy, Acres Saved: TNC Land Protection Statistics (1996).

Landowners are often willing to donate conservation easements on their properties because there are tax advantages in doing so. Under the Internal Revenue Code, a contribution of a "qualified real property interest to a qualified organization exclusively for conservation purposes" is deductible. 26 C.F.R. §1.170A-14(a) (2003). A conservation easement that permanently restricts the land is a "qualified real property interest." *Id.* §1.170A-14(b)(2). If you were representing a group that agrees to take title to a conservation easement, what legal problems might you foresee that the group should consider before it actually receives title? For example, how might you ensure that the group's rights would be enforceable in the event of a dispute in the future? And what about possible tort liability, since your client will now be an owner of a property interest?

In *Johnston v. Sonoma County Agricultural Preservation and Open Space Dist.*, 100 Cal. App. 4th 973 (2000), the district approved the transfer of a utility easement on land subject to a perpetual open space conservation easement. Plaintiffs argued that, under state law, the district could not voluntarily transfer the utility easement. The court, however, disagreed, finding that a transfer could be made because the city had threatened to file a condemnation action.

On conservation easements generally, *see* Peter M. Morrisette, Conservation Easements and the Public Good: Preserving the Environment on Private Lands, 41 Nat. Resources J. 373 (2001); Karen M. White, Note, "Extra" Tax Benefits for Conservation Easements: A Response to Urban Sprawl, 18 Va. Envtl. L. J. 103 (1999).

c. *Agricultural Preservation Easements.* The "agricultural preservation easement" at issue in *Rattee* is a variation on this theme. Instead of situating ownership of the easement in a private party, the state purchases the easement. The easement restricts future land uses on the property, or gives the state the right of approval over those uses. This restriction often leads to interpretive difficulties. In *Twomey v. Commissioner of Food & Agriculture*, 759 N.E.2d 691 (Mass. 2001), the state purchased an "agricultural preservation restriction" from a farm owner. As the court noted, this was a conservation servitude, or easement in gross, that gave the Commisioner authority over future building on the property. The court, however, held that the easement's provisions were inconsistent with the Commissioner's adoption of an "irrebutable presumption" that approval of any dwelling on the farm would defeat the purpose of farmland preservation.

While the court overturned the Commissioner's actions, his reasoning was interesting. The Commissioner was concerned about urbanization of "once rural areas." He reasoned that any new building would make the property unaffordable for farmers to acquire, thus defeating the purpose of the Act. The court referred to this as a "loophole" in the Act; because there was no requirement in the restriction that the property be used as a farm, it could be occupied for purely residential purposes. *Id.* at 694.

d. *Property Tax Incentives.* A key reason why urbanization can force an end to agricultural uses on adjacent land is the effect of that urbanization on property taxes. As nearby land develops, the agricultural property may become more valuable (as the market envisions residential rather than agricultural uses for it), and the property tax on it may increase markedly. Since the financial return of the agricultural operation has not changed, that increase can put severe financial pressure on those operations.

One response is to allow land in agricultural uses to be assessed at agricultural use value for property tax purposes. Many states have adopted provisions that allow for some tax relief of this sort, usually either through a differential assessment or a form of deferred taxation. For example, the Metropolitan Agricultural Preserves Act, Minn. Stat. Ann. §§473H.02-473H.17 (2001), which applies only to certain counties within the state, authorizes differential assessments for lands that meet the definition of an "agricultural preserve."

A key issue in the effectiveness of such legislation is how the protection may be terminated if, for example, a landowner decides that he or she would rather develop the property rather than keep it agricultural. *See Dykstra v. Department of Natural Resources*, 499 N.W.2d 367 (Mich. Ct. App. 1993) (discussing termination of an agreement under the Farmland and Open Space Reservation Act); *Friends of East Willits Valley v. County of Mendocino*, 123 Cal. Rptr. 2d 708 (Ct. App. 2002) (upholding cancellation of "Williamson Act" restrictions that required land to remain agricultural).

e. *Right to Farm Laws.* One typical pattern of agricultural land conversion occurs when a residential development is built next to an agricultural use. The new homeowners may begin complaining about the externalities from the agricultural operations, and those complaints may lead to litigation alleging that the agricultural operations constitute a nuisance, or to local legislation curbing the scope of the agricultural operations.

A common response to this situation is state "right to farm" legislation. *See, e.g.*, Kan Stat. Ann. §§2-3201 to 2-3203 (2002); N.C. Gen. Stat. §§106-701 (2003). In general, "right to farm" statutes attempt to protect agricultural operations that were in place prior to the time that the residential use existed. A principal method of achieving this goal used in the statutes is to codify the so-called coming to the nuisance defense, which prevents nuisance recovery by plaintiffs who knew of the existing agricultural land use, and its nuisance-like conditions, at the time they bought their property. Other state statutes prohibit local governments from enacting laws to restrict agricultural operations.

The "Right to Farm" laws are now starting to receive judicial interpretation. *See Township of Franklin v. Hollander*, 796 A.2d 874 (N.J. 2002) (Right to Farm Act preempts local land use authority over commercial farm producing ornamental plants); *Craig v. County of Chatham*, 565 S.E.2d 172 (N.C. 2002) (state law preempted county "Swine Ordinance" regulating swine farms as well as county zoning ordinance incorporating the swine ordinance).

In *Bormann v. Board of Supervisors*, 584 N.W.2d 309 (Iowa 1998), landowners applied for establishment of an "agricultural area" under state law. A farm in such an area "shall not be found to be a nuisance . . ." Iowa Code §352.11(1)(a) (2001). The Iowa Supreme Court concluded that the application of this law amounted to a facial "taking" of the neighbors' property without just compensation. Accordingly, it concluded that the nuisance immunity provision in the statute was unconstitutional. Does this conclusion comport with your understanding of takings law from Chapter 7?

4. *Farmers as Environmental Stewards?* As you have seen, some of the legislation intended to preserve farms has the effect of at least partially exempting farms from land use regulation. *See Premium Farms v. County of Holt*, 640 N.W.2d 633 (Neb. 2002) (county retained authority, under state statute exempting farm building from regulations, to require a conditional use permit for a confined livestock operation housing over 1,000 "animal units"). In recent years, however, the environmental externalities from farming have generated considerable controversy. For example, large industrialized pig farming operations have caused water pollution. Does this pollution argue for increased regulation of farms, rather than for deregulation? *See, e.g.*, J.B. Ruhl, Farms, Their Environmental Harms, and Environmental Law, 27 Ecol. L.Q. 263 (2000) (documenting the environmental harms caused by farms and arguing for increased regulation of them).

F. ENVIRONMENTAL IMPACT REPORTING LAWS

In 1969, Congress passed the National Environmental Policy Act (NEPA), 42 U.S.C. §4321-4370d (2000), a law that was to have a profound effect on all actions by the federal government. NEPA requires that federal agencies prepare an Environmental Impact Statement (EIS) on all major federal actions which may have a significant effect on the human environment. The EIS examines, among other topics, the significant environmental effects of a project, alternatives to that project, the effects of those alternatives, and significant effects that cannot be avoided if the project is approved. Most significantly, members of the public may bring suit to enjoin a project's implementation on the ground that the project does not comply with NEPA.

NEPA only applies to federal projects and thus has no effect on day-to-day land use decisions made at the local level. However, approximately 20 states have also passed some form of the EIS requirement. In a number of those states, the EIS process plays a significant part in the approval of land use projects. Indeed, practitioners of land use law in states with extensive law in this area must become experts on their state's "little NEPA."

■ MOSS v. CITY OF BELLINGHAM
31 P.3d 703 (Wash. Ct. App. 2001)

BAKER J.

A group of Bellingham citizens filed a land use petition challenging the City of Bellingham's decision to issue a preliminary plat approval for a large subdivision after the City issued a Determination of Nonsignificance (DNS) under the State Environmental Policy Act (SEPA). The citizens argued that the project has significant environmental impacts and requires a full environmental impact statement (EIS). The project developers argued that sweeping regulatory changes in 1995 integrating SEPA project review with the Growth Management Act (GMA) enabled the City's planners to rely on existing laws and regulations, and to mitigate the adverse impacts of the project in order to bring it below the threshold for EIS preparation. The trial court affirmed the City's preliminary plat approval, and the citizens appeal. We affirm.

I

This case involves a citizens' challenge to the City of Bellingham's approval of a preliminary plat for the Birch Street subdivision. The property is owned by Bellingham 88 LLC. Pennbrook Company, an Oregon developer, plans to purchase and develop the property.

The proposed project is a 79 acre, 172 lot subdivision. The site generally slopes downward from south to north and is characterized by ridges and swales, with two creeks running through the property. The property was logged by a previous owner, and is now covered with an immature to semi-mature deciduous coniferous tree canopy. The remnant logging roads are now used as hiking and biking trails. There is a power line on the south boundary, with the adjoining land recently logged. Property to the north is residential, to the west is forested and then residential, and to the east is forested. The project site is located in Area 11 of the Whatcom Falls Neighborhood Comprehensive Plan, adopted by the City of Bellingham in compliance with the Growth Management Act (GMA). The comprehensive plan provides for residential single occupancy in this area with a density of one lot per 20,000 square feet average overall cluster density. Although the area is zoned for residential development, the plan acknowledges that "[t]he steep topography and resultant drainage problems, combined with difficult access routes place limitations on the density of this area. Efforts should be made to mitigate these impacts as this sensitive hillside develops."

The SEPA project review process began when Pennbrook filed an environmental checklist with the City of Bellingham in the fall of 1998. This was soon followed by a formal application for subdivision approval. The Bellingham City Planning and Development Commission held a public meeting to hear concerns about the project and to determine whether additional environmental analysis and mitigation would be necessary. The City's SEPA official, Chris Spens, then mailed a letter to Pennbrook requesting further information in the form of an Environmental Assessment (EA). Pennbrook prepared and submitted an extensive EA detailing the project's environmental impacts, including traffic studies, wetlands assessments, geological engineering reports, and watershed studies. The EA also suggested a number of mitigation measures as part of a revised project proposal. The City circulated the EA to the agencies on its distribution list and requested comments within 14 days.

The day after the City received Pennbrook's EA, Spens issued a Determination of Nonsignificance (DNS) under SEPA. The parties dispute whether the City mailed the DNS to all agencies with jurisdiction. The DNS was published in the Bellingham Herald, and was subject to the same public comment period as the EA. Several agencies submitted comments on the DNS, and more than 200 citizens wrote letters to the City expressing their concern with the DNS and requesting an EIS. . . .

II

A governmental agency's SEPA threshold determination is reviewed under the "clearly erroneous" standard. "A decision is clearly erroneous when the court is 'left with the definite and firm conviction that a mistake has been committed.'" . . .

SEPA FRAMEWORK

SEPA was enacted in 1971 to "promote the policy of fully informed decision making by government bodies when undertaking 'major actions significantly affecting the quality of the environment.'" . . . Contrary to popular belief, "SEPA does not demand a particular substantive result in government decision making[;]" rather, it ensures that environmental values are given appropriate consideration.

Before a local government processes a permit application for a private land use project, it must make a "threshold determination" of whether the project is a "major action significantly affecting the quality of the environment." A threshold determination, made by the "responsible official" of the "lead agency" reviewing the project, is required for any project constituting a SEPA "action" unless it is "categorically exempt." . . .

All threshold determinations must be documented in a determination of nonsignificance (DNS) or a determination of significance (DS). A DS mandates the preparation of a full EIS. Conversely, a DNS means that no EIS is required. Alternatively, under the "mitigated DNS" process, an applicant may avoid EIS preparation by clarifying, changing, or conditioning the project to mitigate its significant adverse environmental impacts. However, if the project continues to have a significant adverse environmental impact, even with mitigation measures, an EIS shall be prepared.

SEPA REGULATORY REFORM

The seeds of SEPA regulatory reform were sown with passage of the Growth Management Act (GMA) in 1990. The GMA requires Urban Growth Areas (UGAs) to be designated only after preparation of an EIS. In 1995, this fundamental policy change came to fruition when the Legislature enacted the Integration of Growth Management and Environmental Review Act. According to Professor Settle, the Integration Act "seeks to avoid duplicative environmental analysis and substantive mitigation of development projects by assigning SEPA a secondary role to (1) more comprehensive environmental analysis in plans and their programmatic environmental impact statements and (2) systematic mitigation of adverse environmental impacts through local development regulations and other local, state, and federal environmental laws."

Several provisions of the Integration Act bear directly on this case. RCW 43.21C.240, as implemented by WAC 197-11-158, substantially streamlines the threshold determination process for cities and counties planning under the GMA by authorizing the SEPA official to rely on existing plans, laws and regulations in meeting SEPA requirements. . . .

The Act further integrates the GMA with the SEPA process in a new chapter entitled "Local Project Review." RCW 36.70B.030 states that "[f]undamental land use planning choices made in adopted comprehensive plans and development regulations shall serve as the foundation for project review" and authorizes local governments to "determine that the requirements for environmental analysis and mitigation measures in development regulations and other applicable laws provide adequate mitigation for some or all of the project's specific adverse environmental impacts to which the requirements apply." In addition, under RCW 36.70B.040, local governments must determine a proposed project's consistency with its development regulations or comprehensive plan during project review by considering the type of land use, level of development, infrastructure, and development characteristics.

ANALYSIS

. . . Appellants do not challenge the trial court's finding that the Birch Street project is consistent with the comprehensive plan and development regulations, but rather contend that those plans and regulations do not, standing alone, sufficiently mitigate the project's impacts.

Though it is quite understandable that local citizens would find it hard to believe that a large subdivision has "no significant impact" and does not require an EIS, the law is on Pennbrook's side. . . .

. . . The MDNS [Mitigated Determination of Nonsignificance] has its roots in *Hayden v. City of Port Townsend.* In *Hayden,* the Washington Supreme Court upheld a DNS issued after officials worked with the project proponents and government agencies to remedy environmental deficiencies in the proposed plan. Although there was nothing in SEPA or its regulations expressly authorizing this process, the court deemed it "eminently sensible" and stated that:

> [w]here it is feasible, it appears reasonable to resolve potential environmental problems before a formal application is made for a building permit. The pertinent question is whether environmental factors were adequately considered before a final decision was made.

Four years after *Hayden,* the MDNS process was "embraced by the SEPA Rules and reined in by process requirements" with the promulgation of WAC 197-11-350. Commentators have stressed the potential for abuse, contending that the MDNS permits agencies to dispense with EIS preparation on the basis of "illusory commitments." Not surprisingly, though, the MDNS has found favor with courts and decisionmakers as "conducive to efficient, cooperative reduction or avoidance of adverse environmental impacts." . . .

We next consider whether there are any facts in the record indicating that the DNS was clearly erroneous. "For the MDNS to survive judicial scrutiny, the record must demonstrate that 'environmental factors were considered in a manner sufficient to amount to prima facie compliance with the procedural requirements of SEPA,' and that the decision to issue an MDNS was based on information sufficient to evaluate the proposal's environmental impacts."

The record indicates that the project received a great deal of review. The environmental checklist was apparently deemed insufficient, and therefore the SEPA official asked for additional information in the form of an EA. The City gathered extensive comments from agencies and the public, held numerous public meetings, and imposed additional mitigation measures on the project before finally approving it. Notably, although appellants complain generally that the impacts were not adequately analyzed, they have failed to cite any facts or evidence in the record demonstrating that the project as mitigated will cause significant environmental impacts warranting an EIS. . . .

IV

RCW 4.84.370 governs fee awards for appeals of land use decisions. The statute provides that "reasonable attorneys' fees and costs shall be awarded to the prevailing party or substantially prevailing party on appeal before the court of appeals" for a local government's decision to issue, condition, or deny a development permit. The court shall award fees and costs if the prevailing party on appeal was also the prevailing party (a) before the local government or (b) in all prior judicial proceedings.

Here, Pennbrook was the prevailing party before the city council and the trial court. Because we hold that Pennbrook prevails on appeal, an award of reasonable attorney fees and costs to Pennbrook is mandatory. These fees and costs are to be paid by appellants Larry Moss, Michael Frome and Concerned Citizens of Park Ridge.

The effects of SEPA regulatory reform, combined with the MDNS process, have created a flexible, streamlined process which allows decisionmakers to rely as much as possible on existing plans and rules in meeting SEPA's procedural requirements. The SEPA official issued the DNS prematurely, before all of the necessary mitigation measures were in place. But appellants have not pointed to any facts or evidence in the record showing that the project, as mitigated, will have significant environmental impacts requiring an EIS. Furthermore, we find no reversible procedural errors. Because Pennbrook prevailed below, it is entitled to attorney fees.

AFFIRMED.

Appelwick., J., and Agid, C.J., concur.

Notes and Comments

1. *Projects and "Threshold Determinations."* State environmental policy acts (SEPAs) typically apply to discretionary decisions made by state or local agencies. If the project "may" have a significant effect on the environment, the agency must examine the environmental consequences of the project in an environmental impact statement. Since most local land use decisions, such as subdivision approvals, rezonings, and the like, are discretionary in nature, they are subject to the state's SEPA. If the agency's decision is ministerial, then no EIS is needed for the simple reason that it could not affect the agency's decision whether to approve the project.

To make the "threshold determination" of whether a project may have a significant effect on the environment, and thus whether an EIS is required, the local agency first prepares an "initial study." In this study, the agency examines a variety of potential impacts to determine whether they *may* be significant. If the agency decides that there is no potential for a significant effect, it prepares a written determination to that end.

The courts require that agencies take a close look at the possible effects before reaching their conclusion about whether an EIS is needed. In New York, for example, the public agency must identify the relevant areas of environmental concern, take a "hard look" at them, and make a "reasoned evaluation" of the basis for any determination not to prepare an EIS. *H.O.M.E.S. v. New York State Urban Development Corp.*, 418 N.Y.S.2d 827 (Sup. Ct. App. Div. 1979).

2. *Dissecting* Moss. How can it be that a 172-unit subdivision, on 79 acres with some apparently sensitive hillsides, will not have a significant environmental effect? Did the court just ignore the possible effects? Or did the plaintiffs, who appeared without counsel in the court of appeal, simply fail to make their case?

The court emphasizes the need to "streamline" the environmental review process. Should the fact that an EIS is done on a plan mean that a later EIS is not needed when the actual regulatory approval is taken? Will the EIS on the plan examine all the possibly significant impacts in detail, or will it necessarily be more general?

Compare Arvin Enterprises, Inc. v. South Valley Area Planning Comm'n, 125 Cal. Rptr. 2d 140 (Ct. App. 2002) (environmental impact report required where developer had 21 houses in various stages of approval in one geographic area). Is the difference here that the developer seemed to "piecemeal" a larger development, and thus disguise its full impact?

3. *Preparation and Content of the EIS.* If the agency determines that an EIS is needed, it will proceed to prepare a draft document. Often the work is done within the public agency; in other instances, the agency contracts the work out to a consultant. Once a draft is prepared, the agency will then circulate the draft for public comment. Both other public agencies with interests in the project and private citizens may submit comments on the discussion in the EIS. The agency considering the project usually must prepare written responses to those comments.

As noted above, the EIS must examine the environmental impacts of the project, alternatives to the project, and mitigation measures that would reduce the project's impacts. In states with EIS requirements, the tests used by courts to examine the adequacy of the discussion in the EIS are relatively uniform. The court does not examine the document for accuracy; instead, it determines whether the EIS was sufficient for informed decisionmaking. The test most widely used is called the "rule of reason." *See, e.g., Orange County v. North Carolina Dep't of Transportation*, 265 S.E.2d 890, 912 (N.C. Ct. App. 1980). The EIS "is to be analytical, not encyclopedic, and the degree of detail with which each factor must be discussed will vary with the circumstances and nature of the proposal"; *Schiff v. Board of Estimate*, 504 N.Y.S.2d 215, 217 (Sup. Ct. App. Div. 1986).

The SEPA case law reveals a wide variety of issues regarding the "adequacy" of the EIS. Plaintiffs may argue that:

(1) The EIS did not adequately describe the project that was being proposed. *See, e.g., San Joaquin Raptor/Wildlife Rescue Ctr. v. County of Stanislaus*, 32 Cal. Rptr. 2d 704, 713 (Ct. App. 1994) ("Sewer expansion was recognized by the DEIR as necessary to the project, yet was excluded from the description of the development project and its effects ignored in the FEIR.");

(2) The discussion of the environmental effects that the project will generate was too skimpy. *Manchester Environmental Coalition v. Stockton*, 441 A.2d 68, 78 (Conn. 1981) ("the impact statement failed to consider air quality");

(3) The EIS did not discuss a sufficient number of alternatives, or the discussion of alternatives that was included was insufficient. *Shellabarger v. Onondaga*

County Water Authority, 482 N.Y.S.2d 610, 611 (Sup. Ct. App. Div. 1984) (the court rejected plaintiff's claim that the alternative of "hydraulic looping" had to be discussed, reasoning that this alternative would not meet the project's objective of providing sufficient hydraulic pressure and secondary storage capacity);

(4) The EIS did not sufficiently analyze the cumulative impacts of the project or improperly "segmented" the project so that the project's impacts seem less than the overall environmental impact that will actually occur. *See, e.g.*, *Cathcart-Maltby-Clearview Community Council*, 634 P.2d 853, 859 (Wash. 1981) (EIS did not have to discuss buildout over 25 years).

4. *Decisionmaking Under SEPAs*. Once the EIS is completed, the public agency then must use the document in making its decision whether to approve the underlying project. In reaching its decision, the agency's obligation is to consider the environmental effects as disclosed in the EIS and to balance those impacts against the benefits of the project in determining whether to approve it. *Town of Henrietta v. Department of Environmental Conservation*, 430 N.Y.S.2d 440, 446 (Sup. Ct. App. Div. 1980) ("SEQRA must also be recognized as not a mere disclosure statement but rather as an aid in an agency's decision-making process to evaluate and balance the competing factors."). The SEPA may require the agency to adopt findings documenting the agency's conclusions.

5. *SEPAs and Land Use*. In states that have enacted SEPAs, those laws are very important to the land use process for a number of reasons. First, the preparation of the SEPA provides a focal point for public participation in the decisionmaking process. The SEPA process is public; there may be initial public hearings and later public hearings on the draft EIS, and all the documents are available to the public. Second, because land use projects are often opposed because of their environmental effects, the EIS is a means of crystallizing the discussion of those effects. Finally, because courts will enjoin projects that do not comply with the state SEPA, those laws give opponents a powerful tool to continue their opposition beyond the hearing room of the local city council and into the courtroom.

The process, however, is certainly not without its defects. For one thing, by focusing so much attention on whether the paperwork discussion of environmental impacts is sufficient, the SEPA process can cause participants to lose sight of the other important issues that underlie the dispute over a particular land use approval. Any subsequent litigation over the project also may focus on whether the EIS adequately addressed a particular impact, rather than on the real concerns of the opponents.

Another problem is generated by the likelihood of litigation over projects for which EISs are prepared. Individuals preparing those documents tend to take a defensive attitude; it is better to discuss even marginally possible environmental effects in detail than to risk a later finding by a court that this impact has been overlooked. As a result, EISs on controversial projects tend to be lengthy and perhaps of only marginal use in the actual decision on the project.

Finally, the procedural structure of EISs has within it distinct limitations on the use of the EIS as a planning tool. SEPAs are an "overlay" law; they attach to decisions made by public agencies under other laws — zoning authority, subdivision approval, permit approval, etc. — which the agency administers. This institutional structure means that, unless the underlying decision is broad enough, the EIS may not be a useful tool for planning purposes.

The problem is well illustrated by a 1992 decision of the New York Court of Appeals, *Long Island Pine Barrens Society, Inc. v. Planning Board*, 606 N.E.2d 1373 (N.Y. 1992). The plaintiffs were concerned about the impacts of regional development on the acquifer system that provides drinking water for Long Island. They filed suit, claiming that the New York SEPA, known as the State Environmental Quality Review Act, required the preparation of a cumulative EIS for a total of 224 development projects currently proposed for the "Central Pine Barrens Region."

The court of appeals rejected the claim. It reasoned:

> [T]here is merely a host of Federal, State, and local statutes designating the region as an ecologically sensitive one and mandating the development of adequate land-use controls. Consequently, there is no cohesive framework for relating the 224 projects in issue to each other.

606 N.E.2d at 1379. The projects did share one common element—their common location within the Pine Barrens. But this element, said the court, "is an insufficient predicate under the present set of administrative regulations for mandatory cumulative impact analysis." *Id.*

15

Urban Redevelopment, Economic Development, and Anticompetitiveness

A. INTRODUCTION

The theme of this chapter is using the land use system to promote economic development in cities and regions. Economic development has long been an element and goal of comprehensive planning as well as an implicit goal of zoning. As urban planning has evolved, economic development has become a central goal of planning in the United States, indeed throughout the world.

1. Economic Development and the Federal Government

In economic development, unlike many other areas of land use, the role of the federal government has been significant. The federal government has long provided the banking, trade, and securities regulation needed to ensure long-term growth. However, most of the actual planning for industrial and commercial development has been left to state and local regulation.

The programs of the federal government most directly affecting local development have been the federal highway program, federal housing subsidies, and grants for community development and other infrastructure. The federal government has also administered programs to encourage small business development, including enterprises for minorities and poor communities. These programs have been supplemental to, and supportive of, local planning.

2. Transportation Planning and Other Themes

The chapter highlights three themes in planning and economic development. First, it investigates the evolution of policy toward urban redevelopment and neighborhood preservation. Second, the materials look at transportation planning. Transportation is fundamental, for it sets the design of community development. For example, lack of transit coupled with low-density zoning will result in automobile-based development with limited access other than by the personal automobile.

Critics have argued that the result of this type of development is often the absence of attractive and vibrant commercial and recreational centers, and the loss of sense of community. They contend that planning which is overly dependent on the automobile will typically be marked by street congestion, proliferation of limited-access highways, and increased air pollution. The more inaccessible or environmentally challenged neighborhoods are left to deterioration and disinvestment.

Nonetheless, while infrastructure needs for water, sewer, and schools are essential to planning for growth, infrastructure planning, other than for transportation, continues to focus largely on capacity rather than design. Such planning, although providing essential services and obviously affecting the cost of growth, plays a secondary role in the day-to-day implementation of land use decisionmaking. Typically, the issue arises only when the traffic and parking effects of proposed projects are considered.

There is another model that could be followed, one which features higher-density, mixed-use projects combining jobs and housing around transit stops in an effort to generate more efficient transportation and more livable, pedestrian-friendly communities. European cities have effectively followed this model in integrating housing with transportation in the planning process, but the model has not been followed in the United States. Here, it is not uncommon to find housing, industrial developments, and commercial developments virtually unserved by public transit. The assumption remains that the automobile, not transit, is to remain the primary means of transportation.

3. Anticompetitiveness and Competition

Finally, the chapter examines the problem of anticompetitiveness in the context of land use regulation. Zoning, like subsidies, can be used to encourage economic development, but it can also be used to gain a competitive advantage for personal gain. Antitrust law plays a role here, and the discussion focuses on the situation in which a most favored developer and a local government join to protect development against undesired competition.

Also examined is the question of whether fostering competition is an appropriate function of zoning and land use planning controls. The use of zoning for economic stabilization raises a fundamental question of economic freedom and democracy. In the United States, the idea of liberty and competition has remained a paramount consideration. In maximizing locational choice, government policy has permitted suburban office and commercial centers to relocate the city's economic core to suburban edge communities, often leaving destabilized central cities.

Once again, Europe provides a sharply contrasting model. European communities have promoted stability over economic freedom, and they have used land use controls to freeze development and protect existing businesses from competition. The student should consider which of these two models is superior. If you conclude that zoning should be used to preserve and revitalize communities, you must remember that this goal may require zoning policies with some anticompetitive effects. Are you willing to accept those effects?

B. THE FEDERAL ROLE IN ECONOMIC DEVELOPMENT

A Note on the Federal Role in Redevelopment

Traditional Urban Renewal. The federal government has traditionally been heavily involved in redevelopment. The original urban renewal program called for slum removal, with the federal government providing funds to administer the program. The federal grant was the amount necessary to make up the difference between the costs of planning, administration, and land acquisition, and the proceeds from the sale of the cleared land to the ultimate developer. Benjamin B. Quinones, Redevelopment Redefined: Revitalizing the Central City With Resident Control, 27 U. Mich. J.L. Ref. 689, 700-709 (1994).

The program was very costly, as the market for redevelopment on the site of former slums was often not great, and land typically sat empty for long periods before redevelopment. Prior site residents were displaced. Typically, they were moved into more expensive housing that was, at the same time, often substandard. In some instances, this housing was in the path of the next clearance or highway improvement, and the displacees were usually poor persons of color. *See, e.g., Garrett v. City of Hamtramck*, 335 F. Supp. 16 (E.D. Mich. 1971), *plan ordered*, 357 F. Supp. 925 (E.D. Mich. 1973), *rev'd in part*, 503 F.2d 1236 (6th Cir. 1974) (redevelopment plan targeting removal of all African-Americans in community). See generally Judith E. Koons, Fair Housing and Community Empowerment: Where the Roof Meets Redemption, 4 Geo. J. on Fighting Poverty 75 (1996).

The 1970 Legislation. In an attempt to improve the system, Congress passed the Uniform Relocation Assistance and Real Property Acquisition Policies Act of 1970, 42 U.S.C. §§4601-4655 (1994). This Act promised relocation planning and benefits to compensate displaced persons for the costs of moving and the higher rents or mortgage payments that a move might require. In practice, however, compliance with the relocation legislation was largely symbolic, as projects were often loosely administered. Adequate relocation payments and proper planning contributed to the cost of acquisition and displacement programs. These costs were enormous, particularly when in many instances the economic life of the community was shifting to the suburban ring, with little demand for cleared slum sites.

In response to criticism, Congress again modified the program, re-targeting resources for neighborhood preservation and rehabilitation. The modified redevelopment program provided grants and loans to owners to finance upgrading. It also expanded the geographical areas where rehabilitation could occur, dissipating limited resources as the expanded project areas raised expectations without increased appropriations. Perversely, the law often hastened disinvestment and abandonment.

The Block Grant Program. In 1974, Congress eliminated most categorical aid programs, such as urban renewal and rehabilitation grants and loans. It replaced them with block grants that local government could spend according to local priorities and plans. The block grant program was notable for reallocating federal community development funding away from the traditional cities to the newly eligible suburbs and smaller cities. Alvin Hirshen and Richard T. LeGates, HUD's Bonanza for Suburbia, 39 Progressive 32 (1975). See generally Charles E. Daye, Jr. *et al.* Housing and Community Development Ch. 5 (3d ed. 1999).

Later Developments. Since the 1970s, funding for community development has rapidly declined. With an increased focus on legislative budget deficits, future community development policy must look to different vehicles and strategies. One concept that has dominated public attention is the enterprise zone (EZ). The concept of an EZ is that taxes are cut within the geographic zone to attract investment. President Clinton signed into law the Empowerment Zones and Enterprise Communities Program. Omnibus Reconciliation Act of 1993, Pub. L. No. 103-66, §§13301-13303, 107 Stat. 312, 543, *codified at* 26 U.S.C. §§1391-1397D (2002 and Supp. 2003).

In the article below, Professor Hyman describes the empowerment and enterprise zone programs that were the centerpieces of the Clinton and Reagan urban policies.

■ WILTON HYMAN, EMPOWERMENT ZONES, ENTERPRISE COMMUNITIES, BLACK BUSINESS, AND UNEMPLOYMENT

53 Wash. U.J. Urb. & Contemp. L. 143 (1998)

The Secretary of HUD [the Department of Housing and Urban Development] and the Secretary of the United States Department of Agriculture (USDA) have designated a total of nine empowerment zones, six of which are located in urban areas and three of which are located in rural areas. Businesses that operate in these empowerment zones are eligible for an employment wage credit and increased section 179 first-year depreciation deductions. The empowerment zone employment wage credit provides a tax credit for wages paid to a "qualified zone employee." A qualified zone employee is any person who performs substantially all of his or her services for an employer within the empowerment zone and who has a principal place of residence within the empowerment zone. The credit, which is gradually phased out, is initially equal to twenty percent of qualified zone wages, up to a maximum credit of three thousand dollars per employee. Under the Taxpayer Relief Act of 1997, federally designated empowerment zones are eligible for the wage credit through the year 2007.

The increased section 179 depreciation deductions are allowed if the business is an "enterprise zone business" as defined in section 1397B of the Internal Revenue Code. Under section 179, small businesses can deduct an additional $18,500 in depreciation deductions on depreciable, tangible, personal property when it is purchased and used in the "active conduct . . . of any trade or business. . . ." The provision is elective and applies only to the first year in which businesses use the property in a trade or business. Businesses that satisfy the requirements of section 1397B can also deduct an additional $20,000 under section 179, allowing them to take up to $38,500 in additional first-year depreciation deductions.

The empowerment zones may also issue tax-exempt facilities bonds, which businesses can use for acquiring or constructing an "enterprise zone facility" and any land "functionally related and subordinate" to the facility. An "enterprise zone facility" is any depreciable, tangible property that has as its principal user an enterprise zone business. In addition, empowerment zones are eligible for EZ/EC [Empowerment Zones and Enterprise Communities] Social Service Block Grants in the amount of $40 million for rural empowerment zones and $100 million for urban empowerment zones.

The Secretaries of HUD and the USDA considered for designation as enterprise communities those areas not selected or designated as empowerment zones. There are a total of ninety-five enterprise communities, sixty-five of which are located in urban areas and thirty of which are located in rural areas. Enterprise communities are not eligible for the employer wage credit or increased section 179 first-year depreciation deductions, but they can issue tax-exempt facilities bonds. Enterprise communities can use the proceeds from these bonds to build and renovate structures for use by businesses operating in the enterprise community. Enterprise communities are also eligible for Social Service Block Grants of $3 million, which they can use to fund activities and projects in their communities. . . .

There is at least one potentially negative effect of the EZ/EC program. By requiring businesses to locate within an economically distressed inner-city community in order to receive the EZ/EC benefits, the federal program creates a bias toward the creation of small-scale traditional line black businesses. This occurs because such businesses are more likely to locate within inner-city areas regardless of the EZ/EC incentives, and because the EZ/ECs do not provide special incentives to encourage the creation of emerging line black businesses that locate outside of EZ/ECs. Thus, the EZ/EC program wastes resources because it targets areas that may lack adequate consumer markets or adequately skilled labor, and because the traditional line businesses that are likely to locate within those areas, even in the absence of EZ/EC incentives, will not provide enough jobs to reduce unemployment significantly. . . .

The present EZ/EC incentive program has the potential to create more small-scale minority-owned businesses within the EZ/ECs, despite the fact that these type[s] of businesses may not have a significant impact on reducing minority unemployment. The federal government should respond to this situation by modifying the current EZ/EC program to allow flexibility in the locations where EZ/EC businesses can operate. The federal government should provide the EZ/EC incentives to businesses located inside and outside of the EZ/ECs, provided that they hire EZ/EC residents. . . .

Notes and Comments

1. *Model Cities.* During the 1960s an initiative called Model Cities was developed as part of President Lyndon Johnson's "Great Society" program. Demonstration Cities and Metropolitan Development Act of 1966, tit. II, 42 U.S.C. §§3301-3313 (1970). See Bernard J. Frieden & Marshall Kaplan, The Politics of Neglect (1975); Charles M. Haar, Between the Idea and the Reality (1975). The Model Cities program was designed to expand revitalization programs and

concentrate resources in selected neighborhoods, allowing funds to address the full gamut of social as well as physical community needs.

Originally, the initiative called for a few experimental neighborhoods to receive all existing federal urban aid, as well as funds to design new programs aimed at improving neighborhood stability. Although the program was often criticized as ineffective, it was never launched as designed. Instead, funding was cut while demand skyrocketed, as many members of Congress wanted a handful of Model Neighborhoods for their constituents. Frieden & Kaplan, *supra* at 214-217, 222-224. Indeed, toward the end of the program, cities were allowed to expand such neighborhoods to cover the entire inner city, dissipating limited funding and frustrating unrealistic aspirations. Ultimately, the program was subsumed by §116(a) of the Housing and Community Development Act of 1974, 42 U.S.C. §5316 (1994).

The failure of the Model Cities program is just one of many government programs that have failed to generate their promised goals. This pattern of failure has, in turn, had important political consequences. For example, it has often been cited as an example of the failure of government intervention and provided a justification for a new agenda of redevelopment policies.

2. *The Results So Far.* The first round of Empowerment Zones generated $8 billion in additional private investment, with the Detroit zone attracting $2 billion, prompting President Clinton to call for a second round. Clinton Calls for Second Empowerment Zone Round, 23 [Current Developments] Hous. & Dev. Rep. (WGL) 643 (1996). The Empowerment Zones and Enterprise Communities Program has yet to generate any audits evaluating whether the program can be termed a success, although some have claimed such success. See also Successful Empowerment Zones Can Help City Financial Ratings, Says Standard & Poor's Report, 25 Hous. & Dev. Rep. (West) 557 (1998) (Detroit's general obligation rating increased from BBB to BBB+, and its limited tax general obligation rating increased from BBB– to BBB as a result of its EZ program, which (1) generated $43.8 billion investment, (2) created 2752 jobs, and (3) reduced city unemployment from 11 to 8.7 percent.) However, a body of criticism does argue that the zones are deceptively expensive due to the significant loss of revenue that they cause, and that the program might be generating a relocation of economic activity rather than stimulating truly new investment.

For commentary on the enterprise and empowerment zones, *see* Edward J. Blakely, Competitive Advantage for the 21st-Century City: Can a Place-Based Approach to Economic Development Survive in a Cyberspace Age?, 67 J. Am. Plan. Ass'n 133, 139 (2001) (arguing that minority business might be better positioned to locate outside declining central cities); *contra*, Karen Chapple, Forsight or Farsight?: It's the Regional Economy Stupid, 67 J. Am. Plan. Ass'n 142 (2001) (arguing that "place" matters more than ever in the New Economy as investment is lured by a sense of "place"). *See also* Jeffrey M. Euston, Clinton's Empowerment Zones: Hope for the Cities or a Failing Enterprise?, 2 Kan. J. L. & Pub. Pol'y 140 (1994); Dan Nnamdi Mbulu, Affordable Housing: How Effective Are Existing Federal Laws in Addressing the Housing Needs of Lower Income Families?, 8 J. Gender, Soc. Pol'y & L. 387 (2000); Audrey G. McFarlane, Race, Space, and Place: The Geography of Economic Development, 36 San Diego L. Rev. 385 (1999) (critical race theory orientation-based critique). For an endorsement of the Enterprise Zone program by Atlanta's mayor, *see* William Campbell, Urban Holism: The

Empowerment Zone and Economic Development in Atlanta, 26 Fordham Urb. L.J. 1411 (1999). Are businesses just outside the enterprise zone the victims of discrimination? *See WDW Properties v. City of Sumpter*, 535 S.E.2d 631 (S.C. 2000) (program served a public purpose as required by South Carolina Constitution).

3. *Displacement.* The experience for many displacees under federal development and transportation programs has been one of tragedy. Despite the requirement that adequate replacement housing be identified, urban renewal and urban highway projects were routinely approved in earlier years despite the failure to undertake relocation planning. Chester W. Hartman, Relocation: Illusory Promises and No Relief, 57 Va. L. Rev. 745 (1971). Even where planning was undertaken, regulations and planning theory too often were violated. For example, in *Tenants & Owners in Opposition to Redevelopment v. HUD*, 406 F. Supp. 1024 (N.D. Cal. 1970), the court rejected, for urban renewal relocation planning, the use of public housing as a planning resource. The court cited long waiting lists for this housing.

C. REDEVELOPMENT THROUGH TAX-INCREMENT FINANCING

Cities have developed renewal programs that do not depend on federal subsidies. The most popular method is through the use of tax-increment financing. Under tax-increment-financed redevelopment, municipal bonds are sold to finance acquisition of property. When the property is later resold for redevelopment, the taxes previously paid to taxing entities are frozen at that level. Development then occurs, enhancing the tax base and generating larger revenues. The tax "increment," that is, the tax revenues in excess of the "frozen" tax obligation, is used to pay off the bond indebtedness.

The funds constituting the increment are then available for making public facility improvements within the project or for rent or mortgage subsidies to generate affordable housing. The use of the tax increment also subsidizes the project, allowing a "write down" on the cost of the acquired land so as to make privately sponsored redevelopment more attractive. "Write down" connotes the sale of land at below the cost of acquisition and administration, often below market value, as a means to attract developers to redevelopment property.

The following case is an example of local, tax increment-financed redevelopment.

CASTEL PROPERTIES, LIMITED v. CITY OF MARION

631 N.E.2d 459 (Ill. App. Ct. 1994)

Justice GOLDENHERSH delivered the opinion of the court: . . .

The major conflict of the parties concerns the Illinois Centre TIF [tax increment financing]. The city first contends that the blight factors noted in the statute and found by the city in ordinance No. 1302 were present and affected the Illinois

Centre tract. Specifically, the city claims that these blight factors impeded the type of development the city desired in that property and that the TIF was necessary to develop this property in accord with the city's comprehensive plan. Plaintiffs, on the other hand, contend that the evidence supports the trial court's findings that the Illinois Centre TIF was not a blighted area as defined by the statute and it therefore failed the "but for" test. We agree with plaintiffs.

The relevant part of the statute concerning its definition of blighting factors and what the city must find is as follows:

> (a) "Blighted area" means any improved or vacant area within the boundaries of a redevelopment project area located within the territorial limits of the municipality where, . . . if vacant, the sound growth of the taxing districts is impaired by, (1) a combination of 2 or more of the following factors: obsolete platting of the vacant land; diversity of ownership of such land; tax and special assessment delinquencies on such land; flooding on all or part of such vacant land; [or] deterioration of structures or site improvements in neighboring areas adjacent to the vacant land. . . .
>
> (n) . . . No redevelopment plan shall be adopted by a municipality without findings that (1) the redevelopment project area on the whole has not been subject to growth and development through investment by private enterprise and would not reasonably be anticipated to be developed without the adoption of the redevelopment plan. . . .
>
> (v) As used in subsection (a) of Section 11-74.4-3 of this Act, "vacant land" means any parcel or combination of parcels of real property without industrial, commercial and residential buildings which has not been used for commercial agricultural purposes within 5 years prior to the designation of the redevelopment project area, unless such parcel is included in an industrial park conservation area or such parcel has been subdivided. (Ill. Rev. Stat. 1989, ch. 24, pars. 11-74.4-3(a), (n), (v) (now see 65 ILCS 5/11-74.4-3(a), (n), (v) (West 1992)).)

The city, in its ordinance, found the following factors concerning blight:

> *Section 1.* That the City Council finds and determines as follows: . . .
>
> (b) There exist conditions which cause the area proposed to be designated as a Redevelopment Project Area to be classified as a "blighted area" as defined in Section 11-74.4-3(a) of the Act.
>
> (c) The proposed Redevelopment Project Area on the whole has not been subject to growth and development through investment by private enterprise and would not be reasonably anticipated to be developed without the adoption of the proposed Redevelopment Plan.

The trial court first considered the question of diversity of ownership. The court noted that 90% of the proposed TIF area is comprised of the Broeking Farm and that various rights of way and easements, including rights of the State, did not present a problem as far as "diversity of ownership" sufficient to constitute a factor of blighting. In essence, the trial court concluded that there was no evidence of diversity of ownership being an impeding factor as far as development is concerned. We agree that this finding is solidly based on the evidence in this record and does not constitute an abuse of discretion.

The second element of blighting that the court addressed was flooding. The trial court specifically found that there was a lack of evidence of any significant flooding. Specifically, the Department of Transportation, in an environmental assessment, stated that the project site was not located in a flood plain, aerial views of the property showed no topographical flood plain characteristics, and there was no evidence in the record that flooding had at any time interfered with the ongoing farming operation on the property. The circuit court did note a statement by Mr. Broeking that on one occasion a small number of acres of his property had flooded, but the flood water quickly subsided. The circuit court concluded, and we agree, that this is insufficient evidence of flooding so as to constitute a blight factor.

The third blighting factor, the presence of deteriorating structures in the neighborhood, was also found insufficient by the circuit court. Those factors were an abandoned motorcycle shop on the south side of Route 13, a cold-storage processing facility to the west of the Broeking Farm, and a wrecking business, also to the west. The circuit court found that these structures are hardly visible from the center of the area and had not been shown to impede development. This finding also meets the clear and convincing standard and does not constitute an abuse of discretion.

The circuit court also found, and the city contests, that the development of this area was likely to occur without TIF treatment. The city essentially argues that the circuit court erred by ignoring two factors in reaching this conclusion. First, the court failed to note evidence of past failures of development, specifically, two commercial projects. Secondly, the city argues the court fails to consider whether this area would have developed in a manner considered appropriate by the city and in conformity with its comprehensive plan. Plaintiffs argue the evidence showed that the history of development in this area indicated the Illinois Centre TIF area would develop commercially, since it was in an area west of Interstate 57 and along Illinois Route 13, a corridor of development in the past and likely to be so in the future. Plaintiffs, in effect, say that this area would develop anyway and therefore fails the "but for" test. The circuit court agreed with plaintiffs and so do we.

According to the city's argument, implicit in the legislative finding that the project area would not develop is the requirement that it develop in a manner contemplated by the city's comprehensive plan. What the statute requires is a finding that the area is not subject to growth or development and it is not reasonably anticipated that the area will be developed. This requirement does not mention, and does not contemplate, the anticipated growth necessarily being in conformity with the city's comprehensive plan for development. The General Assembly has indicated by the Act that any commercial growth or development is the standard. The requirement that development be in conformity with a comprehensive plan applies to the redevelopment plan to be adopted by the city, not to the legislative finding that no growth or development would occur. Given the extensive evidence in this record that growth and development was occurring in this area and that the area was a corridor for growth and development and, specifically as to this project, that the Illinois Centre was being erected without the TIF issue having been finally determined, we cannot say that the trial court was without a sufficient basis in this record to conclude that the city failed to meet the "but for" test as articulated in the statute. Concerning the two prior projects that failed, the circuit court noted, and our review of the record also concludes, that there was no specific evidence given as to the reason for their failures. While naturally all of the relevant evidence concerning a particular point must be considered by the circuit court in reaching its conclusion, we cannot say that the existence of these two business failures was a sufficient basis so that the trial court must, of necessity, hold that plaintiffs failed to meet their standard of clear and convincing evidence to overcome the city's legislative findings. . . .

Notes and Comments

1. *Advice and Strategies re Blight.* How would you advise the principals in *Castel Properties*? Were there litigation strategies or prelitigation strategies that may have generated a different outcome? In *Sweetwater Valley Civic Ass'n v. City of National City*, 555 P.2d 1099 (Cal. 1976), the court rejected an attempt to establish a commercial redevelopment project on the site of a profitable golf course. The city's claim that the site was "blighted" was rejected, absent evidence the site had become an economic liability.

As in the principal case, blight designations may be suspicious or manipulated, particularly if a program designed for revitalizing central cities is employed in a suburban community. *See Friends of Mammoth v. Town of Mammoth Lakes Redev. Agency*, 98 Cal. Rptr. 2d 334 (Ct. App. 2000) (little blight in this affluent, bucolic golf and ski resort, particularly where the redevelopment plan included an existing golf course); *Beach-Courchesne v. City of Diamond Bar*, 95 Cal. Rptr. 2d 265 (Ct. App. 2000) (nonexistent blight in affluent suburban community); *Walser Auto Sales, Inc. v. City of Richfield*, 635 N.W.2d 391 (Minn. Ct. App. 2001), *aff'd mem.*, 644 N.W.2d 425 (Minn. 2002) (rejecting attempt to classify code-complying structures as substandard and therefore blighted). *See* George Lefcoe, Finding the Blight That's Right for California Redevelopment Law, 52 Hastings L.J. 991 (2001).

2. *T.I.F.* Tax-increment financing has been sustained by the state courts that have reviewed the technique for compliance with state law. *See, e.g., In re Advisory Opinion*, 422 N.W.2d 186 (Mich. 1988); *State ex rel. Plaza Properties, Inc. v. Kansas City*, 687 S.W.2d 875 (Mo. 1985). *See also Tax Increment Fin. Comm'n v. J. E. Dunn Constr. Co.*, 781 S.W.2d 70 (Mo. 1989) (tax-increment-financed redevelopment does not involve an increase in tax requiring popular referendum); Craig L. Johnson & Joyce Y. Man (eds.), Tax Increment Financing and Economic Development: Uses, Structures, and Impacts (2001); Marc Jolin, et al., Tax-Increment Financing: Urban Renewal of the 1990s, 32 Clearinghouse Rev. 81 (1998) (suggesting legal, legislative, and local empowerment strategies to advance revitalization without displacement); Susan Mead, Incentives for Downtown Revitalization: Tax Increment Financing Districts, Chapter 380, and Other Tools, 32 Urb. Law. 1013 (2000) (discussing Texas TIF); Michael T. Peddle, TIF in Illinois: The Good, the Bad, and the Ugly, 17 N. Ill. U.L. Rev. 441 (1997) (TIF is a viable economic development tool in need of reform).

3. *Targeting the Expenditure.* Communities may fail to follow statutory obligations to target the expenditure of the "increment," the tax revenue in excess of that needed for bond repayment and the pre-redevelopment tax obligation to state and local government. Courts in general give broad deference to redevelopment planning. However, they will not sustain the use of bonds, secured by funds earmarked for low and moderate income housing, to fund safety-based road

improvements, such as building railroad overpasses, when that use is unrelated to providing affordable housing. *Lancaster Redevelopment Agency v. Dibley*, 25 Cal. Rptr. 2d 593 (Ct. App. 1993).

4. *Local Initiatives.* Local redevelopment strategies are, of course, as diverse as the planning theory that supports them. These strategies run the gamut from land clearance for redevelopment, to rehabilitation loans and grants to homeowners, to simply making public improvements in a community to encourage private investment. Some communities have even provided for establishment of a receivership for substandard properties. *See e,g*,, *Community Renewal Found. v. Chicago Title & Trust*, 255 N.E.2d 908 (Ill. 1970).

D. DISLOCATION AND THE PUBLIC USE REQUIREMENT

Redevelopment can be a catalyst for community renewal, but there are often unavoidable costs. For example, a redevelopment project may cause housing displacement, thereby aggravating a limited, overcrowded housing supply. If the redevelopment is successful, secondary displacement can be generated as private owners upgrade buildings in surrounding streets and neighborhoods. Charles E. Daye, *et al.*, Housing and Community Development Law ch. 5 (2d ed. 1995). Even where the redevelopment area is racially integrated, displacement may exacerbate community segregation patterns. See generally James A. Kushner & Frances E. Werner, Illusory Promises Revisited: Relocation Planning and Judicial Review, 8 Sw. U.L. Rev. 751 (1976).

The following case raises the difficult choice of preserving a stable, low-income, working class residential neighborhood or losing a major employer that may leave the region unless land for expansion can be provided through redevelopment.

POLETOWN NEIGHBORHOOD COUNCIL v. CITY OF DETROIT

304 N.W.2d 455 (Mich. 1981)

PER CURIAM.

This case arises out of a plan by the Detroit Economic Development Corporation to acquire, by condemnation if necessary, a large tract of land to be conveyed to General Motors Corporation as a site for construction of an assembly plant. The plaintiffs, a neighborhood association and several individual residents of the affected area, challenge the project on a number of grounds . . .

I

This case raises a question of paramount importance to the future welfare of this state and its residents: Can a municipality use the power of eminent domain granted to it by the Economic Development Corporations Act, M.C.L. §125.1601 *et seq*; M.S.A. §5.3520(1) *et seq*, to condemn property for transfer to a private corporation to build a plant to promote industry and commerce, thereby adding jobs and taxes to the economic base of the municipality and state?

Const. 1963, Art. 10, §2, states in pertinent part that "[p]rivate property shall not be taken for public use without just compensation therefor being first made or secured in a manner prescribed by law." Art. 10, §2 has been interpreted as requiring that the power of eminent domain not be invoked except to further a public use or purpose. . . .

The Economic Development Corporations Act is a part of the comprehensive legislation dealing with planning, housing and zoning whereby the State of Michigan is attempting to provide for the general health, safety, and welfare through alleviating unemployment, providing economic assistance to industry, assisting the rehabilitation of blighted areas, and fostering urban redevelopment.

Section 2 of the act provides:

> There exists in this state the continuing need for programs to alleviate and prevent conditions of unemployment, and that it is accordingly necessary to assist and retain local industries and commercial enterprises to strengthen and revitalize the economy of this state and its municipalities; that accordingly it is necessary to provide means and methods for the encouragement and assistance of industrial and commercial enterprises in locating, purchasing, constructing, reconstructing, modernizing, improving, maintaining, repairing, furnishing, equipping, and expanding in this state and in its municipalities; and that it is also necessary to encourage the location and expansion of commercial enterprises to more conveniently provide needed services and facilities of the commercial enterprises to municipalities and the residents thereof. *Therefore, the powers granted in this act constitute the performance of essential public purposes and functions for this state and its municipalities.* M.C.L. §125.1602; M.S.A. §5.3520(2). (Emphasis added.)

To further the objectives of this act, the legislature has authorized municipalities to acquire property by condemnation in order to provide industrial and commercial sites and the means of transfer from the municipality to private users. M.C.L. §125.1622; M.S.A. §5.3520(22).

. . . [P]laintiffs-appellants . . . challenge . . . the constitutionality of using the power of eminent domain to condemn one person's property to convey it to another private person in order to bolster the economy. They argue that whatever incidental benefit may accrue to the public, assembling land to General Motors' specifications for conveyance to General Motors for its uncontrolled use in profit making is really a taking for private use and not a public use because General Motors is the primary beneficiary of the condemnation.

The defendants-appellees contend, on the other hand, that the controlling public purpose in taking this land is to create an industrial site which will be used to alleviate and prevent conditions of unemployment and fiscal distress. The fact that it will be conveyed to and ultimately used by a private manufacturer does not defeat this predominant public purpose.

There is no dispute about the law. All agree that condemnation for a public use or purpose is permitted. All agree that condemnation for a private use or purpose is forbidden. Similarly, condemnation for a private use cannot be authorized whatever its incidental public benefit and condemnation for a public purpose cannot be forbidden whatever the incidental private gain. The heart of this dispute is whether the proposed condemnation is for the primary benefit of the public or the private user.

The Legislature has determined that governmental action of the type contemplated here meets a public need and serves an essential public purpose. The Court's role after such a determination is made is limited.

> "The determination of what constitutes a public purpose is primarily a legislative function, subject to review by the courts when abused, and the determination of the legislative body of that matter should not be reversed except in instances where such determination is palpable and manifestly arbitrary and incorrect."

The United States Supreme Court has held that when a legislature speaks, the public interest has been declared in terms "well-nigh conclusive." *Berman v. Parker*, 348 U.S. 26 (1954).

The Legislature has delegated the authority to determine whether a particular project constitutes a public purpose to the governing body of the municipality involved. The plaintiffs concede that this project is the type contemplated by the Legislature and that the procedures set forth in the Economic Development Corporations Act have been followed. This further limits our review.

In the court below, the plaintiffs-appellants challenged the necessity for the taking of the land for the proposed project. In this regard the city presented substantial evidence of the severe economic conditions facing the residents of the city and state, the need for new industrial development to revitalize local industries, the economic boost the proposed project would provide, and the lack of other adequate available sites to implement the project.

As Justice Cooley stated over a hundred years ago "the most important consideration in the case of eminent domain is the necessity of accomplishing some public good which is otherwise impracticable, and . . . the law does not so much regard the means as the need."

When there is such public need, "[t]he abstract right [of an individual] to make use of his own property in his own way is compelled to yield to the general comfort and protection of community, and to a proper regard to relative rights in others." Eminent domain is an inherent power of the sovereign of the same nature as, albeit more severe than, the power to regulate the use of land through zoning or the prohibition of public nuisances.

In the instant case the benefit to be received by the municipality invoking the power of eminent domain is a clear and significant one and is sufficient to satisfy this Court that such a project was an intended and a legitimate object of the Legislature when it allowed municipalities to exercise condemnation powers even though a private party will also, ultimately, receive a benefit as an incident thereto.

The power of eminent domain is to be used in this instance primarily to accomplish the essential public purposes of alleviating unemployment and revitalizing the economic base of the community. The benefit to a private interest is merely incidental.

Our determination that this project falls within the public purpose, as stated by the Legislature, does not mean that every condemnation proposed by an economic development corporation will meet with similar acceptance simply because it may provide some jobs or add to the industrial or commercial base. If the public benefit was not so clear and significant, we would hesitate to sanction approval of such a project. The power of eminent domain is restricted to furthering public uses and purposes and is not to be exercised without substantial proof that the public is primarily to be benefited. Where, as here, the condemnation power is exercised in a way that benefits specific and identifiable private interests, a court inspects with heightened scrutiny the claim that the public interest is the predominant interest being advanced. Such public benefit cannot be speculative or marginal but must be clear and significant if it is to be within the legitimate purpose as stated by the Legislature. We hold this project is warranted on the basis that its significance for the people of Detroit and the state has been demonstrated. . . .

Compare the Michigan Supreme Court's ruling in *Poletown* with the following decision in neighboring Illinois.

■ SOUTHWESTERN ILLINOIS DEVELOPMENT AUTHORITY v. NATIONAL CITY ENVIRONMENTAL, L.L.C.

768 N.E.2d 1 (Ill. 2002), cert. denied, 537 U.S. 880 (2002)

Justice GARMAN delivered the opinion of the court:

The issue in this case is whether the Southwestern Illinois Development Authority (SWIDA) properly exercised the power of eminent domain to take property owned by National City Environmental, L.L.C., and St. Louis Auto Shredding Company (collectively NCE), and convey that property to Gateway International Motorsports Corporation (Gateway). . . .

SWIDA was created in 1987 by the Illinois General Assembly through passage of the Southwestern Illinois Development Authority Act (the Act) . . . SWIDA is a political entity and municipal corporation whose stated purpose is to "promote industrial, commercial, residential, service, transportation and recreational activities and facilities, thereby reducing the evils attendant upon unemployment and enhancing the public health, safety, morals, happiness and general welfare of this State." . . .

The Act mandates that SWIDA "promote development within the geographic confines of Madison and St. Clair counties." It is the duty of SWIDA to assist in the development, construction, and acquisition of industrial, commercial, housing or residential projects within these counties. A "[c]ommercial project" is defined as "any cultural facilities of a for-profit or non-for-profit type including . . . racetracks . . . [and] parking facilities." . . .

To accomplish the purposes of the Act, the legislature empowered SWIDA to issue bonds for the purpose of acquiring, improving or developing projects, including those established by business entities attempting to locate or expand property within Madison and St. Clair Counties. SWIDA also has the authority to acquire property by condemnation. . . .

In June 1996, SWIDA issued $21.5 million in taxable sports facility revenue bonds. The proceeds of the bonds were lent to Gateway to finance the development of a multipurpose automotive sports and training facility in the region (the racetrack). . . .

The racetrack was developed and has flourished. In 1997, the racetrack had a total attendance of 400,000 at various large and small events. Seating included 25,000 grandstand seats and 25,000 portable seats. In 1998, Gateway increased its seating capacity and desired to increase its parking capacity as well. It called upon SWIDA to use its quick-take eminent domain powers to acquire land to the west of the racetrack for the purposes of expanded parking facilities. The adjacent 148.5 acre tract of land sought was owned by NCE.

NCE operates a metal recycling center in an area of St. Clair County that, until recently, was National City, Illinois. NCE employs 80 to 100 persons full time and has been at its present location since 1975. NCE shred cars and appliances and separates the reusable metals. It disposes of nearly 100,000 cars per year. Nonrecyclable by-products of the process, referred to as "fluff," are deposited in NCE's landfill, located to the east of its recycling center. When this landfill site reaches capacity, NCE plans to expand its landfill operations onto the 148.5 acre tract of land it owns to the east of the current landfill. NCE uses clay and dirt from the 148.5 acre tract to fill and cover fluff in the landfill area currently in use.

In early 1998, Gateway attempted to discuss the purchase of NCE's land with NCE's owner. NCE would not discuss the matter and, initially, Gateway made no offer to purchase the land. Instead, Gateway asked SWIDA to exercise its quick-take eminent domain powers to take the 148.5 acres of land and transfer it to Gateway.

Gateway completed a "Quick-Take Application Packet" and stated that it wanted to use the land as a parking lot for the purpose of increasing the value of Gateway's racetrack. Gateway paid SWIDA an application fee of $2,500, and the sum of $10,000 to be applied toward SWIDA's sliding scale fee of 6% to 10% of the acquisition price of property being condemned. In addition, Gateway agreed to pay SWIDA's expenses, including the acquisition price of the property, and other costs associated with quick-take process.

Approval of the county board is required before SWIDA can use its quick-take eminent domain powers within unincorporated areas of a county. On February 23, 1998, the St. Clair County board adopted a resolution authorizing SWIDA to exercise its quick-take eminent domain authority to acquire the NCE tract of land for Gateway parking. The board noted that dramatic attendance increases could be expected at the racetrack and that it was necessary to create additional parking facilities to adequately serve patrons. The board also found that expansion of the racetrack facilities would enhance the public health, safety, morals, happiness, and general welfare of the citizens of southwestern Illinois by increasing the tax base in the area and generating additional tax revenues. . . .

In an effort to acquire the property through a negotiated sale, [SWIDA Executive Director] Ortbals attended a meeting on March 17, 1998, at which he delivered to NCE a written offer to purchase the property for $1 million. By letter dated March 19, 1998, NCE rejected the $1 million offer but indicated its willingness to meet with SWIDA the week of March 30, 1998, following an expected appraisal of the property. On March 20, 1998, SWIDA made another written offer to NCE to purchase the property for $1 million and advised NCE that SWIDA would initiate proceedings to condemn the property if NCE did not accept the offer by 5 p.m. on March 30, 1998. . . .

The State of Illinois, as a sovereign, has the inherent right to condemn property, subject to the state constitutional mandate that private property shall not be taken or damaged for public use without just compensation to its owner . . . The fifth amendment to the United States Constitution (U.S. Const., amend. V), made applicable to the states through the fourteenth amendment (U.S. Const., amend. XIV), also provides that private property shall not be taken for public use without just compensation. . . .

The right of a sovereign to condemn private property is limited to takings for a public use. Clearly, private persons may ultimately acquire ownership of property arising out of a taking and the subsequent transfer to private ownership does not by itself defeat the public purpose. However, that principle alone cannot adequately resolve the issues presented in this case. "Before the right of eminent domain may be exercised, the law, beyond a doubt, requires that the use for which the land is taken shall be public as distinguished from a private use." . . .

It may be impossible to clearly delineate the boundary between what constitutes a legitimate public purpose and a private benefit with no sufficient, legitimate public purpose to support it. "We deal, in other words, with what traditionally has been known as the police power. An attempt to define its reach or trace its outer limits is fruitless, for each case must turn on its own facts." . . . "While, from time to time, the courts have attempted to define public use, there is much disagreement as to its meaning." . . . Great deference should be afforded the legislature and its granting of eminent domain authority. However, the exercise of that power is not entirely beyond judicial scrutiny, and it is incumbent upon the judiciary to ensure that the power of eminent domain is used in a manner contemplated by the framers of the constitutions and by the legislature that granted the specific power in question. "Courts all agree that the determination of whether a given use is a public use is a judicial function." . . .

SWIDA contends that the condemnation and taking of NCE's property is sustainable because a public purpose will be served through (1) the fostering of economic development, (2) the promotion of public safety, and (3) the prevention or elimination of blight. Moreover, once the determination is made that one or all of these requirements is satisfied, "possesory use by the public is not an indispensable prerequisite to the lawful exercise of the power of eminent domain." . . .

SWIDA contends that any distinction between the terms "public purpose" and "public use" has long since evaporated and that the proper test is simply to ask whether a "public purpose" is served by the taking. While the difference between a public purpose and a public use may appear to be purely semantic, and the line between the two terms has blurred somewhat in recent years, a distinction still exists and is essential to this case. We agree that these terms are necessarily somewhat loosely defined. However, that does not mean they are indistinguishable. . . .

If this taking were allowed to stand, it may be true that spectators at Gateway would benefit greatly. Developing additional parking could benefit the members of the public who choose to attend events at the racetrack, as spectators may often have to wait in long lines of traffic to park their vehicles and again to depart the facility. We also acknowledge that a public use or purpose may be satisfied in light of public safety concerns. The public is allowed to park on the property in exchange for the payment of a fee. Gateway's racetrack may be open to the public, but not "by right." It is a private venture designed to result not in a public use, but in private profits. If this taking were permitted, lines to enter parking lots might be shortened and pedestrians might be able to cross from parking areas to event areas in a safer manner. However, we are unpersuaded that these facts alone are sufficient to satisfy the public use requirement, especially in light of evidence that Gateway could have built a parking garage structure on its existing property.

We have also recognized that economic development is an important public purpose. . . . SWIDA presented extensive testimony that expanding Gateway's facilities through the taking of NCE's property would allow it to grow and prosper and contribute to positive economic growth in the region. However, "incidentally, every lawful business does this." . . . Moreover, nearly a century ago, [this court] expressed the long-standing rule that "to constitute a public use, something more than a mere benefit to the public must flow from the contemplated improvement." . . .

Entities such as SWIDA must always be mindful of expediency, cost efficiency, and profitability while accepting the legislature's charge to promote development within their defined parameters. However, these goals must not be allowed to overshadow the constitutional principles that lie at the heart of the power with which SWIDA and similar entities have been entrusted. As Justice Kuehn stated in dissent in the appellate court, "If property ownership is to remain what our forefathers intended it to be, if it is to remain a part of the liberty we cherish, the economic by-products of a private capitalist's ability to develop land cannot justify a surrender of ownership to eminent domain." . . .

While the activities here were undertaken in the guise of carrying out its legislated mission, SWIDA's true intentions were not clothed in an independent, legitimate governmental decision to further a planned public use. SWIDA did not conduct or commission a thorough study of the parking situation at Gateway. Nor did it formulate any economic plan requiring additional parking at the racetrack. SWIDA advertised that, for a fee, it would condemn land at the request of "private developers" for the "private use" of developers. In addition, SWIDA entered into a contract with Gateway to condemn whatever land "may be desired . . . by Gateway." Clearly, the foundation of this taking is rooted not in the economic and planning process with which SWIDA has been charged. Rather, this action was undertaken solely in response to Gateway's expansion goals and its failure to accomplish those goals through purchasing NCE's land at an acceptable negotiated price. It appears SWIDA's true intentions were to act as a default broker of land for Gateway's proposed parking plan.

This point is further emphasized by the fact that other options were available to Gateway that could have addressed many of the problems testified to by Pritchett, Ortbals and others. Gateway could have built a parking garage structure on its existing property rather than develop the land owned by NCE. However, when Gateway discovered that the cost of constructing a garage on land it already owned was substantially higher than using SWIDA as its agent to take NCE's property for open-field parking, Gateway chose the easier and less expensive avenue.

As a result of the acquisition of NCE's property, Gateway could realize an estimated increase of $13 to $14 million in projected revenue per year. While we do not deny that this expansion in revenue could potentially trickle down and bring corresponding revenue increases to the region, revenue expansion alone does not justify an improper and unacceptable expansion of the eminent domain power of the government. Using the power of the government for purely private purposes to allow Gateway to avoid the open real estate market and expand its facilities in a more cost-efficient manner, and thus maximizing corporate profits, is a misuse of the power entrusted by the public. . . .

Notes and Comments

1. *Contrasting* Poletown *with* Southwestern Illinois. Which result do you favor, and did the courts get it right as a matter of law, morality, or policy? How do you explain the Illinois decision in light of the traditional pro-development political and judicial philosophy of that state? For a ruling endorsing the use of tax increment financed redevelopment to finance an automobile race track, *see State ex rel. Tomasic v. Unified Gov't of Wyandotte County/Kansas City, Kansas*, 962 P.2d 543 (Kan. 1998). *See also* Joseph J. Lazzarotti, Public Use or Public Abuse, 68 UMKC L. Rev. 49 (1999) (an important instrument can be abused when courts fail to scrutinize facts and defer to the legislature). Can the state use condemnation power for a public/private venture in which one floor of a five-story building would be devoted to public use? *State ex rel. Washington State Convention & Trade Ctr. v. Evans*, 966 P.2d 1252 (Wash. 1998) (yes for convention center expansion project, as agency condemned no more than necessary for the public use).

2. *Social Equity.* Was the sacrifice required of the displaced citizens in *Poletown* fair so as to allow a private corporation to construct its plant? Are the displacees subsidizing the project? Was there any indication that the property was blighted? Do you punish or reward Detroit for taking this action? *Compare* Frank Aiello, Note, Gambling with Condemnation: An Examination of Detroit's Use of Eminent Domain for Riverfront Casinos, 46 Wayne L. Rev. 1639 (2000) (arguing using condemnation for such a use violates the Michigan Constitution).

3. *Economic Development.* What if a town, to protect its tax base and the economic viability of its commercial district, condemned "blighted" commercial buildings adjacent to an automobile dealership to permit the dealer to expand and not leave its location, as it threatened to do? *City of Center Line v. Chmelko*, 416 N.W.2d 401 (Mich. Ct. App. 1987) (invalid taking, applying the "heightened" judicial scrutiny of *Poletown*). *Compare City of Jamestown v. Leevers Supermarkets*, 552 N.W.2d 365 (N.D. 1996) (city may condemn downtown parking lots for commercial redevelopment for a supermarket when the public purpose is stimulation of commercial growth and removal of economic stagnation).

Can you distinguish *Poletown* and *Jamestown* from *Castel* (read earlier in this chapter) and *Southwestern*? Is the ground for distinction the principle that what is good for General Motors is good for Michigan? What if the developer in *Poletown* built Toyotas? Could the agency in *Southwestern* have cured the problem simply by making a study first?

According to one lawyer for the City of Detroit in *Poletown*:

> The case represented a great victory for the City during a bleak time. Had we lost the case, General Motors would have constructed this assembly plant in the South. Quite possibly, Chrysler would have followed GM out of Detroit (Chrysler did move its headquarters to the suburbs, but kept its assembly plant in Detroit). The "domino" effect would have been catastrophic for the City. All the economic benefits of this condemnation presented at trial were absolutely valid and prophetic.

Letter from William G. Christopher to James A. Kushner, Jan. 21, 1998, at 1.

4. Berman *and* Southwestern. Is the court in *Southwestern* inconsistent with *Berman v. Parker*, 348 U.S. 26 (1954), in which the Supreme Court deferentially endorsed urban renewal land clearance as a public use, even as applied to a

nonblighted, commercial structure? Does *Southwestern* set forth a clear test for determining which projects will pass the "public use" test?

5. *Code Enforcement.* One strategy to stabilize neighborhoods and avoid deterioration to the point of requiring land clearance is enforcement of a housing conditions code. Although virtually every city has a housing conditions code, those codes are typically enforced on an ad hoc basis in response to complaints lodged by a tenant or neighbor.

There are, however, several problems with a systematic code enforcement strategy. Where the economic status of the property owner or of the neighborhood is such that loans cannot be obtained, code enforcement can exacerbate urban problems by causing displacement and, ultimately, abandonment of housing. Additionally, enforcement resources are often limited. Inspectors have little time to engage in proactive inspections rather than simply responding to complaints. One solution is to have all dwellings inspected at the point of sale. *See Butcher v. City of Detroit*, 401 N.W.2d 260 (Mich. 1986), *cert. denied*, 482 U.S. 905 (1987).

A few state courts have ruled that code enforcement can operate as a taking of the landlord's property. *See City of St. Louis v. Brune*, 515 S.W.2d 471 (Mo. 1974) ("hot bath" requirement invalid as applied to terminal, deteriorated housing that could not generate sufficient rent to finance repairs and sufficiently extend the life of the building). Most courts, however, have approved of such local initiatives. *See, e.g., Adamec v. Post*, 7 N.E.2d 120 (N.Y. 1937).

6. *Urban Homesteading.* Detroit created a program of urban "homesteading." Under this program, individuals who did not own the property could occupy and rehabilitate tax-delinquent properties. The homesteader ultimately obtains title through a foreclosure sale. Does the program constitute a regulatory or physical occupation taking? *Moore v. City of Detroit*, 406 N.W.2d 488 (Mich. Ct. App. 1987) (no taking as the program constitutes a creative alternative to demolition).

7. *Literature.* For literature on urban revitalization and community economic development, *see* Joseph Persky & Wim Wiewel, When Corporations Leave Town (2000) (arguing that economic decline is a function of urban sprawl and recommending programs for growth management, regional tax sharing, and urban revitalization along a more compact, transit-served central city); James DeFilippis, The Myth of Social Capital in Community Development, 12 Hous. Pol'y Debate 781 (2001) (discussing community mechanisms to facilitate acquisition of quality of life improvement); Scott L. Cummings, Community Economic Development as Progressive Politics: Toward a Grassroots Movement for Economic Justice, 54 Stan. L. Rev. 399 (2001) (advocating employment and wage reform along with business incubation); Robert E. Suggs, Bringing Small Business Development to Urban Neighborhoods, 30 Harv. C.R.-C.L. L. Rev. 487 (1995) (advocating social capital and tax credits); David Dante Troutt, Ghettos Made Easy: The Metamarket/Antimarket Dichotomy and the Legal Challenges of Inner-City Economic Development, 35 Harv. C.R.-C.L. L. Rev. 427 (2000) (theoretical and structural analysis of lower-income urban markets and the decentralization impacts of American zoning, and a critique of current strategies); Symposium: Revitalizing America's Cities: Searching for Solutions, 8 Stan. L. & Pol'y Rev. 4 (1997). For a description of the significant role played by local Community Development Corporations (CDCs), *see* Paul S. Grogan & Tony Proscio, Comeback Cities: A Blueprint for Urban Neighborhood Revival ch. 4 (2000); William H. Simon, The Community Economic Development Movement, 2002 Wis. L. Rev. 377. On the

need for access to capital at the neighborhood level, *see* Keith N. Hylton, Banks and Inner Cities: Market and Regulatory Obstacles to Development Lending, 17 Yale J. on Reg. 197 (2000); Daniel M. Leibsohn, Community Development: Financial Services Innovation, 8 J. Affordable Housing & Community Dev. L. 122 (1999). For a discussion of the potential role of urban universities in revitalization, *see* Symposium: Universities and Urban Revitalization, 30 Conn. L. Rev. 1199 (1998).

E. TRANSPORTATION PLANNING AND REDEVELOPMENT

Europeans are likely to walk, ride a bicycle, or take public transit for their transportation. In contrast, most Americans rely solely on the automobile.

The dramatic difference in these urban designs has its origins in the aftermath of World War II. As the victor with enormous industrial capacity and pent-up demand for consumer goods and housing, America launched a program of sprawling suburbs patterned on automobile travel and low density, single-family homes. In contrast, Europe was decimated by war and economic chaos, and thus required public transportation and housing. Given limited land available for urban development and the lack of personal automobiles, the only strategy was to build high density apartment blocks linked by train, subway, or bus. The developed pattern became urban villages that were user friendly to transit users, cyclists, and pedestrians.

The excerpts of articles that follow are designed to be provocative. They allow the student to examine the issue of integration of land uses, including transit, with housing, employment, and recreation. The first excerpt argues that opportunities for economic redevelopment and enhanced community design and livability can be obtained through transit-based land use design.

■ JAMES A. KUSHNER, A COMPARATIVE VISION OF THE CONVERGENCE OF ECOLOGY, EMPOWERMENT, AND THE QUEST FOR A JUST SOCIETY

54 U. Miami L. Rev. 301, 309-315 (1998)

. . . The urban poor are a population disproportionately composed of people of color. They are relegated to communities without the tax base to provide safe streets, quality education, or even a semblance of job training and apprenticeship, which could lead to a decent standard of living through secure employment. This is simply unacceptable in the land of a world-class economic and political society. The pattern of community development based upon low-density suburban homes, requiring automobiles for access to employment, is inconsistent with the notion of a just society, if an increasingly significant portion of the population is priced out of that access.

The pattern of development in America's cities also fails to serve the nation's middle class. The suburbs were designed around a $2000 automobile and a house selling for under $10,000. In such a society, a decent wage was earned by the head of the household, while a homemaker was available to supervise and chauffeur children, maintain the home, and serve the family's quest for the pastoral quiet security of the country.

This contrasts sharply with the edge-city village of the twenty-first century. Today, the American suburban family requires a minimum of two cars requiring costly maintenance, insurance, and operation. Where families have two heads of household, both are likely to be employed. . . . The purchase and maintenance of a home is both more costly and time-consuming than desired by modern suburban dwellers. Moreover, automobile use makes living in the suburbs more dangerous for its youth. In fact, the risk of early death is greater in the suburbs than in the central city.[44] . . .

Fair housing can be viewed as a component of what is generally referred to as "sustainable communities." To environmentalists, the term sustainable communities refers to environmental policies of nondegradation and to economic and development decisions that are designed to renew resources and improve air and water quality. On the regional level, sustainable development calls for transit-oriented development patterns, providing for increased trips by pedestrians, bicyclists and transit users, and reduced automobile use. Coincidentally, this is also what many home seekers desire. Sustainable communities envision being able to walk to a village center main street for shopping, along and through attractive parks and pedestrian walkways with bicycle lanes. Ideally, a community should be linked by transit to other transit villages, some of which are higher density with mixed uses of shops, offices, and housing, with vibrant street and cafe life, while others are centers of manufacturing and commerce. . . .

The community of Hellersdorf in Berlin, Germany presents an interesting illustration of a sustainable community at the neighborhood level. Hellersdorf was a socialist suburban village of 130,000 on the northern political boundary of the city of Berlin within the former eastern sector of East Germany. Hellersdorf was not a pretty village, although it was a transit village, lying at the end of an S-Bahn, or surface train line. There was a complete lack of color and foliage in a village of uniformly-drab concrete apartment blocks, each building having at least one flat windowless wall. Hellersdorf had no city services, no telephones, and the apartment units were, like the whole of East Germany, deteriorating and in need of major rehabilitation. A pedestrian-friendly village center was non-existent; by American standards, Hellersdorf lacked even a decent restaurant.

When the Berlin Wall came down in 1989 and millions of East Germans migrated to the West in search of better housing and jobs, a third of Hellersdorf's units were vacated in the exodus. Undoubtedly, if Hellersdorf were located in an American city, it would have become a slum and the market would have awaited its final decline when a developer would purchase the land at low cost,

44. *See* Jane Jacobs, The Death and Life of Great American Cities (1961); James Gerstenzang, Cars Make Suburbs Riskier Than Cities, Study Says, L.A. Times, Apr. 15, 1996, at A1 (Valley ed.) (reporting that more deaths and injuries resulted from cars in suburbs than from guns and drugs in urban settings; in 1995 in the Pacific Northwest, urban deaths occurred at a rate of 16 per 1,000 residents, while the rate was 19.2 in the suburbs; although crime death rates were 10 per 1,000 in cities and only 1 of 1,000 in suburbs, driving death rates were 18.2 per 1,000 in suburbs as compared to 6 of 1,000 in urban settings); Michael E. Lewyn, Are Spread Out Cities Really Safer? (Or, is Atlanta Safer than New York?), 41 Clev. St. L. Rev. 279 (1993).

bulldoze the structures, and perhaps redevelop the community for upper-income housing.

Despite the fact that Berlin was greatly overextended in developing its infrastructure to accommodate the relocation of the German capitol from Bonn following the reunification of Germany, and despite a high unemployment rate and a limited municipal budget, the city never hesitated in acting to stabilize one of its worst neighborhoods. The city planted 15,000 trees, modified building facades to introduce variation and color, and brought in top mural artists to paint attractive varied mural designs on each building. In partnership with a large developer, Berlin rehabilitated the 130,000 housing units and commenced a program to privatize one-quarter of the public housing, offering subsidies to purchasing tenants. The private developer also undertook a massive commercial mixed-use project to build a multi-screen entertainment complex with offices, shops, and restaurants around and over the S-Bahn line.

The Hellersdorf experience demonstrates that, through mixing income groups within public housing, it is possible to bring about the de-stigmatization of neighborhoods. Today, Hellersdorf has a 100% occupancy rate with a waiting list, and each building has families in apartments facing an inner courtyard of new landscaping and modern playground and recreation facilities. Each building has a distinctive and attractive central courtyard. Thus, Hellersdorf has been transformed into a sustainable transit village. Berlin is now more stable and presents an attractive site for private investment, secure that neighborhoods will not be abandoned or investment dishonored.

By comparison, in the last decade, Los Angeles has spent billions of dollars on expensive transit improvements in subways, guideway trams, fixed-rail trolleys, and light-rail trains running on traditional rail corridors. Of nearly 200 transit stops, not one has been replanned as a transit village with shops, restaurants, housing, parks, offices, and pedestrian zones. Every light-rail transit stop is in a stark industrial district with a parking lot for transit users to switch from train to car for the final drive to a typically suburban single-family subdivision.

It is time that federal transit subsidies be conditioned on integrated land-use replanning around transit stops. A comprehensive plan amendment should include decisions on which stops should be high-density, designed around housing and commercial activity. Other stops should be set aside for lower density around new-urbanism-designed communities with single-family homes on small lots with front porches arranged around a New-England-style village town center. Other stops should emphasize mixed-use industrial employment centers.

For areas not served by fixed-rail transit, transit villages can be planned around quality express bus service that would provide superior service, as compared to lower-density areas that might be served by slower local buses or jitneys. In the inner city, transit villages could be linked with empowerment zones to provide industrial centers, and mixed-use neighborhoods of varying densities, affording vibrant community centers containing restaurants, cafes, stores, entertainment, and housing. The time has come to abandon policies of triage, where neighborhoods containing concentrations of the poor are ignored in favor of more affluent communities. . . .

. . . Launching an extensive program of newly constructed villages around transit would create an opportunity under the Fair Housing Act for people of all colors and ethnicities to have some degree of choice in the type of communities in which they would reside. Such a redesigned community development pattern would offer extraordinary opportunity for increased integration, reduced automobile use and dependency, enhanced employment access, the possibility of reconstruction of the city's tax base, and a realistic hope of extending sustainable communities throughout the region. . . .

The following excerpt offers an alternative view of transit-based development that celebrates the benefits of American sprawl development.

PETER GORDON & HARRY W. RICHARDSON, ARE COMPACT CITIES A DESIRABLE PLANNING GOAL?

63 J. Am. Plan. Ass'n 232 (1997)

The revolution in information processing and telecommunications is accelerating the growth and dispersion of both economic activities and population, possibly moving towards the point where "geography is irrelevant." Yet, at the same time, many planners (and policymakers) advocate "compact cities" as an ideal, in contrast to the reality of "increasingly" spread-out metropolitan development. . . .

Density Preferences

LOW-DENSITY SETTLEMENT IS THE OVERWHELMING CHOICE FOR RESIDENTIAL LIVING

Some observers have argued that this is not an unconstrained choice, but influenced by instruments promoting suburbanization, policies such as the preferential income tax treatment of home mortgage interest, subsidies to automobile use, and the ubiquitous interstate highway system. United States-Canadian differences (or similarities) may be a good test of these objections; for example, there is no home mortgage deductibility in Canada. Goldberg and Mercer (1986) marshaled considerable evidence to emphasize the differences. Yet, even their comparisons of the United States and Canada are subject to multiple interpretations, including the hypothesis of a simple time lag in decentralization trends. For example, both countries' cities are shown to have declining (and converging) population density gradients, although central city densities in Canada remain higher than those in the United States.

The policy explanations of United States suburbanization often emphasize the argument that more subsidies are given to auto travel than to public transit. The opposite is true. Federal, state and local expenditures for highways (and parking) were \$66.5 billion in 1991; revenues were \$53.8 billion (81 percent recovery); federal, state and local expenditures for transit were \$20.8 billion, while revenues were \$8.8 billion (42 percent recovery). On a per-passenger-mile basis, the auto subsidy was 0.54 cents; the transit subsidy was 54 times as large, 29.42 cents. Moreover, the transit subsidies have been growing faster: the same calculations for 1981 show that the transit subsidy per passenger-mile was then "only" 33 times the auto subsidy.

The absence of congestion pricing and emissions fees is a widely acknowledged problem; it constitutes an implicit subsidy to auto users. While estimates of these costs cover a wide range, the Environmental Defense Fund suggested that air pollution costs per passenger mile in Southern California in 1991 were 3.6 cents and congestion costs were 7.5 cents. Donald Shoup suggested that there may be up to an additional 11 cents per passenger mile of parking subsidies for Los Angeles automobile commuters. In any event, even with these adjustments (and making the extreme assumption that these costs are "subsidies"), the full auto subsidy adds up to little more than 22 cents per passenger mile and still falls short of the transit subsidy.

Many consumer surveys have shown strong preferences for suburban living, and the link between household preferences and preferred spatial patterns is clear: "[in] evaluating the desirability of existing spatial patterns, revealed preferences of consumers, especially when they have persisted as long as they have in the U.S., must be given some weight." . . .

The Scope for Transit

LOW DENSITIES MAKE HIGH-CAPACITY TRANSIT SYSTEMS UNATTRACTIVE AND THEREFORE WASTEFUL (OF ALL RESOURCES UTILIZED, INCLUDING ENERGY)

Because the spreading out of cities reduces markets for conventional public transit (especially fixed rail, which is spatially inflexible and usually oriented to downtown), it should surprise no one that the United States transit industry has been in decline for most of the twentieth century. Massive subsidies have not helped; they may have made matters worse. The Congressional Budget Office concluded that "despite more than 25 years of federal assistance, mass transit carries only about 5 percent of people who commute to work. The other 95 percent mostly use automobiles. . . . New federally assisted transit systems have not added to mass transit; instead, they have replaced flexible bus routes with costly fixed-route services to a few downtown areas, while the growth in jobs and population has been in the suburbs and in the smaller cities. At the same time, transit costs are rising: transit fleets in general are greatly underused, and the new transit systems have for the most part added to costs and to unused capacity without attracting riders from cars." A large (and still growing) number of studies echo this finding.

It appears that "neotraditional" neighborhoods, pedestrian pockets, mixed land use developments and other features of the New Urbanism do not make much of a difference. Cervero reports: "Over-all, focusing development near transit and designing communities to be more transit-friendly, by themselves, will have little bearing on people's travel choices." Moreover, Crane has suggested it is possible that neotraditional neighborhoods may increase rather than reduce automobile use, depending on case-by-case empirical considerations, because shorter origin-destination distances reduce the average cost per trip. Cheaper trips mean more *vehicle* trips, and it is conceivable, perhaps more probable than not, that total VMT (vehicle miles traveled) may increase. Thus, neotraditional neighborhoods may neither increase transit use nor reduce auto travel. . . .

Technology and Agglomeration-Congestion Trade-Offs

HIGH-RISE OR CONCENTRATED SETTLEMENT IS COSTLY AND ONLY WORTHWHILE IF TRANSPORT OR COMMUNICATIONS COSTS ARE HIGH, YET THESE HAVE BEEN FALLING FOR MANY YEARS, AND COMMUNICATION COSTS, AT LEAST, ARE LIKELY TO CONTINUE TO FALL STEEPLY IN THE MID-TERM FUTURE

High density settlement involves trade-offs between inevitable costs (congestion) and prospective benefits (agglomeration). High-rise buildings exist where they do only because the high costs of erecting and maintaining them were considered to be worth the economies realized through increased accessibility, communication and interaction, and the ease of face-to-face transactions. . . .

For most of the twentieth century, the highway system has been the major force for continued low-density settlement and suburbanization. The barriers of distance continue to "dissolve"; factories and offices continue to move to where employees want to live. Most commuting is now suburb-to-suburb, taking congestion pressures off traditional downtowns and allowing many to drive faster on less congested suburban highways. Suburb-to-central-city commuting continues to diminish. City forms continue to evolve beyond polycentricity to patterns of generalized dispersion. Recent research on the Los Angeles CMSA that compares employment concentrations in the three census years, 1970, 1980, and 1990, shows that all places qualifying as "centers" (based on trip generation densities) accounted for 19 percent of regional employment in 1970, 17 percent in 1980 and only 12 percent in 1990. Also, the number of places qualifying as centers declined from 20 (in 1970) to 12 (in 1990) during a period when the region's employment base grew from 3.6 million to 6.3 million jobs. This dispersion of economic activities, clear-cut in Los Angeles and perhaps evident in other metropolitan areas once the research has been done, is much more radical than implied by the adoption of concepts such as "edge cities," "satellite cities," "polycentricity," and "urban villages."

Rapid advances in telecommunications are now accelerating the decentralization trends set in motion by the advent of the automobile. In 1890, the "effective radius" of U.S. cities was said to be about 2 miles, based largely on pedestrian access. Dyckman reported that this had grown to 8 miles by 1920 because of the development of public transit, to 11 miles by 1950 (the diffusion of automobile ownership), and to 20-24 miles by the 1970s (the construction of urban freeways systems). The centrifugal trends have now accelerated because telecommunications access cannot be measured in terms of geographical distance. The locational choices open to both households and firms have expanded accordingly. In the extreme case, geography might become irrelevant. Peter Drucker suggests that "[o]ffice work, rather than office workers, will do the traveling." Proximity is becoming redundant. . . .

Those who misread these trends do so at considerable cost. For example, Asian real estate investors lost approximately one-half of their $77 billion investment in American cities over the last decade or so by focusing on downtown locations. Americans should not feel too smug, however, because their elected representatives have squandered, in total, even larger sums on dubious downtown renewal schemes. . . .

Notes and Comments

1. *Transit-Based Housing and Sprawl.* Would Gordon and Richardson's thesis be the same if some transit villages were built at densities between 60 and 100 dwelling units per acre as in many European communities? For a general discussion of transit-based housing designed to increase ridership and establish pedestrian villages around transit stops, see Michael Bernick & Robert Cervero, Transit Villages in the 21st Century (1997). "Sprawl" is a general term, while in actuality there exist a range of density and dispersal patterns. *See* George Galster et al., Wrestling Sprawl to the Ground: Defining and Measuring an Elusive Concept, 12 Hous. Pol'y Debate 681 (2001) (offering a conceptual definition considering distinct dimensions of land use patterns — density, continuity, concentration, clustering, centrality, nuclearity, mixed uses, and proximity — with "sprawl" defined as a low value in at least one dimension). *See also* Robert W. Burchell & Naveed Shad, The Evolution of the Sprawl Debate in the United States, 5 Hastings West-N.W. J. Envtl. L. & Pol'y 137 (1999). For support for the Gordon & Richardson thesis, *see* Mark Fina & Leonard Shabman, Some Unconventional Thoughts on Sprawl, 23 Wm. & Mary Envtl. L. & Pol'y Rev. 739 (1999).

Transit systems often neglect bus riders, as expensive subway and light-rail projects are funded and designed to serve the more affluent suburban communities. See Kevin L. Siegel, Discrimination in the Funding of Mass Transit Systems: Formulating a Title VI Challenge to the Subsidization of the Alameda Contra Costa Transit District as Compared to the Bay Area Rapid Transit District, 4 Hastings W.-N.W. J. Envtl. L. & Pol'y 107 (1997). *See also* Michele Casey et al., An Overview of Transportation Issues Affecting the Welfare-to-Work Populations: The TRUC Program, 34 Clearinghouse Rev. 634 (2001) (discussing legal issues and supporting a not-for-profit car dealership as a means to fight inaccessibility); Nicole Stelle Garnett, The Road from Welfare to Work: Informal Transportation and the Urban Poor, 38 Harv. J. on Legis. 173 (2001) (spatial mismatch between employment centers and the jobless makes access for the disabled and the carless problematic).

2. *Modal Splits.* The term "modal splits" describes the methods of trips made by a community's residents. Most Viennese own a transit pass purchased for a few hundred dollars a year, and the average Viennese uses public transit 600 times a year. John Pucher, Urban Travel Behavior as the Outcome of Public Policy: The Example of Modal-Split in Western Europe and North America, 54 J. Am. Plan. Ass'n 509 (1988) (automobile used for 82.3 percent of trips in U.S., 47.6 percent in West Germany, and 38.5 percent in Austria; public transport used for 3.4 percent in U.S., 11.4 percent in West Germany, and 38.5 percent in Austria; bicycle used for 0.7 percent in U.S., 9.6 percent in West Germany, and 38.5 percent in Austria, with walking 10.7 percent in U.S., 30.3 percent in West Germany, and 31.2 percent in Austria). In Jurgen Brunsing, Public Transport and Cycling: Experience of Modal Integration in West Germany, in The Greening of Urban Transport: Planning for Walking and Cycling in Western Cities 231, 232 (Rodney Tolley ed. 1990), the author reports that in Germany in 1982, 17.1 percent used the bicycle as the main means of transport for distances up to three kilometers, and 6.8 percent used public transport. For distances longer than four kilometers, 6.1 percent used the bicycle, and 17.3 used public transport. See also Robert Cervero & Roger Gorham, Commuting in Transit Versus Automobile Neighborhoods, 61 J. Am. Plan. Ass'n 210, 212 (1995) (in San Francisco neighborhoods built before World War II and

originally designed around transit, 23 percent of the trips are on foot and 22 percent by transit, while in newer, auto-oriented neighborhoods, only 9 percent are on foot and 3 percent by transit).

The United States is going in the other direction. Between 1980 and 1990, 22 million new single-occupant drivers were added to the commute, while only 19 million new workers joined the commute during that period. At the same time, transit lost 200,000 riders, four million persons stopped carpooling, and 650,000 stopped walking to work. Department of Transportation, Transportation Statistics: Annual Report 1994 at 53. *See also* Marlon Boarnet & Randall Crane, Travel by Design: The Influence of Urban Form on Travel (2001) (raising doubts on how to build communities and offering a critique of transit-oriented development and New Urbanism); James A. Dunn, Jr., Driving Forces: The Automobile, Its Enemies and the Politics of Mobility (1998) (automobiles rule).

3. *Cities and Suburbs.* Cities are generally experiencing a decline in central city economic activity, a decline in central city population, a decline in suburb to central city commuting, and an increased need for transit between suburbs. Robert Cervero, Suburban Gridlock (1986). Cities have responded with a redistribution of transit subsidies to the suburbs and cities on the edge of the urbanized city (so-called edge cities), often at the expense of higher urban bus and transit fares together with reduced service. The strategy is designed to increase transit ridership and reduce highway congestion. The effect, however, may also be to increase access and demand for even more low density, suburban subdivisions, generating even more traffic.

In *New York Urban League v. State of New York*, 71 F.3d 1031 (2d Cir. 1995) (per curiam), the Second Circuit sustained the denial of a preliminary injunction against a city transit fare increase. The court refused to accept the district court's finding of discrimination based on the disparate impact of fare box recovery ratios. For example, bus and subway fares were raised 12.2 percent, as compared to 2.2 and 2.6 percent increases on suburban transit lines. The Second Circuit noted that other costs of operation were not reflected in the statistics, and the record did not show that suburban fare increases would generate adequate revenues. The court also emphasized that central city residents benefited from suburban transit subsidies in reduced traffic congestion and pollution, and encouragement for central city business location.

4. *Transportation Plans.* The Clean Air Act requires the adoption of state implementation plans (SIPs) designed to reduce air pollution. The SIPs are specifically directed to reducing automobile usage and encouraging alternatives such as carpools and transit, with disincentives such as higher parking and toll costs. Philip Weinberg, Public Transportation and Clean Air: Natural Allies, 21 Envtl. L. 1527 (1991). *See also Conservation Law Found. v. Federal Highway Admin.*, 24 F.3d 1465 (1st Cir. 1994) (Clean Air Act citizen suits available in challenge to highway construction).

5. *Revenue Sharing.* Resistance to transit-based development often comes from local reluctance to develop uses that generate the need for expensive services. Communities prefer to compete for the greatest generator of tax revenues: the shopping mall; the "big box" retail store; the factory outlet; and the commercial, office, or industrial use. Marlon Boarnet & Randall Crane, L.A. Story—A Reality Check for Transit-Based Housing, 63 J. Am. Plan. Ass'n 189 (1997) (explaining the lack of transit villages in the system of 232 existing and proposed southern California rail transit stations as stemming from pressure on local government to

generate sales and business taxes rather than property taxes, and to use transit primarily for economic development goals that call for the retention of industrial land uses).

One proposal to reduce local interjurisdictional competition for tax base would require sharing regional tax revenues. Minnesota, for example, has enacted a scheme of sharing tax revenues from improvements in wealthier communities with those that are less wealthy. See James A. Kushner, The Reagan Urban Policy: Centrifugal Force in the Empire, 2 UCLA J. Envtl. L. & Pol'y 209, 231 (1982). This scheme lowers tax burdens on firms in areas that need an increased tax base by revenue sharing with wealthier areas.

F. ANTICOMPETITIVENESS

Because the promotion of economic development is a centerpiece of contemporary planning, issues of anticompetitiveness necessarily arise in the development and planning process. Indeed, in upcoming years competition among local governments for job development is likely to place anticompetitive behavior even more in the forefront of urban development.

Historically, local government was exposed to federal antitrust liability for zoning and other land use regulation, due to the monopolistic effect of zoning and the fact that the cooperation which often occurs between developers and a city might be characterized as a conspiracy. Later case law and congressional lawmaking have provided local governments with partial immunity from such liability. Nonetheless, some small range of exposure may remain.

The future may see much more concern over intra-regional and inter-regional competition for job development. As recent controversies over attempted moves by professional sports franchises attest, communities are identifying additional reasons for regulating to control the local economic base. As competition for jobs and growth increases, greater focus may be placed on the "pirating" of employers to move to new regions. The future emphasis in this field may look to subsidizing business through public infrastructure finance, such as through tax-supported government improvements. Government policy also may emphasize corporate and below-market industrial bonds where government supplies financing at rates lower than the market rate.

These subsidies may come under fire as constituting a policy that adversely affects competition by using unfair methods to attract employers. The experience under the Common Market (or European Economic Union) and under other international trade agreements such as the General Agreement on Tariffs and Trade (GATT) (equivalent requirements now administered through the World Trade Organization (WTO)) also suggests that policies adversely affecting competition may violate international standards.

1. Federal Antitrust Law

By its very nature, the local government power to regulate land use and development carries the potential for exercising anticompetitive or monopoly power.

Decisions to restrict growth may favor competing landowners or developers, and the danger of local government complicity in monopolization efforts by politically powerful developers is real. Local government acting in its enterprise (or market participant) capacity as a redevelopment sponsor may also be tempted to restrain competing development to obtain a competitive advantage in the pursuit of tax revenues.

Conspiracies in restraint of trade violate the Sherman Act. 15 U.S.C. §§1-2 (2000). Liability requires a conspiracy between local government and a private entity. *See Copperweld Corp. v. Independence Tube Corp.*, 467 U.S. 752 (1984). The conspiracy must be "unreasonable." *Standard Oil Co. v. United States*, 221 U.S. 1, 49 (1911). There does exist, however, an exemption for so-called state action. *Parker v. Brown*, 317 U.S. 341 (1943). Local government is exempt when it acts under state enabling legislation, such as under building codes, outdoor advertising regulation, or zoning. The scope of that exemption is discussed in the next case, *Columbia v. Omni Outdoor Advertising, Inc.*, 499 U.S. 365 (1991).

In addition to the state action exemption, because of tension with the First Amendment, noncriminal organized lobbying to influence public officials in the passage and enforcement of laws to engage in anticompetitive activities is also exempt from antitrust liability. This is the so-called *Noerr-Pennington* doctrine, which applies unless the lobbying is a "sham." *United Mine Workers v. Pennington*, 381 U.S. 657 (1965); *Eastern R.R. Presidents' Conference v. Noerr Motor Freight, Inc.*, 365 U.S. 127 (1961).

CITY OF COLUMBIA v. OMNI OUTDOOR ADVERTISING, INC.

499 U.S. 365 (1991)

Justice SCALIA delivered the opinion of the Court.

This case requires us to clarify the application of the Sherman Act to municipal governments and to the citizens who seek action from them.

I

Petitioner Columbia Outdoor Advertising, Inc. (COA), a South Carolina corporation, entered the billboard business in the city of Columbia, South Carolina (also a petitioner here), in the 1940s. By 1981 it controlled more than 95% of what has been conceded to be the relevant market. COA was a local business owned by a family with deep roots in the community, and enjoyed close relations with the city's political leaders. The mayor and other members of the city council were personal friends of COA's majority owner, and the company and its officers occasionally contributed funds and free billboard space to their campaigns. According to respondent Omni Outdoor Advertising, Inc., these beneficences were part of a "longstanding" "secret anticompetitive agreement" whereby "the City and COA would each use their *[sic]* respective power and resources to protect . . . COA's monopoly position," in return for which "City Council members received advantages made possible by COA's monopoly." Brief for Respondent 12, 16.

In 1981, Omni, a Georgia corporation, began erecting billboards in and around the city. COA responded to this competition in several ways. . . . Finally (and this is what gives rise to the issue we address today), COA executives met with city officials to seek the enactment of zoning ordinances that would restrict billboard construction. COA was not alone in urging this course; concerned about the city's recent explosion of billboards, a number of citizens, including writers of articles and editorials in local newspapers, advocated restrictions.

In the spring of 1982, the city council passed an ordinance requiring the council's approval for every billboard constructed in downtown Columbia. This was later amended to impose a 180-day moratorium on the construction of billboards throughout the city, except as specifically authorized by the council. A state court invalidated this ordinance on the ground that its conferral of unconstrained discretion upon the city council violated both the South Carolina and Federal Constitutions. The city then requested the State's regional planning authority to conduct a comprehensive analysis of the local billboard situation as a basis for developing a final, constitutionally valid, ordinance. In September 1982, after a series of public hearings and numerous meetings involving city officials, Omni, and COA (in all of which, according to Omni, positions contrary to COA's were not genuinely considered), the city council passed a new ordinance restricting the size, location, and spacing of billboards. These restrictions, particularly those on spacing, obviously benefited COA, which already had its billboards in place; they severely hindered Omni's ability to compete.

In November 1982, Omni filed suit against COA and the city in Federal District Court, charging that they had violated §§1 and 2 of the Sherman Act, 26 Stat. 209, as amended, 15 U.S.C. §§1, 2,[1] as well as South Carolina's Unfair Trade Practices Act, S.C. Code Ann. §39-5-140 (1976). Omni contended, in particular, that the city's billboard ordinances were the result of an anticompetitive conspiracy between city officials and COA that stripped both parties of any immunity they might otherwise enjoy from the federal antitrust laws. In January 1986, after more than two weeks of trial, a jury returned general verdicts against the city and COA on both the federal and state claims. It awarded damages, before trebling, of $600,000 on the §1 Sherman Act claim, and $400,000 on the §2 claim.[2] The jury also answered two special interrogatories, finding specifically that the city and COA had conspired both to restrain trade and to monopolize the market. . . .

II

In the landmark case of *Parker v. Brown*, 317 U.S. 341 (1943), we rejected the contention that a program restricting the marketing of privately produced raisins,

1. Section 1 provides in pertinent part: "Every contract, combination in the form of trust or otherwise, or conspiracy, in restraint of trade or commerce among the several States, or with foreign nations, is declared to be illegal." 15 U.S.C. §1.

Section 2 provides in pertinent part: "Every person who shall monopolize, or attempt to monopolize, or combine or conspire with any other person or persons, to monopolize any part of the trade or commerce among the several States, or with foreign nations, shall be deemed guilty of a felony." 15 U.S.C. §2.

2. The monetary damages in this case were assessed entirely against COA, the District Court having ruled that the city was immunized by the Local Government Antitrust Act of 1984, 98 Stat. 2750, as amended, 15 U.S.C. §§34-36, which exempts local governments from paying damages for violations of the federal antitrust laws . . . . Respondent has not challenged that determination in this Court, and we express no view on the matter.

adopted pursuant to California's Agricultural Prorate Act, violated the Sherman Act. Relying on principles of federalism and state sovereignty, we held that the Sherman Act did not apply to anticompetitive restraints imposed by the States "as an act of government." *Id.*, at 352.

Since *Parker* emphasized the role of sovereign *States* in a federal system, it was initially unclear whether the governmental actions of political subdivisions enjoyed similar protection. In recent years, we have held that *Parker* immunity does not apply directly to local governments. We have recognized, however, that a municipality's restriction of competition may sometimes be an authorized implementation of state policy, and have accorded *Parker* immunity where that is the case.

The South Carolina statutes under which the city acted in the present case authorize municipalities to regulate the use of land and the construction of buildings and other structures within their boundaries. It is undisputed that, as a matter of state law, these statutes authorize the city to regulate the size, location, and spacing of billboards. It could be argued, however, that a municipality acts beyond its delegated authority, for *Parker* purposes, whenever the nature of its regulation is substantively or even procedurally defective. On such an analysis it could be contended, for example, that the city's regulation in the present case was not "authorized" by S.C. Code Ann. §5-23-10 (1976), if it was not, as that statute requires, adopted "for the purpose of promoting health, safety, morals or the general welfare of the community." As scholarly commentary has noted, such an expansive interpretation of the *Parker*-defense authorization requirement would have unacceptable consequences.

> To be sure, state law "authorizes" only agency decisions that are substantively and procedurally correct. Errors of fact, law, or judgment by the agency are not "authorized." Erroneous acts or decisions are subject to reversal by superior tribunals because unauthorized. If the antitrust court demands unqualified "authority" in this sense, it inevitably becomes the standard reviewer not only of federal agency activity but also of state and local activity whenever it is alleged that the governmental body, though possessing the power to engage in the challenged conduct, has actually exercised its power in a manner not authorized by state law. . . .

P. Areeda & H. Hovenkamp, Antitrust Law ¶212.3b, p. 145 (Supp. 1989). We agree with that assessment, and believe that in order to prevent *Parker* from undermining the very interests of federalism it is designed to protect, it is necessary to adopt a concept of authority broader than what is applied to determine the legality of the municipality's action under state law. . . . It suffices for the present to conclude that here no more is needed to establish, for *Parker* purposes, the city's authority to regulate than its unquestioned zoning power over the size, location, and spacing of billboards.

Besides authority to regulate, however, the *Parker* defense also requires authority to suppress competition — more specifically, "clear articulation of a state policy to authorize anticompetitive conduct" by the municipality in connection with its regulation. We have rejected the contention that this requirement can be met only if the delegating statute explicitly permits the displacement of competition. It is enough, we have held, if suppression of competition is the "foreseeable result" of what the statute authorizes. That condition is amply met here. The very purpose of zoning regulation is to displace unfettered business freedom in a manner that regularly has the effect of preventing normal acts of competition, particularly on the part of new entrants. A municipal ordinance restricting the size, location, and spacing of billboards (surely a common form of zoning) necessarily protects existing billboards against some competition from newcomers.

The Court of Appeals was therefore correct in its conclusion that the city's restriction of billboard construction was prima facie entitled to *Parker* immunity. The Court of Appeals upheld the jury verdict, however, by invoking a "conspiracy" exception to *Parker* that has been recognized by several Courts of Appeals. . . .

There is no such conspiracy exception. The rationale of *Parker* was that, in light of our national commitment to federalism, the general language of the Sherman Act should not be interpreted to prohibit anticompetitive actions by the States in their governmental capacities as sovereign regulators. . . . [T]his immunity does not necessarily obtain where the State acts not in a regulatory capacity but as a commercial participant in a given market. . . . Since it is both inevitable and desirable that public officials often agree to do what one or another group of private citizens urges upon them, such an exception would virtually swallow up the *Parker* rule: All anticompetitive regulation would be vulnerable to a "conspiracy" charge.

Omni suggests, however, that "conspiracy" might be limited to instances of governmental "corruption," defined variously as "abandonment of public responsibilities to private interests," "corrupt or bad faith decisions," and "selfish or corrupt motives." Ultimately, Omni asks us not to define "corruption" at all, but simply to leave that task to the jury. . . .

A conspiracy exception narrowed along such vague lines is similarly impractical. Few governmental actions are immune from the charge that they are "not in the public interest" or in some sense "corrupt." . . . The fact is that virtually all regulation benefits some segments of the society and harms others; and that it is not universally considered contrary to the public good if the net economic loss to the losers exceeds the net economic gain to the winners. *Parker* was not written in ignorance of the reality that determination of "the public interest" in the manifold areas of government regulation entails not merely economic and mathematical analysis but value judgment, and it was not meant to shift that judgment from elected officials to judges and juries. . . .

III

While *Parker* recognized the States' freedom to engage in anticompetitive regulation, it did not purport to immunize from antitrust liability the private parties who urge them to engage in anticompetitive regulation. However, it is obviously peculiar in a democracy, and perhaps in derogation of the constitutional right "to petition the Government for a redress of grievances," U.S. Const., Amdt. 1, to establish a category of lawful state action that citizens are not permitted to urge. Thus, beginning with *Eastern Railroad Presidents Conference v. Noerr Motor Freight, Inc., supra*, we have developed a corollary to *Parker:* The federal antitrust laws also do not regulate the conduct of private individuals in seeking anticompetitive action from the government. This doctrine, like *Parker*, rests ultimately upon a recognition that the antitrust laws, "tailored as they are for the business world, are not at all appropriate for application in the political arena." That a private party's political motives are selfish is irrelevant: "*Noerr* shields from the Sherman Act a concerted effort to influence public officials regardless of intent or purpose."

Noerr recognized, however, what has come to be known as the "sham" exception to its rule: "There may be situations in which a publicity campaign, ostensibly directed toward influencing governmental action, is a mere sham to cover what is actually nothing more than an attempt to interfere directly with the business relationships of a competitor and the application of the Sherman Act would be justified." The Court of Appeals concluded that the jury in this case could have found that COA's activities on behalf of the restrictive billboard ordinances fell within this exception. In our view that was error.

The "sham" exception to *Noerr* encompasses situations in which persons use the governmental *process* — as opposed to the *outcome* of that process — as an anticompetitive weapon. A classic example is the filing of frivolous objections to the license application of a competitor, with no expectation of achieving denial of the license but simply in order to impose expense and delay. A "sham" situation involves a defendant whose activities are "not genuinely aimed at procuring favorable government action" at all, *Allied Tube & Conduit Corp. v. Indian Head, Inc.*, 486 U.S. 496, 500, n.4 (1988), not one "who 'genuinely seeks to achieve his governmental result, but does so *through improper means*.' "

Neither of the Court of Appeals' theories for application of the "sham" exception to the facts of the present case is sound. The court reasoned, first, that the jury could have concluded that COA's interaction with city officials " 'was actually nothing more than an attempt to interfere directly with the business relations *[sic]* of a competitor.' " This analysis relies upon language from *Noerr*, but ignores the import of the critical word "directly." Although COA indisputably set out to disrupt Omni's business relationships, it sought to do so not through the very process of lobbying, or of causing the city council to consider zoning measures, but rather through the ultimate *product* of that lobbying and consideration, viz., the zoning ordinances. The Court of Appeals' second theory was that the jury could have found "that COA's purposes were to delay Omni's entry into the market and even to deny it a meaningful access to the appropriate city administrative and legislative fora." But the purpose of delaying a competitor's entry into the market does not render lobbying activity a "sham," unless (as no evidence suggested was true here) the delay is sought to be achieved only by the lobbying process itself, and not by the governmental action that the lobbying seeks. . . .

Omni urges that if, as we have concluded, the "sham" exception is inapplicable, we should use this case to recognize another exception to *Noerr* immunity — a "conspiracy" exception, which would apply when government officials conspire with a private party to employ government action as a means of stifling competition. . . .

Giving full consideration to this matter for the first time, we conclude that a "conspiracy" exception to *Noerr* must be rejected. . . . As we have described, *Parker* and *Noerr* are complementary expressions of the principle that the antitrust laws regulate business, not politics; the former decision protects the States' acts of governing, and the latter the citizens' participation in government. Insofar as the identification of an immunity-destroying "conspiracy" is concerned, *Parker* and *Noerr* generally present two faces of the same coin. The *Noerr*-invalidating conspiracy alleged here is just the *Parker*-invalidating conspiracy viewed from the standpoint of the private-sector participants rather than the governmental participants. The same factors which, as we have described above, make it impracticable or beyond the purpose of the antitrust laws to identify and invalidate lawmaking that has been infected by selfishly motivated agreement with private interests likewise make it impracticable or beyond that scope to identify and invalidate lobbying that has produced selfishly motivated agreement with public officials. . . .

Notes and Comments

1. *Home Rule.* While some states and units of local government adhere to "Dillon's Rule" (discussed in Chapter 1) under which cities enjoy only specific powers delegated to them through state enabling legislation, an increasing number of local governments enjoy so-called home rule. Under the variations of home rule, communities possess police powers enjoyed by state legislatures, or in the case of charter cities, those powers contained in a locally adopted charter. The local government, however, remains subject to state legislation preempting the exercise of local regulation. *See* 1 James A. Kushner, Subdivision Law and Growth Management §1:07 (2d ed. 2001 & Supp. 2003).

Does *City of Columbia* discriminate against home rule cities? By requiring specific state enabling legislation that authorizes the anticompetitive activity or regulation, does the Court trample on federalism by not recognizing the autonomy of home rule jurisdictions to adopt regulations authorized by the city charter and not in violation of any state legislation?

2. *Liability After* City of Columbia. Does *City of Columbia* immunize local government from all Sherman Act liability? In what circumstance might a city not be immune? Can the city be liable if it is acting as a market participant as compared to a market regulator? A conspiracy depriving a landowner of a constitutional right, such as a substantive due process right to a nonarbitrary application of land use regulations, can give rise to a civil rights-based action for damages. *See, e.g., Parkway Garage, Inc. v. City of Philadelphia*, 5 F.3d 685 (3d Cir. 1993). However, recent decisions have extended state sovereign immunity under the Tenth and Eleventh Amendments. *See Alden v. Maine*, 527 U.S. 706 (1999) (Tenth Amendment sovereign immunity extended to bar legislation under Article I that would allow employee to utilize state courts to enforce Fair Labor Standards Act violations); *Kimel v. Florida Bd. of Regents*, 528 U.S. 62 (2000) (although Congress expressed its intent to abrogate the Eleventh Amendment in extending the Age Discrimination in Employment Act to state employees, Congress lacked power under Section 5 of the Fourteenth Amendment to enact appropriate legislation to enforce the Equal Protection Clause); *Seminole Tribe v. Florida*, 517 U.S. 44 (1996) (rejecting congressional abrogation of state Eleventh Amendment immunity authority under the Commerce Clause). These decisions raise doubts as to the possibility of municipal damage exposure whether or not the conduct was within the state action doctrine. States remain free to voluntarily waive their immunities. *See generally* E. Thomas Sullivan, Antitrust Regulation of Land Use: Federalism's Triumph Over Competition, The Last Fifty Years, 3 Wash. U. J. L. & Pol'y 473 (2000), *published in* Evolving Voices in Land Use Law ch. 7 (Washington University Journal of Law & Policy 2000).

3. *Anticompetitive Behavior.* Would a community's desire to retain the vitality of an existing retail area justify the denial of rezoning to commercial use to accommodate potential competitors? Would such anticompetitive legislation violate the Sherman Act? *See Jacobs, Visconsi & Jacobs Co. v. City of Lawrence*, 927 F.2d 1111 (10th

Cir. 1991) (anticipating *City of Columbia* by concluding that the zoning enabling act authorizes anticompetitive zoning action). Would a developer surreptitiously financing citizen litigation to halt a competitor's zoning permit be protected under *Noerr-Pennington*? *Baltimore Scrap Corp. v. David J. Joseph Co.*, 237 F.3d 394 (4th Cir. 2000), *cert. denied*, 533 U.S. 916 (2001) (yes, even though the competitor was not a party to the zoning litigation). What if a potential tenant unable to negotiate a deal forms a corporation for the purpose of establishing standing to challenge the project? *Alfred Weissman Real Estate, Inc. v. Big V Supermarkets, Inc.*, 707 N.Y.S.2d 647 (N.Y. Sup. Ct. App. Div. 2000) (shielded under *Noerr-Pennington* where efforts to defeat the rezoning are not a sham nor within the corruption exception). What if riverboat casinos lobby the Gaming Commission to block a casino and an automobile race track? *Harrah's Vicksburg Corp. v. Pennebaker*, 812 So. 2d 163 (Miss. 2001) (immune). Does the grant of exclusive development rights in an urban redevelopment project violate antitrust laws? *Omega Homes, Inc. v. City of Buffalo*, 171 F.3d 755 (2d Cir. 1999) (per curiam), *cert. denied*, 528 U.S. 874 (1999) (state delegation of redevelopment authority contemplates anticompetitive behavior).

4. *Local Government Immunity.* The Local Government Antitrust Act of 1984 bars the recovery of damages, costs, or attorney's fees against local government. 15 U.S.C. §34, 35(a), 36 (2000). The 1984 legislation, however, does not entirely eliminate exposure to antitrust litigation for local government, as injunctive relief remains available as a remedy. The law would not bar a treble damage judgment against private persons who act beyond the cloak of the local government official's action.

5. *State Zoning of Competition.* When a commercial rezoning, subdivision, or site plan is denied, the members of the legislative or administrative body may have opposed the application for a range of reasons. Sorting out the issues before the deciding body can be difficult, as land use matters often present the spectrum of environmental and infrastructure problems. For example, projects can cause increased traffic and parking demands, threaten the retention of the existing community's small town character, pose problems of flood control or surface water, potentially endanger the habitat of flora or fauna, or raise concerns over sewer and school capacity arising from the anticipated demand for housing in the area.

All of these considerations can influence planning decisions, in addition to anticompetitive motives. Like the problems in mixed-motive discrimination cases (*see Arlington Heights* in Chapter 13), the search for a partial improper motive, or the motivating factor, may best be proven by the proverbial "smoking gun" admission. The search for that weapon poses difficult problems for lawyers and judges. *See Ensign Bickford Realty Corp. v. City Council*, 137 Cal. Rptr. 304 (Cal. App. 1977) (holding that the motive of city council person is irrelevant to any inquiry concerning the reasonableness of a zoning ordinance and rejecting plaintiff's claim that the city council denied the rezoning to restrict competition).

If *Ensign Bickford* were decided after *City of Columbia*, would the city lose its antitrust exemption if found to be acting outside the lawful zoning power authorized by the state? Would the outcome differ where a rezoning from business to residential was designed to protect existing business from competition? *See Phillips v. Town of Brookhaven*, 628 N.Y.S.2d 723 (Sup. Ct. App. Div. 1995) (rezoning did not support Sherman Antitrust Act claim). Should communities be allowed to exclude big box retailers by passing "Superstore Laws" that cap maximum floor space? *Great Atlantic & Pac. Tea Co. v. Town of E. Hampton*, 997 F. Supp. 340 (E.D.N.Y. 1998)

("Superstore Law" restricting retail stores over 10,000 square feet to outside of the central business district was not adopted in accordance with a comprehensive plan, and equal protection claim was stated).

2. *State Incentives*

The focus of the anticompetition cases in the land use field has been on discrimination against disfavored developers. Should the focus shift to inter-regional economic moves? For example, do legal theories exist to challenge the pirating of "rust belt" companies by developing "sun belt" cities? As you read the following case, ask whether it is an example of pirating that perhaps should be condemned or just good, proactive planning for economic development that should be praised.

■ MAREADY v. CITY OF WINSTON-SALEM
467 S.E.2d 615 (N.C. 1996)

WHICHARD, Justice.

Plaintiff-appellant, William F. Maready, instituted this action against the City of Winston-Salem, its Board of Aldermen, Forsyth County, its Board of Commissioners, and Winston-Salem Business, Inc. Plaintiff contends that N.C.G.S. §158-7.1, which authorizes local governments to make economic development incentive grants to private corporations, is unconstitutional because it violates the public purpose clause of the North Carolina Constitution. . . .

This action challenges twenty-four economic development incentive projects entered into by the City or County pursuant to N.C.G.S. §158-7.1. The projected investment by the City and County in these projects totals approximately $13,200,000. The primary source of these funds has been taxes levied by the City and County on property owners in Winston-Salem and Forsyth County. City and County officials estimate an increase in the local tax base of $238,593,000 and a projected creation of over 5500 new jobs as a result of these economic development incentive programs. They expect to recoup the full amount of their investment within three to seven years. The source of the return will be revenues generated by the additional property taxes paid by participating corporations. To date, all but one project has met or exceeded its goal.

The typical procedures the City and County observe in deciding to make an economic development incentive expenditure are as follows: A determination is made that participation by local government is necessary to cause a project to go forward in the community. Officials then apply a formula set out in written guidelines to determine the maximum amount of assistance that can be given to the receiving corporation. The amounts actually committed are usually much less than the maximum. The expenditures are in the form of reimbursement to the recipient for purposes such as on-the-job training, site preparation, facility upgrading, and parking. If a proposal satisfies the guidelines as well as community needs, it is submitted to the appropriate governing body for final approval at a regularly scheduled public meeting. If a project is formally approved, it is administered pursuant to a written contract and to the applicable provisions and limitations of N.C.G.S. §158-7.1.

Article V, Section 2(1) of the North Carolina Constitution provides that "[t]he power of taxation shall be exercised in a just and equitable manner, for public purposes only." In *Mitchell v. North Carolina Indus. Dev. Fin. Auth.*, 159 S.E.2d 745 (1968), Justice (later Chief Justice) Sharp, writing for a majority of this Court, stated:

> The power to appropriate money *from* the public treasury is no greater than the power to levy the tax which put the money in the treasury. Both powers are subject to the constitutional proscription that tax revenues may not be used for private individuals or corporations, no matter how benevolent.

In determining whether legislation serves a public purpose, the presumption favors constitutionality. Reasonable doubt must be resolved in favor of the validity of the act. . . .

In exercising the State's police power, the General Assembly may legislate for the protection of the general health, safety, and welfare of the people. It may "experiment with new modes of dealing with old evils, except as prevented by the Constitution." *Redevelopment Comm'n of Greensboro v. Security Nat'l Bank of Greensboro*, 252 N.C. 595, 612, 114 S.E.2d 688, 700 (1960). The initial responsibility for determining what constitutes a public purpose rests with the legislature, and its determinations are entitled to great weight.

The enactment of N.C.G.S. §158-7.1 leaves no doubt that the General Assembly considers expenditures of public funds for the promotion of local economic development to serve a public purpose. Under this statute,

> [e]ach county and city in this State is authorized to make appropriations for the purposes of aiding and encouraging the location of manufacturing enterprises, making industrial surveys and locating industrial and commercial plants in or near such city or in the county; encouraging the building of railroads or other purposes which, in the discretion of the governing body of the city or of the county commissioners of the county, *will increase the population, taxable property, agricultural industries and business prospects of any city or county.* These appropriations may be funded by the levy of property taxes pursuant to G.S. 153A-149 and 160A-209 and by the allocation of other revenues whose use is not otherwise restricted by law.

N.C.G.S. §158-7.1(a) (1994) (emphasis added). When making amendments to chapter 158 and adding other provisions designed to promote economic development, the General Assembly mandated: "This act, being necessary for the prosperity and welfare of the State and its inhabitants, shall be liberally construed to effect these purposes." Act of July 23, 1993, ch. 497, sec. 25, 1993 N.C. Sess. Laws 1932, 1961 (amending the Constitution to permit cities and counties to issue bonds to finance the public portion of economic development projects and to authorize counties and cities to accept as consideration for a conveyance or lease of property to a private party the amount of increased tax revenue expected to be generated by the improvements to be constructed on the property). The General Assembly has further demonstrated its commitment to economic development by enacting several other statutes that permit local governments to appropriate and spend public funds for such purposes. These include, *inter alia:*

N.C.G.S. §158-8 through -15, which establish regional economic development commissions and authorize local governments to create or join economic development commissions and to support them with their funds.

N.C.G.S. §160A-209(c), which provides: "Each city may levy property taxes for one or more of the following purposes . . . : (10b) Economic Development—To provide for economic development as authorized by G.S. 158-12. . . . (17a) Industrial Development—To provide for industrial development as authorized by G.S. 158-7.1."

N.C.G.S. §153A-149(c), which provides: "Each county may levy property taxes for one or more of the purposes listed in this subsection . . . : (10b) Economic Development—To provide for economic development as authorized by G.S. 158-12. . . . (16a) Industrial Development—To provide for industrial development as authorized by G.S. 158-7.1."

These enactments clearly indicate that N.C.G.S. §158-7.1 is part of a comprehensive scheme of legislation dealing with economic development whereby the General Assembly is attempting to authorize exercise of the power of taxation for the perceived public purpose of promoting the general economic welfare of the citizens of North Carolina.

While legislative declarations such as these are accorded great weight, ultimate responsibility for the public purpose determination rests with this Court. . . .

This Court . . . has not specifically defined "public purpose," however; rather, it has expressly declined to "confine public purpose by judicial definition[, leaving] 'each case to be determined by its own peculiar circumstances as from time to time it arises.' " As summarized by Justice Sharp in *Mitchell:*

> A slide-rule definition to determine public purpose for all time cannot be formulated; the concept expands with the population, economy, scientific knowledge, and changing conditions. As people are brought closer together in congested areas, the public welfare requires governmental operation of facilities which were once considered exclusively private enterprises, and necessitates the expenditure of tax funds for purposes which, in an earlier day, were not classified as public. Often public and private interests are so co-mingled that it is difficult to determine which predominates. It is clear, however, that for a use to be public its benefits must be in common and not for particular persons, interests, or estates; the ultimate net gain or advantage must be the public's as contradistinguished from that of an individual or private entity. . . .

Plaintiff also argues, and the trial court apparently agreed, that this question falls squarely within the purview of *Mitchell v. North Carolina Industrial Development Financing Authority.* There we held unconstitutional the Industrial Facilities Financing Act, a statute that authorized issuance of industrial revenue bonds to finance the construction and equipping of facilities for private corporations. . . . We find *Mitchell* distinguishable. . . .

[T]he holding in *Mitchell* clearly indicates that the Court considered private industry to be the primary benefactor of the legislation and considered any benefit to the public purely incidental. Notwithstanding its recognition that any lawful business in a community promotes the public good, the Court held that the "Authority's primary function, to acquire sites and to construct and equip facilities for private industry, is not for a public use or purpose." The Court rightly concluded that direct state aid to a private enterprise, with only limited benefit accruing to the public, contravenes fundamental constitutional precepts. . . .

[T]he Court's focal concern in *Mitchell*, . . . the means used to achieve economic growth, has . . . been removed by constitutional amendment. In 1973 Article V, Section 2(7) was added to the North Carolina Constitution, specifically allowing direct appropriation to private entities for public purposes. This section provides:

> The General Assembly may enact laws whereby the State, any county, city or town, and any other public corporation may contract with and appropriate money to any person, association, or corporation for the accomplishment of public purposes only.

N.C. Const. art. V, §2(7). "[U]nder subsection (7) *direct disbursement* of public funds to private entities is a constitutionally permissible *means* of accomplishing a public purpose provided there is statutory authority to make such appropriation." Hence, the constitutional problem under the public purpose doctrine that the Court perceived in *Mitchell* . . . no longer exists. . . .

The majority in *Mitchell* posed the question: "Is it *today* a proper function of government for the State to provide a site and equip a plant for private industrial enterprise?" This explicit recognition of the importance of contemporary circumstances in assessing the public purpose of governmental endeavors highlights the essential fluidity of the concept. While the *Mitchell* majority answered the question in the negative, the passage of time and accompanying societal changes now suggest a positive response. . . .

The General Assembly may provide for, *inter alia*, roads, schools, housing, health care, transportation, and occupational training. It would be anomalous to now hold that a government which expends large sums to alleviate the problems of its citizens through multiple humanitarian and social programs is proscribed from promoting the provision of jobs for the unemployed, an increase in the tax base, and the prevention of economic stagnation.

This Court most recently addressed the public purpose question in *Madison Cablevision v. City of Morganton*. . . . 386 S.E.2d 200. The Court stated that "[t]wo guiding principles have been established for determining that a particular undertaking by a municipality is for a public purpose: (1) it involves a reasonable connection with the convenience and necessity of the particular municipality; and (2) the activity benefits the public generally, as opposed to special interests or persons." Application of these principles here mandates the conclusion that N.C.G.S. §158-7.1 furthers a public purpose and hence is constitutional.

As to the first prong, whether an activity is within the appropriate scope of governmental involvement and is reasonably related to communal needs may be evaluated by determining how similar the activity is to others which this Court has held to be within the permissible realm of governmental action. We conclude that the activities N.C.G.S. §158-7.1 authorizes are in keeping with those accepted as within the scope of permissible governmental action. . . .

As to the second prong of the *Madison Cablevision* inquiry, under the expanded understanding of public purpose, even the most innovative activities N.C.G.S. §158-7.1 permits are constitutional so long as they primarily benefit the public and not a private party. "It is not necessary, in order that a use may be regarded as public, that it should be for the use and benefit of every citizen in the community." Moreover, an expenditure does not lose its public purpose merely because it involves a private actor. Generally, if an act will promote the welfare of a state or a local government and its citizens, it is for a public purpose.

Viewed in this light, section 158-7.1 clearly serves a public purpose. Its self-proclaimed end is to "increase the population, taxable property, agricultural industries and business prospects of any city or county." N.C.G.S. §158-7.1(a). However, it is the natural consequences flowing therefrom that ensure a net public benefit. The expenditures this statute authorizes should create a more stable local economy by providing displaced workers with continuing employment opportunities, attracting better paying and more highly skilled jobs, enlarging the tax base, and diversifying the economy. Careful planning pursuant to the statute should enable optimization of natural resources while concurrently preserving the local infrastructure. The strict procedural requirements the statute imposes provide safeguards that should suffice to prevent abuse. . . .

We therefore hold that N.C.G.S. §158-7.1, which permits the expenditure of public moneys for economic development in incentive programs, does not violate the public purpose clause of the North Carolina Constitution. Accordingly, the decision of the trial court on this issue is reversed. . . .

Notes and Comments

1. *Government as Land Developer.* In discussing public agency land developers, Professor George Lefcoe points to the potential danger to a community when the agency offers subsidies to industry or a developer:

> [P]rosperous firms are able to buy or lease their sites so cheaply that inquiries can be made about the good judgment or even integrity of local officials. Once a locality does grant land on "give-away" terms, other localities may feel obligated to follow its lead in order to preserve their industrial job bases. Not only do taxpayers suffer, but all the firms that had located in the jurisdiction earlier risk having to compete with newcomers whose rents they have, in effect, subsidized through their own taxes.

George Lefcoe, When Governments Become Land Developers: Notes on the Public-Sector Experience in the Netherlands and California, 51 S. Cal. L. Rev. 165, 169 (1978).

2. *Government as Land Development Catalyst.* The city attorney of Winston-Salem reports:

> Overall, the City of Winston-Salem and Forsyth County invested approximately $13,000,000.00 in economic development incentives which resulted in over $238,000,000.00 in tax base increase and approximately 5,500 new jobs, many of them at relatively high wage rates.

Letter from Ronald Seeber to James A. Kushner, Jan. 27, 1998, at 2. Are you convinced that such economic development expenditures are appropriate? *See also* Rodney R. Akers & Robert W. Oast, Jr., Economic Development North and (New) South: A Tale of Two States, 31 Urb. Law. 793 (1999) (applauding the creativity and success of North Carolina and Pennsylvania as well as inter-regional and inter-city competition).

3. *State Authorization.* While most states authorize locally-sponsored redevelopment with its opportunities for metropolitan entrepreneurship, some states may restrict direct involvement in private industry and development. *State v. Clay County Development Authority*, 140 So. 2d 576 (Fla. 1962) (lack of power to issue bonds to construct an industrial plant for lease to a private corporation); *State v. City of York*, 82 N.W.2d 269 (Neb. 1957) (invalidating the use of revenue bonds to construct and lease industrial buildings); *C.I.V.I.C. Group v. City of Warren*, 723 N.E.2d 106 (Ohio 2000) (state constitution prohibits a public/private affordable housing project where the city would issue bonds and subsidize construction). For cases offering a broader interpretation of local attraction subsidies, *see, e.g., Delogu v. State*, 720 A.2d 1153 (Me. 1998) (sustaining tax incentives to private ship building corporation as serving a public purpose, with 7,000 jobs dependent on modernization). *See* Dale F. Rubin, Public Subsidies to Private Corporations: Are They Constitutional?, 20 State & Local L. News 7 (Winter 1997).

4. *UDAG Pirating.* Pirating problems arose under the short-lived Urban Development Action Grant Program (UDAG), which provided grants to cities to undertake public-private projects, typically for economic development. Attempts by cities to lure employers to participate in the program led HUD to issue anti-pirating regulations. *See Jersey City v. Pierce*, 669 F. Supp. 103 (D.N.J. 1987) (anti-pirating rules sustained under authority of §119(h) of the 1974 Housing and Community Development Act as amended in 1982). The UDAG experience demonstrates congressional power to regulate pirating. *See also* William T. Bogart, "Trading Places": The Role of Zoning in Promoting and Discouraging Intrametropolitan Trade, 51 Case W. Res. L. Rev. 697 (2001) (economic critique of Euclidean zoning as a trade barrier).

5. *Anticompetitiveness and Interstate Commerce.* The United States Supreme Court has extended the reach of the Commerce Clause, authorizing courts to invalidate state and local regulation that carries an anticompetitive impact. *C & A Carbone, Inc. v. Town of Clarkstown*, 511 U.S. 383 (1994). Indeed, the Court has ruled that state subsidies can generate a scheme that discriminates against interstate commerce. *West Lynn Creamery, Inc. v. Healy*, 512 U.S. 186 (1994) (effect of tax on all milk providers and subsidy to in-state dairy farmers constituted discrimination). See generally Dan T. Coenen, Business Subsidies and the Dormant Commerce Clause, 107 Yale L.J. 965 (1998) (arguing that ordinary business subsidies are constitutional and are suspect only when linked to a particular tax policy); Dan T. Coenen & Walter Hellerstein, Suspect Linkage: The Interplay of State Taxing and Spending Measures in the Application of Constitutional Antidiscrimination Rules, 95 Mich. L. Rev. 2167 (1997).

6. *Trade Agreements.* The United States is a member of the World Trade Organization. The requirements of this organization mirror the prior General Agreement on Tariffs and Trade (GATT), an international treaty generally requiring free trade and eliminating discriminatory trade barriers. The United States also is a signer of the Agreements on Subsidies and Countervailing Duties, known as the Uruguay Round Agreements. See Ralph H. Folsom, *et al*, International Business Transactions ch. 7 (3d ed. 1995).

Under the Uruguay Round Agreements covering subsidies, GATT was most concerned with imports and subsidies providing a competitive advantage. Terrence J. McCartin, Red, Yellow or Green: GATT 1994's Traffic Light Subsidies Categories, in Practicing Law Institute, The Commerce Department Speaks on

International Trade and Investment 611 (1994), *reprinted in* Folsom, *supra* at 507 (subsidies impacting imports are "red light" and prohibited, while research and development is a permitted "green light" subsidy, with the remainder characterized as "yellow light" and actionable where a serious adverse impact is generated). *See also* Jennifer Gilbert, Selling the City Without Selling Out: New Legislation on Development Incentives Emphasizes Accountability, 27 Urb. Law. 427, 446 (1995) (arguing that business subsidies are prohibited); Rachel Weber, Do Better Contracts Make Better Economic Development Incentives?, 68 J. Am. Plan. Ass'n 43 (2002) (contracts insufficient to hold firms to promises).

Economic development incentives may often have unexpected and sometimes adverse effects, or may simply be ineffective. John E. Anderson & Robert W. Wassmer, Bidding for Business: The Efficacy of Local Economic Development Incentives in a Metropolitan Area chs. 4-5 (2000) (manufacturing subsidies but not tax increment financing and other tax abatements found effective in Detroit). *See also* Rachel Weber, Why Local Economic Development Incentives Don't Create Jobs: The Role of Corporate Governance, 32 Urb. Law. 97 (2000) (arguing that public participation in corporate governance and alternative dispute resolution are more important than modest subsidies).

Do contemporary American urban boosterism and the luring of employers or sports franchises through lucrative incentives arguably violate the WTO Treaty (formerly GATT)? Should land use lawyers as well as land use casebook authors take a course on international law and trade?

7. *Business Incubation.* A popular economic development strategy is the business incubation program. Under variations of the concept, the government, often in partnership with a university, offers services such as telecommunications, computer access, and academic advice for new business developed on government property with a reduced-rent subsidy. Although designed to offer incentives to new economic development through the use of technical and below-market land subsidies, incubation can be anticompetitive, representing a benefit and subsidy not available to existing businesses and establishments in neighboring communities.

Are incubation subsidies merely research and development subsidies or are they business subsidies under the WTO? Do incubation activities pose a serious adverse impact on trade? *Compare* James A. Kushner, Growth for the Twenty-First Century: Tales from Bavaria and the Vienna Woods — Comparative Images of Urban Planning in Munich, Salzburg, Vienna, and the United States, 29 Urb. Law. 911 (1997), *reprinted as modified*, 6 S.C. Interdisciplinary L.J. 89 (1997) (arguing that incubation subsidies for start-up businesses are valid).

16

Siting Unpopular Land Uses

A. INTRODUCTION

1. NIMBYs, LULUs, and Related Acronyms

As we have seen from previous chapters in this book, two major developments in current land use practice are (1) the empowerment of third-party groups to participate fully in the regulatory process, as well to institute litigation challenging approvals, and (2) the increasing complexity of that regulatory process. Nowhere are these two developments reflected more clearly than in disputes over the siting of land uses that have unquestioned side effects (e.g., prisons, landfills) or that pose significant, long-term environmental risks (e.g., hazardous waste or radioactive waste disposal sites). The apparent inability of government to site such land uses, the so-called siting dilemma, has attracted the attention of legislatures, concerned courts, and prompted a flood of academic commentary.

It has also added to the lexicon of land use law. The acronyms NIMBY ("not in my backyard") and LULU ("locally undesirable land use") are a regular part of the land use dialogue (e.g., "the neighborhood NIMBYs" or "NIMBYism is rampant"). Other acronyms have been semi-facetiously suggested: NOPE ("not on planet earth"), CAVE ("Citizens Against Virtually Everything"), BANANA ("build absolutely nothing anywhere near anything"), or, from the standpoint of local politicians, NIMTOO ("not in my term of office").

How serious is the siting problem? One recent article excerpted below concludes that the NIMBY syndrome "now makes it almost impossible to build or locate vital facilities that the city needs to function." Michael Dear, Understanding and Overcoming the NIMBY Syndrome, 58 J. Am. Plan. Ass'n 288 (1992).

Certainly proposals to site landfills, hazardous waste facilities, mental health facilities, jails, and other similar projects can be counted on to generate fierce opposition from neighbors.

The reason for the state of conflict also seems clear: a mismatch between the benefits from such facilities, which accrue to society generally, and the costs, which tend to fall disproportionately on people who reside nearby. Homeowners located near a hazardous waste site will not be interested in arguments that disposal sites are needed for the good of society. Instead, they will be concerned with the risks, or perceived risks, that are imposed upon them and that are likely to reduce their property values.

At the same time, the sheer intensity of local opposition gives one pause: opponents of unwanted facilities exhibit a passion and dedication to their position that is remarkable. What accounts for this fierceness? Michael Gerrard, in his insightful book Whose Backyard and Whose Risk, suggests two principal reasons. The first is predictable: a dread of the consequences, often unseen and unpredictable, posed by certain kinds of land uses. The second source of the opposition, however, is far less obvious. Gerrard posits that the NIMBY syndrome arises from opposition to "intrusion" into people's lives, intrusion that not only thrusts itself into communities but also seemingly into individual homes. And it is an intrusion without the consent of those upon whom it is inflicted.

Prof. William Fischel, an economist specializing in land use, brings another viewpoint. He sees local opposition as a quite rational response to economic threats. For most homeowners, their homes are the largest single investment in their lives. They respond to perceived threats to this investment, in the form of unwanted nearby land uses, with vigorous opposition intended to protect their investment.

Under the existing land use legal regime, opposition of this nature can make siting such facilities extraordinarily difficult. Opponents can and do use litigation to challenge siting approvals. Even if the litigation is ultimately unsuccessful, the length of time that it may take to resolve the matter in the courts can put a significant financial strain on the applicant. But the pressure that opponents can wield goes far beyond use of the legal system. Because land use remains predominantly a local function, dissatisfaction with a siting proposal arising from a large number of local residents sets off political alarm bells among local elected officials. The result can be a variety of local political efforts designed to gain the attention of those officials.

2. *Responses to the Siting Dilemma*

If we assume that such facilities must be sited somewhere, the question then becomes how to arrange the legal system so that successful siting can occur. Two general types of solutions have been tried. The first is the most obvious: since the opposition centers at the local government level, the state could preempt the field and make the siting decision itself. This method is reflected in a recent Oregon case, *Dunning v. Corrections Facility Siting Authority*, 935 P.2d 1209 (Or. 1997), which summarizes the Oregon system for siting correctional facilities. Often, preemption is coupled with additional procedures that are tacked onto the siting process in an attempt to resolve disputes over scientific issues or to involve broad segments of the community in the siting decision.

Preemption seems a logical way of ensuring that siting occurs, but it has not proved successful. The intensely political nature of the local opposition means that even if the state preempts the field and thus will make the ultimate decision on siting the project, at least some political pressure from opponents can be aimed at state officials. Moreover, state legislatures are reluctant to preempt local powers over land use, even when a regional or statewide perspective over those decisions seems to make sense. The connection between local government and land use runs deep; it is not easily severed for decisions, such as siting unwanted land uses, that are very important to local residents. As a result, relatively few jurisdictions have actually attempted to implement a preemption solution to the siting dilemma.

The second type of solution draws on economic theory in an attempt to remedy the mismatch between the benefits of such facilities and the costs imposed. The premise is that citizens who are impacted locally should be compensated for having to bear the costs, whether real or perceived, of siting unwanted facilities in their community. Under this solution, siting legislation should establish a bargaining process in which the community and the facility negotiate and reach agreement on compensation for locating the facility in that community. The Massachusetts siting law, discussed in *Town of Warren v. Hazardous Waste Facility Site Safety Council*, a principal case in this chapter, is the archetype of this approach.

To date, however, approaches of this nature also have not proved particularly successful. Although applicants in Massachusetts have dropped out of the siting process for a variety of reasons, the bottom line is that the Act has not sited facilities. Although it may be too early to give up on approaches like that tried in Massachusetts, the results are not promising.

This brings us to the last two articles in this chapter that address the NIMBY phenomenon. Perhaps the accepted explanations for NIMBY-like activity, together with the condemnation of those "locals" who oppose facilities that society as a whole needs, are missing the point. Bruce Williams and Albert Matheny, two authors of a leading book, Democracy, Dialogue and Environmental Disputes (1995), suggest that the NIMBY phenomenon does not easily fit within the traditional language in which disputes are categorized. Robert Lake is even more blunt; in a revisionist approach to NIMBY, he suggests that attempts to overcome local opposition are simply not implementing a societal need, but are rather narrow attempts to privilege the use of capital.

3. *The Question of Environmental Justice*

The siting problem is further complicated by a new development, the so-called Environmental Justice movement. The movement started around 1987 with the release of a report by the Commission for Racial Justice of the United Church of Christ. The report argued that the siting of hazardous waste facilities had occurred almost entirely in areas with minority residents. In short, it raised the issue of whether the siting process, to the extent it *had* been successful in the past, was racially biased.

One question raised by the report is why such siting disparities occurred. Are the disparities due to disproportionate siting in minority communities, or is this phenomenon simply market dynamics at work? The dispute over the cause of the siting disparities continues to rage in the flood of academic literature that has addressed the issue over the past few years, and some, including Christopher Boerner *et al.*, directly attack the conclusions in the United Church of Christ report.

Relatively few attempts at solutions to disproportionate siting impacts have been implemented. A presidential executive order directs federal agencies to develop a strategy that identifies and addresses disproportionate adverse environmental effects of its programs on minority and low-income populations. Students will read this enactment and can determine for themselves whether it is useful and workable. Students can also consider a revisionist line of thinking. Given that the siting crisis has dragged on for so many years, is the siting of certain types of facilities (particularly industrial ones) actually indispensable? Or is the opposition to siting facilities in fact forcing industry to create other, perhaps more environmentally benign alternatives to land disposal, such as recycling, and thus actually improving the environmental performance of industry?

This chapter, then, is a work in progress. It is clear that in many instances, determined local opposition to unwanted land uses has prevented the siting of facilities and that the single-purpose legislation designed to ensure siting has not been successful. What is not clear is what solutions, if any, are needed to respond to this situation.

B. NIMBYS, LULUS, AND NEIGHBORHOOD OPPOSITION

In considering opposition to facility siting, the student must focus on the impact of facilities on third parties, such as neighbors who live in the area, and evaluate what legal rights they should have in siting decisions. The chapter starts out by examining a unique group of statutes that gives neighbors enhanced procedural protections when certain local land use decisions may affect them. Why do they merit those additional protections?

■ BOURQUE v. DETTORE

589 A.2d 815 (R.I. 1991)

OPINION

SHEA, Justice. . . .

The petitioner, Steven P. Bourque (Bourque), is the owner of a parcel of real estate located at 61 Pilsudski Street in Providence, Rhode Island. This lot, designated by the Zoning Ordinance of the City of Providence as M-1, general industrial use, is adjacent to an R-3 general residential zone.

On December 12, 1988, Bourque filed an application with the Providence Board of Licenses requesting a license to operate a "white goods" recycling facility. . . White-goods salvage involves the reclamation of large household appliances such as refrigerators, stoves, air conditioners, and microwaves. The operation was to consist of extracting from the appliances capacitors containing polychlorinated biphenyls (PCBs).[1] . . . On April 5, 1989, the board denied the application, relying on its finding that a legal remonstrance existed pursuant to §5-21-2(b). The board explained that according to a report from the Providence police department, 53.7 percent of the neighbors within the statutorily designated radius (200 feet) of the property in question objected to petitioner's application and that, therefore, the issuance of the license must be denied.

Section 5-21-2(b) provides in relevant part:

> No license shall be granted under this chapter to the keeper of any shop or storehouse for the reception of any junk, old metals, or other second-hand articles or to a person establishing, operating or maintaining an automobile junkyard, in any location not lawfully occupied for that purpose at the time of the application for the license, where the owners or occupants of the greater part of the land within two hundred feet (200$) of that building or place shall file with the board, town council, or city council, respectively, having jurisdiction to grant licenses, their objection to the granting of the license.

. . . Bourque asserts that the procedure under §5-21-2 vesting "neighbors" with the right to veto license grants violated his due-process rights because it impermissibly delegated governmental authority to private citizens. . . .

. . . Bourque relies on two cases: *Eubank v. City of Richmond*, 226 U.S. 137 (1912), and *Washington ex rel. Seattle Title Trust Co. v. Roberge*, 278 U.S. 116 (1928). In *Eubank* the United States Supreme Court invalidated a city ordinance that empowered two-thirds of the property owners on any block to establish, within a specified range, a building-setback line. The purpose of the statute was to limit construction in close proximity to streets. However, the Court found that the conferral of authority to those property owners had a tenuous connection to the public safety, convenience, and welfare. . . .

Five years later the United States Supreme Court in *Thomas Cusack Co. v. City of Chicago*, 242 U.S. 526 (1917), upheld a city ordinance that prohibited the construction of billboards in residential areas without the consent of a majority of property owners on the block in which the billboard was to be erected. The Court determined that the ordinance was within the city's police power because regulation of billboards had properly been shown to be "in the interest of the safety, morality, health and decency of the community." *Id.* at 530.

In *Washington ex rel. Seattle Title Trust Co. v. Roberge*, 278 U.S. 116 (1928), the second case upon which Bourque relies, the Court struck down a zoning ordinance that prohibited philanthropic homes for children or old people unless a majority of property owners within the district consented. The Court, relying on *Eubank*, distinguished *Cusack* by characterizing billboards as a potential nuisance to the community since they were "liable to endanger the safety and decency of such districts." 278 U.S. at 122. . . .

Although the land use restrictions under §5-21-2 are matters properly within the scope of the state's police power, we recognize that the promulgation of regulations through private citizens must nevertheless satisfy the requirements

1. Bourque testified at the hearings that the reclamation process solely involved extracting the capacitors from the appliances without touching or exposing the enclosed PCB element. The extracted capacitors are then shipped to another facility for separation and treatment of the PCBs contained therein.

of an otherwise proper delegation of legislative authority. Thus, we bear in mind that "legislative bodies must not abrogate their responsibility to formulate and impose policy regarding matters such as zoning or the issuance of governmental privileges, by delegating this responsibility to private parties 'uncontrolled by any standard or rule prescribed by legislative action.' " *Grendel's Den*, 662 F.2d [1st Cir. 1981] at 93 [88] (quoting *Roberge*, 278 U.S. at 122). In the case at bar we believe that the legislative scheme within §5-21-2 falls entirely within the range of permissible legislative delegations. The statute is braced with specific language and inherent limitations such that the private citizens who are empowered to object to a proposed land use are not formulating governmental policy but rather are implementing the articulated will of the Legislature. Section 5-21-2 is unlike the ordinance in *Eubank* where the Legislature authorized a majority of the neighbors on a block to impose a building-setback restriction at some arbitrarily selected distance from the road. *Eubank* involved a true unconstitutional delegation—"not because of the majority consent procedure but rather because until the majority of owners on the block fixed the property line, there was no normative standard against which to judge the legality of the proposed construction." *Silverman v. Barry*, 851 F.2d 434, 437 (D.C. Cir. 1988). Thus it was not solely the neighbors' authority to impose the setback restriction that constituted an impermissible delegation but rather their authority additionally to determine the setback distance itself. In the case at bar the neighbors who file an objection are not creating the regulation or prescribing conditions for its application. . . .

Bourque contends, nevertheless, that regardless of whether the land use regulations were within the Legislature's exercise of legitimate police power, the delegation in §5-21-2 must fail because a legislative delegation may solely empower private citizens to permit a use otherwise already validly prohibited by the Legislature. . . .

[W]e are not persuaded that such a result is mandated by the United States Supreme Court. . . . Although the legislative delegation in *Eubank* was held unconstitutional, there is no language to suggest that the form of the voting procedure was constitutionally significant. Had the ordinance authorized private citizens to impose a setback restriction at a legislatively predetermined distance, there is reason to believe that the outcome of the Court's decision would have been different—assuming, of course, that the setback restrictions were matters properly within the state's "police power." . . .

Consequently neither do we, nor did the United States Supreme Court hold that *Eubank, Cusack*, and *Roberge* should be construed to mandate that the mitigating consent of private citizens be ascertained in only one particular form—"that modification of a prohibition upon an affirmative expression of 'consent' is valid, whereas modification of the same prohibition upon a 'lack of objection' is constitutionally impermissible." *Grendel's Den*, 662 F.2d at 93. . . . Essentially, *Eubank, Cusack*, and *Roberge* really turn on whether the Supreme Court recognized the protection of a legitimate public-policy interest, and where these interests are protected by validly framed legislative regulations that reflect a clear expression of the governmental policy, this court will not interfere. In the case at bar, there is a clear legislative expression that the regulated land uses under §5-21-2 may well be of such detrimental quality to abutting landowners that any such license should not be granted over their objection. . . .

The judgment of the Providence Board of Licenses is affirmed. . . .

Notes and Comments

1. *Protests and Consents.* The statute at issue in *Bourque* falls into a type of enactment that specially empowers a select class of citizens to block a development. The enactments break down into two classes. The first class encompasses the so-called "consent" provisions, which require the written consent of a certain percentage of landowners or residents before a land use change will be allowed. The second type is a protest provision, which authorizes certain changes in the normal land use approval process if a percentage of landowners or residents file a written protest to a pending change. Such a protest can result either in a requirement that a super-majority of the local legislative body must approve the pending change before it will be enacted, or an outright veto of that change. *See, e.g., McCarty v. City of Kansas City,* 671 S.W.2d 790 (Mo. Ct. App. 1984) (three-fourths majority vote needed where a neighbor protested); *Tippitt v. City of Hernando,* 780 So. 2d 649 (Miss. Ct. App. 2000) (if protest is signed by 20 percent or more of owners, either of the area of the lots or of those immediately adjacent to the rear within a given number of feet, then two-thirds of all the members of the legislative body must approve it).

Some of the laws can be difficult to interpret. *See Morris Communications Corp. v. City of Asheville,* 565 S.E.2d 70 (N.C. 2002) (only protests submitted by lot owners of certain nonconforming signs could be counted in determining whether a "supermajority" provision was triggered by an amendment to a zoning ordinance requiring nonconforming signs to be removed within seven years); *Rock v. Head,* 562 S.E.2d 768 (Ga. App. 2002) (construing provision that required "member of the Commission representing the district in which the subject property is located" to approve the zoning where there were now two separate types of districts: "commissioner districts" and "superdistricts"); *Thomas v. Jensen,* 800 So. 2d 81 (La. Ct. App. 2001) (rejecting argument that a supermajority provision applied only when there was an "appeal" from the planning commission); *Mountain Hill, LLC v. Middletown Tp.,* 801 A.2d 412 (Sup. Ct. App. Div. N.J. 2002) (two-thirds majority of entire township committee—including recused votes—was necessary).

As the *Bourque* case indicates in its review of the relevant U.S. Supreme Court cases on this issue, the case law is sharply divided on the validity of these provisions. *Compare Yanow v. Seven Oaks Park,* 94 A.2d 482 (N.J. 1953) (consent provision requiring 80 percent of owners of frontage of all lots within 200 feet of a proposed private school to consent was invalid) *with O'Brien v. City of St. Paul,* 173 N.W.2d 462 (Minn. 1969) (upholding consent provisions requiring two-thirds of adjacent property owners within 100 feet of premises to consent before property could be rezoned).

2. *The* Bourque *Application.* Did the *Bourque* Court apply the statute properly? More particularly, what does the statutory phrase "owners or occupants of the greater part of the land within 200 feet" mean? Another question is whether the court squarely confronted the "standardless delegation" argument. What exactly was the "standard" that the statute sets forth? The court held that the U.S. Supreme Court's decision in *Eubank v. City of Richmond,* 226 U.S. 137 (1912), was a "true unconstitutional delegation," but distinguished that case on the basis that in *Bourque* the objecting neighbors "are not creating the regulation or proscribing conditions for its application." Are you convinced?

3. *The Nature of Neighbors' Opposition.* What is the rationale for such provisions? A New Jersey court has suggested that their purpose is to give those individuals that would be most affected by a proposed change additional protection against an unwanted or ill-considered change. *Johnson v. Township of Montville*, 264 A.2d 75, 78 (N.J. Super. App. Div. 1970). Why is additional protection of this type needed?

In most situations, consent and protest statutes do not apply. Assuming that they do not, are neighboring property owners entitled to any special procedural protections when they might be affected by a local land use decision? If a quasi-judicial land use decision may affect the neighbors' property, due process may entitle them to a hearing before the decision is reached. *See, e.g., Horn v. County of Ventura*, 596 P.2d 1134 (Cal. 1979) (when approval of a tentative subdivision map will constitute a substantial or significant deprivation of the property of other landowners, the affected persons are entitled to reasonable notice and an opportunity to be heard before the approval occurs).

Another question is whether the neighbors' opposition alone can constitute substantial evidence that will sustain a local jurisdiction's decision to deny a proposed development. The general rule is that opposition, in and of itself, is not a sufficient ground for a denial. *See Ifrah v. Utschig*,774 N.E.2d 732, 734 (N.Y. 2002) ("Although scientific or other expert testimony is not required in every case to support a zoning board's determination, the board may not base its decision on generalized community objections."); *but see Bradley v. Payson City Corp.*, 17 P.3d 1160 (Utah Ct. App. 2001) (although "public clamor doctrine"—idea that public opposition alone cannot be the sole basis for denying a zoning change—applies in an administrative proceeding, this is a legislative proceeding).

4. *The Tools of Opposition.* What legal tools are available to neighbors who wish to oppose a particular development? The obvious ones, of course, are appearances before the local decisionmakers and judicial review of any adverse decision. In some states, the neighbors also may be able to sponsor a referendum that seeks to rescind a quasi-legislative approval. Tim Iglesias, Managing Local Opposition to Affordable Housing: A New Approach to NIMBY, 12 J. of Aff. Housing & Community Dev. L. 78 (2002) ("Opponents' tactics are similarly predictable: distributing flyers; canvassing door to door and holding meetings to organize against the development; circulating petitions to document opposition; demanding meetings with the developer; telling their story to the media; and lobbying local government staff and officials through telephone calls, faxes, e-mails, and private meetings, and at public hearings. If a development appears likely to be approved, some groups threaten a lawsuit or a referendum").

In opposing a power plant proposed for a low and middle-income community in San Francisco, the opponents' strategies included developing a community toxics profile, working with city officials to initiate a community health assessment, presenting testimony before the state commission charged with approving the facility, and seeking a temporary moratorium in the siting of new polluting facilities. See Clifford Rechtschaffen, Fighting Back Against a Power Plant: Some Lessons From the Legal and Organizing Efforts of the Bayview-Hunters Point Community, 3 Hastings W.-N.W. J. Envtl. L. & Pol'y 407 (1996).

5. *The Purpose of Public Participation.* As noted in Chapter 6 of this casebook, one of the most important developments in land use over the past 25 years has been the participation of third-party groups, such as neighborhood and citizens groups, in the land use process. Procedural requirements in the law have often encouraged this development.

Should such public participation be encouraged, or is enhanced public participation, which often leads to litigation, counterproductive to sound land use decisionmaking? To answer this question, you must consider the purposes that public participation serves. See, e.g., Daniel S. Iacofano, Public Involvement as an Organizational Development Process (1990); Daniel S. Fiorino, Environmental Risk and Democratic Process: A Critical Review, 14 Colum. J. Envtl. L. 501, 536 (1989) (summarizing public participation theories). For example, you might ask whether the participation is principally designed to increase the knowledge base of decisionmakers before they act. If so, in what types of situations is this goal likely to be met?

Alternatively, public participation may simply be an exercise in participatory democracy that is intended to contribute to the legitimacy of the ultimate decision. However, are opponents likely to feel that, if they have been heard in a public hearing, the final decision is legitimate and thus should be accepted? Another justification sometimes offered for extensive public participation is that it may build consensus. How likely is consensus to occur in such disputes? Consider here the materials in Chapter 10 on mediation as an alternative means of making land use decisions.

6. *"NIMBYs" and "LULUs."* Whatever your views on the purposes of public participation in the land use decisionmaking process (and the word "participation" includes the right to judicial review), many commentators have concluded that public opposition is adversely affecting society's ability to site important public facilities, such as jails, group homes for the mentally ill, landfills, and hazardous waste facilities. The phenomenon is a relatively new one, having arisen over the last 25 years. The commentary has given rise to new terminology, such as the NIMBY ("not-in-my-backyard") phenomenon and the existence of LULUs ("locally undesirable/unwanted land uses"), which now appears regularly even in the case law. *See, e.g., Harlen Associates v. Incorporated Village of Mineola*, 273 F.3d 494, 500 (2d Cir. 2001) (plaintiff suggests "that the Board's decision was based solely on what Harlen refers to as 'NIMBY (Not In My Back Yard)' community opposition"); and *Families Unafraid to Uphold Rural El Dorado County v. Board of Supervisors*, 94 Cal. Rptr. 2d 205, 213 (2000) (referring to the "County and Cook's 'nimby' argument").

7. *Micro-NIMBY.* The issue generally considered in this chapter is the ability of existing homeowners or residents to collectively oppose unwanted land uses by using the tools provided by the current land use system. Those tools, however, are also available on a micro-level; one landowner can oppose a change to neighboring property. For an extreme example, *see Ayasli v. Armstrong*, 780 N.E.2d 926 (Mass. Ct. App. 2002). In this case the defendant neighbors allegedly used a variety of means, legal and otherwise, to oppose a renovation project on neighboring properties. In addition to one of the defendants stating that she would do everything she could to stop work on the renovation and the various legal appeals, "there were the erection of the sign directing those trying to reach the Ayaslis' property to an impassable way, the threatening dogs at the boundaries of the Ayaslis' property, and the golf balls falling on the Ayaslis' beach where the children swam." *Id.* at 934. In the end, the plaintiffs brought an action under the state civil rights act and recovered $211,000 in damages and $150,000 in attorney's fees.

Academics and commentators have devoted much attention to the repeated instances of local opposition to proposals for unwanted land uses. The following two excerpts explore both the phenomenon and its causes.

The first article discusses the NIMBY syndrome in the context of siting human services facilities. Its analysis, however, applies broadly to opposition to the siting of other types of facilities as well.

■ MICHAEL DEAR, UNDERSTANDING AND OVERCOMING THE NIMBY SYNDROME

58 J. Am. Plan. Ass'n 288 (1992)

. . . Across the country, journalists, scholars, and professionals are reporting the rise of the NIMBY phenomena. In plain language, NIMBY is the motivation of residents who want to protect their turf. More formally, NIMBY refers to the protectionist attitudes of and oppositional tactics adopted by community groups facing an unwelcome development in their neighborhood. . . . Residents usually concede that these "noxious" facilities are necessary, but not near their homes, hence the term "not in my back yard." . . .

Understanding Community Opposition

NIMBY battles tend to arise and progress following certain patterns and consistencies.

EXTERNAL EVENTS

Community opposition tends to be cyclical in nature, with periods of intense and frequent disputes, followed by extended calms. In the field of human services, important national events have formed a backdrop of local events. These include the movement to deinstitutionalize the mentally ill, the extensive restructuring of federal social welfare programs, the collapse of federally assisted affordable housing programs, the widespread restructuring of the U.S. economy toward service employment, and the advent of burgeoning homelessness and AIDS. . . .

INTERNAL RHYTHMS

Each incident of locational conflict seems to follow a three-stage cycle.

- Youth: News of the proposal breaks, lighting the fuse of conflict. Opposition tends to be confined to a small vocal group residing very near to the proposed development. NIMBY sentiments are usually expressed in the rawest, bluntest of terms, often reflecting an irrational, unthinking response by opponents.
- Maturity: Battle lines are solidified as the two sides assemble ranks of supporters. The debate moves away from private complaints and into a public forum. As a consequence, the rhetoric of opposition becomes more rational and objective. Less is heard of the desire to "throw the bums out" of the neighborhood; more measured voices express concerns about property value decline, increased traffic volumes, and the like.
- Old Age: The period of conflict resolution is often long, drawn-out, and sometimes inconclusive. Victory tends to go to those with the persistence

and stamina to last the course. Typically, at this stage, some kind of arbitration process is adopted, using professional or political resources. Both sides make concessions. If positions become sufficiently entrenched, a stalemate can ensue; victory again falling to those with staying power.

OPPOSITION ARGUMENTS

Opposition arguments, after the initial angry phase, usually express three specific concerns: the perceived threat to property values, personal security, and neighborhood amenity. In past decades, the principal concern of opponents has been that property values in their neighborhood would decline. However, none of the studies on real estate transactions in the vicinity of human service facilities has demonstrated a property value decline that could clearly be linked to the facility. . . .

Concerns about personal security are more common in response to certain client groups than to others. The key variables in this category are client dangerousness and unpredictability. Unsurprisingly, substance abusers (particularly drug addicts who might be associated with criminal behavior to support their habits) and exoffenders (with manifest records of lawlessness) figure prominently in this category. But residents have also expressed unease about the mentally disabled, who may display aberrant or aggressive public behavior. Neighborhood concerns about personal security often find expression as questions about facility operating procedures, especially supervision arrangements.

The potential decline of neighborhood quality also worries community members near the proposed facility. This applies equally to the anticipated impact on business as well as on residential amenity. Specific threats to overall neighborhood amenity include the physical appearance of clients, some of whom may appear dirty or unkempt; and antisocial behavior, such as loitering, public urination or defecation, and aggressive panhandling. Businesses complain that clusters of clients drive customers away. Residents worry that their enjoyment of the neighborhood will be undermined by the clients and that certain clients will be a bad influence on children and young people.

■ MICHAEL B. GERRARD, WHOSE BACKYARD, WHOSE RISK: FEAR AND FAIRNESS IN TOXIC AND NUCLEAR WASTE SITING

99-107 (1994)

Many theories have been offered for the widespread public opposition to HW/RW [hazardous waste/radioactive waste] facilities, but I believe that the reasons can be summed up with two words: *dread* and *intrusion*. These have important implications for the siting dilemma.

Dread Polls confirm that by far the most important reason behind opposition to HW/RW facilities is concern over the impact on health, particularly the health of one's children. This is so not only in the United States but in other societies as well. Many educated people (though few if any of the experts in the field) attribute a large percentage of adult and childhood cancers to hazardous waste sites. Worry about health effects is also at the root of the emergence since about 1980 of thousands of grassroots groups of facility opponents and "toxic victims." . . .

Every era has had its own dreads. The Israelites cast out Moses' sister, Miriam, when she contracted leprosy. Successive civilizations have had ample reason to be terrified of plague, smallpox, and polio, until each was eradicated or controlled. These dreads have manifested themselves in disputes over siting; Louis Pasteur's effort to find a laboratory to develop a rabies vaccine was hampered by residents of Paris who feared they would contract the disease. We now have cancer and AIDS. Often people who have been exposed to agents that might cause these diseases, or who simply fear such exposure, become preoccupied with health problems. When wastes are the source of these agents, a further layer of revulsion occurs, at least in the view of Freudians. When the waste is burned, as in incinerators, the complex psychological reaction to fire comes into play.

Yet another layer of horror accrues when the waste is radioactive. Since Hiroshima and Nagasaki, fear of nuclear war has become embedded in the culture. . . .

The distinctions drawn by most members of the public [about HW/RW facilities] tend to be rather sharp. . . .

. . . Many people tend to regard them as horribly dangerous, with no meaningful shades of gray between danger and safety; thus most proposed mitigation measures to reduce dangers will sway few minds. . . .

The sociologist Kai Erikson . . . says that toxic emergencies possess two distinguishing characteristics that add to the dread they induce. First they are unbounded and have no frame or end; the "all clear" is never sounded. Second, "they are without form. You cannot apprehend them through the unaided senses; you cannot taste, touch, smell, or see them. That makes them especially ghostlike and terrifying. Moreover, they invert the process by which disasters normally inflict harm. They do not charge in from outside and batter like a gust of wind or a wall of water. They slink in without warning, do no immediate damage so far as one can tell, and begin their deadly work from within. . . . "

Intrusion The insidiousness of their threat is closely related to the second major reason HW/RW facilities are so hated. The facilities themselves are seen as imposed on communities without consent, and once they arrive they do their damage silently. When forced on unwilling localities, the facilities are seen as colossal intrusions, almost as foreign invasions. Attempts to override local siting authority almost invariably backfire and *increase* local opposition, partly by intensifying the community's perception of risk. Some studies have shown that people will accept voluntary risks approximately 1000 times more hazardous than risks they perceive as involuntarily imposed — they will parachute out of an airplane or smoke a cigarette, but they don't want anyone to build a waste plant miles from their house. . . .

This sense of intrusion is magnified when the waste is imported from other areas. The EPA has acknowledged that public opposition is greater when the facilities would accept out-of-state waste. . . .

A concept closely related to intrusion is trust. Opposition is magnified when the community does not trust the people or institutions seeking to place HW/RW in their midst. The political prospects for several proposed HW facilities were severely damaged when it became known that their proposed developers had histories of environmental or other violations. Other proposals were defeated after the public came to believe that the government was negotiating them in secret with corporate sponsors. . . .

Mistrust is often accompanied by despair. The forces behind hazardous facilities are seen not only as evil, but as invincible. As Peter Sandman has said, "Ironically, nearly everyone is impressed by the community's power of opposition — except the community, which sees itself as fighting a difficult, even desperate uphill battle to stop the siting juggernaut. . . . "

The sense of intrusion is further magnified if the community feels it is being treated unfairly — if, for example, there is no obvious reason why it is being singled out to be exposed to a waste facility. A sense of random victimization increases the outrage felt by the neighbors. . . .

WILLIAM A. FISCHEL, WHY ARE THERE NIMBYS?

77 Land Econ. 144 (2001)

NIMBYs sometimes appear to be irrational in their opposition to projects in the sense that they express far-fetched anxieties or doggedly fight projects whose expected neighborhood effects seem small or even benign. I submit in this note that such anxieties might not be irrational if we consider that most NIMBYs are homeowners, and that homeowners cannot insure their major (and often only) asset against devaluation by neighborhood effects. NIMBYism might better be viewed as a risk-averse strategy. . . .

NIMBYism is weird only if you think solely about the first moment, the rationally expected outcomes from development. NIMBYism makes perfectly good sense if you think about the second moment, the variance in expected outcomes, and the fact that there isn't any way to insure against neighborhood or community-wide decline. . . .

In further support of the idea that the risks of homeownership are the source of the problem, I would point out that both apartment owners and apartment dwellers are rarely NIMBYs, even after accounting for their lower numbers. I don't have numbers on this, but in my ten years experience on a zoning board and my continuous attention to other land-use disputes, it appears that the opposition to land use change is nearly always by homeowners. The only systematic exception is opposition by existing businesses to potential competitors, and even then they usually try to clothe their naked protectionism with appeals to environmental issues that primarily affect homeowners.

Lack of NIMBYism by apartment owners seems strange only if we attribute NIMBYism simply to expected effects of the proposed development rather than the variance of those effects. In absolute dollars, owners of multifamily housing have even more to lose from adverse neighborhood effects than most homeowners. And apartment owners could be pretty effective NIMBYs if they cared to, since they could round up tenants and business allies to oppose the land-use change. But such opposition is rare. The reason is that owners of multifamily homes can spread their risks of ownership much more easily than homeowners. They cannot insure against devaluation of their assets from neighborhood change, but they can divide ownership of rental housing among many owners much more easily by forming a REIT (Real Estate Investment Trust) or some other multi-investor form of ownership.

Homeownership Is a Lopsided Asset

Homeowners are a major political force in all local decisions, not just land-use regulation. Two-thirds of all American homes are owner occupied, but even this understates the importance of homeowners in local affairs. Homeowners vote in municipal elections fifty percent more than renters do. . . .

An owner-occupied home is a peculiar asset in two respects. The more obvious is that the investor is also the consumer. This dual relationship surely contributes to some of the NIMBY syndrome. Consumers get some surplus from most of the goods in their possession — otherwise they would not long remain in their possession. We should not be surprised that owner-occupants are more attached to the same objects that are for distant investors just so many dollars.

The other peculiarity of homeownership is that it is a high-return, high-risk asset that is held by people who have little ability to diversify that risk. Owning a home is financially attractive because the imputed rent on owner-occupied housing is not taxed and because taxation of capital gains on an owner-occupied home has long been deferrable and is now completely avoidable for most owners. The tax treatment of homes makes it an especially desirable asset during inflationary times. But even in the long run, owning a home — in particular, owning a plot of land on which a home can be built, rebuilt, expanded or simply stay put — has had an excellent average return (Gyourko and Voith 1992).

As with other high-return assets, however, homeownership has a good deal of risk. . . .

Personal Attachments and Reluctance to Trade also Fan NIMBYism

There are, of course, other reasons that homeowners are touchier about changes in their neighborhood than about other types of financial risks. Living in a home for a long time creates a personal attachment for which changes in the neighborhood are upsetting. And the well-known (but often ignored) "offer/ask" disparity in economics indicates that people who are already in possession of something need to be paid a great deal more when asked to give it up than those same people would offer to pay for the same entitlement if they did not currently possess it. . . . In short, you ask more (to give up something you own) than you offer (to obtain something not already in your possession).

I am inclined to discount at least the first of these sentiments, long-time residence, as a prime mover for NIMBY anxiety, though. My experience observing NIMBYs is that newcomers are at least as inclined to object to changes in their neighborhoods as long-time residents. . . .

The offer-ask disparity is a better explanation but still not entirely satisfying. The problem isn't the concept itself, which has plenty of empirical evidence in support of it. (This is one of the few areas in economics in which psychological experiments have played an important role.) The problem is how to decide what objectors should regard as the status quo of their neighborhood.

Taken at face value, NIMBYism regards the status quo as the current use (or nonuse) of land in their neighborhood. They want it left the way they found it. But I have had little trouble convincing more disinterested observers that a more reasonable status quo is the long-standing zoning rules that apply to the neighborhood. If zoning creates, as I think it does, a sense of entitlement, then that entitlement belongs as much to the owners of the undeveloped parcels as to the owners of homes that were developed under the same rules many years earlier.

In other words, the NIMBYs are not being asked to give something up. They are demanding that someone else give up a right similar to that which they (or their predecessors in title) had themselves exercised to their advantage. . . .

IF I'M RIGHT, WHY AIN'T I RICH?

I have argued that a major — not the only — source of NIMBYism is home-owners' response to uninsured risks. If I am right about this source, and if NIMBYism is responsible for stopping projects that otherwise would raise aggregate land values in the neighborhood, there must be some potential gains from trade that are unexploited. There is room, in other words, for a smart person to initiate a market for home-value insurance.

Here is the insurance contract that would do the trick: In the event that the insured's property does not rise by the amount that it would have had the development not taken place, the insurer will pay the owner the difference at the time the owner of the property (or his heirs or legatees) chooses to sell it. Once this difference is paid, the succeeding owner acquires no further claim for adverse effects of the development on the property.

The reason the purchaser has no further claim after the insurance claim has been paid to the seller is that the purchaser has been compensated for the adverse effect in the form of the lower price of the house. This is why, incidentally, there is no injustice in the mere fact of differing property tax rates to finance schools in different communities. The higher rates are compensated for by lower housing costs, leaving the owner in the high-rate town with more money to pay taxes. . . .

To state the contract's basic terms is to illustrate why such insurance is difficult to write. . . .

WHAT IS THE RIGHT LEVEL OF NIMBYISM?

. . . NIMBYs are not all bad news. Without neighborhood opposition, some projects that devalue their community and neighborhood would get passed. Even local regulators are often unaware of the micro-neighborhood conditions that might be affected by the proposed development. They depend to a large extent on the willingness of neighborhood residents to take the time and expense of testifying about the possible effects. Thus the real trick in dealing with NIMBYs is motivating them to provide information and opposition when it is appropriate to do so, but not further. . . .

Notes and Comments

1. *The Set of Projects.* As the excerpts suggest, certain kinds of projects are almost always opposed by nearby residents. Do these projects share certain general

characteristics? Or do different types of proposals for locally unwanted land uses — hazardous waste sites, prisons, group homes, and so forth — raise different questions about the legitimate role of local opposition?

2. *Values, Security, and Amenity.* The Dear excerpt suggests that opposition arguments raise three specific concerns: the perceived threats to property values, personal security, and neighborhood amenity. Are some of these concerns more legitimate than others? What criteria do you use, or should the land use system use, to separate legitimate concerns from ones that should be disregarded?

3. *Dread and Intrusion.* The excerpt from the Gerrard book traces the formation of public opposition to two sources: "dread" and "intrusion." Gerrard cites a variety of cultural forces, psychology (reactions to the use of fire) etc., and suggests that each era "has its own dreads." If so, does that mean that opposition to facilities based upon "dread" cannot be overcome?

In a well-known article, William Ruckelshaus, former Administrator of the Environmental Protection Agency, argued that the public must be better educated about risk. William Ruckelshaus, Risk in a Free Society, 14 Envtl. L. Rep. (Envtl. L. Inst.) 10,190 (May 1994). If, as the Gerrard excerpt suggests, there are "no meaningful shades of gray between danger and safety" in the reaction of individuals, does this conclusion mean that efforts to educate the public about risk will necessarily fail?

Gerrard argues that the concepts of intrusion and lack of trust also explain local opposition. Does this idea of intrusion explain why the political system, faced with evidence that many land use problems are of a regional nature and cannot be dealt with locally, has resisted taking control of land use powers away from local government? Another commentator also has emphasized the trust issue, which he terms the "decline of deference" to public decisionmaking institutions. Frank N. Laird, The Decline of Deference: the Political Context of Risk Communication, 9 Risk Anal. 543 (1989). Does this decline of deference mean that it will be nearly impossible to design a process that actually results in the successful siting of needed facilities?

4. *Property Values and Efficiency.* Professor Fischel presents an economic explanation (and justification) for the NIMBY phenomenon. *See also* William A. Fischel, How Home Values Influence Local Government Taxation, School Finance, and Land-Use Policies (2001). The phenomenon is simply wealth-protection. Homeowners, guided by concern for the value of their homes, make political decisions that are more efficient than those that would be made at higher government levels.

Does this theory capture the entirety of local opposition? Or is part of that opposition irrational, the "dread" pointed to by Gerrard? Interestingly, Professor Fischel's theory suggests that from an economic perspective, local opposition is not totally a "bad" thing.

5. *The Developer's Perspective.* In an early, influential book on facility siting, the authors posited that siting proposals follow a set pattern or model:

> In the first stage, the developer makes a series of technical choices with his engineer, market analysts, and lawyers. He typically has no interaction with local government nor those who would be affected by his decisions. . . .
>
> The developer then announces his technology and site package to the public. If he mentions alternatives, they seem factitious. He appears to approach the public

> with a single firm decision camouflaged behind impossible alternatives. His strong position sets the stage for conflict.
>
> Now the permitting process begins. . . . People with strong concerns about the project and those who don't thoroughly understand it approach this opportunity defensively. They have no reason to expect the developer to change his mind, alter his project, choose another site, or heed the public's concern. In fact, they perceive themselves as having power only to delay or stop the project—because the developer has taken an apparently firm position, they must likewise be intransigent in order to protect themselves.

Michael O'Hare, Lawrence Bacow, & Debra Sanderson, Facility Siting and Public Opposition, 6-7 (1983).

Does the model imply that a developer should be required to discuss a project with interested parties *before* deciding to propose it? Even if such a step is not required, would you recommend to your client that it do so?

6. *The Opponents' Perspective.* By their nature, siting decisions present problems of collective action. The benefits of approving land uses such as hazardous waste treatment facilities may well be substantial. Those benefits, however, are spread among a variety of beneficiaries of that site. Individually, each of these beneficiaries has little incentive to participate in an individual siting decision. In contrast, opponents of the project, such as those that live near a site, may feel (rightly or wrongly) that the project will impose specific, large costs upon them. They have a great incentive to organize for the purpose of opposing the project. Thus, even projects with net public benefits may be blocked. See generally, Mancur Olson, The Logic of Collective Action—Public Goods and the Theory of Groups (1965). Any attempt to solve the siting dilemma must consider this organizational aspect of siting controversies.

7. *Siting and Political Theory.* One theory of public decisionmaking that has received much attention in the academic literature is "public choice" theory. Essentially (and in much abbreviated form), public choice theory posits that government decisionmaking has much in common with the operation of a market: "[G]overnment is merely a mechanism for combining private preferences into a social decision." Daniel A. Farber & Philip P. Frickey, Law and Public Choice 44 (1991). The theory posits that participants in that process are motivated by self-interest, much like private participants in a market.

If you employ public choice theory to analyze the siting phenomenon, what will your conclusion be regarding whether government regulation of the sites chosen will be excessive or insufficient? Consider that the benefits of the controls placed on the facility are concentrated, while the costs of those controls are diffuse. See James T. Hamilton, Missing the Mark(et) in Siting Hazardous Waste Facilities, 1 Duke Envtl. L. & Pol. F. 11 (1991) (suggesting that the result will be systematic overregulation).

A competing political theory is known as "civic republicanism." Instead of the individualistic approach found in public choice theory, civic republicanism posits that politics is a sphere in which "citizens rise above their merely private concerns to join in a common enterprise. They put aside their own interests and enter a public-spirited dialogue about the common good." Law and Public Choice, *supra*, at 44. How would those championing civic republicanism view the local opposition to siting found in the NIMBY syndrome? See Peter Margulies, Building

Communities for Virtue: Political Theory, Land Use Policy, and the "Not in My Backyard" Syndrome, 43 Syracuse L. Rev. 945, 947 (1992) (suggesting that such opposition "compromise[s] the civic republican account of community service as a public commitment shared by all").

8. *NIMBY Ineffective?* The assumption has been that local opposition to siting proposals has been very effective, and the anecdotal evidence of that conclusion abounds. However, one article warns against quick conclusions. Anthony P. Matejczyk, Why Not NIMBY? Reputation, Neighbourhood Organisations and Zoning Boards in a US Midwestern City, 38 Urb. Studies 507 (2001). Based on a study of Minnesota zoning decisions, it concluded that "[n]eighborhood organizations that establish reputations for being habitually 'nimby' become, ironically enough, even more vulnerable to the approval of zoning exceptions by the zoning boards in the future." *Id.* at 516.

C. SOLUTIONS TO THE SITING DILEMMA

The following materials set forth several responses to the siting dilemma. The last article, however, suggests that these responses are based on approaches that miss the point about the true nature of the NIMBY phenomenon.

■ DUNNING v. CORRECTIONS FACILITY SITING AUTHORITY

935 P.2d 1209 (Or. 1997)

GILLETTE, Justice. . . .

In 1995, the legislature enacted Oregon Laws 1995, chapter 745, now codified at ORS 421.611 to 421.630. That measure contains legislative findings that "[t]here is a serious and urgent need to construct and operate additional correction[s] facilities in this state" and that "[i]mmediate corrections facility planning and siting requires an expedited process." ORS 421.611(1) and (2). Pursuant to those findings, the balance of the measure creates a special corrections facilities siting process.

The siting process calls, first, for the Department to create by rule "mandatory and desirable criteria" under which potential corrections facility sites can be identified. ORS 421.614. The Department then nominates potential sites for corrections facilities, based on criteria established by rule and certain additional criteria identified in the statute, including local interest and capacity to provide infrastructure and support. ORS 421.616(1).

Nominated sites are then evaluated by a newly created administrative body, the Siting Authority, which is directed to hold hearings concerning each of the nominated sites and to decide which sites should be developed as corrections facilities. ORS 421.621; ORS 421.623. Final authority to approve or disapprove the sites selected by the Siting Authority is reserved to the Governor. ORS 421.626.

The hearing process under which the Siting Authority reviews nominated sites is set out in ORS 421.623. The hearing is to be held within 30 days of site nomination "within the region where each nominated site is located." ORS 421.623(1). Not later than 10 days before the scheduled hearing, "any affected local government or any person" may submit a statement of one or more "proposed conditions" to the Siting Authority. Each such proposed condition is to:

> (a) Be seated separately;
> (b) Be in writing;
> (c) Identify the site to which the condition, if approved, would attach;
> (d) Be specific;
> (e) Directly relate to any site or its proposed development, infrastructure, access thereto or physical condition on or in the immediate vicinity of such site; and
> (f) Be supported by a statement of the need or reasons [for the condition].

ORS 421.623(2).

Within 45 days after site nomination, the Siting Authority is to produce a report selecting and ranking sites. That report is to

> specify site development conditions for each site, based on substantial evidence in the record as a whole and supported by findings, which findings shall address only:
> (a) The criteria specified by the department pursuant to ORS 421.614 and in ORS 421.616.
> (b) The reasons for not adopting any of the proposed conditions that were submitted in accordance with subsection (2) of this section for the selected sites."

ORS 421.623(3) (emphasis added). . . .

TOWN OF WARREN v. HAZARDOUS WASTE FACILITY SITE

466 N.E.2d 102 (Mass. 1984)

Before HENNESSEY, C.J., and WILKINS, ABRAMS and O'CONNOR, JJ.

O'CONNOR, Justice.

In these appeals by the town of Warren and numerous citizen interveners, we consider the constitutionality of St. 1980, c. 508, An Act further regulating the disposal of hazardous waste materials, and the enforceability of town by-laws that would exclude certain hazardous waste facilities from the town. . . .

In 1979 the Legislature established a special commission to "investigate alternative procedures to be utilized by the authorities in granting local and state approval of sites for hazardous waste facilities," and to propose appropriate legislation. St. 1979, c. 704, 4. Draft legislation was submitted by the commission and on July 15, 1980, the Legislature enacted St. 1980, c. 508. The statute's preamble recited that the Legislature's purpose was "to immediately encourage and expedite the process of development of hazardous waste treatment and disposal facilities which provide adequate safeguards to protect the public health, safety, and environment of the commonwealth."

To achieve that purpose, St. 1980, c. 508, §8, inserted in the general laws of the Commonwealth the Massachusetts Hazardous Waste Facility Siting Act (Siting Act), codified as G.L. c. 21D. The Siting Act created the council, which monitors and implements the siting process. G.L. c. 21D, §4.

A developer proposing to construct, maintain, and operate a hazardous waste facility initiates the siting process by submitting a notice of intent to the council and to various other State agencies. The notice may, but need not, propose specific sites. If specific sites are proposed, the notice must be submitted to the communities in which those sites are located. The notice must include, among other items, information about the hazardous wastes that would be treated, the procedures to be used, and any proposed sites. Also, the notice must include preliminary specifications and architectural drawings of the proposed facility. Following the receipt of a completed notice of intent, the council has fifteen days to determine whether the proposal is "feasible and deserving of state assistance." G.L. c. 21D, §7. If the developer has not proposed specific sites, or has done so but is willing to accept alternatives, the council solicits suggestions of sites from various described persons. If more than three sites are suggested, the council reduces the potential sites to three, including the developer's suggested site, if any. G.L. c. 21D, §9.

Within thirty days after receiving either a notice of intent naming a potential site within its borders or, in the case of a site named during the site suggestion period, notice that a site within its borders is on the final list of suggested sites, each community in which such a site is located, referred to in the statute as a "host" community, is required to establish a local assessment committee. The local assessment committee is made up of representatives of the host city or town and may also include representatives of abutting communities. G.L. c. 21D, §5.

The developer must then submit to the council and to the Secretary of the Executive Office of Environmental Affairs a preliminary project impact report for each site under consideration. The report shall consist of (1) the environmental impact report required by G.L. c. 30, 62-62H, to be reviewed by the secretary, and (2) a social and economic appendix, to be reviewed by the council. G.L. c. 21D, §10. The special commission that drafted the Siting Act expressed the hope that the preliminary report would provide the basis for negotiation of a siting agreement between the developer and the host community. 1980 House Doc. No. 6756, at 22.

No facility can be constructed unless a siting agreement has been established by the developer and the host community. G.L. c. 21D, §12. The siting agreement results from negotiations between the local assessment committee and the developer and specifies the terms and conditions under which the facility will be constructed and operated. G.L. c. 21D, §§12 and 13. The agreement is a "nonassignable contract binding upon the developer and the host community, and enforceable against the parties in any court of competent jurisdiction." G.L. c. 21D, §12. A local assessment committee may request technical assistance grants from the council to pay costs incurred in the siting process. G.L. c. 21D, §11.

Sixty days after the determination by the council and the secretary that the preliminary project report is in compliance with the law, if an impasse in negotiations exists, the council may require the local assessment committee and the developer to submit the issues in dispute to final and binding arbitration. Such arbitration is to be conducted in accordance with the provisions of G.L. c. 251, including the provisions for judicial review of an arbitration decision. G.L. c. 21D, §15.

Upon the establishment of a siting agreement, the developer must prepare a final project impact report which incorporates the provisions of the siting agreement. If the secretary and the council find that the final project impact report is in compliance with all applicable provisions of law, the council may then declare that the siting agreement is operative and is to be given full force and effect. G.L. c. 21D, §10. The siting agreement is the final goal of the Siting Act, G.L. c. 21D, which, as we have said, was inserted in the general laws by St. 1980, c. 508, §8. It was designed, at least in part, to mitigate local resistance to the siting of hazardous waste facilities. 1980 House Doc. No. 6756, at 13.

Other sections of St. 1980, c. 508 have a similar purpose. For instance, 2A of St. 1980, c. 508 amended G.L. c. 21C, §7, to provide that the Department of Environmental Quality Engineering "shall grant a license to construct, maintain and operate a [hazardous waste] facility on a site if it determines that said construction, maintenance, and operation does not constitute a significant danger to public health, public safety, or the environment, does not seriously threaten injury to the inhabitants of the area or damage to their property, and does not result in the creation of noisome or unwholesome odors." That determination is subject to judicial review. G.L. c. 21C, §11. General Laws c. 111, §150B, was inserted by §4 of St. 1980, c. 508, to provide that no hazardous waste facility may be operated unless the local board of health has determined that its operation will impose "no significantly greater danger to the public health or public safety from fire, explosion, pollution, discharge of hazardous substances, or other construction or operational factors than the dangers that currently exist in the conduct and operation of other industrial and commercial enterprises in the commonwealth not engaged in the treatment, processing or disposal of hazardous waste, but utilizing processes that are comparable." Any person aggrieved by the board of health action may appeal its decision to the Superior Court.

The Legislature's desire to decrease local resistance to hazardous waste facilities was accompanied by a determination not to permit towns and cities to exclude such facilities from within their borders altogether. . . . In short, the Legislature sought, by means of St. 1980, c. 508, to facilitate the siting of safe facilities for the disposal and treatment of the wastes generated by schools, hospitals, government, and industry in Massachusetts by denying municipalities the right to veto facilities outright. In return, however, the Legislature established a means of involving affected municipalities in the siting process at the earliest possible moment, making available to them the legal, technical, and financial resources necessary for effective participation in that process, and allowing them significant control over the siting of a facility. . . .

BRUCE A. WILLIAMS & ALBERT R. MATHENY, DEMOCRACY, DIALOGUE, AND ENVIRONMENTAL DISPUTES

166-168 (1995)

In this book the authors first identify three "languages" that have evolved for discussing social regulation: (1) the pluralist language, which assumes that conflicting interests are the essence of politics, and that the public interest is served by creating an open political process that allows contending organized interests equal opportunity to influence public policy and assumes that, if the process is open, regulatory outcomes will be fair; (2) managerial language, which emphasizes the technical aspects of regulatory policy and identifies the need for expertise as both a structural barrier to and a substitute for democratic participation; and (3) communitarian language, which argues that the premises of individualism, such as the rational individual who chooses freely, are wrong, and that to discuss individuals one must look first at their communities and their communal languages. They then critique the NIMBY syndrome using each of these three "languages":

. . . Each language conveys an incomplete characterization of a linchpin of [hazardous waste] policy's failure—local opposition to facility siting. . . . [T]he more familiar managerial and pluralist approaches miss the point about NIMBY, and the less-recognized communitarian perspective, while flawed in its own right, casts the phenomenon in a revealing and more favorable light. Neither the managerial nor the pluralist language can account adequately for the widespread, enduring vigor with which grassroots opposition has halted HWDF [Hazardous Waste Disposal Facility] siting and ultimately affected hazardous waste policy in general. Managerial appeals to reason and pluralist references to process miss the mark targeted by the so-called NIMBY protesters and invariably lead to negative characterizations of the phenomenon.

From a managerial perspective, HWDF protesters are simply incapable of appreciating the information they are being given about hazardous waste cleanup and the safety of disposal facilities. Managerial critics often find fault with local siting opponents for failing to compare the "relative risks" of "proper" hazardous waste disposal with, for example, those of ozone depletion or even those of radon in their own homes. The view characterizes popular resistance as either naively ignorant or cynically self-interested. The typical remedy suggested here is the injection of greater expertise into the policy process, either through increased grants of authority to experts or better citizen education, so that the affected public might more rationally evaluate the risks they face with hazardous wastes or at least respect more the expertise of professional decision makers. . . .

The pluralist critique of NIMBY, with its emphasis on interest representation within a fair decision process, stresses the unwillingness of grassroots opponents to accept decisions that have been consummated "democratically." Pluralists argue that, regardless of the risks involved, a constitutionally conceived process providing for adequate group representation should render hazardous waste policy decisions acceptable even to those who do not narrowly benefit from the results. Groups willing to benefit from the political process, so the argument goes, must also be willing to accept unfavorable outcomes in order for that process to serve the public interest. Given its paradigmatic emphasis on compromise, the pluralist remedy for NIMBY generally revolves around some form of environmental mediation in which representatives of the different interest negotiate an appropriate site and settlement.

The communitarian understanding of NIMBY differs fundamentally from these managerial and pluralist assessments and accounts for NIMBY's political impact in ways that neither of the other languages can explain. First, the other languages fail to anticipate NIMBY's raw success in stalling hazardous waste policy implementation. Second, they underestimate the remarkable mobilizing force that the NIMBY phenomenon has brought to local politics—its capacity to inspire and maintain direct citizen participation.

These results are inexplicable in managerial and pluralist terms because neither the managerial emphasis on expertise nor the pluralist focus on process appreciates the role that direct citizen participation has in legitimating or challenging policy outcomes. In contrast, such direct participation is central to the communitarian understanding of legitimate policy-making.

Against the negative characterizations typical of managerial and pluralist commentary, the communitarian perspective constructs NIMBY in a positive light. It locates NIMBY within that long-standing protest tradition of American democratic politics that seeks, however vainly, citizen self-government in the determination of public policy outcomes. Essentially, the communitarian language invokes values that are unrepresented in the other two languages and that seek expression when the operation of market or government (or both) crosses unrecognized barriers of public acceptance. In this light, NIMBY signifies such an occurrence. . . .

Because the communitarian language addresses issues of political cooperation and conflict at the local level, it is relevant precisely at the point where hazardous waste regulation fails. And our dialogic model suggests that ignoring the communitarian language hinders the search for remedies for the problems of social regulation. But communitarian discourse is as incomplete in its conception of politics and policy as are the managerial and pluralist languages. Thus, resolving the policy gridlock surrounding hazardous waste exclusively in communitarian terms also is problematic.

Notes and Comments

1. *Why Not Preemption?* Perhaps the most obvious response to local obstructionism of the NIMBY variety is to take the decision out of the hands of the local jurisdiction and place it at the regional or state level. A number of jurisdictions have taken the preemption approach. The Oregon case, *Dunning v. Corrections Facility Siting Authority*, describes such an approach for the siting of correctional facilities.

These statutes, however, have not always (or, perhaps, even usually) resulted in increased siting of facilities, particularly hazardous waste facilities. Why not? Consider what other avenues of opposition are available to a local government whose local zoning power has been preempted. Most importantly, remember that local government officials are not without political influence at the state level, both in the legislature and before administrative agencies involved in the siting process. Is it possible that preemption only actually serves to intensify local opposition?

Are such proposals more likely to work for some types of "unwanted" land uses (perhaps correctional facilities) than others (hazardous waste sites)?

2. *Compensated Siting: The Academic Proposals.* The compensated siting approach was set forth in several leading academic articles and then implemented in the Massachusetts Hazardous Waste Siting Act, which was described in the *Town of Warren* case. *See* Lawrence S. Bacow & James R. Milkey, Overcoming Local Opposition to Hazardous Waste Facilities: The Massachusetts Approach, 6 Harv. Envtl. L. Rev. 265, 275 (1982). The authors posit that requiring compensation should encourage discussions between the community and the developer, promote efficiency by allowing projects to proceed only if their social benefits outweigh their social costs, and create an incentive for the developer to minimize

costs. *Id.* at 275-276. See also Bernd Holznagel, Negotiation and Mediation: The Newest Approach to Hazardous Waste Facility Siting, 13 B.C. Envtl. Aff. L. Rev. 329 (1986).

What practical difficulties can you foresee in the implementation of compensated siting? Consider, for example, whether it is easy to determine the boundaries of the appropriate "community" that should be compensated. Should the lines be drawn solely on the basis of political jurisdictional boundaries? See Daniel C. Esty, Revitalizing Environmental Federalism, 95 Mich. L. Rev. 570, 597 (1996) (arguing that the sphere of affected interests may expand or contract depending on an evolving definition of community).

Another question is the purpose of compensation. Is the purpose to compensate members of the community for the "damage" caused by siting the facility (that is, to compensate for the reduction in property values caused when the facility is sited in that community)? Alternatively, is it to increase the number and effectiveness of so-called mitigation measures, which might lessen the risks posed by the facility? Or is compensation intended simply to act as an incentive by enticing members of the community to accept the facility?

3. *Compensated Siting: The Experience.* Although much-heralded as the solution to the siting dilemma, "negotiated compensation" has had only limited success in siting facilities. In Massachusetts, the siting law has not resulted in the siting of new facilities. See Mary R. English, The Search for Political Authority in Massachusetts' Toxic Waste Management Law, 16 B.C. Envtl. Aff. L. Rev. 39, 41 (1988). The federal Low-Level Radioactive Waste Policy Act Amendments of 1985 include a provision allowing the imposition of surcharges to be used to mitigate the impact of the waste disposal facilities on the host state. 42 U.S.C. §2021e(d)(2)(E)(i) (2000). To date, however, no new facilities have been sited under the law despite significant efforts. Only the Wisconsin law, which relies on compensation, negotiation, and arbitration to site facilities, has shown some success. Vicki Been, Compensated Siting Proposals: Is it Time to Pay Attention?, 21 Fordham Urb. L.J. 787, 821 (1994) (by the end of 1993, siting agreements had been reached for 5 hazardous waste sites and 41 solid waste sites in Wisconsin).

What is the problem with the theory? One recent article identifies a series of flaws in the Massachusetts approach. Among them, according to the author, were that (1) the compulsory nature of negotiations imparted a strong adversarial cast to the negotiating sessions; (2) the Siting Council was not perceived as neutral and was seldom an effective broker between communities, developers, and agencies; and (3) the law focused too narrowly on compensation as the centerpiece of the negotiating agenda. Michael Wheeler, Negotiating NIMBYs: Learning from the Failure of the Massachusetts Siting Law, 11 Yale J. on Reg. 241, 273-280 (1994). If the article's conclusions are accepted, will it be easy to remedy these flaws by amending the legislation?

4. *"Good Neighbor" Agreements.* Will the incentives change if the facility is an *existing* one and, perhaps, wishes to expand or is charged with violations of environmental permits? In those kinds of situations, the parties in some instances have been able to negotiate so-called Good Neighbor Agreements. These are "agreements between community stakeholders and a polluting industry where the industry agrees, through binding commitments, to eliminate pollution risks in the community." Sara Pirk, Expanding Public Participation in Environmental Justice: Methods, Legislation, Litigation, and Beyond, 17 J. Envtl. L.

& Lit. 207, 237 (2002) (noting that there have been a number of successful "GNAs").

5. *Dispersion.* Some states have attempted to solve the problem of siting group homes, hazardous waste facilities and other unwanted land uses by passing statutes. One approach is to ensure that such homes are not unduly concentrated. In New York, municipalities may refuse to permit a group home for the mentally disabled if establishing the facility "would result in such a concentration of community residential facilities . . . that the nature and character of the areas within the municipality would be substantially altered." N.Y. Mental Hyg. Law §41.34(c)(1)(C) (McKinney 2002).

Can this type of dispersion solution solve all siting problems? For example, do we want more landfills and hazardous waste sites that are spread out among the areas that they serve, or are there strong reasons for siting fewer facilities on more targeted sites? Will the knowledge that other, similarly situated localities will also suffer the same "fate" cause local opposition to a facility to subside?

6. *Public Participation.* What role should public participation play in a successful siting process? One recent article advocated an essential role for such participation, asserting that "having a broad-based public participation process" was one of two features essential to a successful siting process. Howard Kunreuther *et al.*, Risk Perception and Trust: Challenges for Facility Siting, 7 Risk: Health, Safety & Env't 109, 111 (1996). The authors argue that "[p]roject proponents need better advice on how to involve the public earlier in the development cycle."

How would Williams and Matheny respond to this idea?

7. *Safety, Compensation, and "Bribery."* Compensation systems assume that, through bargaining, doubts about the safety of a facility may be resolved. See Douglas J. Amy, The Politics of Environmental Mediation 190 (1987) ("The assumption of the state-mandated mediation process in Massachusetts is that health risks should be negotiable — that the developers can economically compensate the local citizens for any increase in health risks. Thus, the mediation process attempts to portray health as simply another interest, one to which a price can be attached, and one that can be bargained over like any other commodity."). If local citizens will never feel completely safe about a project, however, consider how they will react to suggestions that they should accept the project in any event and, in return, receive some sort of payment for that acceptance. Will they view it as a kind of "bribery," thus adding a moral dimension to the opposition?

8. *NIMBY Reconsidered I.* Are you even sure that the NIMBY phenomenon requires a special legislative response? Consider the following argument by Robert W. Lake:

> These twin assumptions — of societal need and community-society conflict — obfuscate the essential character of LULUs. Rather than necessarily and inherently fulfilling a societal need, LULUs represent a particular solution to a problem. Siting hazardous waste incinerators, for example, constitutes a locational solution to an industrial production problem (hazardous waste generation). But the incinerator siting solution is only one of a number of possible strategies for hazardous waste management. The facility siting strategy concentrates costs on host communities, as compared to the alternative strategy of restructuring production so as to produce less waste, which in the short run concentrates costs on capital. . . .
>
> In short, rather than representing inherent *societal* need, LULUs constitute structurally constrained political solutions to economic problems that privilege the

> needs of *capital*. It follows, then, that rather than reflecting conflict between community and society, local opposition to LULUs expresses conflict between community and capital, and between community and the state, which is constrained in its intervention by the capital-state relationship.

Robert W. Lake, Rethinking NIMBY, 59 J. Am. Plan. Ass'n 87 (1993). Do the solutions to the "NIMBY syndrome" mistakenly identify a "societal need" when one does not really exist?

9. *NIMBY Reconsidered II*. The last few years have brought a new body of literature directed at "localism." You have seen some of it before in this book. For example, as noted in Chapter 10, some have advocated an increased use of neighborhood governance through private land use controls. The positions are, in some ways, quite revolutionary. *See* Richard C. Schragger, The Limits of Localism, 100 Mich. L. Rev. 371, 382 (2001) ("Scholars and policy-makers have increasingly advocated the proliferation of lawmaking authority down to the neighborhood and block level. A burgeoning literature calls for deference to local decisions addressing the quality of life on streets and in particular neighborhoods, and suggests that norms of street (and other behavior) be set locally").

Is this theory inconsistent with the idea that a "solution" to NIMBY behavior is required? Doesn't this theory require acceptance of local control, even when it opposes facilities that might be needed regionally?

D. JUSTICE AND SITING DECISIONS

It may seem that the siting process has been spectacularly unsuccessful and that arranging the legal structure to ensure more successful siting outcomes is difficult. The problem, however, is even more difficult than the material above suggests. In recent years, a movement has emerged, often labeled the "environmental justice" movement, that has added a new voice to the debate. Environmental justice advocates point to evidence that the environmental impacts of sited facilities have fallen overwhelmingly on persons of color. The debate on this issue is summarized in the following articles.

■ COMMISSION FOR RACIAL JUSTICE (UNITED CHURCH OF CHRIST), TOXIC WASTES AND RACE IN THE UNITED STATES: A NATIONAL REPORT ON THE RACIAL AND SOCIO-ECONOMIC CHARACTERISTICS OF COMMUNITIES WITH HAZARDOUS WASTE SITES

xi-xv, 13 (1987)

[T]he United Church of Christ Commission for Racial Justice decided, in 1986, to conduct extensive research on the relationship between the location of sites containing hazardous wastes and the racial and socio-economic characteristics of persons living in close proximity to those sites. . . .

Major Findings

This report presents findings from two cross-sectional studies on demographic patterns associated with (1) commercial hazardous waste facilities and (2) uncontrolled toxic waste sites. The first was an analytical study which revealed a striking relationship between the location of commercial hazardous waste facilities and race. The second was a descriptive study which documented the widespread presence of uncontrolled toxic waste sites in racial and ethnic communities throughout the United States. Among the many findings that emerged from these studies, the following are most important:

DEMOGRAPHIC CHARACTERISTICS OF COMMUNITIES WITH COMMERCIAL HAZARDOUS WASTE FACILITIES

- Race proved to be the most significant among variables tested in association with the location of commercial hazardous waste facilities. This represented a consistent national pattern.
- Communities with the greatest number of commercial hazardous waste facilities had the highest composition of racial and ethnic residents. In communities with two or more facilities or one of the nation's five largest landfills, the average minority percentage of the population was more than three times that of communities without facilities (38 percent vs. 12 percent).
- In communities with one commercial hazardous waste facility, the average minority percentage of the population was twice the average minority percentage of the population in communities without such facilities (24 percent vs. 12 percent).
- Although socio-economic status appeared to play an important role in the location of commercial hazardous waste facilities, race still proved to be more significant. This remained true after the study controlled for urbanization and regional differences. Incomes and home values were substantially lower when communities with commercial facilities were compared to communities in the surrounding counties without facilities.
- Three out of the five largest commercial hazardous waste landfills in the United States were located in predominantly Black or Hispanic communities. These three landfills accounted for 40 percent of the total estimated commercial landfill capacity in the nation.

DEMOGRAPHIC CHARACTERISTICS OF COMMUNITIES WITH UNCONTROLLED TOXIC WASTE SITES

- Three out of every five Black and Hispanic Americans lived in communities with uncontrolled toxic waste sites.
- More than 15 million Blacks lived in communities with one or more uncontrolled toxic waste sites.
- More than 8 million Hispanics lived in communities with one or more uncontrolled toxic waste sites.
- Blacks were heavily over-represented in the populations of metropolitan areas with the largest number of uncontrolled toxic waste sites. . . .

MAJOR CONCLUSIONS AND RECOMMENDATIONS

The findings of the analytical study on the location of commercial hazardous waste facilities suggest the existence of clear patterns which show that communities with greater minority percentages of the population are more likely to be the sites of such facilities. The possibility that these patterns resulted by chance is virtually impossible, strongly suggesting that some underlying factor or factors, which are related to race played a role in the location of commercial hazardous waste facilities. Therefore, the Commission for Racial Justice concludes that, indeed; race has been a factor in the location of commercial hazardous waste facilities in the United States.

The findings of the descriptive study on the location of uncontrolled toxic waste sites suggest an inordinate concentration of such sites in Black and Hispanic communities, particularly in urban areas. This situation reveals that the issue of race is an important factor in describing the problem of uncontrolled toxic waste sites. . . .

RESULTS

This section summarizes the major findings of both studies: the analysis of race and the location of commercial hazardous waste facilities and the descriptive study on the racial composition of communities with uncontrolled toxic waste sites. The first study found that the group of residential ZIP code areas with the highest number of commercial hazardous waste facilities also had the highest mean percentage of residents who belong to a racial and ethnic group. Conversely those residential ZIP codes with no waste facilities had a lower proportion of racial and ethnic residents. . . .

The descriptive study, which focused on closed or uncontrolled toxic waste sites, found their presence in American communities to be highly pervasive. This study found that more than half of the population in the United States lived in residential ZIP code areas with one or more uncontrolled toxic waste sites. The study also found that three out of every five Black and Hispanic Americans lived in communities with uncontrolled toxic waste sites. This figure represents more than 15 million Blacks and 8 million Hispanics. Approximately 2 million Asian/Pacific Islanders and 700,000 American Indians lived in such communities.

■ CHRISTOPHER BOERNER *et al.*, ENVIRONMENTAL JUSTICE?
4-6 (1994)

The first major criticism of the present research centers on the definition of the term "community." Defining minority communities as those areas where the percentage of nonwhite residents exceeds that of the entire population means that a community may be considered "minority" even if the vast majority of its residents are white. Based on this methodology, for example, Staten Island — home of the nation's largest landfill — is considered a minority community even though over 80 percent of its residents are white. In fact, Staten Island is the "whitest" of New York City's five boroughs.

A second, but related, problem is that these studies ignore population densities. Merely citing the proportion of minority or low-income residents in a given host community does not provide information about how many people are actually exposed to environmental harms. For example, given that blacks presently comprise approximately 16 percent of the nation's population, a host community of 1000 residents, 20 percent of whom are black, would be considered "minority," while a host community of 6000 residents, 15 percent of whom are black, would not. By overlooking population density, the studies fail to point out that more blacks (900 versus 200) would be exposed to the pollution in the second, "non-minority" community, than in the first.

In addition to the problems associated with proportionality and population density, the environmental justice studies . . . often define the affected area in geographic terms that are too broad. Much of the prior research is based on ZIP-code areas, which are frequently large units established by the U.S. Postal Service. As a result, the data likely suffer from what statisticians call "aggregation errors." That is to say, the studies reach conclusions from the ZIP-code data which would not be valid if a smaller, more consistent geographic unit were examined. A recent study released by the Social and Demographic Research Institute at the University of Massachusetts, Amherst (UMass) confirms that an analysis of census tracts — small geographic units with relatively fixed boundaries — yields strikingly different results.

The UMass study compared the social and demographic characteristics of census tracts that contain commercial TSDFs [treatment, storage, and disposal facilities] with those tracts that do not have TSDFs. Contrary to conventional wisdom, the UMass researchers found that the percentage of minorities living in neighborhoods with commercial facilities is no greater than in areas without such facilities. Indeed, in the 25 largest metropolitan areas studied, commercial hazardous waste facilities are slightly more likely to be in industrial neighborhoods with a *lower* percentage of minorities and a *higher* percentage of white working-class families. . . . The results of the UMass study — the most comprehensive analysis of environmental justice to date — case serious doubt on much of the [earlier] research.

A third flaw in the existing environmental justice studies is that they imply rather than explicitly state the actual risk presented by commercial TSDFs. While the research attempts to disclose the prevalence of commercial waste plants in poor and minority communities, there is no corresponding information about the dangers associated with living near such facilities. . . .

Finally, existing research on environmental justice fails to establish that discriminatory siting and permitting practices caused present environmental disparities. . . .

Notes and Comments

1. *Conflicting Data.* The Church of Christ excerpt and the Boerner excerpt give you a sense of the debate over whether the empirical research has established a "suspect" siting pattern. Consider carefully Boerner's criticisms of the present research. Do you find each ground convincing? What if the evidence is conflicting about whether market dynamics plays a significant role in the distribution of sites? How conclusive must the proof be before the government should intervene?

2. *Harm from NIMBYism.* Who is harmed by the NIMBY phenomenon? Professor Bullard has argued that the victims of NIMBY are minority communities:

> [T]he cumulative effect of not-in-my-backyard (NIMBY) victories by environmentalists appears to have driven the unwanted facilities toward more vulnerable groups. Black neighborhoods are especially vulnerable to the penetration of unwanted land uses. . . . NIMBY, like white racism, creates and perpetuates privileges for whites at the expense of people of color.

Robert D. Bullard, Dumping in Dixie: Race, Class, and Environmental Quality 46, 108 (1990).

However, a leading practitioner in New York, an excerpt from whose book was reprinted earlier in this chapter, has suggested that the "victims of NIMBY" are "very different from those envisioned by those who either condemn or applaud facility opposition." Michael R. Gerrard, The Victims of NIMBY, 21 Ford. Urb. L.J. 495, 497 (1994). He concluded that local opposition has numerous and complex impacts that vary considerably depending on the nature of the facility that is opposed. For example, he found that opposition to waste disposal facilities "has not generally increased the siting of new landfills and incinerators in minority communities, but it has perpetuated the existence of old, substandard disposal units in those communities." *Id.* at 521. At the same time, it has spurred efforts to recycle and to reduce the creation of waste. In contrast, opposition to housing and social-service facilities "has overwhelmingly negative consequences for society." *Id.* at 522.

3. *Other Evidence*: There has been a variety of studies and articles on the environmental justice issue. See, e.g., U.S. General Accounting Office, Siting of Hazardous Waste Landfills and Their Correlation with Racial and Economic Status of Surrounding Communities (1983) (concluding that a majority of residents in the communities containing three of the four hazardous waste landfills in the EPA's Region IV were African-American). A study of Superfund sites in Florida concluded that blacks and Hispanics are more likely than whites to live near Superfund sites in that state, and that these patterns persist when other variables (housing values, income, percentage of manufacturing employment, urbanization) are controlled. The author concludes that race and ethnicity are the most salient factors in predicting the location of hazardous waste sites. See Paul Stretesky & Michael J. Hogan, Environmental Justice: An Analysis of Superfund Sites in Florida, 45 Soc. Probs. 268-287(1998). Other influential articles broadened the analysis from pure siting decisions to suggest that environmental laws generally have distributed risks unfairly upon minority populations. See, e.g., Richard J. Lazarus, Pursuing "Environmental Justice": The Distributional Effects of Environmental Protection, 87 Nw. U.L. Rev. 787 (1993).

These criticisms challenge the basic tenets of the traditional land use siting process, as well as the premises of the recent attempts to resolve the siting dilemma. For example, one leading advocate in the environmental justice movement has argued that states have established siting processes for waste facilities as a means of stifling local opposition. Luke W. Cole, Remedies for Environmental Racism: A View from the Field, 90 Mich. L. Rev. 1991, 1994 (1992) ("Increasingly, states have set up processes to site toxic waste facilities over local opposition — whether that opposition is by people of color or not.").

4. *The Revisionists.* The initial round of environmental justice literature in turn has produced some revisionist writing. In one recent article, Professor Lynn E. Blais suggested that the political and market determinations leading to the distribution of risks through siting of facilities may reflect rational and legitimate preferences of individuals. Lynn E. Blais, Environmental Racism Reconsidered, 75 N.C. L. Rev. 75, 81 (1996). Others have re-analyzed the data available on siting and reached somewhat different conclusions. Terence J. Centner, Environmental Justice and Toxic Releases: Establishing Evidence of Discriminatory Effect Based on Race and Not Income, 3 Wis. Envtl. L.J. 119 (1996).

Another article reevaluated the United Church of Christ study using census tracts instead of zip codes. It concluded that "there is some statistical evidence" that the higher percentages of minorities near facilities exist "because minorities are more likely to be among those employed in industrial and precision manufacturing operations in those regions." Douglas A. Anderton *et al.*, Environmental Equity: Evaluating TSDF Siting Over the Past Two Decades, Waste Age, July 1994, at 83. The study also found that, although racial composition did not significantly differ between "host" and "non-host" census tracts, there was a statistically significant difference in the percentage of families living below the poverty level. *Id.* at 84. That evidence, of course, would suggest that income rather than race is the key factor. In turn, environmental justice advocates have criticized this study. See, e.g., Benjamin A. Goldman & Laura Fitton, Toxic Wastes and Race Revisited 14-15 (1994).

Professor Blais suggests that, in light of the latest empirical evidence, "we should ask ourselves the very difficult question whether the current distribution of environmentally sensitive land uses represents simply the revealed preferences of a society characterized by substantial and growing disparities in income and opportunities." Blais, Environmental Racism Reconsidered, *supra*, at 93. If the siting disparities are due to factors other than simple racial bias, does this conclusion mean that the present siting system, to the extent that it does site facilities, is equitable?

5. *The Fair Housing Act.* If the discrimination alleged concerns bias against the handicapped rather than racial bias, the Fair Housing Act (which was discussed above in Chapter 13 of this casebook) may provide a remedy. For example, in *Turning Point, Inc. v. City of Caldwell, Idaho*, 74 F.3d 941 (9th Cir. 1996), plaintiffs used two adjacent houses for emergency shelters for homeless individuals, many of whom had mental or physical disabilities. The local commission at first granted a special use permit allowing a maximum of 25 individuals, but after the neighbors complained it lowered the occupancy limit to 15. The plaintiffs then sued, alleging discrimination under the Fair Housing Act. The Court of Appeals for the Ninth Circuit awarded damages based upon a reasonable occupancy rate of 25 individuals. On affordable housing and the NIMBY phenomenon, *see* Peter W. Salsich, Jr., Affordable Housing: Can NIMBYISM Be Transformed into OKIMBYISM?, 19 St. Louis U. Pub. L. Rev. 453 (2000).

Given the extensive debate over the existence and extent of injustice in the siting process, it should come as no surprise that devising solutions to the problem will not be simple.

■ FEDERAL ACTIONS TO ADDRESS ENVIRONMENTAL JUSTICE IN MINORITY POPULATIONS AND LOW-INCOME POPULATIONS

Executive Order No. 12,898, 59 Fed. Reg. 7629 (1994)

§1-103. *Development of Agency Strategies.* (a) Except as provided in section 6-605 of this order, each Federal agency shall develop an agency-wide environmental justice strategy, as set forth in subsections (b)-(e) of this section that identifies and addresses disproportionately high and adverse human health or environmental effects of its programs, policies, and activities on minority populations and low-income populations. The environmental justice strategy shall list programs, policies, planning and public participation processes, enforcement, and/or rule-makings related to human health or the environment that should be revised to, at a minimum: (1) promote enforcement of all health and environmental statutes in areas with minority populations and low-income populations; (2) ensure greater public participation; (3) improve research and data collection relating to the health of and environment of minority populations and low-income populations; and (4) identify differential patterns of consumption of natural resources among minority populations and low-income populations. In addition, the environmental justice strategy shall include, where appropriate, a timetable for undertaking identified revisions and consideration of economic and social implications of the revisions.

The difficulty of securing judicial relief has led plaintiffs to rely on administrative and statutory solutions, such as the executive order signed by President Clinton. The Executive Order is particularly important, for it constitutes governmental recognition that inequities exist in the distribution of risks. Do you think that the processes called for in the order are likely to be effective?

In addition to the executive order, the environmental justice problem appeared to call for a response rooted in the civil rights laws. The federal Environmental Protection Agency has issued interim guidance on how it will respond to complaints, filed under Title VI of the 1964 Civil Rights Act, that state or local agencies issuing permits, which receive funding from EPA, cause discriminatory effects. If EPA accepts a complaint, it will investigate to determine whether the permit under challenge will create or add to a "disparate impact" on minorities. If the agency makes such a finding, then the state or local agency may respond by rebutting the finding, offering a plan for mitigating the disparate impact, or demonstrating that it has a "substantial, legitimate interest that justifies the decision to proceed with the permit, notwithstanding the disparate impact." U.S. EPA, Interim Guidance for Investigating Title VI Administrative Complaints Challenging Permits (Feb.13, 1998), available at http://es.epa.gov/oeca/oej/titlevi.html.

The Interim Guidance takes a broad approach to disparate impact, examining all the circumstances of the particular siting action, including cumulative environmental impacts from the permitting of other facilities. It is enforced by EPA's Office of Civil Rights. The Guidance applies to states with permitting agencies that receive federal funds. (The Executive Order itself applies to EPA's actions.) If EPA makes a finding of "disparate impact," the state agency bears the burden of showing that the impact does not exist, to mitigate the impact, or to justify it.

In short, the Interim Guidance allowed challenges to state and local permitting—an extremely controversial proposition. In response to controversy over how the Interim Guidance was promulgated, EPA created a public consultation process and started redrafting the interim guidance. It then released a draft "Title VI Guidance," which once again was strongly criticized. EPA has not yet finalized that guidance. *See* Michael D. Mathieson, The Effect of Alexander v. Sandoval on Federal Environmental Civil Rights (Environmental Justice) Policy, 13 George Mason Civ. Rights. L.J. 35 (2002); June M. Lyle, Note, Reactions to EPA's Interim Guidance: The Growing Battle for Control Over Environmental Justice Decisionmaking, 75 Ind. L.J. 687 (2000).

One large problem loomed: would private citizens have a cause of action to enforce EPA's "disparate impact" regulations? The original Interim Guidance recognized a private right of action based on EPA's Title VI regulations, which prohibited "disparate impacts" on populations. In *Chester Residents Concerned for Quality Living v. Seif*, 132 F.3d 925 (3d Cir. 1997), *cert. granted sub nom. Seif v. Chester Residents for Quality Living*, 118 S. Ct. 2296 (1998), *judgment vacated*, 119 S. Ct. 22 (1998), plaintiffs challenged Pennsylvania's grant of a permit for a hazardous waste processing facility located in a predominantly black community in Chester, Pennsylvania. The Court of Appeals for the Third Circuit held that plaintiffs had a private right of action under administrative regulations implementing Title VI, which required only the showing of a discriminatory effect. After the Supreme Court granted certiorari in the case, however, the judgment was vacated.

Next, the Supreme Court decided *Alexander v. Sandoval*, 532 U.S. 275 (2001). In that case, the Court held that no private right of action existed to enforce disparate-impact regulations pursuant to Section 602 of Title VI, 42 U.S.C. §2000e. That left one theory to plaintiffs seeking to use Title VI to enforce the disparate-impact regulations in a private case: to argue that a cause of action existed under Section 1983 of the Civil Rights Act. The following case addressed that issue in a siting context.

SOUTH CAMDEN CITIZENS IN ACTION v. NEW JERSEY DEPT. OF ENVTL. PROTECTION

274 F.3d 771 (3d Cir. 2001)

GREENBERG, Circuit Judge.

I. OVERVIEW

This matter comes on before this court on appeals by defendant-appellant New Jersey Department of Environmental Protection ("NJDEP") and intervenor-appellant St. Lawrence Cement Co., L.L.C. ("St. Lawrence") from the district court's order granting preliminary injunctive relief to plaintiffs, South Camden Citizens in Action and ten residents of the Waterfront South neighborhood of Camden, New Jersey. Plaintiffs brought this action pursuant to 42 U.S.C. §1983, as well as on other bases, claiming NJDEP discriminated against them by issuing an air permit to St. Lawrence to operate a facility that would have an adverse disparate racial impact upon them in violation of Title VI of the Civil Rights Act of 1964, 42 U.S.C. §§2000d to 2000d-7.

Our opinion focuses on whether, following the Supreme Court's recent decision in *Alexander v. Sandoval*, 532 U.S. 275, 121 S. Ct. 1511, 149 L.Ed.2d 517 (2000), plaintiffs can maintain this action under section 1983 for disparate impact discrimination in violation of Title VI and its implementing regulations. For the reasons we set forth, we hold that an administrative regulation cannot create an interest enforceable under section 1983 unless the interest already is implicit in the statute authorizing the regulation, and that inasmuch as Title VI proscribes only intentional discrimination, the plaintiffs do not have a right enforceable through a 1983 action under the EPA's disparate impact discrimination regulations. . . .

II. Background and Procedural History

A. Background

[T]he residents of Waterfront South are predominately minorities and the neighborhood is disadvantaged environmentally.[1] Waterfront South contains two Superfund sites, several contaminated and abandoned industrial sites, and many currently operating facilities, including chemical companies, waste facilities, food processing companies, automotive shops, and a petroleum coke transfer station. Moreover, NJDEP has granted permits for operation of a regional sewage treatment plant, a trash-to-steam incinerator and a co-generation power plant in the neighborhood. As a result, Waterfront South, though only one of 23 Camden neighborhoods, hosts 20% of the city's contaminated sites and, on average, has more than twice the number of facilities with permits to emit air pollution than exist in the area encompassed within a typical New Jersey zip code.

St. Lawrence supplies cement materials, primarily to the ready-mix concrete industry. One aspect of St. Lawrence's business is the processing of ground granulated blast furnace slag ("GBFS"), a sand-like by-product of the steel-making industry, used in portland cement. In 1998, St. Lawrence wanted to open a GBFS grinding facility on a site in Camden owned by the South Jersey Port Corporation (the "Port"). In furtherance of this project, in March 1999 St. Lawrence signed a lease with the Port for the site and initiated discussions with NJDEP with respect to obtaining construction and operation permits for the facility, primarily focusing on the air permit that required minimizing the emission of PM10, *i.e.*, particulate matter with a diameter of 10 microns or less. NJDEP required St. Lawrence to conduct an air quality impact analysis for PM10 confirming that there would not be adverse health impacts from operation of the facility and that St. Lawrence's operations complied with the National Ambient Air Quality Standards for PM10. St. Lawrence completed the analysis, and NJDEP accepted the result that the facility's emissions would satisfy the established standards applicable to its operation.

On November 1, 1999, NJDEP notified St. Lawrence that the permit process was "administratively complete." Accordingly, NJDEP permitted St. Lawrence to begin construction of the facility, which it did in late 1999. Then, on July 25, 2000, NJDEP gave notice of a public hearing to be held on August 23, 2000, addressing St. Lawrence's draft air permit. NJDEP stated, however, that it would accept written comments on the draft permit until August 31, 2000. Approximately 120

1. The Waterfront South community is comprised of 63% African-American, 28.3% Hispanic, and 9% white residents.

community members voiced their opinions and concerns about St. Lawrence's facility at the hearing, and several individuals provided NJDEP with written comments.

Thereafter, NJDEP issued a 33-page "Hearing Officer's Report Responses to Public Comments on the Draft Air Permit" for St. Lawrence. In the report, NJDEP addressed the concerns raised by community members, including environmental equity/environmental justice, preexisting local environmental issues, St. Lawrence's emission limits, the results of St. Lawrence's air quality impact analysis, truck emission standards and carbon monoxide air quality evaluation results, and the protection of the health and safety of Waterfront South residents. Plaintiffs, however, filed an administrative complaint with the EPA and a request for a grievance hearing with NJDEP, as they alleged that NJDEP's permit review procedures violated Title VI of the Civil Rights Act of 1964 because the procedures did not include an analysis of the allegedly racially disparate adverse impact of the facility. NJDEP did not respond to the grievance hearing request, and on October 31, 2000, issued St. Lawrence's final air permit.

B. PROCEDURAL HISTORY

On February 13, 2001, plaintiffs filed a complaint against NJDEP and NJDEP Commissioner Robert C. Shinn, Jr., alleging that they violated Title VI by intentionally discriminating against them in violation of section 601, 42 U.S.C. § 2000d, by issuing the air quality permit and further asserting that the facility in operation under the air permit would have an adverse disparate impact on them in violation of section 602, 42 U.S.C. §2000d-1. . . .

. . . On May 10, 2001, the court issued a supplemental opinion and order continuing the preliminary injunction based on plaintiffs' section 1983 claim and again remanding the matter to NJDEP for a Title VI analysis. *See South Camden Citizens in Action v. N.J. Dep't of Envtl. Prot.*, 145 F. Supp. 2d 505 (D.N.J.2001) (South Camden II). In reaching its result the court relied, *inter alia*, on *Powell v. Ridge*, 189 F.3d 387, 403 (3d Cir.), *cert. denied*, 528 U.S. 1046, 120 S. Ct. 579, 145 L. Ed. 2d 482 (1999), in which we held that there was a private right of action available to enforce a regulation implementing Title VI and that a disparate impact discrimination claim could be maintained under section 1983 for a violation of a regulation promulgated pursuant to section 602. *See South Camden II*, 145 F. Supp. 2d at 520, 525, 543. . . .

III. DISCUSSION . . .

[T]he overarching legal issue on this appeal is whether plaintiffs can advance a cause of action to enforce section 602 of Title VI and its implementing regulations through section 1983. If they cannot, then the only basis on which they can obtain relief is to demonstrate that the NJDEP engaged in intentional discrimination. . . .

We start our legal analysis with a consideration of *Sandoval* in which the Court held that a private right of action is not available to enforce disparate impact regulations promulgated under Title VI, thus overruling *Powell* at least to the extent that it held to the contrary. . . . The Court held that "[n]either as originally enacted nor as later amended does Title VI display an intent to create a freestanding private right of action to enforce regulations promulgated under §602. We therefore hold that no such right of action exists." *Id.* at —, 121 S. Ct. at 1523. . . .

. . . However, inasmuch as the plaintiffs in *Sandoval* did not advance a cause of action under section 1983 to enforce Title VI and its implementing regulations, the majority did not consider whether such an action is available.[5]

Resolution of this issue, therefore, requires us to examine whether disparate impact regulations promulgated pursuant to section 602 may, and if so do, create a right that may be enforced through a section 1983 action.

Section 1983 provides, in relevant part:

> Every person who, under color of any statute, ordinance, regulation, custom, or usage, of any State or Territory or the District of Columbia, subjects, or causes to be subjected, any citizen of the United States or other person within the jurisdiction thereof to the deprivation of any rights, privileges, or immunities secured by the Constitution and laws, shall be liable to the party injured in any action at law, suit in equity, or other proper proceeding for redress. . . .

Here, plaintiffs seek to enforce a prohibition on disparate impact discrimination that does not appear explicitly in Title VI, but rather is set forth in EPA regulations. They contend that the regulations are a valid interpretation of Title VI.[6] Section 601 of Title VI provides:

> No person in the United States shall, on the ground of race, color, or national origin, be excluded from participation in, be denied the benefits of, or be subjected to discrimination under any program or activity receiving Federal financial assistance.

42 U.S.C § 2000d. Section 602 provides, in relevant part:

> Each Federal department and agency which is empowered to extend Federal financial assistance to any program or activity, by way of grant, loan, or contract other than a contract of insurance or guaranty, is authorized and directed to effectuate the provisions of section 2000d [Section 601] of this title with respect to such program or activity by issuing rules, regulations, or orders of general applicability which shall be consistent with achievement of the objectives of the statute authorizing financial assistance in connection with which the action is taken.

Id. §2000d-1. Finally, the EPA regulations at issue provide:

5. In his dissent, Justice Stevens stated the following with regard to section 1983:

> [T]o the extent that the majority denies relief to the respondents merely because they neglected to mention 42 U.S.C. §1983 in framing their Title VI claim, this case is something of a sport. Litigants who in the future wish to enforce the Title VI regulations against state actors in all likelihood must only reference §1983 to obtain relief; indeed, the plaintiffs in this case (or other similarly situated individuals) presumably retain the option of re-challenging Alabama's English-only policy in a complaint that invokes §1983 even after today's decision.

Sandoval, 532 U.S. at —, 121 S. Ct. at 1527 (Stevens, J., dissenting). The majority does not address the dissent's statement. Nevertheless, for the reasons that follow, we conclude that the majority's opinion and Supreme Court precedent do not permit the bringing of the section 1983 action that Justice Stevens suggested is available.

6. We assume without deciding that the regulations are valid, as neither NJDEP nor St. Lawrence timely challenged them in the district court and our analysis does not turn on their validity. That being said, like the Court stated in *Sandoval,* we observe that there does seem to be considerable tension between the section 602 regulations proscribing activities that have a disparate impact and section 601's limitation to interdiction only of intentionally discriminatory activities. *See Sandoval,* 532 U.S. at —, 121 S. Ct. at 1517.

> No person shall be excluded from participation in, be denied the benefits of, or be subjected to discrimination under any program or activity receiving EPA assistance on the basis of race, color, [or] national origin. . . .
>
> A recipient shall not use criteria or methods of administering its program which have the effect of subjecting individuals to discrimination because of their race, color, national origin, or sex, or have the effect of defeating or substantially impairing accomplishment of the objectives of the program with respect to individuals of a particular race, color, national origin, or sex.

40 C.F.R. §§7.30 & 7.35(b). According to plaintiffs, these statutory provisions and their complementary regulations prohibiting discriminatory impacts in administering programs create a federal right enforceable through section 1983.

This contention raises the question of whether a regulation can create a right enforceable through section 1983 where the alleged right does not appear explicitly in the statute, but only appears in the regulation. . . .

In considering whether a regulation in itself can establish a right enforceable under section 1983, we initially point out that a majority of the Supreme Court never has stated expressly that a valid regulation can create such a right. . . .

Plaintiffs place much reliance on *Powell v. Ridge*, 189 F.3d at 403, in which we indicated that a disparate impact discrimination claim could be maintained under section 1983 for a violation of a regulation promulgated pursuant to section 602. There, the plaintiffs brought a Title VI action against the Commonwealth of Pennsylvania, challenging its practices in funding public education on the ground that they had a racially discriminatory effect. *See id.* at 391. On appeal, we considered, among other things, whether there was a private right of action available to enforce a regulation implementing Title VI, as well as whether a plaintiff can maintain a claim under section 1983 for a violation of that regulation. *See id.* We answered both questions in the affirmative, stating that section 602 and the Department of Education regulation at issue provided a private right of action, and that plaintiffs also could utilize section 1983 to redress defendants' alleged violation of the statute and regulation. *See id.* at 399-400, 403.

Powell, however, should not be overread. . . . *Powell* did not analyze the foundation issue that is central here, *i.e.*, whether a regulation in itself can create a right enforceable under section 1983. In *Powell*, we seemed simply to assume for section 1983 purposes that it could. . . .

There are cases in other circuits addressing the question of whether a regulation alone may create a right enforceable under section 1983. The Courts of Appeals for the Fourth and Eleventh Circuits concluded that they may not and the Court of Appeals for the Sixth Circuit decided to the contrary. . . .

. . . To start with, we reiterate that in *Sandoval* the Court made the critical point that "[l]anguage in a regulation may invoke a private right of action that Congress through statutory text created, but it may not create a right that Congress has not." 532 U.S. at —, 121 S. Ct. at 1522. . . .

Moreover, it is apparent that in the Court's section 1983 jurisprudence after *Wright* [*v. City of Roanoke Redevelopment & Hous. Auth.*, 479 U.S. 418 (1987)], dealing with whether a plaintiff is advancing an enforceable right, the primary consideration has been to determine if Congress intended to create the particular federal right sought to be enforced. *See Suter*, 503 U.S. at 357, 112 S. Ct. at 1367. . . .

Therefore, we . . . hold that the EPA's disparate impact regulations cannot create a federal right enforceable through section 1983. . . . Since the time of the Supreme Court's decision in *Sandoval*, it hardly can be argued reasonably that the right alleged to exist in the EPA's regulations, namely to be free of disparate impact discrimination in the administration of programs or activities receiving EPA assistance, can be located in either section 601 or section 602 of Title VI.

In reaching our result, we emphasize the following. *Sandoval* made it clear that section 601 proscribes intentional discrimination only. *See Sandoval*, 532 U.S. at —, 121 S. Ct. at 1516. . . .

[T]he Court found that there was no evidence of congressional intent to create new rights under section 602. *See id.* Rather, "§602 limits agencies to 'effectuat[ing]' rights already created by §601." *Id.*

Inasmuch as the Court found previously that the only right conferred by section 601 was to be free of intentional discrimination, it does not follow that the right to be free from disparate impact discrimination can be located in section 602. In fact, it cannot. In sum, the regulations, though assumedly valid, are not based on any federal right present in the statute. . . .

Accordingly, if there is to be a private enforceable right under Title VI to be free from disparate impact discrimination, Congress, and not an administrative agency or a court, must create this right. . . .

We emphasize that the implications of this case are enormous and obviously, as the appearance of the many amici curiae attests, have not been lost on interested parties. It is plain that in view of the pervasiveness of state and local licensing provisions and the likely applicability of Title VI to the agencies involved, the district court's opinion has the potential, if followed elsewhere, to subject vast aspects of commercial activities to disparate impact analyses by the relevant agencies. Indeed, we noted in *Powell* that "[a]t least 40 federal agencies have adopted regulations that prohibit disparate-impact discrimination pursuant to [section 602]." *Powell*, 189 F.3d at 393. While we do not express an opinion on whether that would be desirable, we do suggest that if it is to happen, then Congress and not a court should say so as a court's authority is to interpret rather than to make the law. . . .

McKee, Circuit Judge, dissent[s].

Notes and Comments

1. *Attacking Distributional Inequities.* Assuming that environmental justice, at its core, concerns distributional inequities in the siting of unwanted land uses, the question becomes how to frame a response to that problem. As you can surmise from what you have studied in this book, framing a response is not simple, despite the deluge of academic literature on the subject. One article suggested that the response to environmental injustice in the land use context has taken five forms, "each with corresponding conceptions of, or ways of thinking about, the environmental justice problem":

> (1) to study the evidence and causes of the distribution of environmental hazards and LULUs (evidentiary conceptions); (2) to organize politically against proposed or existing LULUs (power conceptions); (3) to vindicate the constitutional, statutory, or

common-law rights of those affected disproportionately by environmental hazards or LULUs (legal conceptions); (4) to heighten enforcement of environmental laws (environmental conceptions); and (5) to seek or rely on market mechanisms to address the distribution problem (economic conceptions).

Craig Anthony (Tony) Arnold, Land Use Regulation and Environmental Justice, 30 Envtl. L. Rep. 10395 (2000). At its core, isn't the idea of environmental injustice extremely broad? Doesn't it call into question the very foundation of the current land use system?

2. *Litigation as a Tool for Achieving Environmental Justice.* Two laws have been identified as providing possible vehicles for challenging actions by governmental entities that result in allegedly racist siting decisions: the equal protection clause of the Fourteenth Amendment to the United States Constitution and Title VI of the Civil Rights Act of 1964, 42 U.S.C. §2000d (2000) ("[n]o person in the United States shall, on the grounds of race, color or national origin, . . . be subjected to discrimination under any program or activity receiving Federal financial assistance"). These laws, however, have not proven particularly useful to plaintiffs. The few cases that have come down have turned on the plaintiff's inability to meet the evidentiary standards of federal civil rights laws. One important decision was *East Bibb Twiggs Neighborhood Ass'n v. Macon-Bibb County Planning & Zoning Commission*, 706 F. Supp. 880 (M.D. Ga. 1989), *aff'd*, 896 F.2d 1264 (11th Cir. 1989) (rejecting challenge that siting of a landfill in an area where a majority of citizens was black was motivated by racial discrimination). *See also R.I.S.E. v. Kay*, 768 F. Supp. 1144 (E.D. Va. 1991), *aff'd*, 977 F.2d 573 (4th Cir. 1992) (plaintiff failed to establish that placement of landfill in a predominantly black area resulted from intentional discrimination in violation of the Equal Protection Clause); *Bean v. Southwestern Waste Management Corp.*, 482 F. Supp. 673 (S.D. Tex. 1979), *aff'd*, 782 F.2d 1038 (5th Cir. 1986) (plaintiffs did not establish a substantial likelihood of proving that the grant of a permit had been motivated by purposeful racial discrimination).

3. *Taking Stock.* Do you think it is likely that the Supreme Court will recognize a private cause of action to enforce the regulations? How important is such a cause of action? Is it largely symbolic, or is it the only legal tool that has any real "teeth"? *See* Luke W. Cole & Sheila R. Foster, From the Ground Up: Environmental Racism and the Rise of the Environmental Justice Movement 126 (N.Y.U. Press 2001) ("civil rights claims, particularly those based on constitutional principles of equal protection, . . . can be very useful in building morale, raising the profile of a community's struggle, and educating the public about environmental racism").

Assuming that other circuits disagree with *South Camden*, how easy is it for individuals challenging permits to use the procedure in the Interim Guidance? Isn't it a fact-intensive inquiry that can raise a myriad of legal issues? Will most opponents of siting proposals based on disparate impacts have the resources needed to use this procedure? Or will the basis for EPA's jurisdiction over the issue — federal funding of state agencies — be sufficient to cause states to settle any disputes that arise? Will an industry-applicant faced with opposition under the Interim Guidance see years of litigation ahead and drop the proposal?

4. *Reaction v. Proaction.* Is the basic problem with challenging individual permit proposals that citizens are placed in a reactive situation? To resolve disparate impacts, isn't a proactive strategy based on pollution prevention, called for? *See* EPA Advisory Panel Drafting Guidance on Pollution Prevention in Minority Areas,

71 U.S.L.W. 2394 (Dec. 17, 2002) (Members of EPA's National Environmental Justice Advisory Council were considering proposals in which EPA would take steps to address sources of pollution before the pollutants were released, including proposals to facilitate negotiaton of "pollution prevention partnerships" between local communities and industry).

5. *Equity v. Efficiency.* While the legal development of environmental justice principles, at least those based on the civil rights law, appears stalemated, the political and theoretical side of the movement continues. Commentators continue to debate what the movement means. For example, in a recent essay Professor Eileen Gauna suggested that "[p]erhaps the most important contribution the environmental justice movement has made . . . has been to bring to the surface the potential conflict between efficiency and equity and the complicated interplay between the two principles." Eileen Gauna, An Essay on Environmental Justice: The Past, the Present, and Back to the Future, 42 Nat. Res. J. 701, 706 (2002). As she develops the argument, the "willingness to pay" criterion is the foundation upon which efficiency is measured and resources allocated. However, she continues, "it does not necessarily follow that environmental necessities that affect public health can or should be distributed this way. Everyone, regardless of their wealth, should be able to breath clean air and drink uncontaminated water." *Id.*

Do you see any way the two principles can be reconciled, or at least co-exist?

6. *Other State Laws.* A couple of other states have passed legislation dealing with equity in the siting process. Arkansas has passed the Arkansas Environmental Equity Act, Ark. Code Ann. §§8-6-1501 et seq. (1987). The Act establishes a rebuttable presumption against the siting of certain solid waste management facilities located within twelve miles of any existing "high impact solid waste management facility." *Id.* §8-6-1504 (1987).

Assuming that the studies and other literature have demonstrated that siting decisions have a disproportionate impact on minority groups, what solution would you suggest?

17

Protection of Cultural and Aesthetic Values

A. INTRODUCTION

This chapter examines the use of land use regulatory tools to protect cultural and aesthetic values. The material includes regulation to preserve historic buildings and sites, to ban unsightly objects such as billboards and junkyards, and to review proposed architectural changes in neighborhoods for conformity to some predetermined criteria. Like many other areas of land use regulation, the subjects covered in this chapter are marked with controversy, as local governments throughout the nation balance the benefits of regulation versus losses in individual freedom and property rights.

1. Review and Synthesis

In many ways the issues that arise in aesthetic regulation constitute a review for the student of subjects covered previously in this casebook. You will find that the following subjects studied in previous chapters are directly relevant:

- Aesthetic regulation is imposed through tools that you learned about in Chapter 2. They include special permits required for any change in an historic property, and the use of "overlay" zoning techniques.
- Historic preservation litigants often raise takings claims, and the leading case on the applicability of the takings clause in this context is *Penn Central v. City of New York*, which you read in Chapter 7. (Incidentally, you may be interested to know that Grand Central Station was rededicated in October, 1998, after undergoing a 10-year, $200 million restoration.)

- Aesthetic regulation can take the form of conditions placed on project approvals. Conditions of this type are subject to the "*Nollan-Dolan*" constitutional analysis covered in Chapter 4. Furthermore, the California Supreme Court considered the constitutionality of an aesthetic condition — a requirement that a project display public art — in *Ehrlich v. Culver City*, 911 P.2d 429 (Cal. 1996), *cert. denied*, 117 S. Ct. 299 (1996), another case reprinted in that chapter.
- Regulation for aesthetic purposes also often results in claims that the law violates First Amendment rights. For example, regulation of billboard locations raises free expression issues, and the leading case is *Metromedia Inc. v. City of San Diego*, 453 U.S. 490 (1981), another case you read in Chapter 8.
- As you learned in Chapter 10, many communities today are subject to recorded covenants administered by a homeowners association. These covenants often allow the association to regulate the aesthetic features of a development, such as the color used to paint the outside of the units or the types of architectural improvements that an individual owner may construct. Disputes over these types of regulations, however, are private rather than public, as they concern the contractual terms enforced by the covenant.

2. The Rationale for Aesthetic Regulation

As you will recall from *Village of Euclid v. Ambler Realty* in Chapter 2, the original purpose of land use regulation was principally to prevent nuisance-like conflicts. As regulation evolved through the twentieth century, of course, the regulatory system expanded to recognize many other goals, such as ensuring housing, preventing discrimination, protecting the environment, and so forth. However, regulating for purely aesthetic reasons is a significant, perhaps qualitatively different extension of the field of land use regulation. Courts traditionally balked at recognizing aesthetics as a legally justifiable regulatory goal; in the beginning, some flatly rejected the idea. Gradually, and spurred on by the Supreme Court's affirmation of regulation for aesthetic purposes in *Berman v. Parker*, 348 U.S. 26 (1954), courts accepted aesthetic regulation as a legitimate public purpose. At first, the courts included the caveat that the regulation also must serve other purposes, but many jurisdictions later concluded that aesthetics alone could support the regulation.

Nonetheless, the judicial endorsement of purely aesthetic regulation continues to be somewhat cautious, and with good reason. Perhaps the most obvious question that aesthetic regulation raises is one of standards: can we really determine what type of land use violates an aesthetic "norm"? Can we define beauty for community purposes, or is it found only in the eyes of the beholder?

Another question is how far aesthetic regulation should legitimately extend. Let us assume that a certain type of development is in such aesthetic conflict with others in an area that a city may legitimately deny it. A strong argument can be made that property values in the area, as a whole, are bolstered by such a decision. However, once we proceed down the slippery aesthetic slope, where does it stop?

Take, for example, the newspaper article that you will read about regulating the colors that houses may be painted. Opponents argue, with some justification, that the public interest involved in such decisions is so small (or even nonexistent) that the regulation should not stand under the police power. Furthermore, some of the citizens painting in loud colors claim a cultural or even quasi-political motive for their color choice, as the use of loud colors is commonplace in countries from which they immigrated to the United States. Are there First Amendment rights, at least in this community, that should trump the proposed ordinance?

Another example is protection of views. If aesthetics alone is a legitimate goal of the exercise of the police power, then protection of views arguably falls within that goal. But should one person's property rights be restricted simply because her property is situated at a lower height than other property, and those residing higher up wish to preserve their views? A tenable, perhaps strong argument can be made that this type of regulation does not serve the public interest at all.

3. *Historic Preservation*

The rationale for historic preservation, while aesthetic in nature, is less controversial. Academics and others have postulated that societal benefits, both monetary and psychological, accrue from preserving historic sites. Furthermore, a societal consensus seems to support historic regulation; increasingly, even small communities are concerned about preserving the best of their past for future generations. Indeed, the country is in the midst of a long-term historic preservation "boom." One statistic can give you a sense of the growth. In 1957, about 11 communities in the Southeast and Northeast had enacted historic preservation ordinances. By 1983, there were between 8,000 and 10,000 historic preservation commissions throughout the entire country. American Planning Association, Preparing a Historic Preservation Ordinance (1983). In the last twenty years, these efforts have continued to grow.

A singular problem here is the cost involved. When historic districts are created, the concept of "reciprocity of advantage," which underlies the judicial acceptance of zoning, applies. Individual properties benefit from the ambience of the entire district, and burdens as well as benefits are reciprocal. Designation of individual historic landmarks, however, may be quite different. Requiring the preservation of an individual structure can impose significant, specific costs on individual landowners, arguably without the corresponding reciprocity normally found in zoning ordinances. In this respect, the facts in the *Penn Central* litigation may be somewhat atypical, for in that case the plaintiff admitted for purposes of the litigation that it could earn a reasonable return on the railroad station as it then existed. In many cases, the ability to fashion a productive use of a specific "landmarked" property can be difficult; the nature of the property and the inability to make changes in it rule out many uses that would otherwise be appropriate for such property.

These issues often play out when the owner seeks to demolish the building. Demolition may be delayed while the subject is studied, historic preservation officers are consulted, and efforts are made to find alternative uses for the building. At the same time, even when these efforts are exhausted, some laws allow demolition of a historically landmarked structure only if the owner can meet a somewhat stringent statutory standard, such as showing that no economically viable use for the property as it now stands is possible.

The issue of historic preservation, then, is one of those areas of land use regulation where private property rights are often in dramatic conflict with regulation.

Emotions run high. Is historic preservation "almost communism," as the mayor of one small Florida town with an historic preservation ordinance opined? Or is it, as the local newspaper responded, a "well-conceived idea call[ing] for protecting the city against encroaching development, preserving its historic buildings and enhancing the local economy"? Opinion, Don't Tear Down Town History, Orlando Sentinel, June 21, 1998, at K4.

There are, however, at least some rays of hope that historic preservation is economically achievable. We now have good examples of how historic preservation can be coupled with economic vitality and tourism. Not every historic building will become an economic success story, but the economic potential of historic preservation is quite real and cannot be ignored.

Still, while some European countries have made historic preservation a government priority and generously (or at least adequately) funded it, the United States has not done so. Indeed, in recent years funding for preservation at the federal level has declined. Consequently, preservationists have sought private funding. Most recently, where heads of state once dined at George Washington's home in Mount Vernon, they have been replaced by liquor distillery executives and salespeople who rented the facility for the evening. Administrators of the site, which is privately held, cite the need to raise revenue, as traditional tourism declined in 2003. Annie Gowen, Old Places, New Marketing, Washington Post, April 27, 2003, at A01.

The efforts by those in charge of the sites are understandable. Still, these are *historic* sites. At some point, do intrusions by modern economic interests reach a level that is inconsistent with the purpose of preserving the site?

B. HISTORIC PRESERVATION REGULATION

Historic preservation ordinances present a range of issues. The initial question is: what is the rationale for protecting historical landmarks? Specifically, can the law translate aesthetic goals into legal standards? An excerpt from the book by John Costonis looks at this issue. Then, from a legal standpoint, you need to consider the criteria for designation of property as an historical landmark as well as the consequences of "landmarking," that is, how that designation affects the owner's right to use the property. You should read the New York Court of Appeals decision in *Teachers Insurance and Annuity Assn. v. City of New York* with those issues in mind.

■ JOHN J. COSTONIS, ICONS AND ALIENS: LAW, AESTHETICS, AND ENVIRONMENTAL CHANGE

15-19, 76-79 (1989)

The Case for Legal Aesthetics

[W]e are condemned to come to terms with aesthetics, whether we like it or not. Aesthetics considerations are ubiquitous, "underl[ying] *all* zoning, usually in combination with other factors with which they are interwoven," as one judge has accurately observed. Lawmakers therefore must attend to these considerations unless they are prepared to shut down land use regulation in its entirety. To suppose, moreover, that the other values advanced by land use controls are hard, coherent, objective, nonmanipulable, and fully accessible to economics or any other form of analysis is to substitute one kind of tooth fairy logic for another. . . .

If there is a case to be made for legal aesthetics, it must be centered in legal aesthetics' role as a regulator of change in the symbolic environment. Legal aesthetics does for the social system what homeostatic agents do for the human body. Physical health requires the maintenance of key biological constancies within the body. When they go out of balance, biological indicators signal the danger and homeostatic agents swing into action to re-establish equilibrium. Individuals and groups, too, must cope with the threats to their personal and social identity that icon-menacing aliens present. They expect that aesthetics measures will function in a socially homeostatic fashion by precluding, or at least minimizing, the shock of the alien.

The case is not a simple one to make, however. . . .

Little can be said about legal aesthetics in one breath that cannot plausibly be denied in the next. Hence, the necessity of thinking as clearly about legal aesthetics' purpose as this elusive topic allows. The government should not set in motion programs capable of generating such far-flung and contradictory results absent the focused vision of the program's ends and means as envisaged by the substantive due process doctrine. For legal aesthetics, unfortunately, that vision remains blurred to this day. For example, many judges embarrass us and themselves in their clumsy attempts to found legal aesthetics' public purpose in beauty. Those who insist that the government may zone "solely for aesthetics" don't even try. Their formula calls to mind the nineteenth-century Romantics' rallying cry, "art for art's sake," as well as Keats's " 'Beauty is truth, truth beauty,'—that is all/Ye know on earth, and all ye need to know."

Aside from confusing metaphysics with law, these judges beg the question. Even assuming—as I do not—that beauty can be defined for legal purposes, judges are still obligated by the substantive due process doctrine to identify the governmental purpose advanced by measures enacted in beauty's name. Those who attempt this step often sink even further into the mire as, from time to time, the moral theory of art creeps into their discourse. A favorite of Plato and John Ruskin, the claim is that good art makes good citizens, and vice versa. Unfortunately, the theory was praised by Hitler as well, who banished the Bauhaus School from Germany lest it corrupt the Third Reich. The asserted linkage between art and civic virtue is simply too problematic, moreover, to serve as a persuasive justification for aesthetics regulation. . . .

Other judges take refuge in the assertion that beauty's preservation increases property values. Sometimes the facts support the assertion, as in the case of gentrifying areas designated as historic districts. But the facts often cut the other way as well. My own studies in Chicago document that, depending upon the building in question, landmark designation can severely diminish a structure's value and its resulting tax yield to the city. . . .

Fortunately, encouraging signs can be detected in more recent judicial opinions intimating a shift from a beauty- to a stability-based rationale for legal aesthetics. Illustrative is the statement of a District of Columbia court contained in its ruling on a controversy concerning the proposed demolition of Washington's Willard Hotel, a National Register of Historic Places entrant: "The retention of fine architecture, especially in the capitol city of a relatively young country such as ours, lends a certain stability and cultural continuity, which can only contribute over the years to national substance." To like effect is the comment of a Michigan judge in a 1972 opinion sustaining a municipal sign ordinance: "The modern trend is to recognize that a community's aesthetic well-being can contribute to urban man's psychological and emotional stability. . . . We should begin to realize . . . that a visually satisfying city can stimulate an identity and pride which is the foundation for social responsibility and citizenship."

Similar movement is evident on the legislative and administrative fronts, perhaps most clearly in the field of historic preservation. While various statutory or administrative texts could be cited, none better reflects this movement than the following excerpt from a 1981 United States Department of the Interior policy directive: "The historic buildings in a community are tangible links with the nation's past that help provide a sense of identity and stability that is often missing in this era of constant change. . . . Preservation is an anchor that keeps communities together and re-establishes pride and economic vitality."

The reformulation of legal aesthetics' goals suggested in these excerpts . . . affords a cogent response to the substantive due process objection.

■ TEACHERS INSURANCE & ANNUITY ASSOCIATION OF AMERICA v. CITY OF NEW YORK

623 N.E.2d 526 (N.Y. 1993)

KAYE, Chief Judge.

At issue on this appeal is the statutory authority of the Landmarks Preservation Commission to landmark the interior of the Four Seasons restaurant in Manhattan.

Appellant, Teachers Insurance and Annuity Association of America (TIAA), owner of the building that houses the restaurant, argues that the Commission has exceeded its authority under the New York City Landmarks Law. . . .

I.

In 1959, the Four Seasons restaurant opened on the first two floors of the newly constructed Seagram Building on Park Avenue in New York City. The building, designed by the German architectural master Ludwig Mies van der Rohe, is the sole example of his work in New York City. The celebrated American architect Philip Johnson, who assisted Mies van der Rohe in the building design, created the restaurant interior. Both the building exterior and the restaurant interior — which reflects and complements the building's modular design and architectural innovation have been acclaimed as quintessential expressions of the International style. No one disputes their special historical and aesthetic interest.

When TIAA purchased the building from Joseph E. Seagram & Sons in 1980, the portions of the ground and first floors occupied by the restaurant were subject to a 25-year lease that will expire in 1999. By agreement with Seagram, appellant must use its best efforts to continue to lease the space for restaurant use. If it cannot, Seagram has an option until 2025 to find a suitable restaurant tenant. TIAA also agreed to propose the building for landmarking when it became eligible.

In December 1987, appellant proposed the designation of the Seagram Building, including the building lobby and outdoor plaza. Prior to the public hearings before the Commission, and without consulting appellant, the restaurant operators themselves proposed to the Commission that the restaurant interior also be considered for landmark status. The Commission then added that proposal to the calendar and in May and July 1988 conducted public hearings.

Dozens of witnesses and letters before the Commission from prominent architects, artists, community leaders and others supported the designation of the Four Seasons interior. TIAA, several commercial real estate interests and architect Paul Byard opposed the designation.

In October 1989, the Commission unanimously landmarked the building, outdoor plaza, building lobby and the Four Seasons interior. Noting the particular architectural features of the restaurant, including its distinctive design, integral relation to the building architecture and innovative use of new technologies, the Commission found that the restaurant interior "has a special character, special historical and aesthetic interest and value as part of the development, heritage and cultural characteristics of New York City" and that "the Interior is one which is customarily open and accessible to the public, and to which the public is customarily invited." The restaurant designation accords landmark status to the entrance lobby, Grill Room, Pool Room and balcony dining rooms, and includes the marble pool, walnut bar, wall surfaces, floor surfaces, ceiling surfaces, doors, railings, metal draperies and two hanging metal sculptures commissioned by Johnson from the artist. The Board of Estimate, after its own public hearings, approved those designations. . . .

II.

Responding to the loss of a number of its more significant buildings, New York City in 1965 enacted its first historic preservation statute (Administrative Code of City of NY, ch. 8-A [now tit. 25, ch. 3]; *see*, Pyke, Landmark Preservation, at 15 [1969]) for the "protection, enhancement, perpetuation and use of improvements and landscape features of special character or special historical or aesthetic interest or value" (Administrative Code §25-301[b]). In 1973, the Landmarks Law was amended to expand the Commission's jurisdiction by authorizing designation of interior landmarks and by charging the Commission with promoting the use of interior landmarks "for the education, pleasure and welfare of the people of the city" (Administrative Code §25-301[b][g]). . . .

PUBLIC OPENNESS REQUIREMENT

The Commission is authorized to landmark an interior 30 or more years old that is "customarily open or accessible to the public, or to which the public is customarily invited, and which has a special historical or aesthetic interest or value as part of the development, heritage or cultural characteristics of the city, state or nation" (Administrative Code §25-302[m]; §25-303[a][2]). . . .

TIAA's principal argument is that the Landmarks Law must be read to require that interiors subject to landmarking have a "distinctively public character" to bring them within the Commission's jurisdiction. An "ordinary commercial space" that has not been dedicated to public use, TIAA argues, cannot be landmarked over the owner's objection.

At the outset, we note that nothing in the Landmarks Law requires an owner's consent as a prerequisite to designation. While other jurisdictions have required owner consent, the New York City legislature, significantly, has not. Administrative Code §25-313(a) provides only that the owner is entitled to notice of the public hearing, and indeed, failure to give such notice does not invalidate a designation. So long as the statutory criteria are satisfied, the Commission may make a valid designation over an owner's objection. . .

. . . [U]rging "strict construction" of the statute, TIAA asks us to distinguish between a restaurant and "inherently" public interiors, such as railroad stations, lobbies and theaters, which are intrinsically dedicated to public use by their public assemblage purpose. Appellant asserts that the Four Seasons interior has no distinctively public purpose, pointing out that Seagram had considered such uses as an automobile showroom and art gallery before outfitting the space to accommodate the restaurant, and that permitting designations such as this will adversely impact the real estate and economy of New York City.

We reject TIAA's asserted distinction, which on its face is a difficult one. No less than a theater, which generally requires a ticket for public entry, a restaurant by the very nature of its business invites the general public to enter (*see*, *Weinberg v. Barry*, 634 F. Supp. 86, 93 [D.D.C.]). But even if we might agree that it would be prudent policy to adopt the distinction appellant suggests, the argument suffers a more fundamental flaw: the proffered distinction is nowhere part of the unambiguous statute we are obliged to enforce as the City legislature has written it.

The threshold requirement prescribed by the legislature is that an interior be "customarily open or accessible to the public, or [a place] to which the public is customarily invited." The crux of this provision is *customary* openness, accessibility, invitation to the public—words that are readily understood to require usual, ordinary or habitual (rather than rare or occasional) availability to the general public. The legislature did not also specify that an interior must be intended as a place of assemblage—adding an additional dimension to customary public availability—as it might well have done if that were the intention. Consistent with the letter and purpose of the Landmarks Law, the relevant inquiry thus becomes an objective one of whether the interior is habitually open or accessible to the public at large. An interior to which the general public is usually invited, regardless of its intended purpose, falls within the ambit of the statute. . . .

Applying this interpretation, unquestionably the Commission's determination that the Four Seasons "customarily" invites the public is not arbitrary or capricious. The restaurant interior having been provided for the enjoyment of New York City's residents and visitors since it opened more than three decades ago, the Commission now may seek to preserve it for others (*see*, Administrative Code §25-301[b]). . . .

DESIGNATED INTERIOR ITEMS

Even if the designation was authorized, appellant argues, items appurtenant to the interior of the restaurant cannot properly be included in the designation. We find no such limitation in the Landmarks Law.

The City does not challenge appellant's assertion that the Commission's jurisdiction over interior landmark designations extends only to "interior architectural features," defined as the "architectural style, design, general arrangement and components of an interior, including, but not limited to, the kind, color and texture of the building material and the type and style of all windows, doors, lights, signs and other fixtures appurtenant to such interior" (Administrative Code §25-302[*l*]). Emphasizing the word "other," appellant argues that the Commission's jurisdiction extends only to items that qualify as fixtures at common law, and it specifically challenges designation of the hanging sculptures, walnut bar, metal draperies, decorative metal railings and ceiling panels.

We need not pass on whether the designated items are fixtures because the Landmarks Law does not limit the Commission's jurisdiction to fixtures. The language of the statute unambiguously states that interior architectural features are composed of the "architectural style, design, general arrangement and components of an interior" (Administrative Code §25-302[*l*]). We agree with the Appellate Division's construction of the statute that, in authorizing the Commission to designate items appurtenant to an interior, the legislation does not distinguish between personalty and realty.

We defer to the expertise of the Commission in its application of the provision. The Commission found that each of the designated items was created and installed at Philip Johnson's direction as an integral element of the design of the interior. Other items specially created or chosen for the restaurant, although mentioned in the designation report, were not designated by the Commission. As demonstrated by the items chosen for designation, the Commission has drawn a rational distinction between items integral to the design of the interior space, and items that merely enhance the restaurant's ambiance. . . .

Accordingly, the order of the Appellate Division should be affirmed, with costs.

Simons, Titone, Hancock and Bellacosa, JJ., concur, Smith and Levine, JJ., taking no part.

Notes and Comments

1. *Law and Aesthetics*. Professor Costonis argues that other values advanced by land use regulation, like aesthetics, are not "hard, coherent, objective, and nonmanipulable." Do you agree, or do you see qualitative differences between those values and the value of aesthetics? Costonis also suggests that the environment can be thought of as a stage "rich in icons invested with and broadcasting our deepest religious, artistic, social, and personal commitments." If so, does that idea justify aesthetic regulation and advance a coherent principle around which a legal regime of aesthetic regulation may be fashioned? Can a community's aesthetic well-being contribute to "man's psychological and emotional stability" and

stimulate an identity and pride, "which is the foundation for social responsibility and citizenship"? *See, generally*, Arnold R. Alamen and Robert Z. Melnick (eds.), Preserving Cultural Landscapes in America (2000).

Preservation of "cultural heritage" is an issue for international law as well. *See* Lakshman Guruswamy et al., Protecting the Cultural and Natural Heritage: Finding Common Ground, 7 Buff. Envtl. L. J. 47 (2000) ("[T]he reasons for protecting biological diversity apply with even greater force to the cultural heritage. While species and animals facing extinction can reproduce themselves and be raised in captivity, cultural resources are not capable of such renewal").

2. *Over and Under*. In *Metropolitan Dade County v. P.J. Birds, Inc.*, 654 So. 2d 170 (Fla. Dist. Ct. App. 1995), the court considered the county's designation of the "Parrot Jungle and Gardens," a unique tourist attraction, which opened in 1936, as an historic site. The Dade County ordinance divided property into "over fifty" and "under fifty" categories. The ordinance declared that "properties that have achieved significance within the last fifty years, will not normally be considered for designation" as historic. However, the "under fifty" properties will quality if they "are integral parts of districts that do meet the criteria" or are "of exceptional importance." *Id.* at 173.

How important is age to determining whether a property is of historic significance? Is the "over fifty" and "under fifty" line arbitrary? What if, at the time it was built, a structure was "futuristic" to begin with (for instance, the famous Seattle Space Needle)? Should that characteristic affect whether it can be designated as "historic"?

3. *Inside and Outside*. When historic preservation is mentioned, the layperson often thinks of the outside facade of the building. As the *Teachers Insurance* case demonstrates, however, both the outside and the inside of a building can be landmarked. Whether the agency has authority to include both parts in the landmark designation depends upon its statutory authority. *See, e.g., United Artists' Theater Circuit, Inc. v. City of Philadelphia*, 635 A.2d 612, 622 (Pa. 1990) ("[t]he Historical Commission is not explicitly authorized by statute to designate the interior of the building as historically or aesthetically significant").

It may be more likely that the designation of the inside of a building as a landmark will interfere with the actual usage of the building, a factor that can be critical where the designation is challenged on freedom of religion grounds. *See The Society of Jesus of New England v. Boston Landmarks Commn.*, 564 N.E.2d 571, 573 (Mass. 1990) (designation of interior of church as a landmark violated state constitution because "[t]he configuration of the church interior is so freighted with religious meaning that it must be considered part and parcel of the Jesuits' religious worship").

4. *Using Zoning and Subdivison Laws*. Historic preservation laws often use the regulatory tools that you studied in Chapter 2. For example, a city might enact an "overlay" historic zone over its existing zoning. This type of zone creates additional protections for buildings in the district. *See Heithaus v. Planning and Zoning Commn. of the Town of Greenwich*, 779 A.2d 750 (Conn. 2001) (upholding denial of historic overlay zone application and discussing application of historic protection regulation to a particular house).

Subdivision laws also may be pertinent. Could a city deny an application for development approval under its subdivision laws on the grounds that the subdivision would impair a historic district's "streetscape," where the state subdivision statute in question mentions specific factors such as water, drainage, sewage, etc., but does not mention effects on historic preservation efforts? *See Smith v. Zoning Board of Appeals of the Town of Greenwich*, 629 A.2d 1089, 1097 (Conn. 1993), *cert. denied*, 510 U.S. 1164 (1994) ("The defendants argue that public health and safety includes protecting the environment, which, in turn, includes historic preservation. We agree with defendants.").

5. *Historic Districts I.* While some cities denote landmarks on a case-by-case basis, others have designed entire areas as "historic districts." New Orleans, for example, has designed the historic Vieux Carré section of the city (popularly known as the French Quarter), as a historic district. *See Maher v. City of New Orleans*, 516 F.2d 1051 (5th Cir. 1975), *cert. denied*, 426 U.S. 905 (1976) (upholding the ordinance). Some cities, like Corning, New York, and Park City, Utah, have designated their downtown commercial district as historic. Others, like Georgetown in Washington, D.C., and Annapolis, Maryland, include both the commercial district and the surrounding area.

6. *Historic Districts II.* Historic preservation statutes may lay out extensive procedures that must precede designation of historic districts. These often include an investigation and preparation of a report by experts in the field. *See Russell v. Town of Amite City*, 771 So. 2d 289 (La. Ct. App. 2000) (designation of Amite Historic Preservation District invalidated because of failure to follow the required procedures).

One interesting question is whether the local government acts in a quasi-legislative or quasi-judicial capacity in designating the district. As you will recall from the discussion of the *Fasano* case in Chapter 6, this determination has important procedural ramifications. One might think that, because the ordinance covers a particular area, courts are likely to see it as a legislative act. However, in *Billy Graham Evangelistic Assn. v. City of Minneapolis*, 653 N.W.2d 638 (Minn. Ct. App. 2002), the court of appeal found that the city's designation of the Harmon Place Historic District, the heart of the Minneapolis automotive district for over 50 years, was quasi-judicial in nature. The court then held that the designation of the district was arbitrary and capricious. It found that the city's use of an old brick alley, now paved over, as the boundary was arbitrary: "The record is devoid of articulated reasons why certain . . . properties were included based on the use of the alley as a boundary, yet other similarly situated properties were excluded." *Id.* at 644.

In historic districts, the local agency's powers will likely extend beyond the buildings to preserving the entire ambiance of the district. Thus, in *Globe Newspaper Co. v. Beacon Hill Architectural Comm'n*, 659 N.E.2d 710 (Mass. 1996), the Supreme Judicial Court of Massachusetts concluded that the defendant commission's enabling legislation authorized it to regulate newsracks as an "exterior architectural feature" of a "structure" in the Beacon Hill area of Boston.

7. *Replacement and Demolition.* Where a landowner owns a property designated a landmark or included in a historic district, conflict about the effect of the landmark designation often arises when the landowner seeks to change the property. The flash point may be a request to modify the building or to demolish it.

In the case of a modification, the ultimate question is whether a requirement that the building be maintained constitutes a taking. *See, e.g., BSW Development Group v. City of Dayton,* 699 N.E.2d 1271 (Ohio 1998) (no taking because the building was structurally sound and two-thirds of the building had been used by two different businesses for several years just before denial of the demolition permit). In *Harris v. Old King's Highway Regional Historic Comm'n*, 658 N.E.2d 972 (Mass. 1996), the court upheld the denial of certificate of appropriateness to convert the garage on a property in the historic district to a shed or studio. The court reached that conclusion even though the commission had originally granted a certificate of demolition allowing the owner to tear down not only the garage but also a residential house and an outbuilding on the land.

The situation when an owner seeks to demolish a building is more complicated, since the entire structure would vanish. Litigation over proposed demolitions centers on whether the proper procedures have been followed (including, often, consultation with historic preservation officials).

If the procedures have been followed, the principal remaining question is whether officials have the right to deny a demolition permit. *See Donovan v. City of Deadwood*, 538 N.W.2d 790, 793 (S.D. 1995) ("SDCL 1-19B-27 provides that historic properties may be demolished after 180 days notice given to the historic preservation commission and during that 180 day period, the commission may negotiate with the owner in an effort to find a means of preserving the property. However, at the conclusion of the 190 days, the owner of historic property may raze the property."). *Compare The Park Home v. City of Williamsport*, 680 A.2d 835, 837 (Pa. 1996) ("These statements indicate that the Board of Directors [of the Park Home] did not even consider the possibility of selling the property as an alternative to demolition. . . . Appellant did not meet its burden of proving that it has been denied any profitable use of the property.").

8. *New Construction in Historic Districts*. Historic preservation laws also must contend with applications to construct new buildings in areas designated as historic. The obvious criterion here is compatibility with the existing environment. For example, the District of Columbia Historic Landmark and Historic District Protection Act of 1978 declares that a permit for new construction shall be issued unless the Mayor "finds that the design of the building and the character of the historic district . . . are incompatible." *See District Intown Properties, Ltd. v. District of Columbia Dept. of Consumer and Regulatory Affairs*, 680 A.2d 1373, 1378 (D.C. App. 1996) ("In contrast to other. . . . Provisions, which expressly authorize the Mayor to consider unreasonable economic hardship . . . when evaluating applications for permits to demolish, Section 5-1007, which deals with permits for new construction, makes no mention at all of economic hardship").

9. *Federal Historic Preservation Efforts*. The principal federal legislation in this field is the National Historic Preservation Act, 16 U.S.C. §§470-470w-6 (2000), originally enacted in 1966. The act established the National Register of Historic Places, a federally compiled list of historic and cultural resources, as well as a national register including sites of state and local significance. It also established the Advisory Council of Historic Preservation, which provides information on historic properties to federal agencies.

Most significantly, §106 requires that federal agencies must seek comments from the Advisory Council before they take any action that may affect property either on, or eligible for inclusion on, the National Register of Historic Places. The section, however, is procedural rather than substantive in nature. Once the comments are received and the review process is complete, the federal agency maintains full discretion to take whatever action it wishes with respect to the historic resource.

There are other federal laws that affect historic preservation. Perhaps the most important of these is §4(f) of the Department of Transportation Act, 49 U.S.C. §303 (2000). This section bars federal agencies from approving or funding a transportation project that requires the use of an historic site unless (1) there is no feasible and prudent alternative to the action, and (2) the project includes all possible planning to minimize harm to the site. Another important set of federal laws affecting the preservation of historic resources are the tax codes, which provide incentives for the rehabilitation of buildings designated as landmarks. The Tax Reform Act of 1976 allowed owners of historic properties on the National Register of Historic Places to amortize the cost of rehabilitation over a five-year period or to take accelerated depreciation of expenditures. The Economic Recovery Tax Act of 1981 authorized an investment tax credit for rehabilitation of historic structures. *See* Carolyn Ells Cheverine & Charlotte Mariah Hayes, Rehabilitation Tax Credit: Does It Still Provide Incentives?, 10 Va. Tax Rev. 167 (1990).

Another federal law touching on historic preservation is the Native American Grave Protection and Repatriation Act ("NAGPRA"), 25 U.S.C. §3001 et seq. (2000). Applying only to federal lands, NAGPRA requires anyone who discovers "Native American cultural items" to notify the public land manager. The discoverer must also "cease the activity [and] make a reasonable effort to protect the items discovered before resuming the activity. . . ." 25 U.S.C. §3002(d)(1) (2000). *See Yankton Sioux Tribe v. U.S. Army Corps of Engineers*, 194 F. Supp. 2d 977 (D.S.D. 2002) (dispute over remains discovered on shore of a lake behind a dam in South Dakota). *See also* the Archaeological Resources Protection Act, 16 U.S.C. §470aa (2000), and the Archeological and Historic Preservation Act of 1974, 16 U.S.C. §§469-469c (2000).

C. SIGN AND BILLBOARD REGULATION

Regulation of signs and billboards is now commonplace. All of us are familiar with jurisdictions where signs are uniform and non-intrusive. But what, exactly, *is* the problem with signs that are larger in size or that are lit in a certain way? Consider carefully the justifications put forth by the town in the following case.

ASSELIN v. TOWN OF CONWAY
628 A.2d 247 (N.H. 1993)

JOHNSON, Justice.

Michael Asselin, doing business as Mario's restaurant; Barlo Signs, Inc.; and Cardiff & Company (hereinafter Cardiff) appeal from a judgment in Superior Court (*O'Neil*, J.) upholding the validity of the sign illumination provision of the Conway zoning ordinance. . . .

Nestled in the Mount Washington Valley, Conway historically has been a tourist destination for activities in the White Mountain National Forest. Route 16 links the villages of Conway and North Conway and offers striking views of the mountains and ledges to the west. Substantial commercial development, primarily along this highway, has rendered part of the town a shoppers' Mecca. Hundreds of signs draw tourists in the day and evening hours to the shopping centers, lodging facilities, and restaurants clustered in the villages of Conway and North Conway and lining Route 16.

The town passed its first zoning ordinance in 1982, requiring all property owners, with certain exceptions, to obtain a permit from the town zoning officer before erecting a sign. Since 1982, the ordinance has banned signs "illuminated from within," but has allowed the use of signs illuminated by external lights.

Michael Asselin is a town resident who owned Mario's restaurant on Route 16 in North Conway. In December 1988, Asselin acquired a permit to erect an *externally* lit sign. Barlo Signs, Inc. leased to Asselin a sign for Mario's restaurant capable of *internal* illumination. The town notified Asselin that the sign's internal lighting violated the zoning ordinance, and the ZBA denied him permission to use an internally lit sign. Asselin and Barlo Signs, Inc. (hereinafter the Asselin plaintiffs) appealed the ZBA's decision pursuant to RSA 677:4 (1986). The trial court found the sign illumination provision valid and upheld the ZBA's decision.

The trial court's consideration of the Asselin plaintiffs' claims was consolidated with the town's petition for a temporary injunction against Cardiff. Cardiff owns the Indian Head Village Plaza shopping center on Route 16 in North Conway. In February 1990, the town issued Cardiff a permit to erect a sign described in the permit application as externally lit. The two faces of the sign are translucent, and lights in the sign's supporting posts can shine against mirrored surfaces that reflect the light out through the sign faces. Cardiff was convicted in district court in June 1990 of five violations of the sign illumination provision but failed to file a timely appeal. The town petitioned the superior court to enjoin Cardiff from using the lights within the posts to illuminate the sign, and that action was consolidated with the Asselin plaintiffs' action. Following a hearing on the merits, the trial court issued an injunction. . . .

We next consider whether the State zoning enabling act authorized the town to pass the sign illumination provision solely to promote aesthetic values, including preserving scenic vistas, discouraging development from competing with the natural environment, and promoting the character of a "country community." The State zoning enabling act grants municipalities broad authority to pass zoning ordinances for the health, safety, morals, and general welfare of the community. *See* RSA 674:16, I (1986 & Supp. 1992); *Britton v. Town of Chester*, 134 N.H. 434, 441, 595 A.2d 492, 496 (1991). . .

> The concept of the public welfare is broad and inclusive. The values it represents are spiritual as well as physical, aesthetic as well as monetary. It is within the power of the legislature to determine that the community should be beautiful as well as healthy, spacious as well as clean, well-balanced as well as carefully patrolled.

Berman v. Parker, 348 U.S. 26, 33 (1954) (citation omitted). Consistent with this expansive view, we have held that towns may consider, at least among other factors, "aesthetic values, such as preserving rural charm," when passing zoning regulations under State law. *Town of Chesterfield v. Brooks*, 126 N.H. 64, 69, 489 A.2d 600, 604 (1985); *see also* RSA 674:17, II (1986). We now conclude that municipalities may validly exercise zoning power *solely* to advance aesthetic values, because the preservation or enhancement of the visual environment may promote the general welfare. *See* RSA 674:16, I; *Opinion of the Justices*, 103 N.H. 268, 270, 169 A.2d 762, 764 (1961). We hold that the town in this case has not exceeded its authority under RSA 674:16 by relying exclusively on the promotion of aesthetic values for its exercise of zoning power.

The next issue is whether the Conway sign illumination provision is a reasonable exercise of the town's police power. *See* N.H. CONST. pt. I, arts. 2, 12. . . .

. . . The parties challenging the provision in this case argue that it unreasonably burdens "all" sign users and "many" manufacturers. The appropriate inquiry for reviewing this *substantive due process* claim is whether the claimants proved that the provision constitutes a restriction on property rights that is not rationally related to the town's legitimate goals.

. . . The town passed the provision for legitimate purposes, including preserving scenic vistas, discouraging development from competing with the natural environment, and "promoting community character." The community character sought to be promoted is that of a "country community . . . accustomed to having small hanging signs," or a "business community that operated mostly during the daylight hours, not in the evening." There is support for the trial court's finding that "the natural appeal and general atmosphere of the area could well be negatively affected by the unregulated use of nighttime lighting." It is reasonable to infer that the scenic vistas sought to be preserved by the town include the splendor of mountains at twilight and the brilliance of stars at night. Ronald Fleming, an expert witness experienced in planning for the preservation and enhancement of visual environments, testified that . . . internally illuminated signs appear as "disconnected squares of light" at dusk and at night, and that the "overall effect" of "an internally-lit sign is to create a visual block that is seen at some great distance sort of bobbing at the windshield," while external lights "soften the impact" of signs in the darkness. The evidence supports a finding that the restriction on internally lighted signs is rationally related to the town's legitimate, aesthetic goals of preserving vistas, discouraging development that competes with the natural environment, and promoting the character of a "country community."

Furthermore, the evidence supports the finding that the provision does not place oppressive burdens on the private rights of affected businesses. We note that there is no merit to the position that the ordinance impairs the freedom of expression; the provision is merely a content-neutral restriction on one of the myriad ways in which outdoor messages may be conveyed at night. *See State v. Comley*, 130 N.H. 688, 691-92, 546 A.2d 1066, 1068 (1988); *see also Metromedia, Inc. v. San Diego*, 453 U.S. 490, 516 (1981). The provision allows every business owner to erect a sign that may be effectively illuminated. The evidence reflects that a number of manufacturers are capable of constructing signs fit for external lights, and that signs with external lights may be less expensive. We hold that the trial court did not err in finding the provision valid because it is a reasonable regulation consistent with the due process requirements of our Constitution. . . .

Notes and Comments

1. *"Disconnected Squares of Light" at Dusk.* In upholding the regulation, the court relied on testimony by an expert witness regarding the aesthetic problems internally illuminated signs pose. He testified that internally lit signs appear as "disconnected squares of light" at dusk and the effect is to create a visual block that is seen at some great distance "sort of bobbing at the windshield." Were you convinced that this testimony provides a firm enough basis to differentiate internal from external lights?

2. *Rationale for Aesthetic Regulation I.* In a series of articles, Professor Joseph Sax has explored the origins of the idea that the government bears responsibility

to conserve artifacts of historic or aesthetic value. See Joseph L. Sax, Heritage Preservation as Public Duty: The Abbé Gregoire and the Origins of an Idea, 88 Mich. L. Rev. 1142 (1990); Joseph L. Sax, Is Anyone Minding Stonehenge? The Origins of Cultural Property Protection in England, 78 Cal. L. Rev. 1543 (1990). In the Michigan article he notes the seeming oddity of a shared "cultural heritage" in a country that celebrates limited government:

> As uncontroversial as heritage preservation may appear when one thinks of historic monuments and artistic masterworks, the idea of an officially designated culture seems greatly at odds with modern sensibilities. The very idea of government involving itself in cultural life raises the unwelcome specter of censorship on the one side and official propaganda on the other. In addition, there is the more general question of cultural policy as a tool of a paternalistic state that aspires to make its citizens good, a notion that has lost all cachet in our time. In short, state cultural policies appear to be out of harmony with modern ideas about the role of government. Nonetheless, they flourished. Obviously, there is some very strong attraction to the idea of a common heritage: a people and a community bound together in some shared enterprise with shared values.

88 Mich. L. Rev. at 1142. Have the courts sufficiently confronted the specter of propaganda and censorship in generally affirming aesthetic-based regulation?

3. *Rationale for Aesthetic Regulation II.* How does aesthetic regulation serve the public interest? In *Village of Hudson v. Albrecht, Inc.*, 458 N.E.2d 852 (Ohio 1984), the Ohio Supreme Court sustained a regulation that required changes in a specific area to be approved by the village's Architectural and Historic Board of Review. The board was to determine whether the changes would "cause substantial depreciation in the property values" of existing structures or structures currently being built. 458 N.E.2d at 854. The majority reasoned:

> [T]he nature of the police power is elastic, as it must be able to expand or contract in response to changing conditions and needs. *See Euclid v. Ambler Realty*, . . . 272 U.S. at 387. . . . As such, more recent Ohio cases dealing with both zoning and nuisance issues have implied that there is a governmental interest in maintaining the aesthetics of the community and have recognized its role in the exercise of the police power.
>
> One example is the case of *Ghaster Properties, Inc. v. Preston* (1964), 176 Ohio St. 425, 200 N.E.2d 328, which upheld a statute prohibiting the erection or maintenance of advertising devices adjacent to the interstate highways. . . .
>
> Later, in *State v. Buckley* (1968), 16 Ohio St. 2d 128, 133, 243 N.E.2d 66, [this] court upheld a statute requiring junkyards outside a municipality to be obscured from the view of persons passing upon state, county and township roads. The majority reasoned that unfenced or inadequately fenced junkyards are patently offensive, rather than objectionable merely as a matter of taste. . . .
>
> [T]he evolving trend has been to grant aesthetic considerations a more significant role. We believe that this is the correct approach as the appearance of a community relates closely to its citizens' happiness, comfort and general well-being. Accordingly, it is our finding that there is a legitimate governmental interest in maintaining the aesthetics of the community. . . .

458 N.E.2d at 856.

The dissent would have none of it:

> What is aesthetically pleasing to one individual is an affront to the senses of another. . . .

> This zoning case has now placed us in the era of Orwell's "1984" where Big Brother tells us what to do and think in a realm that is protected by the constitutional right of privacy under the first Amendment. . . .
>
> If a zoning code regulation or restriction devoted solely to aesthetic considerations, as in this case, can be bootstrapped to the status of lawfulness by merely adding a provision somewhere in the zoning code that the purpose of the zoning regulation is to protect real estate "from impairment or destruction of value," then any zoning code provision, no matter how absurd, unreasonable or confiscatory can be given the aura of lawfulness.

Id. at 857-858. Who has the better of the argument?

4. *Is an Anchor a "Sign"?* The jurisdictional trigger of sign regulation is, of course, the existence of a "sign." In *Houghtaling v. City of Medina Bd. of Housing Appeals*, 731 N.E.2d 733 (Ohio Ct. App. 1999), plaintiff, who ran a legitimate and legal home business, decided to place a large anchor on his front lawn. The city claimed that the anchor was a "sign" that was not allowed under the local zoning ordinance, which declared that "[n]o sign, advertising the home occupation, will be permitted." Plaintiff admitted that the anchor, which contained no markings, was a "reference point" for people who came to pick up tickets. The court assumed that the anchor was a "sign" but concluded that it did not "advertise" within the ordinance's meaning. The court did so even though the dictionary definition of "advertise" included "[t]o call a matter to the public attention by any means whatsoever."

Was the court right, or did it read an extra requirement into the ordinance: that the sign declare something to a member of the public who is without prior knowledge of that information? *See also* David Montgomery, Coming to a Wall Near You: Arrival of Building-Size Outdoor Ads in D.C. Catches Officials and Residents by Surprise, Washington Post, March 15, 2001, at A01 (discussing whether advertising murals that cover the entire side of a building should be regulated, and noting that advertising executives claim that the signs are not billboards but are wall murals or "wallscapes").

5. *The First Amendment Overtone.* As you saw in Chapter 8, much of the current litigation over sign ordinances tests their legality on First Amendment grounds. The key United States Supreme Court case is *Ladue v. Gilleo*, 512 U.S. 43 (1994), in which the Court invalidated a local ordinance banning all residential signs, with ten exemptions. The Court held that, given the exemptions, the city unconstitutionally discriminated on the basis of content.

For example, in *Cleveland Area Board of Realtors v. City of Euclid*, 88 F.3d 382 (6th Cir. 1996), the court considered a Euclid ordinance that limited placement of real estate "For Sale" signs to the windows of homes in residential areas. The ordinance also limited the size of those signs depending on how far the house was located from the street. The court refused to apply the test for restrictions on commercial speech because the ordinance applied evenhandedly to all types of signs in residential neighborhoods. It also concluded that the regulation was content-neutral because the "time, place, and manner" restriction on signs was justified on the basis of aesthetics. *Id.* at 387.

Nonetheless, the court invalidated the ordinance on the grounds that it was not "narrowly tailored" to serve the significant government interest of aesthetics. The court reasoned: "However, the wholesale ban on lawn signs in the name of aesthetics in this case is, simply, not sufficiently narrowly tailored to withstand constitutional scrutiny. Indeed, it appears that the regulation is not 'tailored' at all." *Id.* at 388. Finally, the court concluded that the ordinance did not leave open ample alternative channels of communication.

The local government initially fared better in *Kroll v. Steere*, 759 A.2d 541 (Conn. Ct. App. 2000). A city ordinance restricted the size of signs to one square foot in area, with certain limited exceptions. The plaintiff, protesting an ordinance allowing deer hunting with bows, arrows, and shotguns, put a sign in her window stating "Who Asked the Deer?" The sign exceeded the size restriction, but the court upheld the local law. It declared that the ordinance "makes no attempt to regulate the content of residential signs" and emphasized the local government's "significant interest" in regulating signs to maintain traffic safety. *Id.* at 546. However, the court remanded the case on the grounds that the city may have selectively enforced the sign ordinance. *See also Desert Outdoor Advertising, Inc. v. City of Moreno Valley*, 103 F.3d 814 (9th Cir. 1996), *cert. denied*, 118 S. Ct. 294 (1997) (overturning a sign ordinance on a variety of constitutional grounds, and concluding that the ordinance could not be justified on grounds of aesthetics); and *Lamar Corp. v. City of Twin Falls*, 981 P.2d 1146 (Idaho 1999) (ordinance in question "contains sufficiently objective and definite standards to guide zoning officials . . . and is therefore not an unconstitutional prior restraint on commercial speech where the ordinance required, among other findings, that the sign would not endanger motorists, will not obstruct the visual quality of public open space, and is compatible with buildings heights of the existing neighborhood).

6. *Time or Money.* As discussed in the Note on Nonconforming Uses in Chapter 2, *supra*, a city that enacts a ban on existing billboards may face a taking claim. *See Odegard Outdoor Advertising, LLC v. Board of Zoning Adjustment of Jackson County*, 6 S.W.3d 148, 150 (Mo. 1999) ("the zoning authority is faced with the choice of allowing the property owners to continue the nonconforming use or compensating the property owner for the value of the taken use"). It can avoid the taking claim by allowing the owner a reasonable time in which to use the billboard and amortize its costs. A steady stream of litigation concerns the sufficiency of the amortization period provided. *See, e.g., Outdoor Graphics, Inc. v. City of Burlington*, 103 F.3d 690 (8th Cir. 1997) (five-year amortization period was sufficient). Some jurisdictions, however, require payment for any billboard that is outlawed. *See Eller Media Co. v. Montgomery County*, 795 A.2d 728 (Md. Ct. Sp. App. 2002) (amortization period could not be used where Maryland statute declared that a city or county "shall pay the fair market value of an outdoor advertising sign removed or required to be removed by the county or municipality").

7. *A Findings Debacle.* If the local government regulates billboards by requiring a conditional use permit, it must make findings of fact if it denies a permit. (The subject of findings was discussed in Chapter 6, *supra*.) Counsel for the parties must take these findings quite seriously. In *Eastern Outdoor Advertising Co. v. Mayor and City Council of Baltimore*, 807 A.2d 49 (Md. Ct. Sp. App. 2002), the city denied a CUP for a billboard within an urban renewal district, and the court remanded. The city again denied and adopted specific findings. The court took a very close look at the city's findings, agreeing with the trial court that "[i]n most instances . . . the statements lacked an adequate factual basis and were merely conclusionary." *Id.* at 68. For example, the city found that the billboard "would disrupt [the] view of the historic fabric of the neighborhood," but the court found that this finding was insufficient. The court explained, "It is impossible for a reviewing court to

determine what view will be disrupted and what is unique to this neighborhood about the alleged disruption." *Id.* The case was remanded, for the second time, for the city to make specific factual findings.

8. *Judicial Evolution.* The judicial attitude toward purely aesthetic regulation has changed markedly during this century. Early cases flatly refused to validate legislation designed to serve aesthetic purposes, often using language that made clear the judges' horror at this possibility. *See, e.g., Spann v. City of Dallas*, 235 S.W. 513, 56 (Tex. 1921) ("it is not the law . . . that a man may be deprived of the lawful use of his property because his tastes are not in accord with those of his neighbors").

Gradually the judicial attitude toward aesthetic regulation changed as land use authority under the police power proved more elastic changed than originally thought. Even here, however, many courts approved regulation for aesthetic purposes only if, in addition to aesthetics, the regulation also served some other purpose. For example, a regulation would be sustained if, in addition to its obvious aesthetic goals, it also served to protect property values. *See, e.g., General Outdoor Advertising Co. v. Indianapolis*, 172 N.E. 309, 312 (Ind. 1930) (while "aesthetic or artistic considerations alone are not considered sufficient to warrant the exercise of the police power," "aesthetic considerations enter in to a great extent as an auxiliary consideration").

The judicial movement toward recognition of regulation aimed solely at aesthetics was greatly bolstered by the Supreme Court's opinion in *Berman v. Parker*, 348 U.S. 26 (1954). In that case, the Court declared "It is within the power of the legislature to determine that the community should be beautiful as well as healthy, spacious as well as clean, well balanced as well as carefully controlled." 348 U.S. at 33.

Finally, from the late 1960s onward, an increasing number of courts have found that aesthetics alone is a sufficient basis for a land use regulation. *See, e.g., State of Tennessee v. Smith*, 618 S.W.2d 474, 477 (Tenn. 1981) ("We are therefore of the opinion that in modern society aesthetic considerations may well constitute a legitimate basis for the exercise of the police power"). *See generally* Elizabeth A. Garvin and Glen S. LeRoy, Design Guidelines: The Law of Aesthetic Controls, Land Use Law and Zoning Dig. (April 2003) 3, 5 (listing 37 states as authorizing regulation based on aesthetics alone).

D. ARCHITECTURAL AND DESIGN REVIEW

Once regulation for aesthetic purposes was found to be within the police power, some local jurisdictions seized the opportunity to regulate architectural design. This type of regulation often raises constitutional claims, such as the claim that the aesthetic "standards" in the ordinance are void for vagueness. The following decision grapples with those issues.

■ ANDERSON v. CITY OF ISSAQUAH
851 P.2d 744 (Wash. Ct. App. 1993)

KENNEDY, Judge.

Appellants M. Bruce Anderson, Gary D. LaChance, and M. Bruce Anderson, Inc. (hereinafter referred to as "Anderson"), challenge the denial of their application for a land use certification, arguing, *inter alia*, that the building design requirements contained in Issaquah Municipal Code (IMC) 16.16.060 are unconstitutionally vague. . . .

FACTS

Anderson owns property located at 145 N.W. Gilman Boulevard in the City of Issaquah (City). In 1988, Anderson applied to the City for a land use certification to develop the property. The property is zoned for general commercial use. Anderson desired to build a 6800 square foot commercial building for several retail tenants.

After obtaining architectural plans, Anderson submitted the project to various City departments for the necessary approvals. The process went smoothly until the approval of the Issaquah Development Commission (Development Commission) was sought. This commission was created to administer and enforce the City's land use regulations. It has the authority to approve or deny applications for land use certification.

Chapter 16.16.060 of the IMC enumerates various building design objectives which the Development Commission is required to administer and enforce. Insofar as is relevant to this appeal, the Development Commission is to be guided by the following criteria:

IMC 16.16.060(B). Relationship of Building and Site to Adjoining Area.

1. Buildings and structures shall be made compatible with adjacent buildings of conflicting architectural styles by such means as screens and site breaks, or other suitable methods and materials.

2. Harmony in texture, lines, and masses shall be encouraged. . . .

IMC 16.16.060(D). Building Design.

1. Evaluation of a project shall be based on quality of its design and relationship to the natural setting of the valley and surrounding mountains.

2. Building components, such as windows, doors, eaves and parapets, shall have appropriate proportions and relationship to each other, expressing themselves as a part of the overall design.

3. Colors shall be harmonious, with bright or brilliant colors used only for minimal accent.

4. Design attention shall be given to screening from public view all mechanical equipment, including refuse enclosures, electrical transformer pads and vaults, communication equipment, and other utility hardware on roofs, grounds or buildings.

5. Exterior lighting shall be part of the architectural concept. Fixtures, standards and all exposed accessories shall be harmonious with the building design.

6. Monotony of design in single or multiple building projects shall be avoided. Efforts should be made to create an interesting project by use of complimentary details, functional orientation of buildings, parking and access provisions and relating the development to the site. In multiple building projects, variable siting of

individual buildings, heights of buildings, or other methods shall be used to prevent a monotonous design.

As initially designed, Anderson's proposed structure was to be faced with off-white stucco and was to have a blue metal roof. It was designed in a "modern" style with an unbroken "warehouse" appearance in the rear, and large retail style windows in the front. The City moved a Victorian era residence, the "Alexander House," onto the neighboring property to serve as a visitors' center. Across the street from the Anderson site is a gasoline station that looks like a gasoline station. Located nearby and within view from the proposed building site are two more gasoline stations, the First Mutual Bank Building built in the "Issaquah territorial style," an Elk's hall which is described in the record by the Mayor of Issaquah as a "box building", an auto repair shop, and a veterinary clinic with a cyclone fenced dog run. The area is described in the record as "a natural transition area between old downtown Issaquah and the new village style construction of Gilman [Boulevard]."

The Development Commission reviewed Anderson's application for the first time at a public hearing on December 21, 1988. Commissioner Nash commented that "the facade did not fit with the concept of the surrounding area." Commissioner McGinnis agreed. Commissioner Nash expressed concern about the building color and stated that he did not think the building was compatible with the image of Issaquah. Commissioner Larson said that he would like to see more depth to the building facade. Commissioner Nash said there should be some interest created along the blank back wall. Commissioner Garrison suggested that the rear facade needed to be redesigned.

At the conclusion of the meeting, the Development Commission voted to continue the hearing to give Anderson an opportunity to modify the building design.

On January 18, 1989, Anderson came back before the Development Commission with modified plans which included changing the roofing from metal to tile, changing the color of the structure from off-white to "Cape Cod" gray with "Tahoe" blue trim, and adding brick to the front facade. During the ensuing discussion among the commissioners, Commissioner Larson stated that the revisions to the front facade had not satisfied his concerns from the last meeting. In response to Anderson's request for more specific design guidelines, Commissioner McGinnis stated that the Development Commission had "been giving direction; it is the applicant's responsibility to take the direction/suggestions and incorporate them into a revised plan that reflects the changes." Commissioner Larson then suggested that "[t]he facade can be broken up with sculptures, benches, fountains, etc." Commissioner Nash suggested that Anderson "drive up and down Gilman and look at both good and bad examples of what has been done with flat facades."

As the discussion continued, Commissioner Larson stated that Anderson "should present a [plan] that achieves what the Commission is trying to achieve through its comments/suggestions at these meetings" and stated that "architectural screens, fountains, paving of brick, wood or other similar method[s] of screening in lieu of vegetative landscaping are examples of design suggestions that can be used to break up the front facade." Commissioner Davis objected to the front facade, stating that he could not see putting an expanse of glass facing Gilman

Boulevard. "The building is not compatible with Gilman." Commissioner O'Shea agreed. Commissioner Nash stated that "the application needs major changes to be acceptable." Commissioner O'Shea agreed. Commissioner Nash stated that "this facade does not create the same feeling as the building [e]nvironment around this site."

Commissioner Nash continued, stating that he "personally like[d] the introduction of brick and the use of tiles rather than metal on the roof." Commissioner Larson stated that he would like to see a review of the blue to be used: "Tahoe blue may be too dark." Commissioner Steinwachs agreed. Commissioner Larson noted that "the front of the building could be modulated [to] have other design techniques employed to make the front facade more interesting."

With this, the Development Commission voted to continue the discussion to a future hearing.

On February 15, 1989, Anderson came back before the Development Commission. In the meantime, Anderson's architects had added a 5-foot overhang and a 7-foot accent overhang to the plans for the front of the building. More brick had been added to the front of the building. Wood trim and accent colors had been added to the back of the building and trees were added to the landscaping to further break up the rear facade.

Anderson explained the plans still called for large, floor to ceiling windows as this was to be a retail premises: "[A] glass front is necessary to rent the space. . . . " Commissioner Steinwachs stated that he had driven Gilman Boulevard and taken notes. The following verbatim statement by Steinwachs was placed into the minutes:

> **"My General Observation From Driving Up and Down Gilman Boulevard."**
> I see certain design elements and techniques used in various combinations in various locations to achieve a visual effect that is sensitive to the unique character of our Signature Street. I see heavy use of brick, wood, and tile. I see minimal use of stucco. I see colors that are mostly earthtones, avoiding extreme contrasts. I see various methods used to provide modulation in both horizontal and vertical lines, such as gables, bay windows, recesses in front faces, porches, rails, many vertical columns, and breaks in roof lines. I see long, sloping, conspicuous roofs with large overhangs. I see windows with panels above and below windows. I see no windows that extend down to floor level. This is the impression I have of Gilman Boulevard as it relates to building design.

Commissioner Nash agreed stating, "[T]here is a certain feeling you get when you drive along Gilman Boulevard, and this building does not give this same feeling." Commissioner Steinwachs wondered if the applicant had any option but to start "from scratch". Anderson responded that he would be willing to change from stucco to wood facing but that, after working on the project for 9 months and experiencing total frustration, he was not willing to make additional design changes.

At that point, the Development Commission denied Anderson's application, giving four reasons:

> 1. After four [sic] lengthy review meetings of the Development Commission, the applicant has not been sufficiently responsive to concerns expressed

by the Commission to warrant approval or an additional continuance of the review.

2. The primary concerns expressed relate to the building architecture as it relates to Gilman Boulevard in general, and the immediate neighborhood in particular.

3. The Development Commission is charged with protecting, preserving and enhancing the aesthetic values that have established the desirable quality and unique character of Issaquah, reference IMC 16.16.010C.[3]

4. We see certain design elements and techniques used in various combinations in various locations to achieve a visual effect that is sensitive to the unique character of our Signature Street. On Gilman Boulevard we see heavy use of brick, wood and tile. We see minimal use of stucco. We see various methods used to provide both horizontal and vertical modulation, including gables, breaks in rooflines, bay windows, recesses and protrusions in front face. We see long, sloping, conspicuous roofs with large overhangs. We see no windows that extend to ground level. We see brick and wood panels at intervals between windows. We see earthtone colors avoiding extreme contrast.

Anderson, who by this time had an estimated $250,000 into the project, timely appealed the adverse ruling to the Issaquah City Council (City Council). After a lengthy hearing and much debate, the City Council decided to affirm the Development Commission's decision by a vote of 4 to 3. . . .

Discussion . . .

2. Constitutionality of IMC 16.16.060 (Building Design Provisions)

[A] statute which either forbids or requires the doing of an act in terms so vague that men [and women] of common intelligence must necessarily guess at its meaning and differ as to its application, violates the first essential of due process of law. . . .

Looking first at the face of the building design sections of IMC 16.16.060, we note that an ordinary citizen reading these sections would learn only that a given building project should bear a good relationship with the Issaquah Valley and surrounding mountains; its windows, doors, eaves and parapets should be of "appropriate proportions," its colors should be "harmonious" and seldom "bright" or "brilliant," its mechanical equipment should be screened from public view; its exterior lighting should be "harmonious" with the building design and "monotony should be avoided." The project should also be "interesting." IMC 16.16.060(D)(1)-(6). If the building is not "compatible" with adjacent buildings, it should be "made compatible" by the use of screens and site breaks "or other suitable methods and materials." "Harmony in texture, lines, and masses [is] encouraged." The landscaping should provide an "attractive . . . transition" to adjoining properties. IMC 16.16.060(B)(1)-(3).

[We] conclude that these code sections "do not give effective or meaningful guidance" to applicants, to design professionals, or to the public officials of

3. IMC 16.16.010(C) provides that one of the purposes of the code is "[to] protect, preserve and enhance the social, cultural, economic, environmental and aesthetic values that have established the desirable quality and unique character of Issaquah[.]"

Issaquah who are responsible for enforcing the code. . . . Although it is clear from the code sections here at issue that mechanical equipment must be screened from public view and that, probably, earth tones or pastels located within the cool and muted ranges of the color wheel are going to be preferred, there is nothing in the code from which an applicant can determine whether his or her project is going to be seen by the Development Commission as "interesting" versus "monotonous" and as "harmonious" with the valley and the mountains. Neither is it clear from the code just what else, besides the valley and the mountains, a particular project is supposed to be harmonious with, although "[h]armony in texture, lines, and masses" is certainly encouraged. IMC 16.16.060(B)(2).

In attempting to interpret and apply this code, the commissioners charged with that task were left with only their own individual, subjective "feelings" about the "image of Issaquah" and as to whether this project was "compatible" or "interesting." The commissioners stated that the City was "making a statement" on its "signature street" and invited Anderson to take a drive up and down Gilman Boulevard and "look at good and bad examples of what has been done with flat facades." One commissioner drove up and down Gilman, taking notes, in a no doubt sincere effort to define that which is left undefined in the code.

The point we make here is that neither Anderson nor the commissioners may constitutionally be required or allowed to guess at the meaning of the code's building design requirements by driving up and down Gilman Boulevard looking at "good and bad" examples of what has been done with other buildings, recently or in the past. We hold that the code sections here at issue are unconstitutionally vague on their face. The words employed are not technical words which are commonly understood within the professional building design industry. Neither do these words have a settled common law meaning.

As they were applied to Anderson, it is also clear the code sections at issue fail to pass constitutional muster. Because the commissioners themselves had no objective guidelines to follow, they necessarily had to resort to their own subjective "feelings." The "statement" Issaquah is apparently trying to make on its "signature street" is not written in the code. In order to be enforceable, that "statement" must be written down in the code, in understandable terms. *See, e.g., Morristown Road Assocs. v. Mayor & Common Council & Planning Bd.*, 163 N.J. Super. 58, 394 A.2d 157 (1978). The unacceptable alternative is what happened here. The commissioners enforced not a building design code but their own arbitrary concept of the provisions of an unwritten "statement" to be made on Gilman Boulevard. The commissioners' individual concepts were as vague and undefined as those written in the code. This is the very epitome of discretionary, arbitrary enforcement of the law. . . .

Conclusion

. . . We order that Anderson's land use certification be issued, provided however, that those changes which Anderson agreed to through the hearing before the City Council may validly be imposed.

Grosse and Scholfield, JJ., concur.

WEBSTER v. TOWN OF CANDIA

146 N.H. 430, 778 A.2d 402 (2001)

DALIANIS, J.

. . . [P]laintiffs Kenneth Webster and Margaret Demos as Trustees of the Kenneth Webster Trust, and Winthrop Sargeant (Webster plaintiffs), appeal the Superior Court's (*Galway*, J.) order affirming the decision of the Town of Candia Planning Board (planning board) denying their application to remove trees from Libbee Road, a designated scenic road. Plaintiff Julee Sanderson, as Trustee of Candia Rangeway Realty Trust (*Sanderson*), appeals the Superior Court's (*Abramsom*, J.) order affirming the planning board's decision denying her application to remove trees from Libbee Road. Sanderson also appeals the Superior Court's (*Coffey*, J.) order denying her motion for reconsideration. We affirm. . . .

1. CONSTITUTIONALITY OF SCENIC ROAD STATUE

The plaintiffs assert that RSA 231:158 (1993), prohibiting cutting trees or destroying stone walls on designated scenic roads absent permission from the planning board (or other "official municipal body"), is impermissibly vague and thus void under the New Hampshire Constitution. . . .

RSA 231:158 provides, in pertinent part:

> Upon a road being designated as a scenic road as provided in RSA 231:157, any repair, maintenance, reconstruction, or paving work done with respect thereto by the state or municipality . . . shall not involve the cutting, damage or removal of trees [of a particular circumference], or the tearing down or destruction of stone walls, or portions thereof, except with the prior written consent of the planning board, or any other official municipal body designated by the meeting [of the town voters] to implement the provisions of this subdivision. . . .

RSA 231:158, II. . . .

The warrant articles by which the town voted to designate Libbee Road as scenic specify that the purpose of so doing was to "protect[] and enhanc[e] . . . the scenic beauty of Candia." *See also N.H.S. Jour.* 708 (1971) (purpose of scenic road statute is to "encourage the tourist attractiveness of our scenic roads in our towns and . . . permit the retention of trees and stone walls so characteristic of our New England scenery"). In context then, RSA 231:158 informs a developer that any plan to cut trees or remove stone walls from a designated scenic road must not destroy the "scenic beauty" of the road. This is sufficient notice to developers of the relevant standards.

The legislature would have been hard pressed to define the concept of "scenic beauty" more specifically. *See Finks v. Maine State Highway Commission*, 328 A.2d 791, 796 (Me. 1974). We agree with the Maine Supreme Judicial Court and the New Jersey Supreme Court that:

> "The Act contemplates that there is a certain basic beauty in natural terrain and vegetation unspoiled by the hands of man, which it proposes to recapture or maintain. Although the extent to which each individual finds a specific landscape beautiful must be determined by a subjective test, this does not denote that there is no catholic

> criterion for the ascertainment of whether *any scenic beauty* exists in a given panorama. 'Scenic beauty' is concerned with such manifold possible situations that it does not lend itself to a more specifically detailed descriptive statement. A tabulation of the various possible elements constituting scenic beauty is well-nigh impossible."

Id. (quoting *Wes Outdoor Advertising Company v. Goldberg*, 55 N.J. 347, 262 A.2d 199, 202 (1970)).

Moreover, the concept of "scenic beauty[ ], although more generally used in a subjective sense, connotes, in terms of [the scenic road statute], a sufficiently definite concrete image . . . to furnish in and of itself an adequate standard." *Id.* . .

Affirmed.

■ KOSALKA v. TOWN OF GEORGETOWN
2000 Me. 106, 752 A.2d 183 (2003)

DANA, J.

Eric and Patricia Kosalka appeal from a judgment entered in the Superior Court (Sagadahoc County, *Calkins, J.*) upholding as constitutional a provision of the Georgetown Shoreland Zoning Ordinance. . .

Here, the Georgetown Ordinance requires that all development "conserve natural beauty." However, all development, to some extent, destroys or impairs "natural beauty." If the provision means that *all* natural beauty must be conserved, then *all* development must be banned. Because the provision cannot reasonably be interpreted to ban all development, the question becomes: How much destruction is okay? Or, put another way[:] How much conservation is required? On this question, however, the Georgetown Ordinance . . . is silent. Neither developers nor the ZBA [Zoning Board of Appeals] are given any guidance on how to interpret the "conserve natural beauty" requirement. Instead, developers are left guessing at how much conservation is necessary. . . .

Because the condition that all proposed developments "conserve natural beauty" is an unmeasurable quality, totally lacking in cognizable, quantitative standards, this condition is an unconstitutional delegation of legislative authority and violative of the due process clause. . . .

Judgment vacated.

■ HUGO MARTIN, HUE AND CRY OVER COLORS OF HOMES IN SOUTH GATE: WHILE THE COUNCIL CONSIDERS BANNING LOUD PAINT JOBS, OTHERS DEFEND THEM AS A TRADITION BROUGHT FROM LATIN AMERICA
L.A. Times, Sept. 22, 1998, at B1

Since Hermila Sanchez and her husband, Miguel, painted their beige South Gate home a light turquoise with white trim, they have noticed some passing neighbors giving the small stucco house disapproving looks.

"I say if they don't like it they can come help us paint it another color," Hermila Sanchez said good-naturedly from her front porch.

Her neighbors may not have a say in the color, but the city of South Gate soon may. This predominantly Latino, blue-collar city in southeast Los Angeles County is considering imposing the kind of color and design restrictions that are usually found only in affluent communities. . . .

At the request of Mayor Henry Gonzalez, the South Gate City Council will vote today on creating a citywide program that limits the colors of homes and businesses to a designated few — most likely not to include the turquoise of the Sanchez home, or the maroon, orange and purple that also dot the landscape.

Gonzalez said the proposed restrictions were prompted by several complaints from residents about garish colors on businesses and homes around the city.

"People are saying, 'It looks like hell,' " he said.

Many homes in this town of 93,000 can best be described as the colors of sorbet: lime green, peach, raspberry and banana yellow. An automotive shop that has drawn the mayor's ire is bright purple with white trim.

But the politics of color may turn into a cultural debate. Many of the property owners who have chosen the lively hues for their homes and businesses may be carrying over a tradition from Mexico or other Latin American countries where vivid colors are embraced and are an expression of individuality.

"It's part of our cultural identity," said Leo Limon, a local artist and co-chairman of the Aztlan Cultural Arts Foundation in Los Angeles. "It's the colors of feathers and birds and trees, and the Latino population sees that and uses that." . . .

Gonzalez said he will ask the council to consider restricting homes and businesses to three or four colors. The city's code enforcement unit would enforce the restrictions, which would apply only when a structure is repainted or rebuilt, he said.

To avoid imposing a financial hardship, Gonzalez said he will ask the city to provide grants to subsidize the cost of the paint and labor.

"I don't want to create a burden, but I want a consistent [color] code where everybody knows what it is," he said. . . .

But most of the dozen or so homeowners and merchants who were interviewed last week said the bright colors they chose for their homes and businesses are a personal expression that should not be restricted by government. . . .

Antonio Rubio, a mechanic and longtime Los Angeles resident, owns that purple, two-story auto shop on the corner of Southern and California avenues that has drawn the ire of Gonzalez and other city officials. Rubio said he painted the building purple about three months ago to grab the attention of potential customers on the nearby busy intersection.

"This is a place where we paint cars and sell exotic rims," he said in Spanish. "The color of the building should be exotic."

Notes and Comments

1. *Authority to Consider Aesthetics*. The local agency must be authorized to regulate for aesthetic purposes. That authorization can come from state zoning enabling legislation or other types of state land use law. *See In re Denio*, 608 A.2d 1166 (Vt. 1992) ("the conditions were based on the Board's finding, under 10 V.S.A. §6086(a)(8), that, in the absence of adherence to the conditions, the subdivision would adversely affect the aesthetics of the surrounding area").

2. *Implementation of Aesthetic Regulation*. Local governments employ a variety of means to implement aesthetic regulation. For example, they may use an "overlay zoning," a zone which overlays the underlying, pre-existing zoning, to ensure that aesthetic goals are met. *See, e.g., Franchise Developers, Inc. v. City of Cincinnati*, 505 N.E.2d 966 (Ohio 1987) (city validly disapproved a permit to construct a "Burger Chef" restaurant in an "environmental quality-urban design zone district," which overlays the existing zoning).

3. *"Harmonious" Development*. Courts are increasingly troubled about the vagueness in local aesthetic regulations. In *Anderson*, the court held that the word "harmonious" did not give sufficient guidance to applicants. However, in *Breneric Associates v. City of Del Mar*, 81 Cal. Rptr. 2d (Cal. Ct. App. 1998), the municipal code required a design review permit and declared that the purpose of design review is to protect the aesthetic quality of the community by "fostering and encouraging good design which encompasses the use of harmonious materials and colors." The court upheld the denial of a permit to construct a two-story addition on the side of an existing residence. Although it did not actually consider a "void for vagueness" claim, the court refused to apply heightened scrutiny to its review. Moreover, it found that the denial did not require expert testimony. The "opinions and objections of neighbors can provide substantial evidence" to support the rejection.

Is *Anderson* or *Breneric* more convincing?

4. *"Scenic" Versus "Natural" Beauty*. In *Webster*, the Supreme Court of New Hampshire concludes that the phrase "scenic beauty" provides sufficient notice to developers of the relevant standards. In support, it cites a 1974 Maine Supreme Court decision, *Finks v. Maine State Highway Comm'n*, 328 A.2d 791, which found that the phrase "scenic beauty" did not lend itself to a more specifically detailed descriptive statement. However, 26 years later in *Kosalka*, the Maine Court concluded that the phrase "conserve natural beauty" did not pass constitutional muster. It thought that this phrase left developers guessing as to how much conservation is necessary. The court did not cite the *Finks* decision.

What do you make of all this? Are both *Webster* and *Kosalka* correct and distinguishable? Is the New Hampshire statute clearer because it lists the specific actions that cannot be taken (cutting, damaging, or removal of trees)? Is "scenic beauty" different from "natural beauty," so that Maine law remains internally consistent? In 30 years, will *Kosalka* be seen as an aberration in the development of law in which courts broadly uphold aesthetic regulation despite definitional difficulties? Or is it part of a judicial sweep back based on the conclusion that aesthetic regulation is simply too uncertain to be upheld?

Aside from constitutional questions, the specific wording of the ordinance can, of course, be very important. In *Cormier v. Town of Danville Zoning Bd. of Adjustment*, the town denied an application for sand and gravel extraction. The trial court accepted the city's argument that the proposal could impact Tuckertown Road, a "natural feature." The court pointed out the obvious: roads are not "natural features"; they are man-made. It reversed.

5. *"Don't Mess with My Pickup Truck."* Even if the courts in a particular state are willing to recognize aesthetics as a permissible purpose for government regulation, the regulatory means must rationally serve that purpose. Would a local ordinance meet this test where it banned the parking of pickup trucks, but not passenger vehicles, in the driveway of private residences between 2:00 and 5:00 A.M.?

In *City of Nichols Hills v. Richardson*, 939 P.2d 17 (Okla. Ct. Crim. App. 1997), the court overturned a conviction under such an ordinance on the grounds that an "ugly, rusted or offensive" vehicle could legally be parked during that period, while a brand new pickup truck could not. The court concluded: "The obvious contradiction belies the City's claim that it has enacted the ordinance to protect the aesthetic integrity of the community." *Id.* at 19. *See also Andrews v. Brown*, 603 A.2d 335, 336 (R.I. 1992) ("There is no evidence in the record that demonstrates that the roof and width standards [for mobile homes] have any impact upon the health, safety, or welfare of the park's residents. Rather these standards appear to reflect the aesthetic preferences of defendants."). *Compare Whaley v. Dorchester County Zoning Bd. of Appeals,* 524 S.E.2d 404 (S.C. 1999) (upholding a regulation prohibiting the long-term parking of commercial vehicles in a residential area and concluding that the prohibition "is reasonably related to protecting property values and maintaining the aesthetic appearance of residential areas").

6. *The Extent of Aesthetic Regulation.* If regulation for aesthetic purposes is within the police power, can local governments be sure that the regulation passed is rationally related to this now-legitimate state interest? Consider the following specific questions:

(1) Can a city mandate that all fences be painted a single color all over, with no designs on the fence? *See* Charity Vogel, Sunflower Fence Casting Shadow over Neighborhood, Buffalo News, Oct. 6, 1997, at B1 (Village charged homeowner with violating local ordinance when she had an artist friend paint sunflowers on the section of her fence along her back lot line).

(2) Can a city pass a "uniformity law" banning white picket fences? Hawke Fracassa, In Sterling Heights: City Considers Fence Uniformity, Detroit News, Jan. 22, 1998, at D5 (Sterling Heights officials are considering imposing a requirement that new fences on private property along some major thoroughfares have the same height, construction material, and color).

(3) Can a city adopt a landscape protection ordinance that restricts business owners from cutting trees into decorative shapes and topiary designs? *See* Monica Richardson, Businesses, JaxPride at Odds Over Tree Law, Florida Times-Union, Apr. 25, 1998, at 1 (councilman proposes amendment to ordinance that would allow business owners to cut and prune their trees so long as they don't kill them).

(4) Can a city pass an ordinance preventing the cutting of trees by developers? *See* Editorial, Clear-Cut Need to Save the Trees, Atlanta Constitution, Jan. 6, 1998, at A:06 ("As forests and shade give way to red dirt and blazing sun, it's essential that residents contact county commissioners and city council members to demand changes in land-use laws to protect trees and reduce the amount of paved surfaces").

7. *The House as a First Amendment Castle*. Should there be First Amendment protection for the exterior design of a private, single-family house? One academic has made the argument, analogizing its design to the protection given to signs in *City of Ladue v. Gilleo*, 512 U.S. 43 (1994). He argues:

> Architecture is entitled to First Amendment protection; in the case of a single-family house, it is entitled to the same protection as Ms. Gilleo was given in posting her

> sign. The exterior design of the house is speech; it can be read by its viewers. The landowner's choice of an exterior design cannot be suppressed simply because a municipality finds it grotesque or appalling or unsightly. If that is the objection, then the viewers must simply turn their heads.

John Nivala, Constitutional Architecture: The First Amendment and the Single Family House, 33 San Diego L. Rev. 291, 339 (1996). Do you agree? *See also* Virginia Postrel, Looking Forward: The Esthetics Police, Forbes, Nov. 1, 1999, 174 (world-renowned architect Frank Gehry's design for a performing arts center at Bard College was moved when neighbors claimed the stainless steel structure would destroy the visual harmony of the local wooded landscape).

8. *View Protection.* Will aesthetic regulation under the police power extend to the protection of views? At least two courts have said yes. *Ross v. City of Rolling Hills Estates*, 238 Cal. Rptr. 561 (Ct. App. 1987) (view protection ordinance was not unconstitutionally vague); *Landmark Land Co., Inc. v. City and County of Denver*, 728 P.2d 1281 (Colo. 1986) (upholding ordinance extending mountain view protection to additional area). But how can we be sure that the aesthetic interest in views should prevail over, for example, those in trees which would have to be cut to preserve the views? See Leslie Earnest, Laguna Beach Plan Unit to Consider Law to Protect Views, L.A. Times, Feb. 11, 1997, at B2 (quoting a member of the "Laguna Landscape Conservancy" to the effect that "[t]he whole thing is anti-tree" and "[w]e're concerned that this whole effort is setting up a negative attitude toward trees").

9. *Beauty and the Eye of the Beholder.* Is it possible for local governments to decide, in a non-arbitrary way, whether excessive use of colors on houses is against the public interest? One person's ugly color is another's fount of beauty (or, perhaps more pragmatically, another's attempt to distinguish his business from other businesses). See Jennifer Brett, Yellow Store Sparks Talk of Color Codes in Pinellas Park, St. Petersburg Times, Jan. 19, 1997, at 10 (while critic found that a pet store painted marigold yellow "looks like a radiation sign" from a distance, the owner declared that "[w]hen I tell people I'm in the yellow building, they know what building I'm in").

Table of Cases

Principal cases are indicated by italic type.

Index

References are to pages.